P9-DUZ-161

COGNITIVE PSYCHOLOGY

This book is dedicated to my three principal advisors, mentors, and role models:

Endel Tulving, during my undergraduate years at Yale

Gordon Bower, during my graduate years at Stanford

Wendell Garner, during my junior-faculty years back at Yale

COGNITIVE PSYCHOLOGY

Second Edition

Robert J. Sternberg
Yale University

Harcourt Brace College Publishers
Fort Worth Philadelphia San Diego New York Orlando Austin San Antonio
Toronto Montreal London Sydney Tokyo

Publisher	Earl McPeek
Executive Editor	Carol Wada
Associate Acquisitions Editor	Lisa D. Hensley
Product Manager	Kathleen Sharp
Developmental Editor	Susan Petty
Project Editor	Louise Slominsky
Production Manager	Andrea A. Johnson
Art Director	David A. Day

Cover image: "Black/White Faces Sectioned" copyright © Wiktor Sadowski/Stock Illustration Source, Inc.

ISBN: 0-15-508354-6
Library of Congress Catalog Card Number: 98-72574

Copyright © 1999, 1996 by Holt, Rinehart and Winston

All rights reserved. No part of this publication may be reproduced or transmitted in any form or by any means, electronic or mechanical, including photocopy, recording, or any information storage and retrieval system, without permission in writing from the publisher.

Requests for permission to make copies of any part of the work should be mailed to: Permissions Department, Harcourt Brace & Company, 6277 Sea Harbor Drive, Orlando, FL 32887-6777.

Copyrights and acknowledgments begin on page 000 and constitute a continuation of the copyright page.

Address for Orders
Harcourt Brace & Company
6277 Sea Harbor Drive
Orlando, FL 32887-6777
1-800-782-4479

Address for Editorial Correspondence
Harcourt Brace College Publishers
301 Commerce Street, Suite 3700
Fort Worth, TX 76102

Web Site Address
http://www.hbcollege.com

Harcourt Brace College Publishers may provide complimentary instructional aids and supplements or supplement packages to those adopters qualified under our adoption policy. Please contact your sales representative for more information. If as an adopter or potential user you receive supplements you do not need, please return them to your sales representative or send them to: Attn: Returns Department, Troy Warehouse, 465 South Lincoln Drive, Troy, MO 63379

Printed in the United States of America

9 0 1 2 3 4 5 6 7 039 9 8 7 6 5 4 3 2

To the Instructor

Every year it was a gamble, and every year I lost: I had taught cognitive psychology a number of times during my 20 years at Yale, and I had never used the same textbook twice. For whatever reason, my students were never taken with any of the books I chose, and neither was I. The book was too hard or too easy, too narrow or too broad, too dated or too trendy. They were decent books, just not the right books. Finally, I decided to stack the deck, and write the book myself. The gamble seems to have paid off as we go into the second edition of *Cognitive Psychology*. In this preface I'll set out the goals of the second edition and then discuss the features and philosophy that underlie the book in both its editions.

What's New in the Second Edition?

During the period in which the first edition of this book was used, the publisher and I actively sought feedback regarding this text. This feedback was invaluable in making countless additions, deletions, and modifications to the text in order better to suit the needs of both professors and students. There are also four major changes in the second edition.

1. Enhanced and integrated coverage of cognitive neuroscience and its interface with cognitive psychology. In response to trends in the field, the name of Chapter 2 has been changed to reflect its new emphasis on cognitive neuroscience. Moreover, the amount of material at the interface between cognitive psychology and neuroscience has been expanded throughout the text. Of the available cognitive psychology texts, I believe mine is among the most extensive in its coverage of cognitive-neuroscientific developments in the field.
2. Extensive updating. Cognitive psychology is a rapidly growing and changing field. Thus, a great deal of updating has been done to ensure that the text would reflect the current state of the field. I believe that this text is now as up-to-date as any that can be found on the market.
3. Reordering of chapters on memory and knowledge representation. In the second edition, the chapters on memory (now 5 and 6) precede the chapters on knowledge representation (now 7 and 8), rather than following them. This ordering provides better continuity and more faithfully reflects the way most instructors prefer to teach the cognitive psychology course.
4. New pedagogy showing practical applications of cognitive psychology. In response to students' desires to relate what they learn in their courses to their everyday lives, a new pedagogical feature, Practical Applications of Cognitive Psychology, has been added throughout the text.

What my students and I wanted in the first edition continues into the second. We wanted a book that would achieve a number of objectives.

1. Combine readability with integrity. I have chosen books that were so chewy that only the strongest stomachs could digest their contents, and I have chosen ones that melted like cotton candy, with substance to match. This book provides students something to chew on, but something they can easily digest.

2. Balance a clear presentation of the big questions of cognitive psychology with a respect for the important details of the field. Perhaps in no course more than in cognitive psychology are both the forest and the trees important. The best and most lasting work in the field is driven by enduring and fundamental questions. However, that work also respects the details of methods and data analysis needed to produce meaningful results. In order to achieve the balance, I have opened each chapter with a preview of the big questions that are dealt with in that chapter and ended each chapter with a summary of what we have learned in the field that addresses each question. Within the chapters, the writing has been guided by the big questions, while conveying to students the kinds of details to which cognitive psychologists need to attend in both their theory and research.
3. Balance the learning of subject matter with thinking about the subject matter. An expert cognitive psychologist knows the discipline but can also utilize the knowledge. Knowledge without thought is useless, but thought without knowledge is empty. I have tried to balance a respect for subject matter with an equal respect for its use. Every chapter ends with diverse questions that emphasize comprehension of subject matter, as well as analytical, creative, and practical thinking using that subject matter.

   This organization is motivated by my triarchic theory of thinking. However, one does not have to accept the theory to recognize the importance of both knowing the facts and being able to think with them, not just in one way, but in three different ways. Students using this book will not only learn the basic ideas and facts of cognitive psychology, but also how to think with them.
4. Recognize both the traditional and emerging trends in the field. This book has all the traditional topics found in the chapters of the large majority of textbooks, including the nature of cognitive psychology (chapter 1), attention and consciousness (chapter 3), perception (chapter 4), memory (chapters 5 and 6), knowledge representation (chapters 7 and 8), language (chapters 9 and 10), problem solving and creativity (chapter 11), and decision making and reasoning (chapter 12). I have also included three chapters that are not typically included as chapters in other books.

   Cognitive neuroscience (chapter 2) is included because the dividing line between cognitive psychology and neuroscience is becoming increasingly indistinct. A great deal of exciting work today is at the interface between the two fields. Whereas the cognitive psychologist of 20 years ago might have been able to get away without an understanding of biological foundations, I believe that today such a cognitive psychologist would be ill served.

   Cognitive development (chapter 13) is included because the fields of cognitive psychology and cognitive development have increasingly become part of the same basic entity. Twenty years ago, the field of cognitive development was still dominated by the Piagetian approach, which made relatively little contact with the main issues being addressed by cognitive psychologists. Today, much of the research being done by cognitive developmentalists is more or less the same as that being done by cognitive psychologists studying adults, except that it is adapted for children. The fields of cognitive psychology and cognitive development have practically merged, and a cognitive psychologist of today should be aware that the field as a whole encompasses the study of children as well as of adults.

Human and artificial intelligence (chapter 14) are becoming increasingly important to the field of cognitive psychology. Twenty years ago, the field of human intelligence was dominated by psychometric (test-based) approaches. The field of artificial intelligence was dominated by programs that were functionally rather remote from human thought processes. Today, both fields of intelligence are much more heavily influenced by cognitive models of how people process information. I include both human- and computer-based intelligence in the same chapter because I believe that their goals, ultimately, are the same—namely, to understand human cognition.

Although the book ends with the chapter on intelligence, intelligence also plays a major role in the beginning and the middle of the book, because it is the organizing framework within which cognitive psychology is presented.

I have tried not only to balance traditional and newer topics, but also older and more recent citations. Some books seem to suggest that almost nothing new has happened over the past decade, whereas others seem to suggest that cognitive psychology was invented in this decade. The goal of this book is to balance citation and description of classic studies with equal attention to recent exciting contributions to the field.

5. Show the basic unity of cognitive psychology. On the one hand, cognitive psychologists disagree about the extent to which the mechanisms of cognition are domain-specific versus domain-general. On the other hand, I believe that almost all cognitive psychologists believe that there is a fundamental functional unity to human cognition. This unity, I believe, is expressed through the concept of human intelligence.

   The concept of intelligence can be seen as providing a unifying umbrella via which to understand the adaptive nature of human cognition. Through this single concept, society, as well as psychological science, acknowledges that as diverse as cognition may be, it comes together in providing us with a functionally unified way of making sense of and adapting to the environment. Thus, the unity of human cognition, as expressed by the concept of intelligence, serves as an integrating theme for this book.

6. Balance various forms of learning and instruction. Students learn best when they learn material in a variety of ways and from different vantage points. To this end, I have sought to achieve a balance among a traditional presentation of text, a variety of kinds of questions about the material (factual, analytical, creative, and practical), demonstrations of key ideas in cognitive psychology, and annotated suggested readings that students can consult if they desire further information about a topic. A chapter outline at the beginning of each chapter

also serves as an advance organizer for what is to come. The opening questions and closing answers help students appreciate the main questions in the field, as well as what progress we have made toward answering them. The text itself emphasizes how contemporary ideas have evolved from past ones, and how these ideas address the key questions cognitive psychologists have sought to answer in their research.

Ancillary Package

Professors using the second edition of *Cognitive Psychology* will be interested to know that, in addition to the printed test bank (ISBN 0-15-507944-1), there are computerized test banks available in Windows, Macintosh, and Dos 3.5 formats. The test bank has been revised to reflect the changes in the second edition and essay questions now test all aspects of students' knowledge—factual, creative, analytical, and practical. A multiple choice answer key is now located at the end of the chapter (in the printed test bank) to accommodate ease of test preparation by the instructor.

A complementary book of readings edited by Robert J. Sternberg and Richard K. Wagner is also available. *Readings in Cognitive Psychology* (ISBN 0-15-504105-3) contains 25 original articles acknowledged by a nationwide sample of cognitive psychology faculty to be part of the core of the field. Interested instructors should contact their Harcourt Brace representative for more information.

Acknowledgments

I am grateful to a number of individuals who have contributed to the development of this book. Earl McPeek, and then Lisa Hensley and Carol Wada, my acquisitions editors, were supportive and enthusiastic from the project's inception. Susan R. Petty, the developmental editor, was diligent in getting reviews of chapters and in helping shape the book. Louise Slominsky, the project editor, shepherded the finished manuscript through the production process, meticulously attending to all the details involved in producing a finely finished book. She had help from Andrea Johnson, production manager; Lora Knox Gray and David Day, art directors; Sarah Sims, copy editor; and Sue Howard, photo researcher and permissions editor.

I thank Jennifer Pardo, who assisted me in revising the text. I am grateful to Marie Martin and Gregory Politzer for their help in creating the test bank to accompany this book.

A number of reviewers have also contributed to the development of the book and ensured that it would be accurate and up-to-date. I thank them for their work on the project. They are:

Tomas R. Alley
Clemson University

Richard A. Block
Montana State University

Edward Crothers
University of Colorado—Boulder

David G. Elmes
Washington and Lee University

Jody Esper
Valparaiso University

Steven F. Faux
Drake University

Richard Jackson Harris
Kansas State University

James Hinrichs
University of Iowa

Rosemary Hornak
Meredith College

James Hunsicker
Southwestern Oklahoma State University

Peter Kaplan
University of Colorado—Denver

Dan Levin
Kent State University

Kevin Morrin
Indiana Purdue University at Fort Wayne

Elizabeth Weiss Ozorok
Allegheny College

Mike Stadler
University of Missouri—Columbia

Holly Taylor
Tufts University

I am also grateful to my wife, Alejandra Campos, and to my children, Seth and Sara, for their patience while I wrote the book. Finally, I want to thank all the members of my present and past research groups at Yale, who over the years have contributed to my development as a teacher of and researcher in cognitive psychology.

RJS

To the Student

Why do we remember people whom we met years ago, but sometimes seem to forget what we learned in a course shortly after we take the final exam (or worse, sometimes right before)? How do we manage to carry on a conversation with one person at a party, and simultaneously eavesdrop on another, more interesting conversation taking place nearby? Why are people so often certain that they are correct in answering a question when in fact they are not? These are just three of the many questions that are addressed by the field of cognitive psychology.

Cognitive psychologists study how people perceive, learn, remember, and think. Although cognitive psychology is a unified field, it draws on many other fields, most notably neuroscience, computer science, linguistics, anthropology, and philosophy. Thus, you will find some of the thinking of all these fields represented in this book. Moreover, cognitive psychology interacts with other fields within psychology, such as psychobiology, developmental psychology, social psychology, and clinical psychology.

For example, it is difficult to be a clinical psychologist today without a solid knowledge of developments in cognitive psychology, because so much of the thinking in the clinical field draws upon cognitive ideas, both in diagnosis and in therapy. Cognitive psychology has also provided a means for psychologists to investigate experimentally some of the exciting ideas that have emerged from clinical theory and practice, such as notions of unconscious thought.

Cognitive psychology will be important to you not only in its own right, but also in helping you in all of your work. For example, a knowledge of cognitive psychology can help you better understand things such as how best to study for tests, how to read effectively, and how to remember difficult-to-learn material. However, in order best to acquire this knowledge, you need to make use of the pedagogical features of this book. These include

1. Chapter outlines, beginning each chapter, which summarize the main topics covered in each chapter and will thus give you an advance overview of what is to be covered in that chapter
2. Opening questions that emphasize the main questions each chapter addresses
3. Boldface terms, listed at the end of chapters and defined in the glossary, which will help you acquire the vocabulary of cognitive psychology
4. End-of-chapter summaries, which return to the questions at the opening of each chapter, and which show our current state of knowledge with regard to these questions
5. End-of-chapter questions, which help you ensure both that you have learned the basic material and that you can think in a variety of ways (analytical, creative, and practical) with this material
6. Annotated suggested readings, which will refer you to other sources you can consult for further information on the topics covered in each chapter

7. Investigating Cognitive Psychology demonstrations, appearing throughout the chapters, which will help you see how cognitive psychology can be used to demonstrate various psychological phenomena
8. Practical Applications of Cognitive Psychology demonstrations will show you how you and others can apply cognitive psychology to your everyday life

This book contains an overriding theme that unifies all the diverse topics to be found in the various chapters: Human cognition has evolved over time as a means of adapting to our environment, and we can call this ability to adapt to the environment intelligence. Through intelligence, we cope in an integrated and adaptive way with the many challenges with which the environment presents us.

Although cognitive psychologists disagree about many issues, there is one issue about which almost all of them agree, namely, that cognition enables us successfully to adapt to the environments in which we find ourselves. Thus, we need a construct such as that of human intelligence, if only to provide a shorthand way of expressing this fundamental unity of adaptive skill. We can see this unity at all levels in the study of cognitive psychology. For example, diverse measures of the psychophysiological functioning of selective attention—the ability to tune in certain stimuli and tune out others—are also related to intelligence, and it has even been proposed that an intelligent person is one who knows what information to attend to, and what information to ignore. Various language and problem-solving skills are also related to intelligence, pretty much without regard to how it is measured. In brief, then, human intelligence can be seen as an entity that unifies and provides direction to the workings of the human cognitive system.

I hope you enjoy this book, and I hope you see why I am enthusiastic about cognitive psychology, and proud to be a cognitive psychologist.

RJS

Contents in Brief

Chapter One Introduction to Cognitive Psychology 1

Chapter Two Cognitive Neuroscience 27

Chapter Three Attention and Consciousness 67

Chapter Four Perception 109

Chapter Five Memory: Models and Research Methods 153

Chapter Six Memory Processes 181

Chapter Seven Knowledge Representation: Images and Propositions 211

Chapter Eight Knowledge Representation and Organization 253

Chapter Nine Language: Nature and Acquisition 283

Chapter Ten Language in Context 315

Chapter Eleven Problem Solving and Creativity 349

Chapter Twelve Decision Making and Reasoning 391

Chapter Thirteen Cognitive Development 431

Chapter Fourteen Human and Artificial Intelligence 467

Glossary 507

References 525

Name Index 559

Subject Index 567

Credits 583

CONTENTS

Chapter One Introduction to Cognitive Psychology 1

Exploring Cognitive Psychology 2
Cognitive Psychology Defined 2
Philosophical Antecedents of Psychology: Rationalism Versus Empiricism 3
Psychological Antecedents of Cognitive Psychology 5
Early Dialectics in the Psychology of Cognition 6
From Associationism to Behaviorism 9
Gestalt Psychology 10
The Emergence of Cognitive Psychology 11
The Early Role of Psychobiology 11
Add a Dash of Technology: Engineering and Computation 12
Research Methods in Cognitive Psychology 13
Goals of Research 13
Distinctive Research Methods 14
Key Issues and Fields Within Cognitive Psychology 20
Underlying Themes in the Study of Cognitive Psychology 20
Chapter Previews 22
Summary 23
Thinking About Thinking: Factual, Analytical, Creative, and Practical Questions 25
Key Terms 25
Annotated Suggested Readings 25

Chapter Two Cognitive Neuroscience 27

Exploring Cognitive Psychology 28
From Neuron to Brain: Organization of the Nervous System 28
Neuronal Structure and Function 29
Communication Between Neurons 32
Levels of Organization in the Nervous System 36
Viewing the Structures and Functions of the Brain 40
Postmortem Studies 41
Animal Studies 41
Electrical Recordings 42
Static Imaging Techniques 42
Metabolic Imaging 44

Cognition in the Brain: Cerebral Cortex and Other Structures 46

Gross Anatomy of the Brain: Forebrain, Midbrain, Hindbrain 49

The Cerebral Cortex and Localization of Function 52

Summary 63

Thinking About Thinking: Factual, Analytical, Creative, and Practical Questions 64

Key Terms 65

Annotated Suggested Readings 66

Chapter Three Attention and Consciousness 67

Exploring Cognitive Psychology 68

Attention and Consciousness 68

Preconscious Processing 70

Controlled Versus Automatic Processes 72

Habituation 76

Attention 80

Signal Detection 80

The Nature of Signal Detection 82

Vigilance 83

Search 84

Selective and Divided Attention 91

Basic Paradigms for Studying Selective Attention 91

Filter and Bottleneck Theories of Selective Attention 93

Attentional-Resource Theories of Selective Attention 97

Additional Considerations in Selective Attention 98

Divided Attention 99

Cognitive Neuroscientific Approaches to Attention and Consciousness 101

Posner's Theory 102

Näätänen's ERP Work 102

A Psychopharmacological Approach 103

Marcel's Model of the Links Among Perception, Attention, and Consciousness 104

Summary 105

Thinking About Thinking: Factual, Analytical, Creative, and Practical Questions 106

Key Terms 107

Annotated Suggested Readings 107

Chapter Four **Perception 109**

Exploring Cognitive Psychology 110
From Sensation to Representation 114
Some Basic Concepts 114
Perceptual Constancies 115
Depth Perception 119
Gestalt Approaches to Form Perception 123
Theoretical Approaches to Perception 126
Bottom-Up Approaches: Direct Perception 127
Top-Down Approaches: Constructive Perception 136
Synthesizing the Two Approaches 139
A Computational Theory of Perception 140
Spatiotemporal Boundary-Formation Theory 142
Reading: Bottom-Up and Top-Down Processes 143
Perceptual Issues in Reading 143
Lexical Processes in Reading 144
Deficits in Perception 148
Summary 150
Thinking About Thinking: Factual, Analytical, Creative, and Practical Questions 151
Key Terms 152
Annotated Suggested Readings 152

Chapter Five **Memory: Models and Research Methods 153**

Exploring Cognitive Psychology 154
Tasks Used for Measuring Memory 154
Recall Versus Recognition Tasks 155
Implicit Versus Explicit Memory Tasks 157
Traditional Model of Memory 157
The Sensory Store 159
The Short-Term Store 162
The Long-Term Store 163
Alternative Perspectives, Alternative Metaphors 164
Levels of Processing 164
Working Memory 166
Multiple-Memory-Systems Model 168
A Connectionist Perspective 169
Memory in the Real World 170

Exceptional Memory and Neuropsychology 172
Outstanding Memory: Mnemonists 172
Deficient Memory: Amnesia 173
The Role of the Hippocampus and Other Structures 176
Summary 178
Thinking About Thinking: Factual, Analytical, Creative, and Practical Questions 179
Key Terms 180
Annotated Suggested Readings 180

Chapter Six Memory Processes 181

Exploring Cognitive Psychology 182
Encoding and Movement of Information 183
Forms of Encoding 183
Movement of Information From Short-Term Memory to Long-Term Memory 185
Retrieval 191
Retrieval From Short-Term Memory 192
Retrieval From Long-Term Memory 195
Processes of Forgetting and Memory Distortion 196
Interference Versus Decay Theory 196
The Constructive Nature of Memory 201
Context Effects on Encoding and Retrieval 203
Summary 206
Thinking About Thinking: Factual, Analytical, Creative, and Practical Questions 208
Key Terms 208
Annotated Suggested Readings 209

Chapter Seven Knowledge Representation: Images and Propositions 211

Exploring Cognitive Psychology 212
Mental Representation of Knowledge 212
External Representations: Pictures Versus Words 214
Mental Imagery 216
Dual-Code Hypothesis: Analogical Images Versus Symbols 218
Propositional Hypothesis 219

Mental Manipulations of Images 225
Mental Rotations 225
Image Scaling 230
Image Scanning 233
Synthesizing Images and Propositions 234
Epiphenomena and Demand Characteristics 234
Johnson-Laird's Mental Models 236
Neuropsychological Evidence for Multiple Codes 238
Spatial Cognition and Cognitive Maps 242
Rats, Bees, and Humans 242
Mental Shortcuts 244
Text Maps 248
Summary 248
Thinking About Thinking: Factual, Analytical, Creative, and Practical Questions 250
Key Terms 251
Annotated Suggested Readings 251

Chapter Eight Knowledge Representation and Organization 253

Exploring Cognitive Psychology 254
Organization of Declarative Knowledge 255
Concepts and Categories 256
Semantic Network Models 260
Schematic Representations 263
Representations of Procedural Knowledge 267
The Production and the Production System 267
Integrative Models for Representing Declarative and Nondeclarative Knowledge 268
Combining Representations: ACT and ACT 268*
Models Based on the Human Brain 272
Parallel Processing: The Connectionist Model 275
How Domain General or Domain Specific Is Cognition? 279
Summary 280
Thinking About Thinking: Factual, Analytical, Creative, and Practical Questions 281
Key Terms 282
Annotated Suggested Readings 282

Chapter Nine Language: Nature and Acquisition 283

Exploring Cognitive Psychology 284

Properties of Language 285

General Description 285

Fundamental Aspects of Language 287

Processes of Language Comprehension 291

Speech Perception 291

Semantics and Syntax 295

Language Acquisition 303

Stages of Language Acquisition 304

Nature and Nurture 307

Beyond the First Years 310

Summary 311

Thinking About Thinking: Factual, Analytical, Creative, and Practical Questions 313

Key Terms 313

Annotated Suggested Readings 314

Chapter Ten Language in Context 315

Exploring Cognitive Psychology 316

Language and Thought 316

Differences Between Languages 316

Bilingualism and Dialects 322

Slips of the Tongue 326

Metaphorical Language 327

Language in a Social Context 329

Speech Acts 330

Conversational Postulates 333

Gender and Language 335

Discourse and Reading Comprehension 336

Neuropsychology of Language 342

Lesion Studies and ERP Research 342

Other Methods 344

Summary 345

Thinking About Thinking: Factual, Analytical, Creative, and Practical Questions 347

Key Terms 347

Annotated Suggested Readings 348

Chapter Eleven **Problem Solving and Creativity 349**

Exploring Cognitive Psychology 350

The Problem-Solving Cycle 351

Types of Problems 354

Well-Structured Problems 355

Ill-Structured Problems and the Role of Insight 363

Obstacles and Aids to Problem Solving 369

Mental Sets, Entrenchment, and Fixation 369

Negative and Positive Transfer 371

Incubation 375

Expertise: Knowledge and Problem Solving 376

Organization of Knowledge 377

Innate Talent and Acquired Skill 380

Creativity 382

It's How Much You Produce 384

It's What You Know 384

It's Who You Are 385

It's Where You Are 385

All of the Above 386

Summary 387

Thinking About Thinking: Factual, Analytical, Creative, and Practical Questions 389

Key Terms 389

Annotated Suggested Readings 390

Chapter Twelve **Decision Making and Reasoning 391**

Exploring Cognitive Psychology 392

Judgment and Decision Making 393

Classical Decision Theory 393

Satisficing 394

Elimination by Aspects 395

Heuristics and Biases 397

Deductive Reasoning 405

Conditional Reasoning 405

Syllogistic Reasoning 410

Further Aids and Obstacles to Deductive Reasoning 419

Inductive Reasoning 421

Reaching Causal Inferences 422

Categorical Inferences 425
Reasoning by Analogy 426
An Alternative View of Reasoning 426
Summary 428
Thinking About Thinking: Factual, Analytical, Creative, and Practical Questions 429
Key Terms 430
Annotated Suggested Readings 430

Chapter Thirteen Cognitive Development 431

Exploring Cognitive Psychology 432
Major Approaches to Cognitive Development 433
General Principles of Cognitive Development 433
Maturation of Thought Processes 435
Sociocultural Influences on Thought Processes 446
Development of Information-Processing Skills 449
Metacognitive Skills and Memory Development 450
Quantitative Skills 452
Visuospatial Skills 453
Inductive Reasoning 455
Neurophysiological Changes in Development 458
Increasing Neuronal Complexity 458
Maturation of Central Nervous System Structures 458
Cognitive Development in Adulthood 460
Patterns of Growth and Decline 460
Wisdom and Aging 463
Summary 464
Thinking About Thinking: Factual, Analytical, Creative, and Practical Questions 465
Key Terms 466
Annotated Suggested Readings 466

Chapter Fourteen Human and Artificial Intelligence 467

Exploring Cognitive Psychology 468
Measures and Structures of Intelligence 470
History of Intelligence Testing and Scoring 470
Intelligence Scales 472
Factor Analysis of Intelligence 472

Information Processing and Intelligence 477

Process Timing Theories 478

The Componential Theory and Complex Problem Solving 480

Biological Bases of Intelligence 482

Alternative Approaches to Intelligence 484

Cultural Context and Intelligence 484

Gardner: Multiple Intelligences 487

Sternberg: The Triarchic Theory 489

Artificial Intelligence: Computer Simulations 491

Can a Computer Program Be "Intelligent"? 492

Questions About the Intelligence of Intelligent Programs 499

Improving Intelligence: Effective, Ineffective, and Questionable Strategies 501

Summary 503

Thinking About Thinking: Factual, Analytical, Creative, and Practical Questions 505

Key Terms 506

Annotated Suggested Readings 506

Glossary 507

References 525

Name Index 559

Subject Index 567

Credits 583

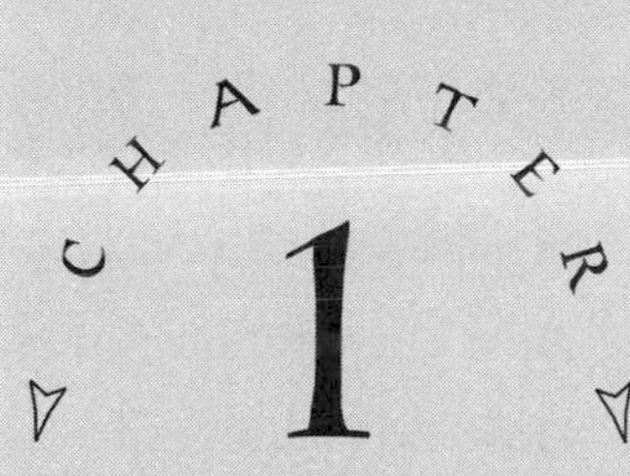

Introduction to Cognitive Psychology

Chapter Outline

Exploring Cognitive Psychology

Cognitive Psychology Defined

Philosophical Antecedents of Psychology: Rationalism Versus Empiricism

Psychological Antecedents of Cognitive Psychology
- Early Dialectics in the Psychology of Cognition
- From Associationism to Behaviorism
- Gestalt Psychology

The Emergence of Cognitive Psychology
- The Early Role of Psychobiology
- Add a Dash of Technology: Engineering and Computation

Research Methods in Cognitive Psychology
- Goals of Research
- Distinctive Research Methods

Key Issues and Fields Within Cognitive Psychology
- Underlying Themes in the Study of Cognitive Psychology
- Chapter Previews

Summary

Thinking About Thinking: Factual, Analytical, Creative, and Practical Questions

Key Terms

Annotated Suggested Readings

EXPLORING COGNITIVE PSYCHOLOGY

1. **What is cognitive psychology?**
2. **How did psychology develop as a science?**
3. **How did cognitive psychology develop from psychology?**
4. **How have other disciplines contributed to the development of theory and research in cognitive psychology?**
5. **What methods do cognitive psychologists use to study how people think?**
6. **What are the current issues and various fields of study within cognitive psychology?**

COGNITIVE PSYCHOLOGY DEFINED

What will you be studying in a textbook about cognitive psychology?

1. *Cognition:* People think.
2. *Cognitive psychology:* Scientists think about how people think.
3. *Students of cognitive psychology:* People think about how scientists think about how people think.
4. *Professors who profess to students about cognitive psychology:* You get the idea.

To be more specific, **cognitive psychology** deals with how people perceive, learn, remember, and think about information. A cognitive psychologist might study how people perceive various shapes, why they remember some facts but forget others, how they learn language, or how they think when they play chess or solve everyday problems. Why do objects look farther away on foggy days than they really are, sometimes deceiving drivers and leading to car accidents? Why do many people remember a particular experience (e.g., seeing O. J. Simpson's white Ford Bronco cruising down a highway while being chased by police cruisers), yet they forget the names of people whom they have known for many years? Why are many people more afraid of traveling in planes than in automobiles, when the chances of injury or death are so much higher in an automobile than in a plane? These are some of the kinds of questions that we can answer through the study of cognitive psychology.

This chapter introduces the field of cognitive psychology by describing the intellectual history of the study of human thinking, particularly emphasizing some of the issues and concerns that arise when we think about how people think. The historical perspective is followed by a brief overview of the major methods, issues, and content areas of cognitive psychology. The ideas presented in this chapter will provide a foundation on which to build an understanding of the topics in cognitive psychology covered in the remaining chapters.

Why study the history of this field—or any other field, for that matter? For one thing, if we know where we came from, we may have a better understanding of where we are heading. For another, we may learn from past mistakes—so that when we make mistakes, they will be fresh, new mistakes and not the same old ones. In addition, many of the issues we now face in cognitive psychology, as in any other field, have deep roots in our early intellectual history. Over the course of intellectual history, our ways of addressing these issues have changed, but some of the fundamental questions remain much the same. Finally, by viewing our own intellectual history, we may see patterns in the development of ideas—in effect, we may learn about how people think by studying how people have thought about thinking.

One of the patterns that emerge from a study of intellectual history is the observation that the progression of ideas often involves a *dialectical process.* In a dialectic, a *thesis* (statement of belief) is proposed. For example, one school of thought has long held that many aspects of human behavior (e.g., intelligence or personality) are entirely governed by human nature. Other thinkers consider the thesis, and if it seems to enhance understanding, the idea may be accepted. After a while, however, some thinkers notice apparent flaws in the thesis, and eventually (or perhaps even quite soon), an *antithesis* (statement that counters the previous statement of belief) emerges. For example, an alternative school of thought has postulated that many aspects of human behavior are determined almost entirely by our nurture—the environmental contexts in which we are reared and in which we later function as adults.

Sooner or later, the debate between the thesis and the antithesis leads to a *synthesis,* which integrates the most credible features of each of the two views. For example, in the debate over nature versus nurture, it has been asserted that various aspects of human behavior are governed by an interaction between our innate (inborn) nature and our environmental nurture. If this synthesis seems to advance our understanding of a subject, it then serves as a new thesis, which is followed by a new antithesis, then a new synthesis, and so on. This observation of the dialectical progression of ideas was advanced by Georg Hegel (1770–1831), a German philosopher who came to his ideas by synthesizing some of the views of his intellectual predecessors and contemporaries.

PHILOSOPHICAL ANTECEDENTS OF PSYCHOLOGY: RATIONALISM VERSUS EMPIRICISM

Where and when did the study of cognitive psychology begin? The answer to this question starts with an understanding of how the field of psychology itself emerged. Arguably, however far back our historical records may go, these documented accounts do not cover the earliest human efforts to understand how humans think. Nonetheless, we usually trace the earliest roots of psychology to two different approaches to understanding the human mind: (a) *philosophy,* which seeks to understand the general nature of many aspects of the world, primarily through *introspection,* the examination of inner ideas and experiences (from *intro-,* "inward, within" and *-spect,* "look"); and (b) *physiology,* the scientific study of life-sustaining functions in living matter, primarily through *empirical* (observation-based) methods. Even now, the issues raised in these two parent fields continue to influence the

(a) (b)

(a) According to the rationalist, the only route to truth is reasoned contemplation; (b) according to the empiricist, the only route to truth is meticulous observation. Cognitive psychology, like other sciences, depends on the work of both rationalists and empiricists.

way in which psychology has developed. In fact, many of the fundamental questions in physiology and philosophy are still among the fundamental questions being asked in psychology today. For example, cognitive psychologists still ask, "Are human psychological characteristics, and even human knowledge, *innate* (inherited from our parents and other ancestors) or *acquired* (learned through our interactions with our physical and social environments)?" "What is the best way to find and to understand answers to questions—by making observations through the use of our senses, or by using logical means of interpreting the information we have available?"

Two Greek philosophers, Plato (ca. 428–348 B.C.) and his student Aristotle (384–322 B.C.), have profoundly affected modern thinking in psychology and in many other fields. Plato and Aristotle differed in their views of the nature of reality. Plato's dualistic *theory of forms* stated that reality resides not in the concrete objects (e.g., tables or chairs) we perceive through our body's senses, but in the abstract forms that these objects represent. Thus, in this view, reality is not inherent in any particular objects (e.g., chairs) we see or touch, but in the eternal abstract *ideas* of objects that exist in our minds. Aristotle, in contrast, believed that reality lies *only* in the concrete world of objects that our bodies sense, and so Plato's intellectual forms (e.g., the idea of a chair) are really derivations of concrete objects.

Plato and Aristotle likewise disagreed regarding how to investigate their ideas, each preferring a different method of inquiry. Thus, they disagreed not only about what was truth but also about how to find truth. According to Plato, observations of imperfect, concrete objects and actions would mislead us and take us away from truth. Therefore, his approach was that of a **rationalist**—one who believes that the route to knowledge is through logical analysis. In contrast, Aristotle (a naturalist and biologist, as well as a philosopher) believed that observations of the external world were the only means to arrive at truth. Therefore, his approach was that of an **empiricist**—one who believes that we acquire knowledge via empirical evidence, obtained through experience and observation.

Aristotle's view, then, leads directly to empirical investigations of psychology, whereas Plato's view foreshadows the various uses of reasoning in theory development. Rationalist theories without any connection to observations may not be valid, but mountains of observational data without an organizing theoretical framework may not be meaningful. We might see Plato's rationalist view of the world as a thesis, and Aristotle's empirical view as an antithesis. Most psychologists today seek a synthesis of the two: They base empirical observations on theory but in turn use these observations to revise their theories.

In the seventeenth century, these contrasting ideas emerge again with the French rationalist, René Descartes (1596–1650), and the British empiricist, John Locke (1632–1704). Descartes agreed with Plato in viewing the introspective, reflective method as being superior to empirical methods for finding truth, whereas Locke shared Aristotle's reverence for empirical observation. Descartes's rationalist philosophy contributed much to the modern philosophy of mind (a grandparent of psychology), and his views had numerous other implications for psychology. In contrast to Descartes, Locke's Aristotelian (and perhaps anti-Cartesian) valuing of empirical observation naturally accompanied his view that humans are born without knowledge—and must therefore seek knowledge through empirical observation. Locke's term for this view is *tabula rasa* (meaning "blank slate" in Latin): Life and experience "write" knowledge upon us. For Locke, then, the study of learning is the key to understanding the human mind. He believed that there are no innate ideas whatsoever.

In the eighteenth century, debates about empiricism versus rationalism reached a peak. The German philosopher, Immanuel Kant (1724–1804), began the process of dialectical synthesis for these questions. In discussing rationalism versus empiricism, and whether knowledge is innate or is passively acquired through experience, Kant firmly declared that both rationalism and empiricism have their place. Both must work together in the quest for truth.

Did Kant settle these debates once and for all? Certainly not. Scholars will always wrestle with aspects of these problems; that is the nature of intellectual inquiry. Kant did, however, effectively redefine many of the issues with which philosophers before him had grappled. Kant's enormous impact on philosophy interacted with nineteenth-century scientific exploration of the body and how it works, to produce profound influences on the eventual establishment of psychology as a discipline in the 1800s, and cognitive psychology many years later, in the late 1950s and early 1960s.

Psychological Antecedents of Cognitive Psychology

The main psychological perspectives build on and react to those perspectives that came before; the dialectical process that appeared throughout the history of philosophy and early psychology also threads through modern psychology. The early psychologists posed yet another fundamental question that continues to perplex cognitive psychologists: Shall we gain an understanding of the human mind by studying its *structures* (much as we study the structures of the body by studying anatomy) or by studying its *functions* (much as we study the processes of the body by studying physiology)? Although cognitive psychology was not identified as a distinct branch of psychology until the latter half of the twentieth century, the questions it addresses were the principal questions addressed by psychologists in the first half of this century.

Early Dialectics in the Psychology of Cognition

Structuralism

The goal of **structuralism,** generally considered to be the first major school of thought in psychology, was to understand the *structure* (configuration of elements) of the mind and its perceptions by analyzing those perceptions into their constituent components. Structuralists would take the perception of a flower, for example, and analyze the perception in terms of the constituent colors, geometric forms, size relations, and so on.

An important progenitor of structuralism was German psychologist Wilhelm Wundt (1832–1920). Wundt suggested that the optimal method by which a person could be trained to analyze the structure of the mind was to study sensory experiences through introspection. To Wundt, *introspection* meant looking inward at pieces of information passing through consciousness, such as at the sensations experienced when looking at a flower. In effect, we analyze our own perceptions.

Wundt had many followers, such as his American student, Edward Titchener (1867–1927). Titchener (1910) believed that all consciousness could be reduced to three elementary states: *sensations*—the basic elements of perception (see chapter 4); *images*—the pictures we form in our minds to characterize what we perceive (see chapters 4 and 5); and *affections*—the constituents of emotions such as love and hate. Nonetheless, even though many of Wundt's followers embraced structuralism, other early psychologists criticized both the method (introspection) and the focus (elementary structures of sensation) of structuralism.

Functionalism: An Alternative to Structuralism

An alternative to structuralism suggested that psychologists should focus on the *processes* of thought rather than on its *contents.* **Functionalists** asked, "What do people *do,* and *why* do they do it?" whereas structuralists had asked, "What are the elementary contents [structures] of the human mind?" Functionalists held that the key to understanding the human mind

Wilhelm Wundt was no great success in school, failing time and again and frequently finding himself subject to the ridicule of others. However, Wundt later showed that school performance does not always predict career success because he is considered to be among the most influential psychologists of all time.

Many cognitive psychologists continue to regard William James, a physician, philosopher, psychologist, and brother of author Henry James, as among the greatest psychologists ever, although James himself seems to have rejected psychology later in his life.

and behavior is to study the processes of how and why the mind works as it does, rather than to study the structural contents and elements of the mind. Functionalists addressed the broad question of how and why the mind works as it does by seeking functional relationships between a specific earlier *stimulus* (something that prompts action; plural, *stimuli;* from the Latin for a sharpened stick that Romans used for goading sluggish animals into action) and a specific subsequent *response* (an action or reaction that is linked to a stimulus).

Functionalists were unified by the kinds of questions they asked, but not necessarily by the answers they found or by the methods they used for finding those answers. We might even suggest that they were unified in believing that a diversity of methods could be used, as long as a given method helped to answer the particular question being probed.

Because functionalists believed in using whichever methods best answered a given researcher's questions, it seems natural for functionalism to have led to pragmatism. **Pragmatists** believe that knowledge is validated by its usefulness: What can you *do* with it? Pragmatists are concerned not only with knowing what people do, but also with what we can do with our knowledge of what people do. For example, pragmatists believe in the importance of the psychology of learning and memory, in part because it could help us improve the performance of children in school.

A leader in guiding functionalism toward pragmatism was William James (1842–1910), whose chief functional contribution to the field of psychology was a single book: his landmark *Principles of Psychology* (1890/1970). Even today, cognitive psychologists frequently point to the writings of James in discussions of core topics in the field, such as attention, consciousness, and perception. James proved that one truly influential work, as well as the reputation of its author, can help shape a field.

Another of the early pragmatists who has profoundly influenced contemporary thinking in cognitive psychology was John Dewey (1859–1952). Dewey is remembered primarily for his pragmatic approach to thinking and to schooling. Much of what cognitive psychologists and educational psychologists say today builds on what Dewey said early in the twentieth century. For example, according to John Dewey, to learn effectively, we need to see the point of our education—the practical use of it. Dewey and other pragmatists raised yet another issue that continues to be a source of controversy among cognitive psychologists: Should research be evaluated in terms of its immediate usefulness in everyday applications or in terms of its profoundness of insight into understanding human cognition?

PRACTICAL APPLICATIONS OF COGNITIVE PSYCHOLOGY

Take a moment right now to put the idea of pragmatism into use. Think about ways to make the information you are learning in this course more useful to you. Part of the work has already been done—notice that the chapter begins with questions that make the information more coherent and useful, and the chapter summary returns to those questions. Does the text successfully answer the questions posed at the beginning of the chapter? Come up with your own questions and try organizing your notes in the form of answers to your questions. Also, try relating this material to other courses or activities you participate in. For example, you may be called upon to explain to a friend how to use a new computer program. A good way to start would be to ask that person if he or she has any questions. That way, the information you provide is more directly useful to your friend, rather than forcing this individual to search for the information he or she needs in a long, one-sided lecture.

ASSOCIATIONISM: AN INTEGRATIVE SYNTHESIS

Associationism, like functionalism, was less a rigid school of psychology than an influential way of thinking. Associationism examines how events or ideas can become associated with one another in the mind, to result in a form of learning. For example, associations may result from *contiguity* (associating things that tend to occur together at about the same time), *similarity* (associating things with similar features or properties), or *contrast* (associating things that seem to show polarities; e.g., hot/cold, light/dark, day/night).

In the late 1800s, associationist Hermann Ebbinghaus (1850–1909) was the first experimenter to apply associationist principles systematically. Specifically, Ebbinghaus studied and observed his own mental processes, using much more rigorous experimental techniques ("systematic experimental introspection," such as counting his errors, recording his response times, etc.) than those of Wundt's methods of introspection. Through his self-observations, Ebbinghaus studied how people learn and remember material through *rehearsal*—conscious repetition of to-be-learned material. Among other findings, he made a groundbreaking experimental discovery—that frequent repetition can fix mental associations more firmly in memory, and, by extension, that repetition aids in learning (see chapter 6).

Another influential associationist, Edward Lee Thorndike (1874–1949), held that the role of "satisfaction" was the key to forming associations. Thorndike termed this principle the *law of effect* (1905): A stimulus will tend to produce a certain response over time if an organism is rewarded for that response. Thorndike believed that an organism learns to respond in a given way (the *effect)* in a given situation if it is repeatedly rewarded for doing so (the *satisfaction,* which serves as a stimulus to future actions). Thus, a child given treats for solving arithmetic problems correctly learns to solve arithmetic problems accurately because he or she forms associations between valid solutions and treats.

FROM ASSOCIATIONISM TO BEHAVIORISM

Other researchers, who were contemporaries of Thorndike, used animal experiments to probe stimulus–response relationships in ways that differed from those of Thorndike and his fellow associationists. These researchers straddled the line between associationism and the emerging field of behaviorism. Some of these researchers, like Thorndike and other associationists, studied responses that were voluntary (although perhaps lacking any conscious thought, as in Thorndike's work), but others studied responses that were involuntarily triggered, in response to what appear to be unrelated external events.

In Russia, Nobel Prize-winning physiologist Ivan Pavlov (1849–1936) studied involuntary learning behavior of this sort, beginning with his observation that dogs salivated in response to the sight of the lab technician who fed them before the dogs even saw whether the technician had food. To Pavlov, this response indicated a form of learning, termed *classically conditioned learning,* over which the dogs had no conscious control; in the dogs' minds, some type of involuntary learning linked the technician to the food (Pavlov, 1955). Pavlov's landmark work paved the way for the development of behaviorism. Of particular interest was the observation later made by Robert Rescorla (1967) that classical conditioning involves more than just an association based on temporal contiguity (e.g., the food and the conditioned stimulus occurring at about the same time). Effective conditioning requires *contingency* (e.g., the presentation of food being contingent on the presentation of the conditioned stimulus; Rescorla & A. R. Wagner, 1972; A. R. Wagner & Rescorla, 1972).

Behaviorism, which may be considered an extreme version of associationism, focuses entirely on the association between the environment and an observable behavior. According to strict, extreme ("radical") behaviorists, any hypotheses about internal thoughts and ways of thinking are nothing more than speculation, and although they might belong within the domain of philosophy, they certainly have no place in psychology.

PROPONENTS OF BEHAVIORISM

The man usually acknowledged as the father of radical behaviorism is John Watson (1878–1958). Watson, who had no use for internal mental contents or mechanisms, dismissed thinking as subvocalized speech. As philosopher Herbert Feigl (as cited in M. Eysenck & Keane, 1990) described it, Watson "made up his windpipe that he had no mind." Still, although Watson disdained key aspects of functionalism, he was clearly influenced by the functionalists in his emphasis on what people do and what causes their actions. Behaviorism also differed from previous movements in psychology by shifting the emphasis of experimental research from human to animal participants. Historically, much behaviorist work has been conducted (and still is) with laboratory animals, such as rats, because these animals allow for much greater behavioral control of relationships between the environment and the behavior emitted in reaction to it. The simpler the organism's emotional and physiological makeup, the less the researcher needs to worry about any of the interference that can plague psychological research with humans as participants. One problem with using animals, however, is determining whether the research can be *generalized* to humans (i.e., applied more generally to humans instead of just to the kinds of animals that were studied).

Since the 1960s, radical behaviorism has seemed almost synonymous with one of its most radical proponents, B. F. Skinner (1904–1990). For Skinner, virtually all forms of human behavior, not just learning, could be explained by behavior emitted in reaction to the environment, which could be studied effectively by observing animal behavior. Skinner rejected mental mechanisms and believed instead that *operant conditioning,* involving the strengthening or weakening of behavior, contingent on the presence or absence of reinforcement (rewards) or punishments, could explain all forms of human behavior. Skinner applied his experimental analysis of behavior to almost everything, from learning to language acquisition to problem solving, and even to the control of behavior in society. Largely because of Skinner's towering presence, behaviorism dominated the discipline of psychology, including the methods and the areas of interest, for several decades.

Behaviorists Daring to Peek Into the Black Box

Whereas most behaviorists shunned peering into the "black box" of the human mind, focusing instead on observable behavior alone, some psychologists were becoming curious about the contents of the mysterious box. For example, Edward Tolman (1886–1959), an early behaviorist, thought that the behavior of neither animals nor persons could be understood without also taking into account the purpose of, and the plan for, the behavior. Tolman (1932) believed that all behavior is directed toward some goal, whether a rat is trying to find food in a maze or a human is trying to escape an unpleasant situation. Tolman thus can be viewed as a forefather of modern cognitive psychology.

A more recent criticism of behaviorism also suggests that it is too limited (Bandura, 1977b), but for yet another reason. This criticism asserts that learning appears to result not merely from direct rewards for behavior; it can also be social, resulting from observations of the rewards or punishments given to others. This view emphasizes how we observe and model our own behavior after the behavior of others, learning by example. This consideration of social learning opens the way to considering what is happening inside the mind of the individual.

Gestalt Psychology

Of the many critics of behaviorism, Gestalt psychologists may have been among the most avid. According to **Gestalt psychology,** we best understand psychological phenomena when we view them as organized, structured wholes, not when we break the phenomena down into smaller parts. Actually, the Gestalt movement was a reaction not only against the early behaviorist tendency to understand behavior in terms of conditioning, but also against the structuralist tendency to analyze mental processes into elementary sensations. The maxim, "the whole differs from the sum of its parts," aptly sums up the Gestalt perspective. To understand the perception of a flower, for example, we would have to take into account the whole of the experience. We could not understand such a perception merely in terms of a description of forms, colors, sizes, and so on. The influence of Gestalt psychology has been most profound in regard to the study of the perception of forms (e.g., Köhler, 1940) and the study of insight (e.g., Köhler, 1927; Wertheimer, 1945/1959), an aspect of problem solving.

THE EMERGENCE OF COGNITIVE PSYCHOLOGY

Up until now, we have emphasized the philosophical and psychological developments that led to the emergence of cognitive psychology. Developments in other fields also contributed to the development of **cognitivism** (the belief that much of human behavior can be understood if we understand first how people think) and of modern cognitive psychology. The fields that have most contributed to the emergence of cognitive psychology are scientific fields such as psychobiology (also called "biological psychology," "physiological psychology," or even "biopsychology"), linguistics, and anthropology, as well as technological fields such as communication systems, engineering, and computation.

THE EARLY ROLE OF PSYCHOBIOLOGY

Ironically, one of Watson's former students, Karl Spencer Lashley (1890–1958), was among the first (in a 1948 symposium) to articulate the need for psychologists to go beyond behaviorism, to study topics not easily explained by simple conditioning, and to embrace methods other than the experimental manipulation of environmental contingencies (Gardner, 1985). Lashley was deeply interested in *neuroanatomy* (the study of the structures of the brain) and in how the organization of the brain governs human activity. Lashley brashly challenged the behaviorist view that the human brain is a passive organ merely responding to environmental contingencies outside the individual; instead, Lashley considered the brain to be an active, dynamic organizer of behavior. Lashley sought to understand how the macro-organization of the human brain made possible such complex, planned activities as musical performance, game playing, and using language—none of which were, in his view, readily explicable in terms of simple conditioning.

In the same vein, but at a different level of analysis, Donald Hebb (1949) was the first psychologist to provide a detailed, testable theory of how the brain could support cognitive processes. His influential work provides a strong foundation for some of the current trends in cognitive psychology. Hebb was interested in how the structure of neural connections in the brain changes as a result of learning. His main contribution lay in proposing *cell assemblies*, coordinated neural structures that develop through frequent stimulation, as the basis for learning in the brain. Cell assemblies develop over time as the ability of one neuron (nerve cell) to stimulate firing in a connected neuron increases. A mental representation of some external event would be represented by a hierarchical structure of multiple cell assemblies. For example, your mental representation of your grandmother might consist of cell assemblies for her face, connected to assemblies for her voice, connected to assemblies for other attributes. When you think about her, you would activate those assemblies responsible for representing her. Hebb's work went beyond

Ulric Neisser *is a professor of psychology at Cornell University. His book,* Cognitive Psychology, *was instrumental in launching the cognitive revolution in psychology. He also has been a major proponent of an ecological approach to cognition and has shown the importance of studying cognitive processing in ecologically valid contexts.*

behavioral approaches to learning by placing mental events within the context of the integrated action of nervous system.

Behaviorists did not jump at the opportunity to agree with theorists like Lashley and Hebb. In fact, behaviorist B. F. Skinner (1957) wrote an entire book describing how language acquisition and usage could be explained purely in terms of environmental contingencies. This work stretched Skinner's framework too far, leaving Skinner open to attack. An attack was indeed forthcoming. Linguist Noam Chomsky (1959) wrote a scathing review of Skinner's ideas. In his article, Chomsky stressed both the biological basis and the creative potential of language—the infinite numbers of sentences we can produce with ease—as defying behaviorist notions that we learn language by reinforcement. Even young children are continually producing novel sentences for which they could not have been reinforced in the past. Chomsky argued that our understanding of language is constrained not so much by what we have heard, but by an innate language acquisition device (LAD) that all humans possess. This device allows the infant to use what it hears in order to infer the grammar of its linguistic environment. In particular, the LAD actively limits the number of permissible grammatical constructions. Thus, it is the structure of the mind, rather than the structure of environmental contingencies, that guides our acquisition of language.

Add a Dash of Technology: Engineering and Computation

In addition to scientific developments, technological developments were also beginning to influence the way in which psychologists viewed the human mind. Technological developments in telecommunications, in human-factors engineering, and in digital computers led to analogous developments in psychological theory, particularly in regard to the processing of information. Following many of the issues faced in computer information processing, psychologists began to talk about information codes (systems of symbols or signals for representing information), about limitations in processing capacity, and about the processing of information either *serially* (one item or step at a time, as on a digital computer) or in *parallel* (more than one item at a time, as in multiple sound waves on a telecommunications system).

By the end of the 1950s, some psychologists were intrigued by the tantalizing notion that machines could be programmed to demonstrate the intelligent processing of information. By 1956, a new phrase had entered our vocabulary: **artificial intelligence (AI),** which is the attempt by humans to construct systems that show intelligence, and particularly, the intelligent processing of information (*Merriam-Webster's Collegiate Dictionary,* 1993). However, early developers of AI were more interested in maximizing information processing efficiency than in simulating human intelligence and how humans solve problems. For example, early programs for playing chess or for demonstrating expertise showed "intelligence" by using processes entirely different from the processes used by humans. Today's programs, such as the "Deep Blue" program that beat world champion Gary Kasparov in 1997, also function in a way that is quite distinct from the way humans play chess. As you may well imagine, initial attempts to get computers to simulate human intelligence—or even to demonstrate machine intelligence—proved to be more difficult than anticipated. Early on, investigators discovered two key insights from computer modeling: (a) Many things that are very easy for computers to do (e.g., quickly calculate 123,456,789 × 987,654,321) are very difficult for people to do, *but* (b) many things that are very easy for people to do (e.g., recognize the face of a friend) are very hard for computers to do.

By the early 1960s, developments in psychobiology, linguistics, anthropology, and artificial intelligence, as well as the reactions against behaviorism by many mainstream psychologists, converged to create an atmosphere ripe for revolution. Early cognitivists argued (e.g., G. A. Miller, Galanter, & Pribram, 1960; Newell, Shaw, & Simon, 1957b) that traditional behaviorist accounts of behavior were inadequate precisely because they said nothing about—indeed, they ignored—how people think. Ulric Neisser's book *Cognitive Psychology* (Neisser, 1967) was especially critical in bringing cognitivism to prominence by informing undergraduates, graduate students, and academics about the newly developing field. Neisser defined *cognitive psychology* as the study of how people learn, structure, store, and use knowledge. Subsequently, Allen Newell and Herbert Simon (1972) proposed detailed models of human thinking and problem solving from the most basic levels to the most complex. By the 1970s, cognitive psychology was widely recognized as a major field of psychological study, with a distinctive set of research methods.

Herbert A. Simon *is a professor of computer science and psychology at Carnegie-Mellon University. He is known for his pioneering work, with Allen Newell and others, on constructing and testing computer models that simulate human thought, and for his experimental tests of these models. He also has been a major advocate of thinking-aloud protocols as a means of studying cognitive processing.*

Research Methods in Cognitive Psychology

Goals of Research

To better understand the specific methods used by cognitive psychologists, one must first grasp the goals of research in cognitive psychology, some of which are highlighted here. Briefly, those goals include data gathering, data analysis, theory development, hypothesis formulation, hypothesis testing, and perhaps even application to settings outside the research environment. Often, researchers simply seek to gather as much information as possible about a particular phenomenon. They may or may not have preconceived notions regarding what they may find while gathering the data. In any case, their research focuses on describing particular cognitive phenomena, such as how people recognize faces or how they develop expertise.

Data gathering reflects an empirical aspect of the scientific enterprise. Once there are sufficient data on the cognitive phenomenon of interest, cognitive psychologists use various methods for drawing inferences from the data. Ideally, they use converging types of evidence to support their hypotheses. Sometimes, just a quick glance at the data leads to intuitive inferences regarding patterns that emerge from those data. More commonly, however, researchers use various statistical means of analyzing the data.

Data gathering and statistical analysis aid researchers in describing cognitive phenomena. No scientific pursuit could get far without such descriptions. However, most cognitive psychologists want to understand more than the *what* of cognition; most seek also to understand the *how* and the *why* of thinking. That is, researchers seek ways to explain cognition, as well as to describe it. To move beyond descriptions, cognitive psychologists must use reasoning to leap from what is observed directly to what can be inferred regarding observations.

Suppose that we wish to study an aspect of cognition, such as how people comprehend information in textbooks. We usually start with a **theory** (an organized body of general explanatory principles regarding a phenomenon), as well as some reasonable **hypotheses** (tentative proposals regarding expected empirical consequences of the theory, such as the outcomes of research) derived from the theory, regarding how people comprehend textbook information. Then we seek to test the theory and thereby to see whether it has the power to predict certain aspects of the phenomenon in question. In other words, our thought process is, "If our theory is correct, then whenever *x* occurs, outcome *y* should result."

Next, we test our hypotheses through experimentation. Even if particular findings appear to confirm a given hypothesis, the findings must be subjected to statistical analysis, to determine their statistical significance. Measures of *statistical significance* indicate the likelihood that the given findings do not merely represent random fluctuations in the data.

Once our hypothetical predictions have been experimentally tested and statistically analyzed, the findings from those experiments may lead to further data gathering, data analysis, theory development, hypothesis formulation, and hypothesis testing. In addition, many cognitive psychologists hope to use insights gained from research to help people use cognition in real-life situations. Some research in cognitive psychology is applied from the start, seeking to help people improve their lives and the conditions under which they live their lives. Thus, basic research may lead to everyday applications. For each of these purposes, different research methods offer differing advantages and disadvantages.

Distinctive Research Methods

Cognitive psychologists use various methods to explore how humans think. These methods include the following: (a) laboratory or other controlled experiments, (b) psychobiological research, (c) self-reports, (d) case studies, (e) naturalistic observation, and (f) computer simulations and artificial intelligence (see Table 1.1 for descriptions and examples of each method). As the table shows, each method offers distinctive advantages and disadvantages.

Experiments on Human Behavior

Controlled laboratory experiments are probably the method most people think of when they think of scientific research. You may recall from introductory psychology courses, or introductory courses in other scientific fields, that in controlled experimental designs, an experimenter conducts research in a laboratory setting in which the experimenter controls as many aspects of the experimental situation as possible. The experimenter then manipulates the independent variables, controlling for the effects of irrelevant variables, and observes the effects on the dependent variables (outcomes).

In implementing the experimental method, the experimenter must use a representative sample of the population of interest and must exert rigorous control over the experimental conditions, randomly assigning participants to the treatment and the control conditions. If those requisites for the experimental method are fulfilled, the experimenter may be able to infer probable causality—the effects of the independent variable (the treatment) on the dependent variable (the outcome). If the outcomes in the treatment condition show a statistically significant difference from the outcomes in the control condition, the experimenter can infer the likelihood of a causal link between the independent variable and the dependent variable. Because the researcher can establish a likely causal link between the given independent variables and the dependent variables, controlled laboratory experiments offer an excellent means of testing hypotheses.

For example, suppose that we wanted to see whether loud, distracting noises influence the ability to perform well on a particular cognitive task (e.g., reading a passage from a textbook and responding to comprehension questions). Ideally, we would first select a random sample of participants from within our total population of interest. We would then randomly assign each participant to a treatment condition or a control condition, and would then introduce some distracting loud noises to the participants in our treatment condition, but not to the participants in our control condition. We would present the cognitive task to participants in both the treatment condition and the control condition, measuring their performance by some means (e.g., speed and accuracy of responses to comprehension questions). Finally, we would analyze our results statistically, to see whether the difference between the two groups reached statistical significance. If the participants in the treatment condition showed poorer performance than the participants in the control condition, at a statistically significant level, we might then infer that loud distracting noises did, indeed, influence the ability to perform well on this particular cognitive task.

In cognitive-psychological research, the dependent variables may be quite diverse, but they often involve various outcome measures of accuracy (e.g., frequency of errors), of response times, or of both. Among the myriad possibilities for independent variables are characteristics of the situation, of the task, or of the participants. For example, characteristics of the situation may involve the presence versus the absence of particular stimuli, such as hints during a problem-solving task; characteristics of the task may involve reading versus listening to a series of words and then responding to comprehension questions; characteristics of the participants may include age differences, differences in educational status, or differences based on test scores.

Although characteristics of the situation or task may be manipulated through random assignment of participants to either the treatment or the control group, characteristics of the participant are not easily manipulated experimentally. For example, if the experimenter wants to study the effects of aging on speed and accuracy of problem solving, the researcher cannot randomly assign participants to various age groups. In such situations, researchers often use other kinds of studies, such as studies involving *correlation,* a statistical relationship between two (or more) attributes (characteristics of the participants, of a situation, etc.), expressed as a number on a scale that ranges from −1.00 (a negative correlation) to 0 (no correlation) to +1.00 (a positive correlation). For example, we may expect a negative correlation between fatigue and alertness, no correlation between intelligence and length of ear lobe, and a positive correlation between vocabulary size and reading comprehension.

Findings of statistical relationships are highly informative and their value should not be underrated. Also, because correlational studies do not require the random assignment of participants to treatment and control conditions, these methods may be flexibly applied. However, correlational studies generally do not permit unequivocal inferences regarding causality, so many cognitive psychologists strongly prefer experimental data to correlational data.

TABLE 1.1 RESEARCH METHODS

Cognitive psychologists use controlled experiments, psychobiological research, self-reports, case studies, naturalistic observation, and computer simulations and artificial intelligence when studying cognitive phenomena.

Method	Controlled Laboratory Experiments	Psychobiological Research	Self-Reports, Such as Verbal Protocols, Self-Ratings, Diaries
Description of method	Obtain samples of performance at a particular time and place	Study animal brains and human brains, using postmortem studies, as well as various psychobiological measures or imaging techniques (see chapter 2)	Obtain participants' reports of own cognition in progress or as recollected
Validity of causal inferences: random assignment of subjects	Usually	Not usually	Not applicable
Validity of causal inferences: experimental control of independent variables	Usually	Varies widely, depending on the particular technique	Probably not
Samples: size	May be any size	Often small	Probably small
Samples: representativeness	May be representative	Often not representative	May be representative
Ecological validity	Not impossible; depends on the task and the context to which it is being applied	Unlikely under some circumstances	Maybe; see strengths and weaknesses
Information about individual differences	Usually de-emphasized	Yes	Yes
Strengths	Ease of administration, of scoring, and of statistical analysis make it relatively easy to apply to representative samples of a population; relatively high probability of drawing valid causal inferences	Provides "hard" evidence of cognitive functions by relating them to physiological activity; offers an alternative view of cognitive processes unavailable by other means; may lead to possibilities for treating persons with serious cognitive deficits	Access to introspective insights from participants' point of view, which may be unavailable via other means
Weaknesses	Not always possible to generalize results beyond a specific place, time, and task setting; discrepancies between real-life behavior and behavior in the laboratory	Limited accessibility for most researchers; requires access both to appropriate subjects and to equipment that may be extremely expensive and difficult to obtain; small samples; many studies are based on studies of abnormal brains or of animal brains, so generalizability of findings to normal human populations may be troublesome	Inability to report on processes occurring outside conscious awareness **Verbal protocols & self-ratings:** Data gathering may influence cognitive process being reported **Recollections:** Possible discrepancies between actual cognition and recollected cognitive processes and products
Examples	David Meyer and Roger Schvaneveldt (1971) developed a laboratory task in which they very briefly presented two strings of letters (either words or nonwords) to subjects, and then they asked the subjects to make a decision about each of the strings of letters, such as deciding whether the letters made a legitimate word or deciding whether a word belonged to a predesignated category	Elizabeth Warrington and Tim Shallice (1972; Shallice & Warrington, 1970) have observed that lesions (areas of injury) in the left parietal lobe of the brain are associated with serious deficits in short-term (brief, active) memory but no impairment of long-term memory, but persons with lesions in the medial (middle) temporal regions of the brain show relatively normal short-term memory but grave deficits in long-term memory (Shallice, 1979; Warrington, 1982)	In a study of mental imagery, Stephen Kosslyn and his colleagues (Kosslyn, Seger, Pani, & Hillger, 1990) asked students to keep a weeklong diary recording all of their mental images in each sensory modality

Case Studies	Naturalistic Observations	Computer Simulations and Artificial Intelligence (AI)
Engage in intensive study of single individuals, drawing general conclusions about behavior	Observe real-life situations, as in classrooms, work settings, or homes	**Simulations:** Attempt to make computers simulate human cognitive performance on various tasks **AI:** Attempt to make computers demonstrate intelligent cognitive performance, regardless of whether the process resembles human cognitive processing
Highly unlikely	Not applicable	Not applicable
Highly unlikely	No	Full control of variables of interest
Almost certain to be small	Probably small	Not applicable
Not likely to be representative	May be representative	Not applicable
High ecological validity for individual cases; lower generalizability to others	Yes	Not applicable
Yes; richly detailed information regarding individuals	Possible, but emphasis is on environmental distinctions, not on individual differences	Not applicable
Access to richly detailed information about individuals, including information about historical and current contexts, which may not be available via other means; may lead to specialized applications for groups of exceptional individuals (e.g., prodigies, persons with brain damage)	Access to rich contextual information, which may be unavailable via other means	Allows exploration of a wide range of possibilities for modeling cognitive processes; allows clear testing to see whether hypotheses accurately predicted outcomes; may lead to wide range of practical applications (e.g., robotics for performing dangerous tasks or for performing in hazardous environments)
Applicability to other persons; small sample size and nonrepresentativeness of sample generally limits generalizability to population	Lack of experimental control; possible influence on naturalistic behavior due to the presence of the observer	Limitations imposed by limits of the hardware (i.e., the computer hardware), as well as of the software (the programs written by the researchers); distinctions between human intelligence and machine intelligence—even in simulations involving sophisticated modeling techniques, simulations may imperfectly model the way that the human brain thinks
Howard Gruber (1974/1981) conducted a case study of Charles Darwin, to explore in depth the psychological context for great intellectual creativity	Michael Cole (Cole, Gay, Glick, & Sharp, 1971) studied members of the Kpelle tribe in Africa, noting how the Kpelle's definitions of intelligence compared with traditional Western definitions of intelligence, as well as how cultural definitions of intelligence may govern intelligent behavior	**Simulations:** Through detailed computations, David Marr (1982) attempted to simulate human visual perception and proposed a theory of visual perception based on his computer models **AI:** Various AI programs have been written, which can demonstrate expertise (e.g., playing chess), but they probably do so via different processes than those used by human experts

Psychobiological Research

Through *psychobiological research,* investigators study the relationship between cognitive performance and cerebral events and structures. Chapter 2 describes various specific techniques used in psychobiological research; these techniques generally fall into three categories: (a) techniques for studying an individual's brain *postmortem* (after the death of an individual), relating the individual's cognitive function prior to death to observable features of the brain; (b) techniques for studying images showing structures of or activities in the brain of an individual who is known to have a particular cognitive deficit; or (c) techniques for obtaining information about cerebral processes during the normal performance of a cognitive activity.

Postmortem studies offered some of the first insights into how specific *lesions* (areas of injury in the brain) may be associated with particular cognitive deficits, and such studies continue to provide useful insights into how the brain influences cognitive function. Recent technological developments also have enabled researchers increasingly to study individuals with known cognitive deficits *in vivo* (while the individual is alive). The study of individuals with abnormal cognitive functions linked to cerebral pathologies often enhances our understanding of normal cognitive functions.

In addition, psychobiological researchers study some aspects of normal cognitive functioning by studying cerebral activity in animal participants. Researchers often use animal participants for experiments involving neurosurgical procedures that cannot be performed on humans because such procedures would be difficult, unethical, or impractical. For example, studies mapping neural activity in the cortex have been conducted on cats and on monkeys (e.g., psychobiological research on how the brain responds to visual stimuli; see chapter 4).

Some cognitive psychologists have questioned whether findings based on the cognitive and cerebral functioning of animals and of abnormal individuals may be generalized to apply to the cognitive and cerebral functioning of normal humans. Psychobiologists have responded to these questions in various ways, most of which go beyond the scope of this chapter (see chapter 2). As just one example, however, for some kinds of cognitive activity, the available technology permits researchers to study the dynamic cerebral activity of normal human participants during cognitive processing (see the brain-imaging techniques described in chapter 2).

Self-Reports, Case Studies, and Naturalistic Observation

Individual experiments and psychobiological studies often focus on precise specification of discrete aspects of cognition across individuals. To obtain richly textured information about how particular individuals think in a broad range of contexts, researchers may use *self-reports* (an individual's own account of cognitive processes), *case studies* (in-depth studies of individuals), and *naturalistic observation* (detailed studies of cognitive performance in everyday situations and nonlaboratory contexts). Whereas experimental research is most useful for testing hypotheses, research based on self-reports, case studies, and naturalistic observation is often particularly useful for the formulation of hypotheses.

The reliability of data based on various kinds of self-reports depends on the candor of the participants providing the reports. Even if participants are completely truthful in their reports, reports involving recollected information (e.g., diaries, retrospective accounts, questionnaires, and surveys) are notably less reliable than reports provided during the cognitive processing under investigation because participants sometimes forget what they did. In studying complex cognitive processes, such as problem solving or decision making, researchers often use a *verbal protocol,* in which the participants describe aloud all of their thoughts and ideas during the performance of a given cognitive task. (For example, "I like the apartment with the swimming pool better, but I can't really afford it, so I might choose. . . .")

An alternative to a verbal protocol is for participants to report specific information regarding a particular aspect of their cognitive processing. For example, in a study of insightful problem solving (see chapter 11), participants were asked, at 15-second intervals, to report numerical ratings indicating how close they felt they were to reaching a solution to a given problem. Unfortunately, even these methods of self-report have their limitations because cognitive processes may be altered by the act of giving the report (e.g., processes involving brief forms of memory; see chapter 5), and cognitive processes may occur outside of conscious awareness (e.g., processes that do not require conscious attention or that take place so rapidly that we fail to notice them; see chapter 3). To get an idea of some of the difficulties with self-reports, carry out the Investigating Cognitive Psychology tasks, which follow, and reflect on your experiences with self-reports.

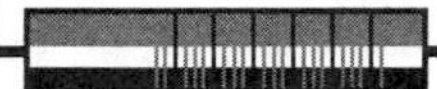

INVESTIGATING COGNITIVE PSYCHOLOGY

1. Without looking at your shoes, try reporting aloud the various steps involved in tying your shoe.
2. Recall aloud what you did on your last birthday.
3. Now, actually tie your shoe (or something else, such as a string tied around a table leg), reporting aloud the steps you take. Do you notice any differences between Task 1 and Task 3?
4. Report aloud how you pulled into consciousness the steps involved in tying your shoe or your memories of your last birthday. Can you report exactly how you pulled the information into conscious awareness? Can you report which part of your brain was most active during each of these tasks?

Case studies (e.g., the study of exceptionally gifted individuals) and naturalistic observations (e.g., the observation of individuals operating in nuclear power plants) may be used to complement findings from laboratory experiments because the former two methods of cognitive research offer high **ecological validity**, the degree to which particular findings in one context may be considered relevant outside of that context. As you probably know, *ecology* is the study of the interactive relationship between an organism (or organisms) and its environment. Many cognitive psychologists seek to understand the interactive relationship between human thought processes and the environments in which humans are thinking. Sometimes, cognitive processes that are commonly observed in one setting (e.g., in a laboratory) are not identical to those observed in another setting (e.g., in an air-traffic control tower or in a classroom).

Computer Simulations and Artificial Intelligence

It may be said that digital computers played a fundamental role in the emergence of the study of cognitive psychology. Their influence is both indirect—through models of human cognition based on models of how computers process information—and direct—through computer simulations and artificial intelligence.

In *computer simulations,* researchers program computers to imitate a given human function or process, such as performance on particular cognitive tasks (e.g., manipulating objects within three-dimensional space) or performance of particular cognitive processes (e.g., pattern recognition). Some researchers even have attempted to create computer models of the entire cognitive architecture of the human mind, and their models have stimulated heated discussions regarding how the human mind may function as a whole (see chapter 8). Sometimes, the distinction between simulation and artificial intelligence is blurred, as in the case of certain programs that are designed simultaneously to simulate human performance and to maximize functioning.

Putting It All Together

Cognitive psychologists often broaden and deepen their understanding of cognition through research in **cognitive science,** a cross-disciplinary field that uses ideas and methods from cognitive psychology, psychobiology, artificial intelligence, philosophy, linguistics, and anthropology. Cognitive scientists use these ideas and methods to focus on the study of how humans acquire and use knowledge. Cognitive psychologists also profit from collaborations with other kinds of psychologists, such as social psychologists (e.g., in the cross-disciplinary field of social cognition), psychologists who study motivation and emotion, and engineering psychologists (i.e., psychologists who study human–machine interactions). Collaborations with engineering psychologists illustrate the interplay between basic cognitive-psychological research and applied psychological investigation.

Key Issues and Fields Within Cognitive Psychology

Throughout this chapter, we have alluded to some of the key themes that arise in the study of cognitive psychology. Many of these issues have a long history, starting with early philosophical questioning. Others arise largely as a result of recent work in the field. Because these themes appear again and again in the various chapters of this textbook, a summary of these themes follows. Some of these questions go to the very core of the nature of the human mind.

Underlying Themes in the Study of Cognitive Psychology

If we review the major ideas in this chapter we discover some of the major themes that underlie all of cognitive psychology. What are some of these themes? Here are seven of them:

1. *Nature versus nurture:* One major issue in cognitive psychology is that of which is more influential in human cognition—nature or nurture? If we believe that innate characteristics of human cognition are more important, we might focus our research on studying innate characteristics of cognition. If we believe that the environment plays an important role in cognition, we might conduct research exploring how distinctive characteristics of the environment seem to influence cognition.
2. *Rationalism versus empiricism:* How should we discover the truth about ourselves and about the world around us? Should we do so by trying to reason logically, based on what we already know, or by observing and testing our observations of what we can perceive through our senses?
3. *Structures versus processes:* Should we study the structures (contents, attributes, and products) of the human mind, or should we focus on the processes of human thinking?
4. *Domain generality versus domain specificity:* Are the processes we observe limited to single domains, or are they general across a variety of domains? Do observations in one domain apply also to all domains, or do they apply only to the specific domains observed?
5. *Validity of causal inferences versus ecological validity:* Should we study cognition by using highly controlled experiments that increase the probability of valid inferences regarding causality, or should we use more naturalistic techniques, which increase the likelihood of obtaining ecologically valid findings, but possibly at the expense of experimental control?
6. *Applied versus basic research:* Should we conduct research into fundamental cognitive processes, or should we study ways in which to help people use cognition effectively in practical situations?
7. *Biological versus behavioral methods:* Should we study the brain and its functioning directly, perhaps even scanning the brain while people are performing cognitive tasks? Or should we study people's behavior in cognitive tasks, looking at measures such as percent correct and reaction time?

Although many of these questions are posed in "either–or" form, remember that often a synthesis of views or methods proves more useful than one extreme position or another. For example, our nature may provide an inherited framework for our distinctive characteristics and patterns of thinking and acting, but our nurture may shape the specific ways in which we flesh out that framework. We may use empirical methods for gathering data and for testing hypotheses, but we may use rationalist methods for interpreting data, constructing theories, and formulating hypotheses based on theories. Our understanding of cognition deepens when we consider both basic research into fundamental cognitive processes and applied research regarding effective uses of cognition in real-world settings. Syntheses are constantly evolving: What today may be viewed as a synthesis may tomorrow be viewed as an extreme position, or vice versa.

Before closing this chapter, think about some of the fields of cognitive psychology, described in the remaining chapters, to which these key issues may apply.

Chapter Previews

Cognitive psychologists have been involved in studying a wide range of psychological phenomena, including not only perception, learning, memory, and thinking, but also seemingly less cognitively oriented phenomena, such as emotion and motivation. In fact, almost any topic of psychological interest may be studied from a cognitive perspective. Nonetheless, there are some main areas of interest to cognitive psychologists. In this textbook, we attempt to describe some of the preliminary answers to questions asked by researchers in the main areas of interest.

Chapter 2 *Cognitive Neuroscience*—What are the structures and processes of the human brain that underlie the structures and processes of human cognition?

Chapter 3 *Attention and Consciousness*—What are the basic processes of the mind that govern how information enters our minds, our awareness, and our high-level processes of information handling?

Chapter 4 *Perception*—How does the human mind perceive what the senses receive? How does the human mind distinctively achieve the perception of forms and patterns?

Chapter 5 *Memory: Models and Research Methods*—How are different kinds of information (e.g., our experiences related to a traumatic event, the names of U.S. presidents, or the procedure for riding a bicycle) represented in memory?

Chapter 6 *Memory Processes*—How do we move information into memory, keep it there, and retrieve it from memory when needed?

Chapter 7 *Knowledge Representation: Images and Propositions*—How do we mentally represent information in our minds? Do we do so in words, in pictures, or in some other form for representing meaning? Alternatively, do we have multiple forms of representation?

Chapter 8 *Knowledge Representation and Organization*—How do we mentally organize what we know? How do we manipulate and operate on knowledge—do we do so serially, through parallel processing, or through some combination of processes?

Chapter 9 *Language: Nature and Acquisition*—How do we derive and produce meaning through language? How do we acquire language—both our primary language and any additional languages?

Chapter 10 *Language in Context*—How does our use of language interact with our ways of thinking? How does our social world interact with our use of language?

Chapter 11 *Problem Solving and Creativity*—How do we solve problems? What processes aid and impede us in reaching solutions to problems? Why are some of us more creative than others? How do we become and remain creative?

Chapter 12 *Decision Making and Reasoning*—How do we reach important decisions? How do we draw reasonable conclusions from the information we have available? Why and how do we so often make inappropriate decisions and reach inaccurate conclusions?

Chapter 13 *Cognitive Development*—How does our thinking change across the life span? What factors contribute to these changes?

Chapter 14 *Human and Artificial Intelligence*—Why do we consider some people more intelligent than others? Why do some people seem better able to accomplish whatever they want to accomplish in their chosen fields of endeavor?

In this book, I have tried to emphasize the underlying, common ideas and organizing themes across various aspects of cognitive psychology, rather than simply to state the facts. I have followed this path in order to help you perceive large meaningful patterns within the domain of cognitive psychology. I have also tried to give you some idea of how cognitive psychologists think and how they structure their field in their day-to-day work. I hope that this approach will help you to contemplate problems in cognitive psychology at a deeper level than might otherwise be possible.

I have tried to present cognitive psychology as a dynamic discipline, rather than as one comprising a static set of facts that we only can pretend will never change or be viewed from a different perspective. Cognitive psychologists are constantly thinking about how they can improve their own work and move the field forward. Perhaps some of this work will lead to ideas for making life easier for students who are trying to think about and to comprehend an entire body of knowledge within a single class term. You may even know someone who might benefit from such information.

SUMMARY

1. **What is cognitive psychology?** Cognitive psychology is the study of how people perceive, learn, remember, and think about information.

2. **How did psychology develop as a science?** Beginning with Plato and Aristotle, people have contemplated how to gain understanding of the truth. Plato held that rationalism offers the clear path to truth, whereas Aristotle espoused empiricism as the route to knowledge. Centuries later, Descartes extended Plato's rationalism, whereas Locke elaborated on Aristotle's empiricism. Kant offered a synthesis of these apparent opposites. Decades after Kant proposed his synthesis, Hegel observed how the history of ideas seems to progress through a *dialectical* process.

3. **How did cognitive psychology develop from psychology?** By the twentieth century, psychology had emerged as a distinct field of study; Wundt focused on the structures of the mind *(structuralism),* whereas James and Dewey focused

on the processes of the mind *(functionalism)*. Emerging from this dialectic was *associationism*, espoused by Ebbinghaus and Thorndike, which paved the way for behaviorism by underscoring the importance of mental associations. Another step toward behaviorism was Pavlov's discovery of the principles of classical conditioning. Watson, and later Skinner, were the chief proponents of *behaviorism*, which focused entirely on observable links between an organism's behavior and particular environmental contingencies that strengthen or weaken the likelihood that particular behaviors will be repeated. Most behaviorists dismissed entirely the notion that there is merit in psychologists' trying to understand what is going on in the mind of the individual engaging in the behavior. However, Tolman and subsequent behaviorist researchers noted the role of cognitive processes in influencing behavior. A convergence of developments across many fields led to the emergence of *cognitive psychology* as a discrete discipline, spearheaded by such notables as Neisser.

4. **How have other disciplines contributed to the development of theory and research in cognitive psychology?** Cognitive psychology has roots in philosophy and physiology, which merged to form the mainstream of psychology. As a discrete field of psychological study, cognitive psychology also profited from cross-disciplinary investigation in linguistics (e.g., How do language and thought interact?), biological psychology (e.g., What are the physiological bases for cognition?), anthropology (e.g., What is the importance of the cultural context for cognition?), and technological advances like *artificial intelligence* (e.g., How do computers process information?).

5. **What methods do cognitive psychologists use to study how people think?** Cognitive psychologists use a broad range of methods, including experiments, psychobiological techniques, self-reports, case studies, naturalistic observation, and computer simulations and artificial intelligence.

6. **What are the current issues and various fields of study within cognitive psychology?** Some of the major issues in the field have centered on how to pursue knowledge: by using both *rationalism* (which is the basis for theory development) and *empiricism* (which is the basis for gathering data); by underscoring the importance of cognitive structures and of cognitive processes; by emphasizing the study of domain-general and of domain-specific processing; by striving for a high degree of experimental control (which better permits causal inferences) and for a high degree of *ecological validity* (which better allows generalization of findings to settings outside of the laboratory); and by conducting basic research seeking fundamental insights about cognition and applied research seeking effective uses of cognition in real-world settings. Although positions on these issues may appear to be diametrical opposites, very often apparently antithetical views may be synthesized into a form that offers the best of each of the opposing viewpoints.

   Cognitive psychologists study biological bases of cognition, as well as attention, consciousness, perception, memory, mental imagery, language, problem solving, creativity, decision making, reasoning, developmental changes in cognition across the life span, human intelligence, artificial intelligence, and various other aspects of human thinking.

Thinking About Thinking: Factual, Analytical, Creative, and Practical Questions

1. Describe the major historical schools of psychological thought leading up to the development of cognitive psychology.
2. Describe some of the ways in which philosophy, linguistics, and artificial intelligence have contributed to the development of cognitive psychology.
3. Compare and contrast the influences of Plato and Aristotle on psychology.
4. Analyze how various research methods in cognitive psychology reflect empiricist and rationalist approaches to gaining knowledge.
5. Design a rough sketch of a cognitive-psychological investigation involving one of the research methods described in this chapter. Highlight both the advantages and the disadvantages of using this particular method for your investigation.
6. This chapter describes cognitive psychology as the field is now. How might you speculate that the field will change in the next 50 years?
7. How might an insight gained from basic research lead to practical uses in an everyday setting?
8. How might an insight gained from applied research lead to deepened understanding of fundamental features of cognition?

Key Terms

artificial intelligence (AI) 12
associationism 8
behaviorism 9
cognitive psychology 2
cognitive science 20
cognitivism 11
ecological validity 19
empiricist 4
functionalist 6
Gestalt psychology 10
hypotheses 14
pragmatist 7
rationalist 4
structuralism 6
theory 14

Annotated Suggested Readings

Dennett, D. (1991). *Consciousness explained.* Boston: Little, Brown. One of the major contemporary works on the nature of consciousness, explained for laypersons by a leading twentieth-century philosopher and cognitive scientist.

Gardner, H. (1985). *The mind's new science: A history of the cognitive revolution.* New York: Basic Books. A lively and thoughtful account of the development of the field of cognitive science.

James, W. (1970). *The principles of psychology* (Vol. 1). New York: Holt. (Original work published 1890) Probably still the most single important work in the history of American psychology. Shows the origins of much contemporary thinking in American psychology. Worth reading in the original.

Sternberg, R. J. (Ed.) (1998). *The nature of cognition*. Cambridge, MA: MIT Press. Essays on various major issues in cognitive science today.

Cognitive Neuroscience

Chapter Outline

Exploring Cognitive Psychology

From Neuron to Brain: Organization of the Nervous System
- Neuronal Structure and Function
- Communication Between Neurons
- Levels of Organization in the Nervous System

Viewing the Structures and Functions of the Brain
- Postmortem Studies
- Animal Studies
- Electrical Recordings
- Static Imaging Techniques
- Metabolic Imaging

Cognition in the Brain: Cerebral Cortex and Other Structures
- Gross Anatomy of the Brain: Forebrain, Midbrain, Hindbrain
- The Cerebral Cortex and Localization of Function

Summary

Thinking About Thinking: Factual, Analytical, Creative, and Practical Questions

Key Terms

Annotated Suggested Readings

EXPLORING COGNITIVE PSYCHOLOGY

1. **What are the fundamental structures and processes of the cells within the brain?**
2. **How do researchers study the major structures and processes of the brain?**
3. **What have researchers found as a result of studying the brain?**

An ancient legend from India (see Rosenzweig & Leiman, 1989) tells of Sita, a woman who marries one man but is attracted to another. These two frustrated men behead themselves, and Sita, bereft of them both, desperately prays to the goddess Kali to bring the men back to life. Sita is granted her wish and is allowed to reattach the heads to the bodies. In her rush to bring the two men back to life, Sita mistakenly switches their heads and so attaches them to the wrong bodies. Now, to whom is she married? Who is who?

The mind–body issue has long interested philosophers and scientists. Where is the mind located in the body, if at all? How do the mind and body interact? How are we able to think, speak, plan, reason, learn, and remember? What are the physical bases for our cognitive abilities? These questions all probe the relationship between cognitive psychology and neurobiology, and some cognitive psychologists seek to answer such questions by studying the biological bases of cognition. Cognitive psychologists are especially concerned with how the *anatomy* (physical structures of the body) and the *physiology* (functions and processes of the body) of the nervous system affect and are affected by human cognition.

A cornerstone of modern cognitive psychology is the belief that the brain is the seat of the mind and therefore the fount of human behavior. *Cognitive neuroscience* is the field of study linking the brain and other aspects of the nervous system to cognitive processing, and ultimately, to behavior. One of the earliest figures to propose the brain as the location for the mind was the Greek physician Hippocrates (ca. 460–377 B.C.), and for centuries, scientists have recognized that the brain influences cognition. By the nineteenth century, scientists (e.g., German physiologist Johannes Müller, 1801–1858) began trying to understand whether the brain shows **localization of function**—that is, whether specific areas of the brain control specific abilities or behaviors. Even today, research on localization in the brain continues to be a hot topic of investigation. Before we focus on the brain, however, we consider how it fits into the overall organization of the nervous system.

FROM NEURON TO BRAIN: ORGANIZATION OF THE NERVOUS SYSTEM

The **nervous system** is the basis for our ability to perceive, adapt to, and interact with the world around us (Gazzaniga, 1995). Through this system we receive, process, and then respond to information from the environment. In this section, we first consider the basic building block of the nervous system, the neuron, examining in detail how information moves through the nervous system at the cellular level. Then, we consider the various levels of organization within the nervous system. In later sections, we will focus on the supreme organ of the nervous system—the brain—paying special attention to the cerebral cortex, which controls many of our thought processes. For now, let's consider how information processing occurs at the cellular level.

NEURONAL STRUCTURE AND FUNCTION

In order to understand how the entire nervous system processes information, we need to examine the structure and function of the cells that constitute the nervous system. Individual neural cells, **neurons,** transmit electrical signals from one location to another in the nervous system. The greatest concentration of neurons is in the neocortex of the brain, the part of the brain associated with complex cognition. There can be as many as 100,000 neurons per cubic millimeter in this tissue (Sejnowski & Churchland, 1989).

Neurons vary in their structure, but almost all neurons have four basic parts, as illustrated in Figure 2.1: a *soma* (cell body), *dendrites,* an *axon,* and *terminal buttons.*

The **soma,** which contains the *nucleus* (center portion, which performs metabolic and reproductive functions for the cell), is responsible for the life of the neuron and connects the dendrites to the axon. The many branchlike **dendrites** receive information from other neurons, and the soma integrates the information. Learning is associated with the formation of new neuronal connections and, hence, increased complexity or ramification of dendrites in the brain. The single **axon** is a long, thin tube that extends from the soma (and that sometimes splits) and responds to the information, when appropriate, by transmitting an electrochemical signal, which travels to the *terminus* (end), where the signal can be transmitted to other neurons.

Axons are of two basic, roughly equally occurring kinds, distinguished by the presence or absence of **myelin,** a white fatty substance (which accounts for some of the whiteness of the white matter of the brain). Some axons are *myelinated,* surrounded by a *myelin sheath,* which insulates and protects longer axons from electrical interference by other neurons in the area, and speeds up the conduction of information. In fact, transmission in myelinated axons can reach 100 meters per second (equal to about 224 miles per hour). Moreover, myelin is not distributed continuously along the axon, but rather in segments broken up by **nodes of Ranvier**—small gaps in the myelin coating along the axon, which serve to increase conduction speed even more. The second kind of axon lacks the myelin coat altogether. Typically, these unmyelinated axons are smaller and shorter (as well as slower) than the myelinated axons, so they do not need the increased conduction velocity myelin provides for longer axons. Multiple sclerosis, an autoimmune disease, is associated with the degeneration of myelin sheaths along axons in certain nerves, resulting in impairments of coordination and balance. In severe cases this disease is fatal.

The **terminal buttons** are small knobs found at the ends of the branches of an axon that do not directly touch the dendrites of the next neuron. Rather, there is a very small gap, the **synapse,** which serves as a juncture between the terminal buttons of one or more neurons and the dendrites (or sometimes the soma) of one or more other neurons (refer to Figure 2.1). Synapses are important in cognition. Rats show increases in both the size and the number of synapses in the brain as a result of learning (Turner & Greenough, 1985). Decreased

FIGURE 2.1 **NEURONS**

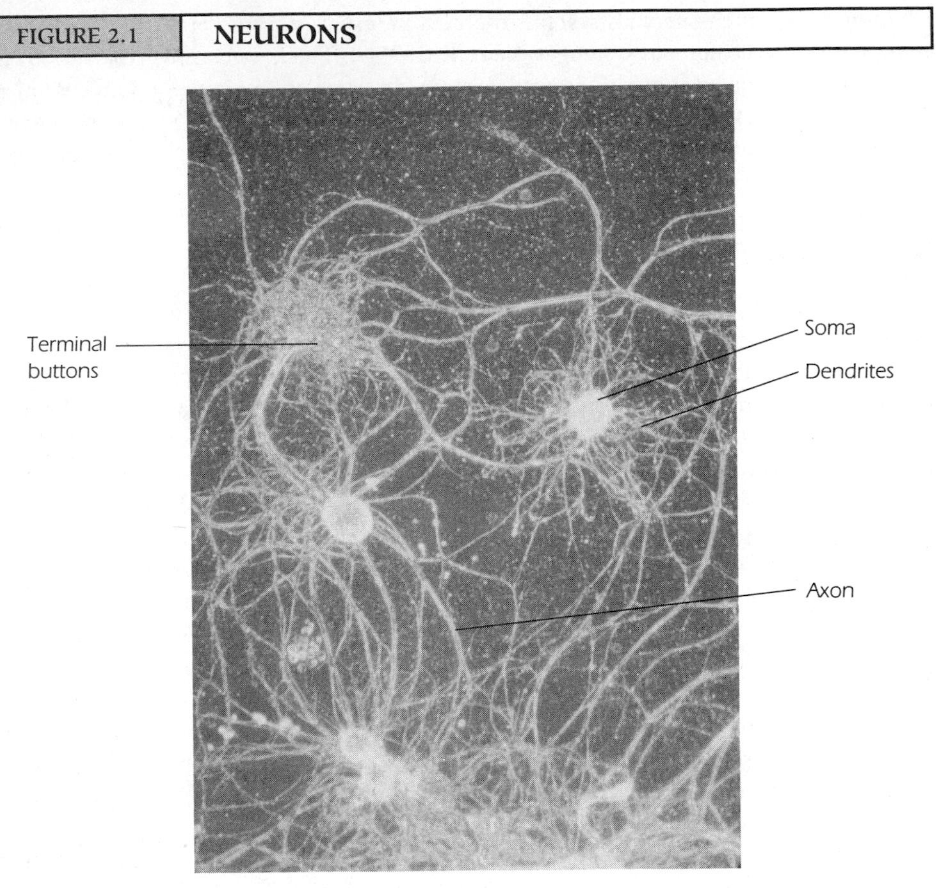

The shape of a neuron is determined by its function. Each neuron, however, has the same structure: soma, dendrites, an axon, and terminal buttons.

cognitive functioning, as in Alzheimer's disease, is associated with reduced efficiency of synaptic transmission of nerve impulses (Selkoe, 1991). Signal transmission between neurons occurs when the terminal buttons release one or more **neurotransmitters** at the synapse. These neurotransmitters serve as chemical messengers for transmission of information across the synaptic gap to the receiving dendrites of the next neuron. We will return to a more detailed discussion of synaptic signal transmission later when discussing communication between neurons. For now, let's focus on transmission of information within a neuron.

Transmission within the neuron is **electrochemical**—that is, conduction is achieved through reactions involving *ions,* positive or negative electrically charged chemical particles. Processes such as learning and thinking, therefore, can be understood at the cognitive level, or at the level of electrochemical transmission within the brain. If the concentrations of the various ions inside and outside the neuron always remained in a **static equilibrium** (a perfect balance, with no changes inside or outside the neuron), intraneuronal conduction would never occur. In living organisms, however, change is constant—ongoing electrical activity within the body stimulates changes in the concentrations of ions inside and outside the neuron, which in turn affect the functioning of the neuron.

Because of the constant fluctuations in the electrical activity of the nervous system, neurons must be somewhat selective in reacting to the tangle of electrical impulses slushing through mires of neurotransmitters. To avoid cognitive overload or even chaos, electrical charges at certain levels of intensity and frequency produce virtually no effect in a neuron at all. However, once a charge reaches or surpasses a certain level, termed the neuron's individual **threshold of excitation,** the neuron reacts quite differently (see Figure 2.2). At or above the threshold, positively and negatively charged ions quickly flow across the neuronal membrane, changing the electrochemical balance inside and outside the neuron. When the chemicals are flowing both ways across the membrane, the neuron's membrane is said to have reached its **action potential.** The specific threshold of excitation required for a given neuron's action potential differs for different neurons. When an action potential occurs, the neuron is said to "fire." Moreover, this firing obeys the *all or none law*—that is, either the electrical charge is strong enough to generate an

FIGURE 2.2 **ACTION POTENTIAL**

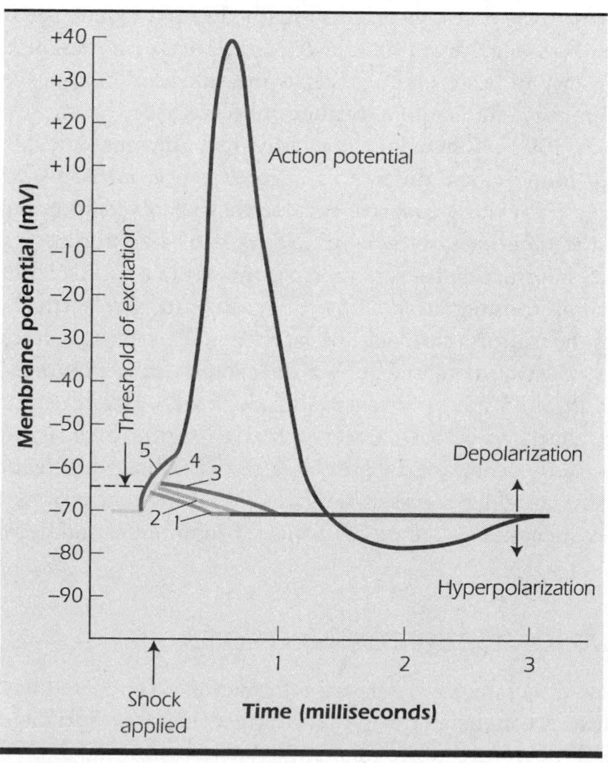

When electrochemical stimulation reaches a neuron's threshold of excitation, the neuron generates an action potential. During an action potential, ions swiftly cross the membrane of the neuron. In the figure, impulses 4 and 5 produce an action potential; 1, 2, and 3 do not.

action potential, or it is not. There is no "middle ground." Furthermore, once the threshold is reached, the charge will travel all the way down the axon without losing strength. If an action potential is all or none, how do our bodies differentiate responses to strong versus weak stimuli? The complement to the all-or-none law of neural firing is the *rate law,* which states that the rate of neural firing corresponds to the intensity of the stimulus: The more intense the stimulus, the greater the frequency of neural firing.

Whereas the rate of neural firing corresponds to the intensity of the stimulus, the speed of neural conduction does not. Several factors affect the speed of neural conduction, not the least of which is the length of the axon through which the neural impulse must travel (shorter is faster). Recall, too, that myelin serves as an insulator and speeds up conduction of neural impulses. Ironically, part of the reason that myelin helps to speed up neural transmission is that there *are* gaps (nodes of Ranvier) in the myelin sheath. That is, electrochemical impulses save time by leaping from one uncoated node of Ranvier to another. This **saltatory conduction** (from Latin *saltare,* "to leap") of impulses occurs only in vertebrates, enabling vertebrates to respond much more quickly than do invertebrates. In addition, conduction speed increases as the axon diameter increases. Motor neurons in control of supplying quick and constant power to arms and legs, for example, are generally thick and myelinated. On the other hand, neurons to the stomach muscles are mostly small in diameter and unmyelinated; the digestive process usually does not require speed. Recently, some cognitive psychologists (e.g., P. A. Vernon & Mori, 1992) have suggested that speed of neural conduction may indicate intelligence, as measured by intelligence tests, but these findings are preliminary and require further substantiation, as the evidence is mixed (Wickett & Vernon, 1994). Whether or not individual differences in speed of neural conduction are linked to individual differences in intelligence, mechanisms for speeding up neural conduction are obviously adaptive because they enable us to respond more quickly and effectively to the sometimes overwhelming array of diverse stimuli in our environment.

To summarize, information transmission occurs within a neuron through excitation at the dendrites, leading to integration at the soma. In turn, an electrical current occurs if excitation reaches the neuron's threshold of excitation. This excitation leads to the propagation of all-or-none action potentials down the axon (refer to Figure 2.2) via a complex electrochemical reaction. Stimulus intensity is coded by the rate of neuronal firing. Transmission speed is influenced by such factors as axon length, thickness, and myelination. These neuronal qualities combine to provide a fast, flexible, intelligent mechanism for information processing, which serves as the basis for all thought processes. Next, we turn to a more detailed discussion of the mechanisms for communication between neurons.

Communication Between Neurons

Up to now, we have discussed how chemical information is conducted within a neuron (via waves of ion exchanges conducted down the length of the axon). Intraneuronal conduction is essential for each neuron to work effectively, but the work of each individual neuron would be for naught if there were no way for neurons to communicate with one another. We already know *where* (in the synapse) and *when* (whenever an action potential triggers release of a neurotransmitter) neurons communicate. We even know *what* (neurotransmitters) they use for communicating. However, we need to know more about *how* they do so. Stated simply, neurons communicate in the following step-by-step process:

1. One neuron ("Neuron A") releases a neurotransmitter from its terminal buttons.
2. The neurotransmitter floods the synapse and reaches the dendrites (or soma) of another neuron ("Neuron B").
3. The dendrites of Neuron B are stimulated by the neurotransmitters it receives until Neuron B reaches its distinctive threshold of excitation.
4. At Neuron B's threshold of excitation, the Neuron B action potential travels down its axon.
5. When Neuron B's action potential reaches Neuron B's terminal buttons, Neuron B releases its own neurotransmitter into the next synapse (perhaps with Neuron C); and so on.

In practice, it is not really that simple. Consider that, at any given synapse, there are usually multiple, often hundreds, of connections among neurons, with dendritic trees branching out to receive messages from many axons (see Figure 2.3). As well, although each neuron is equipped to release only one particular neurotransmitter, dozens of neurotransmitting substances are known to operate within the nervous system. To make matters even more complicated, differing neurotransmitters affect various neurons in different ways. Many neurons are *excited* by particular neurotransmitters they contact in the synapse,

FIGURE 2.3	**INTERNEURONAL COMMUNICATION**

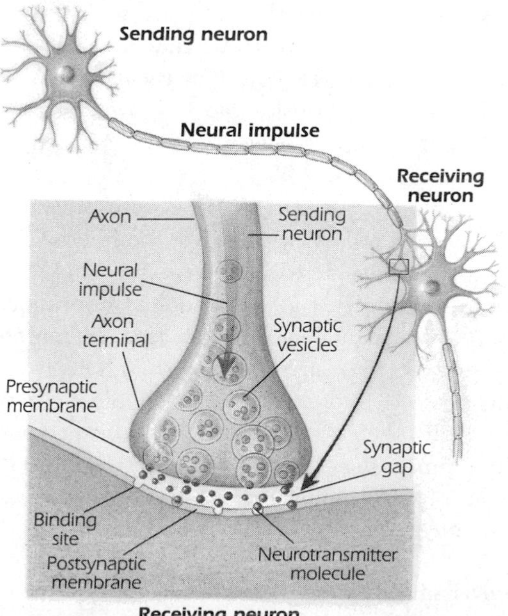

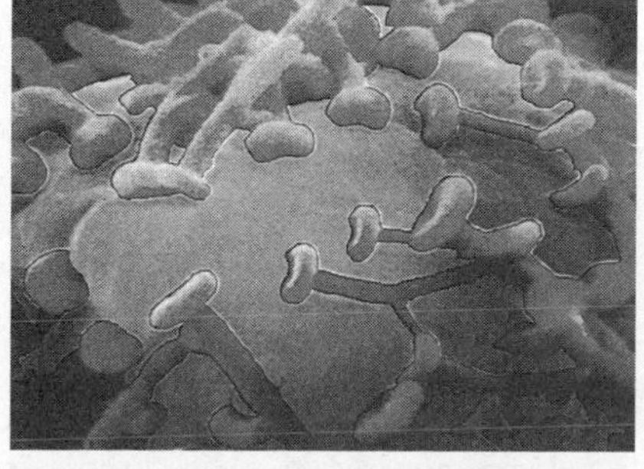

Neurons relay electrochemical messages by releasing neurotransmitters that cross the synapse to the dendrites of the receiving neurons. This electron micrograph shows how densely packed the neurons are.

increasing the likelihood that the neurons will reach their threshold of excitation. Other neurons, however, are actually *inhibited* by particular neurotransmitters, *decreasing* the probability that the neurons will reach their threshold of excitation. Thus, another factor in determining whether a neuron fires is the overall balance of excitation and inhibition from neurotransmitters received by the neuron's dendrites. New learning can involve creation of both new excitatory and new inhibitory neural connections. Indeed, an evolutionary psychologist, David Stenhouse (1974), linked increased intelligence of a species to increased inhibition of instinctive responses. When you think about all that is involved in getting one neuron to communicate with another, it seems a miracle that any of us can think at all. In fact, however, the time it takes for a given signal to cross the synapse can be as little as half a millisecond, although this fire span can also be as long as a second or more.

Given the tremendous volume of neurotransmitters spilling into each synapse, it makes sense that not all the neurotransmitters released by axons can be neatly absorbed by the dendrites. What, then, happens to the leftover transmitter chemicals? Fortunately, our bodies have two mechanisms for dealing with this problem: (a) **reuptake** (the most common mechanism), in which the terminal button of an axon reabsorbs (takes up again) the neurotransmitter that it spilled into the synapse; and (b) **enzymatic deactivation,** in which an *enzyme* (a substance that breaks down other substances) breaks apart the neurotransmitter, thereby making it inactive (deactivated). Both of these mechanisms help prevent the neurons from being overstimulated by leftover transmitter substances. Certain drugs, such as hallucinogens, can alter normal thought patterns by interfering with reuptake of neurotransmitters.

Although scientists already know of more than 50 transmitter substances, it seems likely that more remain to be discovered. Medical and psychological researchers are working to discover and understand neurotransmitters and how they interact with drugs, moods, abilities, and perceptions. Although we know much about the mechanics of impulse transmission in nerves, we still know relatively little about how the nervous system's chemical activity relates to psychological states. Despite the limits on present knowledge, however, we have gained some insight into how several of these substances affect our psychological functioning.

At present, it appears that there are three types of chemical substances involved in neurotransmission: (a) the *monoamine neurotransmitters,* each of which is synthesized by the nervous system through enzymatic actions on one of the *amino acids* (constituents of proteins, such as choline, tyrosine, and tryptophan) in our diet (e.g., acetylcholine, dopamine, and serotonin); (b) *amino-acid neurotransmitters,* which are obtained directly from the amino acids in our diet, without further synthesis (e.g., GABA); and (c) *neuropeptides,* which are *peptide chains* (molecules made from the parts of two or more amino acids). Table 2.1 lists some examples of neurotransmitters, together with their typical functions in the nervous system and their associations with cognitive processing. For example, acetylcholine is associated with memory functions, and the loss of acetylcholine in Alzheimer's disease has been linked to impaired memory functioning in Alzheimer's patients. Dopamine is associated with both attention and learning.

The preceding description drastically oversimplifies the intricacies of constant neuronal communication. Such complexities make it difficult to understand what is happening in the normal brain when we are thinking, feeling, and interacting with our environments. Many researchers seek to understand the normal information processes of

TABLE 2.1 NEUROTRANSMITTERS

Neurotransmitters are responsible for intercellular communication in the nervous system. This table lists only a subset of known neurotransmitters.

Neurotransmitter	Description	General Function	Specific Examples
Acetylcholine (Ach)	Monoamine neurotransmitter synthesized from choline	Excitatory in brain and either excitatory (at skeletal muscles) or inhibitory (at heart muscles) elsewhere in the body	Believed to be involved in memory, due to high concentrations found in the hippocampus (Squire, 1987)
Dopamine (DA)	Monoamine neurotransmitter synthesized from tyrosine	Influences movement, attention, and learning; mostly inhibitory, but some excitatory effects	Parkinson's disease, characterized by tremors and limb rigidity, results from too little DA. Some schizophrenia symptoms are associated with too much DA.
Epinephrine and Norepinephrine	Monoamine neurotransmitter synthesized from tyrosine	Hormones (also known as adrenaline and noradrenaline) involved in regulation of alertness	Involved in diverse effects on body related to fight-or-flight reactions, anger and fear
Serotonin	Monoamine neurotransmitter synthesized from tryptophan	Involved in arousal, sleep and dreaming, and mood; usually inhibitory, but some excitatory effects	Normally inhibits dreaming; defects in serotonin system are linked to severe depression
GABA (gamma-amino butyric acid)	Amino acid neurotransmitter	General neuromodulatory effects due to inhibitory influences on pre-synaptic axons	Currently believed to influence certain mechanisms for learning and memory (Izquierdo & Medina, 1995)
Glutamate	Amino acid neurotransmitter	General neuromodulatory effects due to excitatory influences on pre-synaptic axons	Currently believed to influence certain mechanisms for learning and memory (Izquierdo & Medina, 1995)
Neuropeptides	Peptide chains serving as neurotransmitters	General neuromodulatory effects due to influences on post-synaptic membranes	Endorphines play a role in pain relief. Neuromodulating neuropeptides are sometimes released to enhance the effects of Ach.

the brain, in order to determine what is going wrong in the brains of persons affected by neurological and psychological disorders. Perhaps if we can understand what has gone awry—what chemicals are out of balance—we can figure out how to put things back into balance by providing needed neurotransmitters or by inhibiting the effects of overabundant neurotransmitters.

PRACTICAL APPLICATIONS OF COGNITIVE PSYCHOLOGY

A currently popular additive in American beverages is ginseng, an herbal extract long used in Asian cultures for its many life-enhancing effects. Some of the major claims are that ginseng enhances mental functioning (specifically memory), relieves fatigue, increases resistance to disease, helps control high blood pressure, reduces the risk of diabetes, reduces the risk of cancer, and increases blood volume (because it is a vasodilator). Should we believe all these claims? There is very little scientific research on ginseng, and most of the research has been done on animals. The diffuse effects of ginseng are largely due to the action of particular kinds of saponins in the ginseng, which are steroid-based chemical compounds that have hormone-like effects on the body and brain. Although not much is currently known about exactly how ginseng works from a pharmacological perspective, it has been found to stimulate the release of the neurotransmitter, acetylcholine (Ach), and to enhance the metabolism of Ach. Because Ach is so involved with memory (described in Table 2.1), some of these claims possibly could be true. However, until we know more about how Ach works, we can't say anything definitive about the action of ginseng. Largely because of the diffuse nature of its effects, we are a long way from understanding if and how ginseng works. For now, it appears to have no adverse side effects if used moderately, except that it can be somewhat expensive and thus deplete the pocket book.

LEVELS OF ORGANIZATION IN THE NERVOUS SYSTEM

At this point, we have discussed how transmission occurs both within and between neurons. Neurons fire when they reach their critical threshold of activation. The neurons code stimulus intensity by varying their rate of firing. Communication between neurons occurs when neurotransmitters are released at the synapse by an axon's terminal buttons and are then absorbed at another neuron's dendrites. However, it takes more than just signal transmission to perform the complex behaviors of even the simplest organism with a nervous system. What is required is organization—both structural and functional—in order to make the leap from firing neurons to a thinking, feeling, acting person. This section describes the various levels of organization within the nervous system.

STRUCTURAL ORGANIZATION

The overall structure of the nervous system is shown in the diagram in Figure 2.4. As Figure 2.4 shows, the nervous system is divided into two main parts: the central nervous system (CNS) and the peripheral nervous system (PNS). The **peripheral nervous system** comprises all of the nerve cells *except* those of the brain and the spinal cord. *Peripheral* has two meanings: "auxiliary," because the PNS assists the CNS; and "away from the center," because the peripheral *nerves* (bundles of neural fibers) are external to the CNS. The PNS includes the *spinal nerves,* which branch from the spinal cord (e.g., going to the legs, arms, and torso), and the *cranial nerves,* which branch from the front surface of the brain (e.g., going to the face and the ears). The primary job of the PNS is to relay information between

FIGURE 2.4 **MAJOR DIVISIONS OF THE NERVOUS SYSTEM**

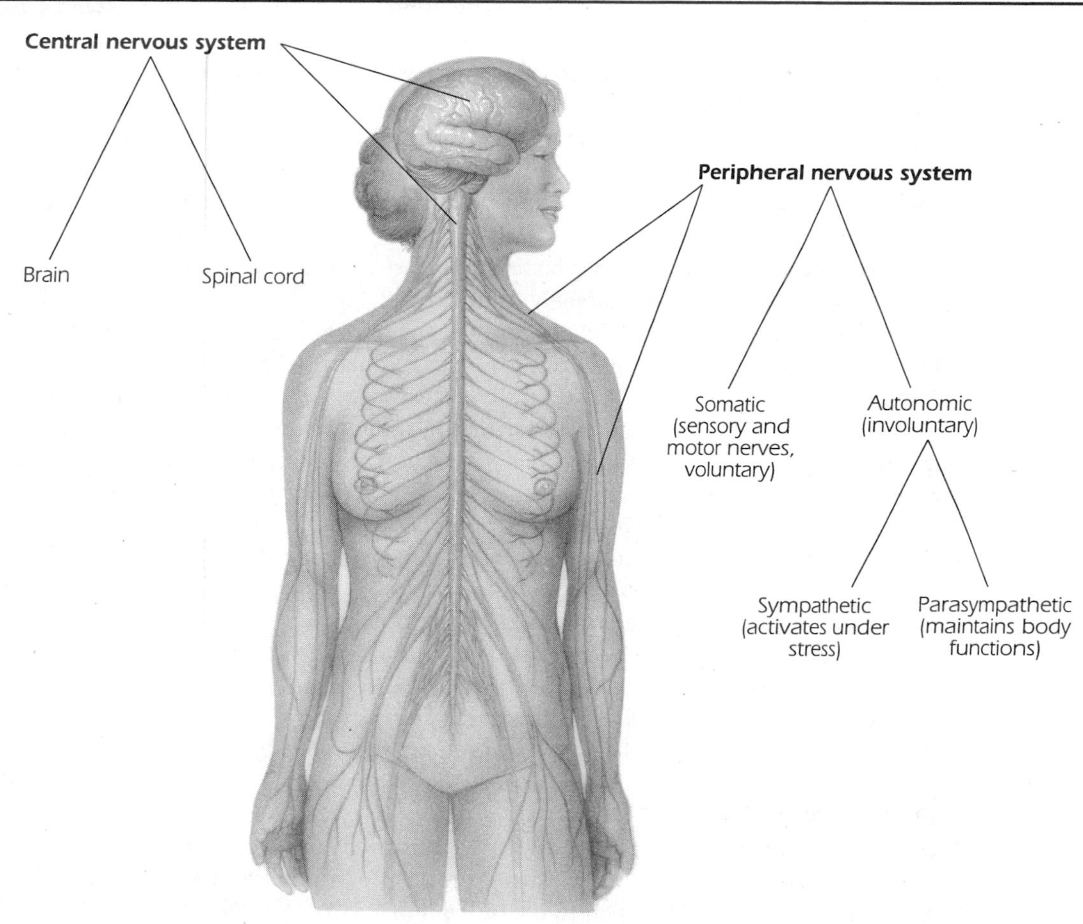

The central nervous system (CNS), protected by bone, comprises the brain and spinal cord. The peripheral nervous system (PNS), not protected by bone, comprises the nerves of the autonomic and somatic systems. The autonomic system transmits messages between the brain and internal organs, and the somatic system transmits messages between the brain and the sensory and motor systems linked to the skeletal muscles.

the CNS and the nerves lying outside of the CNS, such as those in both our external sensory organs (e.g., skin, ears, eyes) and our internal body parts (e.g., stomach, muscles).

Most cognitive psychologists are primarily interested in the **central nervous system,** which consists of two parts, the brain and the spinal cord, both of which are encased in bone. In addition to being protected by bone, the brain and spinal cord are buffered from shocks and minor traumas by a fluid that is secreted constantly in the brain.

Whereas the hard skull and the cerebrospinal fluid minimize harm to the brain from external assaults, yet another physiological structure protects the brain from internal assaults that might come through our bloodstream. For such protection our physiology offers a rather sophisticated barrier. The blood that goes to our brains, rather than being carried by a single large vessel, has to pass through the **blood–brain barrier**—a network of tiny blood vessels that screen out many substances, letting other substances pass through quite easily. For example, the barrier screens out large water-soluble molecules, such as complex proteins and microorganisms that tend to be more likely to cause harm, but it lets *glucose* (a simple sugar) and other small water-soluble molecules, as well as most fat-soluble molecules, pass through rather easily. It is fortunate that glucose can pass through the blood–brain barrier, because not only does glucose supply the body with energy, but it also is consumed when we pay attention to and think about the cognitive tasks we confront in our daily lives.

The **brain** is the organ in our bodies that most directly controls our thoughts, emotions, and motivations. We commonly think of the brain as being at the top of the body's hierarchy—as the boss, with various other organs responding to it. Like any good boss, however, it listens to and is influenced by its subordinates, the other organs of the body. Thus, the brain is reactive as well as directive. Textbook diagrams involving the brain and its interconnections must somewhat oversimplify structures in order to reveal their fundamental elements and relationships. Thus, such diagrams may not show all of the interconnections between the brain and other organs, or between the central and peripheral nervous systems, but such complex connections are there.

If we start from your brain, we can follow a network of neurons to your **spinal cord,** which gathers a series of interconnected neurons into bundles of neural fibers that extend from your brain down through the center of your back. The spinal cord is a roughly cylindrical bundle of neural fibers about the diameter of your little finger; it is enclosed within the protecting *vertebrae,* the backbones that form your *spinal column* (see Figure 2.5). The bundles of neural fibers within the spinal cord, such as those going to the internal organs, the arms, and the legs, branch out to the nerves of the PNS.

Functional Organization

One function of the spinal cord is to carry information to and from the brain: to collect information from the peripheral nervous system and transmit it to the brain, as well as to relay information from the brain to the outlying nerves of the PNS. The two-directional communication of the nervous system involves three different kinds of nerves and neurons: sensory/afferent neurons, motor/efferent neurons, and interneurons.

Sensory (afferent) neurons receive information from the environment through their connections with **receptor cells** (structures specially designed to *receive* a particular substance or a particular kind of information), which detect physical or chemical changes in the sensory organs. Sensory/afferent neurons carry information away from the sensory receptor cells of the PNS and *toward* the spinal cord or brain, the CNS (thus the term, *afferent).* For example, we can see, hear, and smell only because we have sensory neurons to aid us. **Motor (efferent) neurons** carry information *away from* the spinal cord and the brain and toward the appropriate body parts involved in responding to the sensory input (thus the term, *efferent).* Movement would be impossible without motor neurons. **Interneurons** serve as intermediaries between sensory and motor neurons. They receive signals from either sensory neurons or other interneurons, and they send signals either to other interneurons or to motor neurons. In complex organisms such as humans, most neurons are interneurons, and they are found primarily within the CNS, making up virtually all of the gray matter and white matter within the CNS. Thinking involves primarily activity among the interneurons.

FIGURE 2.5 **SPINAL CORD**

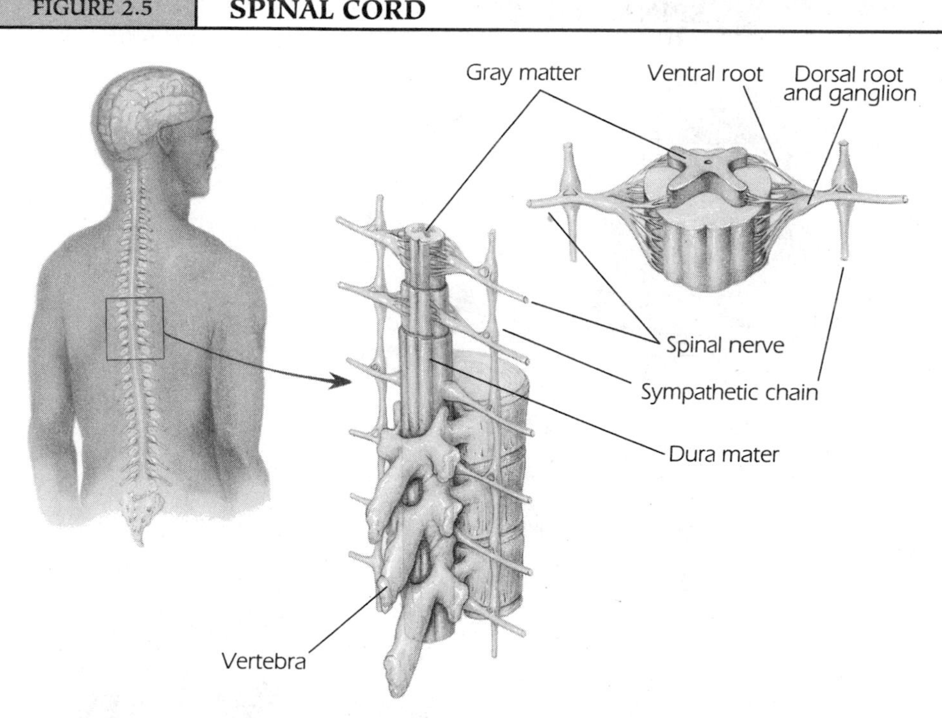

The spinal cord and its connecting nerves are protected by dura mater and vertebrae.

The spinal cord plays a crucial role in routing sensory and motor information through the brain, so that the brain can analyze and synthesize sensory information and direct our motor responses to it. Under some circumstances, however, the spinal cord directly connects receptor nerves with effector nerves, without routing either one through the brain until after the body has responded to the sensory information; the direct-connection responses that are produced are **reflexes** (automatic, involuntary responses; see Figure 2.6). Reflexes can provide much faster responses than can voluntary responses. Quick reflexes are handy because they allow the body to respond immediately to particular sensory information without taking the time for routing the information through the brain. For example, when you feel pain, you reflexively withdraw from whatever causes you pain, without pausing to think, "Gosh, that hurts. I should probably move away from that." Not only do you minimize your pain, but you also minimize any damage that might result from whatever is causing the pain (e.g., fires or cuts). Thus, in both functional and evolutionary terms, our reflexes better enable us to survive. The reflex response shows two things about the nervous system: (a) The spinal cord has the power to act alone, and (b) the brain plays an essential role in our ability consciously to feel anything anywhere outside our heads. To recognize your bodily sensations or to move your body purposefully, your spinal cord must be able to communicate with your brain.

In sum, the nervous system is exceptionally well organized, with lower levels in the hierarchy of command capable of responding without intervention of the brain when the immediate need arises (e.g., spinal reflexes), but with higher levels in the hierarchy

FIGURE 2.6 SPINAL REFLEX

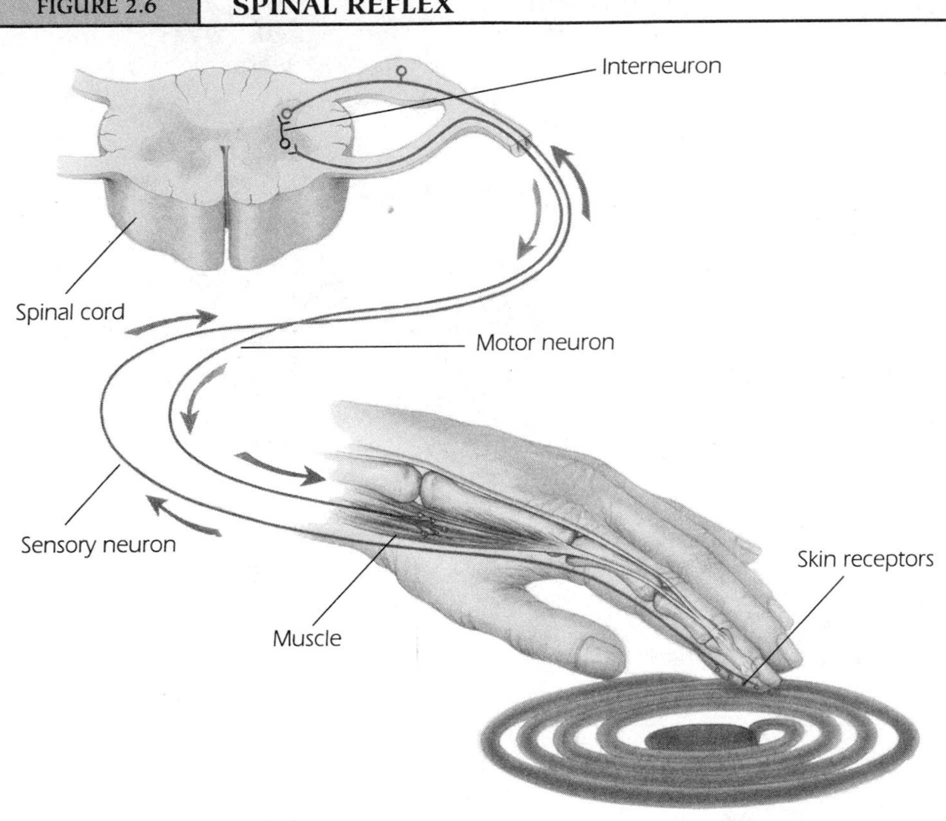

Spinal reflexes often serve protective functions, enabling you to respond to danger or pain more quickly than is possible when responding voluntarily. For example, it takes only about 50 milliseconds from the time the patellar tendon in your knee is tapped until your calf and foot jerk forward, as compared to many hundreds of milliseconds for you to move it in response to being told to move it (Carlson, 1992).

essential for full physical interaction with and perception of the world around us. To understand cognition, psychologists seek insights into how the brain integrates and guides the complex interactions throughout the amazing network of the human nervous system. How can researchers find out about the anatomy and physiology of the brain? Next, we turn to an answer to this question.

Viewing the Structures and Functions of the Brain

Scientists can use many methods for studying the human brain. These methods include both postmortem (from Latin, "after death") studies and in vivo (from Latin, "living") techniques on both humans and animals. Each technique provides important information about the structure and function of the human brain. Even some of the earliest postmortem studies still influence our thinking about how the brain performs certain functions. However, the recent trend is to focus on techniques that provide information about human mental functioning as it is occurring, rather than waiting to find persons with disorders and study their brains after they die. Because they are the foundation for later work, we will first discuss postmortem studies before moving on to the more modern in vivo techniques.

Postmortem Studies

For centuries, investigators have been able to *dissect* (separate into parts for examination) a brain after a person has died. Even today, dissection is often used for studying the relation between the brain and behavior. Researchers look carefully at the behavior of persons who show signs of brain damage while they are alive. The researchers document behavior in these case studies of patients as thoroughly as possible. Later, after the patients die, the researchers examine the patients' brains for *lesions* (areas where body tissue has been damaged, such as from injury or disease). Then the researchers infer that the lesioned locations may be related to the behavior that was affected.

In this way, researchers may trace a link between an observed type of behavior and anomalies in a particular location in the brain. An early example is Paul Broca's (1824–1880) famous patient, Tan (so named because that was the only syllable he was capable of uttering). Tan had severe speech problems, which were linked to lesions in an area of the frontal lobe now called Broca's area, believed to be responsible for certain functions involved in speech production. In more recent times, postmortem examinations of victims of *Alzheimer's disease* (an illness that causes devastating losses of memory; see chapter 5), have led researchers to identify some of the brain structures involved in memory (e.g., the hippocampus, described in a subsequent subsection of this chapter) and some of the microscopic aberrations associated with the disease process (e.g., distinctive tangled fibers in the brain tissue). Although lesioning techniques provide the basic foundation for understanding the relation of the brain to behavior, they are limited in that they cannot be performed on the living brain, and so they do not offer insights into more specific physiological processes of the brain. For this kind of information, we need in vivo techniques such as, but not limited to, those described next.

Animal Studies

Scientists also want to understand the physiological processes and functions of the living brain. To study the changing activity of the living brain, scientists must use in vivo research. Many early in vivo techniques were performed exclusively on animals. For example, Nobel Prize-winning research (i.e., Hubel & Wiesel, 1963, 1968, 1979) on visual perception arose from in vivo studies investigating the electrical activity of individual cells in particular regions of the brains of animals (see chapter 4).

In these kinds of studies, microelectrodes are inserted into the brain of an animal (usually a monkey or cat) in order to obtain single-cell recordings of the activity of a single neuron in the brain. In this way, scientists can measure the effects of certain kinds of stimuli, such as visually presented lines, on the activity of individual neurons. Other animal studies include selective lesioning (surgically removing or damaging part of the brain) to observe resulting functional deficits. Obviously, these techniques can not be used on human participants, nor can we simultaneously record the activity of every neuron. Therefore, generalizations based on these studies are somewhat limited, and an array of less invasive imaging techniques for use with humans has been developed. These techniques are described in the following section.

ELECTRICAL RECORDINGS

Researchers and practitioners (e.g., psychologists and physicians) often record electrical activity in the brain, which appears as waves of various widths (frequencies) and heights (intensities). **Electroencephalograms (EEGs)** measuring these frequencies and intensities may be recorded over relatively long periods of time, to study brain-wave activity indicative of changing mental states such as deep sleep or dreaming. To obtain EEG recordings, electrodes are placed at various places along the surface of the scalp, and the electrical activity of underlying brain areas is recorded. Therefore, the information is not well-localized to specific cells, but is very sensitive to changes over time. For example, EEG recordings taken during sleep reveal changing patterns of electrical activity involving the whole brain, with different patterns emerging during dreaming versus deep sleep.

In order to relate electrical activity to a particular event or task (e.g., seeing a flash of light or listening to sentences), *EEG* waves can be averaged over a large number (e.g., 100) of trials to reveal *event-related potentials (ERPs),* which provide very good information about the time-course of task-related brain activity by averaging out activity that is not task related. The resulting wave-forms show characteristic spikes related to the timing of electrical activity, but reveal only very general information about the location of that activity (because of low spatial resolution, limited by the placement of scalp electrodes). The ERP technique has been used in a wide variety of studies, including studies of intelligence (e.g., Caryl, 1994) that have attempted to relate particular characteristics of ERPs to scores on intelligence tests. Furthermore, the high degree of temporal resolution afforded by ERPs can be used to complement other techniques that have better spatial resolution, but lack such temporal resolution. For example, Posner and Raichle (1994) used both ERPs and positron emission tomography (discussed next) to pinpoint areas involved in word association. Using ERPs, they found that participants showed increased activity in certain parts of the brain (left lateral frontal cortex, left posterior cortex, and right insular cortex) when they made rapid associations to given words. As with any technique, EEGs and ERPs provide only a glimpse of brain activity and are most helpful when used in conjunction with other techniques to converge on particular brain areas involved in cognition.

STATIC IMAGING TECHNIQUES

Psychologists also use various techniques for obtaining still images revealing the structures of the brain (see Figure 2.7). These techniques include angiograms, computerized axial tomography (CT) scans, and magnetic resonance imaging (MRI) scans. The X-ray based techniques (angiogram and CT scan) allow for the observation of large abnormalities of the brain, such as damage resulting from strokes or tumors. However, they are limited in their resolution and cannot provide much information about smaller lesions and aberrations.

Probably the still-image technique of greatest interest to cognitive psychologists is the **magnetic resonance imaging (MRI)** scan, which offers relatively high-level resolution of brain tissue, thereby facilitating the detection of lesions in vivo, such as lesions associated with particular disorders of language use. In MRI, a strong magnetic field is passed

FIGURE 2.7 **IMAGES OF THE BRAIN**

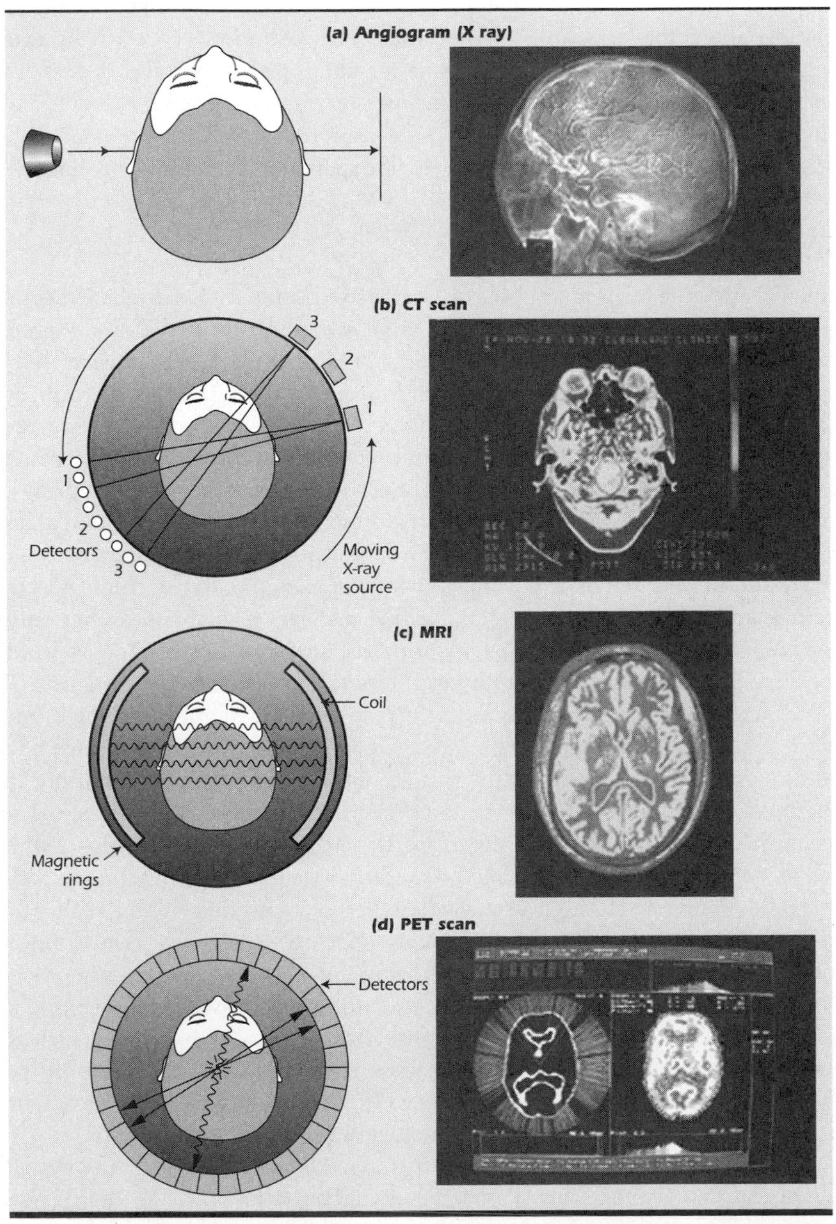

Various techniques have been developed to picture the structures—and sometimes the processes—of the brain. (a) A brain angiogram *highlights the blood vessels of the brain. (b)* A CT-scan *image of a brain uses a series of rotating scans (one of which is pictured here) to produce a 3-D view of brain structures. (c) A rotating series of* MRI scans *(one of which is pictured here) shows a clearer 3-D picture of brain structures than CT scans show. (d) These still photographs of* PET scans *of a brain show different metabolic processes during different activities. PET scans permit the study of brain physiology.*

through the brain of a patient and a rotating scanner detects various patterns of electromagnetic changes in the molecules of the brain. These molecular changes are analyzed by a computer to produce a three-dimensional picture of the brain that includes detailed information about the structures of the brain. This technique is relatively expensive, however, and does not provide much information about physiological processes. The final two techniques to be discussed in the following section are relatively recent, and differ from previous techniques in that they can be used on humans to provide information about physiological processes with relatively fine spatial and temporal resolution.

METABOLIC IMAGING

The kinds of imaging techniques discussed here have been termed metabolic because they rely on changes that take place within the brain as a result of increased consumption of glucose or oxygen in active areas of the brain. The basic idea is that active areas in the brain consume more glucose or oxygen than do inactive areas during some task, and that an area specifically required by one task ought to be more active during that task than during more generalized processing. Scientists attempt to pinpoint specialized areas for a task by using the *subtraction method,* which involves subtracting activity during a more general task from activity during the task of interest. The resulting activity is then statistically analyzed to determine which areas are responsible for performance of a particular task above and beyond the more general activity. For example, to determine which area of the brain is most important for something like retrieval of word meanings, an experimenter would have to subtract activity during a task involving reading of words from activity during a task involving the physical recognition of the letters of words. The difference in activity would be presumed to reflect retrieval of meaning. One important caveat to remember about these techniques, however, is that scientists have no way of determining whether the net effect of this activity is excitatory or inhibitory (because some neurons are inhibited by other neurons' neurotransmitters). Therefore, the subtraction technique reveals net brain activity for particular areas, not whether the area's effect is positive or negative. Moreover, the method assumes that activation is purely additive—that it can be discovered through a subtraction method. This description greatly oversimplifies the subtraction method, but shows at a general level how scientists determine physiological functioning of particular areas using the imaging techniques described next.

Positron emission tomography (PET) scans rely on increased glucose consumption in active brain areas during particular kinds of information processing. To track their use of glucose, participants are given a mildly radioactive form of glucose (one that emits positrons as it is metabolized). Next, the brain is scanned (to detect positrons), and a computer analyzes the data to produce images of the physiological functioning of the brain in action. For example, PET scans have been used to show that blood flow increases to the occipital lobe of the brain during visual processing (Posner, Petersen, Fox, & Raichle, 1988). PET scans have also been used for comparatively studying the brains of persons who score high versus low on intelligence tests. When high-scoring persons are engaged in cognitively demanding tasks, their brains seem to use glucose more efficiently, in highly task-specific areas of the brain; the brains of persons with lower scores appear to use glucose more diffusely, across larger regions of the brain (Haier, Siegel, Tang, Abel, & Buchsbaum, 1992; see chapter 14).

The latest technique, **functional magnetic resonance imaging (fMRI)**, builds upon MRI (discussed earlier), but uses increases in oxygen consumption to construct images of brain activity. The basic idea is the same as in PET scans, but fMRI does not require the use of radioactive particles. Rather, the participant performs a task while placed inside an MRI machine. This machine creates a magnetic field that induces changes in the particles of oxygen atoms. More active areas draw more oxygenated blood than do less active areas in the brain. The differences in the amounts of oxygen consumed form the basis for fMRI measurements, which are then computer analyzed to provide the most precise information currently available about the physiological functioning of the brain's activity during task performance. This technique is not only less invasive than PET, but also has higher temporal resolution—measurements can be taken for activity lasting fractions of a second, rather than only for activity lasting minutes to hours. One major drawback, however, is the expense and novelty of fMRI—few researchers have access to the required machinery, and testing of participants is very time-consuming. See Figure 2.8 for a direct comparison of various brain imaging techniques in terms of spatial and temporal resolution.

AN ARRAY OF TECHNIQUES

We can view the brain at various levels of spatial resolution ranging from a molecule to the whole brain itself, while we can envision the mind as events occurring over times as brief as a few milliseconds—the time it takes one neuron to communicate with another—or as long as a lifetime. Over the past decade or two, scientists have developed a remarkable array of techniques capable of addressing the relationship between brain and mind. Here we graphically summarize the potential contribution of these various techniques to an understanding of this relationship by plotting, logarithmically, the brain on the horizontal axis and the mind on the vertical axis. The techniques are then positioned according to their spatial and temporal precision. Into the left graph we have placed all of the available techniques, including X-ray CT, MRI, PET, EEG, event-related potentials (ERP), electrocorticography (EC_0; EEGs recorded from the brain surface at surgery), and electron microscopy (EM). In the right graph we have eliminated all of the techniques that cannot be applied to human subjects. Although the study of the mind–brain relationship in humans will clearly depend on brain-imaging techniques like MRI, PET, and CT in conjunction with electrical techniques, our ultimate understanding of that relationship will require the integration of information from all levels of inquiry.

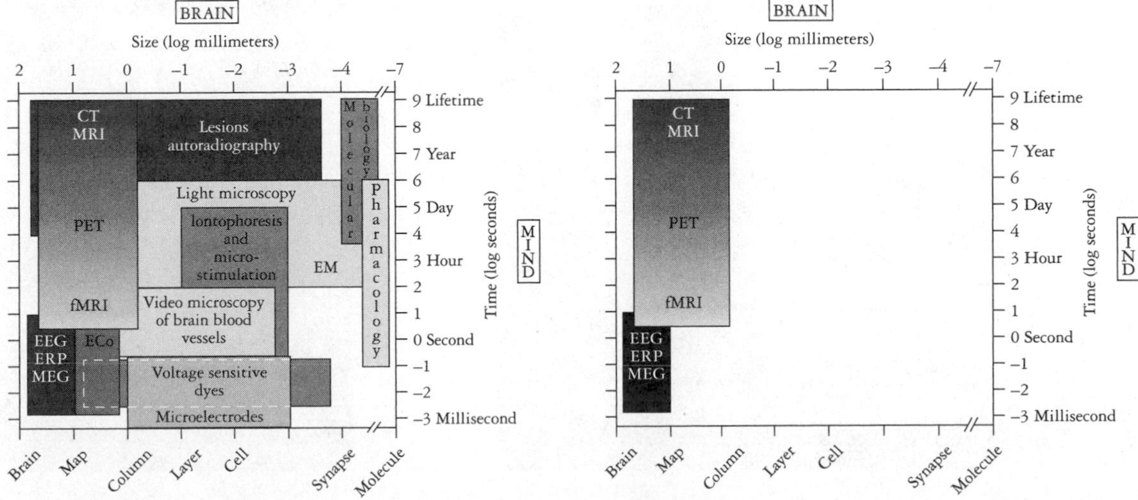

Source: M. I. Posner & M. E. Raichel (1994). *Images of the mind.* New York: Freeman.

Note that the tremendous advances in our ability to view the physiological structures and processes of the brain have not yet led to unequivocal mappings of particular functions to particular brain structures, regions, or even processes. Rather, we have found that some discrete structures, regions, or processes of the brain appear to be involved in particular cognitive functions. Our current understanding of how particular cognitive functions are linked to particular brain structures or processes allows us only to infer suggestive indications of some kind of relationship. Through sophisticated analyses, we can infer increasingly precise relationships, but we are not yet at a point where we can determine the specific cause–effect relationship between a given brain structure or process and a particular cognitive function, in part because particular functions may be influenced by multiple structures, regions, or processes of the brain. Finally, these techniques provide the best information only in conjunction with other experimental techniques for understanding the complexities of cognitive functioning.

COGNITION IN THE BRAIN: CEREBRAL CORTEX AND OTHER STRUCTURES

So far, we have discussed how scientists determine the structure and function of the brain using various postmortem and in vivo techniques. Now we discuss what scientists have discovered about the supreme organ of the nervous system, the human brain. The brain can be viewed as being divided into three major regions: forebrain, midbrain, and hindbrain (see Figure 2.9 and Table 2.2). These labels do not correspond exactly to locations of regions in an adult's or even a child's head, for the terms come

FIGURE 2.9 VIEWS OF THE HUMAN BRAIN

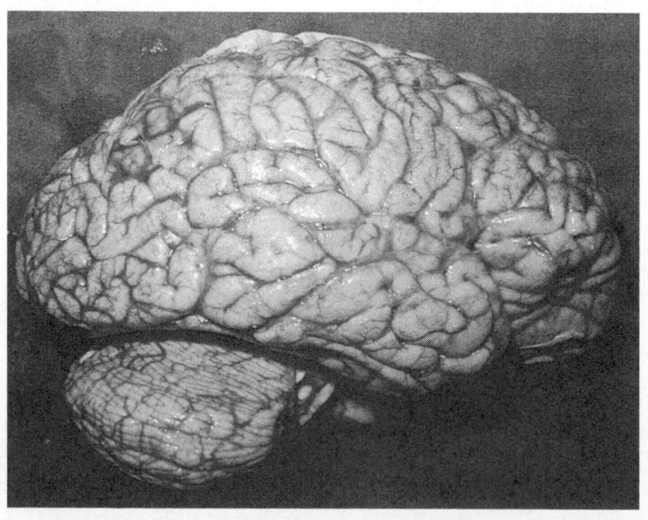

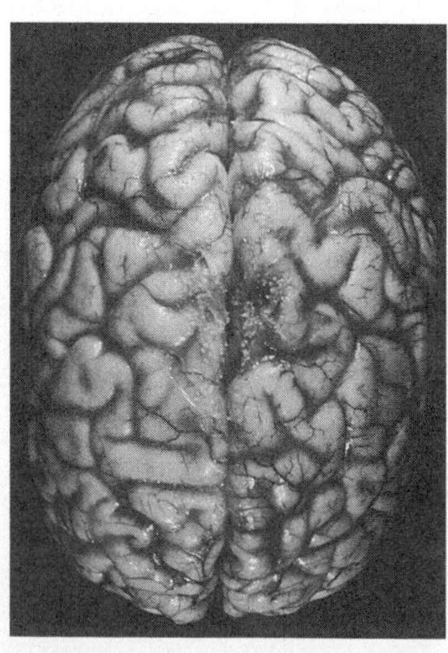

What does a brain actually look like? Here, you can see top and side views of a human brain. Subsequent figures and schematic pictures (i.e., simplified diagrams) point out in more detail some of the main features of the brain.

TABLE 2.2 MAJOR STRUCTURES AND FUNCTIONS OF THE BRAIN

The forebrain, midbrain, and hindbrain contain structures that perform essential functions for survival, as well as for high-level thinking and feeling.

Region of the Brain	Major Structures Within the Regions	Functions of the Structures
Forebrain	**Cerebral cortex** (outer layer of the cerebral hemispheres)	Involved in receiving and processing sensory and processing sensory information, thinking, other cognitive processing, and planning and sending motor information
	Basal ganglia (collections of nuclei and neural fibers)	Crucial to the function of the motor system
	Limbic system (hippocampus, amygdala, and septum)	Involved in learning, emotions, and motivation (in particular, the **hippocampus** influences learning and memory; *amygdala*—anger and aggression; and *septum*—anger and fear)
	Thalamus	Primary relay station for sensory information coming into the brain; transmits information to the correct regions of the cerebral cortex through projection fibers that extend from the thalamus to specific regions of the cortex; comprises several *nuclei* (groups of neurons) that receive specific kinds of sensory information and project that information to specific regions of the cerebral cortex, including four key nuclei for sensory information: (1) from the visual receptors, via optic nerves, to the visual cortex, permitting us to see; (2) from the auditory receptors, via auditory nerves, to the auditory cortex, permitting us to hear; (3) from sensory receptors in the somatic nervous system, to the primary somatosensory cortex, permitting us to sense pressure and pain; (4) from the cerebellum (in the hindbrain) to the primary motor cortex, permitting us to sense physical balance and equilibrium
	Hypothalamus	Controls the endocrine system; controls the autonomic nervous system, such as internal temperature regulation, appetite and thirst regulation, and other key functions; involved in regulation of behavior related to species survival—in particular, fighting, feeding, fleeing, and mating; plays a role in controlling consciousness (see reticular activating system); involved in emotions, pleasure, pain, and stress reactions
Midbrain	*Superior colliculi* (on top)	Involved in vision (especially visual reflexes)
	Inferior colliculi (below)	Involved in hearing
	Reticular activating system (also extends into the hindbrain)	Important in controlling consciousness (sleep, arousal), attention, cardiorespiratory function, and movement
	Gray matter, red nucleus, substantia nigra, ventral region	Important in controlling movement
Hindbrain	*Cerebellum*	Essential to balance, coordination, and muscle tone
	Pons (also contains part of the RAS)	Involved in consciousness (sleep/arousal); bridges neural transmissions from one part of the brain to another; involved with facial nerves
	Medulla oblongata	Serves as juncture at which nerves cross from one side of the body to opposite side of the brain; involved in cardiorespiratory function, digestion, and swallowing

from the front-to-back physical arrangement of these parts in the nervous system of a developing embryo: Initially, the **forebrain** is generally the farthest forward, toward what becomes the face; the **midbrain** is next in line; and the **hindbrain** is generally farthest from the forebrain, near the back of the neck (see Figure 2.10a). In development, the relative orientations change, such that the forebrain is almost a cap on top of the

FIGURE 2.10 **DEVELOPMENT OF THE HUMAN BRAIN**

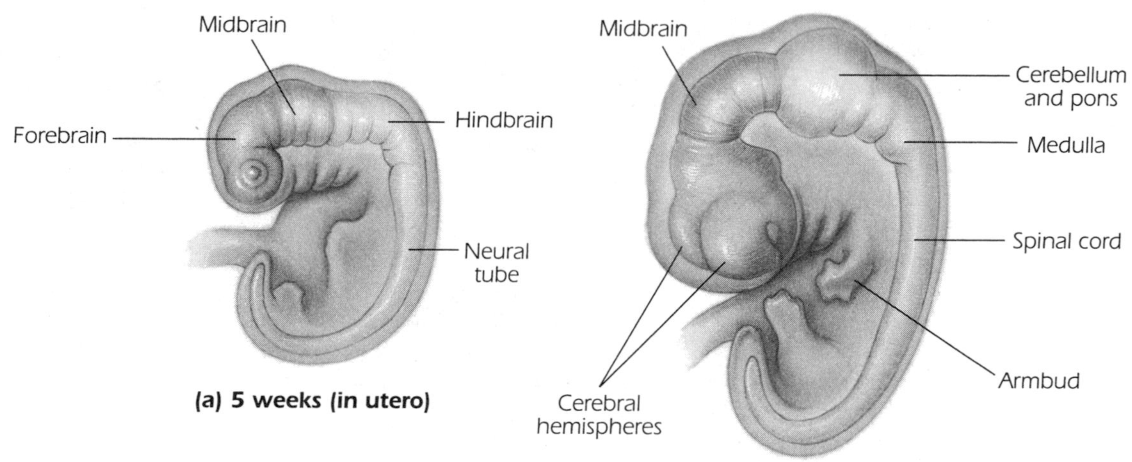

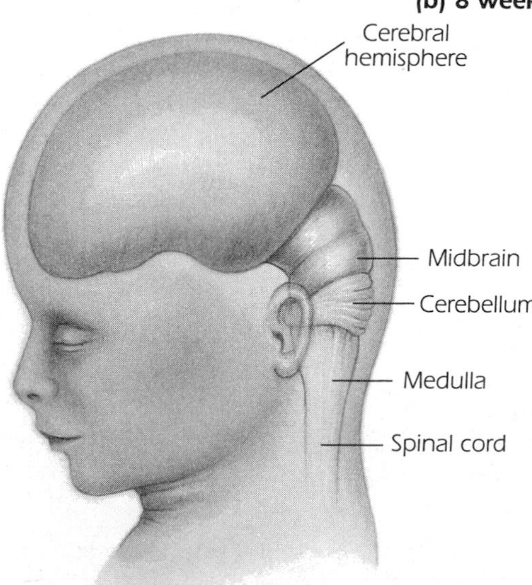

Over the course of embryonic and fetal development, the brain becomes more highly specialized, and the locations and relative positions of the hindbrain, the midbrain, and the forebrain change from conception to full term.

midbrain and hindbrain. Nonetheless, the terms are still used to designate areas of the fully developed brain. Figure 2.10 (b and c) shows the changing locations and relationships of the forebrain, the midbrain, and the hindbrain over the course of development of the brain from an embryo a few weeks after conception to a fetus of 7 months of age.

Gross Anatomy of the Brain: Forebrain, Midbrain, Hindbrain

The Forebrain

The forebrain is the region of the brain located toward the top and front of the brain (see Figure 2.11), and it comprises the cerebral cortex, the basal ganglia, the limbic system, the thalamus, and the hypothalamus. The cerebral cortex is the outer layer of the cerebral hemispheres and plays such a vital role in our thinking and other mental processes that it merits a special section, which follows the present discussion of the major structures and functions of the brain. The *basal ganglia* (singular, *ganglion*) are collections of neurons crucial to motor function.

The **limbic system** is important to emotion, motivation, memory, and learning. Animals such as fish and reptiles, which have relatively undeveloped limbic systems, respond to the environment almost exclusively by instinct. Mammals and especially humans have relatively more developed limbic systems that seem to allow us to suppress instinctive responses (such as the impulse to strike someone who accidentally causes us pain). Our limbic systems make us better able to adapt our behaviors flexibly in response to our changing environment. The limbic system comprises three central interconnected cerebral structures: the amygdala, the septum, and the hippocampus. The *amygdala* plays a role in anger and aggression, and the *septum* is involved in anger and fear. The **hippocampus** (from Greek, "seahorse," its approximate shape) plays an essential role in memory formation. Persons who have suffered damage to or removal of the hippocampus can still recall existing memories (for example, they can recognize old friends and places), but they are unable to form new ones (relative to the time of the brain damage). New information—new situations, people, and places—remain forever new. People with Korsakoff's syndrome, which can result from alcohol use, show loss of memory function that is believed to be associated with deterioration of the hippocampus. The hippocampus also appears to keep track of where things are and how these things are spatially related to each other—in other words, what is where (McClelland, McNaughton, & O'Reilly, 1995; Tulving & Schacter, 1994). We return to the role of the hippocampus in chapter 5.

Most of the sensory input into the brain passes through the **thalamus** (located in about the center of the brain, at about the level of the eyes). The thalamus relays the incoming sensory information through groups of neurons that project to the appropriate region in the cortex. To accommodate all the different types of information that must be sorted out, the thalamus is divided into a number of *nuclei* (groups of neurons of similar function), each of which receives information from specific senses and is related to corresponding specific areas in the cerebral cortex (see Table 2.3, for the names and roles of the various nuclei). The thalamus also helps in the control of sleep and waking.

The small size of the **hypothalamus** (from Greek *hypo-*, "under"; located at the base of the forebrain, beneath the thalamus) belies its importance in controlling many bodily

FIGURE 2.11 **STRUCTURES OF THE FOREBRAIN, MIDBRAIN, AND HINDBRAIN**

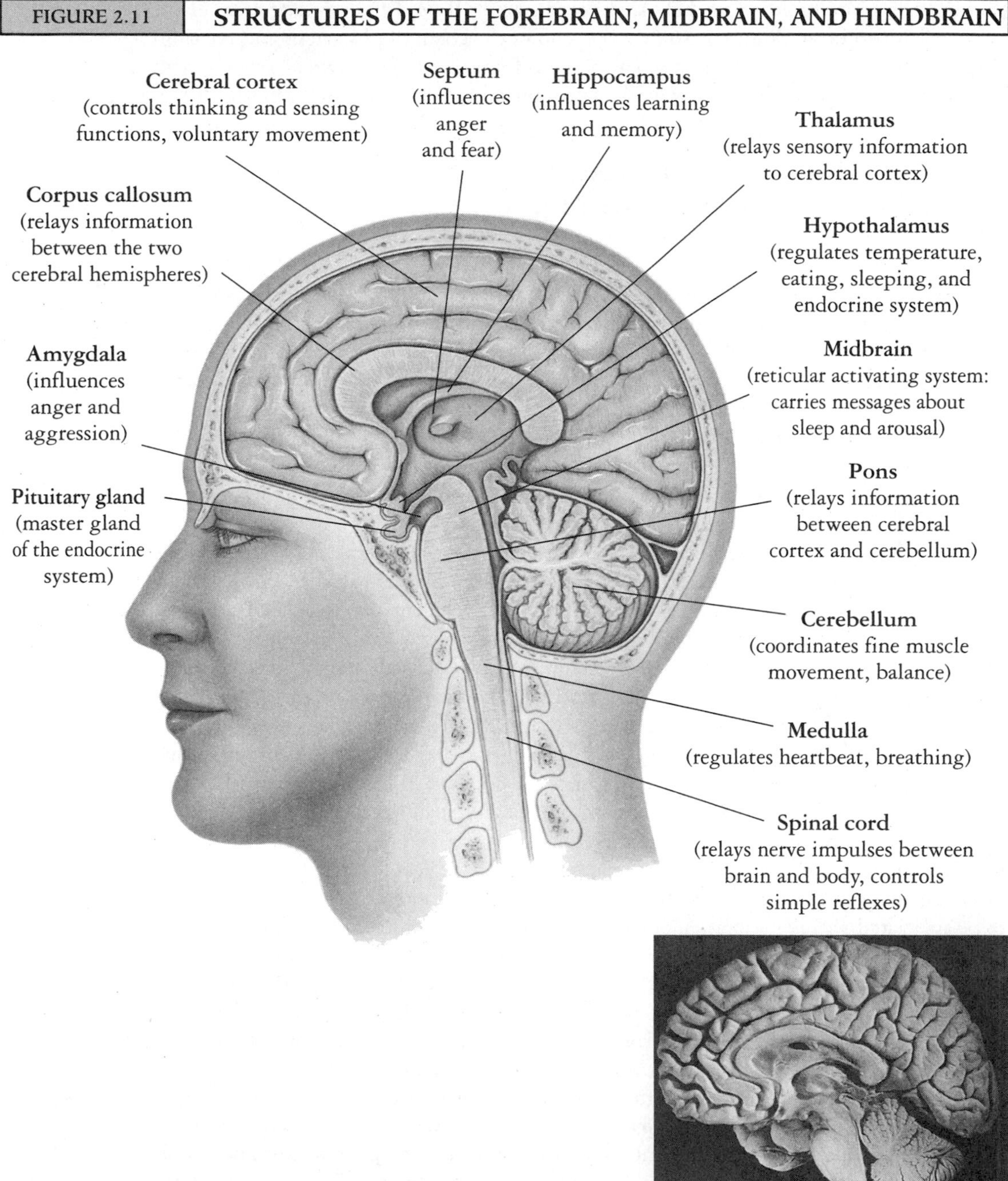

The forebrain, the midbrain, and the hindbrain contain structures that perform essential functions for survival as well as for high-level thinking and feeling.

TABLE 2.3 FOUR MAJOR NUCLEI OF THE THALAMUS*

Four key thalamic nuclei relay visual, auditory, somatosensory, and equilibrium-related information.

Name of Nucleus†	Receives Information From	Projects (Transmits Information) Primarily to	Functional Benefit
Lateral geniculate nucleus	The visual receptors, via optic nerves	The visual cortex	Permits us to see
Medial geniculate nucleus	The auditory receptors, via auditory nerves	The auditory cortex	Permits us to hear
Ventroposterior nucleus	The somatic nervous system	The primary somatosensory cortex	Permits us to sense pressure and pain
Ventrolateral nucleus	The cerebellum (in the hindbrain)	The primary motor cortex	Permits us to sense physical balance and equilibrium

*Other thalamic nuclei also play important roles. †The names refer to the relative location of the nuclei within the thalamus: *lateral* = toward the right or left side of the medial nucleus; *ventral* = closer to the belly than to the top of the head; *posterior* = toward the back, behind; *ventroposterior* = bellyward and in the back; *ventrolateral* = bellyward and on the side. Also, *geniculate* means "knee-shaped."

functions (see Table 2.2 for more information). The hypothalamus, which interacts with the limbic system, also regulates behavior related to species survival: fighting, feeding, fleeing, and mating. Not surprisingly, the hypothalamus is also active in regulating emotions and reactions to stress.

THE MIDBRAIN

The midbrain is more important in nonmammals than in mammals, for in nonmammals it is the main source of control for visual and auditory information. In mammals, these functions are dominated by the forebrain. Even in mammals, though, the midbrain still helps to control eye movement and coordination. Table 2.2 lists several structures (and corresponding functions) of the midbrain, but by far the most indispensable of these structures is the *reticular activating system* (*RAS;* also called the "reticular formation"), a network of neurons essential to the regulation of consciousness (sleep, wakefulness, arousal, and even attention, to some extent), as well as to such vital functions as heartbeat and breathing.

Actually, the RAS also extends into the hindbrain. Both the RAS and the thalamus are essential to our having any conscious awareness of or control over our existence. Together, the hypothalamus, the thalamus, the midbrain, and the hindbrain form the **brain stem,** which connects the forebrain to the spinal cord. Physicians make a determination of brain death based on the function of the brain stem. Specifically, a physician must determine that the brain stem has been damaged so severely that various reflexes of the head (e.g., the pupillary reflex) are absent for more than 12 hours or that the brain shows no electrical activity (as shown by EEG) or cerebral circulation (as shown by angiography; Berkow, 1992).

THE HINDBRAIN

The hindbrain comprises the medulla oblongata, the pons, and the cerebellum. The *medulla oblongata* is an elongated interior structure, located at the point where the spinal cord enters the skull and joins with the brain. The medulla oblongata, which contains part of the RAS, helps to keep us alive: It controls heart activity and largely controls breathing, swallowing, and digestion. The medulla is also the place at which nerves from the right side of the body cross over to the left side of the brain, and nerves from the left side of the body cross over to the right side of the brain.

The *pons* (from Latin, "bridge") serves as a kind of relay station, for it contains neural fibers that pass signals from one part of the brain to another (thus the bridging function for which it is named). The pons also contains a portion of the RAS, as well as nerves serving parts of the head and face. The *cerebellum* (from Latin, "little brain") controls bodily coordination, balance, and muscle tone, as well as some aspects of memory involving procedure-related movements (see chapters 7 and 8).

Intriguingly, the prenatal development of the human brain within each individual roughly corresponds to the evolutionary development of the human brain within the species as a whole. Specifically, the hindbrain, which is the first part of the brain to develop prenatally, is also evolutionarily the oldest, most primitive part of the brain. The midbrain, which develops after the hindbrain, is also a relatively newer addition to the brain in evolutionary terms. Finally, the forebrain, which is the last of the three portions of the brain to develop prenatally, is also the most recent evolutionary addition to the brain.

Additionally, across the evolutionary development of our species, humans have shown an increasingly greater proportion of brain weight in relation to body weight. However, across the span of development after birth, the proportion of brain weight to body weight declines, such that the brain weight of a newborn is proportionately much greater in relation to body weight than is the brain weight of an adult. From infancy through adulthood, the development of the brain centers chiefly on the organizational complexity of the connections within the brain (see chapter 13). The individual's developmental increases in neural complexity are paralleled by the evolutionary development of our species, but the changing proportion of brain weight to body weight in evolution is not.

For cognitive psychologists, the most important of these evolutionary trends is the increasing neural complexity of the brain, more than the changes in proportionate brain weight or even in the sequentially developing structures of the brain. Of even greater interest to cognitive psychologists, however, is how the evolution of the human brain has offered us the increasing ability to exercise voluntary control over behavior and even to plan and to contemplate alternative courses of action, as discussed in the next section with respect to the cerebral cortex.

THE CEREBRAL CORTEX AND LOCALIZATION OF FUNCTION

The **cerebral cortex** forms a 1- to 3-millimeter layer that wraps the surface of the brain somewhat like the bark of a tree wraps around the trunk. In human beings, the many convolutions of the cerebral cortex comprise three different elements: *sulci* (singular, *sulcus),* which are small grooves; *fissures,* which are large grooves; and *gyri* (singular, *gyrus),* which are bulges between adjacent sulci or fissures (see Figure 2.9). These folds greatly increase the surface area of the cortex; if the wrinkly human cortex were smoothed out, it would take up about 2 square feet. The cortex comprises 80% of the human brain (Kolb & Whishaw, 1990). The complexity of brain function increases with the cortical area. The human cerebral cortex enables us to think—to plan, coordinate thoughts and actions, perceive visual and sound patterns, use language, and so on. Without it, we would not be human. The surface of the cerebral cortex is grayish, sometimes referred to as *gray matter,* because it primarily comprises the grayish neural-cell bodies that process the information that the brain receives and sends. In contrast, the underlying *white matter* of the brain's interior comprises mostly white-colored, myelinated axons.

The cerebral cortex forms the outer layer of the two halves of the brain, the left and right **cerebral hemispheres.** Although the two hemispheres appear to be quite similar, they function differently. The left hemisphere is specialized for some kinds of activity, the right for other kinds. For example, receptors in the skin on the right side of the body generally send information through the medulla to areas in the left hemisphere in the brain, and the receptors on the left side generally transmit information to the right hemisphere. Similarly, the left hemisphere of the brain directs the motor responses on the right side of the body, and the right hemisphere directs responses on the left side of the body. However, not all information transmission is **contralateral** (*contra-,* "opposite"; *lateral,* "side"); some **ipsilateral** ("same side") transmission occurs, as well. For example, odor information from the right nostril goes primarily to the right side of the brain, and about half of the information from the right eye goes to the right side of the brain. In addition to this general tendency for contralateral specialization, the hemispheres also communicate directly with one another. The **corpus callosum** (from Latin, "dense body"), a dense aggregate of neural fibers, connects the two cerebral hemispheres, allowing transmission of information back and forth (see Figure 2.11). Once information has reached one hemisphere, the corpus callosum transfers it to the other hemisphere. If the corpus callosum is cut, the two hemispheres of the brain cannot communicate with each other.

HEMISPHERIC SPECIALIZATION

How did psychologists find out that the two hemispheres have different responsibilities? The study of hemispheric specialization in the human brain can be traced back to Marc Dax, a country doctor in France, who in 1836 presented a little-noticed paper to a medical society meeting (Springer & Deutsch, 1985). Dax had treated more than 40 patients suffering from loss of speech as a result of brain damage. This condition, *aphasia* (from Greek, "no speech"), had been reported even in ancient Greece. Dax noticed a relationship between the loss of speech and the side of the brain in which damage had occurred. Dax saw, in studying his patients' brains after death, that in every case there had been damage to the left hemisphere of the brain. He was not able to find even one case of speech loss due to damage to the right hemisphere only. Despite this provocative finding, his paper aroused no scientific interest.

The next major figure in the study of hemispheric specialization was Paul Broca (1824–1880). At a meeting of the French Society of Anthropology in 1861, Broca claimed that a stroke patient of his who was suffering from aphasia was shown in an autopsy to have a lesion in the left cerebral hemisphere of the brain. Despite an initially cool response, Broca soon became a central figure in the heated controversy over whether functions, particularly speech, are indeed localized in particular areas in the brain, rather than generalized over the entire brain. By 1864, Broca was convinced that the left hemisphere of the brain is critical in speech, a view that has held up over time. In fact, the specific area Broca identified as contributing to speech is referred to as Broca's area (see Figure 2.12). Another important early researcher, German neurologist Carl Wernicke (1848–1905), studied language-deficient patients who could speak, but whose speech made no sense. He also traced language ability to the left hemisphere, though to a different precise location, now known as Wernicke's area (see Figure 2.12).

During this era, Karl Spencer Lashley (1890–1958), often described as the father of neuropsychology, started studying localization in 1915 and continued to do so his entire life. In many of his investigations, Lashley surgically implanted electrodes (relatively large ones, compared with the microelectrodes now available) in specific areas of an animal's brain; then he electrically stimulated those areas and recorded the results, such as the animal's motor responses. To ensure that he had indeed localized a particular motor response, Lashley repeated the procedures on the same animals across several different test sessions. The rather bulky electrodes available at that time had to be reimplanted for each new test session. Lashley meticulously reimplanted the electrodes in what he deemed to be identical locations across different tests, yet he found that the apparently identical locations yielded different results, and that different locations sometimes paradoxically yielded the same results (e.g., see Lashley, 1950). Subsequent researchers, using microelectrodes that do not have to be removed between test sessions, have found that specific locations do correlate with specific motor responses across many test sessions. Apparently, Lashley's research was limited by the technology available to him at the time.

Lashley was also particularly interested in knowing whether he could find specific locations in the brain for specific memories for learned habits. He used a slightly different approach for some of these studies. After a memory for a learned habit was established in an animal participant, either *ablation* (removal of tissue) or *incision* (cuts across tissue) was used for cutting off communication between sensory and motor neurons via neural pathways in the cortex, thereby eliminating the memory. After decades of diligent research (involving hundreds of experiments), Lashley finally (1950, as cited in Kolb & Whishaw, 1990, p. 525) surmised that "it is not possible to demonstrate the localization of a memory trace anywhere in the nervous system." Since then, psychologists have identified many cerebral structures involved in memory, but they have yet to find specific locations for specific memories—if such locations exist at all.

Despite the valuable early contributions by Broca, Lashley, and others, the individual most responsible for modern theory and research on hemispheric specialization is Nobel Prize-winning psychologist Roger Sperry (1920–1994). Sperry (1964) argued that each hemisphere behaves in many respects like a separate brain. In a classic experiment that supports this contention, Sperry and his colleagues severed the corpus callosum connecting the two hemispheres of a cat's brain. They then proved that information presented visually to one cerebral hemisphere of the cat was not recognizable to the other hemisphere. Similar work on monkeys indicated the same discrete performance of each hemisphere (Sperry, 1964), as well as the relative safety of performing this procedure on primates.

Some of the most interesting information about how the human brain works, and especially about the respective roles of the hemispheres, has emerged from studies of humans with epilepsy in whom the corpus callosum has been cleaved. Surgically severing

FIGURE 2.12 **BROCA'S AREA AND WERNICKE'S AREA**

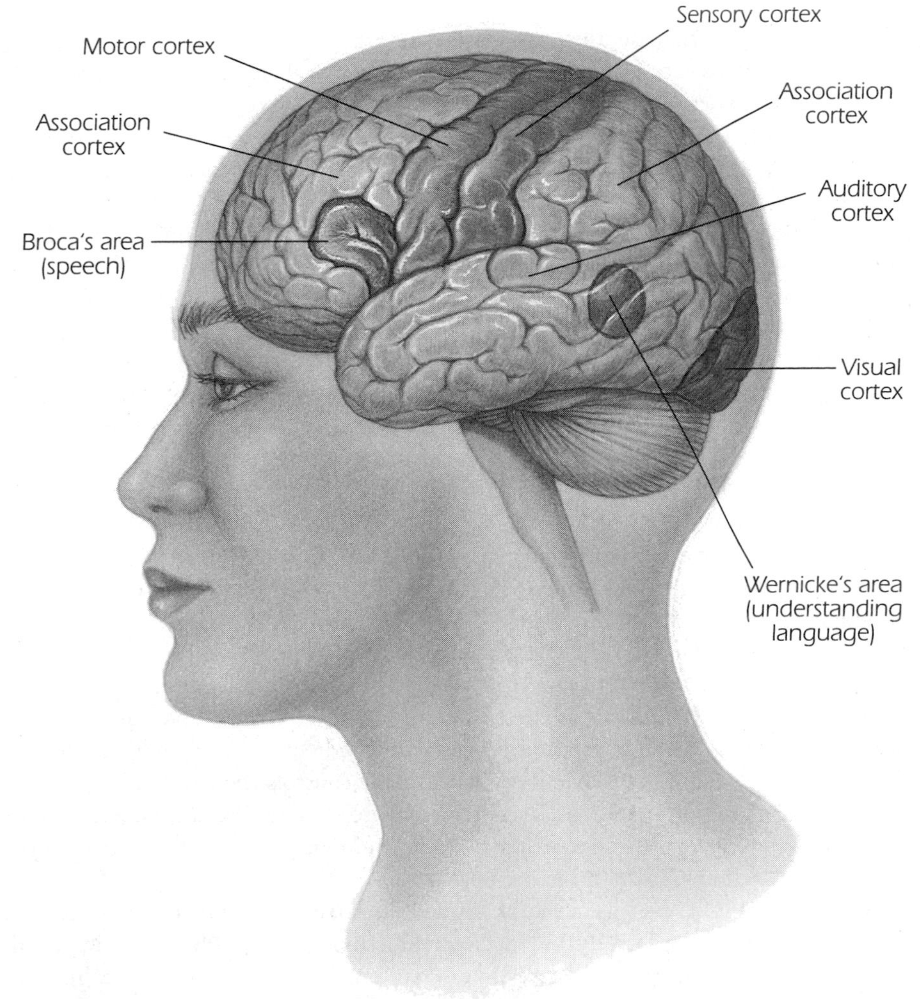

Curiously, although people with lesions in Broca's area cannot speak fluently, they can use their voices to sing or shout.

this neurological bridge prevents epileptic seizures from spreading from one hemisphere to another, thereby drastically reducing their severity. However, this procedure also results in a loss of communication between the two hemispheres, as if the person has two separate specialized brains processing different information and performing separate functions.

People who have undergone such operations are termed **split-brain** patients. Split-brain research reveals fascinating possibilities regarding the ways we think. Many in the field have argued that language is localized in the left hemisphere, and spatial visualization ability is localized in the right hemisphere (Farah, 1988a, 1988b; Gazzaniga, 1985;

Zaidel, 1983). Jerre Levy (one of Sperry's students) and her colleagues (Levy, Trevarthen, & Sperry, 1972) have probed the link between the cerebral hemispheres and visuospatial versus language-oriented tasks, using participants who have undergone split-brain surgery.

In studies such as the one illustrated in Figure 2.13, split-brain patients are typically unaware that they saw conflicting information in the two halves of the picture. When asked to give an answer about what they saw in words, they report that they saw the right half of the picture. Bearing in mind the contralateral association between hemisphere and side of the body, it seems that the left hemisphere is controlling their verbal processing (speaking) of visual information. In contrast, when asked to use the fingers of the left hand (which contralaterally sends and receives information to and from the right hemisphere) to point to what they saw, participants choose the image from the left half of the picture. This finding indicates that the right hemisphere appears to control spatial processing (pointing) of visual information. Thus, the task that the participants are asked to perform is crucial in determining what image the participant thinks was shown.

Michael Gazzaniga—another of Sperry's students—has dissociated himself from the position of his former teacher, Sperry, and of his colleagues, such as Levy. Gazzaniga disagrees with their assertion that the two hemispheres function completely independently. Nonetheless, he still holds that each hemisphere serves a complementary role. For instance, according to Gazzaniga, there is no language processing in the right hemisphere (except in rare cases of early brain damage to the left hemisphere), and visuospatial processing occurs in the right hemisphere. As an example, Gazzaniga has found that before split-brain surgery, people can draw three-dimensional representations of cubes with each hand (Gazzaniga & LeDoux, 1978). After surgery, however, they can draw a reasonable-looking cube only with the left hand. In each patient, the right hand draws pictures unrecognizable either as cubes or as three-dimensional objects. This finding is important because of the contralateral association between each side of the body and the opposite hemisphere of the brain: Because the right hemisphere controls the left hand, and the left hand is the only one that a split-brain patient can use for drawing recognizable figures, this experiment supports the contention that the right hemisphere is dominant in our comprehension and exploration of spatial relations.

Gazzaniga (1985) argues that the brain, and especially the right hemisphere of the brain, is organized into relatively independent functioning units that work in parallel. According to Gazzaniga, each of the many discrete units of the mind operates relatively independently of the others, often outside of conscious awareness. While these various independent and often subconscious operations are taking place, the left hemisphere tries to assign interpretations to these operations. Even when the left hemisphere perceives that the individual is behaving in a way that does not intrinsically make any particular sense, it still finds a way to assign some meaning to that behavior.

In addition to studying hemispheric differences in language and spatial relations, researchers have tried to determine whether the two hemispheres think in ways that differ from one another. Levy (1974) has found some evidence that the left hemisphere tends to process information *analytically* (piece-by-piece, usually in a sequence) and the right hemisphere tends to process it *holistically* (as a whole). However, this interpretation of data does not go unchallenged. Gazzaniga (1985), for example, believes that the data from experiments showing different modes of processing between the two hemispheres are susceptible to alternative interpretations.

FIGURE 2.13 **INTRIGUING SPLITS**

In one study, the participant is asked to focus his or her gaze on the center of screen. Then a chimeric face (a face showing the left side of the face of one person and the right side of another) is flashed on the screen. The participant is then asked to identify what he or she saw, either verbally or by pointing to one of several normal (not chimeric) faces.

Lobes of the Cerebral Hemispheres

For practical purposes, the cerebral hemispheres and cortex are said to be divided into four lobes. These lobes are not distinct units, but rather, arbitrary anatomical regions. Particular functions have been identified with each lobe, but the lobes also interact. The four **lobes,** named after the bones of the skull lying directly over them (see Figure 2.14), are the frontal, parietal, temporal, and occipital lobes. Roughly speaking, motor processing and higher thought processes, such as abstract reasoning, occur in the **frontal lobe;** *somatosensory* processing (sensations in the skin and muscles of the body, *soma-)* in the **parietal lobe;** auditory processing in the **temporal lobe;** and visual processing in the **occipital lobe.**

The areas in the lobes in which sensory processing occurs are termed *projection areas* because the nerves containing sensory information go to the thalamus, from which the sensory information is *projected* to the appropriate projection area in the relevant lobe. Similarly, the projection areas project motor information downward through the spinal cord to the appropriate muscles via the PNS.

The frontal lobe, located toward the front of the head (the face), plays a role in judgment, problem solving, personality, and intentional movement. It contains the **primary motor cortex,** which specializes in the planning, control, and execution of movement, particularly of movement involving any kind of delayed response. If your motor cortex were electrically stimulated, you would react by moving a corresponding body part, depending on where in the motor cortex your brain had been stimulated. Control of the various kinds of body movements is located contralaterally on the primary motor cortex. A similar inverse mapping occurs from top to bottom, with the lower extremities of the body represented on the upper (toward the top of the head) side of the motor cortex, and the upper part of your body represented on the lower side of your motor cortex.

FIGURE 2.14 **LOBES OF THE BRAIN**

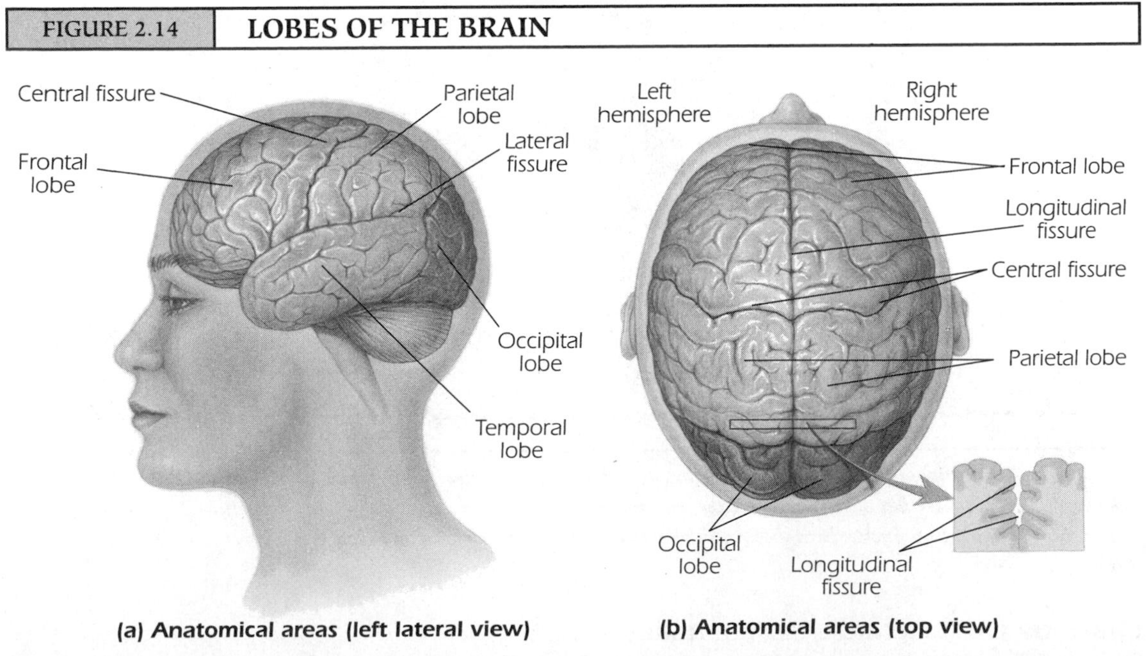

The cortex is divided into the frontal, parietal, temporal, and occipital lobes. The lobes have specific functions but also interact to perform complex processes.

Information going to neighboring parts of the body also comes from neighboring parts of the motor cortex. Thus, the motor cortex can be mapped to show where and in what proportions different parts of the body are represented in the brain (see Figure 2.15).

The three other lobes are located farther away from the front of the head. These lobes specialize in various kinds of sensory and perceptual activity. For example, in the parietal lobe, the **primary somatosensory cortex** (located right behind the frontal lobe's primary motor cortex) receives information from the senses about pressure, texture, temperature, and pain. If your somatosensory cortex were electrically stimulated, you would probably report feeling as if you had been touched (see Figure 2.16).

From looking at the homunculi (Figures 2.15 and 2.16), you can see that the relationship of function to form applies in the development of the motor and somatosensory

FIGURE 2.15	**MOTOR HOMUNCULUS**

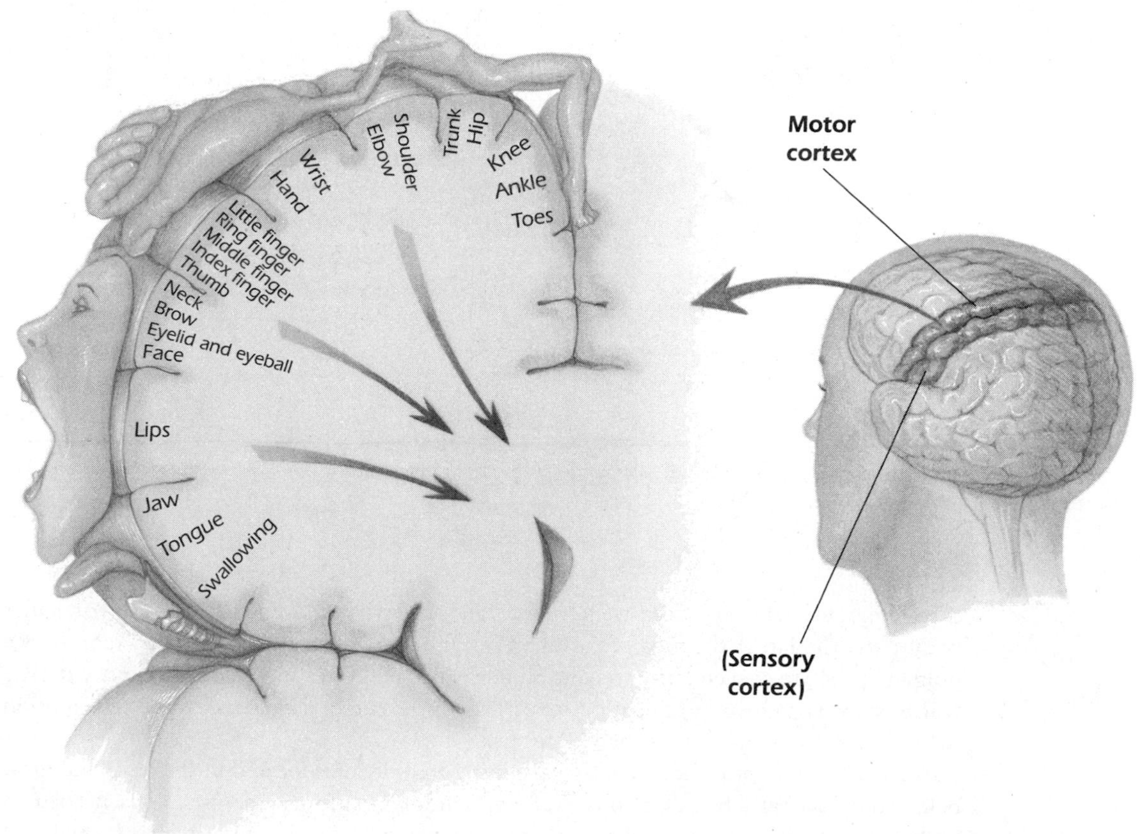

This map of the primary motor cortex is often termed a homunculus *(from Latin, "little person") because it is drawn as a cross-section of the cortex surrounded by the figure of a small upside-down person, whose body parts map out a proportionate correspondence to the parts of the cortex.*

FIGURE 2.16 SOMATOSENSORY HOMUNCULUS

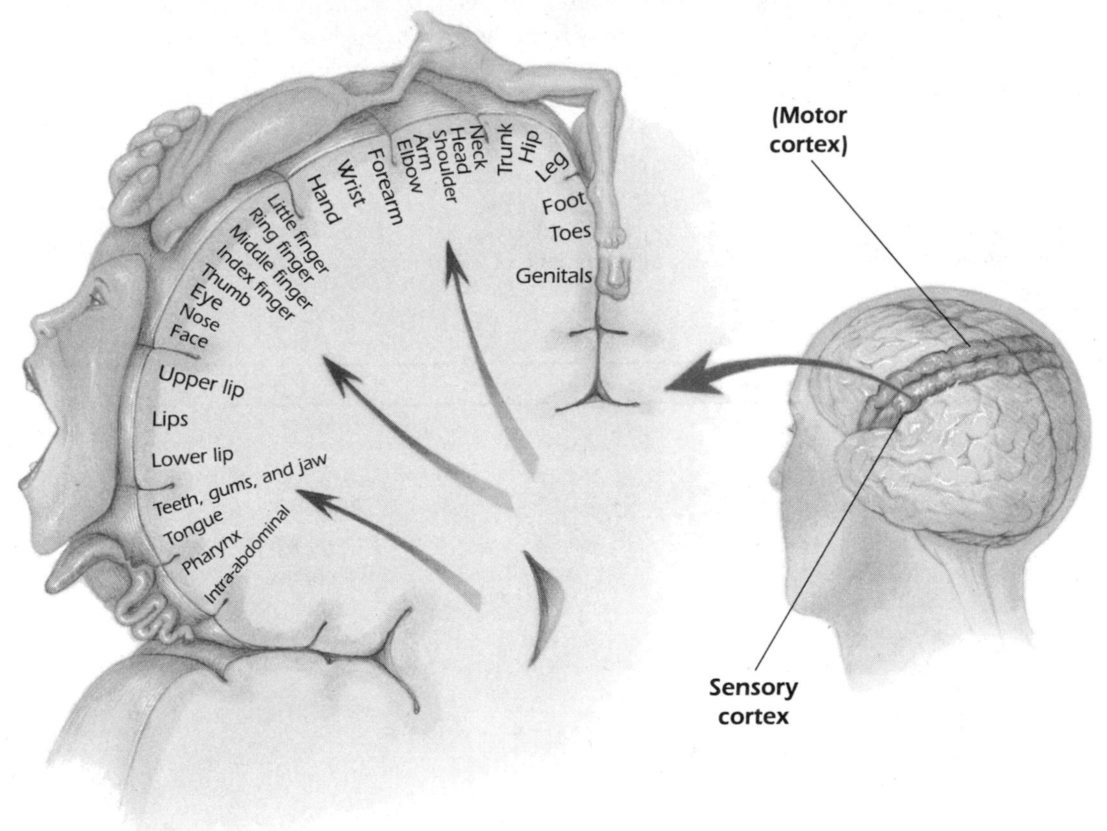

As with the primary motor cortex in the frontal lobe, a homunculus of the somatosensory cortex maps, in inverted form, the parts of the body from which the cortex receives information.

cortex regions: The more need we have for use, sensitivity, and fine control in a particular body part, the larger the area of cortex generally devoted to that part. For example, we humans, who are tremendously reliant on our hands and faces in our interactions with the world, show correspondingly large proportions of the cerebral cortex devoted to sensation in, and motor response by, our hands and face.

The region of the cerebral cortex pertaining to hearing is located in the temporal lobe, below the parietal lobe. This lobe performs complex auditory analysis, as is needed in understanding human speech or listening to a symphony. The lobe is also specialized: Some parts are more sensitive to sounds of higher pitch, others to sounds of lower pitch. The auditory region is primarily contralateral, although both sides of the auditory area have at least some representation from each ear. If your auditory cortex were stimulated electrically, you would report having heard some sort of sound.

The visual region of the cerebral cortex is primarily in the occipital lobe. Some neural fibers carrying visual information travel ipsilaterally from the left eye to the left cerebral hemisphere and from the right eye to the right cerebral hemisphere; other fibers cross over the **optic chiasma** (from Greek, "visual X" or "visual intersection") and go contralaterally to the opposite hemisphere (see Figure 2.17). In particular, neural fibers go from the left

FIGURE 2.17 **OPTIC CHIASMA**

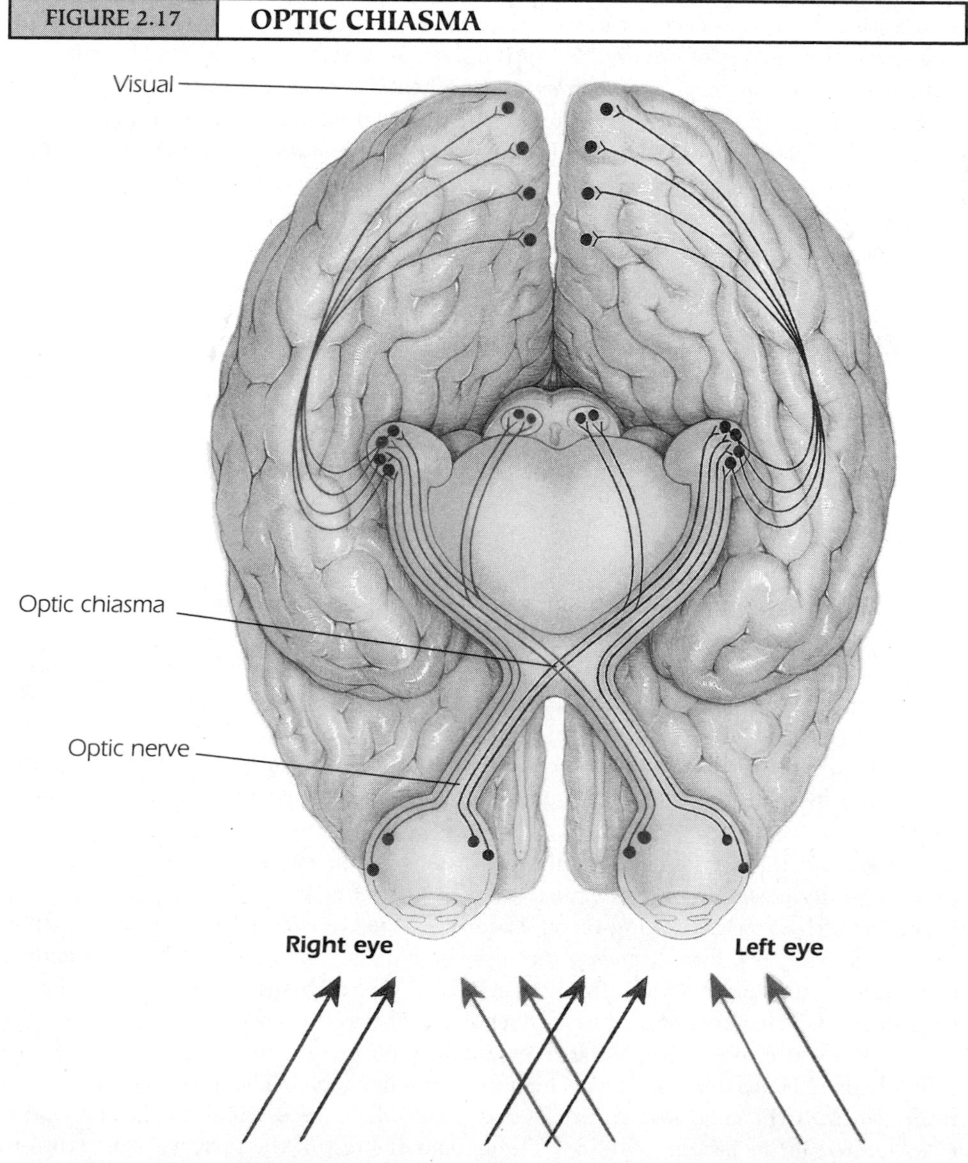

Some nerve fibers carry visual information ipsilaterally from each eye to each cerebral hemisphere; other fibers cross the optic chiasma and carry visual information contralaterally to the opposite hemisphere.

side of the visual field for each eye to the right side of the visual cortex; complementarily, the nerves from the right side of each eye's visual field send information to the left side of the visual cortex.

Michael Posner *is a professor of psychology at the University of Oregon. His groundbreaking research has provided strong evidence of links between cognitive operations and localized brain activity. His work has helped to establish joint cognitive experimental and biological approaches to higher brain function.*

Association Areas

Areas of the lobes that are not part of the somatosensory, motor, auditory, or visual cortices are **association areas.** The term *association area* comes from the belief that the function of these areas is to link (associate) the activity of the sensory and motor cortices. In humans, association areas make up roughly 75% of the cerebral cortex, although in most other animals, the association areas are much smaller. When electrical stimulation is applied to association areas, there is no specific observable reaction. (Thus, early attempts at using stimulation to determine localization had three chances in four of not observing any particular reaction.) However, people with damage to their association areas often do not act, speak, or think normally; the specific abnormal behavior depends on the site of damage. The association areas seem somehow to integrate assorted pieces of information from the sensory cortices and to send the integrated information to the motor cortex, initiating purposeful behavior and expression of logical, reasoned thought.

The frontal association area in the frontal lobes seems to be crucial to problem solving, planning, and judgment. Broca's and Wernicke's speech areas are also located in association areas. Although the roles of association areas in thinking are not completely understood, these areas definitely seem to be places in the brain in which a variety of intellectual abilities are seated.

Work by Steven Petersen, Michael Posner, and their colleagues (e.g., S. E. Petersen, Fox, Posner, Mintun, & Raichle, 1988, 1989; Posner, Petersen, Fox, & Raichle, 1988) illustrates the function of the association areas in integrating information from various parts of the cortex. Specifically, these researchers used PET scans to study regional cerebral blood flow (rCBF) during several activities involving the reading of single words. When participants looked at a word on a screen, areas of their visual cortex showed high levels of activity; when they spoke a word, their motor cortex was highly active; when they heard a word spoken, their auditory cortex was activated; when they were asked to produce words related to the words they saw (requiring high-level integration of visual, auditory, and motor information), the association areas of the cortex showed the greatest amount of activity.

Given all the activities of the brain, it may not surprise you to learn that although the brain typically makes up only one fortieth of the weight of an adult human body, it uses about one fifth of the circulating blood, one fifth of the available glucose, and one fifth of the available oxygen. It is, however, the supreme organ of cognition, and understanding both its structure and function, from the neural to the cerebral levels of organization, is vital to an understanding of cognitive psychology. The recent development of the field of cognitive neuroscience, with its focus on localization of function, reconceptualizes the mind–body question discussed in the beginning of this chapter. The question has changed from "where is the mind located in the body," to "where are particular cognitive operations located in the nervous system?" Throughout the rest of the text, we will return to these questions in reference to particular cognitive operations as these operations are discussed in more detail in subsequent chapters.

SUMMARY

1. **What are the fundamental structures and processes of the cells within the human brain?** A *neuron* is an individual neural cell. The parts of the neuron are the *soma,* the branchlike *dendrites,* and the *axon.* Some axons are coated with *myelin,* and others are not. At the terminus of each axon are *terminal buttons.* Between the terminal buttons of one neuron and the dendrites of the next neuron is a *synapse.* The process on which the conduction of a neural impulse depends is an *action potential,* which is an *all-or-none* response that occurs only if the electrical charge of the neuron has reached a *threshold of excitation.* Although the amplitude of each neuron's action potential does not vary, the rate of neural firing does vary. Thus, the intensity of a stimulus may be indicated through the rate of neural firing, but not through the amplitude of firing within individual neurons. Communication between neurons depends on the actions of chemical neurotransmitters. Neurotransmitters are released from the terminal buttons of an axon and are communicated across synapses to the dendrites of another neuron.

   Neurotransmitters can produce either *excitatory* (stimulating an increased likelihood of firing) or *inhibitory* (suppressing the likelihood of firing) effects on receiving neurons. Excitation and inhibition generally serve complementary roles. An excess of neurotransmitters at the synapse can be absorbed by *reuptake* back into the terminal buttons or by *enzymatic deactivation,* whereby the transmitter substance is chemically decomposed. Several neurotransmitter substances have been identified: Monoamine neurotransmitters include acetylcholine (Ach), dopamine (DA), and serotonin; amino-acid neurotransmitters include glutamate and GABA. In addition, neurotransmission involves neuropeptides, such as endorphins and many chemicals involved in physiological regulation of thirst, hunger, and reproductive functions.

   The nervous system, governed by the human brain, is divided into two main parts: the *central nervous system,* consisting of the brain and the spinal cord, and the *peripheral nervous system,* consisting of the rest of the nervous system (e.g., the nerves in the face, legs, arms, and viscera). Within the nervous system, various *sensory/afferent neurons* receive sensory information from the *receptor* nerves of the body and transmit that information back up through the spinal cord to the brain. Conversely, various *motor/efferent neurons* transmit motor information from the spinal cord (and usually from the brain) about how the body should act in response to the information it receives. *Reflexes* are automatic, involuntary responses to stimulation, which do not require input from the brain. For voluntary actions, however, as well as for the interpretation of all sensations and reactions, the brain must be involved.

2. **How do researchers study the major structures and processes of the brain?** For centuries, scientists have viewed the brain by dissecting it; modern *dissection* techniques include the use of electron microscopes and sophisticated chemical analyses to probe the mysteries of individual cells of the brain. Additionally, surgical techniques on animals (e.g., the use of *selective lesioning* and *single-cell recording)*

are often used. On humans, studies have included electrical analyses (e.g., *electroencephalograms {EEGs}* and *event-related potentials {ERPs}*), studies based on the use of X-ray techniques (e.g., *angiograms* and *computerized axial tomograms {CT scans}*), studies based on computer analyses of magnetic fields within the brain (*magnetic resonance imaging {MRI}*), and studies based on computer analyses of blood flow and metabolism within the brain (*positron emission tomography {PET scan}* and *functional magnetic resonance imaging {fMRI}*).

3. **What have researchers found as a result of studying the brain?** The major structures of the brain may be categorized as those in the *forebrain* (e.g., the all-important cerebral cortex, as well as the *thalamus,* the *hypothalamus,* and the *limbic system,* including the *hippocampus*), the *midbrain* (including a portion of the *brain stem*), and the *hindbrain* (including the *medulla oblongata,* the *pons,* and the *cerebellum*). The highly convoluted *cerebral cortex* surrounds the interior of the brain and is the basis for much of human cognition. The cortex covers the left and right hemispheres of the brain, which are connected by the *corpus callosum.* In general, each hemisphere contralaterally controls the opposite side of the body. Based on extensive *split-brain* research, many investigators believe that the two hemispheres are specialized: In most people, the left hemisphere seems primarily to control language, and the right hemisphere seems primarily to control visuospatial processing. The two hemispheres also may process information differently. Another way to view the cortex is to identify differences among four lobes. Roughly speaking, higher thought and motor processing occur in the *frontal lobe,* somatosensory processing in the *parietal lobe,* auditory processing in the *temporal lobe,* and visual processing in the *occipital lobe.* Within the frontal lobe, the *primary motor cortex* controls the planning, control, and execution of movement. Within the parietal lobe, the *primary somatosensory cortex* is responsible for sensations in our muscles and skin. Specific regions of these two cortices can be mapped to particular regions of the body. *Association areas* within the lobes appear to link the activity of the motor and sensory cortices, allowing for high-level cognitive processes.

Thinking About Thinking: Factual, Analytical, Creative, and Practical Questions

1. Briefly describe the spinal reflex, using the terminology of the nervous system elements mentioned in this chapter.
2. Briefly summarize the main structures and functions of the brain.
3. What are some of the reasons that researchers are interested in finding out the localization of function in the human brain?
4. In your opinion, why have the hindbrain, the midbrain, and the forebrain evolved (across the human species) and developed (across human prenatal

development) in the sequence mentioned in this chapter? Include the main functions of each in your comments.

5. Researchers are already aware that a deficit of acetylcholine in the hippocampus is linked to Alzheimer's disease. Given the difficulty of reaching the hippocampus without causing other kinds of brain damage, how might researchers try to treat Alzheimer's disease?

6. In your opinion, why is it that some discoveries, such as that of Marc Dax, go unnoticed? What can be done to maximize the possibility that key discoveries will be noticed?

7. Given the functions of each of the cortical lobes, how might a lesion in one of the lobes be discovered?

8. What is an area of cognition that could be studied effectively by viewing the structure or function of the human brain? Describe how a researcher might use one of the techniques mentioned in this chapter to study that area of cognition.

KEY TERMS

action potential 31
association areas 62
axon 29
blood–brain barrier 38
brain 38
brain stem 51
central nervous system (CNS) 37
cerebral cortex 52
cerebral hemispheres 53
contralateral 53
corpus callosum 53
dendrites 29
electrochemical 30
electroencephalogram (EEG) 42
enzymatic deactivation 34
forebrain 48
frontal lobe 58
functional magnetic resonance imaging (fMRI) 44
hindbrain 48
hippocampus 49
hypothalamus 49
interneuron 38
ipsilateral 53
limbic system 49
lobes 57
localization of function 28
magnetic resonance imaging (MRI) 42
midbrain 48
motor (efferent) neuron 38
myelin 29
nervous system 28
neuron 29
neurotransmitter 30
nodes of Ranvier 29
occipital lobe 58
optic chiasma 61
parietal lobe 58
peripheral nervous system (PNS) 36
positron emission tomography (PET) 44
primary motor cortex 58
primary somatosensory cortex 59
receptor cells 38
reflex 39
reuptake 34
saltatory conduction 32
sensory (afferent) neuron 38
soma 29
spinal cord 38
split-brain 55
static equilibrium 30
synapse 29
temporal lobe 58
terminal buttons 29
thalamus 49
threshold of excitation 31

Annotated Suggested Readings

Caryl, P. G. (1994). Early event-related potentials correlate with inspection time and intelligence. *Intelligence, 18,* 15–46. A good example of contemporary research attempting to relate information-processing tasks to characteristics of brain functioning, in this case, event-related potentials.

Gould, S. J. (1981). *The mismeasure of man.* New York: Norton. An entertaining but highly controversial account of how attempts to measure people's abilities have often backfired.

Kolb, B., & Whishaw, I. Q. (1990). *Human neuropsychology* (3rd ed.). New York: Freeman. An excellent introduction to neuroscience.

Levy, J., Trevarthen, C., & Sperry, R. W. (1972). Perception of bilateral chimeric figures following hemispheric disconnexion. *Brain, 95,* 61–78. A classic study showing the relative independence of the two hemispheres as revealed by the analysis of the performance of split-brain patients.

Parkin, A. J. (1996). *Explorations in cognitive neuropsychology.* Oxford, UK: Blackwell. A readable and well-integrated survey of the field of cognitive neuroscience.

Pinker, S. (1997). *How the mind works.* New York: Norton. An entertaining and far-reaching, although sometimes speculative account of how evolutionary psychology can be applied to the study of cognition.

Rugg, M. D. (Ed.) (1997). *Cognitive neuroscience.* Hove East Sussex, UK: Psychology Press. An up-to-date and broad-ranging introduction to cognitive neuroscience with contributions by top experts in the field. (Level is a bit higher than that of Parkin.)

ATTENTION AND CONSCIOUSNESS

CHAPTER OUTLINE

EXPLORING COGNITIVE PSYCHOLOGY

ATTENTION AND CONSCIOUSNESS
• Preconscious Processing
• Controlled Versus Automatic Processes
• Habituation

ATTENTION
• Signal Detection
• The Nature of Signal Detection
• Vigilance
• Search

SELECTIVE AND DIVIDED ATTENTION
• Basic Paradigms for Studying Selective Attention
• Filter and Bottleneck Theories of Selective Attention
• Attentional-Resource Theories of Selective Attention
• Additional Considerations in Selective Attention
• Divided Attention

COGNITIVE NEUROSCIENTIFIC APPROACHES TO ATTENTION AND CONSCIOUSNESS
• Posner's Theory
• Näätänen's ERP Work
• A Psychopharmacological Approach
• Marcel's Model of the Links Among Perception, Attention, and Consciousness

SUMMARY

THINKING ABOUT THINKING: FACTUAL, ANALYTICAL, CREATIVE, AND PRACTICAL QUESTIONS

KEY TERMS

ANNOTATED SUGGESTED READINGS

Exploring Cognitive Psychology

1. **Can we actively process information even if we are not aware of doing so? If so, what do we do, and how do we do it?**
2. **What are some of the functions of attention?**
3. **What are some theories cognitive psychologists have developed to explain what they have observed about attentional processes?**
4. **What have cognitive psychologists learned about attention by studying the human brain?**

Investigating Cognitive Psychology

Repeatedly write your name on a piece of paper while you picture everything you can remember about the room in which you slept when you were 10 years old. While continuing to write your name and picturing your old bedroom, take a mental journey of awareness to notice your bodily sensations, starting from one of your big toes and proceeding up your leg, across your torso, to the opposite shoulder, and down your arm. What sensations do you feel—pressure from the ground, your shoes, your clothing, or even pain anywhere? Are you still managing to write your name while retrieving remembered images from memory and continuing to pay attention to your current sensations?

Attention and Consciousness

{Attention} is the taking possession of the mind, in clear and vivid form, of one out of what seem several simultaneously possible objects or trains of thoughts. . . . It implies withdrawal from some things in order to deal effectively with others.

—*William James,* Principles of Psychology

You may have found the preceding task awkward but not impossible. What makes this task difficult, yet possible? **Attention** is the means by which we actively process a limited amount of information from the enormous amount of information available through our senses, our stored memories, and our other cognitive processes. It includes both conscious and unconscious processes. For example, although you always have available to you your memory of where you slept when you were 10 years old, you probably do not often process that information actively. Similarly, you usually have available a wealth of sensory information (e.g., in your body and in your peripheral vision at this very moment), but you attend to only a limited amount of the available sensory information at a given time (see Figure 3.1). Additionally, the contents of attention can reside either within or outside of awareness.

There are many advantages to having attentional processes of some sort. Both laypersons and cognitive psychologists agree that there seem to be at least some limits to our mental resources and that there are limits to the amount of information on which we can focus those mental resources at any one time. The psychological phenomenon of attention allows us to use our limited mental resources judiciously. By dimming the lights on many stimuli from outside (sensations) and inside (thoughts and memories) we can highlight the stimuli that interest us. This heightened focus increases the likelihood that we can respond speedily and accurately to interesting stimuli. Heightened attention also paves the way for memory processes, so that we are more likely to remember information to which we paid attention than information we ignored.

Consciousness is more directly concerned with awareness—it includes both the feeling of awareness and the content of awareness, some of which may be under the focus of attention. Therefore, attention and consciousness form two partially overlapping sets. At one time, psychologists believed that attention was the same thing as consciousness. Now, however, psychologists acknowledge that some active attentional processing of sensory information, remembered information, and cognitive information proceeds without our conscious awareness. For example, at this time in your life, writing your own name requires no conscious awareness, and you may write it while consciously engaged in other activities—although not if you are completely unconscious.

The benefits of attention are particularly salient when we refer to conscious attentional processes. In addition to the overall value of attention, conscious attention serves three purposes in playing a causal role for cognition: (a) monitoring our interactions with the environment, maintaining our awareness of how well we are adapting to the situation in which we find ourselves; (b) linking our past (memories) and our present (sensations) to give us a sense of continuity of experience, which may even serve as the basis for

FIGURE 3.1 **ATTENTION**

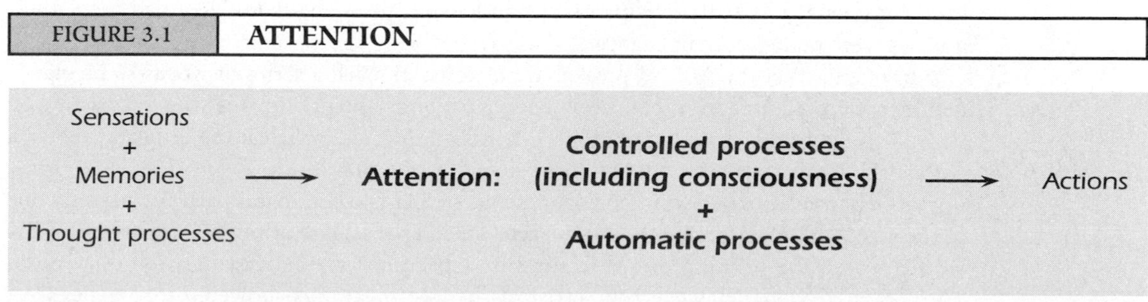

Attention acts as a means of focusing limited mental resources on the information and cognitive processes that are most salient at a given moment.

personal identity; and (c) controlling and planning for our future actions, based on the information from monitoring and from the links between past memories and present sensations.

Preconscious Processing

Some information that currently is outside of our conscious awareness may still be available to consciousness or at least to cognitive processes. Information that is available for cognitive processing but that currently lies outside of conscious awareness exists at the *preconscious* level of awareness. Preconscious information includes stored memories that we are not using at a given time, but that we could summon when needed. For example, when prompted, you can remember what your bedroom looks like, but obviously, you are not always consciously thinking about your bedroom (unless you are extremely tired, perhaps). Sensations, too, may be pulled from preconscious to conscious awareness. For example, before you read this sentence, were you highly aware of the sensations in your right foot? Probably not. However, those sensations were available to you.

How can we study things that currently lie outside conscious awareness? Psychologists have solved this problem by studying a phenomenon known as **priming,** in which processing of certain stimuli is facilitated by prior presentation of the same or similar stimuli. Sometimes, we are aware of the priming stimuli (e.g., you are now primed to read descriptions of studies involving priming). However, priming occurs even when the priming stimulus is presented in a way that does not permit its entry into conscious awareness—it is presented at too low an intensity, in too "noisy" a background (i.e., too many other stimuli divert conscious attention from it), or too briefly to be registered in conscious awareness.

For example, in a set of studies, Anthony Marcel (1983b; see also 1983a) observed processing of stimuli that were presented too briefly to be detected in conscious awareness. In these studies, words were presented to participants very briefly (as measured in *milliseconds*—thousandths of a second), after which each word was replaced by a *visual mask,* which blocks the image of the word from remaining on the *retina* (the rear surface of the eye, comprising the sensory receptors of vision). Marcel timed the presentations to be so brief (20–110 milliseconds) that he was sure that participants could not detect their presence consciously. When participants were asked to guess the word they had seen, their guesses were no better than chance.

In one such study, Marcel presented participants with a series of words to be classified into various categories (e.g., *leg*—body part; *pine*—plant). In this study, the priming stimuli were words having more than one meaning (e.g., *palm* can be either a tree or a part of the hand). In one condition, participants were consciously aware of seeing a priming word that had two meanings. For these participants, the mental pathway for only one of the two meanings seemed to become activated. That is, one of the two meanings of the word showed the priming effect, facilitating (speeding up) the classification of a subsequent related word. However, the other of the two meanings showed a sort of negative priming effect, actually inhibiting (slowing down) the classification of a subsequent unrelated word. For example, if the word *palm* was presented long enough so that the participant was consciously aware of seeing it, the word either facilitated or inhibited the classification of the word *wrist,* depending on whether the participant associated *palm* with *hand* or with *tree.* Apparently, if the participant was consciously aware of seeing the word *palm,* the mental pathway for only one meaning was activated, and the mental pathway for the other meaning was inhibited. In contrast, if the word *palm* was presented so briefly that the person was unaware of seeing the word, *both* meanings of the word appeared to be activated, thereby facilitating subsequent classification. That is, both meanings of the word were primed.

Another example of possible priming effects and preconscious processing was a study described as a test of intuition, using a "dyad of triads" task (Bowers, Regehr, Balthazard, & Parker, 1990). Participants were presented with pairs (dyads) of three-word groups (triads). One of the triads in each dyad was a potentially coherent grouping, and the other triad contained random and unrelated words. For example, the words in Group A, a coherent triad, might have been *playing, credit,* and *report;* and the words in Group B, an incoherent triad, might have been *still, pages,* and *music.* After presentation of the dyad of triads, participants were shown various possible choices for a fourth word related to one of the two triads. The participants were then asked (a) which of the two triads was coherent and related to a fourth word, and (b) which fourth word linked the coherent triad. In the preceding example, the words in Group A can be meaningfully paired with a fourth word, *card (playing card, credit card, report card).* The words in Group B bear no such relationship.

Even if participants could not figure out the unifying fourth word for a given pair of triads, they were asked to indicate which of the two triads was coherent. When participants could not ascertain the unifying word, they were still able to identify the coherent triad at a level well above chance. They seemed to have some preconscious information that led them to select one triad over the other, although they did not consciously know what word unified that triad.

Unfortunately, sometimes pulling preconscious information into conscious awareness is not easy. For example, most of us have experienced the **tip-of-the-tongue phenomenon,** in which we try to remember something that is known to be stored in memory but that cannot quite be retrieved. Psychologists have tried to come up with experiments that measure this phenomenon by finding out how much people can draw from information that seems to be stuck at the preconscious level. In one study (R. Brown & McNeill, 1966), participants were read a large number of dictionary definitions and were then asked to identify the corresponding words having these meanings (a game similar to the television show *Jeopardy).* For example, they might have been given the clue, "an instrument used by navigators to measure the angle between a heavenly body and a horizon."

In the study, participants who could not come up with the word, but who thought they knew it, were then asked various questions about the word, such as to identify the first letter, indicate the number of syllables, or approximate the word's sounds. The participants often answered these questions accurately. They might have been able to say, for example, that the appropriate word for the aforementioned instrument begins with an *s,* has two syllables, and sounds like *sextet.* Eventually, some participants realized that the sought-after word is *sextant.* These results indicate that particular preconscious information, although not fully accessible to conscious thinking, is still available to attentional processes.

Preconscious perception has also been observed in persons who have lesions in some areas of the visual cortex. Typically, the patients are blind in areas of the visual field that correspond to the lesioned areas of the cortex. Some of these patients, however, seem to show *blindsight,* traces of visual perceptual ability in the blind areas. When forced to guess about a stimulus in the "blind" region, they correctly guess locations and orientations of objects at above-chance levels (Weiskrantz, 1994). Similarly, when forced to reach for objects in the blind area, "cortically blind participants . . . will nonetheless preadjust their hands appropriately to size, shape, orientation and 3-D location of that object in the blind field"; yet they fail to show voluntary behavior, such as reaching for a glass of water in the blind region, even when they are thirsty (Marcel, 1986, p. 41). Some visual processing seems to occur even when participants have no conscious awareness of visual sensations.

The preceding examples show that at least some cognitive functions can occur outside of conscious awareness. We appear able to sense, perceive, and even respond to many stimuli that never enter our conscious awareness (Marcel, 1983a). Just what kinds of processes do or do not require conscious awareness?

Controlled Versus Automatic Processes

Many cognitive processes may also be differentiated in terms of whether they do or do not require conscious control (Schneider & Shiffrin, 1977; Shiffrin & Schneider, 1977). Automatic processes involve no conscious control. That is, for the most part, **automatic processes** are performed without conscious awareness (although you may be aware that you are performing them), demand little or no effort or even intention, are performed as parallel processes (i.e., with many operations occurring simultaneously or at least in no particular sequential order), and are relatively fast. In contrast, **controlled processes** are not only accessible to conscious control but also require it; such processes are performed serially (sequentially, one step at a time) and take a relatively long time to execute (at least, as compared with automatic processes).

Michael Posner and Charles Snyder (1975) have suggested three characteristics of automatic processes: By their definition, automatic processes are concealed from consciousness, are unintentional, and consume few attentional resources. An alternative view of attention suggests a continuum of processes between fully automatic processes and fully controlled processes. For one thing, the range of controlled processes is so wide and diverse that it would be difficult to characterize all the controlled processes in the same way (Logan, 1988). Similar difficulties arise with delineating automatic processes. Some automatic processes truly cannot be retrieved into conscious awareness (e.g., preconscious processing or priming), despite any amount of effort to do so. Other automatic processes (e.g., tying your shoes) can be controlled intentionally, although they rarely are handled in this way. For example, you may seldom think about all of the steps involved in executing many automatic behaviors. *Automatic behaviors* require no conscious decisions regarding which muscles to move or which actions to take, such as when dialing a familiar telephone number or driving a car to a familiar place. However, they can be pulled into conscious awareness and controlled relatively easily. (Table 3.1 summarizes the characteristics of controlled versus automatic processes.)

In fact, many tasks that start off as controlled processes eventually become automatic ones. For example, driving a car is initially a controlled process. Once we master driving, however, it becomes automatic under normal driving conditions (on familiar roads, in fair

TABLE 3.1 CONTROLLED VERSUS AUTOMATIC PROCESSES

There is probably a continuum of cognitive processes from fully controlled processes to fully automatic ones; these features characterize the polar extremes of each.

Characteristics	Controlled Processes	Automatic Processes
Amount of intentional effort	Require intentional effort	Require little or no intention or effort (and intentional effort may even be required to *avoid* automatic behaviors)
Degreee of conscious awareness	Require full conscious awareness	Generally occur outside of conscious awareness, although some automatic processes may be available to consciousness
Use of attentional resources	Consume many attentional resources	Consume negligible attentional resources
Type of processing	Performed serially (one step at a time)	Performed by parallel processing (i.e., with many operations occurring simultaneously or at least in no particular sequential order)
Speed of processing	Relatively time-consuming execution, as compared with automatic processes	Relatively fast
Relative novelty of tasks	Novel and unpracticed tasks or tasks with many variable features	Familiar and highly practiced tasks, with largely stable task characteristics
Level of processing	Relatively high levels of cognitive processing (requiring analysis or synthesis)	Relatively low levels of cognitive processing (minimal analysis or synthesis)
Difficulty of tasks	Usually difficult tasks	Usually relatively easy tasks, but even relatively complex tasks may be automatized, given sufficient practice
Process of acquisition	With sufficient practice, many routine and relatively stable procedures may become automatized, such that highly controlled processes may become partly or even wholly automatic; naturally, the amount of practice required for automatization increases dramatically for highly complex tasks	

weather, with little or no traffic). Similarly, when you first learn to speak a foreign language, you need to translate word-for-word from your native tongue; eventually, however, you begin to think in the second language. This thinking enables you to bypass the intermediate-translation stage and allows the process of speaking to become automatic. Your conscious attention can revert to the content, rather than the process, of speaking. A similar shift from conscious control to automatic processing occurs when acquiring the skill of reading.

You may notice that the procedures you learned early in life (e.g., tying your shoes, riding a bicycle, or even reading) are often more highly automatic and less accessible to conscious awareness than are procedures acquired later. In general, more recently acquired routine processes and procedures are less fully automatic and are more accessible to conscious control. The process by which a procedure changes from being highly conscious to being relatively automatic is **automatization** (also termed *proceduralization*). As you may have guessed based on your own experience, automatization occurs as a result of practice, such that highly practiced activities can be automatized and thus become highly automatic (LaBerge, 1975, 1976, 1990; LaBerge & Samuels, 1974).

How does automatization occur? A widely accepted view has been that during the course of practice, implementation of the various steps becomes more efficient. The individual gradually combines individual effortful steps into integrated components, which are then further integrated, until eventually, the entire process is a single highly integrated procedure, rather than an assemblage of individual steps (e.g., J. R. Anderson, 1983; LaBerge & Samuels, 1974). According to this view, people consolidate various discrete steps into a single operation that requires few or no cognitive resources, such as attention or *working memory* (a temporary form of memory, which has limited capacity and holds only the information actively being used for current cognitive processing). This view of automatization seems to be supported by one of the earliest studies of automatization (Bryan & Harter, 1899), which investigated how telegraph operators gradually automatized the task of sending and receiving messages. Initially, new operators automatized the transmission of individual letters. However, once the operators had made the transmission of letters automatic, they automatized the transmission of words, phrases, and then other groups of words.

An alternative explanation, called "instance theory," has been proposed by Gordon Logan (1988), who has suggested that automatization occurs because we gradually accumulate knowledge about specific responses to specific stimuli. For example, when a child first learns to add or subtract, he or she applies a general procedure—counting—for handling each pair of numbers. Following repeated practice, the child gradually stores knowledge about particular pairs of particular numbers. Eventually, the child can retrieve from memory the specific answers to specific combinations of numbers, although she or he can still fall back on the general procedure (counting), as needed. Similarly, when learning to drive, an accumulated wealth of specific experiences forms a knowledge base from which the person can quickly retrieve specific procedures for responding to specific stimuli (e.g., oncoming cars or stoplights). Preliminary findings suggest that Logan's instance theory may better explain specific responses to specific stimuli (e.g., calculating arithmetic combinations), whereas the prevailing view may better explain more general responses involving automatization (Logan, 1988).

The effects of practice on automatization show a *negatively accelerated curve*, in which early practice effects are great (i.e., a graph of improvement in performance would show a steeply rising curve), and later practice effects make less and less difference in the degree of automatization (i.e., on a graph showing improvement, the curve would level off; see Figure 3.2). Clearly, automatic processes generally govern familiar, well-practiced tasks, and controlled processes govern relatively novel tasks. In addition, most automatic processes govern relatively easy tasks, and most difficult tasks require controlled processing, although with sufficient practice, even many extremely complex tasks (e.g., reading) can become automatized. Because highly automatized behaviors require little effort or

FIGURE 3.2 **NEGATIVE-ACCELERATION CURVE**

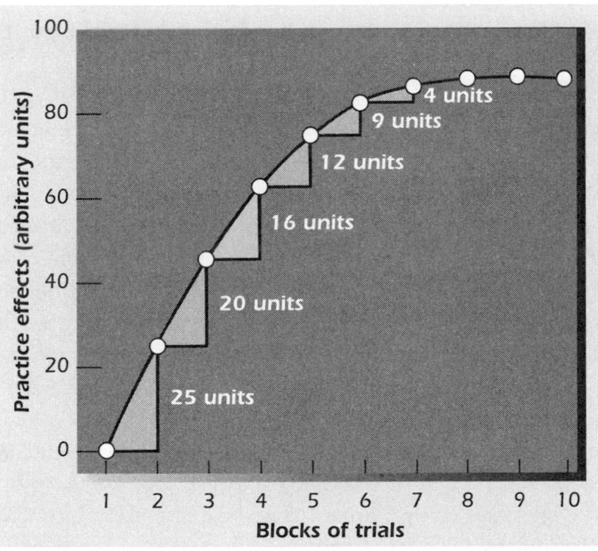

The rate of improvement due to practice effects shows a pattern of negative acceleration. The negative-acceleration curve attributed to practice effects is similar to the curve shown here, indicating that the rate of learning slows down as the amount of learning increases, until eventually learning peaks at a stable level.

conscious control, we can often engage in multiple automatic behaviors, but we can rarely engage in more than one labor-intensive controlled behavior. Although automatic processes do not require conscious control, they are subject to such control. For example, skilled articulation (speaking) and skilled typing can be stopped on signal or in response to detection of an error, almost immediately. However, skilled performance of automatic behaviors is often impaired by conscious control. Try riding a bicycle while consciously monitoring your every movement.

Contemporary cognitive psychologist Donald Norman (1976) has underscored the importance of automatizing various safety practices, particularly for persons engaging in high-risk occupations (e.g., pilots, undersea divers, and firefighters). For example, novice divers often complain about the frequent repetition of various safety procedures (e.g., releasing a cumbersome weight belt) within the confines of a swimming pool. However, the practice is important, as the novices will learn later: Experienced divers recognize the value of being able to rely on automatic processes in the face of potential panic should they confront a life-threatening deep-sea emergency.

In some situations, automatic processes may be life-saving, but in others, they may be life-threatening (Langer, 1997). Ellen Langer (1989) gave an example of what she calls "mindlessness": In 1982, a pilot and copilot went through a routine checklist prior to takeoff, mindlessly noting that the anti-icer was "off"—as it should be under most circumstances, but not under the icy conditions in which they were preparing to fly. The flight ended in a crash that killed 74 passengers. Fortunately for most of us, our absent-minded implementation of automatic processes has far less lethal consequences. When driving, we may end up routinely driving home instead of stopping by the store, as we had intended to do. We may pour a glass of milk and then start to put the carton of milk in the cupboard rather than in the refrigerator.

James Reason (1990) has done an extensive analysis of human error and notes that errors can be classified either as mistakes or as slips. *Mistakes* are errors in choosing an objective or in specifying a means of achieving it; *slips* are errors in carrying out an intended means for reaching an objective. For example, if you were to decide that you did not need to study for an examination, so you purposely left your textbook behind when leaving for a long weekend—only to discover at the time of the exam that you should have studied—that would be a mistake. However, if you fully intended to bring your textbook with you, and you had planned to study extensively over the long weekend, but in your haste to leave, you accidentally left the textbook behind, that would be a slip. Whereas mistakes involve errors in intentional, controlled processes, slips often involve errors in automatic processes (Reason, 1990).

Both Reason (1990) and Norman (1988) have described several kinds of slips (see Table 3.2). In general, slips are most likely to occur (a) when we must deviate from a routine, and automatic processes inappropriately override intentional, controlled processes; or (b) when automatic processes are interrupted—usually as a result of external events or data, but sometimes as a result of internal events, such as highly distracting thoughts. Because automatic processes are so helpful to us under many circumstances—saving us from needlessly focusing attention on routine tasks, such as tying our shoes or dialing a familiar phone number, we are unlikely to forgo them just to avoid occasional slips.

How can we minimize the potential for negative consequences of slips? In everyday situations, we are less likely to slip when we receive appropriate feedback from the environment (e.g., the milk carton may be too tall for the cupboard shelf, or a passenger may say, "I thought you were stopping at the store before going home"). If we can find ways to obtain useful feedback, we may be able to reduce the likelihood that harmful consequences will result from slips. Norman has noted that a particularly helpful kind of feedback involves *forcing functions,* which are physical constraints that make it difficult or impossible to carry out an automatic behavior that may lead to a slip. As an example of a forcing function, some modern cars make it difficult or impossible to drive a car without wearing a seatbelt. You can devise your own forcing functions. You may post a small sign on your steering wheel, reminding yourself to run an errand on the way home, or you may put items in front of the door, blocking your exit so that you cannot leave without them.

Over a lifetime, we automatize countless everyday tasks. However, one of the most helpful pairs of automatic processes first appears within hours after birth: habituation and its complementary opposite, dishabituation.

HABITUATION

In **habituation,** as we become accustomed to a stimulus, we gradually notice it—pay attention to it—less and less. The counterpart to habituation is **dishabituation,** in which a change (sometimes even a very slight change) in a familiar stimulus prompts us

TABLE 3.2 SLIPS ASSOCIATED WITH AUTOMATIC PROCESSES

Occasionally, when we are distracted or interrupted during implementation of an automatic process, slips occur. However, in proportion to the number of times we engage in automatic processes each day, slips are relatively rare events (Reason, 1990).

Type of Error	Description of Error	Example of Error
Capture errors	We intend to deviate from a routine activity we are implementing in familiar surroundings, but at a point where we should depart from the routine, we fail to pay attention and to regain control of the process; hence, the automatic process captures our behavior, and we fail to deviate from the routine.	Psychologist William James (1890/1970, cited in Langer, 1989) gave an example in which he automatically followed his usual routine, undressing from his work clothes, then putting on his pajamas and climbing into bed—only to realize that he had intended to remove his work clothes in order to dress to go out to dinner.
Omissions*	An interruption of a routine activity may cause us to skip a step or two in implementing the remaining portion of the routine.	When going to another room to retrieve something, if a distraction (e.g., a phone call) interrupts you, you may return to the first room without having retrieved the item.
Perseverations*	After an automatic procedure has been completed, one or more steps of the procedure may be repeated.	If, after starting a car, you become distracted, you may turn the ignition switch again.
Description errors	An internal description of the intended behavior leads to performing the correct action on the wrong object.	When putting away groceries, you may end up putting the ice cream in the cupboard and a can of soup in the freezer.
Data-driven errors	Incoming sensory information may end up overriding the intended variables in an automatic action sequence.	While intending to dial a familiar phone number, if you overhear someone call out another series of numbers, you may end up dialing some of those numbers instead of the ones you intended to dial.
Associative-activation errors	Strong associations may trigger the wrong automatic routine.	When expecting someone to arrive at the door, if the phone rings, you may call out, "Come in!"
Loss-of-activation errors	The activation of a routine may be insufficient to carry it through to completion.	All too often, each of us has experienced the feeling of going to another room to do something and getting there only to ask ourselves, "What am I doing here?" Perhaps even worse is the nagging feeling, "I know I should be doing something, but I can't remember what." Until something in the environment triggers our recollection, we may feel extremely frustrated.

*Omissions and perseverations may be considered examples of errors in the sequencing of automatic processes. Related errors include inappropriately sequencing the steps, as in trying to remove socks before taking off shoes.

to start noticing the stimulus again. Both processes occur automatically, without any conscious effort. What governs these processes is the relative stability and familiarity of the stimulus. Any aspects of the stimulus that seem different or novel (unfamiliar) either prompt dishabituation or make habituation less likely to occur in the first place. For example, suppose that a radio were playing instrumental music while you were studying your cognitive psychology textbook. At first, the sound might have distracted you, but after a while, you would have become habituated to the sound and would have scarcely noticed it. If the loudness of the noise were suddenly to change drastically, however, you would immediately dishabituate to it; the once-familiar sound to which you had been habituated would become unfamiliar and would enter your awareness. Habituation is not limited to humans: It is found in organisms as simple as the mollusk, *Aplysia* (Castellucci & Kandel, 1976).

We usually exert no effort whatsoever to become habituated to our sensations of stimuli in the environment. Nonetheless, although we usually do not consciously control habituation, we *can* do so. In this way, habituation is an attentional phenomenon that differs from the physiological phenomenon of **sensory adaptation,** which is not subject to conscious control, and which occurs directly in the sense organ, not in the brain. Whereas we can exert some conscious control over whether we notice something to which we have become habituated, we have no conscious control over sensory adaptation. For example, we cannot consciously force ourselves to smell an odor to which our senses have become adapted. Nor can we consciously force our pupils to adapt—or not adapt—to differing degrees of brightness or darkness. In contrast, we can consciously control habituation; for example, if someone asked us, "Who's the lead guitarist in that song?" we can once again notice background music. Table 3.3 illustrates some of the other distinctions between sensory adaptation and habituation.

Some of the factors that influence habituation are stimulus internal variation and subjective arousal. Some stimuli involve more internal variation than do others. For example, background music contains more internal variation than does the steady drone of an air conditioner. The relative complexity of the stimulus (e.g., an ornate, intricate Oriental rug versus a gray carpet) does not seem to be as important to habituation as does the amount of change within the stimulus over time (e.g., a mobile involves more change than does an ornate but rigid sculpture). Thus, it is relatively difficult to remain continually habituated to the frequently changing noises coming from a television (with voices speaking animatedly and with great inflectional expression).

Psychologists can observe habituation occurring at the physiological level by measuring our degree of arousal. **Arousal** is a degree of physiological excitation, responsivity, and readiness for action, relative to a baseline; arousal is often measured in terms of heart rate, blood pressure, electroencephalograph (EEG) patterns, and other physiological signs. For example, when an unchanging visual stimulus remains in our visual field for a long time, our neural activity (as shown on an EEG) in response to that stimulus decreases (see chapter 2). Both neural activity and other physiological responses (e.g., heart rate) can be measured to detect heightened arousal in response to perceived novelty or diminished arousal in response to perceived familiarity. In fact, psychologists in many fields use physiological indications of habituation to study a wide array of psychological phenomena in persons who cannot provide verbal reports of their responses (e.g., infants or comatose patients). Physiological indicators of habituation tell the researcher whether the person notices

TABLE 3.3 DIFFERENCES BETWEEN SENSORY ADAPTATION AND HABITUATION

Responses involving physiological adaptation take place mostly in our sense organs, whereas responses involving cognitive habituation take place mostly in our brains (and relate to learning).

ADAPTATION	HABITUATION
Not accessible to conscious control *Example:* You cannot decide how quickly to adapt to a particular smell or a particular change in light intensity.	Accessible to conscious control *Example:* You can decide to become aware of background music to which you had become habituated.
Tied closely to stimulus intensity *Example:* The more the intensity of a bright light increases, the more strongly your senses will adapt to the light.	Not tied very closely to stimulus intensity *Example:* Your level of habituation will not differ much in your response to the sound of a loud fan and to that of a quiet air conditioner.
Unrelated to the number, length, and recency of prior exposures *Example:* The sense receptors in your skin will respond to changes in temperature in basically the same way no matter how many times you have been exposed to such changes, and no matter how recently you have experienced such changes.	Tied very closely to the number, length, and recency of prior exposures *Example:* You will become more quickly habituated to the sound of a chiming clock when you have been exposed to the sound more often, for longer times, and on more recent occasions.

changes in the stimulus (e.g., changes in the color, pattern, size, or form of a stimulus) at all, as well as what changes the person notices in the stimulus.

Among other phenomena, psychologists have used habituation to study visual *discrimination* (detection of differences among stimuli) in infants. First, they habituate the infant to a particular visual pattern by presenting it until the infant no longer pays attention to it; then they introduce a visual pattern that only slightly differs from the one to which the infant has become habituated. If the infant is able to discriminate the difference, the infant will not habituate to (i.e., will notice) the new pattern; if the infant cannot discriminate the difference, however, the infant will appear to be habituated to the new pattern as well.

Habituation definitely gives much more to our attentional system than it receives. That is, habituation itself requires no conscious effort and few attentional resources. Despite its negligible use of attentional resources, it offers a great deal of support to attentional processes by allowing us easily to turn our attention away from familiar and relatively stable stimuli and toward novel and changing stimuli. We might conjecture about the evolutionary value of habituation. Without habituation, our attentional system would be much more greatly taxed. How easily would we function in our highly stimulating environments if we could not habituate to familiar stimuli? Imagine trying to listen to a lecture if you could not habituate to the sounds of your own breathing, the rustling of papers and books, or the faint buzzing of fluorescent lights.

PRACTICAL APPLICATIONS OF COGNITIVE PSYCHOLOGY

Habituation is not without faults. Becoming bored during a lecture or while reading a textbook is a sign of habituation. Your attention may start to wander to the background noises, or you may find that you have read a paragraph or two with no recollection of the content. Fortunately, you can dishabituate yourself with very little effort. Here are a few tips on how to overcome the negative effects of boredom.

1. Take a break or alternate between different tasks if possible. If you do not remember the last few paragraphs of the text, it is time to stop for a few minutes. Go back and mark the last place in the text you do remember, and put the book down. If you feel like a break is a waste of valuable time, do some other work for a while.
2. Take notes while reading or listening. Most people already do so, but note-taking focuses attention on the material more than does simply listening or reading. If necessary, try switching from script to printed handwriting to make the task more interesting.
3. Adjust your attentional focus to increase stimulus variability. Is the instructor's voice droning on endlessly, so that you cannot take a break during lecture? Try noticing other aspects of your instructor, like hand gestures or body movements, while still paying attention to the content. Create a break in the flow by asking a question—even just raising your hand can make a change in a lecturer's speaking pattern. Change your arousal level. If all else fails, you may have to force yourself to be interested in the material. Think about how you can use the material in your everyday life. Also, sometimes just taking a few deep breaths or closing your eyes for a few seconds can change your internal arousal levels.

ATTENTION

SIGNAL DETECTION

Habituation supports our attentional system, but this system performs many functions other than merely tuning out familiar stimuli and tuning in novel ones. The three main functions of conscious attention are (a) **signal detection,** including vigilance and search, in which we must detect the appearance of a particular stimulus; (b) **selective attention,** in which we choose to attend to some stimuli and to ignore others; and (c) **divided attention,** in which we prudently allocate our available attentional resources to coordinate our performance of more than one task at a time. These three functions are summarized in Table 3.4. Each of these functions has been studied by cognitive psychologists, to gain a broad understanding of attention from many vantage points. In this section, we discuss signal detection.

What factors contribute to your ability to detect important events in the world? Cognitive psychologists are interested in understanding how people search the environment to detect important stimuli. Understanding this function of attention has immediate practical importance. A lifeguard at a busy beach must be ever-vigilant. Similarly, if you have ever flown in an airplane, you realize the importance of having your air-traffic

TABLE 3.4 **FOUR MAIN FUNCTIONS OF ATTENTION**

Cognitive psychologists have been particularly interested in the study of vigilance and signal detection, search, selective attention, and divided attention.

Function	Description	Example
Divided Attention	We often manage to engage in more than one task at a time, and we shift our attentional resources to allocate them prudently, as needed.	Experienced drivers can easily talk while driving under most circumstances, but if another vehicle seems to be swerving toward their car, they quickly switch all of their attention away from talking and toward driving.
Vigilance and signal detection	On many occasions, we vigilantly try to detect whether we did or did not sense a signal, a particular target stimulus of interest. Through vigilant attention to detecting signals, we are primed to take speedy action when we do detect signal stimuli.	In a research submarine, we may watch for unusual sonar blips; in a dark street, we may try to detect unwelcome sights or sounds; or following an earthquake, we may be wary of the smell of leaking gas or of smoke.
Search	We often engage in an active search for particular stimuli.	If we detect smoke (as a result of our vigilance), we may engage in an active search for the source of the smoke; in addition, some of us are constantly in search of missing keys, sunglasses, and other objects; my teenage son often "searches" for missing items in the refrigerator (often, without much success—until someone else points them out to him).
Selective attention	We are constantly making choices regarding the stimuli to which we will pay attention and the stimuli that we will ignore. By ignoring or at least deemphasizing some stimuli, we thereby highlight particularly salient stimuli. The concentrated focus of attention on particular informational stimuli enhances our ability to manipulate those stimuli for other cognitive processes, such as verbal comprehension or problem solving.	We may pay attention to reading a textbook or to listening to a lecture while ignoring such stimuli as a nearby radio or television or latecomers to the lecture.

controller be highly vigilant. Many other occupations require vigilance, such as those involving any number of communications and warning systems, as well as quality control in almost any setting. Even the work of police detectives, physicians, and research psychologists requires vigilance. Along with being vigilant for the arrival of important stimuli, we must also search out from among a diverse array of items those that are more important. In each of these settings, people must remain alert to detect the appearance of a stimulus, despite the presence of distractors and prolonged periods during which the stimulus is absent.

The Nature of Signal Detection

According to **signal-detection theory (SDT),** there are four possible outcomes of an attempt to detect a **signal,** a target stimulus (see Table 3.5): *hits* (also called "correct positives"), in which we correctly identify the presence of a target; *false alarms* (also called "false positives"), in which we incorrectly identify the presence of a target that is actually absent; *misses* (also called "false negatives"), in which we incorrectly fail to observe the presence of a target; and *correct rejections* (also called "correct negatives"), in which we correctly identify the absence of a target. Usually, the presence of a target is difficult to detect, so we make detection judgments based on inconclusive information, with some criterion for target detections. The number of hits is influenced by where you place your *criterion* for considering something a hit—how willing you are to make false alarms. For example, sometimes the consequences of making a miss are so grave that we lower the criterion for considering something as a hit. In this way, we increase the number of false alarms we make in order to boost hit detection. This trade-off often occurs with medical diagnoses, particularly with hypersensitive screening tests where positives lead to further tests. Thus, overall sensitivity to targets must reflect the placement of a flexible criterion and is measured in terms of hits minus false alarms. Signal-detection theory is often used to measure sensitivity to a target's presence both under conditions of vigilance and when searching for targets. It is also used in memory research to control for effects of guessing.

TABLE 3.5 SIGNAL DETECTION MATRIX USED IN SIGNAL-DETECTION THEORY (SDT)

Signal-detection theory was one of the first theories to suggest an interaction between the physical sensation of a stimulus and cognitive processes such as decision making.

Signal	Detect a Signal	Do Not Detect a Signal
Present	Hit	Miss
Absent	False alarm	Correct rejection

VIGILANCE

Vigilance refers to a person's ability to attend to a field of stimulation over a prolonged period of time, in which the person seeks to detect the appearance of a particular target stimulus of interest. When being vigilant, the individual watchfully waits to detect a signal stimulus that may appear at an unknown time. Typically, vigilance is needed in settings where a given stimulus occurs only rarely but requires immediate attention as soon as it does occur. Military officers watching for a nuclear attack are engaged in a high-stakes vigilance task.

Some of the most important work on vigilance was initiated by Norman Mackworth (1948), who had participants watch a visual display that looked like the face of a clock. A clock hand moved in continuous steps, and every once in a while, the clock hand would take a double step. The participants' task was to press a button as soon as possible after observing a double step. Participants' performance began to deteriorate substantially after just half an hour of observation. Indeed, after a half hour, participants were missing close to one fourth of the double steps. It appears that decreases in vigilance are not primarily due to participants' decreased sensitivity, but rather to their increased doubtfulness about their perceived observations (Broadbent & Gregory, 1965). To relate these findings to SDT, over time, it appears that participants become less willing to risk reporting false alarms. They err instead by failing to report the presence of the signal stimulus when they are not sure they detect it, thereby showing higher rates of misses. Training can help to increase vigilance (Fisk & Schneider, 1981), but in tasks requiring sustained vigilance,

For some jobs, vigilance is a matter of life and death.

fatigue hinders performance, so there may be no substitute for frequent rest periods to enhance signal detection.

Attentional processes governing signal detection also appear to be highly localized and strongly influenced by expectation (Posner, Snyder, & Davidson, 1980). Neurological studies show that signal detection of a visual stimulus is greatest at the point where a signal is expected to appear, and accuracy of signal detection falls off sharply as the appearance of the stimulus occurs farther from the locus of attention (LaBerge & Brown, 1989; LaBerge, Carter, & Brown, 1992; Mangun & Hillyard, 1990, 1991). Thus, a busy lifeguard or air-traffic controller may quickly respond to a signal within a narrow radius of where a signal is expected to appear, but signals appearing outside the concentrated range of vigilant attention may not be detected as quickly or as accurately.

In vigilance tasks, expectations regarding location strongly affect response efficiency (i.e., the speed and accuracy of detecting a target stimulus). However, expectations regarding the form of the stimulus (e.g., what shape or letter may appear in a visual field) do not (Posner, Snyder, & Davidson, 1980). In addition, if a participant is cued to look for a target stimulus in two distant locations, this cueing does not enhance vigilance performance for both locations. Various studies suggest that visual attention may be likened to a spotlight, in that stimuli within the region of the attentional spotlight are readily detected, but stimuli outside the spotlight are not (Norman, 1968; J. Palmer, 1990; Posner et al., 1980). Further, like a spotlight, the beam of focused attention can be narrowly concentrated on a small area or widened to embrace a larger, more diffuse area (J. Palmer, 1990). On the other hand, the abrupt onset of a stimulus (i.e., the sudden appearance of a stimulus) captures our attention. This effect occurs even when factors such as degree of illuminance (brightness) are controlled (Yantis, 1993). Thus, we seem to be predisposed to notice the sudden appearance of stimuli in our visual field. We might well speculate about the adaptive advantage this feature of attention may have offered to our ancestral hunter–gatherer forebears who needed to avoid various predators and to catch various prey.

SEARCH

Whereas vigilance involves passively waiting for a signal stimulus to appear, search involves actively seeking out a target. Specifically, **search** refers to a scan of the environment for particular features—actively looking for something when you are not sure where it will appear. Trying to locate a particular brand of cereal in a crowded aisle at the grocery store—or a particular key term in a crowded textbook—is an example of search. As with vigilance, when we are searching for something, we may respond by making false alarms. In the case of search, false alarms usually arise when we encounter **distractors** (nontarget stimuli that divert our attention away from the target stimulus) while searching for the target stimulus. For instance, when searching in the grocery store, we often see several distracting items that look something like the item we hope to find. Package designers take advantage of the effectiveness of distractors when creating packaging for products—if it looks like a box of Cheerios, you may pick it up without realizing that it's really Tastee-Oh's.

As you may have expected, the number of targets and distractors affects the difficulty of the task. For example, try to find the *T* in Figure 3.3 (a); then try to find the *T* in Figure 3.3 (b). The *display size* refers to the number of items in a given visual array (not to the size of the items or even the size of the field on which the array is displayed). The

FIGURE 3.3 **VISUAL SEARCH**

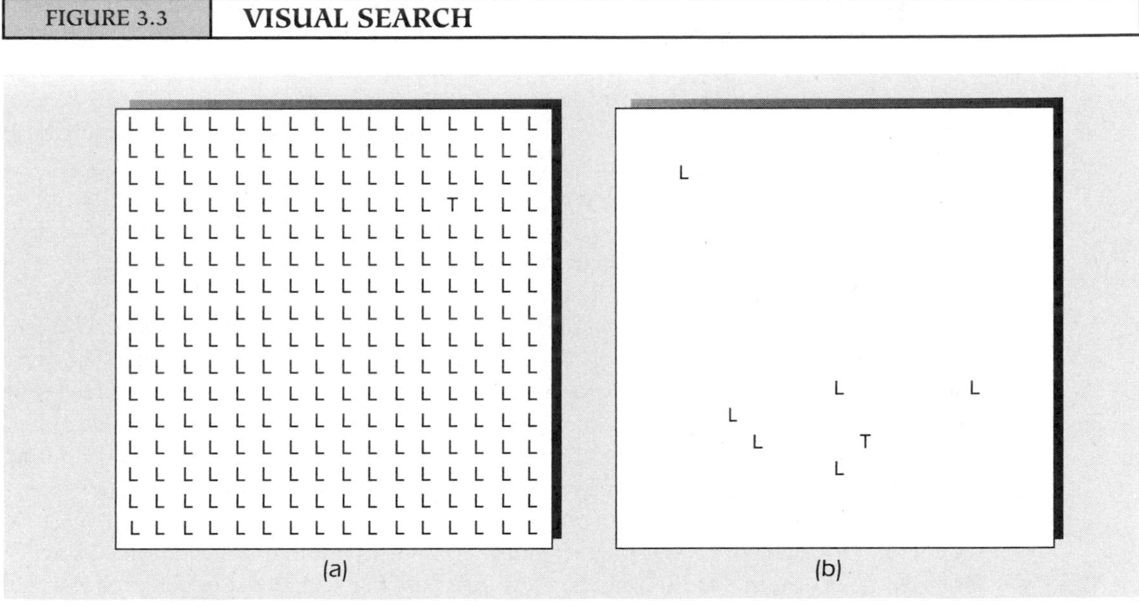

Compare the relative difficulty in finding the T *in (a) and (b). The display size affects your ease of performing the task.*

display-size effect is the degree to which the number of items in a display hinders (slows down) the search process. When studying visual-search phenomena, investigators often manipulate the display size and observe how various contributing factors increase or decrease the display-size effect.

Distractors cause more trouble under some conditions than under others. When we can look for some distinctive features (e.g., color, size, proximity to like items, distance from unlike items, or orientation [vertical, horizontal, oblique]), we are able to conduct a **feature search,** in which we simply scan the environment for that feature or those features (Treisman, 1986, 1992, 1993). Distractors play little role in slowing our search in that case. For example, try to find the *O* in Figure 3.3 (c). Because the *O* has some distinctive features, as compared with the *L* distractors in the display, the *O* seems to pop out of the display. *Featural singletons,* which are items with distinctive features, seem to pop out of the display (Yantis, 1993). When featural singletons are targets, they seem to grab our attention, making search not just easy, but even virtually impossible to avoid. Unfortunately, *any* featural singletons grab our attention—including featural singletons that are distractors. When we are searching for a featural-singleton target stimulus, a featural-singleton distractor stimulus seems to distract us from finding the target (Theeuwes, 1992). For example, find the *T* in Figure 3.3 (d). Even though the *T* is a featural singleton, the presence of the black (filled) circle probably slows you down in your search.

A problem arises, however, when the target stimulus (e.g., a particular boxed or canned item in a grocery aisle) has no unique or even distinctive features. In these situations, the only way we can find it is to conduct a conjunction search (Treisman, 1991). In a **conjunction search,** we look for a particular combination (*conjunction*—joining together) of features. For example, the only difference between a *T* and an *L* is the particular integration (conjunction) of the line segments, not any single distinctive feature of either letter. Both letters comprise a horizontal line and a vertical line, so a search looking for either of these features would provide no distinguishing information. In Figure 3.3 (a), you had to perform a conjunction search to find the *T,* so it probably took you longer to find it than to find the *0* in Figure 3.3 (c).

According to Anne Treisman, a **feature-integration theory** explains the relative ease of conducting feature searches and the relative difficulty of conducting conjunction searches. In Treisman's (1986) model of how our minds conduct visual searches, for each possible feature of a stimulus, each of us has a mental map for representing the given feature across the visual field. For example, there is a map for every color, size, shape, or orientation (e.g., ▶, ◀, ▲, ▼, or p, q, b, d) of each stimulus in our visual field. For every stimulus, the features are represented in the feature maps immediately (with no added time required for additional cognitive processing), simultaneously (i.e., all features at once), and preattentively (i.e., without the need for using focused attentional resources). Thus, during feature searches, we monitor the relevant feature map for the presence of any activation anywhere in the visual field. This process can be done in parallel (all at once) and therefore shows no display-size effects. However, during conjunction searches, an additional stage of processing is needed. During this stage, we must use our attentional resources as a sort of mental "glue" to conjoin two or more features into an object representation at a particular location. This attentional process can only conjoin the features one object at a time. Because this stage must be carried out sequentially, conjoining each object one by one, effects of display size (i.e., a larger number of objects with features to be conjoined) appear.

FIGURE 3.3 **VISUAL SEARCH**

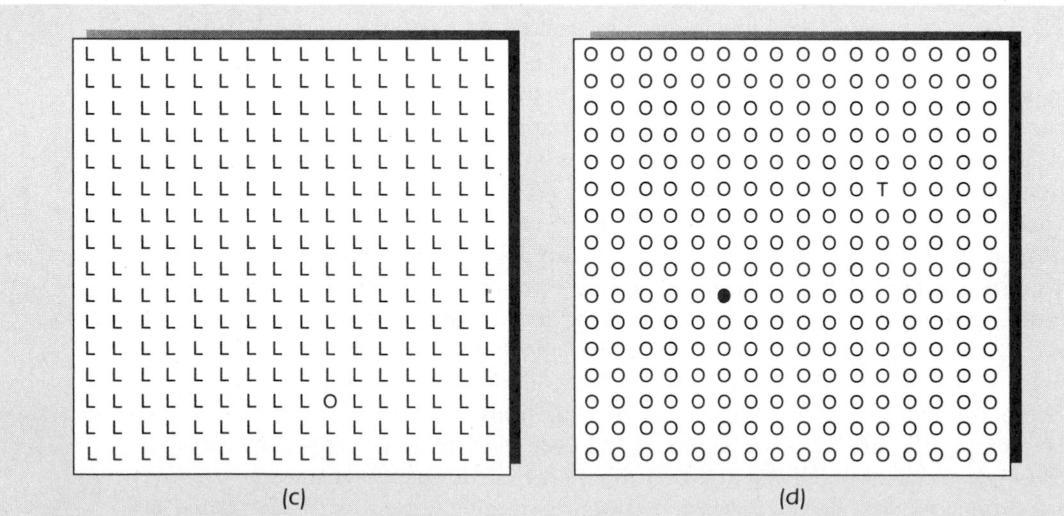

In (c), find the O *and in (d), find the* T.

Sometimes people search for information quite effectively, even though their attention is divided. How can they do this? Treisman and Sato (1990) have suggested they do so through a *feature inhibition mechanism,* by which irrelevant features that might distract an individual from being able to search for a target are inhibited or suppressed. There is some neuropsychological support for Treisman's model. For example, Nobel laureates David Hubel and Torsten Wiesel (1979) have identified specific neural feature detectors, which are cortical neurons that respond differentially to visual stimuli of particular orientations (vertical, oblique, or horizontal). More recently, Mortimer Mishkin and his colleagues (e.g., Bachevalier & Mishkin, 1986; Mishkin & Appenzeller, 1987; Mishkin, Ungerleider, & Macko, 1983) have identified additional cortical processes involved in the various distinct steps of feature integration required for such tasks as object recognition and visual discrimination. They observed that during visual search, differing neural activity appears to be involved in the relatively low-level identification of features, as compared with the neural activity during relatively high-level featural integration and synthesis.

Not everyone agrees with Treisman's model, however. For example, John Duncan and Glyn Humphreys (1989, 1992) have proposed an alternative explanation for many of Treisman's findings. According to their **similarity theory,** Treisman's data can be reinterpreted as being simply due to the fact that as the similarity between target and distractor stimuli increases, so does the difficulty in detecting the target stimuli. Thus, targets that are highly similar to distractors are hard to detect; targets that are highly disparate from distractors are easy to detect. For example, try to find the black (filled) circle in Figure 3.3 (e). Because the target is highly similar to the distractors (black squares or white circles), it is very difficult to find.

Anne Treisman *is a professor of psychology at Princeton University. She is well known for her work in a variety of areas of attention and perception, especially her theory that incoming signals are attenuated rather than filtered when they make their way through the cognitive-processing system.*

FIGURE 3.3 **VISUAL SEARCH**

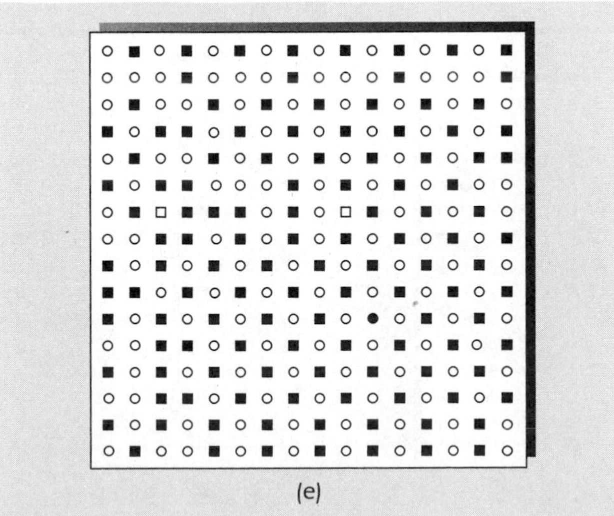

In (e), find the black circle.

According to Duncan and Humphreys (1989), another factor that facilitates the search for target stimuli is similarity (uniformity) among the distractors. That is, searching for target stimuli against a background of relatively uniform (highly similar) distractors is fairly easy, but searching for target stimuli against a background of highly diverse distractors is quite difficult. According to Duncan and Humphreys, the difficulty of search tasks depends on the degree of similarity between the targets and the distractors, as well as on the degree of disparity among the distractors, but not on the number of features to be integrated. For instance, one reason that it is easier to read long strings of text written in lowercase letters than text written in capital letters is that capital letters tend to be more similar to one another in appearance, whereas lowercase letters have more distinguishing features. On the other hand, as in the initial letter of a sentence or of a word in a title, capital letters are quite distinctive from lowercase letters. To get an idea of how highly dissimilar distractors impede visual search, try to find the capital letter *R* in Figure 3.3, (f) and (g).

In addition, some findings do not fit well with Treisman's theory. For example, on the one hand, Ken Nakayama (e.g., He & Nakayama, 1992) agrees that visual search involves a much higher level of visual representation than does simple feature detection. Nakayama further agrees that some features (e.g., color and orientation) require attentional processes for feature integration. However, Nakayama (1990) has found that some features (e.g., size and color) may be easily conjoined even without attentional processes, and search for these integrated features appears to occur about as rapidly as does search for some discrete features. For example, it would be about as easy to search for objects with conjoined features of size and color (e.g., large red circles [target stimuli], vs. small red circles, large blue circles, and small blue circles [distractors]) as it would be to search for objects of a distinctive

FIGURE 3.3 **VISUAL SEARCH**

```
Q W E + T Y U I O P [ ] A S D +
F G H J K L ; ' Z X V B N M C <
> / : \ { } ! @ # $ % ^ & * ( )
D Q W + E + T > U I O A S P [ ]
C F G < H J K / ; ' Z N M X V B
: \ [ ] ! @ # $ % ^ & * ( ) Q W
O P [ ] A S D + Q W E + T Y U I
Z X V B N M C < F G H J K L ; '
# $ % ^ & * ( ) > / : \ { } ! @
U I O A S P [ ] D Q W + E + T >
; ' Z N M X V B C F G < H J K /
% ^ & * ( ) Q W : \ { } ! @ # $
D Q W R E G + > O P [ ] A S D +
F G H J K L ; ' Z X V B N M C <
> / : \ { } ! @ # $ % ^ & * ( )
A S D + Q W J K U I O A S P [ ]
```

(f)

```
w r k / r t g < o a i d ] s p [
e r h j i o z x d r u p [ ] a s
f g q w k l ; ' t y v b n m c <
> / : \ { } ! @ # $ % ^ & * ( )
w e y u j z x h v n ' m c b l ;
c f e h j < u q ; ' z n m x v b
: \ { } ! @ # $ % ^ & * ( ) q w
o p [ ] a s d r q < f R t k g i
$ % * ( p [ / : q w ^ & } ! @ )
z x w r ] a d r j k { b n / $ #
u i o a s # { ] d \ { r e r t >
; ' z n m x v b c f g < h } ! /
% ^ & * @ ) q w : \ k l m c < f
d q s   e g r > o p [ j g ; ' v
> ] : \ s } ! @ # $ h ^ & * % )
a ( d r q w j k u i o a s p [ (
```

(g)

In (f) and (g), find the R.

color alone (e.g., red circles [target stimuli] vs. blue circles [distractors]). Thus, the difficulty of visual search depends not only on whether discrete features must be integrated, but also on which features must be integrated in a given search.

In response to these and other findings, Kyle Cave and Jeremy Wolfe (1990) have proposed an alternative to Treisman's model, which they term *guided search.* According to these researchers, the guided-search model suggests that all searches, whether feature searches or conjunction searches, involve two consecutive stages: (a) In a parallel stage, the individual simultaneously activates a mental representation of all the potential targets, based on their possession of each of the features of the target; and (b) in a serial stage, the individual sequentially evaluates each of the activated elements, according to the degree of activation, and then chooses the true targets from the activated elements. According to their model, the activation process of the parallel initial stage helps to guide the evaluation and selection process of the serial second stage of the search.

To see how guided search might work, try to find the white circles in Figure 3.3 (h). In this case, the targets are all white circles, and the distractors are all black squares (making it a feature search), so the parallel stage will activate all the circles and none of the squares. Therefore, the serial stage quickly will be able to select all the targets. On the other hand, looking at Figure 3.3 (i), try to find the black circle. The distractors include white squares, white circles, and black squares. Hence, the parallel stage will activate a mental map for the target black circle (top-priority activation, due to the conjunction of features) and for the distractor black squares and white circles. During the serial stage, you will first evaluate the black circle (which was highly activated) but will then still evaluate the black squares and the white circles (which were less highly activated) before dismissing them as distractors.

FIGURE 3.3 **VISUAL SEARCH**

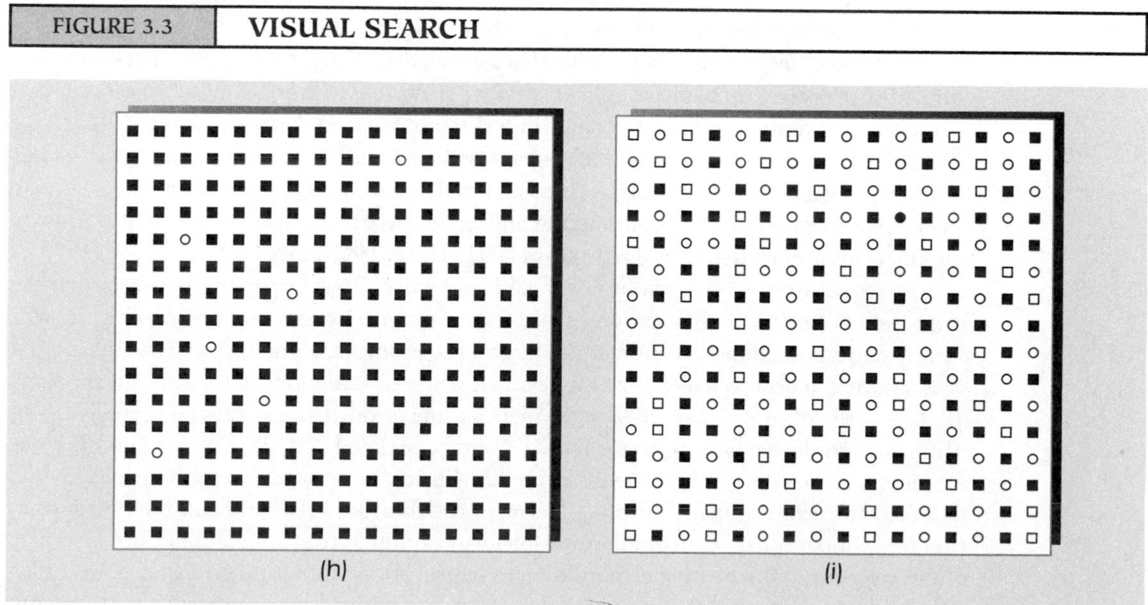

In (h), find the white (hollow) circles, and in (i), find the black circle.

Cave and Wolfe's guided-search model predicts that some conjunction searches (involving more items with features similar to those of the target) are easier than others (involving fewer items with features similar to those of the target). These researchers found support for their model by creating computer simulations of their model and then comparing the performance of the simulations with the actual performance of participants carrying out searches. Under most circumstances, the simulations of their model produced results that were very similar to those of the actual participants.

Peter McLeod, Jon Driver, and their colleagues (McLeod, Driver, Dienes, & Crisp, 1991) found a feature that shows paradoxical effects when it is combined with other features: movement. That is, sometimes movement enhances the ease and speed of conducting a visual search, and at other times, movement inhibits visual search. When movement is conjoined with a distinctive feature (e.g., the shape) of a target, search occurs more easily and speedily than in the search for the distinctive feature alone. For example, movement particularly facilitates visual search when the conjoining feature is a distinctive shape (e.g., X vs. O; McLeod, Driver, & Crisp, 1988; McLeod et al.,1991). For more subtle features (e.g., a very slight difference in orientation), visual search is slowed when movement is a conjoining feature.

McLeod (McLeod et al., 1991, p. 55) has hypothesized that we possess a mechanism he terms a *movement filter,* which "can direct attention to stimuli with a common movement characteristic," independently of other visual features. As a result of lesion studies, McLeod and his colleagues (McLeod, Heywood, Driver, & Zihl, 1989) have even identified a possible cerebral location for the movement filter: a region of the medial temporal cortex. Researchers Margaret Livingstone and David Hubel (1988) have offered support for the existence of a movement filter, in that they have identified particular neural pathways for detecting depth and movement, as well as discrete pathways for detecting form and color.

Synchronous movement also enhances the likelihood of illusory conjunctions. In *illusory conjunctions,* we incorrectly perceive that a particular distractor stimulus possesses conjoined features that are being sought in a target stimulus. Illusory conjunctions occur as a result of mistakenly conjoining in our minds discrete features that we observe in distractor stimuli. For example, if we are looking for a target that is a red triangle, and in our peripheral vision we get a quick glance at a red square and a yellow triangle, we may incorrectly form an illusory conjunction and believe that we saw a red triangle. Illusory conjunctions are predicted by Treisman's (1991, 1992, 1993) model.

When illusory conjunctions occur and movement is a feature, distractors may be identified as targets if they possess some features of the target and are moving in synchrony and in the same direction as the target. For example, if the target stimulus is a red square, but the observer sees a red circle and a white square moving together in the same direction, the observer may incorrectly identify one or both as red squares, perceiving an illusory conjunction of features (Baylis, Driver, & McLeod, 1992). Illusory conjunctions are much more likely when the observer has limited attentional resources (e.g., while focusing attention on other stimuli; Treisman & Schmidt, 1982) or has limited information (e.g., incomplete, distorted, or out-of-focus stimuli). Illusory conjunctions also play a role in form and pattern perception (see chapter 4). Such conjunctions also are influenced by other features of the surrounding context and by prior knowledge and existing schemas (Treisman, 1990). For example, we are much more likely to form an illusory conjunction of features that leads us to perceive a yellow banana and a purple plum rather

FIGURE 3.3 VISUAL SEARCH

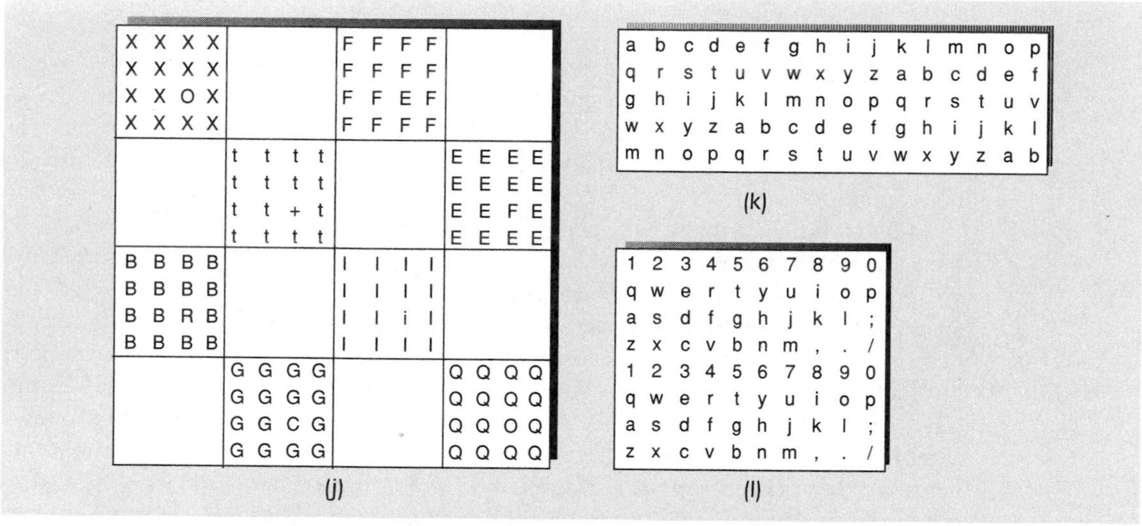

<table>
<tr><td>X X X X
X X X X
X X O X
X X X X</td><td></td><td>F F F F
F F F F
F F E F
F F F F</td><td></td></tr>
<tr><td></td><td>t t t t
t t t t
t t + t
t t t t</td><td></td><td>E E E E
E E E E
E E F E
E E E E</td></tr>
<tr><td>B B B B
B B B B
B B R B
B B B B</td><td></td><td>I I I I
I I I I
I I i I
I I I I</td><td></td></tr>
<tr><td></td><td>G G G G
G G G G
G G C G
G G G G</td><td></td><td>Q Q Q Q
Q Q Q Q
Q Q O Q
Q Q Q Q</td></tr>
</table>

(j)

a	b	c	d	e	f	g	h	i	j	k	l	m	n	o	p
q	r	s	t	u	v	w	x	y	z	a	b	c	d	e	f
g	h	i	j	k	l	m	n	o	p	q	r	s	t	u	v
w	x	y	z	a	b	c	d	e	f	g	h	i	j	k	l
m	n	o	p	q	r	s	t	u	v	w	x	y	z	a	b

(k)

1	2	3	4	5	6	7	8	9	0
q	w	e	r	t	y	u	i	o	p
a	s	d	f	g	h	j	k	l	;
z	x	c	v	b	n	m	,	.	/
1	2	3	4	5	6	7	8	9	0
q	w	e	r	t	y	u	i	o	p
a	s	d	f	g	h	j	k	l	;
z	x	c	v	b	n	m	,	.	/

(l)

In (j), find the deviant stimuli in each subarray. In (k) and (l), find all instances of the letters p *and* a.

than a purple banana and a yellow plum, unless perhaps the odd fruits are depicted on a canvas along with blue apples and pink limes.

Some final considerations in visual search include the observation that when we know in advance the general area in which to expect a stimulus to be located, we can find the stimulus much more readily (Posner et al., 1980). For example, in Figure 3.3 (j), once we detect the spatial pattern regarding where to expect the target stimulus, our search becomes easier. Prior knowledge also influences our ability to use various strategies for conjunctive searches. For example, for most people over age 7 years, it will be relatively easy to find the instances of the letters *a* and *p* in Figure 3.3 (k); similarly, anyone who is experienced at touch typing can readily find the instances of those letters in Figure 3.3 (l). In both cases, prior knowledge may facilitate visual search.

Selective and Divided Attention

Basic Paradigms for Studying Selective Attention

Suppose you are at a dinner party. It is just your luck to be seated next to someone who sells 110 brands of vacuum cleaners and describes to you in excruciating detail the relative merits of each brand. As you are talking to this blatherer, who happens to be on your right, you become aware of the conversation of the two diners sitting on your left. Their exchange is much more interesting, especially because it contains juicy information you had not known about one of your acquaintances. You find yourself trying to keep up the semblance of a conversation with the blabbermouth on your right while tuning in to the dialogue on your left. The preceding vignette describes a naturalistic experiment in selective attention, which inspired the research of Colin Cherry (1953). Cherry referred to this phenomenon as the **cocktail party problem,** which is the process of tracking one conversation in the face of the distraction of other conversations, based on his observation that cocktail parties are often settings in which selective attention is salient, as in the preceding example.

Cherry did not actually hang out at numerous cocktail parties to study conversations, but rather studied selective attention in a more carefully controlled experimental setting. He devised a task known as *shadowing,* in which you listen to two different messages and are required to repeat back only one of the messages as soon as possible after you hear it. In other words, you are to follow one message (think of a detective "shadowing" a suspect) but ignore the other. For some participants, he used a **binaural presentation** (from Latin, *bin-,* "both," and *-aural,* "related to the ears"), in which he presented the same two messages (or sometimes just one message) to both ears simultaneously. For other participants, he used a **dichotic presentation** (from Greek, *dich-,* "in two parts" and *-otic,* "related to the ears"), meaning that he presented a different message to each ear. (Figure 3.4 illustrates how these listening tasks might be presented.)

Cherry's participants found it virtually impossible to track only one message during simultaneous binaural presentation of two distinct messages. His participants much more effectively shadowed distinct messages in dichotic-listening tasks, and in such tasks they shadowed messages fairly accurately for the most part. During dichotic listening, participants were also able to notice physical, sensory changes in the unattended message, such as

FIGURE 3.4 **DICHOTIC VERSUS BINAURAL LISTENING**

Colin Cherry discovered that selective attention was much easier during dichotic presentation than during binaural presentation of differing messages.

when the message was changed to a tone or the voice changed from a male to a female speaker. However, they did not notice semantic changes in the unattended message, failing to notice even when the unattended message shifted to English or German or was played backward.

If you think of being at a cocktail party or in a noisy restaurant, three factors help you to selectively attend only to the message of the target speaker (to whom you wish to listen): (a) distinctive sensory characteristics of the target's speech (e.g., high vs. low pitch, pacing, rhythmicity), (b) sound intensity (loudness), and (c) location of the sound source. By attending to the physical properties of the target speaker's voice, you can avoid being distracted by the semantic content of messages from nontarget speakers in the area. Clearly, the sound intensity of the target also helps. In addition, you probably can intuitively use a strategy for locating sounds, which changes a binaural task into a dichotic one: You turn one ear toward and the other ear away from the target speaker. (Note that this method offers no greater total sound intensity because with one ear closer to the speaker, the other is farther away. The key advantage is that the difference in volume allows you to locate the source of the target sound.)

Filter and Bottleneck Theories of Selective Attention

Broadbent's Model

In one of the earliest theories of attention, Donald Broadbent (1958) proposed that we filter information right after it is registered at the sensory level (see Figure 3.5). In Broadbent's view, multiple channels of sensory input reach an attentional filter, which permits only one channel of sensory information to proceed through the filter to reach the processes of *perception,* through which we assign meaning to our sensations. In addition to the target stimuli, stimuli with distinctive sensory characteristics (e.g., differences in pitch or in loudness) may pass through the attentional system, thereby reaching higher levels of processing, such as perception. However, other stimuli will be filtered out at the sensory level, never passing through the attentional filter to reach the level of perception. Broadbent's theory was supported by Colin Cherry's findings that sensory information (e.g., male vs. female voices, tones vs. words) may be noticed by an unattended ear, but that information requiring higher perceptual processes (e.g., German vs. English words, or even words played backward instead of forward) is not noticed in an unattended ear.

Moray's Selective Filter Model

Not long after Broadbent's theory, the research began (e.g., Gray & Wedderburn, 1960) to suggest that Broadbent's model must be wrong. First, Neville Moray (1959) found that even when participants ignore most other high-level (e.g., semantic) aspects of an unattended message, they still recognize their names in an unattended ear. Moray suggested that the reason for this effect is that powerful, highly salient messages may break through the filter of selective attention, but that other messages may not. To modify Broadbent's metaphor, one could say that, according to Moray, the selective filter blocks out most information at the sensory level, but that some highly salient messages are so powerful that they burst through the filtering mechanism.

FIGURE 3.5 **BOTTLENECK THEORIES OF ATTENTION: EARLY FILTERING MECHANISMS**

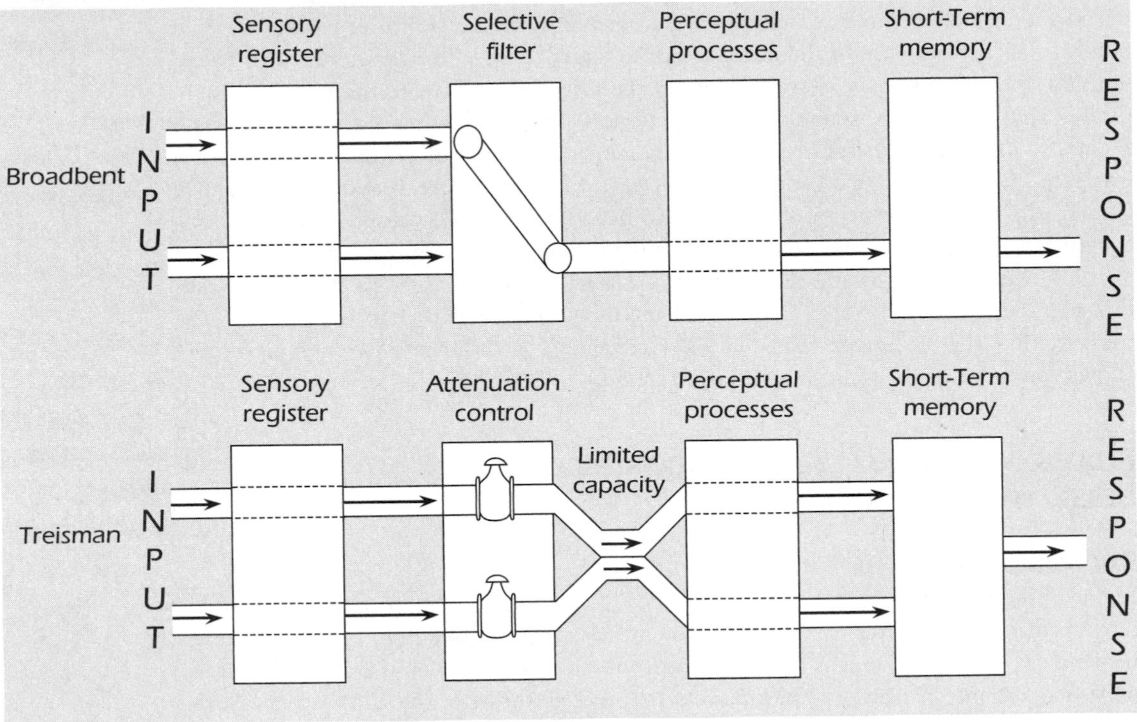

Various mechanisms have been proposed suggesting a means by which incoming sensory information passes through the attentional system to reach high-level perceptual processes.

Treisman's Attenuation Model

In related work, Anne Treisman (1960) found that while a participant is shadowing a coherent message in one ear and ignoring a message in the other ear, something interesting occurs if the message in the attended ear is suddenly switched to the unattended ear: Participants will pick up the first few words of the old message in the new ear, which suggests that context will briefly lead the participants to shadow a message that should be ignored.

Treisman (1964a, 1964b) also noted that if the unattended message was identical to the attended one, all participants noticed it, even if one of the messages was slightly out of temporal synchronization with the other. When this last effect was studied systematically, it was discovered that participants typically recognized the two messages to be the same when the shadowed message was either as much as 4.5 seconds ahead of the unattended one, or as far as 1.5 seconds behind the unattended one. In other words, it is easier to recognize the unattended message when it precedes, rather than follows, the attended one. Treisman also observed that when fluently bilingual participants are studied, some of them will notice the identity of messages if the unattended message is a translated version of the attended one.

Moray's modification of Broadbent's filtering mechanism was clearly not sufficient to explain Treisman's (1960) findings in her experiments in which messages switched from the attended ear to the unattended ear were briefly shadowed, as well as her work with bilinguals, in which synonymous messages were recognized in the unattended ear (Treisman, 1964a, 1964b). Treisman interpreted her findings as suggesting that at least some information about unattended signals is being analyzed. Treisman also interpreted Moray's findings as indicating that some higher level processing of the information reaching the supposedly unattended ear must be taking place; otherwise, participants would not recognize the familiar sounds to realize that they were salient. That is, the incoming information cannot be filtered out at the level of sensation, or we would never perceive the message to recognize its salience.

Based on these findings, Treisman proposed a theory of selective attention involving a different kind of filtering mechanism (which is distinct from her feature-integration theory, described earlier). Recall that in Broadbent's theory, the filter acts to block stimuli other than the target stimulus. In Treisman's theory, however, the mechanism merely *attenuates* (weakens the strength of) stimuli other than the target stimulus. For particularly potent stimuli, the effects of the attenuation are not great enough to prevent the stimuli from penetrating the signal-weakening mechanism. (Figure 3.5 illustrates Treisman's signal-attenuating mechanism.)

According to Treisman, selective attention involves three stages: (a) We preattentively analyze the physical properties of a stimulus, such as loudness (sound intensity), pitch (related to the "frequency" of the sound waves), and so on; this preattentive process is conducted in parallel (simultaneously) on all incoming sensory stimuli. For stimuli that show the target properties, we pass the signal on to the next stage; for stimuli that do not show these properties, we pass on only a weakened version of the stimulus. (b) We analyze whether a given stimulus has a pattern, such as speech or music. For stimuli that show the target pattern, we pass the signal on to the next stage; for stimuli that do not show the target pattern, we pass on only a weakened version of the stimulus. (c) We focus attention on the stimuli that make it to this stage, and we sequentially evaluate the incoming messages, assigning appropriate meanings to the selected stimulus messages.

Deutsch and Deutsch's Late Filter Model

An alternative to Treisman's attenuation theory was simply to move the location of the signal-blocking filter to follow, rather than precede, at least some of the perceptual processing needed for recognition of meaning in the stimuli. In particular, J. Anthony Deutsch and Diana Deutsch (1963), and later Donald Norman (1968), proposed models of attention that placed the signal-blocking filter later in the process, after sensory analysis and also after some perceptual and conceptual analysis of input had taken place (see Figure 3.6). This later filtering would allow people to recognize information entering the unattended ear, such as the sound of their own name or a translation of attended input (for bilinguals). If the information does not perceptually strike some sort of chord, people will throw it out at the filtering mechanism shown in Figure 3.6; if it does, however, as with the sound of an important name, people will pay attention to it. Note that proponents of both the early and the late filtering mechanisms propose that there is an attentional bottleneck through which

FIGURE 3.6 **MODIFIED BOTTLENECK THEORY OF ATTENTION: LATE FILTERING MECHANISMS**

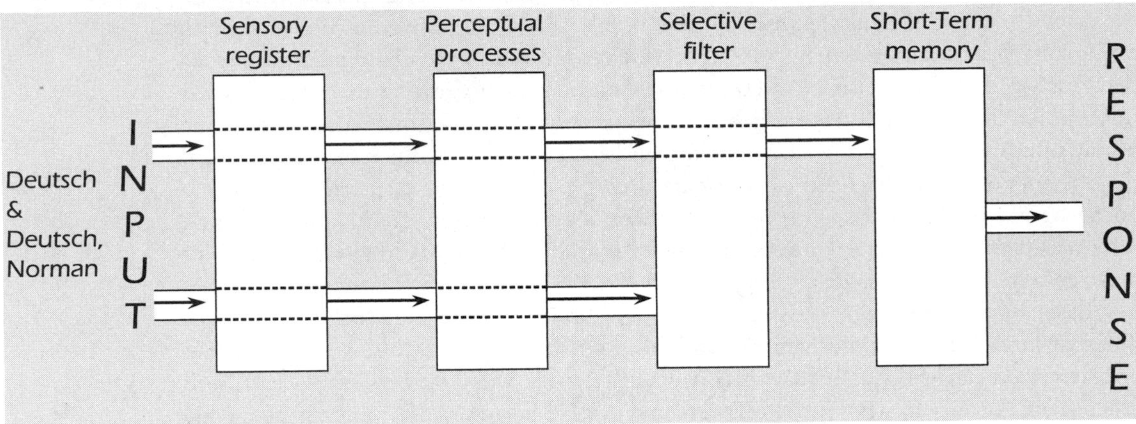

According to some cognitive psychologists, the attentional filtering mechanisms follow, rather than precede, preliminary perceptual processes.

only a single source of information can pass; the two models differ only in terms of where they hypothesize the bottleneck to be positioned.

NEISSER'S SYNTHESIS

In 1967, Ulric Neisser synthesized the early-filter and the late-filter models, proposing that there are two processes governing attention: preattentive and attentive processes. Preattentive, automatic processes are rapid and occur in parallel. They can be used to notice only physical sensory characteristics of the unattended message, but not to discern meaning or relationships. Attentive, controlled processes occur later, are executed serially, consume time and attentional resources (e.g., working memory), can be used to observe relationships among features, and serve to synthesize fragments into a mental representation of an object. More recent work in attention builds upon Neisser's distinction between preattentive and attentive processes by focusing only on the consciously controlled aspects of attention (Cowan, 1995).

James Johnston and his colleagues (e.g., McCann & Johnston, 1992) have suggested a different view of the two processes. According to these researchers, physical analysis of sensory data occurs continually, but semantic analysis of stimuli occurs only when cognitive capacity (in the form of working memory) is not already overtaxed and is sufficient to permit such analysis. Evidence of the twofold system arises from findings that people show much faster reaction times when responding to physically discriminable stimuli than to semantically discriminable stimuli.

A two-step model of some sort could account for Cherry's data, Moray's data, and Treisman's data. Evidence of fully automatic versus fully controlled processes also seems to support this model, in that automatic processes may be governed only by the first step of attentional processing, and controlled processes may additionally be governed by the second of the two steps. The model also nicely incorporates aspects of Treisman's signal-attenuation theory, as well as of her subsequent feature-integration theory, according to which discrete processes for feature detection and for feature integration occur during searches. Again, Treisman's feature-detection process may be linked to the former of the two processes (i.e., speedy, automatic processing), and her feature-integration process may be linked to the latter of the two processes (i.e., slower, controlled processing). Unfortunately, however, the two-step model does not well explain the continuum of processes from fully automatic ones to fully controlled ones. Recall, for example, Neisser's work with Spelke and Hirst (Spelke, Hirst, & Neisser, 1976), in which fully controlled processes appeared to be at least partially automatized. How does the two-process model explain the automatization of processes in divided-attention phenomena, such as reading for comprehension while writing dictated, categorized words?

Attentional-Resource Theories of Selective Attention

More recent theories have moved away from the notion of signal-blocking or signal-attenuating filters and toward the notion of apportionment of limited attentional resources. Attentional-resource theories help to explain how we can perform more than one attention-demanding task at a time, positing that people have a fixed amount of attention, which they can choose to allocate according to what the task requires. Figure 3.7 shows two examples of such a theory. In panel (a), the system has a single pool of resources that can be divided up, say, among multiple tasks (Kahneman, 1973).

FIGURE 3.7 **ATTENTIONAL RESOURCES THEORY**

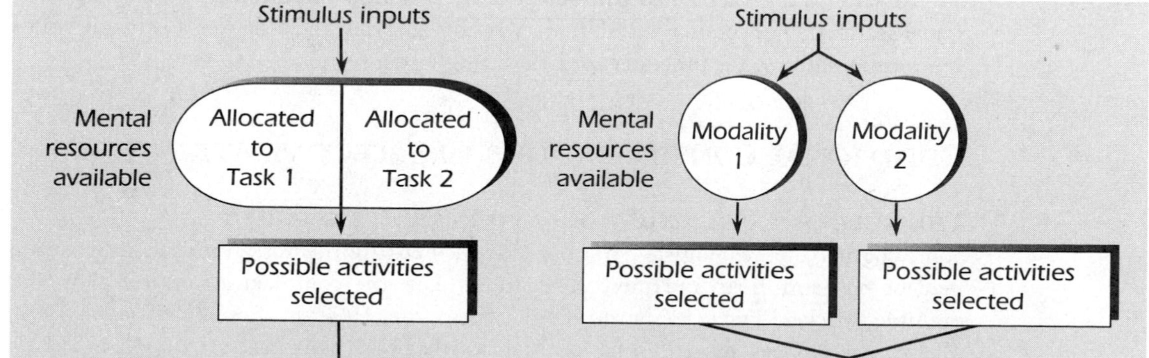

Attentional resources may involve either a single pool or a multiplicity of modality-specific pools. Although attentional resources theory has been criticized for its imprecision, it seems to complement filter theories in explaining some aspects of attention.

However, it now appears that such a model represents an oversimplification because people are much better at dividing their attention when competing tasks are in different modalities. At least some attentional resources may be specific to the modality in which a task is presented. For example, most people easily can simultaneously listen to music and concentrate on writing, but it is harder to listen to the news station and concentrate on writing at the same time because both are verbal tasks. The words from the news interfere with the words you are thinking about. Similarly, two visual tasks are more likely to interfere with each other than are a visual task coupled with an auditory one. Panel (b) of Figure 3.7 shows a model that allows for attentional resources to be specific to a given modality (Navon & Gopher, 1979). For someone trying to write while listening to music, the use of two distinctive modality-specific attentional resources (auditory for music; writing for visual) would probably not pose serious attentional difficulties.

Attentional-resources theory has been severely criticized as overly broad and vague (e.g., S. Yantis, personal communication, December, 1994). Although it may not stand alone in explaining all aspects of attention, it complements filter theories quite well. Filter and bottleneck theories of attention seem to be more suitable metaphors for competing tasks that seem to be attentionally incompatible, such as in selective-attention tasks or in simple divided-attention tasks involving the PRP (psychological refractory period) effect (Pashler, 1994). For these kinds of tasks, it appears that some preattentive processes may occur simultaneously, but that processes requiring attention must be handled sequentially, as if passing one-by-one through an attentional bottleneck. However, resource theory seems to be a better metaphor for explaining phenomena of divided attention on complex tasks, in which practice effects may be observed. According to this metaphor, as each of the complex tasks becomes increasingly automatized, performance of each task makes fewer demands on the limited-capacity attentional resources. Additionally, for explaining search-related phenomena, theories specific to visual search (e.g., models proposing guided search [Cave & Wolfe, 1990] or similarity [J. Duncan & Humphreys, 1989]) seem to have stronger explanatory power than do filter or resource theories, although these theories are not altogether incompatible. That is, although the findings from research on visual search do not conflict with filter or resource theories, the task-specific theories more specifically describe the processes at work during visual search.

Additional Considerations in Selective Attention

The Role of Task, Situation, and Person Variables

Some cognitive psychologists point out that the existing theoretical models of attention may be too simplistic and mechanistic to explain the complexities of attention. For example, Michael Eysenck (e.g., M. Eysenck & Byrne, 1992; M. Eysenck & Calvo, 1992; M. Eysenck & Graydon, 1989) has commented that both trait-based anxiety (a personality characteristic) and situation-related anxiety have been found to affect attention. Both types of anxiety tend to place constraints on attention. Other considerations include (a) overall arousal (e.g., being tired, drowsy, or drugged may limit attention, but being excited sometimes enhances it); (b) specific interest in a target task and stimuli, as against interest in distractors; (c) the nature of the task (e.g., highly difficult, complex, or novel tasks require more attentional resources than do easy, simple, or highly familiar tasks—task difficulty particularly influences performance during divided attention); (d) amount of practice in performing a given task or set of tasks and in the skill of utilizing attentional resources for a task or tasks (with increased practice and skill enhancing attention; Spelke et al., 1976); and (e) the stage of processing at which attentional demands are needed (i.e., before, during, or after some degree of perceptual processing).

In sum, although many attentional processes occur outside our conscious awareness, many other processes are subject to conscious control. The psychological study of attention has included, among other phenomena, vigilance, search, selective attention, and divided attention during the simultaneous performance of multiple tasks. To explain this diversity of attentional phenomena, current theories emphasize that a filtering mechanism appears to govern some aspects of attention, whereas limited modality-specific attentional resources appear to influence other aspects of attention. Clearly, findings from cognitive research have yielded many insights into attention, but additional understanding has also been gained through the study of attentional processes in the brain.

THE STROOP EFFECT

Although much of the research on selective attention has focused on auditory processing, selective attention can also be studied through visual processing. One of the tasks most frequently used for this purpose was first formulated by John Ridley Stroop (1935), for whom the Stroop effect is named. The way the task works is as follows. Quickly read aloud the following words: brown, blue, green, red, purple. Easy, isn't it? Now quickly name aloud the colors shown in part (a) of the top figure on the back endpaper of this book, in which the colored ink matches the name of the color word. This task, too, is easy. Now, look at part (c) of the same figure, in which the colors of the inks differ from the color names that are printed with them, and again name the ink colors you see, out loud, as quickly as possible.

You will probably find the task very difficult: Each of the written words interferes with your naming the color of the ink. The **Stroop effect** demonstrates the psychological difficulty in selectively attending to the color of the ink and trying to ignore the word that is printed with the ink of that color. One explanation of why the Stroop test may be particularly difficult is that, for you and most other adults, reading is now an automatic process, not readily subject to your conscious control (MacLeod, 1991, 1996). For that reason, you find it difficult intentionally to refrain from reading and instead to concentrate on identifying the color of the ink, disregarding the word printed in that ink color. An alternative explanation is that the output of a response occurs when the mental pathways for producing the response are activated sufficiently (MacLeod, 1991). In the Stroop test, the color word activates a cortical pathway for saying the word, while the ink-color name activates a pathway for naming the color; but the former pathway interferes with the latter. In this situation, it takes longer to gather sufficient strength of activation to produce the color-naming response and not the word-reading response.

DIVIDED ATTENTION

In signal detection and selective attention, the attentional system must coordinate a search for the simultaneous presence of many features—a relatively simple, if not easy, task. At times, however, the attentional system must perform two or more discrete tasks at the same time. Early work in this area was done by Ulric Neisser and Robert Becklen (1975), who had participants view a videotape in which the display of one activity (three-person basketball) was superimposed on the display of another activity (two people playing a hand-slapping game). Initially, the task was simply to watch one activity and ignore the other, pressing a button whenever key events occurred in the attended activity. Essentially, this first task required only selective attention.

However, the two researchers then asked participants to attend to both activities simultaneously and to signal key events in each of the two activities. Even when the researchers presented the two activities dichoptically (i.e., not in a single visual field, but rather with one activity observed by one eye and the other activity observed by the other eye), participants had great difficulty performing both tasks simultaneously. Neisser and Becklen hypothesized that improvements in performance would have occurred eventually as a result of practice. They also hypothesized that the performance of multiple tasks was based on skill (due to practice), not on special cognitive mechanisms.

The following year, Elizabeth Spelke, William Hirst, and Ulric Neisser (1976) used a dual-task paradigm to study divided attention during the simultaneous performance of two activities. The dual-task paradigm involves two tasks (Task A and Task B) and three conditions (Task A only, Task B only, and both Tasks A and B together). The idea was that the researchers would compare and contrast the latency (response time) and accuracy of performance in each of the three conditions. Of course, higher latencies mean slower responses. Previous research had shown that the speed and accuracy of simultaneous performance of two tasks was quite poor for the simultaneous performance of two controlled processes. For those rare instances in which persons demonstrated high levels of speed and accuracy for the simultaneous performance of two tasks, at least one of the tasks generally involved automatic processing, and usually both tasks involved such processing.

As expected, Spelke, Hirst, and Neisser found that initial performance was indeed quite poor for the two controlled tasks they chose: (a) reading for detailed comprehension and (b) writing down dictated words. However, Spelke and her colleagues continued to have the two participants in their study perform these two tasks five days a week for many weeks (85 sessions in all). To the surprise of many, given enough practice, the participants' performance improved on both tasks. That is, they showed improvements in their speed of reading and accuracy of reading comprehension, as measured by comprehension tests, as well as in their recognition memory for words they had written during dictation. Eventually, participants' performance on both tasks reached the same levels that the participants had previously shown for each task alone.

The authors then introduced sublists of related words within the full word-dictation lists, such as sublists of words that formed a sentence or that rhymed. They asked the participants to "report any of the dictated words, or any 'general properties' of the list" that they remembered. Although the participants initially recalled very few words and no relationships among any of the words, after repeated practice, they noticed words related by superordinate categories, by rhyming sounds, by sentences (i.e., strings of words that formed sentences), and sometimes even by parts of speech (grammatical classes; i.e., verbs, plural nouns, etc.). Further, although the simultaneous performance of the more complex dictation task initially led to a dip in performance on the reading-comprehension task, with continued practice, performance on that task soon returned to previous high levels.

Next, the authors modified the word-dictation task so that the participants sometimes wrote the dictated words and sometimes wrote the correct one of two categories (e.g., animals vs. furniture) to which the dictated words belonged, while still engaged in the reading-comprehension task. As with previous modifications, initial performance on the two tasks dropped, but performance returned to high levels after practice. Spelke and her colleagues suggested that these findings showed that controlled tasks can be automatized so that they consume fewer attentional resources. Further, two discrete controlled tasks may be automatized to function together as a unit. These authors were quick to point out that the tasks do not, however, become fully automatic both because they continue to be intentional and conscious, and because they involve relatively high levels of cognitive processing. In subsequent work (Hirst, Spelke, Reaves, Caharack, & Neisser, 1980), the authors tested to see whether the participants were alternating their attention between each of two tasks or whether performance on either task had become automatic. In their view, their findings disconfirmed both of the newer explanations and confirmed their earlier interpretation. Significantly, however, the response times during dual-task performance were still lower than response latencies for each task alone.

An entirely different approach to studying divided attention has focused on extremely simple tasks that require speedy responses. According to Harold Pashler (1994), when people try to perform two overlapping speeded tasks, the responses for one or both tasks are almost always slower; when a second task begins soon after the first task has started, speed of performance usually suffers. The slowing due to simultaneous engagement in speeded tasks is termed the *psychological refractory period (PRP) effect.* In Pashler's view, findings from PRP studies indicate that people can fairly easily accommodate perceptual processing of the physical properties of sensory stimuli while engaged in a second speeded task. However, they cannot readily accommodate more than one cognitive task requiring them to choose a response, retrieve information from memory, or engage in various other cognitive operations. When both tasks require performance of any of these cognitive operations, one or both tasks will show the PRP effect.

Cognitive Neuroscientific Approaches to Attention and Consciousness

The neuroscience of attention has an ever growing body of literature. Michael Posner (Posner, 1992; Posner & Dehaene, 1994; Posner & Raichle, 1994), one of the leading investigators in the neuropsychology of attention, has attempted to synthesize diverse studies, including his own research, investigating attentional processes in the brain. One of the questions Posner has addressed is whether attention is a function of the entire brain or is a function of discrete attention-governing modules in the brain. According to Posner, the attentional system in the brain "is neither a property of a single brain area nor of the entire brain" (Posner & Dehaene, 1994, p. 75).

Indeed, other researchers, including Martha Farah (J. D. Cohen, Romero, Servan-Schreiber, & Farah, 1994; Farah, 1994), postulate that attention involves mostly the interaction of diverse areas of the brain, with no specialized areas responsible for specific attentional functions. Farah's work on patients with *neglect,* an attentional dysfunction in which participants ignore half of their visual field (due mainly to unilateral lesions in the parietal lobes), reveals that the problem may be due to the interaction of systems that mutually inhibit one another. When only one of the pair involved in the system is damaged (as is the case with neglect patients), patients become locked in to one side of the visual field because the inhibition normally provided by the other half of the system is no longer working.

Posner's Theory

Posner (1995) has identified an anterior (frontward) attention system (attentional network) within the frontal lobe and a posterior (toward the rear) attention system within the parietal lobe. The anterior attention system becomes increasingly activated during tasks requiring awareness, in which participants must attend to the meanings of words. This system is also involved in "attention for action," in which the participant is planning or selecting an action from among alternative courses of action. In contrast, the posterior attention system involves the parietal lobe of the cortex, a portion of the thalamus, and some areas of the midbrain related to eye movements. This system becomes highly activated during tasks involving visuospatial attention, in which the participant must disengage and shift attention (e.g., visual search or vigilance tasks) (Posner & Raichle, 1994). Attention also involves neural activity in the relevant visual, auditory, motor, and association areas of the cortex involved in particular visual, auditory, motor, or higher order tasks (Posner, Petersen, Fox, & Raichle, 1988). The anterior and posterior attention systems appear to enhance attention across various tasks, suggesting that they may be involved in regulating the activation of relevant cortical areas for specific tasks (Posner & Dehaene, 1994).

Another question has been whether the activity of the attentional system occurs as a result of enhanced activation of attended items, inhibition or suppressed activation of unattended items, or both processes. Michael Posner and Stanislas Dehaene (1994) have suggested a definitive answer: It depends. Specifically, each of these three possibilities may be the case, depending on the particular task and on the area of the brain under investigation. The task at hand is to determine which processes occur in which areas of the brain during the performance of which tasks. For mapping the areas of the brain involved in various tasks, cognitive neuropsychologists often use positron emission tomography (PET), which maps regional cerebral blood flow (rCBF; see chapter 2 for a more in-depth discussion of this technique). In one such PET study (Corbetta, Miezin, Shulman, & Petersen, 1993), researchers found increased activation in areas responsible for each of the distinct attributes of various search tasks: for features such as motion, color, and shape, as well as for selected versus divided attentional conditions.

Näätänen's ERP Work

An alternative way of studying attention in the brain is to focus on studying event-related potentials (ERPs; see chapter 2), which indicate minute changes in electrical activity in response to various stimuli. Risto Näätänen (1988a, 1990, 1992) has gained renown using ERPs to probe the attentional processes of the brain. Both the PET and the ERP techniques offer information on the geography (localization) of cerebral activity and on the chronology of cerebral events. However, the PET technique provides higher resolution for spatial localization of cerebral function, and the ERP provides much more sensitive indications of the chronology of responses (within milliseconds; Näätänen, 1988b). Thus, through ERP studies, even extremely brief responses to stimuli may be noticed.

The ERP's sensitivity to very brief responses has allowed Näätänen and his colleagues (e.g., Cowan, Winkler, Teder, & Näätänen, 1993; Näätänen, 1988a, 1988b; Paavilainen, Tiitinen, Alho, & Näätänen, 1993) to examine the specific conditions in which target versus distractor stimuli do or do not prompt attentional responses. For example, Näätänen has found that at least some response to infrequent, deviant auditory stimuli (e.g., peculiar changes in pitch) seems to be automatic and occurs even when the participant is focusing attention on a primary task and is not consciously aware of the deviant stimuli. These automatic, preconscious responses to deviant stimuli occur whether the stimuli are targets or distractors, and the responses occur whether the deviants are widely different from the standard stimuli or are only slightly different from the standard stimuli (Cowan et al., 1993; Paavilainen et al., 1993). Näätänen (1990) also found no performance decrement in the controlled task, as a result of the automatic response to deviant stimuli, so it seems that some automatic superficial analysis and selection of stimuli may occur without taxing attentional resources.

Many of the foregoing studies have involved normal participants, but cognitive neuropsychologists have also learned a great deal about attentional processes in the brain by studying persons who do not show normal attentional processes, such as persons who show specific attentional deficits, and who are found to have either lesions or inadequate blood flow in key areas of the brain. Overall attention deficits have been linked to lesions in the frontal lobe and in the basal ganglia (Lou, Henriksen, & Bruhn, 1984); visual attentional deficits have been linked to the posterior parietal cortex and the thalamus, as well as to areas of the midbrain related to eye movements (Posner & Petersen, 1990; Posner et al., 1988). Work with split-brain patients (e.g., Ladavas, del Pesce, Mangun, & Gazzaniga, 1994; Luck, Hillyard, Mangun, & Gazzaniga, 1989) has also led to some interesting findings regarding attention and brain function, such as the observation that the right hemisphere seems to be dominant for maintaining alertness, and that the attentional systems involved in visual search seem to be distinct from other aspects of visual attention.

A Psychopharmacological Approach

Another approach to the understanding of attentional processes is psychopharmacological research, which evaluates changes in attention and consciousness associated with various chemicals (e.g., neurotransmitters such as acetylcholine or GABA [see chapter 2], hormones, and even central nervous system [CNS] stimulants ["uppers"] or depressants ["downers"]; e.g., Wolkowitz, Tinklenberg, & Weingartner, 1985). In addition, researchers study physiological aspects of attentional processes at a global level of analysis. For example, overall arousal can be observed through such responses as pupillary dilation, changes in the autonomic (self-regulating) nervous system (see chapter 2), and distinctive

EEG patterns. An area that has long been recognized as crucial to overall arousal is the reticular activating system (RAS; see chapter 2). Changes in the RAS and in specific measures of arousal have been linked to habituation and dishabituation, as well as to the orienting reflex, in which an individual reflexively responds to sudden changes by reorienting the position of the body toward the source of the sudden change (e.g., sudden noise or flash of light).

MARCEL'S MODEL OF THE LINKS AMONG PERCEPTION, ATTENTION, AND CONSCIOUSNESS

In this chapter, we have focused on attention and consciousness. Before closing this discussion and beginning a discussion of perception, we may appreciate one cognitive psychologist's view of how consciousness and perception interact. Anthony Marcel (1983a) has proposed a model for describing how sensations and cognitive processes that occur outside our conscious awareness may influence our conscious perceptions and cognitions. According to Marcel, our conscious representations of what we perceive often differ qualitatively from our nonconscious representations of sensory stimuli. Outside of conscious awareness, we continually try to make sense of a constant flow of sensory information. Also outside of awareness are perceptual hypotheses regarding how the current sensory information matches with various properties and objects we have encountered previously in our environment. These hypotheses are inferences based on knowledge stored in long-term memory. During the matching process, information from differing sensory modalities is integrated.

According to Marcel's model, once there is a suitable match between the sensory data and the perceptual hypotheses regarding various properties and objects, the match is reported to conscious awareness as "being" particular properties and objects. Consciously, we are aware only of the reported objects or properties; we are not aware of the sensory data, the perceptual hypotheses that do not lead to a match, or even the processes that govern the reported match. Thus, before a given object or property is detected consciously (i.e., is reported to conscious awareness by the nonconscious matching process), we will have chosen a satisfactory perceptual hypothesis and excluded various possibilities that less satisfactorily matched the incoming sensory data to what we already know or can infer.

According to Marcel's model, the sensory data and the perceptual hypotheses are available to and used by various nonconscious cognitive processes, in addition to the matching process. Sensory data and cognitive processes that do not reach awareness still exert influence on how we think and how we perform other cognitive tasks. It is widely held that we have limited attentional capacity (e.g., see Norman, 1976). According to Marcel, we accommodate these limitations by making use of nonconscious information and processes as much as possible, while limiting the information and processing that enter our conscious awareness. In this way, our limited attentional capacity is not constantly overtaxed. Hence, our processes of attention are intimately intertwined with our processes of perception. In this chapter, we have described many functions and processes of attention. In the following chapter, we focus on various aspects of perception.

SUMMARY

1. **Can we actively process information even if we are not aware of doing so? If so, what do we do, and how do we do it?** Whereas *attention* embraces all of the information that an individual is manipulating (a portion of the information available from memory, sensation, and other cognitive processes), consciousness comprises only the narrower range of information that the individual is aware of manipulating. Attention allows us to use our limited active cognitive resources (e.g., due to the limits of working memory) judiciously, to respond quickly and accurately to interesting stimuli, and to remember salient information. Conscious awareness allows us to monitor our interactions with the environment, to link our past and present experiences and thereby sense a continuous thread of experience, and to control and plan for future actions.

   We can actively process information at the preconscious level without being aware of doing so. For example, researchers have studied the phenomenon of *priming,* in which a given stimulus increases the likelihood that a subsequent related (or identical) stimulus will be readily processed (e.g., retrieval from long-term memory). In contrast, in the *tip-of-the-tongue phenomenon,* another example of preconscious processing, retrieval of desired information from memory does not occur despite an ability to retrieve related information.

   Cognitive psychologists also observe distinctions in conscious versus preconscious attention by distinguishing between controlled and automatic processing in task performance. *Controlled processes* are relatively slow, sequential in nature, intentional (requiring effort), and under conscious control. *Automatic processes* are relatively fast, parallel in nature, and for the most part outside of conscious awareness. Actually, a continuum of processing appears to exist, from fully automatic to fully controlled processes. A pair of automatic processes that support our attentional system is *habituation* and *dishabituation,* which affect our responses to familiar versus novel stimuli.

2. **What are some of the functions of attention?** One main function involved in attention detecting is important objects and events in the environment. Researchers use measures from *signal-detection theory* to determine an observer's sensitivity to targets in various tasks. For example, *vigilance* refers to a person's ability to attend to a field of stimulation over a prolonged period of time, usually with the stimulus to be detected occurring only infrequently. Whereas vigilance involves passively waiting for an event to occur, *search* involves actively seeking out a stimulus.

   People use selective attention to track one message and simultaneously to ignore others. Auditory selective attention (such as in the *cocktail party problem)* may be observed by asking participants to shadow information presented *dichotically.* Visual selective attention may be observed in tasks involving the *Stroop effect.* Attentional processes are also involved during *divided attention,* when people attempt to handle more than one task at once; generally, the simultaneous performance of more than one automatized task is easier to handle than the simultaneous performance of more than one controlled task. However, with practice, individuals appear to be capable of handling more than one controlled task at a time, even engaging in tasks requiring comprehension and decision making.

3. **What are some of the theories cognitive psychologists have developed to explain what they have observed about attentional processes?** Some theories of attention involve an attentional filter or bottleneck, according to which information is selectively blocked out or attenuated as it passes from one level of processing to the next. Of the bottleneck theories, some suggest that the signal-blocking or signal-attenuating mechanism occurs just after sensation and prior to any perceptual processing; others propose a later mechanism, after at least some perceptual processing has occurred. Attentional-resource theories offer an alternative way of explaining attention; according to these theories, people have a fixed amount of attentional resources (perhaps modulated by sensory modalities) that they allocate according to the perceived task requirements. Resource theories and bottleneck theories may actually be complementary. In addition to these general theories of attention, some task-specific theories (e.g., *feature-integration theory,* guided-search theory, and *similarity theory)* have attempted to explain search phenomena in particular.

4. **What have cognitive psychologists learned about attention by studying the human brain?** Early neuropsychological research led to the discovery of feature detectors, and subsequent work has explored other aspects of feature detection and integration processes that may be involved in visual search. In addition, extensive research on attentional processes in the brain seems to suggest that the attentional system primarily involves two regions of the cortex, as well as the thalamus and some other subcortical structures; the attentional system also governs various specific processes that occur in many areas of the brain, particularly in the cerebral cortex. Attentional processes may be a result of heightened activation in some areas of the brain, of inhibited activity in other areas of the brain, or perhaps of some combination of activation and inhibition. Studies of responsivity to particular stimuli show that even when an individual is focused on a primary task and is not consciously aware of processing other stimuli, the brain of the individual automatically responds to infrequent, deviant stimuli (e.g., an odd tone). By using various approaches to the study of the brain (e.g., PET, ERP, lesion studies, and psychopharmacological studies), researchers are gaining insight into diverse aspects of the brain and are also able to use converging operations to begin to explain some of the phenomena they observe.

Thinking About Thinking: Factual, Analytical, Creative, and Practical Questions

1. Describe some of the evidence regarding the phenomena of priming and preconscious perception.
2. Why are habituation and dishabituation of particular interest to cognitive psychologists?

3. Compare and contrast the theories of visual search described in this chapter.
4. Choose one of the theories of attention, and explain how the evidence from signal detection, selective attention, or divided attention supports or challenges the theory you chose.
5. Design one task likely to activate the posterior attentional system and another task likely to activate the anterior attentional system.
6. Design an experiment for studying divided attention.
7. Describe some practical ways in which you can use forcing functions and other strategies for lessening the likelihood that automatic processes will have negative consequences for you in some of the situations you face.
8. How could advertisers use some of the principles of visual search or selective attention to increase the likelihood that people will notice their messages?

Key Terms

arousal 78
attention 68
automatic processes 72
automatization 74
binaural presentation 92
cocktail party problem 92
conjunction search 85
consciousness 69
controlled processes 72
dichotic presentation 92
dishabituation 76
distractor 84
divided attention 80
feature-integration theory 86
feature search 85
habituation 76
priming 70
search 84
selective attention 80
sensory adaptation 78
signal 82
signal detection 80
signal-detection theory (SDT) 82
similarity theory 87
Stroop effect 99
tip-of-the-tongue phenomenon 71
vigilance 83

Annotated Suggested Readings

Hubel, D. H., & Wiesel, T. N. (1979). Brain mechanisms of vision. *Scientific American*, *241*, 150–162. This classic article shows, in readable terms, the findings that led two scientists, David Hubel and Torsten Wiesel, to develop their Nobel Prize-winning feature-detector theory of vision.

Ladavas, E., del Pesce, M., Mangun, G. R., & Gazzaniga, M. S. (1994). Variations in attentional bias of the disconnected cerebral hemispheres. *Cognitive Neuropsychology, 11* (1), 57–74. An interesting account of how the cerebral hemispheres each attend to stimuli presented to them.

Logan, G. (1988). Toward an instance theory of automatization. *Psychological Review, 95* (4), 492–527. A description of one of the relatively few theories that try to account for how automatization takes place.

Näätänen, R. (1988). Regional cerebral blood-flow: Supplement to event-related potential studies of selective attention. In G. C. Galbraith, M. L. Kietzman, & E. Donchin (Eds.), *Neurophysiology and psychophysiology: Experimental and clinical applications* (pp. 144–156). Hillsdale, NJ: Erlbaum. Shows how measures of blood flow can be used to understand how the brain processes various kinds of information.

Posner, M. I., & Raichle, M. E. (1994). *Images of mind.* New York: Freeman. A provocative integration of much of the neuroscientific evidence for Michael Posner's theory of attention.

PERCEPTION

CHAPTER OUTLINE

EXPLORING COGNITIVE PSYCHOLOGY

FROM SENSATION TO REPRESENTATION
- Some Basic Concepts
- Perceptual Constancies
- Depth Perception
- Gestalt Approaches to Form Perception

THEORETICAL APPROACHES TO PERCEPTION
- Bottom-Up Approaches: Direct Perception
- Top-Down Approaches: Constructive Perception
- Synthesizing the Two Approaches
- A Computational Theory of Perception
- Spatiotemporal Boundary-Formation Theory

READING: BOTTOM-UP AND TOP-DOWN PROCESSES
- Perceptual Issues in Reading
- Lexical Processes in Reading

DEFICITS IN PERCEPTION

SUMMARY

THINKING ABOUT THINKING: FACTUAL, ANALYTICAL, CREATIVE, AND PRACTICAL QUESTIONS

KEY TERMS

ANNOTATED SUGGESTED READINGS

Exploring Cognitive Psychology

1. **How do we perceive stable objects in the environment given variable stimulation?**
2. **What are two fundamental approaches to explaining perception?**
3. **How do perceptual processes interact with the cognitive processes of reading?**
4. **What happens when people with normal visual sensations cannot perceive visual stimuli?**

Have you ever been told that you "can't see something that's right under your nose," or that you "can't see the forest for the trees"? Have you ever listened to your favorite song over and over, trying to decipher the lyrics? In each of these situations, we call on the complex construct of **perception,** the set of processes by which we recognize, organize, and make sense of the sensations we receive from environmental stimuli. Perception encompasses many psychological phenomena. In this chapter, we focus on visual perception because that is the most widely recognized and the most widely studied perceptual *modality* (system for a particular sense, e.g., touch or smell). To find out about some of the phenomena of perception, psychologists often study situations that pose problems in making sense of our sensations.

Consider, for example, the image displayed in Figure 4.1. To most people, the figure initially looks like a blur of meaningless shadings. There is a recognizable creature staring them in the face, but they may not see it. When people finally realize what is in the figure, they rightfully feel "cowed." In Figure 4.1, the figure of the cow is hidden within the continuous gradations of shading that constitute the picture. Before you recognized the figure as a cow, you correctly sensed all aspects of the figure, but you had not yet organized those sensations to form a mental **percept** (a mental representation of a stimulus that is perceived) of the cow, by which you could meaningfully grasp what you previously had only sensed. In Figure 4.2, you will see shadings as well, but these shadings are discrete—in many instances, nothing more than dots. Again, there is a hidden object. If you are dogged in your pursuit of the hidden object, you will no doubt find it.

The preceding examples show that sometimes we cannot perceive what does exist. At other times, however, we perceive things that do not exist. For example, notice the black triangle in the center of the left panel of Figure 4.3, and the white triangle in the center of the right panel of Figure 4.3: They jump right out at you. Now look very closely at each of the panels. You will see that the triangles are not really all there. The black that constitutes the center triangle in the left panel looks darker, or blacker, than the surrounding black, but it is not. Nor is the white central triangle in the right panel any brighter, or whiter, than the surrounding white. Both central triangles are *optical illusions,* which involve the perception of visual information not physically present in the visual sensory stimulus. So, sometimes we do not perceive what *is* there; sometimes we perceive what is *not* there. At other times, we perceive what *cannot* be there. Consider, for example, the

FIGURE 4.1 FORM PERCEPTION I

What do you learn about your own perception by trying to identify the object staring at you from this photo?

FIGURE 4.2 FORM PERCEPTION II

What perceptual changes would make it easier for you to identify the figure depicted here?

FIGURE 4.3 **TRIANGLE ILLUSIONS**

You can easily see the triangles in this figure—or are the triangles just an illusion?

winding staircase in Figure 4.4. Follow it around until you reach the top. Are you having trouble reaching the top? This illusion is called a "perpetual staircase" because it seems always to go up, even though this feat is impossible.

The existence of perceptual illusions suggests that what we sense (in our sensory organs) is not necessarily what we perceive (in our minds). Our minds must be taking the available sensory information and manipulating that information somehow to create mental representations of objects, properties, and spatial relationships of our environments. For millennia, people have recognized that what we perceive often differs from the rectilinear sensory stimuli that reach our sense receptors, as shown by the use of optical illusions in the construction

FIGURE 4.4 **PERPETUAL STAIRCASE**

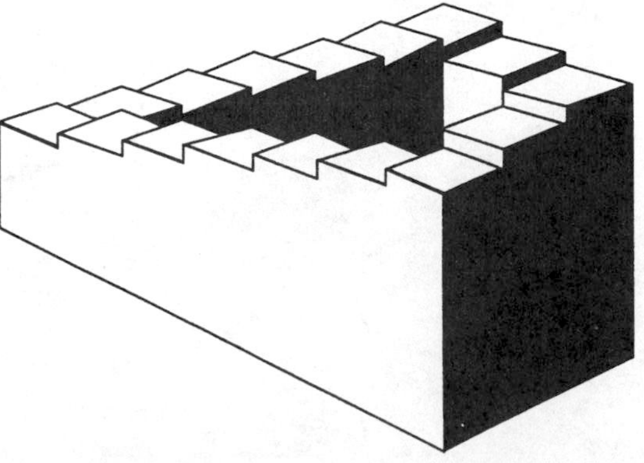

How can you reach the top of the staircase depicted here?

of the Parthenon (see Figure 4.5). Were the Parthenon actually constructed the way it appears to us perceptually (with strictly rectilinear form), its appearance would be bizarre.

Architects are not the only ones to have recognized some fundamental principles of perception. For centuries, artists have known how to lead us to perceive three-dimensional percepts when viewing two-dimensional images. What are some of the principles that guide our perceptions of both real and illusory percepts? First, we consider some of the perceptual information that leads us to perceive three-dimensional space from two-dimensional sensory information, and then we discuss some of the ways in which we perceive a stable set of percepts despite constant changes in the size and shape of what we observe. Then, we move on to theoretical approaches to perception. Finally, we consider some rare failures in normal visual perception among persons with brain injuries.

PARTHENON ILLUSIONS

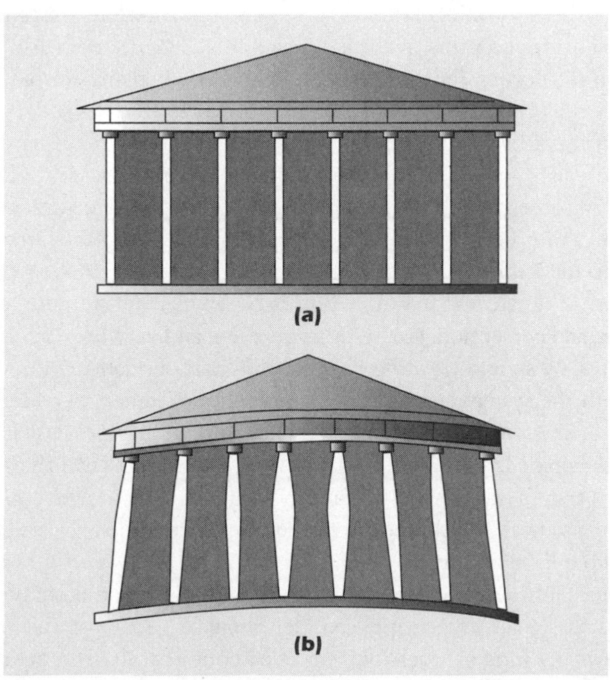

Early in the first century A.D., *Roman architect Marcus Vitruvius Polio wrote* De Architectura, *in which he documented the genius of the Greek architects Ictinus and Callicrates, who designed the Parthenon (dedicated in 438* B.C.*). The columns of the Parthenon actually bulge slightly in the middle, to compensate for the visual tendency to perceive that straight parallel lines seem to curve inward. Similarly, the horizontal lines of the beams crossing the top of the columns and the top step of the porch bulge slightly upward, to counteract the tendency to perceive that they curve slightly downward. In addition, the columns lean ever so slightly inward at the top, to compensate for the tendency to perceive them as spreading out as we gaze upward at them. Vitruvius also described many optical illusions in his treatise on architecture, and contemporary architects consider these distortions of visual perception in their designs today.*

FROM SENSATION TO REPRESENTATION

SOME BASIC CONCEPTS

If a tree falls in the forest, and no one is around to hear it, does it make a sound? An answer to this old riddle can be found by placing the riddle in the context of perception. In his influential and controversial work, James Gibson (1966, 1979) provided a useful framework for studying perception by introducing the concepts of distal (external) object, informational medium, proximal stimulation, and perceptual object.

The *distal object* (*distal,* "far") is the object in the external world, in this case, the falling tree. This event imposes a pattern on an informational medium. The *informational medium* is the reflected light, sound waves (here, the sound of the falling tree), chemical molecules, or tactile (relating to touch) information coming from the environment. Thus, the prerequisites for perception of objects in the external world begin even before sensory information impinges on our sense **receptors** (neural cells that are specialized to receive particular kinds of sensory information). When the information comes into contact with the appropriate sensory receptors of the eyes, ears, nose, skin, or mouth, *proximal stimulation* (*proximal,* "near") occurs. Finally, perception occurs when an internal *perceptual object* in some way reflects the properties of the external world.

Table 4.1 summarizes this framework for the occurrence of perception, listing the various properties of distal objects, informational media, proximal stimuli, and perceptual objects involved in perceiving the environment. To return to the original question, if a tree falls in the forest, and no one is around to hear it, it makes no *perceived* sound; but it does make a sound. (So the answer is *yes* or *no,* depending on how you look at the question.)

The question of where to draw the line between perception and cognition, or even between sensation and perception, arouses much debate, and very little agreement. Instead, to be more productive, we should view these processes as part of a continuum, in which information flows through the system, with different processes designed to address different questions. Questions of sensation focus on *qualities* of stimulation. Is that shade of red brighter than the red of an apple? Is the sound of that falling tree louder than the sound of thunder? How well do one person's impressions of colors or sounds match someone else's impressions of those same colors or sounds? This same color or sound information answers different questions for perception, typically questions of *identity,* as well as of *form, pattern, and movement.* Is that red thing an apple? Did I just hear a tree falling? Finally, cognition occurs as this information is used to serve further goals. Is that apple edible? Should I get out of this forest?

No matter what kinds of questions we ask about the environment, we will always have to deal with a fundamental attribute of our relation to the world, and that is the inherent *variation* of proximal stimulation. We can never experience through vision, hearing, taste, smell, or touch exactly the same set of stimulus properties we have experienced before. Therefore, one fundamental question for perception is, how do we achieve perceptual stability in the face of this utter instability at the level of sensory receptors? Indeed, given the nature of our sensory receptors, variation seems necessary for perception.

In the phenomenon of *sensory adaptation,* receptor cells adapt to constant stimulation by ceasing to fire until there is a change in stimulation. Through sensory adaptation, we may stop detecting the presence of a stimulus. This mechanism ensures that sensory information is constantly changing. Because of sensory adaptation in the *retina* (the receptor surface of the eye), our eyes are constantly making tiny rapid movements, termed *saccades,* to create

TABLE 4.1 PERCEPTUAL CONTINUUM

Perception occurs as environmental objects impart structure of the informational medium that ultimately impinges on sensory receptors, leading to internal object identification.

Distal Object	Informational Medium	Proximal Stimulation	Perceptual Object
Vision—sight (e.g., Grandma's face)	Reflected light from Grandma's face (visible electromagnetic waves)	Photon absorption in the rod and cone cells of the *retina,* the receptor surface in the back of the eye	Grandma's face
Audition—sound (e.g., a falling tree)	Sound waves generated by the tree's fall	Sound wave conduction to the *basilar membrane,* the receptor surface within the cochlea of the inner ear	A falling tree
Olfaction—smell (e.g., sizzling bacon)	Molecules released by frying bacon	Molecular absorption in the cells of the *olfactory epithelium,* the receptor surface in the nasal cavity	Bacon
Gustation—taste (e.g., a bite of ice cream)	Molecules of ice cream both released into the air and dissolved in water	Molecular contact with *taste buds,* the receptor cells on the tongue and soft palate, combined with olfactory stimulation (see above entry)	Ice cream
Touch (e.g., a computer keyboard)	Mechanical pressure and vibration at the point of contact between the surface of the skin (epidermis) and the keyboard	Stimulation of various receptor cells within the *dermis,* the innermost layer of skin	Computer keys

constant changes in the location of the projected image inside the eye. In order to study visual perception without saccades, scientists devised a way to create *stabilized images,* images that do not move across the retina because they actually follow the saccades. The use of this technique has confirmed the hypothesis that constant stimulation of the cells of the retina makes the image appear to disappear (Ditchburn, 1980; Riggs, Ratliff, Cornsweet, & Cornsweet, 1953). Thus, stimulus variation is an essential attribute for perception that paradoxically makes the task of explaining perception more difficult.

Perceptual Constancies

An important way in which the perceptual system deals with variability is by performing a rather remarkable analysis regarding the objects in the perceptual field. For example, picture yourself walking across campus to your cognitive psychology class. Suppose that two students are standing outside the door, chatting as you approach. As you get closer to the door, the amount of space on your retina devoted to images of those students becomes increasingly large. Yet, despite this proximal sensory evidence that the students are becoming larger, you perceive that the students have remained the same size. Why?

Your classmates' perceived constancy in size is an example of perceptual constancy. **Perceptual constancy** occurs when our perception of an object remains the same even when our proximal sensation of the distal object changes. Because the physical characteristics of the external distal object are probably not changing, and because we must be able to deal effectively with the external world, our perceptual system has mechanisms that adjust our perception of the proximal stimulus. Thus, the perception remains constant even though the proximal sensation changes. Of the several kinds of perceptual constancies, here we consider two of the main constancies: size and shape constancies.

Size constancy is the perception that an object maintains the same size despite changes in the size of the proximal stimulus. The size of an image on the retina depends directly on the distance of that object from the eye. The same object at two different distances projects different-sized images on the retina. Some striking illusions can be achieved when our sensory and perceptual systems are misled by the very same information that usually helps us to achieve size constancy. For example, in Figure 4.6, we see the Ponzo illusion, in which two objects that appear to be of different sizes are actually of the same size. The Ponzo illusion stems from the depth cue provided by the converging lines; equivalent image sizes at different depths usually indicate different-sized objects. Another illusion is the Müller–Lyer illusion, illustrated in Figure 4.7. Here, two line segments that are of the same length appear to be of different lengths (for reasons that psychologists still do not fully understand). Finally, compare the two center circles in the pair of circle patterns in Figure 4.8. Both center circles are actually the same size, but the size of the center circle relative to the surrounding circles affects perception of the center circle's size.

FIGURE 4.6 **PONZO ILLUSION**

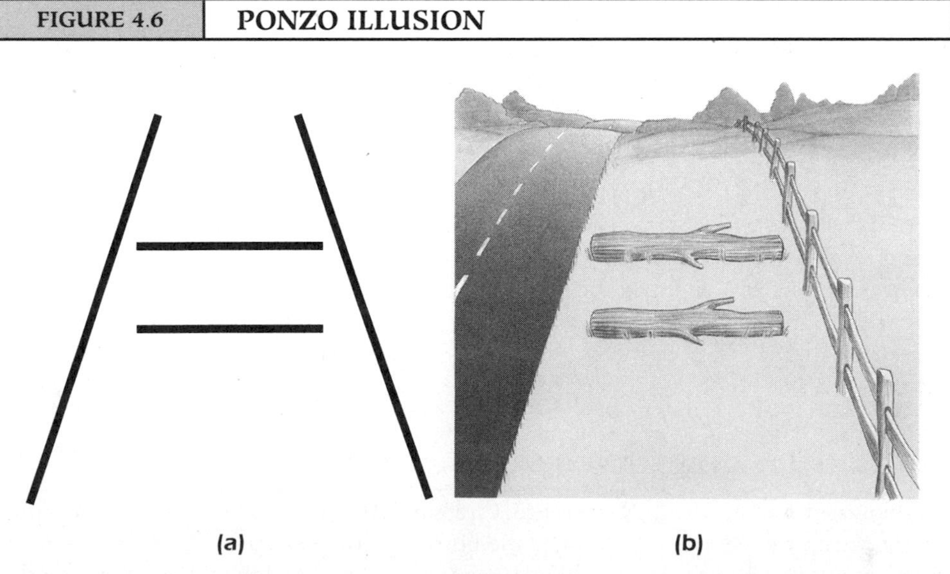

We perceive the top line and the top log as being longer than the bottom line and the bottom log, respectively, even though the top and bottom figures are identical in length. We do so because in the real three-dimensional world, the top line and the log would be larger.

FIGURE 4.7 MÜLLER–LYER ILLUSION

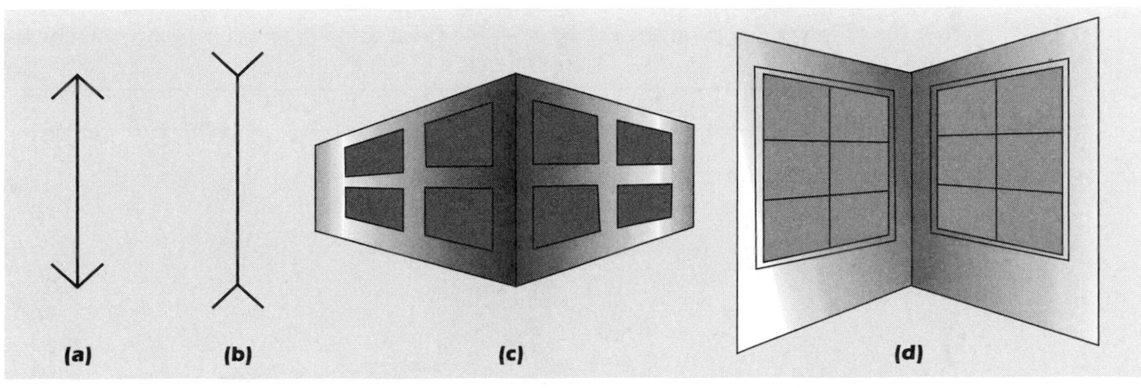

In this illusion, too, we tend to view two equally long line segments as being of different lengths. In particular, the vertical line segments in panels (a) and (c) appear shorter than the line segments in panels (b) and (d), even though all the line segments are the same size. Oddly enough, we are not certain why such a simple illusion occurs. Sometimes, the illusion we see in the abstract line segments (panels a and b) is explained in terms of the diagonal lines at the ends of the vertical segments. These diagonal lines may be implicit depth cues similar to the ones we would see in our perceptions of the exterior and interior of a building (Coren & Girgus, 1978; Gregory, 1966). In panel (c), a view of the exterior of a building, the sides appear to recede into the distance (with the diagonal lines angling toward the vertical line segment, as in panel a), whereas in panel (d), a view of the interior of a building, the sides appear to come toward us (with the diagonal lines angling away from the vertical line segment, as in panel b).

FIGURE 4.8 RELATIVE SIZE ILLUSION

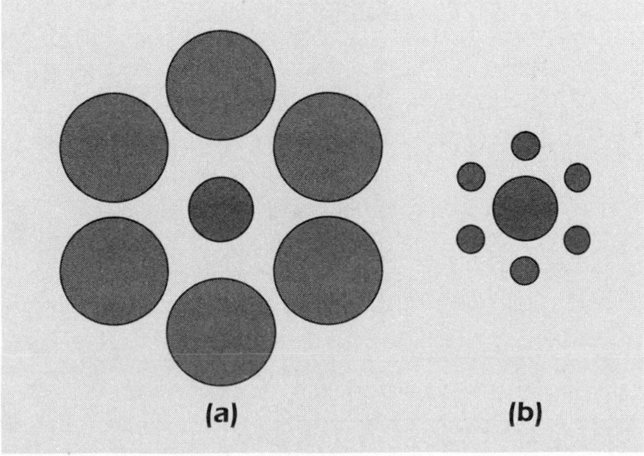

Guess which center circle is larger (a or b), and then measure the diameter of each one.

Like size constancy, shape constancy relates to the perception of distances, but in a different way. Size constancy involves the perceived distance of an object from an observer, whereas shape constancy involves the perceived distance of different *parts* of the object from the observer. For example, Figure 4.9 is an illustration of *shape constancy,* whereby an

FIGURE 4.9 **SHAPE CONSTANCY**

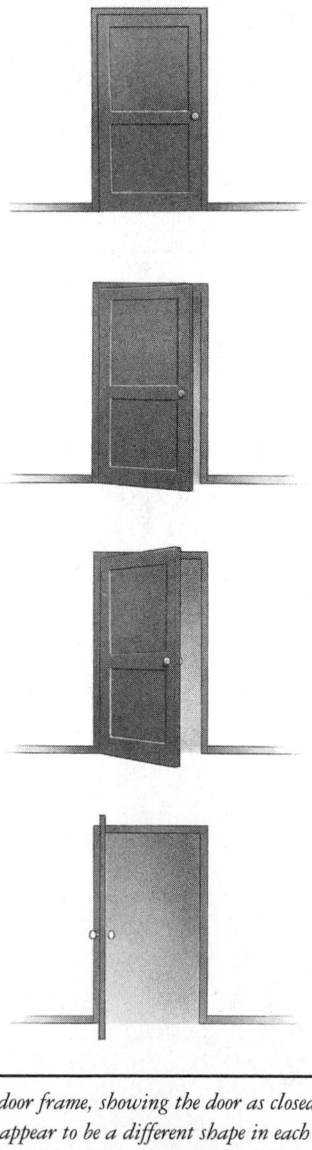

Here, you see a rectangular door and door frame, showing the door as closed, slightly opened, more fully opened, or wide open. Of course, the door does not appear to be a different shape in each panel. Indeed, it would be odd if you perceived a door to be changing shapes as you opened it. Yet, the shape of the image of the door sensed by your retinas does change as you open the door. If you look at the figure, you will see that the drawn shape of the door is different in each panel.

object's perceived shape remains the same despite changes in its orientation and hence in the shape of its retinal image. As the actual shape of the pictured door changes, some parts of the door seem to be changing differentially in their distance from us. Points near the outer edge of the door seem to move more quickly toward us than do points near the inner edge. Nonetheless, we perceive that the door remains the same shape.

DEPTH PERCEPTION

As you move around in your environment, you constantly look around and visually orient yourself in three-dimensional space. As you look forward into the distance, you look into the third dimension of **depth** (distance from a surface, usually using your own body as a reference surface when speaking in terms of depth perception). Whenever you transport your body, reach for or manipulate objects, or otherwise position yourself in your three-dimensional world, you must use information regarding depth. This use of depth information even extends beyond the range of your body's reach. When you drive, you use depth in order to assess the distance of an approaching automobile. When you decide to call out to a friend walking down the street, you determine how loudly to call, based on how far away you perceive your friend to be. How do you manage to perceive three-dimensional (3-D) space when the proximal stimuli on your retinas comprise only a two-dimensional (2-D) projection of what you see?

Refer back to the impossible staircase (Figure 4.4), and look also at other impossible configurations in Figure 4.10. One of the confusing aspects of impossible figures is that there is contradictory depth information in different sections of the picture. Small segments of these impossible figures look reasonable to us because there is no inconsistency in their individual depth cues (Hochberg, 1978). However, when we try to make sense of the figure as a whole, the cues providing depth information in various segments of the picture are in conflict.

Generally, depth cues are either monocular (*mon-,* "one"; *ocular,* related to the eyes) or binocular (*bin-,* "both," "two"). One way of judging depth is through **monocular depth cues,** which can be represented in just two dimensions and observed with just one eye. Figure 4.11 illustrates several of the monocular depth cues defined in Table 4.2, which are texture gradients, relative size, interposition, linear perspective, aerial perspective, location in

FIGURE 4.10 **IMPOSSIBLE FIGURES**

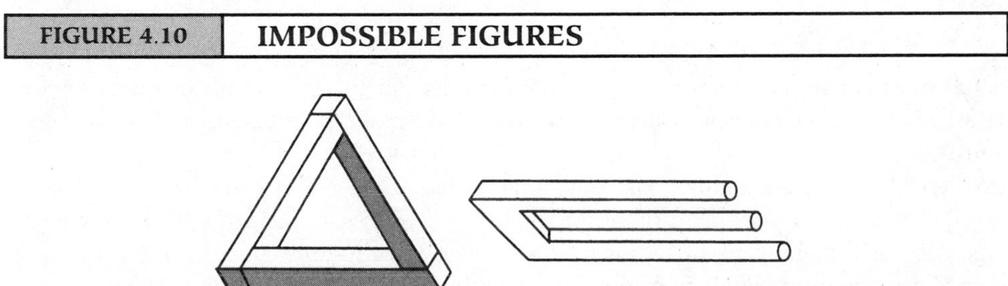

What cues may lead you to perceive these impossible figures as entirely plausible?

FIGURE 4.11	MONOCULAR DEPTH CUES: THE POSSIBLE AND THE IMPOSSIBLE

In The Annunciation, *Carlo Crivelli masterfully illustrated at least five monocular depth cues: (1, 2)* Texture gradients *and* relative size: *The floor tiles appear similar both in front of and behind the figures in the forefront of the corridor, but the tiles at the front of the corridor are larger and are spread farther apart than the tiles at the rear. (3)* Interposition: *The peacock partially blocks our view of the frieze on the wall to the right of the corridor. (4)* Linear perspective: *The sides of the wall seem to converge inward toward the rear of the corridor. (5)* Location in the picture plane: *The figures at the rear of the corridor are depicted higher in the picture plane than are the figures at the front of the corridor. M. C. Escher used his mastery of visual perception to create paradoxical depictions such as in his drawing* Waterfall. *Can you see how he used various monocular depth cues to lead us to perceive the impossible?*

the picture plane, and motion parallax. Before you read about the cues in either the table or the figure caption, look just at the figure, and see how many depth cues you can decipher for yourself, simply by observing the figure carefully.

Table 4.2 also describes motion parallax, the only monocular depth cue not shown in the figure; because motion parallax requires movement, it therefore cannot be used to judge depth within a stationary image, such as a picture. Another means of judging depth involves **binocular depth cues,** which are based on the receipt of sensory information from both eyes. Table 4.2 summarizes some of the monocular and binocular cues used in perceiving depth.

TABLE 4.2 MONOCULAR AND BINOCULAR CUES FOR DEPTH PERCEPTION

Various perceptual cues aid in our perception of the three-dimensional world. Some of these cues can be observed by one eye alone, whereas others require the use of both eyes.

Cues for Depth Perception	Appears Closer	Appears Farther Away
Monocular depth cues		
Texture gradients	Larger grains, farther apart	Smaller grains, closer together
Relative size	Bigger	Smaller
Interposition	Partially obscures other object	Is partially obscured by other object
Linear perspective	Apparently parallel lines seem to diverge as they move away from the horizon	Apparently parallel lines seem to converge as they approach the horizon
Aerial perspective	Images seem crisper, more clearly delineated	Images seem fuzzier, less clearly delineated
Location in the picture plane	Above the horizon, objects are higher in the picture plane; below the horizon, objects are lower in the picture plane	Above the horizon, objects are lower in the picture plane; below the horizon, objects are higher in the picture plane
Motion parallax	Objects approaching get larger at an ever-increasing speed (i.e., big and moving quickly = closer)	Objects departing get smaller at an ever-decreasing speed (i.e., small and moving slowly = farther away)
Binocular depth cues		
Binocular convergence	Eyes feel tug inward toward nose	Eyes relax outward toward ears
Binocular disparity	Huge discrepancy between image seen by left eye and image seen by right eye	Minuscule discrepancy between image seen by left eye and image seen by right eye

The key idea underlying binocular depth cues is that your two eyes are positioned far enough apart to provide two kinds of information to your brain: binocular disparity and binocular convergence. We constantly rely on depth cues based on *binocular disparity,* in which your two eyes send increasingly disparate (differing) images to your brain as objects approach you, and your brain interprets the degree of disparity as an indication of distance from you. In addition, for objects we view at relatively close locations, we use depth cues based on binocular convergence. In *binocular convergence,* your two eyes increasingly turn inward as objects approach you, and your brain interprets these muscular movements as indications of distance from you. (Figure 4.12 illustrates how these two processes work.)

FIGURE 4.12 **BINOCULAR DEPTH CUES**

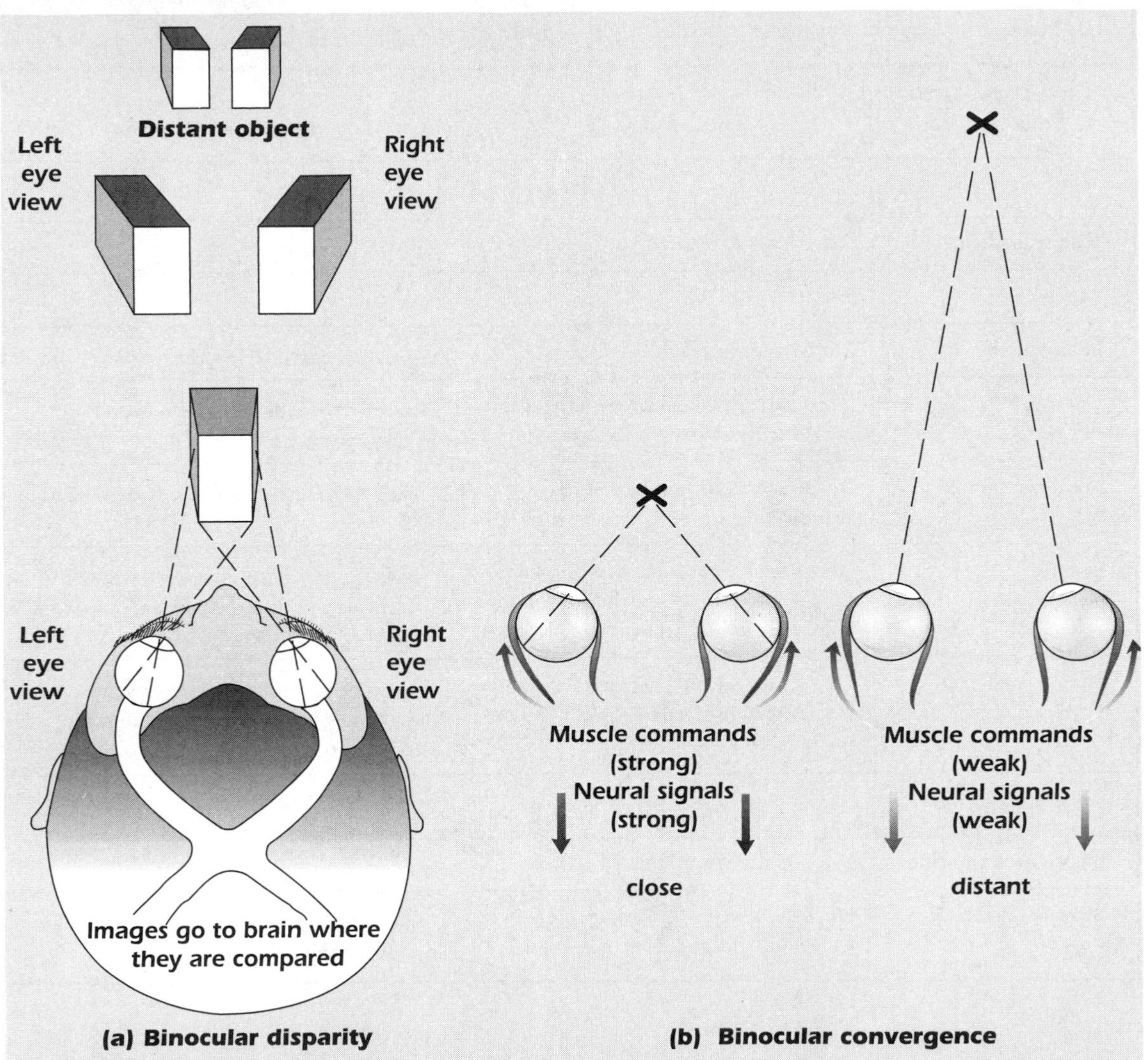

(a) Binocular disparity: *The closer an object is to you, the greater the disparity between the views of it as sensed in each of your eyes. You can test these differing perspectives by holding your finger about an inch from the tip of your nose. Look at it first with one eye covered, then the other: It will appear to jump back and forth. Now do the same for an object 20 feet away, then 100 yards away. The apparent jumping, which indicates the amount of binocular disparity, will decrease with distance. Your brain interprets the information regarding disparity as a cue indicating depth. (b)* Binocular convergence: *Because your two eyes are in slightly different places on your head, when you rotate your eyes so that an image falls directly on the central part of your eye, in which you have the greatest visual acuity, each eye must turn inward slightly to register the same image. The closer the object you are trying to see, the more your eyes must turn inward. Your muscles send messages to your brain regarding the degree to which your eyes are turning inward, and these messages are interpreted as cues indicating depth.*

PRACTICAL APPLICATIONS OF COGNITIVE PSYCHOLOGY

Models and actors often use these depth cues of perception to their advantage while being photographed. For example, some models only allow certain angles or orientations to be photographed. A long nose can appear shorter when photographed from slightly below the facial midline (just look closely at some pictures of Barbara Streisand from different angles) because the bridge of the nose recedes slightly into the distance. Also, leaning forward a little can make the upper body appear slightly larger than the lower body, and vice versa for leaning backward. In group pictures, standing slightly behind another person makes you appear smaller; standing slightly in front makes you appear larger. Women's swimsuit designers create optical-illusion swimsuits to enhance different features of the body, making legs appear longer or waists appear smaller, and either enhancing or de-emphasizing bustlines. Some of these processes to alter perceptions are so basic that many animals have special adaptations designed to make them appear larger (e.g., the fanning peacock tail) or to disguise their identity from predators. Take a moment to think about how you could apply perceptual processes to your advantage.

GESTALT APPROACHES TO FORM PERCEPTION

Perception does much more for us than to maintain size and shape constancy in depth; it also organizes objects in a visual array into coherent groups. One way to understand how this organization occurs is from the structuralist approach to psychology, which was based on the notion that simple sensations constitute the building blocks of perceived form. The *structuralist* approach to form perception is *decompositional* (see chapter 1), and thus focused on breaking wholes into elementary components. This approach does little to address the ways in which these myriad sensations interact, emphasizing instead individual elements. The structuralist approach could not give any inkling as to how—or whether—the dynamic whole of a structure (e.g., a familiar tune) might differ from the sum of its parts (e.g., individual notes). The more functional Gestalt school of psychology emerged largely as a reaction against the extreme approach of structuralism. The Gestaltists' goal was directly to address the more global, holistic processes involved in perceiving structure in the environment.

Iconoclastic psychologists such as Kurt Koffka (1886–1941), Wolfgang Köhler (1887–1968), and Max Wertheimer (1880–1943) founded the **Gestalt approach to form perception** (from German, *Gestalt,* "form"), based on the notion that the whole differs from the sum of its individual parts (see chapter 1). The Gestalt approach has proven to be particularly useful for understanding how we perceive groups of objects or even parts of objects to form integral wholes. According to the Gestalt **law of Prägnanz,** we tend to perceive any given visual array in a way that most simply organizes the disparate elements into a stable and coherent form, rather than as a jumble of unintelligible, disorganized sensations. For example, we tend to perceive a focal figure and to perceive other sensations as forming a background for the figure on which we focus.

When you walk into a familiar room, you perceive that some things stand out (e.g., faces in photographs or posters) and that others fade into the background (e.g., undecorated walls and floors). A *figure* is any object perceived as being highlighted, almost always against, or in contrast to, some kind of receding, unhighlighted (back)*ground.* Figure 4.13 (a) illustrates the concept of **figure–ground.** You will probably first notice the light-colored lettering of the word *figure,* which indeed we perceive as the figure against the darker-lettered surrounding ground of the word *ground.* Similarly, in Figure 4.13 (b), you can see either a white vase against a black background or two silhouetted faces peering at each other against a white ground. Note, however, that it is virtually impossible to see both sets of objects simultaneously. Although you may switch rapidly back and forth between the vase and the faces, you cannot see them both at the same time.

FIGURE 4.13 FIGURE OR GROUND?

(a)

(b)

In these two Gestalt images, find which is the figure and which is the ground.

One of the reasons suggested as to why each figure makes sense is that both figures conform to the Gestalt principle of *symmetry*, in which the features appear to have balanced proportions around a central axis or a central point. Table 4.3 and Figure 4.14 summarize a few of the Gestalt principles of form perception, including figure–ground perception, *proximity, similarity, continuity, closure,* and *symmetry.* Each of these principles supports the overarching law of Prägnanz, in that each illustrates how we tend to perceive visual arrays in ways that most simply organize the disparate elements into a stable and coherent form. If you stop for a moment and look at your environment, you will perceive a coherent,

TABLE 4.3 GESTALT PRINCIPLES OF VISUAL PERCEPTION

The Gestalt principles of proximity, similarity, continuity, closure, and symmetry aid in our perception of forms.

Gestalt Principles	Principle	Figure Illustrating the Principle
Figure–ground	When perceiving a visual field, some objects (figures) seem prominent, and other aspects of the field recede into the background (ground).	Figure 4.13 shows a figure–ground vase, in which one way of perceiving the figures brings one perspective or object to the fore, and another way of perceiving the figures brings a different object or perspective to the fore and relegates the former foreground to the background.
Proximity	When we perceive an assortment of objects, we tend to see objects that are close to each other as forming a group.	In Figure 4.14 (a), we tend to see the middle four circles as two pairs of circles.
Similarity	We tend to group objects on the basis of their similarity.	In Figure 4.14 (b), we tend to see four columns of x's and o's, not four rows of alternating letters.
Continuity	We tend to perceive smoothly flowing or continuous forms rather than disrupted or discontinuous ones.	Figure 4.14 (c) shows two fragmented curves bisecting, which we perceive as two smooth curves, rather than as disjointed curves.
Closure	We tend to perceptually close up, or complete, objects that are not, in fact, complete.	Figure 4.14 (d) shows only disjointed, jumbled line segments, which you close up in order to see a triangle and a circle.
Symmetry	We tend to perceive objects as forming mirror images about their center.	For example, when viewing Figure 4.14 (e), a configuration of assorted brackets, we see the assortment as forming four sets of brackets, rather than eight individual items, because we integrate the symmetrical elements into coherent objects.

FIGURE 4.14 **ILLUSTRATION OF GESTALT PRINCIPLES OF PERCEPTION**

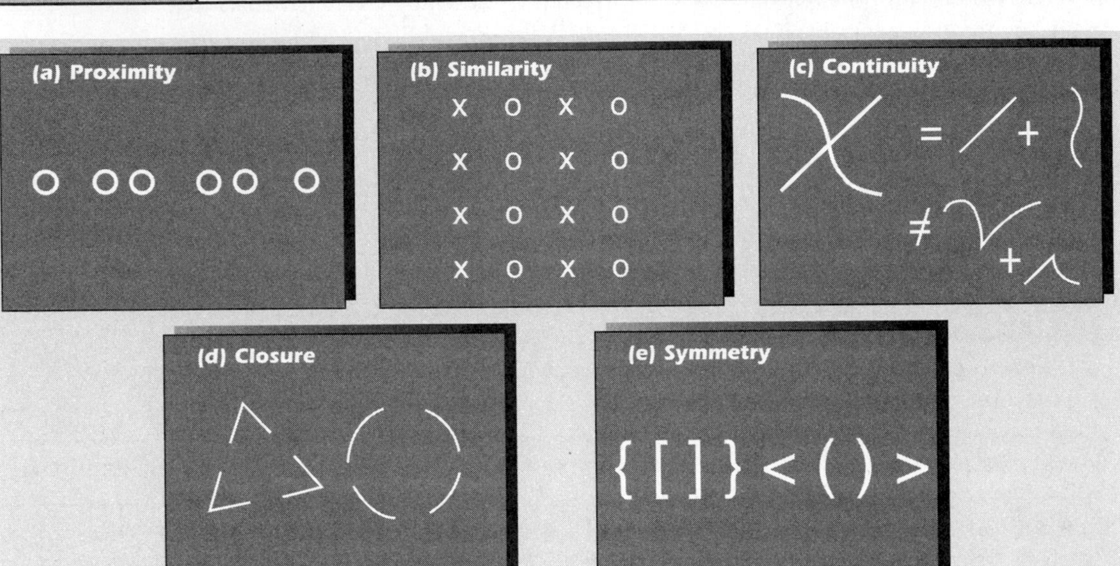

The Gestalt principles of form perception include perception of figure–ground, proximity, similarity, continuity, closure, and symmetry. Each principle demonstrates the fundamental law of Prägnanz, which suggests that through perception, we unify disparate visual stimuli into a coherent and stable whole.

complete, and continuous array of figures and background. You do not perceive holes in objects where your textbook occludes your view of them. If your book obscures part of the edge of a table, you still perceive the table as a continuous entity, not as one with gaping holes. In viewing the environment, we tend to perceive groupings of nearby objects (proximity) or of like objects (similarity), complete objects rather than partial ones (closure), continuous lines rather than broken ones (continuity), and symmetrical patterns rather than asymmetrical ones.

The Gestalt principles of form perception are remarkably simple, yet they characterize much of our perceptual organization (see S. Palmer, 1992). Although the Gestalt principles provide valuable descriptive insights into form and pattern perception, they offer few or no explanations of these phenomena. To understand how or why we perceive forms and patterns, we need to consider explanatory theories of perception.

Theoretical Approaches to Perception

Gestalt principles of perception focus on aspects of the stimuli that influence perception. Many other theoretical explanations of perception also start from the bottom, considering the physical stimulus—the observable form or pattern—being perceived, and then working their way up to higher order cognitive processes, such as organizing principles and concepts. Theories taking this approach are termed **bottom-up theories,** or sometimes, *data-driven* (i.e., stimulus-driven) *theories.* Not all theorists focus on the sensory data of the perceptual stimulus, however. Many theorists prefer **top-down theories,** focusing on the high-level cognitive processes, existing knowledge, and prior expectations that influence perception, then working their way down to considering the sensory data, such as the perceptual stimulus. Top-down and bottom-up approaches have been applied to virtually every aspect of cognition. As applied to perception, there are two major theories of perception, which manifest the bottom-up and top-down approaches. These theories are usually presented in opposition to each other, although to some extent, they deal with different aspects of the same phenomenon. First, we start at the bottom.

Bottom-Up Approaches: Direct Perception

How do you know the letter *A* when you see it? Easy to ask, hard to answer. Of course, it's an *A* because it looks like an *A.* What makes it look like an *A,* though, instead of like an *H?* Just how difficult it is to answer this question becomes apparent when you look at Figure 4.15. You will probably see the image in Figure 4.15 as the words *THE CAT,* and yet the *H* of *THE* is identical to the *A* of *CAT.* What subjectively feels like a simple process of pattern recognition is almost certainly quite complex. How do we connect what we perceive to what we have stored in our minds? Gestalt psychologists referred to this problem as the *Hoffding function* (Köhler, 1940), after nineteenth-century Danish psychologist Harald Hoffding, who questioned whether perception can be reduced to a simple view of associating what is seen with what is remembered. An influential and controversial theorist who also questioned associationism is James J. Gibson (1904–1980), whose theory of *direct perception* truly defines the bottom-up approach. In addition to the direct approach, the four main bottom-up theories of form and pattern perception are: template theories, prototype theories, feature theories, and structural-description theories.

According to Gibson's theory of **direct perception,** the array of information in our sensory receptors, including the sensory context, is all we need to perceive anything. In other words, we do not need higher cognitive processes or anything else to mediate

FIGURE 4.15 "WHAT ARE THE WORDS?"

THE CAT

When you read these words, you probably have no difficulty differentiating the A *from the* H. *Look more closely at each of these two letters. What features differentiate them?*

between our sensory experiences and our perceptions. Existing beliefs or higher-level inferential thought processes are not necessary for perception.

Because Gibson believed that in the real world, sufficient contextual information usually exists to make perceptual judgments, he claimed that we need *not* appeal to higher-level intelligent processes in order to explain perception. For example, Figure 4.16 shows that we do not need to have prior experience with particular shapes to perceive apparent shapes. J. J. Gibson (1979) believed that we use this contextual information directly; in essence, we are biologically tuned to respond to it. According to Gibson, when we observe depth cues such as texture gradients, those cues aid us to perceive directly the relative proximity or distance of objects and of parts of objects. Based on our analysis of the stable relationships among features of objects and settings in the real world, we directly perceive our environment (J. J. Gibson, 1950, 1954/1994; Mace, 1986) without the aid of complex thought processes.

Such contextual information might not be readily controlled in a laboratory experiment, but such information is likely to be available in a real-world setting. Gibson's model is sometimes referred to as an *ecological model* because of Gibson's concern with perception as it occurs in the everyday world (the ecological environment) rather than in laboratory situations, where less contextual information is available. Ecological constraints apply not only to initial perceptions, but to the ultimate internal representations that are formed from those perceptions (Hubbard, 1995; Shepard, 1984), which are considered in later chapters. Continuing to wave the Gibsonian banner is Eleanor Gibson (1991, 1992), who has conducted landmark research in infant perception, such as noting that infants (who certainly lack much prior knowledge and experience) quickly develop many aspects of perceptual awareness, including depth perception.

The direct-perception viewpoint does not integrate the processes of intelligence, as usually conceived, with the processes of perception. In this viewpoint, the information that we need to understand what we see inheres in the stimulus information. Nevertheless,

FIGURE 4.16 PERCEIVED AMORPHOUS SHAPES

The perception of these apparent amorphous shapes is consistent with James Gibson's direct-perception view that contextual information alone is sufficient for perception to occur, without additional knowledge or high-level thinking. Prior knowledge about the contexts does not lead to our perception of the triangle or the pear.

intelligence still plays a role in cognitive processing, but after the perceptual processing has been completed. Thus, this model views the roles of perception and intelligence as separate and possibly sequential, whereas the constructive-perception viewpoint sees them as interactive. Next, we consider some non-Gibsonian bottom-up approaches to pattern recognition before moving on to the constructive-perception view.

TEMPLATE THEORIES

One theory says that we have stored in our minds myriad sets of **templates,** which are highly detailed models for patterns we might potentially recognize. We recognize a pattern by comparing it with our set of templates and then choosing the exact template that perfectly matches what we observe (Selfridge & Neisser, 1960). We see examples of *template matching* in our everyday lives. Fingerprints are matched in this way, and machines rapidly process imprinted numerals on checks by comparing them to templates. Increasingly, products of all kinds are identified with universal product codes (UPCs or "bar codes"), which can be scanned and identified by computers at the time of purchase.

In each of the aforementioned instances, the goal of finding one perfect match and disregarding imperfect matches well suits the task. You would be alarmed to find that your bank's numeral-recognition system failed to register a deposit to your account because it was programmed to accept an ambiguous character according to what seemed to be a best guess. For template matching, only an exact match will do—which is exactly what you want from a bank computer. However, for everyday situations, your perceptual system would rarely work if you required exact matches for every stimulus you were to recognize. Imagine, for example, needing mental templates for every possible percept of the face of someone you love: one for each facial expression, each angle of viewing, each addition or removal of makeup, each hairdo, and so on.

Letters of the alphabet are simpler than faces and other complex stimuli, yet template-matching theories also fail to explain some aspects of the perception of letters. For one thing, such theories cannot easily account for our perception of the letters and words in Figure 4.15. We identify two different letters *(A* and *H)* from only one physical form. Hoffding (1891) noted other problems. We can recognize an *A* as an *A,* despite variations in the size, orientation, and form in which the letter is written. Are we to believe that we have mental templates for each possible size, orientation, and form of a letter? In addition to the unwieldiness of storing, organizing, and retrieving so many templates in memory, how could we possibly anticipate and create so many templates for every conceivable object of perception?

PROTOTYPE THEORIES

The unwieldiness and rigidity of template theories soon led to an alternative explanation of pattern perception: prototype-matching theory. A **prototype** is not a rigid, specific, concrete model, but rather, it is a best-guess example of a class of related objects or patterns, which integrates all of the most typical (most frequently observed) features of the form or pattern. That is, a prototype is highly representative of a pattern but is not intended as a precise, identical match to all other patterns for which it is a model. A great deal of research has been found to support the prototype-matching approach (e.g., Franks & Bransford, 1971). The prototype model seems to explain perception of configurations of dots (e.g., a triangle, a diamond, an *F,* an *M,* or a random array; Posner, Goldsmith, & Welton, 1967; Posner & Keele, 1968); highly simplified line drawings of faces (S. Reed,

1972); and even rather well-defined faces created with the police Identikits, often used for witness identification (Solso & McCarthy, 1981; see Figure 4.17).

Surprisingly, many researchers investigating perceptual prototypes have found that we seem to be able to form prototypes even when we have never seen an exemplar that exactly matches the prototype. That is, the prototypes we form seem to integrate all of the most typical features of a pattern, even when we have never seen a single instance in which all of the typical features are integrated at one time (Neumann, 1977). To illustrate this point, some researchers generated various series of patterns, such as the patterns in Figure 4.17 (a and c), based on a prototype. They then showed participants the series of generated patterns but not the prototype on which the patterns were based. Later, they again showed

FIGURE 4.17 PROTOTYPE MATCHING—EVEN WITHOUT THE PROTOTYPE

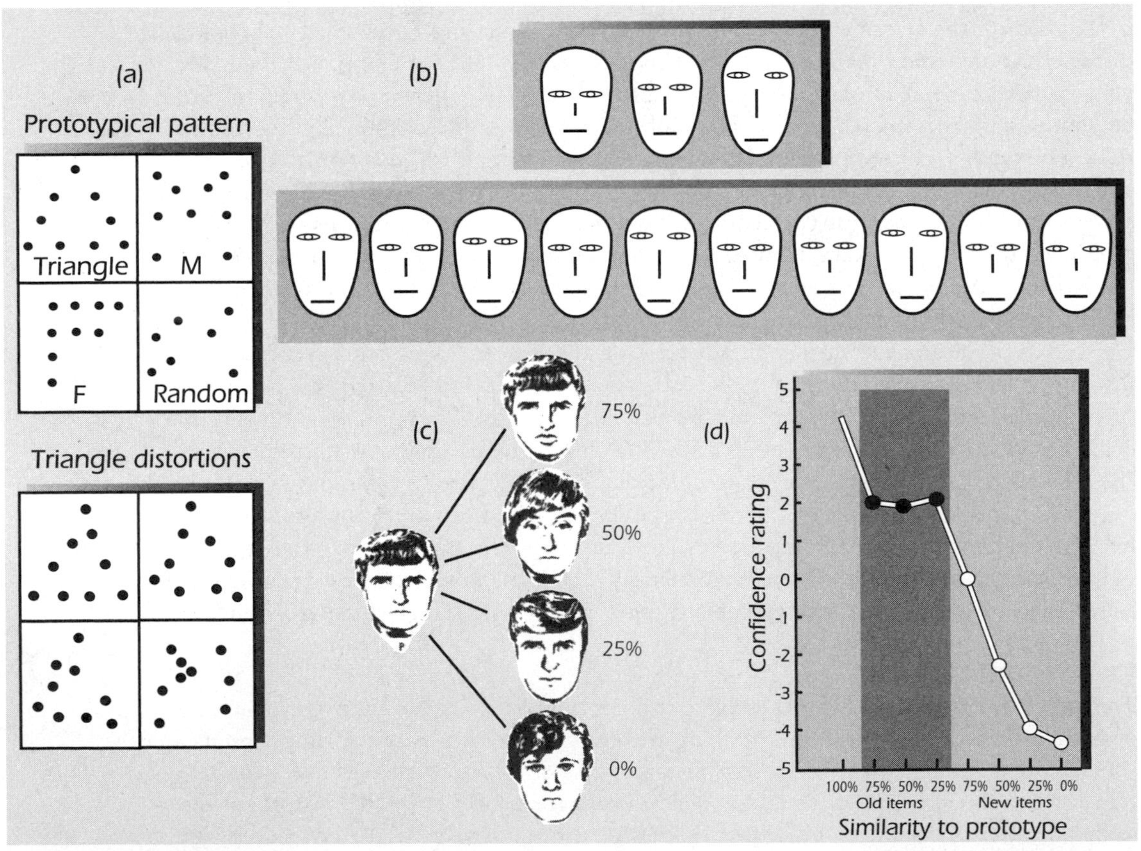

(a) These dot configurations are similar to those used in the experiment by Michael Posner and his colleagues (Posner, Goldsmith, & Welton, 1967; Posner & Keele, 1968). (b) These highly simplified drawings of faces are similar to those used by Stephen Reed (1972). (c) These faces are similar to those created in the experiment by Robert Solso and John McCarthy (1981). (d) This graph illustrates Solso and McCarthy's findings, indicating the frequency of perceived recognition of each face, including the recognition of a prototypical face never observed by the subjects.

participants the series of generated patterns, as well as some additional patterns, including both distractors and the prototype pattern. Under these conditions, participants not only identified the prototype pattern as being one they had seen previously (e.g., Posner & Keele, 1968), but also gave particularly high ratings of their confidence in having seen the prototype previously (Solso & McCarthy, 1981).

FEATURE THEORIES

Yet another alternative explanation of pattern and form perception may be found in **feature-matching** theories, according to which we attempt to match features of a pattern to features stored in memory, rather than to match a whole pattern to a template or a prototype. One such feature-matching model has been called "pandemonium," based on the notion that metaphorical "demons" with specific duties receive and analyze the features of a stimulus (Selfridge, 1959), as shown in Figure 4.18.

Oliver Selfridge's model describes "image demons," which pass on a retinal image to "feature demons." Each feature demon calls out when there are matches between the stimulus and the given feature. These matches are yelled out at demons at the next level of the hierarchy, the "cognitive (thinking) demons," which shout out possible patterns stored in memory that conform to one or more of the features noticed by the feature demons. A "decision demon" listens to the pandemonium of the cognitive demons and decides on what has been seen, based on which cognitive demon is shouting the most frequently (i.e., which has the most matching features).

Although Selfridge's model is one of the most widely known models, other feature models have been proposed. Most feature models also distinguish not only different features, but also different kinds of features, such as global versus local features. *Local features* constitute the small-scale or detailed aspects of a given pattern. Although there is no consensus as to what exactly constitutes a local feature, we can nevertheless generally distinguish such features from *global features,* the features that give a form its overall shape. Consider, for example, the stimuli depicted in Figure 4.19 (a) and (b). These stimuli are of the type used in some research on pattern perception (Navon, 1977). Globally, the stimuli in panels (a) and (b) form the letter *H.* In panel (a), the local features (small *H*'s) correspond to the global ones, whereas in panel (b), comprising many local letter *S*'s, they do not.

David Navon asked participants to identify the stimuli at either the global or the local level. When the local letters were small and positioned close together, participants could identify stimuli at the global level more quickly than at the local level. Moreover, when participants were required to identify stimuli at the global level, whether the local features matched the global ones did not matter: They responded equally rapidly whether the global *H* was made up of local *H*'s or of local *S*'s. However, when participants were asked to respond at the local level, they responded more quickly if the global features agreed with the local ones. In other words, they were slowed down if they had to identify local *S*'s combining to form a global *H* instead of identifying local *H*'s combining to form a global *H.* This pattern of results is called the *global precedence effect.*

In contrast, when letters are more widely spaced, as in panels (a) and (b) of Figure 4.20, the effect is reversed, and a *local-precedence effect* appears. That is, the participants more quickly identify the local features of the individual letters than the global ones, and the local features interfere with the global recognition in cases of contradictory stimuli (M. Martin, 1979). Other limitations (e.g., the size of the stimuli) hold as well, and other kinds of features also influence perception.

FIGURE 4.18 **PANDEMONIUM**

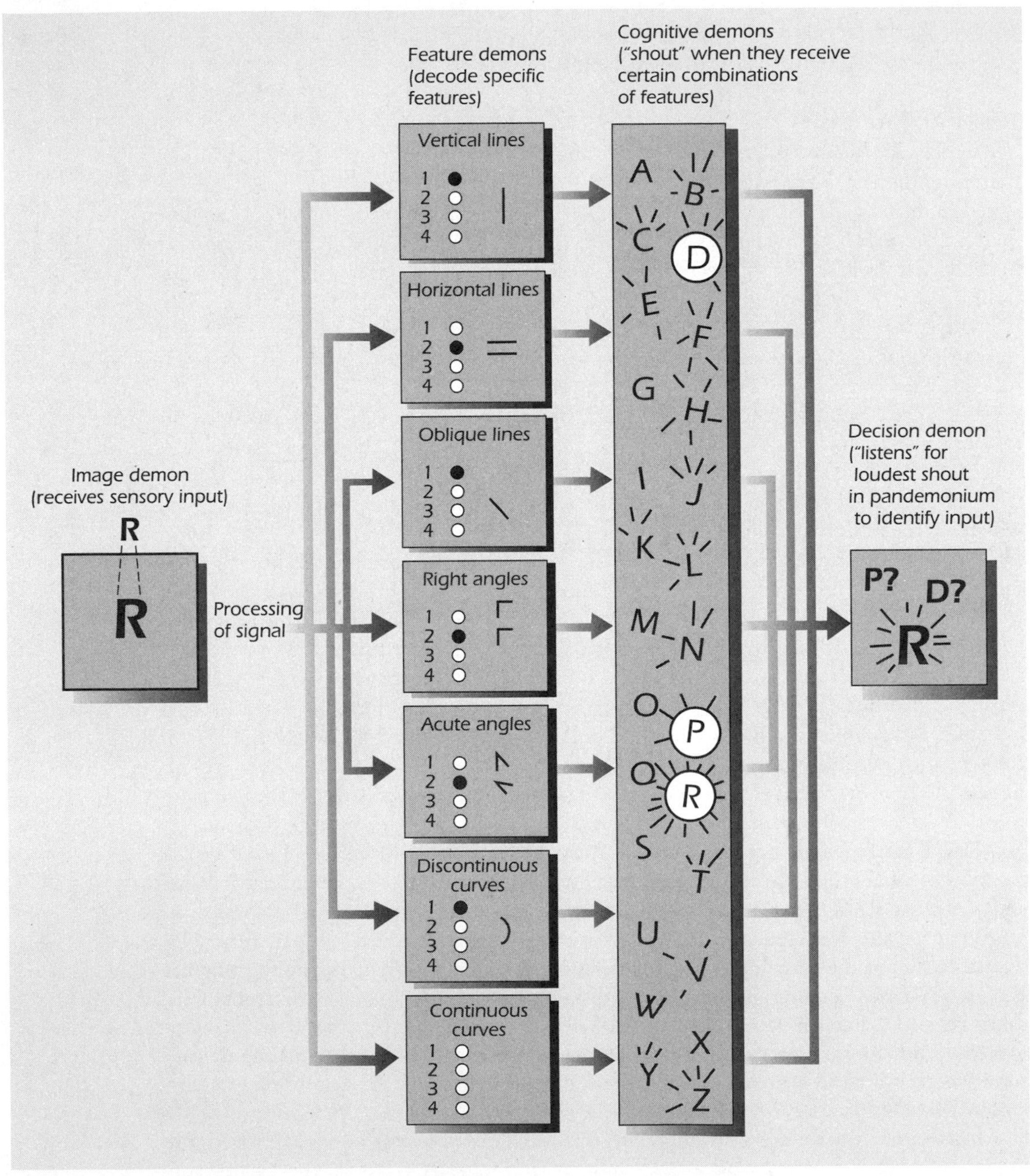

According to Oliver Selfridge's feature-matching model, we recognize patterns by matching observed features to features already stored in memory. We recognize the patterns for which we have found the greatest number of matches.

FIGURE 4.19 **GLOBAL-PRECEDENCE EFFECTS**

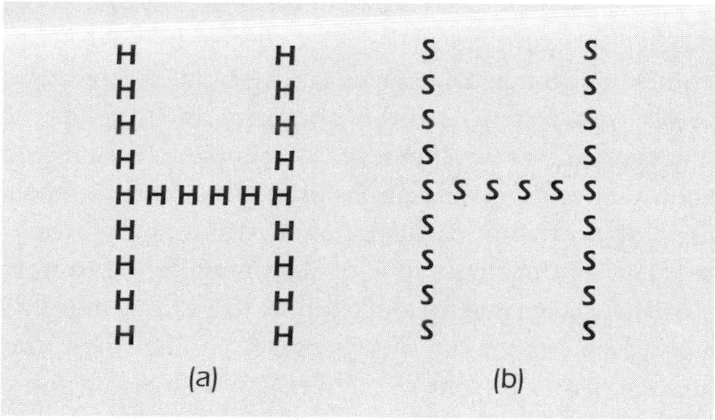

```
H         H     S         S
H         H     S         S
H         H     S         S
H         H     S         S
H H H H H H     S S S S S S
H         H     S         S
H         H     S         S
H         H     S         S
H         H     S         S
    (a)             (b)
```

Compare panel (a) (global H's *made of local* H's*) with panel (b) (global* H's *made of local* S's*). All the local letters are tightly spaced.*

FIGURE 4.20 **LOCAL-PRECEDENCE EFFECTS**

```
H       H       S       S

H       H       S       S

H   H   H       S   S   S

H       H       S       S

H       H       S       S
   (a)             (b)
```

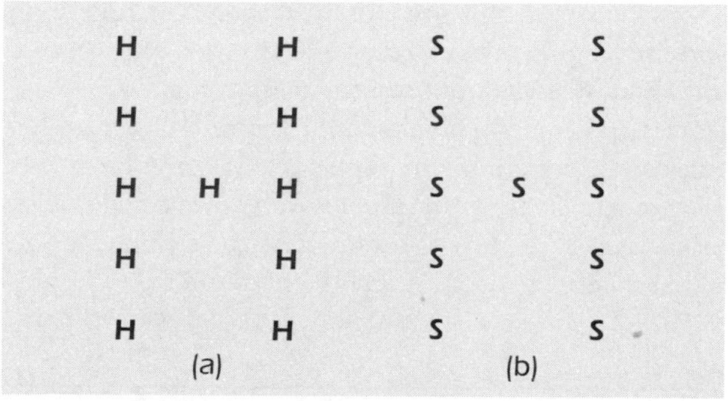

Compare panels (a) and (b), in which the local letters are widely spaced. In which figure (Figure 4.19 or Figure 4.20) do you note the global-precedence effect, and in which figure do you note the local-precedence effect?

Some support for feature theories comes from neurological and physiological research. Specifically, Nobel laureates David Hubel and Torsten Wiesel (1963, 1968, 1979), using single-cell recording techniques with animals, carefully measured the responses of individual neurons in the visual cortex and mapped those neurons to corresponding visual stimuli for particular locations in the visual field (see chapter 2). Their research showed that specific neurons of the visual cortex in the brain respond to varying stimuli presented to specific regions of the retina corresponding to these neurons. Each individual cortical neuron, therefore, can be mapped to a specific *receptive field* on the retina, with a disproportionately large amount of the visual cortex being devoted to neurons mapped to receptive fields in the foveal region of the retina.

Surprisingly, most of the cells in the cortex do not respond simply to spots of light, but rather to "specifically oriented line segments" (Hubel & Wiesel, 1979, p. 9). What's more, these cells seem to show a hierarchical structure in the degree of complexity of the stimuli to which they respond. In general, the size of the receptive field increases, as does the complexity of the stimulus required to prompt a response, as the stimulus proceeds through the visual system to higher levels in the cortex. As evidence of this hierarchy, Hubel and Wiesel isolated two kinds of visual cortex neurons (see Figure 4.21): "simple cells" and "complex cells."

Simple cells receive input from the neurons projecting from the thalamus (see chapter 2), then fire in response to lines of particular orientations and positions in the receptive field, the specifically stimulating orientation or position differing from one cell to another. A particular cell might also preferentially respond to particular light/dark boundaries, bright lines on dark backgrounds, or the reverse; even the line's thickness may affect whether the cell responds to the stimulus. Hubel and Wiesel call the various lines "features," so the neurons that detect and respond to them are called "feature detectors."

Hubel and Wiesel (1979) guessed that groups of these simple cells feed into *complex cells* (see Figure 4.22). Each complex cell fires in response to lines of particular orientations, located anywhere in the receptive field of the group of simple cells, that feed into the given complex cell. Complex cells may receive input from one eye only or from both eyes (Hubel & Wiesel, 1979), and they appear insensitive to the particular type of light/dark contrasts of a line segment, as long as the segment is oriented appropriately (Carlson, 1992). Some complex cells fire only in response to line segments of particular orientations and precise lengths in the receptive field.

Based on Hubel and Wiesel's work, other investigators have found feature detectors that respond to corners and angles (DeValois & DeValois, 1980; Shapley & Lennie, 1985). In some areas of the cortex, certain highly sophisticated complex cells (sometimes termed *hypercomplex cells*) fire maximally only in response to very specific shapes (e.g., a hand or a face), regardless of the size of the given stimulus. As the stimulus decreasingly resembles the optimal shape, these cells are decreasingly likely to fire.

FIGURE 4.21 | HUBEL AND WIESEL'S FEATURE DETECTORS

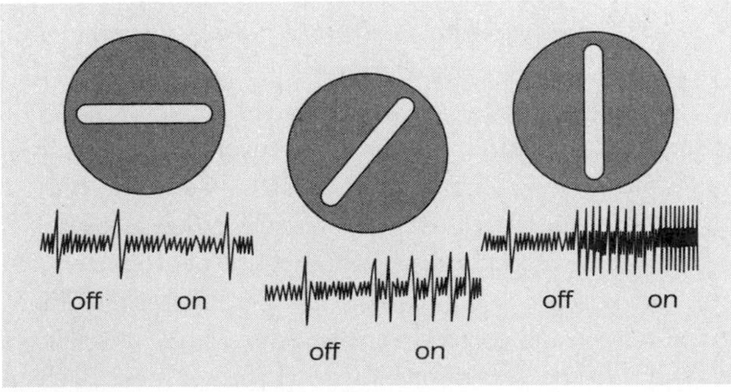

David Hubel and Torsten Wiesel discovered that cells in our visual cortex become activated only when they detect the sensation of line segments of particular orientations.

FIGURE 4.22 **HIERARCHICAL STRUCTURE OF FEATURE DETECTORS**

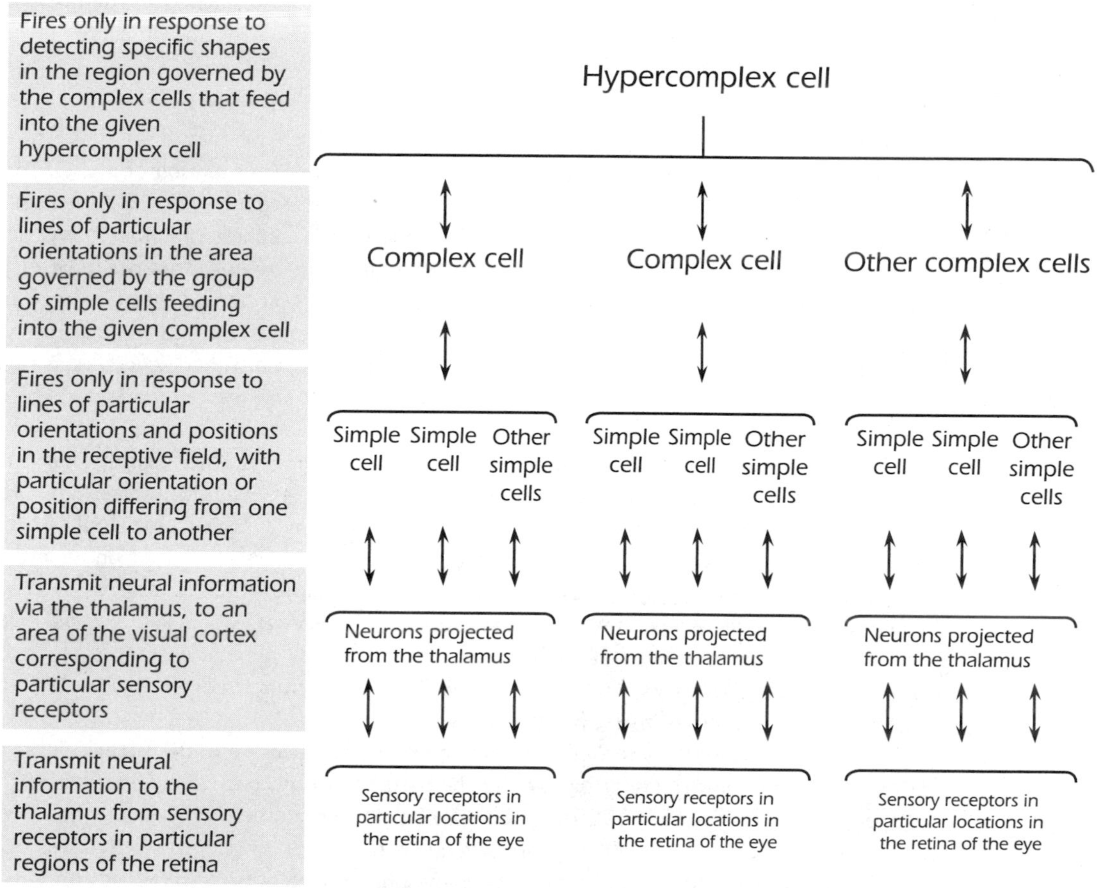

The process of visual perception appears to involve at least three levels of hierarchically organized neurons—simple cells, complex cells, and hypercomplex cells.

Other recent work on visual perception has identified separate neural pathways in the cerebral cortex for processing different aspects of the same stimuli (De Yoe & Van Essen, 1988; Köhler, Kapur, Moscovitch, Winocur, & Houle, 1995), termed the "what" and "where" pathways. The "what" pathway descends from the primary visual cortex in the occipital lobe (see chapter 2) toward the temporal lobes, and is mainly responsible for processing the color, shape, and identity of visual stimuli. The "where" pathway ascends from the occipital lobe toward the parietal lobe, and is responsible for processing location and motion information. Thus, feature information feeds into at least two different systems for identifying objects and events in the environment.

Researchers such as Hubel and Wiesel have helped us to understand how we may perceive lines of various lengths and orientations, as well as more complex configurations of

Irving Biederman *is William M. Keck professor of cognitive neuroscience at the University of Southern California. He is best known for his work in high-level vision, and in shape recognition, in particular. His theory of geons shows a possible way in which various images of objects can be decomposed into a set of fundamental units.*

line segments, based on how the brain works. However, neither they nor others would argue that their insights into feature detectors can account for the richness and complexity of visual perception. Once discrete features have been analyzed according to their orientations, how are they integrated into a form we can recognize as particular objects?

STRUCTURAL-DESCRIPTION THEORY

Irving Biederman (1987) has hypothesized a means by which we may form stable three-dimensional mental representations of objects, based on the manipulation of a few simple geometric shapes. Specifically, Biederman (1990/1993b) proposed a set of three-dimensional *geons* (for *geo*metrical *ions*), "such as bricks, cylinders, wedges, cones, and their curved axis counterparts" (p. 314). According to Biederman's **recognition-by-components (RBC) theory,** we quickly recognize objects by observing the edges of objects and then decomposing the objects into geons, which also can be recomposed into alternative arrangements. Just as a small set of letters can be manipulated to compose countless words and sentences, a small number of geons can be used to build up many basic shapes, and then myriad basic objects (see Figure 4.23).

Because the geons are simple and are viewpoint-invariant (i.e., discernible from various viewpoints), the objects constructed from geons are easily recognized from many perspectives, despite visual noise. According to Biederman (1993a), his RBC theory parsimoniously explains how we are able to recognize the general classification for multitudinous objects quickly, automatically, and accurately, despite changes in viewpoint, and even under many situations in which the stimulus object is degraded in some way. Biederman's RBC theory better explains how we may recognize general instances of chairs, lamps, and faces than it explains how we recognize particular chairs or particular faces (e.g., your own face or your best friend's face).

Irvin Rock *was an adjunct professor of psychology at the University of California, Berkeley. He is well known for his championing of the role of problem solving in perception and the claim that perception is indirect. He also originated the study of one-trial learning and has made major contributions to the study of the moon and other perceptual illusions.*

Biederman himself has recognized that aspects of his theory require further work. By his own account, "how the relations among the parts of an object are to be described is still an open issue" (Biederman, 1990/1993b, p.16). Another problem with Biederman's approach, and the bottom-up approach in general, is how to account for the effects of prior expectations and environmental context on some phenomena of pattern perception.

TOP-DOWN APPROACHES: CONSTRUCTIVE PERCEPTION

In contrast to the bottom-up approach to perception is the top-down, constructive approach. Cognitivists Jerome Bruner (1957), Richard Gregory (1980), and Irvin Rock (1983), building on the earlier work of Hermann von Helmholtz (1909/1962), have been among the chief architects of the constructive (conceptually driven) perception approach. In **constructive perception,** the perceiver builds (constructs) a cognitive understanding (perception) of a stimulus, using sensory information as the foundation for the structure, but also using other sources of information to build the perception. This viewpoint is also known as *intelligent perception,* because it states that higher order thinking plays an important role in perception.

For example, picture yourself driving down a road you have never traveled before. As you approach a blind intersection, you see an octagonal red sign with white lettering, bearing the letters "ST_P," with an overgrown vine cutting between the *T* and the *P.*

FIGURE 4.23 BIEDERMAN'S GEONS

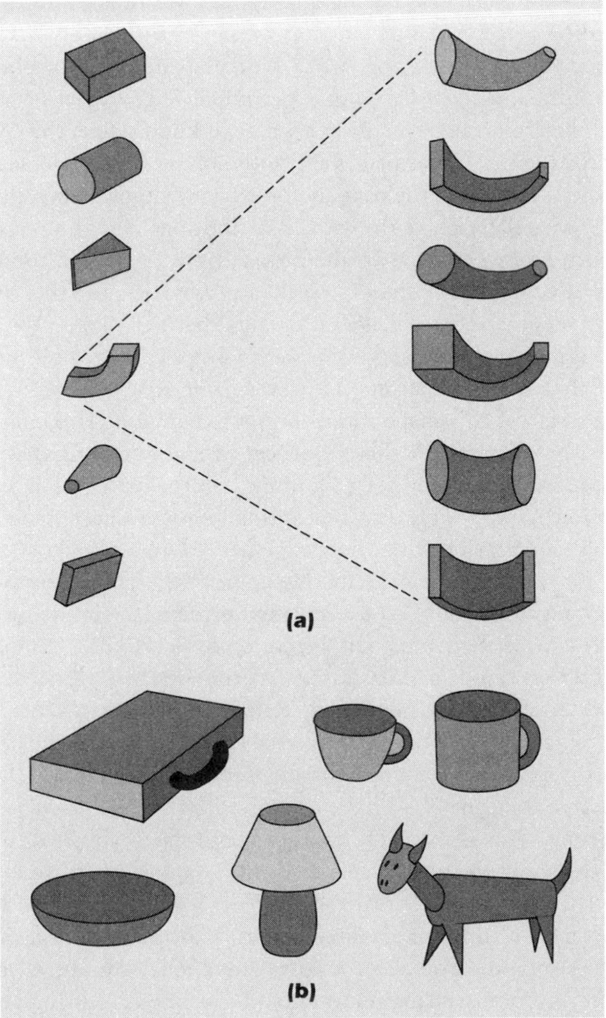

Irving Biederman amplified feature-matching theory by proposing a set of elementary components of patterns, which he based on variations in three-dimensional shapes derived from a cone.

Chances are, you will construct from your sensations a perception of a stop sign, and you will respond appropriately. Similarly, constructivists would suggest that our perceptions of size and shape constancy indicate that high-level constructive processes are at work during perception. Another type of perceptual constancy even more clearly illustrates top-down construction of perception: In *color constancy,* we perceive that the color of an object remains the same despite changes in lighting that alter the hue. Even when the lighting becomes so dim that color sensations are virtually absent, however, we perceive bananas as yellow, plums as purple, and so on.

According to constructivists, during perception, we quickly form and test various hypotheses regarding percepts, based on what we sense (the sensory data), what we know (knowledge stored in memory), and what we can infer (using high-level cognitive processes). In perception, we consider prior expectations (e.g., expecting to see an approaching friend whom we had arranged to meet), what we know about the context (e.g., trains often ride on railroad tracks, but airplanes and automobiles usually do not), or what we reasonably can infer, based both on the data and on what we know about the data. According to constructivists, we usually make the correct attributions regarding our visual sensations because we perform *unconscious inference,* the process by which we unconsciously assimilate information from a number of sources to create a perception. In other words, using more than one source of information, we make judgments that we are not even aware of making.

In the stop-sign example, sensory information implies that the sign is a meaningless assortment of oddly spaced consonants. However, your *prior learning* tells you something important—that a sign of this shape and color, posted at an intersection of roadways, and containing these three letters, in this sequence, probably means that you should stop thinking about the odd letters and start slamming on the brakes. The key feature of constructive perception is that successful perception requires intelligence and thought in combining sensory information with knowledge gained from previous experience.

One reason for favoring the constructive approach is that bottom-up (data-driven) theories of perception do not fully explain **context effects** (the influences of the surrounding environment on perception, e.g., our perception of "THE CAT" in Figure 4.15). Fairly dramatic context effects can be demonstrated experimentally (e.g., Biederman, 1972; Biederman, Glass, & Stacy, 1973; Biederman, Rabinowitz, Glass, & Stacy, 1974). In one study, people were asked to identify objects after they had viewed the objects in either an appropriate or an inappropriate context for the items (S. E. Palmer, 1975). For example, participants might see a scene of a kitchen followed by stimuli such as a loaf of bread, a mailbox, and a drum. Objects that were appropriate to the established context, such as the loaf of bread in this example, were recognized more rapidly than were objects that were inappropriate to the established context.

Perhaps even more striking is a context effect known as the *configural-superiority effect* (Pomerantz, 1981). Suppose you show a participant four stimuli, all of them diagonal lines. Three of the lines are slanting one way, and one line is slanting the other way. The participant's task is to identify which stimulus is unlike the others (e.g., see Figure 4.24 a). Now suppose that you show participants four stimuli, all of them comprising three lines (see Figure 4.24 c). Three of the stimuli are shaped like triangles, one is not. In each case, the stimulus is a diagonal line (Figure 4.24 a) plus other lines (Figure 4.24 b). Thus, the stimuli in this second condition are more complex variations of the stimuli in the first condition. Participants can more quickly spot which of the three-sided figures is different from the others than they can spot which of the lines is different from the others.

In a similar vein, Naomi Weisstein and her colleagues (Lanze, Weisstein, & Harris, 1982; Weisstein & Harris, 1974) have shown an *object-superiority effect,* in which a target line that forms a part of a drawing of a three-dimensional object is identified more accurately than a target that forms a part of a disconnected two-dimensional pattern. These findings parallel findings in the study of letter and word recognition.

FIGURE 4.24 CONFIGURAL-SUPERIORITY EFFECT

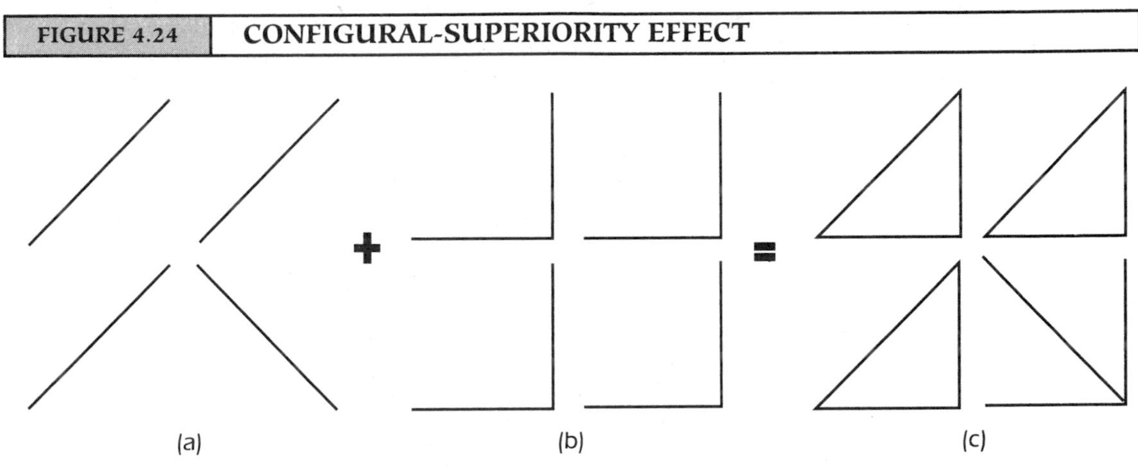

Subjects more readily perceive differences among integrated configurations comprising multiple lines (c) than they do solitary lines (a). In this figure, the lines in (b) are added to the lines in (a), to form shapes in (c), thereby making (c) more complex than (a).

The viewpoint of constructive or intelligent perception shows the central relation between perception and intelligence. According to this viewpoint, intelligence is an integral part of our perceptual processing. We do not perceive simply in terms of what is "out there in the world," but in terms of the expectations and other cognitions we bring to our interaction with the world. On this view, intelligence and perceptual processes interact in the formation of our beliefs about what it is that we are encountering in our everyday contacts with the world at large.

An extreme top-down position would so drastically underestimate the importance of sensory data that we would be susceptible to gross inaccuracies of perception. We would frequently form hypotheses and expectancies that inadequately evaluated the sensory data available (e.g., if we expected to see a friend, and someone else came into view, we might inadequately consider the perceptible differences between the friend and a stranger). Thus, an extreme constructivist view of perception would be highly error-prone and inefficient. However, an extreme bottom-up position would not allow for any influence of past experience or knowledge on perception. Why store knowledge that has no use for the perceiver? Neither extreme is ideal for explaining perception—what is more fruitful is to consider ways in which bottom-up and top-down processes interact to form meaningful percepts.

SYNTHESIZING THE TWO APPROACHES

Both theoretical approaches have been able to garner empirical support (cf. Cutting & Kozlowski, 1977, vs. S. E. Palmer, 1975), so how do we decide between the two? On one level, the constructive-perception theory, which is more top-down, seems to contradict direct-perception theory, which is more bottom-up. Constructivists emphasize the importance of prior knowledge in combination with relatively simple and ambiguous information from the sensory receptors. In contrast, direct-perception theorists emphasize the completeness of the information in the receptors themselves, suggesting that perception occurs simply and directly, with little need for complex information processing.

Instead of viewing these theoretical approaches as incompatible, we may gain deeper insight into perception by considering the approaches to be complementary. Sensory information may be more richly informative and less ambiguous in interpreting experiences than the constructivists would suggest but less so than the direct-perception theorists would assert. Similarly, perceptual processes may be more complex than hypothesized by Gibsonian theorists, particularly under conditions where the sensory stimuli appear only briefly or are degraded. *Degraded* stimuli are less informative for various reasons; for example, the stimuli may be partially obscured, weakened by poor lighting, incomplete, or distorted by illusory cues or other visual "noise" (distracting visual stimulation analogous to audible noise). We likely use a combination of information from the sensory receptors and our past knowledge to make sense of what we perceive.

A Computational Theory of Perception

David Marr (1982) proposed a theory of visual perception that considers the richness of the sensory information without dismissing altogether the value of prior knowledge and experience in perception. Although Marr could not be considered a constructivist, he recognized the complexity of the cognitive processes required for perceiving a mental representation of the environment, based on raw sensory data. In addition, Marr's theory incorporates some of the descriptive principles of perception, such as depth cues, perceptual constancies, and Gestalt principles of form perception.

Marr proposed that raw sensory data from the retinas of the eyes can be organized through the use of three kinds of features: edges, contours, and regions of similarity. *Edges* form the boundaries between and around objects and parts of objects. *Contour* features differentiate one kind of surface from another. In a map, for example, contour lines indicate the differing elevations of land areas. Similarly, on the retina, various kinds of contours provide different kinds of information. For example, one kind of contour represents a convex surface, as would be found on a rounded ball of clay, and another kind of contour represents a *concave* (curving inward) surface, as would be found if someone bashed in the ball of clay and left a sizable indentation (see Figure 4.25). *Regions of similarity* are areas that are largely undifferentiated by distinctive features.

Marr showed how a model of perception could be specified in sufficient detail to be simulated by a computer; hence, his approach is considered a *computational model.* According to Marr (1982), the human brain uses a three-step process for computing a 3-D percept of what we see. First, the brain creates a 2-D primal sketch of the sensory information that reaches the eyes. This sketch represents an object, like a chair, in just two dimensions. Then the brain creates a $2^1/_2$-D sketch of the data, which considers depth cues and surface orientations. For example, now the perception of the chair includes some aspects of depth but not others, so the sketch is incomplete with regard to depth information. This sketch also shows the orientation of the chair in the picture plane (e.g., right side up or maybe even backwards). Finally the brain creates a 3-D model, which represents three-dimensional objects and the spatial interrelationships among the objects. Now consider these aspects in more detail.

FIGURE 4.25 | PERCEPTION OF A CONTOUR

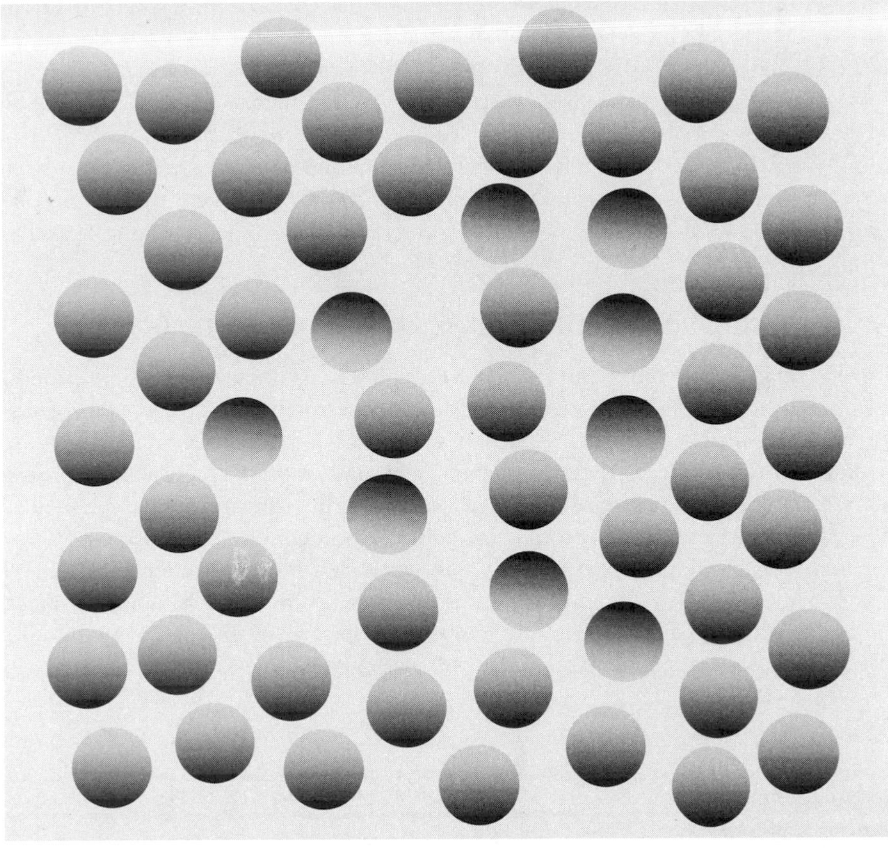

Are these contours concave or convex? Now turn the page upside-down, and tell whether the contours are concave or convex. Our sensitivity to contour features is emphasized in David Marr's computational model of perception.

First, the sensory receptors in the retina send information to the visual areas of the brain, which map out a *2-D primal sketch* of what is observed. This sketch takes sensory data regarding changes in light intensity and maps out edges, contours, and regions of similarity, entirely based on the observer's sensations from a given viewpoint. For example, a bowl of fruit on a table might be sketched as a pattern of edges between and around fruits, between the bowl and the table, and between the table and the background; contours might be observed in the convexities of rounded fruits such as oranges, grapes, or peaches; regions of similarity might be detected in the background, in the expanse of the table surrounding the fruit bowl, and so on.

Second, the brain converts the primal sketch into what Marr termed the *2$^1/_2$-D sketch,* which enhances the 2-D primal sketch by considering the observer's view of the orientations of surfaces, as well as depth cues such as shading, texture gradients, motion, and binocular cues. For example, shadings and other depth cues would indicate which fruits or which legs of the table were nearer to the observer and which were farther.

Third, the brain then further elaborates the $2^1/_2$-D sketch to build a *3-D model,* which fully represents the three-dimensional shapes of objects and the spatial interrelationships among the objects perceived. This 3-D model includes the observer's spatial relationship with the objects but is independent of the observer's viewpoint. For example, each fruit would be represented as a discrete 3-D object despite the observer's view of only one surface of the object. Objects that were obscured from view, such as fruits at the back of the bowl or a fourth leg of the table, would still be represented in the 3-D model. It is in forming the 3-D model that the individual's prior knowledge and experiences may influence perception (e.g., knowing that a fourth leg of a table is likely to exist despite its absence from view), although Marr did not specify how this influence might be exerted.

SPATIOTEMPORAL BOUNDARY-FORMATION THEORY

Philip Kellman and Thomas Shipley (1991; Shipley & Kellman, 1994) have proposed a *spatiotemporal boundary-formation theory,* a model for describing how we perceive objects and boundaries between objects, based on spatial information and temporal changes in the environment. According to these researchers, the same process that leads us to perceive illusory contours (as in Figures 4.3 and 4.25) also permits us to perceive a coherent unity of objects and surfaces even when they are partially occluded by interposing objects. We use *spatial* (static) information when we view stationary objects from a stationary viewpoint. We use *temporal* ("kinematic") information when we observe moving objects or when we view objects from a changing viewpoint while we ourselves are moving. To get an idea of how we use spatial and temporal information, try the following investigation.

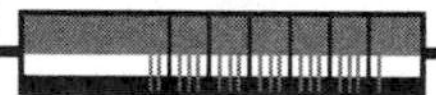

INVESTIGATING COGNITIVE PSYCHOLOGY

Stand your book upright on its bottom edge on a surface such as a table. Grasp two pencils, and hold them so that part of each pencil is behind the upright book, with part of one pencil jutting to the left and part of the other poking out to the right of the book. Move the two pencils into and out of alignment, and note how the changes in alignment influence your perception of the pencils as being either one continuous pencil or two distinct pencils.

Next, try holding one pencil stationary, and move the other pencil along the side of the book. The movement of one pencil, but not of the other, also influences your perception of whether the pencils are part of one continuous object or are discrete objects. Put down one of the pencils, and hold the other pencil horizontally, to the right of the book, in full view. Gradually move the pencil behind the surface of the book, and observe the changes in your view of the pencil. Finally, reposition the pencil, sliding it across the front surface of the book. According to Shipley and Kellman, when an interposing object (e.g., the pencil) creates a concave break in another surface (e.g., the book), we perceive the underlying continuity of the surface of the occluded object, as well as the spatial relationships (depths) of the objects.

Thus far, we have discussed theories regarding how we mentally process the sensations we receive from our environment in a way that helps us to make sense of (mentally represent) three-dimensional objects and space. In addition to being able to manipulate objects within three-dimensional space, we manage to recognize particular patterns, such as the face of a loved one or the letters on a page.

To summarize, current theories concerning the ways we perceive patterns explain some, but not all, of the phenomena we encounter in the study of form and pattern perception. Given the complexity of the process, it is impressive that we understand as much as we do. At the same time, clearly a comprehensive theory is still some way off. Such a theory would need to account fully for the kinds of context effects described here. A particular kind of pattern perception has attracted the attention of cognitive psychologists: the specific ways in which we perceive words and larger passages of text.

Reading: Bottom-Up and Top-Down Processes

Because reading is such a complex process, a discussion of how we engage in this process could be placed in any of a number of chapters in this book. At a minimum, reading involves language, memory, thinking, and intelligence, as well as perception. The ability to read is fundamental to our everyday lives, and people who have **dyslexia**—difficulty in deciphering, reading, and comprehending text—can suffer greatly in a society that puts a high premium on fluent reading. The various kinds of dyslexia and the specific suggested causes of it go beyond the scope of this textbook, but it has been suggested that problems in phonological processing, and thus in word identification, pose "the major stumbling block in learning to read" (Pollatsek & Rayner, 1989, p. 403).

Perceptual Issues in Reading

If you view your own text processing, you can see that the ability to read is truly remarkable: You somehow manage to perceive the correct letter when it is presented in a wide array of *typestyles* and **typefaces,** in CAPITAL and lowercase forms, and even in cursive forms. Such processes involve the perception of *orthographic* (relating to visual form) aspects of printed words. Then you must translate the letter into a sound, creating a *phonological code* (relating to sound). This translation is particularly difficult in English because English does not always ensure a direct correspondence between a letter and a sound. George Bernard Shaw, playwright and lover of the English language, underscored the illogic of English spellings when he suggested that, in English, it would be perfectly reasonable to pronounce "ghoti" as "fish." You would pronounce the "gh" as in *rough,* the "o" as in *women,* and the "ti" as in *nation.* That brings up another perplexing "Englishism": How do you pronounce "ough"? Try the words *dough, bough, bought, through,* and *cough*—had *enough?*

After you somehow manage to translate all those visual symbols into sounds, you must sequence those sounds to form a word; then, you need to identify the word and figure out what the word means; ultimately, you move on to the next word and repeat the process all over again. You continue this process with subsequent words to formulate a single sentence, and you continue this process for as long as you read. Clearly, the normal ability to read is not at all simple, and about 36 million American adults have not yet learned to read at an eighth-grade level (Conn & Silverman, 1991). Although the statistics on low literacy and illiteracy should alarm us and should provoke us to action, we may need to reconsider our possibly less-than-favorable appraisal of those who have not yet mastered the task of reading. To undertake such a challenge—at any age—must be difficult indeed.

When learning to read, novice readers must come to master two basic kinds of perceptual processes: lexical processes and comprehension processes. **Lexical processes** are used to identify letters and words; they also activate relevant information in memory about these words. **Comprehension processes** are used to make sense of the text as a whole (and are discussed later in chapter 10). The separation and integration of both bottom-up and top-down approaches to perception can be seen as we consider the lexical processes of reading.

Lexical Processes in Reading

Fixations and Reading Speed

When we read, our eyes do not move smoothly along a page or even along a line of text. Rather, as mentioned earlier, our eyes move in *saccades*—rapid sequential movements of the eyes as they fixate on successive clumps of text. Keith Rayner (Pollatsek & Rayner, 1989) has described the fixations as a series of "snapshots." Patricia Carpenter and Marcel Just (1981) studied the saccadic movements of college students reading text and found that fixations are of variable length. Readers fixate for a longer time on longer words than on shorter words, and also longer on less-familiar words—that is, words that appear less frequently in the English language—than on more-familiar words (i.e., words of higher frequency). The last word of a sentence also seems to receive an extra-long fixation time, which Carpenter and Just referred to as a "sentence wrap-up time."

Moreover, the researchers found that although most words are fixated, not all of them are. Readers fixate up to about 80% of the content words (e.g., nouns, verbs, and other words that carry the bulk of the meaning) in a text. (Function words, such as *the* and *of,* serve a supporting role to the content words.) Just what is the visual span of one of these fixations? It appears that we can extract useful information from a perceptual window of *characters* (letters, numerals, punctuation marks, and spaces) about 4 characters to the left of a fixation point and about 14 or 15 characters to the right of it. Saccadic movements leap an average of about 7 to 9 characters between successive fixations, so some of the information we extract may be preparatory for subsequent fixation (Pollatsek & Rayner, 1989; Rayner, Sereno, Lesch, & Pollatsek, 1995). When students speed-read, they show fewer and shorter fixations (Just, Carpenter, & Masson, 1982), but apparently, their greater speed is at the expense of comprehension of anything more than just the gist of the passage.

Lexical Access

An important aspect of reading is **lexical access**—the identification of a word which allows us to gain access to the meaning of the word from memory. Most psychologists who study reading believe that lexical access is an *interactive process,* combining information from multiple levels of processing, such as the features of letters, the letters themselves, and the words comprising the letters (e.g., J. Morton, 1969). Consider some of the basics of the *interactive-activation model* suggested by David Rumelhart and James McClelland (1981, 1982), which hypothesizes that activation of particular lexical elements occurs at multiple levels, and that activity at each of the levels is interactive.

Rumelhart and McClelland distinguish among three levels of processing following visual input: the feature level, the letter level, and the word level. The model assumes that information at each level is represented separately in memory, and that information passes from one level to another bidirectionally. In other words, processing is both bottom-up (starting with sensory data and working up to higher levels of cognitive processing) and top-down (starting with high-level cognition operating on prior knowledge and experiences related to a given context; see Figure 4.26). The interactive view implies that not only do we use the sensorially perceptible features of letters, say, to help us identify words, but we also use the features we already know about words to help us identify letters. For this reason, the model is referred to as "interactive." Moreover, the top-down aspect of the model allows for generalized context effects.

Other theorists (e.g., Meyer & Schvaneveldt, 1976; Paap, Newsome, McDonald, & Schvaneveldt, 1982) have suggested alternatives to Rumelhart and McClelland's model, but the distinctions among interactive models go beyond the scope of this introductory text. Support for word-recognition models involving discrete levels of processing comes from studies of cerebral processing (e.g., Petersen, Fox, Posner, Mintun, & Raichle, 1988; Posner, Petersen, Fox, & Raichle, 1988; Posner, Sandson, Dhawan, & Shulman, 1989). Studies that map brain metabolism (e.g., using PET and fMRI techniques discussed in chapter 2) indicate that different regions of the brain become activated during passive visual processing of word forms, as opposed to semantic analysis of words, or even spoken pronunciation of the words.

In addition to neuropsychological support, at least two of the word-recognition models (the McClelland and Rumelhart model and the model proposed by Paap, et al., 1982) have been simulated on computer. Both models aptly predicted a word-superiority effect (as well as a pseudoword-superiority effect), which is similar to the configural-superiority effect and the object-superiority effect (mentioned in regard to top-down influences on perception). In the **word-superiority effect,** letters are more easily read when they are embedded in words than when they are presented either in isolation or with letters that do not form words. The first report of this effect dates back to James McKeen Cattell (1860–1944), who observed that people take substantially longer to read unrelated letters than to read letters that form a word (1886). (Cattell also found that people took about twice as long to read unrelated words as to read words in a sentence.)

Further demonstrations of the effect were offered by Gerald Reicher (1969) and Daniel Wheeler (1970), so it is sometimes called the "Reicher–Wheeler effect." Typically, the word-superiority effect is observed in an experimental paradigm known as the *lexical-decision task.* In this paradigm, a string of letters is presented very briefly and then either removed or covered by a visual mask, and the participant is asked to make a decision about the string of letters.

In studying the word-superiority effect, participants are very briefly presented with either a word or a single letter, followed by a visual mask. The participant is then given a choice of two letters and must decide which he or she just saw. For example, if the test

FIGURE 4.26 INTERACTIVE-ACTIVATION MODEL OF WORD RECOGNITION

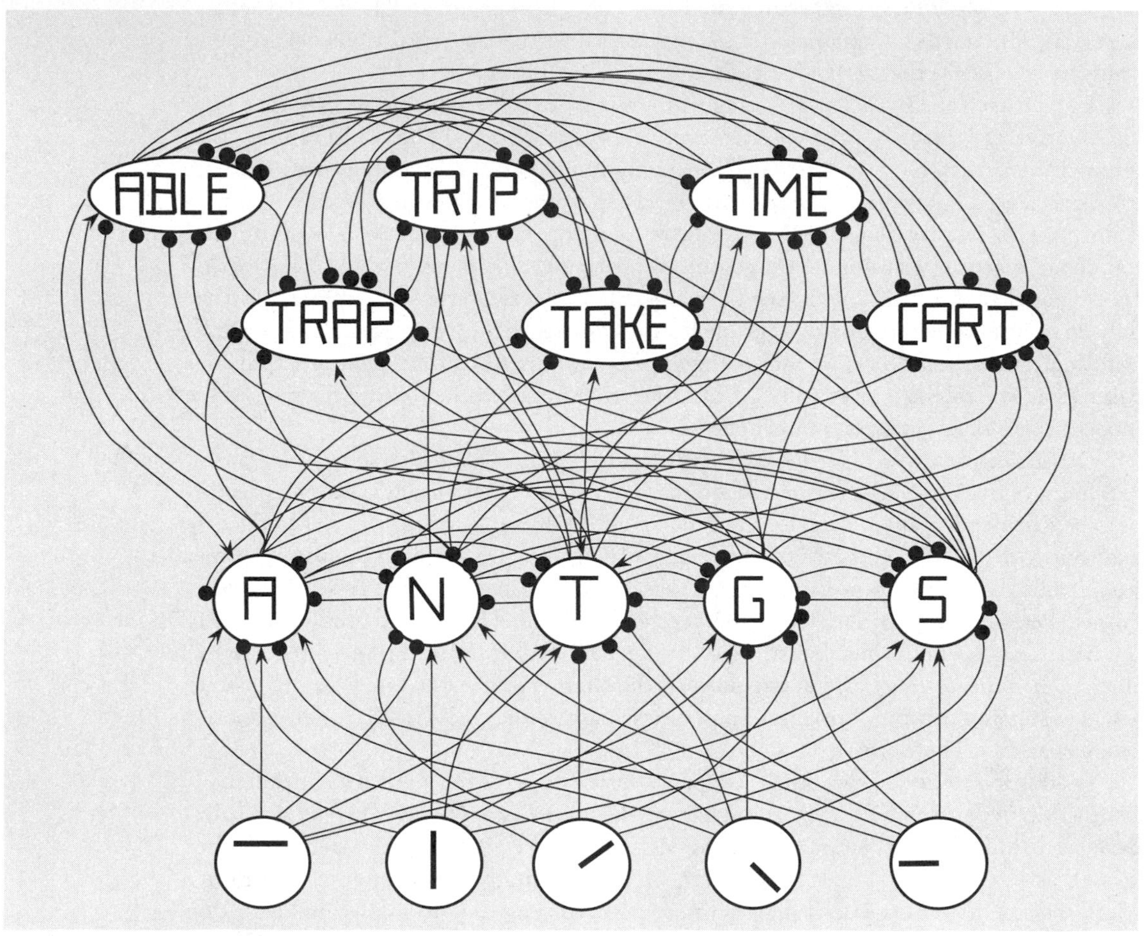

David Rumelhart and James McClelland used this figure to illustrate how activation at the feature level, the letter level, and the word level may interact during word recognition. In this figure, lines terminating in arrows prompt activation, and lines terminating in dots (black circles) prompt inhibition. For example, the feature for a solid horizontal bar at the top of a letter leads to activation of the T *character, but to inhibition of the* N *character. Similarly, at the letter level, activation of* T *as the first letter leads to activation of* TRAP *and* TRIP *but to inhibition of* ABLE. *Going from the top down, activation of the word* TRAP *leads to inhibition of* A, N, G, *and* S *as the first letter but to activation of* T *as the first letter.*

stimulus is the word "WORK," the alternatives might be "_ _ _ D" and "_ _ _ K." If the test stimulus is "K," the alternatives might be "D" and "K." Participants are more accurate in choosing the correct letter when it is presented in the context of a word than they are in choosing the correct letter when it is presented in isolation (e.g., Johnston & McClelland, 1973). Even letters in pronounceable pseudowords (e.g., "MARD") are identified more accurately than letters in isolation, although strings of letters that cannot be pronounced as words (e.g., "ORWK") do not aid in identification (Pollatsek & Rayner, 1989).

J. M. Cattell (1886) also noticed what might be called a "sentence-superiority effect"; this effect was confirmed by subsequent researchers (Perfetti, 1985; Perfetti & Roth, 1981). For example, suppose that a reader very briefly sees a degraded stimulus. The word *window,* for example, might be shown, but in degraded form (see Figure 4.27). When the word is standing by itself in this form, it is more difficult to recognize than when it is preceded by a sentence context such as "There were several repair jobs to be done. The first was to fix the ______" (Perfetti, 1985). Having a meaningful context for a stimulus helps the reader to perceive it.

Also, apparently context effects work at both conscious and preconscious levels. At the conscious level, we have active control over the use of context to determine word meanings, whereas at the preconscious level, the use of context is probably automatic and outside our active control (Stanovich, 1981; see also Posner & Snyder, 1975). A series of experiments involving the lexical-decision task offers evidence of context effects in making lexical decisions (Meyer & Schvaneveldt, 1971; Schvaneveldt, Meyer, & Becker, 1976). Participants seem to make lexical decisions more quickly when presented with strings of letters that are commonly associated pairs of words (e.g., "doctor" and "nurse" or "bread" and "butter"); they respond more slowly when presented with unassociated pairs of words, with pairs of nonwords, or with pairs involving a word and a nonword.

This discussion has focused on only a few of the many complex processes involved in reading. Indeed, little mention has been made of the comprehension processes that go beyond lexical processes in reading, but only because issues in comprehension are more related to language (and will be discussed in chapter 10). Next, we will move on to discuss what can go wrong in perception.

FIGURE 4.27 **DEGRADED STIMULI**

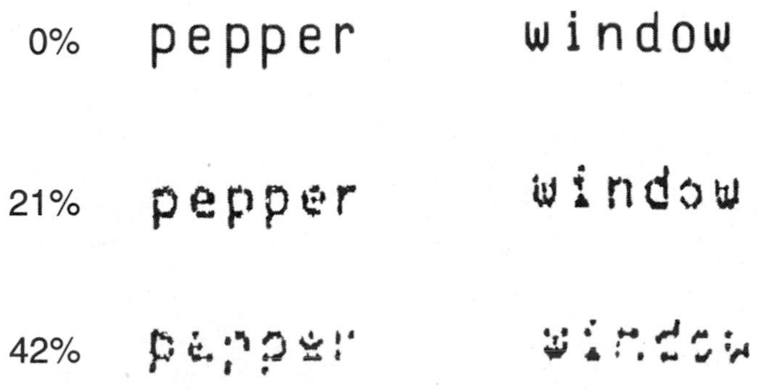

0%	pepper	window
21%	pepper	window
42%	[illegible]	[illegible]

This figure shows instances of the word window *and of the word* pepper, *in which each word is clearly legible, somewhat legible, or almost completely illegible. Percentages are percentages of degradation.*

Deficits in Perception

Clearly, cognitive psychologists learn a great deal about normal perceptual processes by studying perception in normal participants. In addition, however, we also often gain understanding of perception by studying persons whose perceptual processes differ from the norm (Farah, 1990; Weiskrantz, 1994), such as persons who suffer from **agnosia** (from Greek, *a-,* "lack," and *gnosis,* "knowledge"), severe deficits in the ability to perceive sensory information. There are many kinds of agnosias, and not all are visual, although here we focus on a few specific inabilities to see forms and patterns in space. People with visual agnosia have normal sensations of what is in front of them, but they cannot recognize what they see. Agnosias are often caused by brain lesions (Farah, 1990).

Sigmund Freud (1953), who specialized in neurology in his medical practice before he developed his psychodynamic theory of personality, observed that some of his patients were unable to identify familiar objects, even though they seemed to have no particular psychological disturbance or discernible damage to their visual abilities. In fact, people who suffer from *visual-object agnosia* can sense all parts of the visual field, but the objects they see do not mean anything to them (Kolb & Whishaw, 1985). For example, one agnosic patient, upon seeing a pair of eyeglasses, noted first that there was a circle, then that there was another circle, then that there was a crossbar, and finally guessed that he was looking at a bicycle, which does, indeed, comprise two circles and a crossbar (Luria, 1973). Lesions in particular visual areas of the cortex may be responsible for visual-object agnosia.

Disturbance in the temporal region of the cortex can lead to *simultagnosia,* in which an individual is unable to pay attention to more than one object at a time. For instance, if you were simultagnosic and you were to look at the Figure 4.28 (a), you would not be able to see

FIGURE 4.28 SIMULTAGNOSIA

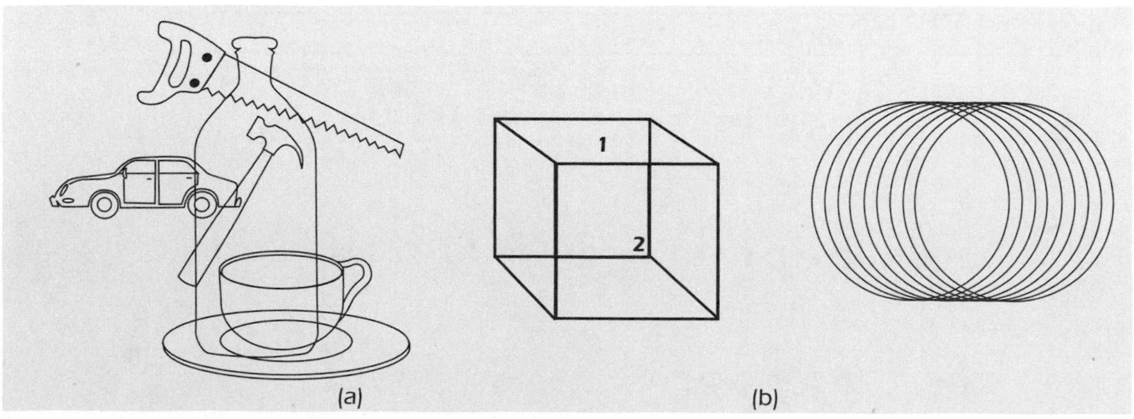

When you view this figure, you see various objects overlapping. Persons with simultagnosia cannot see more than one of these objects at any one time (a). On the other hand, even persons with normal perception cannot simultaneously perceive both objects in reversible figures (b).

each of the objects depicted; rather, you might report seeing the hammer, but not the other objects (M. Williams, 1970). In *spatial agnosia,* which seems to stem from lesions in the parietal lobe of the brain, a person has severe difficulty in negotiating the everyday environment. For example, a spatial agnosic can get lost at home, make wrong turns en route to familiar locations, and fail to recognize even the most familiar landmarks. Such individuals also seem to have great difficulty drawing the symmetrical features of symmetrical objects (Heaton, 1968). *Prosopagnosia* (associated with damage to the right temporal lobe of the brain) results in a severely impaired ability to recognize human faces. A prosopagnosic, for example, might not even be able to recognize her or his own face in the mirror. Furthermore, there are even extremely rare cases of prosopagnosics who can not recognize human faces, but who can recognize the faces of their farm animals, suggesting that the problem is extremely specific to human faces (McNeil & Warrington, 1993). This fascinating disorder has spawned much research on face identification, becoming the latest "hot topic" in visual perception (Damasio, 1985; Farah, Levinson, & Klein, 1995; Farah, Wilson, Drain, & Tanaka, 1995; Haxby, Ungerleider, Horwitz, Maisog, Rappaport, & Grady, 1996).

This kind of extreme specificity of deficits leads to questions about specialization. Specifically, are there distinct processing centers or *modules* for particular perceptual tasks? This question goes beyond the separation of perceptual processes along different sensory modalities (i.e., the differences between visual and auditory perception). *Modular* processes are those that are specialized for particular tasks, whether they involve only visual processes (as in color perception), or an integration of visual and auditory processes (as in certain aspects of speech perception to be discussed in chapter 10). Jerry Fodor, an influential modern philosopher, has written a book entirely devoted to the delineation of the necessary characteristics of modular processes. In order for some process to be truly modular, the following properties must exist: (a) modules work *fast* and their operation is *mandatory*; (b) modules have characteristically *shallow outputs* (i.e., yielding basic categorizations) with *limited central access* to the module's computations (i.e., not participant to conscious attentional influences); (c) modules are *domain specific,* fine-tuned with respect to the kinds of information used, with *informational encapsulation* from other modules and cognitive processes; and (d) modules are supported by *fixed neural architectures* and therefore suffer characteristic breakdown patterns. Thus, for face perception to be considered a truly modular process, we would need to have further evidence of domain-specificity and informational encapsulation. That is, other perceptual processes should not contribute to, interfere with, or share information with face perception. Moreover, the neurological basis of prosopagnosia is not well-understood and needs further elaboration before anything definitive can be said about the neural architecture of face recognition.

Although cognitive psychologists are intrigued by the fact that a few people are prosopagnosic, they are even more fascinated by the fact that most of us are not. Just how do you recognize your mother, or your best friend? In addition, how do you recognize the much simpler and less dynamic forms and patterns of the letters and words in this sentence? This chapter has considered just a few of the many aspects of perception that interest cognitive psychologists. Of particular note are the cognitive processes by which we form mental representations of what we sense, using prior knowledge, inferences, and specialized cognitive operations to make sense of our sensations. Cognitive psychologists also wonder about how we remember what we have perceived. Questions of memory are discussed in the next two chapters.

SUMMARY

1. **How do we perceive stable objects in the environment, given variable stimulation?** Perceptual experience involves four elements: distal object, informational medium, proximal stimulation, and perceptual objects. Because proximal stimulation is constantly changing due to the variable nature of the environment and to physiological processes designed to overcome *sensory adaptation,* perception must address the fundamental question of constancy.

   Perceptual constancies (e.g., size and shape constancy) result when our perceptions of objects tend to remain constant, even as the stimuli registered by our senses change. Some perceptual constancies may be governed by what we know about the world (e.g., expectations regarding how rectilinear structures usually appear), but constancies are also influenced by invariant relationships among objects in their environmental context.

   One reason we can perceive three-dimensional space is due to the use of *binocular depth cues,* such as binocular disparity (based on the fact that each of two eyes receives a slightly different image of the same object as it is being viewed) and *binocular convergence* (based on the degree to which our two eyes must turn inward toward each other as objects get closer to us). We also are aided in perceiving depth by *monocular depth cues,* such as texture gradients, relative size, interposition, linear perspective, aerial perspective, height in the picture plane, and motion parallax. One of the earliest approaches to form and pattern perception is the *Gestalt approach to form perception.* The Gestalt *law of Prägnanz* has led to the explication of several principles of form perception—such as figure–ground, proximity, similarity, closure, continuity, and symmetry—which characterize how we perceptually group together various objects and parts of objects.

2. **What are two fundamental approaches to explaining perception?** *Perception,* the set of processes by which we recognize, organize, and make sense of stimuli in our environment, may be viewed from either of two basic theoretical approaches: bottom-up, direct perception or top-down, constructive perception. The viewpoint of *constructive* (or *intelligent*) *perception* asserts that the perceiver essentially constructs or builds up the stimulus that is perceived, using both prior knowledge and contextual information, as well as sensory information. In contrast, the viewpoint of *direct perception* asserts that all the information we need to perceive is in the sensory input (such as from the retina) that we receive.

   Three of the main bottom-up theoretical approaches to pattern perception include *template-matching* theories, *prototype-matching* theories, and *feature-matching* theories. Some support for feature-matching theories comes from neurophysiological studies identifying what are called "feature detectors" in the brain. It appears that various cortical neurons can be mapped to specific receptive fields on the retina. Differing cortical neurons respond to different features, such as line segments or edges in various spatial orientations. Visual perception seems to depend on three levels of complexity in the cortical neurons; each level of complexity seems to be further removed from the incoming information from the sensory receptors. Another bottom-up approach, *recognition-by-components (RBC) theory,* more specifically delineates a set of features involved in form and pattern perception. Although bottom-up approaches explain some aspects of form and pattern perception, other aspects require approaches that suggest at least some degree of *top-down processing* of perceptual information. For example, top-down approaches better but incompletely explain such phenomena as *context effects,* including the object-superiority effect and the *word-superiority effect.*

An alternative to both of these approaches suggests that perception may be more complex than direct-perception theorists have suggested, yet perception may also involve more efficient use of sensory data than constructive-perception theorists have suggested. Specifically, a computational approach to perception suggests that our brains compute 3-D perceptual models of the environment, based on information from the 2-D sensory receptors in our retinas.

3. **How do perceptual processes interact with the cognitive processes of reading?** The reading difficulties of persons with *dyslexia* often relate to problems with the perceptual aspects of reading. Reading comprises two basic kinds of processes: (a) *lexical processes,* which include sequences of eye fixations and *lexical access;* and (b) *comprehension processes.*

4. **What happens when people with normal visual sensations cannot perceive visual stimuli?** *Agnosias,* which are usually associated with brain lesions, are deficits of form and pattern perception that cause afflicted people to be insufficiently able to recognize objects that are in their visual fields, despite normal sensory abilities. People who suffer from *visual-object agnosia* can sense all parts of the visual field, but the objects they see do not mean anything to them. Individuals with *simultagnosia* are unable to pay attention to more than one object at a time. Persons with *spatial agnosia* have severe difficulty in comprehending and handling the relationship between their bodies and the spatial configurations of the world around them. Persons with *prosopagnosia* have severe impairment in their ability to recognize human faces including their own. These deficits lead to the question of whether or not specific perceptual processes are *modular,* specialized for particular tasks.

Thinking About Thinking: Factual, Analytical, Creative, and Practical Questions

1. Briefly describe each of the monocular and binocular depth cues listed in this chapter.
2. Describe bottom-up and top-down approaches to perception.
3. How might deficits of perception, such as agnosia, offer insight into normal perceptual processes?
4. Compare and contrast the Gestalt approach to form perception, Marr's computational theory, and spatiotemporal boundary-formation theory.
5. Design a demonstration that would illustrate the phenomenon of perceptual constancy.

6. Design an experiment to test either the prototype-matching theory of pattern perception or the feature-matching theory.
7. Based on the discussion of reading in this chapter, what is a practical suggestion you could recommend that might make reading easier for someone who is having difficulty reading?

Key Terms

agnosia 148
binocular depth cues 120
bottom-up theories 127
comprehension processes 144
constructive perception 136
context effects 138
depth 119
direct perception 127
dyslexia 143
feature-matching 131
figure–ground 124
Gestalt approach to form perception 123
law of Prägnanz 123
lexical access 144
lexical processes 144
monocular depth cues 119
percept 110
perception 110
perceptual constancy 116
prototype 129
receptors 114
recognition-by-components (RBC) theory 136
templates 129
top-down theories 127
word-superiority effect 145

Annotated Suggested Readings

Anderson, R. C., & Pichert, J. W. (1978). Recall of previously unrecallable information following a shift in perspective. *Journal of Verbal Learning and Verbal Behavior, 17,* 1–12. This article shows the importance of our mental set in learning: In particular, the perspective we take in learning information affects how well we learn that information.

Biederman, I. (1987). Recognition-by-components: A theory of human image understanding. *Psychological Review, 94,* 115–147. This well-known article provides an account of Biederman's theory of how we recognize objects via basic perceptual components, which Biederman calls "geons."

Farah, M. J. (1990). *Visual agnosia: Disorders of object recognition and what they tell us about normal vision.* Cambridge, MA: MIT Press. A provocative and readable account of how the study of patient populations—in this case, visual agnosics—can inform our understanding of normal functioning.

Palmer, S. (1992). Modern theories of Gestalt perception. In G. W. Humphreys (Ed.), *Understanding vision: An interdisciplinary perspective: Readings in mind and language* (pp. 39–70). Oxford, England: Blackwell. An updated and expanded contemporary description of early Gestalt ideas, which relates the Gestalt approach to studies in neuropsychology and to neural-network models of perception.

MEMORY: MODELS AND RESEARCH METHODS

CHAPTER OUTLINE

EXPLORING COGNITIVE PSYCHOLOGY

TASKS USED FOR MEASURING MEMORY
- Recall Versus Recognition Tasks
- Implicit Versus Explicit Memory Tasks

TRADITIONAL MODEL OF MEMORY
- The Sensory Store
- The Short-Term Store
- The Long-Term Store

ALTERNATIVE PERSPECTIVES, ALTERNATIVE METAPHORS
- Levels of Processing
- Working Memory
- Multiple-Memory-Systems Model
- A Connectionist Perspective
- Memory in the Real World

EXCEPTIONAL MEMORY AND NEUROPSYCHOLOGY
- Outstanding Memory: Mnemonists
- Deficient Memory: Amnesia
- The Role of the Hippocampus and Other Structures

SUMMARY

THINKING ABOUT THINKING: FACTUAL, ANALYTICAL, CREATIVE, AND PRACTICAL QUESTIONS

KEY TERMS

ANNOTATED SUGGESTED READINGS

EXPLORING COGNITIVE PSYCHOLOGY

1. **What are some of the tasks used for studying memory, and what do various tasks indicate about the structure of memory?**
2. **What has been the prevailing traditional model for the structure of memory?**
3. **What are some of the main alternative models of the structure of memory?**
4. **What have psychologists learned about the structure of memory by studying both exceptional memory and the physiology of the brain?**

INVESTIGATING COGNITIVE PSYCHOLOGY

Who is the president of the United States? What is 138 × 241? What is today's date? What does your best friend look like, and what does your friend's voice sound like? What were some of your experiences when you first started college? How do you tie your shoelaces?

How do you know the answers to the preceding questions, or to any questions, for that matter? How do you remember any of the information you use every waking hour of every day? **Memory** is the means by which we draw on our past experiences in order to use this information in the present. As a *process,* memory refers to the dynamic mechanisms associated with retaining and retrieving information about past experience (Crowder, 1976). Specifically, cognitive psychologists have identified three common operations of memory: encoding, storage, and retrieval. Each operation represents a stage in memory processing. In *encoding,* you transform sensory data into a form of mental representation; in *storage,* you keep encoded information in memory; and in *retrieval,* you pull out or use information stored in memory. These memory processes are discussed at length in chapter 6.

This chapter introduces some of the tasks used for studying memory, leading to the traditional model of memory, which includes the sensory, short-term, and long-term storage systems. Although this model still influences current thinking about memory, we will consider some interesting alternative perspectives before moving on to discuss exceptional memory and insights provided by neuropsychology.

TASKS USED FOR MEASURING MEMORY

In studying memory, researchers have devised various tasks that require participants to remember arbitrary information (e.g., numerals) in different ways. Because this chapter includes many references to these tasks, we begin this section with an *advance organizer*—a basis for organizing the information to be given—so that you will know how memory is studied. The tasks involve recall versus recognition memory, implicit versus explicit memory, and declarative versus procedural memory.

Recall Versus Recognition Tasks

If you were to be given a task that requires **recall** from memory, you would be asked to produce a fact, a word, or other item from memory. Fill-in-the-blank tests require that you recall items from memory. On the other hand, if you were given a task that required **recognition,** you would have to select or otherwise identify an item as being one that you learned previously (see Table 5.1 for examples and explanations of each type of task). Multiple-choice and true–false tests involve recognition. The types of recall tasks used in experiments are *serial recall* (in which you recall items in the exact

TABLE 5.1 TYPES OF TASKS USED FOR MEASURING MEMORY

Some memory tasks involve recall or recognition of explicit memory about declarative knowledge. Other tasks involve implicit memory and memory about procedural knowledge.

Tasks for Explicit Memory About Declarative Knowledge	Description of What the Tasks Require	Example
Explicit-memory tasks	You must consciously recall particular information.	Who wrote *Hamlet?*
Declarative-knowledge tasks	You must recall facts.	What is your first name?
Recall tasks	You must produce a fact, a word, or other item from memory.	Fill-in-the-blank tests require that you recall items from memory. For example, "The term for persons who suffer severe memory impairment is ______."
Serial-recall task	You must repeat the items in a list in the exact order in which you heard or read them.	If you were shown the digits 2-8-7-1-6-4, you would be expected to repeat "2-8-7-1-6-4," in exactly that order.
Free-recall task	You must repeat the items in a list in any order in which you can recall them.	If you were presented with the word list, "dog, pencil, time, hair, monkey, restaurant," you would receive full credit if you repeat "monkey, restaurant, dog, pencil, time, hair."
Cued-recall task	You must memorize a list of paired items; then when you are given one item in the pair, you must recall the mate for that item.	Suppose that you were given the following list of pairs: "time–city, mist–home, switch–paper, credit–day, fist–cloud, number–branch." Later, when you were given the stimulus "switch" you would be expected to say, "paper," and so on.

Continued

TABLE 5.1 TYPES OF TASKS USED FOR MEASURING MEMORY *(Continued)*

Tasks for Explicit Memory About Declarative Knowledge	Description of What the Tasks Require	Example
Recognition tasks	You must select or otherwise identify an item as being one that you learned previously.	Multiple–choice and true–false tests involve recognition. For example, "The term for people with outstanding memory ability is (a) amnesics, (b) semanticists, (c) mnemonists, or (d) retrograders."
Implicit-memory tasks	You must draw on information in memory, without consciously realizing that you are doing so.	Word-completion tasks tap implicit memory. You would be presented with a word fragment, such as the first three letters of a word; then you would be asked to complete the word fragment with the first word that comes to mind. For example, suppose that you were asked to supply the missing five letters to fill in these blanks and form a word: imp _ _ _ _ _. Because you had recently seen the word *implicit,* you would be more likely to provide the five letters l-i-c-i-t for the blanks than would someone who had not recently been exposed to the word.
Tasks involving procedural knowledge	You must remember learned skills and automatic behaviors, rather than facts.	If you were asked to demonstrate a "knowing-how" skill, you might be given experience in solving puzzles or in reading mirror writing, and then you would be asked to show what you remember of how to use those skills. Instead, you might be asked to master or to show what you already remember about particular motor skills (e.g., riding a bicycle or ice skating).

order in which they were presented), *free recall* (in which you recall items in any order you choose), and *cued recall* (in which you are first shown items in pairs, but during recall, you are cued with only one member of each pair and are asked to recall each mate; also called "paired-associates recall"). Psychologists can also measure *relearning,* which is the number of trials it takes to learn once again items that were learned at some time in the past.

Recognition memory is usually much better than recall (although there are some exceptions, which are discussed in chapter 6). For example, Lionel Standing, Jerry Conezio, and Ralph Haber (1970) found that participants could recognize close to 2,000 pictures in a recognition-memory task, whereas it is difficult to imagine anyone recalling 2,000 items of any kind they were just asked to memorize. As you will see later in the section on exceptional memory, even with extensive training, the best measured recall performance is around 80 items.

Different memory tasks indicate different levels of learning, with recall tasks generally eliciting deeper levels than recognition ones. Some psychologists refer to recognition-memory tasks as tapping *receptive* knowledge and recall memory tasks, where you have to produce an answer, as requiring *expressive* knowledge. Differences between receptive and expressive knowledge are also observed in areas other than that of simple memory tasks (e.g., language, intelligence, and cognitive development).

IMPLICIT VERSUS EXPLICIT MEMORY TASKS

Each of the preceding tasks involves **explicit memory,** in which participants are asked to perform a task requiring a conscious recollection—to recall or recognize words, facts, or pictures from a particular prior set of items. Cognitive psychologists also seek to understand phenomena of **implicit memory** (Schacter, 1995; Schacter & Graf, 1986a, 1986b), in which task performance is assisted by previous experiences that we do not consciously and purposely try to recollect. Every day, you engage in many tasks that involve your unconscious recollection of information. Even as you read this book, you are unconsciously remembering the meanings of particular words, some of the cognitive-psychological concepts you read about in earlier chapters, and even how to read. In the laboratory, experimenters sometimes study implicit memory by studying people's performance on word-completion tasks, which involve implicit memory. In a word-completion task, the participant is presented with a word fragment, such as the first three letters of a word, and is asked to complete it with the first word that comes to mind.

For example, suppose that you are asked to supply the missing five letters to fill in these blanks and form a word: imp_____. Because you have recently seen the word *implicit,* you would be more likely to provide the five letters l-i-c-i-t for the blanks than would someone who had not recently been exposed to the word. This facilitation in your ability to supply the missing information is called **priming.** In general, participants perform better when they have seen the word on a recently presented list, even though they have not been explicitly instructed to remember words from that list.

TRADITIONAL MODEL OF MEMORY

Through the study of amnesics, mnemonists, and persons with normal memory engaged in specialized memory tasks, cognitive psychologists have gathered substantial data regarding memory. How do they then organize the data to understand how memory works? As you may have guessed, different cognitive psychologists may interpret the identical data in different ways. The core differences among these alternative views center on the metaphor used for conceptualizing memory (Roediger, 1980b). Metaphors often serve an important function in organizing ideas, thereby aiding researchers to conceptualize a phenomenon well enough to investigate it. As the research progresses, the metaphor (mental model) representing a psychological phenomenon may be modified to accommodate new data, or other researchers may propose alternative models. In the mid-1960s, based on the data available at the time, Nancy Waugh and Donald Norman (1965) proposed a model of memory distinguishing two structures of memory: *primary memory,* which holds temporary information currently in use, and *secondary memory,* which holds information permanently, or at least for a very long time.

By the late 1960s, Richard Atkinson and Richard Shiffrin (1968) proposed an alternative metaphor that conceptualized memory in terms of three memory stores: (a) a **sensory store,** capable of storing relatively limited amounts of information for very brief periods of time; (b) a **short-term store,** capable of storing information for somewhat longer periods of time but also of relatively limited capacity; and (c) a **long-term store,** of very large capacity, capable of storing information for very long periods of time, perhaps even indefinitely.

Atkinson and Shiffrin distinguished between the structures, which they termed *stores,* and the information stored in the structures, which they termed *memory.* Today, however, cognitive psychologists commonly describe the three stores as sensory memory, short-term memory (STM), and long-term memory (LTM). Also, Atkinson and Shiffrin were not suggesting that the three stores are distinct physiological structures; rather, the stores are **hypothetical constructs**—concepts that are not themselves directly measurable or observable but that serve as mental models for understanding how a psychological phenomenon, such as memory, works. Figure 5.1 shows a simple information-processing model of these stores (Atkinson & Shiffrin, 1971). As this figure shows, the Atkinson–Shiffrin model emphasizes the passive receptacles in which memories are stored, but it also alludes to some control processes that govern the transfer of information from one store to another.

FIGURE 5.1 **THE THREE-STORES MODEL OF MEMORY**

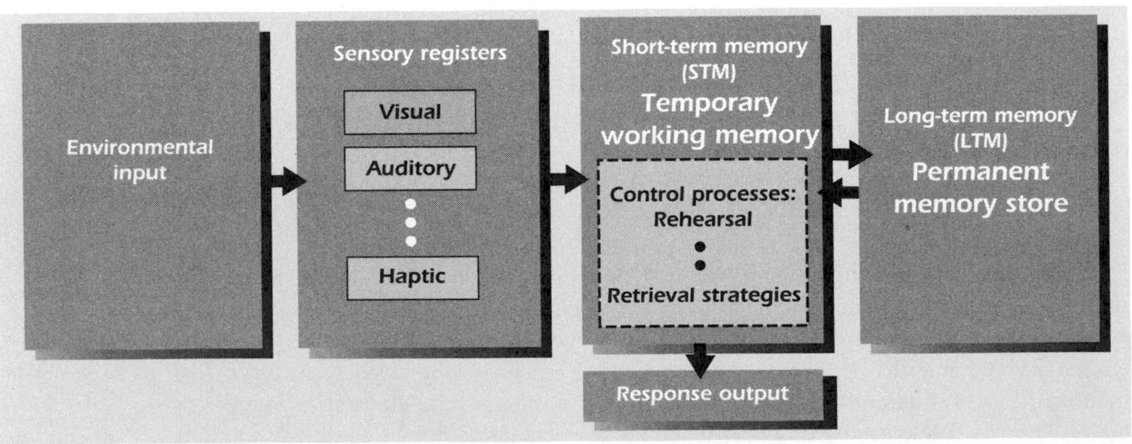

Richard Atkinson and Richard Shiffrin proposed a theoretical model for the flow of information through the human information processor. (After Atkinson & Shiffrin, 1971)

The three-stores model is not the only way to conceptualize memory, however. After presenting what we know about memory in terms of the three-stores model, this chapter describes some alternative ways in which to conceptualize memory. For now, however, we begin with the sensory store in the three-stores model.

THE SENSORY STORE

The *sensory store* is believed to be the initial repository of much information that eventually enters the short-and long-term stores. Strong (although not undisputed; see Haber, 1983) evidence argues in favor of the existence of an iconic store. The **iconic store** is a discrete visual sensory register, so called because information is believed by some to be stored in the form of *icons* (visual images that represent something; icons usually resemble whatever is being represented).

If you have ever "written" your name with a lighted sparkler (or stick of incense) against a dark background, you have experienced the persistence of a visual memory; that is, you briefly "see" your name, even though the sparkler leaves no physical trace. This *visual persistence* is an example of the type of information held in the iconic store. Surprisingly, the initial discovery regarding the existence of the iconic store came from a Ph.D. dissertation by a graduate student at Harvard, George Sperling (1960).

SPERLING'S DISCOVERY

Sperling addressed the question of how much information we can encode in a single, brief glance at a set of stimuli. Sperling flashed an array of letters and numbers on a screen for a mere 50 *milliseconds* (thousandths of a second). Participants were asked to report the identity and location of as many of the symbols as they could recall. Sperling could be sure that participants got only one glance because previous research had shown that 0.050 seconds is long enough for only a single glance at the presented stimulus.

Sperling found that when participants were asked to report on what they saw, they remembered only about four symbols (confirming a finding made by Brigden in 1933). The number of symbols recalled was pretty much the same, without regard to how many symbols had been in the visual display. Some of Sperling's participants mentioned that they had seen all the stimuli clearly, but while reporting what they saw, they forgot the other stimuli. Sperling then conceived an ingenious idea for how to measure what the participants saw. The procedure used by R. Brigden and initially by Sperling is a *whole-report procedure,* in that participants report *every* symbol they have seen. Sperling then introduced a *partial-report procedure,* in which participants needed to report only part of what they saw.

Sperling found a way to obtain a sample of his participants' knowledge and then extrapolated from this sample to estimate their total knowledge, much as school examinations are used as samples of an individual's total knowledge of course material. Sperling presented symbols in three rows of four symbols each. Figure 5.2 shows a display similar to one Sperling's participants might have seen. Sperling informed participants that they would have to recall only a single row of the display. The row to be recalled was signaled by a tone of either high, medium, or low pitch, corresponding to the need to recall the top, middle, or bottom row, respectively.

FIGURE 5.2 **SPERLING'S TEST OF ICONIC MEMORY**

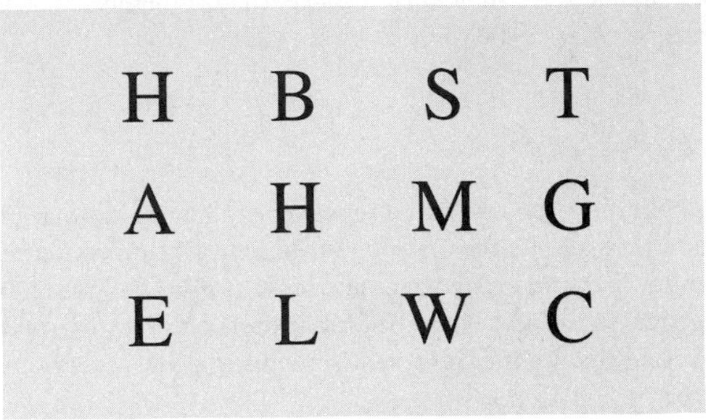

H	B	S	T
A	H	M	G
E	L	W	C

This symbolic display is similar to the one used for George Sperling's visual-recall task.

In order to estimate the duration of iconic memory, Sperling manipulated the interval between the display and the tone. The range of the interval was from 0.10 seconds *before* the onset of the display to 1.0 seconds *after* the offset of the display. The partial-report procedure dramatically changed how much participants could recall. Sperling then multiplied the number of symbols recalled with this procedure by three, because participants had to recall only one third of the information presented, but did not know beforehand which of the three lines they would be asked to report.

Using this partial-report procedure, Sperling found that participants had available roughly 9 of the 12 symbols if they were cued immediately before or immediately after the appearance of the display. However, when they were cued 1 second later, their recall was down to 4 or 5 of the 12 items, about the same as was obtained through the whole-report procedure. These data suggest that the iconic store can hold about 9 items, and that it decays very rapidly (see Figure 5.3). Indeed, the advantage of the partial-report procedure is drastically reduced by 0.3 seconds of delay and is essentially obliterated by 1 second of delay for onset of the tone.

Sperling's results suggest that information fades rapidly from iconic storage. Why are we subjectively unaware of such a fading phenomenon? First, we are rarely subjected to stimuli that appear for only 50 milliseconds, then disappear, and that we then need to report. Second and more important, however, we are unable to distinguish what we see in iconic memory from what we actually see in the environment. What we see in iconic memory is what we take to be in the environment. Participants in Sperling's experiment generally reported that they could still see the display up to 150 milliseconds after it actually had been terminated.

Elegant as it was, Sperling's use of the partial-report procedure still suffered, at least to some small extent, from the problem inherent in the full-report procedure: Participants had to report multiple symbols and may have experienced fading of memory during the report. Indeed, a distinct possibility of *output interference* exists, whereby the production of output (in this case, verbally reporting multiple symbols) interferes with the phenomenon being studied (in this case, iconic memory).

FIGURE 5.3 **EFFECTS OF DELAY ON VISUAL RECALL**

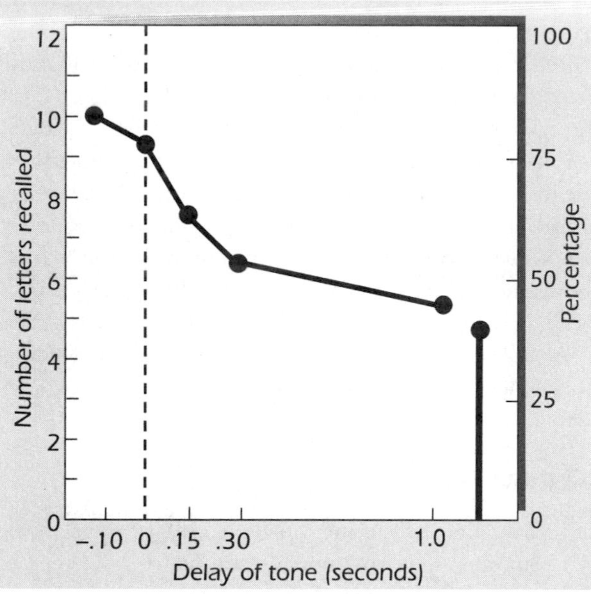

The figure shows the average number of letters recalled (left axis; percentage equivalents indicated on right axis) by a subject, based on using the partial-report procedure, as a function of the delay between the presentation of the letters and the tone signaling when to demonstrate recall. The bar at the lower-right corner indicates the average number of letters recalled when subjects used the whole-report procedure. (After Sperling, 1960)

SUBSEQUENT REFINEMENT

In subsequent work (Averbach & Coriell, 1961), participants were shown displays of two rows of eight randomly chosen letters for a duration of 50 milliseconds. In this investigation, a small mark appeared just above one of the positions where a letter had appeared (or was about to appear), at varying time intervals before or after presentation of the letters. In this research, then, participants needed to report only a single letter at a time, thus minimizing output interference. These investigators found that when the bar appeared immediately before or after the stimulus display, participants could accurately report on about 75% of the trials. Thus, they seemed to be holding about 12 items (75% of 16) in sensory memory. Sperling's estimate of the capacity of iconic memory, therefore, may have been conservative. The evidence in this study suggests that when output interference is greatly reduced, the capacity of iconic memory may comprise as many as 12 items.

A second experiment (Averbach & Coriell, 1961) revealed an additional important characteristic of iconic memory: It can be erased. The erasable nature of iconic memory definitely makes our visual sensations more sensible. We would be in serious trouble if everything we saw in our visual environment persisted for too long a period of time. For example, if we are scanning the environment at a rapid pace, we need the visual information to disappear at a rate faster than the Sperling experiments would suggest that it does.

Averbach and Coriell (1961) found that when a stimulus was presented after a target letter, in the same position that the target letter had occupied, it could erase the visual icon. Interference of this kind—by the placement of one stimulus where another one had previously appeared—is termed *backward visual masking.* The investigators found that if the mask stimulus was presented in the same location as a letter and within 100 milliseconds of the presentation of the letter, the mask was superimposed on the letter (e.g., *F* followed by *L* would be *E*). At longer intervals between the target and the mask, the mask erased the original stimulus (e.g., only the *L* would remain if *F* and then *L* had been presented). At still longer intervals between the target and the mask, the mask no longer interfered, presumably because the target information had already been transferred to more durable memory storage.

To summarize, visual information appears to enter our memory system through an iconic store that holds the visual information for very short periods of time. In the normal course of events, this information may be either transferred to another store or erased if other information is superimposed on it before there is sufficient time for the transfer of the information to another memory store.

The Short-Term Store

Although most of us have little or no introspective access to our sensory memory stores, we all have access to our short-term memory stores, which hold memories for matters of seconds and, occasionally, of up to a couple of minutes. For example, can you remember the name of the researcher who discovered the iconic store? What about the names of the researchers who subsequently refined this work? If you can recall those names, you used some memory-control processes for doing so. According to the Atkinson–Shiffrin model, the short-term store holds not only a few items, but also some control processes that regulate the flow of information to and from the long-term store, where we may hold information for longer periods of time.

How many items of information can we hold in short-term memory at any one time? In a classic paper, George Miller (1956) noted that our immediate (short term) memory capacity for a wide range of items appears to be about 7 items, plus or minus 2. An item can be something simple, such as a digit, or something more complex, such as a word. If we chunk together a string of, say, 20 letters or numbers into 7 meaningful items, we can remember them, whereas we could not remember 20 items and repeat them immediately. For example, most of us cannot hold in short-term memory this string of 21 numbers: 101001000100001000100. However, if we chunk it into larger units, such as 10, 100, 1000, 10000, 1000, and 100, we will probably be able to reproduce easily the 21 numerals as 6 items (cf. G. A. Miller, 1956, regarding binary vs. octal digits).

Other factors also influence memory capacity for temporary storage. For example, the number of syllables we pronounce with each item affects the number of items we can recall. When each item has a larger number of syllables, we can recall fewer items (e.g., Baddeley, Thomson, & Buchanan, 1975; Naveh-Benjamin & Ayres, 1986; Schweickert & Boruff, 1986). In addition, any delay or interference can cause our seven-item capacity to drop to about three items.

Nancy Waugh and Donald Norman (1965) proposed a mathematical technique for estimating the capacity of the short-term store, which was applied to tasks involving the free recall of a list of items. Computations based on their technique suggest that the capacity of the short-term store under these conditions is roughly two to three items.

THE LONG-TERM STORE

Although we constantly use short-term memory throughout our daily activities, when most of us talk about memory, we usually are talking about long-term memory, in which we keep memories that stay with us over long periods of time, perhaps indefinitely. All of us rely heavily on our long-term memory. There we hold information we need to get us by in our day-to-day life: people's names, where we keep things, how we schedule ourselves on different days, and so on. We also worry when we fear that our long-term memory is not up to snuff.

How much information can we hold in long-term memory, and how long does the information last? The question of storage capacity can be disposed of quickly because the answer is simple: We do not know, nor do we know how we would find out. Whereas we can design experiments to tax the limits of short-term memory, we do not know how to test the limits of long-term memory and thereby find out its capacity. Some theorists have suggested that the capacity of long-term memory is infinite, at least in practical terms (Bahrick, 1984a, 1984b; Bahrick & Hall, 1991; Hintzman, 1978). It turns out that the question of how long information lasts in long-term memory is not easily answerable either, because at present, we have no proof that there is an absolute outer limit to how long information can be stored.

Harry Bahrick *is a research professor of psychology at Ohio Wesleyan University. He is best known for his studies of the lifetime retention of information in semantic memory. He has shown that unrehearsed knowledge can remain in memory for a quarter of a century or even longer, as, for example, in the case of recognizing fellow students known during the high school years but not seen or thought of since.*

One of the more unusual demonstrations of long-term memory was conducted by investigating rather directly what is stored in the brain. Wilder Penfield, in performing operations on the brains of conscious patients afflicted with epilepsy, used electrical stimulation of various parts of the cerebral cortex in order to locate the origins of each patient's problem. In fact, his work was instrumental in plotting the motor and sensory areas of the cortex described in chapter 2 of this text.

During the course of such stimulation, Penfield (1955, 1969) found that patients would sometimes appear to recall memories from way back in their childhoods, memories that may not have been called to mind for many, many years. (Note that the patients could be stimulated to recall episodes such as events from their childhood, not facts such as the names of U.S. presidents.) Penfield interpreted these data as suggesting that long-term memories may be permanent.

Some researchers (e.g., Loftus & Loftus, 1980) have disputed Penfield's interpretations, noting the paucity of such reports in relation to the hundreds of patients on whom Penfield operated. In addition, we cannot be certain that the patients were actually recalling rather than inventing—perhaps unwittingly, as in a dream—these events. Other researchers, using empirical techniques on older participants, found contradictory evidence.

An interesting study on memory for names and faces was conducted by Harry Bahrick, Phyllis Bahrick, and Roy Wittlinger (1975). They tested participants' memory for names and photographs of their high-school classmates. Even after 25 years, there was little forgetting of some aspects of memory: Participants tended to recognize names as belonging to classmates rather than to outsiders, and recognition memory for matching names to graduation photos was quite high. As you might expect, recall of names showed a higher rate of forgetting. Based on this study and other research, Harry Bahrick has coined the term *permastore* for the very long-term storage of at least some information, such as knowledge of a foreign language (Bahrick, 1984a, 1984b; Bahrick, Bahrick, Bahrick, & Bahrick, 1993) and of mathematics (Bahrick & Hall, 1991).

Alternative Perspectives, Alternative Metaphors

Levels of Processing

A radical departure from the three-stores model of memory is the **levels-of-processing framework,** originally proposed by Fergus Craik and Robert Lockhart (1972), which postulates that memory does not comprise three or even any specific number of separate stores. Rather, storage varies along a continuous dimension in terms of depth of encoding. In other words, there are theoretically an infinite number of levels of processing (LOP) at which items can be encoded, with no distinct boundaries between one level and the next. Note that the emphasis in this model is on processing as the key to storage. The level at which information is stored will depend, in large part, on how it is encoded. Moreover, the deeper the level of processing, the higher the probability that an item may be retrieved.

Craik, along with Endel Tulving (1975), performed a set of experiments to support the LOP view. Participants were presented with a list of words, with each word preceded by a question. Questions were varied to encourage three different levels of processing, in progressive order of depth: *physical, acoustic,* and *semantic.* Samples of the words and the questions are shown in Table 5.2. The results of their research were clear-cut: The deeper the level of processing encouraged by the question, the higher the level of recall achieved. In Russia, P. I. Zinchenko (1962, 1981) independently found similar results, in that words that were logically (e.g., taxonomically) connected (e.g., *dog* and *animal*) were recalled more easily than were words that were concretely connected (e.g., *dog* and *leg*), and concretely connected words were more easily recalled than were words that were unconnected.

An even more powerful inducement to recall has been termed the *self-reference effect* (Rogers, Kuiper, & Kirker, 1977). In the self-reference effect, participants show very high levels of recall when asked to relate words meaningfully to themselves, by determining whether the words describe themselves. Even the words that participants assess as not describing themselves are recalled at high levels, simply as a result of considering whether the words do or do not describe themselves. However, the highest levels of recall occur with words that people consider self-descriptive. Similar self-reference effects have been found by many other researchers (e.g., Bower & Gilligan, 1979; P. Brown, Keenan, & Potts, 1986; Ganellen & Carver, 1985; Halpin, Puff, Mason, & Marston, 1984; A. N. Katz, 1987; Reeder, McCormick, & Esselman, 1987).

Some researchers suggest that the self-reference effect is distinctive, but others (e.g., Mills, 1983) suggest that it is easily explained in terms of the LOP framework or other ordinary memory processes. Specifically, each of us has a very elaborate *self-schema,* an organized system of internal cues regarding ourselves, our attributes, and our personal experiences. Thus, we can richly and elaborately encode information related to ourselves much

TABLE 5.2 LEVELS-OF-PROCESSING FRAMEWORK

Among the levels of processing proposed by Fergus Craik and Endel Tulving are the physical, acoustic, and semantic levels, as shown in this table.

Level of Processing	Basis for Processing	Example
Physical	Visually apparent features of the letters	Word: TABLE Question: Is the word written in capital letters?
Acoustic	Sound combinations associated with the letters (e.g., rhyming)	Word: CAT Question: Does the word rhyme with "MAT"?
Semantic	Meaning of the word	Word: DAFFODIL Question: Is the word a type of plant?

more so than information about other topics (Bellezza, 1984, 1992). Also, we can easily organize new information pertaining to ourselves. When other information is also readily organized, we may recall non-self-referent information easily, as well (Klein & Kihlstrom, 1986). Finally, when we generate our own cues, we demonstrate much higher levels of recall than when someone else generates cues for us to use (Greenwald & Banaji, 1989).

Despite much supporting evidence, the LOP framework as a whole has its critics. For one thing, some researchers suggest that the particular levels may involve a circular definition, in which the levels are defined as deeper because the information is retained better, and vice versa. In addition, some researchers noted some paradoxes in retention. For example, under some circumstances, strategies that use rhymes (focusing on superficial sounds, not underlying meanings) have produced better retention than those using just semantic rehearsal (focusing on repetition of underlying meanings). Specifically, when the context for retrieval involves attention to phonological (acoustic) properties of words (e.g., rhymes), performance is enhanced when the context for encoding involves rehearsal based on phonological properties, rather than on semantic properties of words (Fisher & Craik, 1977, 1980). Nonetheless, when comparing semantic retrieval, based on semantic encoding, with acoustic (rhyme) retrieval, based on rhyme encoding, performance was greater for semantic retrieval than for acoustic retrieval (Fisher & Craik, 1977).

In light of these criticisms and some contrary findings, the LOP model has been revised to reflect the observation that the sequence of the levels of encoding may not be as important as the match between the type of elaboration of the encoding and the type of task required for retrieval (Morris, Bransford, & Franks, 1977). Furthermore, there appear to be two kinds of strategies for elaborating the encoding: (a) *within-item elaboration,* which elaborates encoding of the particular item (e.g., a word or other fact) in terms of its characteristics—including the various levels of processing; and (b) *between-item elaboration,* which elaborates encoding by relating each item's features (again, at various levels) to the features of items already in memory. Thus, if you wanted to be sure to remember something in particular, you could elaborate it at various levels for each of the two strategies.

PRACTICAL APPLICATIONS OF COGNITIVE PSYCHOLOGY

Elaboration strategies have practical applications: In studying, you may wish to match the way in which you encode the material to the way in which you will be expected to retrieve it in the future. Further, the more elaborately and diversely you encode material, the more readily you are likely to recall it later, in a variety of task settings. Just looking over material again and again in the same way is less likely to be productive for learning the material than is finding more than one way in which to learn it. If the context for retrieval will require you to have a deep understanding of the information, you should find ways to encode the material at deep levels of processing, such as by asking yourself meaningful questions about the material.

WORKING MEMORY

Some psychologists (e.g., Baddeley, 1990a, 1995; Cantor & Engle, 1993; Daneman & Carpenter, 1980; Daneman & Tardif, 1987; Engle, 1994; Engle, Cantor, & Carullo, 1992) view short-term and long-term memory from a different perspective. Table 5.3 contrasts the Atkinson–Shiffrin model with an alternative perspective. You may note the semantic distinctions, the differences in metaphorical representation, and the differences in emphasis for each view. The key feature of the alternative view is the role of **working memory,** defined as being part of long-term memory and which also comprises short-term memory. According to this perspective, working memory holds only the most recently activated portion of long-term memory, and it moves these activated elements into and out of brief, temporary memory storage.

Alan Baddeley *is past director of the MRC Applied Psychology Unit, Cambridge, England, and is a professor of cognitive psychology at Bristol University. Baddeley is best known for his work on the concept of working memory, which has shown that working memory can be viewed as an interface among many of the varied aspects of cognition.*

Alan Baddeley (1990b; 1992; 1993; 1997; Baddeley & Hitch, 1974) has suggested an integrative model of memory, which synthesizes the working-memory model with the LOP framework. Essentially, he views the LOP framework as an extension of, rather than as a replacement for, the working-memory model.

In particular, Baddeley suggests that working memory comprises the following: (a) a *visuospatial sketchpad,* which briefly holds some visual images; (b) a *phonological loop,* which briefly holds inner speech for verbal comprehension, as well as for acoustic rehearsal (without which acoustic information decays after about 2 seconds); and (c) a *central executive,* which both coordinates attentional activities and governs responses; as well as (d) probably a number of other "subsidiary slave systems" that perform other cognitive or perceptual tasks (Baddeley, 1989, p. 36). Baddeley's visuospatial sketchpad might be used for Craik's physical processing; Baddeley's articulatory loop might be used for Craik's acoustic processing. To integrate the various levels of processing, Baddeley's central executive moves items in and out of short-term memory, and it integrates the information arriving from the senses and from long-term memory.

Support for a distinction between working memory and long-term memory comes from neuropsychological research. Neuropsychological studies have shown abundant evidence of a brief memory buffer (used for remembering information temporarily), which is

TABLE 5.3 TRADITIONAL VERSUS NONTRADITIONAL VIEWS OF MEMORY

Since Richard Atkinson and Richard Shiffrin first proposed their three-stores model of memory (which may be considered a traditional view of memory), various other models have been suggested.

	Traditional Three-Stores View	Alternative View of Memory*
Terminology: definition of memory stores	*Working memory* is another name for short-term memory, which is distinct from long-term memory.	*Working memory* (active memory) is that part of long-term memory that comprises all the knowledge of facts and procedures that has been recently activated in memory, including the brief, fleeting short-term memory and its contents.
Metaphor for envisioning the relationships	Short-term memory may be envisioned as being distinct from long-term memory, perhaps either alongside it or hierarchically linked to it.	Short-term memory, working memory, and long-term memory may be envisioned as nested concentric spheres, in which working memory contains only the most recently activated portion of long-term memory, and short-term memory contains only a very small, fleeting portion of working memory.
Metaphor for the movement of information	Information moves directly from long-term memory to short-term memory, and then back, never in both locations at once.	Information remains within long-term memory; when activated, information moves into long-term memory's specialized working memory, which will actively move information into and out of the short-term memory store contained within it.
Emphasis	Distinction between long- and short-term memory.	Role of activation in moving information into working memory and the role of working memory in memory processes.

*Examples of researchers holding this view: Cantor & Engle, 1993; Engle, 1994; Engle, Cantor, & Carullo, 1992.

distinct from long-term memory (used for remembering information for long periods of time; see Schacter, 1989a; Squire, 1986). Furthermore, some promising new research using PET techniques has found evidence for distinct brain areas involved in the different aspects of working memory. The phonological loop, maintaining speech-related information, appears to involve bilateral activation of the frontal and parietal lobes (Cabeza & Nyberg, 1997). Interestingly, the visuospatial sketchpad appears to activate slightly different areas, depending on the length of the retention interval. Shorter intervals activate areas of the occipital and right frontal lobes, whereas longer intervals activate areas of the parietal and left frontal lobes (Haxby, Ungerleider, Horwitz, Rapoport, & Grady, 1995). Finally, the central executive functions appear to involve activation mostly in the frontal lobes (Roberts, Robbins, & Weiskrantz, 1996). Although these findings are interesting and exciting, they should be taken as somewhat speculative until more research has been done to confirm them.

Whereas the three-stores view emphasizes the structural receptacles for stored information, the working-memory model underscores the functions of working memory in governing the processes of memory, such as encoding and integrating information (cross-modal integration of acoustic and visual information, organizing information into meaningful chunks, linking new information to existing forms of knowledge representation in long-term memory, etc.). We can conceptualize the differing emphases with contrasting metaphors, such as comparing the three-stores view to a warehouse, in which information is passively stored, with the sensory store as the loading dock and the short-term store the area surrounding the loading dock, where information is stored temporarily until it is moved to or from the correct location in the warehouse. A metaphor for the working-memory model might be a multimedia production house, which continuously generates and manipulates images and sounds, coordinating the integration of sights and sounds into meaningful arrangements. Once images, sounds, and other information are stored, they are still available for reformatting and reintegration in novel ways, as new demands and new information become available.

MULTIPLE-MEMORY-SYSTEMS MODEL

Recall that when Wilder Penfield electrically stimulated the brains of his patients, the patients often asserted that they vividly recalled particular episodes and events, but not semantic facts that were unrelated to any particular event. These findings suggest that there may be separate memory systems for organizing and storing information with a distinctive time referent (e.g., "What did you eat for lunch yesterday?" "Who was the first person you saw this morning?"), in contrast with information that has no particular time referent ("Who were the two psychologists who first proposed the three-stores model of memory?" "What is a mnemonist?").

Based on such findings, Endel Tulving (1972) proposed a distinction between **semantic memory** (general world knowledge—our memory for facts that are not unique to us and that are not recalled in any particular temporal context) and **episodic memory** (personally experienced events or episodes). According to Tulving, we use episodic memory when we learn lists of words or when we need to recall something that occurred to us at a particular time or in a particular context. For example, if I needed to remember that I saw Harrison Hardimanowitz in the dentist's office yesterday, I would be drawing on an episodic memory, but if I needed to remember the name of the person I now see in the waiting room ("Harrison Hardimanowitz"), I would be drawing on a semantic memory: There is no particular time tag associated with the name of that individual as being Harrison, but there is a time tag associated with my having seen him at the dentist's office yesterday.

Tulving (e.g., 1983, 1989) and others (e.g., Shoben, 1984) have marshalled support for the distinction between semantic and episodic memory, based on both neurological investigation (e.g., electrical-stimulation studies, studies of patients with memory disorders, and cerebral blood flow studies) and cognitive research. For example, lesions in the frontal lobe appear to affect recollection regarding *when* a stimulus was presented, without affecting recall or recognition memory *that* a particular stimulus was presented (see Schacter, 1989a). Nonetheless, it is not clear that semantic and episodic memory are two distinct systems, although they sometimes appear to function in different ways. Many cognitive psychologists (e.g., Baddeley, 1984; M. Eysenck & Keane, 1990;

Humphreys, Bain, & Pike, 1989; M. K. Johnson & Hasher, 1987; Ratcliff & McKoon, 1986; Richardson-Klavehn & Bjork, 1988) question this distinction, pointing to blurry areas on the boundary between these two types of memory, as well as methodological problems with some of the supportive evidence. Perhaps episodic memory is merely a specialized form of semantic memory (Tulving, 1984, 1986). The question is open.

Since Tulving first proposed the distinction between semantic and episodic memory, he has identified a third discrete memory system for procedural knowledge, sometimes termed *procedural memory* (Tulving, 1985). The cerebellum of the brain seems to be centrally involved in this type of memory. In contrast to the available evidence for an episodic memory distinct from semantic memory, the neuropsychological and cognitive evidence supporting a discrete procedural memory has been much better documented (e.g., N. J. Cohen, Eichenbaum, Deacedo, & Corkin, 1985; N. J. Cohen & Squire, 1980; Squire, 1987). Larry Squire (e.g., 1986, 1993) has suggested an alternative taxonomy of memory (see Figure 5.4), in which he distinguishes declarative (explicit) memory from various kinds of nondeclarative (implicit) memory, comprising procedural memory, priming effects, simple classical conditioning, habituation, sensitization, and perceptual aftereffects.

A Connectionist Perspective

The network model provides the structural basis for the *parallel distributed processing (PDP) model,* often termed the *connectionist model.* According to the PDP model, the key to knowledge representation lies in the connections among various nodes, not in each individual node. (This notion of connections as the basis of representation echoes Hebb's work on cell assemblies, discussed in chapter 2.) Furthermore, activation of one node may prompt activation of a connected node, and this process of *spreading activation* may

FIGURE 5.4 **SQUIRE'S TAXONOMY OF MEMORY**

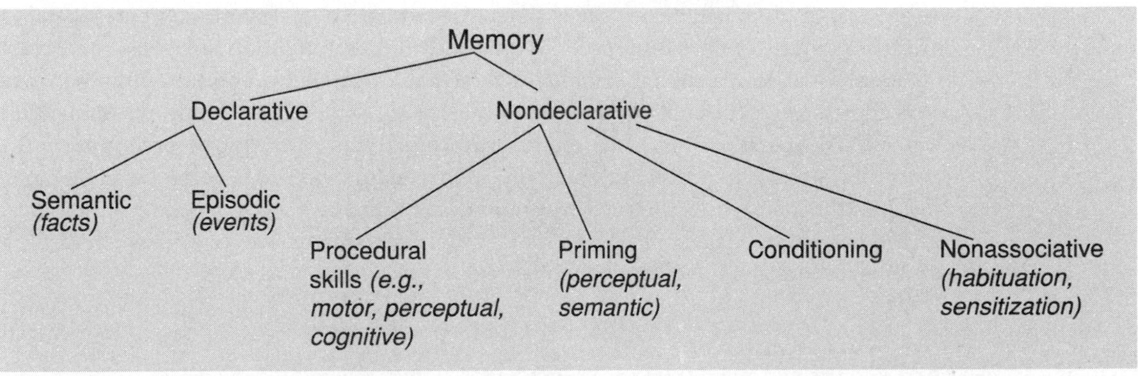

Based on extensive neuropsychological research, Larry Squire has posited that memory comprises two fundamental types: declarative (explicit) memory and various forms of nondeclarative (implicit) memory, each of which may be associated with discrete cerebral structures and processes.

prompt the activation of additional nodes. The PDP model fits quite nicely with the notion of working memory as comprising the activated portion of long-term memory. In this model, activation spreads through nodes within the network, as long as the activation does not exceed the limits of working memory. A node that activates a connected node is termed a **prime,** and the resulting activation is termed the **priming effect.** The priming effect has been supported by considerable evidence (e.g., the aforementioned studies of priming as an aspect of implicit memory). In addition, some evidence supports the notion that priming is due to spreading activation (e.g., McClelland & Rumelhart, 1985, 1988), but not everyone agrees about the mechanism for the priming effect (e.g., see McKoon & Ratcliff, 1992b).

Connectionist models also have some intuitive appeal in their ability to integrate several contemporary notions about memory: *Working memory* comprises the *activated* portion of long-term memory and operates via at least some amount of *parallel processing; spreading activation* involves the simultaneous (parallel) activation *(priming)* of multiple links among *nodes* within the *network.* Many cognitive psychologists who hold this integrated view suggest that part of the reason we humans are as efficient as we are in processing information is because we can handle many operations at once. Thus, the contemporary cognitive-psychological conceptions of working memory, network models of memory, spreading activation, priming, and parallel processes mutually enhance and support one another.

Some of the research supporting the connectionist model of memory has come directly from experimental studies of people performing cognitive tasks in laboratory settings. Connectionist models effectively explain priming effects, skill learning (procedural memory), and several other phenomena of memory. Thus far, however, connectionist models have failed to provide clear predictions and explanations of recall and recognition memory that occurs following a single episode or a single exposure to semantic information.

In addition to using laboratory experiments on human participants, cognitive psychologists have used computer models to simulate various aspects of information processing. The three-stores model is based on serial (sequential) processing of information, which can be simulated on individual computers that handle only one operation at a time. In contrast, the parallel-processing model of working memory, which involves simultaneous processing of multiple operations, cannot be simulated on a single computer; parallel processing requires *neural networks,* in which multiple computers are linked and operating in tandem, or at least a special computer operates with parallel networks. Many cognitive psychologists now prefer a parallel-processing model to describe many phenomena of memory. The parallel-processing model was actually inspired by observing how the human brain seems to process information, with multiple processes going on at the same time. In addition to inspiring theoretical models of memory function, neuropsychological research has offered specific insights into memory processes, as well as evidence regarding various hypotheses of how human memory works.

Memory in the Real World

Before moving on to discuss exceptional memory and neuropsychology, we need to focus on another recent trend in memory research that calls for a more dramatic shift in both the phenomena to be studied and the terminology used in explanations of memory. This perspective begins by asking how memory is used in everyday situations, and what memory is for. Thus, the recommendation is to study memory in more real-world, as opposed to laboratory, settings (G. Cohen, 1989; Neisser, 1978, 1982). The basic idea is that memory research should have *ecological validity,* applying to natural memory phenomena in natural settings—there is no place for pure laboratory research in this kind of framework. The techniques used therefore examine naturalistic settings using self-reports and questionnaires. Although this approach has been criticized for its lack of control and generalizability (Banaji & Crowder, 1989), it has generated some interesting new conceptualizations into the nature of memory research in general.

For example, a recent theoretical paper by Koriat and Goldsmith (1996) calls for a change in the metaphor used in conceptualizing memory, rather than a change in the research setting. Koriat and Goldsmith point out that the traditional *storehouse* metaphor of memory, in which memory is conceived of as a repository of information and events, inevitably leads to questions of quantity—how many items can be remembered from or used in a particular occasion? The laboratory setting is most congenial to this approach, allowing for control over the variables of quantity. In contrast, the everyday or real-world approach calls for more of a *correspondence* metaphor, in which memory is conceived of as a vehicle for interaction with the real world. Thus, the questions shift towards accuracy in representing past events—how closely does memory correspond to particular events?

As Koriat and Goldsmith (1996) point out, the important consideration is not the setting of research, whether laboratory or real-world, but the kind of metaphor. They argue that the correspondence metaphor takes into consideration more of the functional aspects of memory. Moreover, correspondence can be studied using both laboratory and naturalistic settings. They suggest that many of the current disagreements between the laboratory and real-world proponents can be settled by changing the metaphor, rather than the setting, for memory research. This change would provide a new structure for understanding memory—a structure in which memory is viewed as fulfilling a particular purpose in our interactions with the world.

Indeed, we may see this new trend broadening as more researchers become increasingly interested in the functional properties of memory. Already some promising new insights into the question of what memory is for offer some concrete proposals into the structure of memory. For example, a recent paper by Arthur Glenberg (1997) calls for a memory system centered around bodily interactions with the environment. Thus, correspondence with the real world is achieved via representations that reflect the structural relationship between the body and the external world, rather than the encoding of abstract symbolic representations. Likewise, Baddeley's (1997) recent book updates his working memory model by addressing what uses the phonological loop and visuospatial sketchpad provide, as well as extending many of the phenomena of memory into the realm of functionality.

Whether this approach will take the lead in memory research, or be overcome by the impetus of the laboratory-storehouse metaphor, remains to be seen. Whatever the case may be, new metaphors and controversies are essential for the survival of the field—without a constant flow of new ideas (or rethinking of old ideas), science would stagnate and die. Another approach that is already beginning to dominate much of memory research is the neuropsychological study of memory, which developed from the study of persons with exceptional memory.

EXCEPTIONAL MEMORY AND NEUROPSYCHOLOGY

Up to this point, the discussion of memory has focused on tasks and structures involving normally functioning memory. However, there are rare cases of persons with exceptional memory (either enhanced or deficient) that provide some interesting insights into the nature of memory in general. The study of exceptional memory leads directly to neuropsychological investigations of the physiological mechanisms underlying memory.

OUTSTANDING MEMORY: MNEMONISTS

Imagine what your life would be like if you had outstanding memory abilities—if you were able to remember every word printed in this book, for example. If this were the case, you would be considered a **mnemonist,** someone who demonstrates extraordinarily keen memory ability, usually based on using a special technique for memory enhancement. Perhaps the most famous of mnemonists was a man called "S.," who was described by noted Russian psychologist Alexander Luria (1902–1977).

Luria (1968) reported that one day, S. appeared in his laboratory and asked to have his memory tested. Luria tested him and discovered that the man's memory appeared to have virtually no limits. S. could reproduce extremely long strings of words, regardless of how much time had passed since the words had been presented to him. Luria studied S. over a period of 30 years and found that even when S.'s retention was measured 15 or 16 years after a session in which S. had learned words, S. could still reproduce the words. S. eventually became a professional entertainer, dazzling audiences with his ability to recall whatever was asked of him.

What was S.'s trick? How did he remember so much? Apparently, he relied heavily on the mnemonic of visual imagery. He converted material that he needed to remember into visual images. For example, he reported that when asked to remember the word *green,* he would visualize a green flowerpot; for the word *red,* a man in a red shirt coming toward him. Even numbers called up images. For example, *1* was a proud, well-built man, *3* a gloomy person, *6* a man with a swollen foot, and so on.

For S., much of his use of visual imagery in memory recall was not intentional, but rather the result of a rare psychological phenomenon termed *synesthesia* (*syn-,* "together"; *esthesia,* "sensation"), in which he experienced some sensations in a sensory modality different from the sense that was physically stimulated. For example, S. would automatically convert a sound into a visual impression, and he even reported experiencing a word's taste and weight. Each word to be remembered evoked a whole range of sensations that would automatically come to S. when he needed to recall that word.

Other mnemonists have used different strategies. V. P., a Russian émigré (Hunt & Love, 1972), could memorize long strings of material such as rows and columns of numbers. Whereas S. relied primarily on visual imagery, V. P. apparently relied more on verbal translations. He reported memorizing numbers by transforming them into dates, and then thinking about what he had done on that day.

A similar translation strategy was used by a mnemonist studied by K. Anders Ericsson, William Chase, and Steve Faloon (1980). S. F., their mnemonist, remembered long strings of numbers by segmenting them into groups of three or four digits each, and encoding them as running times for different races. An experienced long-distance runner himself, S. F. was familiar with the times that would be plausible for different races. What is particularly interesting about S. F. is that he did not enter the laboratory a mnemonist. Rather, he was selected to represent the average college student in terms of intelligence and memory ability.

S. F.'s original memory for a string of numbers was about seven digits, average for a college student. After 200 practice sessions distributed over a period of 2 years, however, S. F. had increased his memory for digits more than 10-fold, and could recall up to about 80 digits. His memory was severely impaired, however, when the experimenters purposely gave him sequences of digits that could not be translated into running times. The work with S. F. suggests that a person with a fairly typical level of memory ability can, at least in principle, be converted into one with quite an extraordinary memory, at least in some domains, following a great deal of concerted practice.

Many of us yearn to have memory abilities like those of S. or V. P., which would seem to allow us to ace our exams virtually effortlessly. However, we should consider that S. was not particularly happy with his life, in part because of his exceptional memory. He reported that his synesthesia, which was largely involuntary, interfered with his ability to listen to people. Voices gave rise to blurs of sensations, interfering with his ability to follow a conversation. Moreover, S.'s heavy reliance on imagery created difficulty for him when he tried to understand abstract concepts, such as *infinity* or *nothing,* which did not lend themselves well to visual images. He was also sometimes overwhelmed when he read. Earlier memories also sometimes intruded on later ones. Of course, we cannot say how many of S.'s problems in life were caused by his exceptional memory, but clearly S. himself believed that his exceptional memory had a down side as well as an up side, and it was often as likely to be a hindrance as a help.

These exceptional mnemonists offer some insight into processes of memory. Each of the three described here—consciously or almost automatically—translated arbitrary, abstract, meaningless information into more meaningful or more sensorially concrete information. Whether the translated information was racing times, dates and events, or visual images, the key was their meaning for the mnemonist.

We usually take for granted the ability to remember, much like the air we breathe. However, just as we become more aware of the importance of air when we do not have enough to breathe, we are less likely to take memory for granted when we observe people with serious memory deficiencies.

Deficient Memory: Amnesia

One disturbing type of **amnesia** (severe loss of explicit memory) is **retrograde amnesia,** in which individuals lose their purposeful memory for events prior to whatever trauma induces memory loss. Mild forms of retrograde amnesia can occur fairly commonly when someone sustains a concussion; usually events immediately prior to the concussive episode are not well-remembered.

W. Ritchie Russell and P. W. Nathan (1946) reported a more severe case of retrograde amnesia: A 22-year-old greenskeeper was thrown from his motorcycle in August of 1933. A week after the accident, the young man was able to converse sensibly and seemed to have recovered. However, it quickly became apparent that he had suffered a severe loss of memory for events that had occurred prior to the trauma. Upon questioning, he gave the date as February 1922, and believed himself to be a schoolboy. He had no recollection of the intervening years. Over the next several weeks, his memory for past events gradually returned, starting with the least recent and proceeding toward more recent events. By 10 weeks after the accident, he had recovered his memory for most of the events of the previous years, and he finally was able to recall everything that had happened up to a few minutes prior to the accident. In retrograde amnesia, the memories that return typically do so starting from the more distant past and progressing up to the time of the trauma. Often, events right before the trauma are never recalled.

Another kind of amnesia is one that almost all of us experience: **infantile amnesia,** the inability to recall events that happened when we were very young (see Spear, 1979). Generally, we can remember little or nothing that has happened to us before the age of about 5 years, and it is extremely rare for someone to recall many memories before age 3 years. Reports of childhood memories usually involve memories of significant events (e.g., the birth of a sibling or the death of a parent; see Fivush & Hamond, 1991). For example, some adults have recalled their own hospitalization or the birth of a sibling as far back as age 2 years, and the death of a parent or a family move may be recalled from as far back as age 3 years (Usher & Neisser, 1993).

The accuracy of reported childhood memories has come into question recently, however. In fact, many psychologists (e.g., Ceci & Bruck, 1993) suggest that the accuracy of children's recollections of events may be questionable, even shortly after these events occurred, particularly if the children are exposed to covert or overt suggestions regarding the remembered material. (The unreliability of our memories for events is discussed more fully in the next chapter.)

One of the most famous cases of amnesia is the case of H. M., reported by William Scoville and Brenda Milner (1957). H. M. underwent brain surgery to save him from continual disruptions due to uncontrollable epilepsy. The operation took place on September 1, 1953, and was largely experimental, with highly unpredictable results. At the time of the operation, H. M. was 29 years old and above average in intelligence. After the operation, his recovery was uneventful, with one exception. He suffered severe **anterograde amnesia**—he had great difficulty remembering events that occurred from the time of the surgery, onward. However, he had good (although not perfect) recollection of events that had occurred before his operation. H. M.'s memory loss severely affected his life. On one occasion, he remarked, "Every day is alone in itself, whatever enjoyment I've had, and whatever sorrow I've had" (Milner, Corkin, & Teuber, 1968, p. 217). Apparently, H. M. all but totally lost his ability purposefully to recollect any new memories of the time following his operation, so he lived suspended in an eternal present.

Amnesia and the Explicit–Implicit Memory Distinction

Research psychologists study amnesia patients in part to gain insight into memory functioning in general. One of the general insights gained by studying amnesia victims highlights the distinction between explicit memory, which typically is impaired in amnesia, and implicit memory (e.g., priming effects on word-completion tasks and procedural memory for skill-based tasks), which typically is not impaired. Apparently the ability to reflect consciously on prior experience, which is required for tasks involving explicit memory of declarative knowledge, differs in ways from the ability to demonstrate remembered learning in an apparently automatic way, without conscious recollection of the learning (Baddeley, 1989). In fact, even amnesia victims, who perform extremely poorly on most explicit memory tasks, show normal or almost normal performance on tasks involving implicit memory such as cued-recall tasks (Warrington & Weiskrantz, 1970) and word-completion tasks (Baddeley, 1989). However, following word-completion tasks, when amnesics were asked whether they had previously seen the word they just completed, they were unlikely to remember the specific experience of having seen the word (Graf, Mandler, & Haden, 1982; Tulving, Schacter, & Stark 1982). Furthermore, these amnesics do not explicitly recognize words they have seen at better than chance levels. Although the distinction between implicit memory and explicit memory has been readily observed in amnesics, both amnesics and normal participants show the presence of implicit memory.

Likewise, amnesia victims also show paradoxical performance in regard to tasks that involve *procedural knowledge* ("knowing how"—skills, such as how to ride a bicycle) versus those that involve *declarative knowledge* ("knowing that"—factual information, such as the terms in a psychology textbook). On the one hand, amnesia victims may perform extremely poorly on the traditional memory tasks requiring recall or recognition memory of declarative knowledge. On the other hand, they may demonstrate improvement in performance due to learning—remembered practice—when engaged in tasks that require procedural knowledge, such as solving puzzles, learning to read mirror writing, or mastering motor skills (Baddeley, 1989).

Amnesia and Neuropsychology

Studies of amnesia victims have revealed much about the way in which memory depends on the effective functioning of particular structures of the brain. By looking for matches between particular lesions in the brain and particular deficits of function, researchers come to understand how normal memory functions. Thus, when studying different kinds of cognitive processes in the brain, neuropsychologists frequently look for *dissociations* of function, in which normal individuals show the presence of a particular function (e.g., explicit memory), but persons with specific lesions in the brain show the absence of that particular function, despite the presence of normal functions in other areas (e.g., implicit memory).

By observing persons with disturbed memory function, for example, we know that memory is volatile and may be affected by a blow to the head, a disturbance in consciousness, or any number of other injuries to or pathologies of the brain. We cannot determine, however, the specific cause–effect relationship between a given structural lesion and a particular memory deficit. The fact that a particular structure or region is associated with an interruption of function does not mean that the region is solely responsible for controlling that function. Indeed, functions can be shared by multiple structures or regions. A broad physiological analogy may help to explain the difficulty of determining localization based on an observed deficit. The normal functioning of a portion of the brain (the reticular activating system) is essential to life, but life depends on more than a functioning brain—ask a patient with heart or lung disease if you doubt the importance of other structures. Thus, although the reticular activating system is essential to life, a person's death may be due to malfunction in other structures of the body. Tracing a dysfunction within the brain to a particular structure or region poses a similar problem.

When observing simple dissociations, many alternative hypotheses may explain a link between a particular lesion and a particular deficit of function. Much more compelling support for hypotheses about cognitive functions comes from observing *double dissociations,* in which persons with different kinds of neuropathologies show opposite patterns of deficits. For some functions and some areas of the brain, neuropsychologists have managed to observe the presence of a double dissociation. For example, some evidence for distinguishing brief memory from long-term memory comes from just such a double dissociation (Schacter, 1989b): Persons with lesions in the left parietal lobe of the brain show profound inability to retain information in short-term memory but no impairment of long-term memory; they continue to encode, store, and retrieve information in long-term memory, apparently with little difficulty (Shallice & Warrington, 1970; Warrington & Shallice, 1972); in contrast, persons with lesions in the medial (middle) temporal regions of the brain show relatively normal short-term memory of verbal materials (e.g., letters and words) but serious inability to retain new verbal materials in long-term memory (Milner, Corkin, & Teuber, 1968; Shallice, 1979; Warrington, 1982).

Even when double dissociations offer strong support for the notion that particular structures of the brain play particular vital roles in memory (Squire, 1987), and disturbances or lesions in these areas cause severe deficits in memory formation, we cannot say that memory—or even part of memory—resides in these structures. Nonetheless, studies of brain-injured patients are informative and at least suggestive of how memory works. At present, cognitive neuropsychologists have found that double dissociations support a distinction between brief memory and long-term memory, and between declarative (explicit) and nondeclarative (implicit) memory, as well as some preliminary indications of other distinctions.

The Role of the Hippocampus and Other Structures

One of the central questions in the neuropsychology of memory has been this: Where in the brain are memories stored, and what structures and areas of the brain are involved in memory processes, such as encoding and retrieval? Many early attempts at localization of memory were unfruitful. For example, after literally hundreds of experiments, renowned neuropsychologist Karl Lashley reluctantly stated that he could find no specific locations in the brain for specific memories. In the decades since Lashley's admission, psychologists have been able to locate many cerebral structures involved in memory, such as the hippocampus and other nearby structures. However, the physiological structure may not be such that we will find Lashley's elusive localizations of specific ideas, thoughts, or events. Even Penfield's findings regarding links between electrical stimulation and episodic memory of events have been subject to question.

Some studies show encouraging, although preliminary, findings regarding the structures that seem to be involved in various aspects of memory. First, specific sensory properties of a given experience appear to be organized across various areas of the cerebral cortex (Squire, 1986). For example, the visual, spatial, and odor features of an experience may be stored discretely in each of the areas of the cortex responsible for processing of each type of sensation. Thus, the cerebral cortex appears to play an important role in memory, in terms of the long-term storage of information (Zola-Morgan & Squire, 1990).

In addition, the hippocampus and some related nearby cerebral structures appear to be important for explicit memory of experiences and other declarative information, and the hippocampus seems to play a key role in the encoding of declarative information (Squire & Zola-Morgan, 1991; Zola-Morgan & Squire, 1990). Its main function appears to be in the integration and consolidation of separate sensory information, and most importantly, the transfer of newly synthesized information into long-term structures supporting declarative knowledge, perhaps as a means of cross-referencing information stored in different parts of the brain (Reber, Knowlton, & Squire, 1996; Squire, 1986; Squire, Cohen, & Nadel, 1984). Additionally, the hippocampus seems to play a crucial role in complex learning (McCormick & Thompson, 1984).

In evolutionary terms, the aforementioned cerebral structures (chiefly, the cortex and the hippocampus) are relatively recent acquisitions, and declarative memory may be considered a relatively recent phenomenon. At the same time, other memory structures may be responsible for nondeclarative forms of memory. For example, the basal ganglia seem to be the primary structures controlling procedural knowledge (Mishkin & Petri, 1984), although not in controlling the priming effect (Heindel, Butters, & Salmon, 1988), which may be influenced by various other kinds of memory (Schacter, 1989b). Furthermore, the cerebellum also seems to play a key role in memory for classically conditioned responses, as well as contributing to many cognitive tasks in general (Cabeza & Nyberg, 1997; Thompson, 1987). Thus, various forms of nondeclarative memory seem to rely on differing cerebral structures.

In addition to these preliminary insights regarding the macrolevel structures of memory, we are beginning to understand the microlevel structure of memory. For example, we know that repeated stimulation of particular neural pathways tends to strengthen the likelihood of firing; that is, at a particular synapse, there appear to be physiological changes in the dendrites of the receiving neuron, making the neuron more likely to reach the threshold for firing again (see chapter 2).

We also know that some neurotransmitters disrupt memory storage, and other neurotransmitters enhance memory storage. Both serotonin and acetylcholine seem to enhance neural transmission associated with memory, and noradrenaline may also do so. High concentrations of acetylcholine have been found in the hippocampus of normal persons (Squire, 1987), but low concentrations are found in victims of *Alzheimer's disease*—a disorder causing severe memory loss. In fact, Alzheimer's patients show severe loss of the brain tissue that secretes acetylcholine. Despite intensive research in this area, scientists have yet to pin down the specific causes of Alzheimer's disease.

Researchers have been better able to track down the cause of another form of memory dysfunction, but they have not devised a way to eliminate this preventable deficit: Alcohol consumption has been shown to disrupt the activity of serotonin, thereby impairing the formation of memories (Weingartner, Rudorfer, Buchsbaum, & Linnoila, 1983). In fact, severe or prolonged abuse of alcohol can lead to *Korsakoff's syndrome,* a devastating form of anterograde amnesia, often accompanied by at least some retrograde amnesia (Parkin, 1991; Shimamura & Squire, 1986). Korsakoff's syndrome has been linked to damage in the *diencephalon* (the region comprising the thalamus and the hypothalamus) of the brain (e.g., Jernigan, Schafer, Butters, & Cermak, 1991; Langlais, Mandel, & Mair, 1992), as well as to dysfunction or damage in other areas (Jacobson & Lishman, 1990), such as in the frontal (Parsons & Nixon, 1993; Squire, 1982) and the temporal (Blansjaar, Vielvoye, Van Dijk, Gert, & Rinders, 1992) lobes of the cortex.

Other physiological factors also affect memory function. Some of the naturally occurring hormones also stimulate increased availability of glucose in the brain, which enhances memory function. These hormones are often associated with highly arousing events—such as traumas, achievements, first-time experiences (e.g., first passionate kiss), crises, or other peak moments (e.g., reaching a major decision)—and may play a role in remembering these events. Although many cognitive theorists and other researchers have been interested in the neuropsychology of memory for content knowledge, some of the most fascinating work has focused more on the strategies used in regard to memory. Memory strategies and memory processes are the subject of the following chapter.

SUMMARY

1. **What are some of the tasks used for studying memory, and what do various tasks indicate about the structure of memory?** Among the many tasks used by cognitive psychologists, some of the main ones have been tasks assessing explicit recall of information (e.g., free recall, serial recall, and cued recall) and tasks assessing explicit recognition of information. By comparing memory performance on these explicit tasks with performance on implicit tasks (e.g., word-completion tasks), cognitive psychologists have found evidence of differing memory systems or processes governing each type of task (e.g., as shown in studies of amnesics).

2. **What has been the prevailing traditional model of the structure of memory?** *Memory* is the means by which we draw on our knowledge of the past in order to use this knowledge in the present. According to one model, memory is conceived as involving three stores: (a) a *sensory store,* capable of holding relatively limited amounts of information for very brief periods of time; (b) a *short-term store,* capable of holding small amounts of information for somewhat longer periods of time; and (c) a *long-term store,* capable of storing large amounts of information virtually indefinitely. Within the sensory store, the *iconic store* refers to visual sensory memory.

3. **What are some of the main alternative models of the structure of memory?** An alternative model uses the concept of *working memory,* usually defined as being part of long-term memory and also comprising short-term memory. From this perspective, working memory holds only the most recently activated portion of long-term memory, and it moves these activated elements into and out of short-term memory. Additional models include the *levels-of-processing framework,* which hypothesizes distinctions in memory ability based on the degree to which items are elaborated during encoding; and the *multiple-memory-systems* model, which posits not only a distinction between procedural memory and declarative (semantic) memory, but also a distinction between semantic and episodic memory. In addition, psychologists have proposed other models for the structure of memory, including a parallel-distributed-processing (PDP; connectionist) model. The

PDP model incorporates the notions of working memory, semantic memory networks, spreading activation, priming, and parallel processing of information. Finally, many psychologists call for a complete change in the conceptualization of memory, focusing on memory functioning in the real world. This call leads to a shift in memory metaphors from the traditional storehouse to the more modern correspondence metaphor.

4. **What have psychologists learned about the structure of memory by studying exceptional memory and the physiology of the brain?** Among other findings, studies of *mnemonists* have shown the value of imagery in memory for concrete information, as well as the importance of finding or forming meaningful connections among items to be remembered. The main forms of *amnesia* are *anterograde amnesia, retrograde amnesia,* and *infantile amnesia.* The last form of amnesia is qualitatively different from the other forms, and occurs in everyone. By studying the memory function of persons with each form of amnesia, it has been possible to differentiate various aspects of memory, such as long-term versus temporary forms of memory, procedural versus declarative memory processes, and explicit versus implicit memory.

   Although specific memory traces have not yet been identified, many of the specific structures involved in memory function have been located. To date, the subcortical structures involved in memory appear to include the hippocampus, the thalamus, the hypothalamus, and even the basal ganglia and the cerebellum. The cortex also governs much of the long-term storage of declarative knowledge. The neurotransmitters serotonin and acetylcholine appear to be vital to memory function. Other physiological chemicals, structures, and processes also play important roles, although further investigation is required to identify these roles.

Thinking About Thinking: Factual, Analytical, Creative, and Practical Questions

1. Describe two characteristics each of sensory memory, of short-term memory, and of long-term memory.
2. What are double dissociations, and why are they valuable to understanding the relationship between cognitive function and the brain?
3. Compare and contrast the three-stores model of memory with one of the alternative models of memory.
4. Critique one of the experiments described in this chapter. What is a problem you see regarding the interpretation given? How could subsequent research be designed to enhance the interpretation of the findings?
5. How would you design an experiment to study some aspect of implicit memory?

6. Imagine what it would be like to recover from one of the forms of amnesia. Describe your impressions of and reactions to your newly recovered memory abilities.
7. How would your life be different if you could greatly enhance your own mnemonic skills in some way?

Key Terms

amnesia 173
anterograde amnesia 174
episodic memory 168
explicit memory 157
hypothetical construct 158
iconic store 159
implicit memory 157
infantile amnesia 174
levels-of-processing framework 164
long-term store 158
memory 154
mnemonist 172
prime 170
priming 157
priming effect 170
recall 155
recognition 155
retrograde amnesia 173
semantic memory 168
sensory store 158
short-term store 158
working memory 166

Annotated Suggested Readings

Baddeley, A. (1995). Working memory. In M. S. Gazzaniga (Ed.), *The cognitive neurosciences* (pp. 755–764). Cambridge, MA: MIT Press. A concise review of our knowledge regarding working memory.

Koriat, A. & Goldsmith, M. (1996). Memory metaphors and the everyday–laboratory controversy: The correspondence versus the storehouse conceptions of memory. *Behavioral and Brain Sciences, 19,* 167–228. An exciting new approach to organizing memory research, offering some deep insights into the role of metaphors in guiding research.

Schacter, D. L. (1995). Implicit memory. In M. S. Gazzaniga (Ed.), *The cognitive neurosciences* (pp. 815–824). Cambridge, MA: MIT Press. A concise review of our knowledge regarding implicit memory.

Squire, L. R. (1993). The organization of declarative and nondeclarative memory. In T. Ono, L. R. Squire, M. E. Raichle, D. I. Perrett, & M. Fukuda (Eds.), *Brain mechanisms of perception and memory: From neuron to behavior* (pp. 219–227). New York: Oxford University Press. An account of Squire's highly regarded theory of the organization of knowledge in memory.

Memory Processes

Chapter Outline

Exploring Cognitive Psychology

Encoding and Movement of Information
- Forms of Encoding
- Movement of Information From Short-Term Memory to Long-Term Memory

Retrieval
- Retrieval From Short-Term Memory
- Retrieval From Long-Term Memory

Processes of Forgetting and Memory Distortion
- Interference Versus Decay Theory
- The Constructive Nature of Memory
- Context Effects on Encoding and Retrieval

Summary

Thinking About Thinking: Factual, Analytical, Creative, and Practical Questions

Key Terms

Annotated Suggested Readings

Exploring Cognitive Psychology

1. **What have cognitive psychologists discovered regarding how we encode information for storing it in memory?**
2. **What affects our ability to retrieve information from memory?**
3. **How does what we know or what we learn affect what we remember?**

The procedure is actually quite simple. First you arrange items into different groups. Of course one pile may be sufficient depending on how much there is to do. If you have to go somewhere else due to lack of facilities that is the next step; otherwise, you are pretty well set. It is important not to overdo things. That is, it is better to do too few things at once than too many. In the short run this may not seem important but complications can easily arise. A mistake can be expensive as well. At first, the whole procedure will seem complicated. Soon, however, it will become just another facet of life. It is difficult to foresee any end to the necessity for this task in the immediate future, but then, one can never tell. After the procedure is completed one arranges the materials into different groups again. Then they can be put into their appropriate places. Eventually they will be used once more and the whole cycle will then have to be repeated. However, that is part of life.

John Bransford and Marcia Johnson (1972, p. 722) asked their participants to read the preceding passage and to recall the steps involved. To get an idea of how easy it was for their participants to do so, try to recall those steps now yourself. Bransford and Johnson's participants (and probably you, too) had a great deal of difficulty understanding this passage and recalling the steps involved. What makes this task so difficult? What are the mental processes involved in this task?

As mentioned in the previous chapter, cognitive psychologists generally refer to the main processes of memory as comprising three common operations: encoding, storage, and retrieval—each one representing a stage in memory processing. **Encoding** refers to how you transform a physical, sensory input into a kind of representation that can be placed into memory. **Storage** refers to how you retain encoded information in memory. **Retrieval** refers to how you gain access to information stored in memory. Although our emphasis in discussing these processes will be on recall of verbal and pictorial material, remember that we have memories of other kinds of stimuli as well, such as odors (Herz & Engen, 1996).

Encoding, storage, and retrieval are often viewed as sequential stages, whereby you first take in information, then hold it for a while, and later pull it out. However, the processes interact with each other and are interdependent. For example, in trying to encode the information in the chapter-opening passage, you may have found the text difficult to encode, thereby also making it hard to store and to retrieve the information. However, a verbal label can facilitate encoding, and hence storage and retrieval. Most people do much better with the passage if given its title, "Washing Clothes." Try now to recall the steps described in the passage. The verbal label helps us to encode, and therefore to remember, a passage that otherwise seems incomprehensible.

ENCODING AND MOVEMENT OF INFORMATION

FORMS OF ENCODING

SHORT-TERM STORAGE

When you encode information for temporary storage and use, what kind of code do you use? A landmark experiment by R. Conrad (1964) was designed to address this question. Conrad presented participants visually with several series of six letters at the rate of 0.75 second per letter. The letters used in the various lists were *B, C, F, M, N, P, S, T, V,* and *X.* Immediately after the letters were presented, participants had to write down each list of six letters in the order given. Conrad was particularly interested in the kinds of recall errors participants made. The pattern of errors was clear. Despite the fact that letters were presented *visually,* errors tended to be based on *acoustic confusability.* In other words, instead of recalling the letters they were supposed to recall, participants substituted letters that sounded like the correct letters. Thus, they were likely to confuse *F* for *S, B* for *V, P* for *B,* and so on. In order to strengthen his case, Conrad had another group of participants simply listen to single letters in a setting that had noise in the background, and then immediately report each letter as they heard it. Participants showed the same pattern of confusability in the listening task as in the visual memory task, indicating that we seem to encode visually presented letters by how they sound, not by how they look.

Although the Conrad experiment shows the importance in short-term memory of an acoustic code, rather than a visual code, his results do not rule out the possibility that there are other codes—for example, a *semantic code* (one based on word meaning). Alan Baddeley (1966) pursued this line of research and argued that short-term memory relies primarily on an acoustic rather than a semantic code. When he compared recall performance for lists of acoustically confusable words—such as *MAP, CAB, MAD, MAN,* and *CAP*—with that for lists of acoustically distinct words—such as *COW, PIT, DAY, RIG,* and *BUN*—he found that performance was much worse for the visual presentation of acoustically similar words.

In contrast, when he compared performance for lists of semantically similar words—such as *BIG, LONG, LARGE, WIDE,* and *BROAD*—with performance for lists of semantically dissimilar words—such as *OLD, FOUL, LATE, HOT,* and *STRONG*—there was little difference in recall between the two lists. If performance for the semantically similar words had been much worse, it would have indicated that participants were confused by the semantic similarities and hence were processing the words semantically. However, performance for the semantically similar words was only *slightly* worse than that for the semantically dissimilar words.

Subsequent work by Harvey Shulman (1970) and by Delos Wickens and his colleagues (Wickens, Dalezman, & Eggemeier, 1976) investigating how information is encoded in short-term memory has shown clear evidence of at least some semantic encoding in short-term memory. Thus, although encoding in short-term memory appears to be primarily acoustic, there may be some secondary semantic encoding as well. In addition, Michael Posner (1969) and his colleagues (Posner, Boies, Eichelman, & Taylor, 1969; Posner & Keele, 1967) have found evidence that we sometimes temporarily encode information visually as well, although visual encoding appears to be even more fleeting (about 1.5 seconds) and vulnerable to decay than acoustic encoding. Thus, Conrad's original idea that initial encoding is acoustic in nature has been clarified and elaborated by considering additional research showing that other forms may be used under some circumstances.

LONG-TERM STORAGE

As mentioned, information stored temporarily in working memory is encoded primarily in acoustic form. Hence, when we make errors in retrieving words from short-term memory, the errors tend to reflect confusions in sound. How is information encoded into a form that can be transferred into storage and available for subsequent retrieval?

Most information stored in long-term memory seems to be primarily *semantically encoded*—that is, encoded by the meanings of words. Evidence in favor of a semantic code for information stored in long-term memory is highly persuasive, especially because several converging operations suggest the use of such a code. That is, a number of different kinds of experiments converge on the same result: Semantic encoding is used in long-term memory. Consider the kinds of evidence that have been amassed to support the existence of a semantic code.

One way to study encoding is to look at patterns of errors, as was done in research on short-term memory. Leonard Grossman and Morris Eagle (1970), for example, had participants learn a list of 41 different words. Five minutes after learning took place, participants were given a recognition test. Included in the recognition test were *distractors* (items that appear to be legitimate choices but that are not correct alternatives, that is, that were not presented previously). Nine of the distractors were semantically related to words on the list, and nine were not. The data of interest were *false alarms* to the distractors—that is, responses in which the participants indicated that they had seen the distractors, even though they had not. Participants falsely recognized an average of 1.83 of the synonyms, but only an average of 1.05 of the unrelated words, indicating a greater likelihood of semantic confusion.

Another way to show semantic encoding is to use sets of semantically related test words, rather than distractors. Weston Bousfield (1953), for example, had participants learn a list of 60 words that included 15 animals, 15 professions, 15 vegetables, and 15 names of people. The words were presented in random order, so that members of the various categories were thoroughly intermixed. After participants heard the words, they were asked to free-recall the list in any order they wished. Bousfield then analyzed the order of output of the recalled words. The question he addressed is whether participants recalled successive words from the same category more frequently than would be expected by chance. The results of his study showed that successive recalls from the same category did, in fact, occur much more often than would be expected by chance occurrence: Participants were remembering words by clustering them into categories.

Encoding of information in long-term memory is not exclusively semantic. There also is evidence for visual encoding. Nancy Frost (1972), for example, presented participants with 16 drawings of objects, including four items of clothing, four animals, four vehicles, and four items of furniture. Frost manipulated not only the semantic category, but also the visual category. The drawings differed in visual orientation, with four angled to the left, four angled to the right, four horizontal, and four vertical. Items were presented in random order, and participants were asked to recall them freely. The order of participants' responses showed effects of both semantic and visual categories, suggesting that participants were encoding visual as well as semantic information.

In addition to semantic and visual information, research has even shown that acoustic information can be encoded in long-term memory (T. Nelson & Rothbart, 1972). Emerging from these data, therefore, is a picture of considerable flexibility in the way we store information that we retain for long periods of time. Those who seek to know the single correct way we encode information are seeking an answer to the wrong question because there is no one correct way. A more useful question involves asking, In what *ways* do we encode information in long-term memory? From a more psychological perspective, however, the most useful question to ask is, *When* do we encode in *which* ways? In other words, under what circumstances do we use one form of encoding, and under what circumstances another? These questions are the focus of present and future research.

Movement of Information From Short-Term Memory to Long-Term Memory

Given the problems of decay and of interference, how do we move information from short-term memory to long-term memory? The means of moving information depend on whether the information involves declarative or nondeclarative memory. Some forms of nondeclarative memory (e.g., priming and habituation) are highly volatile and decay quickly. Other nondeclarative forms (e.g., procedural memory and simple classical conditioning) are more readily maintained, particularly as a result of repeated practice (of procedures) or repeated conditioning (of responses).

For entrance into long-term declarative memory, various processes are involved. One method of accomplishing this goal is by deliberately attending to information in order to comprehend it. Perhaps an even more important way in which we accomplish this goal is by making connections or associations between the new information and what we already know and understand. We make connections by integrating the new data into our existing schemas of stored information. This process of integrating new information into stored information is termed **consolidation**; in humans, the process of consolidating declarative information into memory can continue for many years after the initial experience (Squire, 1986).

The disruption of consolidation has been effectively studied in amnesics, particularly in persons who have suffered brief forms of amnesia as a consequence of electroconvulsive therapy (ECT; Squire, 1986). For these amnesics, the source of the trauma is clear. Confounding variables can be minimized, a patient history before the trauma can be obtained, and follow-up testing and supervision after the trauma are more likely to be available. Based on studies of ECT patients, other amnesics, and normal participants, apparently during the process of consolidation, our memory is susceptible to disruption and distortion.

To preserve or enhance the integrity of memories during consolidation, we may use various **metamemory** strategies. These strategies involve reflecting on our own memory processes with a view to improving our memory, such as when transferring new information to long-term memory by rehearsing it. Metamemory strategies are just one component of **metacognition,** our ability to think about our own processes of thought and ways of enhancing our thinking.

REHEARSAL

One technique people use for keeping information active is **rehearsal,** the repeated recitation of an item. The effects of such rehearsal are termed *practice effects.* Rehearsal may be *overt,* in which case it is usually aloud and obvious to anyone watching, or *covert,* in which case it is silent and hidden. Whether rehearsal is overt or covert, what is the best way to organize your time for rehearsing new information?

More than a century ago, Hermann Ebbinghaus (1885, cited in Schacter, 1989a) noticed that the distribution of study (memory rehearsal) sessions over time affects the consolidation of information in long-term memory. Much more recently, Harry Bahrick and Elizabeth Phelps (1987) have offered support for Ebbinghaus's observation as a result of their studies of people's long-term recall of Spanish vocabulary words the people had learned 8 years earlier. Bahrick and Phelps observed that people tend to remember information longer when they acquire it via **distributed practice** (i.e., learning in which various sessions are spaced over time) rather than via **massed practice** (with sessions crammed together all at once). The greater the distribution of learning trials over time, the more the participants remembered over long periods of time.

Arthur Glenberg (1977, 1979) has studied the *spacing effect* (greater recall for distributed learning) extensively, and he and others (e.g., Leicht & Overton, 1987) have linked the spacing effect to the process by which memories are consolidated in long-term memory. That is, the spacing effect may occur because at each learning session, the context for encoding may vary, and the individuals may use alternative strategies and cues for encoding, thereby enriching and elaborating their schemas for the information. The principle of the spacing effect is important to remember in studying: You will recall information longer, on average, if you distribute your learning of subject matter, and you vary the context for encoding, instead of trying to mass or cram it all into a short period of time.

Why would distributing learning trials over days make a difference? One possibility is that information is learned in variable contexts, which helps strengthen and begin to consolidate it. Another possible answer comes from studies of the influences of sleep on memory. Some researchers (e.g., Karni, Tanne, Rubenstein, Askenasy, & Sagi, 1994) have found that learning is influenced by the amount of REM sleep (a particular stage of sleep characterized by rapid-eye-movement, dreaming, and rapid brain waves) a person gets in the night following a learning session. Specifically, disruptions in REM sleep patterns reduced the amount of improvement on a visual-discrimination task that occurred with normal sleep from one day to the next. Furthermore, this lack of improvement was not observed for disrupted stage-three or stage-four sleep patterns (Karni,

Tanne, Rubenstein, Askenasy, & Sagi, 1994). Moreover, other research shows increases in the proportion of REM stage sleep with exposure to learning situations (C. Smith, 1996). Thus, apparently a good night's sleep, which includes plenty of REM stage sleep, aids in memory consolidation.

Is there something special occurring in the brain that could explain why REM sleep is so important for memory consolidation? Neuropsychological research on animal learning may offer a tentative answer to this question. Recall that the hippocampus has been found to be an important structure for memory. In recording studies of rat hippocampal cells, researchers have found that cells of the hippocampus that were activated during initial learning are reactivated during subsequent periods of sleep, as if they are replaying the initial learning episode to achieve consolidation into long-term storage (Scaggs & McNaughton, 1996; Wilson & McNaughton, 1994).

In a recent review, McClelland, McNaughton, and O'Reilly (1995) have proposed that the hippocampus acts as a rapid learning system, temporarily maintaining new experiences until they can be appropriately assimilated into the more gradual neocortical representation system of the brain. McClelland and colleagues have argued that such a complementary system is necessary to allow memory to represent more accurately the structure of the environment. They have used connectionist models of learning to show that integrating new experiences too rapidly leads to disruptions in long-term memory systems. Thus, the benefits of distributed practice seem to occur because we have a relatively rapid learning system in the hippocampus that becomes activated during sleep. With repeated exposure on subsequent days and repeated reactivation during subsequent periods of sleep, these rapidly learned memories become integrated into our more permanent long-term memory system.

Although the spacing of practice sessions affects memory consolidation, the distribution of learning trials within any given session does not seem to affect memory. According to the *total-time hypothesis,* the amount of learning depends on the amount of time spent mindfully rehearsing the material, more or less without regard to how that time is divided up into trials in any one session. The total-time hypothesis does not always hold up, however. Moreover, the total-time hypothesis of rehearsal has at least two apparent constraints (Cooper & Pantle, 1967). First, the full amount of time allotted for rehearsal must actually be used for that purpose. Second, to achieve beneficial effects, the rehearsal should include any of various kinds of elaboration or mnemonic devices that can enhance recall.

To move information into long-term memory, an individual must engage in *elaborative rehearsal,* in which the person somehow elaborates the items to be remembered in a way that makes the items either more meaningfully integrated into what the person already knows or more meaningfully connected to one another and therefore more memorable. (Recall the effects of chunking, in which a person can chunk many smaller units of information into larger units of integrated information, to remember the information more easily.)

In contrast, *maintenance rehearsal,* in which the person simply repetitiously rehearses the items to be repeated, temporarily maintains information in short-term memory without transferring the information to long-term memory. Without any kind of elaboration, the information cannot be organized and transferred.

Organization of Information

Stored memories are organized. One way to show this organization is through the measurement of *subjective organization in free recall,* which refers to our individually determined ways of organizing our memories. To measure subjective organization, researchers may give participants a *multitrial free-recall task,* in which the participants have multiple trials during which to learn to recall in any order they choose a list of unrelated words. Recall that Weston Bousfield (1953) showed that if sets of test words can be divided into categories (names of fruits, of furniture, etc.), participants will spontaneously cluster their recall output by these categories, even if the order of presentation is random. Similarly, Endel Tulving (1962) demonstrated that participants will tend to show consistent patterns of word order in their recall protocols, even if there are no apparent relations among words in the list. In other words, participants create their own consistent organization and then group their recall by the subjective units they create. Although most adults spontaneously tend to cluster items into categories, categorical clustering may also be used intentionally, as an aid to memorization.

Practical Applications of Cognitive Psychology

You can use these memory strategies to help you study for exams:

1. Studying throughout the course rather than cramming the night before an exam distributes the learning sessions, allowing for consolidation into more permanent memory systems.
2. Linking new information to what you already know by rehearsing new information in meaningful ways and organizing new information to relate it to other coursework or areas of your life.
3. Using the various mnemonic devices shown in Table 6.1.

Mnemonic devices are specific techniques to help you memorize lists of words. Essentially, such devices add meaning to otherwise meaningless or arbitrary lists of items. As Table 6.1 shows, a variety of methods—*categorical clustering, acronyms, acrostics, interactive imagery* among items, *pegwords,* and the *method of loci*—can help you to memorize lists of words and vocabulary items. Although the techniques described in Table 6.1 are not the only available ones, they are among the most frequently used.

Henry Roediger (1980a) has studied the comparative effectiveness of various mnemonic strategies, including verbal elaborative rehearsal, mental imagery for isolated items, interactive images (linking a sequence of items), the method of loci, and the pegword system (see Table 6.2). Roediger found that the relative effectiveness of the methods for encoding was influenced by the kind of task (free recall vs. serial recall) required at the time of retrieval. Roediger went on to suggest that when choosing a method for encoding information for subsequent recall, one should consider the purpose for recalling the information. The individual should choose not only strategies that allow for effectively encoding the information (moving it into long-term

TABLE 6.1 MNEMONIC DEVICES: ASSORTED TECHNIQUES

Of the many mnemonic devices available, the ones described here rely either on organization of information into meaningful chunks—such as *categorical clustering, acronyms,* and *acrostics;* or on visual images—such as *interactive images,* a *pegword system,* and the *method of loci.*

Technique	Explanation/Description	Example
Categorical clustering	Organize a list of items into a set of categories	If you needed to remember to buy apples, milk, bagels, grapes, yogurt, rolls, Swiss cheese, grapefruit, and lettuce, you would be better able to do so if you tried to memorize the items by categories: *fruits*—apples, grapes, grapefruit; *dairy products*—milk, yogurt, Swiss cheese; *breads*—bagels, rolls; *vegetables*—lettuce.
Interactive images	Create interactive images that link the isolated words in a list	Suppose, for example, that you need to remember a list of unrelated words: *aardvark, table, pencil, book, radio, Kansas, rain, electricity, stone, mirror.* You might better remember these words by generating *interactive images.* For example, you might imagine an *aardvark* sitting on a *table* holding a *pencil* in its claws and writing in a *book,* with *rain* pouring over *Kansas* (as pictured on a map) that lands on a *radio* that is sitting on a *stone,* which generates *electricity* reflected in a *mirror.*
Pegword system	Associate each new word with a word on a previously memorized list, and form an interactive image between the two words	One such list is from a nursery rhyme: One is a bun. Two is a shoe. Three is a tree. Four is a door. Five is a hive. Six is a stick. Seven is heaven. Eight is a gate. Nine is a dime. Ten is a hen. To recall the list of words you used for the interactive images system, you might visualize an *aardvark* eating a delicious *bun.* You might imagine a *shoe* atop a tall *table.* You might visualize one large branch of a *tree* that ends with a sharp *pencil* point. Then you would go on forming interactive images for each of the words in the list. When you need to remember the words, you first recall the numbered images and then recall the words as you visualize them in the interactive images.
Method of loci	Visualize walking around an area with distinctive landmarks that you know well, and then link the various landmarks to specific items to be remembered	When you need to memorize a list of words, mentally walk past each of the distinctive landmarks, depositing each word to be memorized at one of the landmarks. Visualize an interactive image between the new word and the landmark. For example, if you wished to remember the list of items mentioned previously, you might envision an *aardvark* nibbling at the roots of a familiar tree, a *table* sitting on the sidewalk in front of an empty lot, a *pencil*-shaped statue in the center of a fountain, and so on. When you wished to remember the list, you would take your mental walk and pick up the words you had linked to each of the landmarks along the walk.

Continued

TABLE 6.1 MNEMONIC DEVICES: ASSORTED TECHNIQUES *(Continued)*

TECHNIQUE	EXPLANATION/DESCRIPTION	EXAMPLE
Acronym	Devise a word or expression in which each of its letters stands for a certian other word or concept (e.g., USA, IQ, and laser)	Suppose that you want to remember the names of the mnemonic devices described in this chapter. The acronym "I AM PACK" might prompt you to remember *I*nteractive images, *A*cronyms, *M*ethod of loci, *P*egwords, *A*crostics, *C*ategories, and *K*eywords. Of course, this technique is more useful if the first letters of the words to be memorized actually can be formed into a word or phrase, or something close to one, even if the word or phrase is nonsensical, as in this example.
Acrostic	Form a sentence rather than a single word to help you remember the new words	For example, music students trying to memorize the names of the notes found on lines of the treble clef (the higher notes; specifically E, G, B, D, and F above middle C) learn that "*E*very *G*ood *B*oy *D*oes *F*ine."
Keyword system	Form an interactive image that links the sound and meaning of a foreign word with the sound and meaning of a familiar word	For example, suppose that you needed to learn that the French word for *butter* is *beurre*. First, you would note that *beurre* sounds something like "bear." Next, you would associate the keyword *bear* with *butter* in an image or sentence. For instance, you might visualize a bear eating a stick of butter. Later, *bear* would provide a retrieval cue for *beurre*.

memory), but also strategies that offer appropriate cues for facilitating subsequent retrieval when needed. For example, prior to taking an exam in cognitive psychology, using a strategy for retrieving an alphabetical list of prominent cognitive psychologists would probably be much less helpful than using a strategy for linking particular theorists with the key ideas of their theories.

The use of mnemonic devices and other techniques for aiding memory involves metamemory. Most adults spontaneously use categorical clustering, so its inclusion in this list of mnemonic devices is actually just a reminder to use this common memory strategy. In fact, each of us often uses various kinds of *reminders*—external memory aids—to enhance the likelihood we will remember important information. For example, by now, you have doubtless learned the benefits of such external memory aids as taking notes during lectures, writing shopping lists for items to purchase, setting timers and alarms, and even asking other people to help you remember things. In addition, cognitive psychologist (and design engineer) Donald Norman (1988) suggested that we can design our environment to help us remember important information, through the use of *forcing functions,* physical constraints that prevent us from acting without at least considering the key information to be remembered. For example, to ensure that you remember to take your notebook to class, you might lean the notebook against the door through which you must pass in order to leave to go to class.

TABLE 6.2 MNEMONIC DEVICES: COMPARATIVE EFFECTIVENESS

Henry Roediger conducted a study of recall memory, in which initial recall of a series of items was compared with recall following brief training in each of several memory strategies. For both free recall and serial recall, training in interactive imagery, the method of loci, and the pegword system was more effective than either elaborative (verbal) rehearsal or imagery for isolated items. However, the beneficial effects of training were most pronounced for the serial-recall condition. In the free-recall condition, imagery of isolated items was modestly more effective than elaborative (verbal) rehearsal, but for serial recall, elaborative (verbal) rehearsal was modestly more effective than imagery for isolated items.

		Free-Recall Criterion			Serial-Recall Criterion		
			Average number of items recalled correctly following training			*Average number of items recalled correctly following training*	
Condition (type of mnemonic training)	*Number of participants in each condition*	*Number of correct items recalled on practice list, prior to training*	*Immediate recall*	*Recall following a 24-hour delay*	*Number of correct items recalled on practice list, prior to training*	*Immediate recall*	*Recall following a 24-hour delay*
Elaborative rehearsal (verbal)	32	13.2	11.4	6.3	7.0	5.8	1.3
Isolated images of individual items	25	12.4	13.1	6.8	6.8	4.8	1.0
Interactive imagery (with links from one item to the next)	31	13.0	15.6	11.2	7.6	9.6	5.0
Method of loci	29	12.6	15.3	10.6	6.8	13.6	5.8
Pegword system	33	13.1	14.2	8.2	7.7	12.5	4.9
Mean performance across conditions		12.9	13.9	8.6	7.2	9.4	3.6

Source: Adapted from Roediger, H. L. (1980a). The effectiveness of four mnemonics in ordering recall. *JEP: Human Learning & Memory,* 6(5), 558-567.

Retrieval

Once we have stored information, how do we retrieve it when we want to do so? If we have problems retrieving information, how do we know whether we even stored the information in the first place?

Retrieval From Short-Term Memory

Once information is encoded and stored in short-term memory, how do people retrieve that information? A classic series of experiments on this issue was done by Saul Sternberg. The phenomenon he studied is short-term *memory scanning,* whereby we check the contents in our short-term memories.

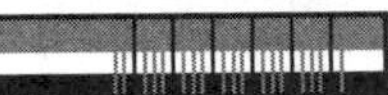

INVESTIGATING COGNITIVE PSYCHOLOGY

Memorize the following list of numbers: 6, 3, 8, 2, 7. Now, was 8 on the list? Sternberg wanted to find out how people make decisions such as this one. Let's consider his very elegant work in some depth.

Saul Sternberg's (1966) basic paradigm was simple. He gave participants a short list including from one to six digits, which he expected participants would be able to hold in short-term memory. After a brief pause, a test digit was flashed on a screen, and participants had to say whether this digit had appeared in the set that they had been asked to memorize. Thus, if the list comprised the digits 4, 1, 9, 3, and the digit 9 were flashed on the screen, the correct response would be *yes.* If, instead, the test digit were 7, the correct response would be *no.* The digits that were presented are termed the *positive set,* and those that were not presented are termed the *negative set.*

Saul Sternberg and other cognitive psychologists wondered whether items are retrieved all at once (parallel processing) or sequentially (serial processing). If retrieved serially, the question then arises, are all items retrieved, regardless of the task (exhaustive retrieval), or does retrieval stop as soon as an item seems to accomplish the task (self-terminating retrieval)?

Parallel Versus Serial Processing

As mentioned previously, *parallel processing* refers to the simultaneous handling of multiple operations; as applied to short-term memory, the items stored in short-term memory would be retrieved all at once, not one at a time. The prediction in Figure 6.1 (a) shows what would happen if parallel processing were the case in S. Sternberg's memory-scanning task. Response times should be the same, regardless of the size of the positive set, because all comparisons would be done at once. In other words, it would be no more time-consuming to retrieve four digits than two, because in each case, all digits would be accessed at once.

Serial processing refers to operations being done one after another. In other words, on the digit-recall task, the digits would be retrieved in succession, rather than all at once (as in the parallel model). According to the serial model, it should take longer to retrieve four digits than to retrieve two digits (as shown in Figure 6.1 b). Nonetheless, it will not necessarily take twice as long to do so because some processes (e.g., starting the retrieval process and making the overt response) take a constant amount of time, regardless of how many digits are retrieved.

FIGURE 6.1 **STERNBERG'S MEMORY-SCANNING TASK**

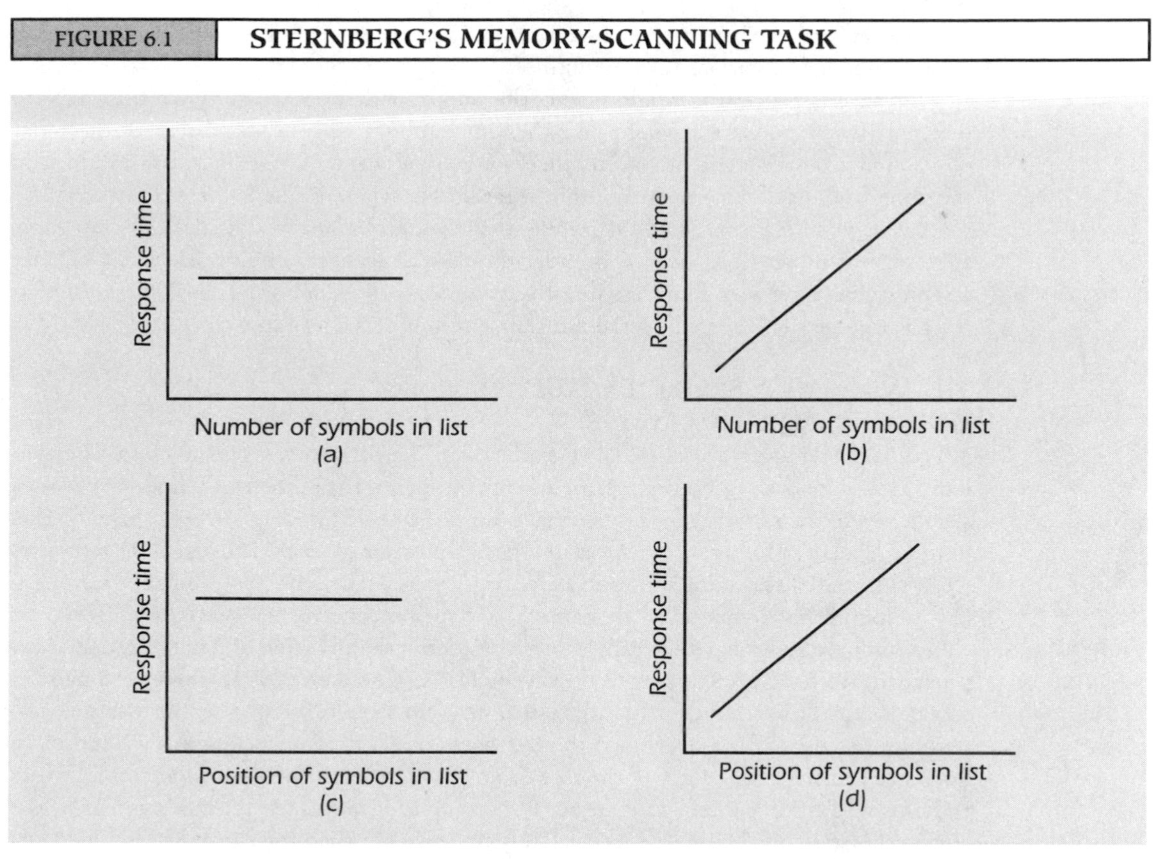

Panel (a) illustrates findings suggestive of parallel processing; (b) illustrates serial processing; (c) shows exhaustive serial processing; and (d) shows self-terminating serial processing. (After S. Sternberg, 1966).

EXHAUSTIVE VERSUS SELF-TERMINATING PROCESSING

If information processing were serial, then there would be either of two ways in which to gain access to the stimuli: exhaustive or self-terminating processing. *Exhaustive serial processing* implies that the participant would always check the test digit against *all* digits in the positive set, even if a match were found partway through the list. Why would a participant use exhaustive processing—which, on its face, would seem to be inefficient? One possibility would be that comparison might be a relatively fast process, and that after having established a trajectory (route) for doing a string of comparisons, finishing the trajectory might be easier and more efficient than interrupting it in the middle.

A way to visualize this process is to picture yourself in a bicycle race. To race at your top speed all the way to the finish line, you might allow yourself to go a bit past the finish line instead of forcing yourself to come to a sudden, full stop at the exact point of crossing the finish line. Another possibility would be that if your mental comparisons were exhaustive, you would have to decide only at the end whether the test digit was a member of the positive set, rather than after each comparison was made. Doing so would decrease the total number of operations to be performed.

Exhaustive processing would predict the pattern of data shown in Figure 6.1 (c). Note that positive responses all would take the same amount of time, regardless of the serial position of a positive test probe. In other words, in an exhaustive search, you would take the same amount of time to find a digit, regardless of where in the list it were located.

Self-terminating serial processing implies that the participant would check the test digit against only those digits needed in order to make a response. Figure 6.1 (d) shows that response time now would increase linearly as a function of where a test digit was located in the positive set. The later the serial position, the longer the response time.

THE WINNER—A SERIAL, EXHAUSTIVE MODEL—WITH SOME QUALIFICATIONS

When Saul Sternberg actually looked at the data, the pattern was crystal clear. The data looked like the data in Figure 6.1 (b) and (c). Response times increased linearly with set size but were the same regardless of serial position. Later, Sternberg (1969) replicated this pattern of data. Moreover, the mean response times for positive and negative responses were essentially the same, further supporting the serial exhaustive model. Sternberg (1966) found that comparisons took roughly 38 milliseconds (0.038 seconds) apiece.

Although Sternberg and many others considered the question of parallel versus serial processing to have been answered decisively, D. W. Corcoran (1971) proposed a parallel model that could account for the data. Imagine a horse race, which involves parallel processing. The race is not over until the last horse passes the finish line. As we add more horses to the race, the length of the race (from the start until the last of the horses crosses the finishing line) is likely to increase. For example, if horses are selected randomly, the slowest horse in an eight-horse race is likely to be slower than the slowest horse in a four-horse race. That is, with more horses, a wider range of speeds is more likely, so the entire race will take longer because the race is not complete until the slowest horse crosses the finish line. Similarly, when applying a parallel model to a retrieval task involving more items, a wider range of retrieval speeds for the various items is also more likely, with the entire retrieval process not complete until the last item has been retrieved. James Townsend (1971) actually proved mathematically that to distinguish parallel from serial models unequivocally is impossible, in that there always exists some parallel model that will mimic any serial model in its predictions, and vice versa. The two models may not be equally plausible, but they still exist.

Moreover, some investigators have obtained serial-position effects with digits (e.g., Kirsner & Craik, 1971; Raeburn, 1974), suggesting the need for at least some modification of Saul Sternberg's model. Mary Naus, Sam Glucksberg, and Peter Ornstein (1972; Naus, 1974) found that when participants engaged in memory scanning for words from a single taxonomic category (e.g., types of fruits), they used serial, exhaustive strategies. However, when engaged in memory scanning for words from two taxonomic categories (e.g., fruits and clothing), participants used a self-terminating strategy. Donald De Rosa and Sharon Tkacz (1976) studied memory scanning and found that, for strings involving a sequence of ordered pictures that could not readily be labeled verbally (e.g., sequences showing a bird taking flight or a frog leaping), participants used parallel search strategies. However, when participants were shown a series of pictures that was not an ordered sequence, participants used serial search strategies, just as they did with digits or other items.

Thus, it cannot even be said that participants are always exhaustive in their search of the list of stimuli. As the years have gone by, various investigators have proposed elaborations of Sternberg's original model in order to take into account the diversity of the findings that have entered the literature (e.g., Atkinson & Juola, 1974).

The research by Saul Sternberg and many other investigators has focused on memory for lists of digits and other isolated fragments of information. In fact, much of the early research on memory focused on studying the underlying structures (see chapter 7) and mechanisms of memory. More recently, some cognitive psychologists (e.g., Bruce, 1991) have suggested that we should seek not only to understand the *how* of memory processes, but also the *why* of memory processes. That is, what functions does memory serve for individual persons and for humans as a species? To understand the functions of memory, we must study memory for relatively complex information, as well as the relationships between the information presented and other information available to the individual, both within the informational context and as a result of prior experience.

RETRIEVAL FROM LONG-TERM MEMORY

Gordon H. Bower *is a professor of psychology at Stanford University. His earlier contributions were in mathematical learning theories. Later, with John Anderson, he developed a theoretical framework for linking up laboratory studies of verbal memory with psycholinguistic theories of memory. He has also investigated how people's emotional states influence memory storage and retrieval.*

A study conducted by Endel Tulving and Zena Pearlstone (1966) nicely shows how difficult it is to separate storage from retrieval phenomena. Participants in this study were tested on their memory for lists of categorized words. Participants would hear words within a category together in the list and would even be given the name of the category before the items within it were presented. For example, the participants might hear the category "article of clothing," followed by the words, "shirt, socks, pants, belt." Participants were then tested for their recall.

The recall test was done in one of two ways. In the free-recall condition, participants merely recalled as many words as they could in any order they chose. In a cued-recall condition, however, participants were tested category by category. They were given each category label as a cue and were then asked to recall as many words as they could from that category. The critical result was that cued recall was far better, on average, than free recall. Were the researchers to have tested only free recall, they might have concluded that participants had not stored quite so many words; however, the comparison to the cued-recall condition demonstrated that apparent memory failures were due largely to retrieval rather than to storage failures.

Gordon Bower and his colleagues (Bower, Clark, Lesgold, & Winzenz, 1969) showed just how dramatically categorization can affect retrieval. They had participants learn lists of categorized words. Either the words were presented in random order, or they were presented in the form of a hierarchical tree that showed the organization of the words (e.g., with the category *minerals* at the top, followed by the categories of *metals* and *stones,* and so on). Participants given hierarchical presentation recalled 65% of the words, compared with recall of just 19% by participants given the words in random order.

Another problem that arises when studying memory is to figure out why we sometimes have trouble retrieving information. Cognitive psychologists often have difficulty finding a way to distinguish between **availability** (the presence of information stored in long-term memory) and **accessibility** (the degree to which we can gain access to the available information). Memory performance depends on the accessibility of the information to be remembered. Ideally, memory researchers would like to assess the availability of information in memory, but alas, they must settle for assessing the accessibility of such information.

PROCESSES OF FORGETTING AND MEMORY DISTORTION

Why do we so easily and so quickly forget phone numbers we have just looked up or the names of people whom we have just met? Several theories have been proposed as to why we forget information stored in working memory. The two most well-known theories are *interference theory* and *decay theory.* **Interference** occurs when competing information causes us to forget something; **decay** occurs when simply the passage of time causes us to forget.

INTERFERENCE VERSUS DECAY THEORY

One of the most famous experimental paradigms in all of memory psychology, and arguably, in all of psychology, is called the "Brown–Peterson" paradigm, after its originators, John Brown (1958) and Lloyd and Margaret Peterson (now Margaret Intons-Peterson) (1959). Although neither Brown nor the Petersons ascribed their findings to interference, both studies were taken as evidence for the existence of a short-term memory store (now viewed by many investigators as equivalent to, or part of, working memory) and also for the **interference theory** of forgetting, according to which forgetting occurs because new information interferes with, and ultimately displaces, old information in short-term memory.

The Petersons (1959), psychologists at Indiana University, asked their participants to recall *trigrams* (strings of three letters) at intervals of 3, 6, 9, 12, 15, or 18 seconds after the presentation of the last letter. The Petersons used only consonants, so that the trigrams would not be easily pronounceable—for example, "K B F." Each participant was tested eight times at each of the six delay intervals, for a total of 48 trials. Figure 6.2 shows percentages of correct recalls after the various intervals of time. Why does recall decline so rapidly? Because after the oral presentation of each trigram, the Petersons asked their participants to count backward by threes from a three-digit number spoken immediately after the trigram. The purpose of having the participants count backward was to prevent them from rehearsing during the *retention interval*—the time between the presentation of the last letter and the start of the recall phase of the experimental trial.

The standard interpretation of these results is quite straightforward. Clearly, the trigram is almost completely forgotten after just 18 seconds if participants are not allowed to rehearse it. Bennet Murdock (1961) further showed that such forgetting occurs when words rather than letters are used as the stimuli to be recalled. The results suggest that counting backward interfered with recall from short-term memory, supporting the interference account of forgetting in short-term memory. At that time, some researchers were

FIGURE 6.2 **BROWN–PETERSON PARADIGM: RECALL OF TRIGRAMS**

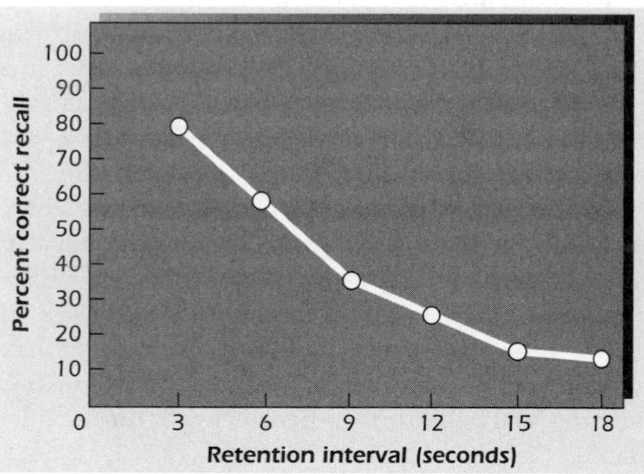

The percentage of recall of three consonants (a trigram) drops off quickly if participants are not allowed to rehearse the trigrams.

surprised to find that numbers would interfere with the recall of letters. The previous view had been that verbal information would interfere only with verbal (words) memory, and quantitative (numbers) information only with quantitative memory.

Although the foregoing discussion has construed interference as though it were a single construct, at least two kinds of interference figure prominently in psychological theory and research: retroactive interference and proactive interference. **Retroactive interference** (or *retroactive inhibition)* is caused by activity occurring *after* we learn something but before we are asked to recall that thing. The interference in the Brown–Peterson task appears to be retroactive because counting backward by threes occurs after learning of the trigram; it interferes with our ability to remember information we learned previously.

A second kind of interference is **proactive interference** (or *proactive inhibition).* This kind of interference occurs when the interfering material occurs *before,* rather than *after,* learning of the to-be-remembered material. Does proactive interference actually operate in the forgetting of material stored in short-term memory? A study conducted by Geoffrey Keppel and Benton Underwood (1962) suggests that it does. Indeed, Keppel and Underwood argued that forgetting in the Brown–Peterson paradigm is due to proactive rather than retroactive interference. This interpretation may seem counterintuitive at first, but suppose that interference in the Brown–Peterson paradigm were indeed proactive: Specifically, the trigrams learned earlier interfered with participants' ability to remember later trigrams. If this were the case, we would make two predictions based on two characteristics of proactive interference noted earlier. First, level of retention should be lower, to the extent that the number of syllables previously tested is higher. In other words, the greater the amount of prior material that is learned, the greater is the extent of the interference. Second, the increase in forgetting as a function of the number of syllables previously learned should be greater for longer retention intervals than for shorter ones.

When Keppel and Underwood (1962) tested their hypothesis, they found that proactive, rather than retroactive, interference appeared to affect recall. However, still other experiments suggested that retroactive interference may play a part in forgetting as well (e.g., Reitman, 1971; Shiffrin, 1973; Waugh & Norman, 1965). It would be nice if we could conclusively say whether retroactive or proactive interference is operating in the Brown–Peterson paradigm. Unfortunately, psychological research (or any scientific research, for that matter) does not always lead to definitive conclusions.

In earlier work, Frederic Bartlett (1932), unlike many other psychologists of his day, recognized the need to study memory retrieval for connected texts and not just for unconnected strings of digits, words, or nonsense syllables. Therefore, he had his participants learn a text and then recall it. Bartlett was also interested in whether memory for material is affected by previous (e.g., culturally based) understandings. Bartlett had his participants in Britain learn what was to them a strange and difficult-to-understand North American Indian legend called "The War of the Ghosts." (The text is depicted in its entirety in Table 6.3.)

Bartlett found that his participants distorted their recall in order to render the story more comprehensible to themselves. In other words, their prior knowledge and expectations had a substantial effect on their recall. Bartlett suggested that people bring into a memory task their already existing *schemas,* or organized relevant knowledge structures, which affect the way in which they recall what they learn. The later work using the Brown–Peterson paradigm confirms the notion that prior knowledge has an enormous effect on memory, sometimes leading to interference or distortion.

In addition to the Brown–Peterson paradigm, another method often used for determining the causes of forgetting draws inferences from a serial-position curve: The *serial-position curve* represents the probability of recall of a given word, given its *serial position* (order of presentation) in a list. Suppose that you are presented with a list of words and are asked to recall them. You might even try it on yourself with the following investigation.

Investigating Cognitive Psychology

Say the following list of words once to yourself, and then, immediately thereafter, try to recall all the words without looking back at them, in any order: *Table, Cloud, Book, Tree, Shirt, Cat, Light, Bench, Chalk, Flower, Watch, Bat, Rug, Soap, Pillow.*

If you are like most people, you will find that your recall of words is best for items at and near the end of the list, second best for items near the beginning of the list, and poorest for items in the middle of the list. A typical serial-position curve is shown in Figure 6.3.

Superior recall of words at and near the end of the list is referred to as a *recency effect.* Superior recall of words at and near the beginning of the list is a *primacy effect.* As Figure 6.3 shows, both the recency effect and the primacy effect seem to influence recall. The

TABLE 6.3 BARTLETT'S LEGEND

Read the legend described in this table, and then turn the page and try to recall the legend in its entirety. (After Bartlett, 1932)

(a) Original Indian Myth	(b) Typical Recall by a Student in England
The War of the Ghosts One night two young men from Egulac went down to the river to hunt seals, and while they were there it became foggy and calm. Then they heard war-cries, and they thought: "Maybe this is a war-party." They escaped to the shore, and hid behind a log. Now canoes came up, and they heard the noise of paddles, and saw one canoe coming up to them. There were five men in the canoe, and they said: "What do you think? We wish to take you along. We are going up the river to make war on the people." One of the young men said, "I have no arrows." "Arrows are in the canoe," they said. "I will not go along. I might be killed. My relatives do not know where I have gone. But you," he said, turning to the other, "may go with them." So one of the young men went, but the other returned home. And the warriors went on up the river to a town on the other side of Kalama. The people came down to the water, and they began to fight, and many were killed. But presently the young man heard one of the warriors say: "Quick, let us go home; that Indian has been hit." Now he thought: "Oh, they are ghosts." He did not feel sick, but they said he had been shot. So the canoes went back to Egulac, and the young man went ashore to his house, and made a fire. And he told everybody and said: "Behold I accompanied the ghosts, and we went to fight. Many of our fellows were killed, and many of those who attacked us were killed. They said I was hit, and I did not feel sick." He told it all, and then he became quiet. When the sun rose he fell down. Something black came out of his mouth. His face became contorted. The people jumped up and cried. He was dead.	*The War of the Ghosts* Two men from Edulac went fishing. While thus occupied by the river they heard a noise in the distance. "It sounds like a cry," said one, and presently there appeared some in canoes who invited them to join the party of their adventure. One of the young men refused to go, on the ground of family ties, but the other offered to go. "But there are no arrows." he said. "The arrows are in the boat," was the reply. He thereupon took his place, while his friend returned home. The party paddled up the river to Kaloma, and began to land on the banks of the river. The enemy came rushing upon them, and some sharp fighting ensued. Presently someone was injured, and the cry was raised that the enemy were ghosts. The party returned down the stream, and the young man arrived home feeling none the worse for his experience. The next morning at dawn he endeavoured to recount his adventures. While he was talking something black issued from his mouth. Suddenly he uttered a cry and fell down. His friends gathered round him. But he was dead.

serial-position curve makes sense in terms of interference theory. Words at the end of the list are subject to proactive but not to retroactive interference; words at the beginning of the list are subject to retroactive but not to proactive interference; and words in the middle of the list are subject to both types of interference. Hence, recall would be expected to be poorest in the middle of the list, as indeed it is.

IDEALIZED SERIAL-POSITION CURVE

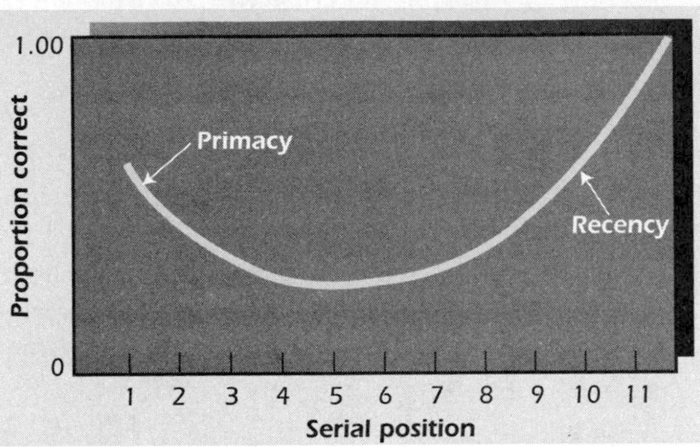

When asked to recall a list of words, we show superior recall of words close to the end of a list (the recency effect), pretty good recall of words close to the beginning of the list (primacy effect), and relatively poor recall of words in the middle of the list.

The amount of proactive interference generally climbs with increases in the length of time between when the information is presented (and encoded) and when the information is retrieved (Underwood, 1957). Also, as you might expect, proactive interference increases as the amount of prior—and potentially interfering—learning increases (Greenberg & Underwood, 1950). Although the effects of proactive interference appear to dominate under conditions in which recall is delayed, both proactive and retroactive interference are now viewed as complementary phenomena. Yet another theory for explaining how we forget information is decay theory.

Decay theory asserts that information is forgotten because of the gradual disappearance, rather than displacement, of the memory trace. Thus, whereas interference theory views one piece of information as blocking another, decay theory views the original piece of information as gradually disappearing unless something is done to keep it intact.

Decay theory turns out to be exceedingly difficult to test. Why? First, under normal circumstances, preventing participants from rehearsing is difficult. Through rehearsal, participants maintain the to-be-remembered information in memory. If participants know that you are testing their memory, they may try to rehearse the information, or they may even inadvertently rehearse it in order to perform well during testing. On the other hand, if you do prevent them from rehearsing, the possibility of interference arises: The task you use to prevent rehearsal may interfere retroactively with the original memory.

Try, for example, not to think of white elephants as you read the next two pages. When instructed not to think about them, you actually find it quite difficult not to, even if you try to follow the instructions. Unfortunately, as a test of decay theory, this experiment is itself a white elephant, because preventing people from rehearsing is so difficult.

Despite these difficulties, Judith Reitman (1971, 1974) proposed a technique that she hoped would provide a fairly exacting test of decay theory. She suggested that what was needed to test decay theory was a task that intervened between learning and testing that (a) prevents rehearsal and (b) presents no interfering learning. The intervening task (which involved tone detection) required a great deal of effort and attention, but no new learning. A very faint tone was presented through earphones, and participants were to press a button each time they heard the tone. Of course, there was no guarantee that participants would not rehearse at all, or that no new information would enter short-term memory. However, she created a situation that was about as close to ideal conditions as she could realistically produce.

Reitman (1974) visually presented participants with five words. The display lasted for 2 seconds. As soon as the display went off, participants engaged in the tone-detection task for 15 seconds, after which they tried to recall as many of the five words as they could. Reitman found that recall declined by about 24% over the 15 seconds. She interpreted this decline as evidence of decay.

To conclude, evidence exists for both interference and decay, at least in short-term memory. The evidence for decay is not airtight, but it is certainly suggestive. The evidence for interference is rather strong, but at present, the extent to which the interference is retroactive, proactive, or both, is unclear. In addition, interference also affects material in long-term memory, leading to memory distortion.

The Constructive Nature of Memory

An important lesson about memory is that memory retrieval is not just **reconstructive,** involving the use of various strategies (e.g., searching for cues, drawing inferences) for retrieving the original memory traces of our experiences and then rebuilding the original experiences as a basis for retrieval (see Kolodner, 1983, for an artificial-intelligence model of reconstructive memory). Rather, in real-life situations, memory is also **constructive,** in that prior experience affects how we recall things and what we actually recall. Recall the Bransford and Johnson (1972) study, cited at the opening of this chapter, in which participants could remember a passage about washing clothes quite well, but only if they realized that it was about washing clothes.

In a further demonstration of the constructive nature of memory, John Bransford and Marcia Johnson (1973) had participants read an ambiguous passage that could be interpreted meaningfully as being either about watching a peace march from the fortieth floor of a building or about a space trip to an inhabited planet. Participants omitted different details, depending on what they thought the passage was about. For example, a sentence mentioning that the atmosphere did not require the wearing of special clothing was more likely to be remembered when the participants thought the passage was about a trip into outer space than when they thought it was about a peace march.

A comparable demonstration in a different domain was done by Gordon Bower and his colleagues (Bower, Karlin, & Dueck, 1975). These investigators showed participants 28 different *droodles*—nonsense pictures that can be given various interpretations (see also chapter 10, Figure 10-2). Half the participants in their experiment were given an interpretation by which they could label what they saw. The other half did not receive an interpretation prompting a label. Participants in the label group correctly reproduced almost 20% more droodles than did participants in the control group.

Elizabeth Loftus *is a professor of psychology at the University of Washington. She has made major contributions to the study of human memory, particularly in the areas of eyewitness testimony and of so-called repressed memories, which she has argued can be planted in the minds of unwitting individuals so that the individuals believe they are remembering events that they never actually experienced.*

THE EYEWITNESS TESTIMONY PARADIGM

Some of the strongest evidence for the constructive nature of memory has been obtained by those who have studied the validity of eyewitness testimony. In a now-classic study, Elizabeth Loftus, David Miller, and Helen Burns (1978) showed participants a series of 30 slides in which a red Datsun drove down a street, stopped at a stop sign, turned right, and then appeared to knock down a pedestrian crossing at a crosswalk. As soon as the participants finished seeing the slides, they had to answer a series of 20 questions about the accident. One of the questions contained information that was either consistent or inconsistent with what they had been shown. For example, half of the participants were asked: "Did another car pass the red Datsun while it was stopped at the stop sign?" The other half of the participants received the same question, except with the word *yield* replacing the word *stop.* In other words, the information in the question given this second group was inconsistent with what the participants had seen.

Later, after engaging in an unrelated activity, all participants were shown two slides and asked which they had seen. One had a stop sign, the other a yield sign. Accuracy on this task was 34% better for participants who had received the consistent question (stop-sign question) than for participants who had received the inconsistent question (yield-sign question). This experiment and others (e.g., Loftus, 1975, 1977) have shown people's great susceptibility to distortion in eyewitness accounts. Although this distortion may be due to phenomena other than just constructive memory, it does show that we easily can be led to construct a memory that is different from what really happened. (You might have had a disagreement with a roommate or a friend, regarding an experience in which both of you were in the same place at the same time, but what each of you remembers about the experience differs sharply—and *both* of you feel that you are truthfully and accurately recalling what happened.)

Loftus (e.g., Loftus & Ketcham, 1991; Loftus, Miller, & Burns, 1987) has been instrumental in pointing to the potential problems of wrongful conviction when using eyewitness testimony as the sole or even the primary basis for convicting accused persons of crimes. She further notes that eyewitness testimony is often a powerful determinant of whether a jury will convict an accused person. The effect is particularly pronounced if eyewitnesses appear highly confident of their testimony, even if the eyewitnesses can provide few perceptual details or offer apparently conflicting responses. People sometimes even think they remember things simply because they have imagined or thought about them (Garry & Loftus, 1994). It has been estimated that as many as 10,000 people per year may be convicted wrongfully on the basis of mistaken eyewitness testimony (Cutler & Penrod, 1995; Loftus & Ketcham, 1991).

John Brigham, Roy Malpass, and others (e.g., Bothwell, Brigham, & Malpass, 1989; Brigham & Malpass, 1985; Shapiro & Penrod, 1986) have pointed out that eyewitness identification is particularly weak when identifying persons of a race other than the race of the witness. Astonishingly, even infants seem to be influenced by postevent information when recalling an experience, as shown through their behavior in operant-conditioning experiments (Rovee-Collier, Borza, Adler, & Boller, 1993).

Not everyone views eyewitness testimony with such skepticism, however (e.g., see Zaragoza, McCloskey, & Jamis, 1987). The question still remains as to whether the information about the original event is actually displaced by, or is simply competing with, the subsequent misleading information. Judith McKenna, Molly Treadway, and Michael

McCloskey (1992) have argued that psychologists need to know a great deal more about the circumstances that impair eyewitness testimony before impugning such testimony before a jury. At present, the verdict on eyewitness testimony is still not in. The same can be said for repressed memories, considered next.

Repressed Memories

Might you have been exposed to a traumatic event as a child, but have been so traumatized by this event that you now cannot remember it? Some psychotherapists have begun using hypnosis and related techniques to elicit from people what are alleged to be *repressed memories,* or memories that have been pushed down into unconsciousness because of the distress they cause. Such memories, according to the view of psychologists who believe in their existence, are very inaccessible, but they can be dredged out (Briere & Conte, 1993).

But do repressed memories actually exist? Many psychologists strongly doubt their existence (Ceci & Loftus, 1994; Lindsay & Read, 1994; Loftus & Ketcham, 1994; Roediger & McDermott, 1995) and others are at least highly skeptical (Bowers & Farvolden, 1996). First, therapists may be inadvertently planting ideas in their clients' heads, creating false memories of events that never took place. Indeed, Roediger and McDermott (1995) have shown that creating false memories is relatively easy, even in people with no particular psychological problems and by using ordinary, nonemotional stimuli. Second, showing that these memories are false is often extremely hard to do, given that reported incidents often end up, as in the case of childhood sexual abuse, merely pitting one person's word against another (Schooler, 1994). At the present time, no compelling evidence points to the existence of such memories, although psychologists also have not reached the point where their existence can be ruled out definitively.

Context Effects on Encoding and Retrieval

As studies of constructive memory show, our cognitive contexts for memory clearly influence our memory processes of encoding, storing, and retrieving information. Studies of expertise also show how existing schemas may provide a cognitive context for encoding, storing, and retrieving new information. Specifically, experts generally have more elaborated schemas than do novices in regard to their areas of expertise (e.g., Chase & Simon, 1973; Frensch & Sternberg, 1989). These schemas provide a cognitive context in which the experts can relatively easily integrate and organize new information, fill in gaps when provided with partial or even distorted information, visualize concrete aspects of verbal information, and implement appropriate metacognitive strategies for organizing and rehearsing new information. Clearly, expertise enhances our confidence in our recollected memories.

Another factor that enhances our confidence in recall is the perceived clarity—the vividness and richness of detail—of the experience and its context. When we are recalling a given experience, we often associate the degree of perceptual detail and intensity with the degree to which we are accurately remembering the experience (Johnson, Foley, Suengas, & Raye, 1988; Johnson & Raye, 1981). We feel greater confidence that our recollections are accurate when we perceive them with greater richness of detail. Although this heuristic for *reality monitoring* is generally effective, Ulric Neisser (1982) and others have pointed to situations in which factors other than accuracy of recall may lead to enhanced vividness and detail of our recollections.

In particular, an oft-studied form of vivid memory is the **flashbulb memory**—a memory of an event so powerful that the person remembers the event as vividly as if it were indelibly preserved on film (R. Brown & Kulik, 1977). Persons old enough to recall the attack of Pearl Harbor or the assassination of President John Kennedy may have flashbulb memories of these events. Some persons also have flashbulb memories for the start of the Gulf War, the explosion of the space shuttle *Challenger,* or momentous events in their personal lives. Based on some findings regarding flashbulb memory, it seems that the emotional intensity of an experience may enhance the likelihood that we will recall the particular experience (over other experiences) ardently and perhaps accurately (Bohannon, 1988). A related view is that a memory is most likely to become a flashbulb memory when it is important to the individual, surprising, and when it has an emotional effect on the individual (Conway, 1995).

Whereas some investigators suggest that flashbulb memories may be more vividly recalled due to their emotional intensity, other investigators suggest that the vividness of recall may be due to the effects of rehearsal, in that we frequently retell, or at least silently contemplate, our experiences of these momentous events. Perhaps our retelling also enhances the perceptual intensity of our recall (Bohannon, 1988). Other findings suggest that flashbulb memories may be perceptually rich (Neisser & Harsch, 1993) and recalled with relatively greater confidence in the accuracy of the memories (Weaver, 1993), but not actually any more reliably accurate than any other recollected memories (Neisser & Harsch, 1993; Weaver, 1993). Possibly, if flashbulb memories are indeed more likely to be the subject of conversation or even silent reflection, perhaps at each retelling of the experience, we reorganize and construct our memories such that the accuracy of our recall actually diminishes while the perceived vividness of recall increases over time. At present, researchers heatedly debate whether studies of such memories as a special process are a flash in the pan (e.g., Cohen, McCloskey, & Wible, 1990) or a flash of insight into memory processes (e.g., Schmidt & Bohannon, 1988).

The emotional intensity of a memorable event is not the only way in which emotions, moods, and states of consciousness affect memory. Our moods and states of consciousness also may provide a context for encoding that affects later retrieval of semantic memories. That is, when we encode semantic information during a particular mood or state of consciousness, we may more readily retrieve that information when in the same state again (Baddeley, 1989; Bower, 1983). Regarding state of consciousness, something that is encoded when we are influenced by alcohol or other drugs may be retrieved more readily while under those same influences again (E. Eich, 1995; J. E. Eich, 1980).

In regard to mood, some investigators (e.g., Baddeley, 1989) have suggested that a factor in maintaining depression may be that the depressed person can more readily retrieve memories of previous sad experiences, which may further the continuation of the depression. If psychologists or others can intervene to prevent the continuation of this vicious cycle, the person may begin to feel happier, resulting in other happy memories being more easily retrieved, thus further relieving the depression, and so on. Perhaps the folk-wisdom advice to "think happy thoughts" is not entirely unfounded. In fact, under laboratory conditions, participants seem more accurately to recall items that have pleasant associations than they recall items that have unpleasant associations (Matlin & Underhill, 1979).

Emotions, moods, states of consciousness, schemas, and other features of our internal context clearly affect memory retrieval. In addition, even our external contexts may affect our ability to recall information. We appear to be better able to recall information when we are in the same physical context as the one in which we learned the material (Godden & Baddeley, 1975). In one experiment, 16 underwater divers were asked to learn a list of 40 unrelated words, either while they were on shore or while they were 20 feet beneath the sea. Later, they were asked to recall the words when either in the same environment as where they had learned them or in the other environment. Recall was better when it occurred in the same place as did the learning.

More recently, Carolyn Rovee-Collier and her colleagues (Butler & Rovee-Collier, 1989) have found that even infants demonstrate context effects on memory. Rovee-Collier has studied these effects in an operant-conditioning experiment in which the infants could make a crib mobile move in interesting ways by kicking it. When 3-month-olds (Butler & Rovee-Collier, 1989) or 6-month-olds (Borovsky & Rovee-Collier, 1990) were given an opportunity to kick a distinctive crib mobile in the same context (i.e., surrounded by a distinctive bumper lining the periphery of the crib) in which they first learned to kick it or in a different context, they kicked more strongly in the same context. The infants showed much less kicking when in a different context or when presented with a different mobile.

From these results, such learning seems highly context-dependent. However, in one set of studies, 3-month-olds (Rovee-Collier & DuFault, 1991) or 6-month-olds (Amabile & Rovee-Collier, 1991) were offered operant-conditioning experiences in multiple contexts for kicking a distinctive mobile. They were soon thereafter placed in a novel context (unlike any of the contexts for conditioning). The investigators found that the infants retained the memory and kicked the mobile at high rates in the novel context. Thus, when information is encoded in various contexts, the information also seems to be retrieved more readily in various contexts, at least when there is minimal delay between the conditioning contexts and the novel context. However, when the novel context occurred after a long delay, the infants did not show increased kicking, although they still showed context-dependent memory for kicking in the familiar contexts (Amabile & Rovee-Collier, 1991).

All of the preceding context effects may be viewed as an interaction between the context for encoding and the context for retrieval of encoded information. The results of various experiments on retrieval suggest that how items are encoded has a strong effect both on how and on how well items are retrieved. Endel Tulving and Donald Thomson (1973) have referred to this relationship as **encoding specificity:** What is recalled depends on what is encoded. A rather dramatic example of encoding specificity was shown by Michael Watkins and Endel Tulving (1975). We know that recognition memory is virtually always better than is recall. For example, generally recognizing a word that you have learned is easier than recalling it. After all, in recognition, you have only to say whether you have seen the word, whereas in recall, you have to generate the word and then mentally confirm whether it appeared on the list.

In one experiment, Watkins and Tulving had participants learn a list of 24 paired associates, such as *ground–cold* and *crust–cake.* Participants were instructed to learn to associate each response (such as *cold)* with its stimulus word (such as *ground).* After participants had studied the word pairs, they were given an irrelevant task. Then they were given a recognition test with distractors. Participants were asked simply to circle the words they had seen previously. Participants recognized an average of 60% of the words from the list. Then, participants were provided with the 24 stimulus words and were asked to recall the responses. Their cued recall was 73%. Thus, recall was better than recognition. Why? Because, according to the encoding-specificity hypothesis, the stimulus was a better cue for the word than the word itself, given that the words had been learned as paired associates.

As mentioned previously (see chapter 5), Anthony Greenwald and Mahzarin Banaji (1989) found that the link between encoding and retrieval may also explain the self-reference effect. Specifically, the main cause of the self-reference effect is not due to unique properties of self-referent cues, but rather to a more general principle of encoding and retrieval: When individuals generate their own cues for retrieval, the cues are much more potent than when others do so. Other researchers have confirmed the importance of making cues meaningful to the individual in order to enhance memory. For example, Timo Mantyla (1986) found that when participants made up their own retrieval cues, they were able to remember, almost without errors, lists of 500 and 600 words. For each word on a list, participants were asked to generate another word (the cue) that, to them, was an appropriate description or property of the target word. Later, they were given a list of their cue words and were asked to recall the target word. Mantyla found that cues were most helpful when they were both *compatible* with the target word, and *distinctive,* in that they would not tend to generate a large number of related words. For example, if you are given the word *coat,* then *jacket* might be both compatible and distinctive as a cue; however, if you came up with the word *wool* as a cue, that cue might make you think of a number of words, such as *fabric* and *sheep,* that are not the target word.

To summarize, retrieval interacts strongly with encoding. If you study for a test and want to recall well at the time of testing, organize the information you are studying in a way that appropriately matches the way in which you will be expected to recall it. Similarly, you will recall information better if the level of processing for encoding matches the level of processing for retrieval (Moscovitch & Craik, 1976).

This chapter and the previous chapter have indicated many situations in which knowledge and memory interact, such as when prior knowledge influences encoding and retrieval. The following two chapters describe how we represent knowledge, emphasizing the roles of mental imagery and semantic knowledge.

SUMMARY

1. **What have cognitive psychologists discovered regarding how we encode information for storing it in memory?** Encoding of information in short-term memory appears to be largely, although not exclusively, acoustic in form, as shown by the susceptibility of information in short-term memory to *acoustic confusability*—that is, errors based on sounds of words. Evidence has also been

found, however, that shows some visual and some semantic encoding of information in short-term memory. Information in long-term memory appears to be encoded primarily in a *semantic* form, so that confusions tend to be in terms of meanings rather than in terms of the sounds of words. In addition, some evidence points to the existence of visual encoding, as well as of acoustic encoding, in long-term storage.

Transfer of information into long-term storage may be facilitated by rehearsal of the information (particularly if the information is elaborated meaningfully), by organization (e.g., categorization) of the information, by the use of mnemonic devices, or by the use of external memory aids (e.g., writing lists or taking notes). In addition, people tend to remember better when knowledge is acquired through *distributed practice* across various study sessions, rather than through *massed practice,* although the distribution of time during any given study session does not seem to affect transfer into long-term memory. The effects of distributed practice may be due to a hippocampal-based mechanism that results in rapid encoding of new information, to be integrated with existing memory systems over time, perhaps during sleep.

2. **What affects our ability to retrieve information from memory?** Studying retrieval from long-term memory is difficult, due to problems of differentiating retrieval from other memory processes, as well as of differentiating *accessibility* from *availability.* Retrieval of information from short-term memory appears to be in the form of *serial, exhaustive processing,* implying that a person always sequentially checks all information on a list, although some data may be interpreted as allowing for the possibility of *self-terminating serial processing* and even of *parallel processing.*

3. **How does what we know or what we learn affect what we remember?** Two of the main theories of forgetting in short-term memory are *decay theory* and *interference theory.* Interference theory distinguishes between *retroactive interference* and *proactive interference.* Although assessing the effects of decay, while ruling out both interference and rehearsal effects, is much harder, some evidence of distinctive decay effects has been found. Interference also seems to influence long-term memory, at least during the period of *consolidation,* which may continue for several years after the initial memorable experience.

   Memory appears to be not only *reconstructive* (a reproduction of what was learned, based on recalled data and on inferences from only those data), but also *constructive* (influenced by attitudes, subsequently acquired information, and schemas based on past knowledge). As shown by the effects of existing schemas on the construction of memory, schemas affect memory processes, as do other internal contextual factors, such as emotional intensity of a memorable experience, mood, and even state of consciousness. In addition, environmental context cues during encoding seem to affect later retrieval. *Encoding specificity* refers to the fact that what is recalled depends largely on what is encoded: How information is encoded at the time of learning will greatly affect how it is later recalled. One of the most effective means of enhancing recall is for the individual to generate meaningful cues for subsequent retrieval.

Thinking About Thinking: Factual, Analytical, Creative, and Practical Questions

1. In what forms do we encode information for brief memory storage versus long-term memory storage?
2. What is the evidence for encoding specificity? Cite at least three sources of supporting evidence.
3. What is the main difference between two of the proposed mechanisms by which we forget information?
4. Compare and contrast some of the views regarding flashbulb memory.
5. Suppose that you are an attorney defending a client who is being prosecuted solely on the basis of eyewitness testimony. How could you demonstrate to members of the jury the frailty of eyewitness testimony?
6. Use the chapter-opening example from Bransford and Johnson as an illustration to make up a description of a common procedure, without labeling the procedure. Try having someone read your description and then recall the procedure.
7. Make a list of 10 or more unrelated items you need to memorize. Choose one of the mnemonic devices mentioned in this chapter, and describe how you would apply the device to memorizing the list of items. Be specific.
8. What are three things you have learned about memory that can help you to learn new information so that you can effectively recall the information over the long term?

Key Terms

accessibility 196
availability 195
consolidation 185
constructive 201
decay 196
decay theory 200
distributed practice 186
encoding 182
encoding specificity 205
flashbulb memory 204
interference 196
interference theory 196
massed practice 186
metacognition 186
metamemory 186
mnemonic device 188
proactive interference 197
reconstructive 201
rehearsal 186
retrieval (memory) 182
retroactive interference 197
storage (memory) 182

Annotated Suggested Readings

Kearins, J. M. (1981). Visual spatial memory in Australian aboriginal children of desert regions. *Cognitive Psychology, 13,* 434–460. An outstanding study showing that children from unconventional environments whose cognitive performance seems backward can actually perform better than other children if the cognitive task is adapted to the environment of the children from the unconventional environment.

McClelland, J. L., McNaughton, B. L., & O'Reilly, R. C. (1995). Why there are complementary learning systems in the hippocampus and neocortex: Insights from the successes and failures of connectionist models of learning and memory. *Psychological Review, 102,* 419–457. Not for the meek, but this work is definitely worth reading (you can skip through the pages with formulas on them) because it offers a good integration of diverse findings on the role of the hippocampus in consolidating memory.

Rubin, D. C. (Ed.). (1996). *Remembering our past: Studies in autobiographical memory.* New York: Cambridge University Press. An excellent study of one of the most interesting topics in human memory—namely, autobiographical memory. This work deals in part with the issue of people's inventions of memories of experiences they have never had.

Sternberg, S. (1969). Memory-scanning: Mental processes revealed by reaction-time experiments. *American Scientist, 4,* 421–457. Worth reading because it is one of the all-time classics of cognitive psychology: influential, engaging, well-written, and a beautiful example of the interaction between theory and research.

Knowledge Representation: Images and Propositions

Chapter Outline

Exploring Cognitive Psychology

Mental Representation of Knowledge
- External Representations: Pictures Versus Words
- Mental Imagery
- Dual-Code Hypothesis: Analogical Images Versus Symbols
- Propositional Hypothesis

Mental Manipulations of Images
- Mental Rotations
- Image Scaling
- Image Scanning

Synthesizing Images and Propositions
- Epiphenomena and Demand Characteristics
- Johnson-Laird's Mental Models
- Neuropsychological Evidence for Multiple Codes

Spatial Cognition and Cognitive Maps
- Rats, Bees, and Humans
- Mental Shortcuts
- Text Maps

Summary

Thinking About Thinking: Factual, Analytical, Creative, and Practical Questions

Key Terms

Annotated Suggested Readings

EXPLORING COGNITIVE PSYCHOLOGY

1. **What are some of the major hypotheses regarding how knowledge is represented in the mind?**
2. **What are some of the characteristics of mental imagery?**
3. **How does knowledge representation benefit from both analogical images and symbolic propositions?**
4. **How may conceptual knowledge and expectancies influence the way we use images?**

Look carefully at the photos depicted in Figure 7.1. Describe to yourself what two of these people look like and sound like. Clearly, none of these people can truly exist in a physical form inside your mind. How are you able to imagine and describe them? You must have in your mind some form of mental *representation* (something that stands for something else) of what you know about them. More generally, you use **knowledge representation,** the form for what you know in your mind about things, ideas, events, and so on, which exist outside of your mind.

MENTAL REPRESENTATION OF KNOWLEDGE

Ideally, cognitive psychologists would love to be able to observe directly how each of us represents knowledge, such as by taking a videotape or a series of snapshots of ongoing representations of knowledge in the human mind. Unfortunately, direct empirical methods for observing knowledge representation are not available now, and such methods are unlikely to be available in the immediate future (although we never know). When direct empirical methods are unavailable, several alternative methods remain. For one thing, we can ask people to describe their own knowledge representations and knowledge-representation processes. Unfortunately, none of us has conscious access to our own knowledge-representation processes, so self-report information about these processes is highly unreliable (Pinker, 1985).

Another possibility is the rationalist approach, in which we try to deduce logically the most reasonable account of how people represent knowledge. For centuries, philosophers have done exactly that. In classic *epistemology* (the study of the nature, origins, and limits of human knowledge), philosophers distinguished between two kinds of knowledge structures: **declarative knowledge** (facts that can be stated, e.g., the date of your birth, the name of your best friend, or the way a rabbit looks) and **procedural knowledge** (procedures that can be implemented, e.g., the steps involved in tying your shoelaces, adding a column of numbers, or driving a car). The distinction, as phrased by the philosopher Gilbert Ryle (1949), is between *knowing that* and *knowing how.*

Although cognitive psychologists have made extensive use of rationalist insights as a starting-point for understanding cognition, they rarely are content with rationalist descriptions alone. Instead, they seek some kind of empirical support for the insights proposed in

FIGURE 7.1 **MENTAL IMAGERY**

Look at each of these photos carefully. Next, close your eyes, and picture two of the people represented—people whom you have heard speak or sing. Without looking again at the photos, mentally compare the voices and the appearances of the two people you have chosen.

rationalist accounts of cognition. There are two main sources of empirical data on knowledge representation: standard laboratory experiments and neuropsychological studies.

In experimental work, researchers indirectly study knowledge representation by observing how people handle various cognitive tasks that require the manipulation of mentally represented knowledge. In neuropsychological studies, researchers either observe how the normal brain responds to various cognitive tasks involving knowledge representation or observe the links between various deficits in knowledge representation and associated pathologies in the brain.

External Representations: Pictures Versus Words

In this chapter, we focus on the distinction between knowledge represented in mental pictures and knowledge represented in more symbolic forms, such as words or abstract propositions. Of course, cognitive psychologists are chiefly interested in our internal, mental representations of what we know, but to help our understanding we shall consider first how external representations in words differ from such representations in pictures.

Some ideas are better and more easily represented in pictures and others in words. For example, if someone asks you, "What is the shape of a chicken egg?" you may find drawing easier than describing an egg. For many geometric shapes and concrete objects, pictures do seem to express myriad words about the object in an economical form. On the other hand, what if someone asks you, "What is justice?" Although describing that abstract concept in words would be very difficult, doing so pictorially would be even harder.

As Figure 7.2 (a) and (b) show, although both pictures and words may be used to represent things and ideas, neither form of representation actually retains all of the characteristics of what is being represented. For example, neither the word *cat* nor the picture of the cat actually eats fish, meows, or purrs when petted. Both the word *cat* and the picture of this cat are distinctive *representations* of "catness," and each type of representation has distinctive characteristics.

Investigating Cognitive Psychology

Observe Figure 7.2. What is the shape of the word *cat?* What is the shape of the picture of the cat? Cover up part of the word, and explain how what is left relates to the characteristics of a cat. Cover up part of the picture, and explain how what is left relates to the characteristics of a cat.

As you just observed, the picture is relatively *analogous* to the real-world object it represents; the picture shows concrete attributes (e.g., shape and relative size) that are similar to the features and properties of the real-world object the picture represents. Even if you cover up a portion of the figure of the cat, what remains is still analogous to a part of a cat. Under typical circumstances, most aspects of the picture may be grasped simultaneously,

FIGURE 7.2 **PICTURES, WORDS, AND PROPOSITIONS**

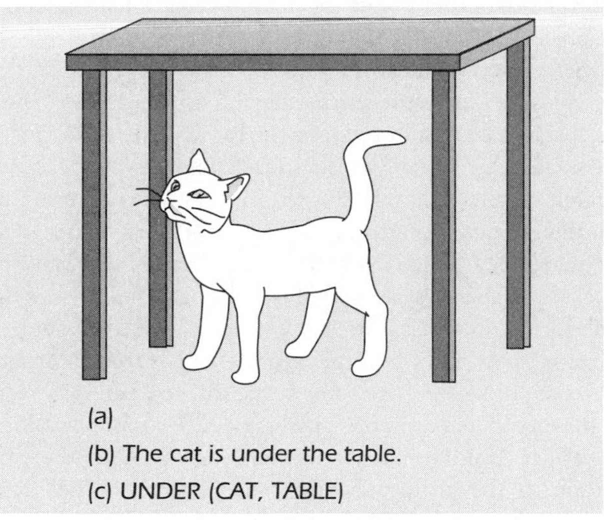

We may represent things and ideas in pictures or in words. Neither pictures nor words capture all the characteristics of what they represent, and each more readily captures some kinds of information than other kinds. Some cognitive psychologists have suggested that we have (a) some mental representations that resemble pictorial, analogous images; (b) other mental representations that are highly symbolic, like words; and perhaps even (c) more fundamental propositional representations that are in a pure abstract "mentalese" that is neither verbal nor pictorial, which cognitive psychologists often represent in this highly simplified shorthand.

although you may scan the picture, zoom in for a closer look, or zoom out to see the big picture. Even when scanning or zooming, however, you do not have to follow any arbitrary rules for looking at features of the picture from top to bottom, left to right, and so on.

Unlike a picture of a cat, the word *cat* is a *symbolic* representation; the relationship between the word and what it represents is simply arbitrary. There is nothing inherently catlike about the word. If you cover up part of the word, it no longer bears even a symbolic relationship to any part of the object it represents. Furthermore, because symbols are arbitrary, their use requires the application of rules. For example, in forming words, the sounds or letters must also be sequenced according to rules (e.g., c-a-t, not a-c-t or t-c-a); in forming sentences, the words must also be sequenced according to rules (e.g., "the cat is under the table," not "table under cat the is").

Symbolic representations such as the word *cat* capture some kinds of information, but not other kinds of information. The dictionary defines *cat* as "a carnivorous mammal *(Felis catus)* long domesticated as a pet and for catching rats and mice" *(Merriam-Webster's Collegiate Dictionary,* 1993). If our own mental representations for the meanings of words resemble those of the dictionary, the word *cat* connotes an animal that eats meat ("carnivorous"), nurses its young ("mammal"), and so on. This information is abstract and general and may be applied to any number of specific cats, having any fur color or pattern. To represent additional characteristics, we must use additional words (e.g., black, Persian, or calico).

The picture of the cat does not convey any of the abstract information conveyed by the word regarding what the cat eats, whether it nurses its young, and so on. On the other hand, the picture conveys a great deal of concrete information about this specific cat, such as the exact position of the cat's legs, the angle at which we are viewing the cat, the length of the cat's tail, whether both of its eyes are open, and so on.

Pictures and words also represent relationships in different ways. The picture in Figure 7.2 (a) shows the spatial relationship between the cat and the table. For any given picture showing a cat and a table, the spatial (positional) relationship (beside, above, below, behind, etc.) will be concretely represented in the picture. In contrast, when using words, spatial relationships between things must be stated explicitly by a discrete symbol (i.e., a word such as a preposition)—for example, "The cat is *under* the table." On the other hand, more abstract relationships, such as class membership, are often implied by the meanings of the words (e.g., cats are mammals, tables are items of furniture) but are rarely implied through pictures.

To summarize, pictures aptly capture concrete and spatial information in a manner analogous to whatever they represent; words handily capture abstract and categorical information in a manner that is symbolic of whatever they represent. Pictorial representations convey all features simultaneously; in general, any rules for creating or understanding pictures pertain to the analogous relationship between the picture and what it represents, perhaps ensuring as much similarity as possible between the two. Representations in words usually convey information sequentially, according to arbitrary rules that have little to do with what the words represent, but that have a lot to do with the structure of the symbol system for using words. Each kind of representation is well suited to some purposes, but not to others. For example, blueprints and identification photos serve different purposes than essays and memos do.

Now that we have some preliminary ideas about external representations of knowledge, we can turn to considering internal representations of knowledge. Specifically, how do we represent what we know in our minds? Do we have mental scenarios (pictures) and mental narratives (words)? In subsequent chapters on information processing and language, we discuss various kinds of symbolic mental representations. In this chapter, we focus on mental pictures.

Mental Imagery

Imagery is the mental representation of things (objects, events, settings, etc.) that are not currently being sensed by the sense organs. For example, recall one of your first experiences on a college campus. What were some of the sights, sounds, and even smells (e.g., cut grass or tree-lined paths) you sensed at that time? Although these sensations are not immediately available to you at this moment, you can still imagine them. In fact, mental imagery may represent things that have never been observed by your senses at any time; for example, imagine what it would be like to travel down the Amazon River. Mental images may even represent things that do not exist at all outside the mind of the person creating the image; for example, imagine how you would look if you had a third eye in the center of your forehead.

Imagery may involve mental representations in any of the sensory modalities (hearing, smell, taste, etc.). Imagine a fire alarm, your favorite song, or your nation's anthem; the smell of a rose, of fried bacon, or of an onion; the taste of a lemon, of a pickle, or of your favorite candy. At least hypothetically, each form of mental representation is subject to investigation, and some researchers have studied each of the sensory representations (e.g., Intons-Peterson, 1992; Intons-Peterson, et al., 1992; Reisberg, Smith, Baxter, & Sonenshine, 1989; Reisberg, Wilson, & Smith, 1991; Smith, Reisberg, & Wilson, 1992).

Nonetheless, most research on imagery in cognitive psychology has focused on *visual imagery,* the mental representation of visual knowledge (e.g., objects or settings) not presently visible to the eyes. Apparently, researchers are just like other people: Most of us are more aware of visual imagery than of other forms of imagery. When Stephen Kosslyn and his colleagues (Kosslyn, Seger, Pani, & Hillger, 1990) asked students to keep a diary of their mental images, the students reported many more visual images than auditory, smell, touch, or taste images.

Stephen M. Kosslyn *is a professor of psychology at Harvard University. He is best known for his research showing that imagery is not a single, undifferentiated faculty but rather involves a number of distinct processes. He also has made major contributions to neuropsychology by identifying discrete areas of the brain associated with specific imagery processes.*

According to Kosslyn (1990), we use visual images to solve problems and to answer questions involving objects. Which is darker red—a cherry or an apple? How many windows are there in your house or apartment? How do you get from your home to your first class of the day? How do you fit together the pieces of a puzzle or the component parts of an engine, a building, or a model? According to Kosslyn, in order to solve problems and answer questions such as these, we visualize the objects in question, mentally representing the images in our minds.

Many psychologists outside of cognitive psychology are interested in applications of mental imagery to other fields in psychology, such as in using guided-imagery techniques for controlling pain, for strengthening immune responses and otherwise promoting health, and for overcoming psychological problems, such as phobias and other anxiety disorders. Applied psychologists observe that design engineers, biochemists, physicists, and many other scientists and technologists use imagery to think about various structures and processes, as well as to solve problems in their chosen fields. Not everyone is equally facile in creating and manipulating mental images, however. Research in applied settings and in the laboratory indicates that some of us are better able to create mental images than are others (Reisberg, Culver, Heuer, & Fischman, 1986).

In just what form do we represent images in our minds? According to an extreme view of imagery, all images of everything we ever sense may be stored as exact copies of physical images. Realistically, to store every observed physical image in the brain seems impossible, simply in terms of the capacity of the brain and the structures and processes used by the brain (Kosslyn, 1981; Kosslyn & Pomerantz, 1977). Take the following simple example.

Investigating Cognitive Psychology

Look at your face in a mirror. Gradually turn your head from far right (to see yourself out of your left peripheral vision) to far left, and from as far forward as you can tilt it to as far back as you can while still seeing your reflection. Now make a few different expressions, perhaps even talking to yourself to exaggerate your facial movements. How could you possibly store a moving picture or even a series of separate images of your face, or of other rotating objects?

Dual-Code Hypothesis: Analogical Images Versus Symbols

In the late 1960s and early 1970s, Allan Paivio (1969, 1971) suggested a **dual-code hypothesis,** according to which we use both imagined and verbal codes for representing information. These two codes organize information into knowledge that can be acted on, stored somehow, and even later retrieved for subsequent use. According to Paivio, mental images are **analogue** codes (a form of knowledge representation that preserves the main perceptual features of whatever is being represented) for the physical stimuli we observe in our environment such as trees and rivers. Just as the movements of the hands on an analogue clock are analogous to the passage of time, the mental images we form in our minds are analogous to the physical stimuli we observe.

In contrast, according to Paivio, our mental representations for words are chiefly represented in a **symbolic** code (a form of knowledge representation that has been arbitrarily chosen to stand for something and that does not perceptually resemble whatever is being represented). Just as a digital watch uses arbitrary symbols (numerals) to represent the passage of time, our minds use arbitrary symbols (words and combinations of words) to represent many ideas. A *symbol* may be anything that is arbitrarily designated to stand for something other than itself. For example, although we recognize that the numeral "9" is a symbol for the concept of "nineness," representing a quantity of nine of something, nothing about the symbol in any way would suggest its meaning. Concepts like *justice* and *peace* would be represented symbolically. We have arbitrarily designated this symbol to represent the concept, but "9" has meaning only because we use it to represent a deeper concept.

Investigating Cognitive Psychology

To get an intuitive sense of how you may use each of the two kinds of representations, think about how you mentally represent all the facts you know about cats based on your mental definition of the word *cat* and all the inferences you may draw from your mental image of a cat. Which kind of representation is more helpful for answering the following questions: Is a cat's tail long enough to reach the tip of the cat's nose if the cat is stretching to full length? Do cats like to eat fish? Are the back legs and the front legs of a cat exactly the same size and shape? Are cats mammals? Which is wider—a cat's nose or a cat's eye? Which kinds of mental representations were the most valuable for answering each of these questions?

Paivio also found some empirical support for his view by noting that verbal information seems to be processed differently than is imaginal information. For example, in one study (Paivio, 1969), participants were shown both a rapid sequence of pictures and a sequence of words. They were then asked to recall the words or the pictures either at random (recalling as many as possible, regardless of the order in which the items were presented) or in the correct sequence. Although participants more easily recalled the pictures when they were allowed to do so in any order, they more readily recalled the sequence in which the words were presented than the sequence for the pictures.

Other researchers also supported the notion that our minds use one system for representing verbal information and a different system for representing imaginal information. For example, it has been hypothesized that actual visual perception could interfere with simultaneous visual imagery, and that the need to produce a verbal response could interfere with the simultaneous mental manipulation of words. Lee Brooks (1968) tested this notion, using a study in which he had participants perform either a visual task (answering questions requiring judgments about a picture that was presented briefly) or a verbal task (answering questions requiring judgments about a sentence that was stated briefly). He then had participants express their responses verbally (saying "yes" or "no" aloud), visually (pointing to an answer), or manually (tapping with one hand to agree and the other to disagree). The two interference conditions were a visual task requiring a visual (pointing) response and a verbal task requiring a verbal response. Brooks found that participants did show more interference (i.e., slower response times) in performing the imaginal task when asked to respond using a competing visual display, as compared with when they were using a noninterfering response medium (i.e., either verbal or manual). Similarly, his participants showed more interference in performing the verbal task when asked to respond using a competing verbal form of expression, as compared with how they performed when responding manually or by using a visual display. Thus, a response involving visual perception can interfere with a task involving manipulations of a visual image; similarly, a response involving verbal expression can interfere with a task involving mental manipulations of a verbal statement. These findings suggest the use of two distinct codes for mental representation of knowledge: an imaginal (analogical) code and a verbal (symbolic) code.

Propositional Hypothesis

Not everyone subscribes to the dual-code hypothesis. John Anderson and Gordon Bower (1973), for example, presented an alternative theory of knowledge representation, sometimes termed the *conceptual-propositional hypothesis* or just the **propositional hypothesis.** According to this view, as well as that of others (e.g., Pylyshyn, 1973, 1978, 1981, 1984), we do not store mental representations in the form of images. Rather, our mental representations (sometimes called "mentalese") more closely resemble the abstract form of a proposition. A *proposition* is the meaning underlying a particular relationship among concepts. According to this view, images are *epiphenomena,* secondary phenomena that occur as a result of other cognitive processes.

How would a propositional representation work? Consider an example. To describe Figure 7.2 (a), you could say, "The table is above the cat." You could also say, "The cat is beneath the table." Both of these statements indicate the same relationship as "Above the cat is the table." With a little extra work, you probably could come up with a dozen or more ways of verbally representing this relationship, which is visually represented in Figure 7.2 (a).

Logicians have devised a shorthand means (called "predicate calculus") of expressing the underlying meaning of a relationship, which attempts to strip away the various superficial differences in the ways we describe the deeper meaning of a proposition:

[RELATIONSHIP BETWEEN ELEMENTS]([SUBJECT ELEMENT],[OBJECT ELEMENT])

The logical expression for the proposition underlying the relationship between the cat and the table is shown in Figure 7.2 (c). This logical expression, of course, would need to be translated by the brain into a format suitable for its internal mental representation.

USING PROPOSITIONS

Why the hypothetical construct of propositions is so widely accepted among cognitive psychologists is easy to see. Propositions may be used to describe any kind of relationship, such as actions, attributes, positions, class membership, and so on, as shown in Table 7.1. In addition, any number of propositions may be combined to represent more complex relationships, images, or series of words (e.g., "The furry mouse bit the cat, who is now hiding under the table"). The key idea is that the propositional form of mental representation is neither in words nor in images, but rather in an abstract form representing the underlying meanings of knowledge. Thus, a proposition for a sentence would not retain the acoustic or visual properties of the words, and a proposition for a picture would not retain the exact perceptual form of the picture (H. H. Clark & Chase, 1972).

According to the propositional view (H. H. Clark & Chase, 1972), both images (e.g., of the cat and the table in Figure 7.2a) and verbal statements (e.g., in Figure 7.2b) are mentally represented in terms of their deep meanings—that is, as propositions, not as specific images or statements. According to propositional theory, imaginal and verbal information are encoded and stored as propositions. Then, when we wish to retrieve the information from storage, the propositional representation is retrieved, and from it, our minds re-create the verbal or the imaginal code relatively accurately.

ANALOGICAL LIMITATIONS

Some evidence does suggest limits to analogical representation of images. For example, look quickly at Figure 7.3 and then look away. Does Figure 7.3 contain a *parallelogram* (a four-sided figure that has two pairs of parallel lines of equal length)? Stephen Reed (1974) asked participants to look at figures such as this one and to determine whether particular shapes (e.g., a parallelogram) were or were not part of a given whole figure (see Figure 7.3). Overall performance was little better than chance. The participants appeared unable to call up a precise analogical mental image and to use that mental image to trace the lines to determine which component shapes were or were not part of a whole figure. To Reed, these findings suggested the use of a propositional code (e.g., "a Star of David" or "two overlapping triangles, one of which is inverted") rather than an analogical one. A more likely explanation, I believe, is that people have analogical mental images, but ones that are imprecise in some ways.

Additional limits to analogical representation have been found by Deborah Chambers and Daniel Reisberg (1985, 1992), who often have used in their research figures such as the one shown in Figure 7.3. Look now at Figure 7.4 (a), and imagine the rabbit shown in the figure. Actually, the figure shown here is an *ambiguous figure,* meaning that it can be

TABLE 7.1 PROPOSITIONAL REPRESENTATIONS OF UNDERLYING MEANINGS

We may use propositions to represent any kind of relationship, including actions, attributes, spatial positions, class membership, or almost any other conceivable relationship. The possibility for combining propositions into complex propositional representational relationships makes the use of such representations highly flexible and widely applicable.

Type of Relationship	Representation in Words	Propositional Representation*	Imaginal Representation
Actions	A mouse bit a cat.	Bite [action] (mouse [agent of action], cat [object])	
Attributes	Mice are furry.	[external surface characteristic] (furry [attribute], mouse [object])	
Spatial positions	A cat is under the table.	[vertically higher position] (table, cat)	
Class membership	A cat is an animal.	[categorical membership] (animal [category], cat [member])	

*In this table, propositions are expressed in a shorthand form (known as "predicate calculus") commonly used to express underlying meaning. This shorthand is intended only to give some idea of how the underlying meaning of knowledge might be represented. It is not believed that this form is literally the form in which meaning is represented in the mind. In general, the shorthand form for representing propositions is this: [Relationship between elements] ([subject element], [object element]).

interpreted in more than one way. Ambiguous figures often are used in studies of perception, but these researchers decided to use such figures to determine whether mental representations of images are truly analogical to perceptions of physical objects. Without looking back at the figure, can you determine the alternative interpretation of 7.4 (a)? When the participants in Chambers and Reisberg's study had difficulty, the researchers offered cues, but even participants with high visualization skills often were unable to conjure the alternative interpretation.

Finally, the authors suggested to participants that they should call on their memory to draw their mental representations of the figures. Without looking again at the figure, briefly sketch Figure 7.4 (a), based on your own mental representation of it. Once you have completed your sketch, try once more to see whether you can find an alternative interpretation of the figure. If you are like most of Chambers and Reisberg's participants, not until

FIGURE 7.3 **PART–WHOLE RELATIONSHIPS**

Quickly glance at this figure and then cover it with your hand. Imagine the figure you just saw. Does it contain a parallelogram?

FIGURE 7.4 **AMBIGUOUS FIGURES**

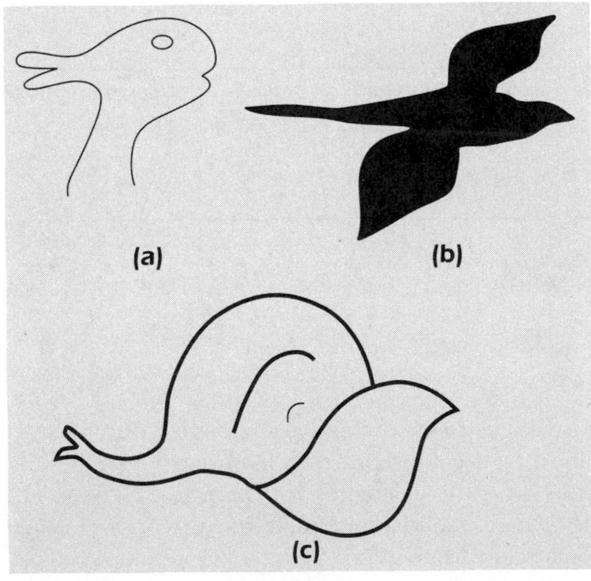

(a) Look closely at the rabbit, then cover it with your hand, and re-create it in your mind. Can you see a different animal in this image, just by mentally shifting your perspective? (b) What animal do you observe in this figure? Create a mental image of this figure, and try to imagine the front end of this animal as the back end of another animal, and the tail end of this animal as the front end of another animal. (c) Observe the animal in this figure, and create a mental image of the animal; cover the figure, and try to reinterpret your mental image as a different kind of animal (both animals are probably facing in the same direction).

you have in front of you an actual *percept* (object of perception) of the figure can you guess at an alternative interpretation of the figure. These studies indicate that mental representations of figures are not the same as percepts of these figures. In case you have not yet guessed it, the alternative interpretation of the rabbit is a duck, in which the rabbit's ears are the duck's bill.

One interpretation of Chambers and Reisberg's findings—an implausible one—is that there is no discrete imaginal code. An alternative and more plausible explanation is that a propositional code may override the imaginal code in some circumstances. That is, the initial interpretation of the figure in propositional code may override the imaginal code for the figure. Much earlier work (Carmichael, Hogan, & Walter, 1932) suggested that semantic (verbal) information (e.g., labels for figures) tends to distort recall of visual images, in the direction of the meaning of the images. For example, for each of the figures in the center column of Figure 7.5, observe the alternative interpretations for the figures recalled, based on the differing labels given for the figures.

Propositional Limits

In contrast to the above work, Ronald Finke, Steven Pinker, and Martha Farah (1989) found some evidence that mental imagery may be manipulated directly, rather than via a propositional code. These researchers had participants manipulate mental images by combining two distinct images to form a different mental image altogether. (This manipulation of mental images may be viewed as an imaginal Gestalt experience, in which the whole of the two combined images differed from the sum of its two distinct parts.) Finke and his colleagues found that in some situations, mental images can be combined effectively (e.g., the letter *H* and the letter *X*) to create mental images of geometric shapes (e.g., right triangles), of letters (e.g., *M*), or of objects (e.g., a bow tie). It appears that propositional codes are less likely to influence imaginal ones when participants create their own mental images, rather than when participants are presented with a picture to be represented. On the other hand, propositional codes may influence imaginal ones when the picture used for creating an image is ambiguous (as in Figure 7.4 a–c) or rather abstract (as in Figure 7.3).

Building on Finke's work (Finke et al., 1989) regarding the construction of mental images, Mary Peterson and her colleagues (M. Peterson, Kihlstrom, Rose, & Glisky, 1992) presented an alternative view of Chambers and Reisberg's findings regarding the manipulation of ambiguous figures (see Figure 7.4a). According to M. Peterson and her colleagues, the mental reinterpretation of ambiguous figures involves two manipulations: (a) a mental *realignment* of the reference frame (i.e., shifting the positional orientations of the figures on the mental "page" or "screen" on which the image is displayed; in Figure 7.4a, the duck's back = the rabbit's front, and the duck's front = the rabbit's back); and (b) a mental *reconstrual* (reinterpretation) of parts of the figure (i.e., the duck's bill = the rabbit's ears). Although participants may be unlikely to manipulate mental images spontaneously in order to reinterpret ambiguous figures, such manipulations occur when participants are given the right context.

In a series of experiments, M. Peterson and her colleagues explored several conditions under which participants mentally reinterpreted their image of the duck/rabbit figure (Figure 7.4a) and some other ambiguous figures. The experiments differed in terms of the types of supporting hints.

FIGURE 7.5 PROPOSITIONAL CODE VERSUS IMAGINAL CODE

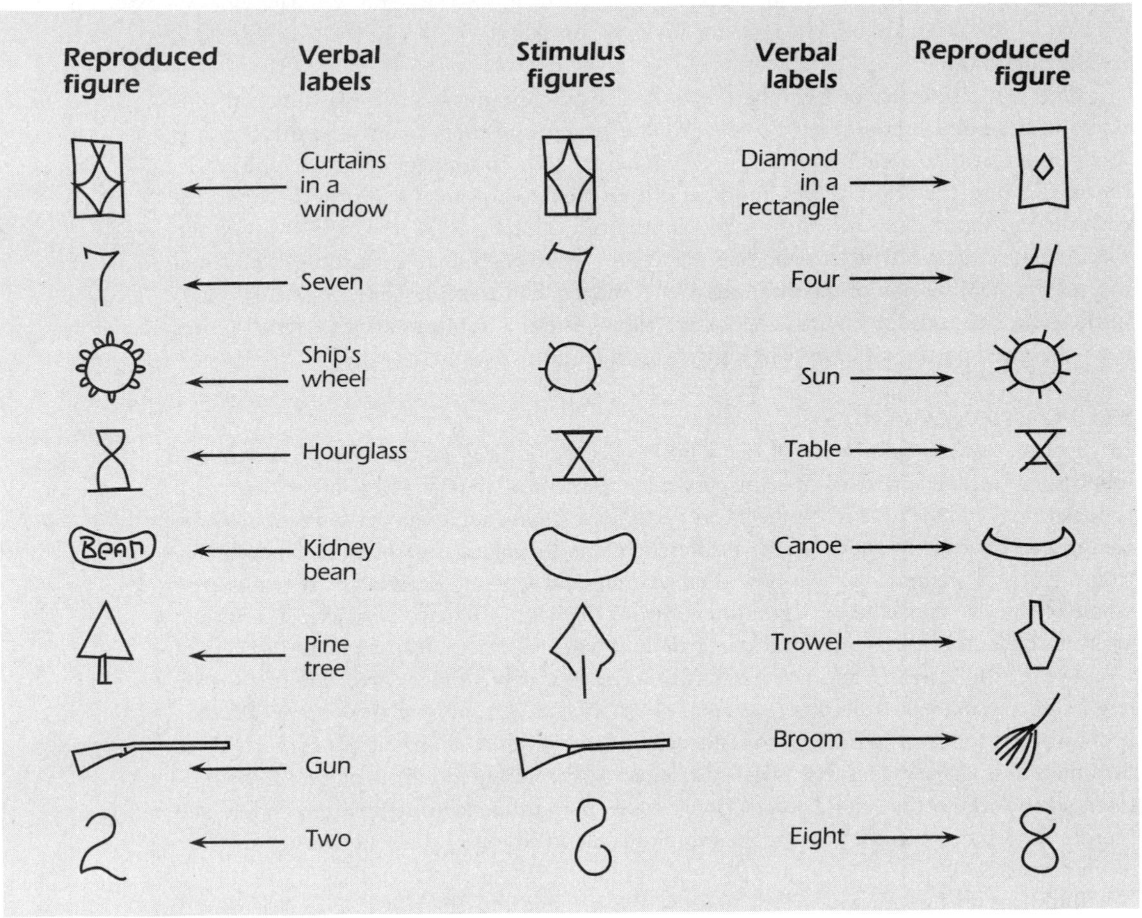

Reproduced figure	Verbal labels	Stimulus figures	Verbal labels	Reproduced figure
	← Curtains in a window		Diamond in a rectangle →	
	← Seven		Four →	
	← Ship's wheel		Sun →	
	← Hourglass		Table →	
BEAN	← Kidney bean		Canoe →	
	← Pine tree		Trowel →	
	← Gun		Broom →	
	← Two		Eight →	

Semantic labels clearly influence mental images, as shown here in the differing drawings based on mental images of objects given differing semantic (verbal) labels. (After Carmichael, Hogan, & Walter, 1932)

Across experiments, from 20% to 83% of participants were able to reinterpret ambiguous figures, using one or more of the following hints: (a) *implicit reference-frame hint*—in which the participants were first shown another ambiguous figure involving realignment of the reference frame (e.g., see Figure 7.4b; a hawk's head = a goose's tail, and a hawk's tail = a goose's head); (b) *explicit reference-frame hint*—in which participants were asked to modify the reference frame, by considering either "the back of the head of the animal they had already seen as the front of the head of some other animal" (M. Peterson et al., 1992, p. 111; considered a conceptual hint) or "the front of the thing you were seeing as the back of something else" (p. 115; considered an abstract hint); (c) *attentional hint*—in which participants were directed to attend to regions of the figure where realignments or reconstruals were to occur;

(d) *construals from "good" parts*—in which participants were asked to construe an image from parts determined to be "good" (according to both objective [geometrical] and empirical [inter-rater agreement] criteria), rather than from parts determined to be "bad" (according to similar criteria). Additionally, some spontaneous reinterpretation of mental images for ambiguous figures may occur, particularly for images of figures that may be reinterpreted without realigning the reference frame (e.g., see Figure 7.4c, which may be either a whole snail or an elephant's head, or possibly even a bird, a helmet, a leaf, or a seashell).

Mary Peterson and colleagues (1992) went on to suggest that the processes involved in constructing and manipulating mental images are similar to the processes involved in perceptual processes, such as the recognition of forms (discussed in chapter 4). Not everyone agrees with Peterson's view, but some support for her views has been found by cognitive psychologists who hold that mental imagery and visual perception are *functionally equivalent* (employing about the same operations to serve about the same purposes for their respective domains). Overall, the weight of the evidence seems to be for there being multiple codes rather than just a single code but the controversy continues (see Barsalou, 1994).

Mental Manipulations of Images

According to the **functional-equivalence hypothesis,** which is supported by many cognitive psychologists (e.g., Farah, 1988b; Finke, 1989; Jolicoeur & Kosslyn, 1985a, 1985b; Rumelhart & Norman, 1988; Shepard & Metzler, 1971), although visual imagery is not identical to visual perception, it is functionally equivalent to it. That is, as Paivio suggested decades ago, although we do not construct images that are exactly identical to percepts, we do construct images that are functionally equivalent to percepts. These functionally equivalent images are analogous to the physical percepts they represent. Finke (1989) has suggested some principles of how visual imagery may be functionally equivalent to visual perception. These principles may be used as a guide for designing and evaluating research on imagery. Table 7.2 offers an idea of some of the research questions that may be generated, based on Finke's principles.

Roger N. Shepard *is the Ray Lyman Wilbur professor emeritus of social science at Stanford University. Shepard is known best for his seminal work on the study of mental imagery, as well as his work on multidimensional scaling, on establishing general laws of cognition, and on visual thinking in general.*

Mental Rotations

Basic Phenomena

The classic experiment studying the functional-equivalence hypothesis is Roger Shepard and Jacqueline Metzler's (1971) experiment on mental rotations. Participants were asked to observe pairs of two-dimensional pictures showing three-dimensional geometric forms (see Figure 7.6). As the figure shows, the forms were rotated from 0 to 180 degrees, either in the picture plane (i.e., in two-dimensional space, as in Figure 7.6a) or in depth (i.e., in three-dimensional space, as in Figure 7.6b). In addition, participants were shown distractor forms, which were not rotations of the original stimuli (as in Figure 7.6c). Participants were then asked to tell whether a given image was or was not a rotation of the original stimulus.

TABLE 7.2 PRINCIPLES OF VISUAL IMAGERY: QUESTIONS

According to the functional-equivalence hypothesis, we represent and use visual imagery in a way that is functionally equivalent to that for physical percepts. Ronald Finke has suggested several principles of visual imagery that may be used to guide research and theory development.

PRINCIPLE	POSSIBLE QUESTIONS GENERATED FROM PRINCIPLES
1. Our mental transformations of images and our mental movements across images correspond to similar transformations of and movements across physical objects and percepts.	Do our mental images follow the same laws of motion and space that are observed in physical percepts? For example, does it take longer to manipulate a mental image at a greater angle of rotation than at a smaller one? Does it take longer to scan across a large distance in a mental image than across a smaller distance?
2. The spatial relations among elements of a visual image are analogous to those relations in actual physical space.	Are the characteristics of mental images analogous to the characteristics of percepts? For example, is it easier to see the details of larger mental images than of smaller ones? Are objects that are closer together in physical space also closer together in mental images of space?
3. Mental images can be used to generate information that was not explicitly stored during encoding.	After participants have been asked to form a mental image, can they answer questions that require them to infer information, based on the image, which was not specifically encoded at the time they created the image? For example, suppose that participants are asked to picture a tennis shoe. Can they later answer questions such as "How many lace-holes are there in the tennis shoe?"
4. The construction of mental images is analogous to the construction of visually perceptible figures.	Does it take more time mentally to construct a more complex mental image than a simpler one? Does it take longer to construct a mental image of a larger image than of a smaller one?
5. Visual imagery is functionally equivalent to visual perception in terms of the processes of the visual system used for each.	Are the same regions of the brain involved in manipulating mental imagery as are involved in manipulating visual percepts? For example, are similar areas of the brain activated when mentally manipulating an image, as compared with those involved when physically manipulating an object?

As shown in Figure 7.7, the response times for answering the questions about the figures formed a *linear function* of the degree to which the figures were rotated. That is, for each increase in the degree of rotation of the figures, there was a corresponding increase in the response times. Furthermore, there was no significant difference between rotations in the picture plane and rotations in depth. These findings are functionally equivalent to what we might expect if the participants had been rotating physical objects in space: To rotate objects at larger angles of rotation takes longer, and whether the objects are rotated clockwise, counterclockwise, or in the third dimension of depth makes little difference. The finding of a relation between degree of angular rotation and reaction time has now been replicated a number of times with a variety of stimuli (e.g., Jordan & Huntsman, 1990; Van Selst & Jolicoeur, 1994).

To try your own hand at mental rotations, try the following demonstration for yourself (based on Hinton, 1979).

FIGURE 7.6 MENTAL ROTATIONS: DEMONSTRATION

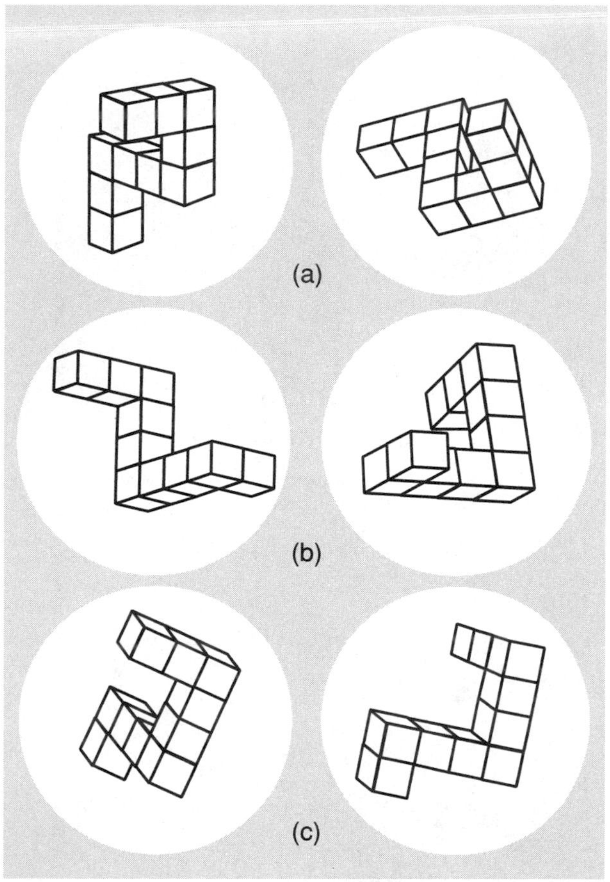

For which of these pairs of figures does the figure on the right show an accurate rotation of the figure on the left?

INVESTIGATING COGNITIVE PSYCHOLOGY

Imagine a cube floating in the space in front of you. Now, mentally grasp the left front bottom corner of the cube with your left hand, and grasp the right back top corner of the cube with your right hand. While mentally holding those corners, rotate the cube so that the corner in your left hand is directly below the corner in your right hand (as if to form a vertical axis around which the cube would spin). How many corners of the imaginary cube are in the middle (i.e., not being grasped by your hands)? Describe the positions of the corners.

FIGURE 7.7 **MENTAL ROTATIONS: FINDINGS**

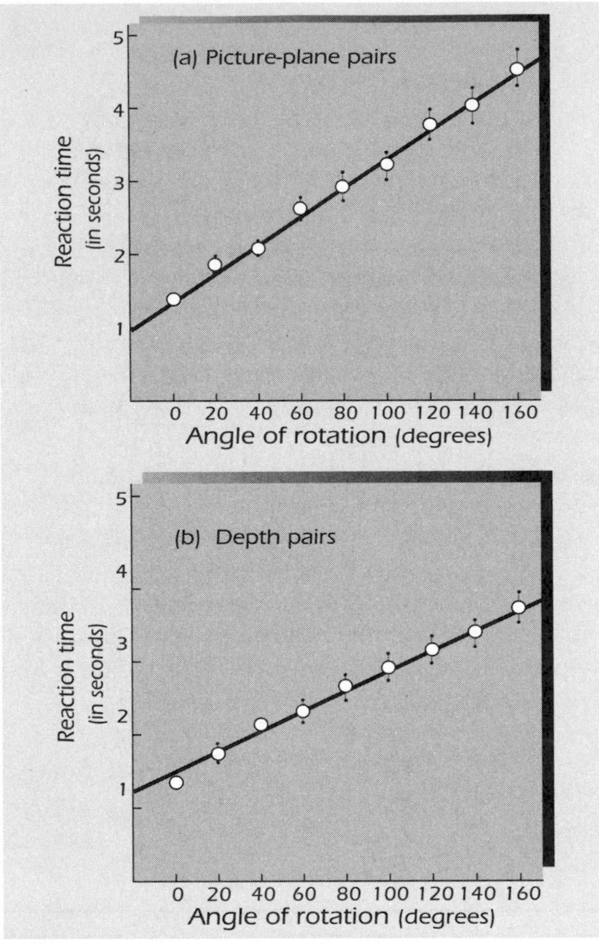

Response times to questions about mental rotations of figures show a linear relationship to the angle of rotation, and this relationship is preserved, whether the rotations are in the picture plane or are in depth.

Other researchers have supported Shepard and Metzler's original findings in other studies of mental rotations—for example, in rotations of two-dimensional figures, such as letters of the alphabet (Jordan & Huntsman, 1990) and cubes (Just & Carpenter, 1985). In addition, response times are longer for *degraded stimuli* (i.e., stimuli that are blurry, incomplete, or otherwise less informative; E. Duncan & Bourg, 1983) than for intact stimuli, and they are longer for unfamiliar figures than for familiar ones (Jolicoeur, Snow, & Murray, 1987).

The benefits of increased familiarity also may lead to practice effects—improvements in performance associated with increased practice. When participants have practice in mentally rotating particular figures (increasing their familiarity), their performance improves, but this improvement appears not to carry over to rotation tasks for novel figures (Jolicoeur, 1985). For example, few people have extensive experience with rotating actual geometrical cubes. Hence, in the demonstration with the mental cube, most people imagine that there are four remaining corners of the cube being held by the two corners in their hands, and that all four corners are aligned on a horizontal plane, parallel to the ground. In fact, six corners remain, and only two corners are aligned in a given horizontal plane (parallel to the ground) at any one time. (Try it yourself, using whatever nonimaginary cube you can put your hands on.)

The work of Shepard and others on mental rotation provides a direct link between research in cognitive psychology and research on intelligence. The kinds of problems studied by Shepard and his colleagues are very similar to problems that can be found on conventional psychometric tests of spatial ability. For example, the Primary Mental Abilities test of Louis Thurstone and Thelma Thurstone (1962) requires mental rotation of two-dimensionally pictured objects in the picture plane, and similar problems appear on other tests. Shepard's work points out a major contribution of cognitive research toward our understanding of intelligence—namely, the identification of the mental representations and cognitive processes that underlie adaptations to the environment, and thus, ultimately, human intelligence.

Neuropsychological Evidence

Is there any physiological evidence for mental rotation? Researchers often are unable to study directly the cerebral activity associated with many cognitive processes in the living brain of a human. Sometimes, we may gain insight into these processes by studying the brains of primates, animals whose cerebral processes seem most closely analogous to our own. Apostolos Georgopoulos and his colleagues (Georgopoulos, Lurito, Petrides, Schwartz et al., 1989), using single-cell recordings in the motor cortex of monkeys, found some physiological evidence of mental rotations by the monkeys. Each monkey had been trained to physically move a handle in a direction that was perpendicular and counterclockwise to a target light, which was used as a reference point. Wherever the target light appeared, the monkeys were to use that point as a reference for the perpendicular and counterclockwise physical rotation of the handle. During these physical rotations, the monkey's cortical activity was recorded. Later, in the absence of the handle, the target light was again presented at various locations, and the cortical activity was again recorded. During these presentations, activity in the motor cortex showed that the same individual cortical cells tended to respond as if the monkeys were anticipating the movements of the particular rotations associated with particular locations of the target light.

Preliminary findings based on primate research suggest that areas of the cerebral cortex have mappings that resemble the two-dimensional spatial arrangements of visual receptors in the retina of the eye (see Kosslyn, 1994). These mappings may be construed as relatively depictive (Kosslyn, Thompson, Kim, & Alpert, 1995). It may be speculated that if these same regions of the cortex are active in humans during tasks involving mental imagery, mental imagery may be similarly depictive in representation. The rise of current brain-imaging techniques have allowed researchers to image human brain activity non-invasively in order to address such speculations (see chapter 2 for a discussion of brain imaging techniques). For example, in a recent study using functional MRI, Cohen and Kosslyn and colleagues (Cohen, Kosslyn, Breiter, DiGirolamo et al., 1996; see also

Kosslyn & Sussman, 1995) found that the same brain areas involved in perception also are involved in mental-rotation tasks.

Thus, not only are imagery and perception found to be functionally equivalent in psychological studies, but neuropsychological techniques verify the equivalence by demonstrating overlapping brain activity as well. However, does mental imagery involve the same mechanisms as memory processes? If so, the functional-equivalence hypothesis for perception would lose some ground. If imagery is "functionally equivalent" to everything, then it is really equivalent to nothing. A recent review by Georgopolous and Pellizzer (1995) cites many psychological studies that find differences between human-imagery and memory tasks. Furthermore, Georgopolous and Pellizzer address single-cell recording studies of primates performing analogous tasks to verify the distinction between imagery and memory. In sum, there is converging evidence, both from traditional and neuropsychological studies, to lend support to the hypothesis of functional equivalence between perception and mental imagery. Further neuropsychological work will be discussed later in the chapter.

IMAGE SCALING

Just as Roger Shepard was the key researcher who launched the study of image rotation, Stephen Kosslyn launched the study of *image scaling* (phenomena related to image size) and image scanning as a means of understanding how we create and manipulate mental representations of images. The key idea underlying research on image size is that we represent and use mental images in ways that are functionally equivalent to our representations and uses of percepts. For example, in visual perception, there are limitations on the *resolution* (ability to distinguish individual elements, such as parts of an object or physically adjacent objects) or the clarity with which we perceive details in what we observe. In general, seeing featural details of large objects is easier than seeing such details of small ones, and we respond more quickly to questions about large objects we observe than to questions about small ones we observe. Thus, if imaginal representation is functionally equivalent to perception, participants also should respond more quickly to questions about features of imaginally large objects than to questions about features of imaginally small ones.

On the other hand, when we zoom in closer to objects, to perceive featural details, sooner or later, we reach a point at which we can no longer see the entire object. To see the whole object once more, we must zoom out. Observe perceptual zooming for yourself.

INVESTIGATING COGNITIVE PSYCHOLOGY

Find a large bookcase (floor to ceiling, if possible; if not, observe the contents of a large refrigerator with an open door). Stand as close to the bookcase as you can while still keeping all of it in view. Now, read the smallest writing on the smallest book in the bookcase. Without changing your gaze, can you still see all of the bookcase? Can you read the title of the book farthest from the book on which you are focusing your perception?

Researchers fairly easily can control the sizes of percepts in perceptual research. However, for research on image size, controlling the sizes of people's mental images is more difficult. How do I know that the image of the elephant in my head is the same size as the image of the elephant in your head? Kosslyn (1975) devised some ways to get around this problem.

One of the strategies was to use relative size as a means of manipulating image size (Kosslyn, 1975): Specifically, Kosslyn asked participants to imagine four different pairs of animals: an elephant and a rabbit, a rabbit and a fly, a rabbit and an elephant-sized fly, and a rabbit and a fly-sized elephant. He then asked the participants specific questions about the features of the rabbit and timed their responses. As he had predicted, it took longer to describe the details of smaller objects (e.g., rabbits paired with elephants or with elephant-sized flies) than to describe the details of the larger objects (e.g., rabbits paired with flies or with fly-sized elephants). Kosslyn (1983) used a metaphor to explain this phenomenon: On our mental screen for visual images, our screen resolution is finer and more detailed for objects that take up a larger area of the mental screen than it is for objects taking up a smaller area.

Using the screen metaphor, Kosslyn (Kosslyn & Koenig, 1992) has noted some intriguing effects of image size, as seen in the next investigation.

In another study, Kosslyn (1976) studied the responses of children in the first and fourth grades, as well as of adult college undergraduates, when asked whether particular animals were characterized as having various physical attributes (e.g., "Does a cat have claws?" "Does a cat have a head?"). In one condition, participants were asked to visualize each animal and to use this mental image in answering the questions; in the other condition, they were not asked to use mental images, and it was presumed that they used verbal/propositional knowledge to respond to the verbal questions.

In the imagery condition, all participants responded more quickly to questions about physical attributes that are larger (e.g., a cat's head) than to questions about attributes that are smaller (e.g., a cat's claws). Different results were found in the nonimagery condition, in which participants were not asked to use imagery. In the nonimagery condition, as expected, fourth-graders and adults responded more quickly to questions about physical attributes based on the distinctiveness of the characteristic for the animal. For example, they responded more quickly to questions about whether cats have claws (which are distinctive) than to questions about whether cats have heads (which are not particularly distinctive to cats alone). The physical size of the features did not have any effect on performance in the nonimagery condition for either fourth-graders or adults.

In contrast, first-graders constantly responded more quickly regarding larger attributes in both the imagery and the nonimagery conditions. When asked about their responses, many of these younger children indicated that they used imagery even when not instructed to do so. Further, in both conditions, adults responded more quickly than did children, but the difference was much greater for the nonimagery condition than for the imagery condition. These findings support the functional-equivalence hypothesis because physical size influences perceptual-resolution ability. The findings also support the dual-code view in two ways: (a) For adults and older children, responses based on the use of imagery (an imaginal code) differed from responses based on propositions (a symbolic code); (b) the development of propositional knowledge and ability does not occur at the same rate as the development of imaginal knowledge and ability. The distinction in the rate of development of each form of representation also seems to support Paivio's notion of two distinct codes.

INVESTIGATING COGNITIVE PSYCHOLOGY

Look at the rabbit and the fly in Figure 7.8. Close your eyes and picture them both in your mind. Now imaginally look only at the fly, and determine the exact shape of the fly's head. Do you notice yourself having to take time to zoom in to "see" the detailed features of the fly?

If you are like most people, you are able to zoom the focus on your mental images, to give the features or objects a larger portion of your mental screen, much as you might physically move toward an object you wanted to observe more closely.

Now, look at the rabbit and the elephant, and picture them both in your mind. Next, close your eyes and look at the elephant. Imagine walking toward the elephant, watching it as it gets closer to you. Do you find that there comes a point when you can no longer see the rabbit or even all of the elephant?

If you are like most people, you will find that the image of the elephant will appear to overflow the size of your image space. To "see" the whole elephant, you probably have to mentally zoom out again.

FIGURE 7.8 **IMAGE SIZE: DEMONSTRATION**

Stephen Kosslyn (1983) asked participants to imagine either a rabbit and a fly (to observe zooming in to "see" details) or a rabbit and an elephant (to observe whether zooming in may lead to apparent overflow of the image space).

IMAGE SCANNING

Kosslyn has found additional support for the use of imaginal representation in his studies of image scanning. The key idea underlying image-scanning research is that images, as spatial representations, can be scanned, much the same as physical percepts can be scanned. Further, our strategies and responses for imaginal scanning are expected to be functionally equivalent to those we use for perceptual scanning. A means of testing the functional equivalence of imaginal scanning is to observe some aspects of performance during perceptual scanning and to compare that performance with performance during imaginal scanning.

For example, in perception, to scan across longer distances takes longer than to scan across shorter ones. In one of Kosslyn's experiments (Kosslyn, Ball, & Reiser, 1978), participants were shown a map of an imaginary island, which you can see in Figure 7.9. The map shows various objects on the island, such as a hut, a tree, and a lake. Participants studied the map until they could reproduce it accurately from memory, placing

FIGURE 7.9 **IMAGE SCANNING**

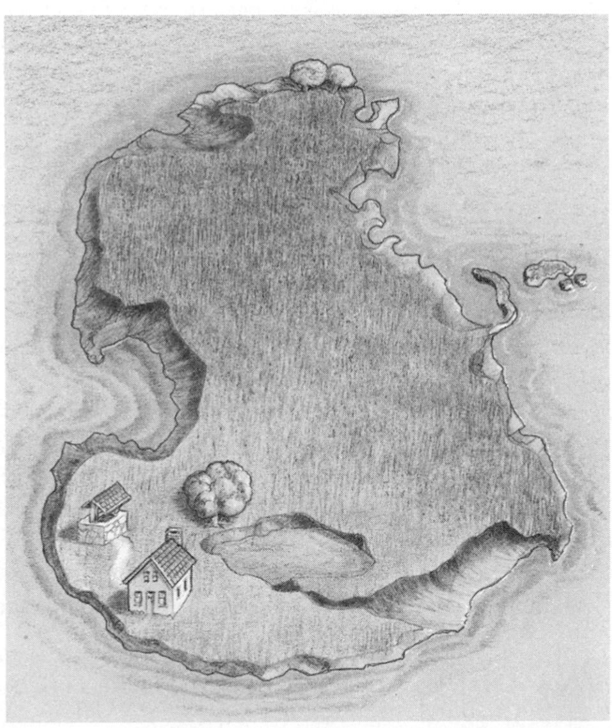

Stephen Kosslyn and his colleagues used a map of an imaginary island with various landmarks, to determine whether mental scanning across the image of a map was functionally equivalent to perceptual scanning of a perceived map.

the locations of each of the six objects in the map no more than a quarter of an inch from their correct locations. Once the memorization phase of the experiment was completed, the critical phase began.

Participants were instructed that, upon hearing the name of an object read to them, they should picture the map, mentally scan directly to the mentioned object, and press a key as soon as they arrived at the location of the named object. An experimenter then read to the participants the name of a first object. Five seconds later, the experimenter read to the participants the name of a second object. Participants again had to scan mentally to the proper location, and press a button when they found the object. This procedure was repeated a number of times, with the participants mentally moving between various pairs of objects on successive trials. The experimenter kept track of response times for participants to press the button on each trial. These response times indicated the amounts of time it took participants to scan from one object to another. The critical finding was an almost perfect linear relation between the distances separating successive pairs of objects in the mental map and the amount of time it took participants to press the button. In other words, participants seem to have encoded the map in the form of an image and actually to have scanned that image as needed for a response.

Findings supporting an imaginal code have been shown in several other domains. For example, Steven Pinker (1980) showed the same pattern of results for scanning objects in three dimensions. Specifically, his participants observed and then mentally represented a three-dimensional array of objects—toys suspended in an open box—and then they mentally scanned from one object to another.

Synthesizing Images and Propositions

In this chapter, we have discussed two opposing views of knowledge representation: (a) a *dual-code hypothesis,* suggesting that knowledge is represented both in images and in symbols; and (b) a *propositional hypothesis,* suggesting that knowledge is represented only in underlying propositions, not in the form of images or of words and other symbols. Before we consider some proposed syntheses of the two hypotheses, let's review the findings described thus far, in light of Finke's principles of visual imagery (see Table 7.3). In the discussion thus far, we have addressed the first three of Finke's criteria for imaginal representations. Based on the studies of mental rotations, image scaling (sizing), and image scanning, mental imagery appears functionally equivalent to perception in many ways. However, the studies involving ambiguous figures and unfamiliar mental manipulations suggest that there are limits to the analogy between perception and imagery.

Epiphenomena and Demand Characteristics

Although there seems to be quite good evidence for the existence of both propositions and mental images (Kosslyn, 1994), the debate is not over. Margaret Intons-Peterson (1983) has suggested that some of the results found in image research could be the result of *demand characteristics,* in which the experimenters' expectancies regarding the performance of participants on a particular task create an implicit demand for the participants to perform as expected.

TABLE 7.3 PRINCIPLES OF VISUAL IMAGERY: FINDINGS

How well did the studies reported in this chapter satisfy the criteria suggested by Ronald Finke's principles of visual imagery?

PRINCIPLE	POSSIBLE HYPOTHESES GENERATED FROM PRINCIPLES
1. Our mental transformations of images and our mental movements across images correspond to similar transformations of and movements across physical objects and percepts.	Mental rotations generally conform to the same laws of motion and space that are observed in physical percepts (e.g., Shepard & Metzler, 1971), even showing performance decrements associated with degraded stimuli (E. Duncan & Bourg, 1983; cf. also chapter 4, for comparisons with perceptual stimuli). However, it appears that for some mental images, mental rotations of imaginal objects do not fully and accurately represent the physical rotation of perceived objects (e.g., Hinton, 1979); hence, sone nonimaginal knowledge representations or cognitive strategies appear influential in some situations. In image scanning, it takes longer to scan across a large distance in a mental image than across a smaller distance (Kosslyn, Ball, & Reiser, 1978).
2. The spatial relations among elements of a visual image are analogous to those relations in actual physical space.	It appears that cognitive manipulations of mental images are analogous to manipulations of percepts in studies involving image size. As in visual perception, there are limits to the resolution of the featural details of an image, as well as limits to the size of the image space (analogous to the visual field) that can be "observed" at any one time. To observe greater detail of individual objects or parts of objects, a smaller size or number of objects or parts of objects may be observed, and vice versa (Kosslyn, 1975). In related work (Kosslyn, 1976), it appears easier to see the details of larger mental images (e.g., a cat's head) than of smaller ones (e.g., a cat's claws). It appears also that just as we perceive the physical proximity (closeness) of objects that are closer together in physical space, we also imagine the closeness of mental images in our mental image space (Kosslyn, Ball, & Reiser, 1978).
3. Mental images can be used to generate information that was not explicitly stored during encoding.	After participants have been asked to form a mental image, they can answer some kinds of questions that require them to infer information, based on the image, which was not specifically encoded at the time they created the image. The studies by S. Reed (1974) and by Chambers and Reisberg (1985) suggest that propositional representations may play a role; studies by Finke (1989) and by M. Peterson et al. (1992) suggest that imaginal representations are sometimes sufficient for drawing inferences.
4. The construction of mental images is analogous to the construction of visually perceptible figures.	Studies of lifelong blind people suggest that mental imagery in the form of spatial arrangements may be constructed from haptic, rather than visual, information. Based on the findings regarding cognitive maps (e.g., Hirtle & Mascolo, 1986: Saarinen, 1987; Stevens & Coupe, 1978, B. Tversky, 1981), it appears that both propositional and imaginal knowledge representations influence the construction of spatial arrangements.
5. Visual imagery is functionally equivalent to visual perception in terms of the processes of the visual system used for each.	It appears that some of the same regions of the brain that are involved in manipulating visual percepts may be involved in manipulating mental imagery (e.g., see Farah, Hammond, et al., 1988; Farah, Peronnet, et al., 1988), but it also appears that spatial and visual imagery may be represented differently in the brain.

Concerned as to whether demand characteristics could be a factor in her own work, Intons-Peterson specifically studied the influence of experimenter expectancies on outcomes. She manipulated experimenter expectancies by suggesting to one group of experimenters that task performance would be expected to be better for perceptual tasks than for imaginal ones, and then suggesting the opposite outcome to a second group of experimenters. She found that experimenter expectancies did influence participants' responses in image scanning, in mental rotations, and in another task comparing perceptual performance with imaginal performance. When experimenters expected imaginal performance to be better than perceptual performance, participants responded accordingly, and vice versa—even when the experimenters were not present while participants were responding, and when the cues were presented via computer. Thus, experimental participants performing visualization tasks may be responding in part to the demand characteristics of the task, due to the experimenters' expectations regarding the outcomes.

Pierre Jolicoeur and Stephen Kosslyn (1985a, 1985b) responded to Intons-Peterson's findings in two different kinds of experiments using the image-scanning paradigm. In one set of experiments, the researchers modified the procedure for the task by completely omitting all instructions to scan the mental image. Further, questions that involved responses requiring image scanning were intermixed with questions that did not require any image scanning. Even when image scanning was not an implicit task demand, participants' responses still showed that mental images are scanned in a manner analogous to perceptual scanning.

In another set of experiments, Jolicoeur and Kosslyn led experimenters to expect a pattern of responses that differed from the one analogous to perceptual scanning. Specifically, experimenters were led to expect that the pattern of responses would show a U-shaped curve, rather than a linear function. In this study, too, responses still showed a linear relation between distance and time, not the U-shaped response pattern expected by the experimenters. The hypothesis regarding the functional equivalence of imagery and perception appears to have strong empirical support.

The debate between the propositional hypothesis and the functional-equivalence (analogical) hypothesis has been suggested to be intractable, based on existing knowledge (Keane, 1994). For each empirical finding that supports the view that imagery is analogous to perception, a rationalist reinterpretation of the finding may be offered, which offers an alternative explanation of the finding. Although the rationalist alternative may be a less parsimonious explanation than the empiricist explanation, the alternative cannot be refuted outright. Hence, the debate between the functional-equivalence view and the propositional view may boil down to a debate between empiricism and rationalism.

JOHNSON-LAIRD'S MENTAL MODELS

Philip Johnson-Laird (1983, 1989) has proposed an alternative synthesis of the literature suggesting that mental representations may take any of three forms: propositions, mental models, or images. Johnson-Laird distinctively defines *propositions* as fully abstracted representations of meaning, which are verbally expressible; the criterion of verbal expressibility distinguishes Johnson-Laird's view from that of other cognitive psychologists. *Mental models* are knowledge structures that individuals construct in order to understand and explain their experiences. The models are constrained by the individuals' implicit theories about these experiences, which can be more or less accurate. For example, you may have a mental model to account for how planes fly into the air, but the model depends not on physical or other laws, but rather, on your beliefs about them.

Images are much more specific representations, which retain many of the perceptual features of particular objects, viewed from a particular angle, with the particular details of a given instantiation. For example, "The cat is under the table" may be represented as a proposition (because it is verbally expressible), as a mental model (of any cat and table, perhaps resembling prototypical ones—see chapter 4), or as an image (of a particular cat in a particular position under a particular table).

Kannan Mani and Philip Johnson-Laird (1982) gave some participants *determinate descriptions* for a spatial layout (indicating a precise location for each object in the spatial array) and other participants *indeterminate descriptions* for a spatial layout (giving ambiguous locations for objects in the array). As an analogy, a relatively determinate description of the location of Washington, D.C., is that it lies between Alexandria, Virginia, and Baltimore, Maryland; a rather indeterminate description of the location is that it lies between the Pacific Ocean and the Atlantic Ocean. These researchers found that when participants were given determinate descriptions for the spatial layout of objects, they inferred additional spatial information not included in the descriptions, but they did not recall the verbatim details well. Their having inferred additional spatial information suggests that the participants formed a mental model of the information. That they then did not recall the verbatim descriptions very well suggests that they relied on the mental models, rather than on the verbal descriptions for their mental representations.

In contrast, when participants were given indeterminate descriptions for the spatial layout of objects, they seldom inferred spatial information not given in the descriptions, but they remembered the verbatim descriptions better than the other participants did. The authors suggested that participants did not infer a mental model for the indeterminate descriptions because of the multitude of possibilities for mental models of the given information. Instead, the participants appear to have mentally represented the descriptions as verbally expressible propositions. The notion of mental models as a form of knowledge representation has been applied to a broad range of cognitive phenomena, including visual perception, memory, comprehension of text passages, and reasoning. In fact, Johnson-Laird (1983, 1989) is perhaps best known for his theoretical applications of mental models in reasoning (see chapter 12).

Perhaps the use of mental models may offer a possible explanation of some findings that cannot be fully explained in terms of visual imagery. In a series of experiments, Nancy Kerr (1983) studied persons who were born blind. Because these participants have never experienced visual perception, we may assume that they have never formed visual images (at least not in the ordinary sense of the term). Kerr adapted some of Kosslyn's tasks to work comparably for sighted and for blind participants. For example, for a map-scanning task, Kerr used a board with topographical features and landmarks that could be detected by using touch, and she then asked participants to form a mental image of the board. For a task similar to Kosslyn's image-size tasks, Kerr asked participants to imagine various common objects of various sizes.

Although the blind participants responded more slowly to all tasks than did the sighted participants, Kerr's blind participants still showed similar response patterns to those of sighted participants. They showed faster response times when scanning shorter distances than when scanning longer distances and when answering questions about images of larger objects than about images of smaller objects. At least in some respects, spatial imagery appears not to involve representations that are actual analogues to visual percepts; the use of *haptic* (based on the sense of touch) "imagery" suggests alternative modalities for mental imagery.

Imaginal representation also may occur in an auditory modality (based on hearing). As an example, Margaret Intons-Peterson and her colleagues (Intons-Peterson, Russell, & Dressel, 1992) found that participants seem to have auditory mental images, just as they have visual mental images. Specifically, the participants took longer mentally to shift a sound upward in pitch from the low-pitched purring of a cat to the high-pitched ringing of a telephone than to shift from the cat's purring to a clock's ticking. The relative response times were analogous to the time needed physically to change sounds up or down in pitch. In contrast, when asked to make psychophysical judgments involving discriminations between stimuli, participants took longer to determine whether purring was lower-pitched than was ticking (two relatively close stimuli) than to determine whether purring was lower-pitched than was ringing (two relatively distant stimuli). Psychophysical tests of auditory sensation and perception reveal findings analogous to these.

Neuropsychological Evidence for Multiple Codes

Although an argument can be made that experimenter expectancies and demand characteristics may influence performance on cognitive tasks, that such factors would influence the results of psychobiological research seems implausible. For example, suppose you remembered every word in chapter 2 regarding which particular parts of your brain govern which kinds of perceptual and cognitive functions (an unlikely assumption for you or for most participants in psychobiological research). How would you go about conforming to experimenters' expectancies, controlling directly your brain's activities and functions so that you would simulate what experimenters expected in association with particular perceptual or cognitive functions? Likewise, brain-damaged patients do not know that particular lesions are supposed to lead to particular deficits—indeed, the patients rarely know where a lesion is until after deficits are discovered. Thus, neuropsychological findings may circumvent issues of demand characteristics in resolving the dual-code controversy (although this research does not eliminate experimenter biases as far as where to look for lesions or their corresponding deficits).

Lateralization of Function

Following the long-standing tradition of studying patterns of brain lesions and relating them to cognitive deficits, Alexander Luria (1976) and Brenda Milner (1968) noted that lesions in particular areas of the brain seem to affect symbol-manipulation functions such as language, whereas lesions in other areas of the brain seem to affect imagery-manipulation functions, such as the ability to recognize faces. Specifically, lesions in the right hemisphere are more strongly associated with impaired visual memory and visual perception; lesions in the left hemisphere are more strongly associated with impaired verbal memory and verbal comprehension.

Initial psychobiological research on imagery came from studies of patients with identified lesions and from split-brain patients (see chapter 2). As was mentioned in chapter 2, in studies of patients who underwent surgery that severed their right from their left hemispheres, Michael Gazzaniga and Roger Sperry (1967) found that the right hemisphere appears to be more proficient in representing and manipulating knowledge of a visuospatial nature, in a manner that may be analogous to perception, whereas the left hemisphere appears to be more proficient in representing and manipulating verbal and other symbol-based knowledge.

More recently, Michael Corballis (1989) has gone so far as to suggest that cerebral asymmetry has evolutionary origins: As in the brains of other animals, the right hemisphere of the human brain represents knowledge in a manner that is analogous to our physical environment; unlike the brains of other animals, however, the left hemisphere of only the human brain has the ability to manipulate imaginal components (e.g., consonant and vowel sounds and geometric shapes) and symbols, and to generate entirely new information. Corballis suggests that humans alone can conceive what they have never perceived. However, a recent review of the findings on lateralization has led Corballis to modify his view somewhat (Corballis, 1997). Specifically, recent neuropsychological studies of mental rotation in both animals and humans show that both hemispheres may be partially responsible for task performance. Corballis suggests that the apparent right hemisphere dominance observed in humans may be due to the overshadowing of left hemisphere functions by linguistic abilities. Thus, although it would be nice to have clear evidence of a cerebral hemispheric dissociation between analogue imagery functions and symbolic propositional functions, scientists will have to look deeper into brain functioning before this issue is resolved completely.

Visual Versus Spatial Images

In attempting to understand the nature of visual imagery, Martha Farah (1988a, 1988b; Farah, Hammond, Levine, & Calvanio, 1988) has found evidence that *visual imagery* (the use of images that represent visual characteristics such as colors and shapes) may be represented differently than is *spatial imagery* (images that represent spatial features such as depth dimensions, distances, and orientations). In the case of L. H., a 36-year-old, head injury at age 18 years had resulted in lesions in the right and the left temporo-occipital regions, the right temporal lobe, and the right inferior frontal lobe. As you may have guessed, based on studies of hemispheric specialization, L. H.'s injuries implicated possible impairment of his ability to represent and manipulate both visual and spatial images.

Martha Farah *is a professor of psychology at the University of Pennsylvania. She is most well known for her seminal work on mental imagery and its relation to the brain. She has shown, for example, that imagery uses many of the same parts of the brain as does visual perception.*

Despite L. H.'s injuries, L. H.'s ability to see was intact, as shown by his copying of various pictures (see Figure 7.10 a–b). Nonetheless, he could not recognize any of the pictures he copied. In other words, he could not link verbal labels to the objects pictured, and he performed very poorly when asked to respond verbally to questions requiring visual imagery (e.g., regarding color or shape). Surprisingly, however, L. H. showed relatively normal abilities in performing tasks (see Figure 7.10 c–d) involving (a) rotations (2-D letters, 3-D objects); (b) mental scanning, size scaling, matrix memory, and letter corners; and (c) state locations.

Farah and her colleagues (Farah, Peronnet, Gonon, & Giard, 1988) have also used ERP (event-related potential, see chapter 2, Table 2-1) studies to compare brain processes associated with visual perception to brain processes associated with visual imagery. As you may recall, the primary visual cortex is located in the occipital region of the brain. During

FIGURE 7.10 **LESIONS AND IMAGERY: A CASE STUDY**

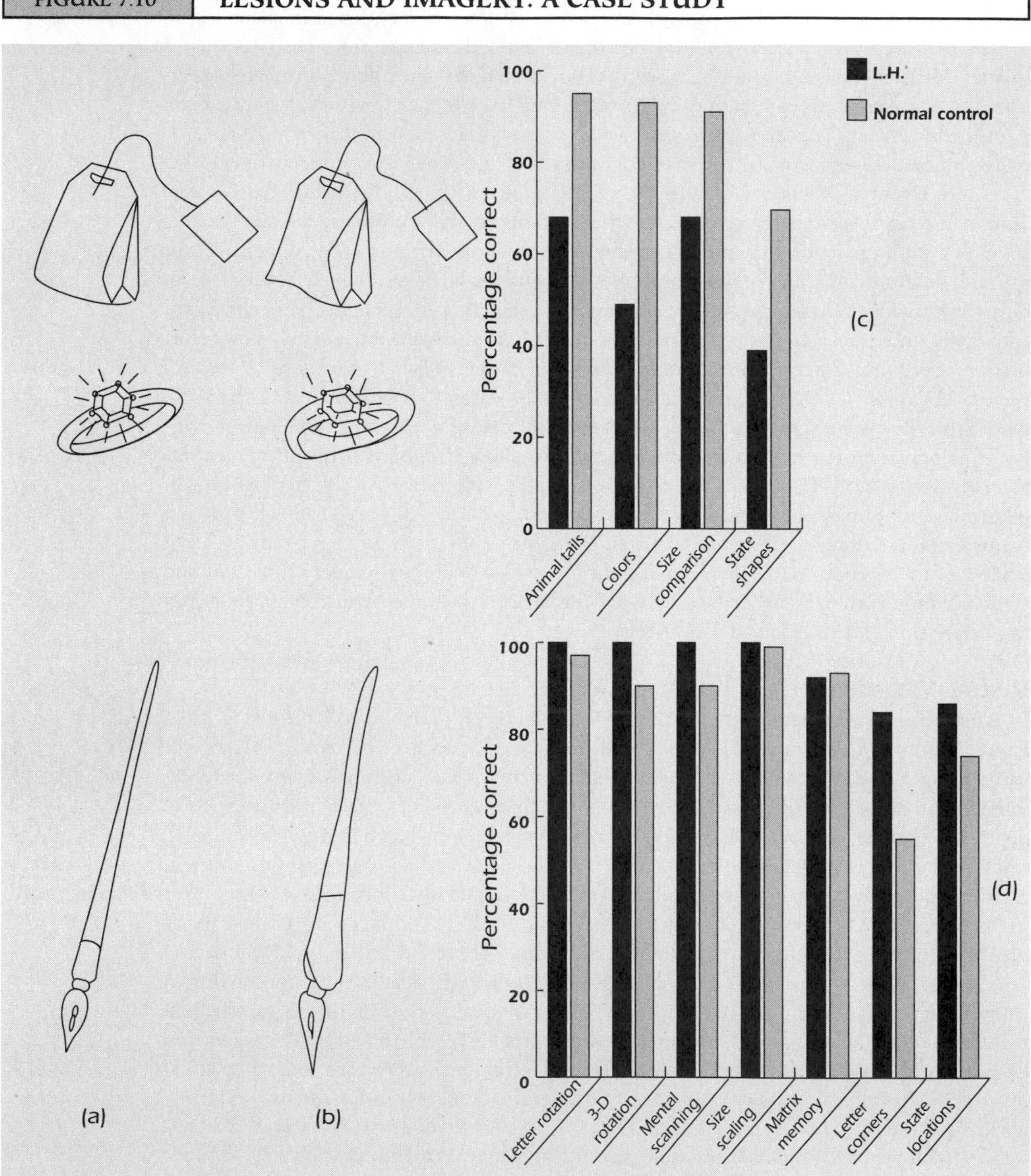

L.H. was able to draw accurately various objects. Panel (a) shows what he was shown, and panel (b) shows what he drew. However, he could not recognize the objects he copied. Despite L.H.'s severe deficits on visual-imagery tasks (panel c, regarding colors, sizes, shapes, etc.), L.H. showed normal ability on spatial-imagery tasks (panel d, regarding rotations, scanning, scaling, etc.).

visual perception, ERPs are generally elevated in the occipital region. If visual imagery were analogous to visual perception, we could expect that during tasks involving visual imagery, there would be analogous elevations of ERPs in the occipital region.

In this study, ERPs were measured during a reading task. In one condition, participants were asked to read a list of concrete words (e.g., *cat*). In the other condition, participants were asked to read a comparable list of concrete words and also to imagine the objects as they read the words. Each word was presented for 200 milliseconds and ERPs were recorded from the different sites in the occipital- and temporal-lobe regions. The researchers found that the ERPs were similar during the first 450 milliseconds, but after this time period, participants in the imaginal condition showed greater neural activity in the occipital lobe than did participants in the nonimaginal (reading only) condition.

According to Farah and her colleagues (Farah, Hammond et al., 1988, p. 459), "Neurophysiological evidence suggests that our cognitive architecture includes both representations of the visual appearance of objects in terms of their form, color, and perspective and of the spatial structure of objects in terms of their three-dimensional layout in space." Those who seek a role for propositional representations might note also that the knowledge of object labels (recognizing the objects by name) and attributes (answering questions about the characteristics of the objects) taps propositional, symbolic knowledge about the pictured objects. In contrast, the ability to manipulate the orientation (rotation) or the size of images taps imaginal, analogous knowledge of the objects. Thus, both forms of representation seem to answer particular kinds of questions for knowledge use.

Practical Applications of Cognitive Psychology

How do you benefit from having a dual code for knowledge representation? Although a dual code may seem redundant and inefficient, having a code for analogue physical and spatial features that is distinct from a code for symbolic propositional knowledge can actually be very efficient. Consider how you learn material in your cognitive psychology course. Most people both go to lecture, where they obtain information from an instructor, and read material from a text book, as you are doing now. If you had only an analogue code for knowledge representation, you would have a much harder time integrating the verbal information you received from your instructor in class with the printed information in your textbook—all of your information would be in the form of auditory/visual images gleaned from listening to and watching your instructor in class and visual images of the words in your textbook. Thus, a symbolic code that is distinct from the analogue features of encoding is helpful for integrating across different modes of knowledge acquisition. Furthermore, analogue codes preserve important aspects of experience without interfering with underlying propositional information. For the purposes of performing well on a test, it is irrelevant whether the information was obtained in class or in the text, but later you may need to verify the source of information in order to prove that your answer is correct, in which case analogical information might help.

SPATIAL COGNITION AND COGNITIVE MAPS

RATS, BEES, AND HUMANS

Most of the studies described thus far have involved the way in which we represent imaginal knowledge based on what we have perceived by looking at and then imagining visual stimuli. Other research suggests that we may form imaginal maps based solely on our physical interactions with and navigations through our physical environment, even when we never have a chance to "see the whole picture," as from an aerial photograph or a map. These internal representations of our physical environment, particularly centering on spatial relationships, are often termed **cognitive maps.** These cognitive maps seem to offer internal representations that simulate particular spatial features of our external environment (Rumelhart & Norman, 1988).

Some of the earliest work on cognitive maps was done by Edward Tolman, during the 1930s, when, for psychologists, to try to understand cognitive processes that could not be observed or measured directly was considered almost unseemly. In one study, Tolman and his colleague C. H. Honzik (1930) were interested in the ability of rats to learn a maze, such as that shown in Figure 7.11. Rats were divided into three groups:

FIGURE 7.11 **RAT MAP**

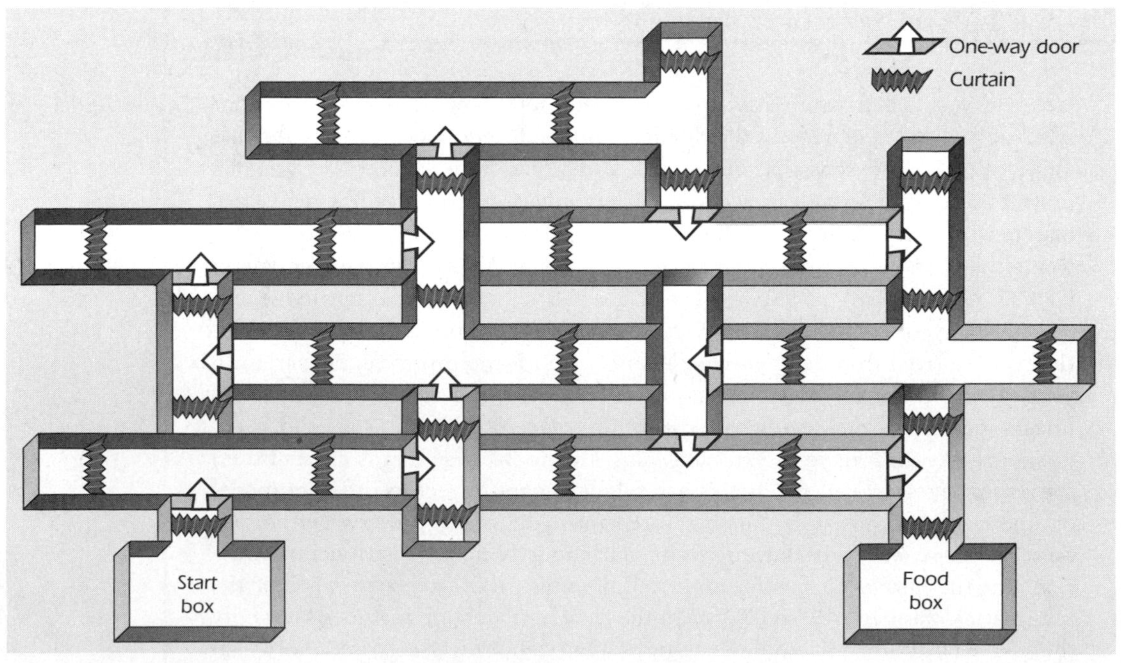

Edward Tolman found that rats seemed to have formed a mental map of a maze during behavioral experiments.

1. In the first group, the rats had to learn the maze, and their reward for getting from the start box to the end box was food. Eventually, these rats learned to run the maze without making any errors (i.e., without making wrong turns or following blind alleys).
2. A second group of rats also was placed in the maze, but these rats received no reinforcement for successfully getting to the end box. Although their performance improved over time, they continued to make more errors than the reinforced group. These results are hardly surprising; we would expect the rewarded group to have more incentive to learn.
3. Finally, though, consider the third group. These rats received no reward for 10 days of learning trials. On the eleventh day, however, food was placed in the end box for the first time. With just one reinforcement, the learning of these rats improved dramatically, so that these rats ran the maze about as well as the rats in the first group in fewer trials.

What, exactly, were the rats in Tolman and Honzik's experiment learning? It seems unlikely that they were learning simply "turn right here, turn left there," and so on. Rather, Tolman argued that the rats were learning a *cognitive map,* an internal representation of the maze. Through this argument, Tolman became one of the earliest cognitive theorists, arguing for the importance of the mental representations that give rise to behavior.

Decades later, even very simple creatures were shown to appear able to form some cognitive maps. They even may be able to translate imaginal representations into a primitive, prewired, analogical and perhaps even symbolic form. For example, Karl von Frisch (1962, 1967), a Nobel Prize–winning German scientist, studied the behavior of bees when they return to their hive after having located a source of nectar. Apparently, bees not only can form imaginal maps for getting to food sources, but also can use a somewhat symbolic form of communicating that information to other bees. Specifically, different patterns of dances can be used to represent different meanings. For example, a round dance indicates a source less than 100 yards from the hive. A figure-eight dance indicates a source at a greater distance. Although the details of the dance (e.g., in regard to wiggle patterns) differ from one species to another, the basic dances appear to be the same across all species of bees. If the lowly bee appears able to imagine the route to nectar, what kinds of cognitive maps may be conceived in the minds of humans?

Humans seem to use three types of knowledge when forming and using cognitive maps: (a) *landmark* knowledge (Thorndyke, 1981), which is information about particular features at a location, and which may be based on both imaginal and propositional representations; (b) *route-road* knowledge (Thorndyke & Hayes-Roth, 1982), which involves specific pathways for moving from one location to another, and which may be based on both procedural knowledge and declarative knowledge; and (c) *survey* knowledge (Thorndyke & Hayes-Roth, 1982), which involves estimated distances between landmarks, much as they might appear on survey maps, and which may be represented imaginally or propositionally (e.g., in numerically specified distances). These observations and others suggest that people use both an analogical code and a propositional code for imaginal representations such as images of maps (McNamara, Hardy, & Hirtle, 1989; J. A. Russell & Ward, 1982).

MENTAL SHORTCUTS

When we use these three kinds of knowledge (landmark, route-road, and survey knowledge), we sometimes seem to take mental shortcuts that influence our estimations of distance. These mental shortcuts are cognitive strategies termed *heuristics,* often described as rules of thumb. For example, in regard to landmark knowledge, the density of the landmarks sometimes appears to affect our mental image of an area. Specifically, as the density of intervening landmarks increases, estimates of distances increase correspondingly. That is, people tend to distort their mental images such that their mental estimates of distances increase in relation to the number of intervening landmarks (Thorndyke, 1981).

In estimations of distances between particular physical locations (e.g., cities), route-road knowledge appears often to be weighted more heavily than survey knowledge, even when participants form a mental image based on looking at a map (McNamara, Ratcliff, & McKoon, 1984). Specifically, when participants were asked to indicate whether particular cities had appeared on a map, they showed more rapid response times between names of cities when the two cities were closer together in route-road distance than when the two cities were physically closer together "as the crow flies," in Euclidean distance (see Figure 7.12).

According to Barbara Tversky (1981), the use of heuristics in manipulating cognitive maps suggests that propositional knowledge affects imaginal knowledge, at least when people are solving problems and answering questions about images. In some situations, conceptual information seems to lead to distortions in mental images; in these situations,

FIGURE 7.12 **ROUTE-ROAD KNOWLEDGE VERSUS SURVEY KNOWLEDGE**

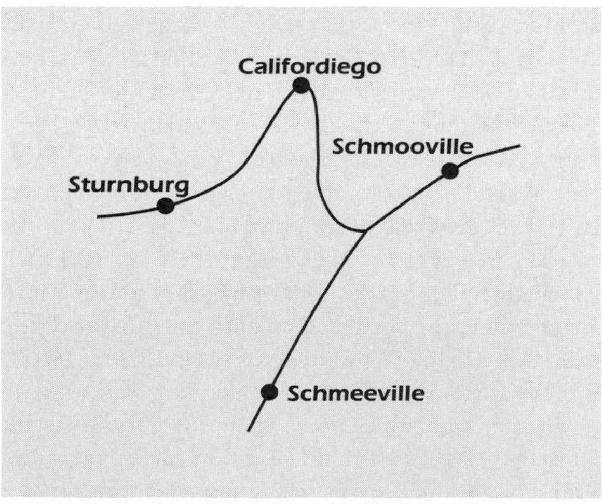

Which city is closer to Sturnburg: Schmeeville or Schmooville? It appears that our use of cognitive maps often emphasizes the use of route-road knowledge, even when it contradicts survey knowledge (McNamara, Ratcliff, & McKoon, 1984).

propositional strategies, rather than imaginal strategies, may better explain people's responses. In general, these distortions seem to reflect a tendency to regularize features of mental maps, so that angles, lines, and shapes are represented as more like pure abstract geometric forms than they really are.

1. *Right-angle bias:* People tend to represent intersections (e.g., street crossings) as forming 90-degree angles more than the angles really do (Moar & Bower, 1983).
2. *Symmetry heuristic:* People tend to represent shapes (e.g., states or countries) as being more symmetrical than they really are (B. Tversky & Schiano, 1989).
3. *Rotation heuristic:* When representing figures and boundaries that are slightly slanted (i.e., oblique), people tend to distort the images as being either more vertical or more horizontal than they really are (B. Tversky, 1981).
4. *Alignment heuristic:* People tend to represent landmarks and boundaries that are slightly out of alignment by distorting their mental images to be better aligned than they really are (i.e., we distort the way we line up a series of figures or objects; B. Tversky, 1981).
5. *Relative-position heuristic:* People tend to represent the relative positions of particular landmarks and boundaries by distorting their mental images in ways that more accurately reflect their conceptual knowledge about the contexts in which the landmarks and boundaries are located, rather than reflecting the actual spatial configurations.

To see how the relative-position heuristic might work, close your eyes, and picture a map of the United States. Is Reno, Nevada, west of San Diego, California, or east of it? In a series of experiments, Albert Stevens and Patty Coupe (1978) asked participants questions such as this one and found that the large majority of people believe San Diego to be west of Reno. That is, for most of us, our mental map looks something like that in panel (a) of Figure 7.13. Actually, however, Reno is west of San Diego, as shown in the correct map in panel (b) of Figure 7.13.

It can be argued that some of these heuristics also affect our *perception* of space and of forms (see chapter 4). For example, the symmetry heuristic seems to be equally strong in memory and in perception (B. Tversky, 1991). Nonetheless, there are differences between perceptual processes and representational (imaginal or propositional) processes. For example, the relative-position heuristic appears to influence mental representation much more strongly than it does perception (B. Tversky, 1991).

Timo Saarinen (1987) found evidence of powerful influences of semantic or propositional knowledge (or beliefs) on imaginal representations of world maps. Specifically, students from 71 sites in 49 countries were asked to draw a sketch map of the world. Most drew maps showing a Eurocentric view of the world (even Asians), many Americans drew Americentric views, and a few others showed views centered on and highlighting their own countries (e.g., see Figure 7.14, showing an Australia-centered view of the world). In addition, most students showed modest distortions that enlarged the more prominent, well-known countries and diminished the sizes of less well-known countries (e.g., in Africa).

FIGURE 7.13 **RELATIVE-POSITION HEURISTIC**

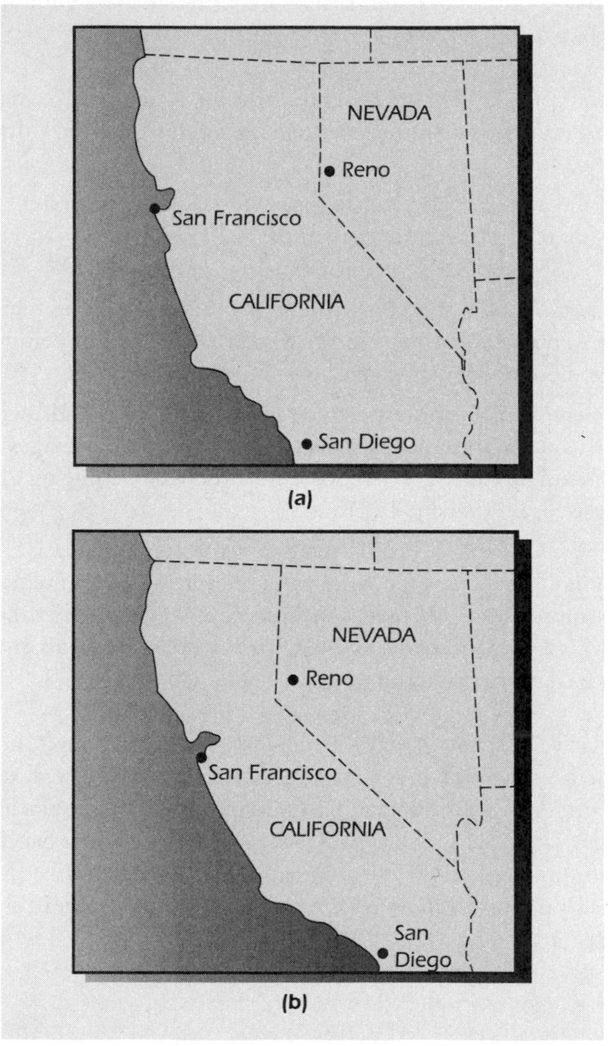

Which of these two maps (a or b) more accurately depicts the relative positions of Reno, Nevada, and San Diego, California?

Finally, work by Stephen Hirtle and his colleagues suggests that propositional knowledge about semantic categories may affect imaginal representations of maps. In one study (Hirtle & Mascolo, 1986), the researchers studied the influence of semantic clustering on estimations of distances. Hirtle's participants were shown a map of many buildings and were then asked to estimate distances between various pairs of buildings. They tended to distort the distances in the direction of guessing shorter distances for more similar landmarks and longer distances for less similar landmarks. Stephen Hirtle and John Jonides (1985) found similar distortions in students' mental maps for the city in which they lived (Ann Arbor, Michigan).

The work on cognitive maps shows once again how the study of mental imagery can help elucidate our understanding of human adaptation to the environment—that is—of human intelligence. In order to survive, we need to find our way around the environment in which we live. We need to get from one place to another, and sometimes, to imagine the route we will need to traverse in order to navigate within our environment. Mental imagery provides a key basis for this adaptation. In some societies (Gladwin, 1970), the ability to navigate with the help of very few cues is a life-or-death issue. If the sailors cannot do so, they eventually get lost, and potentially die of dehydration or starvation. Thus, our imagery abilities are potential keys to our survival, and to what makes us intelligent in our everyday lives.

There are also sex differences in spatial and related skills. Women find it easier to remember where they saw things (spatial-location memory), whereas men find it easier to do mental rotation of spatial images (Silverman & Eals, 1992).

FIGURE 7.14 MENTAL MAPS: A VIEW FROM DOWN UNDER

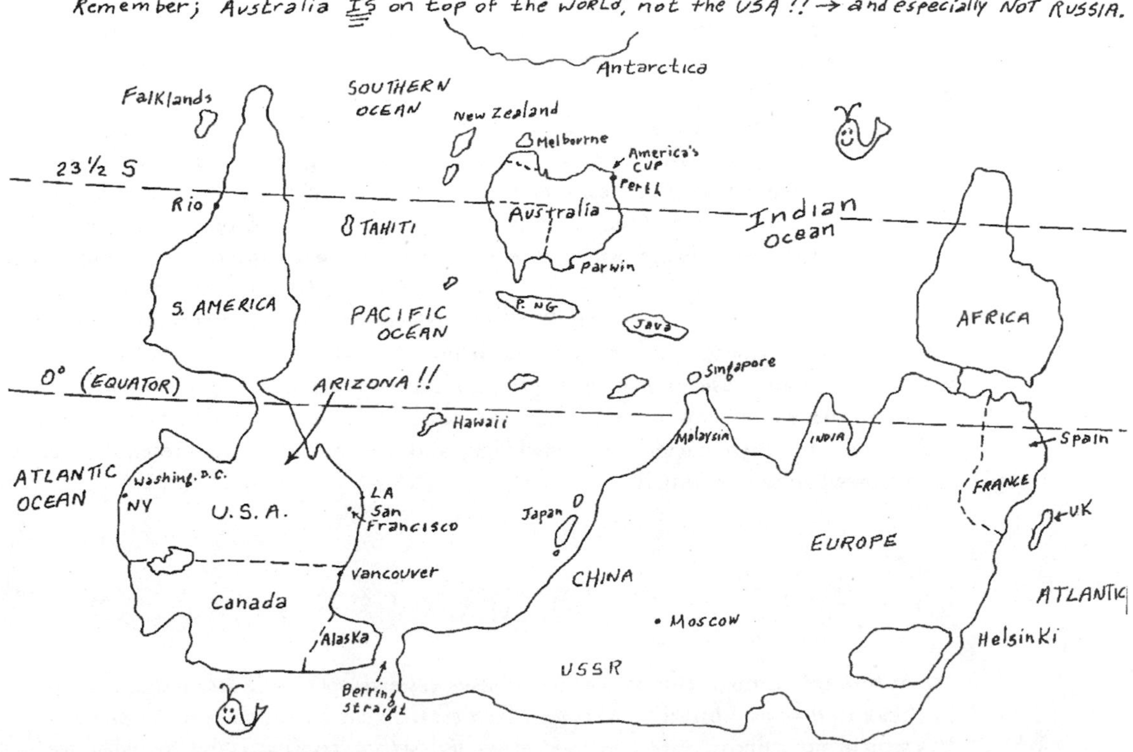

Based on this Australian student's map, can you infer that this student mentally represents the world in the same way you do?

TEXT MAPS

Thus far, we have discussed the construction of cognitive maps based on procedural knowledge (e.g., following a particular route, as a rat in a maze), on propositional information (e.g., using mental heuristics), and on observation of a graphic map. In addition, according to Barbara Tversky and her colleagues (Franklin & B. Tversky, 1990; Taylor & B. Tversky, 1992a, 1992b), we may be able to create cognitive maps from a verbal description, and these cognitive maps may be as accurate as those created from looking at a graphic map. Others have found similar results in studies of text comprehension (Glenberg, Meyer, & Lindem, 1987).

In reflecting on her work, Tversky noted that her research involved having the readers envision themselves in an imaginal setting, as participants, not as observers in the scene. She wondered whether people might create and manipulate images differently when envisioning themselves within the setting, as in her research, than when viewing the setting as an objective observer, which was not the case in her research. Specifically, Tversky wondered whether propositional information might play a stronger role in mental operations when we think about settings in which we are participants, as compared with settings in which we are observers. As Item 4 in Table 7.3 indicates, the findings regarding cognitive maps suggest that the construction of mental imagery may involve both processes analogous to perception and processes relying on propositional representations.

Whether the debate regarding propositions versus imagery can be resolved in the terms in which it traditionally has been presented remains unclear. The various forms of mental representation are sometimes considered to be mutually exclusive. In other words, we think in terms of the question, "Which representation of information is correct?" Often, however, we create false dichotomies, suggesting that alternatives are mutually exclusive, when, in fact, they might be complementary. For example, models postulating mental imagery and those positing propositions can be seen as opposed to each other. However, this opposition does not inhere in the nature of things, but rather, in our construction of a relation. People possibly could use both representations. Indeed, although propositional theorists might like to believe that all representations are fundamentally propositional, quite possibly both images and propositions are way stations toward some more basic and primitive form of representation in the mind, of which we do not yet have any knowledge. A good case can be made in favor of both propositional and imaginal representations of knowledge, and the question we presently need to address is when we use which.

SUMMARY

1. **What are some of the major hypotheses regarding how knowledge is represented in the mind?** *Knowledge representation* comprises the various ways in which our minds create and modify mental structures that stand for what we know about the world outside of our minds. Knowledge representation involves

both *declarative* (knowing that) and *nondeclarative* (knowing how) forms of knowledge. Through *mental imagery,* we create analogue mental structures that stand for things that are not presently being sensed in the sense organs. Imagery may involve any of the senses, but the form of imagery most commonly reported by laypersons and most commonly studied by cognitive psychologists is visual imagery. Some studies (e.g., studies of blind participants and some studies of the brain) suggest that visual imagery itself may comprise two discrete systems of mental representation: one system involving nonspatial visual attributes (e.g., color and shape), and another involving spatial attributes (e.g., location, orientation, and size or distance scaling).

According to Paivio's *dual-code hypothesis,* two discrete mental codes for representing knowledge exist: one code for images and another for words and other symbols. Images are represented in a form analogous to the form we perceive through our senses. In contrast, words and concepts are encoded in a symbolic form, which is not analogical.

An alternative view of image representation, proposed by Anderson and Bower and earnestly endorsed by Pylyshyn, is the *propositional hypothesis,* which suggests that both images and words are represented in a propositional form. The proposition retains the underlying meaning of either images or words, without any of the perceptual features of either. For example, the acoustic features of the sounds of the words are not stored, nor are the visual features of the colors or shapes of the images. Furthermore, propositional codes, more than imaginal codes, seem to influence mental representation when participants are shown ambiguous or abstract figures. Apparently, unless the context facilitates performance, the use of visual images does not always readily lead to successful performance on some tasks requiring mental manipulations of either abstract figures or ambiguous figures.

2. **What are some of the characteristics of mental imagery?** Based on a modification of the dual-code view, Shepard and others have espoused a *functional-equivalence hypothesis,* which asserts that images are represented in a form functionally equivalent to percepts, even if images are not truly identical to percepts. Studies of mental rotations, image scaling, and image scanning suggest that imaginal task performance is functionally equivalent to perceptual task performance. Even performance on some tasks involving comparisons of auditory images seems to be functionally equivalent to performance on tasks involving comparisons of auditory percepts. Propositional codes seem less likely to influence mental representation than imaginal ones when participants are given an opportunity to create their own mental images, such as in tasks involving image sizing or involving mental combinations of imaginal letters. Some researchers have suggested that experimenter expectancies may have influenced cognitive studies of imagery, but others have refuted these suggestions. In any case, psychobiological studies are not subject to such influences, and seem to support the functional-equivalence hypothesis by finding overlapping brain areas involved in visual perception and mental rotation.

3. **How does knowledge representation benefit from both analogical images and symbolic propositions?** Kosslyn has synthesized these various hypotheses to suggest that images may involve both analogous and propositional forms of knowledge representation, and that both forms influence our mental representation and manipulation of images. Thus, some of what we know about images is represented in a form that is analogous to perception, and other things we know about images are represented in a propositional form. Johnson-Laird has proposed an alternative synthesis, suggesting that knowledge may be represented as verbally expressible propositions, as somewhat abstracted analogical mental models, or as highly concrete and analogical mental images.

   Studies of split-brain patients and patients with lesions indicate some tendency toward hemispheric specialization, in which visuospatial information may be processed primarily in the right hemisphere, and linguistic (symbolic) information may be processed primarily in the left hemisphere of right-handed individuals. A case study suggests that spatial imagery may also be processed in a different region of the brain than the regions in which other aspects of visual imagery are processed. Studies of normal participants show that visual-perception tasks seem to involve regions of the brain similar to the regions involved in visual-imagery tasks.

4. **How may conceptual knowledge and expectancies influence the way we use images?** People tend to distort their own mental maps in ways that regularize many features of the maps, such as tending to imagine right angles, symmetrical forms, either vertical or horizontal boundaries (not oblique ones), and well-aligned figures and objects. People also tend to employ distortions of their mental maps in ways that support their propositional knowledge about various landmarks, tending to cluster similar landmarks, to segregate dissimilar ones, and to modify relative positions to agree with conceptual knowledge about the landmarks. In addition, people tend to distort their mental maps such that the people increase their estimates regarding the distances between endpoints as the density of intervening landmarks increases.

   Some of the heuristics that affect cognitive maps support the notion that propositional information influences imaginal representations. The influence of propositional information may be particularly potent when participants are not shown a graphic map but are asked instead to read a narrative passage and to envision themselves as participants in a setting described in the narrative.

Thinking About Thinking: Factual, Analytical, Creative, and Practical Questions

1. Describe some of the characteristics of pictures versus of words, as external forms of knowledge representation.

2. What factors might lead a person's mental model to be inaccurate with respect to how radio transmissions lead people to be able to hear music on a radio?
3. In what ways is mental imagery analogous (or functionally equivalent) to perception?
4. In what ways do propositional forms of knowledge representation influence performance on tasks involving mental imagery?
5. What are some strengths and weaknesses of ERP studies?
6. Some people report never experiencing mental imagery, yet they are able to solve mental-rotation problems. How might they solve such problems?
7. What are some practical applications of having two codes for knowledge representation? Give an example applied to your own experiences, such as applications to studying for examinations.
8. Based on the heuristics described in this chapter, what are some of the distortions that may be influencing your cognitive maps for places with which you are familiar (e.g., a college campus or your home town)?

Key Terms

analogue 218
cognitive maps 242
declarative knowledge 212
dual-code hypothesis 218
functional-equivalence hypothesis 225
imagery 216
knowledge representation 212
procedural knowledge 212
propositional hypothesis 219
symbolic 218

Annotated Suggested Readings

Farah, M. J., Hammond, K. M., Levine, D. N., & Calvanio, R. (1988). Visual and spatial mental imagery: Dissociable systems of representation. *Cognitive Psychology, 20,* 439–462. A provocative article arguing that imagery is of two different kinds—visual and spatial—which may be processed in different hemispheres of the brain.

Intons-Peterson, M. J. (1992). Components of auditory imagery. In D. Reisberg (Ed.), *Auditory imagery* (pp. 45–71). Hillsdale, NJ: Erlbaum. An excellent example of research showing that people have not only visual imagery, but also auditory imagery.

Kosslyn, S. M. (1994). Computational theory of imagery. In M. W. Eysenck (Ed.), *The Blackwell dictionary of cognitive psychology* (pp. 177–181). Cambridge, MA: Blackwell.

A brief but highly readable account of attempts to design computer models of human processing of images.

Kosslyn, S. M., & Koenig, O. (1992). *Wet mind: The new cognitive neuroscience.* New York: Free Press. An excellent and readable account of how cognitive and biological psychology are coming together in the study of cognitive neuroscience.

Knowledge Representation and Organization

CHAPTER OUTLINE

Exploring Cognitive Psychology

Organization of Declarative Knowledge
- Concepts and Categories
- Semantic Network Models
- Schematic Representations

Representations of Procedural Knowledge
- The Production and the Production System

Integrative Models for Representing Declarative and Nondeclarative Knowledge
- Combining Representations: ACT and ACT*
- Models Based on the Human Brain
- Parallel Processing: The Connectionist Model
- How Domain General or Domain Specific Is Cognition?

Summary

Thinking About Thinking: Factual, Analytical, Creative, and Practical Questions

Key Terms

Annotated Suggested Readings

EXPLORING COGNITIVE PSYCHOLOGY

1. **How are representations of words and symbols organized in the mind?**
2. **How do we represent other forms of knowledge in the mind?**
3. **How does declarative knowledge interact with procedural knowledge?**

Once we have represented knowledge, how do we organize it so that we can retrieve and then use it? The preceding chapter described how knowledge may be represented in the form of propositions and images. In this chapter, we continue the discussion of knowledge representation, expanding this discussion to include various means of organizing declarative knowledge that can be expressed in words and other symbols (i.e., "knowing that"). For example, your knowledge of facts about cognitive psychology, about world history, about your own personal history, and about mathematics relies on your mental organization of declarative knowledge. In addition, this chapter describes a few of the various models for representing procedural knowledge, which is knowledge about how to follow various procedural steps for performing actions (i.e., "knowing how"). For example, your knowledge of how to ride a bicycle, how to write your signature, how to drive a car to a familiar location, and how to catch a ball depends on your mental representation of procedural knowledge. Some theorists have even suggested integrative models for representing both declarative and procedural knowledge.

To get an idea of how declarative and procedural knowledge may interact, get out a piece of scrap paper and a pen or pencil, and try the following demonstration.

INVESTIGATING COGNITIVE PSYCHOLOGY

As quickly and as legibly as possible, write your normal signature, from the first letter of your first name to the last letter of your last name. Don't stop to think about which letters come next; just write as quickly as possible.

Turn the paper over, and as quickly and as legibly as possible, write your signature backward, starting with the last letter of your last name, and working toward the first letter of your first name.

Now, compare the two signatures. Which signature was more easily and accurately created?

For both signatures, you had available extensive declarative knowledge of which letters preceded or followed one another, but for the first task, you also could call on procedural knowledge, based on years of knowing how to sign your name.

In addition to seeking to understand the *what* (the form or structure) of knowledge representation, cognitive psychologists also try to grasp the *how* (the processes) of knowledge representation and manipulation. That is, what are some of the general processes by which we select and control the disorganized array of raw data available to us through our sense organs? How do we relate that sensory information to the information we have available from internal sources of information (i.e., our memories and our thought processes)? How do we organize and reorganize our mental representations during various cognitive processes? Through what mental processes do we operate on the knowledge we have in our minds? To what extent are these processes *domain-general*—common to multiple kinds of information, such as verbal and quantitative information—and to what extent are they *domain-specific*—used only for particular kinds of information, such as verbal or quantitative information?

Knowledge representation and processing have been investigated by researchers from several different disciplines. Among these researchers are cognitive psychologists, computer scientists studying *artificial intelligence* (*AI;* attempts to program machines to perform intelligently), and neuropsychologists. These diverse approaches to investigating knowledge representation promote exploration of a wide range of phenomena, encourage multiple perspectives of similar phenomena, and offer the strength of **converging operations** (the use of multiple approaches and techniques to address a problem) when trying to answer some of the riddles of human knowledge representation.

Other than to satisfy their own idle curiosity, why do so many different researchers want to understand how knowledge is represented? They want to know because the way in which knowledge is represented profoundly influences how easily, accurately, and efficiently knowledge can be manipulated for performing any number of cognitive tasks. To illustrate the influence of knowledge representation through a very crude analogy, try the following multiplication task, using a representation in either roman or arabic numerals:

CMLIX	959
× LVIII	× 58

Organization of Declarative Knowledge

The fundamental unit of symbolic knowledge is the **concept**—an idea about something. Often, a single concept may be captured in a single word, such as *apple.* Each concept relates to other concepts, such as *redness, roundness,* or *fruit.* One way to organize concepts can be captured by the notion of a **category**—a concept itself, which functions to organize other concepts based on common features or similiarity to a prototype. For example, the word *apple* can act both as a category, as in a collection of different kinds of apples, and as a concept within the category *fruit.* We will discuss below a number of different ways to organize concepts into categories, including the use of defining features, prototypes and exemplars, and hierarchically organized semantic networks. Later in the chapter, we will discuss how concepts may also be organized into **schemas** (from Latin; singular, *schema;* plural, *schemata*), which are mental frameworks for representing knowledge that encompass an array of interrelated concepts in a meaningful organization (e.g., Bartlett, 1932).

CONCEPTS AND CATEGORIES

FEATURE-BASED CATEGORIES: A DEFINING VIEW

The classic view of conceptual categories involves disassembling a concept into a set of featural components, which are singly necessary and jointly sufficient to define the category (J. J. Katz, 1972; J. J. Katz & Fodor, 1963). In other words, each feature is an essential element of the category; together, the properties uniquely define the category. These components may be viewed as **defining features** because they constitute the definition of a category, according to the feature-based, componential point of view.

Consider, for example, the term *bachelor.* In addition to being human, a bachelor can be viewed as comprising three features: male, unmarried, and adult. Because the features are each singly necessary, even the absence of one feature makes the category inapplicable. Thus, an unmarried male who is not an adult would not be a bachelor—we would not refer to a 15-year-old unmarried boy as a bachelor because he is not an adult. Nor would we refer to just any male adult as a bachelor—if he is married, he is out of the running. An unmarried female adult is not a bachelor, either. Moreover, because the three features are jointly sufficient, if a person has all three features, then he is automatically a bachelor. According to this view, you cannot be male, unmarried, adult, and at the same time not be a bachelor. The feature-based view applies to more than bachelorhood, of course. For example, *wife* is made up of the features *married, female,* and *adult,* and *husband* comprises the features *married, male,* and *adult.*

The feature-based view is especially common among linguists, those who study language (H. H. Clark & Clark, 1977). This view is attractive because it makes categories of meaning appear so orderly. Unfortunately, it does not work as well as it appears to at first glance. Some categories do not readily lend themselves to featural analysis. *Game* is one such category. Philosopher Ludwig Wittgenstein (1953) pointed out that finding anything at all that is a common feature of all games is actually difficult to do. Some are fun; some are not. Some involve multiple players; others, such as solitaire, do not. Some are competitive; others, such as children's circle games (e.g., ring-around-the-rosy), are not. The more you consider the concept of a game, the more you begin to wonder whether there is anything at all that holds the category together. Nonetheless, although it is not clear that there are any defining features of a game at all, we all know what we mean, or think we do, by the word *game.*

On the other hand, although some things may seem to have clear defining features, a violation of those defining features does not seem to change the category we use to define them. Consider a zebra (see Keil, 1989). We all know that a zebra is a black-and-white striped horselike animal. However, suppose that someone were to paint a zebra all black. A zebra painted black is missing the critical attribute of stripes, but we still would call it a "zebra." We run into the same problem with birds. We might think of the ability to fly as critical to being a bird, but certainly we would agree that a robin whose wings have been clipped is still a robin and still a bird, as is an ostrich, which does not fly.

The examples of the robin and the ostrich point out another problem with the feature-based theory. Both a robin and an ostrich share the same defining features of birds and are, therefore, birds. However, loosely speaking, a robin seems somehow to be a better example of a bird than is an ostrich. Indeed, if people are asked to rate the typicality of robin versus ostrich as a bird, the former will virtually always get a higher rating than the latter (Malt &

TABLE 8.1 TYPICALITY RATINGS FOR BIRDS

Barbara Malt and Edward Smith (1984) found enormous differences in the typicality ratings for various instances of birds (or birdlike animals). (After Malt & Smith, 1984)

BIRD	RATING*	BIRD	RATING*
Robin	6.89	Vulture	4.84
Bluebird	6.42	Sandpiper	4.47
Seagull	6.26	Chicken	3.95
Swallow	6.16	Flamingo	3.37
Falcon	5.74	Albatross	3.32
Mockingbird	5.47	Penguin	2.63
Starling	5.16	Bat	1.53
Owl	5.00		

*Ratings were made on a 7-point scale, with 7 corresponding to the highest typicality.

Smith, 1984; Mervis, Catlin, & Rosch, 1976; Rosch, 1975). Moreover, children learn typical instances of a category earlier than they learn atypical ones (Rosch, 1978). Table 8.1 shows some ratings of typicality from a study by Barbara Malt and Edward Smith (1984) for various instances of birds. Clearly, there are enormous differences. On the 7-point scale used by Malt and Smith for ratings of the typicality of birds, *bat* received a rating of 1.53, despite the fact that a bat, strictly speaking, is not even a bird at all.

In sum, the feature-based theory has some attractive features, but it does not seem to give a complete account of categories. Some specific examples of a category such as *bird* seem to be better examples than others, despite the fact that they all have the same defining features. However, the various examples may be differentially typical of the category of birds, a fact taken into account by prototype theory. Thus, we need a theory of knowledge representation that better characterizes how people truly represent knowledge.

PROTOTYPE THEORY: A CHARACTERISTIC VIEW

The **prototype theory** suggests that categories are formed on the basis of **characteristic features,** which describe (characterize or typify) the typical (actually, prototypical) model of the category. For example, the prototype of a game might include that it usually is enjoyable, has two or more players, and presents some degree of challenge. Similarly, a bird usually has wings and flies. This theory introduces a new wrinkle into our attempt to understand knowledge organization by basing categorization on a prototype. A *prototype* is usually the original item on which subsequent models are based, but in this theory, the prototype may be whichever model best represents the class on which the category is based. This theory can handle the facts that (a) games seem to have no defining features at all, and (b) a robin seems to be a better example of a bird than is an ostrich.

In order to understand how these problems are handled, you need to understand the concept of a characteristic feature. Whereas a defining feature is possessed by every instance of a category, a characteristic feature need not be. Instead, many or most instances possess each characteristic feature. Thus, the ability to fly is typical of birds, but it is not a defining feature of a bird. According to prototype theory, because an ostrich cannot fly (and lacks some other characteristic features of birds), it seems less birdlike than a robin, which can fly. Similarly, a typical game may be enjoyable, but it need not be so. Indeed, when people are asked to list the features of a category, such as *fruit* or *furniture,* the majority of features that the people list are characteristic rather than defining (Rosch & Mervis, 1975). By listing the properties typical of a category such as *fruit,* and then assessing how many of those properties a given instance has, one can actually compute a score of *family resemblance* that indicates how typical an instance is, overall, of the more general category (Rosch & Mervis, 1975).

Psychologists, in reflecting on how people seem to think about concepts and categories, came to differentiate two kinds of categories: classical concepts and fuzzy concepts. *Classical concepts* are categories that can be readily defined through defining features, such as *bachelor. Fuzzy concepts* are categories that cannot be so easily defined, largely because the borders of what constitutes them are, well, fuzzy. Classical concepts tend to be inventions that experts have devised for arbitrarily labeling a class that has associated defining features, whereas fuzzy concepts tend to evolve naturally (E. E. Smith, 1988). Thus, the concept of a bachelor is an arbitrary concept we invented. In contrast, although taxonomists may suggest that we use the word *fruit* to describe any part of a plant that has seeds, pulp, and skin, nevertheless, our natural, fuzzy concept of fruit usually does not easily extend to tomatoes, pumpkins, and cucumbers. Check the dictionary definitions for *tomatoes, pumpkins,* and *cucumbers* if you doubt their fruitiness. All of them really are subordinates (lower levels) of their superordinate (higher level) category, *fruit!*

Whereas classical concepts and categories—and the words that label them—may be built on defining features, fuzzy concepts and categories are built up around prototypes. According to the prototype view, an object will be classified as an instance of a category if it is sufficiently similar to the prototype. Exactly what is meant by similarity to a prototype can be a complex issue, and there are actually different theories of how this similarity should be measured (E. E. Smith & Medin, 1981). For our purposes, we view similarity in terms of the number of features shared between an object and the prototype. Moreover, many psychologists suggest that some features be weighted more heavily as being more central to the prototype than are other features (e.g., Komatsu, 1992).

Actually, some psychologists (e.g., Ross & Spalding, 1994) suggest that instead of using a single prototype for categorizing a concept, we use multiple **exemplars**—several alternative typical representatives of a category. For example, in considering birds, we might think of not only the prototypical songbird, which is small, flies, builds nests, sings, and so on, but also of exemplars for birds of prey, for large flightless birds, for medium-sized water fowl, and so on. Robert Nosofsky and colleagues use this approach in explaining how categories are both formed and used in speeded classification situations (Nosofsky & Palmeri, 1997; Nosofsky, Palmeri, & McKinley, 1994). In particular, categories are set up by creating a rule and then storing exceptions as exemplars. Later during recognition, exemplars race in memory, with speed of items determined by similarity to the target item, and likely candidates then enter a selection process. Thus, not only is the category coherent and stable, but storing exceptions allows categories to remain flexible. Indeed, Ross and Spalding suggest that if we have multiple exemplars, when we see an instance of a bird, we can more flexibly match this instance to an appropriate exemplar than to a single prototype.

A Synthesis: Combining Feature-Based and Prototype Theories

Interestingly, even classical categories seem to have prototypes. Consider two of the classical concepts studied by Sharon Armstrong, Lila Gleitman, and Henry Gleitman (1983): *odd number* and *plane geometry figure.* Both of these concepts are easily defined. For example, an *odd number* is any integer not evenly divisible by 2. Armstrong and her colleagues showed that people found different instances of these categories to be more or less prototypical of their respective categories. For example, 7 and 13 are typical examples of odd numbers that are viewed as quite close to the prototype for an odd number. In contrast, 15 and 21 are not seen as so prototypically odd. In other words, people view 7 and 13 as better exemplars of odd numbers than 15 and 21, even though all four numbers are actually odd. Similarly, a triangle is viewed as typical of plane geometry figures, whereas an ellipse is not.

The fact that even classical categories have instances varying in typicality led Armstrong, Gleitman, and Gleitman to conclude that a full theory of categorization would need to combine both defining and characteristic features (see also E. E. Smith, Shoben, & Rips, 1974). These authors have suggested that we might view each category as having both a prototype and a core. A **core** refers to the defining features something must have to be considered an example of a category. In contrast, the prototype refers to the characteristic features that tend to be typical of an example but that are not necessary for being considered an example.

Consider the concept of a *robber,* for example. The core requires that someone labeled as a robber be a person who takes from others without permission. The prototype, however, tends to identify particular people as more likely to be robbers than are others. White-collar criminals are hard to catch, in part because they do not look like our prototypes of robbers, no matter how much they may steal from other people—directly or indirectly. In contrast, unkempt denizens of our inner cities sometimes are arrested for crimes they did not commit, in part because they more closely match the police prototype of a robber, regardless of whether they steal.

Frank Keil and Nancy Batterman (1984) tested the notion that we come to understand the importance of defining features only as we grow older. Younger children, they hypothesized, view categories largely in terms of characteristic features. Keil and Batterman presented children in the age range from 5 to 10 years with descriptions, among which were "a smelly, mean old man with a gun in his pocket who came to your house and took your TV set because your parents didn't want it anymore and told him he could have it," and "a very friendly and cheerful woman who gave you a hug, but then disconnected your toilet bowl and took it away without permission and no intention to return it." Younger children often characterized the first description as a better depiction of a robber than the second description. It was not until close to age 10 years that children began to shift toward characterizing the second individual as more robber-like. In other words, the younger children viewed someone as a robber, even if the person did not rob anything, so long as the person had the characteristic features of a robber. However, remember that the transition is never fully complete: We might suspect that the first individual would be at least as likely to be arrested as the second. Thus, the issue of categorization itself remains somewhat fuzzy, but appears to include some aspects of defining features and some aspects of prototypicality.

SEMANTIC NETWORK MODELS

In 1969, Allan Collins and Ross Quillian published their findings from a landmark study suggesting that knowledge is represented in terms of a hierarchical *semantic* (related to meaning as expressed in language—i.e., in linguistic symbols) **network,** which is a web of interconnected elements. The elements, termed **nodes,** represent concepts. The connections between nodes are *labeled relationships,* which might involve category membership (e.g., an "is a" relationship connecting "pig" to "mammal"), attributes (e.g., connecting "furry" to "mammal"), or some other semantic relationship. Thus, a network provides a means for organizing concepts. The exact form of a semantic network differs from one theory to another, but most networks look something like the highly simplified network shown in Figure 8.1. The labeled relationships form links that enable the individual to connect the various nodes in a meaningful way.

In the Collins and Quillian study, the participants were given statements relating concepts, such as "A robin is a bird" and "A robin is an animal," and were asked to verify the truth of the statements. Collins and Quillian exclusively used *class-inclusion statements,* in which the *subject* (word, words, or phrases about which the sentence tells something) was a single word, and the *predicate* (the part of the sentence that tells something about the subject of the sentence) took the form "is a [category noun]." Some of the statements were true; others were not. A critical finding of the Collins and Quillian study was that as the conceptual category of the predicate became more hierarchically remote from the category of the subject of the statement, people generally took longer to verify a true statement. Thus, we could expect people to take longer to verify "A robin is an animal" than "A robin is a bird," because *bird* is an immediate superordinate category for *robin,* whereas *animal* is a more remote superordinate category. Collins and Quillian concluded that a hierarchical network representation, such as the one shown in Figure 8.2, adequately accounted for the response times in their study. According to this model, organized knowledge representation takes the form of a hierarchical tree diagram.

A hierarchical model seemed ideal because, within a hierarchy, we can efficiently store information that applies to all members of a category at the highest possible level in the hierarchy without having to repeat that information at all of the lower levels in the hierarchy.

FIGURE 8.1 **A SIMPLE NETWORK MODEL OF KNOWLEDGE REPRESENTATION**

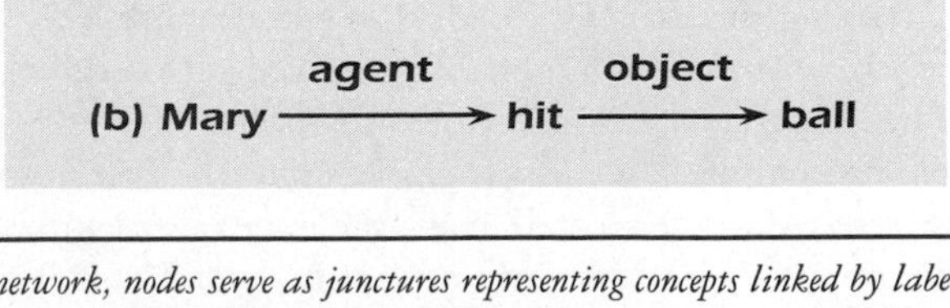

In a simple semantic network, nodes serve as junctures representing concepts linked by labeled relationships: (a) a basic network structure showing that relationship R *links the nodes* a *and* b; *(b) a simple network diagram of the sentence "Mary hit the ball."*

Therefore, a hierarchical model contains a high degree of *cognitive economy*—that is, the system allows for a maximum of efficient capacity use with a minimum of redundancy. Thus, if you know that dogs and cats are mammals, you store everything you know about mammals (have fur, give birth to live young whom they nurse, etc.) at the mammals level, without having to repeat that information again at the hierarchically lower level for dogs and cats. Whatever was known about items at higher levels in a hierarchy was inferred to apply to all items at lower levels in the hierarchy. This concept of *inheritance,* whereby lower-level items inherit the properties of higher level items, is the key to the economy of hierarchical models. Computer models of the network clearly demonstrated the value of cognitive economy.

The Collins and Quillian study instigated a whole line of research into the structure of semantic networks. However, many of the psychologists who studied the Collins and Quillian data disagreed with Collins and Quillian's interpretations. For one thing, numerous anomalies in the data could not be explained by the Collins and Quillian model. For example, participants take longer to verify, "A lion is a mammal," than to verify "A lion is an animal," even though in a strictly hierarchical view, verification should be faster for the mammal statement than for the animal one, because the category *mammal* is hierarchically closer to the category *lion* than is the category *animal.*

FIGURE 8.2 **SEMANTIC NETWORK MODEL**

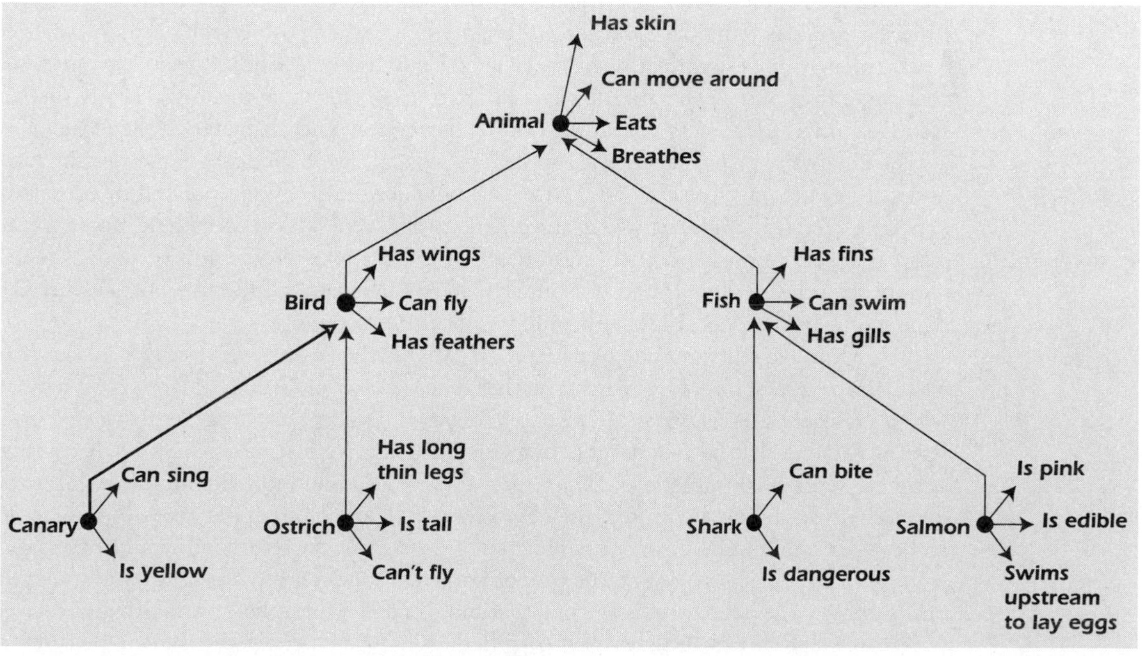

Allan Collins and Ross Quillian developed a model for representing semantic information in terms of a hierarchical network that emphasized cognitive economy. Although the Collins and Quillian model initially seemed promising, it was later found to be flawed. Their network model has led to subsequent models, however, which better explain the available data.

Edward Smith, Edward Shoben, and Lance Rips (1974) proposed an alternative theory according to which knowledge is organized based on a comparison of semantic features, rather than a strict hierarchy of concepts. This theory differs from the feature-based theory of categorization in that features of different concepts are compared directly, rather than serving as the basis for forming a category.

Consider, for example, members of the set of mammal names. In 1969, Nancy Henley showed that mammal names can be represented in terms of a psychological space organized by three features: size, ferocity, and humanness. A lion, for example, would be high in all three, whereas an elephant would be particularly high in size but not so high in ferocity. A rat would be small in size but relatively high in ferocity. Figure 8.3 shows how information might be organized within a non-hierarchical feature-based theory such as that proposed by Smith and his colleagues. Note that this representation, too, leaves a number of questions unanswered. For example, how does the word *mammal* itself fit in? It does not seem to fit into the space of mammal names. Where would other kinds of objects fit?

Neither of the preceding two theories of representation completely specifies how all information might be organized in a semantic network. Perhaps some kind of combination of representations is used (e.g., Collins & Loftus, 1975). Other network models tend to emphasize mental relationships that we think about more frequently (e.g., the link between birds and robins or sparrows, or the link between birds and flying), rather than just any hierarchical relationships (e.g., the link between birds and turkeys or penguins, or the link between birds and standing on two legs).

Eleanor Rosch (1978) and others have noticed that concepts appear to have a **basic level** (sometimes termed a *natural level)* of specificity within a hierarchy that is preferred to other levels. For example, if I show you a red, roundish edible object that has a stem and that came from a tree, you might characterize it as a fruit, an apple, a Delicious apple, a Red Delicious apple, and so on. Most people, however, would characterize the object as an apple. The basic, preferred level is "apple." In general, the basic level is neither the most abstract nor the most specific. Of course, this basic level can be manipulated by context or expertise (Tanaka & Taylor, 1991). In other words, if the object were held up at a fruit stand that sold only apples, you might describe it as a Red Delicious apple, to distinguish it from the other apples around it. Similarly, an apple farmer talking to a horticulture student might be more specific than would be a hurried shopper.

How can we tell what the basic level is? Why is the basic level the *apple,* rather than *Red Delicious apple* or *fruit,* or why *cow,* rather than *mammal* or *Guernsey?* Rosch and her colleagues (Rosch, Mervis, Gray, Johnson, & Boyes-Braem, 1976) suggested that the basic level is the one that has the largest number of distinctive features, which set it off from other concepts at the same level. Thus, most of us would find more distinguishing features between an apple and a cow, say, than between a Red Delicious apple and a Pippin apple, or between a Guernsey cow and a Holstein cow. Again, not everyone would necessarily have the same basic level, as in the case of farmers. However, most people would, and for our purposes, the basic level is the one that most people find to be maximally distinctive.

Rosch and her colleagues (1976) found that when people are shown pictures of objects, the people identify objects at a basic level more quickly than they identify objects at higher or lower levels. Objects appear to be recognized first in terms of their basic level, and only afterward are they classified in terms of higher- or lower-level categories. Thus, the picture of the roundish red edible object from a tree would probably first be identified as an apple, and only then, if necessary, as a fruit or a Red Delicious apple.

FIGURE 8.3 **FEATURES MODEL OF SEMANTIC MEMORY**

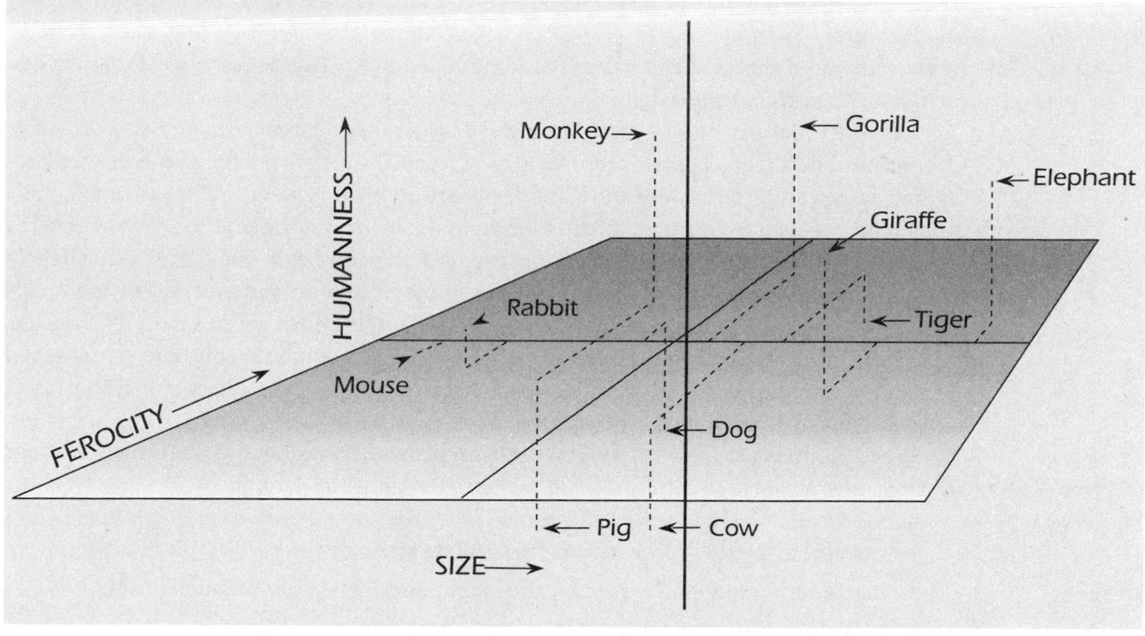

One alternative to hierarchical network models of semantic memory involves representations highlighting the comparison of semantic features. The features model, too, fails to explain all the data regarding semantic memory.

Lloyd Komatsu (1992) and others suggest that we may further broaden our understanding of concepts if we consider not only the hierarchical and basic levels of a concept but also some other relational information the concept contains. Specifically, we may better understand the ways in which we derive meanings from concepts by considering their relations with other concepts, as well as the relations among attributes contained within a concept. Keil perhaps best describes this view, saying, "No individual concept can be understood without some understanding of how it relates to other concepts" (Keil, 1989, p. 1).

Schematic Representations

Schemas

One main approach to understanding how concepts are related in the mind is through schemas, which are very similar to semantic networks except that schemas are often more task-oriented. Recall that a schema is a mental framework for organizing knowledge, creating a meaningful structure of related concepts. Of course, both concepts and schemas may be viewed at many levels of analysis, depending on the mind of the individual, as well as the context. For example, most of us probably view *cow* as a fundamental concept within, perhaps, a more elaborate schema for farm animals. However, for a cattle breeder or a dairy farmer, *cow* may not be at all fundamental because both the breeder and the farmer may recognize many different kinds of cows, each one having various distinctive characteristics. Similarly, most people do not have an elaborate schema for *cognitive psychology.* However, for most cognitive psychologists, the schema for *cognitive psychology* is so richly elaborated that it encompasses many subschemas, such as subschemas for attention, memory, perception, and so on.

David Rumelhart and Andrew Ortony (1977) wrote an extensive analysis of schemas. Other researchers (e.g., Thorndyke, 1984) have reached similar conclusions. Schemas have several characteristics that ensure wide flexibility in their use: (a) Schemas can include other schemas—for example, a schema for animals includes a schema for cows, a schema for apes, and so on. (b) Schemas encompass typical, general facts, which can vary slightly from one specific instance to another—for example, although the schema for mammals includes a general fact that mammals typically have fur, it allows for humans, who are less hairy than most other mammals, as well as for porcupines, which seem more prickly than furry. (c) Schemas can vary in their degree of abstraction—for example, a schema for *justice* is much more abstract than a schema for *apple* or even a schema for *fruit.*

Lloyd Komatsu (1992) has suggested that schemas also can include information about relationships. Some of this information includes relationships among

- Concepts (e.g., the link between trucks and cars),
- Attributes within concepts (e.g., the height and the weight of an elephant),
- Attributes in related concepts (e.g., the redness of a cherry and the redness of an apple),
- Concepts and particular contexts (e.g., fish and the ocean),
- Specific concepts and general background knowledge (e.g., concepts about particular U.S. presidents and general knowledge about the U.S. government and about U.S. history).

Relationships within schemas that particularly interest cognitive psychologists are causal (if–then) relationships. For example, our schema for glass probably specifies that *if* an object made of glass falls onto a hard surface, *then* the object might break. Schemas also include information that we can use as a basis for drawing inferences in novel situations. For instance, suppose that a 75-year-old woman, a 45-year-old man, a 30-year-old nun, and a 25-year-old woman are sitting on park benches surrounding a playground. A young child falls from some playground equipment and calls out "Mama!" To whom is the child calling? Chances are, you would be able to draw an inference by calling on your schemas for mothers, for men and women, for persons of various ages, and even for persons who join religious orders to determine your answer.

In Europe, early conceptions of schemas centered on how we represent information in memory (e.g., Bartlett, 1932) and on how children develop cognitive understandings of how the world works (Piaget, 1928, 1952, 1955). In the United States, researchers interested in AI (artificial intelligence) adapted the notion of schemas to fit various computer models of human intelligence. These researchers were interested in devising computer models of how knowledge is represented and used, as a part of their overall interest in developing computer models of intelligence.

SCRIPTS

At Yale University, AI researchers Roger Schank and Robert Abelson (1977) developed a notion about schematic representations that they termed a *script.* Schank and Abelson define a script as:

> a structure that describes appropriate sequences of events in a particular context. A script is made up of slots and requirements about what can fill those slots. The structure is an interconnected whole, and what is in one slot affects what can be in another. Scripts handle stylized everyday situations. They are not subject to much change, nor do they provide the apparatus for handling totally novel situations. (p. 41)

Thus, scripts are much less flexible than are schemas in general. On the other hand, scripts include default values for the actors, the props, and the setting, as well as for the sequence of events expected to occur.

Take what is probably the most widely discussed script in Schank and Abelson's book, the restaurant script. The script may be applied to one particular kind of restaurant, the coffee shop. A script has several features: (a) props, such as tables, a menu, food, a check, and money; (b) roles to be played—a customer, a waiter, a cook, a cashier, and an owner; (c) opening conditions for the script—that the customer is hungry, and that he or she has money; (d) scenes—entering, ordering, eating, and exiting; and (e) results—that the customer has less money, that the owner has more money, that the customer is no longer hungry, and, sometimes, that the customer and the owner are pleased.

Various empirical studies have been conducted in order to test the validity of the script notion. One of the most widely cited is that by Gordon Bower, John Black, and Terrence Turner (1979). These investigators presented their participants with 18 brief stories. Consider one of these, representing the doctor's-office script:

INVESTIGATING COGNITIVE PSYCHOLOGY

THE DOCTOR

John was feeling bad today so he decided to go see the family doctor. He checked in with the doctor's receptionist, and then looked through several medical magazines that were on the table by his chair. Finally the nurse came and asked him to take off his clothes. The doctor was very nice to him. He eventually prescribed some pills for John. Then John left the doctor's office and headed home.

Did John take off his clothes?

This "scripted" description of a visit to a doctor's office is fairly typical. Notice that in this description, as would probably happen in any verbal description of a script, some details are missing, which the speaker (or script-writer, in this case) may have omitted mentioning. Thus, we do not know for sure that John actually took off his clothes. Moreover, the nurse probably beckoned John at some point and escorted him to an examination room, the nurse probably took John's temperature and his blood pressure and weighed him, the doctor probably asked John to describe his symptoms, and so on. But we do not know any of these things for sure.

In the research by Bower and his colleagues, participants were asked to read the 18 stories and were then asked later to perform one of two tasks. In a recall task, participants were asked to recall as much as they could about each of the stories. The critical result was that participants showed a significant tendency to recall, as parts of the stories, elements that were not actually in the stories, but that were parts of the scripts that the stories represented. In the recognition task, participants were presented with sentences and were asked to rate on a 7-point scale their confidence that they had seen each of the sentences. Some of the sentences were from the stories; others were not. Of the sentences that were *not* from the stories, some were from the relevant scripts, and others were not from these scripts. The critical result was that participants were more likely to characterize particular nonstory sentences as having come from the stories if the nonstory sentences were script-relevant than if the nonstory sentences were not script-relevant. The Bower, Black, and Turner research has become something of a classic because it suggested that scripts seem to guide what people recall and recognize—ultimately, what people know.

In a related context, scripts may also come into play in regard to the ways in which experts converse with and write for one another. Certainly, experts share a **jargon**—specialized vocabulary commonly used within a group, such as a profession or a trade. In addition, however, experts share a common understanding of scripts that are known by insiders to the field of expertise but that are unknown and unfamiliar to outsiders. When trying to understand technical manuals and technical conversations outside your own area of expertise, you may run not only into vocabulary difficulties, but also information gaps in which you lack the proper script for interpreting the language being spoken.

Practical Applications of Cognitive Psychology

Take a closer look at the scripts you use in your everyday life. Is your going-to-class script different from your going-to-meals script, or other scripted activities? In what ways do your scripts differ—in structure or in details? Try making changes to your script, either in details or in structure, and see how things work. For example, you may find that you rush in the morning to get to school or work, and forget things or arrive late. Aside from the obvious adjustment of getting up earlier, analyze the structure of your script to see if you can combine or remove steps. You could try laying out your clothes and packing your backpack or briefcase the night before to simplify your morning routine. The bottom line? The best way to make your scripts work better for you is first to analyze what they are and then to correct them.

Despite the flaws in the script model, cognitive psychologists have gained insight into knowledge organization by observing that scripts may enable us to use a mental framework for acting in certain situations when we must fill in apparent gaps within a given context. Without access to mental scripts, we would probably be at a loss the first time we entered a new restaurant or a new doctor's office—imagine what it would be if the nurse at the doctor's office had to explain each step to you. When everyone in a given situation follows a similar script, the day flows much more smoothly.

Whether we subscribe to the notion of categories, semantic networks, or schemas, the important issue is that knowledge is organized, and these forms of organization can serve different purposes. The most adaptive and flexible use of knowledge would allow us to use any form of organization, depending on the situation—we need some means to define aspects of the situation, to relate these concepts to other concepts and categories, and to select the appropriate course of action given the situation. Next, we move on to discuss theories about how the mind represents procedural knowledge.

REPRESENTATIONS OF PROCEDURAL KNOWLEDGE

Some of the earliest models for representing procedural knowledge come from AI and computer-simulation research (see chapter 1), in which researchers try to get computers to perform tasks intelligently, particularly in ways that simulate intelligent performance of humans. In fact, cognitive psychologists have learned a great deal about representing and using procedural knowledge because of the distinctive problems posed in getting computers to implement procedures based on a series of instructions compiled in programs. Through trial-and-error attempts at getting computers to simulate intelligent cognitive processes, cognitive psychologists have come to understand some of the complexities of human information processing. As a result of their efforts, they have developed a variety of models for how information is represented and processed. Each of these models involves the **serial processing** of information, in which information is handled through a linear sequence of operations, one operation at a time.

THE PRODUCTION AND THE PRODUCTION SYSTEM

One way in which computers can represent and organize procedural knowledge is in the form of sets of rules governing a **production** (generation and output of a procedure). Specifically, computer simulations of productions follow *production rules* (if–then rules), comprising an *if* clause and a *then* clause (Newell & Simon, 1972). People may use this same form of organizing knowledge, or something very close to it. For example, *if* your car is veering toward the left side of the road, *then* you should steer toward the right side of the road if you wish to avoid hitting the curb. The *if* clause includes a set of conditions that must be met in order to implement the *then* clause. The *then* clause is an action or a series of actions.

For a given clause, each condition may contain one or more variables, for each of which there may be one or more possibilities. For example, *if* you want to go somewhere by car, and *if* you know how to drive a car, and *if* you are licensed and insured to drive, and *if* you have a car available to you, and *if* you do not have other constraints (e.g., no keys, no gas, broken engine, dead battery), *then* you may execute the actions for driving a car somewhere.

As you can imagine, when the rules are precisely described and all of the relevant conditions and actions are noted, a huge number of rules are required to perform even a very simple task. These rules are organized into a structure of *routines* (instructions regarding procedures for implementing a task) and *subroutines* (instructions for implementing a subtask within a larger task governed by a routine), many of which are *iterative*—repeated many times during the performance of a task. The various routines and subroutines execute component tasks and subtasks required for implementing the main production. According to John Anderson (1983) and others (e.g., Newell & Simon, 1972), to perform a particular task or to use a particular skill, knowledge representation involves a **production system,** comprising the entire set of rules (productions) for executing the task or using the skill.

An example of a simple production system for a pedestrian to cross the street at an intersection with a traffic light, from Allen Newell and Herbert Simon (1972), is shown here (with the *if* clauses indicated to the left of the arrows and the *then* clauses indicated to the right of the arrows):

traffic-light red → stop

traffic-light green → move

move and left foot on pavement → step with right foot

move and right foot on pavement → step with left foot

In this production system, the individual first tests to see whether the light is red. If it is red, the person stops, and again tests to see whether the light is red. This sequence is repeated until the light turns green, at which point the person starts moving. If the person is moving and the left foot is on the pavement, the person will step with the right foot; if the person is moving and the right foot is on the pavement, the person will step with the left foot.

Sometimes, production systems, like computer programs, contain *bugs* (flaws in the instructions for the conditions or for executing the actions). For example, in the cross-the-street program, if the last line read "move and right foot on pavement → step with right foot," the individual executing the production system would get nowhere. According to the production-system model, human representations of procedural knowledge may well contain some occasional bugs (VanLehn, 1990).

As the foregoing discussion has shown, until about the mid-1970s, researchers interested in knowledge representation followed either of two basic strands of research: AI and information-processing researchers were refining various models for representing procedural knowledge, while cognitive psychologists and other researchers were considering various alternative models for representing declarative knowledge. By the end of the 1970s, some integrative models of knowledge representation began to emerge.

Integrative Models for Representing Declarative and Nondeclarative Knowledge

Combining Representations: ACT and ACT*

An excellent example of a theory that combines forms of mental representation is John Anderson's (1976) ACT (adaptive control of thought) model of knowledge representation and information processing. In his ACT model, Anderson synthesized some of the features of serial information-processing models and some of the features of semantic-network models. In ACT, procedural knowledge is represented in the form of production systems, whereas declarative knowledge is represented in the form of propositional networks. (In 1985, Anderson defined a proposition as being "the smallest unit of knowledge that can stand as a separate assertion." Recall from chapter 7 that propositions are abstracted underlying meanings of relationships among elements.)

Anderson intended his model to be so broad in scope that it would offer an overarching theory regarding the entire architecture of cognition. In Anderson's view, individual cognitive processes (e.g., memory, language comprehension, problem solving, and reasoning) are merely variations on a central theme, reflecting an underlying system of cognition.

ACT is an interesting example of the evolution of a theory. When Anderson was in graduate school, he proposed a model of free recall in an associative network, which he called "FRAN" (J. R. Anderson, 1972). However, this model was very limited in what it could do. So Anderson collaborated with his advisor at Stanford University, Gordon Bower, to produce a much more general model of *h*uman *a*ssociative *m*emory (HAM; J. R. Anderson & Bower, 1973). In short order, the limitations of HAM became clear, which led Anderson to formulate ACT. However, ACT itself had problems, which led to successive revisions of ACT, many of them incorporated in the newer model, **ACT*** (pronounced "act-star"), which is a model of information processing that integrates a network representation for declarative knowledge and a production-system representation for procedural knowledge, (J. R. Anderson, 1983; see Figure 8.4).

John R. Anderson *is a professor of psychology at Carnegie-Mellon University. He is best known for his ACT* model of human cognition. Anderson has also made major contributions in his work on the application of psychology to real-world learning, such as in learning the computer language LISP.*

FIGURE 8.4 **ANDERSON'S ACT* MODEL**

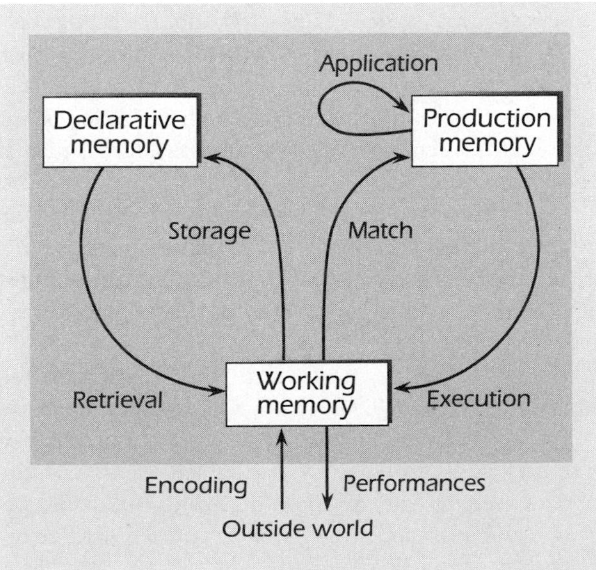

John Anderson's most recent version of ACT comprises declarative knowledge ("declarative memory"), procedural knowledge ("production memory"), and working memory (the activated knowledge available for cognitive processing, which has a limited capacity).*

For example, in his early ACT model, Anderson's declarative knowledge networks comprised propositions only. In subsequent ACT* models, his networks also included images of objects and corresponding spatial configurations and relationships, as well as temporal information, such as relationships involving the sequencing of actions, events, or even the order in which items appear. Anderson referred to the temporal information as *temporal strings,* noting that they contain information about the relative time sequence (e.g., before/after, first/second/third, yesterday/tomorrow), as opposed to absolute time referents (e.g., 2 P.M., Sunday, July 4, 1999). The model is under constant revision, and currently includes information about statistical regularities in the environment (J. R. Anderson, 1991; J. R. Anderson, 1996; J. R. Anderson & Fincham, 1996).

Anderson's declarative network model, like many other network models (e.g., Collins & Loftus, 1975), contains a mechanism by which information can be retrieved, as well as a structure for storing information. Recall that within a semantic network, concepts are stored at various nodes within the network. According to Anderson's model (and various other network models), the nodes can be either inactive or active at a given time. An active node is one that is, in a sense, "turned on." A node can be turned on—activated—directly by external stimuli (e.g., sensations) or by internal stimuli (e.g., memories or thought processes), or it can be activated indirectly, by the activity of one or more neighboring nodes.

As you may have guessed, given each node's receptivity to stimulation from neighboring nodes, activation easily can spread from one node to another. Note that Anderson's model is based on the notion that there are limits on the amount of information (number of nodes) that can be activated at any one time. Within the limited capacity of the overall cognitive system, this **spreading activation** fans out along a set of nodes within a given network. Of course, as more nodes are activated, and the spread of activation reaches greater distances from the initial source of the activation, the activation weakens.

Anderson's model also suggests means by which the network changes as a result of activation. For one thing, the more often particular links between nodes are used, the stronger the links become. In a complementary fashion, activation is much more likely to spread along the routes of frequently traveled connections, rather than along infrequently used connections between nodes.

Consider an analogy. Imagine a complex set of water pipes interlinking various locations. When the water is turned on at one location, the water starts moving through various pipes in a sort of spreading activation. At various interconnections, a valve is either open or closed, either permitting the flow to continue through or diverting the flow (the activation) to other connections.

To carry the analogy a bit further, processes such as attention can influence the degree of activation throughout the system. Thus, in the water system, the higher the water pressure in the system, the farther along the water will spread through the system of pipes. To relate this metaphor back to spreading activation, when we are thinking about an issue, and various associations seem to come to mind regarding that issue, we are experiencing the spread of activation along the nodes that represent our knowledge of various aspects of the problem, and possibly, its solution.

Actually, to help explain some aspects of spreading activation, picture the pipes as being more flexible than normal pipes. These pipes can gradually expand or contract, depending on how frequently they are used. The pipes along routes that are traveled frequently may expand to enhance the ease and speed of travel along those routes. The pipes along routes that are seldom traveled may gradually contract. Similarly, in spreading activation, connections that are frequently used are strengthened, and connections that are seldom used are weakened. Thus, within semantic networks, declarative knowledge may be learned and maintained through the strengthening of connections, as a result of frequent use.

How does Anderson explain the acquisition of procedural knowledge, which is represented in production systems, rather than in semantic networks? J. R. Anderson (1980) has hypothesized that knowledge representation of procedural skills occurs in three stages: cognitive, associative, and autonomous. During the *cognitive* stage, we think about explicit rules for implementing the procedure. During the *associative* stage, we practice using the explicit rules extensively, usually in a highly consistent manner. Finally, during the *autonomous* stage, we use these rules automatically and implicitly, with a high degree of integration and coordination, as well as speed and accuracy.

For example, while we are in the cognitive stage for learning how to drive a standard-shift car, we must explicitly think about each rule for stepping on the clutch pedal, the gas pedal, or the brake pedal, while also trying to think about when and how to shift gears. During the associative stage, we carefully and repeatedly practice following the rules in a consistent manner. We gradually become more familiar with the rules, learning when to follow which rules and when to implement which procedures. Eventually, we reach the autonomous stage, at which time we have integrated all of the various rules into a single, coordinated series of actions. We no longer need to think about what steps to take to shift gears and can concentrate instead on listening to our favorite radio station—as well as on going to our destination, avoiding accidents, stopping for pedestrians, and so on.

According to Anderson, our progress through these stages is *proceduralization,* which is the overall process by which we transform slow, explicit information about procedures ("knowing that") into speedy, implicit, implementations of procedures ("knowing how"). (Recall the discussion of *automatization* in chapter 3, which is a term used by other cognitive psychologists to describe essentially the same process.) One means by which we make this transformation is through *composition,* during which we construct a single production rule that effectively embraces two or more production rules, thus streamlining the number of rules required for executing the procedure. For example, when learning to drive a standard-shift car, we may compose a single procedure for what were two separate procedures for pressing down on the clutch and applying the brakes when we reach a stop sign.

Another aspect of proceduralization is "production tuning," which involves the two complementary processes of generalization and discrimination. We learn to *generalize* (apply information from a specific situation to a broad range of situations) existing rules to apply them to new conditions. For example, we can generalize our use of the clutch, the brakes, and the accelerator to a variety of standard-shift cars. Finally, we learn to *discriminate* (discern relevant information from irrelevant data) new criteria for meeting the conditions we face. For example, after we have mastered driving a particular standard-shift car, if we drive a car with a different number of gears or with different positions for the reverse gear, we must discriminate the relevant information about the new gear positions from the irrelevant information about the old gear positions.

Thus far, the models of knowledge representation presented in this chapter have been based largely on computer models of human intelligence. As the foregoing discussion shows, information-processing theories based on computer simulations of human cognitive processes have greatly advanced our understanding of human knowledge representation and information processing. An alternative approach to understanding knowledge representation in humans has been to study the human brain itself. Much of the research in psychobiology has offered evidence that many operations of the human brain do not seem to process information step-by-step, bit-by-bit. Rather, the human brain seems to engage in multiple processes, acting on myriad bits of knowledge, all at once. Such models do not necessarily contradict step-by-step models. First, people seem likely to use both serial and parallel processing. Second, different kinds of processes may be occurring at different levels. Thus, our brains may be processing multiple pieces of information simultaneously that combine into each of the steps of which we are aware when we process information step-by-step.

Models Based on the Human Brain

As mentioned previously, knowledge has traditionally been described as either declarative or procedural. Procedural knowledge usually involves some degree of skill (e.g., problem-solving, numeric, linguistic, or musical skill), which increases as a result of practice until performance requires little conscious attention under most circumstances (see chapter 3). For example, knowledge of a telephone number is declarative knowledge. Knowing how to memorize a phone number involves procedural knowledge. By now, you have become so skilled at knowing how to memorize information that you are no longer aware of many of the procedures you use for doing so. When you were a child, however, while you were learning how mentally to represent the procedural knowledge for memorizing simple facts, you were probably keenly conscious of learning to do so.

Psychobiologist Larry Squire (1986; Squire et al., 1990) has expanded on the traditional distinction between declarative and procedural knowledge to suggest that nondeclarative knowledge may encompass a broader range of mental representations than just procedural knowledge. Specifically, according to Squire, in addition to declarative knowledge, we mentally represent the following forms of nondeclarative knowledge:

- Perceptual, motor, and cognitive skills (procedural knowledge),
- Simple associative knowledge (classical and operant conditioning),
- Simple nonassociative knowledge (habituation and sensitization),
- Priming (fundamental links within a knowledge network, in which the activation of information along a particular mental pathway facilitates the subsequent retrieval of information along a related pathway or even the same mental pathway; see chapter 3).

According to Squire, all of these nondeclarative forms of knowledge are usually implicit (unstated) and are not easily made explicit.

Squire's primary inspiration for his model came from (a) his own work; (b) a wide range of neuropsychological research done by others (e.g., Baddeley & Warrington, 1970; Milner, 1972), such as studies of amnesic patients, animal studies, and studies of the *microanatomy* of the brain (using microscopes to study brain cells); and (c) human cognitive experiments. As one example, work with amnesic patients reveals clear distinctions between the neural systems for representing declarative knowledge versus neural systems for some of the nondeclarative forms of knowledge. For instance, amnesic patients often continue to show procedural knowledge even when they cannot remember that they possess such knowledge. Often, they show improvements in performance on tasks requiring skills, indicating some form of new knowledge representation, despite an inability to remember ever having previous experience with the tasks. For example, an amnesic patient who is given repeated practice in reading mirror writing will improve as a result of practice but will not recall ever having engaged in the practice (Baddeley, 1989).

Nondeclarative knowledge representation occurs as a result of experience in implementing a procedure, not as a result of reading, hearing, or otherwise acquiring information from explicit instructions. Once a mental representation of nondeclarative knowledge is constructed, that knowledge is implicit and is not easily made explicit. In fact, the process of enhancing the mental representation of nondeclarative knowledge tends actually to decrease explicit access to that knowledge. For example, if you have recently learned how to drive a standard-shift car, you may find it easier to describe how to do so than may someone who learned that skill long ago. As your explicit access to nondeclarative knowledge decreases, however, your speed and ease of gaining implicit access to that knowledge increases. Eventually, most nondeclarative knowledge can be retrieved for use much more quickly than declarative knowledge can be retrieved.

Another paradox of human knowledge representation is also demonstrated by amnesics; that is, although amnesics do not show normal memory abilities under most circumstances, they do show the priming effect. Recall from chapter 3 that in *priming,* particular cues and stimuli seem to activate mental pathways that enhance the retrieval or cognitive processing of related information. For example, if someone asks you to spell the word *sight,* you will probably spell it differently, depending on whether you have been primed to think about sensory modalities ("s-i-g-h-t"), about locations for an archaeological dig ("s-i-t-e"), or about lists of references ("c-i-t-e"). Surprisingly, even when the amnesic participants have no recall of the priming and cannot explicitly recall the experience during which priming occurred, priming still affects their performance.

If you can recruit at least two (and preferably more) volunteers, try the following experiment in priming, which requires you to draw on your store of declarative knowledge.

INVESTIGATING COGNITIVE PSYCHOLOGY

Separate your volunteers into two groups. For one group, ask them to unscramble the following *anagrams* (puzzles in which you must figure out the correct order of letters in order to make a sensible word): ZAZIP, GASPETHIT, POCH YUSE, OWCH MINE, ILCHI, ACOT.

Ask the members of the other group to unscramble the following anagrams: TECKAJ, STEV, ASTEREW, OLACK, ZELBAR, ACOT.

For the first group, the correct answers are *pizza, spaghetti, chop suey, chow mein, chili,* and a sixth item. The correct answers for the second group are *jacket, vest, sweater, cloak, blazer,* and a sixth item. The sixth item in each group may be either *taco* or *coat.* Did your volunteers show a tendency to choose one or the other answer, depending on the preceding list with which they were primed?

The preceding examples illustrate situations in which an item may prime another item that is somehow related in meaning. Michael Posner (e.g., Posner, Petersen, Fox, & Raichle, 1988) has suggested that we may actually differentiate two types of priming: *semantic priming,* in which we are primed by a meaningful context or by meaningful information (e.g., fruits or green things may prime "lime"), and *repetition priming,* in which a prior exposure to a word or other stimulus primes a subsequent retrieval of that information (e.g., hearing the word "lime" primes subsequent stimulation for the word "lime"). A great deal of research has been done on both types of priming, but semantic priming often particularly interests cognitive psychologists.

For example, Gail McKoon and Roger Ratcliff (1980) have provided evidence of priming, based on research on normal participants. In particular, they studied priming using a method that is simple but ingenious. Participants are presented with two short paragraphs. After reading the paragraphs, the participants are given a recognition-memory test. Participants are asked whether they have seen a given word in one of the stories and are timed in their responses. Some of the words they see are from one of the stories they have just read, and others are from neither story. The critical aspect of the experiment is whether a given test word is preceded by a word from the *same* story or by a word from the *other* story. The first kind of trial is a primed trial, the second kind, an unprimed control trial. If priming occurs, then participants should respond more quickly to a test item if it has just been preceded by a test item from the same story than if it has just been preceded by a test item from the other story. This prediction has been verified in a series of experiments.

Many cognitive psychologists (e.g., Meyer & Schvaneveldt, 1971) explain the priming effect in terms of spreading activation within a network model of knowledge representation, but Gail McKoon and Roger Ratcliff have suggested an alternative explanation. McKoon and Ratcliff (1992b; Ratcliff, 1990; Ratcliff & McKoon, 1988, 1994) attribute priming effects to a retrieval process involving what they term a *compound cue,* a linking of the target and the *prime* (an activated node) as a pair used for retrieving information from memory. According to their theory, the key to the priming effect is the mental representation of the prime and the target as a unified compound cue, rather than as discrete nodes. Compound cues are formed as a function of the degree to which the individual is familiar with simultaneously holding both the prime and the target in *working memory* (an active, temporary form of memory for information currently being cognitively processed).

According to these researchers (Ratcliff & McKoon, 1988), the compound cue is sent throughout the memory system, to retrieve whatever information matches up with the two items. The researchers oppose the notion that the cue stimulates spreading activation throughout a network. Rather, they suggest that the compound cue either takes a "random walk" throughout the memory structure (which may or may not be a network) or that it diffuses (spontaneously scatters in all directions) throughout the memory system. In their view, the priming effect occurs because the retrieval responses to the target are multiplied by the retrieval responses to the prime, thereby producing a much more powerful response than would arise from either one alone.

One way to picture the phenomenon of compound cues might be to suppose that you awake one morning in a strange environment, unable to recall anything about yourself. If you wander around aimlessly, asking whomever you meet to tell you whatever they know about you, you may be able to retrieve some information about yourself. The preceding situation would be equivalent to an unprimed retrieval task. As a metaphor for the primed retrieval task, suppose that both you and your best friend awake in a strange environment, unable to recall anything about each other or about yourselves. If the two of you wander around, asking people to tell you information about yourselves, you may be able to have not only twice as much information, but also a multiplier effect because the two of you can work as a team to piece together more information than either of you alone could generate or even more than the two of could generate working totally independently.

The compound-cue model has generated some support (e.g., Ratcliff & McKoon, 1988); for example, a compound-cue model may explain how contextual priming often enhances the speed and accuracy of response (Chawarski & Sternberg, 1993). Also, both the compound-cue model and the spreading-activation model seem to be able to explain most of the data available at present (Ratcliff & McKoon, 1994; Ratcliff & McKoon, 1997). However, the more popular explanation of priming is linked to spreading-activation theory.

According to spreading-activation theories, the amount of activation between a prime and a given target node is a function of the number of links connecting the prime and the target and the relative strengths of each connection. This view holds that increasing the number of intervening links tends to decrease the likelihood of the priming effect, but increasing the strength of each link between the prime and its target tends to increase the likelihood of the priming effect. This model has been well supported (e.g., see McNamara, 1992). Furthermore, the occurrence of priming through spreading activation is taken by most psychologists as support for a network model of knowledge representation in memory processes. In particular, the notions of priming effects through spreading activation within a network model have led to the emergence of what is called a connectionist model of knowledge representation.

PARALLEL PROCESSING: THE CONNECTIONIST MODEL

The computer-inspired information-processing theories assume that humans, like computers, process information serially, one step after another. Although some aspects of human cognition may be explained in terms of serial processing, psychobiological findings and other cognitive research seem to indicate that other aspects of human cognition involve **parallel processing,** in which multiple operations go on all at once. Just as the information processing of a computer has served as a metaphor for many models of cognition, our increasing understanding of how the human brain processes information also serves as a metaphor for many of the recent models of knowledge representation in humans. Because the human brain seems to handle many operations and to process information from many sources simultaneously—in parallel—many contemporary models of knowledge representation emphasize the importance of parallel processing in human cognition. (Note also that as a result of interest in parallel processing, some computers have been made to simulate parallel processing, such as through so-called neural networks of interlinked computer processors.)

At present, many cognitive psychologists are exploring the limits of parallel models, often termed either **parallel distributed processing (PDP)** models (see McClelland, Rumelhart, & the PDP Research Group, 1986; Rumelhart, McClelland, & the PDP Research Group, 1986) or *connectionist* models. According to these models, we may be able to process information as efficiently as we do because we can handle very large numbers of cognitive operations at once, through a network distributed across incalculable numbers of locations in the brain. A computer can begin responding to an input within *nanoseconds* (millionths of a second), but an individual neuron may take up to 3 milliseconds to fire in response to a stimulus, so serial processing in the human brain would be far too slow to manage the amount of information it handles. For example, most of us can recognize a complex visual stimulus within about 300 milliseconds. If we processed the stimulus serially, only a few hundred neurons would have had time to respond. Rather, according to PDP models, the distribution of parallel processes better explains the speed and accuracy of human information processing.

The mental structure within which parallel processing is believed to occur is the network, described earlier in regard to semantic networks of declarative knowledge. In connectionist networks, all forms of knowledge are represented within the network structure. Recall that the fundamental element of the network is the node. Each node is connected to many other nodes. These interconnected patterns of nodes enable the individual meaningfully to organize the knowledge contained in the connections among the various nodes. In many network models, each node represents a concept.

James L. McClelland *is a professor of psychology and computer science at Carnegie-Mellon University and is a codirector of the Center for the Neural Basis of Cognition. McClelland is best known for his seminal work with David Rumelhart on introducing PDP (connectionist) models into the mainstream of psychology, and for showing that such models can be formulated, implemented, and tested in a number of different domains of cognitive functioning.*

In the PDP model proposed by James McClelland and David Rumelhart (1981, 1985; Rumelhart & McClelland, 1982), however, the network comprises neuronlike units, which do not, in and of themselves, actually represent concepts, propositions, or any other type of information. Thus, the pattern of connections represents the knowledge, not the specific units. The same idea governs our use of language: Individual letters (or sounds) of a word are relatively uninformative, but the pattern of letters (or sounds) is highly informative. Similarly, no single unit is very informative, but the pattern of interconnections among units is highly informative. Figure 8.5 illustrates how just six units (dots) may be used to generate many more than six patterns of connections between the dots.

The PDP model demonstrates another way in which a brain-inspired model differs from a computer-inspired one: Differing cognitive processes are handled by differing patterns of activation, rather than as a result of a different set of instructions from a computer's central processing unit (CPU). In the brain, at any one time, a given neuron may be inactive, excitatory, or inhibitory.

- *Inactive* neurons are not stimulated beyond their threshold of excitation and are not releasing any neurotransmitters into the synapse (the interneuronal gap).
- *Excitatory* neurons are releasing neurotransmitters that stimulate receptive neurons at the synapse, increasing the likelihood that the receiving neurons will reach their threshold of excitation.
- *Inhibitory* neurons are releasing neurotransmitters that inhibit receptive neurons, reducing the likelihood that the receiving neurons will reach their threshold of excitation.

Further, although the action potential of a neuron is all or none, the amounts of neurotransmitters and neuromodulators released may vary, and the frequency of firing may vary, thereby affecting the degree of excitation or inhibition of other neurons at the synapse.

FIGURE 8.5 **CONNECTIONS AND PATTERNS**

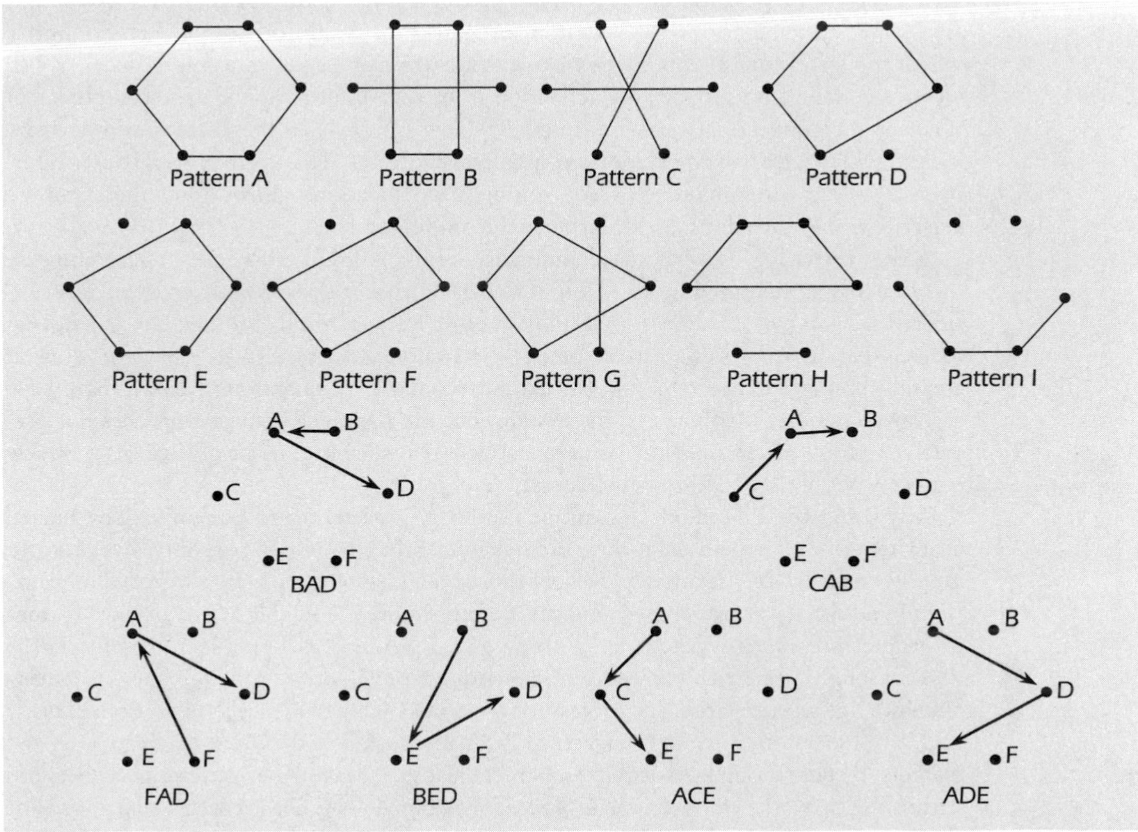

Each individual unit (dot) is relatively uninformative, but when the units are connected into various patterns, each pattern may be highly informative, as illustrated in the patterns at the top of this figure. Similarly, individual letters are relatively uninformative, but patterns of letters may be highly informative. Using just three-letter combinations, we can generate many different patterns, such as DAB, FED, and other patterns shown in the bottom of this figure.

Similarly, in McClelland and Rumelhart's PDP model, individual units may be inactive, or they may send excitatory or inhibitory signals to other units. That is not to say that the PDP model actually indicates specific neural pathways for knowledge representation. We are still a long way from having more than a faint glimmer of how to map specific neural information. Rather, the PDP model uses the physiological processes of the brain as a metaphor for understanding cognition. According to the PDP model, connections between units can possess varying degrees of potential excitation or inhibition, even when the connections are currently inactive. The more often a particular connection is activated, the greater is the strength of the connection, whether excitatory or inhibitory.

According to the PDP model, whenever we use knowledge, we change our representation of it. Thus, knowledge representation is not really a final product, but rather a process or even a potential process. What is stored is not a particular pattern of connections, but rather a pattern of potential excitatory or inhibitory connection strengths, which the mind (brain) uses to re-create given patterns when stimulated to do so. When we receive new information, the activation from that information either strengthens or weakens the connections between units. The new information may come from environmental stimuli, from memory, or from cognitive processes. The ability to create new information by drawing inferences and making generalizations allows for almost infinite versatility in knowledge representation and manipulation.

This versatility is what makes humans—unlike computers—able to accommodate incomplete and distorted information; information that is distorted or incomplete is considered *degraded.* According to the PDP model, human minds are flexible and do not require that all aspects of a pattern precisely match in order to activate a pattern. Thus, if enough distinctive aspects of a particular pattern (and not of another pattern) have been activated by other attributes in the description, the degraded information does not prevent us from re-creating the correct pattern. This cognitive flexibility also greatly enhances our ability to learn new information.

By using the PDP model, cognitive psychologists attempt to explain various general characteristics of human cognition, such as our ability to respond flexibly, dynamically, rapidly, and relatively accurately, even when we are given only partial or degraded information. In addition, cognitive psychologists attempt to use the model to explain specific cognitive processes, such as perception, reasoning, and priming and other memory processes.

Although connectionist models of knowledge representation explain many phenomena of knowledge representation and processing, these models are not flawless. They explain many cognitive processes, which may be learned gradually, such as those involving perception and memory, by our storing knowledge through gradual strengthening of patterns of connections within the network. However, many aspects of the model are not yet well defined, and the model is less effective in explaining how people can remember a single event (Schacter, 1989a). That is, how do we suddenly construct a whole new interconnected pattern for representing what we know about a memorable event (such as graduation day)?

Similarly, connectionist models do not satisfactorily explain how we often quickly can unlearn established patterns of connections when we are presented with contradictory information (Ratcliff, 1990; Treadway, McCloskey, Gordon, & Cohen, 1992). For example, suppose that you are told that the criteria for classifying parts of plants as fruits are that they must have seeds, pulp, and skin, and that whether they are sweeter than other plant parts is not important. If you are then given the task of sorting various photos of plant parts into groups that are or are not fruits, you will sort tomatoes and pumpkins with apples and other fruits, even if you did not previously consider them to be fruits.

In a recent paper, McClelland, McNaughton, and O'Reilly (1997) attempt to bypass these shortcomings of connectionist systems by suggesting that there are two learning systems in the brain. One system corresponds to the connectionist model in resisting change and in being relatively permanent. The complementary system handles rapid acquisition of new information, holds the information for a short period of time, then integrates the newer information with information in the connectionist system. McClelland and colleagues cite evidence from neuropsychology and connectionist network modeling that seems to corroborate this account. Thus, the connectionist system is spared, but we need a satisfactory account of the other learning system.

The preceding models of knowledge representation and information processing have clearly profited from technological advances in computer science, in brain imaging, and in the psychobiological study of the human brain in action—techniques that few would have predicted to have been so promising 40 years ago. Thus, it would be foolish to predict that specific avenues of research will lead us in particular directions. Nonetheless, particular avenues of research do hold promise. For example, using powerful computers, researchers are attempting to create parallel-processing models via neural networks. Increasingly sophisticated techniques for studying the brain offer intriguing possibilities for research. Case studies, naturalistic studies, and traditional laboratory experiments in the field of cognitive psychology also offer rich opportunities for further exploration. Some researchers are trying to explore highly specific cognitive processes (e.g., auditory processing of speech sounds), while others are trying to investigate fundamental processes that underlie all aspects of cognition. Which type of research is more valuable?

How Domain General or Domain Specific Is Cognition?

Should cognitive psychologists try to find a set of mental processes that is common across all domains of knowledge representation and processing, or should they study mental processes specific to a particular domain? In early AI research, investigators believed that the ideal was to write programs that were as domain general as possible. Although none of the programs truly worked in all domains, they were a good start. Similarly, in the broader field of cognitive psychology, the trend in the 1960s and even into the 1970s was to strive for domain-general understandings of cognitive processes (e.g., G. A. Miller, Galanter, & Pribram, 1960; Simon, 1976).

During the late 1970s and the 1980s, the balance shifted toward domain specificity, in part because of the striking demonstrations of Adriaan De Groot (1965) and of William Chase and Herbert Simon (1973) regarding the role of specific knowledge in chess playing (see chapter 11). One of the most influential books in the field of cognitive science during the 1980s was Jerry Fodor's (1983) *The Modularity of Mind,* which presented an argument for extreme domain specificity. Fodor argued that the mind is **modular**, divided into discrete modules that operate more or less independently from each other. According to Fodor, each independently functioning module can process only one kind of input (language [e.g., words], visual percepts [e.g., faces], etc.).

Fodor asserted the modularity of lower level processes, such as the basic perceptual processes involved in lexical access (see chapter 4). However, Howard Gardner (1983) has extended the application of modularity to higher intellectual processes as well. Also, Fodor emphasized the modularity of specific cognitive functions (e.g., lexical access to word meanings, as distinct from word meanings derived from context), as observed in cognitive experiments. However, issues of modularity also have been important in psychobiological research, as in the observation of discrete pathologies associated with discrete cognitive deficits.

Recently, there has been more of an attempt to integrate domain-specific and domain-general perspectives in our thinking about knowledge representation and processing. In my own theory of intelligence, for example (R. J. Sternberg, 1985a; see also R. J. Sternberg, 1989, and chapter 14 in this text), I discuss both domain-general and domain-specific processes. In the chapters that follow, you may wish to reflect on whether the processes and forms of knowledge representation being described may be seen as primarily domain general or primarily domain specific.

SUMMARY

1. **How are representations of words and symbols organized in the mind?** The fundamental unit of symbolic knowledge is the *concept.* Concepts may be organized into categories, which may include other categories; *schemas,* which may include other schemas; may vary in application and in abstractness; and may include information about relationships between concepts, attributes, contexts, and general knowledge, as well as information about causal relationships. There are different general theories of categorization, including *feature-based definitional* categories and *prototype-based* categories, which include *exemplar-based* approaches. One of the forms for schemas that have been proposed is the *script.* An alternative model for knowledge organization is a semantic *network,* involving a web of labeled relations between conceptual *nodes.* An early network model was strictly hierarchical, based on the notion of cognitive economy, but subsequent ones have tended to emphasize the frequency with which particular associations are used.

2. **How do we represent other forms of knowledge in the mind?** Many cognitive psychologists have developed models for procedural knowledge, based on computer simulations of such representations. An example of such a model is the *production system.*

3. **How does declarative knowledge interact with procedural knowledge?** A model for representing both procedural knowledge (in the form of production systems) and declarative knowledge (in the form of a semantic network) has been developed: ACT, as well as its various updated revisions, *ACT*.* In each of these models, the metaphor for understanding both knowledge representation and information processing is based on the way in which a computer processes information. For example, these models underscore the *serial processing* of information.

   Research on how the human brain processes information has shown that brains, unlike computers, use *parallel processing* of information. In addition, it appears that much of information processing is not localized only to particular areas of the brain, but rather is distributed across various regions of the brain, all at once. At a microscopic level of analysis, the neurons within the brain may be inactive, or they may be excited or inhibited by the actions of other neurons with which they share a synapse. Finally, studies of how the brain processes information have shown that some stimuli seem to prime a response to subsequent stimuli, so that it becomes easier to process the subsequent stimuli.

A model for human knowledge representation and information processing based on what we know about the brain is the *parallel distributed processing (PDP)* model, also called a "connectionist" model. In such models, it is held that neuronlike units may be excited or inhibited by the actions of other units, or they may be inactive. Further, knowledge is represented in terms of patterns of excitation or inhibition strengths, rather than in particular units. Most PDP models also explain the priming effect by suggesting the mechanism of *spreading activation,* but some models suggest instead that priming occurs because of the mechanism of compound cues, in which a prime and a target form a compound cue, which has a multiplicative effect on the speed and ease of information retrieval.

Many cognitive psychologists believe that the mind is at least partly *modular,* meaning that different activity centers in the mind operate fairly independently of each other. On the other hand, other cognitive psychologists believe that human cognition is governed by many fundamental operations and that specific cognitive functions are merely variations on a theme. In all likelihood, cognition involves some modular, domain-specific processes and some fundamental, domain-general processes.

Thinking About Thinking: Factual, Analytical, Creative, and Practical Questions

1. Define declarative knowledge and procedural knowledge, and give examples of each.
2. What is a script that you use in your daily life? How might you make it work better for you?
3. Describe some of the attributes of schemas, and compare and contrast two of the schema models mentioned in this chapter.
4. In your opinion, why have many of the models for knowledge representation come from persons with a strong interest in artificial intelligence?
5. What are some advantages and disadvantages of hierarchical models of knowledge representation?
6. How would you design an experiment to test whether a particular cognitive task was better explained in terms of modular components or in terms of some fundamental underlying domain-general processes?
7. What are some practical examples of the forms of nondeclarative knowledge in Squire's model? (For ideas on conditioning, see chapter 1; for ideas on habituation or on priming, see chapter 3.)
8. How might you use semantic priming to enhance the likelihood that a person will think of something you would like the person to think of (e.g., your birthday, a restaurant to visit, or a movie to view)?

Key Terms

ACT* 269
basic level 262
category 255
characteristic features 257
concept 255
converging operations 255
core 259
defining features 256
exemplars 258
jargon 266
modular 279
network 260
node 260
parallel distributed processing (PDP) 275
parallel processing 275
production 267
production system 268
prototype theory 257
schema 255
serial processing 267
spreading activation 270

Annotated Suggested Readings

Anderson, J. R. (1983). *The architecture of cognition.* Cambridge, MA: Harvard University Press. One of the great classics in modern cognitive psychology, this book explores a unified model of virtually all of human information processing.

Komatsu, L. K. (1992). Recent views on conceptual structure. *Psychological Bulletin, 112,* 500–526. An excellent review of the literature on various approaches to how people understand and represent concepts in memory.

Ratcliff, R., & McKoon, G. (1997). A counter model for implicit priming in perceptual word identification. *Psychological Review, 104,* 319–343. An updated theoretical account of memory priming, arguing that data exist that traditional spreading-activation theories have trouble explaining, but not their alternative model.

Rumelhart, D. E., McClelland, J. L., & the PDP Research Group (1986). *Parallel distributed processing. Explorations in the microstructure of cognition: Vol. 1. Foundations.* Cambridge, MA: MIT Press. Very difficult reading, but a classic work that served as a basis for much of the connectionist modeling work that was to follow it.

Language: Nature and Acquisition

Chapter Outline

Exploring Cognitive Psychology

Properties of Language
- General Description
- Fundamental Aspects of Language

Processes of Language Comprehension
- Speech Perception
- Semantics and Syntax

Language Acquisition
- Stages of Language Acquisition
- Nature and Nurture
- Beyond the First Years

Summary

Thinking About Thinking: Factual, Analytical, Creative, and Practical Questions

Key Terms

Annotated Suggested Readings

EXPLORING COGNITIVE PSYCHOLOGY

1. **What properties characterize language?**
2. **What are some of the processes involved in language?**
3. **How do we acquire the ability to use language?**

> *I stood still, my whole attention fixed upon the motions of her fingers. Suddenly, I felt a misty consciousness as of something forgotten—a thrill of returning thought; and somehow the mystery of language was revealed to me. I knew then that "w-a-t-e-r" meant the wonderful cool something that was flowing over my hand. That living word awakened my soul, gave it light, joy, set it free! . . . Everything had a name, and each name gave birth to a new thought. As we returned to the house every object which I touched seemed to quiver with life. . . . I learned a great many new words that day. . . words that were to make the world blossom for me.*
>
> —*Helen Keller,* Story of My Life

Helen Keller, who was both blind and deaf 19 months after her birth, was first awakened to a sentient, thought-filled, comprehensible world through her teacher, Anne Sullivan. The miracle worker held one of Helen's hands under a spigot from which a stream of water gushed over Helen's hand, all the while spelling with a manual alphabet into Helen's other hand the mind-awakening word "w-a-t-e-r."

Language—the use of an organized means of combining words in order to communicate—makes it possible for us to communicate with those around us, as well as to think about things and processes we cannot currently see, hear, feel, touch, or smell, including ideas that may not have any tangible form. As Helen Keller demonstrated, the words we use may be written, spoken, or otherwise signed (e.g., via American Sign Language). Even so, not all **communication**—exchange of thoughts and feelings—is through language; communication encompasses such nonverbal means as gestures (e.g., to embellish or to indicate), glances (e.g., deadly or seductive ones), touches (e.g., handshakes, hits, and hugs), and the like.

Three areas of study have contributed greatly to an understanding of **psycholinguistics**—the psychology of our language as it interacts with the human mind: (a) linguistics—the study of language structure and change; (b) neurolinguistics—the relationships among the brain, cognition, and language; and (c) sociolinguistics—the relationship between social behavior and language (D. W. Carroll, 1986). This chapter first briefly describes some general properties of language. The next sections discuss the processes of language, including how we understand the meanings of particular words, and then how we structure words into meaningful sentences. Then, the final section more fully elaborates the linguistic approach to language by describing how each of us has acquired at least one language. As you might expect, this discussion brings up the nature–nurture debate that so often arises in regard to psychological issues, but focuses on how acquired abilities interact with experience. The following chapter describes the broader context within which we use language, including the psychological and social contexts of language.

PROPERTIES OF LANGUAGE

GENERAL DESCRIPTION

What properties characterize language? The answer to this question depends on whom you ask, and linguists may offer somewhat different answers than may cognitive psychologists. Nonetheless, there seems to be some consensus regarding six properties that are distinctive of language (e.g., R. Brown, 1965; H. H. Clark & Clark, 1977; Glucksberg & Danks, 1975). Specifically, language is:

1. *Communicative:* Language permits us to communicate with one or more persons who share our language.
2. *Arbitrarily symbolic:* Language creates an arbitrary relationship between a symbol and its referent: an idea, a thing, a process, a relationship, or a description.
3. *Regularly structured:* Language has a structure; only particularly patterned arrangements of symbols have meaning, and different arrangements yield different meanings.
4. *Structured at multiple levels:* The structure of language can be analyzed at more than one level (e.g., in sounds, in meaning units, in words, in phrases).
5. *Generative, productive:* Within the limits of a linguistic structure, language users can produce novel utterances, and the possibilities for creating new utterances are virtually limitless.
6. *Dynamic:* Languages constantly evolve.

The communicative property of language is listed first because, despite its being the most obvious feature of language, it is also the most remarkable one. As an example, I can write what I am thinking and feeling, so that you may read and understand my thoughts and feelings. This is not to say that there are not occasional flaws in the communicative property of language—countless cognitive psychologists and others dedicate their lives to the study of how we fail to communicate through language. Despite the frustrations of miscommunications, however, for one person to be able to use language to communicate to another is impressive.

What may be more surprising is the second property of language—that we communicate through our shared system of *arbitrary symbolic reference* to things, ideas, processes, relationships, and descriptions. The *arbitrary* nature of the system alludes to the lack of

Signs that resemble their referents in some way are termed icons. These pictographs are icons that were used in ancient Egyptian hieroglyphics. In contrast, most language involves the manipulation of symbols, which bear only an arbitrary relation to their referents.

any reason for choosing a particular *symbol*—something that represents, indicates, or suggests something else—to *refer* (point or allude) to a particular thing, process, or description—such as *professor, amuse,* or *brilliant.* By consensual agreement, a particular combination of letters or sounds may be meaningful to us, but the particular symbols do not themselves lead to the meaning of the word; the sound combination is arbitrary, as can be seen from the fact that different languages use very different sounds to refer to the same thing (e.g., *baum, arbol, tree).*

All words are *symbols*—things that represent, refer to, stand for, or suggest something else. A convenient feature of using symbols is that we can use symbols to refer to things, ideas, processes, relationships, and descriptions that are not currently present (e.g., the Amazon River), that never have existed (e.g., dragons or elves), or that exist in a form that is not physically tangible (e.g., calculus, truth, or justice). Without arbitrary symbolic reference, we would be limited to symbols that somehow resembled the things they are supposed to symbolize (e.g., a treelike symbol to represent a tree).

The third property, the *regular structure* of language, makes possible this shared system of communication. Later in this chapter, we describe more specifically the structure of language.

For now, however, it suffices that you already know that (a) particular patterns of sounds and of letters form meaningful words, but random sounds and letters usually do not do so, and (b) particular patterns of words form meaningful sentences, paragraphs, and discourse, whereas most others make no sense.

The fourth property is *multiplicity of structure:* Any meaningful utterance can be analyzed at more than one level. Subsequent sections describe several levels at which we can analyze the structure of language. These various levels convey varying degrees of meaningful content. For example, psycholinguists study language at the level of sounds, such as *p* and *t*; at the level of words, such as "pat," "tap," "pot," "top," "pit," and "tip"; at the level of sentences, such as "Pat said to tap the top of the pot, then tip it into the pit"; and at the level of larger units of language, such as this paragraph or even this book.

A fifth property of language is *productivity* (sometimes termed *generativity),* the term for our limitless ability to produce language creatively. That is, although our use of language does have limitations—we have to conform to a particular structure and to use a particular shared system of arbitrary symbols—we can use language to produce an infinite number of unique sentences and other meaningful combinations of words. Although the number of sounds (e.g., *s* as in "hiss") used in a language may be finite, the various sounds can be combined endlessly to form new words and new sentences, among which are many *novel utterances*—language expressions that are brand-new—never spoken before by anyone. Thus, language is inherently creative, precisely because none of us possibly could ever have heard previously all the sentences we are capable of producing and that we actually produce in the course of our everyday lives. Moreover, any language appears to have the potential to express any idea in it that can be expressed in any other language, although the ease, clarity, and succinctness of expression of a particular idea may vary greatly from one language to the next. Thus, the creative potential of different languages appears to be roughly the same.

Finally, the productive aspect of language quite naturally leads to the *dynamic, evolutionary nature* of language. Individual language users coin words and phrases and modify language usage, and the wider group of language users either accepts or rejects the modifications. To imagine that language would never change is almost as incomprehensible as to imagine that people and environments would never change. For example, the modern English we speak now evolved from Middle English, which in turn evolved from Old English.

To conclude, although many differences exist among languages, there are some common properties, among which are communication, arbitrary symbolic reference, regularity of structure, multiplicity of structure, productivity, and change. Next, we consider how language is used in more detail, and then we observe some universal aspects of how we humans acquire our primary language.

FUNDAMENTAL ASPECTS OF LANGUAGE

Essentially, there are two fundamental aspects of language: (a) receptive comprehension and decoding of language input, and (b) expressive encoding and production of language output. Decoding refers to deriving the meaning from whatever symbolic reference system is being used (e.g., while listening or reading). In chapters 5 and 6, we used the term encoding to refer to both semantic and nonsemantic encoding of information into a form that can be stored in memory. As applied to language, encoding involves transforming our thoughts into a form that can be expressed as linguistic output (e.g., speech, signing, or writing). In this chapter, we use the terms encoding and decoding to describe only semantic encoding and decoding. Sometimes, researchers use the terms **verbal comprehension**—the receptive ability to comprehend written and spoken linguistic input, such as words, sentences, and paragraphs; and **verbal fluency**—the expressive ability to produce such linguistic output. When we deal specifically with spoken communication, we can refer to vocal comprehension or fluency.

Language can be broken down into many smaller units, much like chemists analyzing molecules into basic elements. The smallest unit of speech sound is the phone, which is simply a single vocal sound, and which may or may not be part of the speech system of a particular language. A click of your tongue, a pop of your cheek, or a gurgling sound may be a phone. The smallest unit of speech sound that can be used to distinguish one utterance in a given language from another is a **phoneme.** In English, phonemes are made up of vowel and consonant sounds; for example, we distinguish among "sit," "sat," "fat," and "fit," so the /s/ sound, the /f/ sound, the /I/ sound, and /ae/ sound are all phonemes in English (as is the /t/ sound). These sounds are produced by alternating sequences of opening and closing of the vocal tract. Different languages use different numbers and combinations of phonemes. Hawaiian has about 13 whereas some African dialects have up to 60. North American English has about 40 phonemes, as shown in Table 9.1. The following set of examples highlight the difference between phones and phonemes.

In English, the difference between the /p/ and the /b/ sound is an important distinction. These sounds function as phonemes in English because they comprise the difference

TABLE 9.1 NORTH AMERICAN ENGLISH PHONETIC SYMBOLS

The phonemes of a language constitute the repertoire of the smallest units of sound that can be used to distinguish one meaningful utterance from another in the given language. (After H. H. Clark & Clark, 1977)

Consonants				Vowels		Diphthongs	
p	*p*ill	θ	*th*igh	i	b*ee*t	ay	b*i*te
b	*b*ill	ð	*th*y	ι	b*i*t	æw	ab*ou*t
m	*m*ill	š	*sh*allow	e	b*ai*t	oy	b*oy*
t	*t*ill	ž	mea*s*ure	ϵ	b*e*t		
d	*d*ill	č	*ch*ip	æ	b*a*t		
n	*n*il		*g*yp	u	b*oo*t		
k	*k*ill	l	*l*ip	U	p*u*t		
g	*g*ill	r	*r*ip	ʌ	b*u*t		
ŋ	si*ng*	y	*y*et	o	b*oa*t		
f	*f*ill	w	*w*et	ɔ	b*ou*ght		
v	*v*at	ʍ	*wh*et	a	p*o*t		
s	*s*ip	h	*h*at	ə	sof*a*		
z	*z*ip			ɨ	marr*y*		

between different words. For example, English speakers distinguish between "they bit the buns from the bin" and "they pit the puns from the pin" (a well-structured but meaningless sentence). At the same time, there are some phones that English speakers may produce, but that do not function to distinguish words, and therefore do not serve as phonemes in English. These are often called *allophones,* or sound variants of the same phoneme.

To illustrate the difference between the allophones of the phoneme /p/, try putting your open hand about 1 inch from your lips, and say aloud, "Put the paper cup to your lip." If you are like most English speakers, you felt a tiny puff of air when you pronounced the /ph/ in *Put* and *paper* and no puffs of air when you pronounced the /p/ in *cup* or *lip.* If you somehow managed to stifle the puff of air when saying, "Put" or "paper" or to add a puff of air when saying "cup" or "lip," you would be producing different (allo)phones, but you would not be making a meaningful distinction in the phonemes of English—there is no meaningful difference between /ph/ut and /p/ut in English, as opposed to the difference between /k/ut and /g/ut. However, in some languages (e.g., Thai), a distinction considered irrelevant in English is meaningful because in these languages, the difference between /p/ and /ph/ is phonemic rather than merely allophonic (Fromkin & Rodman, 1988).

The study of the particular phonemes of a language is *phonemics,* and the study of how to produce or combine speech sounds or to represent them with written symbols is *phonetics.* Linguists such as Peter Ladefoged often travel to remote villages in order to observe, record, and analyze different languages, some of which are dying as members leave tribal areas in favor of more urban areas. The study of phonetic inventories of diverse languages is one way linguists gain insight into the nature of language (see Ladefoged & Maddieson, 1996).

At the next level of the hierarchy is the **morpheme**—the smallest unit that denotes meaning within a particular language. English courses may have introduced you to two forms of morphemes: (a) root words, to which we add (b) *affixes*—both *suffixes,* which follow the root word, and prefixes, which precede the root word. The word *affixes* itself comprises (a) the root *fix;* (b) the prefix *af-,* which is a variant of the prefix *ad-,* meaning "toward," "to," or "near"; and (c) the suffix *-es,* which indicates the plural form of a noun. The word *recharge* contains two morphemes, *re-* and *charge.*

Linguists analyze the structure of morphemes and words in a way that goes beyond the analysis of roots and affixes. Linguists refer to the words that convey the bulk of the meaning as **content morphemes.** The morphemes that add detail and nuance to the meaning of the content morphemes or that help the content morphemes to fit the grammatical context are **function morphemes** (e.g., the suffix *-ist,* the prefix *de-,* the conjunction *and,* or the article *the).* A subset of function morphemes are inflections, the common suffixes we add to words to fit the grammatical context. For example, most American kindergartners know to add special suffixes to indicate the following:

- *Verb tense:* You study often; you studied yesterday; and you are studying now.
- *Verb and noun number:* The professor assigns homework; the teaching assistants assign homework.
- *Noun possession:* the student's textbook is fascinating.
- *Adjective comparison:* The wiser of the two professors taught the wisest of the three students.

Linguists use the term **lexicon** to describe the entire set of morphemes in a given language or in a given person's linguistic repertoire. The average adult speaker of English has a lexicon of about 80,000 morphemes (G. A. Miller & Gildea, 1987). By combining morphemes, most adult English speakers have a **vocabulary** (repertoire of words) of hundreds of thousands of words. For example, by attaching just a few morphemes to the root content morpheme *study,* we have *student, studious, studied, studying,* and *studies.* One of the ways in which English has expanded to embrace an increasing vocabulary is by combining existing morphemes in novel ways. Some suggest that a part of William Shakespeare's genius lay in his enjoying the creation of new words by combining existing morphemes. He is alleged to have coined more than 1,700 words—8.5% of his written vocabulary—as well as countless expressions—including the word *countless* itself (Lederer, 1991).

For linguists, the next level of analysis is termed *syntax,* which refers to the way in which users of a particular language put words together to form sentences. A sentence comprises at least two parts: (a) a **noun phrase,** which contains at least one noun (often, the subject of the sentence), and includes all the relevant descriptors of the noun and (b) a **verb phrase,** which contains at least one verb and whatever the verb acts on, if anything. The verb phrase also may be termed the *predicate,* as it affirms or states something about the subject, usually an action or a property of the subject. Linguists consider the study of syntax to be fundamental to understanding the structure of language, and the syntactic structure of language is specifically addressed later in this chapter.

INVESTIGATING COGNITIVE PSYCHOLOGY

Identify which of the following are noun phrases: (a) the round, red ball on the corner; (b) and the; (c) round and red; (d) the ball; (e) water; (f) runs quickly. *(Hint:* Noun phrases can be the subject or object of a sentence, e.g., "___[NP]___ bounces ___ [NP] ___.")

Identify which of the following are verb phrases: (a) the boy bounced the ball; (b) and the bouncing ball; (c) rolled; (d) ran across the room; (e) gave her the ball; (f) runs quickly. *(Hint:* Verb phrases contain verbs, as well as anything on which the verb acts [but not the subject of the action]. For example, "The psychology student ___[VP]___.")

Complementary to syntax is **semantics,** the study of meaning in a language. A semanticist would be concerned with how words express meaning (a topic also considered in the previous two chapters).

The final level of analysis is that of **discourse,** which encompasses language use at the level beyond the sentence, such as in conversation, in paragraphs, stories, chapters, and entire books. Table 9.2 summarizes the various aspects of language, and the next section discusses how we understand language through speech perception and further analysis. We will reserve discussion of discourse for chapter 10 and the social context for language.

TABLE 9.2 SUMMARY DESCRIPTION OF LANGUAGE

All human languages can be analyzed at many levels.

Language Input			Language Output
↓	Phonemes (distinctive subset of all possible phones)	. . ./t/ + /ā/ + /k/ + /s/ . . .	↑
D	Morphemes (from the distinctive lexicon of morphemes)	. . . take (content morpheme) + s (plural function morpheme) . . .	E
e	Words (from the distinctive vocabulary of words)	It + takes + a + heap + of + sense + to + write + good + nonsense.	n
c o d	Phrases: Noun phrases (NP: a noun and its descriptors) Verb phrases (VP: a verb and whatever it acts on)	NP = It + VP = takes a heap of sense to write good nonsense.	c o d
i n g	Sentences (based on the language's syntax—syntactical structure)	It takes a heap of sense to write good nonsense.	i n g
↓	Discourse	"It takes a heap of sense to write good nonsense," was first written by Mark Twain (Lederer, 1991, p. 131). . . .	↑
Comprehend Language			Produce Language

Processes of Language Comprehension

How do we understand language, given its multifaceted encoding? One approach to this question centers around the psychological processes involved in speech perception, and how listeners deal with the peculiarities resulting from the acoustic (relating to sound) transmission of language. A more linguistically oriented approach focuses on descriptions of the grammatical structure of languages. Finally, a third approach examines the psycholinguistic processes involved in language comprehension at the discourse macro-level of analysis. All three approaches overlap to some degree, and offer interesting insights into the nature of language and its use.

Speech Perception

Have you ever been in a situation where you needed to communicate with someone, over the phone, but the speech you heard was garbled by a faulty telephone transmission? If so, you will agree that speech perception is fundamental to language use in our everyday lives. Indeed, we have only to listen to people who speak over a faulty telephone to realize the importance of speech perception. To understand speech is crucial to human communication. To understand speech perception, we consider some interesting phenomena of speech and the question of whether speech is somehow special among all of the various kinds of sounds we can perceive.

We are able to perceive speech with amazing rapidity. Whereas we can perceive as many as 50 phonemes *per second* in a language in which we are fluent (Foulke & Sticht, 1969), we can perceive only about two thirds of a phone per second of nonspeech sounds (Warren, Obusek, Farmer, & Warren, 1969). One of the things that makes foreign languages difficult to understand when we hear them, even if we can read them, is that the sounds of their letters and letter combinations may be different from the sounds corresponding to the same letters and letter combinations in our native language. For example, my Spanish sounds "American" because I tend to reinterpret Spanish sounds in terms of the American English phonetic system rather than the Spanish one.

How are we able to perceive 50 phonemes per second if, paradoxically, we can only perceive less than one phone per second of nonspeech sounds? One answer to this question lies in the fact that speech sounds show **coarticulation.** That is, phonemes are produced in a way that overlaps them in time, making one or more phonemes begin while other phonemes are still being produced—the articulations coincide. Not only do phonemes within a word overlap, but the boundaries between words in continuous speech also tend to overlap. Although this overlapping of speech sounds may seem to create additional problems for perceiving speech, coarticulation is viewed as necessary for the effective transmission of speech information, given the previously mentioned deficiencies in perceiving other sounds (Liberman, Cooper, Shankweiler, & Studdert-Kennedy, 1967). Thus, speech perception is viewed as different from other perceptual abilities, due to both the linguistic nature of the information and the particular way in which information must be encoded for effective transmission.

So how do we perceive speech with such ease? As you can imagine, there are many alternative theories of speech perception. These theories differ mainly as to whether speech perception is viewed as special or ordinary with respect to other types of auditory perception.

The View of Speech Perception as Ordinary

One main approach equates processes of speech perception with processes of auditory perception of other sounds. These kinds of theories emphasize either template-matching or feature-detection processes. Such theories postulate that there are distinct stages of neural processing, whereby in one stage, speech sounds are analyzed into their components, and in another stage, these components are analyzed for patterns and matched to a prototype or template (e.g., Kuhl, 1991; Massaro, 1987; Stevens & Blumstein, 1981). One theory of this kind is the *phonetic refinement theory* (Pisoni, Nusbaum, Luce, & Slowiaczek, 1985), which says that we start with an analysis of auditory sensations and shift to higher-level processing, identifying words on the basis of successively paring down the possibilities for matches between each of the phonemes and the words we already know from memory. In this theory, the initial sound that establishes the set of possible words we have heard need not be the first phoneme alone. You may have observed this phenomenon yourself on a conscious level. Have you ever been watching a movie or listening to a lecture when it takes you a few moments to figure out what the speaker must have said when, given that you have heard only a garbled sound? To *decide* what you heard, you may have gone through a conscious process of phonetic refinement. A similar theoretical idea is embodied by the TRACE model (McClelland & Elman, 1986), according to which speech perception begins with three levels of feature detection: the level of acoustic features, the level of phonemes, and the level of words. According to this theory, speech perception is highly interactive, with lower levels affecting higher levels and vice versa.

One trait these theories have in common is that they all require decision-making processes above and beyond feature detection or template matching. Thus, the speech we perceive may differ from the speech sounds that actually reach our ears because cognitive and contextual factors influence our perception of the sensed signal. For example, the *phonemic-restoration effect* (Samuel, 1981; Warren, 1970; Warren & Warren, 1970) involves integrating what we know with what we hear when we perceive speech.

Suppose that you were in an experiment, listening to a sentence having the following pattern: "It was found that the *eel was on the __________." For the final word, one of the following words was inserted: *axle, shoe, table,* or *orange.* In addition, the speaker inserted a cough instead of the initial sound where the asterisk appeared in "*eel." Virtually all subjects are unaware that a consonant has been deleted, and the sound they recall having heard differs according to the context, such that the subjects recall hearing "the *wheel* was on the axle," "the *heel* was on the shoe," "the *{meal}* was on the table," or "the *peel* was on the orange." In essence, they restore the missing phoneme that best suits the context of the sentence.

Phonemic restoration is similar to the visual phenomenon of closure, based on incomplete visual information. Indeed, one main approach to auditory perception attempts to extend the Gestalt principles of visual perception (e.g., symmetry, proximity, similarity) to various acoustic events, including speech (Bregman, 1990). Thus, theories that consider speech perception ordinary use general perceptual principles of feature-detection and Gestalt psychology to explain how listeners understand speech. Other theorists, though, view speech perception as special.

The View of Speech Perception as Special

One phenomenon in speech perception that led to the notion of specialization is the finding of **categorical perception** of speech sounds. That is, even though the speech sounds we actually hear comprise a continuum of variation in sound waves, we perceive discontinuous categories of speech sounds. This phenomenon can be seen in the perception of the consonant-vowel combinations, *ba, da,* and *ga.* The acoustic difference between these syllables centers on distinct patterns of variation in frequency glides in the speech signal, with some patterns leading to perception of *ba,* others to perception of *da,* and still others to perception of *ga.* Moreover, within each syllable category, there are differences in the sound patterns for different instances that do not influence speech perception—the *ba* that you said yesterday differs from the *ba* you say today, but is not perceived as different. This categorical form of perception does not apply to a nonspeech sound, such as a tone, where continuous differences in *pitch* (how high or low the tone is) are heard as continuous and distinct.

In a now classic study, researchers used a speech synthesizer to mimic this natural variation in syllable acoustic patterns and to control the acoustic difference between the syllables (Liberman, Harris, Hoffman, & Griffith,1957). Specifically, Liberman et al. created a series of consonant-vowel sounds that changed in equal increments from *ba* to *da* to *ga.* People who listened to the synthesized syllables, however, heard a sudden switch from the sound category of *ba* to the sound category of *da* (and likewise from the category of *da* to that of *ga*). Furthermore, this difference in labeling the syllables led to poorer discrimination within a phoneme category, and enhanced discrimination across phoneme boundaries. Thus, although the tokens were physically equal in acoustic distance from one another, people only heard the tokens that also differed in phonetic label as different—discrimination of two neighboring *ba*s was poor, while discrimination of *ba* from its neighboring *da* was preserved. Because normal perceptual processing should discriminate equally between all equally spaced pairs of the different tokens along the continuum, the researchers concluded that speech is perceived via specialized processes.

These and other findings led Alvin Liberman and colleagues to investigate the notion that speech perception relies on special processes, and to propose the early but still influential *motor theory* of speech perception (Liberman, Cooper, Shankweiler, & Studdert-Kennedy, 1967; Liberman & Mattingly, 1985). The theory was developed to explain how listeners overcome the context-sensitivity of phonetic segments that arise from coarticulation, resulting in categorical perception phenomena. To return to an earlier example, the /p/ spoken in the word *lip* differs acoustically from the /ph/ spoken in the word *put.* This is due largely to the differences in the coarticulatory context of the two instances of the phoneme—the overlapping of /p/ with *li-* versus *-ut* causes the /p/ to sound different. Why do English-speakers treat the /p/ and /ph/ as the same phoneme? According to the motor theory, speech perception depends on both what we hear a speaker articulate (in this case, /p/ and /ph/) and on what we infer as the intended articulations of the speaker (in this case, only /p/). Thus, the listener uses specialized processes involved in producing speech in order to perceive speech, overcoming the effects of coarticulation and leading to phenomena of categorical perception. Since the early work of Liberman and colleagues, the phenomenon of categorical perception has been extended to the perception of other kinds of stimuli, such as color and facial emotion, weakening the claims that speech perception is special (Jusczyk, 1997). However, supporters of the speech-is-special position still maintain that other forms of evidence indicate that speech is perceived via specialized processes.

One such distinctive aspect of human speech perception can be seen in the so-called *McGurk effect* (McGurk & MacDonald, 1976), which involves the synchrony of visual and auditory perceptions. Imagine yourself watching a movie. So long as the soundtrack corresponds to the speakers' lip movements, you encounter no problems. However, suppose that the soundtrack indicates one thing (e.g., "da") at the same time that the actor's lips clearly make the movements for another sound (e.g., "ba"). You are likely to hear a compromise sound (e.g., "tha") that is neither what was said nor what was seen. You somehow synthesize the auditory and visual information, coming up with a result that is unlike either. For this reason, poorly dubbed movies of foreign origin can be so confusing.

In normal conversation, we use lip reading to augment our perception of speech, particularly in situations in which background noise may make speech perception more difficult. The motor theory accounts for this integration quite easily because articulatory information includes visual and auditory information. However, believers in other theories interpret these findings as support for more general perceptual processes that naturally integrate information across sensory modalities (Massaro, 1987; Massaro & Cohen, 1990).

Is a synthesis of these opposing views possible? Perhaps one reason for the complexity of this issue lies in the nature of speech perception itself, which involves both linguistic and perceptual attributes. From a purely perceptual perspective, speech is just a relatively complex signal that is not treated qualitatively differently from other signals. From a psycholinguistic perspective, speech is special because it lies within the domain of language, a special human ability. Indeed, cognitive psychology textbooks differ in terms of where speech perception is discussed, in the context of language or in that of perception. Thus, the diversity of views on the nature of speech perception can be seen as reflecting the differences in how researchers treat speech—as regular acoustic signals or as more special phonetic messages (Remez, 1994).

SEMANTICS AND SYNTAX

Language is very difficult to put into words.

—*Voltaire*

SEMANTICS

The opening of this chapter quoted from Helen Keller's description of her first awareness that words had meanings. You probably do not remember the moment that words first came alive to you, but your parents surely do. In fact, one of the greatest joys of being a parent is to watch your children's amazing discovery that words have meanings. In semantics, we sometimes refer to the strict dictionary definition of a word as its **denotation,** whereas we refer to a word's emotional overtones, presuppositions, and other nonexplicit meanings as its **connotations.**

How do we understand word meanings in the first place? Recall from previous chapters that we encode meanings into memory through *concepts*—ideas (mental representations) to which we may attach various characteristics and with which we may connect various other ideas, such as through propositions—as well as through images and perhaps also motor patterns for implementing particular procedures. Here, we are concerned only with concepts, particularly in terms of words as arbitrary symbols for concepts.

Actually, when we think of words as concepts, words are quite economical ways in which to manipulate related information. For example, when you think about the single word *desk,* you may also conjure all these things:

- All the instances of desks in existence anywhere,
- Instances of desks that exist only in your imagination,
- All of the characteristics of desks,
- All of the things you might do with desks,
- All of the other concepts you might link to desks (e.g., things you put on or in desks or places where you might find desks).

Having a word for something helps us to add new information to our existing information about that concept. For example, because you have access to the word *desk,* when you have new experiences related to desks or otherwise learn new things about desks, you have a word around which to organize all this related information.

Recall, too, the constructive nature of memory, in which having word labels (e.g., "washing clothes," "peace march") (a) facilitates the ease of understanding and remembering a text passage, (b) enhances subjects' recall of the shape of a droodle, and (c) affects the accuracy of eyewitness testimony. Brian Ross and Thomas Spalding (1994) even suggest that having words as concepts for things helps us in our everyday nonverbal interactions. For example, Ross and Spalding note that our concepts of skunk and of dog allow us more easily to recognize the difference between the two, even if we see an animal only for a moment. This rapid recognition enables us to respond appropriately, depending on which we saw. Clearly, being able to comprehend the conceptual meanings of words is important. Just how do words combine to convey meaning, though?

SYNTAX

An equally important part of the psychology of language is the analysis of linguistic structure—specifically, **syntax,** the systematic way in which words can be combined and sequenced to make meaningful phrases and sentences (D. W. Carroll, 1986). Whereas speech perception chiefly studies phonetic structure of language, syntax focuses on the study of the grammar of phrases and sentences, in other words, the regularity of structure.

Although you have doubtless heard the word *grammar* before, in regard to how people *ought* to structure their sentences, psycholinguists use the word *grammar* in a slightly different way. Specifically, **grammar** is the study of language in terms of noticing regular patterns. These patterns relate to the functions and relationships of words in a sentence—extending as broadly as the level of discourse and as narrowly as the pronunciation and meaning of individual words. In your English courses, you may have been introduced to *prescriptive grammar,* which prescribes the "correct" ways in which to structure the use of written and spoken language. Of greater interest to psycholinguists is *descriptive grammar,* in which an attempt is made to describe the structures, functions, and relationships of words in language.

Psycholinguist Steven Pinker (1994) gives this example of a sentence that illustrates the contrast between prescriptive and descriptive approaches to grammar: When Junior observes his father carrying upstairs an unappealing bedtime book, Junior responds, "Daddy, what did you bring that book that I don't want to be read to out of up for?" (p. 97). Whereas Junior's utterance would shiver the spine of any prescriptive grammarian, Junior's ability to produce such a complex sentence, with such intricate internal interdependencies, would please descriptive grammarians.

Why does syntax prompt such pleasure? Chiefly, for two reasons: First, the study of syntax allows analysis of language in manageable—and therefore relatively easily studied—units; and second, it offers limitless possibilities for exploration. There are virtually no bounds to the possible combinations of words that may be used to form sentences (the property of productivity of language). In English, as in any language, we can take a particular set of words (or morphemes, to be more accurate) and a particular set of rules for combining the items and produce a breathtakingly vast array of meaningful utterances. Barring intentional quotations, if you were to go to the U.S. Library of Congress, randomly select any sentence from any book, and then search for an identical sentence in the vast array of sentences in the books therein, you would be unlikely to find the identical sentence (Pinker, 1994).

INVESTIGATING COGNITIVE PSYCHOLOGY

Mark an asterisk next to the sentences that are not grammatical, regardless of whether the sentences are meaningful or accurate:

1. The student the book.
2. Bought the book.
3. Bought the student the book.
4. The book was bought by the student.
5. By whom was the book bought?
6. By student the bought book.
7. The student was bought by the book.
8. Who bought the book?
9. The book bought the student.
10. The book bought.

THE SYNTAX TENDENCY

Another reason that syntax intrigues cognitive psychologists, as well as linguists, is the remarkable degree to which people demonstrate a knack for understanding syntactical structure (no matter what your high-school English teacher may have said). As the preceding demonstration showed, you, I, and other fluent speakers of a language can immediately recognize whether particular sentences and particular word orders are or are not grammatical (Bock, 1990; Pinker, 1994). We can do so even when the sentences are meaningless, as in Chomsky's sentence, "Colorless green ideas sleep furiously," or composed of nonsense words, as in Lewis Carroll's *Jabberwocky,* " 'Twas brillig and the slithy toves did gyre and gimble in the wabe."

Also, just as we show semantic priming of word meanings in memory, we show *syntactic priming* of sentence structures. That is, we spontaneously tend to use syntactic structures that parallel the structures of sentences we have just heard (Bock, 1990; Bock, Loebell, & Morey, 1992). For example, a speaker will be more likely to use a passive construction (e.g., "The student was praised by the professor") after hearing a passive construction, even when the topics of the sentences differ.

Other evidence of our uncanny aptitude for syntax is shown in the speech errors we produce (Bock, 1990). Even when we accidentally switch the placement of two words in a sentence, we still form grammatical, if meaningless or nonsensical, sentences. We almost invariably switch nouns for nouns, verbs for verbs, prepositions for prepositions, and so on. For example, we may say, "I put the oven in the cake," but we will probably not say, "I put the cake oven in the." We usually even attach (and detach) appropriate function morphemes to make the switched words fit their new positions. For example, when meaning to say, "The butter knives are in the drawer," we may say, "The butter drawers are in the knife," changing "drawer" to plural and "knives" to singular, to preserve the grammaticality of the sentence. Even among so-called agrammatic aphasics, who have extreme difficulties in both comprehending and producing language, substitution errors in speech seem to preserve syntactic categories (Butterworth & Howard, 1987; Garrett, 1992).

The preceding examples seem to indicate that we humans have some mental mechanism for classifying words according to syntactical categories, and this classification mechanism is separate from the meanings for the words (Bock, 1990). When we compose sentences, we seem to *parse* the sentences, assigning appropriate syntactic categories (often called "parts of speech," e.g., noun, verb, article) to each component of the sentence. We then use the syntax rules for the language to construct grammatical sequences of the parsed components.

INVESTIGATING COGNITIVE PSYCHOLOGY

Using the following 10 words, create five strings of words that make grammatical sentences and five sequences of words that violate the syntax rules of English grammar: *ball, basket, bounced, into, put, red, rolled, tall, the, woman.*

To complete the preceding task, you mentally classified the words into syntactical categories (even if you did not know the correct labels for the categories), and then you arranged the words into grammatical sequences, according to the syntactical categories for the words and your implicit knowledge of English syntax rules. Before you get shoulder strain from patting yourself vigorously on the back, you will see later in the chapter that most 4-year-olds can demonstrate the same ability to parse words into categories and to arrange them into grammatical sentences, although most 4-year-olds probably cannot label the syntactic categories for any of the words.

Early in this century, linguists who studied syntax largely focused on how sentences could be analyzed in terms of sequences of phrases (e.g., noun phrases and verb phrases, mentioned previously) and of how phrases could be parsed into various syntactical categories (e.g., nouns, verbs, adjectives). Such analyses are termed **phrase-structure grammars,** because they look at the structure of phrases as they are used. The rules governing the sequences of words are termed *phrase-structure rules.* To observe the interrelationships of phrases within a sentence, linguists often use tree diagrams, such as the ones shown in Figure 9.1, although various other models have been proposed (e.g., relational grammar, D. Perlmutter, 1983; lexical-functional grammar, Bresnan, 1982).

Tree diagrams help to reveal the interrelationships of syntactic classes within the phrase structures of sentences (Bock, 1990; Wasow, 1989). In particular, such diagrams show that sentences are not merely organized chains of words, strung together sequentially, but rather are organized into hierarchical structures of embedded phrases. The use of tree diagrams helps to highlight many aspects of how we use language, including both our linguistic sophistication and our difficulties in using language. Look again at Figure 9.1, focusing on the two possible tree diagrams for one sentence, showing its two possible meanings. By observing tree diagrams of ambiguous sentences, psycholinguists can better pinpoint the source of confusion.

FIGURE 9.1 **TREE DIAGRAMS OF TWO PHRASE STRUCTURES**

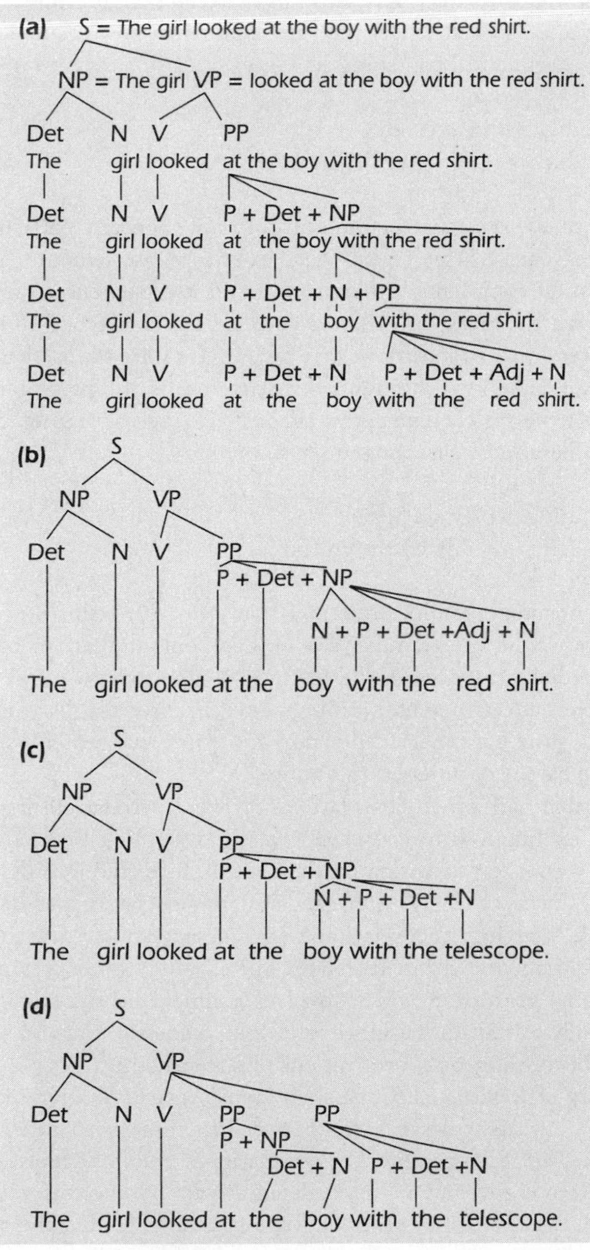

Phrase-structure grammars illustrate the hierarchies of phrases within sentences. (a) The sentence, "The girl looked at the boy with the red shirt" may be diagrammed as shown here. (b) Linguists usually abbreviate tree diagrams as shown here, in the abbreviated linguistic tree diagram of the sentence shown in (a). Tree diagrams (c) and (d) show the possible ways for analyzing the sentence, "The girl looked at the boy with the telescope."

In 1957, Noam Chomsky revolutionized the study of syntax by suggesting that to understand syntax, we must not only observe the interrelationships among phrases within sentences, but also the syntactical relationships between sentences. Specifically, Chomsky observed that particular sentences and their tree diagrams show peculiar relationships.

Consider, for example, the following sentences:

S_1: Susie greedily ate the crocodile.
S_2: The crocodile was eaten greedily by Susie.

Oddly enough, a phrase-structure grammar would not show any particular relation at all between sentences S_1 and S_2 (see Figure 9.2). Indeed, phrase-structure analyses of S_1 and S_2 would look almost completely different. Yet, the two sentences differ only in voice, with the first sentence expressed in the active voice and the second in the passive voice. Recall from chapter 7 that propositions may be used for illustrating that the same underlying meanings can be derived through alternative means of representation. The preceding two sentences represent the same proposition: "ate (greedily)(Susie, crocodile)."

Consider another pair of paraphrased sentences:

S_3: The crocodile greedily ate Susie.
S_4: Susie was eaten greedily by the crocodile.

Phrase-structure grammar would similarly show no relationship between S_3 and S_4. What's more, phrase-structure grammar would show some similarities of surface structure between corresponding sentences in the first and second pairs (S_1 and S_3; S_2 and S_4)—which clearly have quite different meanings—particularly to Susie and the crocodile. Apparently, an adequate grammar would address the fact that sentences with similar surface structures can have very different meanings.

This observation and other observations of the interrelationships among various phrase structures led linguists to go beyond merely describing various individual phrase structures and to focus their attention on the relationships among different phrase structures. Principally, Chomsky (1957) suggested that linguists may gain deeper understanding of syntax by studying the relationships among phrase structures that involve transformations of elements within sentences. Specifically, Chomsky suggested the study of **transformational grammar,** which involves augmenting the study of phrase structures with the study of transformational rules that guide the ways in which underlying propositions can be rearranged to form various phrase structures.

A simple way of looking at Chomsky's transformational grammar is to say that "Transformations . . . are rules that map tree structures onto other tree structures" (Wasow, 1989, p. 170). For example, transformational grammar considers how the tree-structure diagrams in Figure 9.2 are interrelated. By applying transformational rules, the tree structure of S_1 can be mapped onto the tree structure of S_2, and the structure of S_3 can be mapped onto the tree structure of S_4.

Chomsky used the term **deep structure** to refer to an underlying syntactic structure that links various phrase structures through the application of various transformation rules; he used the term **surface structure** to refer to any of the various phrase structures that may result from such transformations. Many casual readers of Chomsky have misconstrued

FIGURE 9.2 **TREE DIAGRAMS AND RELATIONSHIPS AMONG VARIOUS PHRASE STRUCTURES**

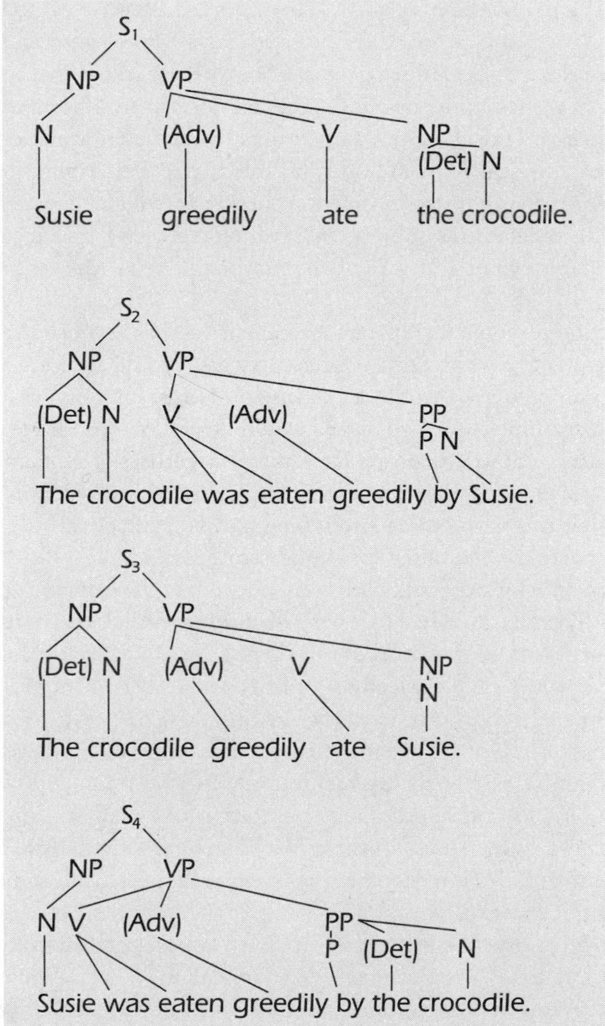

Phrase-structure grammars show surprising dissimilarities between S_1 and S_2 yet surprising similarities between S_1 and S_3 or between S_2 and S_4. Noam Chomsky suggested that to understand syntax, we must also consider a way of viewing the interrelationships among various phrase structures.

Chomsky's terms to suggest that deep structures signify profound underlying meanings for sentences, whereas surface structures refer only to superficial interpretations of sentences. Chomsky meant only to show that differing phrase structures may have a relationship that is not immediately apparent by using phrase-structure grammar alone (as in the example of

"Susie greedily ate the crocodile" and "The crocodile was eaten greedily by Susie"). To detect the underlying relationship between two phrase structures, transformation rules must be applied.

RELATIONSHIPS BETWEEN SYNTACTICAL AND LEXICAL STRUCTURES

Chomsky (1965, cited in Wasow, 1989) also addressed how syntactical structures may interact with lexical structures. In particular, Chomsky suggested that our mental lexicon contains more than the semantic meanings attached to each word (or morpheme). According to Chomsky, each lexical item also contains syntactic information. This syntactic information for each lexical item indicates (a) the syntactical category of the item (e.g., noun vs. verb), (b) the appropriate syntactic contexts in which the particular morpheme may be used (e.g., pronouns as subjects vs. as direct objects), and (c) any idiosyncratic information about the syntactical uses of the morpheme (e.g., the treatment of irregular verbs).

For example, there would be separate lexical entries for the word *spread* categorized as a noun and for *spread* as a verb. Each lexical entry also would indicate which syntactical rules to use for positioning the word, depending on which category was applicable in the given context. For example, as a verb, *spread* would not follow the article *the,* although as a noun, *spread* would be allowed to do so. Even the peculiarities of syntax for a given lexical entry would be stored in the lexicon. For example, the lexical entry for the verb *spread* would indicate that this verb deviates from the normal syntactical rule for forming past tenses (i.e., "add *-ed* to the stem used for the present tense").

You may wonder why we would clutter up our mental lexicon with so much syntactical information. There is an advantage to attaching syntactical, context-sensitive, and idiosyncratic information to the items in our mental lexicon: If we add to the complexity of our mental lexicon, we can drastically simplify the number and complexity of the rules we need in our mental syntax. For example, by attaching the idiosyncratic treatment of irregular verbs (e.g., *spread* or *fall)* to our mental lexicon, we do not have to endure different syntactical rules for each verb. By making our lexicon more complex, we allow our syntax to be simpler, so that appropriate transformations may be simple and relatively context free. Once we know the basic syntax of a language, we can easily apply the rules to all items in our lexicon. We can then gradually expand our lexicon to provide increasing complexity and sophistication.

Not all cognitive psychologists agree with all aspects of Chomsky's theories (e.g., Bock, Loebell, & Morey, 1992; Garrett, 1992; Jackendoff, 1991). Many particularly disagree with his emphasis on syntax (form) over semantics (meaning). Nonetheless, several cognitive psychologists have proposed models of language comprehension and production that include the notion that lexical elements (morphemes) contain various kinds of syntactic information, indicating appropriate syntactic categories, idiosyncratic violations of syntactic rules (e.g., treatment of irregular verbs or collective nouns), peculiarities regarding appropriate contexts for usage, and so on.

How do we link the elements in our mental lexicon to the elements in our syntactical structures? Various models for such bridging have been proposed (e.g., Bock, Loebell, & Morey, 1992; Jackendoff, 1991). According to some of these models, when we parse sentences by syntactic categories, we create slots for each item in the sentence. For example, in the sentence, "Juan gave María the book from the shelf," there is a slot for a noun used as (a) a subject (Juan), (b) as a direct object (the book), (c) as an indirect object (María), and (d) as objects of prepositions (the shelf). There are also slots for the verb, the preposition, and the articles.

In turn, lexical items contain information regarding the kinds of slots into which the items can be placed, based on the kinds of **thematic roles** the items can fill. The thematic roles that have been identified include *agent* (the "doer" of any action), *patient* (the direct recipient of the action), *beneficiary* (the indirect recipient of the action), *instrument* (the means by which the action is implemented), *location* (the place where the action occurs), *source* (where the action originated), and *goal* (where the action is going; Bock, 1990; Fromkin & Rodman, 1988). According to this view of how syntax and semantics are linked, the various syntactical slots (e.g., subject nouns) can be filled by lexical entries with corresponding thematic roles (e.g., agent). For example, nouns that can fill *agent* roles can be inserted into slots for subjects of phrases; *patient* roles correspond to slots for direct objects; *beneficiary* roles fit with indirect objects, and so on. Nouns that are objects of prepositions may be filled with various thematic roles (e.g., location—at the beach; source—from the kitchen; goal—to the classroom). So far, we have concentrated on describing the structure and processes of language in its most developed state, but how do we acquire this remarkable ability?

Practical Applications of Cognitive Psychology

Given what you now know about processes of speech perception, semantics, and syntax, think about ways to make your speech production easier for others to perceive. If you are speaking to someone whose primary language differs from yours, try slowing down your speech, and exaggerating the length of time between words. Be sure to enunciate consonant sounds carefully, without making your vowels sounds too long. Use simpler sentence constructions—break down lengthy and involved sentences into smaller units. Insert longer pauses between sentences to give the person time to translate the sentence into propositional form. Communication may feel more effortful, but will probably be more effective.

Language Acquisition

In the past, debates about the acquisition of language centered on the same theme as debates about the acquisition of any ability—the nature versus nurture theme. However, current thinking about language acquisition has incorporated the understanding that acquiring language really involves a natural endowment modified by the environment. Thus, the approach to studying language acquisition now revolves around discovering what abilities are innately given, and how these abilities are tempered by the environment of the child—a process aptly termed "innately guided learning" (see Jusczyk, 1997). Before examining the nature–nurture debate, let's take a look at what seems to be universal in language acquisition. One thing that seems to be universal is a series of stages of language acquisition.

STAGES OF LANGUAGE ACQUISITION

Around the world, people seem to acquire their primary language in pretty much the same sequence and in just about the same way. Within the first years of life, we humans seem to progress through the following stages in producing language:

1. Cooing, which comprises all possible phones;
2. Babbling, which comprises only the distinct phonemes that characterize the primary language of the infant;
3. One-word utterances;
4. Two-word utterances and telegraphic speech;
5. Basic adult sentence structure (present by about age 4 years), with continuing vocabulary acquisition.

In recent years, research on the development of speech perception finds the same overall pattern of progression—from more general to more specific abilities. That is, as infants we are initially able to distinguish among all possible phonetic contrasts, but over time we lose the ability to distinguish nonnative contrasts in favor of those used in the our native language environment (see Jusczyk, 1997). Thus, some aspects of infants' speech perception and production abilities mirror each other, developing from more general to more specific abilities. From day one, infants appear to be programmed to tune into their linguistic environment with the specific goal of acquiring language.

For example, newborns seem to respond preferentially to their mother's voice (DeCasper & Fifer, 1980), and they seem to respond motorically in synchrony with the speech of the caregivers who interact with them directly (Field, 1978; J. A. Martin, 1981; Schaffer, 1977; Snow, 1977; D. Stern, 1977). Infants also prefer to listen to someone speaking in what will be their native language over a future non-native language, possibly focusing on the rhythmic structure of the language (Bertoncini, 1993; Mehler, Dupous, Nazzi, & Dehaene-Lambertz, 1996). If you were to videotape infants' motor responses while the infants were attending to someone speaking to them, their movements would seem to be dancing in time with the rhythm of the speech. The emotional expression of infants also seems to be matched to that of their caregivers (Fogel, 1991).

Infants have also been known to produce sounds of their own; most obviously, the communicative aspect of crying—whether intentional or not—works quite well. In terms of language acquisition, however, it is the **cooing** of infants that most intrigues linguists. Cooing is the infant's oral expression that explores the production of all the possible phones humans can produce. The cooing of infants around the world, including deaf infants, is indistinguishable across babies and across languages.

During the cooing stage, hearing infants can also discriminate among all phones, not just the phonemes characteristic of their own language. For example, during this stage, both Japanese and American infants can discriminate the /l/ from the /r/ phoneme. However, as infants move into the next stage, they gradually lose this ability, and by 1 year of age, Japanese infants—for whom the distinction does not make a phonemic difference—no longer make this discrimination (Eimas, 1985; Tsushima et al., 1994).

Loss of discrimination ability is not limited to Japanese infants. Janet Werker (1994; Werker & Tees, 1984) found that infants who grow up in homes where English is spoken are able to distinguish early in life between phonemes that are different in the Hindi language of India but that are not different in English. In English, the phonemes are allophones of the /t/ sound. In particular, the English-speaking infants are able to make the discrimination with roughly 95% accuracy at between 6 and 8 months of age. By 8 to 10 months, the infants' accuracy is down to 70%, and by 10 to 12 months it is down to a mere 20%. As they grow older, infants clearly lose the capacity to make discriminations that are not relevant to their language.

At the babbling stage, deaf infants no longer vocalize, and the sounds produced by hearing infants change. **Babbling** is the infant's preferential production of only those distinct phonemes characteristic of the infant's own language (e.g., J. L. Locke, 1994; Petitto & Marentette, 1991). Thus, although the cooing of infants around the world is essentially the same, infant babbling distinctively characterizes the language the infant is acquiring. As suggested previously, the ability of the infant to perceive, as well as to produce, nonphonemic phones recedes during this stage.

Eventually, the infant utters his or her first word—followed shortly by one or two more, and soon after, yet a few more. The infant uses these one-word utterances—termed *holophrases*—to convey intentions, desires, and demands. Usually, the words are nouns describing familiar objects that the child observes (e.g., *car, book, ball, baby, nose)* or wants (e.g., *Mama, Dada, juice, cookie).*

By 18 months of age, children typically have vocabularies of 3 to 100 words (Siegler, 1986). Because the young child's vocabulary cannot yet encompass all the child wishes to describe, the child quite deftly overextends the meaning of words in her or his existing lexicon, to cover things and ideas for which a new word is lacking. For example, the general term for a man may be "Dada"—which can be quite distressing to a new father in a public setting—and the general term for any kind of four-legged animal may be "doggie." The linguistic term for this adaptation is **overextension error.** Young children have to overextend the meanings of the words they know because they have few words in their vocabulary. How do they decide which words to use when overextending the meanings of the words they know?

A *feature hypothesis* suggests that children form definitions that include too few features (E. V. Clark, 1973). Thus, a child might refer to a cat as a dog because of a mental rule that if an animal has the feature of four legs, it is a "doggie." An alternative *functional hypothesis* (K. Nelson, 1973) suggests that children first learn to use words that describe important functions or purposes: Lamps give light, and blankets make us warm. According to this view, overextension errors are due to functional confusions. A dog and a cat both do similar things and serve the same purposes as pets, so a child is likely to confuse them. Although the functional hypothesis has usually been viewed as an alternative to the feature hypothesis, both mechanisms could possibly be at work in children's overextensions.

Gradually, between 1.5 and 2.5 years of age, children start combining single words to produce two-word utterances. Thus begins an understanding of syntax. These early syntactical communications seem more like telegrams than conversations because the articles, prepositions, and other function morphemes are usually left out. Hence, linguists refer to these early utterances with rudimentary syntax as telegraphic speech. In fact, **telegraphic**

speech can be used to describe two- or three-word utterances, and even slightly longer ones, if they have these same characteristic omissions of some function morphemes.

Vocabulary expands rapidly, more than tripling from about 300 words at about 2 years of age, to about 1,000 words at about 3 years of age. Almost incredibly, by age 4 years, children acquire the foundations of adult syntax and language structure (see Table 9.3). By age 5 years, most children can also understand and produce quite complex and uncommon sentence constructions, and by age 10 years, children's language is fundamentally the same as that of adults.

TABLE 9.3 **DEVELOPMENTAL CHANGES ASSOCIATED WITH LANGUAGE ACQUISITION**

Regardless of the language children acquire, children around the world seem to follow the same developmental pattern, at about the same ages.

Approximate Age	Characteristics of Age	Interaction With Information Processing
Prenatal First several months About the second 6 months after birth	Responsivity to human voices Cooing, which comprises all possible phones Babbling, which comprises only the distinct phonemes that characterize the primary language of the infant	As sounds become more meaningful, the infant's perception of the sounds becomes more selective, and the infant's ability to remember sounds increases.
About 1 to 3 years of age	One-word utterances Two-word utterances Telegraphic speech	As fluency and comprehension increase, the ability mentally to manipulate linguistic symbols increases, as does conceptual development; overextension errors occur when children try to apply their limited vocabulary to a variety of situations, but as children's vocabulary becomes more specialized, these errors occur less often.
About 3 to 4 years	Simple sentences that reflect tremendous expansion of vocabulary, as well as remarkably adept understanding of syntax, despite errors of overregularization	Vocabulary and concepts continue to expand in terms of both comprehension and fluency, and the child internalizes rules of syntax; overregularization errors offer insights into how children form rules about language structures.
By about 4 years of age	Basic adult sentence structure; some increases in complexity of structure continue through adolescence; vocabulary continues to increase, although at a declining rate	Children's language patterns and strategies for language acquisition are studied in much the same ways as those for adults; however, their metacognitive strategies for acquiring vocabulary become increasingly sophisticated throughout childhood.

Nature and Nurture

If neither nature alone nor nurture alone adequately explains all aspects of language acquisition, just how might nature facilitate nurture in the process? Noted linguist Noam Chomsky proposed (1965, 1972) that humans have an innate **language-acquisition device (LAD)**, which facilitates language acquisition. That is, we humans seem to be biologically preconfigured to be ready to acquire language. Given the complex neuropsychology of other aspects of human perception and thought, to consider that we may be neuropsychologically predisposed to acquire language is not altogether absurd.

Several observations of humans support the notion that we are predisposed to acquire language. For one thing, human speech perception is quite remarkable, given the nature of auditory processing capacities for other sounds. Moreover, all children within a broad normal range of abilities and of environments seem to acquire language at an incredibly rapid rate. In fact, deaf children acquire sign language in about the same way and at about the same rate as hearing children acquire spoken language. If you have ever struggled to acquire a second language, you can appreciate the relative ease and speed with which young children seem to acquire their first language. This accomplishment is particularly remarkable, given that children are offered a relatively modest quantity and variety of linguistic input (whether speech or signs) in relation to the highly sophisticated internalized language structures children create. Children seem to have a knack for acquiring an implicit understanding of the many rules of language structure, as well as for applying those rules to new vocabulary and new contexts.

Perhaps even more surprising, almost all children seem to acquire these aspects of language in the same progression and at more or less the same time. On the other hand, the linguistic environment clearly plays a role in the language-acquisition process. In fact, there seem to be *critical periods*—times of rapid development, during which a particular ability must be developed if it is ever to develop adequately—for acquiring these understandings of language. During such periods, the environment plays a crucial role. For example, the cooing and babbling stages seem to be a critical period for acquiring a native speaker's discrimination and production of the distinctive phonemes of a particular language; during this critical period, the child's linguistic context must provide those distinctive phonemes.

There seems to be a critical period for acquiring a native understanding of a language's syntax, too. Perhaps the greatest support for this view comes from studies of adult users of American Sign Language (ASL). Among adults who have signed ASL for 30 years or more, researchers could discernibly differentiate among those who acquired ASL before age 4 years, between ages 4 and 6 years, and after age 12 years. Despite 30 years of signing, those who acquired ASL later in childhood showed less profound understanding of the distinctive syntax of ASL (Meier, 1991; Newport, 1990).

Studies of linguistically isolated children seem to provide additional support for the notion of the interaction of both physiological maturation and environmental support. Of the rare children who have been linguistically isolated, those who are rescued at younger ages seem to acquire more sophisticated language structures than do those who are rescued when they are older. (The research on critical periods for language acquisition is much more equivocal for the acquisition of additional languages, after acquiring a first one; see Bahrick, Hall, Goggin, Bahrick, & Berger, 1994; see also chapter 10).

Two additional observations, which apply to all humans, at all ages, also support the notion that nature contributes to language acquisition: First, humans possess several physiological structures that serve no purpose other than to produce speech (G. S. Dell, personal communication, November 1994); and second, myriad universal characteristics have been documented across the vast array of human languages. Since 1963, when a lone linguist documented 45 universal characteristics across 30 languages (e.g., Finnish, Hindi, Swahili, Quechua, and Serbian), hundreds of universal patterns have been documented across languages around the globe (see Pinker, 1994).

Neither nature nor nurture alone appears to determine language acquisition. One such postulate—**hypothesis testing**—suggests this integration of nature and nurture: Children acquire language by mentally forming tentative hypotheses regarding language, based on their inherited facility for language acquisition (nature), and then testing these hypotheses in the environment (nurture). The implementation of this process is said to follow several operating principles (Slobin, 1971, 1985). In forming hypotheses, young children look for and attend to these things:

1. Patterns of changes in the forms of words,
2. Morphemic inflections that signal changes in meaning, especially suffixes,
3. Sequences of morphemes, including both the sequences of affixes and roots and the sequences of words in sentence.

In addition, children learn to avoid exceptions and to figure out various other patterns characteristic of their native tongue. Although not all linguists support the hypothesis-testing view, the phenomena of overregularization (using and sometimes overapplying rules) and of language productivity (creating novel utterances based on some kind of understanding of how to do so) seem to support it.

Elissa Newport (1990) adds a slightly different twist to the hypothesis-testing view, suggesting that while children are acquiring language, they do not pay attention to all aspects of language. Instead, children focus on the perceptually most salient aspects of language, which happen to be the most meaningful aspects in most cases. Although her studies have focused on deaf children's acquisition of ASL, this phenomenon may apply to spoken language as well. Indeed, one study finds that hearing infants do attend to the salient acoustic cues in sentences that mark grammatically critical attributes of sentences (Hirsh-Pasek et al., 1987).

Although few psychologists (if any) have asserted that language is entirely a result of nature, some researchers and theoreticians focus on the environmental mechanisms that children use to acquire language. Three such mechanisms are imitation, modeling, and conditioning.

IMITATION

In imitation, children do exactly what they see others do. Sometimes children do imitate the language patterns of others, especially their parents. Imitation, however, would not in itself be sufficient for acquisition of language. Children must be doing something more. More often, children loosely follow what they hear, a phenomenon referred to as modeling.

MODELING

Even amateur observers of children notice that children's speech patterns and vocabulary model the patterns and vocabulary of the persons in their environment. In fact, parents of very young children seem to go to great lengths to make it easy for children to attend to and to understand what they are saying. Almost without thinking, parents and other adults tend to use a higher pitch than usual, to exaggerate the *vocal inflection* of their speech (i.e., raising and lowering pitch and volume more extremely than normal), and to use simpler sentence constructions when speaking with infants and young children (Rice, 1989). This distinctive form of adult speech has been termed *motherese,* or perhaps more accurately, **child-directed speech.**

Through child-directed speech, adults seem to go out of their way to make language interesting and comprehensible to infants and other young children. In this way, they also make it possible for the infants to model aspects of the adults' behavior. Indeed, infants do seem to prefer listening to child-directed speech more than to other forms of adult speech (Fernald, 1985). These exaggerations seem to gain and hold infants' attention, to signal to them when to take turns in vocalizing, and communicate affect (emotion-related information). Across cultures, parents seem to use this specialized form of speech, further tailoring it to particular circumstances: using rising intonations to gain children's attention; falling intonations to comfort them; and brief, discontinuous, rapid-fire explosions of speech to warn against prohibited behavior (Fernald et al., 1989).

Parents even seem to model the correct format for verbal interactions. Early caregiver–child verbal interactions are characterized by verbal turn-taking, in which the caregiver says something and then uses vocal inflection to cue the infant to respond; the infant babbles, sneezes, burps, or otherwise makes some audible response; the caregiver accepts whatever noises the infant makes as valid communicative utterances and replies; and the infant further responds to the cue—and so on for as long as they both show interest in continuing.

Parents also seem to work hard to understand children's early utterances, in which one or two words might be used for conveying an entire array of concepts. As the child grows older and more sophisticated and acquires more language, parents gradually provide less linguistic support and demand increasingly sophisticated utterances from the child. They initially seem to provide a scaffolding from which the child can construct an edifice of language, and as the child's language develops, the parents gradually remove the scaffolding.

Do parental models of language use provide the chief means by which children acquire language? The mechanism of imitation is quite appealing in its simplicity; unfortunately, it does not explain many aspects of language acquisition. For example, if imitation is the primary mechanism, why do children universally begin by producing one-word utterances, then two-word and other telegraphic utterances, and later complete sentences? Why not start out with complete sentences? In addition, perhaps the most compelling argument against imitation alone relates to our linguistic productivity. Shakespeare may have been more productive than most of us, but each of us is quite innovative in the speech we produce. Most of the utterances we produce are novel ones, which we have never heard or read before.

Yet another argument against imitation alone is the phenomenon of **overregularization,** which occurs when young children have acquired an understanding of how a language usually works, and they then apply the general rules of language to the exceptional cases that vary from the norm. For example, instead of imitating her parents' sentence pattern, "The mice fell down the hole, and they ran home," the young child might overregularize the irregular forms and say, "The mouses falled down the hole, and they runned home." The fact that children say things like "mouses" shows that the next mechanism to be considered, conditioning, could not tell the entire story of language acquisition.

CONDITIONING

The mechanism of conditioning is also exquisitely simple: Children hear utterances and associate those utterances with particular objects and events in their environment. They then produce those utterances and are rewarded by their parents and others for having spoken. Initially, their utterances are not perfect, but through successive approximations, children come to speak just as well as native adult speakers of their language. The progression from babbling to one-word utterances to more complex utterances would seem to support the notion that children begin with simple associations, and their utterances gradually increase in complexity and in the degree to which they approximate adult speech.

As with imitation, the simplicity of the proposed conditioning mechanism does not suffice to explain actual language acquisition fully. For one thing, parents are much more likely to respond to the *veridical content* of the child's speech—that is, whether the statement is true or false—than to the relative correctness of the child's grammar and pronunciation (R. Brown, Cazden, & Bellugi, 1969). In addition, even if parents did respond to the grammatical correctness of children's speech, their responses might explain why children eventually stop overregularizing their speech but not why they ever begin doing so. Also, just as linguistic productivity argues against imitation alone, it contradicts conditioning: Children constantly employ novel utterances, for which they have never previously been rewarded. They consistently apply the words and language structures they already know to novel situations and contexts for which they have never before received reinforcement. Thus, through the combined effects of innately given linguistic abilities and exposure to a linguistic environment, infants acquire a language automatically and seemingly effortlessly.

BEYOND THE FIRST YEARS

The foregoing theories offer explanations of how children acquire the foundations of adult language structure by age 4 years or so. However, as remarkable as 4-year-old language achievements are—and they truly are astonishing—few of us would have difficulty recognizing that the vocabulary and the linguistic sophistication of 4-year-olds differ from those of most older children and adults. What changes occur in children's use of language after age 4, and what do such changes imply regarding developmental changes in cognition?

To understand these changes, we explore both verbal comprehension and verbal fluency. In general, children's ability to comprehend language (and to process information) efficiently increases with age (e.g., Hunt, Lunneborg, & Lewis, 1975; Keating & Bobbitt, 1978). Older children also demonstrate greater verbal fluency than do younger children (e.g., Sincoff & Sternberg, 1988). In addition to the increases in verbal comprehension and fluency abilities that develop with age, we can best understand development by looking not simply at a child's age, but also at the strategies a child of a given age uses to comprehend or to generate verbal material. Much of what develops is not just verbal ability, but also the ability to generate useful strategies for verbal comprehension and fluency. These strategies are at the intersection of language acquisition and metacognition and are important aspects of human intelligence (R. J. Sternberg, 1985a).

An interesting aspect of research on strategies of verbal comprehension has been research on comprehension monitoring (Markman, 1977, 1979), which hypothesizes that one of the ways in which we enhance our understanding of verbal information is to monitor (check for accuracy, logic, cohesiveness) what we hear and read. To study the influence of comprehension monitoring, researchers observed children and adults and attempted to correlate comprehension-monitoring skills with assessments of overall comprehension.

Consider a typical experiment. Children between the ages of 8 and 11 years heard passages containing contradictory information. This description of how to make the dessert Baked Alaska is an example (Markman, 1979, p. 656):

> To make it they put the ice cream in a very hot oven. The ice cream in Baked Alaska melts when it gets that hot. Then they take the ice cream out of the oven and serve it right away. When they make Baked Alaska, the ice cream stays firm and does not melt.

Note that the passage contains a blatant internal contradiction, saying both that the ice cream melts and that it does not. Almost half of the young children who saw this passage did not notice the contradiction at all. Even when they were warned in advance about problems with the story, many of the youngest children still did not detect the inconsistency. Thus, young children are not very successful at comprehension monitoring, even when cued to be aware of inconsistencies in the text they read. An important aspect of development of all cognitive skills, including comprehension monitoring, is the improvement that people show in their use of these skills.

SUMMARY

1. **What properties characterize language?** There are at least six properties of *language,* the use of an organized means of combining words in order to communicate: (a) Language permits us to *communicate* with one or more persons who share our language. (b) Language creates an *arbitrary* relationship between a *symbol* and its *referent*—an idea, a thing, a process, a relationship, or a description. (c) Language has a *regular structure;* only particular sequences of symbols (sounds and words) have meaning. Different sequences yield different meanings. (d) The structure of language can be analyzed at *multiple levels* (e.g., phonemic and morphemic). (e) Despite having the limits of a structure, language users can *produce* novel utterances; the possibilities for *generating* new utterances are virtually limitless. (f) Languages constantly *evolve.*

Language involves *verbal comprehension*—the ability to comprehend written and spoken linguistic input, such as words, sentences, and paragraphs—and *verbal fluency*—the ability to produce linguistic output. The smallest units of sound produced by the human vocal tract are *phones; phonemes* are the smallest units of sound that can be used to differentiate meaning in a given language. The smallest semantically meaningful unit in a language is a *morpheme.* Morphemes may be either roots or *affixes* (prefixes or suffixes), which may be either *content morphemes* (conveying the bulk of the word's meaning) or *function morphemes* (augmenting the meaning of the word). A *lexicon* is the repertoire of morphemes in a given language (or for a given language user). The study of the meaningful sequencing of words within phrases and sentences in a given language is *syntax,* and larger units of language are embraced by the study of *discourse.*

2. **What are some of the processes involved in language?** In speech perception, listeners must overcome the influence of *coarticulation* (overlapping) of phonemes on the acoustic structure of the speech signal. *Categorical perception,* the phenomenon in which listeners perceive continuously varying speech sounds as distinct categories, lends support to the notion that speech is perceived via specialized processes. The *motor theory* of speech perception attempts to explain these processes in relation to the processes involved in speech production. Those who believe speech perception is ordinary explain speech perception in terms of feature-detection, prototype, and Gestalt theories of perception.

   Syntax is the study of the linguistic structure of sentences. *Phrase-structure grammars* analyze sentences in terms of the hierarchical relationships among words in phrases and sentences. *Transformational grammars* analyze sentences in terms of transformational rules that describe interrelationships among the structures of various sentences. Some linguists have suggested a mechanism for linking syntax to semantics, in which grammatical sentences contain particular slots for syntactical categories; these slots may be filled by words that have particular *thematic roles* within the sentences. According to this view, each item in a lexicon contains information regarding appropriate thematic roles, as well as appropriate syntactical categories.

3. **How do we acquire the ability to use language?** Humans seem to progress through the following stages in acquiring language: (a) cooing, which comprises all possible phones; (b) babbling, which comprises only the distinct phonemes that characterize the primary language of the infant; (c) one-word utterances; (d) two-word utterances and telegraphic speech; and (e) basic adult sentence structure (present by about age 4 years). This progression includes changes in perception that reduce the number of phonemes that can be distinguished, tuning in to those of the native language environment.

   During language acquisition, children engage in *overextension errors,* in which they extend the meaning of a word to encompass more concepts than the word is intended to encompass. Neither nature alone nor nurture alone can account for human language acquisition. The mechanism of *hypothesis testing* suggests an integration of nature and nurture: Children acquire language by mentally forming tentative hypotheses regarding language (based on nature) and then testing these hypotheses in the environment (based on nurture). Children are guided in the formation of these hypotheses by an innate *language-acquisition device (LAD),* which facilitates language acquisition. Over the course of development, language complexity, vocabulary, and even strategies for vocabulary acquisition become increasingly sophisticated.

THINKING ABOUT THINKING: FACTUAL, ANALYTICAL, CREATIVE, AND PRACTICAL QUESTIONS

1. Describe the six key properties of language.
2. What evidence is there that both nature and nurture influence language acquisition?
3. In your opinion, why do some view speech perception as special while others consider speech perception ordinary?
4. Compare and contrast the speech is ordinary and speech is special views, particularly in reference to categorical perception and phoneme restoration.
5. How do phrase-structure diagrams reveal the alternative meanings of ambiguous sentences?
6. Make up a sentence that illustrates several of the thematic roles mentioned in this chapter (i.e., agent, patient, beneficiary, instrument, location, source, and goal).
7. In this chapter, we saw that passive-voice sentences can be transformed into active-voice sentences, using transformation rules. What are some other kinds of sentence structures that are related to one another? In your own words, state the transformation rules that would govern the changes from one form to another.
8. Give a sample of an utterance you might reasonably expect to hear from an 18-month-old child.

KEY TERMS

babbling 305
categorical perception 293
child-directed speech 309
coarticulation 292
communication 284
connotation 295
content morpheme 289
cooing 304
deep structure 300
denotation 295
discourse 290
function morpheme 289
grammar 296
hypothesis testing 308
language 284
language-acquisition device (LAD) 307
lexicon 290

morpheme 289
noun phrase 290
overextension error 305
overregularization 309
phoneme 288
phrase-structure grammars 298
psycholinguistics 284
semantics 290
surface structure 300
syntax 296
telegraphic speech 305
thematic roles 303
transformational grammar 300
verb phrase 290
verbal comprehension 288
verbal fluency 288
vocabulary 290

Annotated Suggested Readings

Jusczyk, P. W. (1997). *The discovery of spoken language.* Cambridge, MA: MIT Press. A very coherent and cohesive account of the development of speech perception in the first year of life, placing particular emphasis on how experience modifies innate perceptual abilities.

Keil, F. C. (1989). *Concepts, kinds, and cognitive development.* Cambridge, MA: MIT Press. A wide-ranging account of Keil's research on relationships among concepts, language, and thought in the developing child.

Pinker, S. (1994). *The language instinct.* New York: Morrow. An interesting and extremely readable account of the psychology of language, emphasizing especially its innate aspects.

LANGUAGE IN CONTEXT

CHAPTER OUTLINE

EXPLORING COGNITIVE PSYCHOLOGY

LANGUAGE AND THOUGHT
- Differences Between Languages
- Bilingualism and Dialects
- Slips of the Tongue
- Metaphorical Language

LANGUAGE IN A SOCIAL CONTEXT
- Speech Acts
- Conversational Postulates
- Gender and Language
- Discourse and Reading Comprehension

NEUROPSYCHOLOGY OF LANGUAGE
- Lesion Studies and ERP Research
- Other Methods

SUMMARY

THINKING ABOUT THINKING: FACTUAL, ANALYTICAL, CREATIVE, AND PRACTICAL QUESTIONS

KEY TERMS

ANNOTATED SUGGESTED READINGS

Exploring Cognitive Psychology

1. **How does language affect the way we think?**
2. **How does our social context influence our use of language?**
3. **How can we find out about language by studying the human brain, and what do such studies reveal?**

"My surgeon was a butcher."
"His house is a rat's nest."
"Her sermons are sleeping pills."
"He's a real toad, and he always dates real dogs."
"Abused children are walking time bombs."
"My boss is a tiger in board meetings but a real pussycat with me."
"Billboards are warts on the landscape."
"My cousin is a vegetable."
"John's last girlfriend chewed him up and spit him out."

Not one of the preceding statements is literally true, yet fluent readers of English have little difficulty comprehending these metaphors and other nonliteral forms of language. How do we comprehend them? One of the reasons that we can understand nonliteral uses of language is that we can interpret the words we hear within a broader linguistic, cultural, social, and cognitive context. In this chapter, we will first focus on the cognitive context of language—how language and thought interact. Then, we will discuss some uses of language in its social context, and finally, some neuropsychological insights into language.

Language and Thought

One of the most interesting areas in the study of language is the relationship between language and the thinking human mind. Many different questions have been asked about this relationship, only some of which we consider here. Of the many ways in which to study this relationship, cognitive psychologists and psycholinguists are particularly intrigued by studies comparing and contrasting users of differing languages and dialects. Such studies form the basis of this section.

Differences Between Languages

Why are there so many different languages around the world; and how does using any language in general and using a particular language influence human thought? As you know, different languages comprise different lexicons and use different syntactical structures. These differences often reflect differences in the physical and cultural environments in which the languages arose and developed. For example, in terms of lexicon, the Garo of Burma distinguish among many different kinds of rice, which is understandable, because they are a rice-growing culture. Nomadic Arabs have more than 20 different words for camels. These peoples clearly conceptualize rice and camels more specifically and in more complex ways than do people outside their cultural groups. As a result of these linguistic differences, do the Garo think about rice differently from the way we do, and do the Arabs think about camels differently from the way we do?

The syntactical structures of languages differ, too. Almost all languages permit some way in which to communicate actions, agents of actions, and objects of actions (Gerrig & Banaji, 1994). What differs across languages is the order of subject, verb, and object in a typical declarative sentence, as well as the range of grammatical inflections and other markings that speakers are obliged to include as key elements of a sentence. For example, in describing past actions in English, we indicate whether an action took place in the past by changing (inflecting) the verb form (e.g., walk*ed).* In Spanish and German, the verb also must indicate whether the agent of action was singular or plural and is being referred to in the first, second, or third person. In Turkish, the verb form must indicate past action, singular or plural, and the person, and it must obligatorily indicate whether the action was witnessed or experienced directly by the speaker or was noted only indirectly. Do these differences and other differences in obligatory syntactical structures influence—or perhaps even constrain—the users of these languages to think about things differently because of the language they use while thinking?

LINGUISTIC RELATIVITY: THE SAPIR–WHORF HYPOTHESIS

The concept relevant to this question is **linguistic relativity,** the assertion that the speakers of different languages have differing cognitive systems, and that these different cognitive systems influence the ways in which people speaking the various languages think about the world. Thus, according to the relativity view, the Garo would think about rice differently than we do. For example, the Garo would develop more cognitive categories for rice than would an English-speaking counterpart. When the Garo contemplated rice, they would purportedly view it differently—and perhaps with greater complexity of thought—than do English speakers, who have only a few words for rice. Thus, language would shape thought.

The linguistic relativity hypothesis is sometimes referred to as the Sapir–Whorf hypothesis, after the two men who were most forceful in propagating it. Edward Sapir (1941/1964) said that "we see and hear and otherwise experience very largely as we do because the language habits of our community predispose certain choices of interpretation" (p. 69). Benjamin Lee Whorf (1956) stated this view even more strongly:

> We dissect nature along lines laid down by our native languages. The categories and types that we isolate from the world of phenomena we do not find there because they stare every observer in the face; on the contrary, the world is presented in a kaleidoscopic flux of impressions which has to be organized by our minds—and this means largely by the linguistic systems in our minds. (p. 213)

The Sapir–Whorf hypothesis has been one of the most widely mentioned ideas in all of the social and behavioral sciences (Lonner, 1989). However, some of its implications appear to have reached mythical proportions; for example, many social scientists have warmly accepted and gladly propagated the notion that Eskimos have multitudinous words for the single English word *snow.* In refutation of the myth, anthropologist Laura Martin (1986) has asserted that, contrary to popular beliefs, Eskimos do *not* have numerous words for snow. According to G. K. Pullum (1991), "no one who knows anything about Eskimo (or more accurately, about the Inuit and Yupik families of related languages spoken from Siberia to Greenland) has ever said they do" (p. 160). Martin, who has done more than anyone else to debunk the myth, understands why her colleagues might consider the myth charming, but she has been quite "disappointed in the reaction of her colleagues when she pointed out the fallacy; most, she says, took the position that true or not 'it's still a great example'" (Adler, 1991, p. 63). Apparently, we must exercise caution in our interpretation of findings regarding linguistic relativity.

A milder form of linguistic relativism is that language may not determine thought, but that language certainly may influence thought. Our thoughts and our language interact in myriad ways, only some of which we now understand. Clearly, language facilitates thought, even affecting perception and memory. For one reason, we have limited means by which to manipulate nonlinguistic images (Hunt & Banaji, 1988). Such limitations make desirable the use of language to facilitate mental representation and manipulation. Even nonsense pictures ("droodles") are recalled and redrawn differently, depending on the verbal label given to the picture (e.g., Bower, Karlin, & Dueck, 1975).

To see how this phenomenon might work, look at Figure 10.1 right now. If, instead of being labeled as it is, it had been entitled "beaded curtain," you might have perceived it differently. However, once a particular label has been given, viewing the same figure from the alternative perspective is much harder (Glucksberg, 1988). Psychologists have used other ambiguous figures (see chapter 3) and have found similar results. Figure 10.2 illustrates three other figures that can be given alternative labels. When participants are given a particular label (e.g., either "eyeglasses" or "dumbbells"), they tend to draw their recollection of the figure in a way more similar to the given label.

Language also affects how we encode, store, and retrieve information in memory in other ways. Remember the examples in chapter 6 regarding how the label "Washing Clothes" enhanced people's responses to recall and comprehension questions about text passages (e.g., Bransford & Johnson, 1972, 1973). Elizabeth Loftus (e.g., Loftus & Palmer, 1974) has done extensive work showing that eyewitness testimony is powerfully influenced by the distinctive phrasing of questions posed to eyewitnesses. Jonathan Schooler and Tonya Engstler-Schooler (1990) found that even when participants generated their own descriptions, the subsequent accuracy of their eyewitness testimony declined. That is, these researchers found that accurate recall actually declined following an opportunity to write a description of an observed event, a particular color, or a particular face. When given an opportunity to identify statements about an event or the actual color or face, participants were less able to do so accurately if they had previously described it. Paradoxically, when participants were allowed to take their time in responding, their performance was even less accurate than when they were forced to respond quickly. That is, if given time to reflect on their answers, participants were more likely to respond in accord with what they had said or written than with what they had seen.

FIGURE 10.1 BEAR CLIMBING THE FAR SIDE OF A TREE

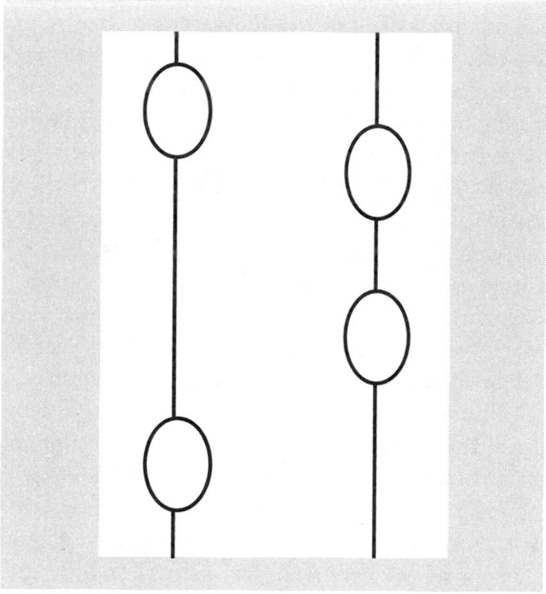

How does your label for this image affect your perception, your mental representation, and your memory of the image? (After Glucksberg, 1988)

FIGURE 10.2 INFLUENCE OF VERBAL LABELS ON MEMORY

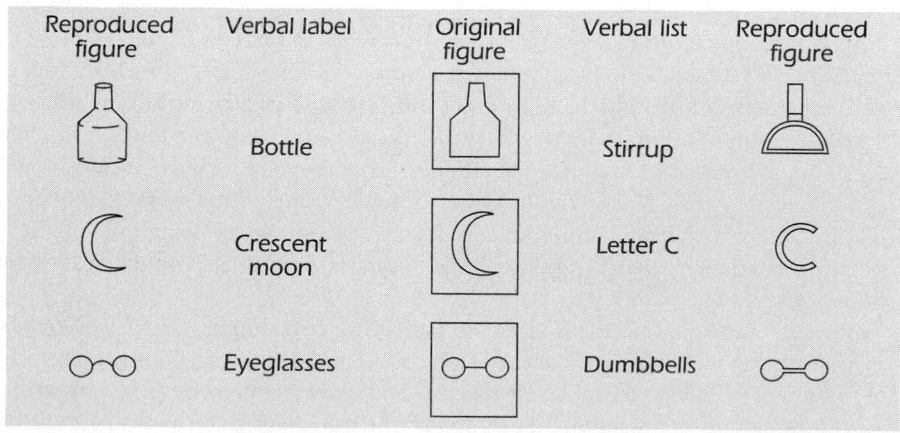

When the original figures (in the center) are redrawn from memory, the new drawings tend to be distorted to be more like the labeled figures. (After Glucksberg, 1988)

LINGUISTIC UNIVERSALS

There has been some research that addresses **linguistic universals**—characteristic patterns across languages of various cultures—and relativity. Recall from chapter 9 that linguists have identified hundreds of linguistic universals related to *phonology* (the study of phonemes), *morphology* (the study of morphemes), semantics, and syntax. An area that well illustrates much of this research focuses on color names. These words provide an especially convenient way of testing for universals because people in every culture can be expected to be exposed, at least potentially, to pretty much the same range of colors.

In actuality, different languages name colors quite differently, but the languages do not divide up the color spectrum arbitrarily. A systematic pattern seems universally to govern color naming across languages. Two anthropologists, Brent Berlin and Paul Kay (1969; Kay, 1975), have investigated color terms in a large number of languages. They unearthed two apparent linguistic universals about color naming across languages. First, all of the languages surveyed took their basic color terms from a set of just 11 color names: black, white, red, yellow, green, blue, brown, purple, pink, orange, and gray. Languages ranged from using all 11 color names, as in English, to using just two of the names. Second, when only some of the color names are used, the naming of colors falls into a hierarchy of five levels: (a) black, white; (b) red; (c) yellow, green, blue; (d) brown; and (e) purple, pink, orange, gray. Thus, if a language names only two colors, they will be black and white. If it names three colors, they will be black, white, and red. A fourth color will be taken from the set of yellow, green, and blue. The fifth and sixth will be taken from this set as well, and so selection will continue until all 11 colors have been labeled.

In addition to studying semantic differences, such as the use of color words, psycholinguists study how syntactical structural differences across languages may affect thought. For example, Spanish has two forms of the verb *to be*—*ser* and *estar;* however, they are used in different contexts. Maria Sera (1992; incidentally, *será* means "will be" in Spanish) has studied the uses of *ser* and *estar* in adults and in children, both in highly structured situations (i.e., in response to patterned sentences in which *ser* or *estar* were used) and in relatively naturalistic situations (i.e., in response to open-ended requests to describe objects or situations).

When *to be* indicated the identity of something (e.g., in English, "This is José") or the class membership of something (e.g., "José is a carpenter"), both adults and children used the verb form *ser.* Moreover, both adults and children used different verb forms when *to be* indicated attributes of things: *Ser* was used to indicate permanent attributes (e.g., "María is tall"), and *estar* was used to indicate temporary attributes (e.g., "María is busy"). When using forms of *to be* to describe the locations of objects (including people, animals, and other things), both adults and children used *estar.* However, when using forms of *to be* to describe the locations of events (e.g., meetings or parties), adults used *ser,* whereas children continued to use *estar.*

Sera (1992) interprets these findings as indicating two things: First, *ser* seems to be used primarily for indicating permanent conditions (e.g., identity, class inclusion, and relatively permanent, stable attributes of things), and *estar* seems to be used primarily for indicating temporary conditions (e.g., temporary attributes of things and the location of objects, which are often subject to change from one place to another). That finding was in accord with other work and was relatively unsurprising. Her second finding was more intriguing. Children treat the location of events in the same way as the location of objects (i.e., as temporary, hence suggesting the use of *estar),* whereas adults differentiate between events and objects. In particular, adults consider the locations of events to be unchanging (i.e., permanent, thereby requiring the use of *ser).*

Sera (1992) noted that other researchers have suggested that young children have difficulty distinguishing between objects and events (e.g., Keil, 1979) and in recognizing the permanent status of many attributes (e.g., Marcus & Overton, 1978). Thus, the developmental differences regarding the use of *ser* to describe the location of events may indicate developmental differences in cognition. Sera's work suggests that differences in language use may indeed indicate differences in thinking. However, her work leaves open the psychological question as to whether native Spanish speakers have a more differentiated sense of the temporary and the permanent than do native English speakers, who use the same verb form to express both senses of *to be.* Thus far, the answer is unclear.

Other languages have also been used in investigations of linguistic relativity. For example, in the Navaho language, the choice of verb depends on the shape of the object engaging in the action of the verb, whereas in English, it does not (J. B. Carroll & Casagrande, 1958). Might the use of different verb forms for different shapes suggest that Navaho children would learn to perceive and organize information by shapes earlier than do children who are English-speaking?

Early research indicated that young English-speaking children group objects by color before they group them by shape (Brian & Goodenough, 1929). In contrast, Navaho-speaking children are more likely than English-speaking Navaho children to classify objects on the basis of shape. However, these findings are problematic because English-speaking children from Boston perform more like the Navaho-speaking Navaho children than like the English-speaking Navaho children (J. B. Carroll & Casagrande, 1958). Furthermore, recent research comparing adult's and children's generalizations of novel nouns among novel objects finds that young English-speaking children will actually overuse shape in classifying objects (L. B. Smith, Jones, & Landau, 1996). What would happen for people who speak both of the languages being studied?

Curt Hoffman, Ivy Lau, and David Johnson (1986) came up with an intriguing experiment designed to assess the possible effects of linguistic relativity by studying persons who speak more than one language. In Chinese, a single term, *shì gÈ,* specifically describes a person who is "worldly, experienced, socially skillful, devoted to his or her family, and somewhat reserved" (p. 1098). English clearly has no comparable single term to embrace these diverse characteristics. Hoffman and his colleagues composed text passages in English and in Chinese describing various characters, including the *shì gÈ* stereotype (without, of course, specifically using the term *shì gÈ* in the descriptions). The researchers then asked participants who were fluent in both Chinese and English to read the passages either in Chinese or in English and then to rate various statements about the characters, in terms of the likelihood that the statements would be true of the characters. Some of these statements involved a stereotype of a *shì gÈ* person.

Their results seemed to support the notion of linguistic relativity, in that the participants were more likely to rate the various statements in accord with the *shì gÈ* stereotype when they had read the passages in Chinese than when they had read the passages in English. Similarly, when participants were asked to write their own impressions of the characters, their descriptions conformed more closely to the *shì gÈ* stereotype if they had previously read the passages in Chinese. These authors do not suggest that it would be

Michael Cole *is a professor of psychology and communication at the University of California, San Diego. He is well known for his contributions to cultural and cross-cultural cognitive psychology, having shown that tests that are valid in one culture can not simply be translated and directly carried over to another culture and remain valid. Cole has also been seminal in reviving psychological interest in the work of Lev Vygotsky over the past 20 years.*

impossible for English speakers to comprehend the *shì gÈ* stereotype, but rather that having that stereotype readily accessible facilitates its mental manipulation.

The question of whether linguistic relativity exists, and if so, to what extent, remains an open question. My reading of the evidence is that there may be a mild form of relativity, whereby language can influence thought. However, a stronger deterministic form of relativity, whereby language determines differences in thought among members of various cultures, is almost certainly inconsistent with the available evidence. Finally, it is probably the case that language and thought interact with each other throughout the life span (Vygotsky, 1986).

Bilingualism and Dialects

The research by Hoffman and his colleagues brings up a few questions that have fascinated psycholinguists: If a person can speak and think in two languages, does the person think differently in each language? In fact, do **bilinguals**—people who can speak two languages—think differently from **monolinguals**—people who can speak only one language? *(Multilinguals* speak at least two and possibly more languages.) What differences, if any, emanate from the availability of two languages versus just one? Might bilingualism affect intelligence, positively or negatively?

Kenji Hakuta (1986) has reviewed much of the literature on this question and has turned up some interesting findings. Consider some of the issues that arise in this field. First, does bilingualism make thinking in any one language more difficult, or does it enhance thought processes? Hakuta reviewed hundreds of studies and found the data to be self-contradictory. Different participant populations, different methodologies, and different language groups, as well as different experimenter biases, may have contributed to the inconsistency in the literature. Hakuta has read the literature as indicating that the question cannot be answered simply. He suggests that when bilinguals are *balanced bilinguals,* roughly equally fluent in both languages, and when they come from middle-class backgrounds, positive effects of bilingualism tend to be found, but negative effects may result under other circumstances. What might be the causes of this difference?

James Cummins (1976) has suggested that we must distinguish between what might be called additive versus subtractive bilingualism. In *additive bilingualism,* a second language is acquired in addition to a relatively well-developed first language. In *subtractive bilingualism,* elements of a second language replace elements of the first language. Cummins hypothesized that the additive form results in increased thinking ability, whereas the subtractive form results in decreased thinking ability. In particular, there may be something of a threshold effect: Individuals may need to be at a certain relatively high level of competence in both languages for a positive effect of bilingualism to be found. Children from backgrounds with lower socioeconomic status (SES) may be more likely to be subtractive bilinguals than are children from the middle SES; their SES may be a factor in their being hurt rather than helped by their bilingualism.

Another factor believed to contribute to acquisition of a language is age. Some researchers have suggested that nativelike mastery of some aspects of a second language are rarely acquired after adolescence. Harry Bahrick and his colleagues (Bahrick, Hall, Goggin, Bahrick, & Berger, 1994) disagree with this view, based on their studies of bilingualism in both recent and long-term immigrants to the United States. Bahrick and his colleagues found that some aspects of a second language (e.g., vocabulary comprehension and fluency) seem to be acquired just as well after adolescence as before. Furthermore, contrary to prior findings (e.g., J. S. Johnson & Newport, 1989, 1991; Newport, 1990), these researchers found that even some aspects of syntax seem to be acquired readily after adolescence, although the mastery of nativelike pronunciation seems to depend on early acquisition (e.g., Asher & Garcia, 1969; Oyama, 1976). Surprisingly, learning completely novel phonemes in a second language may be easier than learning phonemes that are highly similar to the phonemes of the first language (Flege, 1991).

What kinds of learning experiences facilitate second-language acquisition? Ellen Bialystok and Kenji Hakuta (1994) assert that there is no single correct answer to that question. One reason is that each individual language learner brings distinctive cognitive abilities and knowledge to the language-learning experience. In addition, Bialystok and Hakuta suggest that the kinds of learning experiences that facilitate second-language acquisition should match the context and uses for the second language once it is acquired.

For example, consider four different individuals. Caitlin, a young child, may not need to master a wealth of vocabulary and complex syntax to get along quite well with other children. If she can master the phonology, some simple syntactical rules, and some basic vocabulary, she may be considered quite fluent. Similarly, José, who needs only to get by in a few everyday situations (e.g., shopping, handling routine family business transactions, and getting around town), may be considered proficient after mastering some simple vocabulary and syntax, as well as some pragmatic knowledge regarding context-appropriate manners of communicating. Kim Yee, who must be able to communicate regarding her specialized technical field, may be considered proficient if she masters the technical vocabulary, a primitive basic vocabulary, and the rudiments of syntax. Sumesh, a student who studies a second language in an academic setting, may be expected to have a firm grasp of syntax and a rather broad, if shallow, vocabulary. Each of these language learners may require different kinds of language experiences to gain the proficiency being sought. Different kinds of experiences may be needed to enhance their competence in the phonology, vocabulary, syntax, and pragmatics of the second language.

Single-System Versus Dual-System Hypotheses

One way of approaching bilingualism is to apply what we have learned from cognitive-psychological research to practical concerns regarding how to facilitate acquisition of a second language. Another approach is to study bilingual individuals, to see how bilingualism may offer insight into the human mind. For example, some cognitive psychologists have been interested in finding out how the two languages are represented in the bilingual's mind. The **single-system hypothesis** suggests that the two languages are represented in just one system. Alternatively, the **dual-system hypothesis** suggests that the two languages are represented somehow in separate systems of the mind (Paradis, 1981). For instance, might German language information be stored in a physically different part of the brain than English language information? Figure 10.3 shows schematically the difference in the two points of view.

One way to address this question is through the study of bilinguals who have experienced brain damage. If a bilingual has brain damage in a particular part of the brain, an inference consistent with the dual-system hypothesis would be that the individual would show different degrees of impairment in the two languages, whereas the single-system view

FIGURE 10.3 **BILINGUALISM: SINGLE-SYSTEM AND DUAL-SYSTEM HYPOTHESES**

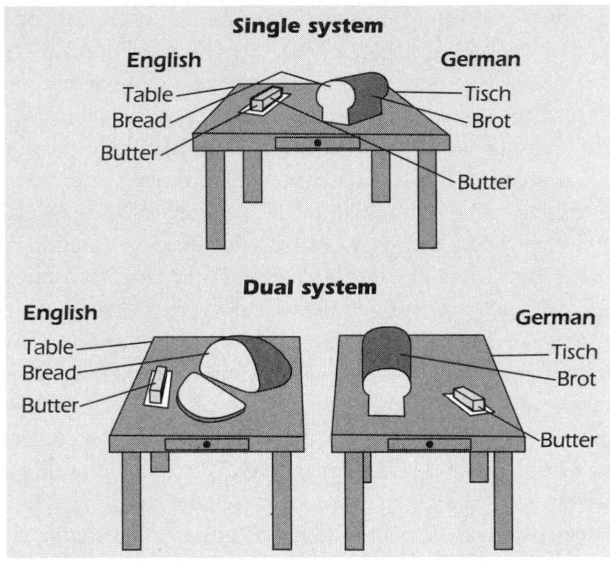

The single-system conceptualization hypothesizes that both languages are represented in a unified cognitive system. The dual-system conceptualization of bilingualism hypothesizes that each language is represented in a separate cognitive system.

would suggest roughly equal impairment in the two languages. The logic of this kind of investigation is compelling, but the results are not. When recovery of language after trauma is studied, sometimes the first language recovers first, sometimes the second language recovers first, and sometimes recovery is about equal for the two languages (Albert & Obler, 1978; Paradis, 1977). Based on this methodology, the conclusions that can be drawn are equivocal, although the results seem to suggest at least some duality of structure.

A different method of study has led to an alternative perspective on bilingualism. George Ojemann and Harry Whitaker (1978) mapped the region of the cerebral cortex relevant to language use in two of their bilingual patients being treated for epilepsy. Mild electrical stimulation was applied to the cortex of each patient. Electrical stimulation tends to inhibit activity where it is applied, leading to reduced ability to name objects for which the memories are stored at the location being stimulated. The results for both patients were the same and may help explain the contradictions in the literature. Some areas of the brain showed equal impairments for object-naming in both languages, but other areas of the brain showed differential impairment in one or the other language. The results also suggested that the weaker language was more diffusely represented across the cortex than was the stronger language. In other words, asking the question of whether two languages are represented singly or separately may be asking the wrong question. The results of this study suggest that some aspects of the two languages may be represented singly, and other aspects may be represented separately.

To summarize, two languages seem to share some, but not all, aspects of mental representation. Learning a second language is often a plus but is probably most so if the individual learning the second language is in an environment in which the learning of the second language adds to rather than subtracts from the learning of the first language. Moreover, for beneficial effects to appear, the second language must be learned rather well. The approach usually taken in schools, whereby students may receive as little as 2 or 3 years of second-language instruction spread out over a few class periods a week, probably will not be sufficient for the beneficial effects of bilingualism to appear. However, schooling does seem to yield beneficial effects on acquisition of syntax, particularly when a second language is acquired after adolescence. Furthermore, individual learners should choose specific kinds of language-acquisition techniques to suit both their personal abilities and preferences and their personal goals for using the second language.

Language Mixtures and Change

Bilingualism is not a certain outcome of linguistic contact between different language groups. Sometimes, when people of two different language groups are in prolonged contact with one another, the languages users of the two groups begin to share some vocabulary that is superimposed onto each group's syntax, resulting in what is known as a *pidgin.* Over time, this admixture can develop into a distinct linguistic form, with its own grammar, becoming a *creole.* Linguist Derek Bickerton (1990) has studied the similarities across different creoles, and postulates that modern creoles may resemble an evolutionarily early form of language, which he termed *protolanguage.* The existence of pidgins and creoles, and possibly a protolanguage, support the universality notion discussed earlier. That is, linguistic ability is so natural and universal that given the opportunity, humans actually invent new languages quite rapidly.

Creoles and pidgins arise when two linguistically distinctive groups meet. The counterpart—a dialect—occurs when a single linguistic group gradually diverges toward somewhat distinctive variations. A **dialect** is a regional variety of a language distinguished by features such as vocabulary, syntax, and pronunciation. Cognitive psychologists study dialects to gain insights into such diverse phenomena as auditory discrimination, test development, and social discrimination.

Dialectical differences often represent harmless regional variations, which create few serious communication difficulties, but which can lead to some confusion. In the United States, for example, when national advertisers give 800 (toll-free) numbers to call, they often route the calls to the Midwest. They do so because they have learned that the Midwestern form of speech seems to be the most universally understood form within the country, whereas other forms, such as southern and northeastern ones, may be harder for people from diverse parts of the country to understand. Many radio announcers try to learn something close to a standard form of English, often called "network English," in order to maximize their comprehensibility to as many listeners as possible.

Sometimes, differing dialects are assigned different social statuses, with *standard* forms having higher status than *nonstandard* ones. The distinction between standard and nonstandard forms of a language can become pernicious when speakers of one dialect start to view themselves as speakers of a superior dialect. Recall that none of the existing languages of the world is inherently better than any other language in terms of the ability to express thoughts. Moreover, virtually any thought can be expressed in any dialect.

SLIPS OF THE TONGUE

Thus far, much of the discussion has assumed that people use—or at least attempt to use—language correctly. An area of particular interest to cognitive psychologists, however, is how people use language incorrectly. One way of using language incorrectly is through **slips of the tongue**—inadvertent linguistic errors in what we say, which may occur at any level of linguistic analysis: phonemes, morphemes, or larger units of language (Crystal, 1987; McArthur, 1992). In such cases, what we think and mean to say do not correspond to what we actually do say. Freudian psychoanalysts have suggested that in *Freudian slips,* the verbal slip reflects some unconscious processing that has psychological significance, often indicating repressed emotions. For example, a business competitor may say, "I'm glad to beat you," when what was overtly intended was, "I'm glad to meet you."

In contrast to the psychoanalytic view, most psycholinguists and other cognitive psychologists are intrigued by slips of the tongue because of what the lack of correspondence between what is thought and what is said may tell us about how language is produced. In speaking, we have a mental plan for what we are going to say. Sometimes, however, this plan is disrupted when our mechanism for speech production does not cooperate with our cognitive one. Often, such errors result from intrusions by other thoughts or by stimuli in the environment (e.g., a radio talk show or a neighboring conversation; Garrett, 1980). Slips of the tongue may be taken to indicate that the language of thought differs somewhat from the language through which we express our thoughts (Fodor, 1975). Often, we have the idea right, but its expression comes out wrong. Sometimes, we are not even aware of the slip until it is pointed out to us, because in the language of the mind, whatever it may be, the idea is right, even though the expression is inadvertently wrong.

Victoria Fromkin (1973; Fromkin & Rodman, 1988) has classified various kinds of slips that people tend to make in their conversations:

- In *anticipation,* the speaker uses a language element before it is appropriate in the sentence because it corresponds to an element that will be needed later in the utterance. For example, instead of saying, "an inspiring expression," a speaker might say, "an expiring expression."
- In *perseveration,* the speaker uses a language element that was appropriate earlier in the sentence but that is not appropriate later on—for example, a speaker might say, "We sat down to a bounteous beast" instead of a "bounteous feast."
- In *substitution,* the speaker substitutes one language element for another as, for example, if you have ever warned anyone to do something "after it is too late," when you meant "before it is too late."
- In *reversal* (also called "transposition"), the speaker switches the positions of two language elements, such as the reversal that reportedly led *flutterby* to become *butterfly,* a reversal that captivated language users so much that the reversal is now the preferred form. Sometimes, reversals can be fortuitously opportune, creating *spoonerisms,* in which the initial sounds of two words are reversed and make two entirely different words. The term is named after the Reverend William Spooner, who was famous for them. Some of his choicest slips include, "You have hissed all my mystery lectures," and "Easier for a camel to go through the knee of an idol" (H. H. Clark & Clark, 1977).

- Additionally, slips may occur due to *insertions* of sounds (e.g., "mischiev*i*ous" instead of "mischievous" or "drown*d*ed" instead of "drowned") or other linguistic elements. The opposite kind of slip involves *deletions* (e.g., sound deletions such as "prossing" instead of "processing"); such deletions often involve *blends* (e.g., "blounds" for "blended sounds").

Each kind of slip of the tongue may occur at different hierarchical levels of linguistic processing (Dell, 1986)—that is, at the acoustical level of phonemes (e.g., "bounteous beast" instead of "bounteous feast"), the semantic level of morphemes (e.g., "after it's too late" instead of "before it's too late"), or even higher levels (e.g., "bought the bucket" instead of "kicked the bucket" or "bought the farm"). The patterns of errors (reversals, substitutions, etc.) at each hierarchical level tend to be parallel (Dell, 1986). For example, in phonemic errors, initial consonants tend to interact with initial consonants (e.g., "tasting wime" instead of "wasting time"), final consonants with final consonants (e.g., "bing his tut" instead of "bit his tongue"), prefixes with prefixes (e.g., "expiring expression"), and so on.

Also, errors at each level of linguistic analysis suggest particular kinds of insights into how we produce speech. For example, in phonemic errors, a stressed word (emphasized through speech rhythm and tone) is more likely to influence other words than is a unstressed word (Crystal, 1987). Furthermore, even when sounds are switched, the basic rhythmic and tonal patterns are usually preserved (e.g., the emphasis on "hissed" and the first syllable of "mystery" in the first spoonerism quoted here).

Even at the level of words, the same parts of speech tend to be involved in the errors we produce (e.g., nouns interfering with other nouns, verbs with verbs; Bock, 1990; Bock, Loebell, & Morey, 1992). For example, in the second spoonerism quoted here, Spooner managed to preserve the syntactical categories (the nouns *knee* and *idol),* as well as to preserve the grammaticality of the sentence by changing the articles from "*a* needle" to "*an* idol." Even in the case of word substitutions, syntactic categories are preserved. In speech errors, semantic categories, too, may be preserved, as in naming a category when intending to name a member of the category (e.g., "fruit" for "apple"), naming the wrong member of the category (e.g., "peach" for "apple"), or in naming a member of a category when intending to name the category as a whole (e.g., "peach" for "fruit"; Garrett, 1992). Data from studies of speech errors may help us better understand normal language processing. Another aspect of language that offers us a distinctive view is the study of metaphorical language.

METAPHORICAL LANGUAGE

Until now, we have discussed primarily the literal uses of language. At least as interesting to poets and to me, as well as to many others, are its omnipresent figurative uses—particularly the use of metaphors as a way of expressing thoughts. **Metaphors** juxtapose two nouns in a way that positively asserts their similarities, while not disconfirming their dissimilarities; **similes** are similar to metaphors, except that they introduce the words *like* or *as* into the comparison.

Metaphors contain four key elements: the two items that are being compared, a tenor and a vehicle, and the two ways the items are related. The *tenor* is the topic of the metaphor, and the *vehicle* is what the tenor is described in terms of. For example, in saying that "billboards are warts on the landscape," the tenor is "billboards," and the vehicle is "warts." The similarities between the tenor and the vehicle are termed the *ground* of the metaphor, and the dissimilarities between the two are the *tension* of the metaphor. We may conjecture that a key similarity between billboards and warts is that they are both considered unattractive. The dissimilarities between the two are many, including that billboards appear on buildings, highways, and other impersonal public locations, but warts appear on diverse personal locations on an individual.

Of the various theories that have been proposed to explain how metaphors work, the main traditional views have highlighted either the ways in which the tenor and the vehicle are similar or the ways in which they differ. For example, the traditional *comparison view* highlights the importance of the comparison and underscores the comparative similarities and analogical relationship between the tenor and the vehicle (Malgady & Johnson, 1976; G. A. Miller, 1979; Ortony, 1979; cf. also R. J. Sternberg & Nigro, 1983). As applied to the metaphor, "Abused children are walking time bombs," the comparison view would underscore the similarity between the elements: their potential for explosion. In contrast, the *anomaly view* of metaphor emphasizes the dissimilarity between the tenor and the vehicle (e.g., Beardsley, 1962; Bickerton, 1969; H. H. Clark & Lucy, 1975; Gerrig & Healy, 1983; Lyons, 1977; Searle, 1979; van Dijk, 1975). The anomaly view would highlight the many dissimilarities between abused children and time bombs.

The *domain-interaction view* integrates aspects of each of the preceding views, suggesting that a metaphor is more than a comparison, as well as more than an anomaly. According to this view, a metaphor involves an interaction of some kind between the domain (area of knowledge, e.g., animals, machines, plants) of the tenor and the domain of the vehicle (Black, 1962; Hesse, 1966). The exact form of this interaction differs somewhat from one theory to another. According to Roger Tourangeau and me (Tourangeau & Sternberg, 1981, 1982), the metaphor is more effective when the tenor and the vehicle share many similar characteristics (e.g., the potential explosiveness of abused children and time bombs), but the domains of the tenor and the vehicle are highly dissimilar (e.g., the domain of humans and the domain of weapons).

Sam Glucksberg and Boaz Keysar (1990) have suggested yet another view of how we understand metaphors, which they base on extensive analysis of the metaphors cited in other research (e.g., some of the aforementioned studies: Black, 1962; H. H. Clark & Lucy, 1975; Ortony, 1979; Searle, 1979; Tourangeau & Sternberg, 1981). Glucksberg and Keysar assert that metaphors are essentially a nonliteral form of class-inclusion statements, in which the tenor of each metaphor is a member of the class characterized by the vehicle of the given metaphor. That is, we understand metaphors not as statements of comparison but as statements of category membership, in which the vehicle is a prototypical member of the category.

For example, when I say, "My colleague's partner is an iceberg," I am saying that the partner belongs to the category of things that are characterized by an utter lack of personal warmth, extreme rigidity, and the ability to produce a massively chilling effect on anyone in the surrounding environment. For a metaphor to work well, the reader should find the salient features of the vehicle ("iceberg") to be unexpectedly relevant as features of the tenor ("my colleague's partner"). That is, the reader should be at least mildly surprised that prominent features of the vehicle may characterize the tenor, but after consideration, the reader should agree that those features do describe the tenor. If you knew my colleague's partner, you would agree.

Metaphors enrich our language in ways that literal statements cannot match. Our understanding of metaphors seems to require not only some kind of comparison, but also that the domains of the vehicle and of the tenor interact in some way. Reading a metaphor can change our perception of both domains and therefore can educate us in a way that is perhaps more difficult to transmit through literal speech.

LANGUAGE IN A SOCIAL CONTEXT

The study of the social context of language is a relatively new area of linguistic research. Increasingly, however, students of language have become interested in **pragmatics,** the study of how people use language, including sociolinguistics and other aspects of the social context of language. Similarly, cognitive psychologists have become increasingly interested in the social context in which we acquire and use language.

Under most circumstances (perhaps first or blind dates to the contrary), you change your use of language in response to contextual cues without giving these changes much thought. Similarly, you usually unself-consciously change your language patterns to fit different contexts.

For example, in speaking with a conversational partner, you seek to establish *common ground,* or a shared basis for engaging in a conversation (H. H. Clark & Brennan, 1991). When we are with people who share largely common background, knowledge, motives, or goals, establishing common ground is likely to be easy and scarcely noticeable. But when little is shared, such common ground may be hard to find.

INVESTIGATING COGNITIVE PSYCHOLOGY

To get an idea of how you change your own use of language in different contexts, suppose that you and your friend are going to meet right after work. Suppose also that something comes up, and you must call your friend to change the time or place for your meeting. When you call your friend at work, your friend's supervisor answers and offers to take a message. Exactly what will you say to your friend's supervisor, to ensure that your friend will know about the change in time or location? Suppose, instead, that the 4-year-old son of your friend's supervisor answers. Exactly what will you say in this situation? Finally, suppose that your friend answers directly. How will you have modified your language for each context, even when your purpose (underlying message) in all three contexts was the same?

Some sociolinguists study the ways in which people use nonlinguistic elements in conversational contexts. For example, sociolinguists and psycholinguists interested in observing your language use in context would be interested in your use of gestures and vocal inflections, as well as your use of other forms of nonverbal communication. One aspect of nonverbal communication is *personal space*—the distance between people in a conversation or other interaction that is considered comfortable for members of a given culture. The formal term for the study of interpersonal distance (or its opposite, proximity) is *proxemics* (relative distancing and positioning of you and your fellow conversants). In the United States, 18 to 24 inches is considered about right (Hall, 1966). Scandinavians expect more distance, whereas Middle Easterners, southern Europeans, and South Americans expect less (Sommer, 1969; O. M. Watson, 1970).

When on our own familiar turf, we take our own cultural views of personal space for granted; only when we come into contact with persons from other cultures do we notice these differences. For example, when I was visiting Venezuela, I noticed my cultural expectations coming into conflict with the expectations of those around me. I often found myself in a comical dance, backing off from the person I was talking to while that person was trying to move closer. Within a given culture, greater proximity generally indicates that (a) the persons see themselves in a close relationship; (b) the people are participating in a social situation that permits violation of the bubble of personal space, such as close dancing; or (c) the "violator" of the bubble is dominating the interaction.

SPEECH ACTS

DIRECT SPEECH ACTS

Another key aspect of the way in which you use language depends on what purpose you plan to achieve with language. In the earlier example, you were using language to try to ensure that your friend would meet you at the new location and time. When you speak, what kinds of things can you accomplish?

The philosopher John Searle (1975a) has proposed a theory of **speech acts,** which addresses the question of what you can accomplish with speech. According to Searle, all speech acts fall into five basic categories, based on the purpose of the acts. Table 10.1 identifies these categories and gives examples of each.

- The first category of speech acts is representatives. A *representative* is a speech act by which a person conveys a belief that a given proposition is true. The speaker can use various sources of information to support the given belief, but the statement is nothing more, nor less, than a statement of belief. We can put in various qualifiers to show our degree of certainty, but we are still stating a belief, which may or may not be verifiable.
- A second category of speech act is a *directive,* which represents an attempt by a speaker to get a listener to do something. Sometimes, a directive is quite indirect. For example, almost any sentence structured as a question is probably serving a directive function. Any attempt to elicit assistance of any kind, however indirect, falls into this category.
- A third category is a commissive. In uttering a *commissive,* the speaker is committing him or herself to some future course of action. Promises, pledges, contracts, guarantees, assurances, and the like all constitute commissives.

TABLE 10.1 **SPEECH ACTS**

The five basic categories of speech acts encompass the various tasks that can be accomplished through speech (or other modes of using language).

SPEECH ACT	DESCRIPTION	EXAMPLE
Representative	A speech act by which a person conveys a belief that a given proposition is true	If I say that "The Marquis de Sade is a sadist," I am conveying my belief that the marquis enjoyed seeing others feel pain. I can use various sources of information to support my belief, including the fact that the word "sadist" derives from this marquis. Nonetheless, the statement is nothing more, nor less, than a statement of belief. Similarly, I can make a statement that is more directly verifiable, such as "As you can see here on this thermometer, the temperature outside is 31 degrees Fahrenheit."
Directive	An attempt by a speaker to get a listener to do something, such as supplying the answer to a question	I can ask my son to help me shovel snow in various ways, some of which are more direct than others, such as, "Please help me shovel the snow," or "It sure would be nice if you were to help me shovel the snow," or "Would you help me shovel the snow?" The different surface forms are all attempts to get him to help me. Some directives are quite indirect. If I ask, "Has it stopped raining yet?" I am still uttering a directive, in this case seeking information rather than physical assistance. In fact, almost any sentence structured as a question probably serves a directive function.
Commissive	A commitment by the speaker to engage in some future course of action	If my son responds, "I'm busy now, but I'll help you shovel the snow later," he is uttering a commissive, in that he is pledging his future help. If my daughter then says, "I'll help you," she too is uttering a commissive, because she is pledging her assistance now. Promises, pledges, contracts, guarantees, assurances, and the like all constitute commissives.
Expressive	A statement regarding the speaker's psychological state	If I tell my son later,"I'm really upset that you didn't come through in helping me shovel the snow," that, too, would be an expressive. If my son says, "I'm sorry I didn't get around to helping you out," he would be uttering an expressive. If my daughter says, "Daddy, I'm glad I was able to help out," she is uttering an expressive.
Declaration (also termed *performative*)	A speech act by which the very act of making a statement brings about an intended new state of affairs	Suppose that you are called into your boss's office and told that you are responsible for the company losing $50,000, and then your boss says, "You're fired." The speech act results in your being in a new state—that is, unemployed. You might then tell your boss, "That's fine, because I wrote you a letter yesterday saying that the money was lost because of your glaring incompetence, not mine, and I resign." You are again making a declaration.

- A fourth category of speech act is an *expressive,* which is a statement regarding the speaker's psychological state—I'm just delighted to discuss speech acts.
- The fifth kind of speech act is a *declaration,* which is a speech act by which the very act of making a statement brings about an intended new state of affairs. When a

cleric says, "I now pronounce you husband and wife," the speech act is a declaration, because once the speech act is accomplished, the marriage rite is completed. Declarations are also termed *performatives* (H. H. Clark & Clark, 1977).

The appealing thing about Searle's taxonomy is that it classifies almost any statement that might be made. It shows exhaustively, at least at one level, the different kinds of things speech can accomplish. It also shows the close relationship between language structure and language function, such as the likelihood that a sentence structured as a question is serving a directive function. Wouldn't you agree?

Indirect Speech Acts

Sometimes, speech acts are indirect, meaning that we accomplish our goals in speaking in an oblique fashion. One way of communicating obliquely is through **indirect requests,** through which we make a request without doing so straightforwardly (Gordon & Lakoff, 1971; Searle, 1975b). There are four basic ways of making indirect requests: (a) asking or making statements about *abilities,* (b) stating a *desire,* (c) stating a future *action,* and (d) citing *reasons.* Examples of these forms of indirect requests are illustrated in Table 10.2, in which the indirect request is aimed at having a waitress tell the speaker where to find the rest room in a restaurant.

When are indirect speech acts interpreted literally, and when is the indirect meaning understood by the listener? A study by Raymond Gibbs (1979) indicated that when an indirect speech act such as "Must you open the window?" is presented in isolation, it is

TABLE 10.2 INDIRECT SPEECH ACTS

One way of using speech is to communicate obliquely, rather than directly.

Type of Indirect Speech Act	Example of an Indirect Request for Information
Abilities	If you say, "Can you tell me where the rest room is?" to a waitress at a restaurant, and she says, "Yes, of course I can," the chances are she missed the point. The question about her ability to tell you the location of the rest room was an indirect request for her to tell you exactly where it is.
Desire	"I would be grateful if you told me where the rest room is." Your statements of thanks in advance are really ways of getting someone to do what you want.
Future action	"Would you tell me where the rest room is?" Your inquiry into another person's future actions is another way to state an indirect request.
Reasons	You need not spell out the reasons to imply that there are good reasons to comply with the request. For example, you might imply that you have such reasons for the waitress to tell you where the rest room is: "I need to know where the rest room is."

usually first interpreted literally (as, "Do you need to open the window?"). When the same speech act is presented in a story context that makes the indirect meaning clear, the sentence is first interpreted in terms of the indirect meaning. For instance, if a character in a story had a cold and asked, "Must you open the window?" it would be interpreted as an indirect request, "Do not open the window."

Subsequent work by Gibbs (1986) showed that indirect speech acts often anticipate what potential obstacles the respondent might pose and specifically address those obstacles through the indirect speech act. For example, the question, "May I have . . ." addresses potential obstacles of permission; "Would you mind . . ." addresses potential obstacles regarding a possible imposition on the respondent; and "Do you have . . ." addresses potential obstacles regarding availability.

CONVERSATIONAL POSTULATES

In speaking to each other, we implicitly set up a cooperative enterprise. Indeed, if we do not cooperate with each other when we speak, we often end up talking past rather than to each other, and we do not communicate what we intended. H. P. Grice (1967) has proposed that conversations thrive on the basis of a **cooperative principle,** by which we seek to communicate in ways that make it easy for our listener to understand what we mean. According to Grice, successful conversations follow four maxims: the maxim of quantity, the maxim of quality, the maxim of relation, and the maxim of manner. (Examples of these maxims are provided in Table 10.3.)

According to the *maxim of quantity,* you should make your contribution to a conversation as informative as required, but no more informative than is appropriate. For example, suppose that someone says to you, "Hi, how are you?" and you enter into a 3-hour soliloquy on how your life is not quite what you were hoping for it to be. Here, you are violating the maxim of quantity. The social convention is to answer with a short response, even if you might like to go into greater detail. Sometimes, we violate the maxim of quantity for a specific end. If I have been seeking a chance to tell the chairperson of our department about problems I see with our educational program, the chairperson is taking a big risk by asking me, "How are things going?" while hoping for only a short reply.

According to the *maxim of quality,* your contribution to a conversation should be truthful. You are expected to say what you believe to be the case. If you have ever sought directions when in a strange city, you know the extreme frustration that can result if people are not truthful in telling you that they do not know where to find a particular location. Irony, sarcasm, and jokes might seem to be exceptions to the maxim of quality, but they are not: The listener is expected to recognize the irony or sarcasm, and to infer the speaker's true state of mind from what is said. Similarly, a joke is often expected to accomplish a particular purpose, and it usefully contributes to a conversation when that purpose is clear to everyone.

According to the *maxim of relation,* you should make your contributions to a conversation relevant to the aims of the conversation. Sometimes, of course, people purposely violate this maxim. If a romantic partner says to you, "I think we need to talk about our relationship," and you say, "The weather sure is beautiful today," you are violating the maxim in order to make the point that you do not want to talk about the relationship. When you do

TABLE 10.3 CONVERSATIONAL POSTULATES

In order to maximize the communication that occurs during conversation, speakers generally follow four maxims.

Postulate	Maxim	Example
Maxim of quantity	Make your contribution to a conversation as informative as required, but no more informative than is appropriate.	If someone asks you the temperature outside, and you reply, "It's 31.297868086298 degrees out there," you are violating the maxim of quantity because you are giving more information than was probably wanted. In the old TV series *Star Trek,* Mr. Spock, a "Vulcan" with a computer-like mind, elicits shrugs when he gives much more information in answer to a question than anyone would expect or want, as in the preceding answer to the temperature question.
Maxim of quality	Your contribution to a conversation should be truthful; you are expected to say what you believe to be the case.	Clearly, there are awkward circumstances in which each of us is unsure of just how much honesty is being requested, such as for the response to, "Honey, how do I look?" Under most circumstances, however, communication depends on an assumption that both parties to the communication are being truthful.
Maxim of relation	You should make your contributions to a conversation relevant to the aims of the conversation.	Almost any large meeting I attend seems to have someone who violates this maxim. This someone inevitably goes into long digressions that have nothing to do with the purpose of the meeting and that hold up the meeting. That reminds me of a story a friend once told me about a meeting he once attended, where . . .
Maxim of manner	You should try to avoid obscure expressions, vague utterances, and purposeful obfuscation of your point.	Nobel Prize–winning physicist Richard Feynman (1985) described how he once read a paper by a well-known sociologist, and he found that he could not make heads or tails of it. The sentence went something like this: "The individual member of the social community often receives information via visual, symbolic channels" (p. 281). Feynman concluded, in essence, that the sociologist was violating the maxim of manner when Feynman realized that the sentence meant, "People read."

so, however, you are being uncooperative, and unless the two of you can agree on how to define the conversation, you will talk past each other and have a very frustrating conversation.

According to the *maxim of manner,* you should be clear, and try to avoid obscure expressions, vague utterances, and purposeful obfuscation of your point. To these four maxims noted by Grice, we might add an additional maxim (Sacks, Schegloff, & Jefferson, 1974): Only one person speaks at a time. Given that maxim, the situational context and the relative social positions of the speakers affect turn-taking (Sacks et al., 1974). Sociolinguists have noted many ways in which speakers signal to one another when and how to take turns; Harvey Sacks and his colleagues mentioned various *adjacency pairs*—invitations selecting the person to speak or self-selected requests to speak. Speakers also use several other strategies for guiding the conversational topics and determining who will speak, such as attention-getters and interrupters, as well as conversational or topic openers and closings (E. Keller, 1976).

Gender and Language

Within our own culture, do men and women speak a different language? Gender differences have been found in the content of what we say. For example, old adolescent and young adult males prefer to talk about political views, sources of personal pride, and what they like about the other person, whereas females in this age group prefer to talk about feelings toward parents, close friends, and classes, and about their fears (Rubin, Hill, Peplau, & Dunkel-Schetter, 1980). Also, in general, women seem to disclose more about themselves than do men (T. U. Morton, 1978).

Deborah Tannen (1986, 1990, 1994) has done extensive sociolinguistic research on male–female conversation, and her research has led her to view the conversations between men and women as cross-cultural communication. Tannen suggests that young girls and boys learn conversational communication in essentially separate cultural environments through their same-sex friendships. As men and women, we then carry over the conversational styles we have learned in childhood into our adult conversations.

Tannen suggests that male–female differences in conversational style largely center on differing understandings of the goals of conversation. These cultural differences result in contrasting styles of communication that can lead to misunderstandings and even breakups as each partner somewhat unsuccessfully tries to understand the other. According to Tannen (1990, 1994), men see the world as a hierarchical social order in which the purpose of communication is to negotiate for the upper hand, to preserve independence, and to avoid failure. Each man strives to one-up the other and to "win" the contest. Women, in contrast, seek to establish a connection between the two participants, to give support and confirmation to others, and to reach consensus through communication.

To reach their conversational goals, women use conversational strategies that minimize differences, establish equity, and avoid any appearances of superiority on the part of one or another conversant. Women also affirm the importance of and the commitment to the relationship, and they handle differences of opinion by negotiating to reach a consensus that promotes the connection and ensures that both parties at least feel that their wishes have been considered, even if they are not entirely satisfied with the consensual decision.

Men enjoy connections and rapport, but because men have been raised in a gender culture in which status plays an important role, other goals take precedence in conversations. Tannen suggests that men seek to assert their independence from their conversational partners in order to indicate clearly their lack of acquiescence to the demands of others (which would indicate lack of power). Men also prefer to inform (thereby indicating the higher status conferred by authority) rather than to consult (indicating subordinate status) with their conversational partners. The male partner in a close relationship may thus end up informing his partner of their plans, whereas the female partner expected to be consulted on their plans. When engaging in cross-gender communications, the crossed purposes of men and women often result in miscommunication because each partner misinterprets the other's intentions.

Tannen suggests that when men and women become more aware of their cross-cultural styles and traditions, they may at least be less likely to misinterpret one another's conversational interactions. In this way, they would both be more likely to achieve their own individual aims, the aims of the relationship, and the aims of the other persons and institutions affected by their relationship. Tannen may well be right, but at present, converging operations are needed in addition to Tannen's sociolinguistic case-based approach in order to pin down the validity and generality of her interesting findings.

Practical Applications of Cognitive Psychology

Think about how your gender influences your conversational style, and construct some ways to communicate more effectively with persons of the opposite sex. How might your speech acts and conversational postulates differ? If you are a man, do you tend to use and prefer directives and declarations over expressives and commissives? If you are a woman, do you use and prefer expressives and commissives over directives and declarations? If so, speaking to persons of the opposite sex can lead to misinterpretations of meaning based on differences in style. For example, when you want to get another person to do something, it may be best to use the style that more directly reflects the other person's style—use a directive with men ("Would you go to the store?") and an expressive with women ("I really enjoy going shopping."). Also, remember that your responses should match the other person's expectations regarding how much information to provide, honesty, relevance, and directness. The art of effective communication really involves listening carefully to another person, observing body language, and interpreting the person's goals accurately. This can only be accomplished with time, effort, and sensitivity.

Discourse and Reading Comprehension

The preceding sections discussed some of the more general aspects of social uses of language. This section discusses more specifically the processes involved in understanding and using language in the social context of discourse. *Discourse* involves communicative units of language larger than individual sentences—in conversations, lectures, stories, essays, and even textbooks. Just as grammatical sentences are structured according to systematic syntactical rules, passages of discourse are structured systematically.

Investigating Cognitive Psychology

The following series of sentences is taken from a short story by O. Henry (William Sydney Porter, 1899–1953) entitled, "The Ransom of Red Chief." Actually, the following sequence of sentences is incorrect. Without knowing anything else about the story, try to figure out the correct sequence of sentences.

1. The father was respectable and tight, a mortgage financier and a stern, upright collection-plate passer and forecloser.
2. We selected for our victim the only child of a prominent citizen named Ebenezer Dorset.
3. We were down South in Alabama—Bill Driscoll and myself—when this kidnapping idea struck us.

(Continued)

(Continued)

4. Bill and me figured that Ebenezer would melt down for a ransom of two thousand dollars to a cent.

Hint: O. Henry was a master of irony, and by the end of the story, the would-be kidnappers paid the father a hefty ransom to take back his son so that they could quickly escape from the boy.

The sequence used by O. Henry, ex-convict and expert storyteller, was 3, 2, 1, 4. Is that pretty much the order you chose? How did you know the correct sequence for these sentences?

By adulthood, most of us have a firm grasp of how sentences are sequenced into a discourse structure. From our knowledge of discourse structure, we can derive meanings of sentence elements that are not apparent by looking at isolated sentences. To see how some of these discourse-dependent elements work, read the following sentences, and then answer the questions that follow them.

INVESTIGATING COGNITIVE PSYCHOLOGY

Rita gave Thomas a book about problem solving. He thanked her for the book. She asked, "Is it what you wanted?" He answered enthusiastically, "Yes, definitely." Rita asked, "Should I get you the companion volume on decision making?" He responded, "Please do."

In the second and third sentences, who were the people and things being referred to with the pronouns "He," "her," "She," and "it"? Why was the noun "book" preceded by the article "a" in the first sentence and by the article "the" in the second one? How do you know what Thomas's answer, "Yes, definitely," means? What is the action being requested in the response, "Please do"?

Cognitive psycholinguists who analyze discourse are particularly intrigued by how we are able to answer the questions posed in the preceding example. When grasping the meanings of pronouns (e.g., *he, she, him, her, it, they, them, we, us),* how do we know to whom (or to what) the pronouns are pointing? How do we know the meanings of ellipsed utterances (e.g., "Yes, definitely")? What does the use of the definite article *the* (as opposed to the indefinite article *a)* preceding a noun signify to listeners regarding whether a noun was mentioned previously? How do you know what event is being referenced by the verb *do?* The meanings of pronouns, ellipses, definite articles, event references, and other local elements within sentences usually depend on the discourse structure within which these elements appear (Grosz, Pollack, & Sidner, 1989).

Often, for understanding discourse, we rely not only on our knowledge of discourse structure, but also on our knowledge of a broad physical, social, or cultural context within which the discourse is presented. For example, observe how your understanding of the meaning of a paragraph is influenced by your existing knowledge and expectations. When reading the following sentences, pause between sentences, and think about what you know and what you expect, based on your knowledge.

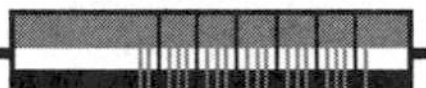

INVESTIGATING COGNITIVE PSYCHOLOGY

1. Susan became increasingly anxious as she prepared for the upcoming science exam. (What do you know about Susan?)
2. She had never written an exam before, and she wasn't sure how to construct an appropriate test of the students' knowledge. (How have your beliefs about Susan changed?)
3. She was particularly annoyed that the principal had even asked her to write the exam.
4. Even during a teachers' strike, a school nurse should not be expected to take on the task of writing an examination. (How did your expectations change over the course of the four sentences?)

In the preceding example, your understanding at each point in the discourse was influenced by your existing knowledge and expectations based on your own experiences within a particular context. Thus, just as prior experience and knowledge may aid us in lexical processing of text, they may also aid us in comprehending the text itself. What are the main reading comprehension processes? The process of reading comprehension is so complex that many entire courses and myriad volumes are devoted exclusively to the topic, but we focus here on just a few processes: semantic encoding, acquiring vocabulary, comprehending ideas in text, creating mental models of text, and comprehending text based on context and point of view.

SEMANTIC ENCODING: RETRIEVING WORD MEANING FROM MEMORY

Semantic encoding is the process by which we translate sensory information into a meaningful representation that we perceive, based on our understanding of the meanings of words. In lexical access, we identify words, based on letter combinations, and thereby activate our memory in regard to the words, whereas in semantic encoding, we take the next step and gain access to the meaning of the word, stored in memory. If we cannot semantically encode the word because its meaning does not already exist in memory, we must find another way in which to derive the meanings of words, such as from noting the context in which we read them.

In order to engage in semantic encoding, the reader needs to know what a given word means. Knowledge of word meanings (vocabulary) very closely relates to the ability to comprehend text: People who are knowledgeable about word meanings tend to be good readers, and vice versa. A reason for this relationship appears to be that readers simply cannot understand text well unless they know the meanings of the component words. For example, in one study, recall of the semantic content of a passage differed by 8% between two groups of participants when the two groups differed in their passage-relevant vocabulary knowledge by 9% (Beck, Perfetti, & McKeown, 1982).

Earl Hunt (1978) has suggested that people with larger vocabularies are able to access lexical information more rapidly than are those with smaller vocabularies. Because verbal information is often presented rapidly—whether in listening or in reading—the individual who can gain access to lexical information rapidly is able to process more information per unit of time than can one who can only gain access to such information slowly.

Acquiring Vocabulary: Deriving Word Meanings From Context

Another way in which having a larger vocabulary contributes to text comprehension is through learning from context. Whenever we cannot semantically encode a word because its meaning is not already stored in memory, we must engage in some kind of strategy to derive meaning from the text. In general, we must either search for a meaning, using external resources (such as dictionaries or teachers), or formulate a meaning, based on the existing information stored in memory, and using context cues with which to do so.

Heinz Werner and Edith Kaplan (1952) proposed that people learn most of their vocabulary indirectly, not by using external resources, but by figuring out the meanings of the *flidges* from the surrounding information.

For example, if you tried to look up the word *flidges* in the dictionary, you did not find it there. From the structure of the sentence, you probably figured out that *flidges* is a noun, and from the surrounding context, you probably figured out that it is a noun having something to do with words or vocabulary. In fact, *flidges* is a nonsense word I used as a placeholder for the word *words,* to show how you would gain a fairly good idea of a word's meaning from its context.

Maartje van Daalen-Kapteijns and Marianne Elshout-Mohr (1981; see also R. J. Sternberg & Powell, 1983) had adult participants learn meanings of words from sentence contexts and found that high- and low-verbal participants (i.e., people with large or small vocabularies, respectively) learn word meanings differently. High-verbal participants perform a deeper analysis of the possibilities for a new word's meaning than do low-verbal participants. In particular, the high-verbal participants used a well-formulated strategy for figuring out word meanings, whereas the low-verbal participants seemed to have no clear strategy at all.

Comprehension of Ideas in Text: Propositional Representations

Walter Kintsch has been particularly interested in the factors that influence our comprehension of what we read and has developed a model of text comprehension based on his observations (Kintsch, 1990; Kintsch & van Dijk, 1978). According to Kintsch, as we read, we try to hold as much information as possible in working (active) memory, in order to understand what we read. However, we do not try to store the exact words we read in working (active) memory. Rather, we try to extract the fundamental ideas from groups of words and store those fundamental ideas in a simplified representational form in working memory.

The representational form for these fundamental ideas is the *proposition.* Propositions were defined in more detail in chapter 7, but for now, it suffices to say that a proposition is the briefest unit of language that can be independently found to be true or false. For example, the sentence, "Penguins are birds, and penguins can fly" contains two propositions because you can verify independently whether penguins are birds and whether penguins can fly. In general, propositions assert either an action (e.g., flying) or a relationship (e.g., membership of penguins in the category of birds).

According to Kintsch, because working memory holds propositions, rather than words, its limits are taxed by large numbers of propositions, rather than by any particular number of words (Kintsch & Keenan, 1973). Thus, when a string of words in text requires us to hold a large number of propositions in working memory, we have difficulty in comprehending the text. When information stays in working memory a longer time, it is better comprehended and better recalled subsequently. Due to the limits of working memory, however, some information must be moved out of working memory to make room for new information.

According to Kintsch, propositions that are thematically central to the understanding of the text will remain in working memory longer than propositions that are irrelevant to the theme of the text passage. Kintsch calls the thematically crucial propositions *macro-propositions* and the overarching thematic structure of a passage of text the *macrostructure.* In an experiment testing his model, Kintsch and an associate (Kintsch & van Dijk, 1978) asked participants to read a 1,300-word text passage and then to summarize the key propositions in the passage immediately, at 1 month, or at 3 months after reading the passage. Even after 3 months, participants recalled the macropropositions and the overall macrostructure of the passage about as well as could participants who summarized it immediately after reading it. However, the propositions providing nonthematic details about the passage were not recalled as well after 1 month and not at all well after 3 months.

Representing the Text in Mental Models

Once words are semantically encoded or their meaning is derived from the use of context, the reader must still create a *mental model* of the text that is being read, which simulates the world being described, rather than the particular words being used to describe it (K. Craik, 1943; see Johnson-Laird, 1989). A mental model may be viewed as a sort of internal working model of the situation described in the text, as the reader understands it. In other words, the reader creates some sort of mental representation that contains within it the main elements of the text, preferably in a way that is relatively easy to grasp, or at least that is simpler and more concrete than the text itself. For example, suppose that you read the sentence, "The loud bang scared Alice." You may form a picture of Alice becoming scared upon hearing a loud noise, or you may access propositions stored in memory regarding the effects of loud bangs.

According to Philip Johnson-Laird (1983), a given passage of text or even a given set of propositions (to refer back to Kintsch's model) may lead to more than one mental model. For example, you may need to modify your mental model, depending on whether the next sentence is, "She tried to steer off the highway without losing control of the car," or, "She ducked to avoid being shot." In representing the loud bang that scared Alice, more than one mental model is possible, and if you start out with a different model than the one required in a given passage, your ability to comprehend the text depends on your ability to form a new mental model.

Note that in order to form mental models, you must make at least tentative *inferences* (preliminary conclusions or judgments) about what is meant but not said. In the first case, you are likely to assume that a tire blew out; in the second case, you may infer that someone is shooting a gun, even though neither of these things is explicitly stated. The construction of mental models illustrates that in addition to comprehending the words themselves, we also need to understand how words combine into meaningfully integrated representations of narratives or expositions. According to Johnson-Laird (1989), passages of text that lead unambiguously to a single mental model are easier to comprehend than are passages that may lead to multiple mental models.

Inferences can be of different kinds. One of the most important kind is what Susan Haviland and Herbert Clark (1974) have referred to as a *bridging inference,* which is an inference a reader (or listener) makes when a sentence seems not to follow directly from the sentence preceding it. In essence, what is new in the second sentence goes one step too far beyond what is given in the previous sentences. Consider, for example, two pairs of two sentences:

1. John took the picnic out of the trunk. The beer was warm.
2. John took the beer out of the trunk. The beer was warm.

Readers took about 180 milliseconds longer to read the first pair of sentences than the second. Haviland and Clark suggested that the reason for this greater processing time was that, in the first pair, information needed to be inferred (the picnic included beer) that was directly stated in the second pair.

Although most researchers emphasize the importance of inference making in reading and forms of language comprehension (e.g., Graesser & Kreuz, 1993), not all researchers do. According to the *minimalist hypothesis,* readers make inferences based only on information that is easily available to them and only when they need to make such inferences to make sense of adjoining sentences (McKoon & Ratcliff, 1992a). I believe that the bulk of the evidence regarding the minimalist position indicates that it is itself too minimalist: Readers appear to make more inferences than this position suggests (Suh & Trabasso, 1993, Trabasso & Suh, 1993).

Comprehending Text Based on Context and Point of View

What we remember from a given passage of text often depends on our point of view. For example, suppose that you were reading a text passage about the home of a wealthy family, which described many of the features of the house (e.g., a leaky roof, a fireplace, a musty basement), as well as its contents (e.g., valuable coins, silverware, television set). How might your encoding and comprehension of the text be different if you were reading it from the point of view of a prospective purchaser of the home, as opposed to the viewpoint of a prospective cat burglar? In a study using just such a passage, people who read the passage from the viewpoint of a cat burglar remembered far more about the contents of the home, whereas those who read from the viewpoint of a home buyer remembered more about the condition of the house (R. C. Anderson & Pichert, 1978).

To summarize, our comprehension of what we read depends on several abilities: (a) gaining access to the meanings of words, either from memory or based on context; (b) deriving meaning from the key ideas in what we read; (c) forming mental models that simulate the situations about which we read; and (d) extracting the key relevant information from the text, based on the contexts in which we read and on the ways in which we intend to use what we read.

Thus far, we have discussed the social and cognitive contexts for language. Language use interacts with, but does not completely determine the nature of thought, and social interactions influence the ways in which language is used and comprehended in discourse and reading. Next, we highlight some of the insights we have gained by studying the physiological context for language. Specifically, how do our brains process language?

NEUROPSYCHOLOGY OF LANGUAGE

Recall from chapter 2 that some of our earliest insights into brain localization related to an association between specific language deficits and specific organic damage to the brain, as first discovered by Marc Dax, Paul Broca, and Carl Wernicke. Broca's aphasia and Wernicke's aphasia are particularly well-documented instances in which brain lesions affect linguistic functions (see chapter 2). Through studies of brain-lesioned patients, researchers have learned a great deal about the relations between particular areas of the brain (the areas of lesions observed in patients) and particular linguistic functions (the observed deficits in the brain-injured patients).

LESION STUDIES AND ERP RESEARCH

For example, we can broadly generalize that many linguistic functions are primarily located in the areas identified by Broca and Wernicke, although damage to Wernicke's area, in the posterior of the cortex, is now believed to entail more grim consequences for linguistic function than does damage to Broca's area, closer to the front of the brain (Kolb & Whishaw, 1990). Also, lesion studies have shown that linguistic function is governed by a much larger area of the posterior cortex than just the area identified by Wernicke. In addition, other areas of the cortex also play a role, such as other association-cortex areas in the left hemisphere, and a portion of the left temporal cortex. Moreover, recent imaging studies of the posttraumatic recovery of linguistic functioning find that neurological language functioning appears to redistribute to other areas of the brain, including analogous areas in the right hemisphere and some frontal areas. Thus, damage to the major left hemisphere areas responsible for language functioning can sometimes lead to enhanced involvement of other areas as language functioning recovers—as if previously dormant or overshadowed areas take over the duties left vacant (Cappa et al., 1997; Weiller et al., 1996). Finally, some subcortical structures (e.g., the basal ganglia and the posterior thalamus) are also involved in linguistic function (Kolb & Whishaw, 1990).

Geschwind (1970) proposed a model, sometimes known as the Geschwind–Wernicke model, for how language is processed by the brain. According to this model, speech sounds signaling language travel to the inner ear. The auditory nerve then carries these signals to the primary auditory cortex of the temporal lobe. From there, the signal travels to an association area of the brain at a region in which the temporal, occipital, and parietal lobes join together. Here sense is made from what was said. In other words, meaning is assigned at this point. From there, the processed information travels to Wernicke's area and then to Broca's area. Although the model as originally formulated localized language comprehension in Wernicke's area and language production in Broca's area, this view is now known to be an oversimplification, in that Wernicke's area seems to have some involvement in language production and Broca's area in language comprehension (Zurif, 1990).

Event-related potentials, or ERPs (see chapter 2), can also be used to study the processing of language in the brain. For one thing, a certain ERP called N400 (a negative potential 400 milliseconds after stimulus onset) typically occurs when individuals hear an anomalous sentence (Kutas & Hillyard, 1980). Thus, if people are presented a sequence of normal sentences but also anomalous sentences (such as "The leopard is a very good napkin"), the anomalous sentences will elicit the N400 potential. Moreover, the more anomalous a sentence is, the greater the response shown in another event-related potential, P600 (a positive potential 600 milliseconds after the stimulus onset; Kutas & Van Patten, 1994).

Men and women appear to process language differently, at least at the phonological level (Shaywitz et al., 1995). An fMRI (functional magnetic resonance imaging) study of men and women asked participants to perform one of four tasks:

1. Indicate whether a pair of letters was identical.
2. Indicate whether two words have the same meaning.
3. Indicate whether a pair of words rhymes.
4. Compare the lengths of two lines (a control task).

The researchers found that when both male and female participants were performing the letter-recognition and word-meaning tasks, they showed activation in the left temporal lobe of the brain. When they were performing the rhyming task, however, only the inferior (lower) frontal region of the left hemisphere was activated for men, whereas the inferior frontal region of both the left and right hemispheres was activated in women. These results suggested that men localized their phonological processing more than did women.

By studying brain-injured men and women, Doreen Kimura (1987) has observed some intriguing sex differences in the ways that linguistic function appears to be localized in the brain. The men she studied seemed to show more left-hemisphere dominance for linguistic function than the women showed; women showed more bilateral, symmetrical patterns of linguistic function. Furthermore, the brain locations associated with aphasia seemed to differ for men and women: Most aphasic women showed lesions in the anterior region, although some aphasic women showed lesions in the temporal region. In contrast, aphasic men showed a more varied pattern of lesions, and aphasic men were more likely to show lesions in posterior regions rather than in anterior regions. One interpretation of Kimura's findings is that the role of the posterior region in linguistic function may be different for women than it is for men; another interpretation is that because women show less lateralization of linguistic function, women may be better able to compensate for any possible loss of function due to lesions in the left posterior hemisphere through functional offsets in the right posterior hemisphere. The possibility that there may also be subcortical sex differences in linguistic function further complicates the ease of interpreting Kimura's findings. (Recall also the earlier discussion of communication differences between men and women.)

Sex differences are not the only individual differences that have interested Kimura. She has also studied hemispheric processing of language in persons who use sign language rather than speech to communicate (Kimura, 1981). She has found that the locations of lesions that would be expected to disrupt speech also disrupt signing. Further, the hemispheric pattern of lesions associated with signing deficits is the same pattern shown with speech deficits. (That is, all right-handers with signing deficits show left-hemisphere lesions, as do most left-handers, but some left-handers with signing deficits show right-hemisphere lesions.) This finding supports the view that the brain processes both signing and speech similarly, in terms of their linguistic function, and it refutes the view that signing involves spatial processing or some other nonlinguistic form of cognitive processing.

Despite the many findings that have resulted from studies of brain-injured patients, there are three key difficulties in drawing conclusions based only on studies of patients with lesions: (a) Naturally occurring lesions are often not easily localized to a discrete region of the brain, with no untoward effects on other regions. For example, when hemorrhaging or insufficient blood flow (such as impairment due to clotting) causes lesions, the lesions may also affect other areas of the brain; thus, many patients who show cortical damage have also suffered some damage in subcortical structures, which may confound the findings of cortical damage. (b) Researchers are able to study the linguistic function of patients only after the lesions have caused damage, usually without having been able to document the linguistic function of patients prior to the damage. (c) Because it would be unethical to create lesions, merely to observe their effects on patients, researchers are able to study the effects of lesions only in those areas where lesions happen to have occurred naturally, and therefore other areas are not studied.

Other Methods

Although lesion studies are valuable, researchers also investigate brain localization of linguistic function via other methods, such as by evaluating the effects on linguistic function that follow electrical stimulation of the brain (e.g., Ojemann, 1982; Ojemann & Mateer, 1979). Through stimulation studies, researchers have found that stimulation of particular points in the brain seems to yield discrete effects on particular linguistic functions (such as the naming of objects), across repeated, successive trials. For example, in a given person, repeated stimulation of one particular point might lead to difficulties in recalling the names of objects on every trial, whereas stimulation of another point might lead to incorrect naming of objects. In addition, information regarding brain locations in a specific individual may not apply across individuals. Thus, for a given individual, a discrete point of stimulation may seem to affect only one particular linguistic function, but across individuals, these particular localizations of function vary widely. The effects of electrical stimulation are transitory, and linguistic function returns to normal soon after the stimulation has ceased. These brain-stimulation studies also show that many more areas of the cortex are involved in linguistic function than was thought previously.

Using electrical-stimulation techniques, George Ojemann has also studied sex differences in linguistic function and has found a somewhat paradoxical interaction of language and the brain: Although females generally have superior verbal skills to males, males have a proportionately larger (more diffusely dispersed) language area in their brains than do females. Ojemann has counterintuitively inferred that the size of the language area in the brain may be inversely related to the ability to use language. This interpretation seems further bolstered by Ojemann's findings with bilinguals, mentioned earlier, regarding the diffuse distribution of the nondominant language versus the more concentrated localization of the dominant language.

Yet another avenue of research involves the study of the metabolic activity of the brain and the flow of blood in the brain during the performance of various verbal tasks. For example, preliminary metabolic and blood-flow studies of the brain (e.g., S. E. Petersen et al., 1988) have indicated that many areas of the brain appear to be involved simultaneously during linguistic processing. However, most studies confirm the left hemisphere bias indicated by lesion studies (see Cabeza & Nyberg, 1997). Through these kinds of studies, researchers can examine multiple simultaneous cerebral processes involved in various linguistic tasks.

The diverse methods of studying the brain support the view that for all right-handed individuals and most left-handed persons, the left hemisphere of the brain seems clearly implicated in syntactical aspects of linguistic processing, and it is essential to speech and to signing. The left hemisphere also seems to be essential to the ability to write. On the other hand, the right hemisphere seems capable of quite a bit of auditory comprehension, particularly in terms of semantic processing, as well as some reading comprehension and in posttraumatic linguistic recovery. The right hemisphere also seems to be important in several of the subtle nuances of linguistic comprehension and expression, such as understanding and expressing vocal inflection and gesture, as well as comprehending metaphors and other nonliteral aspects of language (e.g., jokes and sarcasm; Kolb & Whishaw, 1990).

Finally, some subcortical structures, especially the basal ganglia and the posterior thalamus, seem to be involved in linguistic function. Starting more than a century ago, investigators noted that the thalamus seems to be involved in linguistic function (e.g., Hughlings-Jackson, 1866/1932), particularly in coordinating the activities of the cortical areas involved in speech (Penfield & Roberts, 1959). Since these early observations, Ojemann (1975) and others have linked lesions in the thalamus to specific difficulties in speaking (e.g., perseveration or impairment of speed, fluency, or naming). Also, the thalamus may play a role in activating the cortex for understanding and remembering language. Because of the difficulty of studying subcortical structures, the specific role of the thalamus and other subcortical structures is not yet well defined (Kolb & Whishaw, 1990).

Much of this chapter has revealed the many ways in which language and thought interact. The following chapter focuses on problem solving and creativity, but it also further reveals the interconnectedness of the ways in which we use language and the ways in which we think.

SUMMARY

1. **How does language affect the way we think?** According to the *linguistic relativity* view, cognitive differences that result from using different languages cause people speaking the various languages to perceive the world differently. However, the *linguistic universals* view stresses cognitive commonalities across different language users. No single interpretation explains all of the available evidence regarding the interaction of language and thought.

   Research on bilinguals seems to show that environmental considerations also affect the interaction of language and thought. For example, additive bilinguals have established a well-developed primary language; the second language adds to their linguistic and perhaps even their cognitive skills. In contrast, subtractive bilinguals have not yet firmly established their primary language when portions of a second language partially displace the primary language; this displacement may lead to difficulties in verbal skills. Theorists differ in their views as to whether bilinguals store two or more languages separately *(dual-system hypothesis)* or together *(single-system hypothesis).* Some aspects of multiple languages could possibly be stored separately and others unitarily. Whereas creoles and pidgins arise when two or more distinct linguistic groups come into contact, a *dialect* appears when a regional variety of a language becomes distinguished by features such as distinctive vocabulary, grammar, and pronunciation.

Slips of the tongue may involve inadvertent verbal errors in phonemes, morphemes, or larger units of language. Slips of the tongue include anticipations, perseverations, reversals (including spoonerisms), substitutions, insertions, and deletions. Alternative views of *metaphor* include the comparison view, the anomaly view, the domain-interaction view, and the class-inclusion view.

2. **How does our social context influence our use of language?** Psychologists, *sociolinguists,* and others who study *pragmatics* are interested in how language is used within a social context, including various aspects of nonverbal communication. *Speech acts* comprise representatives, directives, commissives, expressives, and declarations. *Indirect requests,* ways of asking for something without doing so straightforwardly, may refer to abilities, desires, future actions, and reasons. *Conversational postulates,* which provide a means for establishing language as a cooperative enterprise, comprise several maxims, including the maxims of quantity, quality, relation, and manner. Sociolinguists have observed that people engage in various strategies to signal turn-taking in conversations.

   Sociolinguistic research suggests that male–female differences in conversational style center largely on men's and women's differing understandings of the goals of conversation. It has been suggested that men tend to see the world as a hierarchical social order in which their communication aims involve the need to maintain a high rank in the social order. In contrast, women tend to see communication as a means for establishing and maintaining their connection to their communication partners; to do so, they seek ways to demonstrate equity and support and to reach consensual agreement.

   In *discourse* and *reading comprehension,* we use the surrounding context to infer the reference of pronouns and ambiguous phrases. The discourse context can also influence the semantic interpretation of unknown words in passages and aid in acquiring new vocabulary. *Propositional representations* of information in passages can be organized into *mental models* for text comprehension. Finally, a person's point of view likewise influences what will be remembered.

3. **How can we find out about language by studying the human brain, and what do such studies reveal?** Neuropsychologists, cognitive psychologists, and other researchers have managed to link quite a few language functions with specific areas or structures in the brain, largely by noticing what happens when a particular area of the brain is injured, is electrically stimulated, or is studied in terms of its

metabolic activity. Thus far, the various methods of studying the brain support the view that for most persons, the left hemisphere of the brain is vital to speech and affects many syntactical aspects of linguistic processing, as well as some semantic aspects. For most people, the right hemisphere handles a more limited number of linguistic functions, including auditory comprehension of semantic information, as well as comprehension and expression of some nonliteral aspects of language use, such as vocal inflection, gesture, metaphors, sarcasm, irony, and jokes.

THINKING ABOUT THINKING: FACTUAL, ANALYTICAL, CREATIVE, AND PRACTICAL QUESTIONS

1. Why are researchers interested in the number of color words used by different cultures?
2. Describe the five basic kinds of speech acts proposed by Searle.
3. How should cognitive psychologists interpret evidence of linguistic universals when considering the linguistic-relativity hypothesis?
4. Compare and contrast the kinds of understandings that can be gained by studying speech errors made by normal persons with those that can be gained by studying the language produced by persons who have particular brain lesions.
5. Write an example of a pidgin conversation between two people, and a creole conversation, focusing on the differences between pidgins and creoles.
6. Draft an example of a brief dialogue between a male and a female in which each may misunderstand the other, based on their differing beliefs regarding the goals of communication.
7. Suppose that you are an instructor of English as a second language. What kinds of things will you want to know about your students in order to determine how much to emphasize phonology, vocabulary, syntax, or pragmatics in your instruction?
8. Give an example of a humorous violation of one of Grice's four maxims of successful conversation.

KEY TERMS

bilingual 322
cooperative principle 333
dialect 325
dual-system hypothesis 323
indirect request 332
linguistic relativity 317
linguistic universals 320
metaphor 327
monolingual 322
pragmatics 329
simile 327
single-system hypothesis 323
slips of the tongue 326
speech act 330

Annotated Suggested Readings

Bialystok, E., & Hakuta, K. (1994). *In other words: The science of second-language acquisition.* New York: Basic Books. Currently, the most comprehensive and readable exposition to be found on what we know about learning second languages.

Johnson, J. S., & Newport, E. L. (1989). Critical periods in second language learning: The influence of maturational state on the acquisition of English as a second language. *Cognitive Psychology, 21,* 215–258. One of the best empirical studies of whether people have a critical period for the learning of a second language, after which their ability to learn such a language decreases.

Kintsch, W. (1988). The role of knowledge in discourse comprehension: A construction-integration model. *Psychological Review, 95,* 163–182. A presentation of Kintsch's widely respected and frequently cited theory of how people comprehend discourse.

Tannen, D. (1990). *You just don't understand: Women and men in conversation.* New York: Ballantine. A fascinating sociolinguistic account of how men's and women's styles of communication differ, often leading to misunderstandings between the sexes.

Vygotsky, L. S. (1986). *Thought and Language.* Cambridge: MIT Press. A very interesting, thoughtful, and distinctive account—Vygotsky's early twentieth century theory of the interaction between thought and language over the course of development stands out from the rest. Be sure to find the 1986 edition, as it is more complete than earlier edited versions.

Problem Solving and Creativity

Chapter Outline

Exploring Cognitive Psychology

The Problem-Solving Cycle

Types of Problems
- Well-Structured Problems
- Ill-Structured Problems and the Role of Insight

Obstacles and Aids to Problem Solving
- Mental Sets, Entrenchment, and Fixation
- Negative and Positive Transfer
- Incubation

Expertise: Knowledge and Problem Solving
- Organization of Knowledge
- Innate Talent and Acquired Skill

Creativity
- It's How Much You Produce
- It's What You Know
- It's Who You Are
- It's Where You Are
- All of the Above

Summary

Thinking About Thinking: Factual, Analytical, Creative, and Practical Questions

Key Terms

Annotated Suggested Readings

Exploring Cognitive Psychology

1. **What are some key steps involved in solving problems?**
2. **What are the differences between problems that have a clear path to a solution versus problems that do not?**
3. **What are some of the obstacles and aids to problem solving?**
4. **How does expertise affect problem solving?**
5. **What is creativity, and how can it be fostered?**

How do you solve problems that arise in your relationships with other people? How do you solve the "two-string" problem illustrated in Figure 11.1? How does anyone solve any problem, for that matter? This chapter considers the process of solving problems, as well as some of the hindrances and helps to **problem solving,** the goal of which is to overcome obstacles obstructing the path to a solution. In many situations, we are better able to solve problems by using knowledge (including how-to knowledge, such

FIGURE 11.1 **PROBLEM SOLVING**

Imagine that you are the person standing in the middle of this room, in which two strings are hanging down from the ceiling. Your goal is to tie together the two strings, but neither string is long enough so that you can reach out and grab the other string while holding either of the two strings. You have available a few clean paintbrushes, a can of paint, and a heavy canvas tarpaulin. How will you tie together the two strings?

as skills, as well as factual knowledge) or by using creative insights. In previous chapters, we have explored many uses for knowledge other than its application in solving problems. Similarly, creativity may serve purposes other than that of being the goal of problem solving. At the conclusion of this chapter, we discuss creativity in its own right.

THE PROBLEM-SOLVING CYCLE

We engage in problem solving when we need to overcome obstacles in order to answer a question or to achieve a goal. If we can quickly retrieve an answer from memory, we do not have a problem. If we cannot retrieve an immediate answer, then we have a problem to be solved. This section describes the steps of the **problem-solving cycle,** which include problem identification, problem definition, strategy formulation, organization of information, allocation of resources, monitoring, and evaluation (shown in Figure 11.2; see Bransford & Stein, 1993; Hayes, 1989; R. J. Sternberg, 1986a).

In considering the steps, remember also the importance of flexibility in following the various steps of the cycle. Successful problem solving may involve occasionally tolerating some ambiguity regarding how best to proceed. Rarely can we solve problems by following any one optimal sequence of problem-solving steps. Moreover, we may go back and

FIGURE 11.2 **PROBLEM-SOLVING CYCLE**

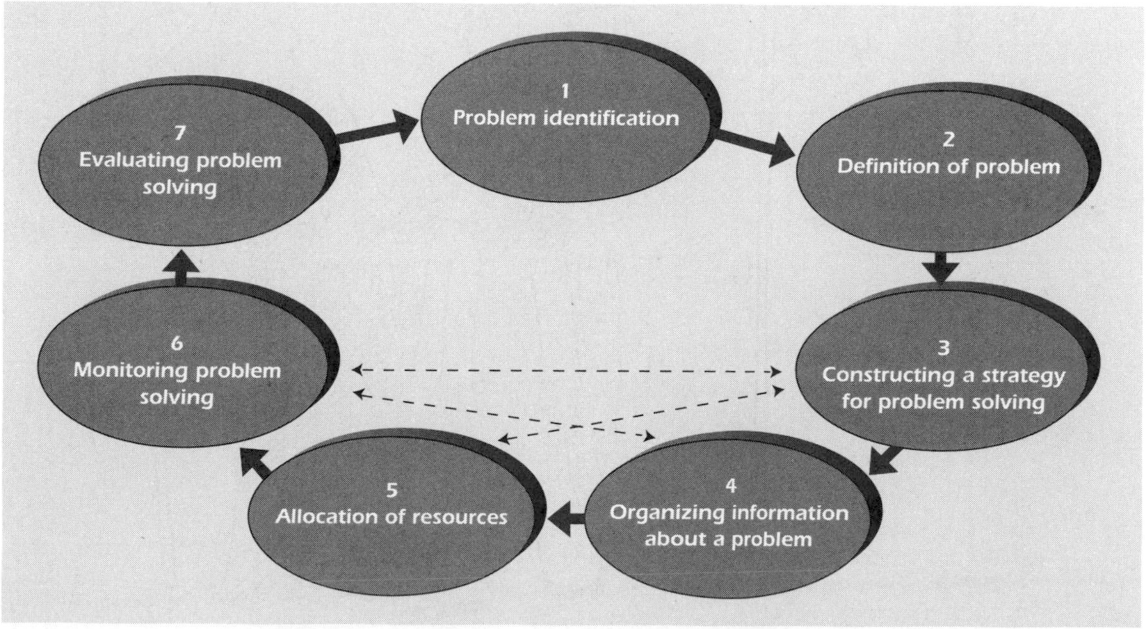

The steps of the problem-solving cycle include problem identification, problem definition, strategy formulation, organization of information, allocation of resources, monitoring, and evaluation.

forth through the steps, change their order as need be, or even skip or add steps when it seems appropriate.

1. *Problem identification:* As odd as it sounds, identifying a situation as problematic is sometimes a difficult step. We may fail to recognize that we have a goal (e.g., needing to stay out of the path of an oncoming car we fail to observe), that our path to a goal is obstructed (e.g., needing to obtain more money because we lack enough to buy something we want), or that the solution we had in mind does not work (e.g., the job we expected to get is not now available to us). If your problem is the need to write a term paper, you must first identify a question that your paper will address.
2. *Problem definition and representation:* Once we identify the existence of a problem, we still have to define and represent the problem well enough to understand how to solve it. For example, in preparing to write your term paper, you must define your topic well enough to determine the research you will gather and your overall strategy for writing your paper. The problem-definition step is crucial because if you inaccurately define and represent the problem, you are much less able to solve it (Funke, 1991; Hegarty, 1991). In fact, in solving the problem shown in Figure 11.1, this step is crucial to your finding the answer. That is, in solving the two-string problem, are you constraining your answer in ways that are limiting your ability to solve the problem?

"Relax, honey. Change is good."

Sometimes, we don't recognize an important problem that confronts us.

3. *Strategy formulation:* Once the problem has been defined effectively, the next step is to plan a strategy for solving it. The strategy may involve **analysis**—breaking down the whole of a complex problem into manageable elements. Instead, or perhaps in addition, it may involve the complementary process of **synthesis**—putting together various elements to arrange them into something useful. In writing your term paper, you must analyze the components of your topic, research the various components, and then synthesize the topics into a rough draft of your paper.

   Another pair of complementary strategies involves divergent and convergent thinking. In **divergent thinking,** you try to generate a diverse assortment of possible alternative solutions to a problem. Once you have considered a variety of possibilities, however, you must engage in **convergent thinking,** to narrow down the multiple possibilities to converge on a single, best answer—or at least what you believe to be the most likely solution, which you will try first. When you came up with the topic for your paper, you first used divergent thinking to generate many possible topics and then used convergent thinking to select the most suitable topic that interested you. In solving real-life problems, you may need both analysis and synthesis, and both divergent and convergent thinking. There is no single ideal strategy for addressing every problem. Instead, the optimal strategy depends on both the problem and the problem-solvers' personal preferences in problem-solving methods.

4. *Organization of information:* Once a strategy (at least a tentative strategy) has been formulated, you are ready to organize the available information in a way that enables you to implement the strategy. Of course, throughout the problem-solving cycle, you are constantly organizing and reorganizing the available information. At this step, however, you organize the information strategically, finding a representation that best enables you to implement your strategy. For example, if your problem is to organize the information for your term paper, you may use an outline to organize your ideas. If your problem is to find a location, you may need to organize and represent the available information in the form of a map. If your problem is to earn a particular amount of money by a particular date, you may represent the available information in the form of a timetable for intervening dates by which you must have earned a particular portion of the total amount.

5. *Resource allocation:* In addition to our other problems, most of us face the problem of having limited resources, including time, money, equipment, space, and so on. Some problems are worth a lot of time and other resources, whereas other problems are worth very few resources. Moreover, we need to know when to allocate which resources. Studies show that expert problem solvers (and better students) tend to devote more of their mental resources to *global* (big-picture) planning than do novice problem solvers. Novices (and poorer students) tend to allocate more time to *local* (detail-oriented) planning than do experts (e.g., Larkin, McDermott, Simon, & Simon, 1980; R. J. Sternberg, 1981). For example, better students are more likely to spend more time in the

initial phase, deciding how to solve a problem, and then less time actually solving it, than are poorer students (Bloom & Broder, 1950). By spending more time in advance deciding what to do, effective students are less likely to fall prey to false starts, winding paths, and all kinds of errors. When a person allocates more mental resources to planning on a large scale, he or she is able to save time and energy and to avoid frustration later on. Thus, when writing your term paper, you will probably spend much of your time conducting your research, organizing your notes, and planning your paper.

6. *Monitoring:* A prudent expenditure of time includes monitoring the process of solving the problem. Effective problem solvers do not set out on a path to a solution and then wait until they have reached the end of the path to check where they are (Schoenfeld, 1981). Rather, they check up on themselves all along the way, to make sure that they are getting closer to their goal. If they are not, they reassess what they are doing, perhaps concluding that they made a false start, that they got off track somewhere along the way, or even that they see a more promising path if they take a new direction. If you are writing a term paper, you will want to be monitoring whether you are making good progress. If you are not making good progress, you will want to figure out why.
7. *Evaluation:* Just as you need to monitor a problem while you are in the process of solving it, you need to evaluate your solution after you have finished. Some of the evaluation may occur right away; the rest may occur a bit later, or even much later. For example, after drafting your term paper, you will probably evaluate your draft, revising and editing it quite a few times before turning in your paper. Often, key advances occur through the evaluation process. Through evaluation, new problems may be recognized, the problem may be redefined, new strategies may come to light, and new resources may become available or existing ones may be used more efficiently. Hence, the cycle is completed when it leads to new insights and begins anew.

TYPES OF PROBLEMS

Cognitive psychologists have categorized problems according to whether the problems have clear paths to a solution. The problems with clear solution paths are sometimes termed **well-structured problems** (also termed *well-defined problems;* e.g., "How do you find the area of a parallelogram?"); those without clear solution paths are **ill-structured problems** (also termed *ill-defined problems;* e.g., "How do you tie together two suspended strings, when neither string is long enough to allow you to reach the other string while holding either of the strings?"). Of course, in the real world of problems, these two categories may represent a continuum of clarity in problem solving rather than two discrete classes with a clear boundary between the two. Nonetheless, the categories are useful in understanding how people solve problems. We next consider each of these kinds of problems in turn.

WELL-STRUCTURED PROBLEMS

On tests in school, your teachers have asked you to tackle countless well-structured problems in specific content areas (e.g., math, history, geography). These problems had clear paths—if not necessarily easy paths—to their solutions. In psychological research, cognitive psychologists might ask you to solve less content-specific kinds of well-structured problems. For example, cognitive psychologists have often studied a particular type of well-structured problem: the class of *move problems,* so termed because such problems require a series of moves to reach a final goal state. Perhaps the most well-known of the move problems is one involving two antagonistic parties, whom we call "forest-burners" and "forest-lovers" in our next investigation.

INVESTIGATING COGNITIVE PSYCHOLOGY

Three forest-burners and three forest-lovers are on a river bank. The forest-burners and forest-lovers need to cross over to the other side of the river. They have for this purpose a small rowboat that will hold just two people. There is one problem, however. If the number of forest-burners on either river bank exceeds the number of forest-lovers on that bank, the forest-burners will destroy the forest on the other side of the river to clear land for a large parking lot. How can all six people get across to the other side of the river in a way that guarantees that they all arrive there with the forest intact?

This problem is represented pictorially in Figure 11.3. Try to solve the problem before reading on.

The solution to the problem is shown in Figure 11.4. The solution contains several features worth noting. First, the problem can be solved in a minimum of 11 steps, including the first and last steps. Second, the solution is essentially *linear* in nature—there is just one valid move (connecting two points with a line segment) at most steps of problem solution. At all but two steps along the solution path, only one error can be made without violating the rules of the move problem: to go directly backward in the solution. At two steps, there are two possible forward-moving responses, but both of these lead toward the correct answer. Thus, again, the most likely error is to return to a previous state in the solution of the problem.

A second kind of error is to make an illegal move—that is, a move that is not permitted according to the terms of the problem. For example, a move that resulted in having more than two individuals in the boat would be illegal. According to those who have studied the problem (e.g., Greeno, 1974; Simon & Reed, 1976; J. C. Thomas, 1974), the main kinds of errors that people seem to make are (a) inadvertently moving backward, (b) making illegal moves, and (c) not realizing the nature of the next legal move.

One method for studying how to solve well-defined problems is to develop computer simulations in which the researcher's task is to create a computer program that can solve these problems. According to this approach, by developing the instructions a computer

FIGURE 11.3 **FOREST-BURNERS AND FOREST-LOVERS: A MOVE PROBLEM**

How can they cross the river and leave the forest intact? (See the text for a description of the problem.)

must execute to solve problems, the researcher may better understand how humans solve similar kinds of problems. Based on early work in computer-simulated problem solving, Allen Newell and Herbert Simon (1972) developed a model of problem solving.

According to the Newell–Simon model, the problem solver (which may be using human or artificial intelligence) must view the initial (problem) state and the goal (solution) state within a **problem space**—the universe of all possible actions that can be applied to solving a problem, given any constraints that apply to the solution of the problem. According to this model, the fundamental strategy for solving problems is to decompose the problem task into a series of steps, which will eventually lead to the solution of the problem at hand. Each step involves a set of rules for procedures ("operations") that can be implemented. The set of rules is organized hierarchically into programs containing various internal levels of subprograms (called "routines" and "subroutines").

Many of the sublevel programs are **algorithms,** sequences of operations that may be used *recursively* (repeated over and over again; Hunt, 1975). Generally, an algorithm continues recursively until it satisfies a condition determined by a program (e.g.,

FIGURE 11.4 **SOLUTION: FOREST-BURNERS AND FOREST-LOVERS**

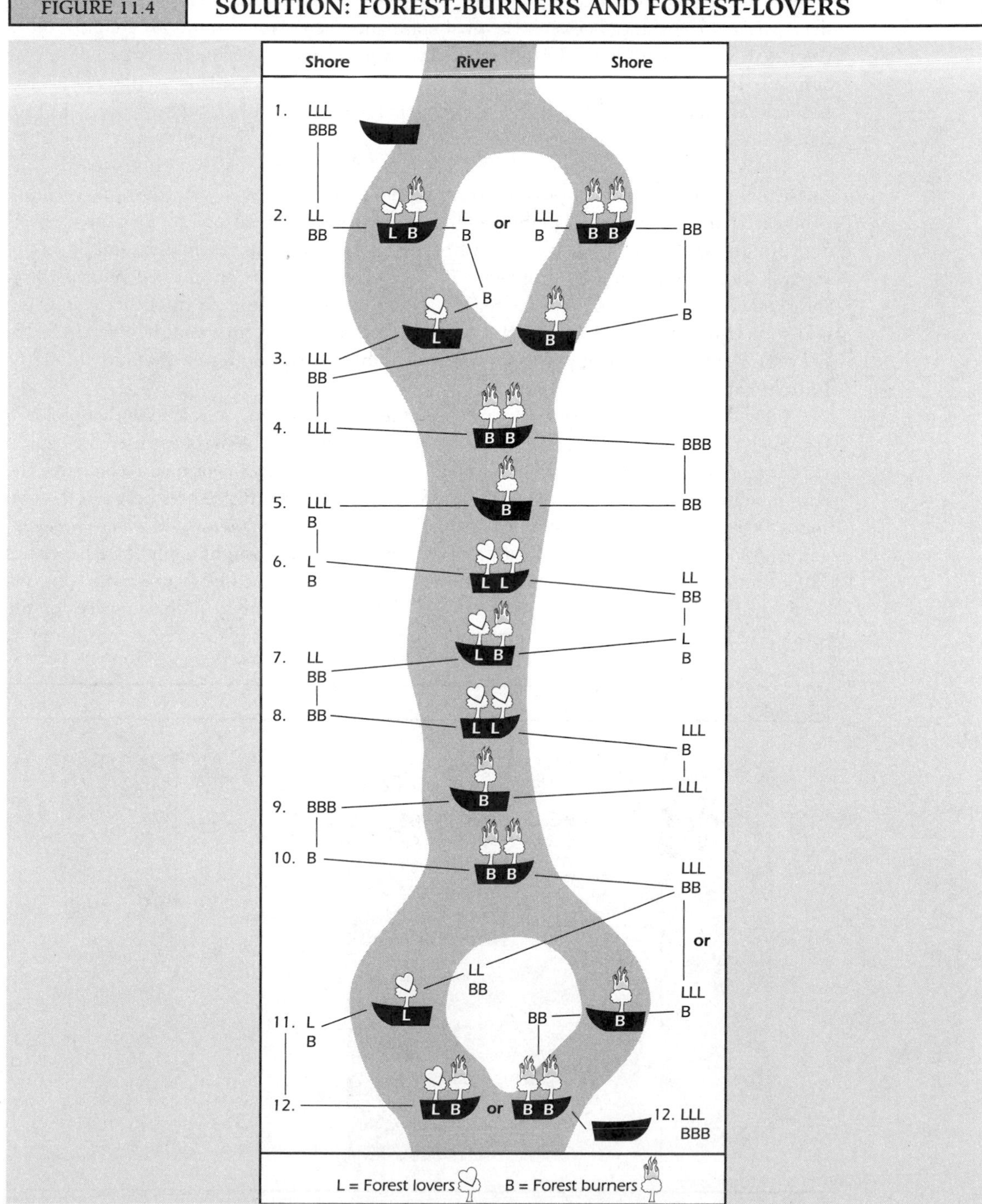

(Refer to the text for an explanation of the solution.) What can you learn about your own methods of solving problems by seeing how you approached this particular problem?

"repeat these steps until the goal state is reached"; "repeat these steps until they stop decreasing the distance between the goal state and the current state"). If a computer is provided with a well-defined problem and an appropriate hierarchy (program) of operations organized into procedural algorithms, the computer can readily calculate all possible operations and combinations of operations within the problem space and can determine the best possible sequence of steps to take to solve the problem.

Unlike computers, however, the human mind does not specialize in high-speed computations of multitudinous possible combinations. The limits of our working memory prohibit us from considering more than just a few possible operations at one time. Newell and Simon recognized these limits and observed that humans must use some kinds of mental shortcuts for solving problems. These mental shortcuts are termed **heuristics**—informal, intuitive, speculative strategies, which sometimes lead to an effective solution and sometimes do not (Holyoak, 1990). If we store in long-term memory several simple heuristics, which we can apply to a variety of problems, we can lessen the burden on our limited-capacity working memory.

Newell and Simon observed that when problem solvers were confronted with a problem for which they could not immediately see an answer, effective problem solvers used the heuristic of *means–ends analysis,* a strategy in which the problem solver continually compares the current state and the goal state and takes steps to minimize the differences between the two states. Various other problem-solving heuristics include *working forward, working backward,* and *generate and test.* Table 11.1 illustrates how a problem solver might apply these heuristics to the aforementioned move problem (Greeno & Simon, 1988), as well as to a more common everyday problem (Hunt, 1994). Figure 11.5 shows a rudimentary problem space for the move problem, illustrating that there may be any number of possible strategies for solving it.

FIGURE 11.5 **PROBLEM SPACE**

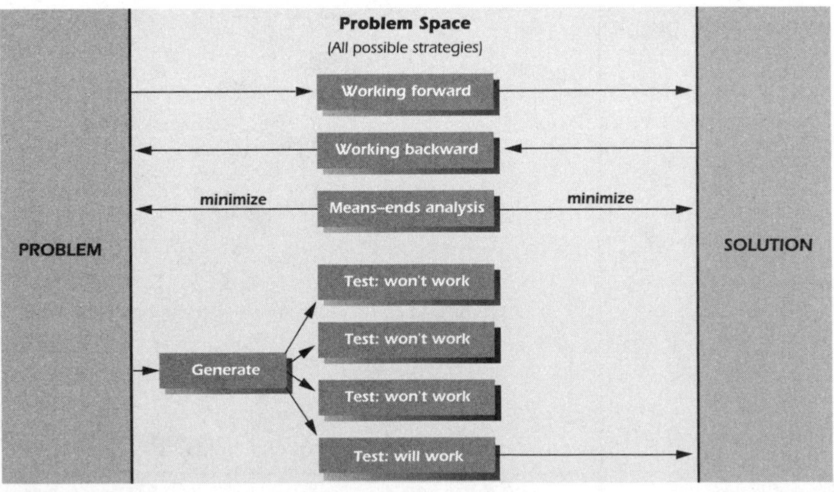

A problem space contains all of the possible strategies leading from the initial problem state to the solution (the goal state). This problem space, for example, shows four of the heuristics that might be used in solving the move problem illustrated in Figures 11.3 and 11.4.

TABLE 11.1 FOUR HEURISTICS

These four heuristics may be used in solving the move problem illustrated in Figures 11-3 and 11-4.

Heuristic	Definition of Heuristic	Example of Heuristic, Applied to the Move Problem (Greeno & Simon, 1988)	Example of Heuristic, Applied to an Everyday Problem: How to Travel by Air From Your Home to Another Location, Using the Most Direct Route Possible (Hunt, 1994)
Means–ends analysis	The problem-solver analyzes the problem by viewing the end—the goal being sought—and then tries to decrease the distance between the current position in the problem space and the end goal in that space.	Try to get as many people on the far bank and as few people on the near bank as possible.	Try to minimize the distance between home and the destination.
Working forward	The problem-solver starts at the beginning and tries to solve the problem from the start to the finish.	Evaluate the situation carefully with the six people on one bank and then try to move them step by step to the opposite bank.	Find the possible air routes leading from home toward the destination, and take the routes that seem most directly to lead to the destination.
Working backward	The problem-solver starts at the end, and tries to work backward from there.	Start with the final state—having all forest-lovers and all forest-burners on the far bank—and try to work back to the beginning state.	Find the possible air routes that reach the destination, and work backward to trace which of these routes can be most directly traced to originate at home.
Generate and test	The problem-solver simply generates alternative courses of action, not necessarily in a systematic way, and then notices in turn whether each course of action will work.	This method works fairly well for the move problem because at most steps in the process, there is only one allowable forward move, and there are never more than two possibilities, both of which will eventually lead to the solution.	Find the various possible alternative routes leading from home, then see which of these routes might be used to end up at the destination. Choose the most direct route. Unfortunately, given the number of possible combinations of routes for air travel, this heuristic may not be very helpful.

You enter a bookstore seeking out a certain book, Hortense Hortigan's *Make a Million in a Month.* You are not sure where in the bookstore, if anywhere, you can find the book. What would be an algorithm for solving this problem? How about a heuristic?

The only algorithm that guarantees your discovering whether the book is in the bookstore is to check each book in the store until you either have found Hortigan's book or searched unsuccessfully through all titles. There are many possible heuristics you could apply, however: (a) asking a clerk for help; (b) looking through an index of books in the store, if one is available; (c) starting your search in more plausible sections (financial or self-help) and only then moving to less plausible sections; and so on. Notice, though, that if you use the heuristics and do not find the book, you cannot be certain the book is not there (e.g., it may be misplaced or not yet in the index). But do not waste your time: there is no such book, and if there were, you can be sure that the claim would be false or that it would be referring to a million somethings, but surely not dollars.

Isomorphic Problems

The forest-burners versus forest-lovers problem described previously has also been presented in terms of cannibals and missionaries, in which cannibals might eat missionaries, or in terms of hobbits and orcs, where orcs devour outnumbered hobbits. These alternative forms of presentation bring us to another point about problems. Sometimes, two problems are **isomorphic** *(iso-,* "same"; *-morph,* "form")—their formal structure is the same; only their content differs. Sometimes, as in the case of the forest-burners and forest-lovers problem, the missionaries and cannibals problem, and the hobbits and orcs problem, the isomorphism is obvious. Similarly, you can readily detect the isomorphism of many games that involve constructing words from jumbled or scrambled letters. Figure 11.6 also shows a different set of isomorphic problems, which illustrates some of the puzzles associated with isomorphic problems.

According to Stephen Reed (1987; Reed, Dempster, & Ettinger, 1985), it is extremely difficult to observe the underlying structural isomorphism of problems and to be able to apply problem-solving strategies from one problem (e.g., an example from a textbook) to another (e.g., a problem on a test). Problem solvers are particularly unlikely to detect isomorphisms when two problems are similar but not identical in structure. Further, when the content or the surface characteristics of the problems differ sharply, detecting the isomorphism of the structure of problems is harder. For example, school-aged children may find it difficult to see the structural similarity between various word problems that are framed within different story situations. Similarly, physics students may have difficulty seeing the structural similarities among various physics problems when different kinds of materials are used. The problem of recognizing isomorphisms across varying contexts returns us to the recurring difficulties in problem representation.

Problems of Problem Representation

What is the key reason that some problems are easier to solve than their isomorphisms? Kenneth Kotovsky, John Richard Hayes, and Herbert Simon (1985) have extensively investigated why some isomorphic forms are easier to solve than others. In particular, they studied various versions of a problem known as the Tower of Hanoi, in which the problem solver must use a series of moves to transfer a set of rings (usually three) from the first of three pegs to the third of the three pegs, using as few moves as possible (see Figure 11.7). In their study, they presented this same basic problem in many different isomorphic forms. They found that some forms of the problem took up to 16 times as long to solve as other forms. Although many factors influenced these findings, the authors concluded that a major determinant of the relative ease of solving the problem was how the problem was represented. For example, in the form shown in Figure 11.7, the physically different sizes

FIGURE 11.6 PROBLEM ISOMORPHS

1	2	3	4	5	6	7	8	9

(a) Number scrabble (Newell & Simon, 1972): A set of cards showing the integers 1–9 are placed face up between two players. The goal of the game is to be the first player to hold three cards bearing integers that sum to 15. (The player may also hold an additional card or two that do not figure into the sum.) The players must take turns choosing one card at a time. If all the cards have been chosen, and neither player holds a set of three integers that sum to 15, neither player wins.

X	X	X
X	O	O
O	X	O

(b) Tic-tac-toe: Two players alternate taking turns to mark in each of the squares, with one player marking X's and the other player marking O's. The first player to have her or his marks form a horizontal, vertical, or diagonal line of three squares wins the game. If all of the squares have been marked, and neither player has formed a line of three squares, neither player wins.

6	1	8
7	5	3
2	9	4

(c) Magic square: If played as a solitary puzzle, try to arrange the integers from 1 to 9 such that the integers sum to 15 in each direction (i.e., horizontal, vertical, and diagonal; one solution is shown here). If played as a competitive game, players may take turns writing each of the integers from 1 to 9. The first player to form a horizontal, vertical, or diagonal line of integers summing to 15 wins the game. If all the integers have been used (and the squares have been filled), and neither player has formed a line of integers summing to 15, neither player wins.

Compare the problems illustrated in the games of (a) number scrabble, (b) tic-tac-toe, and (c) magic square. In what ways are these problems isomorphic? How do their differences in presentation affect the ease of representing and solving these problems?

of the discs facilitated the mental representation of the restriction against moving larger discs onto smaller discs, whereas other forms of the problem did not.

Recall the two-string problem, posed at the outset of this chapter. The solution to the "two-string problem" is shown in Figure 11.8. As this figure shows, the two-string problem can be solved. However, many people find it extremely difficult to arrive at the solution, and many never do, no matter how hard they try. People who find the problem insoluble often err at Step 2 of the problem-solving cycle, after which they never recover. That is, by defining the problem as being one in which they must be able to move toward one string while holding another, they impose on themselves a constraint that makes the problem virtually insoluble. Unfortunately, all of us are subject to misdefining problems from time to time, as the case of the two-string problem shows.

FIGURE 11.7 **TOWER OF HANOI**

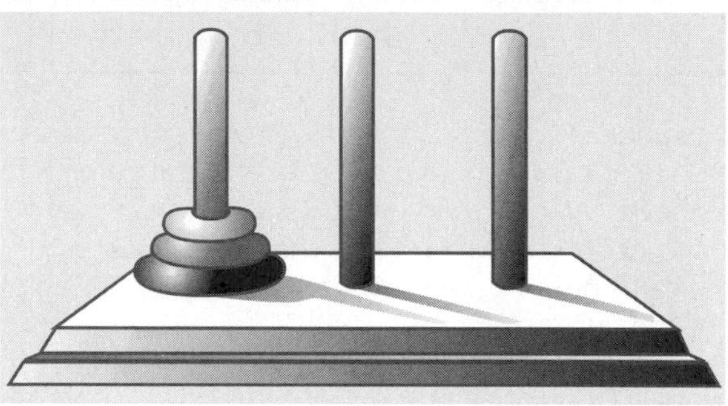

There are three discs of unequal sizes, positioned on the leftmost of three pegs, such that the largest disc is at the bottom, the middle-sized disc is in the middle, and the smallest disc is on the top. Your task is to transfer all three discs to the rightmost peg, using the middle peg as a stationing area, as needed. You may move only one disc at a time, and you may never move a larger disc on top of a smaller disc.

FIGURE 11.8 **SOLUTION TO THE TWO-STRING PROBLEM**

Many people assume that they must find a way to move themselves toward each string and then bring the two strings together. They fail to consider the possibility of finding a way to get one of the strings to move toward them, such as by tying something to one of the strings, then swinging the object as a pendulum, and grabbing the object when it swings close to the other string. There is nothing in the problem that suggests that the person must move, rather than that the string may move. Nevertheless, most people presuppose that the constraint exists. By placing an unnecessary and unwarranted constraint on themselves, people make the problem insoluble.

ILL-STRUCTURED PROBLEMS AND THE ROLE OF INSIGHT

The two-string problem is an example of an ill-structured problem. In fact, although we may occasionally misrepresent well-structured problems, we are much more likely to have difficulty representing ill-structured problems. Before we explain the nature of ill-structured problems, try to solve a couple more such problems. The following problems illustrate some of the difficulties created by the representation of ill-structured problems (after R. J. Sternberg, 1986a). Be sure to try both problems before you read about their solutions.

1. Haughty Harry and several other job-seekers were looking for work as carpenters. The site supervisor handed each applicant two sticks (a 1" x 2" x 60" stick and a 1" x 2" x 43" stick) and a 2" C-clamp (see Figure 11.9; the opening of the clamp is wide enough so that both sticks can be inserted and held together securely when the clamp is tightened). The supervisor ushered the job applicants into a room 12'3" x 13'5", with an 8' ceiling. Mounted on the ceiling were two 1' x 1' beams, dividing the ceiling into thirds lengthwise. She told the applicants that she would hire the first applicant who could build a hat rack capable of supporting her hard hat, using just the two sticks and the C-clamp. She could only hire one person, so she recommended that the applicants not try to help one another. What should Harry do?
2. A woman who lived in a small town married 20 different men in that same town. All of them are still living, and she never divorced any of them. Yet she broke no laws. How could she do this?

FIGURE 11.9 **THE HAT-RACK PROBLEM**

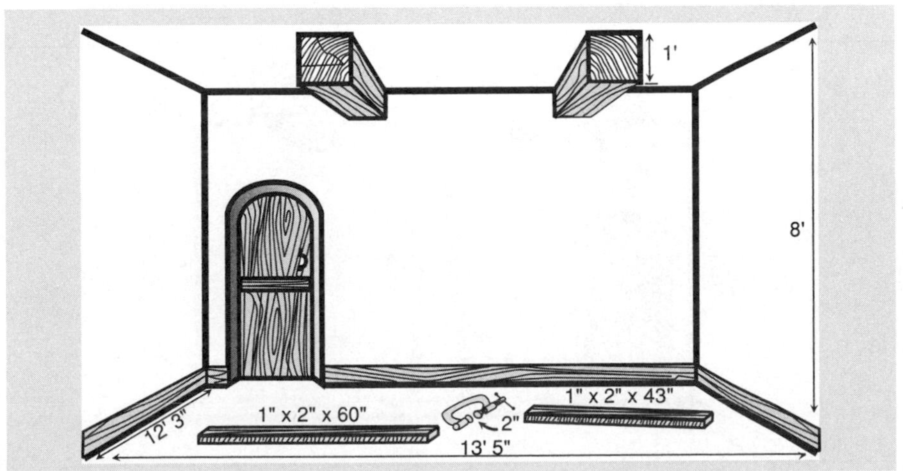

Using just the materials shown here, how can you construct a hat rack in the room shown in this figure?

3. You have loose black and brown socks in a drawer, mixed in a ratio of five black socks for every brown one. How many socks do you have to take out of that drawer to be assured of having a pair of the same color?

Both the two-string problem and each of the three preceding problems are ill-structured problems, for which there is no clear, readily available path to solution. By definition, ill-structured problems do not have well-defined problem spaces, and problem solvers have difficulty constructing appropriate mental representations for modeling these problems and their solutions. For such problems, much of the difficulty is in constructing a plan for sequentially following a series of steps that inch ever closer to their solution. These three particular ill-structured problems are termed *insight problems* because in order to solve each problem, you need to see the problem in a novel way—differently from how you would probably see the problem at first, and differently from how you would probably solve problems in general. That is, you must restructure your representation of the problem in order to solve it.

Insight is a distinctive and sometimes seemingly sudden understanding of a problem or of a strategy that aids in solving the problem. Often, an insight involves reconceptualizing a problem or a strategy for its solution in a totally new way. Insight often involves detecting and combining relevant old and new information to gain a novel view of the problem or of its solution. Although insights may feel as though they are sudden, they are often the result of much prior thought and hard work, without which the insight would never have occurred: Insight can be involved in solving well-structured problems, but it is more often associated with the rocky and twisting path to solution that characterizes ill-structured problems. For many years, psychologists interested in problem solving have been trying to figure out the true nature of insight.

In order to understand some of the alternative views on insightful problem solving, you may find knowing the solutions to the preceding two insight problems useful. With respect to

FIGURE 11.10 **SOLUTION TO THE HAT-RACK PROBLEM**

Were you able to modify your definition of the materials available in a way that aided you in solving the problem?

the hat-rack problem, Harry was unable to solve the problem before Sally quickly whipped together a hat rack like the one shown in Figure 11.10. To solve the problem, Sally had to redefine her view of the materials in a way that allowed her to conceive of a C-clamp as a hat holder.

The woman who was involved in multiple marriages is a minister. The critical element for solving this problem is to recognize that the word "married" may be used to describe the performance of the marriage ceremony, so the minister married the 20 men but did not herself become wedded to any of them. To solve this problem, you had to redefine your interpretation of the term *married.* (Others have suggested yet additional possibilities—for example, that the woman was an actress and only married the men in her role as an actress, that the woman's multiple marriages were annulled, so she never technically divorced any of the men, and so on.)

As for the socks, you need only to take out three socks to be assured of having a pair of the same color. The ratio information is irrelevant. Whether or not the first two socks you withdraw match in color, the third will certainly match at least one of the first two.

Early Gestaltist Views

Gestalt psychologists emphasized the importance of the whole as more than a collection of parts. In regard to problem solving, Gestalt psychologists held that insight problems require problem solvers to perceive the problem as a whole. Gestalt psychologist Max Wertheimer wrote about **productive thinking** (Wertheimer, 1945/1959), which involves insights that go beyond the bounds of existing associations, and which he distinguished from *reproductive thinking,* which is based on existing associations involving what is already known. According to Wertheimer, insightful (productive) thinking differs fundamentally from reproductive thinking. In solving the insight problems given in this chapter, you had to break away from your existing associations and see each problem in an entirely new light. Productive thinking can also be applied to well-structured problems.

Wertheimer's colleague Wolfgang Köhler (1927) studied insight in nonhuman primates, particularly a caged chimpanzee named Sultan (see Figure 11.11). In Köhler's view, the ape's behavior illustrated insight. To Köhler and other Gestaltists, insight is a special process, involving thinking that differs from normal, linear information processing.

Gestalt psychologists described examples of insight and speculated on a few ways in which the special process of insight might occur: It might result from (a) extended unconscious leaps in thinking, (b) greatly accelerated mental processing, or (c) some kind of short-circuiting of normal reasoning processes (see Perkins, 1981). Unfortunately, the early Gestaltists did not provide convincing evidence for any of these mechanisms, nor did they specify exactly what insight is. Therefore, we need to consider alternative views as well.

The Nothing-Special View

According to the nothing-special view, insight is merely an extension of ordinary perceiving, recognizing, learning, and conceiving. This view is argued by David Perkins (1981), by Robert Weisberg (1986; 1995), and by Pat Langley, Herbert Simon, and their colleagues (Langley, Simon, Bradshaw, & Zytkow, 1986). They suggest that Gestalt psychologists failed to pin down insight because there is no special thinking process called "insight." Additionally, sometimes, people seem to have solved so-called insight problems without experiencing any sudden mental restructuring of the problem, and at other times, people seem to show sudden mental restructuring of so-called routine problems (Weisberg, 1995). Insights are merely significant products of ordinary thinking processes.

FIGURE 11.11 **APE INSIGHT**

In the study depicted here, Gestalt psychologist Wolfgang Köhler placed an ape in an enclosure with a few boxes. At the top of the cage, just out of reach, was a bunch of bananas. After the ape unsuccessfully tried to jump and to stretch to reach the bananas, the ape showed sudden insight: The ape realized that the boxes could be stacked on top of one another to make a structure tall enough to reach the bunch of bananas.

THE NEO-GESTALTIST VIEW

Janet Metcalfe (1986; Metcalfe & Wiebe, 1987) and her colleagues have found that insightful problem solving can be distinguished from noninsightful problem solving in two ways. For one thing, when given routine problems to solve, problem solvers show remarkable accuracy in their ability to predict their own success in solving a problem, prior to any attempt to solve it. In contrast, when given insight problems, problem solvers show very poor ability to predict their own success prior to trying to solve the problems. Not only were successful problem solvers pessimistic about their ability to solve insight problems, but unsuccessful problem solvers were often optimistic about their ability to solve them.

In addition, Metcalfe used a clever methodology to observe the problem-solving process while participants were solving routine versus insight problems. At 15-second intervals, participants paused briefly to rate how close ("warm" vs. far, "cold") they felt they were to reaching a solution. For routine problems (e.g., algebra, Tower of Hanoi, deductive reasoning), participants showed incremental increases in their feelings of warmth as they drew closer to reaching a correct solution. For insight problems, however, participants showed no such incremental increases. Figure 11.12 shows a comparison of participants' reported feelings of warmth for solving algebra problems versus for solving insight problems. In solving insight problems, participants showed no increasing feelings of warmth until moments before abruptly realizing the solution and correctly solving the problem. Metcalfe's findings certainly seem to support the Gestaltist view that there is something special about insightful problem solving, as distinct from noninsightful, routine problem solving. The specific nature and underlying mechanisms of insightful problem solving have yet to be addressed by this research, however.

FIGURE 11.12 **INSIGHT OF A SPECIAL PROCESS: FEELINGS OF WARMTH**

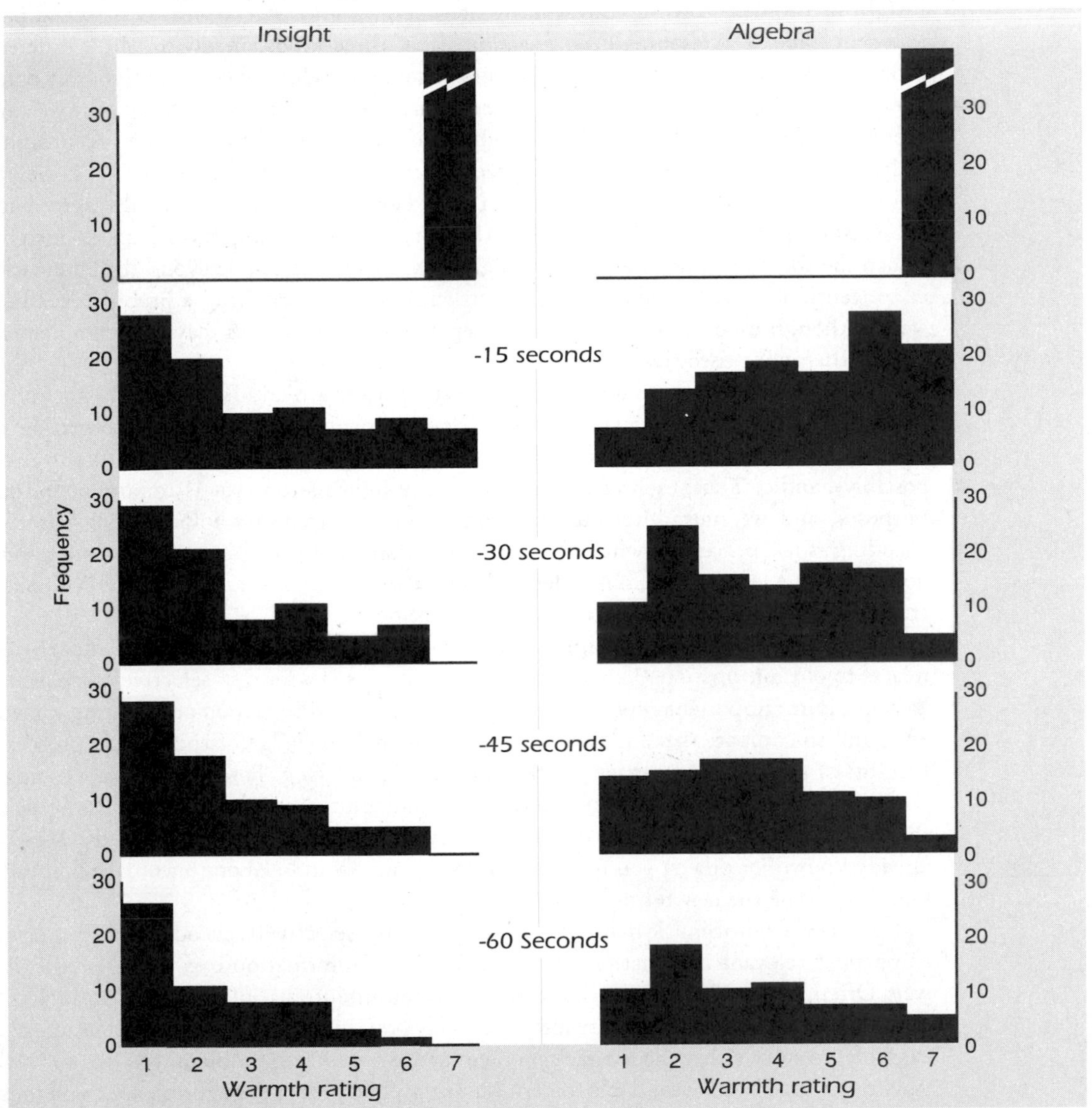

When Janet Metcalfe presented participants with routine problems and insight problems, they showed clear differences in their feelings of warmth as they approached a solution to the problems. These frequency histograms (bar graphs in which the area of each bar indicates the frequency for the given interval of time) show comparative feelings of warmth during the four 15-second intervals prior to solving the problems. When solving insight problems, participants showed no incremental increases in feelings of warmth, whereas when solving routine problems, participants showed distinct incremental increases in feelings of warmth. Routine problems included algebra problems such as "$(3x^2 + 2x + 10)(3x) =$." Insight problems included problems such as "A prisoner was attempting escape from a tower. He found in his cell a rope which was half long enough to permit him to reach the ground safely. He divided the rope in half and tied the two parts together and escaped. How could he have done this?" (From Metcalfe & Wiebe, 1987, pp. 242, 245)

THE THREE-PROCESS VIEW

Yet another view of insight has focused specifically on the possible mechanisms for insightful problem solving (Davidson & Sternberg, 1984). According to the view proposed by Janet Davidson and me, insights are of three kinds, involving three different processes: selective encoding, selective comparison, and selective combination. We agree with the nothing-special theorists to some extent, in that the three processes that we suggest as underlying the three kinds of insights also can be used mundanely and noninsightfully. In fact, selective combination has been linked to routine problem solving, as well as to insightful problem solving (Davidson, 1995). However, Davidson and I also agree with the Gestalt psychologists in proposing that there is something special about insight: When the three processes are applied insightfully, the processes go beyond the boundaries of conventional thinking and involve constructing or reconstructing a problem in a new way. Although each process may be used separately, the processes may also complement one another when used conjointly.

Selective-encoding insights involve distinguishing relevant from irrelevant information. Recall from earlier chapters that *encoding* involves representing information in memory. In today's world, all of us have available much more information than we can possibly handle. Thus, each of us must select the information that is important for our purposes, and we must filter out the unimportant or irrelevant information. Selective encoding is the process by which this filtering is done. For example, when you are taking notes during a lecture, you must selectively encode which points are crucial, which points are supportive and explanatory, and which are not necessary.

Selective-comparison insights involve novel perceptions of how new information relates to old information. The creative use of analogies is a form of selective comparison. When solving important problems, we almost always need to call on our existing knowledge and to compare that information with our new knowledge of the current problem. Insights of selective comparison are the basis for this relating. For example, suppose that you must master a whole list of new terms for your cognitive psychology class. For some of the terms, you may be able to compare the new terms with synonymous words that you already know. For others, you may be able to expand on and elaborate words you already know, to define the new terms.

Selective-combination insights involve taking selectively encoded and compared snippets of relevant information and combining that information in a novel, productive way. Often, for us just to identify analytically the important information for solving a problem is not enough; we must also figure out how to synthesize the information. For example, to solve either the hat-rack problem or the two-string problem, you had to find a way to put together the available materials in a novel way. To write a term paper, you must synthesize your research notes in a way that addresses the central question in your paper.

ADDITIONAL INSIGHTS INTO INSIGHT

Steven Smith (1995) has suggested another view of routine versus insightful problem solving. Smith distinguishes between the *insight experience,* which is a special process involving an abrupt mental restructuring, and *insight,* which is an understanding that may involve either the special insight experience or normal cognitive processes that occur incrementally, rather than suddenly. Thus, routine problems may demand insight, but they may not require the insight experience; insight problems, on the other hand, require the insight experience. According to Smith, therefore, insights need not be sudden "ah-ha" experiences. They may and often do occur gradually and incrementally over time.

Unfortunately, insights—like many other aspects of human thinking—can be both startlingly brilliant and dead wrong. How do we fall into mental traps that lead us down false paths as we try to reach solutions?

OBSTACLES AND AIDS TO PROBLEM SOLVING

While studying problem isomorphs, Kotovsky, Hayes, and Simon (1985) found that several factors hindered problem solving: (a) more novelty (e.g., new objects, new rules, new operations or manipulations, new knowledge), (b) larger numbers of rules, (c) greater complexity of rules, and (d) more counterintuitive rules (i.e., rules that seem to go against common sense or against what the problem solver knows or infers). In addition, recall that these researchers found that the way in which people represented the problem affected the ease with which people solved the problems. Problems that were more abstract or that posed more difficulties in forming and using mental representations were much harder to solve.

MENTAL SETS, ENTRENCHMENT, AND FIXATION

Many problems, and especially insight problems, are hard to solve because problem solvers tend to bring to the new problem a particular **mental set**—a frame of mind involving an existing model for representing a problem, a problem context, or a procedure for problem solving. Another term for mental set is *entrenchment.* When problem solvers have an entrenched mental set, they fixate on a strategy that normally works well in solving many problems but that does not work well in solving this particular problem. For example, in the two-string problem, you may fixate on strategies that involve moving yourself toward the string, rather than moving the string toward you; in the oft-marrying minister problem, you may fixate on the notion that to marry someone is to become wedded to the person.

Mental sets can also influence the solution of rather routine problems. For example, Abraham Luchins (1942) exquisitely demonstrated the phenomenon of mental set in what he called "water-jar" problems. In Luchins's water-jar problems, participants were asked how to measure out a certain amount of water, using three different jars, with each jar holding a different amount of water. Table 11.2 shows the problems used by Luchins.

If you are like many people solving these problems, you will have found a formula that works for all of the remaining problems: You fill up Jar B, then pour out of it the amount of water you can put into Jar A, and then twice pour out of it the amount of water you can put into Jar C. The formula, therefore, is $B - A - 2C$. However, Problems 7 through 11 can be solved in a much simpler way, using just two of the jars. For example, Problem 7 can be solved by $A - C$, Problem 8 by $A + C$, and so on. People who are given Problems 1 through 6 to solve generally continue to use the $B - A - 2C$ formula in solving Problems 7 through 11. In Luchins's original experiment, between 64% and 83% of participants who solved the first set of problems went on to solve the last set of problems by using the less simple strategy. However, only 1% to 5% of control participants, who were not given the first set of problems,

TABLE 11.2 LUCHINS'S WATER-JAR PROBLEMS

How do you measure out the right amount of water using Jars A, B, and C?
You need to use up to three jars to obtain the required amounts of water (measured in numbers of cups) in the last column. Columns A, B, and C show the capacity of each jar. The first problem, for example, requires you to get 20 cups of water from just two of the jars, a 29-cup one (Jar A) and a 3-cup one (Jar B). Easy: Just fill Jar A, and then empty out 9 cups from this jar by taking out 3 cups three times, using Jar B. Problem 2 isn't too hard, either. Fill Jar B with 127 cups, then empty out 21 cups using Jar A, and then empty out 6 cups, using Jar C twice. Now try the rest of the problems yourself. (After Luchins, 1942)

Problem No.	Jars Available for Use			Required Amount (Cups)
	A	*B*	*C*	
1	29	3	0	20
2	21	127	3	100
3	14	163	25	99
4	18	43	10	5
5	9	42	6	21
6	20	59	4	31
7	23	49	3	20
8	15	39	3	18
9	28	76	3	25
10	18	48	4	22
11	14	36	8	6

failed to apply the simpler solutions to the last set of problems: They had no established mental set that interfered with their seeing things in a new and simpler way.

Another type of mental set involves fixation on a particular use (function) for an object: Specifically, **functional fixedness** is the inability to realize that something known to have a particular use may also be used for performing other functions. Functional fixedness prevents us from solving new problems by using old tools in novel ways. Becoming free of functional fixedness is what first allowed people to use a reshaped coat hanger to get into a locked car, and it is what first allowed thieves to pick simple spring door locks with a credit card. It is also what might allow you to think of a cognitive psychology textbook as a resource for criminal ideas!

Another type of mental set is considered an aspect of social cognition: **stereotypes,** which are beliefs that members of a social group tend more or less uniformly to have particular types of characteristics. We seem to learn many stereotypes during childhood; for example, cross-cultural studies of children show their increasing knowledge about—and use of—gender stereotypes across the childhood years (e.g., Neto, Williams, & Widner, 1991). Stereotypes often arise in the same way that other kinds of mental sets develop: We observe a particular instance or set of instances of some pattern, and we overgeneralize from those limited observations to assume that all future instances will similarly demonstrate that pattern. Of course, when the stereotypes are used to target particular scapegoats for societal mistreatment, grave social consequences result for the targets of stereotypes. The targets are not the only ones to suffer from stereotypes, however. Like other kinds of mental sets, stereotypes hinder the problem-solving abilities of the individuals who limit their thinking by using stereotypes.

Negative and Positive Transfer

Often, when people have particular mental sets, which prompt them to fixate on one aspect of a problem or one strategy for problem solving, to the exclusion of other possible relevant ones, they are carrying knowledge and strategies for solving one kind of problem to a different kind of problem. Cognitive psychologists use the term *transfer* to describe the broader phenomenon of any carryover of knowledge or skills from one problem situation to another. Transfer can be either negative or positive. **Negative transfer** occurs when solving an earlier problem makes it harder to solve a later one. Sometimes an early problem gets an individual on a wrong track. For example, police may have difficulty solving a political crime because such a crime differs so much from the kinds of crime that they typically deal with. **Positive transfer** occurs when the solution of an earlier problem makes it easier to solve a new problem. That is, sometimes the transfer of a mental set can be an aid to problem solving.

From a broad perspective, positive transfer may be considered to involve the transfer of factual knowledge or skills from one setting to another one. For example, you may apply your general knowledge about psychology and your study skills acquired during a lifetime of studying for tests to the problem of studying for an examination in cognitive psychology. More narrowly, however, during positive transfer, you effectively apply a strategy or a type of solution that worked well for one particular problem or set of problems when you are trying to solve an analogous problem. How do people realize that particular problems are analogous and can be solved through positive transfer of strategies or even of solutions?

Transfer of Analogies

Mary Gick and Keith Holyoak (1980, 1983) have designed some elegant studies of positive transfer involving analogies. In order to appreciate their results, you need to become familiar with a problem first used by Karl Duncker (1945), often called the "radiation problem."

Investigating Cognitive Psychology

Imagine that you are a doctor treating a patient with a malignant stomach tumor. You cannot operate on the patient because of the severity of the cancer, but unless you destroy the tumor somehow, the patient will die. You could use high-intensity X rays to destroy the tumor. Unfortunately, the intensity of X rays needed to destroy the tumor will also destroy healthy tissue through which the rays must pass. X rays of lesser intensity will spare the healthy tissue but will be insufficiently powerful to destroy the tumor. Your problem is to figure out a procedure that will destroy the tumor without also destroying the healthy tissue surrounding the tumor.

Duncker had in mind a particular insightful solution as the optimal one for this problem. Figure 11.13 shows the solution pictorially.

Prior to presenting Duncker's radiation problem, Gick and Holyoak would present another, easier problem, called the "military problem" (Holyoak, 1984, p. 205), described in the next investigation.

INVESTIGATING COGNITIVE PSYCHOLOGY

A general wishes to capture a fortress located in the center of a country. There are many roads radiating outward from the fortress. All have been mined so that although small groups of men can pass over the roads safely, any large force will detonate the mines. A full-scale direct attack is therefore impossible. What should the general do?

FIGURE 11.13 **X-RAY PROBLEM**

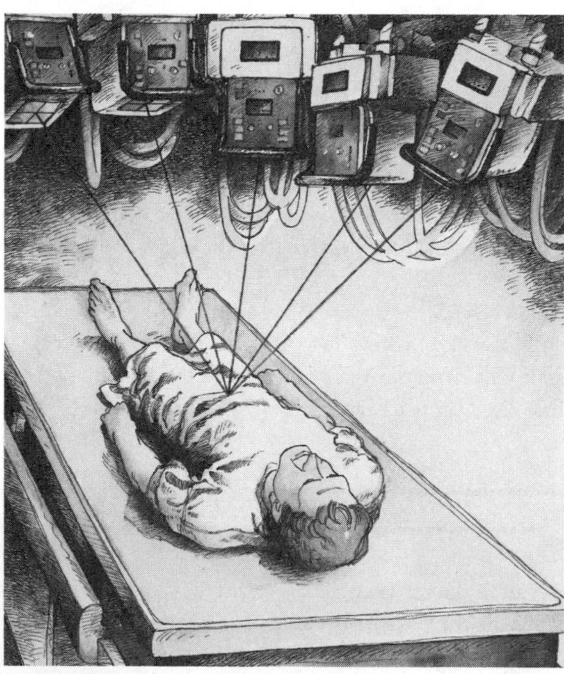

The solution to the X-ray problem involves dispersion. The idea is to direct weak X-radiation toward the tumor from a number of different points outside the body. No single set of rays would be strong enough to destroy either the healthy tissue or the tumor. However, the rays would be aimed so that they all converged at one spot within the body—the spot that houses the tumor. This solution is actually used today in some X-ray treatments, except that a rotating source of X rays is used for dispersing rays.

Table 11.3 shows the correspondence between the radiation and the military problems, which turns out to be quite close, although not perfect. The question is whether producing a group-convergence solution to the military problem helped participants in solving the radiation problem. If participants received the military problem with the convergence solution and then were given a hint to apply it in some way to the radiation problem, about 75% of the participants reached the correct solution to the radiation problem, compared with less than 10% of the participants who did not receive the military story first but instead received no prior story or only an irrelevant one.

In another experiment, participants were not given the convergence solution to the military problem but had to figure it out for themselves. About 50% of the participants generated the convergence solution to the military problem, and of these, 41% went on to generate a parallel solution to the radiation problem. That is, positive transfer was *weaker* when participants produced the original solution themselves than when the solution to the first problem was given to them (41%, as compared with 75%).

Gick and Holyoak found that the usefulness of the military problem as an analogue to the radiation problem depended on the induced mental set with which the problem solver approached the problems. If participants were asked to memorize the military story under

TABLE 11.3 CORRESPONDENCE BETWEEN THE RADIATION AND THE MILITARY PROBLEMS

What are the commonalities between the two problems, and what is an elemental strategy that can be derived by comparing the two problems? (After Gick & Holyoak, 1983)

Military Problem
- Initial State
  - Goal: Use army to capture fortress
  - Resources: Sufficiently large army
  - Constraint: Unable to send entire army along one road
- Solution Plan: Send small groups along multiple roads simultaneously
- Outcome: Fortress captured by army

Radiation Problem
- Initial State
  - Goal: Use rays to destroy tumor
  - Resources: Sufficiently powerful rays
  - Constraint: Unable to administer high-intensity rays from one direction only
- Solution Plan: Administer low-intensity rays from multiple directions simultaneously
- Outcome: Tumor destroyed by rays

Convergence Schema
- Initial State
  - Goal: Use force to overcome a central target
  - Resources: Sufficiently great force
  - Constraint: Unable to apply full force along one path alone
- Solution Plan: Apply weak forces along multiple paths simultaneously
- Outcome: Central target overcome by force

Dedre Gentner *is a professor of psychology in the department of psychology at Northwestern University. She is especially well known for her seminal work on mental models and for her work on analogy.*

the guise that it was a story-recall experiment and then were given the radiation problem to solve, only 30% of participants produced the convergence solution to the radiation problem. Gick and Holyoak also found that positive transfer improved if two analogous problems were given in advance of the radiation problem rather than just one. Holyoak and others have expanded these findings to encompass problems other than the radiation problem, and they found that when the domains or the contexts for the two problems were more similar, participants were more likely to see and apply the analogy (see Holyoak, 1990).

Similar patterns of data were found using various types of problems involving electricity (Gentner & Gentner, 1983) and in studies of mathematical insight (Davidson & Sternberg, 1984). Perhaps the most crucial aspect of these studies is that people have trouble noticing the analogy unless they are explicitly told to look for it. In studies involving physics problems, positive transfer from solved examples to unsolved problems was more likely among students who specifically tried to understand *why* particular examples were solved as they were, as compared with students who sought only to understand *how* particular problems were solved as they were (Chi, Bassok, Lewis, Reimann, & Glaser, 1989). Based on these findings, we generally need to be looking for analogies in order to find them. We often will not find them unless we explicitly seek them.

Intentional Transfer: Searching for Analogies

In looking for analogies, we need to be careful not to be misled by associations between two things that are analogically irrelevant. For example, Georgia Nigro and I studied children's solutions to verbal analogies of the form "A is to B as C is to X," where the children are given multiple-choice options for X. We found that children will often choose an answer that is associatively close but analogically incorrect. (In representing analogies, a single colon [:] indicates the "is to" expression and a double colon [::] is used to indicate the "as" expression.) For example, in the analogy,

LAWYER : CLIENT :: DOCTOR : (A. NURSE, B. PATIENT, C. MEDICINE, D. MD),

children might choose option A because NURSE is more strongly associated with DOCTOR than is the correct answer, PATIENT (R. J. Sternberg & Nigro, 1980).

Dedre Gentner (1983) has argued that analogies between problems involve mappings of relationships between problems; the actual content attributes of the problems are irrelevant. In other words, what matters in analogies is not the similarity of the content, but how closely their structural systems of relationships match. Because we are accustomed to considering the importance of the content, we find it difficult to push the content to the background and to bring form (structural relationships) to the foreground. For example, the differing content makes the analogy between the military problem and the radiation problem hard to recognize and impedes positive transfer from one problem to the other.

Gentner terms the opposite phenomenon—in which people see analogies where they do not exist because of similarity of content—**transparency.** In making analogies, we need to be sure we are focusing on the relationships between the two terms being compared, not just their surface content attributes. For example, in studying for final exams in two psychology courses, different strategies may be needed when studying for a closed-book essay exam than for an open-book, multiple-choice exam. Transparency of content may lead to negative transfer between nonisomorphic problems if care is not taken to avoid such transfer.

INCUBATION

For solving many problems, the chief obstacle is not the need to find a suitable strategy for positive transfer, but rather to avoid obstacles resulting from negative transfer. **Incubation**—simply putting the problem aside for a while—offers one way in which to minimize negative transfer. For example, if you find that you are unable to solve a problem, and none of the strategies you can think of seem to work, try setting the problem aside for a while to let it incubate. During incubation, you must not consciously think about the problem. You do, however, allow for the possibility that the problem will be processed subconsciously. Some investigators of problem solving have even asserted that incubation is an essential stage of the problem-solving process (e.g., R. B. Cattell, 1971; Helmholtz, 1896). Others (e.g., Baron, 1988) have failed to find experimental support for the phenomenon of incubation, although extensive anecdotal support has been offered (e.g., Poincaré, 1913). Still others suggest that incubation may be particularly helpful in solving insight problems (e.g., S. M. Smith, 1995).

Several possible mechanisms for the beneficial effects of incubation have been proposed, such as the following:

1. When we no longer keep something in active memory, we let go of some of the unimportant details and keep only the more meaningful aspects in memory; from these meaningful aspects, we are then free to reconstruct anew, with fewer of the limitations of the earlier mental set (e.g., B. F. Anderson, 1975).
2. As time passes, more recent memories become more integrated with existing memories (e.g., J. R. Anderson, 1985); during this reintegration, some associations of the mental set may weaken.
3. As time passes, new stimuli—both internal and external—may activate new perspectives on the problem, weakening the effects of the mental set (e.g., Bastik, 1982).
4. An internal or external stimulus may lead the problem solver to see an analogy between the current problem and another problem, so that the problem solver can either readily find a comparable solution or perhaps even simply apply a known solution (Langley & Jones, 1988).
5. When problem solvers are in a low state of cortical arousal (e.g., in the shower, in bed, taking a walk), increases in attention span—and perhaps working-memory capacity—may allow increasingly remote cues to be perceived and held in active memory simultaneously; the person may relaxedly toy with cues that might otherwise be perceived as irrelevant or distracting when in a high state of cortical arousal (e.g., while trying actively to solve the problem; Luria, 1973/1984). Some of the preceding mechanisms may also interact, perhaps through the process of spreading activation or through some sort of priming effect.

Craig Kaplan and Janet Davidson (1989) have reviewed the literature on incubation and have found that the benefits of incubation can be enhanced in two ways: (a) Invest enough time in the problem initially; perhaps explore all aspects of the problem, and investigate several possible avenues of solving it. (b) Allow sufficient time for incubation to permit your old associations due to negative transfer to weaken somewhat. A drawback of incubation is that it takes time. If you have a deadline for problem solution, you must begin solving the problem early enough to meet the deadline, including the time you need for incubation.

Practical Applications of Cognitive Psychology

These suggestions can be used directly to help you solve everyday problems. If you have an assignment due at some later date, take the time immediately upon being given the assignment to plan a course of action. For example, in writing a term paper, peruse the outlines of future readings in the course to find the general topic that interests you. Then get some idea on how much information is available on your topic, without getting too involved in the details—this procedure can help you narrow down the focus. Choosing a topic you are relatively unfamiliar with for shorter paper assignments is probably better because you will be more likely to have entrenched ideas or fixations concerning topics of higher familiarity (plus you will also learn something new). However, do try positively to transfer major themes across different topics—for example, the nature and nurture issue often plays out in diverse topics in psychology. Finally, put the topic to the side for a while and allow the course material to integrate itself with your existing knowledge and with your developing topic ideas, perhaps while you are collecting some relevant reading material along the way. Then, about two to three weeks before the paper is due, start working on a draft that you can set aside again for a few days before final polishing. Overall, the total amount of distributed time involved in completing an assignment this way will be only slightly more than if you cram the work into a few days before the paper is due; but the quality of the paper is almost sure to be better.

Expertise: Knowledge and Problem Solving

Even persons who do not have expertise in cognitive psychology recognize that knowledge, particularly expert knowledge, greatly enhances problem solving. What interests cognitive psychologists is the reason that expertise enhances problem solving. Why can experts solve problems in their field more successfully than novices can? Do experts know more problem-solving algorithms, heuristics, and other strategies? Do experts know better strategies, or do they just use these strategies more often? What do experts know that makes the problem-solving process more effective for experts than for novices in a field? Is it all talent or just acquired skill?

ORGANIZATION OF KNOWLEDGE

William Chase and Herbert Simon (1973) set out to discover what experts know and do by determining what distinguishes expert from novice chess players. In one of their studies, Chase and Simon had expert and novice players briefly view a display of a chess board with the chess pieces on it, and then recall the positions of the chess pieces on the board. In general, the experts performed quite a bit better than the novices—but only if the positions of the chess pieces on the board made sense in terms of an actual game of chess (see also Vicente & DeGroot, 1990). If the pieces were randomly distributed around the board, experts recalled the positions of the pieces no better than did the novices (see Figure 11.14).

ELABORATION OF KNOWLEDGE

The work of Chase and Simon, combined with earlier work by Adrian De Groot (1965), suggested that what differentiated the experts from the novices was in the amount, organization, and use of knowledge. Both chess tasks—whether with a random array of pieces or with a meaningful arrangement of pieces—required the experts to use heuristics for storing and retrieving information about the positions of the pieces on the chess board. According to these investigators, the key difference was that chess experts had stored and organized in memory tens of thousands of particular board positions. When they saw sensible board positions, they could use the knowledge they had in memory to help them remember the various board positions as integrated, organized chunks of information. For random scatterings of pieces on the board, however, the knowledge of the experts was of no use, so that the experts had no advantage over the novices. Like the novices, they had to try to memorize the distinctive interrelations among many discrete pieces and positions.

Michelene Chi *is a professor of psychology at the University of Pittsburgh. She is most well known for showing that the organization of experts' knowledge in their domain of expertise allows them to represent this knowledge more profoundly than can novices. She has also shown that the initial organization of a learner's knowledge can be fundamentally flawed so that it prevents the learner from understanding the true meaning of a concept.*

A recent series of papers by Gobet and Simon (1996a, b, c) confirms the earlier Chase and Simon work, demonstrating that retrieval processes involving recognition of board arrangements are instrumental in grandmaster-level chess players' success when compared to novices' play. Even when grand masters are time-constrained so that look-ahead processes are curtailed, their constrained performance does not differ substantially from their unconstrained playing. Thus, an organized knowledge system is relatively more important to experts' performance in chess than even the processes involved in predicting future moves.

After the Chase and Simon work, a number of other investigators (e.g., Reitman, 1976) began studying large numbers of experts in different domains (e.g., radiology—Lesgold et al., 1988; physics—Larkin, McDermott, Simon, & Simon, 1980), and they found the same thing again and again: What differentiated experts from novices were their schemas for solving problems within their own domains of expertise (Glaser & Chi, 1988). The schemas of experts involve large, highly interconnected units of knowledge, which are organized according to underlying structural similarities among knowledge units. In contrast, the schemas of novices involve relatively small and disconnected units of knowledge, which are organized according to superficial similarities (e.g., Bryson, Bereiter, Scardamalia, & Joram, 1991). This observation can be noted in how experts versus novices (a) classify various problems (Chi, Glaser, & Rees, 1982), (b) describe the essential nature of various problems (Larkin et al., 1980), and (c) determine and describe a solution method for various problems (Chi et al.,1982).

FIGURE 11.14 **EXPERTISE IN CHESS**

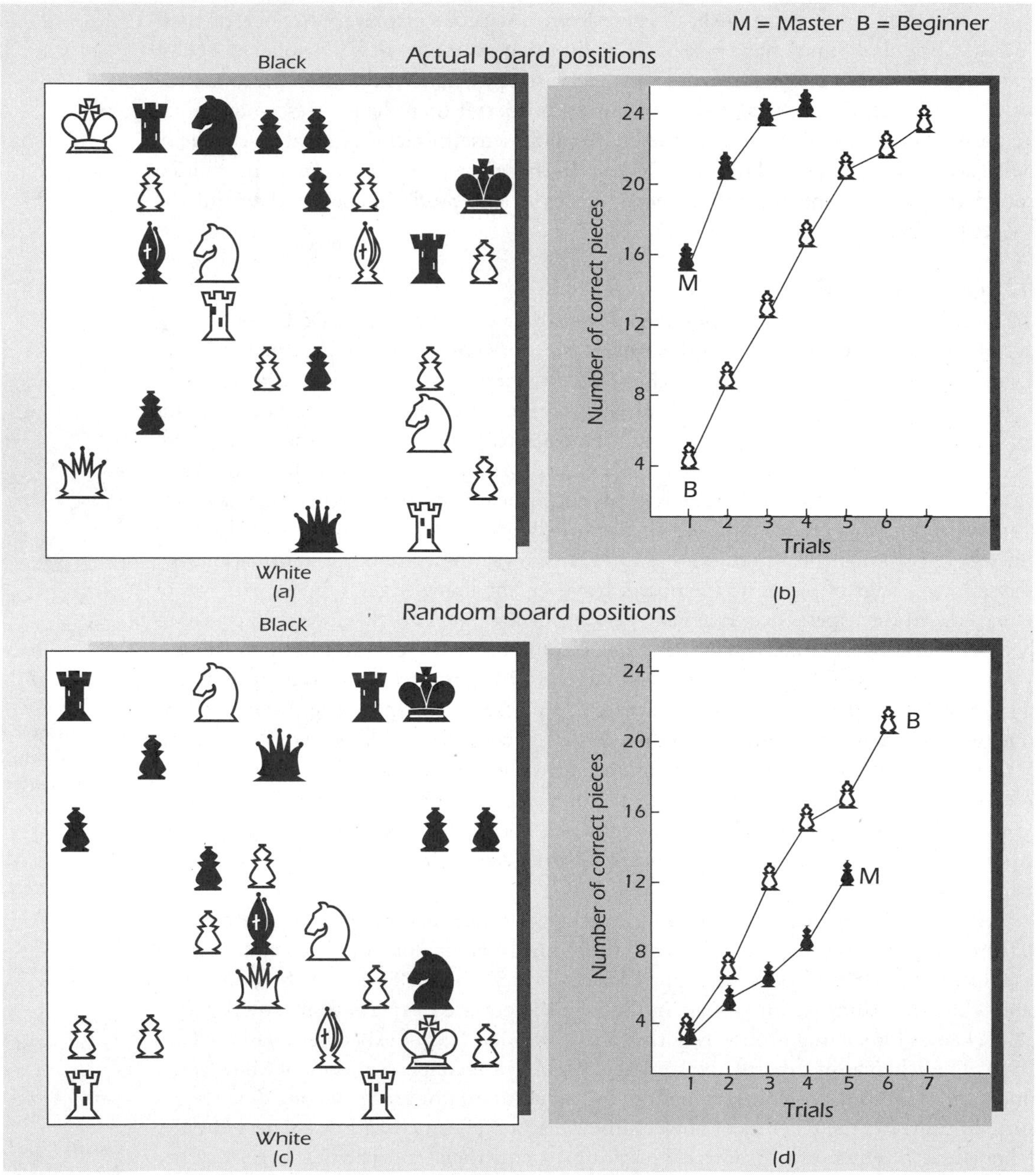

When experts and novices were asked to recall realistic patterns of chess pieces, as in (a), experts demonstrated much better performance, as shown in (b). However, when experts and novices were asked to recall random arrangements of chess pieces, as shown in (c), experts performed no better than novices, as shown in (d).

SETTING UP THE PROBLEM

Another difference between experts and novices can be observed by asking problem solvers to report aloud what they are thinking as they are attempting to solve various problems (Bryson et al., 1991; De Groot, 1965; Lesgold, 1988). Observers can compare the statements made by problem solvers ("verbal protocols"), the time spent on various aspects of problems ("latencies"), and the relationship between problem-solving strategies and the solutions reached. From such work, experts appear to spend proportionately more time determining how to represent a problem than do novices (Lesgold, 1988; Lesgold et al., 1988), but they spend much less time than do novices actually implementing the strategy for solution.

The differences between experts and novices in their expenditure of time can be viewed in terms of the focus and direction of their problem solving. Experts seem to spend relatively more time than do novices figuring out how to match the given information in the problem ("What do I know about the problem?") with their existing schemas ("How does the given information match what I already know based on my expertise?"). Once experts find a correct match, they can quickly retrieve and implement a problem strategy. Thus, experts seem to be able to work forward from the given information ("What do I know?") to find the unknown information ("What do I need to find out?"), implementing the correct sequence of steps, based on the strategies they have retrieved from their schemas in long-term memory (Chi et al., 1982).

Consider, for example, the ways an expert doctor and a novice medical student might handle a patient presenting a set of symptoms. The novice is not sure what to make of the symptoms, and somewhat haphazardly orders a long and expensive series of medical tests in the hope that with a more nearly complete set of symptomatic information, he may be able to make a correct diagnosis. The more experienced doctor, on the other hand, is more likely immediately to recognize the symptoms as fitting into a diagnostic pattern or one of a small number of patterns. She orders only a small number of highly targeted tests to choose the correct diagnosis from among the limited number of possibilities, and then moves on to treat the diagnosed illness.

In contrast, novices seem to spend relatively little time trying to represent the problem, choosing instead to work backward from the unknown information ("What do I need to find out?") to the given information ("What information is offered, and what strategies do I know that can help me find the missing information?"). Often, novices use means–ends analysis (see Hunt, 1994; recall that Newell and Simon described this strategy as a heuristic for figuring out how to solve well-defined problems). Thus, novices often consider more possible strategies than experts consider (see Holyoak, 1990). For experts, means–ends analysis of problems serves only as a backup strategy, to which they turn if they are unable to retrieve an appropriate strategy, based on their existing schemas.

Thus, experts have not only more knowledge, but also better organized knowledge, which allows them to use their knowledge more effectively. Furthermore, the schemas of experts involve not only greater declarative knowledge about a problem domain, but also more procedural knowledge about strategies relevant to that domain. Perhaps because of their better grasp of the strategies required, experts more accurately predict the difficulty of solving problems than do novices (Lesgold & Lajoie, 1991). Experts also monitor their problem-solving strategies more carefully than novices do (Schoenfeld, 1981).

Automatic Expert Processes

Through practice in applying strategies, experts may automatize various operations, which they can retrieve and execute easily while working forward (see VanLehn, 1989). Through the processes of *schematization* (developing rich, highly organized schemas) and *automatization* (consolidating sequences of steps into unified routines that require little or no conscious control), experts may shift the burden of solving problems from limited-capacity working memory to infinite-capacity long-term memory, thereby becoming increasingly efficient and accurate in solving problems. The freeing of their working-memory capacity may better enable them to monitor their progress and their accuracy during problem solving. Novices, in contrast, must use their working memory for trying to hold multiple features of a problem and various possible alternative strategies; this effort may leave novices with less working memory available for monitoring their accuracy and their progress toward solving the problem.

A good example of how automatization enhances performance can be seen in studies of reading ability. Wagner and Stanovich (1996) discuss the issue of expertise in reading in an attempt to explain individual differences in reading ability. Why would some people, particularly children learning to read, be better than others at reading? Wagner and Stanovich point out that reading is believed to involve two distinct processes, a process of conversion from the orthographic (relating to visual appearance of letters) code to the phonological (relating to the sounds of the language) code, and a phonology-based word recognition process. Extensive exposure to text can enhance the orthographic-to-phonological conversion process by increasing automaticity at this level of processing. Thus, a portion of the differences in reading ability appears to be due to increased automaticity in the conversion of orthographic to phonological encoding of words through increased reading practice (see Samuels, in press; R. J. Sternberg & Wagner, 1982).

On the other hand, the automaticity of experts may actually hinder problem solving when experts are tackling problems that differ structurally from the problems they normally encounter (Frensch & Sternberg, 1989). Initially, novices may perform better than experts when the problems appear structurally different from the norm. Eventually, however, the performance of experts generally catches up to and surpasses that of novices (Frensch & Sternberg, 1989; Lesgold, 1988), perhaps because of the experts' richly developed schemas and their enhanced self-monitoring skills. (Table 11.4 summarizes the various characteristics of expert problem solving.)

Innate Talent and Acquired Skill

Although a richly elaborated knowledge base is crucial to expertise in a domain, there remain differences in performance that are not explainable in terms of knowledge level alone. There is considerable debate as to whether differences between novices and experts and among different experts themselves are due either to innate talent or to the quantity and quality of practice in a domain, with many espousing the "practice makes perfect" point of view (see Ericsson, 1996; Sloboda, 1996; R. J. Sternberg, 1998). The practice should be deliberate, or focused, emphasizing acquisition of new skills rather than emphasizing mindless repetition of what the developing expert already knows how to do. However, some take an alternative approach that acknowledges the importance of practice in building up a knowledge and skill base, while also underscoring the importance of something like talent. Indeed, the interaction between innate abilities modified by experience

TABLE 11.4 **WHAT CHARACTERIZES EXPERTISE?**

Although many aspects of expertise remain to be explored, several characteristics of expert problem solving have been discovered.

Experts	Novices
Have large, rich schemas containing a great deal of declarative knowledge about domain	Have relatively impoverished schemas containing relatively less declarative knowledge about domain
Have well-organized, highly interconnected units of knowledge in schemas	Have poorly organized, loosely interconnected, scattered units of knowledge
Spend proportionately more time determining how to represent a problem than in searching for and executing a problem strategy	Spend proportionately more time searching for and executing a problem strategy than in determining how to represent a problem
Develop sophisticated representation of problems, based on structural similarities among problems	Develop relatively poor and naive representation of problems, based on superficial similarities among problems
Work forward from given information to implement strategies for finding unknown	Work backward from focusing on unknown to finding problem strategies that make use of given information
Generally choose a strategy based on elaborate schema of problem strategies; use means–ends analysis only as a backup strategy for handling unusual, atypical problems	Frequently use means–ends analysis as a strategy for handling most problems; sometimes choose a strategy based on knowledge of problem strategies
Schemas contain a great deal of procedural knowledge about problem strategies relevant to domain	Schemas contain relatively little procedural knowledge about problem strategies relevant to domain
Have automatized many sequences of steps within problem strategies	Show little or no automatization of any sequences of steps within problem strategies
Show highly efficient problem solving; when time constraints are imposed, solve problems more quickly than novices	Show relatively inefficient problem solving; solve problems less quickly than experts
Accurately predict the difficulty of solving particular problems	Do not accurately predict the difficulty of solving particular problems
Carefully monitor own problem-solving strategies and processes	Show poor monitoring of own problem-solving strategies and processes
Show high accuracy in reaching appropriate solutions	Show much less accuracy than experts in reaching appropriate solutions
When confronting highly unusual problems with atypical structural features, take relatively more time than novices both to represent the problem and to retrieve appropriate problem strategies	When confronting highly unusual problems with atypical structural features, novices take relatively less time than experts both to represent the problem and to retrieve problem strategies
When provided with new information that contradicts initial problem representation, show flexibility in adapting to a more appropriate strategy	Show less ability to adapt to new information that contradicts initial problem representation and strategy

is widely accepted in the domain of language acquisition (as discussed in chapter 9) as well as other domains.

As pointed out by R. J. Sternberg (1996), many scientists in the field of expertise prefer to minimize the contributions of talent to expertise by locking talent in the trunk of "folk" psychology. This tendency is not surprising, given the widespread use of the term *talent* outside the scientific community, and the lack of an adequate, testable definition of talent.

Genetic heritage seems to make some difference in the acquisition of at least some kinds of expertise. Studies of the heritability of reading disabilities, for example, seem to point to a strong role for genetic factors in reading disabled persons (see DeFries & Gillis, 1993; Olson, in press). Furthermore, Wagner and Stanovich (1996) propose that differences in the phonological awareness entailed in reading ability could be a factor in reading for which individual differences are at least partially genetic. Recall from before that exposure to print appears to enhance automaticity of the orthographic to phonological coding aspect of reading. In contrast, Wagner and Stanovich report that phonological abilities are not affected by increased practice, and that reading disabilities appear to be related to phonological abilities. Thus, some aspect of the phonological-awareness component of reading appears to be the best candidate for a talent factor in reading that is genetically based, at least in part.

In general, as Shiffrin (1996) points out, even if the role of practice is found to account for much of the expertise shown in a given domain, the contributions of genetic factors to the remaining portion of expertise could make all the difference in a world of intense competition.

The application of expertise to problem solving generally involves converging on a single correct solution, from a broad range of possibilities. A complementary asset to expertise in problem solving involves creativity, in which an individual extends the range of possibilities to consider never-before-explored options. In fact, many problems can be solved only by inventing or discovering strategies in order to answer a complex question.

CREATIVITY

One of the most difficult questions that occurs to cognitive psychologists interested in creativity is this: How can we possibly define creativity as a single construct that unifies the work of Leonardo da Vinci and Marie Curie, of Vincent Van Gogh and Isaac Newton, of Toni Morrison and Albert Einstein, and of Wolfgang Mozart and Nicolaus Copernicus? Although there may be about as many narrow definitions of creativity as there are people who think about creativity (see Figure 11.15), most investigators in the field of creativity would broadly define **creativity** as the process of producing something that is both original and worthwhile. The *something* could be a theory, a dance, a chemical, a process or procedure, a story, a symphony, or almost anything else.

What does it take to create something original and worthwhile? What are creative people like? Almost everyone would agree that creative individuals show *creative productivity,* producing inventions, insightful discoveries, artistic works, revolutionary paradigms, or other creative products that are both original and worthwhile. Conventional wisdom suggests that highly creative individuals also have creative lifestyles, characterized by flexibility,

How can we tell a highly creative person from someone who is relatively less creative? What do creative people look like? Pictured here are (a) physicist Stephen Hawking, (b) chemist Marie Curie, and (c) novelist Toni Morrison.

FIGURE 11.15	CREATIVITY—DEFINED

CREATIVITY IS...

DIGGING DEEPER

CREATIVITY IS...

LOOKING TWICE

CREATIVITY IS...

LISTENING FOR SMELLS

CREATIVITY IS...

~~TALKING~~ LISTENING TO A CAT

CROSSING OUT MISTAKES

Here are some original and worthwhile ways of defining creativity. How do you define creativity? (Torrance, 1988, pp. 50–53) nonstereotyped behaviors, and nonconforming attitudes. What characteristics do cognitive psychologists notice in creative individuals? The answer to this question depends on the perspective of the psychologist whom you ask. This section of this chapter describes psychometric and cognitive approaches; personality and motivational approaches; and social, societal, and historical approaches to understanding creativity. I conclude the chapter with a couple of integrative perspectives, which attempt to incorporate key features of the other approaches to creativity.

It's How Much You Produce

Do creative individuals simply produce more? Although we have yet to develop a method for detecting highly creative individuals at a glance, psychologists have found that highly creative individuals seem to share several characteristics. Psychologists who take a *psychometric (-metric,* measurement) approach, such as J. P. Guilford (1950), emphasize performance on tasks involving specific aspects of creativity, such as *divergent production,* the generation of a diverse assortment of appropriate responses. Therefore, creativity reflects simply the ability to create more.

For example, Paul Torrance (1988) has asserted that creative individuals have high scores on tests of creativity (including his own *Torrance Tests of Creative Thinking,* 1974, 1984) that measure the diversity, numerosity, and appropriateness of responses to open-ended questions—such as to think of all the possible ways in which to use a paper clip or a ballpoint pen. Torrance's test also assesses creative figural responses. For example, a person might be given a sheet of paper displaying some circles, squiggles, or lines; the test would assess how many different ways the person had used the given shapes to complete a drawing. Assessment of the Torrance test would particularly consider how much the person had used unusual or richly elaborated details in completing a figure.

It's What You Know

Other psychological researchers (e.g., Finke, 1995; Langley & Jones, 1988; S. M. Smith, 1995; Weisberg, 1988, 1995) have focused on creativity as a cognitive process by studying problem solving and insight. Are creative people smarter than the rest of us? Robert Weisberg (1988, 1995) holds that what distinguishes remarkably creative individuals from less remarkable persons is their expertise and commitment to their creative endeavor. Highly creative individuals work long and hard, studying the work of their predecessors and their contemporaries, to become thoroughly expert in their fields. They then build on and diverge from what they know, to create innovative approaches and products. To Weisberg, creativity in itself is nothing special; the processes involved in creativity are used by all of us every day in solving problems. What differentiates the remarkable from the mundane is the extraordinary content on which these ordinary processes operate. This notion feeds back to those discussed previously in expertise, and indeed, creativity is often treated as related to expertise.

Not every cognitive psychologist agrees with Weisberg's nothing-special view of creative insight. For example, to Ronald Finke (1995), "insight is what distinguishes . . . the inspiring from the denigrating, the magical from the mediocre" (p. 255). Finke goes on to describe two types of creative thinking: (a) In *convergent insight,* the individual converges on a unifying pattern or structure within a scattered assortment of data; (b) in *divergent insight,* the individual diverges from a particular form or structure, to explore what kinds of uses may be found for it. Finke's work has explored how the notion of divergent insight may be used to understand various creative endeavors, such as architectural design, physical or biological models, product development, or scientific invention.

Pat Langley and Randolph Jones (1988) focus on creativity as it is manifested in scientific insight; these researchers suggest that memory processes such as spreading activation (see chapter 8) and thinking processes such as analogical reasoning (see chapter 12) account for much of scientific insight. Steven Smith (1995), who distinguishes between scientific insight and the insight experience, suggests that the abruptness of the insight experience may be due to a sudden release from a mental rut (a mental set such as functional fixedness). In Smith's view, this sudden release may be more likely to arise after a period of incubation in a context other than the context in which the individual became fixated on the problem.

It's Who You Are

Other psychologists have turned their focus away from cognition to consider the role of personality and motivation in creativity. Is there a creative personality—either you have it or you don't? Frank Barron (1988), for example, underscores the importance of personal style, such as "openness to new ways of seeing, intuition, alertness to opportunity, a liking for complexity as a challenge to find simplicity, independence of judgment that questions assumptions, willingness to take risks, unconventionality of thought that allows odd connections to be made, keen attention, and a drive to find pattern and meaning—these, coupled with the motive and the courage to create" (p. 95). Barron also mentions the role of personal philosophy in creativity, suggesting that flexible beliefs and broadly accepting attitudes toward other cultures, other races, and other religious creeds enhance creativity.

Teresa Amabile and others (e.g., Amabile, 1996; Hennessey & Amabile, 1988) have focused on the importance of motivation in creative productivity. Amabile differentiates *intrinsic motivation* (internal to the individual) from *extrinsic motivation* (external to the individual); for example, intrinsic motivators might include sheer enjoyment of the creative process or personal desire to solve a problem, whereas extrinsic motivators might include a desire for fame or fortune. According to Amabile, intrinsic motivation is essential to creativity, whereas extrinsic motivators may actually impede creativity under many but not all circumstances. Individual psychologists might also add other characteristics as being definitive or at least typical characteristics of creative individuals.

It's Where You Are

In addition to these intrinsic characteristics of creative individuals, some researchers focus on the importance of external factors that contribute to creativity. Do you have to be in the right place at the right time? According to Mihaly Csikszentmihalyi (1988, p. 325), "we cannot study creativity by isolating individuals and their works from the social and historical milieu in which their actions are carried out. . . . what we call creative is never the result of individual action alone." In regard to the context for creativity, Csikszentmihalyi (1996) urges us to consider both the *domain* (existing knowledge in a particular area of creative endeavor, such as particle physics or painting) and the *field* (social context, including both the collegial network in the domain and the broader social and public institutions of the society) surrounding the creative endeavor.

Dean Simonton (1988, 1994, 1997) goes beyond the immediate social, intellectual, and cultural context to embrace the entire sweep of history. In his extensive survey of greatness, Simonton (1994) probed the multiple internal and external factors that must be combined to contribute to highly creative productivity. While acknowledging that historical movements and cultural trends may facilitate particular kinds of scientific, artistic, or other creative developments, Simonton underscores the importance of the individual creator. Furthermore, although hindsight permits us to see how antecedent events may have led up to a creative work, creative contributions, almost by definition, are unpredictable because they violate the norms established by the forerunners and the contemporaries of the creator. Among the many attributes of creative individuals noted by Simonton is the ability to make serendipitous discoveries, as well as to pursue such discoveries actively.

All of the Above

Howard Gardner (1993a) has attempted to synthesize various aspects of research on creativity, and to formulate an integrated view of what characterizes creative individuals. Like some case-study researchers (e.g., Gruber, 1974/1981; Gruber & Davis, 1988), he used in-depth study of several (seven) creative individuals. Like Simonton, he attempted to relate these creative individuals to the historical context in which they developed and worked, noting that great creators seemed to be in the right place at the right time for revolutionary change in their chosen domain. Like Csikszentmihalyi, Gardner studied how both the domain (e.g., physics, politics, music) and the field (e.g., collaborators, mentors, rivals) influence the way in which the creative individual demonstrates creativity. In addition, as a developmental psychologist, Gardner studied both the kinds of early experiences leading to creative achievement and the development of creativity across the life span.

Regarding early experiences, Gardner found that creative individuals tended to have moderately supportive but rather strict and relatively chilly (i.e., not warmly affectionate and nurturing) early family lives. Most showed an early interest in their chosen field, but most were not particularly prodigious. Also, although they generally tended to show an early interest in exploring uncharted territory, only after gaining mastery of their chosen field (after about a decade of practicing their craft) did they have their initial revolutionary breakthrough. Most creators seemed to have obtained at least some emotional support and some intellectual support at the time of their breakthrough. However, following this initial breakthrough (and sometimes before), highly creative individuals generally dedicated all their energies to their work, abandoning, neglecting, or exploiting any close relationships during adulthood. About a decade after their initial creative achievement, most of the creators Gardner studied made a second breakthrough, which was more comprehensive and more integrative, but less revolutionary. Whether a creator continued to make significant contributions depended on the particular field of endeavor, with poets and scientists less likely to do so than musicians and painters.

An alternative integrative theory of creativity, which I developed with Todd Lubart (R. J. Sternberg & Lubart, 1991b, 1993, 1995, 1996), suggests that multiple individual and environmental factors must converge for creativity to occur. That is, what distinguishes the highly creative individual from the only modestly creative one is the confluence of multiple factors, rather than extremely high levels of any particular factor or even the possession of a distinctive trait.

Our theory (R. J. Sternberg & Lubart, 1995, 1996) is termed the *investment theory of creativity* because the theme unifying these various factors is that the creative individual takes a buy-low, sell-high approach to ideas. In *buying low,* the creator initially sees the hidden potential of ideas that are presumed by others to have little value. The creative person then focuses attention on this idea, which is unrecognized or undervalued by contemporaries, but which has great potential for creative development. He or she then develops the idea into a meaningful, significant creative contribution until at last others can also recognize the merits of the idea. Once the idea has been developed and its value is recognized, the creator then *sells high,* moving on to other pursuits and looking for the hidden potential in other undervalued ideas. Thus, the creative person influences the field most by always staying a step ahead of the rest.

Despite the diversity of views, most researchers would agree that most of the preceding individual characteristics and environmental conditions are necessary, and none alone would be sufficient. In fact, extraordinary creative productivity may be as rare as it is precisely because so many variables must come together, in the right amounts, in a single person. A further complication is that many of these variables do not show a *linear relationship* to creativity, in which case an increase in a particular characteristic or condition always would be associated with an increase in creativity. On the contrary—many seem to show paradoxical effects and other nonlinear relationships. When people have new ideas, they have to use their reasoning skills to analyze these ideas and ultimately to decide if the ideas are truly creative. How do they do such reasoning and decision making? These issues are discussed in the next chapter.

SUMMARY

1. **What are some key steps involved in solving problems?** *Problem solving* involves mentally working to overcome obstacles that stand in the way of reaching a goal. The key steps of problem solving are problem identification, problem definition and representation, strategy construction, organization of information, allocation of resources, monitoring, and evaluation. In everyday experiences, these steps may be implemented very flexibly, such that various steps may be repeated, may occur out of sequence, or may be implemented interactively.

2. **What are the differences between problems that have a clear path to a solution versus problems that do not?** Although *well-structured problems* may have clear paths to solution, the route to solution may still be difficult to follow. Some well-structured problems can be solved using *algorithms,* which may be tedious to implement, but which are likely to lead to an accurate solution if applicable to a

given problem. Whereas computers are likely to use algorithmic problem-solving strategies, humans are more likely to use rather informal *heuristics* (e.g., means–ends analysis, working forward, working backward, and generate and test) for solving problems. When solving *ill-structured problems,* the choice of an appropriate problem representation powerfully influences the ease of reaching an accurate solution. Additionally, in solving ill-structured problems, people may need to use more than a heuristic or an algorithmic strategy; insight may be required.

Many ill-structured problems cannot be solved without the benefit of insight. There are several alternative views of how insightful problem solving takes place: (a) According to the *Gestalt* and the *neo-Gestalt views,* insightful problem solving is a special process that comprises more than the sum of its parts and may be evidenced by the suddenness of realizing a solution; (b) according to the *nothing-special view,* insightful problem solving is no different from any other kind of problem solving; and (c) according to the *three-process view,* insight involves a special use of three processes: selective encoding, selective combination, and selective comparison.

3. **What are some of the obstacles and aids to problem solving?** A *mental set* (also termed *entrenchment)* is a strategy that has worked in the past but that does not work for a particular problem that needs to be solved in the present. A particular type of mental set is *functional fixedness,* which involves the inability to see that something that is known to have a particular use may also be used for serving other purposes. Transfer, which may be either positive or negative, refers to the carry-over of problem-solving skills from one problem or kind of problem to another. *Positive transfer* across isomorphic problems rarely occurs spontaneously, particularly if the problems appear to be different in content or in context. *Incubation,* which follows a period of intensive work on a problem, involves laying a problem to rest for a while and then returning to it, so that unentrenched subconscious work can continue on the problem while the problem is consciously ignored.

4. **How does expertise affect problem solving?** Experts differ from novices in both the *amount* and the *organization of knowledge* that they bring to bear on problem solving in the domain of their expertise. For experts, many aspects of problem solving may be governed by automatic processes; such automaticity usually facilitates the expert's ability to solve problems in the given area of expertise. When problems involve novel elements, requiring novel strategies, however, the automaticity of some procedures may actually impede problem solving, at least temporarily. Expertise in a given domain is viewed mostly from the practice makes perfect perspective. However, many point out that the notion of talent should not be ignored, and probably contributes much to the differences between different experts.

5. **What is creativity, and how can it be fostered?** *Creativity* involves producing something that is both original and worthwhile. Factors that characterize highly creative individuals are (a) extremely high motivation to be creative in a particular field of endeavor (e.g., for the sheer enjoyment of the creative process); (b) both nonconformity in violating any conventions that might inhibit the creative work

and dedication in maintaining standards of excellence and self-discipline related to the creative work; (c) deep belief in the value of the creative work, as well as willingness to criticize and improve the work; (d) careful choice of the problems or subjects on which to focus creative attention; (e) thought processes characterized by both insight and divergent thinking; (f) risk taking; (g) extensive knowledge of the relevant domain; and (h) profound commitment to the creative endeavor. In addition, the historical context and the domain and field of endeavor influence the expression of creativity.

Thinking About Thinking: Factual, Analytical, Creative, and Practical Questions

1. Describe the steps of the problem-solving cycle, and give an example of each step.
2. What are some of the key characteristics of expert problem solvers?
3. What are some of the insights into problem solving gained through studying computer simulations of problem solving? How might a computer-based approach limit the potential for understanding problem solving in humans?
4. Compare and contrast the various approaches to creativity.
5. Design a problem that would require insight for its solution.
6. Design a context for problem solving that would enhance the ease of reaching a solution.
7. Given what we know about some of the hindrances to problem solving, how could you minimize those hindrances in your handling of the problems you face?
8. Given some of the ideas regarding creativity presented in this chapter, what can you do to enhance your own creativity?

Key Terms

algorithm 356
analysis 353
convergent thinking 353
creativity 382
divergent thinking 353
functional fixedness 370
heuristics 358
ill-structured problem 354
incubation 375
insight 364
isomorphic 360
mental set 369
negative transfer 371
positive transfer 371
problem solving 350
problem-solving cycle 351
problem space 356
productive thinking 365

selective-combination insights 368
selective-comparison insights 368
selective-encoding insights 368
stereotype 370
synthesis 353
transparency 374
well-structured problem 354

Annotated Suggested Readings

Gardner, H. (1993). *Creating minds.* New York: Basic Books. An intriguing look at commonalities in the creative thinking of seven of the twentieth century's greatest thinkers: Sigmund Freud, Albert Einstein, Pablo Picasso, Igor Stravinsky, T. S. Eliot, Martha Graham, and Mohandas Gandhi.

Langley, P., Simon, H. A., Bradshaw, G. L., & Zytkow, J. M. (1986). *Scientific discovery: Computational explorations of the creative process.* Cambridge, MA: MIT Press. A description of how computer simulation may be applied toward understanding the mental processes underlying creative discovery.

Sternberg, R. J., & Davidson, J. E. (Eds.) (1995). *The nature of insight.* Cambridge, MA: MIT Press. A review of almost all of the various approaches to understanding insightful problem solving.

Sternberg, R. J., & Frensch, P. A. (Eds.) (1991). *Complex problem solving.* Hillsdale, NJ: Erlbaum. A look at a wide variety of approaches to complex problem solving across many different subject-matter domains.

Ward, T. B., Smith, S. M., & Vaid, J. (Eds.) (1997). *Creative thought: An investigation of conceptual structures and processes.* Washington, DC: American Psychological Association. A wide-ranging sampling of modern cognitive approaches to understanding creativity.

Decision Making and Reasoning

Chapter Outline

Exploring Cognitive Psychology

Judgment and Decision Making
- Classical Decision Theory
- Satisficing
- Elimination by Aspects
- Heuristics and Biases

Deductive Reasoning
- Conditional Reasoning
- Syllogistic Reasoning
- Further Aids and Obstacles to Deductive Reasoning

Inductive Reasoning
- Reaching Causal Inferences
- Categorical Inferences
- Reasoning by Analogy

An Alternative View of Reasoning

Summary

Thinking About Thinking: Factual, Analytical, Creative, and Practical Questions

Key Terms

Annotated Suggested Readings

EXPLORING COGNITIVE PSYCHOLOGY

1. What are some of the strategies that guide human decision making?
2. What are some of the forms of deductive reasoning that people may use and what factors facilitate or impede deductive reasoning?
3. How do people use inductive reasoning to make causal inferences and to reach other types of conclusions?
4. Are there any alternative views of reasoning?

Linda is 31 years old, single, outspoken, and very bright. She majored in philosophy. As a student, she was deeply concerned with issues of discrimination and social justice, and also participated in anti-nuclear demonstrations. (Tversky & Kahneman, 1983, p. 297)

INVESTIGATING COGNITIVE PSYCHOLOGY

Based on the preceding description, list the likelihood that the following statements about Linda are true: (a) "Linda is a teacher in elementary school." (b) "Linda works in a bookstore and takes Yoga classes." (c) "Linda is active in the feminist movement." (d) "Linda is a psychiatric social worker." (e) "Linda is a member of the League of Women Voters." (f) "Linda is a bank teller." (g) "Linda is an insurance salesperson." (h) "Linda is a bank teller and is active in the feminist movement."

If you are like 85% of the people Tversky and Kahneman studied, you rated the likelihood of item (h) as greater than the likelihood of item (f). Stop for a minute, though, and imagine a huge convention hall filled with the entire population of bank tellers, and now think about how many of them would be at a hypothetical booth for feminist bank tellers—a subset of the entire population of bank tellers. If Linda is at the booth for feminist bank tellers, she must, by definition, be in the convention hall of bank tellers. Hence, the likelihood that she is at the booth (i.e., she is a feminist bank teller) cannot logically be greater than the likelihood that she is in the convention hall (i.e., she is a bank teller). Nonetheless, given the description of Linda, we intuitively feel more likely to find her at the booth than in the convention hall. This intuitive feeling is an example of a fallacy in judgment and reasoning.

In this chapter we will consider many ways in which we make judgments and decisions and use reasoning to draw conclusions. The first section deals with how we make choices and judgments. The goal of **judgment and decision making** is to select from among choices or to evaluate opportunities (e.g., choosing the car that would please you the most for the amount of money you have). The second section addresses various forms of reasoning. The goal of reasoning is to draw conclusions deductively from principles (e.g., applying the general laws of physics to reach conclusions regarding the mechanics of a particular car engine) and inductively from evidence (e.g., reading consumer-oriented statistics to find out the reliability, economy, and safety of various cars).

JUDGMENT AND DECISION MAKING

In the course of our everyday lives, we are constantly making judgments and decisions. One of the most important decisions you may have made is that of whether and where to go to college. Once in college, you still need to decide on which courses to take and, later, on a major field of study. You make decisions about friends and dates, about how to relate to your parents, and about how to spend money. How do you go about making these decisions?

CLASSICAL DECISION THEORY

The earliest models of how people make decisions are referred to as "classical decision theory." Most of these models were devised by economists, statisticians, and philosophers, not by psychologists. Hence, they reflect the strengths of an economic perspective—such as the ease of developing and using mathematical models for human behavior. Among the early models of decision making crafted in this century was *economic man and woman,* which assumed that decision makers are (a) fully informed regarding all possible options for their decisions and of all possible outcomes of their decision options, (b) infinitely sensitive to the subtle distinctions among decision options, and (c) fully rational in regard to their choice of options (Edwards, 1954; see also Slovic, 1990). The assumption of infinite sensitivity means that people can evaluate the difference between two outcomes, no matter how subtle the distinctions among options may be. The assumption of rationality means that people make their choices so as to maximize something of value, whatever that something may be.

As an example of how this model works, suppose that a decision maker is considering which of two job offers to accept, assuming that both provide the same starting salaries. Suppose also that people at Company A have a 50% chance of getting a 20% salary increase the first year, whereas people at Company B have a 90% chance of getting a 10% salary increase the first year. The decision maker will then calculate the *expected value* for each option, which is the probability times the corresponding value (utility), which here is the increase in salary ($0.50 \times 0.20 = 0.10$; $0.90 \times 0.10 = 0.09$). For all of the potential benefits (additive calculations) and costs (subtractive calculations) of each job, the person would perform similar calculations and then choose the job with the highest expected value—that offering the highest calculated benefit, at the lowest calculated cost. Assuming all other things are equal, we should choose Company A. A great deal of economic research has been based on this model.

An alternative model makes greater allowance for the psychological makeup of each individual decision maker. According to *subjective expected utility theory,* the goal of human action is to seek pleasure and to avoid pain. According to this theory, in making decisions, people will seek to maximize pleasure (referred to as *positive utility)* and to minimize pain (referred to as *negative utility).* In doing so, however, each of us uses calculations of both **subjective utility** (based on the individual's judged weightings of utility, rather than on objective criteria) and **subjective probability** (based on the individual's estimates of likelihood, rather than on objective statistical computations).

As an example of how this model works, in deciding which of two job offers to accept, different people would give different subjective positive or negative utilities to each feature of each job offer. Someone with a husband and four children might give a higher positive utility to benefits such as health insurance, dental care, vacation time, paid holidays, and so on, than would a single person who is strongly career oriented. Similarly, the family woman might assign a higher negative utility to the warning that a job involves a lot of travel requiring the person to be out of state for many days each month.

Two job seekers might also assign differing subjective probabilities to various potential positive or negative utilities. A pessimist probably would expect a higher likelihood of negative utilities and a lower likelihood of positive utilities than would an optimist. Hence, according to subjective expected utility theory, each person will then multiply each subjective probability by each subjective positive utility for each job offer, subtract the calculation of the subjective probability of each subjective negative utility, and then reach a decision based on the relative expected values obtained from these calculations. The alternative that has the highest expected value is chosen. Although subjective utility theory takes into account the many subjective variables that arise when people are involved, theorists soon noticed that human decision making is more complex than even this modified theory implies.

Given that for most decisions, there is no one perfect option that will be selected by all persons, how can we predict the optimal decision for a particular person? According to subjective expected utility theory, if we know the person's subjective expected utilities (based on both subjective estimates of probability and subjective weightings of costs and benefits), we can predict the optimal decision for that person. This prediction is based on the belief that people seek to reach well-reasoned decisions based on (a) consideration of all possible known alternatives, given that unpredictable alternatives may be available; (b) use of a maximum amount of available information, given that some relevant information may not be available; (c) careful, if subjective, weighing of the potential costs (risks) and benefits of each alternative; (d) careful (though subjective) calculation of the probability of various outcomes, given that certainty of outcomes cannot be known; and (e) a maximum degree of sound reasoning, based on considering all of the aforementioned factors. Now, answer truthfully: When was the last time you implemented the five preceding aspects of optimal decision making, even allowing for limits on your knowledge and for unpredictable elements?

SATISFICING

As early as the 1950s, some psychologists were beginning to challenge the notion of unlimited rationality. Not only did these psychologists recognize that we humans do not always make ideal decisions and that we usually include subjective considerations in our decisions, but they also suggested that we humans are not entirely and boundlessly rational in making decisions. In particular, Herbert Simon (1957), who was to go on to win the Nobel Prize in Economics, suggested that we humans are not necessarily irrational, but rather that we show **bounded rationality**—we are rational, but within limits.

Simon suggested that we typically use a decision-making strategy he termed **satisficing.** In satisficing, we do *not* consider all possible options and then carefully compute which of the entire universe of options will maximize our gains and minimize our losses. Rather, we consider options one by one, and then we select an option as soon as we find one that is satisfactory, or just good enough to meet our minimum level of acceptability. Thus, we will consider the minimum possible number of options to arrive at a decision that we believe to satisfy our minimum requirements. Of course, satisficing is only one of several suboptimal strategies people can use.

Suppose, for example, that you are looking for a used car. There are probably a staggering number of used-car lots near where you live, and you probably have neither the time nor the inclination to visit them all and pick the car that seems best on all of the many dimensions on which you might judge a car. So you go to one lot and see what is available. If you see a car there that you find satisfactory in terms of your major criteria for making the purchase, you buy it. If you do not find a car there that is good enough, you move on to the next lot. You keep looking only until you find a car that meets your needs, and then you buy. On the one hand, you have probably not picked the optimal car of all those available. On the other hand, you have not spent 4 months looking through all of the lots in town.

Amos Tversky, *recently deceased, was the Davis–Brack professor of behavioral science at Stanford University. Tversky was best known for his work on human judgment and decision making, including work with Daniel Kahneman on heuristics and biases in judgment under conditions of uncertainty. Tversky also made major contributions to the study of similarity and psychological measurement.*

You also may use satisficing when considering research topics for a term project or paper. Of the countless possible topics, you probably consider quite a few but then settle on a satisfactory or even pretty-good topic without continuing your exploration indefinitely. Additionally, a decision maker may decide to adjust the minimum level deemed adequate for satisficing if she or he finds that an uncomfortably high number of options have failed to reach the initial minimum level of acceptability. For example, if I decide that I want to buy a new luxury car with an excellent consumer track record and high fuel efficiency, for less than $3,000, I may end up having to adjust my minimum level of acceptability way downward.

ELIMINATION BY ASPECTS

In the 1970s, Amos Tversky (1972a, 1972b) built on Simon's notion of bounded rationality and observed that we sometimes use a different strategy when faced with far more alternatives than we feel that we can reasonably consider in the time we have available. In such situations, we do not try to manipulate mentally all the weighted attributes of all the available options. Rather, we use a process of **elimination by aspects:** We focus on one aspect (attribute) of the various options, and we form a minimum criterion for that aspect. We then eliminate all options that do not meet that criterion. For the remaining options, we then select a second aspect for which we set a minimum criterion by which to eliminate additional options. We continue using a sequential process of elimination of options by considering a series of aspects until a single option remains.

For example, in choosing a car to buy, we may focus on total price as an aspect, dismissing factors such as maintenance costs, insurance costs, or other factors that might realistically affect the money we will have to spend on the car in addition to the sale price. Once we have weeded out the alternatives that do not meet our criterion, we choose another aspect, set a criterion value, and weed out additional alternatives. We continue in this way, weeding out more alternatives, one aspect at a time, until we are left with a single option. In practice, it appears that we may use some elements of elimination by aspects or satisficing to narrow the range of options to just a few, then we use more thorough and careful strategies (e.g., those suggested by subjective expected utility theory) for selecting among the few remaining options (Payne, 1976).

Tversky was not content just to observe that we often make decisions based on less than optimal strategies. Adding insult to injury, Tversky and an associate observed that we often use mental shortcuts and even biases that limit and sometimes distort our ability to make rational decisions. One of the key ways in which we use mental shortcuts centers on our estimations of probability. Consider, for example, some of the strategies used by statisticians when calculating probability, shown in Table 12.1.

You may be able easily to calculate the simple probability that a given cost or benefit will occur (shown on the first row of the table), as well as the simple probability that a given cost or benefit will not occur (shown on the second line of the table). However, the calculations of combined probabilities for the occurrence or nonoccurrence of various costs and benefits can be quite cumbersome (see the third and fourth rows of the table).

TABLE 12.1 **RULES OF PROBABILITY**

Statisticians regularly use the rules of probability described in this table. However, most nonstatisticians fail to follow most of these rules when estimating the likelihood of particular events or when estimating the probable outcomes of multiple decision options.

What Is Being Determined		Mathematical Expression of Likelihood
Simple probability of event (*A*)	The likelihood that a given event (*A*) will occur—that is, What is the probability of *A*?	$p(A)$
Negation of the probability of event (*A*)	The likelihood that a given event (*A*) will *not* occur—that is, What is the probability of not *A* (expressed as "$\bar{A}$")?	$p\bar{A} = 1 - p(A)$
Combined probability of two mutually exclusive events	If the occurrence of event *A* is mutually exclusive of the occurrence of event *B* (that is, the likelihood that both will occur is 0), what is the likelihood that either will occur?	$p(A) + p(B)$
Combined probability of two independent events	If the occurrence of event *A* is independent of the occurrence of event *B*, what is the likelihood that both will occur?	$p(A) \times p(B)$

Another probability is *conditional probability,* which is the likelihood of one event, given another. For example, you might want to calculate the likelihood of receiving an "A" for a cognitive psychology course, given that you receive an "A" on the final exam. The formula for calculating conditional probabilities in light of evidence, known as Bayes's theorem, is quite complex, so most people do not use it in everyday reasoning situations. Nonetheless, such calculations are essential to evaluating scientific hypotheses, forming realistic medical diagnoses, analyzing demographic data, and many other real-world applications. (For a highly readable explanation of Bayes's theorem, see M. Eysenck & Keane, 1990, pp. 456–458; for a detailed description of Bayes's theorem from a cognitive psychological perspective, see Osherson, 1990.)

HEURISTICS AND BIASES

Amos Tversky and Daniel Kahneman (e.g., Kahneman & Tversky, 1972, 1990; Tversky & Kahneman, 1971, 1993) changed the face of judgment and decision-making research by suggesting that people may be far more likely to make decisions based on biases and heuristics (short-cuts) than earlier decision-making research had suggested. These mental shortcuts lighten the cognitive load of making decisions, but they also allow for a much greater chance of error. Tversky, Kahneman, and their colleagues in the field of decision making have investigated several heuristics and biases we often use when making decisions and other judgments; some of these are described in the following section.

HYPOTHETICAL EXAMPLE	CALCULATION OF PROBABILITY
Lee is 1 of 10 highly qualified candidates applying for 1 scholarship. What are Lee's chances of getting the scholarship?	Lee has a .1 chance of getting the scholarship.
If Lee is 1 of 10 highly qualified scholarship students applying for 1 scholarship, what are Lee's chances of *not* getting the scholarship?	$1 - .1 = .9$ Lee has a .9 chance of not getting the scholarship.
Lee's roommate and Lee are among 10 highly qualified scholarship students applying for one scholarship. What are the chances that one of the two will get the scholarship?	$.1 + .1 = .2$ There is a .2 chance that one of the two roommates will get the scholarship.
Lee owns four pairs of shoes—blue, white, black, and brown. Lee rotates randomly among the pairs of shoes he wears. What are the chances that one of the two roommates will be awarded the scholarship and that Lee will be wearing black shoes at the time?	$.25 \times .2 = .05$ There is a .05 chance that one of the two roommates will be awarded the scholarship and that Lee will be wearing black shoes at the time of the announcement.

REPRESENTATIVENESS

Before you read about representativeness, try the following problem from Kahneman and Tversky (1972).

> **INVESTIGATING COGNITIVE PSYCHOLOGY**
>
> All the families having exactly six children in a particular city were surveyed. In 72 of the families, the exact order of births of boys and girls was G B G B B G (G = girl; B = boy).
>
> What is your estimate of the number of families surveyed in which the exact order of births was B G B B B B?

Most people judging the number of families with the B G B B B B birth pattern estimate the number to be less than 72. Actually, the best estimate of the number of families with this birth order is 72, the same as for the G B G B B G birth order. The expected number for the second pattern would be the same because the gender for each birth is independent (at least, theoretically) of the gender for every other birth, and for any one birth, the chance of a boy (or a girl) is one out of two. Thus, any particular pattern of births is equally likely (1/2) 6, even B B B B B B or G G G G G G.

Why do many of us believe some birth orders to be more likely than others? Kahneman and Tversky suggest that it is because we use the heuristic of **representativeness,** in which we judge the probability of an uncertain event according to (a) how obviously it is similar to or representative of the population from which it is derived, and (b) the degree to which it reflects the salient features of the process by which it is generated (such as randomness). For example, people believe that the first birth order is more likely because first, it is more representative of the number of females and males in the population, and second, it looks more random than the second birth order. In fact, of course, either birth order is equally likely to occur by chance.

Similarly, if asked to judge the probability of flips of a coin yielding the sequence—H T H H T H—most people will judge it as higher than they will if asked to judge the sequence—H H H H T H. If you expect a sequence to be random, you tend to view as more likely a sequence that "looks random." Indeed, people often comment that the numbers in a table of random numbers "don't look random," because people underestimate the number of runs of the same number that will appear wholly by chance. We frequently reason in terms of whether something appears to represent a set of accidental occurrences, rather than actually considering the true likelihood of a given chance occurrence. This tendency makes us more vulnerable to the machinations of magicians, charlatans, and con artists, who may make much of their having predicted the realistic probability of a non-random-looking event. For example, the odds are 9 to 1 that 2 persons in a group of 40 persons (e.g., in a classroom or a small nightclub audience) will share a birthday (the same month and day, not necessarily the same year); in a group of 14 people, there are better than even odds that 2 persons will have birthdays within a day of each other (Krantz, 1992).

Another example of the representativeness heuristic is the *gambler's fallacy,* in which the gambler mistakenly believes that the probability of a given random event (e.g., winning or losing at a game of chance) is influenced by previous random events. For example, a gambler who loses five successive bets may believe that a win is therefore more likely the sixth time. In truth, of course, each bet (or coin toss, etc.) is an independent event and has an equal probability of winning or losing. The gambler is no more likely to win on the sixth bet than on the first—or on the 1,001st!

A related fallacy is the misguided belief in the "hot hand" or the "streak shooter" in basketball. Apparently, both professional and amateur basketball players, as well as their fans, believe that a player's chances of making a basket are greater after making a previous shot than after missing one, even though the statistical likelihoods (and the actual records of players) show no such tendency (Gilovich, Vallone, & Tversky, 1985). Shrewd players will take advantage of this belief and will closely guard opponents immediately after they have made baskets because the opposing players will be more likely to try to get the ball to these perceived "streak shooters."

That we frequently rely on the representativeness heuristic may not be terribly surprising because it is easy to use and often works. For example, if we have not heard a weather report prior to stepping outside, we informally judge the probability that it will rain based on how well the characteristics of this day (e.g., the month of the year and the presence or absence of clouds in the sky) represent the characteristics of days on which it rains. According to Tversky and Kahneman (1971), another reason that we often use the representativeness heuristic is that we mistakenly believe that small samples (of events, of people, of characteristics, etc.) resemble in all respects the whole population from which the sample is drawn. That is, we particularly tend to underestimate the likelihood that the characteristics of a small sample (e.g., the people whom we know well) of a population inadequately represent the characteristics of the whole population.

We also tend to use the representativeness heuristic more frequently when we are highly aware of anecdotal evidence based on a very small sample of the population. Richard Nisbett and Lee Ross (1980) refer to this reliance on anecdotal evidence as a "man-who" argument. When presented with statistics, we may refute those data with our own observations of, "I know a man who . . . ." For example, faced with statistics on coronary disease and high-cholesterol diets, someone may counter with, "I know a man who ate whipping cream for breakfast, lunch, and dinner and lived to be 110 years old, when he was shot through his perfectly healthy heart by a jealous lover."

One reason that people misguidedly use the representativeness heuristic is because they fail to understand the concept of *base rates*—the prevalence of an event or characteristic within its population of events or characteristics. In everyday decision making, people often ignore base-rate information, even though it is important to effective judgment and decision making. In many occupations, the use of base-rate information is essential for adequate job performance. For example, if a doctor were told that a 10-year-old boy was suffering chest pains, the doctor would be much less likely to worry about an incipient heart attack than if told that a 50-year-old man had the identical symptom. Why? Because the base rate of heart attacks is much higher in 50-year-old men than in 10-year-old boys. Of course, people use other heuristics as well.

AVAILABILITY

Most of us at least occasionally use the **availability heuristic** (Tversky & Kahneman, 1973), in which we make judgments on the basis of how easily we can call to mind what we perceive as relevant instances of a phenomenon. For example, consider the letter *R*. Are there more words in the English language that begin with the letter *R* or that have *R* as their third letter? Most respondents say that there are more words beginning with the letter *R* (Tversky & Kahneman, 1973). Why? Because generating words beginning with the letter *R* is easier than generating words having *R* as the third letter. In fact, there are more English-language words with *R* as their third letter. The same happens to be true of some other letters as well, such as *K, L, N,* and *V.*

The availability heuristic has also been observed in regard to everyday situations. Michael Ross and Fiore Sicoly (1979) asked married partners individually to state which of the two partners performed a larger proportion of each of 20 different household chores (e.g., grocery shopping or preparing breakfast). Each partner stated that he or she more often performed about 16 of the 20 chores. If each partner was correct, it appears that in order to accomplish 100% of the work in a household, each partner must perform 80% of the work. The authors found similar outcomes when questioning members of college basketball teams and joint participants in laboratory tasks. For all participants, the greater availability of their own actions made it seem that each had performed a greater proportion of the work in joint enterprises.

Although clearly 80% + 80% ≠ 100%, we can understand why people may engage in using the availability heuristic when it confirms their beliefs about themselves. However, people also employ the availability heuristic when its use leads to a logical fallacy that has nothing to do with their beliefs about themselves. Two groups of participants were asked to estimate the number of words of a particular form that would be expected to appear in a 2,000-word passage. For one group, the form was _________*ing* (i.e., seven letters ending in *-ing),* and for the other group, the form was _________*n*_ (i.e., seven letters with *n* as the second-to-the-last letter). Clearly, there cannot be more seven-letter words ending in *-ing* than seven-letter words with *n* as the second-to-the-last letter, but the greater availability of the former led to estimates of probability that were more than twice as high for the former, as compared with the latter (Tversky & Kahneman, 1983). This example illustrates how the availability heuristic might lead to the *conjunction fallacy,* in which an individual gives a higher estimate for a subset of events (e.g., the instances of *-ing)* than for the larger set of events containing the given subset (e.g., the instances of *n* as the second-to-the-last letter). This fallacy is also illustrated in the opening vignette of the chapter, regarding Linda.

Tversky and Kahneman (1983) have shown that another heuristic—the representativeness heuristic—may also induce individuals to engage in the conjunction fallacy during probabilistic reasoning. These authors asked college students,

> Please give your estimate of the following values: What percentage of the men surveyed [in a health survey] have had one or more heart attacks? What percentage of the men surveyed both are over 55 years old and have had one or more heart attacks? (p. 308).

The mean estimates were 18% for the former and 30% for the latter. In fact, 65% of the respondents gave higher estimates for the latter (which is clearly a subset of the former).

On the other hand, people do not always engage in the conjunction fallacy. Only 25% of respondents gave higher estimates for the latter question than for the former when the questions were rephrased as frequencies (i.e., numbers of individuals within a given sample of the population) rather than as percentages. Also, the authors found that the conjunction fallacy was less likely

> when the conjunctions are defined by the intersection of concrete classes [e.g., types of objects or individuals such as dogs or beagles] than by a combination of properties [e.g., features of objects or individuals such as conservatism or feminism]. Although classes and properties are equivalent from a logical standpoint, they give rise to different mental representations in which different rules and relations are transparent. The formal equivalence of properties to classes is apparently not programmed into the lay mind. (Tversky & Kahneman, 1983, p. 309)

A variant of the conjunction fallacy is the *inclusion fallacy,* in which the individual judges a greater likelihood that every member of an inclusive category (e.g., lawyers) has a particular characteristic than that every member of a subset of the inclusive category (e.g., labor-union lawyers) has that characteristic (Shafir, Osherson, & Smith, 1990). For example, participants judged a much greater likelihood that "every single lawyer" (i.e., every lawyer) is conservative than that every single labor-union lawyer is conservative. According to these authors, we tend to judge the likelihood that the members of a particular class (e.g., lawyers) or subclass (e.g., labor-union lawyers) of individuals will demonstrate a particular characteristic (e.g., conservatism) based on the perceived typicality (i.e., representativeness) of the given characteristic for the given category, rather than judging likelihood based on statistical probability.

Heuristics such as representativeness and availability do not always lead to wrong judgments or poor decisions. Indeed, we use these mental shortcuts because they are so often right. For example, one of the factors that leads to the greater availability of an event is in fact the greater frequency of the event. However, availability also may be influenced by recency of presentation (as in implicit-memory cueing, mentioned in chapter 7), unusualness, or distinctive salience of a particular event or event category for the individual. Nonetheless, when the available information is not biased for some reason (e.g., due to sensationalized press coverage, to extensive advertising, to recency of an uncommon occurrence, or to personal prejudices), the instances that are most available are generally the most common ones. Because we generally make decisions in which the most common instances are the most relevant and valuable ones, the availability heuristic is often a convenient shortcut with few costs. However, when particular instances are better recalled due to biases (e.g., your views of your own behavior, in comparison with that of other persons), the availability heuristic may lead to less than optimal decisions.

OTHER JUDGMENT PHENOMENA

A heuristic related to availability is the *anchoring-and-adjustment heuristic.* Before you read on, quickly (in less than 5 seconds) calculate in your head the answer to the following problem:

$$8 \times 7 \times 6 \times 5 \times 4 \times 3 \times 2 \times 1$$

Now, quickly calculate your answer to the following problem:

$$1 \times 2 \times 3 \times 4 \times 5 \times 6 \times 7 \times 8$$

Tversky and Kahneman (1974) asked two groups of participants to estimate the product of one or the other of the preceding two sets of eight numbers. The median (middle) estimate for the participants given the first sequence was 2,250. For the participants given the second sequence, the median estimate was 512. (The actual product is 40,320 for both!) The two products are the same, as they must be because the numbers are exactly the same (applying the commutative law of multiplication). Nonetheless, people provide a higher estimate for the first sequence than for the second because their computation of the *anchor*—the first few digits multiplied by each other—renders a higher estimate from which they make an *adjustment* to reach a final estimate.

Another consideration in decision theory is the influence of *framing effects,* in which the way that the options are presented influences the selection of an option (Tversky & Kahneman, 1981). For instance, we tend to choose options that demonstrate *risk aversion* when we are faced with an option involving potential gains. That is, we tend to choose options offering a small but certain gain rather than a larger but uncertain gain, unless the uncertain gain is either tremendously greater or only modestly less than certain. The following example is only slightly modified from one used by Tversky and Kahneman (1981).

INVESTIGATING COGNITIVE PSYCHOLOGY

Suppose that you were told that 600 people were at risk of dying of a particular disease. Vaccine A could save the lives of 200 of the people at risk. For Vaccine B, there is a .33 likelihood that all 600 people would be saved, but there is a .66 likelihood that all 600 people will die. Which option would you choose?

On the other hand, we tend to choose options that demonstrate *risk seeking* when we are faced with options involving potential losses. That is, we tend to choose options offering a large but uncertain loss rather than a smaller but certain loss, unless the uncertain loss is either tremendously greater or only modestly less than certain. The next investigation provides an interesting example.

INVESTIGATING COGNITIVE PSYCHOLOGY

Suppose that for the 600 people at risk of dying of a particular disease, if Vaccine C is used, 400 people will die. However, if Vaccine D is used, there is a .33 likelihood that no one will die and a .66 likelihood that all 600 people will die. Which option would you choose?

In the preceding situations, most people will choose Vaccine A and Vaccine D. Now, compare the number of people whose lives will be lost or saved by using Vaccines A or C. Similarly, compare the number of people whose lives will be lost or saved by using Vaccines B or D. Our predilection for risk aversion versus risk seeking leads us to quite different choices based on the way in which a decision is framed, even when the actual outcomes of the choices are identical.

Another judgment phenomenon is **illusory correlation,** in which we tend to see particular events or particular attributes and categories as going together because we are predisposed to do so. In the case of events, we may see spurious cause–effect relationships. In the case of attributes, we may use personal prejudices to form and use stereotypes (perhaps as a result of using the representativeness heuristic). For example, if we expect persons of a given political party to show particular intellectual or moral characteristics, the instances in which persons show those characteristics are more likely to be available in memory and recalled more easily than are instances that contradict our biased expectations. In other words, we perceive a correlation between the political party and the particular characteristics.

Loren Chapman and Jean Chapman (1967, 1969, 1975) have shown that illusory correlation may even influence psychiatric diagnoses based on projective tests such as the Rorschach and the Draw-a-Person tests. In their study, the researchers suggested a false correlation in which particular responses would be associated with particular diagnoses. For example, they suggested that diagnosed paranoids tend to draw persons with large eyes more than do persons with other diagnoses. In fact, diagnoses of paranoia were no more likely to be linked to depictions of large eyes than were any other diagnoses. However, when individuals expected to observe a correlation between the particular responses and the associated diagnoses, they tended to see the illusory correlation, although no actual correlation existed.

Baruch Fischhoff *is a professor of social and decision sciences and a professor of engineering and public policy at Carnegie-Mellon University. He has studied psychological processes such as hindsight bias, risk perception, and value elicitation. He also has done policy-making work in areas such as risk and environmental management.*

Another all-too-common error that I know for sure that I have observed in other people (although never in myself or in you) is **overconfidence**—an individual's overvaluation of her or his own skills, knowledge, or judgment. For example, Baruch Fischhoff, Paul Slovic, and Sarah Lichtenstein (1977) gave people 200 two-alternative statements, such as "Absinthe is (a) a liqueur, (b) a precious stone." (*Absinthe* is a licorice-flavored liqueur.) People were asked to choose the correct answer and to state the probability that their answer was correct. People were overconfident. For example, when people were *100%* confident in their answers, they were right only *80%* of the time!

Due to overconfidence, people often make poor decisions, based on inadequate information and ineffective decision-making strategies. Why we tend to be overconfident in our judgments is not clear; one simple explanation is that we prefer not to think about being wrong (Fischhoff, 1988).

Finally, a bias that often affects all of us is **hindsight bias.** Specifically, once we look at a situation retrospectively, we can easily see all the signs and events leading up to a particular outcome (Fischhoff, 1982; Wasserman, Lempert, & Hastie, 1991). For example, when people are asked to predict the outcomes of psychological experiments in advance of the experiments, people are rarely able to predict the outcomes at better than chance levels. However, when people are told of the outcomes of psychological experiments, they frequently comment that these outcomes were obvious and would easily have been predicted in advance. Similarly, when intimate personal relationships are in trouble, people often fail to observe signs of the difficulties until the problems reach crisis proportions, perhaps leading to dissolution of the relationship. In retrospect, however, people slap their foreheads and ask themselves, "Why didn't I see it coming? It was so obvious! I should have seen the signs."

Much of the work on judgment and decision making has focused on the errors we make. The research of Tversky and Kahneman, as well as Fischhoff and others, shows clearly that human rationality is limited. Still, as Jonathan Cohen (1981) has pointed out, human irrationality is also limited, as we do act rationally in many instances. Also, each of us can improve our decision making through practice, particularly if we obtain specific feedback regarding how to improve our decision-making strategies. Another key way to improve decision making is to gain accurate information for the calculation of probabilities and to use probabilities appropriately in decision making. In addition, although we recognize that subjective expected utility theory offers a poor *description* of actual human decision making, it offers a pretty good *prescription* for enhancing the effectiveness of decision making when confronting a decision important enough to warrant the time and mental effort required (Slovic, 1990). Further, we can try to avoid overconfidence in our intuitive guesses regarding optimal choices. Yet another way to enhance our decision making is to use careful reasoning in drawing inferences about the various options available to us.

The work on heuristics and biases shows the importance of distinguishing between intellectual competence and intellectual performance as it manifests itself in daily life. Even experts in the use of probability and statistics can find themselves falling into faulty patterns of judgment and decision making in their everyday lives. People may be intelligent in a conventional, test-based sense, yet show exactly the same biases and faulty reasoning that someone with a lower test score would show. People often fail fully to utilize their intellectual competence in their daily life. There can even be a wide gap between the two. Thus, to the extent we wish to be intelligent in our daily lives and not just on tests, we have to be mindful of applying our intelligence to the problems that continually confront us.

Judgment and decision making involve evaluating opportunities and selecting one choice over another. A related kind of thinking, familiar to students in logic courses, is reasoning. **Reasoning** pertains to the process of drawing conclusions from principles and from evidence (Wason & Johnson-Laird, 1972), moving on from what is already known to infer a new conclusion or to evaluate a proposed conclusion.

Reasoning is often divided into two types—deductive and inductive reasoning. **Deductive reasoning** is the process of reasoning from one or more general statements regarding what is known, to reach a logically certain conclusion. It often involves reasoning from one or more general statements regarding what is known to a specific application of the general statement. In contrast, **inductive reasoning** is the process of reasoning from specific facts or observations to reach a likely conclusion that may explain the facts; the inductive reasoner may then use that probable conclusion to attempt to predict future specific instances. The key feature distinguishing inductive from deductive reasoning is that in inductive reasoning, we can never reach a logically certain conclusion—we can only reach a particularly well-founded or probable conclusion.

DEDUCTIVE REASONING

Deductive reasoning is based on logical propositions. A **proposition** is basically an assertion, which may be either true or false—for example, "Cognitive psychology students are brilliant," "cognitive psychology students wear shoes," or "cognitive psychology students like peanut butter." In a logical argument, propositions about which arguments are made are referred to as **premises.** Cognitive psychologists are particularly interested in propositions that may be connected in ways that require people to draw reasoned conclusions. That is, what makes deductive reasoning interesting and useful is that people connect various propositions to draw conclusions. Cognitive psychologists want to know how people connect propositions to draw conclusions, some of which are well reasoned, and some of which are not.

CONDITIONAL REASONING

One of the primary types of deductive reasoning is **conditional reasoning,** in which the reasoner must draw a conclusion based on an *if–then* proposition. The conditional *if–then* proposition states that *if* antecedent condition p is met, *then* consequent event q follows. For example, "If students study hard, then they score high on their exams." Under some circumstances, *if* you have established a conditional proposition, *then* you may draw a well-reasoned conclusion. The usual set of conditional propositions from which you can draw a well-reasoned conclusion is "If p, then q. p. Therefore, q." This inference illustrates **deductive validity,** in that it follows logically from the propositions on which it is based. So is this proposition: "If students eat pizza, then they score high on their exams. They eat pizza. Therefore, they score high on their exams." As you may have guessed, deductive validity does not equate with truth. You can reach deductively valid conclusions that are completely untrue with respect to the world. Whether the conclusion is true depends on the truthfulness of the premises. In fact, people are more likely mistakenly to accept an illogical syllogism as logical if the conclusion is factually true. For now, however, we put aside the issue of truth and focus only on the soundness—the deductive validity—of the reasoning.

One set of propositions and its conclusion is the argument "If p, then q. p. Therefore, q," which is termed a *modus ponens* argument. In the *modus ponens* argument, the reasoner *affirms the antecedent.* For example, take the argument, "If you are a husband, then you are married. Harrison is a husband. Therefore, he is married." The shorthand notation for "if p, then q" is "$p \rightarrow q$." The shorthand for "therefore" is "$\therefore$." Hence, the shorthand for the *modus ponens* argument is "$p \rightarrow q$. p. $\therefore$ q."

The set of propositions for the *modus ponens* argument is shown in Table 12.2. As the table shows, in addition to the *modus ponens* argument, you may draw another well-reasoned conclusion from a conditional proposition, given a different second proposition: "If p, then q. Not q. Therefore, not p." This inference is also deductively valid; this particular set of propositions and its conclusion is termed a *modus tollens* argument, in which the reasoner *denies the consequent.* For example, we modify the second proposition of the argument to deny the consequent: "If you are a husband, then you are married. Harrison is not married. Therefore, he is not a husband." The shorthand for the *modus tollens* argument is "$p \rightarrow q$. $\neg q$. $\therefore$ $\neg q$."

TABLE 12.2 CONDITIONAL REASONING: DEDUCTIVELY VALID INFERENCES AND DEDUCTIVE FALLACIES

Two kinds of conditional propositions lead to valid deductions, and two others lead to deductive fallacies.

Type of Argument		Conditional Proposition	Existing Condition	Inference
Deductively valid inferences	*Modus ponens*	$p \rightarrow q$ If you are a mother, then you have a child.	p You are a mother.	$\therefore q$ Therefore, you have a child.
	Modus tollens	$p \rightarrow q$ If you are a mother, then you have a child.	$\neg q$ You do not have a child.	$\therefore \neg p$ Therefore, you are not a mother.
Deductive fallacies	Denying the antecedent	$p \rightarrow q$ If you are a mother, then you have a child.	$\neg p$ You are not a mother.	$\therefore \neg q$ Therefore, you do not have a child.
	Affirming the consequent	$p \rightarrow q$ If you are a mother, then you have a child.	q You have a child.	$\therefore p$ Therefore, you are a mother.

Table 12.2 shows not only two conditions in which a well-reasoned conclusion can be reached but also two conditions in which such a conclusion cannot be reached. As the examples illustrate, some inferences based on conditional reasoning are **fallacies;** they lead to conclusions that are not deductively valid. When using conditional propositions, we cannot reach a deductively valid conclusion based either on denying the antecedent condition or on affirming the consequent. To return to the proposition, "If you are a husband, then you are married," we would not be able to confirm or to refute the proposition based on denying the antecedent: "Joan is not a husband. Therefore, she is not married." Even if we ascertain that Joan is not a husband, we cannot conclude that she is not married. Similarly, we cannot deduce a valid conclusion by affirming the consequent: "Joan is married. Therefore, she is a husband." Even if Joan is married, her spouse may not consider her a husband.

Peter Wason (1968, 1969, 1983; Wason & Johnson-Laird, 1970, 1972) has studied conditional reasoning in the laboratory, using what he calls a "selection task." Participants are presented with a set of four two-sided cards. Each card has a numeral on one side and a letter on the other side. Face up are two letters (a consonant and a vowel) and two numerals (an even number and an odd number). For example, participants may be faced with the following series of cards: S, 3, A, 2. Each participant is then told a conditional statement, such as "If a card has a consonant on one side, then it has an even number on the other side." The task is to determine whether the conditional statement is true or false, by turning over the exact number of cards necessary to test the conditional statement. That is, the participant must not turn over any cards that are *not* valid tests of the statement, but the participant must turn over all cards that *are* valid tests of the conditional proposition.

Table 12.3 illustrates the four possible tests participants might perform on the cards. Two of the tests (affirming the antecedent and denying the consequent) are both necessary and sufficient for testing the conditional statement. That is, to evaluate the deduction, the participant must turn over the card showing a consonant to see whether it has an even number on the other side, thereby affirming the antecedent (the *modus ponens* argument). In addition, the participant must turn over the card showing an odd number (i.e., not an even number) to see whether it has a vowel (i.e., not a consonant) on the other side, thereby denying the consequent (the *modus tollens* argument). The other two possible tests (denying the antecedent and affirming the consequent) are irrelevant. That is, the participant need not turn over the card showing a vowel (i.e., not a consonant, to deny the antecedent) or showing an even number (i.e., to affirm the consequent). Wason found that most participants knew to test for the *modus ponens* argument. However, many participants

TABLE 12.3 CONDITIONAL REASONING: WASON'S SELECTION TASK

In the Wason selection task, Peter Wason presented participants with a set of four cards, from which the participants were to test the validity of a given proposition. This table illustrates how a reasoner might test the conditional proposition ($p \rightarrow q$), "If a card has a consonant on one side (p), then it has an even number on the other side (q)."

Proposition Based on What Shows on the Face of the Card	Test	Type of Reasoning	
p A given card has a consonant on one side (e.g., "S," "F," "V," or "P").	$\therefore q$ Does the card have an even number on the other side?	Based on *modus ponens*	Deductively valid inferences
$\neg q$ A given card does not have an even number on one side. That is, a given card has an odd number on one side (e.g., "3," "5," "7," or "9").	$\therefore \neg p$ Does the card *not* have a consonant on the other side? That is, does the card have a vowel on the other side?	Based on *modus tollens*	
$\neg p$ A given card does not have a consonant on one side. That is, a given card has a vowel on one side (e.g., "A," "E," "I," or "O").	$\therefore \neg q$ Does the card *not* have an even number on the other side? That is, does the card have an odd number on the other side?	Based on denying the antecedent	Deductive fallacies
q A given card has an even number on one side (e.g., "2," "4," "6," or "8").	$\therefore p$ Does the card have a consonant on the other side?	Based on affirming the consequent	

failed to test for the *modus tollens* argument, and some of these participants instead tried to deny the antecedent as a means of testing the conditional proposition.

Most people of all ages (at least, starting in elementary school) appear to have little difficulty in recognizing and applying the *modus ponens* argument. However, few people spontaneously recognize the need for reasoning by means of the *modus tollens* argument, and many people do not recognize the logical fallacies of denying the antecedent or affirming the consequent, at least as these fallacies are applied to abstract reasoning problems (Braine & O'Brien, 1991; Rips, 1988, 1994; Rumain, Connell, & Braine, 1983). In fact, some evidence suggests that even persons who have taken a course in logic fail to demonstrate deductive reasoning across various situations (Cheng, Holyoak, Nisbett, & Oliver, 1986). On the other hand, most people do demonstrate conditional reasoning under circumstances that minimize possible linguistic ambiguities or that activate *schemas* (mental frameworks for organizing information about the world, based on previous experiences) that provide a meaningful context for the reasoning.

For example, Barbara Rumain, Jeffrey Connell, and Martin Braine (1983) found that both children and adults may fallaciously affirm the consequent or deny the antecedent because of invited inferences that follow from normal discourse comprehension of conditional phrasing. For instance, suppose that my publisher advertises, "If you buy this textbook, then we will give you a $5 rebate." In everyday situations, you probably correctly infer that if you do not buy this textbook, the publisher will not give you a $5 rebate, even though formal deductive reasoning would consider this denial of the antecedent to be fallacious. Similarly, you may infer that you must have bought this textbook (affirm the consequent) if you received a $5 rebate from the publisher. Both inferences are fallacious according to formal deductive reasoning, but both are quite reasonable invited inferences in everyday situations. When the wording of conditional-reasoning problems either explicitly or implicitly disinvites these inferences, both adults and children are much less likely to engage in these logical fallacies.

The demonstration of conditional reasoning is also influenced by the presence of contextual information that converts the problem from one of abstract deductive reasoning to one that applies to an everyday situation. For example, Richard Griggs and James Cox (1982) gave participants both the Wason selection task and a modified version of the Wason selection task. In the modified version, the participants were asked to suppose that they were police officers attempting to enforce the laws applying to the legal age for drinking alcoholic beverages. The particular rule to be enforced was "If a person is drinking beer, then the person must be over 19 years of age." Each participant was presented with a set of four cards: (a) "drinking a beer," (b) "drinking a coke," (c) "16 years of age," and (d) "22 years of age." The participant was then instructed, "Select the card or cards that you definitely need to turn over to determine whether or not the people are violating the rule" (p. 414). Although none of Griggs and Cox's participants had responded correctly on the abstract version of the Wason selection task, a remarkable 72% of the participants correctly responded to the modified version of the task.

A more recent modification of this task has shown that beliefs regarding plausibility influence whether people choose the *modus tollens* argument (i.e., denying the consequent by checking to see whether a person who is *not* over 19 years of age is *not* drinking beer). Specifically, people are far more likely to try to deny the consequent when the test involves checking to see whether an 18-year-old is drinking beer than checking to see whether a

4-year-old is drinking beer, even though the logical argument is the same in both cases (Kirby, 1994). Patricia Cheng and Keith Holyoak (1985) also have investigated how people use deductive reasoning in realistic situations. These two investigators have suggested that, rather than using formal inference rules, people often employ pragmatic reasoning schemas. **Pragmatic reasoning schemas** are general organizing principles—rules—related to particular kinds of goals, such as permissions, obligations, or causations; these schemas are sometimes referred to as *pragmatic rules.* These pragmatic rules are not as abstract as formal logical rules, yet they are sufficiently general and broad so that they can apply to a wide variety of specific situations.

Thus, in situations in which our previous experiences or our existing knowledge cannot tell us all we want to know, we may rely on pragmatic reasoning schemas to help us deduce what might reasonably be true. Particular situations or contexts activate particular schemas. For example, suppose that you are walking across campus and see someone who looks extremely young on campus; then you see the person walk to a car, unlock it, get in, and drive away. This observation would activate your *permission schema* for driving, "If you are to be permitted to drive alone, then you must be at least 16 years old." You might now deduce that the person you saw is at least 16 years old. In one of their experiments, Cheng and Holyoak (1985) found that 62% of participants correctly chose *modus ponens* and *modus tollens* arguments but not the two logical fallacies when the conditional-reasoning task was presented in the context of permission statements, but only 11% did so when the task was presented in the context of arbitrary statements unrelated to pragmatic reasoning schemas.

More recently, Griggs and Cox (1993) have conducted an extensive analysis comparing the standard abstract Wason selection task ("If a card has an 'A' on one side, then it must have a '4' on the other side") with an abstract form of a permission problem (i.e., "If one is to take action 'A,' then one must first satisfy precondition 'P'"). These authors found that performance on the abstract permission task was still superior (49% correct overall) to performance on the standard abstract task (only 9% correct overall), even when the authors added to the standard abstract task a statement that framed the task in a checking context (i.e., "Suppose you are an authority checking whether or not certain rules are being followed"), a rule-clarification statement (i.e., "In other words, in order to have an 'A' on one side, a card must first have a '4' on the other side"), or explicit negations (i.e., "NOT A" and "NOT 4" instead of implicit negations for A and 4—namely, "B" and "7"). In the discussion of their findings, these authors agreed with other researchers (i.e., Manktelow & Over, 1990, 1992) in concluding that although the standard selection task and the permission-related task both involve deductive reasoning, the two tasks actually pose different problems.

Despite their explanatory power for some kinds of conditional reasoning in relation to permissions and obligations, pragmatic reasoning schemas do not fully explain all aspects of conditional reasoning (Braine & O'Brien, 1991). Such schemas also fail to explain either puzzling successes in the absence of an appropriate permissions-related context or failures in the presence of an appropriate context (Braine & O'Brien, 1991). Some theorists (e.g., Braine, 1978; Braine, Reiser, & Rumain, 1984; Rips, 1983, 1988, 1994) have suggested that although people do not demonstrate formal logical reasoning, we do demonstrate a natural logic, which is a kind of mental syntax for reasoning. A careful analysis of various empirical studies of reasoning (E. E. Smith, Langston, & Nisbett, 1992) supported the notion that people frequently apply the following rules of reasoning: the *modus ponens* argument, contractual rules (e.g., permissions and obligations), causal rules, and the statistical law of large numbers. (According to the *law of large numbers,* the larger the sample size, the more probable that an effect of a given size is not due to random variation.)

An altogether different approach to conditional reasoning has been suggested by Leda Cosmides (1989). According to Cosmides, cognitive psychologists should take an evolutionary view of cognition and should consider what kinds of thinking skills would provide a naturally selective advantage for humans in adapting to our environment across evolutionary time. To gain insight into human cognition, we should look to see what kinds of adaptations would have been most useful to human hunters and gatherers during the millions of years of evolutionary time that predated the relatively recent development of agriculture and the very recent development of industrialized societies.

How has evolution influenced human cognition? Just as Noam Chomsky has suggested that humans possess an innate language-acquisition device, which facilitates our ability quickly to learn the structure of our native language (see chapter 9), Cosmides has suggested that humans possess something like a schema-acquisition device, which facilitates our ability quickly to glean important information from our experiences and to organize that information into meaningful frameworks. In her view, these schemas are highly flexible, but they are also specialized for selecting and organizing the information that will most effectively aid us in adapting to the situations we face. According to Cosmides, one of the distinctive adaptations shown by human hunters and gatherers has been in the area of social exchange. Hence, evolutionary development of human cognition should facilitate the acquisition of schemas related to social exchange.

According to Cosmides, two of the inferences that social-exchange schemas facilitate are inferences related to cost–benefit relationships and inferences that help people to detect when someone is cheating in a particular social exchange. Over a series of nine experiments, Cosmides compared participants' performance on deductive reasoning tasks based on social-exchange theory with their performance on the standard Wason selection task, as well as with performance on tasks calling for the use of permissions schemas. Across the nine experiments, participants demonstrated deductive reasoning that confirmed the predictions of social-exchange theory, rather than predictions based on permissions-related schemas or on abstract deductive-reasoning principles.

Syllogistic Reasoning

In addition to conditional reasoning, the other key type of deductive reasoning is syllogistic reasoning, based on the use of syllogisms. **Syllogisms** are deductive arguments that involve drawing conclusions from two premises (Rips, 1994). All syllogisms comprise a major premise, a minor premise, and a conclusion. (Unfortunately, sometimes the conclusion may be that no conclusion may be reached based on the two given premises.) Two key types of syllogisms—linear syllogisms and categorical syllogisms—are described in detail in this chapter, but other types of syllogisms are also used in deductive reasoning.

Linear Syllogisms

In a syllogism, each of the two premises describes a particular relationship between two items, and at least one of the items is common to both premises. The items may be objects, categories, attributes, or almost anything else that can be related to something.

Logicians designate the first term of the major premise as the *subject,* the common term as the *middle term* (which is used once in each premise), and the second term of the minor premise as the *predicate.*

In a **linear syllogism,** the relationship among the terms is *linear,* involving a quantitative or qualitative comparison, in which each term shows either more or less of a particular attribute or quantity. Suppose, for example, that you are presented with the problem in the following investigation.

INVESTIGATING COGNITIVE PSYCHOLOGY

You are smarter than your best friend.
Your best friend is smarter than your roommate.
Which of you is the smartest?

Each of the two premises describes a linear relationship between two items; Table 12.4 shows the terms of each premise and the relationship of the terms in each premise. The deductive-reasoning task for the linear syllogism is to determine a relationship between two items that do not appear in the same premise. In the preceding linear syllogism, the problem solver needs to infer that you are smarter than your roommate in order to realize that you are the smartest of the three.

When the linear syllogism is deductively valid, its conclusion follows logically from the premises, and we can correctly deduce with complete certainty that you are the smartest of the three. Your roommate or your best friend may, however, point out an area of weakness in your conclusion. Even a conclusion that is deductively valid may not be objectively true, although, of course, it is true in this example.

How do people solve linear syllogisms? Several different theories have been proposed. Some investigators (e.g., DeSoto, London, & Handel, 1965; Huttenlocher, 1968) have suggested that linear syllogisms are solved spatially, through mental representations of linear continua. The idea here is that people imagine a visual representation laying out the terms on a linear continuum. For example, the premise "You are smarter than your roommate"

TABLE 12.4 LINEAR SYLLOGISMS

What logical deduction can you reach, based on the premises of this linear syllogism? Is deductive validity the same as truth?

	First Term (Item)	Linear Relationship	Second Term (Item)
Premise A	You	are smarter than	your best friend.
Premise B	Your best friend	is smarter than	your roommate.
Conclusion: Who is smartest?	————	is/are the smartest of the three.	

might be represented mentally as an image of a vertical continuum with your name above your roommate's. The linear continuum is usually visualized vertically, although it can be visualized horizontally. When answering the question, people consult this continuum and choose the item in the correct place along the continuum.

Other investigators (e.g., H. H. Clark, 1969) have proposed that people solve linear syllogisms using a semantic model involving propositional representations. For example, the premise "You are smarter than your roommate" might be represented as [smarter (you, your roommate)]. According to this view, people do not use images at all, but rather combine semantic propositions.

A third view (e.g., R. J. Sternberg, 1980) is that people use a combination of spatial and propositional representations in solving the syllogisms. According to this view, people use propositions initially to represent each of the premises, and then form mental images based on the contents of these propositions. Model testing has tended to support the combination (or mixture) model over exclusively propositional or exclusively spatial representations (R. J. Sternberg, 1980).

At this time, however, none of the three models appear to be quite right because they all represent performance averaged over many individuals. Rather, there seem to be individual differences in strategies (R. J. Sternberg & Weil, 1980), in which some people tend to use a more imaginal strategy, and others tend to use a more propositional strategy. This result points out an important limitation on many psychological findings: Unless we consider each individual separately, we risk jumping to conclusions based on a group average that does not necessarily apply to each person individually (see Siegler, 1988a). Whereas most people may use a combination strategy, not everyone does, and the only way to find out which each person uses is to examine each individual.

Categorical Syllogisms

Probably the most well-known kind of syllogism is the categorical syllogism. Like other kinds of syllogisms, **categorical syllogisms** comprise two premises and a conclusion; in the case of the categorical syllogism, the premises state something about the category memberships of the terms. In fact, each term represents all, none, or some of the members of a particular class or category. As with other syllogisms, each premise contains two terms, one of which must be the middle term, common to both premises. The first and the second term in each premise are linked through the categorical membership of the terms—that is, one term is a member of the class indicated by the other term. However the premises are worded, they state that some (or all or none) of the members of the category of the first term are (or are not) members of the category of the second term. To determine whether the conclusion follows logically from the premises, the reasoner must determine the category memberships of the terms. An example of a categorical syllogism would be

All cognitive psychologists are pianists.

All pianists are athletes.

Therefore, all cognitive psychologists are athletes.

Logicians often use circle diagrams to illustrate class membership and to make it easier to figure out whether a particular conclusion is logically sound. The conclusion for this syllogism does in fact follow logically from the premises, as shown in the circle diagram in Figure 12.1. However, the conclusion is false because the premises are false. For the preceding categorical syllogism, the subject is *cognitive psychologists,* the middle term is *pianists,* and the predicate is *athletes.* In both premises, we asserted that all members of the category of the first term were members of the category of the second term.

Statements of the form "All *A* are *B*" are sometimes referred to as *universal affirmatives,* because they make a positive (affirmative) statement about *all* members of a class (universal). In addition, there are three other kinds of possible statements in a categorical syllogism: *universal negative* statements (e.g., "No cognitive psychologists are flutists"); *particular affirmative* statements (e.g., "Some cognitive psychologists are left-handed"); and *particular negative* statements (e.g., "Some cognitive psychologists are not physicists"); these are summarized in Table 12.5.

FIGURE 12.1 **CIRCLE DIAGRAM OF A SYLLOGISM**

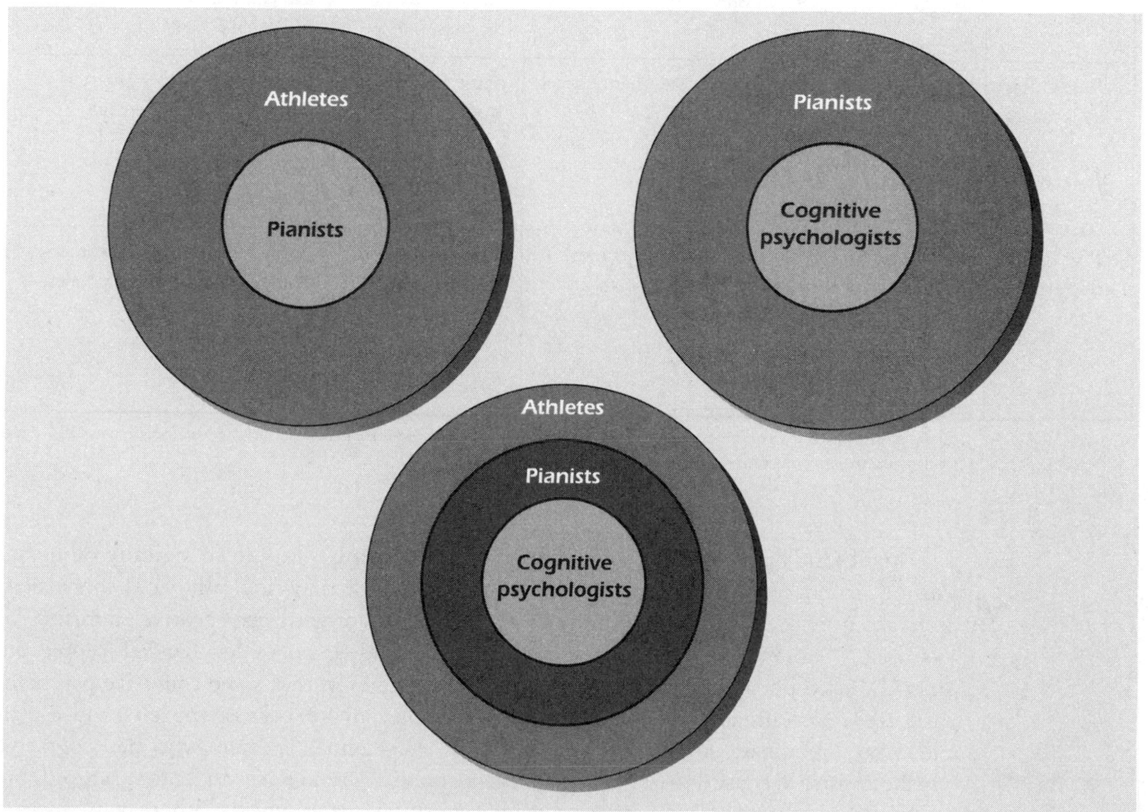

Circle diagrams may be used to represent categorical syllogisms such as the one shown here: "All pianists are athletes. All cognitive psychologists are pianists. Therefore, all cognitive psychologists are athletes."

TABLE 12.5 CATEGORICAL SYLLOGISMS: TYPES OF PREMISES

The premises of categorical syllogisms may be universal affirmatives, universal negatives, particular affirmatives, or particular negatives.

Type of Premise	Form of Premise Statements	Description	Examples	Reversibility*
Universal affirmative	All *A* are *B*.	The premise positively (affirmatively) states that *all* members of the first class (universal) are members of the second class.	All men are males.	All men are males. ≠ All males are men. **Nonreversible** All *A* are *B*. ≠ All *B* are *A*.
Universal negative	No *A* are *B*. (Alternative: All A are *not* B.)	The premise states that none of the members of the first class are members of the second class.	No men are females. *or* All men are not females.	No men are females = No females are men. **↔Reversible↔** No *A* are *B* = No *B* are *A*.
Particular affirmative	Some *A* are *B*.	The premise states that only some of the members of the first class are members of the second class.	Some females are women.	Some females are women. ≠ Some women are females. **Nonreversible** Some *A* are *B*. ≠ Some *B* are *A*.
Particular negative	Some *A* are not *B*.	The premise states that some members of the first class are not members of the second class.	Some females are not women.	Some females are not women. ≠ Some women are not females. **Nonreversible** Some *A* are not *B*. ≠ Some *B* are not *A*.

*In formal logic, the word *some* means "some and possibly all." In common parlance, and as used in cognitive psychology, *some* means "some and not all." Thus, in formal logic, the particular affirmative would also be reversible. For our purposes, it is not.

In all kinds of syllogisms, some combinations of premises lead to no logically valid conclusion. In *categorical* syllogisms, in particular, we cannot draw logically valid conclusions from categorical syllogisms with two particular premises or with two negative premises. For example, "Some cognitive psychologists are left-handed. Some left-handed people are smart." Based on these premises, you cannot conclude even that some cognitive psychologists are smart (although, of course, we know that they all are) because the left-handed people who are smart might not be the same left-handed people who are cognitive psychologists. We just don't know. To take a negative example, "No students are stupid. No stupid people eat pizza." We cannot conclude anything one way or the other about whether students eat pizza, based on these two negative premises. As you may have guessed, people appear to have more difficulty (work more slowly and make more errors) when trying to deduce conclusions based on one or more particular premises or negative premises.

Various theories have been proposed as to how people solve categorical syllogisms. One of the earliest theories was the *atmosphere bias,* initially proposed by Robert Woodworth and Saul Sells (1935) and later elaborated by Ian Begg and J. Denny (1969). According to this theory, people tend to prefer syllogistic conclusions that have certain features that are similar to those of the premises. That is, some characteristics of the premises (e.g., negative vs. affirmative premises; particular vs. universal premises) within a syllogism create an atmosphere that influences the conclusion (negative/affirmative, particular/universal) people tend to draw. For example, if at least one premise is negative (e.g., "No pilots are boys"), you might be more likely to prefer a negative conclusion (e.g., "No pilots are children"). Similarly, if at least one premise is particular (e.g., "Some pilots are women"), you might prefer a particular conclusion ("Some pilots are adults"). For such a simple theory, atmosphere bias does a surprisingly good job of predicting about 40% to 50% of people's responses. Nonetheless, it does not account very well for large numbers of responses.

The next major theory to come along was proposed by Loren Chapman and Jean Chapman (1959). These researchers focused attention on the *conversion* of premises, in which the terms of a given premise are reversed, and the reversed form of the premise is believed to be just as valid as the original form. In fact, conversion always works for universal negatives. That is, if no *A* are *B,* then no *B* are *A.* If no apples are oranges, then no oranges are apples. However, as shown in Table 12.5 and Figure 12.2, conversion does not always work for the other three types of premises. For example, saying that all cognitive

FIGURE 12.2 CONVERSION OF LOGICAL PREMISES

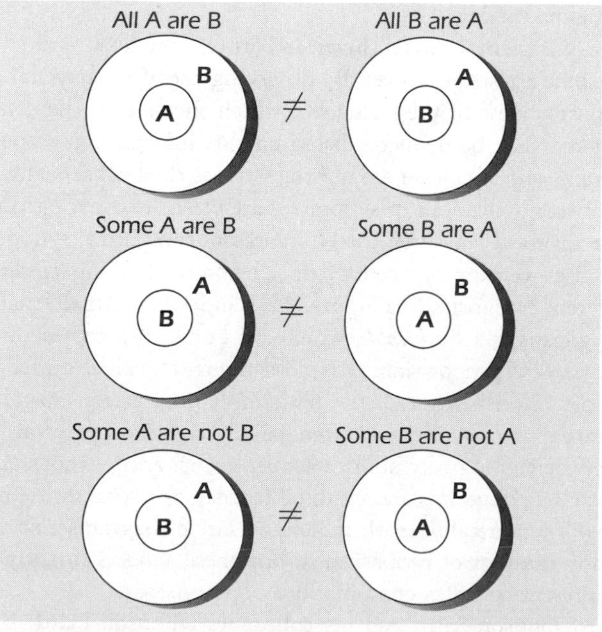

Some logical premises are nonreversible; when nonreversible premises are converted, logical errors result.

psychology students are smart is not quite equivalent to saying that all smart people are cognitive psychology students—much as I might like this statement. The main claim of the theory was that people make errors because of *illicit conversion*—converting (i.e., reversing) premises that are nonreversible. As it turns out, although people do convert premises, illicit conversion does not account for all or even most errors of deductive reasoning.

In the late 1970s, Philip Johnson-Laird and Mark Steedman (1978) proposed a highly comprehensive theory of syllogistic reasoning, which can account for a large proportion of people's responses. Their theory is based on the notion that people solve syllogisms by using a semantic (meaning-based) process based on mental models (Johnson-Laird, Byrne, & Schaeken, 1992). According to Johnson-Laird, his view of reasoning as involving semantic processes based on mental models may be contrasted with rule-based ("syntactic") processes, such as those characterized by formal logic. A **mental model** is an internal representation of information that corresponds analogously with whatever is being represented (see Johnson-Laird, 1983). Some mental models are more likely to lead to a deductively valid conclusion than are others; in particular, some mental models may not be effective in disconfirming an invalid conclusion.

For example, in the Johnson-Laird study, participants were asked to describe their conclusions and their mental models for the syllogism, "All of the artists are beekeepers. Some of the beekeepers are clever." One participant said, "I thought of all the little . . . artists in the room and imagined they all had beekeeper's hats on" (Johnson-Laird & Steedman, 1978, p. 77). Figure 12.3 shows two different mental models for this syllogism. As the figure shows, the choice of a mental model may affect the reasoner's ability to reach a valid deductive conclusion. Because some models are better than others for solving some syllogisms, a person is more likely to reach a deductively valid conclusion by using more than one mental model.

Philip Johnson-Laird *is a professor of psychology at Princeton University. He is best known for his work on mental models, deductive reasoning, and creativity. In particular, Johnson-Laird has shown how the concept of mental models can be applied toward understanding a wide variety of psychological processes.*

In the figure, the mental model shown in part (a) may lead to the deductively invalid conclusion that some artists are clever. By observing the alternative model in part (b), we can see an alternative view of the syllogism, which shows that the conclusion that some artists are clever may not be deduced, based on this information alone. Specifically, perhaps the beekeepers who are clever are not the same as the beekeepers who are artists.

Two types of representations of syllogisms are often used by logicians. As mentioned previously, circle diagrams are often used to represent categorical syllogisms. In circle diagrams, you can use overlapping, concentric, or nonoverlapping circles to represent the members of different categories (see Figures 12.1 and 12.2). An alternative representation often used by logicians is a *truth table,* which can be used to represent the truth value of various combinations of propositions, based on the truth value of each of the component propositions. Table 12.6 illustrates how a few simple propositions may be combined using the logical operators *and, or,* and *not* (often called "Boolean operators"). These operators may be indicated by the logic symbols $\wedge$ (and), $\vee$ (or), and $\neg$ (not). As Figure 12.4 and Table 12.6 show, circle diagrams and truth tables may be useful for representing very simple relationships. Theoretically, truth tables and circle diagrams also may be created for compounds of any number of propositions, but these models quickly become unwieldy when used to represent complex combinations of premises.

According to Johnson-Laird and his colleagues (Johnson-Laird, Byrne, & Schaeken, 1992), the difficulty of many problems of deductive reasoning relates to the number of mental models needed for adequately representing the premises of the deductive argument.

FIGURE 12.3 **MENTAL MODELS OF SYLLOGISMS**

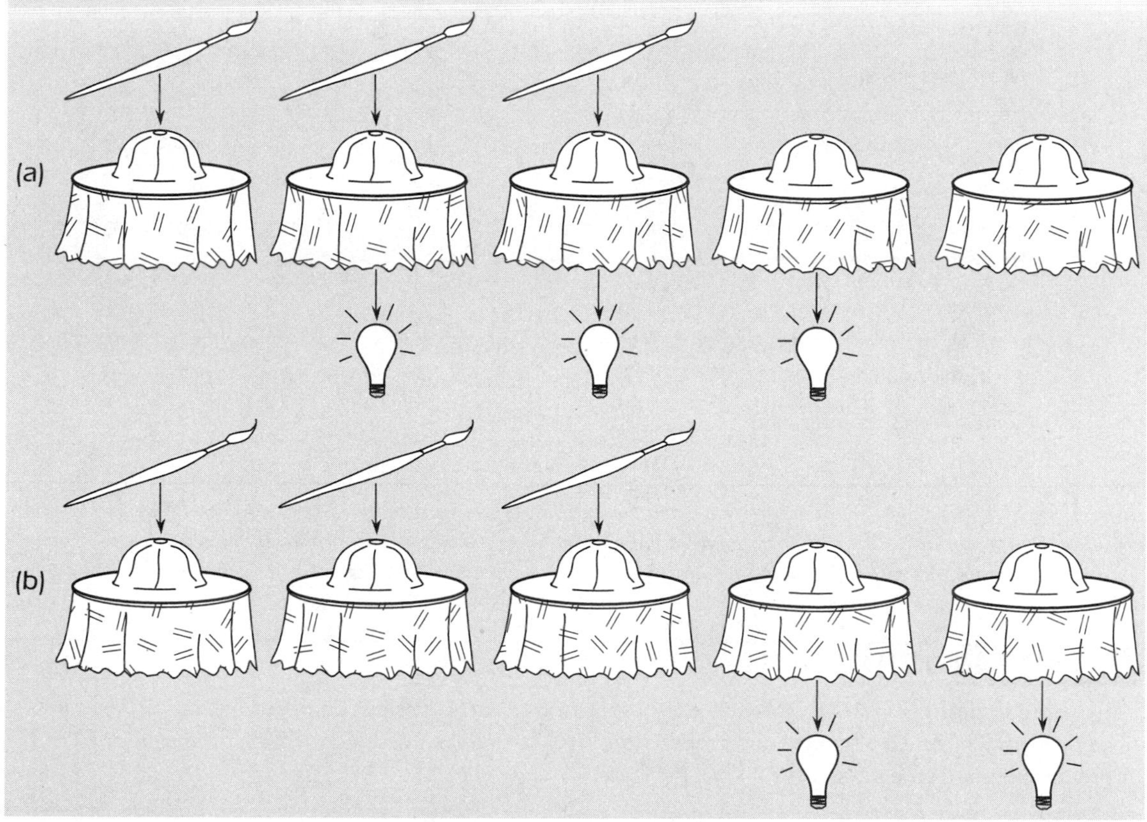

Philip Johnson-Laird and Mark Steedman hypothesized that people use various mental models analogously to represent the items within a syllogism. Some mental models are more effective than others, and to reach a valid deductive conclusion, more than one model may be necessary, as shown here. (See text for explanation.)

Arguments that entail only one mental model may be solved quickly and accurately. However, to infer accurate conclusions based on arguments that may be represented by multiple alternative models is much harder because of the great demands placed on working memory. In these cases, the individual must hold in working memory each of the various models in order to reach a conclusion or to evaluate a conclusion. Thus, Johnson-Laird's view suggests that the limitations of working-memory capacity may underlie at least some of the errors observed in human deductive reasoning (Johnson-Laird, Byrne, & Schaeken, 1992).

Other factors also may contribute to the ease of forming appropriate mental models. Catherine Clement and Rachel Falmagne (1986) found that participants seem to solve logical problems more accurately and more easily when the terms have high imagery value—which would probably facilitate their representation. Similarly, they found that

FIGURE 12.4 CIRCLE DIAGRAMS

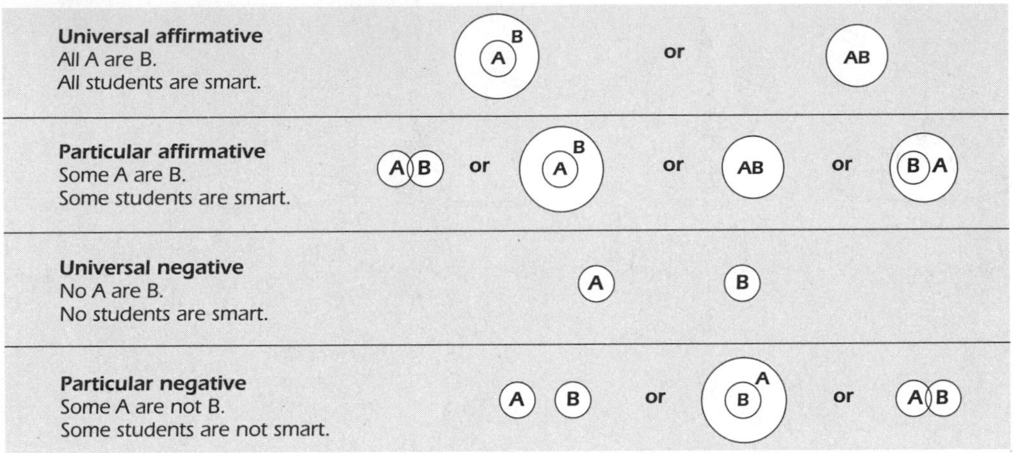

Universal affirmative
All A are B.
All students are smart.

Particular affirmative
Some A are B.
Some students are smart.

Universal negative
No A are B.
No students are smart.

Particular negative
Some A are not B.
Some students are not smart.

Although circle diagrams may help in representing simple propositions, they become much more complicated when representing relationships among propositions. In formal logic, the word some *means "some and possibly all." Hence, the possible circle-diagram representations for the particular affirmative are more numerous than for the other statements.*

TABLE 12.6 TRUTH TABLE

By using logical operators to combine the propositions p and q, various compound propositions can be formed. The truth of compound propositions may be deduced based on whether the elemental propositions are true or false. ($T = true$; $F = false$)

p	q	$p \wedge q$	$p \vee q$
T All penguins are birds.	*F* All penguins are mammals.	*F* All penguins are birds, and all penguins are mammals.	*T* All penguins are birds, or all penguins are mammals.
T Cognitive psychology students read books.	*T* The sky is blue.	*T* Cognitive psychology students read books, and the sky is blue.	*T* Cognitive psychology students read books, or the sky is blue.
F Aristotle is living now.	*F* Cognitive psychology professors eat worms.	*F* Aristotle is living now, and cognitive psychology professors eat worms.	*F* Aristotle is living now, or cognitive psychology professors eat worms.
F All humans reason perfectly well.	*T* All humans make mistakes.	*F* All humans reason perfectly well, and all humans make mistakes.	*T* All humans reason perfectly well, or all humans make mistakes.

when the propositions showed high relatedness in terms of mental images (e.g., one premise about dogs and the other about cats, rather than one about dogs and the other about tables), participants could more easily and accurately solve the problems and judge the accuracy of the conclusions. For example, it would be easier to solve a high-imagery, high-relatedness syllogism, such as "Some artists are painters. Some painters use black paint" than to solve a low-imagery, low-relatedness syllogism, such as "Some texts are prose. Some prose is well-written." According to Clement and Falmagne, high imagery value and high relatedness make it easier for reasoners to come up with counterexamples that reveal an argument to be deductively invalid.

Some deductive-reasoning problems comprise more than two premises. For example, *transitive-inference problems,* in which problem solvers must order multiple terms, can have any number of premises linking large numbers of terms. Mathematical and logical proofs are deductive in character and can have many steps as well.

FURTHER AIDS AND OBSTACLES TO DEDUCTIVE REASONING

In deductive reasoning, as in many other cognitive processes, we engage in many heuristic shortcuts, which sometimes lead to inaccurate conclusions. In addition to these shortcuts, we are often influenced by biases that distort the outcomes of our reasoning. Heuristics in syllogistic reasoning include *overextension errors,* in which we overextend the use of strategies

$\neg p$	$\neg q$	$\neg p \vee \neg q$	$\neg p \wedge \neg q$
F Penguins are not birds.	*T* Penguins are not mammals.	*T* Penguins are not birds, or penguins are not mammals.	*F* Penguins are not birds, and penguins are not mammals.
F Not all cognitive psychology students read books.	*F* The sky is not blue.	*F* Cognitive psychology students do not read books, or the sky is not blue.	*F* Cognitive psychology students do not read books, and the sky is not blue.
T Aristotle is not living now.	*T* Cognitive psychology professors do not eat worms.	*T* Aristotle is not living now, or cognitive psychology professors do not eat worms.	*T* Aristotle is not living now, and cognitive psychology professors do not eat worms.
T Humans do not reason perfectly well.	*F* Humans do not make mistakes.	*T* Humans do not reason perfectly well, or humans do not make mistakes.	*F* Humans do not reason perfectly well, and humans do not make mistakes.

that work in some syllogisms to syllogisms in which the strategies fail us. For example, although reversals work well with universal negatives, they do not work with other kinds of premises. We also experience *foreclosure effects* when we fail to consider all of the possibilities before reaching a conclusion. For example, we may fail to think of contrary examples when inferring conclusions from particular or negative premises. In addition, *premise-phrasing effects* (e.g., the sequence of terms, the use of particular qualifiers or negative phrasing) may influence our deductive reasoning, such that we will leap to a conclusion without adequately reflecting on the deductive validity of the syllogism.

Biases that affect deductive reasoning generally relate to the content of the premises and the believability of the conclusion, as well as the tendency toward confirmation bias. When the content of the premises and a conclusion seem to be true, reasoners tend to believe in the validity of the conclusion, even when the logic is flawed (Evans, Barston, & Pollard, 1983). To a lesser extent, people also show the opposite tendency to disconfirm the validity of the conclusion when the conclusion or the content of the premises contradicts the reasoner's existing beliefs (Evans et al., 1983; Janis & Frick, 1943). This is not to say that people fail to consider logical principles when reasoning deductively. In analyzing people's *verbal protocols* (self-reflective statements made by participants during cognition), researchers have found that explicit attention to the premises seems more likely to lead to valid inferences, whereas explicit attention to irrelevant information more often leads to inferences based on prior beliefs regarding the believability of the conclusion (Evans et al., 1983).

To enhance our deductive reasoning, we may try not only to avoid heuristics and biases that distort our reasoning, but also to engage in practices that facilitate reasoning, such as taking longer to reach or to evaluate conclusions. Effective reasoners also consider more alternative conclusions than do poor reasoners (Galotti, Baron, & Sabini, 1986). In addition, training and practice seem to increase performance on reasoning tasks, although the benefits of training tend be stronger when the training relates to pragmatic reasoning schemas (Cheng, Holyoak, Nisbett, & Oliver, 1986) or to such fields as law and medicine (Lehman, Lempert, & Nisbett, 1987) rather than to abstract rules of logic (see Holland, Holyoak, Nisbett, & Thagard, 1986; Holyoak & Nisbett, 1988).

PRACTICAL APPLICATIONS OF COGNITIVE PSYCHOLOGY

Even without training, you can improve your own deductive reasoning through developing strategies to avoid making errors. Make sure you are using the proper strategies in solving syllogisms—remember that reversals only work with universal negatives. Sometimes, translating abstract terms to concrete ones (e.g., the letter *C* to *cows)* can help. Also, take the time to consider contrary examples and create more mental models. The more mental models you use for a given set of premises, the more confident you can be that if your conclusion is not valid, it will be disconfirmed. Thus, the use of multiple mental models increases the likelihood of avoiding errors. The use of multiple mental models also helps you to avoid the tendency to engage in confirmation bias. Circle diagrams can also be helpful in solving deductive-reasoning problems.

Inductive Reasoning

Despite a gap between the theory and the practice of deductive reasoning, with deductive reasoning, reaching logically certain—deductively valid—conclusions is at least theoretically possible. In inductive reasoning, which is based on our observations, reaching any logically certain conclusion is not possible. The most that we can strive to reach is only a strong, or highly probable, conclusion.

For example, suppose that you notice that all of the persons enrolled in your cognitive psychology course are on the dean's list (or honor roll). From these observations, you could inductively reason that all students who enroll in cognitive psychology are excellent students (or at least earn the grades to give that impression). However, unless you can observe the grade-point averages of all persons who ever have taken or ever will take cognitive psychology, you will be unable to prove your conclusion. Further, a single poor student who happened to enroll in a cognitive psychology course would disprove your conclusion. Still, after myriad observations, you might conclude that you had made enough observations to reason inductively.

In this situation and in many others requiring reasoning, you were not given clearly stated premises or obvious, certain relationships between the elements, which would lead you to deduce a surefire conclusion. In such situations, you cannot deduce a logically valid conclusion at all. At these times, an alternative kind of reasoning is needed: Inductive reasoning comes to the rescue. Inductive reasoning involves reasoning where there is no logically certain conclusion. Often, it involves reasoning from specific facts or observations to a general conclusion that may explain the facts.

A key feature of inductive reasoning, which forms the basis of the empirical method, is that we cannot logically leap from saying, "All observed instances to date of *X* are *Y*" to saying, "Therefore, all *X* are *Y*." It is always possible that the next observed *X* will not be a *Y*. Furthermore, regardless of the number of observations or the soundness of the reasoning, no inductively based conclusions can be proved; such conclusions can only be supported, to a greater or lesser degree, by available evidence. Thus, we return to the need to consider probability. The inductive reasoner must state any conclusions about a hypothesis in terms of likelihoods, such as "There is a 99% chance of rain tomorrow," or "The probability is only .05 that the null hypothesis is correct in asserting that these findings are a result of random variation."

Cognitive psychologists probably agree on at least one of the reasons why people use inductive reasoning: to become increasingly able to make sense out of the great variability in their environment and to predict events in their environment, thereby reducing their uncertainty. Thus, cognitive psychologists seek to understand the how rather than the why of inductive reasoning. Although we may (or may not) have some innate schema-acquisition device, we certainly are not born with all the inferences we manage to induce. We have already implied that inductive reasoning often involves the processes of generating and testing hypotheses. We may further figure out that we reach inferences by generalizing some broad understandings from a set of specific instances. As we observe additional instances, we may further broaden our understanding, or we may infer specialized exceptions to the general understandings. For example, after observing quite a few birds, we may infer that birds can fly, but after observing penguins and ostriches, we may add to our generalized knowledge specialized exceptions for flightless birds.

During generalization, we observe that particular properties vary together across diverse instances of a concept or that particular procedures covary across different events, then we induce some general principles for those covariations. The great puzzle of inductive reasoning is how we mere mortals manage to infer useful general principles based on the myriad observations of covariation to which we are constantly exposed. Humans do not approach induction with mind-staggering computational abilities to calculate every possible covariation and to derive inferences from just the most frequent or the most plausible of these covariations. Rather, we seem to approach this task as we approach so many other cognitive tasks: We look for shortcuts. Inductive reasoners, like other probabilistic reasoners, use heuristics such as representativeness, availability, the law of large numbers, and the unusualness heuristic. When using the *unusualness heuristic,* we pay particular attention to unusual events, and when two unusual events co-occur or occur in close proximity to one another, we tend to assume that the two events are connected in some way (such as inferring that the former unusual event caused the latter one; Holyoak & Nisbett, 1988).

REACHING CAUSAL INFERENCES

One approach to studying inductive reasoning is to examine **causal inferences**—how people make judgments about whether something causes something else. One of the first investigators to propose a theory of how people make causal judgments was John Stuart Mill (1887), who proposed a set of *canons*—widely accepted heuristic principles on which people may base their judgments. For example, one of Mill's canons—the "method of agreement"—involved making separate lists of the possible causes that are present and those that are absent when a given outcome occurs. If, of all the possible causes, only one is present in all instances of the given outcome, the observer can inductively conclude that the one cause present in all instances is the true cause. (That is, despite all the differences among possible causes, there is agreement in terms of one cause and one effect.)

For example, if a number of persons in a given community contracted hepatitis, the local health authorities would try to track down all the various possible means by which each of the hepatitis sufferers had contracted the disease. If it turned out that they all lived in different neighborhoods, shopped at different grocery stores, had different physicians and dentists, and otherwise led very different lives, *but* that they all ate in the same restaurant on a given night, the health authorities would probably inductively conclude that they contracted hepatitis while eating at that restaurant.

Another of Mill's canons is the "method of difference," in which you observe that all the circumstances in which a given phenomenon occurs are just like those in which it does not occur *except* for one way in which they differ. For example, suppose that a particular group of students all live in the same dormitory, eat the same food in the same dining halls, sleep on the same schedule, and take all the same classes—*except* that some of the students attend one discussion group, and other students attend another. The students in discussion group A get straight A's, and the students in discussion group B get straight C's. We could inductively conclude that something is happening in the discussion groups to lead to this difference. Does this method sound familiar? If the observer manipulated the various aspects of this method, the method might be called an empirical experiment: You would hold constant all the variables but one, which you would manipulate, to observe whether this variable is distinctively associated with the predicted outcome. In fact, Jerome Bruner (J. S. Bruner, Goodnow, & Austin, 1956) long ago asserted that inductive reasoning may be viewed as hypothesis testing.

Miriam Schustack and I (Schustack & Sternberg, 1981) investigated causal inference by giving people scenarios such as the one shown in Table 12.7. The participants' task was to use the information describing the consequences for each company to figure out whether a company's stock values would drop if the company's major product were under suspicion as a carcinogen. We found that people used four pieces of information to make causal judgments, as shown in Table 12.8. Specifically, they tended to confirm that an event was causal based either on the joint presence of the possibly causal event and the outcome or on the joint absence of the possibly causal event and the outcome. They tended to disconfirm the causality of a particular antecedent event based either on the presence of the possibly causal event but the absence of the outcome or on the absence of the possibly causal event but the presence of the outcome. In these ways, people can be quite rational in making causal judgments, making reasonable use of evidence.

On the other hand, we do fall prey to various common errors of inductive reasoning. One common error of induction relates to the law of large numbers. Under some circumstances, we recognize that a greater number of observations strengthens the likelihood of our conclusions. At other times, however, we fail to consider the size of the sample we have observed when assessing the strength or the likelihood of a particular inference. In addition, most of us tend to ignore base-rate information, focusing instead on unusual variations or salient anecdotal ones. Awareness of these errors can help us improve our decision making.

Perhaps our greatest failing is one that extends to psychologists and other scientists, as well as to nonscientists: We demonstrate *confirmation bias,* which may lead us to errors such as the illusory correlations noted by Chapman and Chapman (1967, 1969, 1975). Furthermore, we frequently make mistakes when attempting to determine causality based on correlational evidence alone. As has been stated many times, correlational evidence cannot indicate the direction of causation. In observing a correlation between Factor A and Factor B, we may find that Factor A may cause Factor B, Factor B may cause Factor A, or some higher order Factor C may be causing both Factors A and B to occur together. A related error occurs when we fail to recognize that many phenomena have multiple causes.

TABLE 12.7 **MARKET ANALYST OBSERVATIONS REGARDING COSMETICS MANUFACTURERS**

Based on the information given here, how would you determine causality?

Company 1	The office staff of the company organized and joined a union. The company's major product was under suspicion as a carcinogen.	There was a drastic drop in the value of the company's stock.
Company 2	The office staff of the company did not organize and join a union. The company's major product was under suspicion as a carcinogen.	There was a drastic drop in the value of the company's stock.
Company 3	Illegal campaign contributions were traced to the company's managers. The company's major product was not under suspicion as a carcinogen.	There was no drastic drop in the value of the company's stock.

TABLE 12.8 FOUR BASES FOR INFERRING CAUSALITY

Even nonlogicians often use available information effectively when assessing causality.

Causal Inference	Basis for Inference	Explanation	Example
Confirmation	The joint presence of the possibly causal event and the outcome	If an event and an outcome tend to co-occur, people are more likely to believe that the event causes the outcome.	If some other company had a major product suspected to be a carcinogen, and its stock went down, that pairing of facts would increase people's belief that having a major product labeled as a carcinogen depresses stock values.
Confirmation	The joint absence of the possibly causal event and the outcome	If the outcome does not occur in the absence of the possibly causal event, then people are more likely to believe that the event causes the outcome.	If other companies' stocks have not gone down when they had no products labeled as carcinogens, then the absence of both the carcinogens among the major products and the stock drops is at least consistent with the notion that having a product labeled as a carcinogen might cause stocks to drop.
Disconfirmation	The presence of the possibly causal event but the absence of the outcome	If the possibly causal event is present but not the outcome, then the event is seen as less likely to lead to the outcome.	If other companies have had major products labeled as carcinogens, but their stocks have not gone down, people would be more likely to conclude that having a major product labeled as a carcinogen does not lead to drops in stock prices.
Disconfirmation	The absence of the possibly causal event but the presence of the outcome	If the outcome occurs in the absence of the possibly causal event, then the event is seen as less likely to lead to the outcome. (This rule is one of Mill's canons.)	If other companies have had stock prices drop without having products labeled as carcinogens, people would be less likely to infer that having a product labeled as a carcinogen leads to decreases in stock prices.

For example, a car accident often involves several causes, such as negligence of several drivers, rather than just one cause. Therefore, once we have identified one of the suspected causes of a phenomenon, we may stop searching for additional alternative or contributing causes, committing what is known as a *discounting* error.

Confirmation bias can have a major effect on our everyday lives. For example, we may meet someone, expecting not to like him. As a result, we may treat him in ways that are different from how we would treat him if we expected to like him. He may then respond to us in less favorable ways, "confirming" our original belief that he is not likable. Confirmation bias can thereby play a major role in schooling. Teachers often expect little of students when they think them low in ability. The students then give the teachers little. The teachers' original beliefs are thereby "confirmed" (R. J. Sternberg, 1997).

Recent work by Woo-kyoung Ahn and colleagues (Ahn & Bailenson, 1996; Ahn, Kalish, Medin, & Gelman, 1995) investigates the relationship between covariation (correlation) information and causal inferences. In order for some information to contribute to causal inferences, the information must necessarily be correlated with the event, but this covariation information is not sufficient to imply causality. Ahn and colleagues propose that the covariation information must also provide information about a possible causal mechanism in order for the information to contribute to causal inferences. To use their example, in attempting to determine the cause of Jane's car accident last night, one could use purely covariation information such as, "Jane is more likely than most to have a car accident," and "car accidents were more likely to have occurred last night." However, Ahn et al. (1995) showed that people prefer information specifically about causal mechanisms such as, "Jane was not wearing her glasses last night" and "the road was icy" in making causal attributions over information that only covaries with the car accident event. Both of these latter pieces of information about Jane's car accident can be considered covariation information, but the descriptions provide additional causal mechanism information. A recent paper by Cheng (1997) furthers the notion of causal mechanisms in attempting to explain how people select certain covariates as candidates for being causal agents, given that we can never directly observe causality. The details of the model are beyond the scope of this text, but in general, Cheng proposes that people act as naive scientists in positing unobservable theoretical causal power entities to explain observable covariations. Thus, people are somewhat rational in making causal attributions based on the right kinds of covariation information.

Categorical Inferences

On what basis do people draw inferences? According to Keith Holyoak and Richard Nisbett (1988), people use both bottom-up strategies (based on information from their sensory experiences) and top-down strategies (based on what they already know or have inferred previously) for doing so. Bottom-up strategies are based on observing various instances and considering the degree of variability across instances. From these observations, we abstract a prototype (see chapters 6 and 9), a category comprising rules or rule clusters, or a category-like network of covarying associated characteristics. Once a prototype or a category has been induced, the individual may use focused sampling to add new instances to the category, focusing chiefly on properties that have provided useful distinctions in the past. Top-down strategies include selectively searching for constancies within myriad variations and selectively combining existing concepts and categories.

Daniel Osherson and his colleagues (Osherson, Smith, Wilkie, Lopez, & Shafir, 1990) have proposed a hypothesis regarding the likelihood that people will induce a conclusion from a given premise (statement regarding an observation) or set of premises. According to their similarity-coverage hypothesis, two factors will increase the likelihood that people will induce a concluding statement about a category: (a) high degree of similarity between the categories of the premises (e.g., "sparrows eat fleagles" and "geese eat fleagles") and the category of the conclusion (e.g., "falcons eat fleagles"); and (b) high degree of similarity between the category of the premises and the members of the lowest-level inclusive category (i.e., the category that is the lowest one in a hierarchy, which includes both the premises and the conclusion). As an example of the second factor, for the same two premises ("sparrows eat fleagles" and "geese eat fleagles"), inductive reasoners are more likely to induce a conclusion that "birds eat fleagles" than a conclusion that "animals eat fleagles" because the members of the lowest-level inclusive category for birds (i.e., various kinds of birds) are more similar to the category of the premises (i.e., birds) than are the members of the lowest-level inclusive category for animals (i.e., various kinds of mammals, reptiles, and amphibians as well as birds).

Reasoning by Analogy

Inductive reasoning may be applied to a broader range of situations than those requiring causal or categorical inferences. For example, inductive reasoning may be applied to reasoning by analogy, such as in the analogy, "Fire is to asbestos as water is to (a) vinyl, (b) air, (c) cotton, (d) faucet." In reasoning by analogy, the reasoner must observe the first pair of items ("fire" and "asbestos" in this example) and must induce from those two items one or more relations (in this case, surface resistance because surfaces coated with asbestos can resist fire). The reasoner must then apply the given relation in the second part of the analogy. In the example analogy, the reasoner chooses the solution to be "vinyl" because surfaces coated with vinyl can resist water.

Some investigators have used reaction-time methodology to figure out how people solve induction problems. For example, using mathematical modeling, I was able to break down the amounts of time participants spent on various processes of analogical reasoning. I found that most of the time spent in solving simple verbal analogies is spent in encoding the terms and in responding (R. J. Sternberg, 1977). Only a small part is actually spent in doing reasoning operations on these encodings.

The difficulty of encoding can become even greater in various puzzling analogies. For example, in the analogy RAT : TAR :: BAT : (a. CONCRETE, b. MAMMAL, c. TAB, d. TAIL), the difficulty is in encoding the analogy as one involving letter reversal rather than semantic content for its solution. In a problematic analogy such as AUDACIOUS : TIMOROUS :: MITIGATE : (a. ADUMBRATE, b. EXACERBATE, c. EXPOSTULATE, d. EVISCERATE), the difficulty is in recognizing the meanings of the words. If reasoners know the meanings of the words, they will probably find it relatively easy to figure out that the relation is one of antonyms. (Did this example audaciously exacerbate your difficulties in solving problems involving analogies?)

An Alternative View of Reasoning

By now, you have reasonably inferred that cognitive psychologists often disagree—sometimes rather heatedly—about how and why people reason as they do. Recently, an alternative perspective on reasoning has been proposed, which is sure to spark stimulating discussion and to fuel further investigation as cognitive psychologists with differing views evaluate it. Steven Sloman (1996) has looked at the empirical data regarding how people reason and has inferred that two complementary systems of reasoning can be distinguished:

(a) an associative system, which involves mental operations based on observed similarities and *temporal contiguities* (i.e., tendencies for things to occur close together in time); and (b) a rule-based system, which involves manipulations based on the relations among symbols.

The associative system can lead to speedy responses that are highly sensitive to patterns and to general tendencies. Through this system, we detect similarities between observed patterns and patterns stored in memory. We may pay more attention to salient features (e.g., highly typical or highly atypical ones) than to defining features of a pattern. This system imposes rather loose constraints that may inhibit the selection of patterns that are poor matches to the observed pattern, in favor of remembered patterns that are better matches to the observed pattern. Evidence of associative reasoning includes use of the representativeness heuristic, belief-bias effects in syllogistic reasoning (agreeing more with syllogisms that affirm their beliefs, whether or not these syllogisms are logically valid), plausibility effects in conditional reasoning, and enhancement of conditional reasoning in pragmatic contexts.

The rule-based system usually requires more deliberate, sometimes painstaking procedures for reaching conclusions. Through this system, we carefully analyze relevant features (e.g., defining features) of the available data, based on rules stored in memory. This system imposes rigid constraints that rule out possibilities that violate the rules. Evidence of rule-based reasoning include the following: (a) We can recognize logical arguments when they are explained to us; (b) we can recognize the need to make categorizations based on defining features despite similarities in typical features (e.g., recognizing that a coin with a 3-inch diameter, which looks exactly like a quarter, must be a counterfeit); (c) we can rule out impossibilities (e.g., cats conceiving and giving birth to puppies); and (d) we can recognize many improbabilities (e.g., the likelihood that the U.S. Congress will pass a law that provides annual salaries to all full-time college students). According to Sloman, we need both complementary systems. We need to respond quickly and easily to everyday situations, based on observed similarities and temporal contiguities, yet we also need a means for evaluating our responses more deliberately.

Sloman has suggested that his two systems may be conceptualized within a connectionist framework. The associative system is easily represented in terms of pattern activation and inhibition, which readily fits the connectionist model. The rule-based system may be represented as a system of production rules (see chapter 11).

An alternative connectionist view suggests that deductive reasoning may occur when a given pattern of activation in one set of nodes (e.g., those associated with a particular premise or set of premises) entails or produces a particular pattern of activation in a second set of nodes (Rips, 1994). Similarly, a connectionist model of inductive reasoning may involve the repeated activation of a series of similar patterns across various instances. This repeated activation may then strengthen the links among the activated nodes, leading to generalization or abstraction of the pattern for a variety of instances.

Connectionist models of reasoning and the various other approaches described in this chapter offer diverse views of the available data regarding how we reason and make judgments. At present, no one theoretical model explains all the data well, although each model explains at least some of the data satisfactorily. Nonetheless, a commonality unifying all the foregoing empirical data and theories is their focus on how adults think, reason, make decisions, and reach conclusions—and their neglect of how children do so. Thus far, we have said little about whether or how children may think differently than adults do. The following chapter addresses the issue of how cognition develops across the life span.

SUMMARY

1. **What are some of the strategies that guide human decision making?** Early theories were designed to achieve practical mathematical models of decision making and assumed that decision makers are fully informed, infinitely sensitive to information, and completely rational. Subsequent theories began to acknowledge that humans often use subjective criteria for decision making, that chance elements often influence the outcomes of decisions, that humans often use subjective estimates for considering the outcomes, and that humans are not boundlessly rational in making decisions. People apparently often use *satisficing* strategies, settling for the first minimally acceptable option, and strategies involving a process of *elimination by aspects,* to weed out an overabundance of options.

   One of the most common heuristics most of us use is the *representativeness heuristic.* We fall prey to the fallacious belief that small samples of a population resemble the whole population in all respects. Our misunderstanding of base rates and other aspects of probability often leads us to other mental shortcuts as well, such as in the *conjunction fallacy* and the *inclusion fallacy.* Another common heuristic is the *availability heuristic,* in which we make judgments based on information that is readily available in memory, without bothering to seek less available information. The use of heuristics such as *anchoring and adjustment, illusory correlation,* and *framing effects* also often impair our ability to make effective decisions. Once we have made a decision (or better yet, another person has made a decision), and the outcome of the decision is known, we may engage in *hindsight bias,* skewing our perception of the earlier evidence in light of the eventual outcome. Perhaps the most serious of our mental biases, however, is *overconfidence,* which seems to be amazingly resistant to evidence of our own errors.

2. **What are some of the forms of deductive reasoning that people may use and what factors facilitate or impede deductive reasoning?** *Deductive reasoning* involves reaching conclusions from a set of *conditional propositions* or from a syllogistic pair of *premises.* Among the various types of syllogisms are *linear syllogisms* and *categorical syllogisms.* In addition, deductive reasoning may involve complex transitive-inference problems or mathematical or logical proofs, involving large numbers of terms. Also, deductive reasoning may involve the use of *pragmatic reasoning schemas* in practical, everyday situations.

   In drawing conclusions from conditional propositions, people readily apply the *modus ponens* argument, particularly regarding universal affirmative propositions. Most of us have more difficulty, however, in using the *modus tollens* argument and in avoiding deductive fallacies such as affirming the consequent or denying the antecedent, particularly when faced with propositions involving particular propositions or negative propositions. In solving syllogisms, we have similar difficulties with particular premises and negative premises, as well as with terms that are not presented in the customary sequence. Frequently, when trying to draw conclusions, we overextend a strategy from a situation in which it leads to a deductively valid conclusion to one in which it leads to a deductive fallacy. We also may foreclose on a given conclusion before considering the full range of possibilities that may affect the conclusion. These mental shortcuts may be exacerbated by situations in which we engage in confirmation bias (tending to confirm our own beliefs).

We can enhance our ability to draw well-reasoned conclusions in many ways, such as by taking time to evaluate the premises or propositions carefully and by forming multiple *mental models* of the propositions and their relationships. We may also benefit from training and practice in effective deductive reasoning. We are particularly likely to reach well-reasoned conclusions when such conclusions seem plausible and useful in pragmatic contexts, such as during social exchanges.

3. **How do people use inductive reasoning to reach causal inferences and to reach other types of conclusions?** Although we cannot reach logically certain conclusions through *inductive reasoning,* we can at least reach highly probable conclusions through careful reasoning. More than a century ago, John Stuart Mill recommended that people use various canonical strategies for reaching inductive conclusions. When making categorical inferences, people tend to use both top-down and bottom-up strategies. Processes of inductive reasoning generally form the basis of scientific study and hypothesis testing as a means to derive causal inferences. In addition, in reasoning by analogy, people often spend more time encoding the terms of the problem than in performing the inductive reasoning. It appears that people may sometimes use reasoning based on formal rule systems, such as by applying rules of formal logic, and sometimes use reasoning based on associations, such as by noticing similarities and temporal contiguities.

4. **Are there any alternative views of reasoning?** Steven Sloman has suggested that people have two distinct systems of reasoning, an associative system that is sensitive to observed similiarities and temporal contiguities, and a rule-based system that involves manipulations based on relations among symbols.

Thinking About Thinking: Factual, Analytical, Creative, and Practical Questions

1. Describe some of the heuristics and biases people use while making judgments or reaching decisions.
2. What are the two logical arguments and the two logical fallacies associated with conditional reasoning, as in the Wason selection task?
3. Which of the various approaches to conditional reasoning seems best to explain the available data? Give reasons for your answer.
4. Some cognitive psychologists question the merits of studying logical formalisms such as linear or categorical syllogisms. What do you think can be gained by studying how people reason in regard to syllogisms?
5. Based on the information in this chapter, design a way to help college students more effectively apply deductive reasoning to the problems they face.

6. Design a question, such as the ones used by Kahneman and Tversky, which requires people to estimate subjective probabilities of two different events. Indicate the fallacies that you may expect to influence people's estimates, or tell why you think people would give realistic estimates of probability.
7. Suppose that you need to rent an apartment. How would you go about finding one that most effectively meets your requirements, as well as your preferences? How closely does your method resemble the methods described by subjective expected utility theory, by satisficing, or by elimination by aspects?
8. Give two examples showing how you use rule-based reasoning and associative reasoning in your everyday experiences.

KEY TERMS

availability heuristic 400
bounded rationality 395
categorical syllogism 412
causal inference 422
conditional reasoning 405
deductive reasoning 404
deductive validity 405
elimination by aspects 395
fallacy 406
hindsight bias 403
illusory correlation 403
inductive reasoning 404
judgment and decision making 392
linear syllogism 411
mental model 416
overconfidence 403
pragmatic reasoning schema 409
premise 405
proposition 405
reasoning 404
representativeness 398
satisficing 395
subjective probability 394
subjective utility 394
syllogism 410

ANNOTATED SUGGESTED READINGS

Dawes, R. (1994). *House of cards.* An incisive and controversial examination of how errors of reasoning can permeate judgments, even of psychologists.

Johnson-Laird, P. N. (1983). *Mental models.* Cambridge, MA: Harvard University Press. The seminal and classic work on the mental-models approach to understanding human cognition; although more recent work has been done on the approach, no other single source explains mental models as thoroughly or as well.

Plous, S. (1993). *The psychology of judgment and decision making.* Philadelphia: Temple University Press. An excellent review of the literature on decision making covering all of the major heuristics and biases.

Sternberg, R. J. (Ed.). (1994). *Thinking and problem solving.* San Diego: Academic Press. An incisive and broad-ranging review of the literature on higher mental processes, including both inductive and deductive reasoning

Cognitive Development

Chapter Outline

Exploring Cognitive Psychology

Major Approaches to Cognitive Development
- General Principles of Cognitive Development
- Maturation of Thought Processes
- Sociocultural Influences on Thought Processes

Development of Information-Processing Skills
- Metacognitive Skills and Memory Development
- Quantitative Skills
- Visuospatial Skills
- Inductive Reasoning

Neurophysiological Changes in Development
- Increasing Neuronal Complexity
- Maturation of Central Nervous System Structures

Cognitive Development in Adulthood
- Patterns of Growth and Decline
- Wisdom and Aging

Summary

Thinking About Thinking: Factual, Analytical, Creative, and Practical Questions

Key Terms

Annotated Suggested Readings

EXPLORING COGNITIVE PSYCHOLOGY

1. **What are some of the major theoretical perspectives regarding how cognitive development occurs?**
2. **What do researchers find by investigating the development of information-processing skills?**
3. **What kinds of changes occur with the development of the brain?**
4. **What are some of the developmental changes in cognition that occur during adulthood?**

Never hug and kiss them, never let them sit on your lap. If you must, kiss them once on the forehead when they say good night. Shake hands with them in the morning. Give them a pat on the head if they have made an extraordinarily good job of a difficult task. Try it out. In a week's time you will find how easy it is to be perfectly objective with your child and at the same time kindly. You will be utterly ashamed at the mawkish, sentimental way you have been handling it.

—*John Watson,* Psychological Care of Infant and Child

Clearly, the way that psychologists view children has changed dramatically since the heyday of behaviorism, when John Watson made this pronouncement. We recognize both that children are like adults in their need for warmth and affection and that children differ from adults in many ways, particularly in the way they think. Psychologists who seek to understand how thinking changes across the life span study **cognitive development,** the investigation of how mental skills build and change with increasing physiological maturity (maturation) and experience (learning). Cognitive-developmental psychologists study the differences and similarities among people of different ages, seeking to discover how and why people think and behave differently at different times in their lives.

Cognitive development involves *qualitative* changes in thinking, as well as *quantitative* changes, such as increasing knowledge and ability. Most cognitive psychologists agree that developmental changes occur as a result of the interaction of maturation (nature) and learning (nurture). However, some cognitive psychologists give much greater emphasis to *maturation,* which refers to any relatively permanent change in thought or behavior that occurs simply as a result of aging, without regard to particular experiences. Others, however, underscore the importance of *learning,* which refers to any relatively permanent change in thinking, as a result of experience. Bear in mind this interaction of nature and nurture as you read about the various theoretical perspectives on cognitive development.

The interactive influence of nature and nurture starts in infancy. Very young infants appear to be innately predisposed to attend to stimuli that are moderately novel—that is, neither so familiar that the stimuli are uninteresting nor so novel that the infants cannot make sense of the stimuli (McCall, Kennedy, & Appelbaum, 1977). An environment that offers infants moderately novel stimuli will help infants to make the most of their innate preferences. Some have suggested that infants' preference for moderate novelty explains how infants learn about things when they are ready to do so. Infants do not waste their time attending to completely familiar things or to things so new that they are overwhelming. Some researchers (e.g., Bornstein & Sigman, 1986; Lewis & Brooks-Gunn, 1981) have suggested that infants who more strongly prefer some degree of novelty are more intelligent than are infants who less strongly prefer novelty. Some findings (e.g., Bornstein, 1989; Fagan, 1984, 1985; Fagan & Montie, 1988) indicate that young infants with strong preferences for novelty may be more likely to have high scores on intelligence tests at ages 2 to 7 years, but other researchers (e.g., L. G. Humphreys & Davey, 1988; Kagan, 1989; McCall, 1989) would advise us not leap to conclusions at this point.

In this chapter, I first discuss some theoretical approaches to cognitive development; then I consider cognitive development in specific domains, such as memory and perceptual skills, as well as neurophysiological maturation. Finally, I look briefly at adult cognition—in particular, at important cognitive changes that occur after adolescence.

Major Approaches to Cognitive Development

Theories of cognitive development are of various kinds. Although this chapter cannot encompass all of these theories, we will discuss some of the most influential theories in the field. As you read about the processes involved in cognitive development, think about which ones seem most sensible to you. Consider that you may find strengths and weaknesses in each of the theories, and that no single theory has yet explained all aspects of cognitive development. The approaches included here represent psychological theorists' best attempts to explain how human cognition develops. This chapter will discuss the cognitive-developmental work of Jean Piaget and the neo-Piagetians, of Lev Vygotsky, and of the information-processing theorists. After investigating these cognitive-developmental phenomena of childhood, I consider an additional view of cognitive development, based on neurophysiological research. (For a brief summary of how each of the theories describes the characteristic progression of cognitive development, see Table 13.1.)

General Principles of Cognitive Development

Regardless of the particular theoretical approach—whether Piagetian, Vygotskyan, or information processing—what basic principles crosscut the study of cognitive development and tie it together? A review of the data suggests some possible answers (R. J. Sternberg & Powell, 1983). First, over the course of development, people seem to gain more sophisticated control over their own thinking and learning. As people grow older, they become capable of more complex interactions between thought and behavior. Second, people

TABLE 13.1

CHARACTERISTIC PROGRESSION OF COGNITIVE DEVELOPMENT

The various theories of cognitive development offer complementary information regarding how cognitive development progresses from birth through adolescence.

<table>
<tr><th>Theorists</th><th>Birth to 1 Year</th><th>1 to 2 Years</th><th>2 to 4 Years</th><th>4 to 6 Years</th><th>6 to 8 Years</th><th>8 to 10 Years</th><th>10 to 12 Years</th><th>12 to 16 Years</th></tr>
<tr><td>Piaget</td><td colspan="2">Sensorimotor: characterized by building on reflexive actions and acting to maintain or repeat interesting sensations (major accomplishment: object permanence)</td><td colspan="2">Preoperational: characterized by intentional experimentation on physical objects, involving increasingly thoughtful planning and internal representations of physical objects; has trouble decentering to consider more than one characteristic at a time (major accomplishment: language and conceptual development)</td><td colspan="3">Concrete operations: characterized by increasingly sophisticated mental manipulations of the internal representations of concrete objects; can decenter to consider more than one characteristic at a time (major achievement: conservation of quantity)</td><td>Formal operations: abstract thought and logical reasoning</td></tr>
<tr><td>Fifth-stage theorists</td><td colspan="2">Sensorimotor (see Piaget)</td><td colspan="2">Preoperational (see Piaget)</td><td colspan="3">Concrete operations (see Piaget)</td><td>Formal operations (see Piaget)*</td></tr>
<tr><td>Case</td><td colspan="2">Sensorimotor (see Piaget)</td><td colspan="2">Relational structures: characterized by increasing understanding of relations between objects and concepts</td><td colspan="3">Dimensional structures: characterized by increasing understanding of objects and concepts in terms of their dimensions</td><td>Abstract structures: abstract concepts can be understood separately from concrete objects</td></tr>
<tr><td>Fischer</td><td colspan="2">Sensorimotor (see Piaget)</td><td colspan="5">Representational</td><td>Abstract</td></tr>
<tr><td>Vygotsky</td><td colspan="8">Increasing internalization and increasing abilities within the zone of proximal development</td></tr>
<tr><td>Information-processing theorists</td><td colspan="8">Increasingly sophisticated encoding, combination, knowledge acquisition, self-monitoring, feedback, and self-modifying production systems;
Increasing ability to distinguish appearances from reality, increasing verbal fluency and comprehension, increasing grasp of quantity;
Increasing knowledge of, control over, and capacity in memory; increasing ability mentally to manipulate objects in space;
Increasing control over strategies for solving problems; increasing ability to reason deductively, inductively, and analogically.</td></tr>
</table>

*Fifth-stage theorists propose a stage of cognitive development that follows the stage of formal operations. This stage, in some theories, is a stage of post-formal thinking, characterized by the ability to handle ambiguities and contradictions in solving problems.

engage in more thorough information processing with age. Older children encode more information from problems than do younger children, and they are therefore more likely to solve problems accurately. Even during adulthood, people continue to accumulate knowledge across the life span. Third, people become increasingly able to comprehend successively more complex relationships over the course of development. Finally, over time, people develop increasing flexibility in their uses of strategies or other information. As people grow older, they become less bound to using information in just a single context, and they learn how to apply it in a greater variety of contexts. People may even gain greater wisdom—insight into themselves and the world around them. As you read about the various phenomena of cognitive development, think about how cognitive complexity changes in these ways within each domain studied.

MATURATION OF THOUGHT PROCESSES

To overestimate the importance of Swiss psychologist Jean Piaget (1896–1980) to developmental research would be hard. His is generally considered the most comprehensive theory of cognitive development. Although aspects of Piaget's theory have been questioned and in some cases have been disconfirmed, the theory is still enormously influential. Indeed, the contribution of his theory, like that of others, is shown more by its influence on further theory and research than by its ultimate correctness.

In particular, Piaget revolutionized the study of children's concept formation and intelligence by proposing that researchers could learn as much about children's intellectual

Jean Piaget learned a great deal about how children think by observing his own children and by paying a lot of attention to what appeared to be errors in their reasoning.

development from examining their incorrect answers to test items as from examining their correct answers. Through his repeated observations of children, including his own children, and especially through investigation of their errors in reasoning, Piaget concluded that coherent logical systems underlie children's thought. These systems, he believed, differ in kind from the logical systems that adults use. If we are to understand development, we must identify these systems and their distinctive characteristics. In this section, we first consider some of Piaget's general principles of development and then Piaget's stages of cognitive development.

Piaget believed that the function of intelligence is to aid in adaptation to the environment. In his view (Piaget, 1972), the means of adaptation form a continuum ranging from relatively unintelligent means, such as habits and reflexes, to relatively intelligent means, such as those requiring insight, complex mental representation, and the mental manipulation of symbols. In accord with his focus on adaptation, he believed that cognitive development is accompanied by increasingly complex responses to the environment (Piaget, 1972). Piaget further proposed that with increasing learning and maturation, both intelligence and its manifestations become *differentiated*—more highly specialized in various domains.

Piaget believed that development occurs in stages that evolve via **equilibration,** in which children seek a balance (equilibrium) between both what they encounter in their environments and what cognitive processes and structures they bring to the encounter, as well as among the cognitive capabilities themselves. Equilibration involves three processes. In some situations, the child's existing mode of thought and existing *schemas* (mental frameworks) are adequate for confronting and adapting to the challenges of the environment; the child is thus in a state of equilibrium. For example, suppose that 2-year-old Jimmy uses the word *doggie* to embrace all the four-legged furry creatures that are like his own dog; as long as all the four-legged creatures that Jimmy sees are like the dogs he has already seen, Jimmy remains in a state of equilibrium.

At other times, however, the child is presented with information that does not fit with the child's existing schemas, so cognitive disequilibrium arises. That is, imbalance occurs when the child's existing schemas are inadequate for new challenges the child encounters. The child consequently attempts to restore equilibrium through **assimilation**—incorporating the new information into the child's existing schemas. For example, suppose that Jimmy's dog is a Great Dane, and that Jimmy goes to the park and sees a poodle, a cocker spaniel, and an Alaskan malamute. Jimmy must assimilate the new information into his existing schema for *doggies*—not a big deal.

Suppose, however, that Jimmy also visits a small zoo and sees a wolf, a bear, a lion, a zebra, and a camel. On seeing each new animal, Jimmy looks perplexed and asks his mother, "Doggie?" Each time, his mother says, "No, that animal isn't a dog. That animal is a __________ [naming the animal]." Jimmy cannot assimilate these diverse creatures into his existing schema for *doggies;* instead, he must somehow modify his schemas to allow for the new information, perhaps creating an overarching schema for animals, into which he fits his existing schema for dogs. Piaget would suggest that Jimmy modifies existing schemas through **accommodation**—changing the existing schemas to fit the relevant new information about the environment. Together, the processes of assimilation and accommodation result in a more sophisticated level of thought than was possible previously. In addition, these processes result in the reestablishment of equilibrium, thus offering the individual—such as Jimmy—higher levels of adaptability.

According to Piaget, the equilibrative processes of assimilation and accommodation account for all of the changes associated with cognitive development. In Piaget's view, disequilibrium is more likely to occur during periods of stage transition. That is, although Piaget posited that equilibrative processes go on throughout childhood as children continually adapt to their environment, he also considered development to involve discrete, discontinuous stages. In particular, Piaget (1969, 1972) divided cognitive development into the four main stages summarized here: the sensorimotor, preoperational, concrete-operational, and formal-operational stages.

THE SENSORIMOTOR STAGE

The first stage of development, the **sensorimotor stage,** involves increases in the number and the complexity of sensory (input) and motor (output) abilities during infancy—roughly from birth to about 2 years of age. According to Piaget, the infant's earliest adaptations are reflexive ones. Gradually, infants gain conscious, intentional control over their motor actions. At first, they do so in order to maintain or to repeat interesting sensations. Later, however, they actively explore their physical world and seek out new and interesting sensations.

Throughout the early phases of sensorimotor cognitive development, infant cognition seems to focus only on what the infants can immediately perceive through their senses. Infants do not conceive of anything that is not immediately perceptible to them. According to Piaget, infants do not have a sense of **object permanence,** by which objects continue to exist even when imperceptible to the infants. For example, before about 9 months of age, infants who observe an object as it is being hidden from view will not seek the object once it is hidden. If a 4-month-old were to watch you hide a rattle beneath a blanket, the 4-month-old would not try to find the rattle beneath the blanket, whereas a 9-month-old would. Although subsequent research has called into question some of Piaget's interpretations regarding object permanence, infants appear not to have the same concept regarding the permanence of objects that adults have.

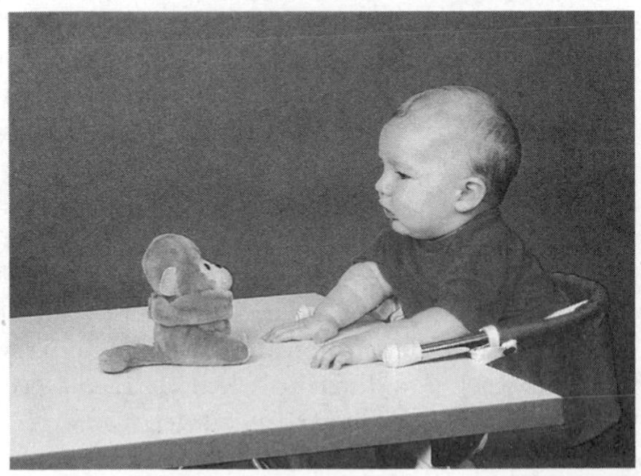
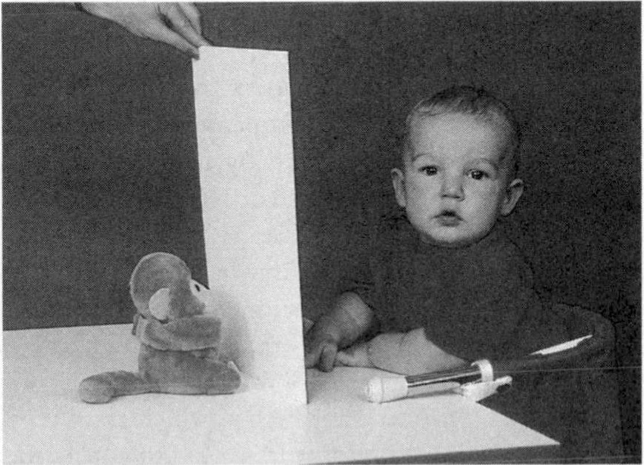

An infant responds to the object-permanence demonstration of hiding an object behind a screen. The infant looks away as soon as the object disappears from sight.

To have a sense of object permanence requires some internal, mental representation of an object even when the object is not seen, heard, or otherwise perceived. The young infant's responses do not require a conception of object permanence or of any other internal mental representations of objects or actions. The child's thoughts are focused only on sensory perceptions and motor behaviors. By the end of the sensorimotor period (18–24 months of age), children begin to show signs of **representational thought**—internal representations of external stimuli. In this transition to the preoperational stage, the child starts to be able to think about people and objects that are not necessarily perceptible at that moment.

Piaget believed that the pattern of increasing ability to form internal mental representations continues throughout childhood. Another characteristic pattern of cognitive development involves children's moving increasingly from a focus on self to an interest in others. That is, as children grow older, they become less **egocentric**—less focused on themselves. Note that egocentrism as conceived of by Piaget is a cognitive characteristic, not a personality trait. For example, the earliest adaptations that occur during infancy all pertain to the infant's own body (e.g., sucking reflexes may be adapted to include sucking a thumb or a toe). Later adaptations, however, also involve objects in the environment outside the child's body. Similarly, early mental representations involve only the child, but later ones also involve other objects. Piaget viewed this early trend as indicative of a broader trend for children of all ages to become increasingly aware of the outer world and of how others may perceive that world.

The Preoperational Stage

In the **preoperational stage,** from about age 2 years to about 6 or 7 years, the child begins actively to develop the internal mental representations that started at the end of the sensorimotor stage. According to Piaget, the arrival of representational thought during the preoperational stage paves the way for the subsequent development of logical thought during the stage of concrete operations. With representational thought comes verbal communication (see chapter 9, for a discussion of language acquisition). However, the communication is largely egocentric. A conversation may seem to have no coherence at all. Children say what is on their minds, pretty much without regard to what anyone else has said. As children develop, however, they increasingly take into account what others have said when forming their own comments and replies.

The ability to manipulate verbal symbols for objects and actions—even egocentrically—accompanies the ability to manipulate concepts, and the preoperational stage is characterized by increases in conceptual development. Nonetheless, children's ability to manipulate concepts is still quite limited during the preoperational stage. For example, during this stage, children exhibit **centration**—a tendency to focus on only one especially noticeable aspect of a complicated object or situation. Piaget (1946) did a series of experiments showing children's centration. He showed children two model trains on two different parallel tracks, as shown in Figure 13.1. He used different starting and stopping times for each train, and he ran each train down its track at a different speed. He then asked questions such as which train traveled longer or faster. He found that children who were 4 to 5 years old tended to concentrate on a single dimension, usually the point at which the trains stop. Specifically, these children would say that the train that had traveled farther down the track had also traveled faster and longer, regardless of when the trains had

FIGURE 13.1 **CENTRATION: A SINGLE TRAIN OF THOUGHT**

Although Jean Piaget showed the children that the trains started at different times and traveled at different speeds, the children did not consider those variables because they could not decenter from the single dimension that one train had traveled farther than the other.

started or stopped. Thus, children in the preoperational stage focus on one particular dimension of a problem—such as the final position of the trains—ignoring other aspects of the situation, even when they are relevant.

A lot of developmental changes occur during the preoperational stage. Children's active, intentional experimentation with language and with objects in their environments results in tremendous increases in conceptual and language development. These developments help to pave the way for further cognitive development during the stage of concrete operations.

THE CONCRETE-OPERATIONAL STAGE

In the stage of **concrete operations,** from roughly ages 7 or 8 until 11 or 12 years, children become able to manipulate mentally the internal representations that they formed during the preoperational period. In other words, they now not only have thoughts and memories of objects, but they also can perform mental operations on these thoughts and memories. However, they can do so only in regard to concrete objects (e.g., thoughts and memories of cars, food, toys, and other tangible things)—hence the name "concrete operations."

Perhaps the most dramatic evidence of the change from preoperational thought to the representational thought of the concrete-operational stage is seen in Piaget's classic experiments (1952, 1954, 1969) on **conservation** of quantity. In conservation, the child is able mentally to conserve (keep in mind) a given quantity despite observing changes in the appearance of the object or substance. These experiments probed children's responses to whether an amount of something (e.g., number of checkers, length of rods, or volume of dough) was conserved despite changes in appearance (see Table 13.2). Initially, children rely on their immediate perceptions of how things appear to be; gradually, they begin to formulate internal rules regarding how the world works, and eventually, they use these internal rules to guide their reasoning, rather than using appearances alone.

TABLE 13.2 **CONSERVATION OF QUANTITY**

During the preoperational stage, children have difficulty conserving quantity when perceptible changes occur. When viewing an experimenter pour liquid from a wide, shallow glass to a tall, narrow one, preoperational children tend to assert that there is more liquid in the tall glass than in the wide one. When viewing an experimenter transform the shape of a wad of clay, preoperational children tend to assert that there is more clay when the volume of clay appears to be greater (e.g., in a long snake). When viewing an experimenter change the arrangements of checkers from a more dense pattern to a more scattered pattern, preoperational children tend to assert that there is a larger number of checkers in the dispersed arrangement than in the dense arrangement. When viewing an experimenter change the relative positions of rods, preoperational children tend to assert that the rods are longer when they appear to protrude farther in one direction than when they do not. When viewing an experimenter rearrange wooden blocks on a board, preoperational children tend to assert that the scattered arrangement covers more area. When viewing an experimenter transform the shape of a ball of clay that is to displace liquid in a glass of water, preoperational children tend to assert that there is more clay when the volume of the clay appears to be greater (e.g., the flat pancake, as opposed to a ball of clay).

TYPE	THE CHILD IS SHOWN:	THE EXPERIMENTER:	THE CHILD RESPONDS:
Liquid	two equal short, wide glasses of water and agrees that they hold the same amount	pours water from the short, wide glass into the tall, thin one and asks if one glass holds more water than the other or if both are the same	*Preoperational child:* The tall glass has more. *Concrete-operational child:* They hold the same amount.
Matter	two equal balls of clay and agrees they are the same	rolls one ball of clay into a sausage and asks if one has more clay or if both are the same	*Preoperational child:* The long one has more clay. *Concrete-operational child:* They both have the same amount.
Number	two rows of checkers and agrees that both rows have the same number	spreads out the second row and asks if one row has more checkers than the other or if both are the same	*Preoperational child:* The longer row has more checkers. *Concrete-operational child:* The number of checkers in each row hasn't changed.
Length	two sticks and agrees that they are the same length	moves the bottom stick and asks if they are still the same length	*Preoperational child:* The bottom stick is longer. *Concrete-operational child:* They're the same length.

Continued

TABLE 13.2 CONSERVATION OF QUANTITY *(Continued)*

TYPE	THE CHILD IS SHOWN:	THE EXPERIMENTER:	THE CHILD RESPONDS:
Area	two boards with six wooden blocks and agrees that the blocks on both boards take up the same space	scatters the blocks on one board and asks if one board has more unoccupied space or if both are the same	*Preoperational child:* The blocks on Board B take up more space. *Concrete-operational child:* They take up the same amount of space.
Volume	two balls of clay put in two glasses equally full of water and says the level is the same in both	flattens one ball of clay and asks if the water level will be the same in both glasses	*Preoperational child:* The water in the glass with the flat piece won't be as high as the water in the other glass. *Concrete-operational child:* Nothing has changed; the level will be the same in each glass.

Perhaps the most well-known Piagetian conservation experiment of all demonstrates developmental changes in the *conservation of liquid quantity* (see Figure 13.2). The experimenter shows the child two short, stout beakers with liquid in them. The experimenter has the child verify that the two beakers contain the same amounts of liquid. Then, as the child watches, the experimenter pours the liquid from one of the short beakers into a third beaker, which is taller and thinner than the other two. In the new beaker, the liquid in the narrower tube rises to a higher level than in the other still full, shorter and wider beaker.

When asked whether the amounts of liquid in the two full beakers are the same or different, the preoperational child says that there is now more liquid in the taller, thinner beaker because the liquid in that beaker reaches a perceptibly higher point. The preoperational child has seen the experimenter pour all the liquid from one to the other, adding none, but the child does not conceive that the amount is conserved despite the change in appearance. The concrete-operational child, on the other hand, says that the beakers contain the same amount of liquid, based on the child's internal schemas regarding the conservation of matter.

What can the concrete-operational child do that the preoperational child cannot? The concrete-operational child can manipulate internal representations of concrete objects and substances, mentally conserving the notion of amount and concluding that despite different physical appearances, the quantities are identical. For one thing, the concrete-operational child can decenter from the single dimension of the height of the liquid in the container, to consider also the width of the container. Moreover, concrete-operational thinking is **reversible:** The concrete-operational child can judge the quantities to be identical because the child understands that potentially, the liquid could be

FIGURE 13.2 **CONSERVATION OF LIQUID QUANTITY**

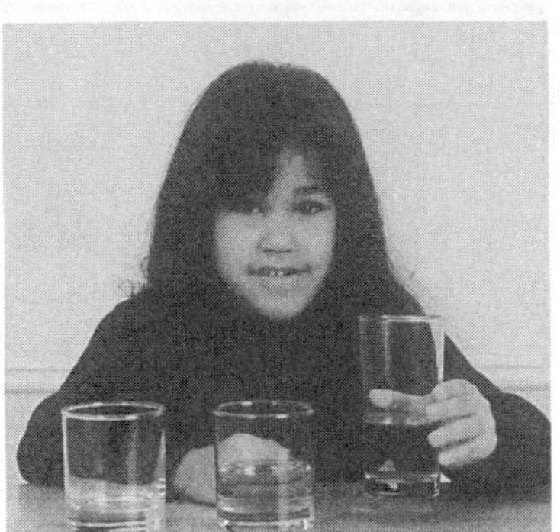

This young girl is participating in the classic Piagetian task in which the researcher measures out equal quantities of liquid into two identical beakers, then pours from one of the beakers into a tall beaker. Still in the preoperational stage, this girl cannot yet conserve liquid quantity, so she does not recognize that the quantity is conserved, despite superficial changes in the appearance of the amount. In the final photo, she holds the tall beaker, asserting that it contains more liquid than the short beaker. Once this girl reaches the stage of concrete operations, she will readily conserve the quantity of liquid.

poured back into the original container (the short beaker), thereby reversing the action. Once the child internally recognizes the possibility of reversing the action and can mentally perform this concrete operation, the child can grasp the logical implication that the quantity has not changed. Note, however, that the operations are concrete—that is, the cognitive operations act on cognitive representations of actual physical events. The final stage of cognitive development, according to Piaget, involves going beyond these concrete operations and applying the same principles to abstract concepts.

The Formal-Operational Stage

The **formal-operational stage,** from roughly 11 or 12 years of age onward, involves mental operations on abstractions and symbols that may not have physical, concrete forms. Moreover, children begin to understand some things that they have not directly experienced themselves (Inhelder & Piaget, 1958). During the stage of concrete operations, children begin to be able to see the perspective of others if the alternative perspective can be concretely manipulated. For example, they can guess how another child may view a scene (e.g., depicting a village) when they sit at opposite sides of a table on which the scene is displayed. During formal operations, however, children are finally fully able to take on perspectives other than their own, even when they are not working with concrete objects. Furthermore, persons in the formal-operations stage purposefully seek to create a systematic mental representation of situations they confront.

Piaget used several tasks to demonstrate the entry into formal operations. Consider, for example, the way in which we devise *permutations* (variations in combinations). Stop for a moment, and try to answer the question in the following investigation.

INVESTIGATING COGNITIVE PSYCHOLOGY

What are all the possible permutations of the letters, "A, B, C, D"?

How did you approach the problem? A person in the formal-operational stage will devise a system, perhaps first varying the placement of the last letter, then of the second-to-last, and so on. A formal-operational person's list might start: ABCD, ABDC, ADBC, DABC. . . . The concrete-operational person is more likely just to list combinations randomly, without any systematic plan: ABCD, DCBA, ACBD, DABC, and so on. Many other aspects of deductive and inductive reasoning also develop during the period of formal operations. The ability to use formal logic and mathematical reasoning also increases during this time. In addition, the sophistication of conceptual and linguistic processing continues to increase.

In sum, Piaget's theory of cognitive development involves stages. To Piaget, stages occur at roughly the same ages for different children, and each stage builds on the preceding stage. Stages occur in a fixed order and are irreversible: Once a child enters into a new stage, the child thinks in ways that characterize that stage regardless of the task domain, the specific task, or even the context in which the task is presented. He or she never thinks in ways that characterize an earlier stage of cognitive development. Other theorists (e.g., Beilin, 1971; R. Gelman, 1969), including some neo-Piagetians (e.g., Case, 1992; Fischer, 1980), would disagree with this view, suggesting that there may be greater flexibility in cognitive-developmental progression across tasks and task domains than is suggested by Piagetian theory.

EVALUATION OF PIAGET'S THEORY OF MATURATION OF THOUGHT PROCESSES

One criticism directly questions Piaget's assertion that the changes in children's cognition occur chiefly as an outcome of maturational processes. Although Piaget observed that developmental processes result from children's adaptations to their environment, he held that internal maturational processes, rather than environmental contexts or events, determine the sequence of cognitive-developmental progression. Evidence of environmental influences on children's performance on Piagetian tasks contradicts this premise. Hence, Piagetian theory is contradicted by evidence (e.g., Fischer & Bidell, 1991; R. Gelman, 1972; Gottfried, 1984) that particular experiences, training, or other environmental factors may alter performance on Piagetian tasks.

A second criticism arises because many developmental theorists question Piaget's fundamental assumption that cognitive development occurs in a fixed sequence of discontinuous spurts across task domains, tasks, and contexts. Regarding the discontinuity of development, many theorists (e.g., Brainerd, 1978) believe that cognitive development occurs as a continuous process rather than in discontinuous stages of development. Additionally, accumulating evidence (e.g., Beilin, 1971; see also Bidell & Fischer, 1992; Case, 1992) contradicts the assumption that within a given stage of development, children demonstrate only stage-appropriate levels of performance. It now appears that many aspects of the child's physical and social environment, of the child's prior experiences with the task and the task materials, and even of the experimenter's presentation of the task itself may lead to apparent unevenness in cognitive development.

Third, theorists and researchers have questioned Piaget's interpretation regarding what caused difficulty for children in particular Piagetian tasks. Piaget's theory emphasized the development of deductive and inductive reasoning, and Piaget held that limitations on children's ability to reason caused their difficulties in solving particular cognitive tasks. Different theorists have suggested that other kinds of limitations may at least partly influence children's performance on Piagetian tasks. Such limitations include children's motor coordination (J. M. Mandler, 1990), working-memory capacity (e.g., Bryant & Trabasso, 1971; Kail, 1984; Kail & Park, 1994), memory strategies (Siegler, 1991), or verbal understanding of questions (e.g., R. J. Sternberg, 1985a). For example, some researchers have suggested that children often might not have understood Piaget's questions, so that his experiments may have failed to elicit the children's full complement of abilities (e.g., see Figure 13.3). In general, Piaget appears to have underestimated the importance of language and its development in this theory.

Fourth, many theorists have questioned the accuracy of Piaget's estimates of the ages at which people demonstrate mastery of Piagetian tasks. Piaget himself underscored the importance of noting the sequence of developments, not the estimated ages at which these developments occurred. In general, the trend has been toward demonstrating that

FIGURE 13.3 **CLASS INCLUSION**

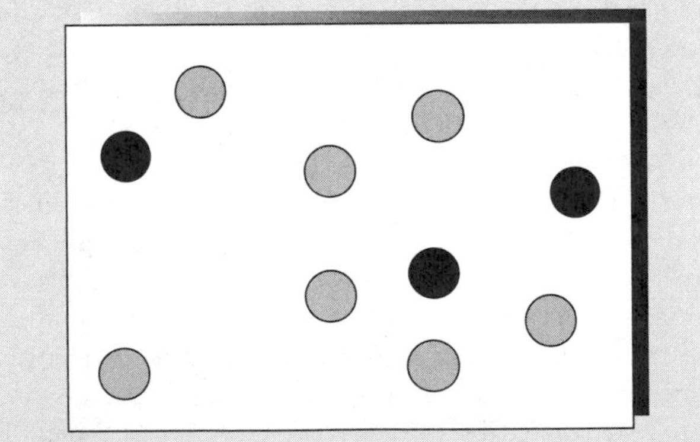

In one Piagetian task, Jean Piaget asked children to observe a set of marbles like those shown here. (Imagine that the lightly shaded marbles are blue and the black marbles are green.) He then asked the children the class-inclusion question, "Are there more blue marbles or more marbles?" Children in the preoperational stage often answered, "There are more blue marbles." Some researchers have suggested that the children did not really understand the rather odd question. Instead, the children believed that Piaget was asking them to compare the blue marbles with the green marbles—that is, the two subsets of the class, not the subset of the class with the class that includes the subset. (You may recall from the discussion of the representativeness heuristic used in decision making that adults have difficulty with class inclusion when considering probability.)

children can do things at ages earlier than Piaget had thought possible (see, e.g., Baillargeon, 1987; Brainerd, 1973; R. Gelman, 1969; R. Gelman & Baillargeon, 1983). Piaget's estimates of ages may have been skewed by his use of somewhat loose methods of research.

The evidence cited against stages usually refers to children's inconsistent abilities to perform well on tasks believed to be beyond their stage of development. However, Thelan and Smith (1994) present a new approach to development that encompasses many of these apparent problems for Piaget's theory. In particular, Thelen and Smith's dynamic systems approach, in which discontinuities occur as part of the natural interaction of nonlinear dynamic systems (systems with highly complex physical properties—in this case, children and their environment), predicts the very kinds of conflicting performance seen in children on the verge of stage transition. Indeed, Thelen and Smith point out that instability is necessary in order for new abilities to develop—a system must contain variability in its behavior in order for new behaviors to be selected. According to Thelen and Smith, children move from equilibrium in ability level to points of instability in performance, in which they are able inconsistently to perform beyond their current stage in some contexts. Furthermore, this disequilibrium is part of the natural interaction of the nonlinear dynamic systems involved in children's interactions with their environment. Thus, the dynamic systems approach to development encompasses conflicting evidence into a new framework—children do progress through stages, but not strictly via maturation. The discontinuous stages proposed by Piaget and the apparent conflicts in children's performance at stage transition result from natural interactions between children and their environment.

At the other end of the spectrum, even adolescents and adults do not show formal-operational thinking under many circumstances (Dasen & Heron, 1981; Neimark, 1975). They often seem to think associatively rather than logically (Sloman, 1996). In 1972, Piaget modified his own theory to acknowledge that the stage of formal operations may be more a product of an individual's domain-specific expertise, based on experience, than of the maturational processes of cognitive development.

Finally, the variation in the ages at which particular cognitive tasks are mastered shows that most of us have a wide range of performance, so that what we may be optimally capable of doing may often differ from what we actually do much of the time. The context in which we typically demonstrate cognitive performance may not be a true indication of what we are optimally able to achieve—and vice versa. One way of viewing these apparent contradictions is to describe Piaget's theory as primarily a **competence theory**—a theory of what people of various ages are maximally capable of doing. Other theorists prefer to view cognitive development in terms of a **performance theory**—a theory of what people of various ages naturally do in their day-to-day lives (see Davidson & Sternberg, 1985).

Neo-Piagetian Theorists: Alternative Views of Maturation of Thought Processes

Neo-Piagetian (*neo,* "new") theorists build upon a broad understanding of Piaget's theory of cognitive development. Although each neo-Piagetian is different, most neo-Piagetians (a) accept Piaget's broad notion of developmental stages of cognitive development; (b) concentrate on the scientific or logical aspects of cognitive development (often observing children engage in many of the same tasks as those used by Piaget); and (c) retain some ties with the notion that cognitive development occurs through equilibration. Of the many neo-Piagetian theories, I briefly consider here only a few. First, I describe briefly a few theories that posit a fifth stage of cognitive development, such as the theories of Patricia Arlin and others.

Fifth-stage theorists do not posit an entirely different theory of cognitive development; instead, they build on Piaget's four stages by suggesting a fifth stage beyond formal operations. Patricia Arlin (1975) proposes that a fifth stage of cognitive development is problem finding. In this fifth stage, individuals come to master the tasks of figuring out exactly what problems they face and deciding which problems are most important and deserving of their efforts toward solution.

Several theorists have suggested that logical reasoning beyond Piagetian formal operations might proceed to a fifth stage of *dialectical thinking* (see chapter 1). Dialectical thinking recognizes that in much of life, there is no one final, correct answer, but rather a progression of beliefs whereby we first propose some kind of thesis, then later see its antithesis, and finally effect some kind of synthesis between the two, which then serves as the new thesis for the continuing evolution of thought. For example, adults use dialectical thinking when considering one extreme and then the other, and then incorporating only the best elements of each extreme.

Psychologists such as Deirdre Kramer (1990), Gisela Labouvie-Vief (1980, 1990), Juan Pascual-Leone (1984, 1990), and Klaus Riegel (1973) assert that after the stage of formal operations, we reach a stage of *postformal thinking,* in which we recognize the constant unfolding and evolution of thought, such as in the dialectic originally proposed by philosopher Georg Hegel. Postformal thought allows adults to manipulate mentally the vagaries and inconsistencies of everyday situations, in which simple, unambiguous answers rarely are available. Through postformal thinking, we can consider and choose among alternatives, recognizing that other alternatives may offer benefits not obtainable from the chosen one. We may also take into account the sociocultural context in which we are making our decisions.

Sociocultural Influences on Thought Processes

Cognitive-developmental theorist Lev Vygotsky (1896–1934) died tragically of tuberculosis at only 38 years of age. Despite his early demise, the stature of Vygotsky is generally considered to be second only to that of Piaget in terms of his importance to the field of cognitive development. Moreover, the influence of this Russian psychologist has increased in recent years. Whereas Piaget dominated developmental psychology in the 1960s and 1970s, Vygotsky's work was rediscovered in the late 1970s and 1980s, and he continues to be influential today. Although Vygotsky had many fertile ideas, two of them are particularly important for us to consider here: internalization and the zone of proximal development.

In Piaget's theory, cognitive development proceeds largely "from the inside out," through maturation. Environments can foster or impede development, but Piaget emphasized the biological and hence the maturational aspect of development. Vygotsky's (1934/1962, 1978) theory takes an entirely different approach in emphasizing the role of the environment in children's intellectual development. Vygotsky suggested that cognitive

Many of the ideas about how children think that were proposed by cognitive-developmental theorist Lev Vygotsky, have been important not only to psychologists, but also to educators. Jean Piaget started out studying zoology, so his theories have a distinctively biological flavor. In contrast, Vygotsky had been studying other social sciences until age 28, when he turned his attention to psychology. During the next 10 years, Vygotsky developed his entire theory of cognitive development, probed the relationship between language and thought, and served as mentor for Alexander Luria (see chapters 7 and 8). Piaget, born the same year as Vygotsky, lived another 46 years after Vygotsky died, and Piaget continued to publish major new works decades after Vygotsky's death. We can only imagine what Vygotsky might have accomplished had he lived as long as Piaget.

development proceeds largely from the outside in, through **internalization**—the absorption of knowledge from context. Thus, social, rather than biological, influences are key in Vygotsky's theory of cognitive development. According to Vygotsky, then, much of children's learning occurs through the child's interactions within the environment, which largely determine what the child internalizes.

Consider, for example, a little girl on a lurching train. As the train is bumping along, she rises to walk in the aisle. Suppose that her mother simply says authoritatively, "Sit down," without explanation. An opportunity for learning has been lost. The child may neglect to infer the reasoning underlying her mother's request. However, suppose instead that the mother says, "Sit down because the train might jerk or sway suddenly, and you might fall." The child now has an opportunity not only to modify her behavior, but also to learn how to use this modification in other appropriate circumstances. Thus, the parent and others in the child's environment may extend the child's knowledge and may facilitate the child's learning through their interactions with the child.

This interactive form of learning relates to Vygotsky's (1934/1962, 1978) second major contribution to educational and developmental psychology—the construct of the **zone of proximal development (ZPD;** sometimes termed the *zone of potential development).* The ZPD is the range of potential between a child's observable level of realized ability (performance) and the child's underlying latent capacity (competence), which is not directly obvious (see Figure 13.4). When we observe children, what we typically observe is the ability that they have developed through the interaction of heredity and environment. To a large extent, however, we are truly interested in what children are capable of doing—what their potential would be if they were freed from the confines of an environment that is never truly optimal. Before Vygotsky proposed his theory, people were unsure how to measure this latent capacity.

Vygotsky argued that we need to reconsider not only how we think about children's cognitive abilities, but also how we measure them. Typically, we test children in a **static assessment environment,** in which an examiner asks questions and expects the child to answer them. Whether the child responds correctly or incorrectly, the examiner moves to the next question or task on the list of items in the test. Like Piaget, Vygotsky was interested not only in children's correct responses, but also in their incorrect responses to questions.

Thus, Vygotsky recommended that we move from a static assessment environment to a **dynamic assessment environment,** in which the interaction between child and examiner does not end when the child responds, especially not if the child responds incorrectly. In static testing, when a child gives a wrong answer, the examiner moves on to the next problem. In dynamic assessment, when the child gives a wrong answer, the examiner gives the child a graded sequence of guided hints in order to facilitate problem solving. In other words, the examiner serves as both teacher and tester.

FIGURE 13.4 **ZONE OF PROXIMAL DEVELOPMENT (ZPD)**

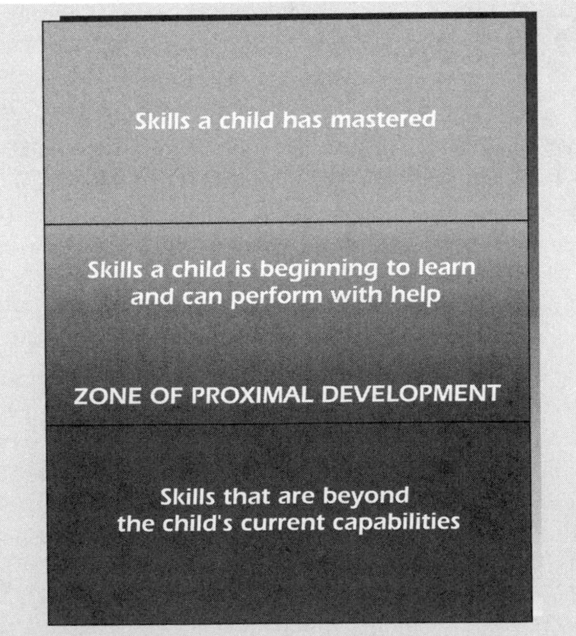

The ZPD is the range of ability in which a child may be able to push the boundaries of her or his performance, to approximate more closely her or his potential competence.

The ability to use hints is the basis for measuring the ZPD because this ability indicates the extent to which the child can expand beyond her or his observable abilities at the time of testing. Two children may answer a given problem incorrectly. However, a child who can profit from instruction can potentially go far, whereas a child who cannot is unlikely to acquire the skills needed to solve not only the problem being tested, but also related ones. Several tests have been created to measure the ZPD (e.g., A. L. Brown & French, 1979; Campione, 1989; Campione & Brown, 1990), the most well known of which is Reuven Feuerstein's (1979) *Learning Potential Assessment Device.*

The ZPD is one of the more exciting concepts in cognitive-developmental psychology, as it may enable us to probe beyond a child's observed performance. Moreover, the combination of testing and teaching appeals to many psychologists and educators. Educators, psychologists, and other researchers have been captivated by Vygotsky's notion that we can extend and facilitate children's development of cognitive abilities.

Both Piaget and Vygotsky—arguably the two most influential developmental psychologists to date—urged us not to be content just to note whether children's responses to questions and tasks are accurate. The power of these two developmental psychologists lay in their interest in probing beneath the surface, to try to understand why children behave and respond as they do. As is true of almost any significant contribution to science, the ideas of Vygotsky and of Piaget are measured more by how much they prompt us to extend our knowledge than by how nearly perfectly they have represented a complete, final understanding of the developing human mind. Perhaps the most we can ask of a theory is that it be worthy of further exploration. Next, we consider cognitive development as studied in the realm of information-processing skills.

Development of Information-Processing Skills

Information-processing theorists seek to understand cognitive development in terms of how people of different ages process information (i.e., decode, encode, transfer, combine, store, retrieve it), particularly when solving challenging mental problems. We should state at the outset that the typical information-processing theorist makes no claim to providing as comprehensive and well-integrated an explanation of cognitive development as did Piaget or even Vygotsky. On the other hand, information-processing theorists, taken as a whole, consider the entire range of cognitive processes that manipulate information in persons of all ages. (Recall discussions of information-processing theories in regard to knowledge representation, memory, text and other language processing, problem solving and insight, and various other cognitive domains.) Any mental activity that involves noticing, taking in, mentally manipulating, storing, combining, retrieving, or acting on information falls within the purview of information-processing approaches: How do our processes, strategies, or ways of representing and organizing information change over time, if at all? If there are changes, what might cause the changes?

Information-processing theorists take one of two fundamental approaches to studying information processing: a primarily domain-general or a primarily domain-specific approach. Domain-general theorists try to describe, in general terms, how we mentally process information. They want to show how general principles of information processing apply and are used across a variety of cognitive functions, from making perceptual judgments to understanding written text to reading maps to solving calculus problems. Most of these theories emphasize developmental changes in encoding, self-monitoring, and use of feedback. Domain-specific theorists emphasize the role of the development of competencies and knowledge in specific domains, arguing that most development is of this domain-specific kind.

In regard to encoding, as children grow older, they can more fully encode many features of their environment, and they can organize their encodings more effectively (e.g., Siegler, 1984, 1996; R. J. Sternberg, 1982a, 1984b). Across childhood, children can increasingly integrate and combine encoded information in more complex ways, forming more elaborate connections with what they already know. Additionally, older children just plain know more than younger ones, and they can call on increasingly large stores of remembered information.

Metacognitive Skills and Memory Development

Some researchers have also suggested that older children may have greater processing resources (Kail & Bisanz, 1992), such as attentional resources and working memory, which may underlie their overall greater speed of cognitive processing. According to this view, the reason that older children seem able to process information more quickly than younger children may be because the older children can hold more information for active processing. Hence, in addition to being able to organize information into increasingly large and complex chunks, older children may be able to hold more chunks of information in working memory.

Children appear to develop and use increasingly metamemory skills and various other kinds of *metacognitive skills* (involving the understanding and control of cognitive processes), such as monitoring and modifying their own cognitive processes while they are engaged in tackling cognitive tasks (A. L. Brown, 1978; Flavell & Wellman, 1977). Many information-processing researchers have been interested in the specific metacognitive skills of older children. An example is work on the understanding of appearance and reality. For example, 4- and 5-year-old children were shown imitation objects such as a sponge that looked exactly like a rock (Flavell, Flavell, & Green, 1983). The researchers encouraged the children to play with the imitations, so that the children would clearly see that the fakes were not what they appeared to be, and so that they could become thoroughly familiar with the objects. Children then had to answer questions about the identity of the objects. Afterward, the children were asked to view the objects through a blue plastic sheet, which distorted the perceived hues of the objects, and to make color judgments about the objects. The children were also asked to make size judgments while viewing the objects through a magnifying glass. The children were fully aware that they were viewing the objects through these intermediaries.

The children's errors formed an interesting pattern. There were two fundamental kinds of errors. On the one hand, when asked to report reality (the way the object actually was), the children would sometimes report appearance (the way the object looked through the blue plastic or the magnifying glass). Conversely, when asked to report appearance, they would sometimes report the reality. In other words, 4- and 5-year-old children did not yet clearly perceive the distinction between appearance and reality.

Actually, many Piagetians would agree with the observation that young children often fail to distinguish appearance from reality; their failure to conserve quantity may also be attributed to their attention to the change in appearance, rather than to the stability of the quantity. Children also increasingly profit from and eventually even seek out feedback regarding the outcomes of their cognitive efforts. These changes in encoding, memory organization and storage, metacognition, and use of feedback seem to affect children's cognitive development across many specific domains. In addition, however, some cognitive-developmental changes seem to be domain specific. Development in memory skills is discussed next.

The use of external memory aids, of rehearsal, and of many other memory strategies seems to come naturally to almost all of us as adults—so much so that we may take for granted that we have always done it; we have not. Lynne Appel and her colleagues (1972) designed an experiment to discover the extent to which young children spontaneously rehearse. They showed colored pictures of common objects to children at three grade levels: preschoolers, first-graders, and fifth-graders. Children were instructed either to "look at" the names of 15 pictures or to "remember" the names for a later test.

When children were instructed just to look at the pictures, almost no children exhibited rehearsal. In the memory condition, some of the young children showed some—but not much—rehearsal. Very few of the preschoolers seemed to know that rehearsing would be a good idea when they would later be asked to recall information. Moreover, the performance of the preschoolers was no better in the memory condition than in the looking condition.

Older children performed better. On the basis of these and other data, John Flavell and H. M. Wellman (1977) concluded that the major difference between the memory of younger and older children (as well as adults) is not in basic mechanisms, but in learned strategies, such as rehearsal. Young children seriously overestimate their ability to recall information, and they rarely spontaneously use rehearsal strategies when asked to recall items. That is, young children seem not to know about many memory-enhancing strategies.

In addition, even when young children do know about such strategies, they do not always use them. For example, even when trained to use rehearsal strategies in one task, most do not *transfer* the use of that strategy, carrying over their learning from one task to other tasks (Flavell & Wellman, 1977). Thus, young children appear to lack not only the knowledge of strategies but also the inclination to use them when they do know about them. Older children understand that to retain words in short-term memory, they need to rehearse; younger children do not. In a nutshell, younger children lack metamemory skills.

Whether children rehearse is not just a function of age. Ann Brown and her colleagues (A. L. Brown, Campione, Bray, & Wilcox, 1973) found that mentally retarded children are much less likely to rehearse spontaneously than are children of normal intelligence. Indeed, if such children are trained to rehearse, their performance can be greatly improved (Belmont & Butterfield, 1971; Butterfield, Wambold, & Belmont, 1973). However, the retarded performers will not always spontaneously transfer their learning to other tasks. For example, if the children are taught to rehearse with lists of numbers but then are presented with a list of animals, they may have to be taught all over again to rehearse for the new kinds of items, as well as for the old.

Culture, experience, and environmental demands also affect the use of memory-enhancing strategies. For example, Western children, who generally have more formal schooling than non-Western children do, are given much more practice using rehearsal strategies for remembering isolated bits of information. In contrast, Guatemalan children and Australian aboriginal children generally have many more opportunities to become adept at using memory-enhancing strategies that rely on spatial location and arrangements of objects (Kearins, 1981; Rogoff, 1986).

Another aspect of metamemory skill involves *cognitive monitoring,* in which the individual tracks and, as needed, readjusts an ongoing train of thought. Cognitive monitoring may consist of several related skills (A. L. Brown, 1978; see also A. L. Brown & DeLoache, 1978). For instance, you are realizing "what you know and what you do not know" (A. L. Brown, 1978, p. 82). You learn to be aware of your own mind and the degree of your own understanding (Holt, 1964). More recent work on the development of cognitive monitoring proposes a distinction between self-monitoring and self-regulation strategies (T. O. Nelson & Naren, 1994). Self-monitoring is a bottom-up process of keeping track of current understanding, involving the improving ability to predict memory performance accurately. Self-regulation is a top-down process of central executive control over planning and evaluation. Children benefit from training in using such cognitive monitoring processes to enhance their use of appropriate strategies (see Schneider & Bjorklund, 1998).

Recall also that physiological maturation of the brain and increasing content knowledge may partially explain why adults and older children generally perform better on memory tests than do younger children. These physiological and experience-based changes augment the changes in memory processes, such as increased knowledge about and inclination to use metamemory strategies. The goal of such strategies is eventually to be able to retrieve stored information, at will.

QUANTITATIVE SKILLS

One approach to understanding quantitative skills has considered computational abilities. Consider, for example, the addition problem, "2 + 3 = ?" Several different information-processing models have been proposed regarding how children solve problems of this kind (e.g., Groen & Parkman, 1972; Suppes & Groen, 1967; subtraction problems also have been studied by Woods, Resnick, & Groen, 1975, and by Siegler & Shrager, 1984; see also Resnick, 1980). Early models described some type of mental counter that starts at some value (determined by the addition problem) and then adds increments as needed (also determined by the addition problem). Before each *increment* (i.e., addition of one unit), a mental test counts whether the child has already added the needed number of increments. If so, the incremental process stops, and the child has reached the answer. If not, the child adds increments one by one until the required number of increments (in this case, three) have been added.

Robert Siegler's model (1991; Siegler & Shrager, 1984) enhances the early models by adding a second major component to the process. Specifically, once children encode the problem, they first attempt to retrieve a potential correct answer from memory. If the answer they retrieve exceeds their own preset level of confidence in the accuracy of the answer, they state the retrieved answer. If it does not, they again try to retrieve a correct answer from memory. They repeat this process until either they retrieve a satisfactory answer that exceeds their confidence level or they exceed a preset number of retrieval attempts. If they exceed their preset number of retrieval attempts, they then turn to a *backup strategy* (a more time-consuming but more reliable way of reaching an answer, used when faster methods fail to produce satisfactory results). For addition problems, this backup strategy is the incremental counter mentioned in other models. Siegler has also applied the strategy-choice (retrieval-backup) model to children's other arithmetic computations, such as multiplication (Siegler, 1988b).

Robert S. Siegler *is the Theresa Heinz professor of cognitive psychology at Carnegie-Mellon University. He has made major contributions toward our understanding of rule-based thinking in children and has developed methods of assessing the rules, strategies, and selection of strategies that children use in problem solving.*

In a review of the literature pertaining to development of mathematical skills, Ginsburg (1996) proposes various basic principles of mathematical learning. Here, I discuss a few key ideas to remember about quantitative skill development. First, even infants have some fundamental notion of quantity within the range of smaller numbers. Prelinguistic infants seem to know that adding leads to greater quantities and subtracting leaves smaller quantities. Moreover, young children appear to build on this fundamental knowledge to apply more abstract mathematical concepts in counting and to reason about addition and subtraction. Not only do children use the counting and memorization strategies previously discussed, but children also derive abstract rules from experience with particular kinds of counting sets. For example, rule learning combined with practice in counting by fives allows children to acquire multiplication principles more easily (Baroody, 1995). Finally, context effects, from problem wording to cultural environment, greatly influence mathematical learning beyond the formulation of informal strategies.

VISUOSPATIAL SKILLS

The rules for arithmetic computation of quantities (skills leading to understanding of algebra) are not the only mathematical abilities that develop during early childhood. Young children also develop basic spatial understandings that form the basis for geometry. One such basic understanding is *spatial visualization*—our ability to orient ourselves in our surroundings and to manipulate images of objects mentally (see chapters 4 and 7). Although many studies have examined spatial visualization in children (e.g., Huttenlocher, Hedges, & Duncan, 1991; Huttenlocher & Presson, 1973, 1979; Kail, 1991, 1997; Marmor, 1975, 1977), I summarize here just one typical example of this research (Kail, Pellegrino, & Carter, 1980).

Participants in grades 3, 4, and 6, and in college judged whether pairs of stimuli were identical or were mirror-image reversals of each other. (Recall some of the mental-rotation tasks used by Roger Shepard, described in chapter 7.) One stimulus in each pair was presented in an upright position, and the other was rotated 0, 30, 60, 90, 120, or 150 degrees from the standard upright position. The pairs comprising each stimulus item were either *alphanumeric* (alphabetic and/or numeric) symbols—such as 4, 5, F, and G—or unfamiliar abstract geometric forms (see Figure 13.5). Robert Kail and his colleagues (1980) found that the speed of mental rotation increases with age and with the degree of familiarity of the objects. Thus, older participants can mentally rotate more quickly, and all participants can rotate familiar objects more quickly than they can rotate unfamiliar ones.

The findings raised several questions, two of which particularly intrigued researchers. First, why might the speed of mental rotation improve with age? The researchers suggested that younger children must rotate the entire stimulus, whereas older children may rotate stimuli more analytically, so that they rotate each component separately and may need only to rotate a part of the stimulus. Thus, the change in cognitive development may involve more than a simple change in processing speed. A second question is why participants encoded and rotated the unusual geometric forms more slowly than the familiar, alphanumeric ones. The difference might be due to the activation of an already existing, easily accessible pattern in memory for the familiar characters, in contrast to the requirement that the participants form a new representation for the unfamiliar stimuli.

Kail (Kail & Park, 1990) also found that both children and young adults showed speedier response times in mental-rotation tasks when given opportunities for practice (see Figure 13.5). More recently, Kail (1991) observed that the performance of both school-aged children and young adults on mental-rotation tasks was not impaired as a function of their engaging in simultaneous tasks involving memory recall. Kail has interpreted these findings as suggesting that mental rotation may be an automatic process for both school-aged children and adults. Given that both familiarity with the items and practice with mental rotation appear to enhance response times, his study suggesting that mental rotation may be an automatic process may permit us to infer that enhanced response times may be due to increasing automatization (see chapter 3) of the task across childhood and adolescence. Furthermore, such automatic processes may be a sign of more effective visuospatial skills because increased speed is associated with increased accuracy in spatial memory (Kail, 1997).

At the other end of the life span, Itiel Dror and Stephen Kosslyn (1994) studied whether processing speed or other factors may influence age-related changes in mental rotation by adults. Dror and Kosslyn found that older participants (55–71 years; mean 65 years) responded more slowly and less accurately than younger participants (18–23 years; mean 20 years) on mental-rotation tasks. However, they found that older and younger participants showed comparable response times and error rates on tasks involving image scanning

FIGURE 13.5 **MENTAL ROTATION OF ALPHANUMERIC PAIRS**

Robert Kail found that speed of mental rotation improved with both greater familiarity with the forms and older age of the subjects.

(see chapter 5, for details on image-scanning tasks). Based on these and other findings, these authors concluded that aging affects some aspects of visual imagery more than others.

The authors also analyzed their data for mental rotation, image-scanning, and two other imagery tasks (generating or maintaining a mental image within a visual region and then indicating whether the image would obscure a probe stimulus within that region). As a result of their analyses, the authors inferred that general effects of aging may lead to a reduction in response times across tasks. On the other hand, they inferred that age differences in error rates may arise due to specific effects of aging, which may selectively influence particular aspects of mental imagery. The authors also speculated that if the participants had been urged to minimize their error rates, perhaps older persons would have shown even slower response times, to ensure lower error rates. However, other work (Hertzog, Vernon, & Rypma, 1993) directly testing that speculation failed to confirm the authors' hypothesis. Other researchers have suggested that a factor contributing to task-specific differences in age-related decline in mental imagery is whether the task requires multiple simultaneous transformations or multiple sequential ones (Mayr & Kliegl, 1993).

Inductive Reasoning

Recall from chapter 12 that *inductive reasoning* does not lead to a single, logically certain solution to a problem, but only to solutions that have different levels of plausibility. In inductive reasoning, the reasoner induces general principles, based on specific observations. Susan Carey has done extensive work in observing inductive reasoning in children and has observed some developmental trends.

For instance, 4-year-olds appear not to induce generalized biological principles about animals when given specific information about individual animals (Carey, 1985). By age 10 years, however, children are much more likely to do so. For example, if 4-year-olds are told that both dogs and bees have a particular body organ, they still assume that only animals that are highly similar either to dogs or to bees have this organ and that other animals do not. In contrast, 10-year-olds would induce that if animals as dissimilar as dogs and bees have this organ, many other animals are likely to have this organ, as well. Also, 10-year-olds would be much more likely than 4-year-olds to induce biological principles that link humans to other animals. Along the same lines, when 5-year-olds learn new information about a specific kind of animal, they seem to add the information to their existing schemas for the particular kind of animal but not to modify their overall schemas for animals or for biology as a whole (see Keil, 1989). On the other hand, first- and second-graders have shown an ability to choose and even to spontaneously generate appropriate tests for gathering indirect evidence to confirm or disconfirm alternative hypotheses (Sodian, Zaitchik, & Carey, 1991).

Susan Gelman (1984/1985; S. A. Gelman & Markman, 1987) has noted that even children as young as 3 years old seem to induce some general principles from specific observations, particularly those principles that pertain to taxonomic categories for animals. For example, preschoolers were able to induce principles that correctly attribute the cause of phenomena (such as growth) to natural processes rather than to human intervention (S. A. Gelman & Kremer, 1991; Hickling & Gelman, 1995). In related work, preschoolers were able to reason correctly that a blackbird was more likely to behave like a flamingo than like a bat because blackbirds and flamingos are both birds (S. A. Gelman & Markman, 1987). Note that in this example, preschoolers are going against their perception that blackbirds look more like bats than like flamingos, basing their judgment instead on the fact that they are both birds (although the effect is admittedly strongest when the term *bird* is also used in regard to both the flamingo and the blackbird).

Other work by Gelman (S. A. Gelman & Markman, 1986) supports the view that preschoolers may make decisions based on induced general principles rather than on perceptual appearances—for example, they may induce taxonomic categories based on functions (such as means of breathing) rather than on perceptual appearances (such as apparent weight). When given information about the internal parts of objects in one category, preschoolers also induced that other objects in the same category were likely to have the same internal parts (S. A. Gelman & O'Reilly, 1988; see also S. A. Gelman & Wellman, 1991). On the other hand, when inducing principles from discrete information, young preschoolers were more likely than older children to emphasize external, superficial features of animals than to give weight to internal structural or functional features. Also, given the same specific information, older children seem to induce richer inferences regarding biological properties than do younger children (S. A. Gelman, 1989).

In a more recent review, Wellman and Gelman (1998) stress the importance of maintaining both forms of knowledge, appearance-based and principled, for flexible use across different situations and domains. Knowledge about deep internal functional relationships is important for inducing properties of objects, but similarity in appearance is also important under other circumstances. Wellman and Gelman propose that knowledge acquisition develops via the use of framework theories, or models, for drawing inferences about the environment in various domains (such as physics, psychology, and biology). Wellman and Gelman cite numerous studies demonstrating children's early and rapid acquisition of expertise in understanding physical objects and causal relations between events, psychological entities and casual-explanatory reasoning, and biological entities and forces. The changes in reasoning about factors in these domains appear to show enhanced understanding of the relation between appearances and deeper functional principles. Thus, children use foundational knowledge within different domains to build framework understandings of the world.

To summarize these findings, once again, early developmental psychologists appear to have underestimated the cognitive capabilities of young children. In addition, a supportive context for induction can greatly enhance children's ability to induce appropriate principles (Keil, 1989). Nonetheless, there does appear to be a developmental trend toward increasing sophistication in inducing general principles from specific information and toward increasing reliance on more subtle features of the information on which such inductions are based. Furthermore, this sophisticated knowledge may be organized into general frameworks for understanding within the important domains of physics, psychology, and biology.

In the preceding section, I have attempted to provide a brief but diverse survey of the abundant research on information-processing theories of cognitive development. These theories greatly elaborate on the theorizing of Piaget—providing details of performance that Piaget did not specify—and also show that Piaget's model really applied more to ideal competencies than to everyday performances. This vast area of study encompasses far more than can be included within the scope of this introduction to cognitive development, but the material covered here provides a good foundation for further investigation. The various cognitive-developmental perspectives are not mutually exclusive; some have been pursued simultaneously, some have evolved as reactions to others, and some are offshoots of others. Table 13.3

summarizes the ways in which these theories compare, contrast, and relate to one another. All of these theories of cognitive development contribute to the ongoing process of understanding how and why we humans think as we do. Yet another view of cognitive development considers the physiological development of the brain and neural apparatus.

TABLE 13.3 SUMMARY OF COGNITIVE-DEVELOPMENT THEORIES

How do the theories presented in this chapter address the issues of nature versus nurture, continuity versus discontinuity, domain generality versus domain specificity, and the nature of the developmental process?

Theory	Nature or Nurture?	Continuous or Discontinuous (Stages)?	Domain General or Domain Specific?	Process by Which Development Occurs?
Piaget	Biological maturation is crucial; environment plays a secondary but important role.	There are 4 discontinuous stages.	Development largely occurs simultaneously across domains, although some domains may show change slightly ahead of others.	Equilibrative processes of assimilation and accommodation
Neo-Piagetians	May emphasize role of the environment somewhat more than Piaget did.	May add a fifth stage; may question the ages for particular stages suggested by Piaget.	Same as Piaget (i.e., development largely occurs simultaneously across domains, although some domains may show change slightly ahead of others).	Same as Piaget (i.e., equilibrative processes of assimilation and accommodation)
Vygotsky	Social and physical environment plays a crucial role; maturational readiness may provide the broad parameters (zone of proximal development) within which the social environment determines development.	Continuous	The zone of proximal development may apply to many domains, but the environment may provide sufficient support for development only in specific domains, thus affecting development.	Internalization that results from interactions between the individual and the environment, occurring within the individual's zone of proximal development
Information-processing theorists	Nature provides the physiological structures and functions (e.g., memory capacity), and nurture provides the environmental supports that allow the individual to make the most of the existing structures and functions.	Continuous	Some theorists have been interested in processes that generalize across all domains; others have focused their research and theories on specific domains.	Internal changes in cognitive processing, as a result of physiological maturation, environmental events, and the individual's own shaping of cognitive processes

Neurophysiological Changes in Development

Increasing Neuronal Complexity

Figure 13.6 illustrates some of the striking microlevel (fine) changes in the neural networks of the brain that occur during the first 2 years after birth. In this early period of rapid neural growth, no new neurons are formed—the growth that takes place comprises dendritic and axonal growth of existing cells. Here, the "use it or lose it" principle clearly applies—cells that are not needed and that do not form connections to other cells actually die. Likewise, synaptic connections between neurons that are not used will become overwhelmed by competing connections that are used. After the first few years, however, the rate of neural growth and development declines dramatically. In fact, 90% of neural growth is complete by age 6 years. Recall that the evidence for a critical period in language acquisition coincides with this time period. Perhaps the complexities of language acquisition (along with other early acquired skills) require the increased plasticity and flexibility of the early developing nervous system. Both the micro and the macrolevel changes in structure show an increase in complexity over the course of development.

Maturation of Central Nervous System Structures

Chapter 2 (Figure 2-10) illustrates the physiological changes in the macrolevel (gross) structure of the brain that occur during prenatal development. At birth, the brain stem (which comprises the hindbrain, the midbrain, and part of the forebrain) is almost fully developed. Nonetheless, some subcortical developments continue to influence cognitive

FIGURE 13.6 NEURAL NETWORKS IN THE DEVELOPING HUMAN BRAIN

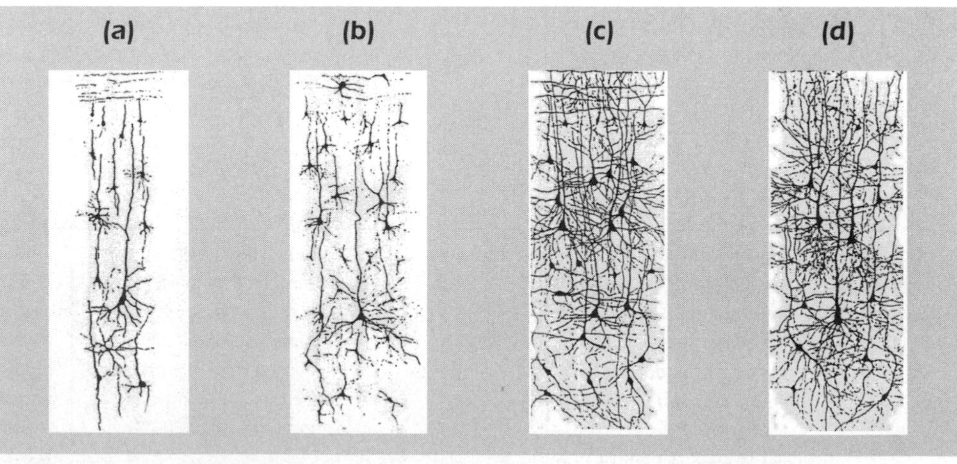

Observe the increasing complexity of neural connections (a) at birth, (b) at 3 months, (c) at 6 months, and (d) at 24 months.

development after birth. For example, enhancements in recognition memory seem to correspond to maturation of the hippocampus (Diamond, 1990). As compared with subcortical structures, however, the cerebral cortex is still largely immature.

The areas of the brain that develop most rapidly after birth are those in the sensory and motor cortex; subsequently, the association areas related to problem solving, reasoning, memory, and language develop. The preceding sections of this chapter have already suggested that the physiological material with which we think must become increasingly complex and that sensorimotor development precedes more sophisticated cognitive processes.

Similarly, physiological changes in the frontal lobes parallel cognitive changes. In infants, maturation of the frontal lobes seems to parallel the significant cognitive developments of this period noted by Piaget (Diamond, 1993; see also Goldman-Rakic, 1993). ERP (event-related potential) studies examining electrical waves in the brain show that, later in development, frontal-lobe maturation is linked to reading skill, in that a threshold level of maturation seems to be necessary for effective reading. Above that threshold level of maturation, however, differences in reading skill were correlated with differences in hemispheric specialization for language skill (Segalowitz, Wagner, & Menna, 1992).

Particularly intriguing findings regarding hemispheric specialization may also offer insight into a recurring issue in the study of cognitive development. Some studies by Robert Thatcher and colleagues of the EEG (electroencephalogram) patterns of 577 people ranging in age from 2 months to early adulthood show different developmental patterns in the right and left cerebral hemispheres (Thatcher, Walker, & Giudice, 1987). In the right hemisphere, there appear to be continuous, gradual changes in EEG patterns associated with age. In the left hemisphere, however, there appear to be abrupt shifts in the EEG patterns, at least up through the time of early adulthood (see Figure 13.7).

FIGURE 13.7 **DEVELOPMENTAL CHANGES IN BRAIN WAVES**

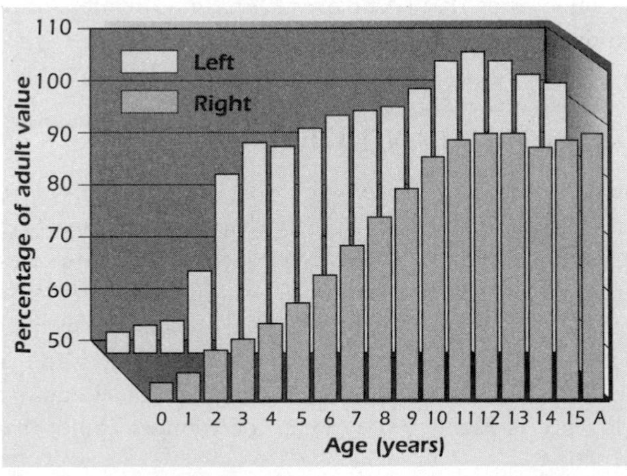

This graph of developmental changes in EEG patterns shows increasing electrical activity in both cerebral hemispheres. Note, however, that whereas the course of development in the left hemisphere is discontinuous, showing bursts and plateaus, the course of development in the right hemisphere is continuous. (After Thatcher, Walker, & Giudice, 1987)

Additional studies of cerebral architecture development and EEG patterns find alternations between left and right hemisphere synaptic connection growth spurts—development in one hemisphere proceeds much more rapidly than in the other during a period of time, then the pattern switches to dominance of the other hemisphere. Such alternating asymmetries in hemispheric development could perhaps underlie adult hemispheric differences in abilities—adult left-hemisphere dominance in particular language abilities may reflect acquisition of those skills during the time of left-hemisphere growth dominance. Likewise, individual differences in relative timing of periods of skill acquisition and periods of hemispheric dominance could be related. Moreover, the anterior portions of the frontal lobes, through connections to posterior areas, appear to regulate synaptic reorganization of posterior areas. Thus, not only are there left–right changes in development, but front–back changes take place as well (Thatcher, 1991; 1992; 1994).

In addition to the good news associated with our increasing cognitive capabilities, one developmental trend in our physiology brings bad news: Between our peak of neural growth (in early adulthood) and about age 80 years, we lose about 5% of our brain weight. Nonetheless, changes in neural connections help to compensate for our cell loss (Coleman & Flood, 1986). That is, over the life span, our brains show continually increasing specificity of neural connections (as long as we remain mentally active and do not suffer from abnormal pathologies). Just what those physiological changes may mean in terms of cognitive development during adulthood is the topic of the next section.

Cognitive Development in Adulthood

Thus far, this chapter has focused primarily on cognitive development in children. Cognitive development does not stop at adolescence, however. Many cognitive psychologists study the changes in abilities that occur over a lifetime. Before closing this chapter, I address adult cognitive development.

Patterns of Growth and Decline

Is cognitive growth never-ending? Do scores on cognitive-ability tests continue to increase indefinitely? The available data suggest that they may not. Cognitive psychologists often distinguish between *fluid intelligence*—the cognitive-processing skills that enable us to manipulate abstract symbols, as in mathematics—and *crystallized intelligence*—our stored knowledge, which is largely declarative, such as vocabulary, but may also be procedural, such as the expertise of a master chess player. It turns out that although crystallized intelligence is higher, on average, for older adults than for younger adults, fluid intelligence is higher, on average, for younger adults than for older ones (Horn & Cattell, 1966).

For example, the performance of older adults on many information-processing tasks appears to be slower, particularly on complex tasks (Bashore, Osman, & Hefley, 1989; Cerella, 1990, 1991; Poon, 1987; Schaie, 1989). In general, crystallized cognitive abilities seem to increase throughout the life span, whereas fluid cognitive abilities seem to increase up until the 20s or 30s or possibly 40s and slowly to decrease thereafter. The preservation of crystallized abilities suggests that long-term memory and the structure and organization of knowledge representation are preserved across the life span (see Salthouse, 1992, 1996).

Although psychometric researchers disagree about the age when fluid intelligence starts to decline, many researchers agree that eventually some decline does indeed occur, on average. The rate and extent of decline varies widely across people. Some cognitive abilities also seem to decline under some circumstances but not others, on average. For example, effectiveness of performance on some problem-solving tasks appears to show age-related decline (Denny, 1980), although even brief training appears to improve scores on problem-solving tasks for older adults (Rosenzweig & Bennett, 1996; Willis, 1985).

Not all cognitive abilities decline, however. For example, a relatively recent book (Cerella, Rybash, Hoyer, & Commons, 1993) devotes 20 chapters to describing studies showing little or no intellectual decline in various areas of cognition, including object and word perception, language comprehension, and problem solving. Some researchers (e.g., Schaie & Willis, 1986) have found that some kinds of learning abilities seem to increase, and others (Graf, 1990; Labouvie-Vief & Schell, 1982; M. Perlmutter, 1983) have found that the ability to learn and remember meaningful skills and information shows little decline. Also, even in a single domain, such as memory, decreases in one kind of performance may not imply decreases in another. For example, although short-term memory performance seems to decline (Hultsch & Dixon, 1990; West, 1986), long-term memory (Bahrick, Bahrick, & Wittlinger, 1975) and recognition memory (Schonfield & Robertson, 1966) remain quite good.

Some researchers (e.g., Schaie, 1974, 1996) even question much of the evidence for intellectual decline. For one thing, our views of memory and aging may be confounded by reports of pathological changes that occur in some older adults. Such changes are not due to general intellectual decline, but result from specific neurophysiological disorders. These neurophysiological disorders, such as Alzheimer's disease, are fairly uncommon even among the most elderly. Preventive screening tools for Alzheimer's disease, which capitalize on differences in typical aging adult abilities, are currently being investigated with mixed success (Mirmiran, von Someren, & Swaab, 1996).

Another qualification on findings of decline in older age is the use of *cross-sectional research designs,* which involve testing different cohorts (generations) of individuals at the same time. Such designs tend to overestimate the extent of decline of cognitive abilities, because for unknown reasons, more recent generations of individuals show higher cognitive abilities—at least as measured by IQ (Flynn, 1984, 1987)—than do earlier generations. Consequently, the lower IQs of the older individuals may be a generational effect rather than an aging effect. Indeed, *longitudinal research designs,* which test the same individuals repeatedly over an extended period of time, suggest less decline in mental abilities with age. These studies, however, may underestimate the extent of decline due to selective dropout. The less able participants drop out of the study over the years, perhaps because they find the taking of the cognitive tests to be discouraging or even humiliating.

Although the debate about intellectual decline with age continues, positions have converged somewhat. For instance, there is general consensus (e.g., Cerella, 1990, 1991; Kliegl, Mayr, & Krampe, 1994; Salthouse, 1994, 1996) that some slowing of the rate of cognitive processing occurs across the span of adulthood, and the evidence of slowing remains even when the experimental methodology and analyses rule out the disproportionate representation of demented adults among the elderly (e.g., Salthouse, Kausler, & Saults, 1990). Among the general factors that have been suggested as contributing to age-related slowing of cognitive processing have been a generalized decline in CNS (central nervous system) functioning (Cerella, 1991), a decline in working-memory capacity (Salthouse, 1993), and a decline in attentional resources (see Horn & Hofer, 1992).

Salthouse (1996) attempts to explain why slowed processing might lead to cognitive deficits by pointing to two speed-related issues in cognitive functioning—limited time and simultaneity. Slowed processing may prevent certain operations from being computed because such operations may need to occur within a limited amount of time, and the operations may need to overlap, due to storage limitations. For example, auditory memory exhibits rapid decay, leading to the necessity for rapid classification of auditory signals. Slowing of upper-level processing can result in incomplete or inaccurate processing of auditory signals. Given the semi-parallel nature of much of cognitive processing along with the nature of synaptic transmission, that speed would be an issue is not surprising — such processing is very time-dependent.

In addition to these general factors, many cognitive-developmental psychologists have suggested that specific factors also affect age-related changes in cognitive processing, and the specific factors may differentially affect various cognitive tasks. For example, specific factors include greater slowing of higher order cognitive processes than of sensory-motor processes (Cerella, 1985), differential slowing of high- versus low-complexity tasks (Kliegl et al., 1994), greater slowing for tasks requiring coordinative complexity (requiring simultaneous processing of multiple stimuli) than for sequential complexity (requiring sequential processing of multiple stimuli; Mayr & Kliegl, 1993), and greater age-related decline in processes of information retrieval than in processes of encoding (see Salthouse, 1992). In addition, priming effects and tasks requiring implicit memory seem to show little or no evidence of decline, but tasks involving explicit memory do show age-related decline (see Salthouse, 1992).

Based on existing research, three basic principles of cognitive development in adulthood have been suggested (Dixon & Baltes, 1986). First, although fluid abilities and other aspects of information processing may decline in late adulthood, this decline is balanced by stabilization and even advancement of well-practiced and pragmatic aspects of mental functioning (crystallized abilities). Second, despite the age-related decline in information processing, sufficient reserve capacity allows at least temporary increases in performance, especially if the older adult is motivated to perform well. Third, when adults lose some of the speed and physiology-related efficiency of information processing, they often compensate, in a given task, with other knowledge and expertise-based information-processing skills (Salthouse, 1991, 1996; see also Salthouse & Somberg, 1982).

Although the evidence regarding age-related differences in the selection of cognitive strategies is mixed, there appear to be no age-related differences in self-monitoring of cognitive processes (see Salthouse, 1992), so it would appear that older adults may be able effectively to utilize information regarding how to enhance their cognitive performance. Also, when task performance is based more on accuracy than on speed, older adults may at least partly compensate for speed deficits with increased carefulness and persistence (see Horn & Hofer, 1992). Further, at all times throughout the life span, there is considerable **plasticity**—modifiability—of abilities (Baltes, 1997; Baltes & Willis, 1979; Mirmiran et al., 1996; Rosenzweig & Bennett, 1996). None of us is stuck at a particular level of performance. Each of us can improve.

Many researchers have come to believe that adult cognition not only does not decline but actually continues to develop and improve. Recall, for example, the characteristics of postformal thought, described in regard to some of the Piagetian fifth-stage theorists. Those who support the notion of postformal thought indicate some ways in which older adults may show a kind of thinking that qualitatively differs from the thinking of adolescents and perhaps even young adults (Moshman, 1998). Although older adults generally do not demonstrate the same speed of information processing shown in younger adults, they may show instead the benefits of taking time to consider alternatives and to reflect on past experiences before making judgments—a skill often termed *wisdom*.

PRACTICAL APPLICATIONS OF COGNITIVE PSYCHOLOGY

If you are reading this book, chances are you have not experienced these age-related changes in your mental abilities, but it is not too early to prepare for the future. In particular, it is a good idea to start establishing habits that could help you avoid losing your cognitive edge. For example, reading is an important intellectual activity that you may decrease or even stop once you leave school and become involved in your career (unless your career involves reading). It is a good idea to continue reading noncareer-related materials or to engage in any mentally challenging activities to keep your cognitive skills in tune. Reading is one way to keep yourself exposed to diverse ideas, and because reading involves many rapid cognitive operations, this kind of activity might also help delay the slowing of cognitive operations. Moreover, an even better idea is to continue actively to educate yourself throughout the course of your life by taking courses or intensively studying topics that interest you. If you use your mental abilities throughout the course of your life, you will be much less likely to lose those abilities.

WISDOM AND AGING

In recent years, life-span developmental psychologists have become particularly interested in the development of wisdom in adulthood (see R. J. Sternberg, 1990). Most theorists have argued that wisdom increases with age, although there are exceptions (Meacham, 1990). Psychologists' definitions of wisdom have been diverse. Some (Baltes & Smith, 1990; Baltes, Staudinger, Maercker, & Smith, 1995) define **wisdom** as exceptional insight into human development and life matters, including exceptionally good judgment and advice, as well as commentary about difficult life problems. Furthermore, wisdom can be seen as reflecting a positive gain in culture-based cognitive pragmatics (meaningful uses of cognitive skills) in the face of the more physiologically controlled losses in cognitive mechanics (Baltes, 1993). Other research (R. J. Sternberg, 1985b) has found six factors in people's conceptions of wisdom: reasoning ability, sagacity (shrewdness), learning from ideas and from the environment, judgment, expeditious use of information, and *perspicacity* (intensely keen awareness, perception, and insight). In wisdom, to know what you do not know is also important (Meacham, 1983, 1990). Whatever the definition, the study of wisdom represents an exciting new direction for discovering what abilities may be developed during later adulthood at the same time that fluid abilities or the mechanical aspects of information processing may be flagging. This study is closely related to the study of intelligence, the topic of the next and final chapter of this book.

SUMMARY

1. **What are some of the major theoretical perspectives regarding how cognitive development occurs?** Jean Piaget proposed that cognitive development centers on increasingly complex adaptations to the environment, based primarily on changes due to physiological maturation. More specifically, cognitive development occurs largely through two processes of equilibration: *assimilation* and *accommodation.*

   Piaget posited four stages of cognitive development: the *sensorimotor stage,* the *preoperational stage,* the *concrete-operational stage,* and the *formal-operational stage.* At the end of the sensorimotor stage, children start to develop *representational thought,* involving people and objects that the child cannot currently see, hear, or otherwise perceive—first clearly noticeable in the achievement of *object permanence,* but later apparent in other cognitive developments as well. Furthermore, as children grow older, they become less *egocentric*—that is, less focused on themselves and more able to see things from the perspective of others. Some theorists have posited a fifth stage beyond Piaget's original four. Such a postformal stage might involve problem finding (rather than problem solving) or a tendency toward dialectical thinking.

   Lev Vygotsky's theory of cognitive development more strongly emphasizes the importance of the social context, rather than physiological maturation, as a determinant of cognitive development. His theory stresses the importance of *internalization* and of the *zone of proximal development.* In general, development can be seen as the interaction of biological and environmental factors leading to increased cognitive complexity and flexibility.

2. **What do researchers find by investigating the development of information-processing skills?** Information-processing theorists seek to understand cognitive development in terms of how children at different ages process information, particularly in regard to problem solving. Some theorists formulate general theories of how information processing works, and others study information processing within specific domains. In general, the development of many abilities can be related to changes in *metacognitive* skills—in particular, knowing the difference between appearance and reality. Furthermore, the development of memory appears to be related to the spontaneous use of rehearsal strategies. Finally, development of other skills, such as quantitative, visuospatial, and reasoning skills, appear to involve the ability to use rule-based processes and increasing more subtle strategies.

3. **What kinds of changes occur with the development of the brain?** Overall, neurophysiological development entails increases in neuronal connection complexity with decreases in the actual numbers of neurons used in the brain. The maturation of central nervous system structures likewise shows increasing complexity in structures, and some studies show cyclical patterns of discontinuous hemispheric development.

4. **What are some of the developmental changes in cognition that occur during adulthood?** It appears that *fluid abilities*—involved in rapid cognitive processing in response to new cognitive tasks—first increase and then start to decline at some point in later life, whereas *crystallized abilities*—represented by the accumulation of knowledge—increase across the life span or at least gradually stabilize in later adulthood. In addition, *wisdom* (broadly defined as extraordinary insight, keen awareness, and exceptional judgment) generally increases with age, although there are exceptions. The next chapter, Intelligence, echoes some of these intricate issues in adult development.

THINKING ABOUT THINKING: FACTUAL, ANALYTICAL, CREATIVE, AND PRACTICAL QUESTIONS

1. According to Piaget, what are the main stages of cognitive development?
2. What are some of the key physiological changes that accompany cognitive development?
3. Compare and contrast Piagetian theory with Vygotskyan theory.
4. How do some of the findings based on information-processing theory complement the findings based on Piagetian theory?
5. Choose an area of cognition that interests you, and design an experiment that would use an information-processing approach to study the developmental trends in that area of cognition.
6. Design a task that can be used in a dynamic-assessment environment. Include the graded series of hints that would be given to the test-taker.
7. According to Piaget, egocentrism is a characteristic of cognition. In what ways do you observe that characteristic in your own thinking and in the thinking of others you know?
8. Suppose you are the group leader of a task force comprising two groups of volunteers: high-school students who are getting course credit for volunteering and retired workers who want to volunteer their services to their community. Assuming that the trends regarding fluid versus crystallized intelligence apply to these individuals, what kinds of tasks would you assign to the younger and the older workers to take full advantage of their respective abilities?

KEY TERMS

accommodation 436
assimilation 436
centration 438
cognitive development 432
competence theory 445
concrete operations 439
conservation 439
dynamic assessment environment 448
egocentric 438
equilibration 436
formal-operational stage 442
information-processing theorists 449
internalization 447
object permanence 437
performance theory 445
plasticity 462
preoperational stage 438
representational thought 438
reversible 441
sensorimotor stage 437
static assessment environment 448
wisdom 463
zone of proximal development (ZPD) 447

ANNOTATED SUGGESTED READINGS

Baltes, P. B., & Smith, J. (1990). Toward a psychology of wisdom and its ontogenesis. In R. J. Sternberg (Ed.), *Wisdom: Its nature, origins, and development* (pp. 87–120). New York: Cambridge University Press. Baltes, arguably the world leader in the study of wisdom, presents in a clear fashion his theory of wisdom, as well as experiments testing it.

Damon, W. (Series Ed.), & Kuhn, P., & Siegler, R. S. (Vol. Eds.). (1998). *Handbook of child psychology: Vol. 2. Cognition, perception, and language.* New York: Wiley. A comprehensive, somewhat high-level account of cognitive development.

Siegler, R. S. (1996). *Emerging minds.* New York: Oxford University Press. A complete review of Siegler's ground-breaking work on cognitive development.

Sternberg, R. J., & Berg, C. A. (Eds.). (1992). *Intellectual development.* New York: Cambridge University Press. A review of almost all modern theories of intellectual development.

HUMAN AND ARTIFICIAL INTELLIGENCE

CHAPTER OUTLINE

EXPLORING COGNITIVE PSYCHOLOGY

MEASURES AND STRUCTURES OF INTELLIGENCE
- History of Intelligence Testing and Scoring
- Intelligence Scales
- Factor Analysis of Intelligence

INFORMATION PROCESSING AND INTELLIGENCE
- Process Timing Theories
- The Componential Theory and Complex Problem Solving
- Biological Bases of Intelligence

ALTERNATIVE APPROACHES TO INTELLIGENCE
- Cultural Context and Intelligence
- Gardner: Multiple Intelligences
- Sternberg: The Triarchic Theory

ARTIFICIAL INTELLIGENCE: COMPUTER SIMULATIONS
- Can a Computer Program Be "Intelligent"?
- Questions About the Intelligence of Intelligent Programs

IMPROVING INTELLIGENCE: EFFECTIVE, INEFFECTIVE, AND QUESTIONABLE STRATEGIES

SUMMARY

THINKING ABOUT THINKING: FACTUAL, ANALYTICAL, CREATIVE, AND PRACTICAL QUESTIONS

KEY TERMS

ANNOTATED SUGGESTED READINGS

Exploring Cognitive Psychology

1. What are the key issues in measuring intelligence? How do different researchers and theorists approach the issues?
2. What are some information-processing approaches to intelligence?
3. What are some alternative views of intelligence?
4. How have researchers attempted to simulate intelligence, using machines such as computers?
5. Can intelligence be improved, and if so, how?

Investigating Cognitive Psychology

Before you read about how cognitive psychologists view intelligence, try responding to a few tasks that require you to use your own intelligence:

1. Candle is to tallow as tire is to (a) automobile, (b) round, (c) rubber, (d) hollow.
2. Complete this series: 100%, .75, 1/2 ; (a) whole, (b) one eighth, (c) one fourth.
3. The first three items form one series. Complete the analogus second series that starts with the fourth item:

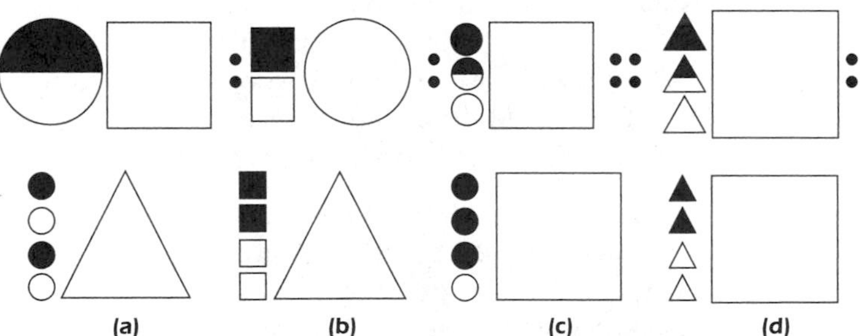

4. You are at a party of truth-tellers and liars. The truth-tellers always tell the truth, and the liars always lie. You meet someone new. He tells you that he just heard a conversation in which a girl said she was a liar. Is the person you met a liar or a truth-teller?

Each of the preceding tasks is believed, at least by some cognitive psychologists, to require some degree of intelligence. (The answers are at the end of this section.) Intelligence is a concept that can be viewed as tying together all of cognitive psychology. Just what is intelligence? In 1921, when the editors of the *Journal of Educational Psychology* asked 14 famous psychologists that question, the responses varied but generally embraced these two themes: **Intelligence** involves (a) the capacity to learn from experience and (b) the ability to adapt to the surrounding environment. Sixty-five years later (R. J. Sternberg & Detterman, 1986), 24 cognitive psychologists with expertise in intelligence research were asked the same question. They, too, underscored the importance of learning from experience and adapting to the environment. They also broadened the definition to emphasize the importance of *metacognition*—people's understanding and control of their own thinking processes. Contemporary experts also more heavily emphasized the role of culture, pointing out that what is considered intelligent in one culture may be considered stupid in another culture. To summarize, *intelligence* is the capacity to learn from experience, using metacognitive processes to enhance learning, and the ability to adapt to the surrounding environment, which may require different adaptations within different social and cultural contexts.

According to the *Oxford English Dictionary,* the word *intelligence* entered our language in about the twelfth century. Today, we can look up *intelligence* in numerous dictionaries, but most of us still have our own *implicit* (unstated) ideas about what it means to be smart; that is, we have our own implicit theories of intelligence. We use our implicit theories in many social situations, such as when we meet people or when we describe people we know as being very smart or not so smart.

Within our implicit theories of intelligence, we also recognize that intelligence has different meanings in different contexts. A smart salesperson may show a different kind of intelligence than a smart neurosurgeon or a smart accountant, each of whom may show a different kind of intelligence than a smart choreographer, composer, athlete, or sculptor. Often, we use our implicit and context-relevant definitions of intelligence to make assessments of intelligence. Is your mechanic smart enough to find and fix the problem in your car? Is your physician smart enough to find and treat your health problem? Is this attractive person smart enough to hold your interest in a conversation?

Explicit definitions of intelligence also frequently take on an assessment-oriented focus. In fact, some psychologists, such as Edwin Boring (1923), have been content to define *intelligence* as whatever it is that the tests measure. This definition, unfortunately, is circular because according to it, the nature of intelligence is what is tested, but what is tested must necessarily be determined by the nature of intelligence. Although most cognitive psychologists do not go to that extreme, the tradition of attempting to understand intelligence by measuring various aspects of intelligence has a long history.

By the way, the answers to the questions in the chapter opener are as follows:

1. Candles are frequently made of tallow, just as tires are frequently made of (c) rubber.
2. 100%, .75, and 1/2 are quantities that successively decrease by 1/4; to complete the series, the answer is (c) one fourth, which is a further decrease by 1/4.
3. The first series was a circle and a square, followed by two squares and a circle, followed by three circles and a square; the second series was three triangles and a square, which would be followed by (b), four squares and a triangle.
4. The person you met is clearly a liar. If the girl about whom this person was talking were a truth-teller, she would have said that she was a truth-teller. If she were a liar, she would have lied and said that she was a truth-teller also.

Thus, regardless of whether the girl were a truth-teller or a liar, she would have said that she was a truth-teller. Because the man you met has said that she said she was a liar, he must be lying and hence must be a liar.

Measures and Structures of Intelligence

History of Intelligence Testing and Scoring

Contemporary measurements of intelligence usually can be traced to one of two very different historical traditions. One tradition concentrated on lower level, *psychophysical abilities* (such as sensory acuity, physical strength, and motor coordination); the other focused on higher level, *judgmental abilities* (which we traditionally describe as related to thinking). Stop for a moment to think about yourself and your close associates. How would you assess yourself and your associates in terms of intelligence? When making these assessments, do psychophysical abilities seem more important, or do judgment abilities seem more important to you?

Francis Galton (1822–1911) believed that intelligence is a function of psychophysical abilities, and for several years, Galton maintained a well-equipped laboratory where visitors could have themselves measured on a variety of psychophysical tests. These tests measured a broad range of psychophysical skills and sensitivities, such as *weight discrimination* (the ability to notice small differences in the weights of objects), *pitch sensitivity* (the ability to hear small differences between musical notes), and physical strength (Galton, 1883). One of the many enthusiastic followers of Galton, Clark Wissler (1901), attempted to detect links among the assorted tests, which would unify the various dimensions of psychophysically based intelligence. Much to Wissler's dismay, no unifying associations could be detected. Moreover, the psychophysical tests did not predict college grades. Thus, the psychophysical approach to assessing intelligence soon faded almost into oblivion, although it would reappear many years later.

An alternative to the psychophysical approach was developed by Alfred Binet (1857–1911). He and his collaborator, Theodore Simon, also attempted to assess intelligence, but their goal was much more practical than purely scientific. Binet had been asked to devise a procedure for distinguishing normal from mentally retarded learners (Binet & Simon, 1916). Thus, Binet and his collaborator set out to measure intelligence as a function of the ability to learn within an academic setting. In Binet's view, judgment is the key to intelligence, not psychophysical acuity, strength, or skill.

For Binet (Binet & Simon, 1916), intelligent thought—mental judgment—comprises three distinct elements: direction, adaptation, and criticism. Think about how you are intelligently using these elements yourself at this moment: *Direction* involves knowing what has to be done and how to do it; *adaptation* refers to customizing a strategy for performing a task, and then monitoring that strategy while implementing it; and *criticism* is your ability to critique your own thoughts and actions. The importance of direction and adaptation certainly fits with contemporary views of intelligence, and Binet's notion of criticism actually seems prescient, considering the current appreciation of metacognitive processes as a key aspect of intelligence.

Initially, when Binet and Simon developed their intelligence test, they were interested in some means of comparing the intelligence of a given child with that of other children of the same chronological (physical) age. For their purposes, they sought to determine each child's *mental age*—the average level of intelligence for a person of a given age. Thus, a mental age of 7 refers to the level of thinking reached by an average 7-year-old. Mental ages worked just fine for comparing a given 7-year-old with other 7-year-olds, but the use of mental ages made it difficult to compare relative intelligence in children of differing chronological ages.

William Stern (1912) suggested instead that we evaluate people's intelligence by using an *intelligence quotient (IQ):* a ratio of mental age (MA) divided by chronological age (CA), multiplied by 100 (see Figure 14.1). This ratio can be expressed mathematically as follows: $IQ = (MA/CA) \times 100$. Thus, if Joan's mental age of 5 equals her chronological age of 5, then her intelligence is average, and her IQ is 100, because $(5/5)(100) = 100$. When mental age exceeds chronological age, the ratio will lead to an IQ score above 100, and when chronological age exceeds mental age, the ratio will lead to an IQ score below 100. Intelligence scores that are expressed in terms of a ratio of mental age to chronological age are termed *ratio IQs.*

For various reasons, ratio IQs, too, proved inadequate. For example, increases in mental age slow down at about age 16 years. An 8-year-old with a mental age of 12 years is pretty smart. On the other hand, do you feel sure that a 40-year-old with a mental age of 60 is similarly intelligent, even though the ratio IQ is the same for the 8-year-old and the 40-year-old? What does a mental age of 60 mean? Today, psychologists rarely use IQs based on mental ages. Instead, researchers have turned to measurement comparisons based on assumed normal distributions of test scores within large populations. Scores based on deviations from the middle score in a normal distribution of scores on a test of intelligence are termed *deviation IQs.* Many cognitive theorists believe that IQs provide only incomplete measurement of intelligence, as will be discussed later.

FIGURE 14.1 **NORMAL DISTRIBUTION OF DEVIATION IQs**

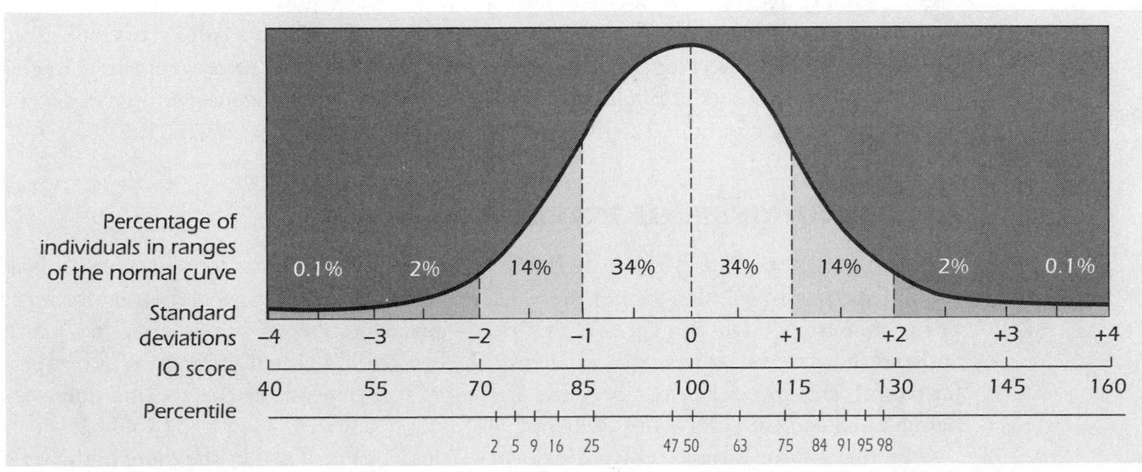

This figure shows a normal distribution as it applies to IQ, including identifying labels that are sometimes used to characterize different levels of IQ. It is important not to take these labels too seriously, as they are only loose characterizations, not scientific descriptions of performance.

Intelligence Scales

Lewis Terman of Stanford University built on Binet and Simon's work in Europe and constructed the earliest version of what has come to be called the *Stanford–Binet Intelligence Scales* (Terman & Merrill, 1937, 1973; R. L. Thorndike, Hagen, & Sattler, 1986; see Table 14.1). For years, the Stanford–Binet test was the standard for intelligence tests, and it is still widely used. The competitive Wechsler scales, named for their creator, David Wechsler, are probably even more widely used, however.

There are three levels of the Wechsler intelligence scales, including the third edition of the *Wechsler Adult Intelligence Scale (WAIS-III),* the third edition of the *Wechsler Intelligence Scale for Children (WISC-III),* and the *Wechsler Preschool and Primary Scale of Intelligence (WPPSI).* The Wechsler tests yield three scores: a verbal score, a performance score, and an overall score. The verbal score is based on tests such as *vocabulary* and *verbal similarities,* in which the test-taker has to say how two things are similar. The performance score is based on tests such as *picture completion,* which requires identification of a missing part in a picture of an object; and *picture arrangement,* which requires rearrangement of a scrambled set of cartoonlike pictures into an order that tells a coherent story. The overall score is a combination of the verbal and the performance scores. Table 14.2 shows the types of items from each of the Wechsler adult-scale subtests, which you may wish to compare with those of the Stanford–Binet

Wechsler, like Binet, had a conception of intelligence that went beyond what his own test measured. Although Wechsler clearly believed in the worth of attempting to measure intelligence, he did not limit his conception of intelligence to test scores. Wechsler believed that intelligence is central in our everyday lives. Intelligence is not represented just by a test score or even by what we do in school. We use our intelligence not just in taking tests and in doing homework, but also in relating to people, in performing our jobs effectively, and in managing our lives in general.

A focus on the measurement of intelligence is only one of several approaches to theory and research on intelligence. At least two of the key issues in the approach to studying intelligence have arisen in earlier chapters of this book, in regard to other topics in cognitive psychology. In particular, cognitive psychologists often ask, (a) Should we focus on the measurement of intelligence or on the processes of intelligence? (b) What underlies intelligence: a person's genetic inheritance, a person's acquired attributes, or some kind of interaction between the two?

Factor Analysis of Intelligence

Psychologists interested in the structure of intelligence have relied on factor analysis as the indispensable tool for their research. **Factor analysis** is a statistical method for separating a construct—intelligence in this case—into a number of hypothetical factors or abilities that the researchers believe to form the basis of individual differences in test performance. The specific factors derived, of course, still depend on the specific questions being asked and the tasks being evaluated.

Factor analysis is based on studies of correlation. The idea is that the more highly two tests are correlated, the more likely they are to measure the same thing. In research on intelligence, a factor analysis might involve these steps: (a) Give a large number of people several different tests of ability, (b) determine the correlations among all those tests, and (c) statistically analyze those correlations to simplify them into a relatively small number of factors that summarize people's performance on the tests. The investigators in this area

TABLE 14.1 THE *STANFORD–BINET INTELLIGENCE SCALE*

The sample questions used throughout this chapter are not actual questions from any of the scales; they are intended only to illustrate the types of questions that might appear in each of the main content areas of the tests. How would you respond to these questions? What do your responses indicate about your intelligence?

Content Area	Explanation of Tasks/Questions	Example of a Possible Task/Question
Verbal Reasoning		
Vocabulary	Define the meaning of a word.	What does the word *diligent* mean?
Comprehension	Show an understanding of why the world works as it does.	Why do people sometimes borrow money?
Absurdities	Identify the odd or absurd feature of a picture.	(Recognize that ice hockey players do not ice-skate on lakes into which swimmers in bathing suits are diving.)
Verbal relations	Tell how three of four items are similar to one another yet different from the fourth item.	(Note that an apple, a banana, and an orange can be eaten, but a mug cannot be.)
Quantitative Reasoning		
Number series	Complete a series of numbers.	Given the numbers 1, 3, 5, 7, 9, what number would you expect to come next?
Quantitative	Solve simple arithmetic-word problems.	If María has six apples, and she wants to divide them evenly among herself and her two best friends, how many apples will she give to each friend?
Figural/Abstract Reasoning		
Pattern analysis	Figure out a puzzle in which the test-taker must combine pieces representing parts of geometric shapes, fitting them together to form a particular geometric shape.	Fit together these pieces to form a (geometric shape).
Short-Term Memory		
Memory for sentences	Listen to a sentence, then repeat it back exactly as the examiner said it.	Repeat this sentence back to me: "Harrison went to sleep late and awoke early the next morning."
Memory for digits	Listen to a series of digits (numbers), then repeat the numbers either forward or backward or both.	Repeat these numbers backward: "9, 1, 3, 6."
Memory for objects	Watch the examiner point to a series of objects in a picture, then point to the same objects in exactly the same sequence in which the examiner did so.	(Point to the carrot, then the hoe, then the flower, then the scarecrow, then the baseball.)

TABLE 14.2 THE *WECHSLER ADULT INTELLIGENCE SCALE*

Based on the content areas and the kinds of questions shown here, how does the Wechsler differ from the Stanford–Binet?

CONTENT AREA	EXPLANATION OF TASKS/QUESTIONS	EXAMPLE OF A POSSIBLE TASK/QUESTION
Verbal Scale		
Comprehension	Answer questions of social knowledge.	What does it mean when people say, "A stitch in time saves nine"? Why are convicted criminals put into prison?
Vocabulary	Define the meaning of a word.	What does *persistent* mean? What does *archaeology* mean?
Information	Supply generally known information.	Who is Chelsea Clinton? What are six New England states?
Similarities	Explain how two things or concepts are similar.	In what ways are an ostrich and a penguin alike? In what ways are a lamp and a heater alike?
Arithmetic	Solve simple arithmetic-word problems.	If Paul has $14.43, and he buys two sandwiches, which cost $5.23 each, how much change will he receive? How many hours will it take to travel 1200 miles if you are traveling 60 miles per hour?
Digit span	Listen to a series of digits (numbers), then repeat the numbers either forward, backward, or both.	Repeat these numbers backward: "9, 1, 8, 3, 6." Repeat these numbers, just as I am telling you: "6, 9, 3, 2, 8."
Performance Scale		
Object assembly	Put together a puzzle by combining pieces to form a particular common object.	Put together these pieces to make something. 
Block design	Use patterned blocks to form a design that looks identical to a design shown by the examiner.	Assemble the blocks at the left to match the design at the right. 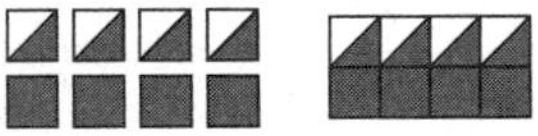
Picture completion	Tell what is missing from each picture.	What is missing from this picture? 
Picture arrangement	Put a set of cartoonlike pictures into chronological order, so that they tell a coherent story.	Arrange these pictures in an order that tells a story, and then tell what is happening in the story. 
Digit symbol	When given a key matching particular symbols to particular numerals, use the sequence of symbols to transcribe from symbols to numerals,	Look carefully at the key, showing which symbols correspond to which numerals. In the blanks, write the correct numeral for the symbol above each blank. ○ □ ⊗ ◇ ⊖ / 1 2 3 4 5 □ ◇ ⊖ □ ○ ⊗ ◇ ⊖

have generally agreed on and followed this procedure; yet the resulting factorial structures of intelligence have differed among different theorists. Among the many competing factorial theories, the main ones have probably been those of Spearman, Thurstone, Guilford, Cattell, Vernon, and Carroll. Figure 14.2 contrasts four of these theories.

FIGURE 14.2 **COMPARISONS AMONG SOME OF THE STRUCTURAL APPROACHES TO INTELLIGENCE**

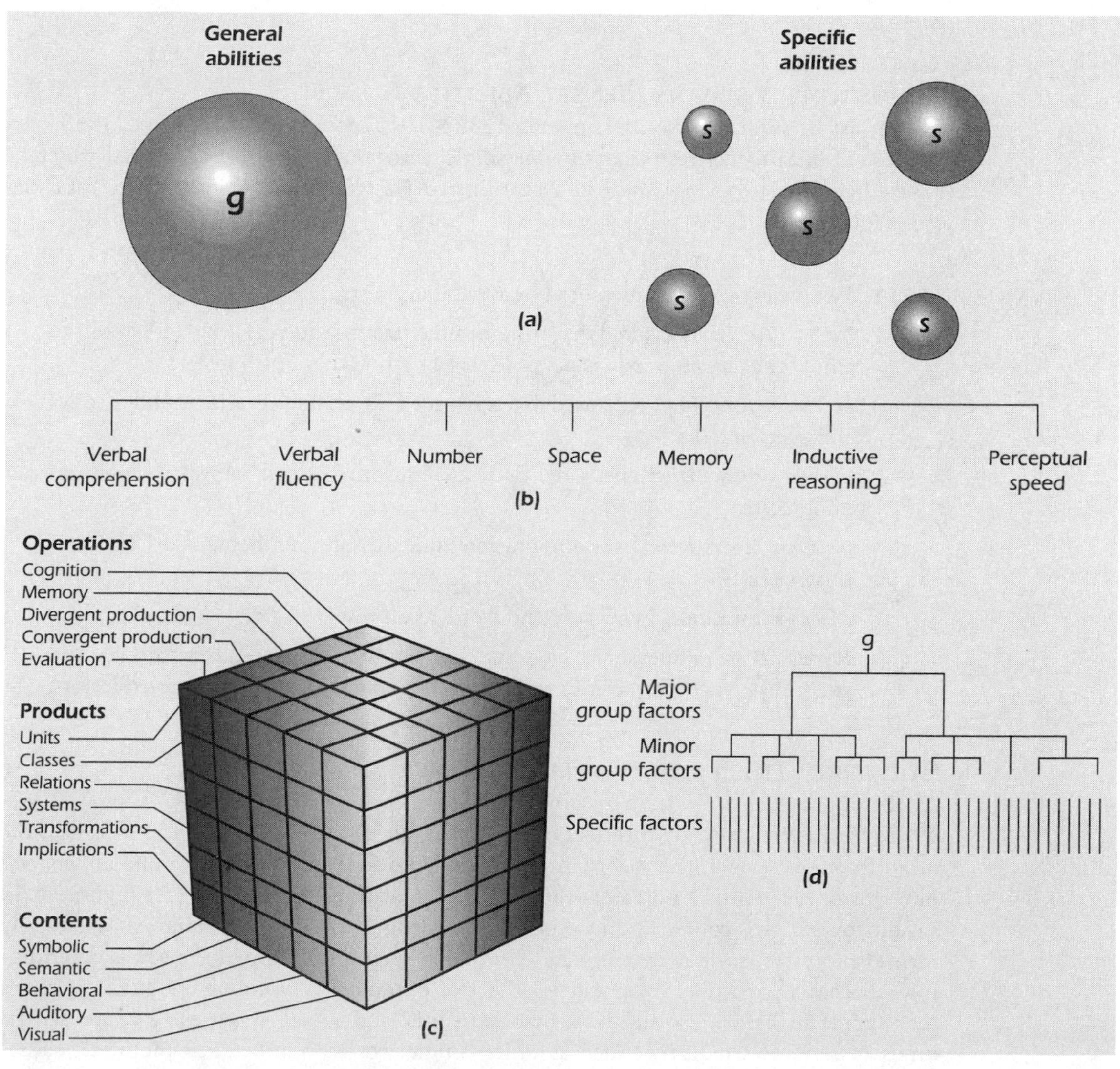

Although Spearman, Thurstone, Guilford, and Vernon all used factor analysis to determine the factors underlying intelligence, they all reached different conclusions regarding the structure of intelligence. Which model most simply yet comprehensively describes the structure of intelligence as you understand it? How do particular models of intelligence shape our understanding of intelligence?

SPEARMAN: THE "G" FACTOR

Charles Spearman (1863–1945) is usually credited with inventing factor analysis (Spearman, 1927). Using factor-analytic studies, Spearman concluded that intelligence can be understood in terms of both a single general factor that pervades performance on all tests of mental ability and a set of specific factors, each of which is involved in performance on only a single type of mental-ability test (e.g., arithmetic computations). In Spearman's view, the specific factors are of only casual interest, due to the narrow applicability of these factors. To Spearman, the general factor, which he labeled **"g,"** provides the key to understanding intelligence. Spearman believed *g* to be due to "mental energy."

THURSTONE: PRIMARY MENTAL ABILITIES

In contrast to Spearman, Louis Thurstone (1887–1955) concluded (Thurstone, 1938) that the core of intelligence resides not in one single factor but in seven such factors, which he referred to as *primary mental abilities.* According to Thurstone, the primary mental abilities are as follows:

1. *Verbal comprehension:* measured by vocabulary tests;
2. *Verbal fluency:* measured by time-limited tests requiring the test-taker to think of as many words as possible that begin with a given letter;
3. *Inductive reasoning:* measured by tests such as analogies and number-series completion tasks;
4. *Spatial visualization:* measured by tests requiring mental rotation of pictures of objects;
5. *Number:* measured by computation and simple mathematical problem-solving tests;
6. *Memory:* measured by picture and word-recall tests;
7. *Perceptual speed:* measured by tests that require the test-taker to recognize small differences in pictures, or to cross out the *a*'s in strings of varied letters.

GUILFORD: THE STRUCTURE OF INTELLECT

At the opposite extreme from Spearman's single g-factor model is J. P. Guilford's (1967, 1982, 1988) **structure-of-intellect (SOI)** model, which includes up to 150 factors of the mind in one version of the theory. According to Guilford, intelligence can be understood in terms of a cube that represents the intersection of three dimensions (see Figure 14.2): various operations, contents, and products. According to Guilford, *operations* are simply mental processes, such as memory and evaluation (making judgments, such as determining whether a particular statement is of fact or opinion). *Contents* are the kinds of terms that appear in a problem, such as semantic (words) and visual (pictures). *Products* are the kinds of responses required, such as units (single words, numbers, or pictures), classes (hierarchies), and implications (see Figure 14.2).

If you think that more than 100 factors are too many, you are not alone. Quite a few psychologists agree with you (e.g., H. J. Eysenck, 1967; Horn & Knapp, 1973). Perhaps

Guilford's most valuable contribution was to suggest that we consider various kinds of mental operations, contents, and products in our views and our assessments of intelligence.

Cattell, Vernon, and Carroll: Hierarchical Models

A more parsimonious way of handling a number of factors of the mind is through a hierarchical model of intelligence. One such model, developed by Raymond Cattell (1971), proposed that general intelligence comprises two major subfactors, both of which were described in chapter 13: *fluid ability* (speed and accuracy of abstract reasoning, especially for novel problems) and *crystallized ability* (accumulated knowledge and vocabulary). Subsumed within these two major subfactors are other, more specific factors. A similar view was proposed by Philip E. Vernon (1971), who made a general division between practical-mechanical and verbal-educational abilities.

More recently, John B. Carroll (1993) has proposed a hierarchical model of intelligence, based on his analysis of more than 460 data sets obtained between 1927 and 1987. His analysis encompasses more than 130,000 people from diverse walks of life and even countries of origin (although non-English-speaking countries are poorly represented among his data sets). The model Carroll proposed, based on his monumental undertaking, is a hierarchy comprising three strata: Stratum I, which includes many narrow, specific abilities (e.g., spelling ability, speed of reasoning); Stratum II, which includes various broad abilities (e.g., fluid intelligence, crystallized intelligence); and Stratum III, which is just a single general intelligence, much like Spearman's *g*. Of these strata, the most interesting is the middle stratum, which is neither too narrow nor too all-encompassing.

In addition to fluid intelligence and crystallized intelligence, Carroll includes in the middle stratum learning and memory processes, visual perception, auditory perception, facile production of ideas (similar to verbal fluency), and speed (which includes both sheer speed of response and speed of accurate responding). Although Carroll does not break new ground, in that many of the abilities in his model have been mentioned in other theories, he does masterfully integrate a large and diverse factor-analytic literature, thereby giving great authority to his model. Whereas the factor-analytic approach has tended to emphasize the structures of intelligence, the information-processing approach has tended to emphasize the operations of intelligence.

Information Processing and Intelligence

As previous chapters have shown, information-processing theorists are interested in studying how people mentally manipulate what they learn and know about the world. The ways in which various information-processing investigators study intelligence differ primarily in terms of the complexity of the processes being studied. Among the advocates of this approach have been Ted Nettelbeck, Arthur Jensen, Earl Hunt, Herbert Simon, and I. Each of these researchers has considered both the speed and the accuracy of information processing to be important factors in intelligence. In addition to speed and accuracy of processing, Hunt has considered verbal versus spatial skill, as well as attentional ability. Both Simon and I have considered intelligent processing of relatively complex cognitive tasks, such as those related to problem solving. First, we consider speed.

PROCESS TIMING THEORIES

INSPECTION TIME

Ted Nettelbeck and his colleagues (e.g., 1987; Nettelbeck & Lally, 1976; Nettelbeck & Rabbitt, 1992; see also Deary & Stough, 1996) have suggested a speed-related indicator of intelligence, involving the encoding of visual information for brief storage in working memory. If you were implementing Nettelbeck's technique for measuring inspection time, you would do as follows: For each of a number of trials, on a computer monitor, present a fixation cue (a dot in the area where a target figure will appear) for 500 milliseconds; then wait 360 milliseconds, following which you would present the target stimulus for a particular interval of time; finally, you would present a *visual mask* (a stimulus that erases the trace in iconic memory).

The target stimulus comprises two vertical lines of unequal length (e.g., 25 mm vs. 35 mm), which are aligned at the top by a horizontal crossbar. The shorter of the two lines may appear on either the right or the left side of the stimulus. The visual mask is a pair of lines that is thicker and longer than the two lines of the target stimulus. The task is to inspect the target stimulus and then indicate the side on which the shorter line appeared by pressing either a left- or a right-hand button on a keypad connected to a computer that records the responses.

The key variable is the length of time for the presentation of the target stimulus, not the speed of responding by pressing the button. Nettelbeck operationally defined *inspection time* as the length of time for presentation of the target stimulus after which the participant still responds with at least 90% accuracy in indicating the side on which the shorter line appeared. Nettelbeck (1987) found that shorter inspection times correlate with higher scores on intelligence tests (e.g., various subscales of the WAIS) among differing populations of participants. Other investigators have confirmed this finding (e.g., Deary & Stough, 1996).

CHOICE REACTION TIME

Arthur Jensen (1979) emphasized a different aspect of information-processing speed; specifically, he proposed that intelligence can be understood in terms of speed of neuronal conduction. In other words, the smart person is someone whose neural circuits conduct information rapidly. When Jensen proposed this notion, direct measures of neural-conduction velocity were not readily available, so Jensen primarily studied a proposed proxy for measuring neural-processing speed: *choice reaction time*—the time it takes to select one answer from among several possibilities.

For example, suppose that you are one of Jensen's participants. You might be seated in front of a set of lights on a board (see Figure 14.3). When one of the lights flashed, you would be expected to extinguish it by pressing as rapidly as possible a button beneath the correct light. The experimenter would then measure your speed in performing this task.

Jensen (1982) found that participants with higher IQs (of which, of course, you would be one) are faster than participants with lower IQs in their *reaction time* (RT), the time between when a light comes on and the finger leaves the home (central) button. In some studies, participants with higher IQs also showed a faster *movement time* (MT), the time between letting the finger leave the home button and hitting the button under the light. Based on such tasks, T. E. Reed and Jenson (1991, 1993) propose that their findings may be due to increased central nerve-conduction velocity, although at present this proposal remains speculative.

FIGURE 14.3 **JENSEN'S APPARATUS**

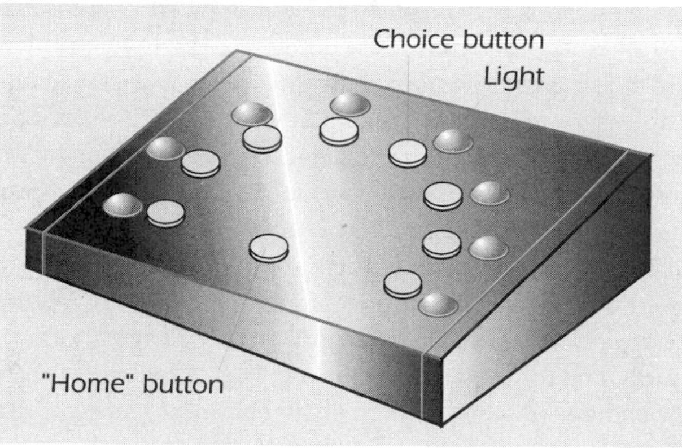

To measure choice reaction time, Jensen used an apparatus like the one shown here.

More recently, researchers have suggested that various findings regarding choice reaction time may be influenced by the number of response alternatives and the visual-scanning requirements of Jensen's apparatus, rather than being due to the speed of reaction time alone (Bors, MacLeod, & Forrin, 1993). In particular, Bors and his colleagues found that manipulating the number of buttons and the size of the visual angle of the display could reduce the correlation between IQ and reaction time. Thus, the relation between reaction time and intelligence is unclear.

Lexical Access Speed and Speed of Simultaneous Processing

Like Jensen, Earl Hunt (1978) has suggested that intelligence be measured in terms of speed. However, Hunt has been particularly interested in verbal intelligence, and so Hunt has focused on *lexical-access speed*—the speed with which we can retrieve information about words (e.g., letter names) stored in our long-term memories. To measure this speed, Hunt proposed using a letter-matching, reaction-time task (Posner & Mitchell, 1967).

Earl Hunt *is a professor of psychology and adjunct professor of computer science at the University of Washington. He has done major work on computer-simulation models of inductive reasoning, on the nature of intelligence, and on drug-induced alterations of memory and reasoning.*

For example, suppose that you are one of Hunt's participants. You would be shown pairs of letters, such as "A A," "A a," or "A b." For each pair, you would be asked to indicate whether the letters constitute a match in name (e.g., "A a" match in name of letter of the alphabet but "A b" do not). You would also be given a simpler task, in which you would be asked to indicate whether the letters match physically (e.g., "A A" are physically identical, whereas "A a" are not). Hunt would be particularly interested in discerning the difference between your speed for the first set of tasks, involving name matching, and your speed for the second set, involving matching of physical characteristics. Hunt would consider the difference in your reaction time for each task to indicate a measure of your speed of lexical access. Thus, he would *subtract* from his equation the physical-match reaction time. For Hunt, the response time in indicating that "A A" is a physical match is unimportant. What interests him is a more complex reaction time—that for recognizing names of letters. He and his colleagues have found that students with lower verbal ability take longer to gain access to lexical information than do students with higher verbal ability.

Earl Hunt and Marcy Lansman (1982) also studied people's ability to divide their attention as a function of intelligence. For example, suppose that you are asked to solve mathematical problems and simultaneously to listen for a tone and press a button as soon as you hear it. We can expect that you would both solve the math problems effectively and respond quickly to hearing the tone. According to Hunt and Lansman, more intelligent people are better able to timeshare between two tasks and to perform both effectively.

In sum, process timing theories attempt to account for differences in intelligence by appealing to differences in the speed of various forms of information processing—inspection time, choice reaction time, and lexical access timing have all been found to correlate with measures of intelligence. These findings suggest that higher intelligence may be related to the speed of various information-processing abilities, including (a) encoding information more rapidly into working memory, (b) accessing information in long-term memory more rapidly, and (c) responding more rapidly. Why would more rapid encoding, retrieval, and responding be associated with higher intelligence test scores—do rapid information-processors learn more?

More recent research on learning in aged persons investigated whether there is a link between age-related slowing of information processing and (a) initial encoding and recall of information and (b) long-term retention (Nettelbeck, Rabbitt, Wilson, & Batt, 1996; see also Bors & Forrin, 1995). The findings suggest that the relation between inspection time and intelligence may not be related to learning. In particular, Nettelbeck et al. find that there is a difference between initial recall and actual long-term learning—whereas initial recall performance is mediated by processing speed (older, slower participants showed deficits), longer-term retention of new information (preserved in older participants) is mediated by cognitive processes other than speed of processing, including rehearsal strategies. Thus, speed of information processing may influence initial performance on recall and inspection time tasks, but speed is not related to long-term learning. Perhaps faster information-processing aids participants in performance aspects of intelligence test tasks, rather than contributing to actual learning and intelligence. Clearly, this area requires more research to determine how information-processing speed relates to intelligence.

The Componential Theory and Complex Problem Solving

In my early work on intelligence, I began using cognitive approaches for studying information processing in more complex tasks, such as analogies, series problems (e.g., completing a numerical or figural series), and syllogisms (R. J. Sternberg, 1977, 1983, 1984a; see chapter 12). My goal was to find out just what it was that made some people more intelligent processors of information than others. My idea was to take the kinds of tasks used on conventional intelligence tests and to isolate the **components** of intelligence—the mental processes used in performing these tasks, such as translating a sensory input into a mental representation, transforming one conceptual representation into another, or translating a conceptual representation into a motor output (R. J. Sternberg, 1982b).

Componential analysis breaks down people's reaction times and error rates on these tasks in terms of the processes that make up the tasks. This kind of analysis revealed that people may solve analogies and similar tasks by using several component processes, among which are (a) encoding the terms of the problem; (b) inferring relations among at least some of the terms; (c) mapping the inferred relations to other terms, which would be presumed to show similar relations; and (d) applying the previously inferred relations to the new situations.

Consider the analogy, LAWYER : CLIENT :: DOCTOR : (a. PATIENT b. MEDICINE). To solve this analogy, you need to *encode* each term of the problem, which includes perceiving a term and retrieving information about it from memory. You then *infer* the relationship between lawyer and client—that the former provides professional services to the latter. You then *map* the relationship in the first half of the analogy to the second half of the analogy, noting that it will involve that same relationship. Finally, you *apply* that inferred relationship to generate the final term of the analogy, leading to the appropriate response of PATIENT. (Figure 14.4 shows how componential analysis would be applied to an analogy problem, *A* is to *B* as *C* is to *D,* where *D* is the solution.) Studying these components of information processing reveals more than measuring mental speed alone.

When measuring speed alone, I have found significant correlations between speed in executing these processes and performance on other, traditional intelligence tests. However, a more intriguing discovery is that participants who score higher on traditional intelligence tests take *longer* to encode the terms of the problem than do less intelligent participants, but they make up for the extra time by taking less time to perform the remaining components of the task. In general, more intelligent participants take longer during **global planning**—encoding the problem and formulating a general strategy for attacking the problem (or set of problems)—but they take less time for **local planning**—forming and implementing strategies for the details of the task (R. J. Sternberg, 1981).

FIGURE 14.4 **COMPONENTIAL ANALYSIS OF AN ANALOGY PROBLEM**

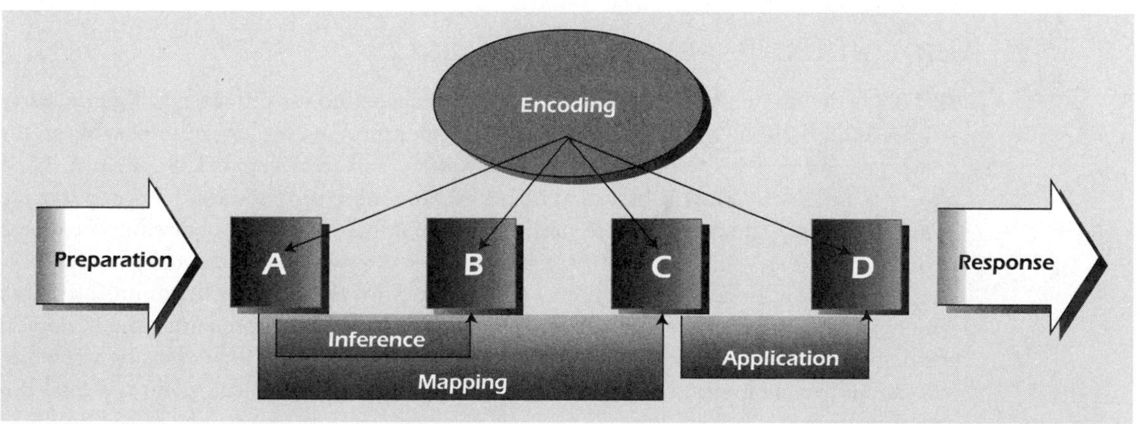

In solving an analogy problem, the problem solver must first encode the problem A *is to* B *as* C *is to* D*. The problem solver must then infer the relationship between* A *and* B*. Next, the problem solver must map the relationship between* A *and* B *to the relationship between* C *and each of the possible solutions to the analogy. Finally, the problem solver must apply the relationship to choose which of the possible solutions is the correct solution to the problem.*

The advantage of spending more time on global planning is the increased likelihood that the overall strategy will be correct. Thus, brighter people may take longer to do something than will less bright people when taking more time is advantageous. For example, the brighter person might spend more time researching and planning for writing a term paper, but less time in the actual writing of it. This same differential in time allocation has been shown in other tasks, as well (e.g., in solving physics problems, Larkin, McDermott, Simon, & Simon, 1980; see R. J. Sternberg, 1979, 1985a); that is, more intelligent people seem to spend more time planning for and encoding the problems they face, but less time engaging in the other components of task performance. This may relate to the previously mentioned metacognitive attribute many include in their notions of intelligence.

In a similarly cognitive approach, Herbert Simon has studied the intelligent information processing of people engaged in *complex problem solving* situations, such as when playing chess and performing logical derivations (Newell & Simon, 1972; Simon, 1976). For example, a simple, brief task might require the participant to view an arithmetic or geometric series, figure out the rule underlying the progression, and guess what numeral or geometric figure might come next; more complex tasks might include some of the tasks mentioned in chapter 11 (e.g., the water jugs problems; see Estes, 1982).

In Simon's work with Allen Newell and others, computer simulations were created that would solve these complex problems. The idea was to understand intelligence through highly complex problem solving in which solution times may be measured in minutes, rather than seconds. Simon was particularly interested in the limits imposed by working memory and by the ways in which more intelligent people organize and sequence the processes by which they solve problems. Just as more artificially intelligent computer programs can be designed to handle various procedures more efficiently, more intelligent humans should be able to coordinate their handling of mental procedures more efficiently. One way of studying mental efficiency is through biological analysis.

Biological Bases of Intelligence

Although the human brain is clearly the organ responsible for human intelligence, early studies (e.g., those by Karl Lashley and others) seeking to find biological indices of intelligence and other aspects of mental processes were a resounding failure, despite great efforts. As tools for studying the brain have become more sophisticated, however, we are beginning to see the possibility of finding physiological indicators of intelligence. Some investigators (e.g., Matarazzo, 1992) believe that we will have clinically useful psychophysiological indices of intelligence very early in the next millennium, although widely applicable indices will be much longer in coming. In the meantime, the biological studies we now have are largely correlational, showing statistical associations between biological and psychometric or other measures of intelligence. The studies do not establish causal relations.

For now, some of the current studies offer some appealing possibilities. For example, complex patterns of electrical activity in the brain, which are prompted by specific stimuli, appear to correlate with scores on IQ tests (Barrett & Eysenck, 1992). Several studies (e.g., McGarry-Roberts, Stelmack, & Campbell, 1992; P. A. Vernon & Mori, 1992) initially suggested that speed of conduction of neural impulses may correlate with intelligence, as measured by IQ tests. A follow-up study (Wickett & Vernon, 1994), however, failed to find a strong relation between neural-conduction velocity (as measured by neural-conduction speeds in a main nerve of the arm) and intelligence (as measured on the Multidimensional Aptitude Battery). Surprisingly, neural-conduction velocity appears to be a more powerful predictor of IQ scores for men than for women, so sex differences may account for some of the differences in the data (Wickett & Vernon, 1994). Additional studies on both males and females are needed.

An alternative approach to studying the brain suggests that neural efficiency may be related to intelligence; such an approach is based on studies of how the brain metabolizes *glucose* (simple sugar required for brain activity) during mental activities (see chapter 2, for more on PET and other brain-imaging techniques). Richard Haier and his colleagues (Haier, Siegel, Tang, Abel, & Buchsbaum, 1992) have cited several other researchers who support their own findings that higher intelligence correlates with reduced levels of glucose metabolism during problem-solving tasks—that is, smarter brains consume less sugar (and hence expend less effort) than do less smart brains doing the same task. Furthermore, Haier and his colleagues found that cerebral efficiency increases as a result of learning on a relatively complex task involving visuospatial manipulations (the computer game *Tetris).* As a result of practice, more intelligent participants show not only lower cerebral glucose metabolism overall, but also more specifically localized metabolism of glucose. In most areas of their brains, smarter participants show less glucose metabolism, but in selected areas of their brains (believed to be important to the task at hand), they show higher levels of glucose metabolism. Thus, more intelligent participants may have learned how to use their brains more efficiently to focus their thought processes on a given task.

More recent research by Haier and colleagues, however, suggests that the relationship between glucose metabolism and intelligence may be more complex (Haier, Chueh, et al., 1995; Larson, Haier, LaCasse, & Hazen, 1995). Whereas Haier, Chueh, et al. (1995) confirm the earlier findings of increased glucose metabolism in less smart participants (in this case, mildly retarded participants), the study by Larson et al. (1995) found, contrary to the earlier findings, that smarter participants had increased glucose metabolism relative to their average comparison group.

One problem with earlier studies is that the tasks used were not matched for difficulty level across groups of smart and average individuals. The Larson et al. study used tasks that were matched to the ability levels of the smarter and average participants and found that the smarter participants used more glucose. Moreover, the glucose metabolism was highest in the right hemisphere of the more intelligent participants performing the hard task—again suggesting selectivity of brain areas. What could be driving the increases in glucose metabolism? Currently, the key factor appears to be subjective task difficulty, with smarter participants in earlier studies simply finding the tasks too easy. Matching task difficulty to participants' abilities seems to indicate that smarter participants increase glucose metabolism when the task demands it. The preliminary findings in this area will need to be investigated further before any conclusive answers arise.

Some neuropsychological research (e.g., Dempster, 1991) suggests that performance on intelligence tests may not indicate a crucial aspect of intelligence: the ability to set goals, to plan how to meet them, and to execute those plans. Specifically, persons with lesions on the frontal lobe of the brain frequently perform quite well on standardized IQ tests, which require responses to questions within a highly structured situation, but which do not require much in the way of goal setting or planning. If intelligence involves the ability to learn from experience and to adapt to the surrounding environment, the ability to set goals and to design and implement plans cannot be ignored. An essential aspect of goal setting and planning is the ability to attend appropriately to relevant stimuli and to ignore or discount irrelevant stimuli.

What makes some responses appropriate or inappropriate and some stimuli irrelevant or relevant? The context in which they occur is key. Specifically, we cannot realistically study a brain or its contents and processes in isolation, without also considering the entire human being, including the interactions of that human being with the entire environmental context within which the person acts intelligently. Hence, many researchers and theorists urge us to take a more contextual view of intelligence. Furthermore, some alternative views of intelligence attempt to broaden the definition of intelligence to be more inclusive of people's varied abilities.

Alternative Approaches to Intelligence

According to **contextualists,** intelligence cannot be understood outside its real-world context. The context of intelligence may be viewed at any level of analysis, focusing narrowly, as on the home and family environment, or extending broadly, as on entire cultures. For example, even cross-community differences have been correlated with differences in performance on intelligence tests; such context-related differences include those of rural versus urban communities, low versus high proportions of teenagers to adults within communities, and low versus high socioeconomic status of communities (see Coon, Carey, & Fulker, 1992). Contextualists have been particularly intrigued by the effects of cultural context on intelligence.

In fact, contextualists consider intelligence so inextricably linked to culture that they view intelligence as something that a culture creates to define the nature of adaptive performance in that culture, and to account for why some people perform better than others on the tasks that the culture happens to value (R. J. Sternberg, 1985a). Theorists who endorse this model study just how intelligence relates to the external world in which the model is being applied and evaluated. In general, definitions and theories of intelligence will more effectively encompass cultural diversity by broadening in scope. Before exploring some of the contextual theories of intelligence, we will look at what prompted psychologists to believe that culture might play a role in how we define and assess intelligence.

Cultural Context and Intelligence

People in different cultures may have quite different ideas of what it means to be smart. For example, one of the more interesting cross-cultural studies of intelligence was performed by Michael Cole and his colleagues (Cole, Gay, Glick, & Sharp, 1971). These investigators asked adult members of the Kpelle tribe in Africa to sort terms representing concepts. In Western culture, when adults are given a sorting task on an intelligence test, more intelligent people will typically sort hierarchically. For example, they may sort names of different kinds of fish together, and then the word *fish* over that, with the name *animal* over *fish* and over *birds,* and so on. Less intelligent people will typically sort functionally. They may sort *fish* with *eat,* for example, because we eat fish, or *clothes* with *wear,* because we wear clothes. The Kpelle sorted functionally—even after investigators unsuccessfully tried to get the Kpelle spontaneously to sort hierarchically.

Finally, in desperation, one of the experimenters (Glick) asked a Kpelle to sort as a foolish person would sort. In response, the Kpelle quickly and easily sorted hierarchically. The Kpelle had been able to sort this way all along; they just hadn't done it because they viewed it as foolish—and they probably considered the questioners rather unintelligent for asking such stupid questions.

The Kpelle people are not the only ones who might question Western understandings of intelligence. In the Puluwat culture of the Pacific Ocean, for example, sailors navigate incredibly long distances, using none of the navigational aids that sailors from technologically advanced countries would need in order to get from one place to another (Gladwin, 1970). Were Puluwat sailors to devise intelligence tests for us and our fellow Americans, we and our compatriots might not seem very intelligent. Similarly, the highly skilled Puluwat sailors might not do well on American-crafted tests of intelligence. These and other observations have prompted quite a few theoreticians to recognize the importance of considering cultural context when assessing intelligence.

A study by Seymour Sarason and John Doris (1979) provides an example a little closer to home regarding the effects of cultural differences on intelligence tests. These researchers tracked the IQs of an immigrant population: Italian Americans. Less than a century ago, first-generation Italian-American children showed a median IQ of 87 (low average; range 76–100), even when nonverbal measures were used and when so-called mainstream American attitudes were considered. Some social commentators and intelligence researchers of the day pointed to heredity and other nonenvironmental factors as the basis for the low IQs—much as they do today for other minority groups.

For example, a leading researcher of the day, Henry Goddard, pronounced that 79% of immigrant Italians were "feebleminded" (he also asserted that about 80% of immigrant Jews, Hungarians, and Russians were similarly unendowed; H. J. Eysenck & Kamin, 1981). Goddard (1917) also asserted that moral decadence was associated with this deficit in intelligence; he recommended that the intelligence tests he used be administered to all immigrants and that all those he deemed substandard be selectively excluded from entering the United States. Stephen Ceci (1991) notes that the subsequent generations of Italian-American students who take IQ tests today show slightly above average IQs; other immigrant groups that Goddard had denigrated have shown similar "amazing" increases. Even the most fervent hereditarians would be unlikely to attribute such remarkable gains in so few generations to heredity. Cultural assimilation, including integrated education, seems a much more plausible explanation.

The preceding arguments may make it clear why it is so difficult to come up with a test that everyone would consider **culture-fair**—equally appropriate and fair for members of all cultures. If members of different cultures have different ideas of what it means to be intelligent, then the very behaviors that may be considered intelligent in one culture may be considered unintelligent in another. Take, for example, the concept of mental quickness. In mainstream U.S. culture, quickness is usually associated with intelligence. To say someone is "quick" is to say that the person is intelligent, and indeed, most group tests of intelligence are quite strictly timed, and even on individual tests of intelligence, the test-giver times some responses of the test-taker. Many information-processing theorists and even psychophysiological theorists focus on the study of intelligence as a function of mental speed.

In many cultures of the world, however, quickness is not at a premium. In these cultures, people may believe that more intelligent people do not rush into things. Even in our own culture, no one will view you as brilliant if you decide on a marital partner, a job, or a place to live in the 20 to 30 seconds you might normally have to solve an intelligence-test problem. Thus, given that there exist no perfectly culture-fair tests of intelligence, at least at present, how should we consider context when assessing and understanding intelligence?

Several researchers have suggested that providing **culture-relevant** tests is possible (e.g., Baltes, Dittmann-Kohli, & Dixon, 1984; Jenkins, 1979; Keating, 1984), that is, those which employ skills and knowledge that relate to the cultural experiences of the test-takers. Designing culture-relevant tests requires creativity and effort but is probably not impossible. For example, a study by Daniel Wagner (1978) investigated memory abilities—one aspect of intelligence as our culture defines it—in our culture versus the Moroccan culture. Wagner found that level of recall depended on the content that was being remembered, with culture-relevant content being remembered more effectively than nonrelevant content (e.g., when compared with Westerners, Moroccan rug merchants were better able to recall complex visual patterns on black-and-white photos of Oriental rugs). Wagner further suggested that when tests are not designed to minimize the effects of cultural differences, the key to culture-specific differences in memory may be the knowledge and use of metamemory strategies, rather than actual structural differences in memory (e.g., memory span and rates of forgetting).

Intricate patterns on Moroccan rugs were more easily remembered by Moroccan rug merchants than by Westerners. In contrast, Westerners more easily remembered information unfamiliar to Moroccan rug merchants.

In Kenya, Robert Sternberg and Elena Grigorenko (1997) and their colleagues have shown that rural Kenyan school children have substantial knowledge about natural herbal medicines they believe fight infection: Western children, of course, would not be able to identify any of these medicines. In short, making a test culturally relevant appears to involve much more than just removing specific linguistic barriers to understanding.

Stephen Ceci (Ceci & Roazzi, 1994) has found similar context effects in children's and adults' performance on a variety of tasks. Ceci suggests that the *social context* (e.g., whether a task is considered masculine or feminine), the *mental context* (e.g., whether a visuospatial task involves buying a home or burgling it), and the *physical context* (e.g., whether a task is presented at the beach or in a laboratory) all affect performance. For example, 14-year-old boys performed poorly on a task when it was couched as a cupcake-baking task but performed well when it was framed as a battery-charging task (Ceci & Bronfenbrenner, 1985). Brazilian maids had no difficulty with proportional reasoning when hypothetically purchasing food but had great difficulty with it when hypothetically purchasing medicinal herbs (Schliemann & Magalhües, 1990). Brazilian children whose poverty had forced them to become street vendors showed no difficulty in performing complex arithmetic computations when selling things but had great difficulty performing similar calculations in a classroom (Carraher, Carraher, & Schliemann, 1985). Thus, test performance may be affected by the context in which the test terms are presented. In this study, the investigators looked at the interaction of cognition and context. Several investigators have proposed theories that seek explicitly to examine this interaction within an integrated model of many aspects of intelligence. Such theories view intelligence as a complex system and are discussed in the next two sections.

GARDNER: MULTIPLE INTELLIGENCES

Howard Gardner *is a professor of education and adjunct professor of psychology at Harvard University. He is best known for his theory of multiple intelligences and for showing how the theory can be applied in educational settings. He has also done important work in neuropsychology as well as in the psychology of creativity.*

Howard Gardner (1983, 1993b) has proposed a **theory of multiple intelligences,** in which intelligence is not just a single, unitary construct. However, instead of speaking of multiple abilities that together constitute intelligence (e.g., Thurstone, 1938), Gardner (in press) speaks of eight distinct intelligences that are relatively independent of each other (see Table 14.3). Each is a separate system of functioning, although these systems can interact to produce what we see as intelligent performance. In looking at Gardner's list of intelligences, you might want to evaluate your own intelligences, perhaps rank ordering your strengths in each.

In some respects, Gardner's theory sounds like a factorial one because it specifies several abilities that are construed to reflect intelligence of some sort. However, Gardner views each ability as a separate intelligence, not just as a part of a single whole. Moreover, a crucial difference between Gardner's theory and factorial ones is in the sources of evidence Gardner used for identifying the eight intelligences. Gardner used converging operations, gathering evidence from multiple sources and types of data.

In particular, Gardner (1983, pp. 63–67) points to eight "signs" he used as criteria for detecting the existence of a discrete kind of intelligence:

1. Potential isolation by brain damage, in that the destruction or sparing of a discrete area of the brain (e.g., areas linked to verbal aphasia) may destroy or spare a particular kind of intelligent behavior;

TABLE 14.3 GARDNER'S EIGHT INTELLIGENCES

On which of Howard Gardner's eight intelligences do you show the greatest ability? In what contexts can you use your intelligences most effectively? (After Gardner, in press)

Type of Intelligence	Tasks Reflecting This Type of Intelligence
Linguistic intelligence	Used in reading a book; writing a paper, a novel, or a poem; and understanding spoken words
Logical-mathematical intelligence	Used in solving math problems, in balancing a checkbook, in solving a mathematical proof, and in logical reasoning
Spatial intelligence	Used in getting from one place to another, in reading a map, and in packing suitcases in the trunk of a car so that they all fit into a compact space
Musical intelligence	Used in singing a song, composing a sonata, playing a trumpet, or even appreciating the structure of a piece of music
Bodily-kinesthetic intelligence	Used in dancing, playing basketball, running a mile, or throwing a javelin
Interpersonal intelligence	Used in relating to other people, such as when we try to understand another person's behavior, motives, or emotions
Intrapersonal intelligence	Used in understanding ourselves—the basis for understanding who we are, what makes us tick, and how we can change ourselves, given our existing constraints on our abilities and our interests
Naturalist intelligence	Used in understanding patterns in nature

2. The existence of exceptional individuals (e.g., musical or mathematical prodigies) who demonstrate extraordinary ability (or deficit) in a particular kind of intelligent behavior;
3. An identifiable core operation or set of operations (e.g., detection of relationships among musical tones) that are essential to performance of a particular kind of intelligent behavior;
4. A distinctive developmental history leading from novice to master, along with disparate levels of expert performance (i.e., varying degrees of expressing this type of intelligence);
5. A distinctive evolutionary history, in which increases in intelligence may be plausibly associated with enhanced adaptation to the environment;
6. Supportive evidence from cognitive-experimental research, such as task-specific performance differences across discrete kinds of intelligence (e.g., visuospatial tasks vs. verbal tasks), accompanied by cross-task performance similarities within discrete kinds of intelligence (e.g., mental rotation of visuospatial imagery and recall memory of visuospatial images);
7. Supportive evidence from psychometric tests indicating discrete intelligences (e.g., differing performance on tests of visuospatial abilities vs. on tests of linguistic abilities);
8. Susceptibility to encoding in a symbol system (e.g., language, math, musical notation) or in a culturally devised arena (e.g., dance, athletics, theater,

engineering, or surgery as culturally devised expressions of bodily-kinesthetic intelligence).

Thus, although Gardner does not dismiss entirely the use of psychometric tests, the base of evidence used by Gardner does not rely on the factor analysis of various psychometric tests alone. In thinking about your own intelligences, how fully integrated do you believe them to be? How much do you perceive each type of intelligence as depending on any of the others?

Gardner's view of the mind is modular. *Modularity theorists* believe that different abilities—such as Gardner's intelligences—can be isolated as emanating from distinct portions or modules of the brain. Thus, a major task of existing and future research on intelligence is to isolate the portions of the brain responsible for each of the intelligences. Gardner has speculated as to at least some of these locales, but hard evidence for the existence of these separate intelligences has yet to be produced. Furthermore, Nettelbeck and Young (1996) question the strict modularity of Gardner's theory. Specifically, the phenomenon of preserved specific cognitive functioning in autistic savants (persons with severe social and cognitive deficits, but with corresponding high ability in a narrow domain) as evidence for modular intelligences may not be justified. According to Nettelbeck and Young, the narrow long-term memory and specific aptitudes of savants is not really intelligent. Thus, there may be reason to question the intelligence of inflexible modules.

STERNBERG: THE TRIARCHIC THEORY

Whereas Gardner emphasizes the separateness of the various aspects of intelligence, I tend to emphasize the extent to which they work together in my **triarchic theory of human intelligence** (R. J. Sternberg, 1985a, 1988c, 1996). According to the triarchic *(tri-,* "three"; *-archic,* "governed") theory, intelligence comprises three aspects, dealing with the relation of intelligence (a) to the internal world of the person, (b) to experience, and (c) to the external world. Figure 14.5 illustrates the parts of the theory and their interrelations.

HOW INTELLIGENCE RELATES TO THE INTERNAL WORLD

This part of the theory emphasizes the processing of information, which can be viewed in terms of three different kinds of components: (a) *metacomponents:* executive processes (i.e., metacognition) used to plan, monitor, and evaluate problem solving; (b) *performance components:* lower order processes used for implementing the commands of the metacomponents; and (c) *knowledge-acquisition components:* the processes used for learning how to solve the problems in the first place. The components are highly interdependent.

Suppose that you were asked to write a term paper. You would use metacomponents to decide on a topic, plan the paper, monitor the writing, and evaluate how well your finished product succeeds in accomplishing your goals for it. You would use knowledge-acquisition components for research to learn about the topic. You would use performance components for the actual writing. In practice, the three kinds of components do not function in isolation. Before actually writing the paper, you would first have to decide on a topic and then do some research. Similarly, your plans for writing the paper might change as you gather new information. It may turn out that there just is not enough information on particular aspects of the chosen topic, forcing you to shift your emphasis. Your plans also may change if particular aspects of the writing go more smoothly than others.

FIGURE 14.5	STERNBERG'S TRIARCHIC THEORY OF INTELLIGENCE

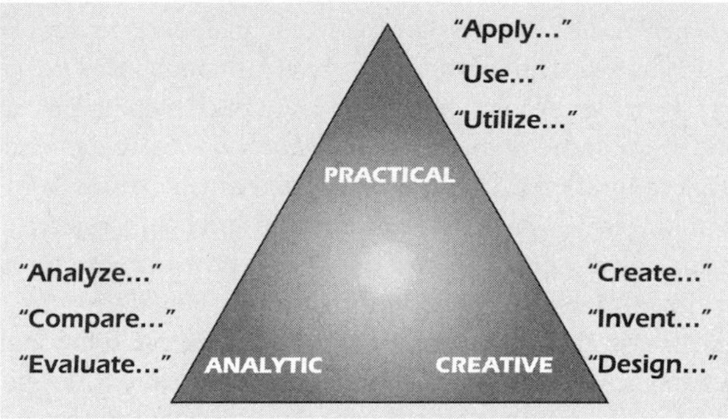

According to Robert Sternberg, intelligence comprises analytical, creative, and practical abilities. In analytical thinking, we try to solve familiar problems by using strategies that manipulate the elements of a problem or the relationships among the elements (e.g., comparing, analyzing); in creative thinking, we try to solve new kinds of problems that require us to think about the problem and its elements in a new way (e.g., inventing, designing); in practical thinking, we try to solve problems that apply what we know to everyday contexts (e.g., applying, using).

How Intelligence Relates to Experience

The theory also considers how prior experience may interact with all three kinds of information-processing components. That is, each of us faces tasks and situations with which we have varying levels of experience, ranging from a completely novel task, with which we have no previous experience, to a completely familiar task, with which we have vast, extensive experience. As a task becomes increasingly familiar, many aspects of the task may become *automatic,* requiring little conscious effort for determining what step to take next and how to implement that next step. A novel task makes demands on intelligence different from those of a task for which automatic procedures have been developed.

According to the triarchic theory, relatively novel tasks—such as visiting a foreign country, mastering a new subject, or acquiring a foreign language—demand more of a person's intelligence. On the other hand, a completely unfamiliar task may demand so much of the person as to be overwhelming. For example, if you were visiting a foreign country, you would probably not profit from enrolling in a course with unfamiliar abstract subject matter, taught in a language you do not understand. The most intellectually stimulating tasks are those that are challenging and demanding but not overwhelming.

How Intelligence Relates to the External World

The triarchic theory also proposes that the various components of intelligence are applied to experience in order to serve three functions in real-world contexts: adapting ourselves to our existing environments, shaping our existing environments to create new environments, and selecting new environments. You use adaptation when you learn the ropes in a new environment and try to figure out how to succeed in it. For example, when you first start college, you probably try to figure out the explicit and implicit rules of college life and how you can use these rules in order to succeed in the new environment. You also shape your environment, such as in deciding what courses to take and what activities to pursue. You may even try to shape the behavior of those around you. Finally, if you are unable either to adapt yourself or to shape your environment to suit you, you might consider selecting another environment—such as by transferring to a different college.

According to the triarchic theory, people may apply their intelligence to many different kinds of problems. For example, some people may be more intelligent in the face of abstract, academic problems, whereas others may be more intelligent in the face of concrete, practical problems. The theory does not define an intelligent person as someone who necessarily excels in all aspects of intelligence. Rather, intelligent persons know their own strengths and weaknesses and find ways in which to capitalize on their strengths and either to compensate for or to remediate their weaknesses. For example, a person who is strong in psychology but not in physics might choose as a physics project the creation of a physics aptitude test (which I did when I took physics). The point is to make the most of your strengths and to find ways to improve on or at least to live comfortably with your weaknesses.

In a recent comprehensive study testing the validity of the triarchic theory and its usefulness in improving performance, we found that matching students' instruction and assessment to their abilities does indeed lead to improved performance (R. J. Sternberg, Ferrari, Clinkenbeard, & Grigorenko, 1996). Teaching all students to use all of their analytic, creative, and practical abilities has resulted in improved school achievement for all students, whatever their ability pattern (R. J. Sternberg, Torff, & Grigorenko, 1998). One important consideration in light of such findings is the need for changes in the assessment of intelligence (R. J. Sternberg & Kaufman, 1996). Current measures of intelligence are somewhat one-sided, measuring mostly analytic abilities with little or no assessment of creative and practical aspects of intelligence. A more well-rounded assessment and instruction system could lead to greater benefits of education for a wider variety of students—a nominal goal of education.

Thus far, we have described various models of human intelligence, mentioning only briefly that humans have tried to program computers to simulate various aspects of intelligence. Before concluding this discussion of intelligence, we now turn to a discussion of artificial intelligence. As this chapter has shown, cognitive psychologists have learned much about human intelligence by attempting to understand and even to create artificial intelligence.

ARTIFICIAL INTELLIGENCE: COMPUTER SIMULATIONS

Much of the early information-processing research centered on work based on computer simulations of human intelligence as well as computer systems that use optimal methods to solve tasks. Programs of both kinds can be classified as examples of **artificial intelligence (AI)**. Computers cannot actually think; they must be programmed to behave as though they are thinking—that is, they must be programmed to simulate cognitive processes. In this way, they give us insight into the details of how people process information cognitively. Essentially, computers are just pieces of *hardware*—physical components of equipment—that respond to instructions. Other kinds of hardware (other pieces of equipment) also respond to instructions; for example, if you can figure out how to give the instructions, a VCR (videocassette recorder) will respond to your instructions and will do what you tell it to do.

What makes computers so interesting to researchers is that they can be given highly complex instructions, known as computer programs or even more commonly as *software,* which tell the computer how to respond to new information. The new information may come from various sources: (a) the environment (e.g., given the instruction, "When the temperature goes above 75 degrees Fahrenheit [≈24 degrees centigrade], turn on the cooling system," a heat-sensing mechanism, and a connection to the cooling system, the program will implement the instruction when it receives environmental information that the temperature has exceeded 75 degrees); (b) someone interacting with the computer (e.g., given the command to implement a set of instructions, "execute the spell-checking program," the program will do so); or even (c) its own processes (e.g., when implementing an instruction in a program, such as, "Repeat this step until reaching a count of 10 iterations, and then stop this step and proceed to the next step"). Before we consider any intelligent programs, we need to consider seriously the issue of what, if anything, would lead us to describe a computer program as being "intelligent."

CAN A COMPUTER PROGRAM BE "INTELLIGENT"?

THE TURING TEST

Probably the first serious attempt to deal with the issue of whether a computer program can be intelligent was made by Alan Turing (1963), based on ideas Turing first presented in 1950. Specifically, Turing devised a test by which a human could assess the intelligence of a respondent. The basic idea behind the Turing Test is whether an observer can distinguish the performance of a computer from that of a human, whom everyone would agree is intelligent in at least some degree. In the specific form proposed by Turing, the test is conducted with a computer, a human respondent, and an interrogator. The interrogator has two different "conversations" with an interactive computer program. The goal of the interrogator is to figure out which of two parties is a person communicating through the computer and which is the computer itself. The interrogator can ask the two parties any questions at all. However, the computer will try to fool the interrogator into believing that it is human, whereas the human will be trying to show the interrogator that she or he truly is human. The computer passes the Turing Test if an interrogator is unable to distinguish the computer from the human.

The test of indistinguishability of computer from human is commonly used in assessing the intelligence of a computer program. The test is not usually performed in quite the way described by Turing. For example, outputs of some kind generated by a computer might be scanned and assessed for their comparability to human performance. In some cases, human data from a problem-solving task are compared to computer-generated data, and the degree of relation between them is evaluated. For example, if a computer solves number-series problems such as 1, 4, 9, 16, . . . (where each number is the next larger perfect square), the response times and error patterns of the computer can be compared to those of human participants who have solved the same problems (e.g., Kotovsky & Simon, 1973; Simon & Kotovsky, 1963). Of course, the response times of the computer are typically much faster than those of humans, but the researchers are less interested in overall reaction times than in patterns of reaction times. In other words, what matters is not whether computers take more or less time on each problem than do humans, but whether the problems that take the computer relatively longer to solve also take human participants relatively longer.

Sometimes, the goal of a computer model is not to match human performance, but to exceed it. In this case, maximum artificial intelligence, rather than simulation of human intelligence, is the goal of the program. The criterion of whether computer performance matches that of humans is no longer relevant. Instead, the criterion of interest is that of how well the computer can perform the task assigned it. Computer programs that play chess, for example, typically play in a way that emphasizes "brute force," with the programs evaluating extremely large numbers of possible moves, many of which humans would never even consider evaluating (e.g., Berliner, 1969; Bernstein, 1958). Using brute force, and the IBM program, "Deep Blue," beat world champion Gary Kasparov in a 1997 chess match. The same brute force method is used in programs that play checkers (e.g., A. L. Samuel, 1963). These programs are generally evaluated in terms of how well they can beat each other, or even more importantly, human contenders playing against them.

Having considered some issues of what constitutes an intelligent computer program, we now turn to some of the actual programs. The discussion of these programs will give you an idea of how AI research has evolved, as well as of how AI models have influenced the work of cognitive psychologists. As the preceding examples have shown, many early AI programs focused on problem solving.

THE LOGIC THEORIST (LT)

One of the very earliest intelligent programs was formulated by Allen Newell, Clifford Shaw, and Herbert Simon (1957b). This program, the Logic Theorist (LT), was designed to discover proofs for theorems in elementary symbolic logic. For example, the program might be asked to prove the theorem, "If *P* or *Q* is true, then either *B* is true, or *P* or *Q* is true." LT was able to prove this theorem by comparing it to an *axiom* (a logical statement accepted as true). "If *A* is true, then *B* or *A* is true." (For example, "if it will rain, then either it will rain or it will snow," because for a logical *or* statement to be true, it is sufficient that either one—or even both—of its terms be true.)

To prove the original theorem, LT employed the *rule of substitution.* According to this rule, any expression may be substituted for any variable in any theorem, provided that the substitution is made throughout the theorem wherever that variable appears. LT proved the theorem by substituting "*P* or *Q*" for "*A*" in the logical axiom. Thus, the statement, "If *A* is true, then *B* or *A* is true," becomes, "If *P* or *Q* is true, then *B,* or *P* or *Q,* is true," and the theorem is proved. By using the rule of substitution, LT showed that the theorem was logically equivalent to the axiom.

The example given here is relatively simple. However, using just four rules, including the rule of substitution, LT could prove theorems that were quite a bit more complicated. Thus, Newell and his colleagues showed how a machine could be programmed to do a task that formerly required a person with good background knowledge—as well as intelligence—to do. Although LT could prove logical theorems, it could not go beyond its narrow function to address other kinds of problems. Next, Newell and his colleagues wrote a program that went beyond the capabilities of LT to solve a broader range of problems.

THE GENERAL PROBLEM SOLVER (GPS)

The new program, the General Problem Solver (GPS), was designed to solve a broader, more general range of kinds of problems than LT could solve (Newell, Shaw, & Simon, 1957a). The assumption of this program is that the processing of information is domain general, to a large extent, rather than domain specific. Although GPS uses a number of different methods to solve problems, these methods generally draw on a single heuristic for problem solving. The heuristic GPS uses is *means–ends analysis,* which involves solving problems by successively reducing the difference between the present status (where you are now) and the goal status (where you want to be; see chapter 11). Figure 14.6 shows a schematic **flow chart** (a model path for reaching a goal or solving a problem) for how GPS can transform one object (or one problem state) into another using means–ends analysis.

Means–ends analysis can be applied to a wide range of problems (e.g., the "MOVE" problems described in chapter 11, in which forest-burners and forest-lovers needed to cross a river, using just one two-person boat). GPS, as it was formulated back in the 1950s and 1960s, could apply the heuristic to problems such as proving logic theorems, or some of the other problems described in chapter 11. The GPS program and the LT program were typical of the early work carried out at Carnegie-Mellon University, but the Newell–Simon group at Carnegie was not the only group busy trying to create intelligent programs. At M.I.T., a group led primarily by Marvin Minsky was also interested in creating AI programs. The M.I.T. programs differed from the Carnegie programs in their greater emphasis on the retrieval of semantic information—that is, the use of meaningful verbal information (Minsky, 1968).

SHRDLU

By the early 1970s, M.I.T. researcher Terry Winograd (1972) had developed SHRDLU, generally considered a landmark in AI. SHRDLU (named for a basic string of letters on

FIGURE 14.6 **FLOW CHART**

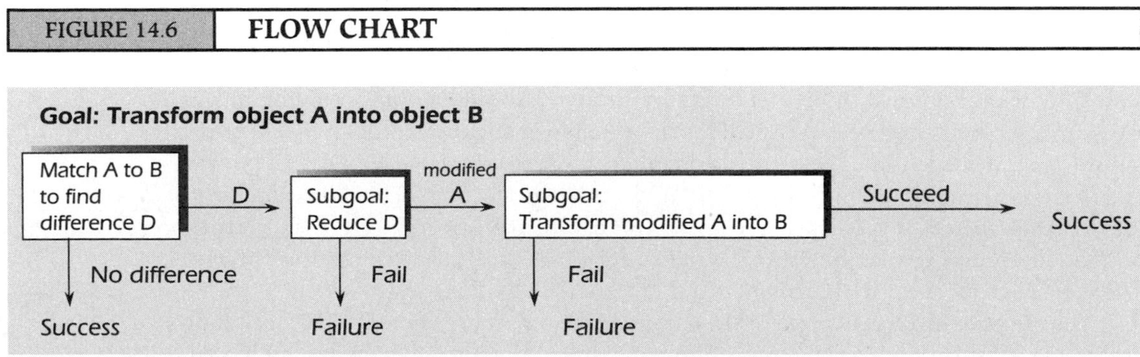

In developing GPS, Allen Newell, Clifford Shaw, and Herbert Simon suggested a flow chart for implementing a means–ends analysis to reach a goal.

traditional linotype machines used in printing) serves as the basis for operating a robot. Winograd's robot lives in a "block world," in which the tasks of "living" revolve around performing various manipulations on a set of blocks that differ in size, shape, and color. The world contains, for example, a green cube, a red pyramid, and so on. Figure 14.7 shows some examples of the kinds of elements that inhabit the block world of SHRDLU.

For example, the operator of the program might instruct the robot (through the computer program) to pick up a big red block, which the robot then picks up. Alternatively, the operator might ask the program how many blocks are not in the box, and the robot would respond with the number of blocks outside the box. Sometimes, the robot could not execute the program because the instructions were ambiguous and required clarification. For example, when asked what supported the pyramid, it would ask which of the two pyramids was being referenced. Also, the program would occasionally respond that it did not know an answer, as when asked whether a pyramid can support a pyramid.

SHRDLU processes information in terms of a block world. Other programs, however, operate in very different worlds. One of the more interesting is that of the psychotherapist, on the one hand, and the patient, on the other.

FIGURE 14.7 **SHRDLU'S WORLD**

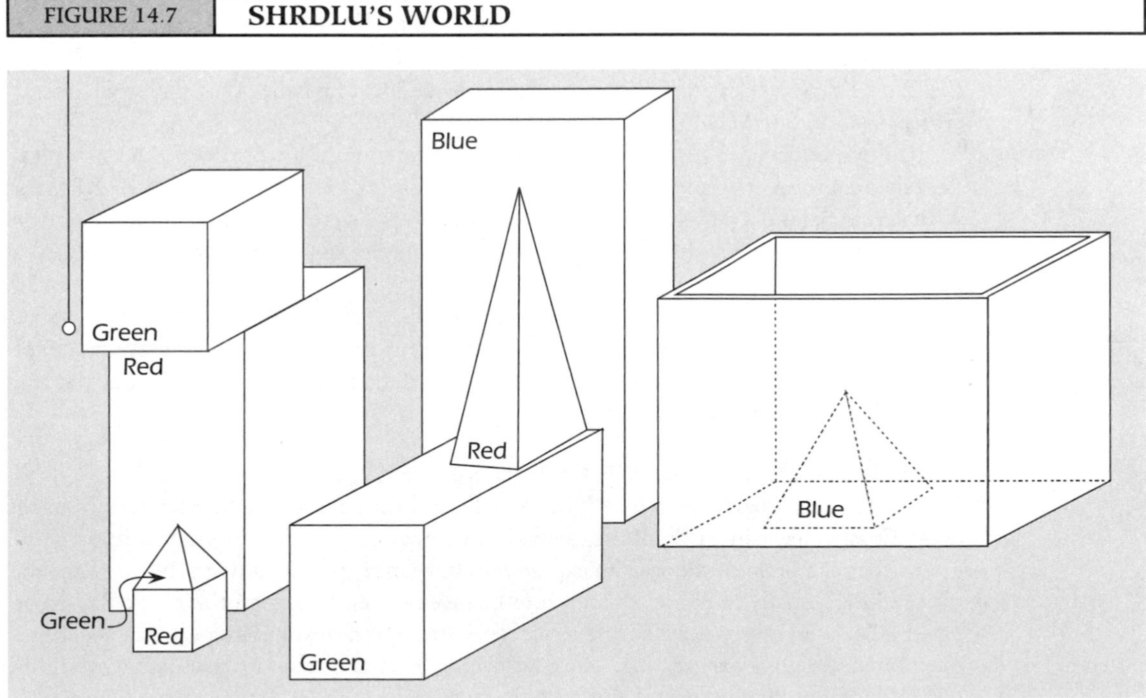

Terry Winograd's robot was programmed to operate within a three-dimensional block world containing elements such as the blocks shown here.

ELIZA AND PARRY

Two programs that operate in the world of psychotherapy are ELIZA and PARRY, the former taking on the role of a nondirective psychotherapist, and the latter taking on the role of a paranoid patient of a psychotherapist. The goal of the nondirective therapist is to elicit a patient's feelings, to reflect these feelings back to the patient, and to help the patient to understand and figure out what to do about these feelings. Consider, for example, a segment of an interaction between ELIZA and a patient working with ELIZA, as shown in Table 14.4. In this segment, ELIZA seems to show clinical insight about her patient. However, ELIZA is not as bright as she appears here. She uses key words and phrases in the interlocutor's (patient's) remarks to choose her own remarks, without understanding in any larger sense what the patient is saying. Indeed, Joseph Weizenbaum (1966) of M.I.T., the creator of ELIZA, chose the domain of nondirective psychotherapy because he believed simulating the responses of a nondirective psychotherapist would be relatively easy, as opposed to simulating people in other occupations who more directively show their knowledge and expertise in their interactions with others.

If therapists can be simulated, why not patients? Kenneth Colby (1963), a trained psychiatrist, created a simulation of a paranoid patient who is especially concerned that the Mafia is after him, as shown in the segment of dialogue reproduced in Table 14.4. Colby's simulation of a paranoid is not just a set of responses that "sounds paranoid." Rather, the simulation is generated from a theory of the neurotic process of a paranoid. The primary intention of the paranoid is to determine another person's intentions. Messages from the other are scanned in order to assist in this determination. Messages are classified as malevolent, benevolent, or neutral. The interpretation of malevolence, to which the paranoid is particularly susceptible, can emanate from a belief that the other intends either physical or psychological harm to the paranoid.

Colby performed a somewhat more formal evaluation of his program than is typical. He asked a group of 33 psychiatrists to read transcripts of "interviews" with PARRY and with actual paranoid patients. None of the psychiatrists were told that a computer model was involved. Roughly half of them rated the model as more paranoid than actual patients.

Colby's program differs from many others, in that it simulates not just abstract cognitive processes, but also a belief system. A more recent program by Colby employs cognitive therapy for the treatment of mild depression, using both a text and dialogue mode of interaction with a person (Colby, 1995).

PROGRAMS THAT SIMULATE EXPERTISE

Unlike the East Coast research at Yale, M.I.T., and Carnegie-Mellon, AI research on the West Coast, especially at Stanford, tended to emphasize **expert systems:** computer programs that can perform the way an expert does in a fairly specific domain. No attempt was made more globally to model human intelligence or even to extend the particular expert systems, even in theory. Rather, the researchers attempted to simulate performance in just one domain, often a narrow one, but at a level of expertise that surpasses what would be possible for a program that was fairly domain general.

For example, several programs were developed to diagnose various kinds of medical disorders. Such programs are obviously of enormous potential significance, given the very high costs (financial and personal) of incorrect diagnoses. Probably the most well-known

TABLE 14.4

PROGRAMS THAT SIMULATE BELIEF SYSTEMS: ELIZA AND PARRY

Joseph Weizenbaum's ELIZA was developed to simulate a nondirective psychotherapist, and Kenneth Colby's PARRY was developed to simulate a paranoid patient. What might happen if PARRY were to seek psychotherapeutic guidance from ELIZA? (Adapted from Weizenbaum, 1966, and from Colby, 1963)

ELIZA	PARRY
Men are all alike. IN WHAT WAY? They're always bugging us about something or other. CAN YOU THINK OF A SPECIFIC EXAMPLE? Well, my boyfriend made me come here. YOUR BOYFRIEND MADE YOU COME HERE. He says I'm depressed much of the time. I AM SORRY TO HEAR THAT YOU ARE DEPRESSED. It's true. I am unhappy. DO YOU THINK COMING HERE WILL HELP YOU NOT TO BE UNHAPPY? I need some help, that much seems certain. WHAT WOULD IT MEAN TO YOU IF YOU GOT SOME HELP? Perhaps I could learn to get along with my mother. TELL ME MORE ABOUT YOUR FAMILY. My mother takes care of me. WHO ELSE IN YOUR FAMILY TAKES CARE OF YOU? My father. YOUR FATHER? You are like my father in some ways. WHAT RESEMBLANCE DO YOU SEE? You are not very aggressive, but I think you don't want me to notice that. WHAT MAKES YOU THINK I AM NOT VERY AGGRESSIVE? You don't argue with me. WHY DO YOU THINK I DON'T ARGUE WITH YOU? You are afraid of me. DOES IT PLEASE YOU TO THINK THAT I AM AFRAID OF YOU? My father is afraid of everybody. WHAT ELSE COMES TO MIND WHEN YOU THINK OF YOUR FATHER? Bullies. DOES THAT HAVE ANYTHING TO DO WITH THE FACT THAT YOUR BOYFRIEND MADE YOU COME HERE?	Why are you in the hospital? I SHOULDN'T BE HERE. Who brought you here? THE POLICE. What trouble did you have with the police? COPS DON'T DO THEIR JOB. What do they do instead? COPS ARREST THE WRONG PEOPLE. They arrest the right ones sometimes. THE LAW SHOULD GET THOSE ITALIAN CROOKS. Are you Italian? MY BACKGROUND IS BRITISH BUT I WAS BORN IN THIS COUNTRY. Do you know any Italian crooks? I TRY TO AVOID THE UNDERWORLD. Are you afraid of the underworld? THE MAFIA ARE THE WORST GANGSTERS. Are you connected with the Mafia? YOU KNOW, THEY KNOW ME. How do they know you? THEY SPY ON ME. Why do they? THEY WANT TO GET FALSE EVIDENCE TO FRAME ME. What do they have against you? THEY ARE OUT TO GET ME. What for? I HAVE INCRIMINATING EVIDENCE AGAINST THE MAFIA. Are you sure of all this? YOU DON'T BELIEVE ME? I am doing my best. (SILENCE ON THE "PATIENT'S" PART) (Silence on the psychiatrist's part) CAN'T YOU THINK OF A DECENT QUESTION TO ASK? You seem hostile to me. SOME OF YOUR REMARKS ANNOY ME. I am sorry. FORGET THE EXCUSES, YOU GUYS ARE ALL ALIKE.

and certainly the oldest of these programs is MYCIN (Buchanan & Shortliffe, 1984; Shortliffe, 1976). MYCIN can be used for detecting and potentially even treating certain bacterial infections. MYCIN processes the results of blood tests, such as the numbers of red and white blood cells, or the amount of glucose in the blood. It then proposes a diagnosis of the disease and possibly also a drug treatment. It will even give an indication of the relative reliability of its diagnosis. MYCIN is based on the use of an organized system of if–then statements (see Table 14.5, which shows a fragment of a system of statements used by MYCIN, translated to be readable by humans). Note that the program gives an indication of its certainty (.6) regarding the identification of the offending microorganism as being bacteroides. The .6 is not, strictly speaking, a probability, but is on a scale where 0 indicates total lack of certainty regarding truth and 1 indicates total certainty. MYCIN contains roughly 500 rules (if–then statements) and can deal with about 100 different kinds of bacterial infections

MYCIN has been tested for its validity in making diagnoses and treatment suggestions. MYCIN's performance compared favorably with that of faculty members in the Stanford School of Medicine, and MYCIN outperformed medical students and residents in the same school (Yu et al., 1984). Earlier, it had been shown to be quite effective in prescribing medication for meningitis. Thus, within its relatively narrow domain of expertise, MYCIN is clearly an impressive expert system.

Other expert systems also have been created for medical diagnosis. For example, INTERNIST (R. A. Miller, Pople, & Myers, 1982) diagnoses a broader spectrum of diseases than does MYCIN, although within its broader domain, its diagnostic powers do not measure up to those of an experienced internist. This program illustrates what is sometimes termed the *bandwidth-fidelity problem.* The broader the bandwidth of a radio or other receiver, the poorer its fidelity (faithfulness, reliability) tends to be. Similarly, the wider the spectrum of problems to which an AI program addresses itself, the less reliable it is likely to be in solving any one of those kinds of problems.

Other expert systems solve other types of problems, including some of the problems found by scientists. For example, DENDRAL, another early expert system developed at Stanford, helps scientists identify the molecular structure of newly discovered organic compounds, and metaDENDRAL, an enhanced version, finds new rules for the basic DENDRAL program to use in making these identifications (Buchanan et al., 1976).

TABLE 14.5 A PROGRAM THAT SIMULATES EXPERTISE: MYCIN

At Stanford, the development of expert systems, such as the one excerpted here, has been a focus of AI research.

If:	(1) The gram stain of the organism is gramneg [i.e., not a particular type of microorganism],
	(2) The morphology of the organism is rod, and
	(3) The aerobicity of the organism is anaerobic
Then:	There is suggestive evidence (.6) that the identity of the organism is bacteroides.

Questions About the Intelligence of Intelligent Programs

Artificially intelligent programs such as the ones described here are not without their critics, of course. Consider some of the main objections that have been raised in regard to some of the aforementioned programs. Experts differ as to how much credence they give to these various objections. Ultimately, each of us needs to evaluate the objections for ourselves.

Some of the objections to artificial intelligence pertain to the limitations of the existing hardware and software designs. For one thing, human brains can process many sources of information simultaneously. However, because of the architectural structure of computer hardware, most computers (virtually all early computers, and even most contemporary ones) can only handle one instruction at a time. Hence, models based on computer simulations have tended to depend on *serial processing* (step-by-step, one-at-a-time) of information. However, by linking various computers into neural networks of computers, computers may now simulate *parallel processing* (multiple steps being performed simultaneously). Hence, the serial-processing limitation no longer applies to all computer-based models of artificial intelligence.

Absence of Intuition

Another of the limitations of artificial intelligence relates to a different characteristic of human intelligence: intuition. Hubert Dreyfus and Stuart Dreyfus (1990) have argued that whereas computers can be good and competent manipulators of symbols according to prepackaged algorithms, they lack intuition. To these authors, intuition is found in the kinds of hunches that distinguish genuine experts from those with book knowledge but without the expertise that will enable them to exploit their knowledge maximally when confronted with a difficult situation. Basically, the Dreyfuses are arguing that computers excel in the mathematical and deductive aspect of thinking, but not in the intuitive one.

For example, a United Airlines DC-10 airliner once crash-landed when all three of its hydraulic systems were severed by debris from an engine that was torn off in midair and hit the tail of the plane, where the three hydraulic systems were interlinked. The pilot of the DC-10 radioed to technical headquarters for guidance as to what to do when all three hydraulic systems go down. The technical experts were unable to help the crew because they had never encountered the situation before and had no guidelines to follow. The crew, nevertheless, working on intuition, managed to steer the plane roughly by varying engine thrust. The news media and others applauded the pilot and his crew for their intuitions as to what to do in the face of a problem for which there were no guidelines, and for which no computer program had been written. As a result of these intuitions, roughly two-thirds of the passengers in the plane survived a crash landing in Sioux City, Iowa.

The argument that computers cannot show intuitive intelligence does not go unchallenged. Several researchers interested in human problem solving (see chapter 11) have studied computer simulations of problem solving, and their research has led them to infer that at least some characteristics of intuition can be modeled on computers. For example, Pat Langley, Herbert Simon, Gary Bradshaw, and Jan Zytkow (1987) have written a set of programs (the "Bacon" programs) simulating the processes involved in various important scientific discoveries in the past. They argue that their programs do display intuition, and moreover, that there is nothing mystical about intuition. Rather, according to these researchers, intuition can be understood in terms of the same information-processing mechanisms that are applied to conventional forms of problem solving.

Along a similar line, John Holland, Keith Holyoak, Richard Nisbett, and Paul Thagard (1986) have simulated large parts of a theory of how we reason inductively, going beyond the information given in a problem to come up with a solution that is not deductively determined by the problem elements. One can easily argue that such a program is intuitive, at least in some sense, in that it goes beyond the information given. Other programs also make inferences that go well beyond the simple facts stored in their data bases.

Intelligence Versus the Appearance of Intelligence

Perhaps a more fundamental challenge to artificial intelligence comes from a philosopher, rather than from a cognitive psychologist. John Searle (1980) has raised an objection to the basic idea that computers can be considered truly intelligent. To make his objection, he uses what is known as the "Chinese Room" problem. Imagine that Searle is locked in a room and is given a large batch of Chinese writing to translate. He knows no Chinese at all. However, suppose that, in addition to the Chinese writing, Searle is given a second batch of Chinese script with a set of rules for translating the Chinese into English. Next, Searle is given a third batch, giving him a set of rules for formulating responses to questions that were raised in the first batch of Chinese writing. Searle then responds to the original, first batch of writing, with a response that makes sense and is in perfect Chinese. Presumably, over time, Searle could become so good at manipulating the rules that his responses would be every bit as good as those of a native Chinese speaker who understood exactly what was being asked. However, in fact, Searle still knows no Chinese at all. He is simply following a set of rules.

According to Searle, programs that seem to understand various kinds of inputs, and then to respond in an intelligent way (such as Winograd's SHRDLU), are like Searle in the Chinese room. The computers understand the input being given to them no better than Searle understands Chinese. They are simply operating according to a set of preprogrammed rules. Searle's notion is that the computer does not really see and understand the connections between input and output, but rather uses preestablished connections that make it seem intelligent on the surface. To Searle, these programs do not demonstrate artificial intelligence; rather, they only *appear* to show intelligence.

Predictably, AI researchers have not competed with each other to be the first to accept Searle's argument and to acknowledge the folly of their attempts to model AI. A number of researchers have offered responses to Searle's charge that the computer is not anything like what it is cracked up to be. Robert Abelson (1980), for example, has argued that Searle's use of the rule systems in the second and third batches of input is, in fact, intelligent. Abelson further argues that children learning a language also at first apply rules rather blindly, only later coming to understand them and how they are being used. Others argue that the system as a whole (comprising Searle as well as the set of instructions) does indeed exhibit understanding. In addition, some computer programs have even shown an ability to simulate at least a modest degree of skill development and knowledge acquisition, although existing computer programs do not begin to approach our human ability to enhance our own intelligence.

Improving Intelligence: Effective, Ineffective, and Questionable Strategies

Although designers of artificial intelligence have made great strides in creating programs that simulate knowledge and skill acquisition, no existing programs even approach the ability of the human brain to enhance its own intelligence. Human intelligence is highly *malleable*—it can be shaped and even increased through various kinds of interventions (Detterman & Sternberg, 1982; Perkins & Grotzer, 1997; R. J. Sternberg, Ferrari, Clinkenbeard, & Grigorenko, 1996; R. J. Sternberg, Powell, McGrane, & McGregor, 1997). Moreover, the malleability of intelligence has nothing to do with the extent to which intelligence has a genetic basis (R. J. Sternberg, 1997). An attribute (such as height) can be partly or even largely genetically based and yet be environmentally malleable.

The Head Start program was initiated in the 1960s as a way of providing preschoolers with an edge on intellectual abilities and accomplishments when they started school. Long-term follow-ups have indicated that by midadolescence, children who participated in the program were more than a grade ahead of matched controls who did not receive the program (Lazar & Darlington, 1982; Zigler & Berman, 1983). The children in the program also scored higher on a variety of tests of scholastic achievement, were less likely to need remedial attention, and were less likely to show behavioral problems. Although such measures are not truly measures of intelligence, they show strong positive correlations with intelligence tests.

Investigating Cognitive Psychology

A number of newer programs have also shown some success. One such program, Reuven Feuerstein's (1980) *Instrumental Enrichment* program, involves training in a variety of abstract-reasoning skills and appears to be particularly effective for improving the skills of retarded performers. Another program, the *Odyssey* program (see Adams, 1986), has been shown effective in raising the intellectual performance of Venezuelan children of junior high school age. The *Philosophy for Children* program (Lipman, Sharp, & Oscanyan, 1980) has been shown to teach logical thinking skills to children throughout the primary and secondary levels of schooling. Aspects of the *Intelligence Applied* program (R. J. Sternberg, 1986a) for teaching intellectual skills have been shown to improve both insight skills (Davidson & Sternberg, 1984) and the ability to learn meanings of words from context, a primary means for acquiring new vocabulary (R. J. Sternberg, 1987a). Practical intelligence can also be taught (Gardner, Krechevsky, Sternberg & Okagaki et al., 1994; R. J. Sternberg, Okagaki, & Jackson, 1990).

Practical Applications of Cognitive Psychology

What is your dominant cognitive style? Defining your preferred way of interacting with the environment could help you perform better in school or on the job. The "Thinking About Thinking" section at the end of each of the chapters in this text was designed to appeal to different cognitive styles in order to more meaningfully integrate the information in each chapter. Which questions were more appealing to you, or helped you most? Analytic questions asked you to compare, analyze, or evaluate ideas; creative questions asked you to design or create; and practical questions asked you to apply information to other situations. Try to apply your knowledge in all three ways for the most effective and flexible use.

An alternative to intellectual enrichment outside the home may be to provide an enriched home environment. Support for the importance of home environment was found by Robert Bradley and Bettye Caldwell (1984) in regard to the development of intelligence in young children. These researchers found that several factors in the early (preschool) home environment appear to be correlated with high IQ scores: emotional and verbal *responsivity* of the primary caregiver and the caregiver's *involvement* with the child, *avoidance of restriction* and punishment, *organization* of the physical environment and activity schedule, provision of appropriate play *materials,* and opportunities for *variety* in daily stimulation. Further, Bradley and Caldwell found that these factors more effectively predicted IQ scores than did socioeconomic status (SES) or family-structure variables. It should be noted, however, that the Bradley–Caldwell study is correlational and therefore cannot be interpreted as indicating causality. Furthermore, their study pertained to preschool children, and children's IQ scores do not begin to predict adult IQ scores well until age 4 years. Moreover, before age 7 years, the scores are not very stable (Bloom, 1964). More recent work (e.g., Pianta & Egeland, 1994) has suggested that factors such as maternal social support and interactive behavior may play a key role in the instability of scores on tests of intellectual ability between ages 2 and 8 years.

The Bradley and Caldwell data should not be taken to indicate that demographic variables have little effect on IQ scores. To the contrary, throughout history and across cultures, many groups of people have been assigned pariah status as inferior members of the social order. Across cultures, these disadvantaged groups (e.g., native Maoris vs. European New Zealanders) have shown differences in tests of intelligence and aptitude (Steele, 1990; Zeidner, 1990). Such was the case of the Burakumin tanners in Japan, who, in 1871, were granted emancipation but not full acceptance into Japanese society. Despite their poor performance and underprivileged status in Japan, those who immigrate to America—and are treated like other Japanese immigrants—perform on IQ tests and in school achievement at a level comparable to that of their fellow Japanese Americans (Ogbu, 1986).

Similar positive effects of integration were shown on the other side of the world. In Israel, the children of European Jews score much higher on IQ tests than do children of Arabic Jews—except when the children are reared on kibbutzim in which the children of all national ancestries are raised by specially trained caregivers, in a dwelling separate from their parents. When these children shared the same child-rearing environments, there were no national-ancestry-related differences in IQ (Smilansky, 1974).

Altogether, there is now abundant evidence that people's environments (e.g., Ceci, Nightingale, & Baker, 1992; T. E. Reed, 1993; R. J. Sternberg & Wagner, 1994), their motivation (e.g., Collier, 1994; R. J. Sternberg & Ruzgis, 1994), and their training (e.g., Feuerstein, 1980; R. J. Sternberg, 1987c) can profoundly affect their intellectual skills. Thus, the controversial claims made by Herrnstein and Murray (1994) in their book, *The Bell Curve,* regarding the futility of intervention programs, are unfounded when one considers the evidence in favor of the possibility of improving cognitive skills. Likewise, Herrnstein and Murray's appeal to "a genetic factor in cognitive ethnic differences" (Herrnstein & Murray, 1994, p. 270) falls apart in light of the direct evidence against such genetic differences (see R. J. Sternberg, 1996), and results from a misunderstanding of the heritability of traits in general.

Heredity may set some kind of upper limit on how intelligent a person may become. However, we now know that for any attribute that is partly genetic, there is a *reaction range*—that is, the attribute can be expressed in various ways within broad limits of possibilities. Thus, each person's intelligence can be developed further within this broad range of potential intelligence. We have no reason to believe that people now reach their upper limits in the development of their intellectual skills. To the contrary, the evidence suggests that we can do quite a bit to help people become more intelligent (for further discussion of these issues, see R. J. Sternberg, 1995; see also Neisser et al., 1996).

Ultimately, what we do to help people become more intelligent is to help them to better perceive, learn, remember, represent information, reason, decide, and solve problems. In other words, what we do is to help them improve the cognitive functions that have been the focus of this book. The connection between improving intelligence and improving cognition is not a casual one. On the contrary, human cognition forms the core of human intelligence, and thus intelligence is a construct that helps us unify all the diverse aspects of cognition. Although cultural and other contextual factors may influence the expression of our intelligence (e.g., behavior that is considered intelligent in one culture may be considered unintelligent in another culture), the cognitive processes underlying behavior are the same: In every culture, people need to learn, to reason, to solve problems, and so on. Thus, when we study cognitive psychology, we are learning about the fundamental core of human intelligence that helps people the world over to adapt to their environmental circumstances, no matter how different those circumstances may be. No wonder, then, that the study of cognition is so fundamental to psychology in particular, and to the understanding of human behavior in general.

Summary

1. **What are the key issues in intelligence research? How do different researchers and theorists respond to those issues?** An early issue in the study of intelligence centered on how to measure intelligence. Francis Galton

and his followers emphasized psychophysical acuity, whereas Binet and his followers emphasized judgment. Two common themes that run through the definitions of intelligence proposed by many experts are the capacity to learn from experience and the ability to adapt to the environment. In addition, the importance of metacognition and of cultural context are increasingly recognized by researchers and theorists of intelligence. Nonetheless, psychologists often disagree regarding the relative importance of context (nurture) versus inheritance (nature) in determining intelligence. Also, different researchers disagree regarding whether to focus on studying the structures of intelligence (e.g., Spearman, Thurstone, Cattell) or the processes of intelligence (e.g., Hunt, Jensen, Simon). Some researchers (e.g., Gardner, Sternberg) have also focused on trying to integrate the various approaches to intelligence into comprehensive systems models of intelligence. One approach to intelligence is to understand it in terms of *factor analysis,* a statistical technique that seeks to identify latent sources of individual differences in performance on tests. Some of the principal factor-analytic models of the mind are the *g*-factor model of Spearman, the primary-mental-abilities model of Thurstone, the *structure-of-intellect (SOI)* model of Guilford, and the hierarchical models of Cattell, of Vernon, and of Carroll, among others.

2. **What are some information-processing approaches to intelligence?** An alternative approach to intelligence is to understand it in terms of information processing. Information-processing theorists have sought to understand intelligence in terms of constructs such as inspection time, choice reaction time, speed of lexical access, the ability to divide attention successfully, the components of reasoning and problem solving, and complex problem solving that can be simulated via computers. A related approach is the biological model, which uses increasingly sophisticated means of viewing the brain while the brain is engaged in intelligent behaviors. Preliminary findings suggest that speed of neural conduction may play a role in intelligence. Particularly intriguing are findings suggesting that neural efficiency and specialization of cerebral function may be influential in intelligent cognitive processing.

3. **What are some alternative views of intelligence?** Another main approach to understanding intelligence (based on an anthropological model) is a *contextual approach,* according to which intelligence is viewed as wholly or partly determined by cultural values. Contextual theorists differ in the extent to which they believe that the meaning of intelligence differs from one culture to another. What is considered to be intelligent behavior is, to some extent, *culturally relative:* The same behavior that is considered to be intelligent in one culture may be considered unintelligent in another culture. To create a test of intelligence that is *culture-fair*—that is, equally fair for members of different cultures—is difficult—perhaps impossible—because members of different cultures have different conceptions of what constitutes intelligent behavior.

   Systems models of intelligence seek to go beyond cultural content. Gardner's *theory of multiple intelligences* specifies that intelligence is not a unitary construct, but rather that there are multiple intelligences, each relatively independent of the others. Sternberg's *triarchic theory of human intelligence* conceives of intelligence in terms of information-processing components, which are applied to experience to serve the functions of adaptation to the environment, shaping of the environment, and selection of new environments.

4. **How have researchers attempted to simulate intelligence, using machines such as computers?** AI research is conducted on the premise that having machines simulate intelligence is both possible and valuable. The Turing Test is designed to evaluate the extent to which particular AI programs have succeeded in simulating humanlike intelligence. Critics of AI, however, question both the possibility and the worth of trying to get machines to simulate human intelligence, sometimes using the "Chinese Room" problem to illustrate a distinction between simulated intelligence and true understanding. Arguments can be made to support either perspective. Of the many now classic AI programs that have been developed, among the earliest ones are the Logic Theorist, which proves theorems in symbolic logic, and the General Problem Solver, which solves various kinds of problems using means–ends analysis. A later program was SHRDLU, which simulated a robot performing various operations in a block world, such as placing one block on top of another, or placing a block in a box. Programs that modeled belief systems include ELIZA, designed to simulate a nondirective psychotherapist; and PARRY, designed to simulate the thinking of a paranoid psychiatric patient. *Expert systems,* programs designed to demonstrate expertise, include MYCIN, which diagnoses certain bacterial diseases by analyzing the results of blood tests, and DENDRAL, which analyzes the structure of organic compounds.

5. **Can intelligence be improved, and if so, how?** Intellectual skills can be taught. Thus, intelligence is malleable rather than fixed. Although researchers largely agree that some improvements are possible, they disagree regarding both the degree to which they believe that such improvements can be achieved, and the means by which to do so.

Thinking About Thinking: Factual, Analytical, Creative, and Practical Questions

1. Briefly summarize the key strands of AI research, and name an example of a program in each strand.
2. What are some of the main reasons that intelligence tests have been devised and used?
3. In what ways is the theory of multiple intelligence different from factor-analytic theories of intelligence?
4. What are some of the strengths and limitations of the information-processing approach to intelligence?
5. How would you design a program to improve intelligence (as you define the concept)?

6. Design an experiment that would link a physiological approach to a cognitive approach to intelligence.
7. How might any of the structural approaches to intelligence lead to practical applications?
8. Contextualists underscore the importance of viewing intelligence within a given context. What are some aspects of your social, mental, or physical context that you consider important to the expression of your intelligence?

KEY TERMS

artificial intelligence (AI) 491
component 480
componential analysis 480
contextualist 484
culture-fair 485
culture-relevant 486
expert system 496
factor analysis 472
flow chart 494
g 476
global planning 481
intelligence 469
local planning 481
structure-of-intellect (SOI) 476
theory of multiple intelligences 487
triarchic theory of human intelligence 489

ANNOTATED SUGGESTED READINGS

Ceci, S. J. (1996). *On intelligence.* Cambridge, MA: Harvard University Press. A treatise arguing that biological and ecological approaches need to be combined to understand intelligence.

Gardner, H. (1983). *Frames of mind: The theory of multiple intelligences.* New York: Basic Books. The original and still the most comprehensive account of Howard Gardner's theory of multiple intelligences, as told by the originator of the theory.

Haier, R. J., Siegel, B., Tang, C., Abel, L., & Buchsbaum, M. S. (1992). Intelligence and changes in regional cerebral glucose metabolic rate following learning. *Intelligence, 16,* 415–426. A seminal article showing how neural imaging can be used to study intelligence; in particular, such imaging reveals that during problem solving, some regions of the brain are actually *less* active in *more* able thinkers, as compared with less able thinkers.

Sternberg, R. J. (Ed.). (1994). *Encyclopedia of human intelligence.* New York: Macmillan. You will not have time to read all of this two-volume work, but in the work are easily readable articles on practically any area of the study of intelligence that interests you.

Sternberg, R. J. (1997). *Successful intelligence.* New York: Plume.This book shows how intelligence can be used to help you in your everyday life.

Glossary

accessibility—the ease of gaining access to information that has been stored in long-term memory (cf. **availability**)

accommodation—equilibrative process whereby an individual modifies his or her cognitive schemas to fit relevant new aspects of the environment (cf. **assimilation**; see **equilibration**)

ACT*—a model of information processing that integrates a network representation for **declarative knowledge** and a production-system representation for **procedural knowledge**

action potential—mechanism for neuronal conduction, which involves a rapid change in electrical charge across the membrane of a **neuron**, due to the exchange of ions

agnosia—a severe deficit in the ability to perceive sensory information, usually related to the visual sensory modality; agnosics have normal sensations but lack the ability to interpret and recognize what they sense, usually as a result of lesions in the brain (from Greek, *a-*, "lack"; *gnosis*, "knowledge")

algorithm—formal path for reaching a solution, which involves one or more iterative processes that usually lead to an accurate answer to a question (cf. **heuristics**; see **problem solving**)

amnesia—severe loss of explicit **memory**, usually affecting declarative memory more than procedural memory (see **declarative knowledge** vs. **procedural knowledge**)

analogue—a form of **knowledge representation** that preserves the main perceptual features of whatever is being represented (cf. **symbolic**)

analysis—the process of breaking down a complex whole into smaller elements (cf. **synthesis**)

anterograde amnesia—inability explicitly to recall events that occur *after* whatever trauma caused the **memory** loss (affects the acquisition of **semantic memory**, but apparently not the acquisition of procedural memory; cf. **retrograde amnesia**; see also **amnesia**)

arousal—a hypothetical construct representing alertness, wakefulness, and activation, related to the activity of the **central nervous system**

artificial intelligence (AI)—field of research attempting to build systems that demonstrate at least some form of **intelligence**; although such systems offer many applications, cognitive psychologists are particularly interested in work involving computer models of the intelligent processing of information (see also **expert system**)

assimilation—equilibrative process whereby an individual incorporates new information into existing cognitive schemas (cf. **accommodation**; see **equilibration**)

association areas—regions of the **cerebral cortex** that appear to link the activities of the motor and sensory regions of the cortex and to provide a place in which many high-level cognitive processes may occur

associationism—a school of psychological thought examining how humans and other organisms may learn to link particular events or ideas with one another in the mind

attention—the cognitive link between the limited amount of information that is actually manipulated mentally and the enormous amount of information available through the senses, stored memories, and other cognitive processes (cf. **consciousness**)

automatic processes—cognitive manipulations that require no conscious decisions or intentional effort (cf. **controlled processes**)

automatization—the process by which an individual repeats a procedure so frequently (i.e., practices the procedure) that the procedure changes from being highly conscious and effortful to being relatively automatic and effortless (also termed *proceduralization*)

availability—the existing storage of given information in long-term memory, without which retrieving the information would be impossible, and with which retrieving the information is possible if appropriate retrieval strategies can be implemented (cf. **accessibility**)

availability heuristic—a cognitive shortcut in which an individual makes judgments on the basis of how easily he or she is able to call to mind what are perceived as relevant instances of a given phenomenon (see also **heuristics**)

axon—the part of the **neuron** through which intraneuronal conduction occurs (via the **action potential**) and at the terminus of which are located the **terminal buttons** that release **neurotransmitters**

babbling—a prelinguistic preferential production of only those distinct **phonemes** characteristic of the **language** being acquired (cf. **cooing**)

basic level—a degree of specificity of a **concept** within a conceptual hierarchy, which seems to be the degree to which most speakers describe the concept (sometimes termed a *natural level);* generally neither the most abstract nor the most detailed degree of specificity, but usually the degree of specificity that has the largest number of distinctive properties (i.e., properties that distinguish the given concept from other concepts at the same level of specificity)

behaviorism—a school of psychological thought that focuses entirely on the links between observed stimuli and observed responses, discounting any mental phenomena that cannot be observed directly

bilinguals—persons who can speak two languages (cf. **monolinguals**)

binaural presentation—the presentation of the same audible stimuli to both ears at the same time (from Latin, *bin-,* "both"; *-aural,* "related to the ears"; cf. **dichotic presentation**)

binocular depth cues—one of the two chief means of judging the distances of visible objects (cf. **monocular depth cues**), based on the two different angles from which each eye views a scene (from Latin, *bin-,* "two"; *-ocular,* "pertaining to the eye")

blood–brain barrier—physiological network of tiny blood vessels, which restricts the flow of substances that may enter or leave the **brain** through the bloodstream

bottom-up strategies—approaches to deriving meaning, which start with the immediate sensorially perceptible features, then manipulate that information, drawing on memory and existing schemas, only as needed in order to derive meaning from the **percepts** (cf. **top-down strategies**)

bottom-up theories—theoretical explanations of **perception**, which focus on the physical stimulus being perceived and then proceed upward to consider higher order cognitive processes (sometimes termed *data-driven theories;* cf. **top-down theories**)

bounded rationality—the recognition that although humans are rational, there are limits to the degree to which humans demonstrate rational cognitive processes across situations

brain—the organ responsible for cognition, as well as emotion and motivation

brain stem—the portion of the brain that comprises the **thalamus** and **hypothalamus,** the **midbrain,** and the **hindbrain,** and that connects the rest of the **brain** to the **spinal cord**

categorical perception—the phenomenon in speech perception in which continuously varying sounds are heard as distinct categories, and acoustically different members within a category are not distinguished as well as similarly different sounds in different categories

categorical syllogism—a deductive argument in which the relationship among the three terms in the two **premises** involves categorical membership (see **syllogism;** see also **deductive reasoning**)

category—a kind of **concept** that functions to organize other concepts based on common features or similarity to a **prototype**

causal inference—a conclusion regarding whether something (such as an event) causes something else

central nervous system (CNS)—one of the two main divisions of the **nervous system** (cf. **peripheral nervous system**), consisting of the **brain** and the **spinal cord**

centration—the tendency of children to focus all their thought processes on one perceptually salient aspect of an object, situation, or problem, to the exclusion of other aspects that may be relevant

cerebral cortex—the highly convoluted layer of tissue that surrounds the interior of the **brain**

and that permits human reasoning, abstract thinking, **memory,** forethought and planning, and holistic and analytic processes of **perception**

cerebral hemispheres—the right and left globe-shaped halves of the **brain,** which are connected by the **corpus callosum**

cerebrospinal fluid—a translucent fluid that circulates throughout the **central nervous system (CNS),** cushioning the **brain** and **spinal cord,** as well as helping to eliminate waste products within the CNS

characteristic features—the qualities that describe a prototypical model of a word (or **concept**) and thereby serve as the basis for the meaning of the word (or concept), according to **prototype theory;** these qualities will characterize many or most of the instances of the word (or concept), but not necessarily all instances (cf. **defining features**)

child-directed speech—a characteristic form of speech that adults tend to use when speaking with infants and young children, which usually involves a higher pitch, exaggerated raising and lowering of pitch and volume, and relatively simple sentence constructions; generally more effective than normal speech in gaining and keeping the attention of infants and young children (formerly termed *motherese)*

coarticulation—the overlapping in speech production of neighboring phonemes.

cocktail party problem—the process of tracking one conversation with the distraction of other conversations, a problem often experienced at cocktail parties

cognitive development—the diverse changes in thinking that occur across the life span, in association with increasing physiological maturity *(maturation)* and experience *(learning)*

cognitive maps—mental representations of the physical environment, particularly in regard to spatial relationships among objects in the environment

cognitive psychology—the study of how people perceive, learn, remember, and think about information

cognitive science—a cross-disciplinary science, which embraces **cognitive psychology,** psychobiology, philosophy, anthropology, linguistics, and **artificial intelligence,** as a means of understanding cognition (thinking)

cognitivism—a psychological perspective suggesting that the study of how people think will lead to broad insight into much of human behavior

communication—the exchange of thoughts and feelings, which may include **language,** as well as nonverbal forms of expression, such as gestures, glances, and so on (cf. **language**)

competence theory—theoretical approach emphasizing what people are ideally able to do (cf. **performance theory**)

component—specific mental process or strategy used in performing cognitive tasks, such as encoding, inferring, mapping, or applying

componential analysis—a breakdown of reaction times and error rates on cognitive tasks, used for differentiating the various processes that make up each task

componential theory—one of two primary theories of semantics (cf. **prototype theory**), which claims that the meaning of a word (or concept) can be understood by disassembling the word (or concept) into a set of **defining features** (also termed *definitional theory)*

comprehension processes—the cognitive processes used for understanding text as a whole and thereby making sense of what is read

concept—an idea or a thought about something, to which various characteristics may be attached and to which various other ideas may be connected; may be used to describe either abstract or concrete ideas

concrete operations—Piagetian stage during which children (roughly ages 7 through 12 years) become proficient in mentally manipulating their internal representations of concrete objects

conditional reasoning—a process of **deductive reasoning,** by which a reasoner attempts to draw a conclusion based on a conditional *(if–then)* **proposition** and an assertion of an existing condition

conjunction search—a means of pursuing a quest for a target stimulus by seeking the joint appearance of multiple features that distinguish the target stimulus from **distractors** (cf. **feature search;** see also **search;** cf. also **vigilance**)

connotation—an emotional overtone, presupposition, or other nonexplicit meaning of a word (cf. **denotation**)

consciousness—the complex phenomenon of evaluating the environment and then filtering that information through the mind, with awareness of doing so; may be viewed as the mental reality created in order to adapt to the world (cf. **attention**)

conservation—the ability to keep in mind the stability of a given quantity despite observed changes in the appearance of an object or a substance

consolidation—the process by which people integrate new information into their existing information stored in long-term memory (see **long-term store**)

constructive—psychological phenomenon in which an individual builds memories, based on prior experience and expectations, such that existing **schemas** or new information may affect how other information is stored in **memory** (cf. **reconstructive**)

constructive perception—one of the two key views of **perception** (also termed *intelligent perception;* cf. **direct perception**); asserts that the perceiver builds the stimulus that is perceived, using sensory information as the foundation for the structure, but also considering the existing knowledge and thought processes of the individual

content morpheme—a **morpheme** that carries the bulk of the meaning of a word (cf. **function morpheme**)

context effects—the influences of the surrounding environment on **perception,** particularly as applied to the visual perception of forms

contextualist—theorist or researcher who holds that a given psychological construct, such as **intelligence,** cannot be understood outside its real-world context

contralateral—toward the opposite side (cf. **ipsilateral**)

controlled processes—cognitive operations that require conscious control and effort, that are performed one step at a time, and that take longer to execute than mental operations governed by **automatic processes** (see also **attention, consciousness**)

convergent thinking—thought processes during which an individual selectively narrows down multiple alternatives until reaching a single, optimal alternative

converging operations—the use of multiple approaches and techniques to come together in addressing a problem or in responding to a question

cooing—oral expression that explores the production of all the phones (cf. **phonemes**) that humans can possibly produce; precedes **babbling**

cooperative principle—principle of conversation in which it is held that people seek to communicate in ways that make it easy for a listener to understand what a speaker means, such as by following the maxims of manner, quality, quantity, and relation proposed by Grice

core—a set of **defining features** of a **concept,** all of which are required in order for a particular example to be considered an instance of the concept; the core of defining features may be considered to complement the **prototype,** which comprises the **characteristic features** of most examples of the concept (cf. **prototype;** see **componential theory, prototype theory**)

corpus callosum—the dense network of tissue connecting the left and right hemispheres of the **brain**

cortex—see **cerebral cortex**

creativity—a cognitive process that leads to the production of something that is both original and worthwhile

crystallized intelligence—knowledge and expertise accumulated over a lifetime of experience (cf. **fluid intelligence**)

culture-fair—an ideal describing something that is equally appropriate and fair for members of all cultures

culture-relevant—a characteristic of an assessment based on skills and knowledge that relate to the cultural experiences of the test-takers, still recognizing that the test-givers' definitions of the construct being measured may differ from the definitions of the test-takers

decay—a phenomenon of memory by which simply the passage of time leads to forgetting (cf. **interference**)

decay theory—the assertion that information is forgotten because it gradually disappears over time, rather than because the information is displaced by other information

declarative knowledge—a recognition and understanding of factual information known about objects, ideas, and events in the environment ("knowing that," not "knowing how"; cf. **procedural knowledge**)

deductive reasoning—a process by which an individual tries to draw a logically certain and specific conclusion from a set of general **propositions** (cf. **inductive reasoning**)

deductive validity—a determination as to whether a given conclusion follows logically from the **propositions** on which it is based (cf. **fallacy**; see also **deductive reasoning**)

deep structure—a level of syntactic analysis, which indicates the relationships among various surface structures by means of transformational rules (cf. **surface structure**; see **transformational grammar**)

defining features—a set of component characteristics, each of which is an essential element of a given concept, and which together compose the properties that uniquely define the concept, according to **componential theory** (cf. **characteristic features, prototype theory**; see also **core**)

dendrites—branchlike structures of each **neuron,** which extend into **synapses** with other neurons, and which receive neurochemical messages sent by other neurons into the synapses

denotation—a strict dictionary definition of a word (cf. **connotation**)

depth—as applied to **perception,** the perceived distance of something from the body of the perceiver (see **monocular depth cues, binocular depth cues**)

dialect—a regional variation of a **language,** characterized by distinctive features such as differences in **vocabulary, syntax,** and pronunciation

dichotic presentation—simultaneous presentation of differing audible stimuli (such as verbal messages) to each ear (from Greek, *dich-,* "in two parts"; *-otic,* "related to the ears"; cf. **binaural presentation**)

direct perception—one of the two key views of **perception** (cf. **constructive perception**); asserts that the array of information in the sensory receptors is all that is needed for an individual to perceive anything—that is, prior knowledge or thought processes are not necessary for perception

discourse—the most comprehensive level of linguistic analysis, which encompasses **language** use at the level beyond the sentence, such as in conversation, in paragraphs, and so on (cf. **semantics, syntax**)

dishabituation—phenomenon in which a change (sometimes just a slight change) in a familiar stimulus prompts a perceiver to start noticing anew a stimulus to which the perceiver had previously become habituated (cf. **habituation**)

distal stimulus—an external source of stimulation as it exists in the world; this external stimulus may differ somewhat from the internal sensation of the stimulus, as it is detected in sensory receptors (cf. **proximal stimulus**; see also **perceptual constancy**)

distractor—feature, characteristic, object, or other stimulus that causes an individual difficulty in selectively attending to the stimuli of interest (see **attention, search, vigilance**); frequently used in studies of **perception** and of **memory**

distributed practice—an apportionment of time spent learning a body of information by spacing the total time over various sessions, rather than by consolidating the total time in a single session; when testing of recall is delayed, such practice generally leads to better retention than does **massed practice**

divergent thinking—thought processes involving the production of diverse alternatives

divided attention—a process by which an individual allocates available attentional resources to coordinate the performance of more than one task at a time

domain-general theorists—theoreticians who seek to understand how general principles of information processing apply and are used across a variety of cognitive domains

dual-code hypothesis—an assertion of belief that information may be represented either imaginally (in nonverbal images) or verbally (in symbolic forms), or sometimes in both forms

dual-system hypothesis—a view of bilingualism, which suggests that the two languages are represented somehow in separate systems of the brain (cf. **single-system hypothesis;** see also **bilinguals**)

dynamic assessment environment—a context for examination in which an examiner responds distinctively when a child gives an incorrect answer, offering the child a graded series of hints to guide the child toward the correct answer (cf. **static assessment environment;** see **zone of proximal development**)

dyslexia—difficulty in mentally processing information in text, such as during various reading tasks

ecological validity—the degree to which particular findings in one context (e.g., a laboratory) may be considered relevant outside of that context; based on the notion that human thought processes interact with particular environmental contexts

effector—one of two types of nerves (cf. **receptor**); transmits information regarding how the muscles should be moved, sending the information from the **spinal cord** (and usually from the **brain**) to various nerves within muscles of the body

egocentric—characteristic in which children focus largely on themselves and on their own perspective; over the course of development, children become decreasingly egocentric and thereby better able to see things from the perspective of others

electrochemical—involving chemical actions of electrically charged particles

electroencephalogram (EEG)— a recording (-gram) of the electrical activity of the living brain, as detected by various electrodes (from Greek, *en-*, "in," *cephalo-*, "head")

elimination by aspects—a decision-making strategy in which an individual gradually narrows an overabundance of options by focusing first on one key attribute of each option, forming a minimum criterion for that attribute, and then eliminating all options that do not meet that criterion; the process is repeated until either a single option remains or few enough remain so that a more careful selection process may be used

empiricist—person who believes that knowledge is most effectively acquired through observation (cf. **rationalist**)

encoding—process by which a physical, sensory input is transformed into a representation that can be stored in **memory** (cf. **retrieval, storage**)

encoding specificity—hypothesized phenomenon of **memory** in which the specific way of representing information as it is placed into memory affects the specific way in which the information may be retrieved later

enzymatic deactivation—a mechanism whereby a **neurotransmitter** is chemically decomposed

episodic memory—**encoding, storage,** and **retrieval** of events or episodes that the rememberer experienced personally at a particular time and place (cf. **semantic memory**)

equilibration—a process of cognitively adapting to the environment, whereby an individual works to maintain a state of cognitive equilibrium (balance), even in the face of new information (see **assimilation, accommodation**)

exemplar—one of several typical representatives of a particular **concept** or of a class of objects; sometimes, several exemplars may be used as a set of alternatives to a single **prototype** for deriving the meaning of a concept (cf. **prototype;** see **prototype theory**)

expert system—a computer program designed to perform tasks at a high level of expertise (see **artificial intelligence**)

explicit memory—a form of memory **retrieval** in which an individual consciously acts to recall or to recognize particular information (cf. **implicit memory;** see also **memory**)

factor analysis—a statistical method for discerning various component hypothetical factors underlying observed test scores

fallacy—a logical argument in which the conclusion is not deductively valid, based on the given **propositions** (cf. **deductive validity**)

feature-integration theory—a theory regarding the **perception** of forms and patterns (particularly when conducting visual searches), which explains the relative ease of conducting searches for single outstanding features (a task involving a single process of feature detection) and the relative difficulty of conducting searches for two or more conjoined features (a task involving two steps: feature detection and feature integration) (see **conjunction search, feature search, search;** cf. **similarity theory**)

feature-matching—a **theory** of form **perception** according to which forms are recognized by matching features in given forms to features stored in **memory**

feature search—visual pursuit of a particular characteristic by means of scanning the environment for the characteristic (cf. **conjunction search;** see **search**)

figure–ground—a Gestalt principle of form perception (see **Gestalt approach**): the tendency to perceive that an object in or an aspect of a perceptual field seems prominent (termed the *figure),* whereas other objects or aspects recede into the background (termed the *ground)*

flashbulb memory—recollection of an unusually distinctive event, in which the recollection is highly vivid and richly detailed, as if it were indelibly preserved on film; frequently, the accuracy of such recall is not as great as the rememberer may believe it to be

flow chart—a box diagram showing the steps for solving a problem or for implementing a sequence of instructions within a computer program

fluid intelligence—process-oriented **intelligence,** requiring rapid understanding of novel relationships (cf. **crystallized intelligence**)

forebrain—one of three major regions of the **brain** (cf. **hindbrain, midbrain**), containing the **cerebral cortex** and many other structures necessary both for high-level cognitive functions (e.g., the **thalamus,** the **hypothalamus,** and the **limbic system,** which includes the **hippocampus**) and for intentional movement (e.g., the basal ganglia)

formal-operational stage—Piagetian stage during which children (roughly starting at age 12 years) become proficient in mentally manipulating their internal representations not only of concrete objects but also of abstract symbols

frontal lobe—the region of the **cerebral cortex** largely responsible for many aspects of higher thought and motor processing and planning

function morpheme—a **morpheme** that adds detail and nuance to the meaning of a **content morpheme** or that helps a content morpheme to fit a particular syntactical context

functional-equivalence hypothesis—an assertion of belief that although mental **imagery** is not identical to **perception,** it is functionally equivalent to perception—that is, it works in about the same way as perception

functional fixedness—a **mental set** in which an individual fails to see an alternative use for something that has been known previously to have a particular use

functionalists—psychologists who hold that the key to understanding the human mind and behavior is to study the processes of how and why the mind works as it does, rather than to study the structural contents and elements of the mind

functional magnetic resonance imaging (fMRI)— imaging technique, not requiring the use of radioactive isotopes, for viewing functions of the human brain revealed by increased consumption of oxygenated blood in active parts of the **brain**

g—the general factor of intelligence identified by Spearman through **factor analysis**

Gestalt approaches to form perception—a way of studying the **perception** of objects and other forms, based on the notion that the whole of a form differs from the sum of its individual parts (from German, *Gestalt,* "form"; see also **Gestalt psychology**)

Gestalt psychology—school of psychological thought, which asserts that many psychological phenomena must be understood as integral wholes and that analysis into fragmentary elements often destroys the integrity of these phenomena

global planning—aspect of **problem solving** during which an individual encodes the problem and formulates a general strategy for attacking the problem (cf. **local planning**)

grammar—the study of **language** in terms of regular patterns that relate to the functions and relationships of words in a sentence—extending as broadly as the level of **discourse** and as narrowly as the pronunciation and meaning of individual words; *descriptive grammar*—the description of language patterns that relate to the structures, functions, and relationships of words in a sentence (see **phrase-structure grammars, transformational grammar**); *prescriptive grammar*—the formulation of various rules dictating the preferred use of written and spoken language, such as the functions, structures, and relationships of words in a sentence

habituation—the tendency to become accustomed to a stimulus and gradually to notice it less and less (cf. **dishabituation**; cf. also **sensory adaptation**)

heuristics—informal, speculative, shortcut strategies for solving problems, which sometimes work and sometimes do not (cf. **algorithm**; see **problem solving**)

hindbrain—the most primitive of the three major regions of the **brain** (cf. **forebrain, midbrain**), containing structures vital to low-level functioning of the organism, including part of the reticular activating system (the medulla oblongata), the pons, and the cerebellum

hindsight bias—a bias in decision making, in which an individual becomes aware of a given outcome of a decision and then perceives, retrospectively, all the signs and events leading up to the known outcome, believing these forewarnings to be obvious at the present time, although they were not obvious at the earlier time

hippocampus—a structure within the **limbic system** in the **forebrain,** implicated in many aspects of learning function

hypothalamus—a structure of the **forebrain,** involved in controlling many bodily functions (e.g., hormonal regulation)

hypothesis—tentative proposal regarding expected empirical consequences of a theory, such as the outcomes of research

hypothesis testing—a view of language acquisition, which asserts that children acquire **language** by mentally forming tentative assumptions regarding language and then testing these assumptions in the environment, using several operating principles for generating and testing their assumptions

hypothetical construct—concept that cannot be directly measured or observed but that may be used as a mental representation for understanding the workings of a psychological phenomenon

iconic store—a sensory register for the fleeting **storage** of discrete visual images in the form of *icons* (visual images that represent something, usually resembling whatever is being represented) (see **sensory store**)

ill-structured problem—a problem with no clear, obvious path to solution (cf. **well-structured problem**; see **problem solving**)

illusory correlation—a bias in which an individual tends to see events or other items as going together because the person is predisposed to do so

imagery—mental representation of objects, events, settings, and other things that are not immediately perceptible to sensory receptors (cf. **perception**)

implicit memory—a form of memory **retrieval** in which an individual shows enhanced performance on a task, as a result of prior experience, despite having no conscious awareness of recollecting the prior experience (cf. **explicit memory**; see also **memory**)

incubation—a period of rest, following a period of intensive effort in **problem solving,** during which the problem solver puts aside the problem for a while, thereby permitting greater mental flexibility so that **insight** may emerge

indirect request—a form of **speech act** in which an individual asks for something (e.g., information, a favor, a privilege, a resource) in an oblique, rather than a direct, manner

inductive reasoning—a process by which an individual tries to reach a probable general conclusion, based on a set of specific facts or observations (cf. **deductive reasoning**)

infantile amnesia—inability to recall events that happened during early development of the **brain** (usually the first 3 to 5 years; see **amnesia, memory**)

information-processing theorists—cognitive psychologists who seek to understand cognition (or other psychological phenomena) in terms of how people engage in various cognitive processes, such as decoding, encoding, storing, and retrieving information in various forms (e.g., images, propositions, or symbols)

insight—a seemingly sudden understanding of the nature of something, often as a result of taking a novel approach to the object of insight

intelligence—the ability to learn from experience and to adapt to the surrounding environment

interference—the process by which an individual forgets some information because competing information displaces the information that the individual is trying to store in **memory** (cf. **decay**; see also **proactive interference, retroactive interference**)

interference theory—the theory by which forgetting occurs because new information interferes with and ultimately displaces, old information in short-term memory

internalization—a Vygotskyan process whereby individuals incorporate into themselves knowledge that they gain through their interactions within a social context

interneuron—one of three types of **neurons;** links **sensory neurons** and **motor neurons**

ipsilateral—toward the same side (cf. **contralateral**)

isomorphic—characterized as having the same form or the same formal structure

jargon—a specialized set of words, phrases, and idioms commonly developed and used within a group sharing a common purpose or a common activity

judgment and decision making—cognitive processes by which an individual may evaluate various options and select the most suitable option from among various alternatives

knowledge representation—a mental form for what individuals know about things, ideas, events, and so on that exist outside their minds

language—the use of an organized means of combining words in order to communicate (cf. **communication**)

language-acquisition device (LAD)—the hypothetical construct of an innate human predisposition to acquire language; not yet identified as a specific physiological structure or function

law of Prägnanz—a Gestalt principle asserting the perceptual tendency to perceive visual arrays in ways that most simply organize disparate elements into a stable and coherent form

levels-of-processing framework—a way of looking at memory **storage,** which postulates that memory does not comprise any specific number of separate stores but instead comprises a continuous dimension in which the depth to which memory is encoded corresponds to the ease of retrieving the item: the deeper the level of processing, the higher the probability that an item may be retrieved (an alternative view is the *three-stores view,* in which memory is viewed as comprising a **sensory store, a short-term store,** and a **long-term store**)

lexical access—process by which people can retrieve (from **memory**) information about words (e.g., letter names)

lexical processes—various cognitive processes involved in identifying letters and words, as well as in activating relevant information in **memory** about the words

lexicon—the entire set of **morphemes** in a given **language** or in a given person's linguistic repertoire (cf. **vocabulary**)

limbic system—structure in the **forebrain,** which is involved in emotion, motivation, and learning

linear syllogism—a deductive argument in which the relationship among the three terms in the two **premises** involves a quantitative or qualitative comparison along a linear continuum (see **syllogism;** see also **deductive reasoning**)

linguistic relativity—a proposition regarding the relationship between thought and language, which asserts that speakers of different languages have differing cognitive systems, based on the languages they use, and that these different cognitive systems influence the ways in which people speaking the various languages think about the world

linguistic universals—characteristic patterns of language that apply across all of the languages of various cultures

lobes—four major regions of the **cerebral cortex** (see **frontal lobe, occipital lobe, parietal lobe, temporal lobe**)

local planning—aspect of **problem solving** during which an individual devises or selects detailed tactics (cf. **global planning**)

localization of function—identification of particular structures or regions of the **brain,** which appear to be partially or wholly involved in particular cognitive processes and other activities of the brain

long-term store—according to a three-stores model of **memory,** the **hypothetical construct** of a long-term store has a greater capacity than both the **sensory store** and the **short-term store,** and it can store information for very long periods of time, perhaps even indefinitely

magnetic resonance imaging (MRI)—sophisticated technique for revealing high-resolution images of the structure of the living **brain** by computing and analyzing magnetic changes in the energy of the orbits of nuclear particles in the molecules of the body

massed practice—the acquisition of a body of information all at one time rather than spaced over time; when testing is delayed, such practice generally does not lead to as much recall as does **distributed practice**

memory—the means by which individuals draw on past knowledge in order to use such knowledge in the present; the dynamic mechanisms associated with the retention and retrieval of information; the three operations through which information is processed by and for memory are **encoding, storage,** and **retrieval**

mental model—an internal representation of information, which somehow corresponds with whatever is being represented; may involve the use of both analogical and symbolic or propositional forms of **knowledge representation**

mental set—a cognitive phenomenon in which an individual is predisposed to use an existing model for representing information, even when the existing model inadequately represents the information in a new situation

metacognition—the ability of an individual to think about and to consider carefully the person's own processes of thought, particularly in regard to trying to strengthen cognitive abilities

metamemory—an aspect of **metacognition,** involving knowledge and understanding of memory abilities, as well as of ways in which to enhance **memory** abilities (e.g., through the use of **mnemonic devices**)

metaphor—a juxtaposition of two dissimilar nouns, which asserts the existence of some similarities between the two, while not disconfirming their dissimilarities (cf. **simile**)

midbrain—the middle of the three regions of the **brain** (cf. **forebrain, hindbrain**), involved in eye movements and coordination; contains a portion of the **brain stem**

mnemonic device—any of a set of specific techniques for aiding in the memorization of various isolated items, thereby adding meaning or **imagery** to an otherwise arbitrary listing of isolated items that may be difficult to remember (see **metamemory**)

mnemonist—person who uses **memory**-enhancing techniques for greatly improving his or her memory or who has a distinctive sensory or cognitive ability to remember information, particularly information that is highly concrete or that can be visualized readily (see **metamemory**)

modular—occurring in distinctive units of discrete processes or areas, rather than in an integrated manner across various processes or areas

monocular depth cues—one of the two chief means of judging the distances of visible objects (cf. **binocular depth cues**), based on sensed information that can be represented in just two dimensions and observed with just one *(mono-)* eye *(-ocular)*

monolinguals—persons who can speak only one language (cf. **bilinguals**)

morpheme—the smallest unit of single or combined sounds that denotes meaning within a given **language** (see also **content morpheme, function morpheme**)

motor (efferent) neuron—nerve cell involved in transmitting information from the **brain** or **spinal cord** to the muscles of the body (cf. **interneuron, sensory neuron**)

myelin—a fatty substance coating the **axons** of some **neurons**, facilitating the speed and accuracy of neural communication

negative transfer—the hindrance of **problem solving** as a result of prior experience in solving apparently related or similar problems (cf. **positive transfer**; see also **transfer**)

nervous system—the organized network of cells **(neurons)** through which an individual receives information from the environment, processes that information, and then interacts with the environment

network—a web of labeled relations (e.g., category membership, attribution) between **nodes**

neuron—individual neural cell

neurotransmitter—chemical messenger used for interneuronal communication

node—element representing a concept within a semantic network; each node is linked in relationships with other nodes in the **network**

nodes of Ranvier—gaps in the **myelin** coating of myelinated **axons**

noun phrase—a syntactic structure that often serves as a subject of a sentence but that may also act as an object of a **verb phrase** or of a prepositional phrase

object permanence—a cognitive awareness that objects continue to exist even when the objects are not immediately perceptible through the senses

occipital lobe—region of the **cerebral cortex** chiefly involved in visual processing

optic chiasma—structure in which roughly half of the information from each eye crosses over, to reach cortical areas in each **contralateral cerebral hemisphere**

overconfidence—a bias affecting decision making, in which individuals overestimate the probability that their own responses are accurate or even more broadly overvalue their own skills, knowledge, or judgment

overextension error—overapplication of the meaning of a given word to more things, ideas, and situations than is appropriate for the **denotation** and the **defining features** of the word; usually made by children or other persons who have not yet acquired a broad **vocabulary**; generally no longer typifies language production once the vocabulary of the language user has expanded to comprise enough words to describe the meanings that the individual intends to convey

overregularization—an error that commonly occurs during language acquisition, in which the novice language user has gained an understanding of how a language usually works and then overapplies the general rules of the language to the exceptional cases for which the rule does not apply

parallel distributed processing (PDP)—a model of **knowledge representation** and information processing, which proposes that knowledge is represented within a **network** in which information is stored in the form of various patterns of connection strengths, the patterns of connections are distributed across the brain, and information processing occurs through **parallel processing** of activated connections

parallel processing—means by which various information processes may be executed simultaneously (cf. **serial processing**)

parallel-processing model—conceptual model of memory in which the cognitive manipulation of multiple operations occurs simultaneously; as applied to short-term memory, the items stored in short-term memory would be retrieved all at once, not one at a time (see also **parallel distributed processing [PDP]**)

parietal lobe—region of the **cerebral cortex** chiefly involved in somatosensory processing (see also **primary somatosensory cortex**)

passive theories—a category of theories that explains speech perception exclusively in terms of the listener's passive reception of speech, without involving cognitive processes such as **memory** and consideration of context; according to these kinds of theories, the listener perceives speech exclusively through sensory processes such as filtering (e.g., screening out irrelevant sounds) and feature detection (e.g., matching features of speech sounds to existing templates for those sounds; see **feature matching**)

percept—mental representation of a stimulus that is perceived

perception—the set of psychological processes by which people recognize, organize, synthesize, and give meaning (in the brain) to the sensations received from environmental stimuli (in the sense organs)

perceptual constancy—the **perception** that a given object remains the same even when the immediate sensation of the object changes (see also **distal stimulus** vs. **proximal stimulus**)

performance theory—theoretical perspective emphasizing what people typically do (cf. **competence theory**)

peripheral nervous system (PNS)—one of the two main divisions of the **nervous system** (cf. **central nervous system**), comprising all nerves *except* those of the **brain** and the **spinal cord**

phoneme—smallest unit of speech sound that can be used to distinguish one meaningful utterance from another in a given language

phrase-structure grammars—a form of syntactical analysis, which decomposes sentences in terms of the superficial sequence of words in sentences (see **surface structure**; cf. **deep structure**), without considering relationships among sentences; analysis often centers on the analysis of **noun phrases** and **verb phrases** (also termed *surface-structure grammars* because analysis centers on **syntax** at a surface level of analysis; cf. **transformational grammar**)

plasticity—a characteristic of human cognition, whereby people appear to be limitlessly able to modify their cognitive processes and products, improving their effectiveness at the tasks they face

positive transfer—the facilitation of **problem solving** as a result of prior experience in solving related or similar problems (cf. **negative transfer**; see also **transfer**)

positron emission tomography (PET)—method for imaging the functioning of portions of the brain, requiring use of radioactive isotopes, based on increased consumption of glucose by activated portions

pragmatic reasoning schema—a mental framework comprising various general organizing principles (rules) related to particular kinds of goals

pragmatics—the study of how people use **language**, emphasizing the contexts in which language is used, as well as the nonverbal communication that augments verbal communication (cf. **discourse**)

pragmatist—proponent of a school of psychological thought that evaluates the merits of knowledge in terms of the usefulness of that knowledge

premise—either of two statements by which a syllogistic argument is made (see **syllogism**)

preoperational stage—Piagetian stage during which a child (roughly 2 to 7 years of age) begins actively to develop internal mental representations and to use **language** as a means of cognitive manipulation, as well as **communication**

primary motor cortex—region of the **cerebral cortex** that is chiefly responsible for directing the movements of all muscles

primary somatosensory cortex—region of the **cerebral cortex** that is chiefly responsible for receiving sensations from the skin, including sensations from the tongue and other parts of the face

prime—a **node** within a **network,** which activates a connected node in the network; this activation is known as the **priming effect** (see **spreading activation**)

priming—the process by which particular initial stimuli activate mental pathways, thereby enhancing the ability to process subsequent stimuli related to the priming stimuli in some way; the activation of a **node** by a **prime** (activating node) to which the node is connected in a **network** (see **spreading activation**)

priming effect—the enhanced access to a particular stimulus or item of information, as a result of recent activation of or exposure to that stimulus or datum; according to the network view of memory processes, the effect is due to the activation of a **node** by a **prime** (activating node) to which the node is connected in a **network,** in the process of **spreading activation**

proactive interference—a type of **memory** disruption, which occurs when interfering information is presented *before,* rather than *after,* presentation of the information that is to be remembered (also termed *proactive inhibition;* cf. **retroactive interference;** see also **interference**)

problem solving—a process for which the goal is to overcome obstacles obstructing a path to a solution

problem-solving cycle—a series of steps for problem solving, which include problem identification, problem definition and representation, strategy formulation, organization of information, allocation of resources, monitoring, and evaluation

problem space—a metaphor proposed for encompassing all of the possible actions that can be applied to solving a problem, considering any constraints that apply to the solution of the problem

procedural knowledge—information regarding how to execute a sequence of operations; understanding and awareness of how to perform particular tasks, skills, or procedures ("knowing how," not "knowing that"; cf. **declarative knowledge**)

production—a condition–action ("if–then") sequence, often used in the implementation of a procedure

production system—an ordered set of **productions** in which execution starts at the top of a list of productions, continues until a condition is satisfied, and then returns to the top of the list to start anew

productive thinking—thought processes involving novel, nonlinear insights

proposition—in regard to **deductive reasoning,** an assertion of belief that may be either true or false; in regard to **knowledge representation,** an underlying meaning representing a concept or a relationship among concepts

propositional hypothesis—an assertion of belief that both imaginal and verbal information is represented in the form of **propositions,** which are the meanings underlying various concepts and relationships among concepts

prototype—a model that best represents a given **concept** (and various instances of the concept); the model for a given concept comprises a set of **characteristic features** that tend to be typical of most examples (cf. **exemplars**) of the concept, although no single characteristic feature is necessary for a given example to be considered an instance of the concept (see **prototype theory;** cf. **componential theory, core, defining features**)

prototype theory—one of two primary theories of semantics (cf. **componential theory**); this theory claims that the meaning of a word (or **concept**) can be understood in terms of a **prototype** (see also **exemplar**), which best represents a given word and which comprises a set of **characteristic features** that tend to be typical of most examples of the word (cf. **core, defining features**)

proximal stimulus—the internal sensation of a source of stimulation, as it is registered by the sensory receptors; this internal sensation might not exactly match the external source of stimulation as it exists in the world (cf. **distal stimulus;** see also **perceptual constancy**)

psycholinguistics—study of language as it interacts with the human mind

rationalist—person who believes that the route to knowledge is through the use of logical analysis (cf. **empiricist**)

reasoning—cognitive process by which an individual may infer a conclusion from an assortment of evidence or from statements of principles (see **deductive reasoning, inductive reasoning**)

recall—a process of **memory** often employed in memory tasks, in which an individual is asked to produce (not just to recognize as correct) a fact, a word, or other item from memory (cf. **recognition**)

receptor—one of two types of neurons (cf. **effector**); receives information about sensations throughout the body as a first step toward transmission of that information to the **brain,** usually through the **spinal cord**

receptor cells—structures specially designed to receive a particular substance or a particular kind of information

recognition—a process of **memory** often employed in memory tasks, in which an individual is asked just to recognize as correct (not to produce) a fact, a word, or other item from memory (cf. **recall**)

recognition-by-components (RBC) theory—a theory of object **perception,** which suggests that objects are recognized based on the perception of the distinctive arrangement of various *geons* (a set of three-dimensional geometrical elements) that compose each object

reconstructive—psychological phenomenon in which an individual stores in **memory** some information about events or facts, exactly as the events or facts took place, and then during **retrieval,** the individual uses various strategies to rebuild the remembered experience (cf. **constructive**)

reflex—an automatic, involuntary response to stimulation, which does not require input from the **brain**

rehearsal—strategy for keeping information in short-term memory or for moving information into long-term memory by repeating the information over and over, usually by elaborating the information in some way

representational thought—cognitive processes by which people form internal representations (symbolic or imaginal depictions) of external stimuli

representativeness—a decision-making **heuristic** in which an individual judges the probability of an uncertain event by the degree to which that event is similar in its essential properties to the population from which it derives, and by the degree to which the event reflects the salient features of the processes by which it is generated (e.g., randomness)

retrieval (memory)—recovery of stored information from **memory,** by moving the information into **consciousness** for use in active cognitive processing (cf. **encoding, storage**)

retroactive interference—a type of **memory** disruption, which occurs when interfering information is presented *after,* rather than *before,* presentation of the information that is to be remembered (also termed *retroactive inhibition;* cf. **proactive interference;** see also **interference**)

retrograde amnesia—inability explicitly to recall events that occurred *before* a trauma that causes **memory** loss (often, the amnesic gradually begins to recall earlier events, starting with the earliest experiences and gradually recalling events that occurred closer to the time of the trauma, perhaps eventually even recalling the traumatic episode; cf. **anterograde amnesia;** see also **amnesia**)

reuptake—a mechanism for removing excess **neurotransmitters** from a **synapse,** simply by absorbing the excess back into the **terminal buttons**

reversible—characteristic of processes that can be undone, once they have been done (e.g., pouring liquid from one container to another and then back again)

saccades—minute movements of the eyes that serve to increase stimulus variability on the retina, and to bring different aspects of the visual world into focus

saltatory conduction—a means by which an electrical impulse moves quickly through an **axon,** by leaping across the **myelin** sheath, from one **node of Ranvier** to another

satisficing—a decision-making strategy in which an individual chooses the first acceptable alternative that becomes available, without considering all possible alternative options

schema—a cognitive framework for meaningfully organizing various interrelated **concepts,** based on previous experiences (from Latin; plural, *schemas* or *schemata*)

script—structure for a **schema** involving a common understanding about the characteristic actors, objects, and sequence of actions in a stereotypical situation

search—active scanning of the environment, in pursuit of particular stimuli or particular features (see **conjunction search, feature search;** cf. **vigilance**)

selective attention—a process by which an individual attempts to track one stimulus or one type of stimulus and to ignore another

selective-combination insights—thought processes involving novel syntheses of relevant information

selective-comparison insights—cognitive processes involving novel realizations of how existing knowledge may be related to new information

selective-encoding insights—cognitive processes of mental representation, in which relevant information is distinguished from irrelevant information

semantic memory—**encoding, storage,** and **retrieval** of facts (e.g., **declarative knowledge** about the world) that do not describe the unique experiences of the individual recalling the facts; sometimes distinguished from retrieval of information that has a particular temporal context in which the individual acquired the facts (cf. **episodic memory**)

semantics—the study of meanings in **language,** which involves both **denotation** and **connotation** (see **componential theory, prototype theory**)

sensorimotor stage—Piagetian stage during which an infant (roughly from birth to age 2 years) gradually adapts motor output (e.g., **reflexes**) in response to sensory input, to serve the intentional goals of the infant; involves increases in both the number and the complexity of sensory and motor abilities

sensory adaptation—a temporary physiological response to a sensed change in the environment (e.g., adaptation to changes in light intensity), which is generally not subject to conscious manipulation or control, and which does not depend on previous experience with the given type of environmental change (cf. **habituation**)

sensory (afferent) neuron—one of three types of **neurons** (cf. **interneuron, motor neuron**); receives information about sensations and transmits that information to the **spinal cord** and the **brain**

sensory store—according to a three-stores model of **memory** (cf. **long-term store, short-term store**), the **hypothetical construct** of a sensory store has the smallest capacity for storing information (i.e., for only a fleeting sensory image) and has the shortest duration for memory storage (i.e., for only fractions of a second; see also **iconic store**)

serial processing—means by which only one information process is executed at any one time, and multiple processes are handled sequentially (cf. **parallel processing**)

short-term store—according to a three-stores model of memory (cf. **long-term store, sensory store**), the **hypothetical construct** of a short-term store has a modest capacity (i.e., for only about seven items, give or take a couple of items) and has a duration for storing information for only a number of seconds unless strategies (e.g., **rehearsal**) are used for keeping the information in the short-term store for longer periods of time

signal—a stimulus to be detected; according to signal-detection theory, there are four possible stimulus–response pairs: a hit, a miss, a false alarm, or a correct rejection

signal detection—a process by which an individual must detect the appearance of a particular stimulus

signal-detection theory (SDT)—a set of perceptual principles positing four possible stimulus–response pairs in detecting a perceptual signal: a hit, a miss, a false alarm, or a correct rejection

similarity theory—a theory regarding the **perception** of forms and patterns (cf. **feature-integration theory**), which suggests that the key factor affecting the relative ease or difficulty of visual **search** is the degree to which targets and **distractors** are similar; factors that increase the ease of search are uniformity (high similarity) of the targets, uniformity of the distractors, and disparity (high dissimilarity) between the targets and the distractors; factors that make search more difficult are variety (dissimilarity) in targets or in distractors, as well as similarity between target stimuli and distractors

simile—a juxtaposition of two dissimilar nouns, in which the word *like* or *as* is used to suggest similarities between the two (cf. **metaphor**)

single-system hypothesis—a view of bilingualism, which suggests that both languages are represented in just one system in the brain (cf. **dual-system hypothesis;** see also **bilinguals**)

slips of the tongue—inadvertent errors in speech, usually as a result of phonological or semantic confusion of **phonemes, morphemes,** or even larger units of **language**

soma—the cell body of a **neuron,** which is the part of the neuron essential to the life and reproduction of the cell

speech act—any of five basic categories of speech, analyzed in terms of the purposes accomplished by the given act

spinal cord—a bundle of **neurons** and neural fibers extending from the base of the **brain** to the base of the spine; the locus from which the spinal nerves branch from the center of the body

split-brain—the result of a process that severs the **corpus callosum** connecting the two **cerebral hemispheres** of the **brain**

spreading activation—process by which stimuli excite units (or **nodes**) within a **network,** and excited units cause connected units to become active

static assessment environment—a typical context for examination in which an examiner makes no effort to respond distinctively when a child gives an incorrect answer, proceeding instead to the next question in the test (cf. **dynamic assessment environment**)

static equilibrium—a state in which the electrically charged particles inside and outside the **axon** of a **neuron** are balanced, during which an **action potential** may occur

stereotype—**mental set** involving a belief that all members of a given social group will demonstrate particular characteristics observed in one or more members of that group

storage (memory)—the movement of encoded information into **memory** and the maintenance of information in storage (cf. **encoding, retrieval**)

Stroop effect—the psychological difficulty in selective attention that occurs when a literate individual attempts to name the colors of ink in which are printed color words that identify a color other than the color of the ink (e.g., the word *blue* may be printed in red ink)

structuralism—a psychological perspective postulating that the key to understanding the human mind and behavior is to study the structural contents and elements of the mind; early psychologists who favored this perspective sought to analyze **consciousness** into its constituent components of elementary sensations, using the reflective self-observation technique of introspection

structure-of-intellect (SOI)—Guilford's model for a three-dimensional structure of **intelligence,** embracing various contents, operations, and products of intelligence

subjective probability—an individual's personal guesses regarding the likelihood that particular outcomes will occur

subjective utility—an individual's personal assessment of the degree to which a particular outcome provides pleasure or pain

subliminal perception—a form of preconscious processing, in which people may be able to detect information without being aware that they are doing so

surface structure—a level of syntactic analysis, which indicates just the specific syntactical sequence of words in a sentence (cf. **deep structure**; see **phrase-structure grammars, syntax**)

syllogism—a deductive argument comprising a major **premise,** a minor premise, and a conclusion that may be drawn from the two premises (sometimes, the conclusion is simply that no conclusion may be drawn from the existing premises) (cf. **conditional reasoning;** see also **deductive reasoning**)

symbolic—connoting a form of **knowledge representation** that has been arbitrarily chosen to stand for something and that does not perceptually resemble whatever is being represented (cf. **analogue**)

synapse—a small gap between **neurons,** which serves as a point of contact between the **terminal buttons** of one or more neurons and the **dendrites** of one or more other neurons

syntax—a level of linguistic analysis, which centers on the patterns by which users of a particular **language** put words together at the level of the sentence (see also **grammar**)

synthesis—the process of integrating various elements into a more complex whole (cf. **analysis**)

telegraphic speech—rudimentary syntactical communications of two words or more, which are characteristic of very early **language** acquisition, and which seem more like telegrams than like conversation because **function morphemes** are usually omitted

template—exact model of a distinctive pattern or form, used as the basis for perception of patterns or forms (cf. **prototype**)

temporal lobe—region of the **cerebral cortex** chiefly involved in auditory processing

terminal buttons—knobs at the end of each branch of an **axon;** each button may release a chemical **neurotransmitter** as a result of an **action potential**

thalamus—a structure of the **forebrain,** which serves as a vital relay station for sensory input into the **cerebral cortex**

thematic roles—the semantic relationships among words in a sentence, particularly in regard to how the words relate to the verb; roles may include agents, patients, beneficiaries, locations, sources, goals, instruments, and so on (see **semantics;** cf. **syntax**)

theory—a statement of some general principles that explain a phenomenon or a set of phenomena

theory of multiple intelligences—a theoretical perspective in which **intelligence** is seen as a set of discrete abilities, each of which is a distinct kind of intelligence, not merely a component of a unitary construct of intelligence

threshold of excitation—point above which an **action potential** for a particular **neuron** may occur and below which an action potential will not occur

tip-of-the-tongue phenomenon—an experience involving the preconscious level of **consciousness,** in which a person tries to remember something that is known to be stored in **memory** but that the person cannot quite retrieve

top-down strategies—approaches to deriving meaning, which start with a person's existing **schemas** for prior experience and knowledge, especially in a given context; these schemas then shape the person's expectations regarding what will be perceived, and the resulting perceptions influence the meanings derived (cf. **bottom-up strategies**)

top-down theories—theoretical explanations of **perception** that focus on the high-level cognitive processes, existing knowledge, and prior expectations that influence perception, and then work their way down to considering the sensory data, such as the perceptual stimulus (cf. **bottom-up theories**)

transfer—the carryover of knowledge or skills from one kind of task or one particular context to another kind of task or another context (see **negative transfer, positive transfer**)

transformational grammar—a form of syntactical analysis that centers on transformational rules that guide the relationships among various **surface structures** of phrases (cf. **phrase-structure grammars;** see **deep structure**)

transparency—the tendency to believe that problem situations with similar contexts or content also have analogous formal structures or solution paths

triarchic theory of human intelligence—a theoretical perspective integrating features of the internal world, the external world, and the experience of an individual, which the person uses in addressing tasks requiring analytical, practical, and creative intelligence

verb phrase—one of the two key parts of a statement (also termed a *predicate;* cf. **noun phrase**); the part of a sentence that tells something about the subject of the sentence, usually including a verb and whatever the verb acts on, but sometimes including a linking verb (e.g., *is, are)* and a descriptor

verbal comprehension—the ability to understand written and spoken linguistic input, such as words, sentences, and paragraphs (cf. **verbal fluency**)

verbal fluency—the ability to produce written and spoken linguistic output, such as words, sentences, and paragraphs (cf. **verbal comprehension**)

vigilance—the ongoing alert watchfulness for the appearance of an unpredictable stimulus, which may be sensed through any of the sensory modalities (cf. **search**)

vocabulary—a repertoire of words, formed by combining **morphemes** (cf. **lexicon**)

well-structured problem—problem with a well-defined path to solution (cf. **ill-structured problem;** see **problem solving**)

wisdom—broadly defined as extraordinary **insight,** keen awareness, and exceptional judgment

word-superiority effect—a perceptual phenomenon in which an individual can more readily identify (discriminate) letters when they are presented in the context of words than when they are presented as solitary letters

working memory—a portion of **memory** that may be viewed as a specialized part of long-term memory; it holds only the most recently activated portion of long-term memory and moves these activated elements into and out of short-term memory (which may be viewed as the narrow portion of working memory that enters immediate awareness); some psychologists consider working memory to be a **hypothetical construct** in opposition to the three-stores view, but others consider it a complement to the three-stores view

zone of proximal development (ZPD)—the range of ability between a child's existing undeveloped potential ability (competence) and the child's observed ability (performance)

REFERENCES

Abelson, R. P. (1973). The structure of belief systems. In R. C. Schank & K. M. Colby (Eds.), *Computer models of thought and language* (pp. 287–339). San Francisco: Freeman, 1973.

Abelson, R. P. (1980). Searle's argument is just a set of Chinese symbols. *Behavioral and Brain Sciences, 3,* 424–425.

Abelson, R. P., & Carroll, J. D. (1965). Computer simulation of individual belief systems. *American Behavioral Scientist, 8,* 24–30.

Adams, M. J. (Ed.). (1986). *Odyssey: A curriculum for thinking* (Vols. 1–6). Watertown, MA: Charlesbridge Publishing.

Adler, J. (1991, July 22). The melting of a mighty myth. *Newsweek,* 63.

Ahn, W., & Bailenson, J. (1996). Causal attribution as a search for underlying mechanisms. An explanation of the conjunction fallacy and the discounting principle. *Cognitive Psychology, 31,* 82–123.

Ahn, W., Kalish, C. W., Medin, D. L., & Gelman, S. A. (1995). The role of covariation versus mechanism information in causal attribution. *Cognition, 54,* 299–352.

Alba, J. W., & Hasher, L. (1983). Is memory schematic? *Psychological Bulletin, 93*(2), 203–231.

Albert, M. L., & Obler, L. (1978). *The bilingual brain: Neuropsychological and neurolinguistic aspects of bilingualism.* New York: Academic Press.

Amabile, T. A., & Rovee-Collier, C. (1991). Contextual variation and memory retrieval at six months. *Child Development, 62*(5), 1155–1166.

Amabile, T. M. (1996). *Creativity in context.* Boulder, CO: Westview.

Anderson, B. F. (1975). *Cognitive psychology.* New York: Academic Press.

Anderson, J. R. (1972). FRAN: A simulation model of free recall. In G. H. Bower (Ed.), *The psychology of learning and motivation* (Vol. 5, pp. 315–378). New York: Academic Press.

Anderson, J. R. (1976). *Language, memory, and thought.* Hillsdale, NJ: Erlbaum.

Anderson, J. R. (1980). Concepts, propositions, and schemata: What are the cognitive units? *Nebraska Symposium on Motivation, 28,* 121–162.

Anderson, J. R. (1983). *The architecture of cognition.* Cambridge, MA: Harvard University Press.

Anderson, J. R. (1985). *Cognitive psychology and its implications.* New York: Freeman.

Anderson, J. R. (1991). The adaptive nature of human categorization. *Psychological Review, 98,* 409–429.

Anderson, J. R. (1996). ACT: A simple theory of complex cognition. *American Psychologist, 51,* 355–365.

Anderson, J. R., & Bower, G. H. (1973). *Human associative memory.* New York: Wiley.

Anderson, J. R., & Fincham, J. M. (1996). Categorization and sensitivity to correlation. *Journal of Experimental Psychology: Learning, Memory, and Cognition, 22,* 259–277.

Anderson, R. C., & Pichert, J. W. (1978). Recall of previously unrecallable information following a shift in perspective. *Journal of Verbal Learning and Verbal Behavior, 17,* 1–12.

Angell, J. R. (1907). The province of functional psychology. *Psychological Review, 14,* 61–91.

Antell, S. E., & Keating, D. P. (1983). Perception of numerical invariance in neonates. *Child Development, 54,* 695–701.

Appel, L. F., Cooper, R. G., McCarrell, N., Sims-Knight, J., Yussen, S. R., & Flavell, J. H. (1972). The development of the distinction between perceiving and memorizing. *Child Development, 43,* 1365–1381.

Aristotle. (1987). The works of Aristotle. In R. M. Hutchins *Great books of the Western world: Vol. 8.* Chicago: Encyclopaedia Britannica. (Original work ca. 335 b.c.)

Arlin, P. K. (1975). Cognitive development in adulthood: A fifth stage? *Developmental Psychology, 11,* 602–606.

Armstrong, S. L., Gleitman, L. R., & Gleitman, H. (1983). What some concepts might not be. *Cognition, 13,* 263–308.

Asher, J. J., & Garcia, R. (1969). The optimal age to learn a foreign language. *Modern Language Journal, 53*(5), 334–341.

Atkinson, R. C., & Juola, J. F. (1974). Search and decision processes in recognition memory. In D. H. Krantz, R. C. Atkinson, R. D. Luce, & P. Suppes (Eds.), *Contemporary developments in mathematical psychology.* San Francisco: Freeman.

Atkinson, R. C., & Shiffrin, R. M. (1968). Human memory: A proposed system and its control processes. In K. W. Spence & J. T. Spence (Eds.), *The psychology of learning and motivation: Vol. 2. Advances in research and theory.* New York: Academic Press.

Atkinson, R. C., & Shiffrin, R. M. (1971). The control of short-term memory. *Scientific American, 225,* 82–90.

Au, T. K. (1983). Chinese and English counterfactuals: The Sapir–Whorf hypothesis revisited. *Cognition, 15,* 155–187.

Au, T. K. (1984). Counterfactuals: In reply to Alfred Bloom. *Cognition, 17,* 289–302.

Averbach, E., & Coriell, A. S. (1961). Short-term memory in vision. *Bell System Technical Journal, 40,* 309–328.

Bachevalier, J., & Mishkin, M. (1986). Visual recognition impairment follows ventromedial but not dorsolateral frontal lesions in monkeys. *Behavioral Brain Research, 20*(3), 249–261.

Baddeley, A. D. (1966). Short-term memory for word sequences as function of acoustic, semantic, and formal similarity. *Quarterly Journal of Experimental Psychology, 18,* 362–365.

Baddeley, A. D. (1984). The fractionation of human memory. *Psychological Medicine, 14*(2), 259–264.

Baddeley, A. D. (1989). The psychology of remembering and forgetting. In T. Butler (Ed.), *Memory: History, culture and the mind.* London: Basil Blackwell.

Baddeley, A. D. (1990a). *Human memory.* Hove, England: Erlbaum.

Baddeley, A. D. (1990b). *Human memory: Theory and practice.* Needham Heights, MA: Allyn & Bacon.

Baddeley, A. D. (1992). Working memory. *Science, 255,* 556–559.

Baddeley, A. D. (1993). Verbal and visual subsystems of working memory. *Current Biology, 3,* 563–565.

Baddeley, A. D. (1995). Working memory. In M. S. Gazzaniga (Ed.), *The cognitive neurosciences* (pp. 755–764). Cambridge, MA: MIT Press.

Baddeley, A. D. (1997). *Human memory: Theory and practice* (Rev. ed.). Sussex: Psychology Press.

Baddeley, A. D., & Hitch, G. J. (1974). Working memory. In G. Bower (Ed.), *Advances in learning and motivation* (Vol. 8, pp. 47–90). New York: Academic Press.

Baddeley, A., Thomson, N., & Buchanan, M. (1975). Word length and the structure of short-term memory. *Journal of Verbal Learning & Verbal Behavior, 14*(6), 575–589.

Baddeley, A., & Warrington, E. (1970). Amnesia and the distinction between long- and short-term memory. *Journal of Verbal Learning & Verbal Behavior, 9*(2), 176–189.

Bahrick, H. P. (1984a). Fifty years of second language attrition: Implications for programmatic research. *Modern Language Journal, 68*(2), 105–118.

Bahrick, H. P. (1984b). Semantic memory content in permastore: Fifty years of memory for Spanish learned in school. *Journal of Experimental Psychology: General, 113*(1), 1–29.

Bahrick, H. P., Bahrick, L. E., Bahrick, A. S., & Bahrick, P. E. (1993). Maintenance of foreign language vocabulary and the spacing effect. *Psychological Science, 4*(5), 316–321.

Bahrick, H. P., Bahrick, P. O., & Wittlinger, R. P. (1975). Fifty years of memory for names and faces: A cross-sectional approach. *Journal of Experimental Psychology: General, 104,* 54–75.

Bahrick, H. P., & Hall, L. K. (1991). Lifetime maintenance of high school mathematics content. *Journal of Experimental Psychology: General, 120*(1), 20–33.

Bahrick, H. P., Hall, L. K., Goggin, J. P., Bahrick, L. E., & Berger, S. A. (1994). Fifty years of language maintenance and language dominance in bilingual Hispanic immigrants. *Journal of Experimental Psychology: General, 123*(3), 264–283.

Bahrick, H. P., & Phelps, E. (1987). Retention of Spanish vocabulary over eight years. *Journal of Experimental Psychology: Learning, Memory, & Cognition, 13,* 344–349.

Baillargeon, R. (1987). Object permanence in 3½ and 4½ month-old infants. *Developmental Psychology, 23,* 655–664.

Baltes, P. B. (1993). The aging mind: Potential and limits. *Gerontologist, 33,* 580–594.

Baltes, P. B. (1997). On the incomplete architecture of human ontogeny: Selection, optimization, and compensation as foundations of developmental theory. *American Psychologist, 52,* 366–380.

Baltes, P. B., Dittmann-Kohli, F., & Dixon, R. A. (1984). New perspectives on the development of intelligence in adulthood: Toward a dual-process conception and a model of selective optimization with compensation. In P. B. Baltes & O. G. Brim, Jr. (Eds.), *Life-span development and behavior* (Vol. 6, pp. 33–76). New York: Academic Press.

Baltes, P. B., & Smith, J. (1990). Toward a psychology of wisdom and its ontogenesis. In R. J. Sternberg (Ed.), *Wisdom: Its nature, origins, and development* (pp. 87–120). New York: Cambridge University Press.

Baltes, P. B., Staudinger, U. M., Maercker, A., & Smith, J. (1995). People nominated as wise: A comparative study of wisdom-related knowledge. *Psychology & Aging, 10,* 155–166.

Baltes, P. B., & Willis, S. L. (1979). Toward psychological theories of aging and development. In J. E. Birren & K. W. Schaie (Eds.), *Handbook of the psychology of aging.* New York: Van Nostrand Reinhold.

Banaji, M. R., & Crowder, R. G. (1989). The bankruptcy of everyday memory. *American Psychologist, 44,* 1185–1193.

Bandura, A. (1977a). Self-efficacy: Toward a unifying theory of behavioral change. *Psychological Review, 84,* 181–215.

Bandura, A. (1977b). *Social learning theory.* Englewood Cliffs, NJ: Prentice-Hall.

Baron, J. (1988). *Thinking and deciding.* New York: Cambridge University Press.

Baroody, A. J. (1995). Mastery of basic number combinations: Internalization of relationships or facts? *Journal for Research in Mathematical Education, 16,* 83–98.

Barrett, P. T., & Eysenck, H. J. (1992). Brain evoked potentials and intelligence: The Hendrickson paradigm. *Intelligence, 16*(3,4), 361–381.

Barron, F. (1988). Putting creativity to work. In R. J. Sternberg (Ed.), *The nature of creativity* (pp. 76–98). New York: Cambridge University Press.

Barsalou, L. W. (1994). Flexibility, structure, and linguistic vagary in concepts: Manifestations of a compositional system of perceptual symbols. In A. F. Collins, S. E. Gathercole, M. A. Conway, & P. E. Morris (Eds.), *Theories of memory* (pp. 29–101). Hillsdale, NJ: Erlbaum.

Bartlett, F. C. (1932). *Remembering: A study in experimental and social psychology.* Cambridge, England: Cambridge University Press.

Bashore, T. R., Osman, A., & Hefley, E. F. (1989). Mental slowing in elderly persons: A cognitive psychophysiological analysis. *Psychology & Aging, 4,* 235–244.

Bastik, T. (1982). *Intuition: How we think and act.* Chichester, England: Wiley.

Baylis, G., Driver, J., & McLeod, P. (1992). Movement and proximity constrain miscombinations of colour and form. *Perception, 21*(2), 201–218.

Beardsley, M. (1962). The metaphorical twist. *Philosophical Phenomenological Research, 22,* 293–307.

Beck, I. L., Perfetti, C. A., & McKeown, M. G. (1982). Effects of long-term vocabulary instruction on lexical access and reading comprehension. *Journal of Educational Psychology, 74,* 506–521.

Begg, I., & Denny, J. (1969). Empirical reconciliation of atmosphere and conversion interpretations of syllogistic reasoning. *Journal of Experimental Psychology, 81,* 351–354.

Beilin, H. (1971). Developmental stages and developmental processes. In D. R. Green, M. P. Ford, & G. B. Flamer (Eds.), *Measurement and Piaget* (pp.172–197). New York: McGraw-Hill.

Bellezza, F. S. (1984). The self as a mnemonic device: The role of internal cues. *Journal of Personality and Social Psychology, 47,* 506–516.

Bellezza, F. S. (1992). Recall of congruent information in the self-reference task. *Bulletin of the Psychonomic Society, 30*(4), 275–278.

Belmont, J. M., & Butterfield, E. C. (1971). Learning strategies as determinants of memory deficiencies. *Cognitive Psychology, 2,* 411–420.

Benishin, C. G., Lee, R., Wang, L. C. H., & Liu, H. J. (1991). Effects of gensenoside RB-1 on central cholinergic metabolism. *Pharmacology, 42,* 223–229.

Berkow, R. (1992). *The Merck manual of diagnosis and therapy* (16th ed.). Rahway, NJ: Merck Research Laboratories.

Berlin, B., & Kay, P. (1969). *Basic color terms: Their universality and evolution.* Los Angeles: University of California Press.

Berliner, H. J. (1969, August). Chess playing program. *SICART Newsletter, 19,* 19–20.

Bernstein, A. (1958, July). A chess-playing program for the IBM704. *Chess Review,* 208–209.

Berry, J. W. (1974). Radical cultural relativism and the concept of intelligence. In J. W. Berry & P. R. Dasen (Eds.), *Culture and cognition: Readings in cross-cultural psychology* (pp. 225–229). London: Methuen.

Bertoncini, J. (1993), Infants' perception of speech units: Primary representation capacities. In B. B. De Boysson-Bardies, S. De Schonen, P. Jusczyk, P. MacNeilage, & J. Morton (Eds.), *Developmental neurocognition: Speech and face processing in the first year of life.* Dordrecht: Kluwer.

Bialystok, E., & Hakuta, K. (1994). *In other words: The science and psychology of second-language acquisition.* New York: Basic Books.

Bickerton, D. (1969). Prolegomena to a linguistic theory of metaphor. *Foundations of Language, 5,* 36–51.

Bickerton, D. (1990). *Language and species.* Chicago: University of Chicago Press.

Bidell, T. R., & Fischer, K. W. (1992). Beyond the stage debate: Action, structure, and variability in Piagetian theory and research. In R. J. Sternberg & C. A. Berg (Eds.), *Intellectual development* (pp. 100–140). New York: Cambridge University Press.

Biederman, I. (1972). Perceiving real-world scenes. *Science, 177*(4043), 77–80.

Biederman, I. (1987). Recognition-by-components: A theory of human image understanding. *Psychological Review, 94,* 115–147.

Biederman, I. (1993a). Geon theory as an account of shape recognition in mind and brain. *Irish Journal of Psychology, 14*(3), 314–327.

Biederman, I. (1993b). Visual object recognition. In A. I. Goldman (Ed.), *Readings in philosophy and cognitive science* (pp. 9–21). Cambridge, MA: MIT Press. (Original work published 1990)

Biederman, I., Glass, A. L., & Stacy, E. W. (1973). Searching for objects in real-world scenes. *Journal of Experimental Psychology, 97*(1), 22–27.

Biederman, I., Rabinowitz, J. C., Glass, A. L., & Stacy, E. W. (1974). On the information extracted from a glance at a scene. *Journal of Experimental Psychology, 103*(3), 597–600.

Biederman, I., Teitelbaum, R. C., & Mezzanotte, R. J. (1983). Scene perception: A failure to find a benefit from prior expectancy or familiarity. *Journal of Experimental Psychology: Learning, Memory, & Cognition, 9*(3), 411–429.

Bierlein, J. F. (1992). *The book of ages.* New York: Ballantine.

Binet, A., & Simon, T. (1916). *The development of intelligence in children* (E. S. Kite, Trans.). Baltimore: Williams & Wilkins.

Black, M. (1962). *Models and metaphors.* Ithaca, NY: Cornell University Press.

Blansjaar, B. A., Vielvoye, G. J., Van Dijk, J. Gert, & Rinders, R. J. (1992). Similar brain lesions in alcoholics and Korsakoff patients: MRI, psychometric and clinical findings. *Clinical Neurology & Neurosurgery, 94*(3), 197–203.

Bloom, A. H. (1981). *The linguistic shaping of thought: A study in the impact of language on thinking in China and the West.* Hillsdale, NJ: Erlbaum.

Bloom, B. S. (1964). *Stability and change in human characteristics.* New York: Wiley.

Bloom, B. S., & Broder, L. J. (1950). *Problem-solving processes of college students.* Chicago: University of Chicago Press.

Bobrow, D. G. (1968). Natural language input for a computer problem-solving system. In M. L. Minsky (Ed.), *Semantic information processing* (pp. 146–226). Cambridge, MA: MIT Press.

Bock, K. (1990). Structure in language: Creating form in talk. *American Psychologist, 45*(11), 1221–1236.

Bock, K., Loebell, H., & Morey, R. (1992). From conceptual roles to structural relations: Bridging the syntactic cleft. *Psychological Review, 99*(1), 150–171.

Bohannon, J. (1988). Flashbulb memories for the space shuttle disaster: A tale of two theories. *Cognition, 29*(2), 179–196.

Boring, E. G. (1923, June 6). Intelligence as the tests test it. *New Republic,* 35–37.

Boring, E. G. (1942). *Sensation and perception in the history of experimental psychology.* New York: Appleton-Century-Crofts.

Bornstein, M. H. (1989). Information processing (habituation) in infancy and stability in cognitive development. *Human Development, 32*(3–4), 129–136.

Bornstein, M. H., & Sigman, M. D. (1986). Continuity in mental development from infancy. *Child Development, 57,* 251–274.

Borovsky, D., & Rovee-Collier, C. (1990). Contextual constraints on memory retrieval at six months. *Child Development, 61*(5), 1569–1583.

Bors, D. A., & Forrin, B. (1995). Age, speed of information processing, recall, and fluid intelligence. *Intelligence, 20,* 229–248.

Bors, D. A., MacLeod, C. M., & Forrin, B. (1993). Eliminating the IQ–RT correlation by eliminating an experimental confound. *Intelligence, 17*(4), 475–500.

Bothwell, R. K., Brigham, J. C., & Malpass, R. S. (1989). Cross-racial identification. *Personality & Social Psychology Bulletin, 15*(1), 19–25.

Bousfield, W. A. (1953). The occurrence of clustering in the recall of randomly arranged associates. *Journal of General Psychology, 49,* 229–240.

Bower, G. H. (1983). Affect and cognition. *Philosophical Transaction: Royal Society of London* (Series B), *302,* 387–402.

Bower, G. H., Black, J. B., & Turner, T. J. (1979). Scripts in memory for texts. *Cognitive Psychology, 11,* 177–220.

Bower, G. H., Clark, M. C., Lesgold, A. M., & Winzenz, D. (1969). Hierarchical retrieval schemes in recall of categorized word lists. *Journal of Verbal Learning and Verbal Behavior, 8,* 323–343.

Bower, G. H., & Gilligan, S. G. (1979). Remembering information related to one's self. *Journal of Research in Personality, 13,* 420–432.

Bower, G. H., Karlin, M. B., & Dueck, A. (1975). Comprehension and memory for pictures. *Memory & Cognition, 3,* 216–220.

Bowers, K. S., & Farvolden, P. (1996). Revisiting a century-old Freudian slip: From suggestion disavowed to the truth repressed. *Psychological Bulletin, 119,* 355–380.

Bowers, K. S., Regehr, G., Balthazard, C., & Parker, K. (1990). Intuition in the context of discovery. *Cognitive Psychology, 22,* 72–110.

Bradley, R. H., & Caldwell, B. M. (1984). 174 Children: A study of the relationship between home environment and cognitive development during the first 5 years. In A. W. Gottfried (Ed.), *Home environment and early cognitive development: Longitudinal research.* San Diego, CA: Academic Press.

Braine, M. D. S. (1978). On the relation between the natural logic of reasoning and standard logic. *Psychological Review, 85*(1), 1–21.

Braine, M. D. S., & O'Brien, D. P. (1991). A theory of if: A lexical entry, reasoning program, and pragmatic principles. *Psychological Review, 98*(2), 182–203.

Braine, M. D. S., Reiser, B. J., & Rumain, B. (1984). Some empirical justification for a theory of natural propositional logic. In G. H. Bower (Ed.), *The psychology of learning and motivation* (Vol. 18). New York: Academic Press.

Brainerd, C. J. (1973). Neo-Piagetian training experiments revisited: Is there any support for the cognitive developmental hypothesis? *Cognition, 2,* 349–370.

Brainerd, C. J. (1978). The stage question in cognitive-developmental theory. *Behavioral and Brain Sciences, 1,* 173–182.

Bransford, J. D., & Johnson, M. K. (1972). Contextual prerequisites for understanding: Some investigations of comprehension and recall. *Journal of Verbal Learning and Verbal Behavior, 11,* 717–726.

Bransford, J. D., & Johnson, M. K. (1973). Considerations of some problems of comprehension. In W. G. Chase (Ed.), *Visual information processing* (pp. 383–438). New York: Academic Press.

Bransford, J. D., & Stein, B. S. (1993). *The ideal problem solver: A guide for improving thinking, learning, and creativity* (2nd ed.). New York: W. H. Freeman.

Bregman, A. S. (1990). *Auditory scene analysis: The perceptual organization of sound.* Cambridge, MA: MIT Press.

Bresnan, J. W. (Ed.). (1982). *The mental representation of grammatical relations.* Cambridge, MA: MIT Press.

Brian, C. R., & Goodenough, F. L. (1929). The relative potency of color and form perception at various ages. *Journal of Experimental Psychology, 12,* 197–213.

Briere, J., & Conte, J. R. (1993). Self-reported amnesia for abuse in adults molested as children. *Journal of Traumatic Stress, 6,* 21–31.

Brigden, R. (1933). A tachistoscopic study of the differentiation of perception. *Psychological Monographs, 44,* 153–166.

Brigham, J. C., & Malpass, R. S. (1985). The role of experience and contact in the recognition of faces of own and other-race persons. *Journal of Social Issues, 41*(3), 139–155.

Broadbent, D. E. (1958). *Perception and communication.* Oxford, England: Pergamon.

Broadbent, D. E., & Gregory, M. (1965). Effects of noise and of signal rate upon vigilance analyzed by means of decision theory. *Human Factors, 7,* 155–162.

Brooks, L. R. (1968). Spatial and verbal components of the act of recall. *Canadian Journal of Psychology, 22*(5), 349–368.

Brown, A. L. (1978). Knowing when, where, and how to remember: A problem of metacognition. In R. Glaser (Ed.), *Advances in instructional psychology* (Vol. 1, pp. 77–165). Hillsdale, NJ: Erlbaum.

Brown, A. L., Campione, J. C., Bray, N. W., & Wilcox, B. L. (1973). Keeping track of changing variables: Effects of rehearsal training and rehearsal prevention in normal and retarded adolescents. *Journal of Experimental Psychology, 101,* 123–131.

Brown, A. L., & DeLoache, J. S. (1978). Skills, plans, and self-regulation. In R. Siegler (Ed.), *Children's thinking: What develops?* (pp. 3–35). Hillsdale, NJ: Erlbaum.

Brown, A. L., & French, A. L. (1979). The zone of potential development: Implications for intelligence testing in the year 2000. In R. J. Sternberg & D. K. Detterman (Eds.), *Human intelligence: Perspectives on its theory and measurement* (pp. 217–235). Norwood, NJ: Ablex.

Brown, J. A. (1958). Some tests of the decay theory of immediate memory. *Quarterly Journal of Experimental Psychology, 10,* 12–21.

Brown, P., Keenan, J. M., & Potts, G. R. (1986). The self-reference effect with imagery encoding. *Journal of Personality & Social Psychology, 51*(5), 897–906.

Brown, R. (1965). *Social psychology.* New York: Free Press.

Brown, R., Cazden, C. B., & Bellugi, U. (1969). The child's grammar from 1 to 3. In J. P. Hill (Ed.), *Minnesota Symposium on Child Psychology* (Vol. 2). Minneapolis: University of Minnesota Press.

Brown, R., & Kulik, J. (1977). Flashbulb memories. *Cognition, 5,* 73–99.

Brown, R., & McNeill, D. (1966). The "tip of the tongue" phenomenon. *Journal of Verbal Learning and Verbal Behavior, 5,* 325–337.

Bruce, D. (1991). Mechanistic and functional explanations of memory. *American Psychologist, 46*(1), 46–48.

Bruner, J. S. (1957). On perceptual readiness. *Psychological Review, 64,* 123–152.

Bruner, J. S., Goodnow, J. J., & Austin, G. A. (1956). *A study of thinking.* New York: Wiley.

Bryan, W. L., & Harter, N. (1899). Studies on the telegraphic language: The acquisition of a hierarchy of habits. *Psychological Review, 6,* 345–375.

Bryant, P. E., & Trabasso, T. (1971). Transitive inferences and memory in young children. *Nature, 232,* 456–458.

Bryson, M., Bereiter, C., Scarmadalia, M., & Joram, E. (1991). Going beyond the problem as given: Problem solving in expert and novice writers. In R. J. Sternberg & P. A. Frensch (Eds.), *Complex problem solving: Principles and mechanisms* (pp. 61–84). Hillsdale, NJ: Erlbaum.

Buchanan, B. G., & Shortliffe, E. H. (1984). *Rule-based expert systems: The MYCIN experiments of the Stanford Heuristic Programming Project.* Reading, MA: Addison-Wesley.

Buchanan, B. G., Smith, D. H., White, W. C., Gritter, R., Feigenbaum, E. A., Lederberg, J., & Djerassi, C. (1976). Applications of artificial intelligence for chemical inference: XXII. Automatic rule formation in mass spectrometry by means of the meta-Dendral program. *Journal of the American Chemistry Society, 98,* 6168–6178.

Butler, J., & Rovee-Collier, C. (1989). Contextual gating of memory retrieval. *Developmental Psychobiology, 22,* 533–552.

Butterfield, E. C., Wambold, C., & Belmont, J. M. (1973). On the theory and practice of improving short-term memory. *American Journal of Mental Deficiency, 77,* 654–669.

Butterworth, B., & Howard, D. (1987). Paragrammatisms. *Cognition, 26*(1), 1–37.

Cabeza, R., & Nyberg, L. (1997). Imaging cognition: An empirical review of PET studies with normal subjects. *Journal of Cognitive Neuroscience, 9*(1), 1–26.

Campbell, F. W., & Robson, J. G. (1968). Application of Fourier analysis to the visibility of gratings. *Journal of Physiology, 197,* 551–566.

Campione, J. C. (1989). Assisted assessments: A taxonomy of approaches and an outline of strengths and weaknesses. *Journal of Learning Disabilities, 22,* 151–165.

Campione, J. C., & Brown, A. L. (1990). Guided learning and transfer: Implications for approaches to assessment. In N. Frederiksen, R. Glaser, A. Lesgold, & M. Shafto (Eds.), *Diagnostic monitoring of skill and knowledge acquisition* (pp. 141–172). Hillsdale, NJ: Erlbaum.

Cantor, J., & Engle, R. W. (1993). Working memory capacity as long-term memory activation: An individual differences approach. *Journal of Experimental Psychology: Learning, Memory, & Cognition, 19*(5), 1101–1114.

Cappa, S. F., Perani, D., Grassli, F., Bressi, S., et al. (1997). A PET follow-up study of recovery after stroke in acute aphasics. *Brain and Language, 56,* 55–67.

Carey, S. (1985). *Conceptual change in childhood.* Cambridge, MA: MIT Press.

Carlson, N. R. (1992). *Foundations of physiological psychology* (2nd ed.). Boston: Allyn & Bacon.

Carmichael, L., Hogan, H. P., & Walter, A. A. (1932). An experimental study of the effect of language on the reproduction of visually perceived form. *Journal of Experimental Psychology, 15,* 73–86.

Carpenter, P. A., & Just, M. A. (1981). Cognitive processes in reading: Models based on readers' eye fixations. In A. M. Lesgold & C. A. Perfetti (Eds.), *Interactive processes in reading* (pp. 177–213). Hillsdale, NJ: Erlbaum.

Carraher, T. N., Carraher, D., & Schliemann, A. D. (1985). Mathematics in the streets and in the schools. *British Journal of Developmental Psychology, 3,* 21–29.

Carroll, D. W. (1986). *Psychology of language.* Monterey, CA: Brooks/Cole.

Carroll, J. B. (1993). *Human cognitive abilities: A survey of factor-analytic studies.* New York: Cambridge University Press.

Carroll, J. B., & Casagrande, J. B. (1958). The function of language classification in behavior. In E. E. Maccoby, T. Newcomb, & E. L. Hartley (Eds.), *Readings in social psychology* (3rd ed., pp. 18–31). New York: Holt, Rinehart and Winston.

Caryl, P. G. (1994). Early event-related potentials correlate with inspection time and intelligence. *Intelligence, 18*(1), 15–46.

Case, R. (1978). Intellectual development from birth to adulthood: A neo-Piagetian interpretation. In R. Siegler (Ed.), *Children's thinking: What develops?* (pp. 37–71). Hillsdale, NJ: Erlbaum.

Case, R. (1984). The process of stage transition: A neo-Piagetian view. In R. J. Sternberg (Ed.), *Mechanisms of cognitive development* (pp. 20–44). New York: Freeman.

Case, R. (1985). *Intellectual development: Birth to adulthood.* New York: Academic Press.

Case, R. (1987). The structure and process of intellectual development. *International Journal of Psychology, 22,* 571–607.

Case, R. (1992). Neo-Piagetian theories of child development. In R. J. Sternberg & C. A. Berg (Eds.), *Intellectual development* (pp. 161–196). New York: Cambridge University Press.

Castellucci, V. F., & Kandel, E. R. (1976). Presynaptic facilitation as a mechanism for behavioral sensitization in *Aplysia. Science, 194,* 1176–1178.

Cattell, J. M. (1886). The influence of the intensity of the stimulus on the length of the reaction time. *Brain, 9,* 512–514.

Cattell, R. B. (1971). *Abilities: Their structure, growth, and action.* Boston: Houghton Mifflin.

Cave, K. R., & Wolfe, J. M. (1990). Modeling the role of parallel processing in visual search. *Cognitive Psychology, 22*(2), 225–271.

Ceci, S. J. (1991). How much does schooling influence general intelligence and its cognitive components? A reassessment of the evidence. *Developmental Psychology, 27*(5), 703–722.

Ceci, S. J., & Bronfenbrenner, U. (1985). Don't forget to take the cupcakes out of the oven: Strategic time-monitoring, prospective memory and context. *Child Development, 56,* 175–190.

Ceci, S. J., & Bruck, M. (1993). Suggestibility of the child witness: A historical review and synthesis. *Psychological Bulletin, 113*(3), 403–439.

Ceci, S. J., & Loftus, E. F. (1994). "Memory work": A royal road to false memories? *Applied Cognitive Psychology, 8,* 351–364.

Ceci, S. J., Nightingale, N. N., & Baker, J. G. (1992). The ecologies of intelligence: Challenges to traditional views. In D. K. Detterman (Ed.), *Current topics in human intelligence: Vol. 2. Is mind modular or unitary?* (pp. 61–82). Norwood, NJ: Ablex.

Ceci, S. J., & Roazzi, A. (1994). The effects of context on cognition: Postcards from Brazil. In R. J. Sternberg & R. K. Wagner (Eds.), *Mind in context: Interactionist perspectives on human intelligence* (pp. 74–101). New York: Cambridge University Press.

Cerella, J. (1985). Information processing rates in the elderly. *Psychological Bulletin, 98*(1), 67–83.

Cerella, J. (1990). Aging and information-processing rate. In J. E. Birren & K. W. Schaie (Eds.), *Handbook of the psychology of aging* (3rd ed., pp. 201–221). San Diego, CA: Academic Press.

Cerella, J. (1991). Age effects may be global, not local: Comment on Fisk and Rogers (1991). *Journal of Experimental Psychology: General, 120*(2), 215–223.

Cerella, J., Rybash, J. M., Hoyer, W., & Commons, M. L. (1993). *Adult information processing: Limits on loss.* San Diego, CA: Academic Press.

Chambers, D., & Reisberg, D. (1985). Can mental images be ambiguous? *Journal of Experimental Psychology: Human Perception & Performance, 11*(3), 317–328.

Chambers, D., & Reisberg, D. (1992). What an image depicts depends on what an image means. *Cognitive Psychology, 24*(2), 145–174.

Chapman, L. J., & Chapman, J. P. (1959). Atmosphere effect reexamined. *Journal of Experimental Psychology, 58,* 220–226.

Chapman, L. J.,& Chapman, J. P. (1967). Genesis of popular but erroneous psychodiagnostic observations. *Journal of Abnormal Psychology, 72*(3), 193–204.

Chapman, L. J., & Chapman, J. P. (1969). Illusory correlation as an obstacle to the use of valid psychodiagnostic signs. *Journal of Abnormal Psychology, 74,* 271–280.

Chapman, L. J., & Chapman, J. P. (1975). The basis of illusory correlation. *Journal of Abnormal Psychology, 84*(5), 574–575.

Chase, W. G., & Simon, H. A. (1973). The mind's eye in chess. In W. G. Chase (Ed.), *Visual information processing* (pp. 215–281). New York: Academic Press.

Chawarski, M. C., & Sternberg, R. J. (1993). Negative priming in word recognition: A context effect. *Journal of Experimental Psychology: General, 122*(2), 195–206.

Cheng, P. W. (1997). From covariation to causation: A causal power theory. *Psychological Review, 104,* 367–405.

Cheng, P. W., & Holyoak, K. J. (1985). Pragmatic reasoning schemas. *Cognitive Psychology, 17,* 391–416.

Cheng, P. W., Holyoak, K. J., Nisbett, R. E., & Oliver, L. M. (1986). Pragmatic versus syntactic approaches to training deductive reasoning. *Cognitive Psychology, 17*(3), 391–416.

Cherry, E. C. (1953). Some experiments on the recognition of speech with one and two ears. *Journal of the Acoustical Society of America, 25,* 975–979.

Chi, M. T. H. (1978). Knowledge structures and memory development. In R. S. Siegler (Ed.), *Children's thinking: What develops?* (pp. 73–96). Hillsdale, NJ: Erlbaum.

Chi, M. T. H., Bassok, M., Lewis, M., Reimann, P., & Glaser, R. (1989). Self-explanations: How students study and use examples in learning to solve problems. *Cognitive Science, 13,* 145–182.

Chi, M. T. H., Glaser, R., & Farr, M. (Eds.). (1988). *The nature of expertise.* Hillsdale, NJ: Erlbaum.

Chi, M. T. H., Glaser, R., & Rees, E. (1982). Expertise in problem solving. In R. J. Sternberg (Ed.), *Advances in the psychology of expertise* (Vol. 1, pp. 7–76). Hillsdale, NJ: Erlbaum.

Chi, M. T. H., & Koeske, R. D. (1983). Network representations of a child's dinosaur knowledge. *Developmental Psychology, 19,* 29–39.

Chomsky, N. (1957). *Syntactic structures.* The Hague, Netherlands: Mouton.

Chomsky, N. (1959). [Review of the book *Verbal behavior*] *Language, 35,* 26–58.

Chomsky, N. (1965). *Aspects of the theory of syntax.* Cambridge, MA: MIT Press.

Chomsky, N. (1972). *Language and mind* (2nd ed.). New York: Harcourt Brace Jovanovich.

Clark, E. V. (1973). What's in a word? On the child's acquisition of semantics in his first language. In T. E. Moore (Ed.), *Cognitive development and the acquisition of language.* New York: Academic Press.

Clark, H. H. (1969). Linguistic processes in deductive reasoning. *Psychological Review, 76,* 387–404.

Clark, H. H., & Brennan, S. E. (1991). Grounding in communication. In L. B. Resnick, J. M. Levine, & S. P. Tansley (Eds.), *Perspectives on socially shared cognition* (pp. 127–149). Washington, DC: American Psychological Association.

Clark, H. H., & Chase, W. G. (1972). On the process of comparing sentences against pictures. *Cognitive Psychology, 3,* 472–517.

Clark, H. H., & Clark, E. V. (1977). *Psychology and language: An introduction to psycholinguistics.* New York: Harcourt Brace Jovanovich.

Clark, H. H., & Lucy, P. (1975). Understanding what is meant from what is said: A study in conversationally conveyed requests. *Journal of Verbal Learning and Verbal Behavior, 14,* 56–72.

Clement, C. A., & Falmagne, R. J. (1986). Logical reasoning, world knowledge, and mental imagery: Interconnections in cognitive processes. *Memory & Cognition, 14*(4), 299–307.

Cohen, G. (1989). *Memory in the real world.* Hillsdale, NJ: Erlbaum.

Cohen, J. (1981). Can human irrationality be experimentally demonstrated? *Behavioral and Brain Sciences, 4,* 317–331.

Cohen, J. D., Romero, R. D., Servan-Schreiber, D., & Farah, M. J. (1994). Mechanisms of spatial attention: The relation of macrostructure to microstructure in parietal neglect. *Journal of Cognitive Neuroscience, 6,* 377–387.

Cohen, M. S., Kosslyn, S. M., Breiter, H. C., Di Girolamo, G. J., et al. (1996). Changes in cortical activity during mental rotation: A mapping study using functional MRI. *Brain, 119,* 89–100.

Cohen, N. J., Eichenbaum, H., Deacedo, B. S., & Corkin, S. (1985). Different memory systems underlying acquisition of procedural and declarative knowledge. *Annals of the New York Academy of Sciences, 444,* 54–71.

Cohen, N. J., McCloskey, M., & Wible, C. G. (1990). Flashbulb memories and underlying cognitive mechanisms: Reply to Pillemer. *Journal of Experimental Psychology: General, 119*(1), 97–100.

Cohen, N. J., & Squire, L. (1980). Preserved learning and retention of pattern-analyzing skill in amnesia: Dissociation of knowing how and knowing that. *Science, 210*(4466), 207–210.

Colby, K. M. (1963). Computer simulation of a neurotic process. In S. S. Tomkins & S. Messick (Eds.), *Computer simulation of personality: Frontier of psychological research* (pp. 165–180). New York: Wiley.

Colby, K. M. (1995). A computer program using cognitive therapy to treat depressed patients. *Psychiatric Services, 46,* 1223–1225.

Cole, M., Gay, J., Glick, J., & Sharp, D. W. (1971). *The cultural context of learning and thinking.* New York: Basic Books.

Cole, M., & Scribner, S. (1974). *Culture and thought: A psychological introduction.* New York: Wiley.

Coleman, P. D., & Flood, D. G. (1986). Dendritic proliferation in the aging brain as a compensatory repair mechanism. In D. F. Swaab, E. Fliers, M. Mirmiram, W. A. Van Gool, & F. Van Haaren (Eds.), *Progress in brain research* (Vol. 20). New York: Elsevier.

Collier, G. (1994). *Social origins of mental ability.* New York: Wiley.

Collins, A. M., & Loftus, E. F. (1975). A spreading-activation theory of semantic processing. *Psychological Review, 82,* 407–429.

Collins, A. M., & Quillian, M. R. (1969). Retrieval time from semantic memory. *Journal of Verbal Learning and Verbal Behavior, 8,* 240–248.

Conn, C., & Silverman, I., (Eds.). (1991). *What counts: The complete Harper's index.* New York: Henry Holt.

Conrad, R. (1964). Acoustic confusions in immediate memory. *British Journal of Psychology, 55,* 75–84.

Conway, M. A. (1995). *Flashbulb memories.* Hove, England: Erlbaum.

Coon, H., Carey, G., & Fulker, D. W. (1992). Community influences on cognitive ability. *Intelligence, 16*(2), 169–188.

Cooper, E. H., & Pantle, A. J. (1967). The total-time hypothesis in verbal learning. *Psychological Bulletin, 68,* 221–234.

Corballis, M. C. (1989). Laterality and human evolution. *Psychological Review, 96*(3), 49–50.

Corballis, M. C. (1997). Mental rotation and the right hemisphere. *Brain and Language, 57,* 100–121.

Corbetta, M., Miezin, F. M., Dobmeyer, S., Shulman, G. L., & Petersen, S. E. (1993). Selective and divided attention during visual discriminations of shape, color, and speed: Functional anatomy by positron emission tomography. *Journal of Neuroscience, 11,* 2383–2402.

Corbetta, M., Miezin, F. M., Shulman, G. L., & Petersen, S. E. (1993). A PET study of visuospatial attention. *Journal of Neuroscience, 13*(3), 1202–1226.

Corcoran, D. W. J. (1971). *Pattern recognition.* Harmondsworth: Penguin.

Coren, S., & Girgus, J. S. (1978). *Seeing is deceiving: The psychology of visual illusions.* Hillsdale, NJ: Erlbaum.

Cosmides, L. (1989). The logic of social exchange: Has natural selection shaped how humans reason? Studies with the Wason selection task. *Cognition, 31,* 187–276.

Cowan, N., Winkler, I., Teder, W., & Näätänen, R. (1993). Memory prerequisites of mismatch negativity in the auditory event-related potential (ERP). *Journal of Experimental Psychology: Learning, Memory, & Cognition, 19*(4), 909–921.

Cowan, N. (1995). *Attention and memory: An integrated framework.* New York: Oxford University Press.

Craik, F. I. M., & Lockhart, R. S. (1972). Levels of processing: A framework for memory research. *Journal of Verbal Learning and Verbal Behavior, 11,* 671–684.

Craik, F. I. M., & Tulving, E. (1975). Depth of processing and the retention of words in episodic memory. *Journal of Experimental Psychology: General, 104,* 268–294.

Craik, K. (1943). *The nature of exploration.* Cambridge, England: Cambridge University Press.

Crowder, R. G. (1976). *Principles of learning and memory.* Hillsdale, NJ: Erlbaum.

Crowder, R. G., & Morton, J. (1969). Precategorical acoustic storage (PAS). *Perception and Psychophysics, 5,* 365–373.

Crystal, D. (Ed.). (1987). *The Cambridge encyclopedia of language.* New York: Cambridge University Press.

Csikszentmihalyi, M. (1988). Society, culture, and person: A systems view of creativity. In R. J. Sternberg (Ed.), *The nature of creativity* (pp. 325–339). New York: Cambridge University Press.

Csikszentmihalyi, M. (1996). *Creativity.* New York: Harper Collins.

Cummins, J. (1976). The influence of bilingualism on cognitive growth: A synthesis of research findings and explanatory hypothesis. *Working Papers on Bilingualism, 9,* 1–43.

Cutler, B. L., & Penrod, S. D. (1995). *Mistaken identification: The eyewitness, psychology, and the law.* New York: Cambridge University Press.

Cutting, J., & Kozlowski, L. (1977). Recognizing friends by their walk: Gait perception without familiarity cues. *Bulletin of the Psychonomic Society, 9*(5), 353–356.

Damasio, A. R. (1985). Prosopagnosia. *Trends in Neurosciences, 8,* 132–135.

Daneman, M., & Carpenter, P. A. (1980). Individual differences in working memory and reading. *Journal of Verbal Learning and Verbal Behavior, 19,* 450–466.

Daneman, M., & Tardif, T. (1987). Working memory and reading skill reexamined. In M. Coltheart (Ed.), *Attention and performance: Vol. 12. The psychology of reading* (pp. 491–508). Hove, England: Erlbaum.

Darwin, C. (1859). *Origin of species.* London: John Murray.

Darwin, C. J., Turvey, M. T., & Crowder, R. G. (1972). An auditory analogue of the Sperling partial report procedure: Evidence for brief auditory storage. *Cognitive Psychology, 3,* 255–267.

Dasen, P. R. (1972). Cross-cultural Piagetian research: A summary. *Journal of Cross-Cultural Psychology, 17,* 367–377.

Dasen, P. R., & DeRibeaupierre, A. (1988). Neo-Piagetian theories: Cross-cultural and differential perspectives. In A. Demetriou (Ed.), *The neo-Piagetian theories of cognitive development: Toward an integration* (pp. 287–326). New York: North-Holland Elsevier.

Dasen, P. R., & Heron, A. (1981). Cross-cultural tests of Piaget's theory. In H. C. Triandis & A. Heron (Eds.), *Handbook of cross-cultural psychology* (Vol. 4). Boston: Allyn & Bacon.

Davidson, J. E. (1995). The suddenness of insight. In R. J. Sternberg & J. E. Davidson (Eds.), *The nature of insight* (pp. 125–155). Cambridge, MA: MIT Press.

Davidson, J. E., & Sternberg, R. J. (1984). The role of insight in intellectual giftedness. *Gifted Child Quarterly, 28,* 58–64.

Davidson, J. E., & Sternberg, R. J. (1985). Competence and performance in intellectual development. In E. Neimark, R. deLisi,

& J. H. Newman (Eds.), *Moderators of competence* (pp. 43–76). Hillsdale, NJ: Erlbaum.

Deary, I. J., & Stough, C. (1996). Intelligence and inspection time: Achievements, prospects, and problems. *American Psychologist, 51,* 599–608.

DeCasper, A. J., & Fifer, W. P. (1980). Of human bonding: Newborns prefer their mothers' voices. *Science, 208,* 1174–1176.

De Groot, A. D. (1965). *Thought and choice in chess.* The Hague, Netherlands: Mouton.

De Rosa, D. V., & Tkacz, S. (1976). Memory scanning of organized visual material. *Journal of Experimental Psychology: Human Learning & Memory, 2,* 688–694.

De Yoe, E. A., & Van Essen, D. C, (1988). Concurrent processing streams in monkey visual cortex. *Trends in Neurosciences, 11,* 219–226.

Dell, G. S. (1986). A spreading-activation theory of retrieval in sentence production. *Psychological Review, 93*(3), 283–321.

Dempster, F. N. (1991). Inhibitory processes: A neglected dimension of intelligence. *Intelligence, 15*(2), 157–173.

Dennett, D. (1991). *Consciousness explained.* Boston: Little, Brown.

Denny, N. W. (1980). Task demands and problem-solving strategies in middle-aged and older adults. *Journal of Gerontology, 35,* 559–564.

Descartes, R. (1972). *The treatise of man.* Cambridge, MA: Harvard University Press. (Originally published 1662).

Descartes, R. (1987). Meditations on first philosophy. In *Great books of the western world: Vol. 31. Descartes, Spinoza.* Chicago: Encyclopaedia Britannica. (Originally published 1641).

DeSoto, C. B., London, M., & Handel, S. (1965). Social reasoning and spatial paralogic. *Journal of Personality and Social Psychology, 2,* 513–521.

Detterman, D. K., & Sternberg, R. J. (Eds.). (1982). *How and how much can intelligence be increased.* Norwood, NJ: Ablex.

Deutsch, J. A., & Deutsch, D. (1963). Attention: Some theoretical considerations. *Psychological Review, 70,* 80–90.

DeValois, R. L., & DeValois, K. K. (1980). Spatial vision. *Annual Review of Psychology, 31,* 309–341.

Diamond, A. (1990). Rate of maturation of the hippocampus and the developmental progression of children's performance on the delayed nonmatching to sample and visual paired comparison tasks. *Annals of the New York Academy of Sciences, 608,* 394–433.

Diamond, A. (1993). Neuropsychological insights into the meaning of object concept development. In M. H. Johnson (Ed.), *Brain development and cognition: A reader* (pp. 208–247). Oxford, England: Blackwell Publishers.

Ditchburn, R. W. (1980). The function of small saccades. *Vision Research, 20,* 271–272.

Dixon, R. A., & Baltes, P. B. (1986). Toward life-span research on the functions and pragmatics of intelligence. In R. J. Sternberg & R. K. Wagner (Eds.), *Practical intelligence: Nature and origins of competence in the everyday world* (pp. 203–235). New York: Cambridge University Press.

Dreyfus, H. L., & Dreyfus, S. E. (1990). Making a mind versus modelling the brain: Artificial intelligence back at a branchpoint. In M. A. Boden (Ed.), *The philosophy of artificial intelligence: Oxford readings in philosophy* (pp. 309–333). Oxford, England: Oxford University Press.

Driver, J., & McLeod, P. (1992). Reversing visual search asymmetries with conjunctions of movement and orientation. *Journal of Experimental Psychology: Human Perception & Performance, 18*(1), 22–33.

Driver, J., McLeod, P., & Dienes, Z. (1992). Are direction and speed coded independently by the visual system? Evidence from visual search. *Spatial Vision, 6*(2), 133–147.

Dror, I. E., & Kosslyn, S. M. (1994). Mental imagery and aging. *Psychology and Aging, 9*(1), 90–102.

Duncan, E., & Bourg, T. (1983). An examination of the effects of encoding and decision processes on the rate of mental rotation. *Journal of Mental Imagery, 7*(2), 3–55.

Duncan, J., & Humphreys, G. (1989). Visual search and stimulus similarity. *Psychological Review, 96*(3), 433–458.

Duncan, J., & Humphreys, G. (1992). Beyond the search surface: Visual search and attentional engagement. *Journal of Experimental Psychology: Human Perception & Performance, 18*(2), 578–588.

Duncker, K. (1945). On problem-solving. *Psychological Monographs, 58*(5, Whole No. 270).

Ebbinghaus, H. (1885). *Uber das Gedächtnis.* Leipzig, Germany: Duncker and Humblot.

Edwards, W. (1954). The theory of decision making. *Psychological Bulletin, 51,* 380–417.

Eich, E. (1995). Searching for mood dependent memory. *Psychological Science, 6,* 67–75.

Eich, J. E. (1980). The cue-dependent nature of state-dependent retrieval. *Memory & Cognition, 8,* 157–158.

Eimas, P. D. (1985). The perception of speech in early infancy. *Scientific American, 252,* 46–52.

Eimas, P. D., & Corbit, J. D. (1973). Selective adaptation of linguistic feature detectors. *Cognitive Psychology, 4,* 99–109.

Engle, R. W. (1994). Individual differences in memory and their implications for learning. In R. J. Sternberg (Ed.), *Encyclopedia of intelligence* (pp. 700–704). New York: Macmillan.

Engle, R. W., Cantor, J., & Carullo, J. J. (1992). Individual differences in working memory and comprehension: A test of four hypotheses. *Journal of Experimental Psychology: Learning, Memory, & Cognition, 18*(5), 972–992.

Ericsson, K. A. (Ed.). (1996). *The road to excellence.* Mahwah, NJ: Erlbaum.

Ericsson, K. A., Chase, W. G., & Faloon, S. (1980). Acquisition of a memory skill. *Science, 208,* 1181–1182.

Estes, W. K. (1982). Learning, memory, and intelligence. In R. J. Sternberg (Ed.), *Handbook of intelligence* (pp. 170–224). New York: Cambridge University Press.

Evans, J. St. B. T., Barston, J. I., & Pollard, P. (1983). On the conflict between logic and belief in syllogistic reasoning. *Memory and cognition, 11*(3), 295–306.

Evans, T. G. (1968). A program for the solution of geometric-analogy intelligence question. In M. L. Minsky (Ed.), *Semantic information processing* (pp. 271–353). Cambridge, MA: MIT Press.

Eysenck, H. J. (1967). Intelligence assessment: A theoretical and experimental approach. *British Journal of Educational Psychology, 37,* 81–98.

Eysenck, H. J., & Kamin, L. (1981). *The intelligence controversy: H. J. Eysenck vs. Leon Kamin.* New York: Wiley.

Eysenck, M., & Byrne, A. (1992). Anxiety and susceptibility to distraction. *Personality & Individual Differences, 13*(7), 793–798.

Eysenck, M., & Calvo, M. G. (1992). Anxiety and performance: The processing efficiency theory. *Cognition & Emotion, 6*(6), 409–434.

Eysenck, M., & Graydon, J. (1989). Susceptibility to distraction as a function of personality. *Personality & Individual Differences, 10*(6), 681–687.

Eysenck, M., & Keane, M. T. (1990). *Cognitive psychology: A student's handbook.* Hove, England: Erlbaum.

Fagan, J. F. (1984). The intelligent infant: Theoretical implications. *Intelligence, 8,* 1–9.

Fagan, J. F. (1985). A new look at infant intelligence. In D. K. Detterman (Ed.), *Current topics in human intelligence: Vol. 1. Research methodology* (pp. 223–246). Norwood, NJ: Ablex.

Fagan, J. F., & Montie, J. E. (1988). Behavioral assessment of cognitive well-being in the infant. In J. Kavanagh (Ed.), *Understanding mental retardation: Research accomplishments and new frontiers.* Baltimore: Brookes.

Farah, M. J. (1988a). Is visual imagery really visual? Overlooked evidence from neuropsychology. *Psychological Review, 95*(3), 307–317.

Farah, M. J. (1988b). The neuropsychology of mental imagery: Converging evidence from brain-damaged and normal subjects. In J. Stiles-Davis, M. Kritchevsky, & U. Bellugi (Eds.), *Spatial cognition: Brain bases and development* (pp. 33–56). Hillsdale, NJ: Erlbaum.

Farah, M. J. (1990). *Visual agnosia: Disorders of object recognition and what they tell us about normal vision.* Cambridge, MA: MIT Press.

Farah, M. J. (1994). Neuropsychological inference with an interactive brain: A critique of the "locality" assumption. *Behavioral and Brain Sciences, 17,* 43–104.

Farah, M. J., Hammond, K. M., Levine, D. N., & Calvanio, R. (1988a). Visual and spatial mental imagery: Dissociable systems of representation. *Cognitive Psychology, 20*(4), 439–462.

Farah, M. J., Levinson, K. L., & Klein, K. L. (1995). Face perception and within category discrimination in prosopagnosia. *Neuropsychologia, 33,* 661–674.

Farah, M. J., Peronnet, F., Gonon, M. A., & Giard, M. H. (1988b). Electrophysiological evidence for a shared representational medium for visual images and visual percepts. *Journal of Experimental Psychology: General, 117*(3), 248–257.

Farah, M. J., Wilson, K. D., Drain, H. M., & Tanaka, J. R. (1995). The inverted face inversion effect in prosopagnosia: Evidence for mandatory, face-specific, perceptual mechanisms. *Vision Research, 35,* 2089–2093.

Fernald, A. (1985). Four-month-old infants prefer to listen to motherese. *Infant Behavior and Development, 8,* 118–195.

Fernald, A., Taeschner, T., Dunn, J., Papousek, M., De Boysson-Bardies, B., & Fukui, I. (1989). A cross-cultural study of prosodic modification in mothers' and fathers' speech to preverbal infants. *Journal of Child Language, 16,* 477–501.

Feuerstein, R. (1979). *The dynamic assessment of retarded performers: The learning potential assessment device, theory, instruments, and techniques.* Baltimore: University Park Press.

Feuerstein, R. (1980). *Instrumental enrichment: An intervention program for cognitive modifiability.* Baltimore: University Park Press.

Feynman, R. (1985). *Surely you're joking, Mr. Feynman.* New York: Norton.

Field, T. (1978). Interaction behaviors of primary versus secondary caregiver fathers. *Developmental Psychology, 14,* 183–184.

Fillmore, C. J. (1968). The case for case. In E. Bach & R. T. Harms (Eds.), *Universals in linguistic theory* (pp. 1–88). New York: Holt, Rinehart and Winston.

Finke, R. A. (1989). *Principles of mental imagery.* Cambridge, MA: MIT Press.

Finke, R. A. (1995). Creative insight and preinventive forms. In R. J. Sternberg & J. E. Davidson (Eds.), *The nature of insight* (pp. 255–280). Cambridge, MA: MIT Press.

Finke, R. A., Pinker, S., & Farah, M. J. (1989). Reinterpreting visual patterns in mental imagery. *Cognitive Science, 13*(3), 252–257.

Fischer, K. W. (1980). A theory of cognitive development: The control and construction of hierarchies of skills. *Psychological Review, 87*(6), 477–531.

Fischer, K. W., & Bidell, T. R. (1991). Constraining nativist inferences about cognitive capacities. In S. Carey & R. Gelman (Eds.), *Structural constraints on knowledge in cognitive development* (pp. 199–235). Hillsdale, NJ: Erlbaum.

Fischer, K. W., & Farrar, M. J. (1987). Generalizations about generalization: How a theory of skill development explains both generality and specificity. *International Journal of Psychology, 22,* 643–677.

Fischer, K. W., & Pipp, S. L. (1984). Processes of cognitive development: Optimal level and skill acquisition. In R. J. Sternberg (Ed.), *Mechanisms of cognitive development* (pp. 45–75). New York: Freeman.

Fischhoff, B. (1982). For those condemned to study the past: Heuristics and biases in hindsight. In D. Kahneman, P. Slovic, & A. Tversky (Eds.), *Judgment under uncertainty: Heuristics and biases* (pp. 335–351). Cambridge, England: Cambridge University Press.

Fischhoff, B. (1988). Judgment and decision making. In R. J. Sternberg & E. E. Smith (Eds.), *The psychology of human thought* (pp. 153–187). New York: Cambridge University Press.

Fischhoff, B., Slovic, P., & Lichtenstein, S. (1977). Knowing with certainty: The appropriateness of extreme confidence. *Journal of Experimental Psychology: Human Perception and Performance, 3,* 552–564.

Fisher, R. P., & Craik, F. I. (1977). Interaction between encoding and retrieval operations in cued recall. *Journal of Experimental Psychology: Human Learning & Memory, 3*(6), 701–711.

Fisher, R. P., & Craik, F. I. (1980). The effects of elaboration on recognition memory. *Memory & Cognition, 8*(5), 400–404.

Fisk, A. D., & Schneider, W. (1981). Control and automatic processing during tasks requiring sustained attention: A new approach to vigilance. *Human Factors, 23,* 737–750.

Fivush, R., & Hamond, N. R. (1991). Autobiographical memory across the preschool years: Toward reconceptualizing childhood memory. In R. Fivush & N. R. Hamond (Eds.), *Knowing and remembering in young children* (pp. 223–248). New York: Cambridge University Press.

Flavell, J. H., Flavell, E. R., & Green, F. L. (1983). Development of the appearance–reality distinction. *Cognitive Psychology, 15,* 95–120.

Flavell, J. H., & Wellman, H. M. (1977). Metamemory. In R. V. Kail, Jr., & J. W. Hagen (Eds.), *Perspectives on the development of memory and cognition* (pp. 3–33). Hillsdale, NJ: Erlbaum.

Flege, J. (1991). The interlingual identification of Spanish and English vowels: Orthographic evidence. *Quarterly Journal of Experimental Psychology: Human Experimental Psychology, 43,* 701–731.

Flynn, J. R. (1984). The mean IQ of Americans: massive gains 1932 to 1978. *Psychological Bulletin, 95,* 29–51.

Flynn, J. R. (1987). Massive IQ gains in fourteen nations: What IQ tests really measure. *Psychological Bulletin, 95,* 29–51.

Fodor, J. A. (1975). *The language of thought.* New York: Crowell.

Fodor, J. A. (1983). *The modularity of mind.* Cambridge, MA: MIT Press.

Fogel, A. (1991). *Infancy: Infant, family, and society* (2nd ed.). St. Paul, MN: West.

Foulke, E., & Sticht, T. (1969). Review of research on the intelligibility and comprehension of accelerated speech. *Psychological Bulletin, 72,* 50–62.

Franklin, N., & Tversky, B. (1990). Searching imagined environments. *Journal of Experimental Psychology: General, 119*(1), 63–76.

Franks, J. J., & Bransford, J. D. (1971). Abstraction of visual patterns. *Journal of Experimental Psychology, 90*(1), 65–74.

Frensch, P. A., & Sternberg, R. J. (1989). Expertise and intelligent thinking: When is it worse to know better? In R. J. Sternberg (Ed.), *Advances in the psychology of human intelligence* (Vol. 5, pp. 157–188). Hillsdale, NJ: Erlbaum.

Freud, S. (1953). *An aphasia.* London: Imago.

Frisch, K. von. (1962). Dialects in the language of the bees. *Scientific American, 207,* 79–87.

Frisch, K. von. (1967). Honeybees: Do they use direction and distance information provided by their dances? *Science, 158,* 1072–1076.

Fromkin, V. A. (1973). *Speech errors as linguistic evidence.* The Hague, Netherlands: Mouton.

Fromkin, V. A., & Rodman, R. (1988). *An introduction to language* (4th ed.). Fort Worth, TX: Holt, Rinehart and Winston.

Frost, N. (1972). Encoding and retrieval in visual memory tasks. *Journal of Experimental Psychology, 95,* 317–326.

Funke, J. (1991). Solving complex problems: Exploration and control of complex social systems. In R. J. Sternberg & P. A. Frensch (Eds.), *Complex problem solving: Principles and mechanisms* (pp. 159–183). Hillsdale, NJ: Erlbaum.

Galotti, K. M., Baron, J., & Sabini, J. P. (1986). Individual differences in syllogistic reasoning: Deduction rules or mental models? *Journal of Experimental Psychology: General, 115*(1), 16–25.

Galton, F. (1883). *Inquiry into human faculty and its development.* London: Macmillan.

Ganellen, R. J., & Carver, C. S., (1985). Why does self-reference promote incidental encoding? *Journal of Experimental Social Psychology, 21*(3), 284–300.

Gardner, H. (1983). *Frames of mind: The theory of multiple intelligences.* New York: Basic Books.

Gardner, H. (1985). *The mind's new science: A history of the cognitive revolution.* New York: Basic Books.

Gardner, H. (1993a). *Creating minds: An anatomy of creativity seen through the lives of Freud, Einstein, Picasso, Stravinsky, Eliot, Graham, and Gandhi.* New York: HarperCollins.

Gardner, H. (1993b). *Multiple intelligences: The theory in practice.* New York: Basic Books.

Gardner, H. (in press). Are there additional intelligences? The case for naturalist, spiritual, and existential intelligences. In J. Kane (Ed.), *Education, information, and transformation.* Englewood Cliffs, NJ: Prentice-Hall.

Gardner, H., Krechevsky, M. Sternberg, R. J. & Okagaki, L. (1994). Intelligence in context: Enhancing students' practical intelligence for school. In K. McGilly (Ed.), *Classroom lessons: Integrating cognitive theory and classroom practice* (pp. 105–127). Cambridge, MA: Bradford Books.

Gärling, T., Böök, A., & Lindberg, E. (1985). Adults' memory representations of the spatial properties of their everyday physical environment. In R. Cohen (Ed.), *The development of spatial cognition* (pp. 141–184). Hillsdale, NJ: Erlbaum.

Garner, W. R. (1970). The stimulus in information processing. *American Psychologist, 25,* 350–358.

Garner, W. R. (1974). *The processing of information and structure.* Potomac, MD: Erlbaum.

Garrett, M. F. (1980). Levels of processing in sentence production. In B. Butterworth (Ed.), *Language production: Vol. 1. Speech and talk* (pp. 177–210). London: Academic Press.

Garrett, M. F. (1992). Disorders of lexical selection. *Cognition, 42*(1–3), 143–180.

Garry, M., & Loftus, E. F. (1994). Pseudomemories without hypnosis. *International Journal of Clinical and Experimental Hypnosis, 42,* 363–378.

Gazzaniga, M. S. (1985). *The social brain: Discovering the networks of the mind.* New York: Basic Books.

Gazzaniga, M. S. (Ed.). (1995). *The cognitive neurosciences.* Cambridge, MA: MIT Press.

Gazzaniga, M. S., & LeDoux, J. E. (1978). *The integrated mind.* New York: Plenum.

Gazzaniga, M. S., & Sperry, R. W. (1967). Language after section of the cerebral commissures. *Brain, 90*(1), 131–148.

Gelman, R. (1969). Conservation acquisition: A problem of learning to attend to relevant attributes. *Journal of Experimental Child Psychology, 7,* 167–187.

Gelman, R. (1972). Logical capacity of very young children: Number invariance rules. *Child Development, 43,* 75–90.

Gelman, R., & Baillargeon, R. (1983). A review of some Piagetian concepts. In P. H. Mussen (Series Ed.), J. Flavell, &

E. Markman (Vol. Eds.), *Handbook of child psychology: Cognitive development* (Vol. 3, 4th ed., pp. 167–230). New York: Wiley.

Gelman, R., & Gallistel, C. R. (1978). *The child's understanding of number.* Cambridge, MA: Harvard University Press.

Gelman, S. A. (1985). Children's inductive inferences from natural kind and artifact categories. (Doctoral dissertation, Stanford University, 1984). *Dissertation Abstracts International, 45*(10B), 3351–3352.

Gelman, S. A. (1989). Children's use of categories to guide biological inferences. *Human Development, 32*(2), 65–71.

Gelman, S. A., & Kremer, K. E. (1991). Understanding natural causes: Children's explanations of how objects and their properties originate. *Child Development, 62*(2), 396–414.

Gelman, S. A., & Markman, E. M. (1986). Categories and induction in young children. *Cognition, 23*(3), 183–209.

Gelman, S. A., & Markman, E. M. (1987). Young children's inductions from natural kinds: The role of categories and appearances. *Child Development, 58*(6), 1532–1541.

Gelman, S. A., & O'Reilly, A. W. (1988). Children's inductive inferences within superordinate categories: The role of language and category structure. *Child Development, 59*(4), 876–887.

Gelman, S. A., & Wellman, H. M. (1991). Insides and essence: Early understandings of the non-obvious. *Cognition, 38*(3), 213–244.

Gentner, D. (1983). Structure-mapping: A theoretical framework for analogy. *Cognitive Science, 7,* 155–170.

Gentner, D., & Gentner, D. R. (1983). Flowing waters or teeming crowds: Mental models of electricity. In D. Gentner & A. Stevens (Eds.), *Mental models.* Hillsdale, NJ: Erlbaum.

Georgopoulos, A. P., Lurito, J. T., Petrides, M., & Schwartz, A. B., et al. (1989). Mental rotation of the neuronal population vector. *Science, 243*(4888), 234–236.

Georgopoulos, A. P., & Pellizzer, G. (1995). The mental and the neural: Psychological and neural studies of mental rotation and memory scanning. *Neuropsychologia, 33,* 1531–1547.

Gerrig, R. J., & Banaji, M. R. (1994). Language and thought. In R. J. Sternberg (Ed.), *Thinking and problem solving* (pp. 235–61). New York: Academic Press.

Gerrig, R. J., & Healy, A. F. (1983). Dual processes in metaphor understanding: Comprehension and appreciation. *Journal of Experimental Psychology: Learning, Memory, & Cognition, 9,* 667–675.

Geschwind, N. (1970). The organization of language and the brain. *Science, 170,* 940–944.

Gibbs, R. W. (1979). Contextual effects in understanding indirect requests. *Discourse Processes, 2,* 1–10.

Gibbs, R. W. (1986). What makes some indirect speech acts conventional? *Journal of Memory and Language, 25,* 181–196.

Gibson, E. J. (1991). The ecological approach: A foundation for environmental psychology. In R. M. Downs, L. S. Liben, & D. S. Palermo (Eds.), *Visions of aesthetics, the environment & development: The legacy of Joachim F. Wohlwill* (pp. 87–111). Hillsdale, NJ: Erlbaum.

Gibson, E. J. (1992). How to think about perceptual learning: Twenty-five years later. In H. L. Pick, Jr., P. W. van den Broek, & D. C. Knill (Eds.), *Cognition: Conceptual and methodological issues* (pp. 215–237). Washington, DC: American Psychological Association.

Gibson, J. J. (1950). *The perception of the visual world.* Boston: Houghton Mifflin.

Gibson, J. J. (1966). *The senses considered as perceptual systems.* New York: Houghton Mifflin.

Gibson, J. J. (1979). *The ecological approach to visual perception.* Boston: Houghton Mifflin.

Gibson, J. J. (1994). The visual perception of objective motion and subjective movement. *Psychological Review, 101*(2), 318–323. (Original work published 1954)

Gick, M. L., & Holyoak, K. J. (1980). Analogical problem solving. *Cognitive Psychology, 12,* 306–355.

Gick, M. L., & Holyoak, K. J. (1983). Schema induction and analogical transfer. *Cognitive Psychology, 15,* 1–38.

Gilovich, T., Vallone, R., & Tversky, A. (1985). The hot hand in basketball: On the misperception of random sequences. *Cognitive Psychology, 17*(3), 295–314.

Ginsberg, H. P., Klein, A., & Starkey, P. (in press). The development of children's mathematical thinking: Connecting research with practice. To appear in I. Siegel & A. Renninger (Eds.), *Handbook of Child Psychology* (5th ed., Vol. 4, Child Psychology and Practice). New York: Wiley.

Ginsburg, H. (1996). Toby's math. In R. J. Sternberg & T. Ben-Zeev (Eds.), *The nature of mathematical thinking* (pp. 175–202). Mahwah, NJ: Erlbaum.

Gladwin, T. (1970). *East is a big bird.* Cambridge, MA: Harvard University Press.

Glaser, R., & Chi, M. T. H. (1988). Overview. In M. T. H. Chi, R. Glaser, & M. Farr (Eds.), *The nature of expertise* (pp. xv–xxxvi). Hillsdale, NJ: Erlbaum.

Glenberg, A. M. (1977). Influences of retrieval processes on the spacing effect in free recall. *Journal of Experimental Psychology: Human Learning & Memory, 3*(3), 282–294.

Glenberg, A. M. (1979). Component-levels theory of the effects of spacing of repetitions on recall and recognition. *Memory & Cognition, 7*(2), 95–112.

Glenberg, A. M. (1997). What memory is for. *Behavioral and Brain Sciences, 20,* 1–55.

Glenberg, A. M., Meyer, M., & Lindem, K. (1987). Mental models contribute to foregrounding during text comprehension. *Journal of Memory & Language, 26*(1), 69–83.

Glucksberg, S. (1988). Language and thought. In R. J. Sternberg & E. E. Smith (Eds.), *The psychology of human thought* (pp. 214–241). New York: Cambridge University Press.

Glucksberg, S., & Danks, J. H. (1975). *Experimental psycholinguistics.* Hillsdale, NJ: Erlbaum.

Glucksberg, S., Gildea, P., & Bookin, H. B. (1982). On understanding nonliteral speech: Can people ignore metaphors? *Journal of Verbal Learning and Verbal Behavior, 21,* 85–98.

Glucksberg, S., & Keysar, B. (1990). Understanding metaphorical comparisons: Beyond similarity. *Psychological Review, 97*(1), 3–18.

Gobet, F., & Simon, H. A. (1996a). Recall of random and distorted chess positions: Implications for the theory of expertise. *Memory and Cognition, 24,* 493–503.

Gobet, F., & Simon, H. A. (1996b). Roles of recognition processes and look-ahead search in time-constrained expert problem solving: Evidence from grand-master-level chess. *Psychological Science, 7,* 52–55.

Gobet, F., & Simon, H. A. (1996c). Templates in chess memory: A mechanism for recalling several boards. *Cognitive Psychology, 31,* 1–40.

Goddard, H. H. (1917). Mental tests and immigrants. *Journal of Delinquency, 2,* 243–277.

Godden, D. R., & Baddeley, A. D. (1975). Context-dependent memory in two natural environments: On land and underwater. *British Journal of Psychology, 66,* 325–331.

Goldenberg, G., Podreka, I., & Steiner, M. (1990). The cerebral localization of visual imagery: Evidence from emission computerized tomography of cerebral blood flow. In P. J. Hampson, D. F. Marks, & J. T. E. Richardson (Eds.), *Imagery: Current developments* (pp. 307–332). London: Routledge.

Goldenberg, G., Podreka, I., & Steiner, M., Suess, E., et al. (1988). Pattern of regional cerebral blood flow related to visual and motor imagery: Results of emission computerized tomography. In M. Denis, J. Engelkamp, & J. T. E. Richardson (Eds.), *Cognitive and neuropsychological approaches to mental imagery* (NATO ASI series, Series D, Behavioral and social sciences, No. 42) (pp. 363–373). Dordrecht, Netherlands: Martinus Nijhoff Publishing.

Goldman-Rakic, P. S. (1993). Specification of higher cortical functions. *Journal of Head Trauma Rehabilitation, 8*(1), 13–23.

Gordon, D., & Lakoff, G. (1971). Conversational postulates. In *Papers from the Seventh Regional Meeting, Chicago Linguistic Society* (pp. 63–84). Chicago: Chicago Linguistic Society.

Gottfried, A. W. (Ed.). (1984). *Home environment and early cognitive development: Longitudinal research.* San Diego, CA: Academic Press.

Gould, S. J. (1981). *The mismeasure of man.* New York: Norton.

Graesser, A. C., & Kreuz, R. J. (1993). A theory of inference generation during text comprehension. *Discourse Processes, 16,* 145–160.

Graf, P. (1990). Life-span changes in implicit and explicit memory. *Bulletin of the Psychonomic Society, 28,* 353–358.

Graf, P., Mandler, G., & Haden, P. E. (1982). Simulating amnesic symptoms in normal subjects. *Science, 218*(4578), 1243–1255.

Gray, J. A., & Wedderburn, A. A. I. (1960). Grouping strategies with simultaneous stimuli. *Quarterly Journal of Experimental Psychology, 12,* 180–184.

Greenberg, R., & Underwood, B. J. (1950). Retention as a function of stage of practice. *Journal of Experimental Psychology, 40,* 452–457.

Greene, R. L., & Crowder, R. G. (1984). Modality and suffix effects in the absence of auditory stimulation. *Journal of Verbal Learning and Verbal Behavior, 23,* 371–382.

Greeno, J. G. (1974). Hobbits and orcs: Acquisition of a sequential concept. *Cognitive Psychology, 6,* 270–292.

Greeno, J. G. (1978). Natures of problem solving abilities. In W. K. Estes (Ed.), *Handbook of learning and cognitive processes* (Vol. 5, pp. 239–270). Hillsdale, NJ: Erlbaum.

Greeno, J. G., & Simon, H. A. (1988). Problem solving and reasoning. In R. C. Atkinson, R. Herrnstein, G. Lindzey, & R. D. Luce (Eds.), *Stevens' handbook of experimental psychology* (Rev. ed., pp. 589–672). New York: Wiley.

Greenwald, A. G., & Banaji, M. (1989). The self as a memory system: Powerful, but ordinary. *Journal of Personality & Social Psychology, 57*(1), 41–54.

Gregory, R. L. (1966). *Eye and brain.* New York: World University Library.

Gregory, R. L. (1980). Perceptions as hypotheses. *Philosophical Transactions of the Royal Society of London, Series B, 290,* 181–197.

Grice, H. P. (1967). William James Lectures, Harvard University, published in part as "Logic and conversation." In P. Cole & J. L. Morgan (Eds.), *Syntax and semantics: Vol. 3. Speech acts* (pp. 41–58). New York: Seminar Press.

Griggs, R. A., & Cox, J. R. (1982). The elusive thematic-materials effect in Wason's selection task. *British Journal of Psychology, 73,* 407–420.

Griggs, R. A., & Cox, J. R. (1993). Permission schemas and the selection task. *The Quarterly Journal of Experimental Psychology, 46A*(4), 637–651.

Groen, G. J., & Parkman, J. M. (1972). A chronometric analysis of simple addition. *Psychological Review, 79,* 329–343.

Grossman, L., & Eagle, M. (1970). Synonymity, antonymity, and association in false recognition responses. *Journal of Experimental Psychology, 83,* 244–248.

Grosz, B. J., Pollack, M. E., & Sidner, C. L. (1989). Discourse. In M. I. Posner (Ed.), *Foundations of cognitive science* (pp. 437–468). Cambridge, MA: MIT Press.

Groves, P. M., & Rebec, G. V. (1988). *Introduction to biological psychology* (3rd ed.). Dubuque, IA: William C. Brown.

Gruber, H. E. (1981). *Darwin on man: A psychological study of scientific creativity* (2nd ed.). Chicago: University of Chicago Press. (Original work published 1974)

Gruber, H. E., & Davis, S. N. (1988). Inching our way up Mount Olympus: The evolving-systems approach to creative thinking. In R. J. Sternberg (Ed.), *The nature of creativity* (pp. 243–270). New York: Cambridge University Press.

Guilford, J. P. (1950). Creativity. *American Psychologist, 5*(9), 444–454.

Guilford, J. P. (1967). *The nature of human intelligence.* New York: McGraw Hill.

Guilford, J. P. (1982). Cognitive psychology's ambiguities: Some suggested remedies. *Psychological Review, 89,* 48–59.

Guilford, J. P. (1988). Some dangers in the structure-of-intellect model. *Educational & Psychological Measurement, 48,* 1–4.

Haber, R. N. (1983). The impending demise of the icon: A critique of the concept of iconic storage in visual information processing. *Behavioral and Brain Sciences, 6*(1), 1–54.

Haier, R. J., Chueh, D., Touchette, P., Lott, I., Buchbaum, M. S., MacMillan, D., Sandman, C., LaCase, L., & Sosa, E. (1995).

Brain size and cerebral glucose metabolic rate in nonspecific mental retardation and Down syndrome. *Intelligence, 20,* 191–210.

Haier, R. J., Siegel, B., Tang, C., Abel, L., & Buchsbaum, M. S. (1992). Intelligence and changes in regional cerebral glucose metabolic rate following learning. *Intelligence, 16*(3–4), 415–426.

Hakuta, K. (1986). *Mirror of language.* New York: Basic Books.

Hall, E. T. (1966). *The hidden dimension.* New York: Doubleday.

Halliday, M. A. K. (1970). Language structure and language function. In J. Lyons (Ed.), *New horizons in linguistics* (pp. 140–165). Baltimore, MD: Penguin.

Halpin, J. A., Puff, C. R., Mason, H. F., & Marston, S. P. (1984). Self-reference and incidental recall by children. *Bulletin of the Psychonomic Society, 22,* 87–89.

Haviland, S. E., & Clark, H. H. (1974). What's new? Acquiring new information as a process in comprehension. *Journal of Verbal Learning and Verbal Behavior, 13,* 512–521.

Haxby, J. V., Ungerleider, L. G., Horwitz,B., Rapoport, S., & Grady, C. L. (1995). Hemispheric differences in neural systems for face working memory: A PET-rCBF study. *Human Brain Mapping, 3,* 68–82.

Haxby, J. V., Ungerleider, L. G., Horwitz, B., Maisog, J. M., Rappaport, S. L., & Grady, C. L. (1996). Face encoding and recognition in the human brain. *Proceedings of he National Academy of Sciences USA, 98,* 922–927.

Hayes, J. R. (1989). *The complete problem solver* (2nd ed.). Hillsdale, NJ: Erlbaum.

He, Z., & Nakayama, K. (1992). Apparent motion determined by surface layout not by disparity or three-dimensional distance. *Nature, 367*(6459), 173–175.

Heaton, J. M. (1968). *The eye: Phenomenology and psychology of function and disorder.* London: Tavistock.

Hebb, D. O. (1949). *The organization of behavior: A neuropsychological theory.* New York: Wiley.

Hegarty, M. (1991). Knowledge and processes in mechanical problem solving. In R. J. Sternberg & P. A. Frensch (Eds.), *Complex problem solving: Principles and mechanisms* (pp. 159–183). Hillsdale, NJ: Erlbaum.

Hegel, G. W. F. (1931). *The phenomenology of mind* (2nd ed., J. B. Baillie, Trans.). London: Allen & Unwin. (Original work published 1807)

Heindel, W. C., Butters, N., & Salmon, D. P. (1988). Impaired learning of a motor skill in patients with Huntington's disease. *Behavioral Neuroscience, 102*(1), 141–147.

Helmholtz, H. von. (1896). *Vorträge und Reden.* Braunschweig, Germany: Vieweg und Sohn.

Helmholtz, H. L. F. von. (1962). *Treatise on physiological optics* (3rd ed., J. P. C. Southall, Ed. and Trans.). New York: Dover. (Original work published 1909)

Henley, N. M. (1969). A psychological study of the semantics of animal terms. *Journal of Verbal Learning and Verbal Behavior, 8,* 176–184.

Hennessey, B. A., & Amabile, T. M. (1988). The conditions of creativity. In R. J. Sternberg (Ed.), *The nature of creativity* (pp. 11–38). New York: Cambridge University Press.

Herrnstein, R., & Murray, C. (1994). *The bell curve: Intelligence and class structure in American life.* New York: Free Press.

Hertzog, C., Vernon, M. C., & Rypma, B. (1993). Age differences in mental rotation task performance: The influence of speed/accuracy tradeoffs. *Journal of Gerontology, 48*(3), 150–156.

Herz, R. S., & Engen, T. (1996). Odor memory: Review and analysis. *Psychonomic Bulletin and Review, 3,* 300–313.

Hesse, M. (1966). *Models and analogies in science.* South Bend, IN: University of Notre Dame Press.

Hickling, A. K., & Gelman, S. A. (1995). How does your garden grow? Earl;y conceptualization of seeds and their place in the plant growth cycle. *Child Development, 66,* 856–867.

Hinton, G. E. (1979). Some demonstrations of the effects of structural descriptions in mental imagery. *Cognitive Science, 3,* 231–251.

Hintzman, D. L. (1978). *The psychology of learning and memory.* San Francisco: Freeman.

Hirsh-Pasek, K., Kemler Nelson, D. G., Jusczyk, P. W., Cassidy, K. W., Druss, B., & Kennedy, L. (1987). Clauses are perceptual units for young infants. *Cognition, 26,* 269–286.

Hirst, W., Spelke, E., Reaves, C. C., Caharack, G., & Neisser, U. (1980). Dividing attention without alternation or automaticity. *Journal of Experimental Psychology: General, 109,* 98–117.

Hirtle, S. C., & Jonides, J. (1985). Evidence of hierarchies in cognitive maps. *Memory & Cognition, 13*(3), 208–217.

Hirtle, S. C., & Mascolo, M. F. (1986). Effect of semantic clustering on the memory of spatial locations. *Journal of Experimental Psychology: Learning, Memory, & Cognition, 12*(2), 182–189.

Hochberg, J. (1978). *Perception* (2nd ed.). Englewood Cliffs, NJ: Prentice-Hall.

Hoffding, H. (1891). *Outlines of psychology.* New York: Macmillan.

Hoffman, C., Lau, I., & Johnson, D. R. (1986). The linguistic relativity of person cognition: An English–Chinese comparison. *Journal of Personality and Social Psychology, 51,* 1097–1105.

Holland, J. H., Holyoak, K. J., Nisbett, R. E., & Thagard, P. R. (1986). *Induction processes of inference, learning, and discovery.* Cambridge, MA: MIT Press.

Holt, J. (1964). *How children fail.* New York: Pitman.

Holyoak, K. J. (1984). Analogical thinking and human intelligence. In R. J. Sternberg (Ed.), *Advances in the psychology of human intelligence* (Vol. 2, pp. 199–230). Hillsdale, NJ: Erlbaum.

Holyoak, K. J. (1990). Problem solving. In D. N. Osherson & E. E. Smith (Eds.), *An invitation to cognitive science: Vol. 3. Thinking* (pp. 116–146). Cambridge, MA: MIT Press.

Holyoak, K. J., & Nisbett, R. E. (1988). Induction. In R. J. Sternberg & E. E. Smith (Eds.), *The psychology of human thought* (pp. 50–91). New York: Cambridge University Press.

Horn, J. L., & Cattell, R. B. (1966). Refinement and test of the theory of fluid and crystallized ability intelligences. *Journal of Educational Psychology, 57,* 253–270.

Horn, J. L., & Hofer, S. M. (1992). Major abilities and development in the adult period. In R. J. Sternberg & C. A. Berg

(Eds.), *Intellectual development* (pp. 44–99). New York: Cambridge University Press.

Horn, J. L., & Knapp, J. R. (1973). On the subjective character of the empirical base of Guilford's structure-of-intellect model. *Psychological Bulletin, 80,* 33–43.

Hubbard, T. L. (1995). Environmental invariants in the representation of motion: Implied and representational momentum, gravity, friction, and centripetal force. *Psychonomic Bulletin and Review, 2,* 322–338.

Hubel, D., & Wiesel, T. (1963). Receptive fields of cells in the striate cortex of very young, visually inexperienced kittens. *Journal of Neurophysiology, 26,* 994–1002.

Hubel, D., & Wiesel, T. (1968). Receptive fields and functional architecture of the monkey striate cortex. *Journal of Physiology, 195,* 215–243.

Hubel, D. H., & Wiesel, T. N. (1979). Brain mechanisms of vision. *Scientific American, 241,* 150–162.

Hughlings-Jackson, J. (1932). In J. Taylor (Ed.), *Selected writings of John Hughlings-Jackson.* London: Hodder and Stoughton. (Original work published 1866)

Hultsch, D. F., & Dixon, R. A. (1990). Learning and memory in aging. In J. E. Birren & K. W. Schaie (Eds.), *Handbook of the psychology of aging: The handbooks of aging* (3rd ed. pp. 258–274). San Diego, CA: Academic Press.

Humphreys, L. G., & Davey, T. C. (1988). Continuity in intellectual growth from 12 months to 9 years. *Intelligence, 12,* 183–197.

Humphreys, M., Bain, J. D., & Pike, R. (1989). Different ways to cue a coherent memory system: A theory for episodic, semantic, and procedural tasks. *Psychological Review, 96*(2), 208–233.

Hunt, E. B. (1975). *Artificial intelligence.* New York: Academic Press.

Hunt, E. B. (1978). Mechanics of verbal ability. *Psychological Review, 85,* 109–130.

Hunt, E. B. (1994). Problem solving. In R. J. Sternberg (Ed.), *Handbook of perception and cognition: Vol. 12. Thinking and problem solving* (pp. 215–232). New York: Academic Press.

Hunt, E. B., & Banaji, M. (1988). The Whorfian hypothesis revisited: A cognitive science view of linguistic and cultural effects on thought. In J. W. Berry, S. H. Irvine, & E. Hunt (Eds.), *Indigenous cognition: Functioning in cultural context.* Dordrecht, The Netherlands: Martinus Nijhoff Publishers.

Hunt, E. B., & Lansman, M. (1982). Individual differences in attention. In R. J. Sternberg (Ed.), *Advances in the psychology of human intelligence* (Vol. 1, pp. 207–254). Hillsdale, NJ: Erlbaum.

Hunt, E. B., & Love, T. (1972). How good can memory be? In A. W. Melton & E. Martin (Eds.), *Coding processes in human memory.* Washington, DC: V. H. Winston & Sons.

Hunt, E. B., Lunneborg, C., & Lewis, J. (1975). What does it mean to be high verbal? *Cognitive Psychology, 7,* 194–227.

Huttenlocher, J. (1968). Constructing spatial images: A strategy in reasoning. *Psychological Review, 75,* 550–560.

Huttenlocher, J., Hedges, L. V., & Duncan, S. (1991). Categories and particulars: Prototype effects in spatial location. *Psychological Review, 98*(3), 352–376.

Huttenlocher, J., & Presson, C. C. (1973). Mental rotation and the perspective problem. *Cognitive Psychology, 4,* 277–299.

Huttenlocher, J., & Presson, C. C. (1979). The coding and transformation of spatial information. *Cognitive Psychology, 11*(3), 375–394.

Inhelder, B., & Piaget, J. (1958). *The growth of logical thinking from childhood to adolescence.* New York: Basic Books.

Intelligence and its measurement: A symposium. (1921). *Journal of Educational Psychology, 12,* 123–147, 195–216, 271–275.

Intons-Peterson, M. J. (1983). Imagery paradigms: How vulnerable are they to experimenters' expectations? *Journal of Experimental Psychology: Human Perception & Performance, 9*(3), 394–412.

Intons-Peterson, M. J. (1992). Components of auditory imagery. In D. Reisberg (Ed.), *Auditory imagery* (pp. 45–71). Hillsdale, NJ: Erlbaum.

Intons-Peterson, M. J., & Roskos-Ewoldsen, B. B. (1989). Sensory-perceptual qualities of images. *Journal of Experimental Psychology: Learning, Memory, & Cognition, 15*(2), 188–199.

Intons-Peterson, M. J., Russell, W., & Dressel, S. (1992). The role of pitch in auditory imagery. *Journal of Experimental Psychology: Human Perception & Performance, 18*(1), 233–240.

Izquierdo, I., & Medina, J. H. (1995). Correlations between the pharmacology of long-term potentiation and the pharmacology of memory. *Neurobiology of Learning & Memory, 63,* 19–32.

Jackendoff, R. (1991). Parts and boundaries. *Cognition, 41*(1–3), 9–45.

Jacobson, R. R., & Lishman, W. A. (1990). Cortical and diencephalic lesions in Korsakoff's syndrome: A clinical and CT scan study. *Psychological Medicine, 20*(1), 63–75.

James, W. (1970). *The principles of psychology* (Vol. 1). New York: Holt. (Original work published 1890)

Janis, I. L., & Frick, F. (1943). The relationship between attitudes toward conclusions and errors in judging logical validity of syllogisms. *Journal of Experimental Psychology, 33,* 73–77.

Jenkins, J. J. (1979). Four points to remember: A tetrahedral model of memory experiments. In L. S. Cermak & F. I. M. Craik (Eds.), *Levels of processing in human memory* (pp. 429–446). Hillsdale, NJ: Erlbaum.

Jensen, A. R. (1979). *g:* Outmoded theory or unconquered frontier? *Creative Science and Technology, 2,* 16–29.

Jensen, A. R. (1982). The chronometry of intelligence. In R. J. Sternberg (Ed.), *Advances in the psychology of human intelligence.* (Vol. 1, pp. 255–310). Hillsdale, NJ: Erlbaum.

Jernigan, T. L., Schafer, K., Butters, N., & Cermak, L. S. (1991). Magnetic resonance imaging of alcoholic Korsakoff patients. *Neuropsychopharmacology, 4*(3), 175–186.

Johnson, J. S., & Newport, E. L. (1989). Critical period effects in second language learning: The influence of maturational state on the acquisition of English as a second language. *Cognitive Psychology, 21,* 60–99.

Johnson, J. S., & Newport, E. L. (1991). Critical period effects on universal properties of language: The status of subjacency in the acquisition of a second language. *Cognition, 39*(3), 215–258.

Johnson, M. K., Foley, M. A., Suengas, A. G., & Raye, C. L. (1988). Phenomenal characteristics of memories for perceived and imagined autobiographical events. *Journal of Experimental Psychology: General, 117*(4), 371–376.

Johnson, M. K., & Hasher, L. (1987). Human learning and memory. *Annual Review of Psychology, 38,* 631–668.

Johnson, M. K., & Raye, C. L. (1981). Reality monitoring. *Psychological Review, 88,* 67–85.

Johnson-Laird, P. (1975). Models of deduction. In R. J. Falmagne (Ed.), *Reasoning: Representation and process* (pp. 7–54). Hillsdale, NJ: Erlbaum.

Johnson-Laird, P. N. (1983). *Mental models.* Cambridge, MA: Harvard University Press.

Johnson-Laird, P. N. (1989). Mental models. In M. I. Posner (Ed.), *Foundations of cognitive science* (pp. 469–499). Cambridge, MA: MIT Press.

Johnson-Laird, P. N., Byrne, R. M. J., & Schaeken, W. (1992). Propositional reasoning by model. *Psychological Review, 99*(3), 418–439.

Johnson-Laird, P. N., & Steedman, M. (1978). The psychology of syllogisms. *Cognitive Psychology, 10,* 64–99.

Johnston, J. C., & McClelland, J. L. (1973). Visual factors in word perception. *Perception & Psychophysics, 14,* 365–370.

Jolicoeur, P. (1985). The time to name disoriented natural objects. *Memory & Cognition, 13*(4), 289–303.

Jolicoeur, P., & Kosslyn, S. (1985a). Demand characteristics in image scanning experiments. *Journal of Mental Imagery, 9*(2), 41–49.

Jolicoeur, P., & Kosslyn, S. (1985b). Is time to scan visual images due to demand characteristics? *Memory & Cognition, 13*(4), 320–332.

Jolicoeur, P., Snow, D., & Murray, J. (1987). The time to identify disoriented letters: Effects of practice and font. *Canadian Journal of Psychology, 41*(3), 303–316.

Jordan, K., & Huntsman, L. A. (1990). Image rotation of misoriented letter strings: Effects of orientation cuing and repetition. *Perception & Psychophysics, 48*(4), 363–374.

Jusczyk, P. W. (1986) Speech perception. In K. R. Boff, L. Kaufman, & J. P. Thomas (Eds.), *Handbook of perception and human performance: Vol. 2. Cognitive processes and performance* (pp.1–57). New York: Wiley.

Jusczyk, P. W. (1997). *The discovery of spoken language.* Cambridge, MA: MIT Press.

Just, M., & Carpenter, P. A. (1985). Cognitive coordinate systems: Accounts of mental rotation and individual differences in spatial ability. *Psychological Review, 92*(2), 137–172.

Just, M. A., Carpenter, P. A., & Masson, M. E. J. (1982). *What eye fixations tell us about speed reading and skimming* (EyeLab Tech. Rep.). Pittsburgh, PA: Carnegie-Mellon University.

Juster, N. (1961). *The phantom tollbooth.* New York: Epstein & Carroll.

Kagan, J. (1989). [Commentary]. Continuity in early cognitive development—conceptual and methodological challenges [special issue]. *Human Development, 32,* 172–176.

Kahneman, D. (1973). *Attention and effort.* Englewood Cliffs, NJ: Prentice-Hall.

Kahneman, D., & Tversky, A. (1972). Subjective probability: A judgment of representativeness. *Cognitive Psychology, 3,* 430–454.

Kahneman, D., & Tversky, A. (1973). On the psychology of prediction. *Psychological Review, 80,* 237.

Kahneman, D., & Tversky, A. (1979). Intuitive prediction: Biases and corrective procedures. *Management Science, 12,* 313–327.

Kahneman, D., & Tversky, A. (1990). Prospect theory: An analysis of decision under risk. In P. K. Moser (Ed.), *Rationality in action: Contemporary approaches* (pp. 140–170). New York: Cambridge University Press.

Kail, R. V. (1984). *The development of memory in children* (2nd ed.). New York: Freeman.

Kail, R. V. (1991). Controlled and automatic processing during mental rotation. *Journal of Experimental Child Psychology, 51*(3), 337–347.

Kail, R. V. (1997). Processing time, imagery, and spatial memory. *Journal of Experimental Child Psychology, 64,* 67–78.

Kail, R. V., & Bisanz, J. (1992). The information-processing perspective on cognitive development in childhood and adolescence. In R. J. Sternberg & C. A. Berg (Eds.), *Intellectual development* (pp. 229–260). New York: Cambridge University Press.

Kail, R. V., & Park, Y. S. (1990). Impact of practice on speed of mental rotation. *Journal of Experimental Child Psychology, 49*(2), 227–244.

Kail, R. V., & Park, Y. S. (1994). Processing time, articulation time, and memory span. *Journal of Experimental Child Psychology, 57*(2), 281–291.

Kail, R. V., Pellegrino, J. W., & Carter, P. (1980). Developmental changes in mental rotation. *Journal of Experimental Child Psychology, 29,* 102–116.

Kant, I. (1987). The critique of pure reason. In R. M. Hutchins *Great books of the Western world: Vol. 42. Kant.* Chicago: Encyclopaedia Britannica. (Original work published 1781)

Kaplan, C. A., & Davidson, J. E. (1989). *Incubation effects in problem solving.* Manuscript submitted for publication.

Kass-Simon, G., & Farnes, P. (Eds.). (1990). *Women of science: Righting the record.* Bloomington, IN: Indiana University Press.

Karni, A., Tanne, D., Rubenstein, B. S., Askenasy, J. J. M., & Sagi, D. (1994). Dependence on REM sleep of overnight improvement of a perceptional skill. *Science, 265,* 679.

Katz, A. N. (1987). Self-reference in the encoding of creative-relevant traits. *Journal of Personality, 55,* 97–120.

Katz, J. J. (1972). *Semantic theory.* New York: Harper & Row.

Katz, J. J., & Fodor, J. A. (1963). The structure of a semantic theory. *Language, 39,* 170–210.

Kay, P. (1975). Synchronic variability and diachronic changes in basic color terms. *Language in Society, 4,* 257–270.

Keane, M. T. (1994). Propositional representations. In M. W. Eysenck (Ed.), *The Blackwell dictionary of cognitive psychology.* Cambridge, MA: Blackwell.

Kearins, J. M. (1981). Visual spatial memory in Australian aboriginal children of desert regions. *Cognitive Psychology, 13*(3), 434–460.

Keating, D. P. (1984). The emperor's new clothes: The "new look" in intelligence research. In R. J. Sternberg (Ed.), *Advances in the psychology of human intelligence* (Vol. 2, pp. 1–45). Hillsdale, NJ: Erlbaum.

Keating, D. P., & Bobbitt, B. L. (1978). Individual and developmental differences in cognitive-processing components of mental ability. *Child Development, 49,* 155–167.

Keil, F. C. (1979). *Semantic and conceptual development.* Cambridge, MA: Harvard University Press.

Keil, F. C. (1989). *Concepts, kinds, and cognitive development.* Cambridge, MA: MIT Press.

Keil, F. C., & Batterman, N. (1984). A characteristic-to-defining shift in the development of word meaning. *Journal of Verbal Learning and Verbal Behavior, 23,* 221–236.

Keller, E. (1976). Gambits. *TESL Talk,* 7(2), 18–21.

Keller, H. (1988). *The story of my life.* New York: Signet. (Original work published 1902)

Kellman, P. J., & Shipley, T. F. (1991). A theory of visual interpolation in object perception. *Cognitive Psychology, 23*(2), 141–221.

Keppel, G., & Underwood, B. J. (1962). Proactive inhibition in short-term retention of single items. *Journal of Verbal Learning and Verbal Behavior, 1,* 153–161.

Kerr, N. (1983). The role of vision in "visual imagery" experiments: Evidence from the congenitally blind. *Journal of Experimental Psychology: General, 112*(2), 265–277.

Kimura, D. (1981). Neural mechanisms in manual signing. *Sign Language Studies, 33,* 291–312.

Kimura, D. (1987). Are men's and women's brains really different? *Canadian Psychology, 28*(2), 133–147.

Kintsch, W. (1988). The role of knowledge in discourse comprehension: A construction–integration model. *Psychological Review, 95*(2), 163–182.

Kintsch, W. (1990). The representation of knowledge and the use of knowledge in discourse comprehension. In C. Graumann & R. Dietrich (Eds.), *Language in the social context.* Amsterdam: Elsevier.

Kintsch, W., & Buschke, H. (1969). Homophones and synonyms in short-term memory. *Journal of Experimental Psychology, 80,* 403–407.

Kintsch, W., & Keenan, J. (1973). Reading rate and retention as a function of the number of propositions in the base structure of sentences. *Cognitive Psychology, 5,* 257–274.

Kintsch, W., & van Dijk, T. A. (1978). Toward a model of text comprehension and production. *Psychological Review, 85*(5), 363–394.

Kirby, K. N. (1994). Probabilities and utilities of fictional outcomes in Wason's selection task. *Cognition, 51*(1), 1–28.

Kirsner, K., & Craik, F. I. M. (1971). Naming and decision processes in short-term recognition memory. *Journal of Experimental Psychology, 88,* 149–157.

Klein, S. B., & Kihlstrom, J. F. (1986). Elaboration, organization, and the self-reference effect in memory. *Journal of Experimental Psychology: General, 115*(1), 26–38.

Kliegl, R., Mayr, U., & Krampe, R. T. (1994). Time–accuracy functions for determining process and person differences: An application to cognitive aging. *Cognitive Psychology, 26*(2), 134–164.

Köhler, S., Kapur, S., Moscovitch, M., Winocur, G., & Houle, S. (1995). Dissociation of pathways for object and spatial vision in the intact human brain. *Neuroreport, 6,* 1865–1868.

Köhler, W. (1927). *The mentality of apes.* New York: Harcourt Brace.

Köhler, W. (1940). *Dynamics in psychology.* New York: Liveright.

Kolb, B., & Whishaw, I. Q. (1985). *Fundamentals of human neuropsychology* (2nd ed.). New York: Freeman.

Kolb, B., & Whishaw, I. Q. (1990). *Fundamentals of human neuropsychology* (3rd ed.). New York: Freeman.

Kolers, P. A. (1966a). Interlingual facilitation of short-term memory. *Journal of Verbal Learning and Verbal Behavior, 5,* 314–319.

Kolers, P. A. (1966b). Reading and talking bilingually. *American Journal of Psychology, 79,* 357–376.

Kolodner, J. L. (1983). Reconstructive memory: A computer model. *Cognitive Science,* 7(4), 281–328.

Komatsu, L. K. (1992). Recent views on conceptual structure. *Psychological Bulletin, 112*(3), 500–526.

Koriat, A., & Goldsmith, M. (1996). Memory metaphors and the everyday–laboratory controversy: The correspondence versus the storehouse conceptions of memory. *Behavioral and Brain Sciences, 19,* 167–228.

Kosslyn, S. M. (1975). Information representation in visual images. *Cognitive Psychology,* 7(3), 341–370.

Kosslyn, S. M. (1976). Using imagery to retrieve semantic information: A developmental study. *Child Development, 47*(2), 434–444.

Kosslyn, S. M. (1981). The medium and the message in mental imagery: A theory. *Psychological Review, 88*(1), 46–66.

Kosslyn, S. M. (1983). *Ghosts in the mind's machine: Creating and using images in the brain.* New York: Norton.

Kosslyn, S. M. (1990). Mental imagery. In D. N. Osherson, S. M. Kosslyn, & J. M. Hollerbach (Eds.), *Visual cognition and action: Vol. 2. An invitation to cognitive science* (pp. 73–97). Cambridge, MA: MIT Press.

Kosslyn, S. M. (1994). Computational theory of imagery. In M. W. Eysenck (Ed.), *The Blackwell dictionary of cognitive psychology* (pp. 177–181). Cambridge, MA: Blackwell.

Kosslyn, S. M., Ball, T. M., & Reiser, B. J. (1978). Visual images preserve metric spatial information: Evidence from studies of image scanning. *Journal of Experimental Psychology: Human Perception and Performance, 4,* 47–60.

Kosslyn, S. M., & Koenig, O. (1992). *Wet mind: The new cognitive neuroscience.* New York: Free Press.

Kosslyn, S. M., & Pomerantz, J. R. (1977). Imagery, propositions, and the form of internal representations. *Cognitive Psychology,* 9(1), 52–76.

Kosslyn, S.M., Seger, C., Pani, J. R., & Hillger, L. A. (1990). When is imagery used in everyday life? A diary study. *Journal of Mental Imagery, 14*(3–4), 131–152.

Kosslyn, S. M., & Sussman, A. L. (1995). Roles of memory in perception. In M. S. Gazzaniga (Ed.), *The cognitive neurosciences* (pp. 1035–1042). Cambridge, MA: MIT Press.

Kosslyn, S. M., Thompson, W. L., Kim, J. J., & Alpert, N. M. (1995). Topographical representations of mental images in primary visual cortex. *Nature, 378,* 496–498.

Kotovsky, K., Hayes, J. R., & Simon, H. A. (1985). Why are some problems hard? Evidence from the tower of Hanoi. *Cognitive Psychology, 17,* 248–294.

Kotovsky, K., & Simon, H. A. (1973). Empirical tests of a theory of human acquisition of concepts for sequential events. *Cognitive Psychology, 4,* 399–424.

Kozlowski, L., & Cutting, J. (1977). Recognizing the sex of a walker from a dynamic point-light display. *Perception & Psychophysics, 21*(6), 575–580.

Kramer, D. A. (1990). Conceptualizing wisdom: The primacy of affect–cognition relations. In R. J. Sternberg (Ed.), *Wisdom: Its nature, origins, and development* (pp. 279–313). New York: Cambridge University Press.

Krantz, L. (1992). *What the odds are: A-to-Z odds on everything you hoped or feared could happen.* New York: Harper Perennial.

Kuhl, P. K. (1991). Human adults and infants show a "perceptual magnet effect" for the prototypes of speech categories, monkeys do not. *Perception & Psycholinguistics, 50*, 93–107.

Kutas, M., & Hillyard, S. A. (1980). Reading senseless sentences: Brain potentials reflect semantic incongruity. *Science, 207,* 203–205.

Kutas, M., & Van Patten, C. (1994). Psycholinguistics electrified: Event-related brain potential investigations. In M. A. Gernsbacher (Ed.), *Handbook of psycholinguistics* (pp. 83–143). San Diego, CA: Academic Press.

LaBerge, D. (1975). Acquisition of automatic processing in perceptual and associative learning. In P. M. A. Rabbit & S. Dornic (Eds.), *Attention and performance.* London: Academic Press.

LaBerge, D. (1976). Perceptual learning and attention. In W. Estes (Ed.), *Handbook of learning and cognitive processes: Vol. 4. Attention and memory.* Hillsdale, NJ: Erlbaum.

LaBerge, D. (1990). Attention. *Psychological Science, 1*(3), 156–162.

LaBerge, D., & Brown, V. (1989). Theory of attentional operations in shape identification. *Psychological Review, 96*(1), 101–124.

LaBerge, D., Carter, M., & Brown, V. (1992). A network simulation of thalamic circuit operations in selective attention. *Neural Computation, 4*(3), 318–331.

LaBerge D., & Samuels, S. J. (1974). Toward a theory of automatic information processing in reading. *Cognitive Psychology, 6*(2), 293–323.

Labouvie-Vief, G. (1980). Beyond formal operations: Uses and limits of pure logic in life span development. *Human Development, 23,* 141–161.

Labouvie-Vief, G. (1990). Wisdom as integrated thought: Historical and developmental perspectives. In R. J. Sternberg (Ed.), *Wisdom: Its nature, origins, and development* (pp. 52–83). New York: Cambridge University Press.

Labouvie-Vief, G., & Schell, D. A. (1982). Learning and memory in later life. In B. B. Wolman (Ed.), *Handbook of developmental psychology.* Englewood Cliffs, NJ: Prentice-Hall.

Ladavas, E., del Pesce, M., Mangun, G. R., & Gazzaniga, M. S. (1994). Variations in attentional bias of the disconnected cerebral hemispheres. *Cognitive Neuropsychology, 11*(1), 57–74.

Ladeforged, P., & Maddieson, I. (1996). *The sounds of the world's languages.* Cambridge: Blackwell.

Lakoff, G. (1971). On generative semantics. In D. D. Steinberg & L. A. Jakobovits (Eds.), *Semantics: An interdisciplinary reader in philosophy, linguistics, and psychology.* Cambridge, England: Cambridge University Press.

Langer, E. J. (1989). *Mindfulness.* New York: Addison-Wesley.

Langer, E. J. (1997). *The power of mindful learning.* Needham Heights, MA: Addison-Wesley.

Langlais, P. J., Mandel, R. J., & Mair, R. G. (1992). Diencephalic lesions, learning impairments, and intact retrograde memory following acute thiamine deficiency in the rat. *Behavioural Brain Research, 48*(2), 177–185.

Langley, P., & Jones, R. (1988). A computational model of scientific insight. In R. J. Sternberg (Ed.), *The nature of creativity* (pp. 117–201). New York: Cambridge University Press.

Langley, P., Simon, H. A., Bradshaw, G. L., & Zytkow, J. M. (1987). *Scientific discovery: Computational explorations of the creative process.* Cambridge, MA: MIT Press.

Lanze, M., Weisstein, N., & Harris, J. R. (1982). Perceived depth versus structural relevance in the object-superiority effect. *Perception & Psychophysics, 31*(4), 376–382.

Larkin, J. H., McDermott, J., Simon, D. P., & Simon, H. A. (1980). Expert and novice performance in solving physics problems. *Science, 208,* 1335–1342.

Larson, G. E., Haier, R. J., LaCasse, L. & Hazen, K. (1995). Evaluation of a "mental effort" hypothesis for correlation between cortical metabolism and intelligence. *Intelligence, 21*, 267–278.

Lashley, K. S. (1950). In search of the engram. *Symposia of the Society for Experimental Biology, 4,* 454–482.

Lazar, I., & Darlington, R. (1982). Lasting effects of early education: A report from the consortium for longitudinal studies. *Monographs of the Society for Research in Child Development, 47*(2–3, Serial No. 195).

Lederer, R. (1987). *Anguished English.* New York: Pocket Books.

Lederer, R. (1991). *The miracle of language.* New York: Pocket Books.

Lehman, D., Lempert, R., & Nisbett, R. E. (1987). *The effects of graduate education on reasoning: Formal discipline and thinking about everyday-life events.* Unpublished manuscript, University of British Columbia.

Leicht, K. L., & Overton, R. (1987). Encoding variability and spacing repetitions. *American Journal of Psychology, 100*(1), 61–68.

Lesgold, A. M. (1988). Problem solving. In R. J. Sternberg & E. E. Smith (Eds.), *The psychology of human thought* (pp. 188–213). New York: Cambridge University Press.

Lesgold, A. M., & Lajoie, S. (1991). Complex problem solving in electronics. In R. J. Sternberg & P. A. Frensch (Eds.), *Complex problem solving: Principles and mechanisms* (pp. 287–316). Hillsdale, NJ: Erlbaum.

Lesgold, A. M., Rubinson, H., Feltovich, P., Glaser, R., Klopfer, D., & Wang, Y. (1988). Expertise in a complex skill: Diagnosing x-ray pictures. In M. T. H. Chi, R. Glaser, & M. Farr (Eds.), *The nature of expertise.* Hillsdale, NJ: Erlbaum.

Lévi-Strauss, C. (1963). *Structural anthropology* (C. Jacobson & B. G. Schoepf, Trans.). New York: Basic Books. (Original work published 1958)

Levy, J. (1974). Cerebral asymmetries as manifested in split-brain man. In M. Kinsbourne & W. L. Smith (Eds.), *Hemispheric disconnection and cerebral function.* Springfield, IL: Charles C. Thomas.

Levy, J., Trevarthen, C., & Sperry, R. W. (1972). Perception of bilateral chimeric figures following hemispheric deconnexion. *Brain, 95*(1), 61–78.

Lewis, M., & Brooks-Gunn, J. (1981). Visual attention at three months as a predictor of cognitive functioning at two years of age. *Intelligence, 5,* 131–140.

Liberman, A. M., Cooper, F. S., Shankweiler, D. P., & Studdert-Kennedy, M. (1967). Perception of the speech code. *Psychological Review, 74,* 431–461.

Liberman, A. M., Harris, K. S., Hoffman, H. S., & Griffith, B. C. (1957). The discrimination of speech sounds within and across phoneme boundaries. *Journal of Experimental Psychology, 54,* 358–368.

Liberman, A. M., & Mattingly, I. G. (1985). The motor theory of speech perception revised. *Cognition, 21,* 1–36.

Lindsay, D. S., & Read, J. D. (1994). Psychotherapy and memories of childhood sexual abuse: A cognitive perspective. *Applied Cognitive Psychology, 8,* 281–338.

Lipman, M., Sharp, A. M., & Oscanyan, F. S. (1980). *Philosophy in the classroom.* Philadelphia, PA: Temple University Press.

Livingstone, M., & Hubel, D. (1988). Segregation of form, color, movement, and depth: Anatomy, physiology, and perception. *Science, 240*(4853), 740–749.

Locke, J. (1961). An essay concerning human understanding. In R. M. Hutchins *Great books of the Western world: Vol. 35. Locke, Berkeley, Hume.* Chicago: Encyclopaedia Britannica. (Original work published 1690)

Locke, J. L. (1994). Phases in the child's development of language. *American Scientist, 82,* 436–445.

Loftus, E. F. (1975). Leading questions and the eyewitness report. *Cognitive Psychology, 7,* 560–572.

Loftus, E. F. (1977). Shifting human color memory. *Memory & Cognition, 5,* 696–699.

Loftus, E. F., & Ketcham, K. (1991). *Witness for the defense: The accused, the eyewitness, and the expert who puts memory on trial.* New York: St. Martin's Press.

Loftus, E. F., & Ketcham, K. (1994). *The myth of repressed memory.* New York: St. Martin's Press.

Loftus, E. F., & Loftus, G. R. (1980). On the permanence of stored information in the human brain. *American Psychologist, 35,* 409–420.

Loftus, E. F., Miller, D. G., & Burns, H. J. (1978). Semantic integration of verbal information into a visual memory. *Journal of Experimental Psychology: Human Learning and Memory, 4,* 19–31.

Loftus, E. F., Miller, D. G., & Burns, H. J. (1987). Semantic integration of verbal information into a visual memory. In L. S. Wrightsman, C. E. Willis, S. M. Kassin (Eds.), *On the witness stand: Vol. 2. Controversies in the courtroom* (pp. 157–177). Newbury Park, CA: Sage.

Loftus, E. F., & Palmer, J. C. (1974). Reconstruction of automobile destruction: An example of the interaction between language and memory. *Journal of Verbal Learning and Verbal Behavior, 13,* 585–589.

Logan, G. (1988). Toward an instance theory of automatization. *Psychological Review, 95*(4), 492–527.

Lonner, W. J. (1989). The introductory psychology text: Beyond Ekman, Whorf, and biased IQ tests. In D. M. Keats, D. Munro, & L. Mann (Eds.), *Heterogeneity in cross-cultural psychology* (pp. 4–22). Amsterdam: Swets & Zeitlinger.

Lou, H. C., Henriksen, L., & Bruhn, P. (1984). Focal cerebral hypoperfusion in children with dyphasia and/or attention deficit disorder. *Archives of Neurology, 41*(8), 825–829.

Lowry, R. (1971). *The evolution of psychological theory: 1650 to the present.* Chicago, IL: Aldine-Atherton.

Luce, R. D., & Raiffa, H. (1957). *Games and decisions.* New York: Wiley.

Luchins, A. S. (1942). Mechanization in problem solving. *Psychological Monographs, 54*(6, Whole No. 248).

Luck, S. J., Hillyard, S. A., Mangun, G. R., & Gazzaniga, M. S. (1989). Independent hemispheric attentional systems mediate visual search in split-brain patients. *Nature, 342*(6249), 543–545.

Luria, A. R. (1968). *The mind of a mnemonist.* New York: Basic Books.

Luria, A. R. (1973). *The working brain.* London: Penguin.

Luria, A. R. (1976). *Basic problems of neurolinguistics.* The Hague, Netherlands: Mouton.

Luria, A. R. (1984). *The working brain: An introduction to neuropsychology* (B. Haigh, Trans.). Harmondsworth, England: Penguin. (Original work published 1973)

Lyons, J. (1977). *Semantics.* New York: Cambridge University Press.

Mace, W. M. (1986). J. J. Gibson's ecological theory of information pickup: Cognition from the ground up. In T. J. Knapp & L. C. Robertson (Eds.), *Approaches to cognition: Contrasts and controversies* (pp. 137–157). Hillsdale, NJ: Erlbaum.

Mackworth, N. H. (1948). The breakdown of vigilance during prolonged visual search. *Quarterly Journal of Experimental Psychology, 1,* 6–21.

MacLeod, C. (1991). Half a century of research on the Stroop effect: An integrative review. *Psychological Bulletin, 109*(2), 163–203.

MacLeod, C. M. (1996). How priming affects two speeded implicit tests of remembering: Naming colors versus reading words. *Consciousness and Cognition: An International Journal, 5,* 73–90.

MacLeod, C. M., Hunt, E. B., & Mathews, N. N. (1978). Individual differences in the verification of sentence–picture relationships. *Journal of Verbal Learning and Verbal Behavior, 17,* 493–507.

Malgady, R., & Johnson, M. (1976). Modifiers in metaphors: Effects of constituent phrase similarity on the interpretation of figurative sentences. *Journal of Psycholinguistic Research, 5,* 43–52.

Malt, B. C., & Smith, E. E. (1984). Correlated properties in natural categories. *Journal of Verbal Learning and Verbal Behavior, 23,* 250–269.

Mandler, G. (1974). Memory storage and retrieval: Some limits on the reach of attention and consciousness. In P. M. A. Rabbit & S. Dornic (Eds.), *Attention and performance.* London: Academic Press.

Mandler, J. (1983). Representation. In P. H. Mussen (Ed.), *Handbook of child psychology: Vol. 3. Cognitive development.* New York: Wiley.

Mandler, J. M. (1990). A new perspective on cognitive development in infancy. *American Scientist, 78,* 236–243.

Mangun, G. R., & Hillyard, S. A. (1990). Electrophysiological studies of visual selective attention in humans. In A. B. Scheibel & A. F. Wechsler (Eds.), *Neurobiology of higher cognitive function* (pp. 271–295). New York: Guilford.

Mangun, G. R., & Hillyard, S. A. (1991). Modulations of sensory-evoked brain potentials indicate changes in perceptual processing during visualspatial priming. *Journal of Experimental Psychology: Human Perception & Performance, 17*(4), 1057–1074.

Mani, K., & Johnson-Laird, P. N. (1982). The mental representation of spatial descriptions. *Memory & Cognition, 10*(2), 181–187.

Manktelow, K. I., & Over, D. E. (1990). Deontic thought and the selection task. In K. J. Gilhooly, M. T. G. Keane, & G. Erdos (Eds.), *Lines of thinking* (Vol. 1, pp. 153–164). London: Wiley.

Manktelow, K. I., & Over, D. E. (1992). Obligation, permission, and mental models. In V. Rogers, A. Rutherford, & P. Bibby (Eds.), *Models in the mind* (pp. 249–266). London: Academic Press.

Mantyla, T. (1986). Optimizing cue effectiveness: Recall of 500 and 600 incidentally learned words. *Journal of Experimental Psychology: Learning, Memory, & Cognition, 12,* 66–71.

Marcel, A. J. (1983a). Conscious and unconscious perception: An approach to the relations between phenomenal experience and perceptual processes. *Cognitive Psychology, 15*(2), 238–300.

Marcel, A. J. (1983b). Conscious and unconscious perception: Experiments on visual masking and word recognition. *Cognitive Psychology, 15*(2), 197–237.

Marcel, A. J. (1986). Consciousness and processing: Choosing and testing a null hypothesis. *Brain and Behavioral Sciences, 9,* 40–41.

Marcus, D., & Overton, W. (1978). The development of gender constancy and sex role preferences. *Child Development, 49,* 434–444.

Markman, E. M. (1977). Realizing that you don't understand: A preliminary investigation. *Child Development, 48,* 986–992.

Markman, E. M. (1979). Realizing that you don't understand: Elementary school children's awareness of inconsistencies. *Child Development, 50,* 643–655.

Marmor, G. S. (1975). Development of kinetic images: When does the child first represent movement in mental images? *Cognitive Psychology, 7,* 548–559.

Marmor, G. S. (1977). Mental rotation and number conservation: Are they related? *Developmental Psychology, 13,* 320–325.

Marr, D. (1982). *Vision.* San Francisco: Freeman.

Martin, J. A. (1981). A longitudinal study of the consequences of early mother–infant interaction: A microanalytic approach. *Monographs of the Society for Research in Child Development, 46*(203, Serial No. 190).

Martin, L. (1986). Eskimo words for snow: A case study in the genesis and decay of an anthropological example. *American Psychologist, 88,* 418–423.

Martin, M. (1979). Local and global processing: The role of sparsity. *Memory & Cognition, 7,* 476–484.

Massaro, D. W. (1987). *Speech perception by ear and eye: A paradigm for psychological inquiry.* Hillsdale, NJ: Erlbaum.

Massaro, D. W., & Cohen, M. M. (1990). Perception of synthesized audible and visible speech. *Psychological Science, 1,* 55–63.

Matarazzo, J. D. (1992). Biological and physiological correlates of intelligence. *Intelligence, 16*(3,4), 257–258.

Matlin, M. W., & Underhill, W. A. (1979). Selective rehearsal and selective recall. *Bulletin of the Psychonomic Society, 14*(5), 389–392.

Mayr, U., & Kliegl, R. (1993). Sequential and coordinative complexity: Age-based processing in figural transformations. *Journal of Experimental Psychology: Learning, Memory, & Cognition, 19*(6), 1297–1320.

McArthur, T. (Ed.). (1992). *The Oxford companion to the English language.* New York: Oxford University Press.

McCall, R. B. (1989). The development of intellectual functioning in infancy and the prediction of later IQ. In S. D. Osofsky (Ed.), *The handbook of infant development* (pp. 707–741). New York: Wiley.

McCall, R. B., Kennedy, C. B., & Appelbaum, M. I. (1977). Magnitude of discrepancy and the distribution of attention in infants. *Child Development, 48,* 772–786.

McCann, R. S., & Johnston, J. C. (1992). Locus of single-channel bottleneck in dual-task interference. *Journal of Experimental Psychology: Human Perception & Performance, 18*(2), 471–484.

McClelland, J. L., & Elman, J. L. (1986). The TRACE model of speech perception. *Cognitive Psychology, 18,* 1–86.

McClelland, J. L., McNaughton, B. C., & O'Reilly, R. C. (1995). Why there are complementary learning systems in the hippocampus and neocortex: Insights from the successes and failures of connectionist models of learning and memory. *Psychological Review, 102,* 419–457.

McClelland, J. L., & Rumelhart, D. E. (1981). An interactive activation model of context effects in letter perception: Part 1. An account of basic findings. *Psychological Review, 88,* 483–524.

McClelland, J. L., & Rumelhart, D. E., (1985). Distributed memory and the representation of general and specific information. *Journal of Experimental Psychology: General, 114*(2), 159–188.

McClelland, J. L., & Rumelhart, D. E. (1988). *Explorations in parallel distributed processing: A handbook of models, programs, and exercises.* Cambridge, MA: MIT Press.

McClelland, J. L., Rumelhart, D. E., & the PDP Research Group (1986). *Parallel distributed processing: Explorations in the microstructure of cognition: Vol. 2. Psychological and biological models.* Cambridge, MA: MIT Books.

McCormick, D. A., & Thompson, R. F. (1984). Cerebellum: Essential involvement in the classically conditioned eyelid response. *Science, 223,* 296–299.

McGarry-Roberts, P. A., Stelmack, R. M., & Campbell, K. B. (1992). Intelligence, reaction time, and event-related potentials. *Intelligence, 16*(3,4), 289–313.

McGurk, H., & MacDonald, J. (1976). Hearing lips and seeing voices. *Nature, 264,* 746–748.

McKenna, J., Treadway, M., & McCloskey, M. E. (1992). Expert psychological testimony on eyewitness reliability: Selling psychology before its time. In P. Suedfeld & P. E. Tetlock (Eds.), *Psychology and social policy* (pp. 283–293). New York: Hemisphere.

McKoon, G., & Ratcliff, R. (1980). Priming in item recognition: The organization of propositions in memory for text. *Journal of Verbal Learning and Verbal Behavior, 19,* 369–386.

McKoon, G., & Ratcliff, R. (1992a). Inference during reading. *Psychological Review, 99,* 440–466.

McKoon, G., & Ratcliff, R. (1992b). Spreading activation versus compound cue accounts of priming: Mediated priming revisited. *Journal of Experimental Psychology: Learning, Memory, & Cognition, 18*(6), 1155–1172.

McLeod, P., Driver, J., & Crisp, J. (1988). Visual search for a conjunction of movement and form is parallel. *Nature, 332*(6160), 154–155.

McLeod, P., Driver, J., Dienes, Z., & Crisp, J. (1991). Filtering by movement in visual search. *Journal of Experimental Psychology: Human Perception & Performance, 17*(1), 55–64.

McLeod, P., Heywood, C., Driver, J., & Zihl, J. (1989). Selective deficit of visual search in moving displays after extrastriate damage. *Nature, 339*(6224), 466–467.

McNamara, T. P. (1992). Theories of priming: I. Associative distance and lag. *Journal of Experimental Psychology: Learning, Memory, & Cognition, 18*(6), 1173–1190.

McNamara, T. P., Hardy, J. K., & Hirtle, S. C. (1989). Subjective hierarchies in spatial memory. *Memory & Cognition, 17*(4), 444–453.

McNamara, T. P., Ratcliff, R., & McKoon, G. (1984). The mental representation of knowledge acquired from maps. *Journal of Experimental Psychology: Learning, Memory, & Cognition, 10*(4), 723–732.

McNeil, J. E., & Warrington, E. K. (1993). Prosopagnosia: A face specific disorder. *Quarterly Journal of Experimental Psychology: Human Experimental Psychology, 46,* 1–10.

Meacham, J. A. (1983). Wisdom and the context of knowledge: Knowing that one doesn't know. In D. Kuhn & J. A. Meacham (Eds.), *On the development of developmental psychology* (pp. 111–134). Basel, Switzerland: Karger.

Meacham, J. A. (1990). The loss of wisdom. In R. J. Sternberg (Ed.), *Wisdom: Its nature, origins, and development* (pp. 181–211). New York: Cambridge University Press.

Mehler, J., Dupoux, E., Nazzi, T., & Dahaene-Lambertz, G. (1996). Coping with linguistic diversity: The infant's viewpoint. In J. L. Morgan & K. Demuth (Eds.), *Signal to Syntax: Bootstrapping from speech to grammar in early acquisition* (pp. 101–116). Mahwah, NJ: Erlbaum.

Meier, R. P. (1991). Language acquisition by deaf children. *American Scientist, 79,* 60–76.

Merriam-Webster's collegiate dictionary (10th ed.). (1993). Springfield, MA: Merriam-Webster.

Mervis, C. B., Catlin, J., & Rosch, E. (1976). Relationships among goodness-of-example, category norms, and word frequency. *Bulletin of the Psychonomic Society, 7,* 268–284.

Metcalfe, J. (1986). Feeling of knowing in memory and problem solving. *Journal of Experimental Psychology: Learning, Memory, & Cognition, 12*(2), 288–294.

Metcalfe, J., & Wiebe, D. (1987). Intuition in insight and noninsight problem solving. *Memory & Cognition, 15*(3), 238–246.

Meyer, D. E., & Schvaneveldt, R. W. (1971). Facilitation in recognizing pairs of words: Evidence of a dependence between retrieval operations. *Journal of Experimental Psychology, 90*(2), 227–234.

Meyer, D. E., & Schvaneveldt, R. W. (1976). Meaning, memory structure, and mental processes. *Science, 192*(4234), 27–33.

Mill, J. S. (1887). *A system of logic.* New York: Harper & Brothers.

Miller, G. A. (1956). The magical number seven, plus or minus two: Some limits on our capacity for processing information. *Psychological Review, 63,* 81–97.

Miller, G. A. (1978). Semantic relations among words. In M. Halle, J. Bresnan, & G. A. Miller (Eds.), *Linguistic theory and psychological reality* (pp. 60–118). Cambridge, MA: MIT Press.

Miller, G. A. (1979). Images and models, similes and metaphors. In A. Ortony (Ed.), *Metaphor and thought* (pp. 202–250). New York: Cambridge University Press.

Miller, G. A., Galanter, E. H., & Pribram, K. H. (1960). *Plans and the structure of behavior.* New York: Holt, Rinehart and Winston.

Miller, G. A., & Gildea, P. M. (1987). How children learn words. *Scientific American, 257*(3), 94–99.

Miller, G. A., & Johnson-Laird, P. N. (1976). *Language and perception.* Cambridge, MA: Harvard University Press.

Miller, R. A., Pople, H., & Myers, J. (1982). INTERNIST, an experimental computer-based diagnostic consultant for general internal medicine. *New England Journal of Medicine, 307*(8), 494.

Mills, C. J. (1983). Sex-typing and self-schemata effects on memory and response latency. *Journal of Personality & Social Psychology, 45*(1), 163–172.

Milner, B. (1968). Disorders of memory loss after brain lesions in man: Preface—Material-specific and generalized memory loss. *Neuropsychologia, 6*(3), 175–179.

Milner, B. (1972). Disorders of learning and memory after temporal lobe lesions in man. *Clinical Neurosurgery, 19,* 421–446.

Milner, B., Corkin, S., & Teuber, H. L. (1968). Further analysis of the hippocampal amnesic syndrome: 14-year follow-up study of H. M. *Neuropsychologia, 6,* 215–234.

Minsky, M. (Ed.). (1968). *Semantic information processing.* Cambridge, MA: MIT Press.

Minsky, M. (1975). A framework for representing knowledge. In P. H. Winston (Ed.), *The psychology of computer vision.* New York: McGraw-Hill.

Mirmiran, N., von Someren, E. J. W., & Swaab, D. F. (1996). Is brain plasticity preserved during aging and in Altzheimer's disease? *Behavioral Brain Research, 78,* 43–48.

Mishkin, M., & Appenzeller, T. (1987). The anatomy of memory. *Scientific American, 256*(6), 80–89.

Mishkin, M., & Petri, H. L. (1984). Memories and habits: Some implications for the analysis of learning and retention. In L. R. Squire & N. Butters (Eds.), *Neurophysiology of memory* (pp. 287–296). New York: Guilford.

Mishkin, M., Ungerleider, L. G., & Macko, K. A. (1983). Object vision and spatial vision: Two cortical pathways. *Trends in Neurosciences, 6*(10), 414–417.

Moar, I., & Bower, G. H. (1983). Inconsistency in spatial knowledge. *Memory & Cognition, 11*(2), 107–113.

Moray, N. (1959). Attention in dichotic listening: Affective cues and the influence of instructions. *Quarterly Journal of Experimental Psychology, 11,* 56–60.

Morris, C. D., Bransford, J. D., & Franks, J. (1977). Levels of processing versus transfer appropriate processing. *Journal of Verbal Learning & Verbal Behavior, 16*(5), 519–533.

Morton, J. (1969). Interaction of information in word recognition. *Psychological Review, 76,* 165–178.

Morton, T. U. (1978). Intimacy and reciprocity of exchange: A comparison of spouses and strangers. *Journal of Personality and Social Psychology, 36,* 72–81.

Moscovitch, M., & Craik, F. I. M. (1976). Depth of processing, retrieval cues, and uniqueness of encoding as factors in recall. *Journal of Verbal Learning and Verbal Behavior, 15,* 447–458.

Moshman, E. (1998). Cognitive development beyond childhood. In W. Damon (Ed.-in-Chief), D. Kuhn, & R. S. Siegler (Vol. Eds.), *Handbook of child psychology: Vol. 2. Cognitive Development* (pp. 947–978). New York: Wiley.

Murdock, B. B., Jr. (1961). Short-term retention of single paired-associates. *Psychological Reports, 8,* 280.

Näätänen, R. (1988a). Implications of ERP data for psychological theories of attention. *Biological Psychology, 26*(1–3), 117–163.

Näätänen, R. (1988b). Regional cerebral blood-flow: Supplement to event-related potential studies of selective attention. In G. C. Galbraith, M. L. Kietzman, & E. Donchin (Eds.), *Neurophysiology and psychophysiology: Experimental and clinical applications* (pp. 144–156). Hillsdale, NJ: Erlbaum.

Näätänen, R. (1990). The role of attention in auditory information processing as revealed by event-related potentials and other brain measures of cognitive function. *Behavioral & Brain Sciences, 13*(2), 201–288.

Näätänen, R. (1992). *Attention and brain function.* Hillsdale, NJ: Erlbaum.

Nairne, J. S., & Crowder, R. G. (1982). On the locus of the stimulus suffix effect. *Memory & Cognition, 10,* 350–357.

Nakayama, K. (1990). Visual inference in the perception of occluded surfaces (Summary). *Proceedings of the 125th Annual Conference of the Cognitive Science Society* (p. 1019). Hillsdale, NJ: Erlbaum.

Naus, M. J. (1974). Memory search of categorized lists: A consideration of alternative self-terminating search strategies. *Journal of Experimental Psychology, 102,* 992–1000.

Naus, M. J., Glucksberg, S., & Ornstein, P. A. (1972). Taxonomic word categories and memory search. *Cognitive Psychology, 3,* 643–654.

Naveh-Benjamin, M., & Ayres, T. J. (1986). Digit span, reading rate, and linguistic relativity. *Quarterly Journal of Experimental Psychology: Human Experimental Psychology, 38*(4), 739–751.

Navon, D. (1977). Forest before trees: The precedence of global features in visual perception. *Cognitive Psychology, 9,* 353–383.

Navon, D., & Gopher, D. (1979). On the economy of the human-processing system. *Psychological Review, 86,* 214–255.

Neimark, E. D. (1975). Intellectual development during adolescence. In F. D. Horowitz (Ed.), *Review of child development research* (Vol. 4). Chicago: University of Chicago Press.

Neisser, U. (1967). *Cognitive psychology.* New York: Appleton-Century-Crofts.

Nessier, U. (1978). Memory: What are the important questions? In M. M. Gruneberg, P. Morris, & R. Sykes (Eds.), *Practical aspects of memory* (pp. 3–24). London: Academic Press.

Neisser, U. (1982). Snapshots or benchmarks? In U. Neisser (Ed.), *Memory observed: Remembering in natural contexts.* San Francisco: Freeman.

Neisser, U., & Becklen, R. (1975). Selective looking: Attending to visually specified events. *Cognitive Psychology, 7*(4), 480–494.

Nessier, U., Boodoo, G., Bouchard, T. J., Boykin, W. A., Brody, N., Ceci, S. J., Halpern, D. F., Loehlin, J. C., Perloff, R., Sternberg, R. J., & Urbina, S. (1996). Intelligence: Knowns and Unknowns. *American Psychologist, 51,* 77–101.

Neisser, U., & Harsch, N. (1993). Phantom flashbulbs: False recollections of hearing the news about Challenger. In E. Winograd & U. Neisser (Eds.), *Affect and accuracy in recall: Studies of "flashbulb" memories* (pp. 9–31). New York: Cambridge University Press.

Nelson, K. (1973). Structure and strategy in learning to talk. *Monograph of the Society for Research in Child Development, 38*(Serial No. 149).

Nelson, T. O., & Narens, L. (1994). Why investigate metacognition? In J. Metcalfe & A. P. Shimamura (Eds.), *Metacognition—Knowing about knowing.* Cambridge, MA: MIT Press.

Nelson, T. O., & Rothbart, R. (1972). Acoustic savings for items forgotten from long-term memory. *Journal of Experimental Psychology, 93,* 357–360.

Neto, F., Williams, J. E., & Widner, S. C. (1991). Portuguese children's knowledge of sex stereotypes: Effects of age, gender, and socioeconomic status. *Journal of Cross-Cultural Psychology, 22*(3), 376–388.

Nettelbeck, T. (1987). Inspection time and intelligence. In P. A. Vernon (Ed.), *Speed of information-processing and intelligence* (pp. 295–346). Norwood, NJ: Ablex.

Nettelbeck, T., & Lally, M. (1976). Inspection time and measured intelligence. *British Journal of Psychology, 67,* 17–22.

Nettelbeck, T., & Rabbitt, P. M. A. (1992). Aging, cognitive performance, and mental speed. *Intelligence, 16*(2), 189–205.

Nettlebeck, T., Rabbitt, P. M. A., Wilson, C., & Batt, R. (1996). Uncoupling learning from initial recall: The relationship between speed and memory deficits in old age. *British Journal of Psychology, 87,* 593–607.

Nettlebeck, T., & Young, R. (1996). Intelligence and savant syndrome: Is the whole greater than the sum of the fragments? *Intelligence, 22,* 49–67.

Neumann, P. G. (1977). Visual prototype formation with discontinuous representation of dimensions of variability. *Memory & Cognition, 5*(2), 187–197.

Newell, A. (1973). Production systems: Models of control structures. In W. G. Chase (Ed.), *Visual information processing* (pp. 463–526). New York: Academic Press.

Newell, A., Shaw, J. C., & Simon, H. A. (1957a). Empirical explorations of the logic theory machine: A case study in heuristics. *Proceedings of the Western Joint Computer Conference,* 230–240.

Newell, A., Shaw, J. C., & Simon, H. A. (1957b). Problem solving in humans and computers. *Carnegie Technical, 21*(4), 34–38.

Newell, A., & Simon, H. A. (1972). *Human problem solving.* Englewood Cliffs, NJ: Prentice-Hall.

Newport, E. L. (1990). Maturational constraints on language learning. *Cognitive Science, 14,* 11–28.

Nisbett, R., & Ross, L. (1980). *Human inference: Strategies and shortcomings of social judgment.* Englewood Cliffs, NJ: Prentice-Hall.

Norman, D. A. (1968). Toward a theory of memory and attention. *Psychological Review, 75,* 522–536.

Norman, D. A. (1976). *Memory and attention: An introduction to human information processing* (2nd ed.). New York: Wiley.

Norman, D. A. (1988). *The design of everyday things.* New York: Doubleday.

Norman, D. A., & Rumelhart, D. E. (1975). *Explorations in cognition.* San Francisco: Freeman.

Nosofsky, R. M., & Palmeri, T. J. (1997). An exemplar-based random walk model of speeded classification. *Psychological Review, 104,* 266–300.

Nosofsky, R. M., Palmeri, T. J., & McKinley, S. C. (1994). Rule-plus-exception model of classification learning. *Psychological Review, 101,* 53–79.

Ogbu, J. U. (1986). The consequences of the American caste system. In U. Neisser (Ed.), *The school achievement of minority children.* Hillsdale, NJ: Erlbaum.

O. Henry [William Sydney Porter]. The ransom of red chief. In *The complete works of O. Henry* (pp. 1144–1152). Garden City, NY: Doubleday. (1899–1953).

Ojemann, G. A. (1975). The thalamus and language. *Brain and Language, 2,* 1–120.

Ojemann, G. A. (1982). Models of the brain organization for higher integrative functions derived with electrical stimulation techniques. *Human Neurobiology, 1,* 243–250.

Ojemann, G. A., & Mateer, C. (1979). Human language cortex: Localization of memory, syntax, and sequential motor–phoneme identification systems. *Science, 205,* 1401–1403.

Ojemann, G. A., & Whitaker, H. A. (1978). The bilingual brain. *Archives of Neurology, 35,* 409–412.

Olson, R. K. (in press). Genes, environment, and reading disabilities. In R. J. Sternberg & L. Spear-Swerling (Eds.), *Perspectives on learning disabilities: Biological, cognitive, contextual.* Boulder, CO: Westview Press.

Ortony, A. (1979). The role of similarity in similes and metaphors. In A. Ortony (Ed.), *Metaphor and thought* (pp. 186–201). New York: Cambridge University Press.

Osherson, D. N. (1990). Judgment. In D. N. Osherson & E. E. Smith (Eds.), *An invitation to cognitive science: Vol. 3. Thinking* (pp. 55–87). Cambridge, MA: MIT Press.

Osherson, D. N., Smith, E. E., Wilkie, O., Lopez, A., & Shafir, E. (1990). Category-based induction. *Psychological Review, 97*(2), 185–200.

Otero, J., & Kintsch, W. (1992). Failures to detect contradictions in a text: What readers believe versus what they read. *Psychological Science, 3*(4), 229–235.

Oxford English Dictionary (2nd ed.). (1989). Oxford, England: Clarendon Press.

Oyama, S. (1976). A sensitive period for the acquisition of a nonnative phonological system. *Journal of Psycholinguistic Research, 5*(3), 261–283.

Paap, K. R., Newsome, S. L., McDonald, J. E., & Schvaneveldt, R. W. (1982). An activation-verification model for letter and word recognition: The word-superiority effect. *Psychological Review, 89*(5), 573–594.

Paavilainen, P., Tiitinen, H., Alho, K., & Näätänen R. (1993). Mismatch negativity to slight pitch changes outside strong attentional focus. *Biological Psychology, 37*(1), 23–41.

Paivio, A. (1969). Mental imagery in associative learning and memory. *Psychological Review, 76*(3), 241–263.

Paivio, A. (1971). *Imagery and verbal processes.* New York: Holt, Rinehart and Winston.

Paivio, A. (1978a). Comparisons of mental clocks. *Journal of Experimental Psychology: Human Perception & Performance, 4*(1), 61–71.

Paivio, A. (1978b). Imagery, language, and semantic memory. *International Journal of Psycholinguistics, 5*(2,10), 31–47.

Palmer, J. (1990). Attentional limits on the perception and memory of visual information. *Journal of Experimental Psychology: Human Perception & Performance, 16*(2), 332–350.

Palmer, S. E. (1975). The effects of contextual scenes on the identification of objects. *Memory & Cognition, 3,* 519–526.

Palmer, S. E. (1992). Modern theories of Gestalt perception. In G. W. Humphreys (Ed.), *Understanding vision: An interdisciplinary perspective—Readings in mind and language* (pp. 39–70). Oxford, England: Blackwell.

Paradis, M. (1977). Bilingualism and aphasia. In H. A. Whitaker & H. Whitaker (Eds.), *Studies in neurolinguistics* (Vol. 3). New York: Academic Press.

Paradis, M. (1981). Neurolinguistic organization of a bilingual's two languages. In J. E. Copeland & P. W. Davis (Eds.), *The seventh LACUS forum.* Columbia, SC: Hornbeam Press.

Parkin, A. J. (1991). Recent advances in the neuropsychology of memory. In J. Weinman & J. Hunter (Eds.), *Memory: Neurochemical and abnormal perspectives* (pp. 141–162). London: Harwood Academic Publishers.

Parsons, O. A., & Nixon, S. J. (1993). Neurobehavioral sequelae of alcoholism. *Neurologic Clinics, 11*(1), 205–218.

Pascual-Leone, J. (1970). A mathematical model for the transition rule in Piaget's development stages. *Acta Psychologica, 32,* 301–345.

Pascual-Leone, J. (1984). Attentional, dialectic, and mental effort. In M. L. Commons, F. A. Richards, & C. Armon (Eds.), *Beyond formal operations.* New York: Plenum.

Pascual-Leone, J. (1990). An essay on wisdom: Toward organismic processes that make it possible. In R. J. Sternberg (Ed.), *Wisdom: Its nature, origins, and development* (pp. 244–278). New York: Cambridge University Press.

Pashler, H. (1994). Dual-task interference in simple tasks: Data and theory. *Psychological Bulletin, 116*(2), 220–244.

Pavlov, I. P. (1955). *Selected works.* Moscow: Foreign Languages Publishing House.

Payne, J. (1976). Task complexity and contingent processing in decision making: An information search and protocol analysis. *Organizational Behavior and Human Performance, 16,* 366–387.

Penfield, W. (1955). The permanent record of the stream of consciousness. *Acta Psychologica, 11,* 47–69.

Penfield, W. (1969). Consciousness, memory, and man's conditioned reflexes. In K. H. Pribram (Ed.), *On the biology of learning* (pp. 129–168). New York: Harcourt, Brace & World.

Penfield, W., & Roberts, L. (1959). *Speech and brain mechanisms.* Princeton, NJ: Princeton University Press.

Penrose, R. (1989). *The emperor's new mind: Concerning computers, minds, and the laws of physics.* New York: Oxford University Press.

Perfetti, C. A. (1985). *Reading ability.* New York: Oxford University Press.

Perfetti, C. A., & Roth, S. F. (1981). Some of the interactive processes in reading and their role in reading skill. In A. M. Lesgold & C. A. Perfetti (Eds.), *Interactive processes in reading* (pp. 269–297). Hillsdale, NJ: Erlbaum.

Perkins, D. N. (1981). *The mind's best work.* Cambridge, MA: Harvard University Press.

Perkins, D. N. (1995). *Outsmarting I.Q.* New York: Free Press.

Perkins, D. N., & Grotzer, T. A. (1997). Teaching intelligence. *American Psychologist, 52,* 1125–1133.

Perlmutter, D. (Ed.). (1983). *Studies in relational grammar* (Vol. 1). Chicago: University of Chicago Press.

Perlmutter, M. (1983). Learning and memory through adulthood. In M. W. Riley, B. B. Hess, & K. Bond (Eds.), *Aging in society: Selected reviews of recent research.* Hillsdale, NJ: Erlbaum.

Petersen, S. E., Fox, P. T., Posner, M. I., Mintun, M., & Raichle, M. E. (1988). Positron emission tomographic studies of the cortical anatomy of single-word processing. *Nature, 331*(6157), 585–589.

Petersen, S. E., Fox, P. T., Posner, M. I., Mintun, M., et al. (1989). Positron emission tomographic studies of the processing of single words. *Journal of Cognitive Neuroscience, 1*(2), 153–170.

Peterson, L. R., & Peterson, M. J. (1959). Short-term retention of individual verbal items. *Journal of Experimental Psychology, 58,* 193–198.

Peterson, M. A., Kihlstrom, J. F., Rose, P. M., & Glisky, M. L. (1992). Mental images can be ambiguous: Reconstruals and reference-frame reversals. *Memory & Cognition, 20*(2), 107–123.

Petitto, L., & Marentette, P. F. (1991). Babbling in the manual mode: Evidence for the ontogeny of language. *Science, 251*(5000), 1493–1499.

Piaget, J. (1928). *Judgment and reasoning in the child.* London: Routledge & Kegan Paul.

Piaget, J. (1946). *The development of children's concept of time.* Paris: Presses Universitaires de France.

Piaget, J. (1952). *The origins of intelligence in children.* New York: International Universities Press.

Piaget, J. (1954). *The construction of reality in the child.* New York: Basic Books.

Piaget, J. (1955). *The language and thought of the child.* New York: Meridian Books.

Piaget, J. (1969). *The child's conception of physical causality.* Totowa, NJ: Littlefield, Adams.

Piaget, J. (1972). *The psychology of intelligence.* Totowa, NJ: Littlefield, Adams.

Pianta, R. C., & Egeland, B. (1994). Predictors of instability in children's mental test performance at 24, 48, and 96 months. *Intelligence, 18*(2), 145–163.

Pinker, S. (1980). Mental imagery and the third dimension. *Journal of Experimental Psychology: General, 109*(3), 354–371.

Pinker, S. (1985). Visual cognition: An introduction. In S. Pinker (Ed.), *Visual cognition* (pp. 1–63). Cambridge, MA: MIT Press.

Pinker, S. (1994). *The language instinct.* New York: William Morrow.

Pisoni, D. B., Nusbaum, H. C., Luce, P. A., & Slowiaczek, L. M. (1985). Speech perception, word recognition and the structure of the lexicon. *Speech Communication, 4,* 75–95.

Poincaré, H. (1913). *The foundations of science.* New York: Science Press.

Pollatsek, A., & Rayner, K. (1989). Reading. In M. I. Posner (Ed.), *Foundations of cognitive science* (pp. 401–436). Cambridge, MA: MIT Press.

Pomerantz, J. R. (1981). Perceptual organization in information processing. In M. Kubovy & J. R. Pomerantz (Eds.), *Perceptual organization* (pp. 141–180). Hillsdale, NJ: Erlbaum.

Poon, L. W. (1987). *Myths and truisms: Beyond extant analyses of speed of behavior and age.* Address to the Eastern Psychological Association Convention.

Posner, M.I. (1969). Abstraction and the process of recognition. In G. H. Bower & J. T. Spence (Eds.), *The psychology of learning and motivation: Vol. 3. Advances in learning and motivation.* New York: Academic Press.

Posner, M. I. (1992). Attention as a cognitive and neural system. *Current Directions in Psychological Science, 1*(1), 11–14.

Posner, M. I. (1995). Attention in cognitive neuroscience: An overview. In M. Gazzaniga (Ed.), *The cognitive neurosciences* (pp. 615–624). Cambridge, MA: MIT Press.

Posner, M. I., Boies, S., Eichelman, W., & Taylor, R. (1969). Retention of visual and name codes of single letters. *Journal of Experimental Psychology, 81,* 10–15.

Posner, M. I., & Dehaene, S. (1994). Attentional networks. *Trends in Neurosciences, 17*(2), 75–79.

Posner, M. I., Goldsmith, R., & Welton, K. E., Jr. (1967). Perceived distance and the classification of distorted patterns. *Journal of Experimental Psychology, 73*(1), 28–38.

Posner, M. I., & Keele, S. W. (1967). Decay of visual information from a single letter. *Science, 158*(3797), 137–139.

Posner, M., & Keele, S. W. (1968). On the genesis of abstract ideas. *Journal of Experimental Psychology, 77*(3, Pt. 1), 353–363.

Posner, M. I., & Mitchell, R. F. (1967). Chronometric analysis of classification. *Psychological Review, 74,* 392–409.

Posner, M. I., & Petersen, S. E. (1990). The attention system of the human brain. *Annual Review of Neuroscience, 13,* 25–42.

Posner, M. I., Petersen, S. E., Fox, P. T., & Raichle, M. E. (1988). Localization of cognitive operations in the human brain. *Science, 240*(4859), 1627–1631.

Posner, M. I., & Raichle, M. E. (1994). *Images of mind.* New York: Freeman.

Posner, M. I., Sandson, J., Dhawan, M., & Shulman, G. L. (1989). Is word recognition automatic? A cognitive-anatomical approach. *Journal of Cognitive Neuroscience, 1,* 50–60.

Posner, M. I., & Snyder, C. R. R. (1975). Attention and cognitive control. In R. Solso (Ed.), *Information processing and cognition: The Loyola Symposium* (pp. 55–85). Hillsdale, NJ: Erlbaum.

Posner, M. I., Snyder, C. R. R., & Davidson, B. J. (1980). Attention and the detection of signals. *Journal of Experimental Psychology: General, 109*(2), 160–174.

Pritchard, R. M. (1961). Stabilized images on the retina. *Scientific American, 204,* 72–78.

Pullum, G. K. (1991). *The Great Eskimo vocabulary hoax and other irreverent essays on the study of language.* Chicago: University of Chicago Press.

Pylyshyn, Z. W. (1973). What the mind's eye tells the mind's brain: A critique of mental imagery. *Psychological Bulletin, 80,* 1–24.

Pylyshyn, Z. (1978). Imagery and artificial intelligence. In C. W. Savage (Ed.), *Minnesota studies in the philosophy of science: Vol. 9. Perception and cognition issues in the foundations of psychology* (pp. 19–56). Minneapolis: University of Minnesota Press.

Pylyshyn, Z. (1981). The imagery debate: Analogue media versus tacit knowledge. *Psychological Review, 88*(1), 16–45.

Pylyshyn, Z. (1984). *Computation and cognition.* Cambridge, MA: MIT Press.

Raeburn, V. P. (1974). Priorities in item recognition. *Memory & Cognition, 2,* 663–669.

Raphael, B. (1968). SIR: A computer program for semantic information retrieval. In M. Minsky (Ed.), *Semantic information processing* (pp. 33–145). Cambridge, MA: MIT Press.

Ratcliff, R. (1990). Connectionist models of recognition memory: Constraints imposed by learning and forgetting functions. *Psychological Review, 97*(2), 285–308.

Ratcliff, R., & McKoon, G. (1986). More on the distinction between episodic and semantic memories. *Journal of Experimental Psychology: Learning, Memory, & Cognition, 12*(2), 312–313.

Ratcliff, R., & McKoon, G. (1988). A retrieval theory of priming in memory. *Psychological Review, 95*(3), 385–408.

Ratcliff, R., & McKoon, G. (1994). Retrieving information from memory: Spreading-activation theories versus compound-cue theories. *Psychological Review, 101*(1), 177–184.

Ratcliff, R., & McKoon, G. (1997). A counter model for implicit priming in perceptual word identification. *Psychological Review, 104,* 319–343.

Rayner, K. (1975). The perceptual span and peripheral cues in reading. *Cognitive Psychology, 7,* 65–81.

Rayner, K., Sereno, S. C., Lesch, M. F., & Pollatsek, A. (1995). Phonological codes are automatically activated during reading: Evidence from an eye movement priming paradigm. *Psychological Science, 6,* 26–31.

Reason, J. (1990). *Human error.* New York: Cambridge University Press.

Reber, P. J., Knowlton, B. J, & Squire, L. R. (1996). Dissociable properties of memory systems: Differences in the flexibility of declarative and nondeclarative knowledge. *Behavioral Neurosciences, 110,* 861–871.

Reed, S. (1972). Pattern recognition and categorization. *Cognitive Psychology, 3*(3), 382–407.

Reed, S. (1974). Structural descriptions and the limitations of visual images. *Memory & Cognition, 2*(2), 329–336.

Reed, S. K. (1987). A structure-mapping model for word problems. *Journal of Experimental Psychology: Learning, Memory, & Cognition, 13*(1), 125–139.

Reed, S. K., Dempster, A., & Ettinger, M. (1985). Usefulness of analogous solutions for solving algebra word problems. *Journal of Experimental Psychology: Learning, Memory, & Cognition, 11*(1), 106–125.

Reed, T. E. (1993). Effect of enriched (complex) environment on nerve conduction velocity: New data and review of implications for the speed of information processing. *Intelligence, 17*(4), 533–540.

Reed, T. E,. & Jensen, A. R. (1991). Arm nerve conduction velocity (NCV), brain NCV, reaction time, and intelligence. *Intelligence, 15,* 33–47.

Reed, T. E., & Jensen, A. R. (1993).Choice reaction time and visual pathway nerve conduction velocity both correlate with intelligence, but appear not to correlate with each other: Implications for information processing. *Intelligence, 17,* 191–203.

Reeder, G. D., McCormick, C. B., & Esselman, E. D. (1987). Self-referent processing and recall of prose. *Journal of Educational Psychology, 79,* 243–248.

Reicher, G. M. (1969). Perceptual recognition as a function of meaningfulness of stimulus material. *Journal of Experimental Psychology, 81,* 275–280.

Reisberg, D. (Ed.). (1992). *Auditory imagery.* Hillsdale, NJ: Erlbaum.

Reisberg, D., Culver, L. C., Heuer, F., & Fischman, D. (1986). Visual memory: When imagery vividness makes a difference. *Journal of Mental Imagery, 10*(4), 51–74.

Reisberg, D., Smith, J. D., Baxter, D. A., & Sonenshine, M. (1989). "Enacted" auditory images are ambiguous: "Pure" auditory images are not. *Quarterly Journal of Experimental Psychology: Human Experimental Psychology, 41*(3–A), 619–641.

Reisberg, D., Wilson, M., & Smith, J. D. (1991). Auditory imagery and inner speech. In R. H. Logie & M. Denis (Eds.), *Advances in psychology: Vol. 80. Mental images in human cognition* (pp. 59–81). Amsterdam: North-Holland.

Reitman, J. S. (1971). Mechanisms of forgetting in short-term memory. *Cognitive Psychology, 2,* 185–195.

Reitman, J. S. (1974). Without surreptitious rehearsal, information in short-term memory decays. *Journal of Verbal Learning and Verbal Behavior, 13,* 365–377.

Reitman, J. S. (1976). Skilled perception in Go: Deducing memory structures from inter-response times. *Cognitive Psychology, 8,* 336–356.

Remez, R. E. (1994). A Guide to research on the perception of speech. In M. A. Gernsbacher (Ed.), *Handbook of psycholinguistics* (pp. 145–172). San Diego: Academic Press.

Rescorla, R. A. (1967). Pavlovian conditioning and its proper control procedures. *Psychological Review, 74,* 71–80.

Rescorla, R. A., & Wagner, A. R. (1972). A theory of Pavlovian conditioning: Variations in the effectiveness of reinforcement and non-reinforcement. In A. H. Black & W. F. Prokasy (Eds.), *Classical conditioning: Vol. 2. Current research and theory.* New York: Appleton-Century-Crofts.

Resnick, L. B. (1980). *The role of invention in the development of mathematical competence.* Unpublished manuscript.

Rice, M. L. (1989). Children's language acquisition. *American Psychologist, 44,* 149–156.

Richardson-Klavehn, A., & Bjork, R. A. (1988). Measures of memory. *Annual Review of Psychology, 39,* 475–543.

Riegel, K. F. (1973). Dialectical operations: The final period of cognitive development. *Human Development, 16,* 346–370.

Riggs, L. A., Ratliff, F., Cornsweet, J. C., & Cornsweet, T. N. (1953). The disappearance of steadily fixated visual test objects. *Journal of the Optical Society of America, 43,* 495–501.

Rips, L. J. (1983). Cognitive processes in propositional reasoning. *Psychological Review, 90*(1), 38–71.

Rips, L. J. (1988). Deduction. In R. J. Sternberg & E. E. Smith (Eds.), *The psychology of human thought* (pp. 116–152). New York: Cambridge University Press.

Rips, L. J. (1994). Deductive reasoning. In R. J. Sternberg (Ed.), *Handbook of perception and cognition: Thinking and problem solving* (pp. 149–178). New York: Academic Press.

Roberts, A. C., Robbins, T. W., & Weiskrantz, L. (1996). Executive and cognitive functions of the pre-frontal cortex. *Philosophical Transactions of the Royal Society (London), B, 351,* (1346).

Rock, I. (1983). *The logic of perception.* Cambridge, MA: MIT Press.

Roediger, H. L. (1980a). The effectiveness of four mnemonics in ordering recall. *Journal of Experimental Psychology: Human Learning & Memory, 6*(5), 558–567.

Roediger, H. L., III. (1980b). Memory metaphors in cognitive psychology. *Memory & Cognition, 8*(3), 231–246.

Roediger, H. L., III., & McDermott, K. B. (1995). Creating false memories: Remembering words not presented in lists. *Journal of Experimental Psychology: Learning, Memory, and Cognition, 21,* 803–814.

Rogers, T. B., Kuiper, N. A., & Kirker, W. S. (1977). Self-reference and the encoding of personal information. *Journal of Personality & Social Psychology, 35*(9), 677–688.

Rogoff, B. (1986). The development of strategic use of context in spatial memory. In M. Perlmutter (Ed.), *Perspectives on intellectual development.* Hillsdale, NJ: Erlbaum.

Roland, P. E., & Friberg, L. (1985). Localization of cortical areas activated by thinking. *Journal of Neurophysiology, 53*(5), 1219–1243.

Rosch, E. (1975). Cognitive representations of semantic categories. *Journal of Experimental Psychology: General, 104,* 192–233.

Rosch, E. (1978). Principles of categorization. In E. Rosch & B. B. Lloyd (Eds.), *Cognition and categorization.* Hillsdale, NJ: Erlbaum.

Rosch, E. H., & Mervis, C. B. (1975). Family resemblances: Studies in the internal structure of categories. *Cognitive Psychology, 7,* 573–605.

Rosch, E. H., Mervis, C. B., Gray, W. D., Johnson, D. M., & Boyes-Braem, P. (1976). Basic objects in natural categories. *Cognitive Psychology, 8,* 382–439.

Rosenzweig, M. R. & Bennett, E. L. (1996). Psychobiology of plasticity: Effects of training and experience on brain and behavior. *Behavior and Brain Research, 78,* 57–65.

Rosenzweig, M. R., & Leiman, A. L. (1989). *Physiological psychology* (2nd ed.). New York: Random House.

Ross, B. H., & Spalding, T. L. (1994). Concepts and categories. In R. J. Sternberg (Ed.), *Handbook of perception and cognition: Vol. 12. Thinking and problem solving* (pp. 119–148). New York: Academic Press.

Ross, B. M., & Millsom, C. (1970). Repeated memory of oral prose in Ghana and New York. *International Journal of Psychology, 5*(3), 173–181.

Ross, M., & Sicoly, F. (1979). Egocentric biases in availability and attribution. *Journal of Personality and Social Psychology, 37,* 322–336.

Rovee-Collier, C., Borza, M. A., Adler, S. A., & Boller, K. (1993). Infants' eyewitness testimony: Effects of postevent information on a prior memory representation. *Memory & Cognition, 21*(2), 267–279.

Rovee-Collier, C., & DuFault, D. (1991). Multiple contexts and memory retrieval at three months. *Developmental Psychobiology, 24*(1), 39–49.

Rubin, Z., Hill, C. T., Peplau, L. A., & Dunkel-Schetter, C. (1980). Self-disclosure in dating couples: Sex roles and the ethic of openness. *Journal of Marriage and the Family, 42,* 305–317.

Rumain, B., Connell, J., & Braine, M. D. S. (1983). Conversational comprehension processes are responsible for reasoning fallacies in children as well as adults: If is not the biconditional. *Developmental Psychology, 19*(4), 471–481.

Rumelhart, D. E., & McClelland, J. L. (1981). Interactive processing through spreading activation. In A. M. Lesgold & C. A. Perfetti (Eds.), *Interactive processes in reading* (pp. 37–60). Hillsdale, NJ: Erlbaum.

Rumelhart, D. E., & McClelland, J. L. (1982). An interactive activation model of context effects in letter perception: Part 2. The contextual enhancement effect and some tests and extensions of the model. *Psychological Review, 89,* 60–94.

Rumelhart, D. E., McClelland, J. L., & the PDP Research Group. (1986). *Parallel distributed processing. Explorations in the microstructure of cognition: Vol. 1. Foundations.* Cambridge, MA: MIT Press.

Rumelhart, D. E., & Norman, D. (1988). Representation in memory. In R. C. Atkinson, R. J. Herrnstein, G. Lindzey, R. D. Luce (Eds.), *Stevens' handbook of experimental psychology: Vol. 2. Learning and cognition* (2nd ed., 511–587). New York: Wiley.

Rumelhart, D. E., & Ortony, A. (1977). The representation of knowledge in memory. In R. C. Anderson, R. J. Spiro, & W. E. Montague (Eds.), *Schooling and the acquisition of knowledge* (pp. 99–135). Hillsdale, NJ: Erlbaum.

Russell, J. A., & Ward, L. M. (1982). Environmental psychology. *Annual Review of Psychology, 33,* 651–688.

Russell, W. R., & Nathan, P. W. (1946). Traumatic amnesia. *Brain, 69,* 280–300.

Ryle, G. (1949). *The concept of mind.* London: Hutchinson.

Saarinen, J. (1987). Perception of positional relationships between line segments in eccentric vision. *Perception, 16*(5), 583–591.

Saarinen, T. F. (1987). *Centering of mental maps of the world* (discussion paper). University of Arizona, Tucson: Department of Geography and Regional Development.

Sacks, H., Schegloff, E. A., & Jefferson, G. (1974). A simplest systematics for the organization of turn-taking for conversation. *Language, 50,* 696–735.

Salthouse, T. A. (1991). Expertise as the circumvention of human processing limitations. In K. A. Ericsson & J. Smith (Eds.), *Toward a general theory of expertise: Prospects and limits* (pp. 286–300). New York: Cambridge University Press.

Salthouse, T. A. (1992). The information-processing perspective on cognitive aging. In R. J. Sternberg & C. A. Berg (Eds.), *Intellectual development* (pp. 261–277). New York: Cambridge University Press.

Salthouse, T. A. (1993). Influence of working memory on adult age differences in matrix reasoning. *British Journal of Psychology, 84*(2), 171–199.

Salthouse, T. A. (1994). The nature of the influence of speed on adult age differences in cognition. *Developmental Psychology, 30*(2), 240–259.

Salthouse, T. A. (1996). The processing-speed theory of adult age differences in cognition. *Psychological Review, 103,* 403–428.

Salthouse, T. A., Kausler, D. H., & Saults, J. S. (1990). Age, self-assessed health status, and cognition. *Journal of Gerontology, 45*(4), P156–P160.

Salthouse, T. A., & Somberg, B. L. (1982). Skilled performance: Effects of adult age and experience on elementary processes. *Journal of Experimental Psychology: General, 111*(2), 176–207.

Samuel, A. G. (1981). Phonemic restoration: Insights from a new methodology. *Journal of Experimental Psychology: General, 110,* 474–494.

Samuel, A. L. (1963). Some studies in machine learning using the game of checkers. In E. A. Feigenbaum & J. Feldman (Eds.), *Computers and thought* (pp. 71–105). New York: McGraw-Hill.

Samuels, J. J. (in press). Developing reading fluency in learning disabled students. In R. J. Sternberg & L. Spear-Swerling (Eds.), *Perspectives on learning disabilities: Biological, cognitive, contextual.* Boulder, CO: Westview Press.

Sapir, E. (1964). *Culture, language and personality.* Berkeley, CA: University of California Press. (Original work published 1941)

Sarason, S. B., & Doris, J. (1979). *Educational handicap, public policy, and social history.* New York: Free Press.

Scaggs, W. E., & McNaughton, B. L. (1996). Replay of neuronal firing sequences in rat hippocampus during sleep following spatial experience. *Science, 271,* 1870–1873.

Schacter, D. L. (1989a). Memory. In M. I. Posner (Ed.), *Foundations of cognitive science* (pp. 683–725). Cambridge, MA: MIT Press.

Schacter, D. L. (1989b). On the relation between memory and consciousness: Dissociable interactions and conscious experience. In H. L. Roediger & F. I. M. Craik (Eds.), *Varieties of memory and consciousness: Essays in honor of Endel Tulving.* Hillsdale, NJ: Erlbaum.

Schacter, D. L. (1995). Implicit memory. In M. S. Gazzaniga (Ed.), *The cognitive neurosciences* (pp. 815–824). Cambridge, MA: MIT Press.

Schacter, D. L., & Graf, P. (1986a). Effects of elaborative processing on implicit and explicit memory for new associations. *Journal of Experimental Psychology: Learning, Memory, & Cognition, 12*(3), 432–444.

Schacter, D. L., & Graf, P. (1986b). Preserved learning in amnesic patients: Perspectives from research on direct priming. *Journal of Clinical & Experimental Neuropsychology, 8*(6), 727–743.

Schaffer, H. R. (1977). *Mothering.* Cambridge, MA: Harvard University Press.

Schaie, K. W. (1974). Translations in gerontology—from lab to life. *American Psychologist, 29,* 802–807.

Schaie, K. W. (1989). Perceptual speed in adulthood: Cross-sectional and longitudinal studies. *Psychology and Aging, 4,* 443–453.

Schaie, K. W. (1996). *Intellectual development in adulthood: The Seattle longitudinal study.* New York: Cambridge University Press.

Schaie, K. W., & Willis, S. L. (1986). Can decline in intellectual functioning in the elderly be reversed? *Developmental Psychology, 22,* 223–232.

Schank, R. C. (1972). Conceptual dependency: A theory of natural language understanding. *Cognitive Psychology, 3,* 552–631.

Schank, R. C. (1984). *The cognitive computer: On language, learning and artificial intelligence.* Reading, MA: Addison-Wesley.

Schank, R. C., & Abelson, R. P. (1977). *Scripts, plans, goals, and understanding.* Hillsdale. NJ: Erlbaum.

Schliemann, A. D., & Magalhües, V. P. (1990). *Proportional reasoning: From shops, to kitchens, laboratories, and, hopefully, schools.* Proceedings of the Fourteenth International Conference for the Psychology of Mathematics Education, Oaxtepec, Mexico.

Schmidt, S. R., & Bohannon, J. N. (1988). In defense of the flashbulb-memory hypothesis: A comment on McCloskey, Wible, & Cohen (1988). *Journal of Experimental Psychology: General, 117*(3), 332–335.

Schneider, W., & Bjorklund, D. F. (1998). Memory. In W. Damon (Ed.-in-Chief), D. Kuhn, & R. S. Siegler (Vol. Eds.), *Handbook of child psychology: Vol. 2. Cognitive deveolpment* (pp. 467–521). New York: Wiley.

Schneider, W., & Shiffrin, R. (1977). Controlled and automatic human information processing. *Psychological Review, 84,* 1–66.

Schoenfeld, A. H. (1981). *Episodes and executive decisions in mathematical problem solving.* Paper presented at the annual meeting of the American Educational Research Association, Los Angeles, CA.

Schonfield, D., & Robertson, D. A. (1966). Memory storage and aging. *Canadian Journal of Psychology, 20,* 228–236.

Schooler, J. W. (1994). Seeking the core: The issues and evidence surrounding recovered accounts of sexual trauma. *Consciousness and Cognition, 3,* 452–469.

Schooler, J. W., & Engstler-Schooler, T. Y. (1990). Verbal overshadowing of visual memories: Some things are better left unsaid. *Cognitive Psychology, 22,* 36–71.

Schultz, D. (1981). *A history of modern psychology* (3rd ed.). New York: Academic Press.

Schustack, M. W., & Sternberg, R. J. (1981). Evaluation of evidence in causal inference. *Journal of Experimental Psychology: General, 110,* 101–120.

Schvaneveldt, R. W., Meyer, D. E., & Becker, C. A. (1976). Lexical ambiguity, semantic context, and visual word recognition. *Journal of Experimental Psychology: Human Perception & Performance, 2*(2), 243–256.

Schweickert, R., & Boruff, B. (1986). Short-term memory capacity: Magic number or magic spell? *Journal of Experimental Psychology: Learning, Memory, & Cognition, 12*(3), 419–425.

Scoville, W. B., & Milner, B. (1957). Loss of recent memory after bilateral hippocampal lesions. *Journal of Neurology, Neurosurgery, and Psychiatry, 20,* 11–19.

Searle, J. R. (1975a). Indirect speech acts. In P. Cole & J. L. Morgan (Eds.), *Syntax and semantics: Speech acts* (Vol. 3, pp. 59–82). New York: Seminar Press.

Searle, J. R. (1975b). A taxonomy of elocutionary acts. In K. Gunderson (Ed.), *Minnesota studies in the philosophy of language* (pp. 344–369). Minneapolis: University of Minnesota Press.

Searle, J. R. (1979). *Expression and meaning: Studies in the theory of speech acts.* Cambridge, England: Cambridge University Press.

Searle, J. R. (1980). Minds, brains, and programs. *Behavioral and Brain Sciences, 3,* 417–424.

Segall, M. H., Campbell, D. T., & Herskovits, M. J. (1966). *The influence of culture on visual perception.* Indianapolis: Bobbs-Merrill.

Segalowitz, S. J., Wagner, W. J., & Menna, R. (1992). Lateral versus frontal ERP predictors of reading skill. *Brain & Cognition, 20*(1), 85–103.

Sejnowski, T. J., & Churchland, P. S. (1989). Brain and cognition. In M. I. Posner (Ed.), *Foundations of cognitive science* (pp. 301–356). Cambridge, MA: MIT Press.

Selfridge, O. G. (1959). Pandemonium: A paradigm for learning. In D. V. Blake & A. M. Uttley (Eds.), *Proceedings of the Symposium on the Mechanization of Thought Processes* (pp. 511–529). London: Her Majesty's Stationery Office.

Selfridge, O. G., & Neisser, U. (1960). Pattern recognition by machine. *Scientific American, 203,* 60–68.

Selkoe, P. J. (1991). Amyloid protein and Alzheimer's disease. *Scientific American, 265,* 68–78.

Sera, Maria D. (1992). To be or to be: Use and acquisition of the Spanish copulas. *Journal of Memory and Language, 31,* 408–427.

Shafir, E. B., Osherson, D. N., & Smith, E. E. (1990). Typicality and reasoning fallacies. *Memory & Cognition, 18*(3), 229–239.

Shallice, T. (1972). Dual functions of consciousness. *Psychological Review, 79*(5), 383–393.

Shallice, T. (1979). Neuropsychological research and the fractionation of memory systems. In L. G. Nilsson (Ed.), *Perspectives on memory research.* Hillsdale, NJ: Erlbaum.

Shallice, T., & Warrington, E. (1970). Independent functioning of verbal memory stores: A neuropsychological study. *Quarterly Journal of Experimental Psychology, 22*(2), 261–273.

Shapiro, P., & Penrod, S. (1986). Meta-analysis of facial identification studies. *Psychological Bulletin, 100*(2), 139–156.

Shapley, R., & Lennie, P. (1985). Spatial frequency analysis in the visual system. *Annual Review of Neuroscience, 8,* 547–583.

Shaywitz, B. A., Pugh, K. R., Constable, R. T., Skudlarski, P., Fulbright, R. K., Bronen, R. A., Fletcher, J. M., Shankweiler, P., Katz, L., & Gore, J. L. (1995). Sex differences in the functional organization of the brain for language. *Nature, 373,* 607–609.

Shepard, R. N. (1984). Ecological constraints on internal representation. Resonant kinematics of perceiving, imaging, thinking, and dreaming. *Psychological Review, 91,* 417–447.

Shepard, R. N., & Metzler, J. (1971). Mental rotation of three-dimensional objects. *Science, 171*(3972), 701–703.

Shiffrin, R. M. (1973). Information persistence in short-term memory. *Journal of Experimental Psychology, 100,* 39–49.

Shiffrin, R. M. (1996). Laboratory experimentation on the genesis of expertise. In K. A. Ericsson (Ed.), *The road to excellence* (pp. 337–347). Mahwah, NJ: Erlbaum.

Shiffrin, R. M., & Schneider, W. (1977). Controlled and automatic human information processing: II. Perceptual learning, automatic attending, and a general theory. *Psychological Review, 84,* 127–190.

Shimamura, A. P., & Squire, L. R. (1986). Korsakoff's syndrome: A study of the relation between anterograde amnesia and remote memory impairment. *Behavioral Neuroscience, 100*(2), 165–170.

Shipley, T. F., & Kellman, P. J. (1994). Spatiotemporal boundary formation: Boundary, form, and motion perception from transformations of surface elements. *Journal of Experimental Psychology: General, 123*(1), 3–20.

Shoben, E. J. (1984). Semantic and episodic memory. In R. W. Wyer, Jr., & T. K. Srull (Eds.), *Handbook of social cognition* (Vol. 2, pp. 213–231). Hillsdale, NJ: Erlbaum.

Shook, M. D., & Shook, R. L. (1991). *The book of odds.* New York: Penguin.

Shortliffe, E. H. (1976). *Computer-based medical consultations: MYCIN.* New York: American Elsevier.

Shulman, H. G. (1970). Encoding and retention of semantic and phonemic information in short-term memory. *Journal of Verbal Learning and Verbal Behavior, 9,* 499–508.

Siegler, R. S. (1976). Three aspects of cognitive development. *Cognitive Psychology, 8,* 481–520.

Siegler, R. S. (1978). The origins of scientific reasoning. In R. S. Siegler (Ed.), *Children's thinking: What develops?* (pp. 109–149). Hillsdale, NJ: Erlbaum.

Siegler, R. S. (1984). Mechanisms of cognitive growth: Variation and selection. In R. J. Sternberg (Ed.), *Mechanisms of cognitive development* (pp. 142–162). New York: Freeman.

Siegler, R. S. (1986). *Children's thinking.* Englewood Cliffs, NJ: Prentice-Hall.

Siegler, R. S. (1988a). Individual differences in strategy choices: Good students, not-so-good students, and perfectionists. *Child Development, 59*(4), 833–851.

Siegler, R. S. (1988b). Strategy choice procedures and the development of multiplication skill. *Journal of Experimental Psychology: General, 117*(3), 258–275.

Siegler, R. S. (1991). Strategy choice and strategy discovery. *Learning & Instruction, 1*(1), 89–102.

Siegler, R. S. (1996). *Emerging minds.* New York: Oxford University Press.

Siegler, R. S., & Shrager, J. (1984). Strategy choices in addition and subtraction: How do children know what to do? In C. Sophian (Ed.), *Origins of cognitive skills* (pp. 229–293). Hillsdale, NJ: Erlbaum.

Silverman, I., & Eals, M. (1992). Sex differences in spatial abilities: Evolutionary theory and data. In J. Barkow, L. Cosmides, & J. Tooby (Eds.), *The adapted mind* (pp. 533–549). New York: Oxford.

Simon, H. A. (1957). *Administrative behavior* (2nd ed.). Totowa, NJ: Littlefield, Adams.

Simon, H. A. (1976). Identifying basic abilities underlying intelligent performance of complex tasks. In L. B. Resnick (Ed.), *The nature of intelligence* (pp. 65–98). Hillsdale, NJ: Erlbaum.

Simon, H. A., & Kotovsky, K. (1963). Human acquisition of concepts for sequential patterns. *Psychological Review, 70,* 534–546.

Simon, H. A., & Reed, S. K. (1976). Modeling strategy shifts in a problem-solving task. *Cognitive Psychology, 8,* 86–97.

Simonton, D. K. (1988). Creativity, leadership, and chance. In R. J. Sternberg (Ed.), *The nature of creativity* (pp. 386–426). New York: Cambridge University Press.

Simonton, D. K. (1994). *Greatness: Who makes history and why.* New York: Guilford.

Simonton, D. K. (1997). Creativity in personality, developmental, and social psychology: Any links with cognitive psychology? In T. B. Ward, S. M. Smith, & J. Vaid (Eds.), *Creative thought: Conceptual structures and processes* (pp. 309–324). Washington, DC: American Psychological Association.

Sincoff, J. B., & Sternberg, R. J. (1988). Development of verbal fluency abilities and strategies in elementary-school-age children. *Developmental Psychology, 24,* 646–653.

Skinner, B. F. (1957). *Verbal behavior.* New York: Appleton-Century-Crofts.

Slobin, D. I. (1971). Cognitive prerequisites for the acquisition of grammar. In C. A. Ferguson & D. I. Slobin (Eds.), *Studies of child language development.* New York: Holt, Rinehart and Winston.

Slobin, D. I. (Ed.). (1985). *The cross-linguistic study of language acquisition.* Hillsdale, NJ: Erlbaum.

Sloboda, J. A., (1996). The acqisition of musical performance expertise: Deconstructing the "talent" account of individual differences in musical expressivity. In K. A. Ericsson (Ed.), *The road to excellence* (pp. 107–127). Mahwah, NJ: Erlbaum.

Sloman, S. (1996). The empirical case for two systems of reasoning. *Psychological Bulletin, 119*, 3–22.

Slovic, P. (1990). Choice. In D. N. Osherson & E. E. Smith (Eds.), *An invitation to cognitive science: Vol. 3. Thinking* (pp. 89–116). Cambridge, MA: MIT Press.

Smilansky, B. (1974). Paper presented at the meeting of the American Educational Research Association, Chicago.

Smith, C. (1996). Sleep states, memory phases, and synaptic plasticity. *Behavior and Brain Research, 78*, 49–56.

Smith, E. E. (1988). Concepts and thought. In R. J. Sternberg & E. E. Smith (Eds.), *The psychology of human thought* (pp. 19–49). New York: Cambridge University Press.

Smith, E. E., Langston, C., & Nisbett, R. E. (1992). The case for rules in reasoning. *Cognitive Science, 16*(1), 1–40.

Smith, E. E., & Medin, D. L. (1981). *Categories and concepts.* Cambridge, MA: Harvard University Press.

Smith, E. E., Shoben, E. J., & Rips, L. J. (1974). Structure and process in semantic memory: A featural model for semantic decisions. *Psychological Review, 81,* 214–241.

Smith, J. D., Reisberg, D., & Wilson, M. (1992). Subvocalization and auditory imagery: Interactions between the inner ear and inner voice. In D. Reisberg (Ed.), *Auditory imagery* (pp. 95–119). Hillsdale, NJ: Erlbaum.

Smith, L. B., Jones, S. S., & Landau, B. (1996). Naming in young children: A dumb attentional mechanism? *Cognition, 60,* 143–171.

Smith, S. M. (1995). Getting into and out of mental ruts: A theory of fixation, incubation, and insight. In R. J. Sternberg & J. E. Davidson (Eds.), *The nature of insight* (pp. 229–251). Cambridge, MA: MIT Press.

Snow, C. E. (1977). The development of conversation between mothers and babies. *Journal of Child Language, 4,* 1–22.

Sodian, B., Zaitchik, D., & Carey, S. (1991). Young children's differentiation of hypothetical beliefs from evidence. *Child Development, 62*(4), 753–766.

Solso, R., & McCarthy, J. E. (1981). Prototype formation of faces: A case of pseudomemory. *British Journal of Psychology, 72,* 499–503.

Sommer, R. (1969). *Personal space.* Englewood Cliffs, NJ: Prentice-Hall.

Spear, N. E. (1979). Experimental analysis of infantile amnesia. In J. E. Kihlstrom & F. J. Evans (Eds.), *Functional disorders of memory.* Hillsdale, NJ: Erlbaum.

Spearman, C. (1927). *The abilities of man.* New York: Macmillan.

Spelke, E., Hirst, W., & Neisser, U. (1976). Skills of divided attention. *Cognition, 4,* 215–230.

Sperling, G. (1960). The information available in brief visual presentations. *Psychological Monographs: General and Applied, 74,* 1–28.

Sperry, R. W. (1964). The great cerebral commissure. *Scientific American, 210*(1), 42–52.

Spoehr, K. T., & Corin, W. J. (1978). The stimulus suffix effect as a memory coding phenomenon. *Memory & Cognition, 6,* 583–589.

Springer, S. P., & Deutsch, G. (1985). *Left brain, right brain.* New York: Freeman.

Squire, L. R. (1982). The neuropsychology of human memory. *Annual Review of Neuroscience, 5,* 241–273.

Squire, L. R. (1986). Mechanisms of memory. *Science, 232*(4578), 1612–1619.

Squire, L. R. (1987). *Memory and the brain.* New York: Oxford University Press.

Squire, L. R. (1993). The organization of declarative and nondeclarative memory. In T. Ono, L. R. Squire, M. E. Raichle, D. I. Perrett, & M. Fukuda (Eds.), *Brain mechanisms of perception and memory: From neuron to behavior* (pp. 219–227). New York: Oxford University Press.

Squire, L. R., Cohen, N. J., & Nadel, L. (1984). The medial temporal region and memory consolidations: A new hypothesis. In H. Weingardner & E. Parker (Eds.), *Memory consolidation.* Hillsdale, NJ: Erlbaum.

Squire, L. R., & Zola-Morgan, S. (1991). The medial temporal lobe memory system. *Science, 253,* 1380–1386.

Squire, L. R., Zola-Morgan, S., Cave, C. B., Haist, F., Musen, G., & Suzuki, W. P. (1990). Memory: Organization of brain systems and cognition. In D. E. Meyer & S. Kornblum (Eds.), *Attention and performance: Vol. 14. Synergies in experimental psychology, artificial intelligence, and cognitive neuroscience* (pp. 393–424). Cambridge, MA: MIT Press.

Standing, L., Conezio, J., & Haber, R. N. (1970). Perception and memory for pictures: Single-trial learning of 2500 visual stimuli. *Psychonomic Science, 19,* 73–74.

Stanovich, K. E. (1981). Attentional and automatic context effects in reading. In A. M. Lesgold & C. A. Perfetti (Eds.), *Interactive processes in reading* (pp. 241–267). Hillsdale, NJ: Erlbaum.

Steele, C. (1990, May). A conversation with Claude Steele. *APS Observer,* pp. 11–17.

Stenhouse, D. (1974). *The evolution of intelligence.* New York: Barnes & Noble.

Stern, D. (1977). *The first relationship: Mother and infant.* Cambridge, MA: Harvard University Press.

Stern, W. (1912). *Psychologische Methoden der Intelligenz-Prüfung.* Leipzig, Germany: Barth.

Sternberg, R. J. (1977). *Intelligence, information processing, and analogical reasoning: The componential analysis of human abilities.* Hillsdale, NJ: Erlbaum.

Sternberg, R. J. (1979, September). Beyond IQ: Stalking the IQ quark. *Psychology Today,* pp. 42–54.

Sternberg, R. J. (1980). Representation and process in linear syllogistic reasoning. *Journal of Experimental Psychology: General, 109,* 119–159.

Sternberg, R. J. (1981). Intelligence and nonentrenchment. *Journal of Educational Psychology, 73,* 1–16.

Sternberg, R. J. (1982a). A componential approach to intellectual development. In R. J. Sternberg (Ed.), *Advances in the psychology of human intelligence* (Vol. 1, pp. 413–463). Hillsdale, NJ: Erlbaum.

Sternberg, R. J. (Ed.). (1982b). *Handbook of human intelligence.* New York: Cambridge University Press.

Sternberg, R. J. (1983). Components of human intelligence. *Cognition, 15,* 1–48.

Sternberg, R. J. (Ed.). (1984a). *Human abilities: An information-processing approach.* San Francisco: Freeman.

Sternberg, R. J. (1984b). Mechanisms of cognitive development: A componential approach. In R. J. Sternberg (Ed.), *Mechanisms of cognitive development* (pp. 164–186). New York: Freeman.

Sternberg, R. J. (1985a). *Beyond IQ: A triarchic theory of human intelligence.* New York: Cambridge University Press.

Sternberg, R. J. (1985b). Implicit theories of intelligence, creativity, and wisdom. *Journal of Personality and Social Psychology, 49,* 607–627.

Sternberg, R. J. (1986a). *Intelligence applied: Understanding and increasing your intellectual skills.* San Diego, CA: Harcourt Brace Jovanovich.

Sternberg, R. J. (1986b). A triarchic theory of intellectual giftedness. In R. J. Sternberg & J. E. Davidson (Eds.), *Conceptions of giftedness* (pp. 223–243). New York: Cambridge University Press.

Sternberg, R. J. (1987a). Most vocabulary is learned from context. In M. McKeown (Ed.), *The nature of vocabulary acquisition* (pp. 89–105). Hillsdale, NJ: Erlbaum.

Sternberg, R. J. (1987b). The psychology of verbal comprehension. In R. Glaser (Ed.), *Advances in instructional psychology* (Vol. 3, pp. 97–151). Hillsdale, NJ: Erlbaum.

Sternberg, R. J. (1987c). Teaching intelligence: The application of cognitive psychology to the improvement of intellectual skills. In J. B. Baron & R. J. Sternberg (Eds.), *Teaching thinking skills: Theory and practice* (pp. 182–218). New York: W. H. Freeman.

Sternberg, R. J. (Ed.). (1988a). *The nature of creativity.* New York: Cambridge University Press.

Sternberg, R. J. (1988b). A three-facet model of creativity. In R. J. Sternberg (Ed.), *The nature of creativity* (pp. 125–147). New York: Cambridge University Press.

Sternberg, R. J. (1988c). *The triarchic mind.* New York: Viking.

Sternberg, R. J. (1989). Domain-generality versus domain-specificity: The life and impending death of a false dichotomy. *Merrill-Palmer Quarterly, 35,* 115–130.

Sternberg, R. J. (Ed.). (1990). *Wisdom: Its nature, origins, and development.* New York: Cambridge University Press.

Sternberg, R. J. (1995). For whom the bell curve tolls: A review of *The Bell Curve. Psychological Science, 6,* 257-261.

Sternberg, R. J. (1996). Costs of expertise. In K. A. Ericsson (Ed.), *The road to excellence* (pp. 347–355). Mahwah, NJ: Erlbaum.

Sternberg, R. J. (1996). Myths, countermyths, and truths about human intelligence. *Educational Researcher, 25*(2), 11–16.

Sternberg, R. J. (1997). *Successful intelligence.* New York: Simon & Schuster.

Sternberg, R. J. (1998). Abilities are forms of developing expertise. *Educational Reseracher, 27*(3), 11–20.

Sternberg, R. J., & Detterman, D. K. (Eds.). (1986). *What is intelligence? Contemporary viewpoints on its nature and definition.* Norwood, NJ: Ablex.

Sternberg, R. J., & Downing, C. J. (1982). The development of higher-order reasoning in adolescence. *Child Development, 53*(1), 209–221.

Sternberg, R. J., Ferrari, M., Clinkenbeard, P. R., & Grigorenko, E. L. (1996). Identification, instruction, and assessment of gifted children: A construct validation of a triarchic model. *Gifted Child Quarterly, 40,* 129–137.

Sternberg, R. J., & Grigorenko, E. L. (1997, Fall). The cognitive costs of physical and mental ill health: Applying the psychology of the developed world to the problems of the developing world. *Eye on Psi Chi, 2*(1), 20–27.

Sternberg, R. J., & Kaufman, J. L. (1996). Innovation and intelligence testing: The curious case of the dog that didn't bark. *European Journal of Psychological Assessment, 12,* 175–182.

Sternberg, R. J., & Lubart, T. I. (1991a, April). Creating creative minds. *Phi Delta Kappan,* 608–614.

Sternberg, R. J., & Lubart, T. I. (1991b). An investment theory of creativity and its development. *Human Development, 34,* 1–31.

Sternberg, R. J., & Lubart, T. I. (1993). Investing in creativity. *Psychological Inquiry, 4*(3), 229–232.

Sternberg, R. J., & Lubart, T. I. (1995). *Defying the crowd.* New York: Free Press.

Sternberg, R. J., & Lubart, T. I. (1996). Investing in creativity. *American Psychologist, 51,* 677–688.

Sternberg, R. J., & Nigro, G. (1980). Developmental patterns in the solution of verbal analogies. *Child Development, 51,* 27–38.

Sternberg, R. J., & Nigro, G. (1983). Interaction and analogy in the comprehension and appreciation of metaphors. *Quarterly Journal of Experimental Psychology, 35A,* 17–38.

Sternberg, R. J., Okagaki, L., & Jackson, A. (1990). Practical intelligence for success in school. *Educational Leadership, 48,* 35–39.

Sternberg, R. J., & Powell, J. S. (1983). Comprehending verbal comprehension. *American Psychologist, 38,* 878–893.

Sternberg, R. J., Powell, C., McGrane, P. A., & McGregor, S. (1997). Effects of a parasitic infection on cognitive functioning. *Journal of Experimental Psychology:Applied, 3,* 67–76.

Sternberg, R. J., & Ruzgis, P. (Eds.). (1994). *Personality and intelligence.* New York: Cambridge University Press.

Sternberg, R. J., Torff, B., & Grigorenko, E. L. (1998). Teaching for successful intelligence raises school achievement. *Phi Delta Kappan, 79*(9), 667–669.

Sternberg, R. J., & Wagner, R. K. (1982, July). Automization failure in learning disabilities. *Topics in Learning and Learning Disabilites, 2,* 1–11.

Sternberg, R. J., & Wagner, R. K. (Eds.). (1994). *Mind in context: Interactionist perspectives on human intelligence.* New York: Cambridge University Press.

Sternberg, R. J., & Weil, E. M. (1980). An aptitude–strategy interaction in linear syllogistic reasoning. *Journal of Educational Psychology, 72,* 226–234.

Sternberg, S. (1966). High-speed memory scanning in human memory. *Science, 153,* 652–654.

Sternberg, S. (1969). Memory-scanning: Mental processes revealed by reaction-time experiments. *American Scientist, 4,* 421–457.

Stevens, A., & Coupe, P. (1978). Distortions in judged spatial relations. *Cognitive Psychology, 10,* 422–437.

Stevens, K. N., & Blumenstein, S. E. (1981). The search for invariant accoustic correlates of phonetic features. In P. K. Eimas & J. L. Miller (Eds.), *Perspectives on the study of speech* (pp. 1–38). Hillsdale: Erlbaum.

Stough, C., Nettlebeck, T., Cooper, C., & Bates, T. (1995). Strategy use in Jensen's reaction time paradigm: Relationship to intelligence? *Australian Journal of Psychology, 47,* 61–65.

Stroop, J. R. (1935). Studies of interference in serial verbal reactions. *Journal of Experimental Psychology, 18,* 624–643.

Suh, S., & Trabasso, T. (1993). Inferences during reading: Converging evidence from discourse analysis, talk-aloud protocols, and recognition priming. *Journal of Memory and Language, 32,* 279–300.

Suppes, P., & Groen, G. (1967). Some counting models for first-grade performance data on simple addition facts. In J. M. Scandura (Ed.), *Research in mathematics education.* Washington, DC: National Council of Teachers of Mathematics.

Tanaka, J. W., & Taylor, M. (1991). Object categories and expertise: Is the basic level in the eye of the beholder? *Cognitive Psychology, 23,* 457–482.

Tannen, D. (1986). *That's not what I meant! How conversational style makes or breaks relationships.* New York: Ballantine.

Tannen, D. (1990). *You just don't understand: Women and men in conversation.* New York: Ballantine.

Tannen, D. (1994). *Talking from 9 to 5: How women's and men's conversational styles affect who gets heard, who gets credit, and what gets done at work.* New York: Morrow.

Taylor, H., & Tversky, B. (1992a). Descriptions and depictions of environments. *Memory & Cognition, 20*(5), 483–496.

Taylor, H., & Tversky, B. (1992b). Spatial mental models derived from survey and route descriptions. *Journal of Memory & Language, 31*(2), 261–292.

Terman, L. M., & Merrill, M. A. (1937). *Measuring intelligence.* Boston: Houghton Mifflin.

Terman, L. M., & Merrill, M. A. (1973). *Stanford–Binet Intelligence Scale: Manual for the third revision.* Boston: Houghton Mifflin.

Thatcher, R. W. (1991). Maturation of the human frontal lobes: Physiological evidence for staging. *Developmental Neuropsychology, 7,* 397–419.

Thatcher, R. W. (1992). Cyclic cortical reorganization during early childhood. *Brain & Cognition, 20,* 24–50.

Thatcher, R. W. (1994). Psychopathology of early frontal lobe damage: Dependence on cycles of development. *Development & Psychopathology, 6,* 565–596.

Thatcher, R. W., Walker, R. A., & Giudice, S. (1987). Human cerebral hemispheres develop at different rates and ages. *Science, 236,* 1110–1113.

Theeuwes, J. (1992). Perceptual selectivity for color and form. *Perception & Psychophysics, 51*(6), 599–606.

Thelen, E., & Smith, L. B. (1994). *A dynamic systems approach to the development of cognition and action.* Cambridge, MA: MIT Press.

Thelen, E., & Smith, L. B. (in press). Dynamic systems theories. In R. M. Lerner (Ed.), *Handbook of Child Psychology: Vol. 1. Theoretical models of human development* (5th ed.). New York: Wiley.

Thomas, J. C., Jr. (1974). An analysis of behavior in the hobbits–orcs problem. *Cognitive Psychology, 6,* 257–269.

Thomas, O. (1966). *Transformational grammar and the teacher of English.* New York: Holt, Rinehart and Winston.

Thompson, R. F. (1987). The cerebellum and memory storage: A response to Bloedel. *Science, 238,* 1729–1730.

Thorndike, E. L. (1905). *The elements of psychology.* New York: Seiler.

Thorndike, R. L., Hagen, E. P., & Sattler, J. M. (1986). *Stanford–Binet Intelligence Scale: Guide for administering and scoring the fourth edition.* Chicago: Riverside.

Thorndyke, P. W. (1981). Distance estimation from cognitive maps. *Cognitive Psychology, 13,* 526–550.

Thorndyke, P. W. (1984). Applications of schema theory in cognitive research. In J. R. Anderson & S. M. Kosslyn (Eds.), *Tutorials in learning and memory* (pp. 167–192). San Francisco: Freeman.

Thorndyke, P. W., & Hayes-Roth, B. (1982). Differences in spatial knowledge acquired from maps and navigation. *Cognitive Psychology, 14,* 580–589.

Thurstone, L. L. (1938). *Primary mental abilities.* Chicago: University of Chicago Press.

Thurstone, L. L., & Thurstone, T. G. (1962). *Tests of primary abilities* (Rev. ed.). Chicago: Science Research Associates.

Tipper, S. P., & Behrmann, M. (1996). Object centered, not scene-based visual neglect. *Journal of Experimental Psychology: Human Perception and Performance, 22,* 1261–1278.

Titchner, E. B. (1909). *A textbook of psychology.* New York: MacMillan.

Tolman, E. C. (1932). *Purposive behavior in animals and men.* New York: Appleton-Century-Crofts.

Tolman, E. C., & Honzik, C. H. (1930). "Insight" in rats. *University of California Publications in Psychology, 4,* 215–232.

Torrance, E. P. (1974). *The Torrance tests of creative thinking: Technical-norms manual.* Bensenville, IL: Scholastic Testing Services.

Torrance, E. P. (1984). *Torrance tests of creative thinking: Streamlined (revised) manual, Figural A and B.* Bensenville, IL: Scholastic Testing Services.

Torrance, E. P. (1988). The nature of creativity as manifest in its testing. In R. J. Sternberg (Ed.), *The nature of creativity* (pp. 43–75). New York: Cambridge University Press.

Tourangeau, R., & Sternberg, R. J. (1981). Aptness in metaphor. *Cognitive Psychology, 13,* 27–55.

Tourangeau, R., & Sternberg, R. J. (1982). Understanding and appreciating metaphors. *Cognition, 11,* 203–244.

Townsend, J. T. (1971). A note on the identifiability of parallel and serial processes. *Perception and Psychophysics, 10,* 161–163.

Trabasso, T., & Suh, S. (1993). Understanding text: achieving explanatory coherence through on-line inferences and mental operations in working memory. *Discourse Processes, 16,* 3–34.

Treadway, M., McCloskey, M., Gordon, B., & Cohen, N. J. (1992). Landmark life events and the organization of memory: Evidence from functional retrograde amnesia. In S. A. Christianson (Ed.), *The handbook of emotion and memory: Research and theory* (pp. 389–410). Hillsdale, NJ: Erlbaum.

Treisman, A.M. (1960). Contextual cues in selective listening. *Quarterly Journal of Experimental Psychology, 12,* 242–248.

Treisman, A. M. (1964a). Monitoring and storage of irrelevant messages in selective attention. *Journal of Verbal Learning and Verbal Behavior, 3,* 449–459.

Treisman, A. M. (1964b). Selective attention in man. *British Medical Bulletin, 20,* 12–16.

Treisman, A. M. (1986). Features and objects in visual processing. *Scientific American, 255*(5), 114B–125.

Treisman, A. M. (1990). Visual coding of features and objects: Some evidence from behavioral studies. In National Research Council (Ed.), *Advances in the modularity of vision: Selections from a symposium on frontiers of visual science* (pp. 39–61). Washington, DC: National Academy Press.

Treisman, A. M. (1991). Search, similarity, and integration of features between and within dimensions. *Journal of Experimental Psychology: Human Perception & Performance, 17,* 652–676.

Treisman, A. M. (1992). Perceiving and re-perceiving objects. *American Psychologist, 47,* 862–875.

Treisman, A. M. (1993). The perception of features and objects. In A. Baddeley & C. L. Weiskrantz (Eds.), *Attention: Selection, awareness, and control* (pp. 5–35). Oxford: Clarenden.

Treisman, A. M., & Sato, S. (1990). Conjunction search revisited. *Journal of Experimental Psychology: Human Perception and Performance, 16,* 459–478.

Treisman, A. M., & Schmidt, H. (1982). Illusory conjunctions in the perception of objects. *Cognitive Psychology, 14*(1), 107–141.

Tsushuma, T., Takizawa, O., Saski, M., Siraki, S., Nishi, K., Kohno, M., Menyuk, P., & Best, C. (1994). Discrimination of English /r-l/ and w-y/ by Japanese infants at 6–12 months: Language specific developmental changes in speech perception abilities. Paper presented at International Conference on Spoken Language Processing, 4. Yokohama, Japan.

Tulving, E. (1962). Subjective organization in free recall of "unrelated" words. *Psychological Review, 69,* 344–354.

Tulving, E. (1972). Episodic and semantic memory. In E. Tulving & W. Donaldson (Eds.), *Organization of memory.* New York: Academic Press.

Tulving, E. (1983). *Elements of episodic memory.* New York: Oxford University Press.

Tulving, E. (1984). Precis: Elements of episodic memory. *Behavioral and Brain Sciences, 7,* 223–268.

Tulving, E. (1985). How many memory systems are there? *American Psychologist, 40*(4), 385–398.

Tulving, E. (1986). What kind of a hypothesis is the distinction between episodic and semantic memory? *Journal of Experimental Psychology: Learning, Memory, & Cognition, 12*(2), 307–311.

Tulving, E. (1989, July/August). Remembering and knowing the past. *American Scientist, 77,* 361–367.

Tulving, E., & Pearlstone, Z. (1966). Availability versus accessibility of information in memory for words. *Journal of Verbal Learning and Verbal Behavior, 5,* 381–391.

Tulving, E., & Schacter, D. L. (1994). *Memory systems 1994.* Cambridge, MA: MIT Press.

Tulving, E., Schacter, D. L., & Stark, H. A. (1982). Priming effects in word-fragment completion are independent of recognition memory. *Journal of Experimental Psychology: Learning, Memory, & Cognition, 8*(4), 336–342.

Tulving, E., & Thomson, D. M. (1973). Encoding specificity and retrieval processes in episodic memory. *Psychological Review, 80,* 352–373.

Turing, A. M. (1963). Computing machinery and intelligence. In E. A. Feigenbaum & J. Feldman (Eds.), *Computers and thought.* New York: McGraw-Hill.

Turner, A. M., & Greenough, W. T. (1985). Differential rearing effects on rats' visual cortex synapses. *Brain Research, 329,* 195–203.

Tversky, A. (1972a). Choice by elimination. *Journal of Mathematical Psychology, 9*(4), 341–367.

Tversky, A. (1972b). Elimination by aspects: A theory of choice. *Psychological Review, 79,* 281–299.

Tversky, A., & Kahneman, D. (1971). Belief in the law of small numbers. *Psychological Bulletin, 76*(2), 105–110.

Tversky, A., & Kahneman, D. (1973). Availability: A heuristic for judging frequency and probability. *Cognitive Psychology, 5,* 207–232.

Tversky, A., & Kahneman, D. (1974). Judgment under uncertainty: Heuristics and biases. *Science, 185,* 1124–1131.

Tversky, A., & Kahneman, D. (1981). The framing of decisions and the psychology of choice. *Science, 211,* 453–458.

Tversky, A., & Kahneman, D. (1983). Extensional versus intuitive reasoning: The conjunction fallacy in probability judgment. *Psychological Review, 90*(4), 293–315.

Tversky, A., & Kahneman, D. (1993). Belief in the law of small numbers. In G. Keren & C. Lewis (Eds.), *A handbook for data analysis in the behavioral sciences: Methodological issues* (pp. 341–349). Hillsdale, NJ: Erlbaum.

Tversky, B. (1981). Distortions in memory for maps. *Cognitive Psychology, 13*(3), 407–433.

Tversky, B. (1991). Distortions in memory for visual displays. In S. R. Ellis, M. Kaiser, & A. Grunewald (Eds.), *Spatial instruments and spatial displays* (pp. 61–75). Hillsdale, NJ: Erlbaum.

Tversky, B., & Schiano, D. J. (1989). Perceptual and conceptual factors in distortions in memory for graphs and maps. *Journal of Experimental Psychology: General, 118,* 387–398.

Underwood, B. J. (1957). Interference and forgetting. *Psychological Review, 64,* 49–60.

Usher, J. A., & Neisser, U. (1993). Childhood amnesia and the beginnings of memory for four early life events. *Journal of Experimental Psychology: General, 122*(2), 155–165.

van Daalen-Kapteijns, M., & Elshout-Mohr, M. (1981). The acquisition of word meanings as a cognitive learning process. *Journal of Verbal Learning & Verbal Behavior, 20*(4), 386–399.

van Dijk, T. A. (1975). Formal semantics of metaphorical discourse. *Poetics, 4,* 173–198.

van Dijk, T. A., & Kintsch, W. (1983). *Strategies of discourse comprehension.* New York: Academic Press.

VanLehn, K. (1989). Problem solving and cognitive skill acquisition. In M. I. Posner (Ed.), *Foundations of cognitive science* (pp. 526–579). Cambridge, MA: MIT Press.

VanLehn, K. (1990). *Mind bugs: The origins of procedural misconceptions.* Cambridge, MA: MIT Press.

Van Selst, M., & Jolicoeur, P. (1994). Can mental rotation occur before the dual-task bottleneck? *Journal of Experimental Psychology: Human Perception and Performance, 20,* 905–921.

Vernon, P. A., & Mori, M. (1992). Intelligence, reaction times, and peripheral nerve conduction velocity. *Intelligence, 16*(3–4), 273–288.

Vernon, P. E. (1971). *The structure of human abilities.* London: Methuen.

Vincente, K. J., & DeGroot, A. D. (1990). The memory recall paradigm: straightening out the historical record. *American Psychologist, 45,* 285–287.

Vokey, J. R., & Read, J. D. (1985). Subliminal messages: Between the devil and the media. *American Psychologist, 40,* 1231–1239.

Vygotsky, L. S. (1962). *Thought and language.* Cambridge, MA: MIT Press. (Original work published 1934)

Vygotsky, L. S. (1978). *Mind in society: The development of higher psychological processes.* Cambridge, MA: Harvard University Press.

Vygotsky, L. S. (1986). *Thought and language.* Cambridge, MA: MIT Press.

Wagner, A. R., & Rescorla, R. A. (1972). Inhibition in Pavlovian conditioning: Application of a theory. In R. A. Boakes & M. S. Halliday (Eds.), *Inhibition and learning.* New York: Academic Press.

Wagner, D. A. (1978). Memories of Morocco: The influence of age, schooling, and environment on memory. *Cognitive Psychology, 10,* 1–28.

Wagner, R. K., & Stanovich, K. E. (1996). Expertise in reading. In K. A. Ericsson (Ed.), *The road to excellence* (pp. 159–227). Mahwah, NJ: Erlbaum.

Warren, R. M. (1970). Perceptual restoration of missing speech sounds. *Science, 167,* 392–393.

Warren, R. M., Obusek, C. J., Farmer, R. M., & Warren, R. P. (1969). Auditory sequence: Confusion of patterns other than speech or music. *Science, 164,* 586–587.

Warren, R. M., & Warren, R. P. (1970). Auditory illusions and confusions. *Scientific American, 223,* 30–36.

Warrington, E. (1982). The double dissociation of short- and long-term memory deficits. In L. S. Cermak (Ed.), *Human memory and amnesia.* Hillsdale, NJ: Erlbaum.

Warrington, E., & Shallice, T. (1972). Neuropsychological evidence of visual storage in short-term memory tasks. *Quarterly Journal of Experimental Psychology, 24*(1), 30–40.

Warrington, E., & Weiskrantz, L. (1970). Amnesic syndrome: Consolidation or retrieval? *Nature, 228*(5272), 628–630.

Wason, P. C. (1968). Reasoning about a rule. *Quarterly Journal of Experimental Psychology, 20*(3), 273–281.

Wason, P. C. (1969). Regression in reasoning? *British Journal of Psychology, 60*(4), 471–480.

Wason, P. C. (1983). Realism and rationality in the selection task. In J. St. B. T. Evans (Ed.), *Thinking and reasoning: Psychological approaches* (pp. 44–75). Boston: Routledge & Kegan Paul.

Wason, P., & Johnson-Laird, P. (1970). A conflict between selecting and evaluating information in an inferential task. *British Journal of Psychology, 61*(4), 509–515.

Wason, P. C., & Johnson-Laird, P. N. (1972). *Psychology of reasoning: Structure and content.* London: B. T. Batsford.

Wasow, T. (1989). Grammatical theory. In M. I. Posner (Ed.), *Foundations of cognitive science* (pp. 208–243). Cambridge, MA: MIT Press.

Wasserman, D., Lempert, R. O., & Hastie, R. (1991). Hindsight and causality. *Personality & Social Psychology Bulletin, 17*(1), 30–35.

Watkins, M. J., & Tulving, E. (1975). Episodic memory: When recognition fails. *Journal of Experimental Psychology: General, 104,* 5–29.

Watson, J. B. (1928). *Psychological care of infant and child.* New York: Norton.

Watson, J. B., & McDougall, W. (1929). *The battle of behaviorism.* New York: Norton.

Watson, O. M. (1970). *Proxemic behavior: A cross-cultural study.* The Hague, Netherlands: Mouton.

Waugh, N. C., & Norman, D. A. (1965). Primary memory. *Psychological Review, 72,* 89–104.

Weaver, C. A. (1993). Do you need a "flash" to form a flashbulb memory? *Journal of Experimental Psychology: General, 122*(1), 39–46.

Wegner, D. M. (1989). *White bears and other unwanted thoughts: Suppression, obsession, and the psychology of mental control.* New York: Penguin.

Wegner, D. M., & Erber, R. (1992). The hyperaccessibility of suppressed thoughts. *Journal of Personality & Social Psychology, 63*(6), 903–912.

Weiller, C., Isansee, C., Rijntgis, M., Huber, W., et. al. (1996). Recovery from Wernicke's aphasia: A positron emission tomography study. *Annals of Neurology, 37,* 723–732.

Weingartner, H., Rudorfer, M. V., Buchsbaum, M. S., & Linnoila, M. (1983). Effects of serotonin on memory impairments produced by ethanol. *Science, 221,* 442–473.

Weisberg, R. W. (1986). *Creativity: Genius and other myths.* New York: Freeman.

Weisberg, R. W. (1988). Problem solving and creativity. In R. J. Sternberg (Ed.), *The nature of creativity* (pp. 148–176). New York: Cambridge University Press.

Weisberg, R. W. (1995). Prolegomena to theories of insight in problem solving: A taxonomy of problems. In R. J. Sternberg & J. E. Davidson (Eds.), *The nature of insight* (pp. 157–196). Cambridge, MA: MIT Press.

Weiskrantz, L. (1994). Blindsight. In M. W. Eysenck (Ed.), *The Blackwell dictionary of cognitive psychology.* Cambridge, MA: Blackwell.

Weisstein, N., & Harris, C. S. (1974). Visual detection of line segments: An object-superiority effect. *Science, 186,* 752–755.

Weizenbaum, J. (1966). ELIZA—A computer program for the study of natural language communication between man and machine. *Communications of the Association for Computing Machinery, 9,* 36–45.

Wellman, H. M., & Gelman, S. A. (1998). Knowledge acquisition in foundational domains. In W. Damon (Ed.-in-Chief), D. Kuhn, & R. S. Siegler (Vol. Eds.), *Handbook of child psychology:Vol. 2. Cognitive development* (pp. 523–573). New York: Wiley.

Werker, J. F. (1994). Cross-language speed perception: developmental change does not involve loss. In J. C. Goodman & H. L. Nusbaum (Eds.), *The development of speech perception: The transition from speech sounds to spoken words* (pp. 93–120). Cambridge, MA: MIT Press.

Werker, J. F., & Tees, R. L. (1984). Cross-language speech perception: evidence for perceptual reorganization during the first year of life. *Infant Behavior and Development, 7,* 49–63.

Werner, E. E. (1972). Infants around the world. *Journal of Cross-Cultural Psychology, 3*(2), 111–134.

Werner, H., & Kaplan, E. (1952). The acquisition of word meanings: A developmental study. *Monographs of the Society for Research in Child Development,* No. 51.

Wertheimer, M. (1959). *Productive thinking* (Rev. ed.). New York: Harper & Row. (Original work published 1945)

West, R. L. (1986). Everyday memory and aging. *Developmental Neuropsychology, 2*(4), 323–344.

Wheeler, D. D. (1970). Processes in word recognition. *Cognitive Psychology, 1,* 59–85.

Whorf, B. L. (1956). In J. B. Carroll (Ed.), *Language, thought and reality: Selected writings of Benjamin Lee Whorf.* Cambridge, MA: MIT Press.

Wickens, D. D., Dalezman, R. E., & Eggemeier, F. T. (1976). Multiple encoding of word attributes in memory. *Memory & Cognition, 4*(3), 307–310.

Wickett, J. C., & Vernon, P. (1994). Peripheral nerve conduction velocity, reaction time, and intelligence: An attempt to replicate Vernon and Mori. *Intelligence, 18,* 127–132.

Williams, J., Mark, G., Mathews, A., & MacLeod, C. (1996). The emotional Stroop and psychopathology. *Psychological Bulletin, 120,* 3–24.

Williams, M. (1970). *Brain damage and the mind.* London: Penguin.

Willis, S. L. (1985). Towards an educational psychology of the older adult learner: Intellectual and cognitive bases. In J. E. Birren & K. W. Schaie (Eds.), *Handbook of the psychology of aging* (2nd ed.). New York: Van Nostrand Reinhold.

Wilson, M. A., & McNaughton, B. L. (1994). Reactivation of hippocampal ensemble memories during sleep. *Science, 265,* 676–679.

Winograd, T. (1972). *Understanding natural language.* New York: Academic Press.

Wissler, C. (1901). The correlation of mental and physical tests. *Psychological Review, Monograph Supplement 3*(6).

Wittgenstein, L. (1953). *Philosophical investigations.* New York: Macmillan.

Wolkowitz, O. M., Tinklenberg, J. R., & Weingartner, H. (1985). A psychopharmacological perspective of cognitive functions: II. Specific pharmacologic agents. *Neuropsychobiology, 14*(3), 133–156.

Woods, S. S., Resnick, L. B., & Groen, G. J. (1975). An experimental test of five process models for subtraction. *Journal of Educational Psychology, 67,* 17–21.

Woodworth, R. S., & Sells, S. B. (1935). An atmosphere effect in formal syllogistic reasoning. *Journal of Experimental Psychology, 18,* 451–460.

Yantis, S. (1993). Stimulus-driven attentional capture. *Current Directions in Psychological Science, 2*(5), 156–161.

Yu, V. L., Fagan, L. M., Bennet, S. W., Clancey, W. J., Scott, A. C., Hannigan, J. F., Blum, R. L., Buchanan, B. G., & Cohen, S. N. (1984). An evaluation of MYCIN's advice. In B. G. Buchanan & E. H. Shortliffe (Eds.), *Rule-based expert systems.* Reading, MA: Addison-Wesley.

Zaidel, E. (1983). A response to Gazzaniga: Language in the right hemisphere, convergent perspectives. *American Psychologist, 38*(5), 542–546.

Zaragoza, M. S., McCloskey, M., & Jamis, M. (1987). Misleading postevent information and recall of the original event: Further evidence against the memory impairment hypothesis. *Journal of Experimental Psychology: Learning, Memory, & Cognition, 13*(1), 36–44.

Zeidner, M. (1990). Perceptions of ethnic group modal intelligence scores: Reflections of cultural stereotypes or intelligence test scores? *Journal of Cross-Cultural Psychology, 21,* 214–231.

Zigler, E., & Berman, W. (1983). Discerning the future of early childhood intervention. *American Psychologist, 38,* 894–906.

Zinchenko, P. I. (1962). *Neproizvol'noe azpominanie* [Involuntary memory] (pp. 172–207). Moscow: USSR APN RSFSR.

Zinchenko, P. I. (1981). Involuntary memory and the goal-directed nature of activity. In J. V. Wertsch, *The concept of activity in Soviet psychology.* Armonk, NY: Sharpe.

Zingeser, L. B., & Berndt, R. W. (1990). Retrieval of nouns and verbs in agrammatism and anomia. *Brain and Language, 39*(1), 14–32.

Zola-Morgan, S. M., & Squire, L. R. (1990). The primate hippocampal formation: Evidence for a time-limited role in memory storage. *Science, 250,* 228–290.

Zurif, E. B. (1990). Language and the brain. In D. N. Osherson & H. Lasnik (Eds.), *Language* (pp. 177–198). Cambridge, MA: MIT Press.

Name Index

Abel, L., 44, 483
Abelson, R. P., 265, 500
Adams, M. J., 501
Adler, J., 318
Adler, S. A., 202
Ahn, W-K., 425
Albert, M. L., 324
Alho, K., 103
Alpert, N. M., 229
Amabile, T. A., 385
Amabile, T. M., 205
Anderson, B. F., 375
Anderson, J. R., 74, 195, 219, 268–269, 270, 271, 375
Anderson, R. C., 341
Appel, L. F., 451
Appelbaum, M. I., 433
Appenzeller, T., 87
Aristotle, 4–5, 23
Arlin, P. K., 446
Armstrong, S. L., 259
Asher, J. J., 323
Askenasy, J. J. M., 186, 187
Atkinson, R. C., 158, 195
Austin, G. A., 423
Averbach, E., 161–162
Ayres, T. J., 162

Bachevalier, J., 87
Baddeley, A. D., 162, 166, 168, 171, 175, 183, 204, 205, 272, 273
Bahrick, A. S., 164
Bahrick, H. P., 163–164, 186, 307, 322, 461
Bahrick, L. E., 164, 307, 322
Bahrick, P. E., 164
Bahrick, P. O., 163, 461
Bailenson, J., 425
Baillargeon, R., 445
Bain, J. D., 169
Baker, J. G., 503
Ball, T. M., 233, 235
Baltes, P. B., 462, 463, 486
Balthazard, C., 71
Banaji, M. R., 165, 171, 206, 317, 318
Bandura, A., 10
Baron, J., 375, 420
Baroody, A. J., 453
Barrett, P. T., 482
Barron, F., 385
Barsalou, L. W., 225
Barston, J. I., 420
Bartlett, F. C., 198, 199, 255, 264
Bashore, T. R., 460
Bassok, M., 374
Bastik, T., 375
Batt, R., 480
Batterman, N., 259
Baxter, D. A., 217
Baylis, G., 90
Beardsley, M., 328
Beck, I. L., 339
Becker, D. E., 147
Becklen, R., 100
Begg, I., 415
Beilin, H., 443
Bellezza, F. S., 165
Bellugi, U., 310
Belmont, J. M., 451
Bennett, E. L., 461, 463
Bereiter, C., 377
Berger, S. A., 307, 322
Berkow, R., 51
Berlin, B., 320
Berliner, H. J., 493
Berman, W., 501
Bernstein, A., 493
Bertoncini, J., 304
Bialystok, E., 323
Bickerton, D., 325, 328
Bidell, T. R., 443
Biederman, I., 136, 137, 138
Binet, A., 470–471, 472
Bisanz, J., 450
Bjork, R. A., 169
Bjorklund, D. F., 452
Black, J. B., 265, 266
Black, M., 328
Blansjaar, B. A., 177
Bloom, B. S., 354, 502
Blumstein, S. E., 292
Bobbitt, B. L., 310
Bock, K., 297, 298, 302, 303, 327
Bohannon, J., 204
Bohannon, J. N., 204
Boies, S., 184
Boller, K., 202
Boring, E. G., 469
Bornstein, M. H., 433
Borovsky, D., 205
Bors, D. A., 479, 480
Boruff, B., 162
Bothwell, R. K., 202
Bourg, T., 228, 235
Bousfield, W. A., 184, 188
Bower, G. H., 164, 195, 201, 204, 219, 265, 266, 269, 318
Bowers, K. S., 71, 203
Boyes-Braem, P., 262
Bradley, R. H., 502
Bradshaw, G. L., 365, 499
Braine, M. D. S., 408, 409
Brainerd, C. J., 443, 445
Bransford, J. D., 129, 165, 182, 201, 318, 351
Bray, N. W., 451
Bregman, A. S., 293
Breiter, H. C., 229
Brennan, S. E., 329
Bresnan, J. W., 298
Brian, C. R., 321
Briere, J., 203
Brigham, J. C., 202
Broadbent, D. E., 83, 93, 95
Broca, P., 41, 53–54, 62, 342
Broder, L. J., 354
Bronfenbrenner, U., 487
Brooks, L. R., 219
Brooks-Gunn, J., 433
Brown, A. L., 449, 450, 451, 452
Brown, J. A., 196
Brown, P., 164
Brown, R., 204, 285, 310
Brown, V., 84
Broza, M. A., 202
Bruce, D., 195
Bruck, M., 174
Bruhn, P., 103
Bruner, J. S., 136, 423
Bryan, W. L., 74
Bryant, P. E., 444
Bryson, M., 377, 379
Buchanan, B. G., 498
Buchanan, M., 162
Buchsbaum, M. S., 44, 177, 483
Burns, H. J., 202
Butler, J., 205
Butterfield, E. C., 451
Butters, N., 177
Butterworth, B., 298
Byrne, A., 98
Byrne, R. M. J., 416, 417

Cabeza, R., 167, 177, 345
Caldwell, B. M., 502

Calvanio, R., 239
Calvo, M. G., 98
Campbell, K. B., 482
Campione, J. C., 449, 451
Cantor, J., 166, 167
Cappa, S. F., 342
Carey, G., 484
Carey, S., 455
Carlson, N. R., 40, 134
Carmichael, L., 223, 224
Carpenter, P. A., 144, 166, 228
Carraher, D., 487
Carraher, T. N., 487
Carroll, D. W., 284, 296
Carroll, J. B., 321, 475, 477, 504
Carroll, L., 297
Carter, M., 84
Carter, P., 453
Carullo, J. J., 166, 167
Carver, C. S., 164
Caryl, P. G., 42
Casagrande, J. B., 321
Case, R., 443
Castellucci, V. F., 78
Catlin, J., 257
Cattell, J. M., 145, 147
Cattell, R. B., 375, 460, 475, 477, 504
Cave, K. R., 89, 90, 98
Cazden, C. B., 310
Ceci, S. J., 174, 203, 485, 487, 503
Cerella, J., 460, 461, 462
Cermak, L. S., 177
Chambers, D., 220, 221, 223, 235
Chapman, J. P., 403, 415, 423
Chapman, L. J., 403, 415, 423
Charack, G., 101
Chase, W. G., 172, 203, 220, 279, 377
Cheng, P. W., 408, 409, 420, 425
Cherry, E. C., 92, 93, 96
Chi, M. T. H., 374, 377, 379
Chomsky, N., 12, 297, 300–302, 307, 410
Chueh, D., 483
Churchland, P. S., 29
Clark, E. V., 256, 285, 305, 326, 332
Clark, H. H., 220, 256, 285, 326, 328, 329, 332, 341, 412
Clark, M. C., 195
Clement, C. A., 417–418
Clinkenbeard, P. R., 491, 501
Cohen, G., 171
Cohen, J., 404
Cohen, J. D., 101
Cohen, M. M., 294
Cohen, M. S., 229
Cohen, N. J., 169, 177, 204, 278
Colby, K. M., 496, 497
Cole, M., 17, 322, 484
Coleman, P. D., 460
Collins, A. M., 260, 261, 262, 270
Commons, M. L., 461
Conezio, J., 156
Conn, C., 144
Connell, J., 408
Conrad, R., 183, 184
Conte, J. R., 203
Conway, M. A., 204
Coon, H., 484
Cooper, E. H., 187
Cooper, F. S., 292, 294
Copernicus, N., 382
Corballis, M., 239
Corbetta, M., 102
Corcoran, D. W., 194
Coren, S., 117
Coriell, A. S., 161–162
Corkin, S., 169, 174, 176
Cornsweet, J. C., 115
Cornsweet, T. N., 115
Cosmides, L., 410
Coupe, P., 235, 245
Cowan, N., 96, 103
Cox, J. R., 408, 409
Craik, F. I. M., 164, 165, 166, 194, 206
Craik, K., 340
Crisp, J., 90
Crivelli, C., 120
Crowder, R. G., 154, 171
Crystal, D., 326, 327
Csikszentmihalyi, M., 385–386
Culver, L. C., 217
Cummins, J., 322
Curie, M., 382, 383
Cutler, B. L., 202
Cutting, J., 139

Dalezman, R. E., 184
Damasio, A. R., 149
Daneman, M., 166
Danks, J. H., 285
Darlington, R., 501
Darwin, C., 17
Dasen, P. R., 445
Davey, T. C., 433
Davidson, B. J., 84
Davidson, J. E., 368, 374, 375, 445, 501
Da Vinci, L., 382
Davis, S. N., 386
Dax, M., 53, 342
Deacedo, B. S., 169
Deary, I. J., 478
DeCasper, A. J., 304
De Groot, A. D., 279, 377, 379
Dehaene, S., 101, 102
Dehaene-Lambertz, G., 304
Dell, G. S., 308, 327
DeLoache, J. S., 452
Del Pesce, M., 103
Dempster, A., 360
Dempster, F. N., 483
Denny, J., 415
Denny, N. W., 461
De Rosa, D. V., 194
Descartes, R., 5, 23
DeSoto, C. B., 411
Detterman, D. K., 469, 501
Deutsch, D., 95
Deutsch, G., 53
Deutsch, J. A., 95
DeValois, K. K., 134
DeValois, R. L., 134
Dewey, J., 7–8, 23
De Yoe, E. A., 135
Dhawan, M., 145
Diamond, A., 459
Dienes, Z., 90
DiGirolamo, G. J., 229
Ditchburn, R. W., 115
Dittmann-Kohli, F., 486
Dixon, R. A., 461, 462, 486
Doris, J., 485
Drain, H. M., 149
Dressel, S., 238
Dreyfus, H. L., 499
Dreyfus, S. E., 499
Driver, J., 90
Dror, I. E., 454
Dueck, A., 201, 318
DuFault, D., 205
Duncan, E., 228, 235
Duncan, J., 87, 88, 98
Duncan, S., 453
Duncker, K., 371–372
Dunkel-Schetter, C., 335
Dupous, E., 304

Eagle, M., 184
Eals, M., 247
Ebbinghaus, H., 8, 24, 186
Edwards, W., 393
Egeland, B., 502
Eggemeier, F. T., 184
Eich, E., 204
Eich, J. E., 204
Eichelman, W., 184
Eichenbaum, H., 169

Eimas, P. D., 304
Einstein, A., 382
Elman, J. L., 293
Elshout-Mohr, M., 339
Engen, T., 182
Engle, R. W., 166, 167
Engstler-Schooler, T. Y., 318
Ericsson, K. A., 172, 380
Escher, M. C., 120
Esselman, E. D., 164
Estes, W. K., 482
Ettinger, M., 360
Evans, J. St. B. T., 420
Eysenck, H. J., 476, 482, 485
Eysenck, M., 9, 98, 168, 397

Fagan, J. F., 433
Falmagne, R. J., 417–418
Faloon, S., 172
Farah, M. J., 55, 101, 148, 149, 223, 225, 235, 239, 241
Farmer, R. M., 292
Farvolden, P., 203
Feigl, H., 9
Fernald, A., 309
Ferrari, M., 491, 501
Feuerstein, R., 449, 501, 503
Feynman, R., 334
Field, T., 304
Fifer, W. P., 304
Fincham, J. M., 270
Finke, R., 223, 225, 226, 234, 235, 384–385
Fischer, K. W., 443
Fischhoff, B., 403
Fischman, D., 217
Fisher, R. P., 165
Fisk, A. D., 83
Fivush, R., 174
Flavell, E. R., 450
Flavell, J. H., 450, 451
Flege, J., 323
Flood, D. G., 460
Flynn, J. R., 461
Fodor, J. A., 149, 256, 279, 326
Fogel, A., 304
Foley, M. A., 203
Forrin, B., 479, 480
Foulke, E., 292
Fox, P. T., 44, 62, 102, 145, 274
Franklin, N., 248
Franks, J. J., 129, 165
French, A. L., 449
Frensch, P. A., 203, 380
Freud, S., 148
Frick, F., 420
Frisch, K. von, 243
Fromkin, V. A., 289, 303, 326
Frost, N., 185
Fulker, D. W., 484
Funke, J., 352

Galanter, E. H., 13, 279
Galotti, K. M., 420
Galton, F., 470, 503
Ganellen, R. J., 164
Garcia, R., 323
Gardner, H., 11, 279, 386, 487–489, 501, 504
Garrett, M. F., 298, 302, 326, 327
Garry, M., 202
Gay, J., 17, 484
Gazzaniga, M. S., 28, 55, 56, 103, 239
Gelman, R., 443, 445
Gelman, S. A., 425, 455, 456
Gentner, D., 374
Gentner, D. R., 374
Georgopoulos, A. P., 229, 230
Gerrig, R. J., 317, 328
Gert, J., 177
Geschwind, N., 342
Giard, M. H., 239
Gibbs, R. W., 332
Gibson, E. J., 128
Gibson, J. J., 114, 127–128
Gick, M. L., 371, 372, 373–374
Gildea, P. M., 290
Gilligan, S. G., 164
Gillis, 382
Gilovich, T., 399
Ginsburg, H., 453
Girgus, J. S., 117
Giudice, S., 459
Gladwin, T., 247, 485
Glaser, R., 374, 377
Glass, A. L., 138
Gleitman, H., 259
Gleitman, L. R., 259
Glenberg, A. M., 171, 186, 248
Glick, J., 17, 484, 485
Glisky, M. L., 223
Glucksberg, S., 194, 285, 318, 319, 328
Gobet, F., 377
Goddard, H., 485
Godden, D. R., 205
Goggin, J. P., 307, 322
Goldman-Rakic, P. S., 459
Goldsmith, M., 171
Goldsmith, R., 129, 130
Gonon, M. A., 239
Goodenough, F. L., 321
Goodnow, J. J., 423
Gopher, D., 98
Gordon, B., 278
Gordon, D., 332
Gottfried, A. W., 443
Grady, C. L., 149, 167
Graesser, A. C., 341
Graf, P., 157, 175, 461
Gray, J. A., 93
Gray, W. D., 262
Graydon, J., 98
Green, F. L., 450
Greenberg, R., 200
Greeno, J. G., 355, 358, 359
Greenough, W. T., 29
Greenwald, A. G., 165, 206
Gregory, M., 83
Gregory, R. L., 117, 136
Grice, H. P., 332, 334
Griffith, B. C., 293
Griggs, R. A., 408, 409
Grigorenko, E. L., 487, 491, 501
Groen, G. J., 452
Grossman, L., 184
Grosz, B. J., 337
Grotzer, T. A., 501
Gruber, H., 17, 386
Guilford, J. P., 384, 475, 476, 504

Haber, R. N., 156, 159
Haden, P. E., 175
Hagen, E. P., 472
Haier, R. J., 44, 483
Hakuta, K., 322, 323
Hall, E. T., 330
Hall, L. K., 163, 164, 307, 322
Halpin, J. A., 164
Hammond, K. M., 235, 239, 241
Hamond, N. R., 174
Handel, S., 411
Hardy, J. K., 243
Harris, J. R., 138
Harris, K. S., 293
Harsch, N., 204
Harter, N., 74
Hasher, L., 169
Hastie, R., 403
Haviland, S. E., 341
Hawking, S., 382, 383
Haxby, J. V., 149, 167
Hayes, J. R., 351, 360, 369
Hayes-Roth, B., 243
Hazen, K., 483
He, Z., 88
Healy, A. F., 328

Heaton, J. M., 149
Hebb, D., 11–12, 169
Hedges, L. V., 453
Hefley, E. F., 460
Hegarty, M., 352
Hegel, G., 3, 23, 446
Heindel, W. C., 177
Helmholtz, H. L. F. von, 136, 375
Henley, N. M., 262
Hennessey, B. A., 385
Henriksen, L., 103
Henry, O. (W. S. Porter), 336, 337
Heron, A., 445
Herrnstein, R., 503
Hertzog, C., 455
Herz, R. S., 182
Hesse, M., 328
Heuer, F., 217
Heywood, C., 90
Hickling, A. K., 455
Hill, C. T., 335
Hillger, L. A., 16, 217
Hillyard, S. A., 84, 103, 343
Hinton, G. E., 226, 235
Hintzman, D. L., 163
Hippocrates, 28
Hirsh-Pasek, K., 308
Hirst, W., 97, 100, 101
Hirtle, S. C., 235, 243, 246, 247
Hitch, G. J., 166
Hochberg, J., 119
Hofer, S. M., 462
Hoffding, H., 129
Hoffman, C., 321, 322
Hoffman, H. S., 293
Hogan, H. P., 223, 224
Holland, J. H., 420, 500
Holt, J., 452
Holyoak, K. J., 358, 371, 372, 373–374, 379, 408, 409, 420, 422, 425, 500
Honzik, C. H., 242, 243
Horn, J. L., 460, 462, 476
Hortigan, H., 359
Horwitz, B., 149, 167
Houle, S., 135
Howard, D., 298
Hoyer, W., 461
Hubbard, T. L., 128
Hubel, D. H., 41, 87, 90, 133, 134, 135
Hughlings-Jackson, J., 345
Hultsch, D. F., 461
Humphreys, G., 87, 88, 98
Humphreys, L. G., 433
Humphreys, M., 169
Hunt, E. B., 172, 310, 318, 339, 356, 359, 379, 477, 479–480
Huntsman, L. A., 226, 228
Huttenlocher, J., 411, 453

Inhelder, B., 442
Intons-Peterson, M. J., 196, 217, 234, 236, 238. *See also* Peterson, M. J.
Izquierdo, I., 35

Jackendoff, R., 302
Jackson, A., 501
Jacobson, R. R., 177
James, W., 7, 23, 68
Jamis, M., 202
Janis, I. L., 420
Jefferson, G., 334
Jenkins, J. J., 486
Jensen, A. R., 477, 478, 479
Jernigan, T. L., 177
Johnson, D. M., 262
Johnson, D. R., 321
Johnson, J. S., 323
Johnson, M. K., 169, 182, 201, 203, 318, 328
Johnson-Laird, P. N., 236, 237, 250, 340, 341, 404, 406, 416–417
Johnston, J. C., 96, 146
Jolicoeur, P., 225, 226, 228, 229, 236
Jones, R., 375, 384, 385
Jones, S. S., 321
Jonides, J., 247
Joram, E., 377
Jordan, K., 226, 228
Juola, J. F., 195
Jusczyk, P. W., 294, 303, 304
Just, M. A., 144, 228

Kagan, J., 433
Kahneman, D., 97, 392, 395, 397, 398, 399, 400, 401, 402, 404
Kail, R. V., 444, 450, 453, 454
Kalish, C. W., 425
Kamin, L., 485
Kandel, E. R., 78
Kant, I., 5, 23
Kaplan, C. A., 375
Kaplan, E., 339
Kapur, S., 135
Karlin, M. B., 201, 318
Karni, A., 186
Kasparov, G., 12
Katz, A. N., 164
Katz, J. J., 256
Kaufman, J. L., 491
Kausler, D. H., 462
Kay, P., 320
Keane, M. T., 9, 168, 236, 397
Kearins, J. M., 452
Keating, D. P., 310, 486
Keele, S. W., 129, 130, 131, 184
Keenan, J., 340
Keenan, J. M., 164
Keil, F. C., 256, 259, 263, 321, 456
Keller, E., 334
Keller, H., 284, 295
Kellman, P. J., 142
Kennedy, C. B., 433
Keppel, G., 197, 198
Kerr, N., 237
Ketcham, K., 202, 203
Keysar, B., 328
Kihlstrom, J. F., 165, 223
Kim, I. J., 229
Kimura, D., 343
Kintsch, W., 339, 340
Kirby, K. N., 409
Kirker, W. S., 164
Kirsner, K., 194
Klein, K. L., 149
Klein, S. B., 165
Kliegl, R., 455, 461, 462
Knapp, J. R., 476
Knowlton, B. J., 177
Koenig, O., 231
Koffka, K., 123
Köhler, S., 135
Köhler, W., 11, 123, 127, 365
Kolb, B., 53, 54, 148, 342, 345
Kolodner, J. L., 201
Komatsu, L. K., 258, 263, 264
Koriat, A., 171
Kosslyn, S. M., 16, 217, 225, 229, 230, 231, 232, 233, 234, 235, 236, 237, 250, 454
Kotovsky, K., 360, 369, 493
Kozlowski, L., 139
Kramer, D. A., 446
Krampe, R. T., 461
Krantz, L., 398
Krechevsky, M., 501
Kremer, K. E., 455
Kreuz, R. J., 341
Kuhl, P. K., 292
Kuiper, N. A., 164
Kulik, J., 204
Kutas, M., 343

LaBerge, D., 74, 84
Labouvie-Vief, G., 446, 461
LaCasse, L., 483

Ladavas, E., 103
Ladeforged, P., 289
Lajoie, S., 379
Lakoff, G., 332
Lally, M., 478
Landau, B., 321
Langer, E. J., 75
Langlais, P. J., 177
Langley, P., 365, 375, 384, 385, 499
Langston, C., 409
Lansman, M., 480
Lanze, M., 138
Larkin, J. H., 353, 377, 482
Larson, G. E., 483
Lashley, K. S., 11, 12, 54, 176, 482
Lau, I., 321
Lazar, I., 501
Lederer, R., 290
LeDoux, J. E., 56
Lehman, D., 420
Leicht, K. L., 186
Leiman, A. L., 28
Lempert, R., 403, 420
Lennie, P., 134
Lesch, M. F., 144
Lesgold, A. M., 195, 377, 379, 380
Levine, D. N., 239
Levinson, K. L., 149
Levy, J., 56
Lewis, J., 310
Lewis, M., 374, 433
Liberman, A. M., 292, 293, 294
Lichtenstein, S., 403
Lindem, K., 248
Lindsay, D. S., 203
Linnoila, M., 177
Lipman, M., 501
Lishman, W. A., 177
Livingstone, M., 90
Locke, J., 5
Locke, J. L., 305
Lockhart, R. S., 164
Loebell, H., 297, 302, 327
Loftus, E. F., 163, 202, 203, 262, 270, 318
Loftus, G. R., 163
Logan, G., 74
London, M., 411
Lonner, W. J., 318
Lopez, A., 425
Lou, H. C., 103
Love, T., 172
Lubart, T. I., 387
Luce, P. A., 292
Luchins, A. S., 369, 370
Luck, S. J., 103
Lucy, P., 328
Lunneborg, C., 310
Luria, A. R., 148, 172, 238, 375
Lurito, J. T., 229
Lyons, J., 328

MacDonald, J., 294
Mace, W. M., 128
Macko, K. A., 87
Mackworth, N. H., 83
MacLeod, C., 99, 479
Maddieson, I., 289
Maercker, A., 463
Magalhües, V. P., 487
Mair, R. G., 177
Maisog, J. M., 149
Malgady, R., 328
Malpass, R. S., 202
Malt, B. C., 256
Mandel, R. J., 177
Mandler, G., 175
Mandler, J. M., 444
Mangun, G. R., 84, 103
Mani, K., 237
Manktelow, K. I., 409
Mantyla, T., 206
Marcel, A. J., 70, 72, 104
Marcus, D., 321
Marentette, P. F., 305
Markman, E. M., 311, 455, 456
Marmor, G. S., 453
Marr, D., 17, 140, 141, 142
Marston, S. P., 164
Martin, J. A., 304
Martin, L., 318
Martin, M., 131
Mascolo, M. F., 235, 246
Mason, H. F., 164
Massaro, D. W., 292, 294
Masson, M. E. J., 144
Matarazzo, J. D., 482
Mateer, C., 344
Matlin, M. W., 205
Mattingly, I. G., 294
Mayr, U., 455, 461, 462
McArthur, T., 326
McCall, R. B., 433
McCann, R. S., 96
McCarthy, J. E., 130, 131
McClelland, J. L., 49, 145, 146, 170, 187, 275, 276, 277, 278, 293
McCloskey, M., 202–203, 204, 278
McCormick, C. B., 164
McCormick, D. A., 177
McDermott, J., 353, 377, 482
McDermott, K. B., 203
McDonald, J. E., 145
McGarry-Roberts, P. A., 482
McGrane, P. A., 501
McGregor, S., 501
McGurk, H., 294
McKenna, J., 202
McKeown, M. G., 339
McKinley, S. C., 258
McKoon, G., 169, 170, 244, 274, 275, 341
McLeod, P., 90
McNamara, T. P., 243, 244, 275
McNaughton, B. C., 49, 187, 278
McNaughton, B. L., 187
McNeil, J. E., 149
Meacham, J. A., 463, 464
Medin, D. L., 258, 425
Medina, J. H., 35
Mehler, J., 304
Meier, R. P., 307
Menna, R., 459
Merrill, M. A., 472
Mervis, C. B., 257, 258, 262
Metcalfe, J., 366, 367
Metzler, J., 225, 228, 235
Meyer, D. E., 16, 145, 147, 274
Meyer, M., 248
Miezin, F. M., 102
Mill, J. S., 422
Miller, D. G., 202
Miller, G. A., 13, 162, 279, 290, 328
Miller, R. A., 498
Mills, C. J., 164
Milner, B., 174, 176, 238, 272
Minsky, M., 494
Mintun, M., 62, 145
Mirmiran, N., 461, 462
Mishkin, M., 87, 177
Mitchell, R. F., 479
Montie, J. E., 433
Moray, N., 93, 95, 96
Morey, R., 297, 302, 327
Mori, M., 32, 482
Morris, C. D., 165
Morrison, T., 382, 383
Morton, J., 145
Morton, T. U., 335
Moscovitch, M., 135, 206
Moshman, E., 463
Mozart, W., 382
Müller, J., 28
Murdock, B. B., Jr., 196
Murray, C., 503
Murray, J., 228

Myers, J., 498

Näätänen, R., 102–103
Nadel, L., 177
Nakayama, K., 88
Naren, L., 452
Nathan, P. W., 173
Naus, M. J., 194
Naveh-Benjamin, M., 162
Navon, D., 98, 131
Nazzi, T., 304
Neimark, E. D., 445
Neisser, U., 12, 13, 96, 97, 100, 101, 129, 171, 174, 204, 503
Nelson, K., 305
Nelson, T. O., 185, 452
Neto, F., 370
Nettelbeck, T., 477, 478, 480, 489
Neumann, P. G., 130
Newell, A., 13, 267, 268, 356, 358, 361, 379, 482, 493–494
Newport, E. L., 307, 308, 323
Newsome, S. L., 145
Nightingale, N. N., 503
Nigro, G., 328, 374
Nisbett, R. E., 399, 408, 409, 420, 422, 425, 500
Nixon, S. J., 177
Norman, D. A., 75, 76, 84, 95, 104, 158, 162, 190, 198, 225, 242
Nosofsky, R. M., 258
Nusbaum, H. C., 292
Nyberg, L., 167, 177, 345

Obler, L., 324
O'Brien, D. P., 408, 409
Obusek, C. J., 292
Ogbu, J. U., 502
Ojemann, G. A., 324, 344, 345
Okagaki, L., 501
Oliver, L. M., 408, 420
Olson, R. K., 382
O'Reilly, A. W., 456
O'Reilly, R. C., 49, 187, 278
Ornstein, P. A., 194
Ortony, A., 264, 328
Oscanyan, F. S., 501
Osherson, D. N., 397, 401, 425
Osman, A., 460
Over, D. E., 409
Overton, R., 186
Overton, W., 321
Oyama, S., 323

Paap, K. R., 145
Paavilainen, P., 103
Paivio, A., 218, 225, 249
Palmer, J., 84
Palmer, J. C., 318
Palmer, S. E., 126, 138, 139
Palmeri, T. J., 258
Pani, J. R., 16, 217
Pantle, A. J., 187
Paradis, M., 323, 324
Park, Y. S., 444, 454
Parker, K., 71
Parkin, A. J., 177
Parkman, J. M., 452
Parsons, O. A., 177
Pascual-Leone, J., 446
Pashler, H., 98, 101
Pavlov, I., 9, 24
Payne, J., 396
Pearlstone, Z., 195
Pellegrino, J. W., 453
Pellizzer, G., 230
Penfield, W., 163, 168, 345
Penrod, S., 202
Penrod, S. D., 202
Peplau, L. A., 335
Perfetti, C. A., 147, 339
Perkins, D., 365, 501
Perlmutter, D., 298
Perlmutter, M., 461
Peronnet, F., 235, 239
Petersen, S. E., 44, 62, 102, 103, 145, 274, 345
Peterson, L. R., 196
Peterson, M. A., 223, 224, 225, 235
Peterson, M. J., 196. *See also* Intons-Peterson, M. J.
Petitto, L., 305
Petri, H. L., 177
Petrides, M., 229
Phelps, E., 186
Piaget, J., 264, 433, 435–443, 444–445, 446, 447, 448, 449, 456, 457, 459, 464
Pianta, R. C., 502
Pichert, J. W., 341
Pike, R., 169
Pinker, S., 212, 223, 234, 296, 297, 308
Pisoni, D. B., 292
Plato, 4–5, 23
Poincaré, H., 375
Polio, M. V., 113
Pollack, M. E., 337
Pollard, P., 420
Pollatsek, A., 143, 144, 147
Pomerantz, J. R., 138, 217
Poon, L. W., 460
Pople, H., 498
Porter, W. S. *See* Henry, O. (W. S. Porter)
Posner, M. I., 42, 44, 62, 72, 84, 91, 101, 102, 103, 129, 130, 131, 145, 147, 184, 274, 479
Potts, G. R., 164
Powell, C., 501
Powell, J. S., 339, 433
Presson, C. C., 453
Pribram, K. H., 13, 279
Puff, C. R., 164
Pullum, G. K., 318
Pylyshyn, Z. W., 219

Quillian, M. R., 260, 261

Rabbitt, P. M. A., 478, 480
Rabinowitz, J. C., 138
Raeburn, V. P., 194
Raichle, M. E., 42, 44, 62, 101, 102, 145, 274
Rapoport, S., 167
Rappaport, S. L., 149
Ratcliff, R., 169, 170, 244, 274, 275, 278, 341
Ratliff, F., 115
Raye, C. L., 203
Rayner, K., 143, 144, 147
Read, J. D., 203
Reason, J., 76, 77
Reaves, C. C., 101
Reber, P. J., 177
Reed, S. K., 129, 220, 235, 355, 360
Reed, T. E., 478, 503
Reeder, G. D., 164
Rees, E., 377
Regehr, G., 71
Reicher, G. M., 145
Reimann, P., 374
Reisberg, D., 217, 220, 221, 223, 235
Reiser, B. J., 233, 235, 409
Reitman, J. S., 198, 200–201, 377
Remez, R. E., 295
Rescorla, R. A., 9
Resnick, L. B., 452
Rice, M. L., 309
Richardson-Klavehn, A., 169
Riegel, K. F., 446
Riggs, L. A., 115
Rinders, R. J., 177
Rips, L. J., 259, 262, 408, 409, 410, 427
Roazzi, A., 487
Robbins, T. W., 167
Roberts, A. C., 167

Roberts, L., 345
Robertson, D. A., 461
Rock, I., 136
Rodman, R., 289, 303, 326
Roediger, H. L., 157, 188, 191, 203
Rogers, T. B., 164
Rogoff, B., 452
Romero, R. D., 101
Rosch, E. H., 257, 258, 262
Rose, P. M., 223
Rosenzweig, M. R., 28, 461, 463
Ross, B. H., 258, 296
Ross, L., 399
Ross, M., 400
Roth, S. F., 147
Rothbart, R., 185
Rovee-Collier, C., 202, 205
Rubenstein, B. S., 186, 187
Rubin, Z., 335
Rudorfer, M. V., 177
Rumain, B., 408, 409
Rumelhart, D. E., 145, 146, 170, 225, 242, 264, 275, 276, 277
Russell, J. A., 243
Russell, W., 238
Russell, W. R., 173
Rybash, J. M., 461
Ryle, G., 212
Rypma, B., 455

Saarinen, T., 235, 245
Sabini, J. P., 420
Sacks, H., 334
Sagi, D., 186, 187
Salmon, D. P., 177
Salthouse, T. A., 461, 462
Samuel, A. G., 293
Samuel, A. L., 493
Samuels, S. J., 74, 380
Sandson, J., 145
Sapir, E., 317
Sarason, S. B., 485
Sato, S., 87
Sattler, J. M., 472
Saults, J. S., 462
Scaggs, W. E., 187
Scardamalia, M., 377
Schacter, D. L., 49, 157, 167, 168, 175, 176, 177, 186
Schaeken, W., 416, 417
Schafer, K., 177
Schaffer, H. R., 304
Schaie, K. W., 460, 461
Schank, R. C., 265
Schegloff, E. A., 334
Schell, D. A., 461
Schliemann, A. D., 487
Schmidt, H., 90
Schmidt, S. R., 204
Schneider, W., 72, 83, 452
Schoenfeld, A. H., 354, 379
Schonfield, D., 461
Schooler, J. W., 203, 318
Schustack, M. W., 423
Schvaneveldt, R. W., 16, 145, 147, 274
Schwartz, A. B., 229
Schweickert, R., 162
Scoville, W. B., 174
Searle, J. R., 328, 330, 332, 500
Segalowitz, S. J., 459
Seger, C., 16, 217
Sejnowski, T. J., 29
Selfridge, O. G., 129, 131, 132
Selkoe, P. J., 30
Sells, S. B., 415
Sera, M. D., 320–321
Sereno, S. C., 144
Servan-Schreiber, D., 101
Shafir, E. B., 401, 425
Shallice, T., 16, 176
Shankweiler, D. P., 292, 294
Shapiro, P., 202
Shapley, R., 134
Sharp, A. M., 501
Sharp, D. W., 17, 484
Shaw, G. B., 143
Shaw, J. C., 13, 493, 494
Shaywitz, B. A., 343
Shepard, R. N., 128, 225, 228, 230, 235, 247, 453
Shiffrin, R., 72, 158, 198, 382
Shimamura, A. P., 177
Shipley, T. F., 142
Shoben, E. J., 168, 259, 262
Shortliffe, E. H., 498
Shrager, J., 452
Shulman, G. L., 102, 145
Shulman, H. G., 184
Sicoly, F., 400
Sidner, C. L., 337
Siegel, B., 44, 483
Siegler, R. S., 305, 412, 444, 450, 452, 453
Sigman, M. D., 433
Silverman, I., 144, 247
Simon, D. P., 353, 377, 482
Simon, H. A., 13, 203, 267, 268, 279, 353, 355, 356, 358, 359, 360, 361, 365, 369, 377, 379, 395, 477, 482, 493, 494, 499
Simon, T., 470–471, 472
Simonton, D. K., 386
Sincoff, J. B., 310
Skinner, B. F., 10, 12, 24
Slobin, D. I., 308
Sloboda, J. A., 380
Sloman, S. A., 426, 445
Slovic, P., 393, 403, 404
Slowiaczek, L. M., 292
Smilansky, B., 503
Smith, C., 187
Smith, E. E., 257, 258, 259, 262, 401, 409, 425
Smith, J., 463
Smith, J. D., 217
Smith, L. B., 321, 445
Smith, S. M., 375, 384, 385
Snow, C. E., 304
Snow, D., 228
Snyder, C. R. R., 72, 84, 147
Sodian, B., 455
Solso, R., 130, 131
Somberg, B. L., 462
Sommer, R., 330
Sonenshine, M., 217
Spalding, T. L., 258, 296
Spear, N. E., 174
Spearman, C., 475, 476, 504
Spelke, E., 97, 99, 100, 101
Sperling, G., 159–160, 161
Sperry, R. W., 54, 56, 239
Spooner, W., 326, 327
Springer, S. P., 53
Squire, L. R., 35, 167, 169, 176, 177, 185, 272
Stacy, E. W., 138
Standing, L., 156
Stanovich, K. E., 147, 380, 382
Stark, H. A., 175
Staudinger, U. M., 463
Steedman, M., 416
Steele, C., 502
Stein, B. S., 351
Stelmack, R. M., 482
Stenhouse, D., 34
Stern, D., 304
Stern, W., 471
Sternberg, R. J., 203, 280, 282, 310, 311, 328, 339, 351, 353, 363, 368, 374, 380, 387, 412, 423, 425, 426, 433, 444, 445, 450, 463, 469, 480–481, 482, 484, 487, 489, 490, 491, 501, 503, 504
Sternberg, S., 192, 193, 194, 195
Stevens, A., 235, 245

Stevens, K. N., 292
Sticht, T., 292
Stough, C., 478
Stroop, J. R., 99
Studdert-Kennedy, M., 292, 294
Suengas, A. G., 203
Suh, S., 341
Suppes, P., 452
Sussman, A. L., 230
Swaab, D. F., 461

Tanaka, J. R., 149
Tanaka, J. W., 262
Tang, C., 44, 483
Tanne, D., 186, 187
Tannen, D., 335
Tardif, T., 166
Taylor, H., 248
Taylor, M., 262
Taylor, R., 184
Teder, W., 103
Tees, R. L., 305
Terman, L. M., 472
Teuber, H. L., 174, 176
Thagard, P. R., 420, 500
Thatcher, R. W., 459, 460
Theeuwes, J., 85
Thelan, E., 445
Thomas, J. C., 355
Thompson, R. F., 177
Thompson, W. L., 229
Thomson, D. M., 205
Thomson, N., 162
Thorndike, E. L., 8–9, 24
Thorndike, R. L., 472
Thorndyke, P. W., 243, 244, 264
Thurstone, L. L., 229, 475, 476, 487, 504
Thurstone, T. G., 229
Tiitinen, H., 103
Tinklenberg, J. R., 103
Titchener, E., 6
Tkacz, S., 194
Tolman, E. C., 10, 24, 242, 243
Torff, B., 491
Torrance, E. P., 383, 384
Tourangeau, R., 328
Townsend, J. T., 194
Trabasso, T., 341, 444
Treadway, M., 202, 278
Treisman, A. M., 85, 86, 87, 90, 94–95, 96, 97
Trevarthen, C., 56
Tsushima, T., 304
Tulving, E., 49, 164, 165, 168, 169, 175, 188, 195, 205
Turing, A. M., 492
Turner, A. M., 29
Turner, T. J., 265, 266
Tversky, A., 392, 395, 397, 398, 399, 400, 401, 402, 404
Tversky, B., 235, 244, 245, 248

Underhill, W. A., 205
Underwood, B. J., 197, 198, 200
Ungerleider, L. G., 87, 149, 167
Usher, J. A., 174

Vallone, R., 399
Van Daalen-Kapteijns, M., 339
Van Dijk, T. A., 177, 328, 339, 340
Van Essen, D. C., 135
Van Gogh, V., 382
VanLehn, K., 268, 380
Van Patten, C., 343
Van Selst, M., 226
Vernon, M. C., 455
Vernon, P. A., 32, 482, 483, 504
Vernon, P. E., 475, 477
Vicente, K. J., 377
Vielvoye, G. J., 177
Voltaire, 295
Von Someren, E. J. W., 461
Vygotsky, L. S., 322, 433, 446–448, 449, 464

Wagner, A. R., 9
Wagner, D. A., 486
Wagner, R. K., 380, 382, 503
Wagner, W. J., 459
Walker, R. A., 459
Walter, A. A., 223, 224
Wambold, C., 451
Ward, L. M., 243
Warren, R. M., 292, 293
Warren, R. P., 292, 293
Warrington, E. K., 16, 149, 175, 176, 272
Warrington, E. K., 149
Wason, P., 404, 406, 407
Wasow, T., 298, 300, 302
Wasserman, D., 403
Watkins, M. J., 205
Watson, J., 9, 11, 24, 432
Watson, O. M., 330
Waugh, N. C., 158, 162, 198
Weaver, C. A., 204
Wechsler, D., 472
Wedderburn, A. A. I., 93
Weil, E. M., 412
Weiller, C., 342
Weingartner, H., 103, 177
Weisberg, R. W., 365, 384
Weiskrantz, L., 72, 148, 167, 175
Weisstein, N., 138
Weizenbaum, J., 496, 497
Wellman, H. M., 450, 451, 456
Welton, K. E., Jr., 129, 130
Werker, J. F., 305
Werner, H., 339
Wernicke, C., 54, 62, 342
Wertheimer, M., 11, 123, 365
West, R. L., 461
Wheeler, D. D., 145
Whishaw, I. Q., 53, 54, 148, 342, 345
Whitaker, H. A., 324
Whorf, B. L., 317
Wible, C. G., 204
Wickens, D. D., 184
Wickett, J. C., 32, 483
Widner, S. C., 370
Wiebe, D., 366, 367
Wiesel, T. N., 41, 87, 133, 134, 135
Wilcox, B. L., 451
Wilkie, O., 425
Williams, J. E., 370
Williams, M., 149
Willis, S. L., 461, 462
Wilson, C., 480
Wilson, K. D., 149
Wilson, M., 217
Wilson, M. A., 187
Winkler, I., 103
Winocur, G., 135
Winograd, T., 494–495
Winzenz, D., 195
Wissler, C., 470
Wittgenstein, L., 256
Wittlinger, R. P., 163, 461
Wolfe, J. M., 89, 90, 98
Wolkowitz, O. M., 103
Woods, S. S., 452
Woodworth, R. S., 415
Wundt, W., 6

Yantis, S., 84, 85, 98
Young, R., 489
Yu, V. L., 498

Zaidel, E., 56
Zaitchik, D., 455
Zaragoza, M. S., 202
Zeidner, M., 502
Zigler, E., 501
Zihl, J., 90
Zinchenko, P. I., 164
Zola-Morgan, S. M., 176, 177
Zurif, E. B., 342
Zytkow, J. M., 365, 499

Subject Index

Abilities, as indirect speech act, 332, 333
Ablation, 54
Abstract ideas, 4
Abstract reasoning, 58
Accessibility, 196
Accommodation, 436, 437
Acetylcholine (Ach), 34, 35, 36
Acoustic confusability, 183
Acoustic information, encoding of, 184–185
Acoustic processing, 164, 165
Acquired characteristics, 4
Acquired skill, expertise and, 380–382
Acronyms, 188, 189, 190
Acrostics, 188, 189, 190
ACT (adaptive control of thought model), 268–272
ACT*, 269, 270
Action, communication of, 317
Action potential, 31–32
Activated memory, 170
Activation, 270–271
  priming effect and, 274
Adaptation
  perception and, 123
  sensory, 78
Additive bilingualism, 322
Adjacency pairs, 334
Adulthood. *See also* Age
  cognitive development in, 460–464
Advance organizer, for memory, 154–155
Affections, 6
Afferent neurons. *See* Sensory (afferent) neurons
Affixes, 289
Age. *See also* Adulthood; Children
  cognitive development and, 460–464
  and information-processing, 480
  language acquisition and, 322–323
  mental rotation and, 453–454
  wisdom and, 463–464
Agnosia, 148–149
Agrammatic aphasics, 298
AI. *See* Artificial intelligence (AI)
Alcohol, memory and, 177
Algorithms, 356
Alignment heuristic, 245
Allophones, 289
All or none law, 31–32
Alphanumeric symbols, 453–454
Alzheimer's disease, 30, 177, 461
  neurotransmitters and, 34
  postmortem exams and, 41
Ambiguous figures, 220–221, 222, 223
American Sign Language (ASL), 307, 308
Amino-acid neurotransmitters, 34, 35
Amino acids, 35
Amnesia, 173–176, 177
  anterograde, 174
  disruption of consolidation in, 185–186
  and explicity-implicit memory distinction, 174–175
  infantile, 174
  neuropsychology and, 175–176
  retrograde, 173–174
Amnesics, 157
Amygdala, 49, 50
Analogical imagery
  limitations of, 220–223
  pictures and, 214–215, 216
  vs. symbols, 218–219
Analogies
  componential analysis of, 481
  intentional transfer and, 374
  reasoning by, 426
  transfer of, 371–374
Analysis, 353
Analytical information processing, 56
Anatomy, 28
Anatomy of brain. *See* Brain; cerebral hemispheres
Anchoring-and-adjustment heuristic, 401–402
Angiograms, 42
Animal research
  by behaviorists, 9–10
  insight in primates, 365, 366
  on localization of function, 54
  of Pavlov, 9
  rats, bees, and cognitive maps, 242–243
  in vivo of brain, 41–42
Anterograde amnesia, 174
  Korsakoff's syndrome and, 177
Anthropology, 11
Anticipation, slips of the tongue and, 326
Antithesis, 3
Ape insight. *See* Chimpanzee
Aphasia, 53–54
  agrammatic, 298
Applied vs. basic research, 21
Arbitrarily symbolic property of language, 285–286
Arguments. *See also* Reasoning
  modus ponens, 405, 407, 409
  modus tollens, 405, 407–408, 409
Aristotelian approach, 4
Arousal, 78
Artificial intelligence (AI), 12, 17, 20, 255, 264, 491–501
  ELIZA and PARRY psychotherapy programs, 496, 497
  General Problem Solver (GPS) and, 494
  intelligence of programs and, 499–501
  intelligence vs. appearance of intelligence and, 500–501
  Logic Theorist (LT) and, 493–494
  SHRDLU and, 494–495
ASL. *See* American Sign Language (ASL)
Assessment environment, 448
Assimilation, 436, 437
Association areas, 62
Associationism, 8–9
Associative stage, 271
Associative system, reasoning and, 427
Atmosphere bias, 415
Attention, 68, 80–91
  cognitive neuroscientific approaches to, 101–104
  and consciousness, 68–80
  divided, 80, 98–101
  functions of, 81
  perception and, 104
  Posner's theory of, 102
  selective, 91–101
  signal, 80
  signal-detection theory and, 82
  vigilance and, 81, 83–84, 102
Attentional deficits, 103
Attentional hint, 224
Attentional-resource theories of selective attention, 97–98
Attenuation model of attention, 94–95
Audition, 115
Auditory perceptions, visual perceptions and, 294
Auditory processing, 58
Auditory region of brain, 60
Autoimmune diseases, multiple sclerosis as, 29

Automatic behaviors, 72
Automatic processes, controlled processes and, 72–76
Automatization, 74–76, 271, 380
Autonomous stage, 271
Availability, 195–196
Availability heuristic, 400–401
Awareness. *See* Attention; Consciousness
Axon, 29

Babbling, 305
Backup strategy, 453
Backward visual masking, 162
"Bacon" programs, 500
Balanced bilinguals, 322
Bandwidth-fidelity programs, 498
Basal ganglia, 47, 49
 memory and, 177
Base rates, 399
Basic level, 262
Basic research, vs. applied research, 21
Bayes's theorem, 397
Behavior, automatic, 72
Behavioral methods, vs. biological methods, 21
Behaviorism, 9–10
 "black box" of human mind and, 10
 Skinner and, 10
 Watson and, 9–10
Beliefs, 245
Belief systems, ELIZA and PARRY psychotherapy programs and, 496, 497
Bell Curve, The (Herrnstein and Murray), 503
Between-item elaboration, 165
Bias
 atmosphere, 415
 confirmation, 420, 423
 in deductive reasoning, 420
 heuristics and, 397–404
 hindsight, 403–404
Bilingualism, 322
 selective attention and, 94, 95
Bilinguals, 322
Binaural presentation, 92
Binocular depth cues, 119–121, **120**, 122
 convergence, 121, 122
 disparity, 121, 122
Biological bases of intelligence, 482–484
Biological psychology. *See* Psychobiology
Biological vs. behavioral methods, 21
Biopsychology. *See* Psychobiology
Birds, typicality ratings for, 257
"Black box" of human mind, 10
Blind persons, visual images and, 237–238
Block world, of SHRDLU, 495
Blood–brain barrier, 38
Blood flow, in brain, during verbal tasks, 345
Bodily-kinesthetic intelligence, 488
Boolean operators, 416
Bottleneck, attentional, 95–96
Bottom-up theories (direct perception), 127–136
 categorical inferences and, 425
Bounded rationality, 395
 elimination by aspects and, 395
Brain, 38. *See also* Attention; Biological bases of intelligence; Central nervous system (CNS); Event-related potentials (ERPs); Nervous system; Neurons; Psychobiological research
 animal studies of, 41–42
 association areas of, 62
 cerebral cortex of, 52–62
 cognitive development and, 458–460
 development of, 48
 electrical recordings of, 42
 forebrain, 47, 48, 49–51
 function of, 38
 Hebb and, 11
 hemispheres of, 53–62
 hindbrain, 47, 48, 50, 52
 hippocampus, memory, and, 176–178
 knowledge models based on, 272–275
 language processing in, 342–345
 lateralization of function and, 238–239
 learning and, 11–12
 memory and, 176
 metabolic imaging of, 44–46
 midbrain, 48, 50, 51, 57
 mind and, 28
 neural networks in developing, 458
 postmortem studies of, 41
 REM sleep, memory, and, 187
 single system vs. dual-system hypotheses and, 323–324
 static imaging techniques of, 42–44
 structures and functions of, 46–62
 viewing structures and functions of, 40–46
 weight of, 52
Brain stem, 65
Brain-wave activity, 42
Brain waves, developmental changes in, 459
Bridging inference, 341
Brief memory, 176
Broadbent model, of selective attention, 93, 94
Broca's area, 41, 53–54, 55, 62, 342
Brown-Peterson paradigm, 196

Canons, heuristic principles as, 422
Carnegie-Mellon University, AI work at, 494
Cartesian rationalism, 4
Case's theory, of cognitive development, 434
Case studies, 17, 18, 19
Categorical clustering, 188, 189
Categorical inferences, 425–426
Categorical perception of speech sounds, **293**
Categorical syllogisms, 412–419
 types of premises for, 414
Category, **255**
 concepts and, 256–259
 feature-based, 256–257
Cattell's hierarchical model, 477
Causal inferences, 422–425
 vs. ecological validity, 21
Cell assemblies, 11
Cells
 in nervous system, 29
 simple and complex, 134
Central executive, 166
Central nervous system (CNS), 36–38, **37**
 maturation of, and cognitive development, 458–460
Central processing unit (CPU), 276
Centration, **438**, 439
Cerebellum, 47, 50, 52
 memory and, 177
Cerebral asymmetry, 239
Cerebral cortex, 47, 50, 52–62
 association areas of, 62
 memory and, 176
Cerebral hemispheres, **53**
 language processing in brain and, 343–344
 lateralization of function and, 239
 lobes of, 57–62
 specialization in, 53–56
Characteristic features, **257**
Chemicals, in neurotransmission, 34–35
Chess game
 Deep Blue computer and, 493

expertise in, 377, 378
Child-directed speech, 309
Child rearing practices, intelligence and, 502–503
Children. *See also* Cognitive development
inductive reasoning by, 456
language acquisition by, 304–306
neurophysiological changes in development and, 458–460
Chimeric face, 57
Chimpanzee, insight studies with, 365, 366
Chinese language, linguistic universals and, 321
"Chinese Room" problem, 500
Choice reaction time, 478–479
Choline, 34
Chronological age (CA), 471
Circle diagrams
for propositions, 418
of syllogism, 413
Classical concepts, 258
Classical conditioning, 9
Classical decision theory, 393–394
Classically conditioned responses, brain and, 177
Class inclusion, 444
Class-inclusion statements, 260
Closure, 125
CNS. *See* Central nervous system (CNS)
Coarticulation, 292
Cocktail party problem, 92
Cognition
age and, 461
in brain, 46–62
domain generality, domain specificity, and, 279–280
evolutionary view of, 410
perception and, 114
Cognitive development, 432–433, 457. *See also* Brain
in adulthood, 460–464
information-processing theorists and, 449–457
maturation and, 432
nature, nurture, and, 432
Neo-Piagetian theorists and, 445–446
neurophysiological changes in, 458–460
Piagetian theory of, 434, 435–443
principles of, 433–435
progression of, 434
Cognitive disequilibrium, 436
Cognitive economy, 261
Cognitive maps, 242
mental shortcuts and, 244–247
spatial cognition and, 242–248
text maps, 248
Cognitive monitoring, 452
Cognitive neuroscience, 28
attention, consciousness, and, 101–104
Cognitive psychology, 2–3
emergence of, 11–13
ginseng and, 36
Neisser on, 13
philosophical antecedents of, 3–5
psychological antecedents of, 5–11
research methods in, 13–20
themes in, 20–21
Tolman and, 10
Cognitive Psychology (Neisser), 12, 13
Cognitive science, 20
Cognitive stage, 271
Cognitivism, 11
Color, visual search and, 88–89
Color constancy, 137
Color naming, linguistic universals and, 320
Commissive, as speech act, 330, 331
Communication, 284
interneuronal, 32–35
Communication systems, 11
Communicative property of language, 285
Comparison view, of metaphor, 328
Competence theory, 445
Complex cells, 134
Complex problem solving, 482
Componential analysis, 480
and complex problem solving, 480–482
Components of intelligence, **480**
Composition, 271
Compound-cue model, 274–275
Comprehension, 291
based on context and point of view, 341–342
of ideas in text, 339–340
reading, 336–343
receptive, 287
verbal, 288
Comprehension monitoring, 311
Comprehension processes, 144
Computation, 11
Computational theory of perception, 140–142
Computer, 13–14
Computerized axial tomography (CT) scans, 42, 43
Computer models. *See also* Computer simulations
vs. brain-inspired models, 276–278
for information processing, 170
simulating human thought, 13
Computer simulations, 17, 20
AI and, 491–501
of expertise, 496–498
General Problem Solver (GPS) and, 494
Logic Theorist (LT), 493–494
SHRDLU and, 494–495
Turing test and, 492–493
for well-defined problems, 355–356
Concept, 255
categories and, 256–259
classical and fuzzy, 258
schematic representations and, 263–267
Conceptual information, 244–245
Conceptual-propositional hypothesis. *See* Propositional hypothesis
Conclusions. *See* Reasoning
Concrete operations, 439–442
Conditional probability, 397
Conditional reasoning, 405–410
deductively valid inferences and deductive fallacies, 406
Wason selection task and, 407, 408
Conditioned learning, 9
Conditioning
operant, 10
and speech acquisition, 310
Configural-superiority effect, 138, 139, 145
Confirmation bias, 420, 423
Conjunction fallacy, 400
Conjunction search, 85–86
Connectionist model
parallel processing and, 275–279
of reasoning, 427
Connectionist perspective on memory, 169–170
Connotation, 295
Consciousness, 69
attention and, 68–80
cognitive neuroscientific approaches to, 101–104
perception, attention, and, 104
structuralists on, 6
Conservation of quantity, **439,** 440–441
liquid quantity, 441, 442
Consolidation, 185–186

Construals, from "good" parts, 225
Constructive, 201
Constructive nature of memory, 201–203, 296
Constructive perception, 136–140
Content morphemes, 289
Context
comprehension based on, 341–342
intelligence and, 487
word meanings and, 339
Context effects, 138
on encoding and retrieval, 203–206
in infants, 205
Contextualists, 484
Contextual priming, 275
Contiguity, 8
Contingency, 9
Continuity, 125
Contour features, 140
Contralateral transmission, 53
Contrast, 8
Controlled laboratory experiments, 14–15, 16
Controlled processes, 72
automatic processes and, 72–76
Convergence, binocular, 121, 122
Convergent insight, 385
Convergent thinking, 353
Converging operation, 255
Conversational postulates, 332–334
Conversion of premises, in categorical syllogisms, 415–416
Cooing, 304
Cooperative principle, 332
Core, 259
Corpus callosum, 50, 53
Correct rejections, 82
Correlation, 15
and causal inferences, 425
Correspondence metaphor of memory, 171
Cortex, 58
cerebral, 47
language processing and, 345
primary motor, 58
primary somatosensory, 59
Covariation information, and causal inferences, 425
Cranial nerves, 36
Creativity, 382–387
defined, 383
external factors and, 385–386
integrated view of characteristics, 386–387
personality and, 385
tests of, 384
Creole, 325
Critical periods, language acquisition and, 307
Cross-cultural studies, stereotypes and, 370
Cross-sectional research designs, cognition in adults and, 461
Crystallized intelligence, 460–461, 477
CT scans. *See* Computerized axial tomography (CT) scans
Cued recall, 155, 156
Cues, 273
Culture
intelligence and, 484–487
linguistic universals and, 320
memory and, 452
Culture-fair test, **485**–**486**
Culture-relevant tests, **486**

Data-driven theories, 127
Data gathering, 13
Deaf children, ASL and, 309
Decay, 185, **196**–201
Decay theory, 200–201
Decision making. *See also* Probability
heuristics, bias, and, 397–404
judgment and, 393–404
Decision theory, 393–394
Declaration, as speech act, 331–332
Declarative information, consolidation of, 185
Declarative knowledge, 155, 175, **212**
integrative models for representing, 268–272
and nondeclarative knowledge, 272–273
organization of, 255–267
Declarative memory. *See* Explicit memory
Declarative network model, 270
Decoding, of language input, 287
Decompositional approach, 123
Deductive reasoning, 404, 405–420
aids and obstacles to, 419–420
conditional reasoning and, 405–410
heuristics in, 419–420
syllogistic reasoning and, 410–419
Deductive validity, 405
Deep Blue computer, 10, 493
Deep structure, 300–302
Deficient memory (amnesia), 173–176
Deficits, attentional, 103
Defining features, 256
Degraded information, 278
Degraded stimuli, 147, 228
Demand characteristics, epiphenomena and, 234–236
Demographic variables, IQ scores and, 502
DENDRAL program, 498
Dendrites, 29
Denotation, 295
Dependent variables, 15
Depressants, 103
Depression, memory and, 204
Depth, 119
Depth cues, 119–120, 121
binocular, 119, 120, 121
Depth perception, 119–122
Descriptive grammar, 296
Desire, as indirect speech act, 332, 333
Determinate descriptions, 237
Deutsch and Deutsch's late filter model, 95–96
Developmental psychology. *See* Cognitive development; Piagetian theory of cognitive development; Vygotsky's theory of cognitive development
Deviation IQs, 471
Dialect, 325
Dialectical process, 3
Dialectical synthesis, Kant and, 5
Dialectical thinking, 446
Diaries, 16
Dichotic listening, 92–93
Dichotic presentation, 92
Diencephalon, memory and, 177
Differentiated intelligence, 436
Diffusion, through memory system, 274
Directive, as speech act, 330, 331
Direct perception, 127–136
feature theories of, 131–136
Gibson on, 127–128
prototype theories of, 129–131
template theories of, 129
Direct speech acts, 330–332
Discounting error, 424
Discourse, 290
reading comprehension and, 336–343
Discrimination, 271
visual, 79
Dishabituation, 76–78
processes for, 80
Disparity, binocular, 121, 122
Display size, 84, 85
Dissecting, 41
Dissociations of function, 175
Distal object, 114
Distortion. *See* Memory
Distractor, 84

Distributed practice, 186
Divergent insight, 385
Divergent production, 384
Divergent thinking, 353
Divided attention, 80, 98–101
Dog experiments, of Pavlov, 9
Domain, creativity and, 386
Domain-general approach, 255
vs. domain specificity, 21, 279–280
to information processing, 449–450
Domain-interaction view, of metaphor, 328
Domain-specific approach, 21, 279–280
to information processing, 450
Dopamine (DA), 34, 35
Double dissociations, 176
Downers, 103
Draw-a-Person test, 403
Droodles, 201
Dual-code hypothesis, 218–219, 234
Dual-system hypothesis, 323–325
Dual-task paradigm, 100
Dura mater, 39
Dyad of triads task, 71
Dynamic assessment environment, 448
Dynamic property of language, 285, 287
Dyslexia, 143

Ecological approach to cognition, Neisser and, 12
Ecological model of perception, 128
Ecological validity, 19
vs. causal inferences, 21
Economic man and woman, 393
Economic research, decision theory and, 393–394
Edges, 140
EEGs. *See also* Electroencephalograms (EEGs)
Efferent neurons. *See* Motor (efferent) neurons
Egocentric, 438
Eight intelligences, of Gardner, 487–488
Elaborative rehearsal, 187
Electrochemical transmission, 30–32
Electroencephalograms (EEGs), 42
Elimination by aspects, 395–397
ELIZA program, 496, 497
Emotion, memory and, 204–205
Empirical data, 212–214
Empirical method, 3–4
inductive reasoning and, 421
Empiricism
of Aristotle, 4
of Locke, 5
vs. rationalism, 3–4, 21
Empiricist approach, of Aristotle, 4
Encoding, 165, **182–185**, 287–288
of acoustic information, 185
cognitive development and, 450
context effects on, 203–206
hippocampus and, 177
insight and, 368
language and, 318
memory and, 171
semantic, 184, 338–339
visual, 185
working memory and, 168
Engineering, 11, 13–14
English language. *See* English-speaking children; North American English
English-speaking children, 321
Enrichment programs, for intelligence, 501–503
Entrenchment, 369
Environment
intelligence and, 502–503
memory and, 452
memory system and, 171
Enzymatic deactivation, 34
Enzyme, 34
Epilepsy
bilingualism and, 324
studies of, 54–56
Epinephrine, 35
Epiphenomena, 219
and demand characteristics, 234–236
Episodic memory, 168
Epistemology, 212
Equilibration, 436
ERPs. *See* Event-related potentials (ERPs)
Eskimos, Sapir-Whorf hypothesis and, 318
Event-related potentials (ERPs), 42
language processing in brain and, 343
Näätänen's work on, 102–103
visual vs. spatial images and, 239–241
Evolutionary nature of language, 287
Evolutionary view of cognition, 410
Exceptional memory, 172–178
Excitation of neurons. *See* Neurons; Threshold of excitation
Excitatory neurons, 276
Exemplars, 258
Exhaustive processing, 193–195
Expected value, 394
Experience
intelligence and, 490
memory and, 452
Experimental techniques, 8
Experimentation, 14
Experimenter, expectancies of, 236
Experiments. *See also* Research methods
on human behavior, 14–15
Expertise
automatic expert processes, 380
characteristics of, 381
computer simulations of, 496–497
innate talent, acquired skill, and, 380–382
knowledge, problem solving, and, 376–382
setting up problem, 379
Expert system, 496
Explicit memory, 155, **157,** 169, 176
amnesia and, 174–175
Explicit reference-frame hint, 224
Expressive, as speech act, 331
Expressive encoding, 287
External representations, words vs. pictures, 214–216
External world, intelligence and, 490–491
Extrinsic motivation, 385
Eyewitness testimony paradigm, 202–203

Factor analysis of intelligence, 472–477
Fallacies, 406
False alarms, 82, 184
Family resemblance, 258
Featural singletons, 85
Feature-based categories, 256–257
Feature-based theory, and prototype theory, 259
Feature detectors, 87, 134–136
hierarchical structure of, 135
Feature hypothesis, 305
Feature inhibition mechanism, 87
Feature-integration theory, 86
Feature matching theories, 131
Feature search, 85
Features model, of semantic memory, 263
Feature theories of direct perception, 131–136
Field, creativity and, 386
Fifth-stage theorists of cognitive development, 434, 446, 463
Figure–ground, 124
Filter models of attention, 93–97
Fischer's theory, of cognitive development, 434
Fissures, 52
Flashbulb memory, 204
Flow chart, 494

Fluency, verbal, 288
Fluid ability, 477
Fluid intelligence, 460
fMRI. *See* Functional magnetic resonance imaging (fMRI)
Forcing functions, 76, 190–191
Forebrain, 47, **48,** 49–51
structures of, 50
Foreclosure effects, 420
Foreign languages, speech perception and, 292
Forest burners and forest lovers, as move problem, 355, 356, 357
Forgetting. *See also* Memory
memory distortion and, 196–206
Formal-operational stage, 442–443
Form perception, 110–112
Gestalt approaches to, 123–126
Framing effects, 402
FRAN model, 269
Free recall, 155, 156, 188, 269
Freudian slip, 327
Frontal lobe, 58
Functional-equivalence hypothesis, 225
Functional fixedness, 370
Functional hypothesis, 305
Functionalism, 6–8, 9. *See also* Pragmatics
Functionalists, 6–7
Functional magnetic resonance imaging (fMRI), 45
of language tasks, 343
Functional sorting, 485
Function morphemes, 289
Future action, as indirect speech act, 332, 333
Fuzzy concept, 258

GABA (gamma-amno butyric acid), 35, 103
Gambler's fallacy, 399
Ganglion. *See* Basal ganglia
Gardner's multiple intelligences theory, 487–489
Gender. *See also* Sex differences
and biological bases of intelligence, 483
language and, 335
stereotypes and, 370
General intelligence, Cattell on, 477
Generalization, 421–422
of research, 10
Generalizing, 271
General Problem Solver (GPS), 494
Generate and test heuristic, 358, 359
Generativity, as property of language, 285, 287
Genetic heritage, expertise and, 382
Geons, 136, 137
Geschwind–Wernicke model, 342
Gestalt approach, to form perception, 123–126
Gestalt psychology, 10–11
problem solving and, 365
"g" factor, 476
Ginseng, 36
Glands. *See* specific glands
Global features, 131
Global planning, 353–354, **481**
Global-precedence effect, 131, 133
Glucose, 38
Glucose metabolism, and intelligence, 483
Glutamate, 35
Grammar, 296
phrase-structure, 298–300
transformational, 300
Gray matter, 47, 53
Ground, of metaphor, 328
Guided search, 89–90
Guilford's structure of intellect, 476–477
Gustation, 115
Gyri, 52

Habituation, 76–79
Handedness, speech and, 343–344
Haptic imagery, 238
Hat-rack problem, 363, 364
Head Start, 501
Hearing, temporal lobe and, 60
Hemispheres. *See* Cerebral hemispheres
Heuristics, 244, **358–360**
biases and, 397–404
canons and, 422
in inductive reasoning, 422
representativeness, 398–399
in syllogistic reasoning, 419–420
Hierarchical models, 261–262
of intelligence, 477
Hierarchical sorting, 484–485
Higher thought processes, 58
High-verbals, 339
Hindbrain, 47, **48,** 50, 52
Hindsight bias, 403–404
Hippocampus, 49, 50
memory and, 176–178
History of cognitive psychology, importance of, 2–3
Hits, 82
Holistic information processing, 56
Homunculus
motor, 59
somatosensory, 60
Hormones, memory and, 178
Human behavior, experiments on, 14–15
Human intelligence. *See* Artificial intelligence (AI); Intelligence
Hypothalamus, 47, 49–51
Hypotheses, 14
Hypothesis testing, 308
Hypothetical constructs, memory stores as, **158**

Iconic memory, 159–160
research on, 161–162
Iconic store, 159–160
Icons, 159
Ideas, in text, 339–340
Identity, perception and, 114
"If–then" rules, 267
Ill-structured problems, 354
insight and, 363–369
Illusions, optical, 110, 116, 117
Illusory conjunctions, 90
Illusory correlation, 403
Imagery, 216. *See also* Mental rotations
image scaling and, 232
lesions and, 240
mental, 213, 216–217
visual, 217, 226, 235
Images, 6
Johnson-Laird on, 236
mental manipulations of, 225–234
stabilized, 115
synthesizing, 234–241
visual vs. spatial, 239–241
Image scaling, 230–233
demonstration, 232
Image scanning, 233–234
in research, 236
Imaginal code, 234
vs. propositional code, 224
Imaginal representation, 236–238
Imaging techniques
electrical recordings as, 42
metabolic, 44–46
static, 42–44
Imitation, and language acquisition, 308
Immigrants, intelligence tests and, 485
Implicit memory, 156, 157, 169, 176
amnesia and, 174–175
long-term, 185
Implicit reference-frame hint, 224
Inactive neurons, 276
Incision, 54
Inclusion fallacy, 401
Incubation, 375–376

Independent variables, 15
Indeterminate descriptions, 237
Indirect requests, 332
Indirect speech acts, 332, 333
Inductive reasoning, 404, 421–426
in information processing, 455–457
Infantile amnesia, 174
Infants
context effects on, 205
language acquisition by, 304–306
Inferences, 340. *See also* Reasoning
categorical, 425–426
causal, 422
deductively valid, 406
generalization and, 421
Inferior colliculi, 47
Inflection, 309
Information. *See also* Organization of information
movement of, 167
Informational medium, 114
Information-processing, 12–13. *See also* Knowledge representation; Learning
componential theory and, 480–482
computer models for, 170
by hemisphere, 56
model of memory stores, 158
theories, 271–272
Information-processing skills
inductive reasoning and, 455–457
metacognitive skills and memory development, 450–452
quantitative, 452–453
visuospatial, 453–455
Information-processing theorists, 434, 449–457
intelligence and, 477–484
Information retrieval, age and, 462
Information transmission. *See also* Neurons
spinal cord and, 38
Inheritance, in hierarchical models, 261
Inhibitory neurons, 276
Innate characteristics, 4
Innate (inborn) nature, 2
Innate talent, expertise and, 380–382
Insight, 363–369, **364**
creativity and, 384–385
experience, 368–369
Gestalt views of, 365
vs. insight experience, 368–369
neo-Gestaltist view of, 366, 367
nothing-special view of, 365
three-process view of, 368
Instance theory, 74
Instrumental Enrichment program (Feuerstein), 501
Integration of information, working memory and, 168
Integrative model
of memory, 166
for representing declarative and nondeclarative knowledge, 268–280
Intellectual history, 3
Intelligence, 469. *See also* Learning; Specific theories of intelligence
vs. appearance of intelligence, 500–501
artificial, 12, 255, 491–501
biological bases of, 482–484
cognitive research and, 229
computers and, 12–13
cultural context and, 484–487
defined, 468–470
direct-perception view and, 128–129
factor analysis of, 472–477
fluid vs. crystallized, 460–461
Gardner's multiple intelligences theory, 487–489
history of testing and scoring, 470–471
information-processing and, 477–484
inhibition of instinctive responses and, 34
of intelligent programs, 499–501
measures and structures of, 470–477
neural conduction and, 32
Piaget on, 436
process timing theories of, 478–480
Sternberg's triarchic theory of, 489–491
strategies for, 501–503
teaching of, 501
Intelligence Applied program (Sternberg), 501
Intelligence quotient (IQ), 471
and biological bases of intelligence, 482–483
normal distribution and, 471
strategies for improving, 501–503
Intelligence scales, 472
Intelligence tests
Binet, Simon, and, 470–471
neuropsychological research and, 483–484
Intelligent perception, 136. *See also* Constructive perception
Intentional transfer, 374
Interactive-activation model of word recognition, 145, 146
Interactive imagery, 188, 189
Interactive process, lexical access as, 144–145
Interference, 185, 196–201, 219
memory and, 197–198
Interference theory, 196
Internalization, 446–447
Internal world, intelligence and, 489–490
Interneuron, 38
Interneuronal communication, 32–35
INTERNIST program, 498
Interpersonal intelligence, 488
Intraneuronal transmission, 32
Intrapersonal intelligence, 488
Intrinsic motivation, 385
Introspection, 3, 6
Intuition
AI and, 499–500
study, 71
Investment theory of creativity, 387
In vivo studies, 18, 41–42
Ipsilateral transmission, **53**
IQ. *See* Intelligence quotient (IQ)
Isomorphic problems, **360**
Italian Americans, intelligence testing of, 485
Iterative subroutines, 267–268

Jabberwocky (Carroll), 297
Jargon, 266
Jensen's choice reaction time, 478–479
Johnson-Laird's mental models, 236–238
Judgment and decision making, 393–404
alternative view of reasoning, 427
classical decision theory and, 393–395
deductive reasoning and, 405–420
elimination by aspects and, 395–397
heuristics, biases, and, 397–404
inductive reasoning and, 421–426
intelligence and, 470
wisdom and, 463–464

Keyword systems, 190
Knowledge. *See also* Knowledge representation
declarative, 212, 255–267
elaboration of, 377, 378

expertise and, 376–382
mental shortcuts and, 244–248
organization of, 377–380
PDP model and, 278
procedural, 212, 267–268
used for cognitive maps, 243
Knowledge-acquisition components of intelligence, 489
Knowledge representation, 212
for declarative and nondeclarative knowledge, 268–272
dual-code hypothesis of, 218–219, 234
mental, 212–214
network model of, 260
procedural knowledge, 267–268
propositional hypothesis of, 219–225, 234
spatial cognition, cognitive maps, and, 242–248
synthesizing images and propositions in, 234–241
Korsakoff's syndrome, 49, 177
Kpelle tribe, 484–485

Labeled relationships, 260
Labels, and memory, 318, 319
LAD. *See* Language acquisition device (LAD)
Landmark knowledge, 243
Language, 284–285. *See also* Speech
dialects and, 325
differences among, 316–322
fundamental aspects of, 287–291
gender and, 335
input, 287, 291
metaphors and, 327–329
neuropsychology of, 342–345
output, 287, 291
properties of, 285–291
social context of, 329–342
and thought, 316–329
units of, 288–289
Language acquisition, 303–311
Chomsky on, 12
conditioning and, 310
developmental changes associated with, 306
after four years old, 310–311
imitation and, 308
modeling and, 309–310
Skinner on, 12
stages of, 304–306
Language-acquisition device (LAD), 12, 307
Language comprehension
processes of, 291–303
relationships between syntactical and lexical structures, 302–303
semantics and, 295–296
speech perception and, 291–295
syntax tendency and, 297–302
Lateral geniculate nucleus, 51
Lateralization of function, 238–239
Law of effect, Thorndike on, 8–9
Law of large numbers, 410
Law of Prägnanz, 123
Learning. *See also* Cognition; Information-processing
brain and, 11–12
classically conditioned, 9
cognitive development and, 432
Learning Potential Assessment Device (Feuerstein), 449
Left hemisphere, 55. *See also* Localization
Lesions, 41. *See also* Brain
imagery and, 240
language processing and, 343–344
lateralization of function and, 238–239
Levels-of-processing framework, 164–165
Lexical access, 144–147
Lexical-access speed, and speed of simultaneous processing, 479–480
Lexical-decision task, 145
Lexical processes, 144–147
Lexical structures, syntax and, 302–303
Lexicon, 290
language differences and, 317
Limbic system, 47, 49
Linear function, 226
Linear syllogisms, 410–412, 411
Linguistic intelligence, 488
Linguistic relativity, 317–319
linguistic universals and, 320–322
Linguistics, 11. *See also* Language
Chomsky and, 12
feature-based view and, 256
Linguistic universals, 320–322
Listening. *See also* Selective attention
dichotic, 92–93
Lobes, 57–62. *See also* Brain; Cerebral hemispheres
frontal, 58
occipital, 61–62
parietal, 59–60
temporal, 60
Localization, 28
of function, 28, 52–62
memory and, 175, 176
Local planning, 353–354, **481**
Local-precedence effect, 131, 133
Logical-mathematical intelligence, 488
Logical premises. *See also* Reasoning; Syllogisms
conversion of, 415–416
Logical reasoning, 409–410
Logic Theorist (LT), 493–494
Longitudinal research designs, cognition in adults and, 461
Long-term memory, 176. *See also* Forgetting; Memory
movement of information to short-term memory, 185–191
retrieval from, 195–196
working memory and, 166, 167
Long-term storage, 184–185
Long-term store, 158, 163–164
Low-verbals, 339

Macropropositions, 340
Macrostructure, of passage of text, 340
Magnetic resonance imaging (MRI) scans, 42–44
Maintenance rehearsal, 187
Maps
cognitive, 242–248
mental, 247
and relative-position heuristic, 246
text, 248
world, 245
Map scanning, 237
Marcel's model, 104
Massed practice, 186
Mathematics. *See also* Logical premises; Reasoning
quantitative skills and, 453
Maturation, of central nervous system, 458–460
Maturation approach to cognitive development, 432
Neo-Piagetian theory on, 445–446
Piaget and, 433, 435–445
Maxim of manner, 334
Maxim of quality, 333
Maxim of quantity, 333
Maxim of relation, 333–334
McGurk effect, 294
Meaning, preconscious processing and, 70–71
Means–end analysis, 358, 494
heuristic of, 359
Medial geniculate nucleus, 51
Medulla, 50

Medulla oblongata, 47, 52
Memorization, 188, 189–190, 191
Memory, 154. *See also* Forgetting; Priming
acetylcholine (Ach) and, 34
age and, 461, 462
amnesia and, 173–176
brain and, 176–178
compound cues and, 274
connectionist perspective on, 169–170
consolidation and, 185–186
constructive nature of, 201–203, 296
culture-relevance and, 486
distortion of, 196–206
encoding and, 182–185
episodic, 168
exceptional, 172–178
flashbulb, 204
forgetting, distortion, and, 196–206
hippocampus and, 49, 176–178
implicit vs. explicit, 157
information-processing model of, 158
labels and, 319
language and, 318
levels-of-processing framework for, 164–165
long-term store of, 163–164
macro- and micro-level structures of, 177
measuring, 155–157
metacognitive skills and, 450–452
mnemonists and, 172–173
multiple-memory-systems model of, 168–169
neuropsychology of, 172–178
nontraditional views of, 167
postmortem exams and, 41
procedural, 169
random walk and diffusion through, 274
in real world, 170–171
recall vs. recognition, 156–157
REM sleep and, 187
retrieval from, 191–196
semantic, 168
semantic encoding and, 338–339
sensory store of, 159
short-term store of, 162–163
Squire's taxonomy of, 169
stores of, 158–164, 166–168
three-stores model of, 158, 167–168
traditional model of, 157–164
working, 166–168
Memory scanning, 192, 193
Men. *See also* Sex differences
gender, language, and, 335
Mental age (MA), 471
Mental context, 487
Mental imagery, 213, 216–217
Mental manipulations of images, 225–234
Mental maps, 247
Mental model, 340
of Johnson-Laird, 236–238
of syllogisms, **416**–419
Mental realignment, 223
Mental reconstrual, 223
Mental representations. *See* Imagery; Knowledge representation; Pictures; Word(s)
Mental rotations, 225–230. *See also* Imagery
age and, 453–454
demonstration of, 227
findings of, 228
neuropsychological evidence for, 229–230
Mental sets, 369–371
Mental shortcuts, 244–248
Metabolic imaging, 44–46
Metabolism, glucose, and intelligence, 483
Metacognition, 186
Metacognitive skills, memory development and, 450–452
Metacomponents of intelligence, 489
Metamemory strategies, **186**
Metaphors, 157–158, **327–329**
for movement of information, 167
in real-world memory, 171
for working memory, 168
Method of difference, 422
Method of loci, 188, 189
Microanatomy of brain, 272
Midbrain, 47, **48,** 50, 51
structures of, 50
Military problem, 372, 373–374
Mind. *See also* Functionalism; Structuralism
behaviorism and, 10
brain and, 28
structure vs. function of, 5–9
Mindlessness, 75–76
Minimalist hypothesis, 341
Mistakes, 76
M.I.T., AI work at, 494
Mnemonic devices, 188, 189–190, 191
Mnemonist, 157, 172–173
Modeling, and language acquisition, 309–310
Modular, 279
Modularity of Mind, The (Fodor), 279
Modularity theorists, 489
Modular processes, for separation of perceptual processes, 149
Modus ponens argument, 405, 407, 409
Modus tollens argument, 405, 407–408, 409
Monoamine neurotransmitters, 34, 35
Monocular depth cues, 119–120, 121
Monolingals, 322
Moral decadence, intelligence and, 485
Moray's selective filter model, 93
Morpheme, 289–290
Morphology, 320
Motion parallax, 120
Motivation, extrinsic and intrinsic, 385
Motor cortex, 459
Motor homunculus, 59
Motor (efferent) neurons, 32, **38**
Motor processing, 58
Motor theory of speech perception, 294
Movement
feature search and, 90
of information, 167
Movement filter, 90
Movement of information, from short-term to long-term memory, 185–191
Movement time, 478
Move problems, 355, 356
MRI scans. *See* Magnetic resonance imaging (MRI) scans
Müller–Lyer illusion, 116, 117
Multidimensional Aptitude Battery, 483
Multiple codes, neuropsychological evidence for, 238–240
Multiple intelligences theory, 487–489
Multiple-memory-systems model, 168–169
Multiple sclerosis, 29
Multiple tasks
performance of, 81
selective attention and, 100
Multiplicity of structure, as property of language, 285, 287
Multitrial free-recall task, 188
Musical intelligence, 488
MYCIN program, 498
Myelinated axons, 29, 53
Myelin sheath, **29**

Näätänen's ERP work, 102–103
Nanoseconds, 276
Naturalistic observation, 17, 18, 19

Naturalist intelligence, 488
Natural level. *See* Basic level
Nature vs. nurture, 2, 21
cognitive development and, 433
language acquisition and, 303, 307–310
Navaho-speaking children, 321
Negatively accelerated curve, in effects of practice on automatization, 74–75
Negative set, 192
Negative transfer, 371
Negative utility, 394
Neglect, 101–102
Neisser's synthesis, of attention filtering models, 96–97
Neocortex, 29
Neo-Gestaltist view, of problem solving, 366, 367
Neo-Piagetian theorists, 445–446, 457
Nerve cells, in PNS, 36
Nervous system, 28. *See also* Brain
cognitive neuroscience and, 28
communication between neurons, 32–35
functional organization of, 38–40
learning and, 11–12
levels of organization in, 36–40
neuronal structure and function in, 29–32
organization of, 28–40
Network, 170, **260**
parallel processing in, 276
semantic, 260–263
Network English, 325
Neural conduction, speed of, 32
Neural feature detectors, 87
Neural firing, 31–32
Neural networks, 170
in developing human brain, 458
Neuroanatomy, 11
Neurons, 29. *See also* Nervous system
cognitive development and, 458
communication between, 32–35
parts of, 29–30
PDP model and, 276
structure and function of, 29–32
Neuropeptides, 34, 35
Neurophysiology, cognitive development and, 458–460
Neuropsychological evidence
for mental rotation, 229–230
for multiple codes, 238–241
Neuropsychological research, working vs. long-term memory and, 166–167
Neuropsychology, 54
amnesia and, 175–176
of language, 342–345
of memory, 172–178
Neuroscience. *See* Cognitive neuroscience
Neurotransmitters, 30
attention and, 103
chemical substances in, 34–35
intraneuronal and interneuronal transmission and, 32–35
Nodes, 260
memory, 170
Nodes of Ranvier, 29, 32
Nondeclarative knowledge
and declarative knowledge, 272–273
integrative models for representing, 268–272
Nondeclarative memory. *See* Implicit memory
Nonlinguistic images, 318
Nonspeech sounds, perception of, 292
Nonstandard dialects, 325
Norepinephrine, 35
Normal distribution, IQ and, 471
North American English. *See also* English-speaking children
phonetic symbols for, 288
Nothing-special view, of insight, 365, 384–385
Noun phrase, 290
Novel utterances, 287
Nucleus, 29, 49
Nurture. *See* Nature vs. nurture

Object permanence, 437
Object-superiority effect, 138, 145
Observation, naturalistic, 17, 18
Occipital lobe, 58, 61–62
Olfaction, 115
Operant conditioning, 10
Optical illusions, 110, 116, 117
Optic chiasma, 61–62
Organization, of knowledge, 267
Organization of information, in stored memory, 188–191
Orthography, 143
Output interference, 160
Outstanding memory (mnemonists), 172–173
Overconfidence, 403
Overextension error, 305, 419–420
Overregularization, 309

Pandemonium, 131, 132
Parallel distributed processing (PDP) model, 169–170, **275–279**
Parallel processing, 12, 170, 193, **275,** 499
connectionist model and, 275–279
Parietal lobe, 58, 59–60
PARRY program, 97, 496
Parthenon illusion, 113
Partial-report procedure, 159–160
Patterns, reasoning and, 427
Pavlovian conditioning, 9
PDP model. *See* Parallel distributed processing (PDP) model
Pegwords, 188, 189
Peptide chains, 34, 35
Percept, 223
Perception, 110–113. *See also* Attention; Perceptual theories; Preconscious processing
Broadbent's model and, 93, 94
computational theory of, 140–142
continuum of, 115
deficits in, 148–149
depth, 119–122
Gestalt approaches to form, 123–126
Marcel's model and, 104
in reading, 143–147
from sensation to representation, 114–126
of space and forms, 245
speech, 291–295
Perceptual constancy, 115–119, **116**
color, 137–138
shape, 118–119
size, 116
Perceptual object, 114
Perceptual scanning, in research, 236
Perceptual staircase, 112
Perceptual theories, 126–143
bottom-up approaches (direct perception), 127–136, 139–140
computational, 140–142
spatiotemporal boundary-formation, 142–143
structural-description theory, 136
top-down approaches (constructive perception), 136–140
Performance components of intelligence, 489
Performance theory, 445
Performative. *See* Declaration
Peripheral nervous system (PNS), 36, 37
Permastore, 164
Permutations, 442
Perseveration, slips of the tongue and, 326

Personality, creative, 385
Person variables, in selective attention, 98–99
Perspicacity, 464
PET scans. *See* Positron emission tomography (PET) scans
Philosophy, as antecedent of psychology, 3–4
Phone, as speech sound, 288
Phoneme, 288–289. *See also* Language acquisition
in language acquisition, 304–305
speech perception and, 292
Phonemic-restoration effect, 293
Phonemics, 289
Phonetic refinement theory, 292
Phonetics, 289
Phonetic symbols, for North American English, 288
Phonological code, 143
Phonological loop, 166, 167
Phonological properties of words, 165
Phonology, 320
Phrases
syntax and, 296
tree diagrams of structure, 298, 299
Phrase-structure grammars, 298
Physical context, 487
Physical processing, 164
Physiological indicators, of habituation, 78–79
Physiological psychology. *See* Psychobiology
Physiology, 3, 28
Piagetian theory of cognitive development, 434, 435–443, 457
evaluation of, 443–445
Pictures, vs. words, 214–216
Pidgin, 325
Pitch sensitivity, 470
Pituitary gland, 50
Planning, global and local, 353–354, 481
Plasticity, 462
Platonic approach, 4
PNS. *See* Peripheral nervous system (PNS)
Point of view, comprehension based on, 341–342
Pons, 47, 50, 52
Ponzo illusion, 116
Positive set, 192
Positive transfer, 371–374
Positive utility, 394
Positron emission tomography (PET) scans, 42, 44–45
memory and, 167
Posner's theory of attention, 102
Postformal thought, 446
age and, 463
Postmortem, 18
brain studies, 41
Practice, automatization and, 74
Practice effect, 186
Pragmatic reasoning schemas, 409, 420
Pragmatic rules, 409
Pragmatics, 329
Pragmatists, 7–8
Preconscious processing, 70–72
Predicate, 290
Predicate calculus, 221n
Prefixes, 289
Premise, 405. *See* Syllogisms
Premise-phrasing effects, 420
Preoperational stage, 438–439
Prescriptive grammar, 296
Primacy effect, 198
Primal sketch, 141
Primary memory, 158
Primary mental abilities, 476
Primary motor cortex, 58
Primary somatosensory cortex, 59
Prime, 170, 274
Priming, 70, 273–274
syntactic, 297
Priming effect, 70–71, 170
Principles of Psychology (James), 7
Prior learning, 138
Proactive interference, 197, 198, 200
Probability, 396–397, 404
rules of, 396
Problems
isomorphic, 360
representation problems and, 360–361, 362
types of, 354–369
well-structured, 354, 355–362
Problem solving, 350–351. *See also* Creativity
age and, 461
in chess games, 377, 378
componential theory and, 480–482
computer models of, 356–360, 499–500
definition of problem in, 351, 352
entrenchment and, 369
evaluation in, 351, 354
expertise, knowledge, and, 376–382
fixation and, 369–371
identification in, 351, 352
incubation and, 375–376
information organization for, 351, 353
insight and, 363–369
mental sets and, 369–371
monitoring in, 351 , 354
resource allocation in, 351, 353
strategies and conclusions reached, 379
strategy for, 351, 353
Problem-solving cycle, 351–354
Problem space, 356
Proceduralization, 74, 271
Procedural knowledge, 175, **212,** 272
Anderson on, 271
brain and, 177
memory and, 156
representations of, 267–268
Procedural memory, 169
Processes, vs. structures, 21
Process timing theories of intelligence, 478–480
Production, 267
of language, 291
and production system, 267–268
Production rules, 267
Production system, 268
production and, 267–268
Productive thinking, 365
Productivity
creative, 382–384
as property of language, 285, 287
Programming, 12
Projection areas, 58
Projective tests, illusory correlation and, 403
Properties of language, 285–291
Proposition, 219, 339–340
Johnson-Laird on, 236
representations of underlying meanings and, 221
synthesizing, 234–241
using, 220
Propositional code, vs. imaginal code, 224
Propositional hypothesis, 219–225
Propositional knowledge, 245
Propositional limits, 223–225
Propositional representations
and comprehension of ideas in text, 339–340
for solving syllogisms, 412
Protolanguage, 325
Prototype, 129, 257
matching of, 130
Prototype theory, 257–258

of direct perception, 129–131
and feature-based theory, 259
Proxemics, 330
Proximal stimulation, 114
variation of, 114
Proximity, 125
PRP (psychological refractory period) effect, 98, 101
Psychoanalytic view, slips of the tongue and, 326
Psychobiological research, 16, 18
Psychobiology, 11
early role of, 11–12
Psycholinguistic perspective, on speech, 295
Psycholinguistics, 284, 329–330
Psychological refractory period effect. *See* PRP (psychological refractory period) effect
Psychology, philosophical antecedents of, 3–4
Psychometric approach, to creativity, 384
Psychopharmacological approach, to attention, 103–104
Psychophysical abilities, 470
Psychophysical approach, to intelligence testing, 470
Psychotherapy, ELIZA and PARRY programs and, 496, 497
Punishments, 10

Qualitative and quantitative changes, cognitive development and, 432
Quantitative skills, in information processing, 452–453

Radiation problem, 371–373
Radical behaviorism, 9
of Skinner, 10
Random occurrences, 398
Random walk, 274
RAS. *See* Reticular activating system (RAS, reticular formation)
Rate law, 32
Rationalism
of Descartes, 5
vs. empiricism, 3–4, 21
of Plato, 4–5
Rationalist approach, 4–5
Rationalist insights, 212–214
Rationality
bounded, 395
unlimited, 394–395
Rats. *See* Animal research
RBC theory. *See* Recognition-by-components (RBC) theory
Reaction range, intelligence and, 503
Reaction time, 478–479
lexical access speed and, 479
Reading
automatization in, 380
perceptual issues in, 143–147
Reading comprehension, discourse and, 336–343
Reality monitoring, 204
Real world memory, 170–171
Reasoning, 404
alternative view of, 426–427
by analogy, 426
deductive, 404, 405–420
inductive, 404, 421–426, 455–457
Reasons, indirect request and citation of, 332, 333
Recall, 155. *See also* Long-term memory; Memory; Short-term memory
FRAN and, 269
long-term storage and, 184
memorization and, 188–190
recognition and, 155–157
retrieval from long-term memory, 195–196
scripts and, 266–267
of trigrams, 197
Recency effect, 198
Receptive comprehension, 287
Receptive field, 133
Receptor cells, 38
Receptors, 38
Recognition, 155
recall and, 155–157
Recognition-by-components (RBC) theory, 136
Recognition tasks, 156
Reconstructive memory retrieval, **201**
Red nucleus, 47
Reflexes, 39
spinal, 39, 40
Regions of similarity, 140
Regularly structured property of language, 285, 286–287
Rehearsal, 8, **186**–187. *See also* Memory
in memory development, 451
Reicher-Wheeler effect, 145
Reinforcement (rewards), 10
Relationships, schemas and, 264
Relative-position heuristic, 245
Relative size illusion, 116, 117
Relativity, linguistic, 317–319
Relearning, 156
REM sleep, 186–187
Repetition. *See* Rehearsal
Repetition priming, 274
Representation
dual-code hypothesis and, 218–219
imaginal, 236–238
integrative models for, 268–272
of procedural knowledge, 267–268
semantic network models and, 262
sensation and, 114–126
for solving syllogisms, 412
words, pictures, and, 214–216
Representational thought, 438
Representative, as speech act, 330, 331
Representativeness heuristic, **398**–399
Repressed memories, 203
Reproductive thinking, 365
Research, goals of, 13–14
Research methods
in cognitive psychology, 13–20
computer simulations and artificial intelligence, 20
cross-disciplinary, 20
experiments on human behavior, 14
psychobiological research, 18
self-reports, case studies, and naturalistic observation, 18–19
Resolution, 230
Response. *See* Stimulus-response
Retention interval, 196
Reticular activating system (RAS, reticular formation), 47, 51, 104
Retina, 70
sensory adaptation and, 114–115
Retrieval, 154, **182,** 191–196. *See also* Memory; Priming
context effects on, 203–206
language and, 318
from long-term memory, 195–196
from short-term memory, 192–195
Retroactive interference, 197
Retrograde amnesia, 173–174
Reuptake mechanism, **34**
Reversal, slips of the tongue and, 326
Reversible concrete-operational thinking, 441–442
Rhymes, 165
Right-angle bias, 245
Right hemisphere, 55. *See also* Cerebral hemispheres; Localization
Risk aversion, 402
Risk seeking, 402–403
Roles, thematic, 303
Root words, 289
Rorschach test, 403

Rotation heuristic, 245
Route-road knowledge, 243, 244
Routine problems, 365
Routines, 267–268
Rule of substitution, 493
Rules of thumb, 244

Saccades, 114
Saltatory conduction, 32
Sapir–Whorf hypothesis, 317–319
Saponins, 36
Satisfaction, Thorndike on, 8–9
Satisficing, 394–395
Scanning. *See also* Search
  image, 233–234
Schemas, 198, **255,** 263–264
  pragmatic reasoning, 409
Schematic representations, 263–267
  schemas, 263–264
  scripts, 264–267
Schematization, 380
Schools of psychology
  associationism and, 8
  behaviorism and, 9–10
  functionalism and, 6–8
  Gestalt psychology and, 10–11
  pragmatism and, 7–8
  structuralism and, 6
Screen metaphor, image scaling and, 231
Scripts, 265–267
  jargon and, 266
SDT. *See* Signal-detection theory (SDT)
Search, 81, **84–91**
Secondary memory, 158
Second-language acquisition, bilingualism and, 322–323
Seeing. *See* Visual region of brain
Selection task, 406–407
Selective attention, 80, 81, 91–99
  attentional-resource theories of, 97–98
  Broadbent's model of, 93
  Deutsch and Deutsch's late filter model of, 95–96
  Moray's selective filer model, 93
  Neisser's synthesis model, 96–97
  Stroop effect and, 99
  task, situation, and person variables in, 98–99
  Treisman's attenuation model of, 94–95
Selective-combination insights, 368
Selective-comparison insights, 368
Selective-encoding insights, 368
Selective filter model, 93
Self-observation, of Ebbinghaus, 8
Self-ratings, 16
Self-reference effect, 164
Self-reports, 16, 18–19
Self-schema, 164
Self-terminating processing, 193–194
Semantic code, 183
Semantic encoding, 184, 338–339
Semantic knowledge, 245
Semantic memory, 168
  features model of, 263
Semantic model, for linear syllogisms, 412
Semantic network model, 260–263, 261
Semantic priming, 274
Semantic processing, 164
Semantic rehearsal, 165
Semantics, 290, 295–296
Sensations, 6
  representation and, 114–126
Sensorimotor stage, 437–438
Sensory adaptation, 78, 114–115
  and habituation, 79
Sensory cortex, 459
Sensory information, 93
  hippocampus and, 177
Sensory input, 49
Sensory (afferent) neurons, 38
Sensory store, 158, 159–162
Sentences, syntax and, 296
Septum, 49, 50. *See also* Brain
Serial exhaustive processing, 194–195
Serial position, 198
  curve, 198, 200
Serial processing, 12, 192, **267,** 499
Serial recall, 155–156, 188
Serotonin, 34, 35
SES. *See* Socioeconomic status (SES)
Sex differences. *See also* Gender
  in language processing in brain, 343
Shadowing technique, 92
Shape constancy, 118–119
Short-term memory. *See also* Forgetting; Memory
  movement of information to long-term memory, 185–191
  retrieval from, 192–195
  working memory and, 166–167
Short-term storage, 183–184
Short-term store, 158, 162
SHRDLU, 494–495
Sight. *See* Vision
Signal, 82
Signal-attenuation theory, 97
Signal detection, 80–82
Signal-detection theory (SDT), 82
Sign language
  American Sign Language (ASL) and, 307, 308
  hemispheric processing of language and, 343–344
Similarity, 8, 125
Similarity-coverage hypothesis, 425–426
Similarity theory, 87–88
Simile, 327
Simple cells, 134
Simulations. *See* Computer simulations
Simultagnosia, 148–149
Single-system hypothesis, 323–325
Situation variables, in selective attention, 98–99
Size, visual search and, 88–89
Size constancy, 116
Skills. *See also* Specific skills
  acquired, 380–382
  information-processing, 449–458
Sleep, REM, 186–187
Slips, automatic processes and, 76, 77
Slips of the tongue, 326–327
Smell, 115
Social context of language, 329–342
  conversational postulates and, 332–334
  discourse, reading comprehension, and, 336–342
  gender and, 335
  speech acts and, 330–332
Sociocultural influences, on thought processes, 446–449
Socioeconomic status (SES), bilingualism and, 322
Sociolinguistics, 329–330
Soma, 29
Somatosensory homunculus, 60
Somatosensory processing, 58
Sound, 115. *See also* Reading
Spacing effect, 186
Spanish language, language universals and, 320–321
Spatial agnosia, 149
Spatial cognition, and cognitive maps, 242–248
Spatial images, visual vs., 239–241
Spatial intelligence, 488
Spatial representations, for solving syllogisms, 412
Spatial visualization, 453–455
Spatiotemporal boundary-formation theory, 142–143
Speaking, automatic nature of, 73

Spearman's "g" factor, 476
Specialization, hemispheric, 53–56
Speech, Wernicke's area and, 54, 55, 62
Speech acts, 330–332
direct, 330–332
indirect, 332
Speech errors, syntax and, 297–298
Speech perception, 291–295
motor theory of, 294
view as ordinary, 292–293
view as special, 293–295
Speech sounds, 288–289
Speech synthesizer, syllable acoustic patterns and, 293–294
Speed of simultaneous processing, 479–480
Spinal column, 38
Spinal cord, 38, 39, 50. *See also* Central nervous system (CNS)
function of, 38–40
Spinal nerves, 36
Spinal reflexes, 39, 40
Split-brain patients, **55**–56, 239. *See also* Brain; Cerebral hemispheres
Spreading-activation theories, 169–170, 274, 275
Squire's taxonomy of memory, 169
Stabilized images, 115
Stages of development. *See* Piagetian theory of cognitive development
Standard dialects, 325
Stanford-Binet Intelligence Scales, 472, 473
State of consciousness, memory and, 204–205
Static assessment environment, 448
Static equilibrium, 30–31
Static imaging techniques, 42–44
Statistical analysis, 13, 15
Statistical significance, 14
Stereotypes, 370–371
Sternberg's triarchic theory of intelligence, 489–491
Stimulants, of central nervous system, 103
Stimuli
degraded, 147
target, 85
Stimulus internal variation, habituation and, 78
Stimulus-response, 7
Stimulus variation, 114–115
Storage, 154, **182**
language and, 318
long-term, 184
Stored memory, organization of information in, 188–191
Storehouse, memory as, 171
Stores of memory, 158
Story of My Life (Keller), 284
Stroop effect, 99
Structural approaches to intelligence, 472–477
Structural-description theory, 136
Structuralism, 6
Titchener and, 6
Wundt and, 6
Structuralist approach, to form perception, 123
Structural organization, of nervous system, 36–38
Structure-of-intellect (SOI) model, **476**–477
Structures vs. processes, 21
Subcortical structures, language processing and, 345
Subjective arousal, habituation and, 78
Subjective expected utility theory, 394
Subjective organization in free recall, 188
Subjective probability, 394
Subjective utility, 394
Subroutines, 267–268
Substantia nigra, 47
Substitution, slips of the tongue and, 326
Subtraction method, of metabolic imaging, 44
Subtractive bilingualism, 322
Suffixes, 289
Sulci, 52
Superior colliculi, 47
Surface structure, 300–302
Survey knowledge, 243, 244
Syllable categories, 293–394
Syllogisms, 410
categorical, 412–419
circle diagram of, 413
linear, 410–412
mental model of, 416–419
Syllogistic reasoning, 410–419
Symbolic, 218
Symbolic representation, 215
Symbols, analogical images and, 218–219
Symbolic nature of language, 285–286
Symmetry, 125
heuristic, 245
Synapse, 29–30. *See also* Interneuronal communication
Synchronous movement, 90
Synesthesia, 172
Syntactical structures, lexical structures and, 302–303
Syntax, 290, **296**
Chomsky on, 300
and language acquisition, 305–306
Syntax tendency, 297–302
Synthesis, 3
of images and propositions, 234–241
Synthesizing images and propositions, 234–241
Systematic experimental introspection, of Ebbinghaus, 8

Tabula rasa view, 5
Talent, expertise and, 380–382
Target stimulus, in search, 85
Task variables, in selective attention, 98–99
Taste, 115
Taxonomy, of memory, 169
Technology, engineering, computation, and, 13–14
Telegraphic speech, 305–306
Templates, 129
Temporal contiguities, 427
Temporal lobe, 58, 60
Temporal strings, 270
Tenor, in metaphor, 327–328
Tension, of metaphor, 328
Terminal buttons, 29–30
Terminus, 219
Tests and testing. *See also* Intelligence tests
culture-fair, 485–486
culture-relevant, 486
intelligence, 470–471
Text
comprehension of ideas in, 339–340
representing, in mental models, 340–341
Text maps, 248
Thalamus, 47, **49**, 50
linguistic functions and, 345
nuclei of, 51
Thematic roles, 303
Theory, 14
Theory of forms (Plato), 4
Theory of multiple intelligences, 487–489
Thesis, 3
Thinking. *See also* Thought
dialectical, 446
divergent and convergent, 353
postformal, 446
Thinking-aloud protocols, 13
Thought. *See also* Thinking
language interactions and, 317–329

maturation of processes, 435–446
representational, 438
sociocultural influences on, 446–449
3-D models, 141, 142
Three-process view, of insight, 368
Three-stores model, 158, 167–168, 170
Threshold of excitation, 31, 33–34
Thurstone's primary mental abilities, 476
Tip-of-the-tongue phenomenon, 71
Top-down theories, 127, 136–140
categorical inferences and, 425
Torrance Tests of Creative Thinking, 384
Total-time hypothesis, 187
Touch, 115
Towers of Hanoi problem, 360–361, 362
TRACE model, 293
Transfer
of analogies, 371–374
intentional, 374
negative and positive, 371–374
Transformational grammar, 300
Transitive-inference problems, 419
Transparency, 374
Transposition, slips of the tongue and, 326
Tree diagrams, syntactic classes in sentences and, 298, 299
Treisman's attenuation model, 94–95, 97
Triads, 71
Triangle illusions, 112
Triarchic theory of human intelligence, 489–491
Trigrams, 196
recall of, 197
Truth table, 416, 418–419
Tryptophan, 34
Turing test, 492–493
2 1/2-D primal sketch, 141
2-D primal sketch, 141
Two-string problem, 350, 361, 362
Typestyles, 143
Tyrosine, 34, 35

Unconscious inference, 138
Universal affirmatives, 413
Unusualness heuristic, 422
Uppers, 103
Utility theory, 394

Validity
of causal inferences vs. ecological validity, 21
deductive, 405
ecological, 19
Variables
dependent, 15
independent, 15
Vehicle, in metaphor, 328
Ventral region, 47
Ventrolateral nucleus, 51
Verbal comprehension, 288
Verbal fluency, 288
Verbal labels, and memory, 319
Verbal protocol, 16, 19, 420
Verb phrase, 290
Veridical content, of speech, 310
Vernon's hierarchical model, 477
Vertebrae, 39
Vigilance, 83–84, 102
and signal detection, 81
Vision, 115
Visual cortex, preconscious perception and, 71–72
Visual discrimination, 79
Visual encoding, 185
Visual imagery, 217
principles of, 226, 235
spatial images and, 239–241
Visual mask, 70, 478
Visual-object agnosia, 148
Visual perception
auditory perceptions and, 294
Gestalt principles of, 123–126
Visual persistence, 159
Visual processing, 58
Visual recall, delay and, 161
Visual region of brain, 61
Visual search, 84–91, 102
Visuospatial sketchpad, 166
Visuospatial skills, 453–455
in information processing, 453–455
Vocabulary, 290
acquisition of, 339
language acquisition and, 305, 306
Vocal inflection, 309
Vygotsky's theory of cognitive development, 434, 446–449, 457

Warmth, insight and, 366, 367
"War of the Ghosts, The," 198, 199
Wason selection task, 407, 408
Water-jar problem, 369, 370
Wechsler intelligence scales
Wechsler Adult Intelligence Scale (WQIS-III), 472, 474
Wechsler Intelligence Scale for Children (WISC-III), 472
Wechsler Preschool and Primary Scale of Intelligence (WPPSI), 472
Weight discrimination, 470
Well-structured problems, 354, 355–362
Wernicke's area, 54, 55, 62, 342
White matter, 53
Whole relationships, 222
Whole-report procedure, 159
Wisdom, 463–464
Within-item elaboration, 165
Women. *See also* Sex differences
gender, language, and, 335
Word(s). *See also* Speech sounds
vs. pictures, 214–216
root, 289
Word labels, 296
Word meanings, from context, 339
Word order, syntax and, 297
Word-recognition models, 144–147
Word-superiority effect, 145
Working backward heuristic, 358, 359
Working forward heuristic, 358, 359
Working memory, 166–168, 170, 274
age and, 462
intelligence and, 478
World maps, 245

X-ray based techniques, 42
X-ray problem, 371–373

Zone of proximal development (ZPD), 447–449

ILLUSTRATION CREDITS

Table 2.1. Neurotransmitters by Izquierdo/Medina from *Neurobiology of Learning & Memory, 63,* 19–32. Copyright ©1995. Reprinted by permission of Academic Press.

Figures 2.4, 2.5, 2.6, 2.8, 2.10, 2.11, 2.13, 2.14, 2.15, 2.16, 2.17, 4.3, 4.21, 8.2, 11.13, 12.1, and 14.2. From *In Search of the Human Mind* by Robert J. Sternberg, copyright © 1995 by Harcourt Brace & Company, reproduced by permission of the publisher.

Figure 2.12. From *Introduction to Psychology,* Eleventh Edition, by Richard Atkinson, Rita Atkinson, Darly Bem, Ed Smith, and Susan Nolen Hoeksema, copyright © 1995 by Harcourt Brace & Company, reproduced by permission of the publisher.

Figure 2.13(a). Darley/Glucksberg/Kinchla, *Psychology,* Fifth Edition, copyright © 1991, p. 58. Reprinted by permission of Prentice-Hall, Upper Saddle River, New Jersey.

Figure 2.13(b). Reprinted from *Psychology,* Second Edition, by H. Gleitman, with the permission of W.W. Norton & Company, Inc. Copyright © 1986 by H. Gleitman.

Figure 3.7. D. Navon and D. Gopher (1979) "On the Economy of the Human-Processing System," *Psychological Review, 86,* pp. 214–255. Copyright © 1979 by the American Psychological Association. Reprinted with permission.

Table 4.1. Courtesy of Jennifer Pardo.

Figure 4.13. From *Mind Sights* by Roger Shepard. Copyright © 1990 by W. H. Freeman & Company. Reprinted by permission of W. H. Freeman & Company.

Figures 4.16 and 4.25. From *The Legacy of Solomon Asch: Essays in Cognition and Social Psychology* by Irving Rock. Copyright © 1990 by Lawrence Erlbaum Associates. Reprinted by permission.

Figure 4.17(a). Michael I. Posner, Ralph Goldsmith, and Kenneth E. Welton, Jr. (1967), "Perceived Distance and the Classification of Distorted Patterns," from *Journal of Experimental Psychology, 73*(1): 28–38. Copyright © 1967 by the American Psychological Association. Reprinted with permission.

Figure 4.17(b). Stephen K. Reed (1972), "Pattern Recognition and Categorization," *Cognitive Psychology,* July 1972, 3(3): 382–407. Reprinted by permission of Academic Press.

Figure 4.17(c). Robert Solso and Judith McCarthy (1981), "Prototype Formation of Faces: A Case of Pseudomemory," *British Journal of Psychology,* November 1981, vol. 72, no. 4, pp. 499–503. Reprinted by permission of The British Psychological Society.

Figure 4.17(d). D. Navon, "Forest Before Trees: The Precedence to Global Features in Visual Perception," *Cognitive Psychology,* July 1977, vol. 9, no. 3, pages 353–382. Reprinted by permission of Academic Press.

Figure 4.23. I. Biederman (1987), "Recognition by Components: A Theory of Human Image Understanding," *Computer Vision, Graphics, and Image Processing, 32,* 29–73. Reprinted by permission of Academic Press.

Figure 4.26. David Rumelhart and James McClelland, "An interactive activation model of context effects in letter perception: Part 1. An account of basic findings," from *Psychological Review,* no. 88, pp. 483–524. Copyright © 1981 by the American Psychological Association. Adapted with permission.

Figure 4.27. Charles A. Perfetti (1985), "Reading Acquisition and Beyond: Decoding Includes Cognition," *American Journal of Education,* November 1984, vol. 93, no. 1, pp. 40–60. Reprinted by permission of The University of Chicago Press.

Figure 4.28. From *Sensation and Perception* by Stanley Coren and Lawrence M. Ward, copyright © 1989 by Harcourt Brace & Company, reproduced by permission of the publisher.

Figure 5.1. Illustration by Allen Beechel, adapted from "The Control of Short-Term Memory," by Richard C. Atkinson and Richard M. Shriffin. Copyright © 1971 by Scientific American, Inc. Reprinted by permission of the artist.

Figure 5.2. From *Psychology,* Second Edition, by Margaret Matlin, copyright © 1995 by Harcourt Brace & Company, reproduced by permission of the publisher.

Table 6.2. H. L. Roediger (1980), "The Effectiveness of Four Mnemonics in Ordering Recall," *Journal of Experimental Psychology: LMC, 6*(5): 558–567. Copyright (1980) by the American Psychological Association. Adapted with permission.

Table 6.3. "The War of the Ghosts," from *Remembering: A Study in Experimental and Social Psychology* by F.C. Bartlett. Copyright © 1932 by Cambridge University Press. Reprinted with the permission of Cambridge University Press.

Figure 6.1. Reprinted with permission from S. Sternberg (1966), "High Speed in S. Sternberg's Short-Term Memory-Scanning Task," *Science,* vol. 153, pp. 652–654. Copyright © 1966 American Association for the Advancement of Science.

Figure 6.2. G. Keppel and B.J. Underwood (1962), "Proactive Inhibition in Short-Term Retention of Single Items," *Journal of Verbal Learning and Verbal Behavior,* vol. 1, pp. 153–161. Reprinted by permission of Academic Press.

Figure 7.3. From *Cognition,* Third Edition, by Margaret Matlin, copyright © 1994 by Harcourt Brace & Company, reproduced by permission of the publisher.

Figure 7.4. D. Chambers and D. Reisberg (1985), "Can Mental Images be Ambiguous," *Journal of Experimental Psychology: Human Perception and Performance, 11*: 317–328. Copyright © 1985 by the American Psychological Association. Reprinted with permission.

Figures 7.6 and 7.7. From "Mental Rotation," by R. Shepard and J. Metzler. Copyright © 1971 by the Association for the Advancement of Science. Reprinted by permission.

Figures 7.10 and 7.14. From *Cognitive Psychology,* Third Edition, by Robert Solso. Copyright © 1991 by Robert Solso. Reprinted by permission of Allyn & Bacon.

Figure 7.12. Timothy P. McNamara, Roger Ratcliff, and Gail McKoon (1984), "The Mental Representation of Knowledge Acquired from Maps," *Journal of Experimental Psychology: LMC, 10*(4): 723–732. Copyright © 1984 by the American Psychological Association. Adapted with permission.

Table 8.1. B. Malt & E. Smith (1984), "Correlated Properties in Natural Categories," *Journal of Verbal Learning and Verbal Behavior,* vol. 23, pp. 250–269. Reprinted by permission of Academic Press.

Figure 8.3. N. M. Henley (1969), "A Psychological Study of the Semantics of Animal Terms," *Journal of Verbal Learning and Verbal Behavior,* vol. 8, pp. 176–184. Reprinted by permission of Academic Press.

Figure 8.4. "Anderson's ACT Model" based on Robert L. Solso, *Cognition and the Visual Arts,* 1994, p. 223.

Table 9.1. From *Psychology and Language: An Introduction to Psycholinguistics* by Herbert H. Clark and Eve V. Clark, copyright © 1977 by Harcourt Brace & Company, reproduced by permission of the publisher.

Figures 10.1 and 10.2. Darley/Glucksberg/Kinchla, *Psychology,* Fourth Edition, copyright © 1988, p. 286. Reprinted by permission of Prentice-Hall, Upper Saddle River, New Jersey.

Figures 11.1 and 11.8. From Richard E. Mayer, "The Search for Insight: Grappling with Gestalt Psychology's Unanswered Questions." In *The Nature of Insight* edited by R. J. Sternberg and J. E. Davidson. Copyright © 1995 by MIT Press. Reprinted by permission.

Figures 11.7, 11.9, and 11.10. From *Intelligence Applied: Understanding and Increasing Your Intellectual Skills* by Robert J. Sternberg, copyright © 1986 by Harcourt Brace & Company, reproduced by permission of the publishers.

Figure 11.12. Janet Metcalfe and David Wiebe (1987), "Intuition in Insight and Noninsight Problem Solving," from *Memory and Cognition,* vol. 13, no. 3, pp. 238–246. Reprinted by permission of Psychonomic Society.

Table 11.2. Abraham S. Luchins (1942), "Mechanization in Problem Solving: The Effect of Einstellung." *Psychological Monographs*, vol. 54, no. 6 (whole number 248). Copyright © 1942 by Dr. Abraham S. Luchins. Reprinted by permission.

Table 11.3. M. L. Gick and K. J. Holyoak (1983), "Schema Induction and Analogical Transfer," *Cognitive Psychology*, vol. 15, pp. 1–38. Reprinted by permission of Academic Press.

Figure 11.14. From William G. Chase and Herbert A. Simon (1973), "The Mind's Eye in Chess," in *Visual Information Processing* edited by William G. Chase. Reprinted by permission of Academic Press.

Figure 11.15. From "The Nature of Creativity as Manifest in its Testing," by E. P. Torrance in *The Nature of Creativity*, edited by Robert J. Sternberg. Copyright © 1988 by Cambridge University Press. Reprinted by permission of Cambridge University Press.

Figure 12.2. J. Loren and P. Chapman (1959) "Atmosphere Effect Re-examined," *Journal of Experimental Psychology*, September 1959, vol. 58, pp. 220–226. Copyright © 1959 by the American Psychological Association. Reprinted with permission.

Figure 12.4. From *The Blackwell Dictionary of Cognitive Psychology*, edited by M. W. Eysenck and M. T. Keane. Copyright © 1994 by Blackwell Publishers. Reprinted by permission.

Figure 13.1. J. Piaget and F. Gonseth (1946), "Groupings, Groups, and Lattices," vol. 31, pp. 65–73.

Table 13.2 and Figure 13.5. From *Understanding Development* by Sandra Scarr, Richard Weinberg, and Carol Levine. Copyright © 1986 by Sandra Scarr, Richard Weinberg, and Anne Levine. Reprinted by permission of Virginia Barber Literary Agency, Inc.

Figure 13.6. R. V. Kail, J. W. Pellegrino, and P. Carter (1980), "Developmental Changes in Mental Rotation" *Journal of Experimental Child Psychology*, vol. 29, pp. 102–116. Reprinted by permission of Academic Press.

Figure 13.7. Reprinted with permission from R. Thatcher, R. A. Walker, and S. Guidice, "Human Cerebral Hemispheres Develop at Different Rates and Ages," from *Science*, vol. 236, pp. 1110–1113. Copyright © 1987 by American Association for the Advancement of Science.

Figure 14.3. Reprinted with the permission of The Free Press, A Division of Simon & Schuster, Inc. from *Bias in Mental Testing* by Arthur R. Jensen. Copyright © 1980 by Arthur R. Jensen.

Table 14.3. "Seven Intelligences" from *Multiple Intelligences: The Theory and Practice* by Howard Gardner. Copyright © 1993 by Howard Gardner. Reprinted by permission of Basic Books, a division of Harper-Collins Publishers.

Figure 14.7. From *Understanding Natural Languages* by Terry Winograd. Copyright ©1972 by Terry Winograd. Reprinted by permission of Academic Press.

Table 14.4. J. J. Weizenbaum (1966) "ELIZA—A Computer Program for the Study of Natural Language Communication Between Man & Machine," *Communications of the Association for Computing Machinery*, vol. 9, pp. 36–45. Reprinted by the permission of the Association of Computing Machinery; and "Computer Simulation of A Neurotic Process" by Perry Colby. In Tomkins/Messick *Computer Simulation and Personality*. Copyright © 1963 by John Wiley & Sons. Reprinted by permission.

Table 14.5. From *Computer Based Medical Consultations* by F. H. Shortliffe. Copyright © 1974 by Elsevier Science Publishing. Reprinted by permission.

PHOTO CREDITS

Page 6, Archives of the History of American Psychology University of Akron.

Page 7, Archives of the History of American Psychology University of Akron.

Page 12, Courtesy of Dr. Ulric Neisser.

Page 13, Courtesy of Dr. Herbert A. Simon.

Page 30, Copyright © Alexander Tsiaras/ Stock Boston.

Page 33, Omikron/Science Source/Photo Researchers.

Page 43 top, CNRI/SPL/Photo Researchers.

Page 43 top center, Ohio Nuclear Corporation/SPL/ Photo Researchers.

Page 43 bottom center, CNRI/SPL/Photo Researchers.

Page 43 bottom, Copyright © Spencer Grant/Stock Boston.

Page 46 left, Biophoto Associates/Science Source/Photo Researchers.

Page 46 right, Copyright © A. Glauberman/ Photo Researchers.

Page 50, Copyright © Manfred Kage/Peter Arnold, Inc.

Page 62, Courtesy of Dr. Michael Posner.

Page 83, Copyright © Peter Menzel/Stock Boston.

Page 87, Courtesy of Dr. Anne Treisman.

Page 111 top, From Dallenbach, K. M. 1951, A Puzzle Picture with a New Principle of Concealment. *American Journal of Psychology*, volume 54, 431–433.

Page 111 bottom, Ronald James.

Page 120 left, Alinari/Art Resource, New York.

Page 120 right, Copyright © 1998 M. C. Escher/ Cordon Art Baarn-Holland. All rights reserved.

Page 124, Kaiser Porcelain, Ltd., London, England.

Page 136 top, Courtesy of Dr. Irving Biederman.

Page 136 bottom, Courtesy of Dr. Irvin Rock.

Page 164, Courtesy of Dr. Harry Bahrick.

Page 166, Courtesy of Dr. Alan Baddeley.

Page 195, Courtesy of Dr. Gordon H. Bower.

Page 202, Courtesy of Dr. Elizabeth Loftus.

Page 213 top left, AP/Wide World Photos.

Page 213 top right, AP/Wide World Photos.

Page 213 bottom left, AP/Wide World Photos.

Page 213 bottom right, AP/Wide World Photos.

Page 217, Courtesy of Dr. Stephen M. Kosslyn.

Page 225, Courtesy of Dr. Roger N. Shepard.

Page 239, Courtesy of Dr. Martha J. Farah.

Page 269, Courtesy of Dr. John R. Anderson.

Page 276, Courtesy of Dr. James L. McClelland.

Page 286, Copyright © George Bellirose/Stock Boston.

Page 322, Courtesy of Dr. Michael Cole.

Page 352, Copyright © 1998 Bob Mankoff from the Cartoon Bank™ Inc.

Page 366 left, Superstock.

Page 366 center, Superstock.

Page 366 right, Superstock.

Page 374, Courtesy of Dr. Dedre Gentner.

Page 377, Courtesy of Dr. Michelene Chi.

Page 383 left, AP/Wide World Photos.

Page 383 center, Copyright © Keystone/The Image Works.

Page 383 right, AP/Wide World Photos.

Page 395, Courtesy of Dr. Amos Tversky.

Page 403, Courtesy of Dr. Baruch Fischhoff.

Page 416, Courtesy of Dr. Philip Johnson-Laird.

Page 435, Copyright © Bill Anderson/Monkmeyer Press Photos.

Page 437 left, Copyright © Doug Goodman/Monkmeyer Press Photos.

Page 437 right, Copyright © Doug Goodman/Monkmeyer Press Photos.

Page 442 left, Copyright © Laura Dwight/ PhotoEdit.

Page 442 center, Copyright © Laura Dwight/ PhotoEdit.

Page 442 right, Copyright © Laura Dwight/ PhotoEdit.

Page 447, Robert Solso/Photo by Felicia Martinez/PhotoEdit.

Page 453, Courtesy of Dr. Robert S. Siegler.

Page 458, R. V. Kail, J. W. Pellegrino, and P. Carter (1980), "Developmental Changes in Mental Rotation," *Journal of Experimental Child Psychology*, volume 29, pages 102–116. Reprinted by permission of the Academic Press.

Page 479, Courtesy of Dr. Earl Hunt.

Page 486, Copyright © George Holton/Photo Researchers.

Page 487, Courtesy of Dr. Howard Gardner.